International Law

Selected Documents

International Law

Selected Documents

2013-2015 Edition

Barry E. Carter
Professor of Law
Georgetown University

About Wolters Kluwer Law & Business

Wolters Kluwer Law & Business is a leading global provider of intelligent information and digital solutions for legal and business professionals in key specialty areas, and respected educational resources for professors and law students. Wolters Kluwer Law & Business connects legal and business professionals as well as those in the education market with timely, specialized authoritative content and information-enabled solutions to support success through productivity, accuracy and mobility.

Serving customers worldwide, Wolters Kluwer Law & Business products include those under the Aspen Publishers, CCH, Kluwer Law International, Loislaw, ftwilliam.com and MediRegs family of products.

CCH products have been a trusted resource since 1913, and are highly regarded resources for legal, securities, antitrust and trade regulation, government contracting, banking, pension, payroll, employment and labor, and healthcare reimbursement and compliance professionals.

Aspen Publishers products provide essential information to attorneys, business professionals and law students. Written by preeminent authorities, the product line offers analytical and practical information in a range of specialty practice areas from securities law and intellectual property to mergers and acquisitions and pension/benefits. Aspen's trusted legal education resources provide professors and students with high-quality, up-to-date and effective resources for successful instruction and study in all areas of the law.

Kluwer Law International products provide the global business community with reliable international legal information in English. Legal practitioners, corporate counsel and business executives around the world rely on Kluwer Law journals, looseleafs, books, and electronic products for comprehensive information in many areas of international legal practice.

Loislaw is a comprehensive online legal research product providing legal content to law firm practitioners of various specializations. Loislaw provides attorneys with the ability to quickly and efficiently find the necessary legal information they need, when and where they need it, by facilitating access to primary law as well as state-specific law, records, forms and treatises.

ftwilliam.com offers employee benefits professionals the highest quality plan documents (retirement, welfare and non-qualified) and government forms (5500/PBGC, 1099 and IRS) software at highly competitive prices.

MediRegs products provide integrated health care compliance content and software solutions for professionals in healthcare, higher education and life sciences, including professionals in accounting, law and consulting.

Wolters Kluwer Law & Business, a division of Wolters Kluwer, is headquartered in New York. Wolters Kluwer is a market-leading global information services company focused on professionals.

Contents

Alphabetical List of Documents   *xiii*
Abbreviations List   *xvii*
Preface   *xix*

Chapter 1. What Is International Law?   **1**

United Nations Charter   1
Statute of the International Court of Justice   28
International Emergency Economic Powers Act [See Chapter 3]
Materials on September 11, 2001, case study
  [See Chapter 11]
N.Y. Convention on the Recognition and Enforcement of
  Foreign Arbitral Awards [See Chapter 4]

Chapter 2. Treaties and Customary International Law   **43**

Vienna Convention on the Law of Treaties   43

Chapter 3. International Law in the United States   **69**

The Constitution of the United States   69
Trading with the Enemy Act   86
National Emergencies Act   88
International Emergency Economic Powers Act (IEEPA)   93
Alien Tort Statute (ATS) or Alien Tort Claims Act (ATCA)   99
Torture Victim Protection Act (TVPA)   99

Chapter 4.   International Dispute Resolution   **101**

International Court of Justice Statute [See Chapter 1]
Rome Statute of the International Criminal Court
  [See end of Chapter 12]
ICC Rules of Arbitration   101
N.Y. Convention on the Recognition and Enforcement of
  Foreign Arbitral Awards   118
Convention on the Settlement of Investment
  Disputes Between States and Nationals of Other
  States (ICSID Convention)   123
North American Free Trade Agreement (NAFTA)   137
GATT Articles XXII and XXIII   165
Uruguay Round Final Act   167
• World Trade Organization (WTO) Agreement   168
• Annex 2. Dispute Settlement Understanding   177

Chapter 5.   States and Other Major International Entities   **201**

U.N. Charter [See Chapter 1]
Treaty on European Union   201
Treaty on the Functioning of the European Union   225
Charter of Fundamental Rights of the European Union   273
North Atlantic Treaty (NATO)   284
Charter of the Organization of American States (OAS)   288

**Chapter 6.   Foreign Sovereign Immunity and the Act
            of State Doctrine**   **301**

U.S. Foreign Sovereign Immunities Act (FSIA)   301
Vienna Convention on Diplomatic Relations   317
Vienna Convention on Consular Relations   331
Optional Protocol to the Vienna Convention Concerning
  Compulsory Settlement of Disputes   353

Chapter 7.   Allocation of Legal Authority Among States   **355**

Some U.S. Anti-Terrorism Statutes   355

Contents

**Chapter 8. State Responsibility—Injuries to Aliens and
International Human Rights**   361

U.S.-Ukraine Bilateral Investment Treaty   361
International Law Commission, Draft Articles on
  Responsibility of States for Internationally Wrongful Acts   372
Charter of Fundamental Rights of the European Union
  [See Chapter 5]
Universal Declaration of Human Rights   384
International Covenant on Civil and Political Rights   390
U.S. Senate Resolution of Advice and Consent to
  Ratification of the Covenant on Civil and Political Rights   406
First Optional Protocol to the ICCPR   409
International Covenant on Economic, Social and Cultural Rights   412
Genocide Convention   421
U.S. Reservations and Understandings to the Genocide
  Convention   423
Convention on Elimination of Racial Discrimination   425
U.S. Reservations, Understanding, and Declaration to the
  Convention on Racial Discrimination   433
Convention on Discrimination Against Women   435
Convention Against Torture   446
U.S. Reservations, Understandings, and Declaration to the
  Torture Convention   456
Convention on the Rights of the Child   458
Optional Protocol on the Involvement of Children in
  Armed Conflict   467
Optional Protocol on the Sale of Children, Child Prostitution
  and Child Pornography   473
European Convention for the Protection of Human Rights
  and Fundamental Freedoms   481
Protocols to the European Human Rights Convention
  (Nos. 1, 4, 6, 7, 12, 13, 14)   494
American Convention on Human Rights   505
Constitutive Act of the African Union   524
African Charter on Human and Peoples' Rights   529

Chapter 9. Law of the Sea   539

UNCLOS Resolution on Preparatory Commission   539
Law of the Sea Convention (1982)   541
Agreement Relating to Part XI of the LOS Convention   639
Antarctic Treaty   653

Chapter 10. International Environmental Law   659

Stockholm Declaration   659
Rio Declaration on Environment and Development   664
Vienna Ozone Convention   669
Helsinki Declaration on the Ozone Layer   679
Montreal Ozone Protocol (as amended)   681
Framework Convention on Climate Change   704
Kyoto Protocol to Climate Change Convention   718

Chapter 11. Use of Force and Arms Control   739

U.N. Charter [See Chapter 1]
NATO Treaty [See Chapter 5]
OAS Charter [See Chapter 5]
U.N. "Uniting for Peace" Resolution   739
U.N. Definition of Aggression Resolution   745
U.N. Participation Act   749
War Powers Resolution   752
Materials re: Iraq   759
U.N. Security Council Res. 660 (August 2, 1990)   759
U.N. Security Council Res. 661 (August 6, 1990)   759
U.N. Security Council Res. 678 (November 29, 1990)   761
Congressional Authorization for Use of Military Force
     Against Iraq (AUMF) (1991)   762
President Bush's Letter to Congress re: Attack on Iraq (1991)   763
U.N. Security Council Res. 687 (April 3, 1991)   764
U.N. Security Council Res. 688 (April 5, 1991)   770
Congressional Authorization for Use of Military Force
     Against Iraq (2002)   770
U.N. Security Council Res. 1441 (November 8, 2002)   774
Letter from President Bush to Congressional Leaders
     (March 21, 2003)   778
Letter from U.S. Permanent Representative to the
     U.N. Security Council (March 20, 2003)   779
U.K. Government Statement on Legal Basis for Use of Force
     against Iraq (March 2003)   780
U.N. Security Council Res. 1483 (May 22, 2003)   781
Materials re: Kosovo   786
U.S. Ambassador Burleigh, Statement to Security Council
     (March 24, 1999)   786
Sir Jeremy Greenstock (U.K.), Statement to Security Council
     (March 24, 1999)   787
President Clinton's Letter to Congress re: Kosovo
     (March 26, 1999)   788

Contents

Written Answer from Prime Minister Blair (April 29, 1999)   789

U.N. Security Council Res. 1244 (June 10, 1999)   790

Materials on September 11   793

U.N. General Assembly Res. 56/1 (September 12, 2001)   793

U.N. Security Council Res. 1368 (September 12, 2001)   793

Congressional Joint Resolution: Authorization of Use
of Force (September 14, 2001)   794

U.N. Security Council Res. 1373 (September 28, 2001)   795

Letter from President Bush to Congressional Leaders
on Afghanistan (October 9, 2001)   798

Letter from U.S. Permanent Representative to the
U.N. Security Council (October 7, 2001)   799

U.N. Security Council Res. 1378 (November 14, 2001)   800

U.N. Security Council Res. 1383 (December 6, 2001)   801

U.N. Security Council Res. 1386 (December 20, 2001)   802

Materials re: International Humanitarian Law   805

Geneva Convention Relative to the Treatment of
Prisoners of War (III) (1949)   805

Geneva Convention Relative to the Protection of Civilian
Persons in Time of War (IV) (1949)   819

Protocol I to the Geneva Conventions of 1949   833

President Obama, Ensuring Lawful Interrogations
(January 22, 2009)   858

President Obama, Review of Individuals Detained at
Guantanamo Bay (March 7, 2011)   862

Materials re: Proliferation, Including North Korea and Iran   867

U.N. Security Council Res. 1540 (April 28, 2004)   867

U.N. Security Council Res. 1718 [re: North Korea]
(October 14, 2006)   870

U.N. Security Council Statement Condemning North Korean
Missile Launch (April 13, 2009)   874

U.N. Security Council Res. 2087 [re: North Korea]
(January 22, 2013)   875

U.N. Security Council Res. 2094 [re: North Korea]
(March 7, 2013)   877

U.N. Security Council Res. 1737 [re: Iran] (December 23, 2006)   883

U.N. Security Council Res. 1747 [re: Iran] (March 24, 2007)   887

U.N. Security Council Res. 1803 [re: Iran] (March 3, 2008)   889

U.N. Security Council Res. 1929 [re: Iran] (June 9, 2010)   892

Materials re: Libya   902

U.N. Security Council Res. 1970 (February 26, 2011)   902

U.N. Security Council Res. 1973 (March 17, 2011)   909

Chapter 12. International Criminal Law   **917**

Treaty on Mutual Legal Assistance in Criminal Matters
   Between France and U.S.   917
U.S.-U.K. Extradition Treaty (2003)   929
U.N. Security Council Resolutions Establishing
   War Crimes Tribunals for the Former Yugoslavia and Rwanda   938
U.N. Security Council Res. 827 (May 25, 1993)   938
U.N. Security Council Res. 955 (November 8, 1994)   940
Rome Statute of the International Criminal Court   942

Alphabetical List of Documents

African Charter on Human and Peoples' Rights	529
Agreement Relating to Part XI of the LOS Convention	639
Alien Tort Statute (or Alien Tort Claims Act)	99
American Convention on Human Rights	505
Antarctic Treaty	653
Anti-Terrorism Laws, Some U.S.	355
Charter of Fundamental Rights of the European Union	273
Constitutive Act of the African Union	524
Convention Against Torture	446
Convention on Discrimination Against Women	435
Convention on Elimination of Racial Discrimination	425
Convention on the Rights of the Child	458
Convention on the Settlement of Investment Disputes Between States and Nationals of Other States (ICSID Convention)	123
European Convention for the Protection of Human Rights and Fundamental Freedoms	481
European Union Treaty	201
First Optional Protocol to the International Covenant on Civil and Political Rights	409
Foreign Sovereign Immunities Act (FSIA)	301
Framework Convention on Climate Change	704
Functioning of the European Union Treaty	225
GATT Articles XXII and XXIII	165
Geneva Convention Relative to the Treatment of Prisoners of War (III) (1949)	805
Geneva Convention Relative to the Protection of Civilian Persons in Time of War (IV) (1949)	819
Genocide Convention	423

Helsinki Declaration on the Ozone Layer 679
ICC Rules of Arbitration 101
International Court of Justice Statute 28
International Covenant on Civil and Political Rights 390
International Covenant on Economic, Social and Cultural Rights 412
International Emergency Economic Powers Act (IEEPA) 93
International Humanitarian Law Materials 805
Iraq Materials 759
Kosovo Materials 786
Kyoto Protocol to Climate Change Convention 718
Law of the Sea Convention (1982) 541
Libya Materials 902
Montreal Ozone Protocol (as amended) 681
Mutual Legal Assistance in Criminal Matters Between France and
    U.S. 917
National Emergencies Act 88
North American Free Trade Agreement (NAFTA) 137
North Atlantic Treaty 284
N.Y. Convention on the Recognition and Enforcement of Foreign
    Arbitral Awards 118
Optional Protocol on the Involvement of Children in Armed
    Conflict 467
Optional Protocol on the Sale of Children, Child Prostitution and
    Child Pornography 473
Optional Protocol to the Vienna Consular Convention
    Concerning the Compulsory Settlement of Disputes 353
Organization of American States (OAS) Charter 288
President Obama, Ensuring Lawful Interrogations 858
President Obama, Review of Individuals Detained at
    Guantanamo Bay 862
Proliferation Materials, including North Korea and Iran 867
Protocol I to the Geneva Conventions of 1949 833
Protocols to the European Human Rights Convention (Nos. 1, 4,
    6, 7, 12, 13, 14) 494
Rio Declaration on Environment and Development 664
Rome Statute of the International Criminal Court 942
September 11 Materials 793
Stockholm Declaration 659
Torture Victim Protection Act 99
Trading with the Enemy Act 86
Treaty on European Union 201
Treaty on the Functioning of the European Union 225
UNCLOS Resolution on Preparatory Commission 539
U.N. Charter 1
U.N. Definition of Aggression Resolution 745
U.N. Participation Act 749

Alphabetical List of Documents

U.N. Security Council Resolutions Establishing War Crimes
    Tribunals in the Former Yugoslavia and Rwanda   938
U.N. "Uniting for Peace" Resolution   739
U.S. Constitution   69
U.S. Reservations and Understandings to the Genocide
    Convention   423
U.S. Reservations, Understanding, and Declaration to the
    Convention on Racial Discrimination   433
U.S. Reservations, Understandings, and Declarations to the
    Torture Convention   456
U.S. Senate Resolution of Advice and Consent to Ratification of
    the International Covenant on Civil and Political Rights   406
U.S.-U.K. Extradition Treaty (2003)   929
U.S.-Ukraine Bilateral Investment Treaty   361
"Uniting for Peace" Resolution   739
Universal Declaration of Human Rights   384
Uruguay Round Final Act   167
Vienna Convention on Consular Relations   331
Vienna Convention on Diplomatic Relations   317
Vienna Convention on the Law of Treaties   43
Vienna Ozone Convention   669
War Powers Resolution   752
World Trade Organization (WTO) Agreement   168
World Trade Organization Dispute Settlement Understanding   177

Abbreviations List

A.J.I.L.	American Journal of International Law
Bevans	Bevans, Treaties and Other International Agreements of the United States of America, 1776-1949 (1968-76)
C.E.T.S.	Council of Europe Treaty Series
E.T.S.	European Treaty Series
G.A.Res.	United Nations General Assembly Resolution
I.L.M.	International Legal Materials
L.N.T.S.	League of Nations Treaty Series
O.A.S.	Organization of American States
Stat.	Statutes at Large, United States
T.I.A.S.	Treaties and Other International Acts Series
T.S.	Treaty Series
U.N. Doc.	United Nations Document
U.N.T.S.	United Nations Treaty Series
U.S.C.	United States Code
U.S.T.	United States Treaties and Other International Agreements

Preface

These documents should be useful for anyone working in the international law field who needs a compilation of the basic documents. They have been collected for use as a supplement to Barry E. Carter and Allen S. Weiner, International Law (Wolters Kluwer 6th ed. 2011).

The documents are organized according to the chapters in that casebook. Background information about a document's date of signing and entry into force, as well as the countries that have become parties to it, are provided in a footnote to each document. Unless indicated otherwise, these footnotes at the start of each document are current through at least February 2013. Information about treaties and other agreements is often from the Web sites that are provided with the document or in the footnote below it. Other sources include International Legal Materials; U.S. Department of State, Treaties in Force: A List of Treaties and Other International Agreements of the United States in Force on January 1, 2012; United Nations, Multilateral Treaties Deposited with the Secretary General; and from other published sources. Web sites provide a valuable and usually the most up-to-date source for recent documents and for the new parties to treaties and other documents. For example, the United Nations has an excellent online treaty collection at <http://treaties.un.org>.

Because this collection is a reference book, the substantive provisions of each document are usually printed in full. When deemed peripheral, however, materials have been omitted—for example, some of the preambles and the final paragraphs containing mere formalities. There has been substantial editing of some of the longer documents, whose complex provisions go well beyond what is needed here. These long documents include the 1982 Law of the Sea Convention and the Treaty on the Functioning of the European Union. All omissions are indicated by ellipses. The tables of contents for some of the treaties have been substantially edited as well; they might reflect the provisions presented in this book as well as additional sections from the entire treaties.

I have been responsible for preparing this collection of documents. Professor Phillip R. Trimble, who contributed constructively to this collection through 2001, has left the academic world. My present active co-author on the casebook, Professor Allen S. Weiner, made very helpful recommendations about changes in this and three previous editions of the document collection. I also want to acknowledge the valuable assistance on this edition of Cynthia Rockwell at Georgetown and the help of very supportive people at Wolters Kluwer, including John Devins, as well as Troy Froebe at The Froebe Group.

I encourage any suggestions about possible additions or deletions in future editions.

Barry E. Carter

June 2013

1

What Is International Law?

CHARTER OF THE UNITED NATIONS
(as amended)

June 26, 1945, 59 Stat. 1031, T.S. No. 993, 3 Bevans 1153*

We the peoples of the United Nations determined to save succeeding generations from the scourge of war, which twice in our lifetime has brought

---

*Signed at San Francisco on June 26, 1945. Entered into force on October 24, 1945. The latest amendments are at 24 U.S.T. 2225, T.I.A.S. 7739.

The following were the 193 parties to the Charter and Member States of the United Nations as of April 2013: Afghanistan, Albania, Algeria, Andorra, Angola, Antigua and Barbuda, Argentina, Armenia, Australia, Austria, Azerbaijan, Bahamas, Bahrain, Bangladesh, Barbados, Belarus, Belgium, Belize, Benin, Bhutan, Bolivia, Bosnia and Herzegovina, Botswana, Brazil, Bruni Darussalam, Bulgaria, Burkina Faso, Burundi, Cambodia, Cameroon, Canada, Cape Verde, Central African Republic, Chad, Chile, China, Colombia, Comoros, Congo, Congo (Democratic Republic of), Costa Rica, Côte d'Ivoire, Croatia, Cuba, Cyprus, Czech Republic, Denmark, Djibouti, Dominica, Dominican Republic, Ecuador, Egypt, El Salvador, Equatorial Guinea, Eritrea, Estonia, Ethiopia, Fiji, Finland, France, Gabon, Gambia, Georgia, Germany, Ghana, Greece, Grenada, Guatemala, Guinea, Guinea-Bissau, Guyana, Haiti, Honduras, Hungary, Iceland, India, Indonesia, Iran, Iraq, Ireland, Israel, Italy, Jamaica, Japan, Jordan, Kazakhstan, Kenya, Kiribati, Korea (Democratic People's Republic of), Korea (Republic of), Kuwait, Kyrgyzstan, Lao People's Democratic Republic, Latvia, Lebanon, Lesotho, Liberia, Libyan Arab Jamahiriya, Liechtenstein, Lithuania, Luxembourg, Macedonia (the former Yugoslav Republic of), Madagascar, Malawi, Malaysia, Maldives, Mali, Malta, Marshall Islands, Mauritania, Mauritius, Mexico, Micronesia, Moldova, Monaco, Mongolia, Montenegro, Morocco, Mozambique, Myanmar, Namibia, Nauru, Nepal, Netherlands, New Zealand, Nicaragua, Niger, Nigeria, Norway, Oman, Pakistan, Palau, Panama, Papua New Guinea, Paraguay, Peru, Philippines, Poland, Portugal, Qatar, Romania, Russian Federation, Rwanda, Saint Kitts and Nevis, Saint Lucia, Saint Vincent and the Grenadines, Samoa, San Marino, Sao Tome and Principe, Saudi Arabia, Senegal, Serbia, Seychelles, Sierra Leone, Singapore, Slovakia, Slovenia, Solomon Islands, Somalia, South Africa, South Sudan, Spain, Sri Lanka, Sudan, Suriname, Swaziland, Sweden, Switzerland, Syrian Arab Republic, Tajikistan, Tanzania, Thailand, Timor-Leste, Togo, Tonga, Trinidad and Tobago, Tunisia, Turkey, Turkmenistan, Tuvalu, Uganda, Ukraine, United Arab Emirates, United Kingdom, United States of America, Uruguay, Uzbekistan, Vanuatu, Venezuela, Viet Nam, Yemen, Zambia, and Zimbabwe. See the U.N. Web site at <http://treaties.un.org>.

untold sorrow to mankind, and to reaffirm faith in fundamental human rights, in the dignity and worth of the human person, in the equal rights of men and women and of nations large and small, and to establish conditions under which justice and respect for the obligations arising from treaties and other sources of international law can be maintained, and to promote social progress and better standards of life in larger freedom, and for these ends to practice tolerance and live together in peace with one another as good neighbors, and to unite our strength to maintain international peace and security, and to ensure, by the acceptance of principles and the institution of methods, that armed force shall not be used, save in the common interest, and to employ international machinery for the promotion of the economic and social advancement of all peoples, have resolved to combine our efforts to accomplish these aims.

Accordingly, our respective Governments, through representatives assembled in the city of San Francisco, who have exhibited their full powers found to be in good and due form, have agreed to the present Charter of the United Nations and do hereby establish an international organization to be known as the United Nations.

Chapter I. Purposes and Principles

Article 1

The Purposes of the United Nations are:

1. To maintain international peace and security, and to that end: to take effective collective measures for the prevention and removal of threats to the peace, and for the suppression of acts of aggression or other breaches of the peace, and to bring about by peaceful means, and in conformity with the principles of justice and international law, adjustment or settlement of international disputes or situations which might lead to a breach of the peace;

2. To develop friendly relations among nations based on respect for the principle of equal rights and self-determination of peoples, and to take other appropriate measures to strengthen universal peace;

3. To achieve international cooperation in solving international problems of an economic, social, cultural, or humanitarian character, and in promoting and encouraging respect for human rights and for fundamental freedoms for all without distinction as to race, sex, language, or religion; and

4. To be a center for harmonizing the actions of nations in the attainment of these common ends.

Article 2

The Organization and its Members, in pursuit of the Purposes stated in Article 1, shall act in accordance with the following Principles.

1. The Organization is based on the principle of the sovereign equality of all its Members.

Weat phal -
Indepers -

2. All Members, in order to ensure to all of them the rights and benefits resulting from membership, shall fulfill in good faith the obligations assumed by them in accordance with the present Charter. *Charter political doct treaty w/ binding legal ob.*

3. All Members shall settle their international disputes by peaceful means in such a manner that international peace and security, and justice, are not endangered.

4. All Members shall refrain in their international relations from the threat or use of force against the territorial integrity or political independence of any state, or in any other manner inconsistent with the Purposes of the United Nations.

5. All Members shall give the United Nations every assistance in any action it takes in accordance with the present Charter, and shall refrain from giving assistance to any state against which the United Nations is taking preventive or enforcement action.

6. The Organization shall ensure that states which are not Members of the United Nations act in accordance with these Principles so far as may be necessary for the maintenance of international peace and security.

7. Nothing contained in the present Charter shall authorize the United Nations to intervene in matters which are essentially within the domestic jurisdiction of any state or shall require the Members to submit such matters to settlement under the present Charter, but this principle shall not prejudice the application of enforcement measures under Chapter VII.

Chapter II.   Membership

Article 3

The original Members of the United Nations shall be the states which, having participated in the United Nations Conference on International Organization at San Francisco, or having previously signed the Declaration by United Nations of January 1, 1942, sign the present Charter and ratify it in accordance with Article 110.

Article 4

1. Membership in the United Nations is open to all other peace-loving states which accept the obligations contained in the present Charter and, in the judgment of the Organization, are able and willing to carry out these obligations.

2. The admission of any such state to membership in the United Nations will be effected by a decision of the General Assembly upon the recommendation of the Security Council.

Article 5

A Member of the United Nations against which preventive or enforcement action has been taken by the Security Council may be suspended from the exercise of the rights and privileges of membership by the General Assembly upon the recommendation of the Security Council. The exercise of these rights and privileges may be restored by the Security Council.

Article 6

A Member of the United Nations which has persistently violated the Principles contained in the present Charter may be expelled from the Organization by the General Assembly upon the recommendation of the Security Council.

Chapter III.   Organs

Article 7

1. There are established as the principal organs of the United Nations: a General Assembly, a Security Council, an Economic and Social Council, a Trusteeship Council, an International Court of Justice, and a Secretariat.
2. Such subsidiary organs as may be found necessary may be established in accordance with the present Charter.

Article 8

The United Nations shall place no restrictions on the eligibility of men and women to participate in any capacity and under conditions of equality in its principal and subsidiary organs.

Chapter IV.   The General Assembly

Composition

Article 9

1. The General Assembly shall consist of all the Members of the United Nations.
2. Each Member shall have not more than five representatives in the General Assembly.

Functions and Powers

Article 10

The General Assembly may discuss any questions or any matters within the scope of the present Charter or relating to the powers and functions of any organs provided for in the present Charter, and, except as provided in Article 12, may make recommendations to the Members of the United Nations or to the Security Council or to both on any such questions or matters.

Article 11

1. The General Assembly may consider the general principles of co-operation in the maintenance of international peace and security, including the principles governing disarmament and the regulation of armaments, and may make recommendations with regard to such principles to the Members or to the Security Council or to both.

2. The General Assembly may discuss any questions relating to the maintenance of international peace and security brought before it by any Member of the United Nations, or by the Security Council, or by a state which is not a Member of the United Nations in accordance with Article 35, paragraph 2, and, except as provided in Article 12, may make recommendations with regard to any such questions to the state or states concerned or to the Security Council or to both. Any such question on which action is necessary shall be referred to the Security Council by the General Assembly either before or after discussion.

3. The General Assembly may call the attention of the Security Council to situations which are likely to endanger international peace and security.

4. The powers of the General Assembly set forth in this Article shall not limit the general scope of Article 10.

Article 12

1. While the Security Council is exercising in respect of any dispute or situation the functions assigned to it in the present Charter, the General Assembly shall not make any recommendation with regard to that dispute or situation unless the Security Council so requests.

2. The Secretary-General, with the consent of the Security Council, shall notify the General Assembly at each session of any matters relative to the maintenance of international peace and security which arc being dealt with by the Security Council and shall similarly notify the General Assembly, or the Members of the United Nations if the General Assembly is not in session, immediately the Security Council ceases to deal with such matters.

Article 13

1. The General Assembly shall initiate studies and make recommendations for the purpose of:

a. promoting international cooperation in the political field and encouraging the progressive development of international law and its codification;

b. promoting international cooperation in the economic, social, cultural, educational, and health fields, and assisting in the realization of human rights and fundamental freedoms for all without distinction as to race, sex, language, or religion.

2. The further responsibilities, functions, and powers of the General Assembly with respect to matters mentioned in paragraph 1(b) above are set forth in Chapters IX and X.

Article 14

Subject to the provisions of Article 12, the General Assembly may recommend measures for the peaceful adjustment of any situation, regardless of origin, which it deems likely to impair the general welfare or friendly relations among nations, including situations resulting from a violation of the provisions of the present Charter setting forth the Purposes and Principles of the United Nations.

Article 15

1. The General Assembly shall receive and consider annual and special reports from the Security Council; these reports shall include an account of the measures that the Security Council has decided upon or taken to maintain international peace and security.

2. The General Assembly shall receive and consider reports from the other organs of the United Nations.

Article 16

The General Assembly shall perform such functions with respect to the international trusteeship system as are assigned to it under Chapters XII and XIII, including the approval of the trusteeship agreements for areas not designated as strategic.

Article 17

1. The General Assembly shall consider and approve the budget of the Organization.

2. The expenses of the Organization shall be borne by the Members as apportioned by the General Assembly.

3. The General Assembly shall consider and approve any financial and budgetary arrangements with specialized agencies referred to in Article 57 and shall examine the administrative budgets of such specialized agencies with a view to making recommendations to the agencies concerned.

Voting

Article 18

1. Each member of the General Assembly shall have one vote.

2. Decisions of the General Assembly on important questions shall be made by a two-thirds majority of the members present and voting. These questions shall include: recommendations with respect to the maintenance

of international peace and security, the election of the non-permanent members of the Security Council, the election of the members of the Economic and Social Council, the election of members of the Trusteeship Council in accordance with paragraph 1(c) of Article 86, the admission of new Members to the United Nations, the suspension of the rights and privileges of membership, the expulsion of Members, questions relating to the operation of the trusteeship system, and budgetary questions.

3. Decisions on other questions, including the determination of additional categories of questions to be decided by a two-thirds majority, shall be made by a majority of the members present and voting.

Article 19

A Member of the United Nations which is in arrears in the payment of its financial contributions to the Organization shall have no vote in the General Assembly if the amount of its arrears equals or exceeds the amount of the contributions due from it for the preceding two full years. The General Assembly may, nevertheless, permit such a Member to vote if it is satisfied that the failure to pay is due to conditions beyond the control of the Member.

Procedure

Article 20

The General Assembly shall meet in regular annual sessions and in such special sessions as occasion may require. Special sessions shall be convoked by the Secretary-General at the request of the Security Council or of a majority of the Members of the United Nations.

Article 21

The General Assembly shall adopt its own rules of procedure. It shall elect its President for each session.

Article 22

The General Assembly may establish such subsidiary organs as it deems necessary for the performance of its functions.

Chapter V.   The Security Council

Composition

Article 23

1. The Security Council shall consist of fifteen Members of the United Nations. The Republic of China, France, the Union of Soviet Socialist Republics, the United Kingdom of Great Britain and Northern Ireland, and

the United States of America shall be permanent members of the Security Council. The General Assembly shall elect ten other Members of the United Nations to be non-permanent members of the Security Council, due regard being specially paid, in the first instance to the contribution of Members of the United Nations to the maintenance of international peace and security and to the other purposes of the Organization, and also to equitable geographical distribution.

2. The non-permanent members of the Security Council shall be elected for a term of two years. In the first election of the non-permanent members after the increase of the membership of the Security Council from eleven to fifteen, two of the four additional members shall be chosen for a term of one year. A retiring member shall not be eligible for immediate re-election.

3. Each member of the Security Council shall have one representative.

Functions and Powers

Article 24

1. In order to ensure prompt and effective action by the United Nations, its Members confer on the Security Council primary responsibility for the maintenance of international peace and security, and agree that in carrying out its duties under this responsibility the Security Council acts on their behalf.

2. In discharging these duties the Security Council shall act in accordance with the Purposes and Principles of the United Nations. The specific powers granted to the Security Council for the discharge of these duties are laid down in Chapters VI, VII, VIII, and XII.

3. The Security Council shall submit annual and, when necessary, special reports to the General Assembly for its consideration.

Article 25

The Members of the United Nations agree to accept and carry out the decisions of the Security Council in accordance with the present Charter.

Article 26

In order to promote the establishment and maintenance of international peace and security with the least diversion for armaments of the world's human and economic resources, the Security Council shall be responsible for formulating, with the assistance of the Military Staff Committee referred to in Article 47, plans to be submitted to the Members of the United Nations for the establishment of a system for the regulation of armaments.

Voting

Article 27

1. Each member of the Security Council shall have one vote.

2. Decisions of the Security Council on procedural matters shall be made by an affirmative vote of nine members.

3. Decisions of the Security Council on all other matters shall be made by an affirmative vote of nine members including the concurring votes of the permanent members; provided that, in decisions under Chapter VI, and under paragraph 3 of Article 52, a party to a dispute shall abstain from voting.

Veto

Procedure

Article 28

1. The Security Council shall be so organized as to be able to function continuously. Each member of the Security Council shall for this purpose be represented at all times at the seat of the Organization.

2. The Security Council shall hold periodic meetings at which each of its members may, if it so desires, be represented by a member of the government or by some other specially designated representative.

3. The Security Council may hold meetings at such places other than the seat of the Organization as in its judgment will best facilitate its work.

Article 29

The Security Council may establish such subsidiary organs as it deems necessary for the performance of its functions.

Article 30

The Security Council shall adopt its own rules of procedure, including the method of selecting its President.

Article 31

Any Member of the United Nations which is not a member of the Security Council may participate, without vote, in the discussion of any question brought before the Security Council whenever the latter considers that the interests of that Member are specially affected.

Article 32

Any Member of the United Nations which is not a member of the Security Council or any state which is not a Member of the United Nations, if it is a party to a dispute under consideration by the Security Council, shall be invited to participate, without vote, in the discussion relating to the dispute.

The Security Council shall lay down such conditions as it deems just for the participation of a state which is not a Member of the United Nations.

Chapter VI. Pacific Settlement of Disputes

Article 33

1. The parties to any dispute, the continuance of which is likely to endanger the maintenance of international peace and security, shall, first of all, seek a solution by negotiation, enquiry, mediation, conciliation, arbitration, judicial settlement, resort to regional agencies or arrangements, or other peaceful means of their own choice.

2. The Security Council shall, when it deems necessary, call upon the parties to settle their dispute by such means.

Article 34

The Security Council may investigate any dispute, or any situation which might lead to international friction or give rise to a dispute, in order to determine whether the continuance of the dispute or situation is likely to endanger the maintenance of international peace and security.

Article 35

1. Any Member of the United Nations may bring any dispute, or any situation of the nature referred to in Article 34, to the attention of the Security Council or of the General Assembly.

2. A state which is not a Member of the United Nations may bring to the attention of the Security Council or of the General Assembly any dispute to which it is a party if it accepts in advance, for the purposes of the dispute, the obligations of pacific settlement provided in the present Charter.

3. The proceedings of the General Assembly in respect of matters brought to its attention under this Article will be subject to the provisions of Articles 11 and 12.

Article 36

1. The Security Council may, at any stage of a dispute of the nature referred to in Article 33 or of a situation of like nature, recommend appropriate procedures or methods of adjustment.

2. The Security Council should take into consideration any procedures for the settlement of the dispute which have already been adopted by the parties.

3. In making recommendations under this Article the Security Council should also take into consideration that legal disputes should as a general rule be referred by the parties to the International Court of Justice in accordance with the provisions of the Statute of the Court.

Article 37

1. Should the parties to a dispute of the nature referred to in Article 33 fail to settle it by the means indicated in that Article, they shall refer it to the Security Council.

2. If the Security Council deems that the continuance of the dispute is in fact likely to endanger the maintenance of international peace and security, it shall decide whether to take action under Article 36 or to recommend such terms of settlement as it may consider appropriate.

Article 38

Without prejudice to the provisions of Articles 33 to 37, the Security Council may, if all the parties to any dispute so request, make recommendations to the parties with a view to a pacific settlement of the dispute.

Chapter VII. Action with Respect to Threats to the Peace, Breaches of the Peace, and Acts of Aggression

Article 39

The Security Council shall determine the existence of any threat to the peace, breach of the peace, or act of aggression and shall make recommendations, or decide what measures shall be taken in accordance with Articles 41 and 42, to maintain or restore international peace and security.

Article 40

In order to prevent an aggravation of the situation, the Security Council may, before making the recommendations or deciding upon the measures provided for in Article 39, call upon the parties concerned to comply with such provisional measures as it deems necessary or desirable. Such provisional measures shall be without prejudice to the rights, claims, or position of the parties concerned. The Security Council shall duly take account of failure to comply with such provisional measures.

Article 41

The Security Council may decide what measures not involving the use of armed force are to be employed to give effect to its decisions, and it may call upon the Members of the United Nations to apply such measures. These may include complete or partial interruption of economic relations and of rail, sea, air, postal, telegraphic, radio, and other means of communication, and the severance of diplomatic relations.

Article 42

Should the Security Council consider that measures provided for in Article 41 would be inadequate or have proved to be inadequate, it may take such action by air, sea, or land forces as may be necessary to maintain or restore international peace and security. Such action may include demonstrations, blockade, and other operations by air, sea, or land forces of Members of the United Nations.

used force

Article 43

1. All Members of the United Nations, in order to contribute to the maintenance of international peace and security, undertake to make available to the Security Council, on its call and in accordance with a special agreement or agreements, armed forces, assistance, and facilities, including rights of passage, necessary for the purpose of maintaining international peace and security.

2. Such agreement or agreements shall govern the numbers and types of forces, their degree of readiness and general location, and the nature of the facilities and assistance to be provided.

3. The agreement or agreements shall be negotiated as soon as possible on the initiative of the Security Council. They shall be concluded between the Security Council and Members or between the Security Council and groups of Members and shall be subject to ratification by the signatory states in accordance with their respective constitutional processes.

Article 44

When the Security Council has decided to use force it shall, before calling upon a Member not represented on it to provide armed forces in fulfillment of the obligations assumed under Article 43, invite that Member, if the Member so desires, to participate in the decisions of the Security Council concerning the employment of contingents of that Member's armed forces.

Article 45

In order to enable the United Nations to take urgent military measures, Members shall hold immediately available national air-force contingents for combined international enforcement action. The strength and degree of readiness of these contingents and plans for their combined action shall be determined, within the limits laid down in the special agreement or agreements referred to in Article 43, by the Security Council with the assistance of the Military Staff Committee.

Article 46

Plans for the application of armed force shall be made by the Security Council with the assistance of the Military Staff Committee.

Article 47

1. There shall be established a Military Staff Committee to advise and assist the Security Council on all questions relating to the Security Council's

military requirements for the maintenance of international peace and security, the employment and command of forces placed at its disposal, the regulation of armaments, and possible disarmament.

2. The Military Staff Committee shall consist of the Chiefs of Staff of the permanent members of the Security Council or their representatives. Any Member of the United Nations not permanently represented on the Committee shall be invited by the Committee to be associated with it when the efficient discharge of the Committee's responsibilities requires the participation of that Member in its work.

3. The Military Staff Committee shall be responsible under the Security Council for the strategic direction of any armed forces placed at the disposal of the Security Council. Questions relating to the command of such forces shall be worked out subsequently.

4. The Military Staff Committee, with the authorization of the Security Council and after consultation with appropriate regional agencies, may establish regional subcommittees.

Article 48

1. The action required to carry out the decisions of the Security Council for the maintenance of international peace and security shall be taken by all the Members of the United Nations or by some of them, as the Security Council may determine.

2. Such decisions shall be carried out by the Members of the United Nations directly and through their action in the appropriate international agencies of which they are members.

Article 49

The Members of the United Nations shall join in affording mutual assistance in carrying out the measures decided upon by the Security Council.

Article 50

If preventive or enforcement measures against any state are taken by the Security Council, any other state, whether a Member of the United Nations or not, which finds itself confronted with special economic problems arising from the carrying out of those measures shall have the right to consult the Security Council with regard to a solution of those problems.

Article 51

Nothing in the present Charter shall impair the inherent right of individual or collective self-defense if an armed attack occurs against a Member of the United Nations, until the Security Council has taken the measures necessary to maintain international peace and security. Measures taken by Members in the exercise of this right of self-defense shall be

13

immediately reported to the Security Council and shall not in any way affect the authority and responsibility of the Security Council under the present Charter to take at any time such action as it deems necessary in order to maintain or restore international peace and security.

Chapter VIII.   Regional Arrangements

Article 52

1. Nothing in the present Charter precludes the existence of regional arrangements or agencies for dealing with such matters relating to the maintenance of international peace and security as are appropriate for regional action, provided that such arrangements or agencies and their activities arc consistent with the Purposes and Principles of the United Nations.

2. The Members of the United Nations entering into such arrangements or constituting such agencies shall make every effort to achieve pacific settlement of local disputes through such regional arrangements or by such regional agencies before referring them to the Security Council.

3. The Security Council shall encourage the development of pacific settlement of local disputes through such regional arrangements or by such regional agencies either on the initiative of the states concerned or by reference from the Security Council.

4. This Article in no way impairs the application of Articles 34 and 35.

Article 53

1. The Security Council shall, where appropriate, utilize such regional arrangements or agencies for enforcement action under its authority. But no enforcement action shall be taken under regional arrangements or by regional agencies without the authorization of the Security Council, with the exception of measures against any enemy state, as defined in paragraph 2 of this Article, provided for pursuant to Article 107 or in regional arrangements directed against renewal of aggressive policy on the part of any such state, until such time as the Organization may, on request of the Governments concerned, be charged with the responsibility for preventing further aggression by such a state.

2. The term enemy state as used in paragraph 1 of this Article applies to any state which during the Second World War has been an enemy of any signatory of the present Charter.

Article 54

The Security Council shall at all times be kept fully informed of activities undertaken or in contemplation under regional arrangements or by regional agencies for the maintenance of international peace and security.

Chapter IX. International Economic and Social Cooperation

Article 55

With a view to the creation of conditions of stability and well-being which are necessary for peaceful and friendly relations among nations based on respect for the principle of equal rights and self-determination of peoples, the United Nations shall promote:

a. higher standards of living, full employment, and conditions of economic and social progress and development;

b. solutions of international economic, social, health, and related problems; and international cultural and educational cooperation; and

c. universal respect for, and observance of, human rights and fundamental freedoms for all without distinction as to race, sex, language, or religion.

Article 56

UN can articulate HR prin statement obligations to give effect

All Members pledge themselves to take joint and separate action in cooperation with the Organization for the achievement of the purposes set forth in Article 55.

Article 57

1. The various specialized agencies, established by intergovernmental agreement and having wide international responsibilities, as defined in their basic instruments, in economic, social, cultural, educational, health, and related fields, shall be brought into relationship with the United Nations in accordance with the provisions of Article 63.

2. Such agencies thus brought into relationship with the United Nations are hereinafter referred to as specialized agencies.

Article 58

The Organization shall make recommendations for the coordination of the policies and activities of the specialized agencies.

Article 59

The Organization shall, where appropriate, initiate negotiations among the states concerned for the creation of any new specialized agencies required for the accomplishment of the purposes set forth in Article 55.

Article 60

Responsibility for the discharge of the functions of the Organization set forth in this Chapter shall be vested in the General Assembly and, under the authority of the General Assembly, in the Economic and Social Council, which shall have for this purpose the powers set forth in Chapter X.

Chapter X.   The Economic and Social Council

Composition

Article 61

1. The Economic and Social Council shall consist of fifty-four Members of the United Nations elected by the General Assembly.

2. Subject to the provisions of paragraph 3, eighteen members of the Economic and Social Council shall be elected each year for a term of three years. A retiring member shall be eligible for immediate re-election.

3. At the first election after the increase in the membership of the Economic and Social Council from twenty-seven to fifty-four members, in addition to the members elected in place of the nine members whose term of office expires at the end of that year, twenty-seven additional members shall be elected. Of these twenty-seven additional members, the term of office of nine members so elected shall expire at the end of one year, and of nine other members at the end of two years, in accordance with arrangements made by the General Assembly.

4. Each member of the Economic and Social Council shall have one representative.

Functions and Powers

Article 62

1. The Economic and Social Council may make or initiate studies and reports with respect to international economic, social, cultural, educational, health, and related matters and may make recommendations with respect to any such matters to the General Assembly, to the Members of the United Nations, and to the specialized agencies concerned.

2. It may make recommendations for the purpose of promoting respect for, and observance of, human rights and fundamental freedoms for all.

3. It may prepare draft conventions for submission to the General Assembly, with respect to matters falling within its competence.

4. It may call, in accordance with the rules prescribed by the United Nations, international conferences on matters falling within its competence.

Article 63

1. The Economic and Social Council may enter into agreements with any of the agencies referred to in Article 57, defining the terms on which the agency concerned shall be brought into relationship with the United Nations. Such agreements shall be subject to approval by the General Assembly.

2. It may coordinate the activities of the specialized agencies through consultation with and recommendations to such agencies and through

recommendations to the General Assembly and to the Members of the United Nations.

Article 64

1. The Economic and Social Council may take appropriate steps to obtain regular reports from the specialized agencies. It may make arrangements with the Members of the United Nations and with the specialized agencies to obtain reports on the steps taken to give effect to its own recommendations and to recommendations on matters falling within its competence made by the General Assembly.

2. It may communicate its observations on these reports to the General Assembly.

Article 65

The Economic and Social Council may furnish information to the Security Council and shall assist the Security Council upon its request.

Article 66

1. The Economic and Social Council shall perform such functions as fall within its competence in connection with the carrying out of the recommendations of the General Assembly.

2. It may, with the approval of the General Assembly, perform services at the request of Members of the United Nations and at the request of specialized agencies.

3. It shall perform such other functions as are specified elsewhere in the present Charter or as may be assigned to it by the General Assembly.

Voting

Article 67

1. Each member of the Economic and Social Council shall have one vote.

2. Decisions of the Economic and Social Council shall be made by a majority of the members present and voting.

Procedure

Article 68

The Economic and Social Council shall set up commissions in economic and social fields and for the promotion of human rights, and such other commissions as may be required for the performance of its functions.

Article 69

The Economic and Social Council shall invite any Member of the United Nations to participate, without vote, in its deliberations on any matter of particular concern to that Member.

Article 70

The Economic and Social Council may make arrangements for representatives of the specialized agencies to participate, without vote, in its deliberations and in those of the commissions established by it, and for its representatives to participate in the deliberations of the specialized agencies.

Article 71

The Economic and Social Council may make suitable arrangements for consultation with nongovernmental organizations which are concerned with matters within its competence. Such arrangements may be made with international organizations and, where appropriate, with national organizations after consultation with the Member of the United Nations concerned.

Article 72

1. The Economic and Social Council shall adopt its own rules of procedure, including the method of selecting its President.

2. The Economic and Social Council shall meet as required in accordance with its rules, which shall include provision for the convening of meetings on the request of a majority of its members.

Chapter XI.   Declaration Regarding Non-Self-Governing Territories

Article 73

Members of the United Nations which have or assume responsibilities for the administration of territories whose peoples have not yet attained a full measure of self-government recognize the principle that the interests of the inhabitants of these territories are paramount, and accept as a sacred trust the obligation to promote to the utmost, within the system of international peace and security established by the present Charter, the well-being of the inhabitants of these territories, and, to this end:

a. to ensure, with due respect for the culture of the peoples concerned, their political, economic, social, and educational advancement, their just treatment, and their protection against abuses;

b. to develop self-government, to take due account of the political aspirations of the peoples, and to assist them in the progressive development of their free political institutions, according to the particular circumstances of each territory and its peoples and their varying stages of advancement;

c. to further international peace and security;

d. to promote constructive measures of development, to encourage research, and to cooperate with one another and, when and where appropriate, with specialized international bodies with a view to the practical achievement of the social, economic, and scientific purposes set forth in this Article; and

e. to transmit regularly to the Secretary-General for information purposes, subject to such limitation as security and constitutional considerations may require, statistical and other information of a technical nature relating to economic, social, and educational conditions in the territories for which they are respectively responsible other than those territories to which Chapters XII and XIII apply.

Article 74

Members of the United Nations also agree that their policy in respect of the territories to which this Chapter applies, no less than in respect of their metropolitan areas, must be based on the general principle of good-neighborliness, due account being taken of the interests and well-being of the rest of the world, in social, economic, and commercial matters.

Chapter XII.   International Trusteeship System

Article 75

The United Nations shall establish under its authority an international trusteeship system for the administration and supervision of such territories as may be placed thereunder by subsequent individual agreements. These territories are hereinafter referred to as trust territories.

Article 76

The basic objectives of the trusteeship system, in accordance with the Purposes of the United Nations laid down in Article 1 of the present Charter, shall be:

a. to further international peace and security;

b. to promote the political, economic, social, and educational advancement of the inhabitants of the trust territories, and their progressive development towards self-government or independence as may be appropriate to the particular circumstances of each territory and its peoples and the freely expressed wishes of the peoples concerned, and as may be provided by the terms of each trusteeship agreement;

c. to encourage respect for human rights and for fundamental freedoms for all without distinction as to race, sex, language, or religion, and to encourage recognition of the interdependence of the peoples of the world; and

d. to ensure equal treatment in social, economic, and commercial matters for all Members of the United Nations and their nationals, and also equal treatment for the latter in the administration of justice, without prejudice to the attainment of the foregoing objectives and subject to the provisions of Article 80.

Article 77

1. The trusteeship system shall apply to such territories in the following categories as may be placed thereunder by means of trusteeship agreements:
    a. territories now held under mandate;
    b. territories which may be detached from enemy states as a result of the Second World War; and
    c. territories voluntarily placed under the system by states responsible for their administration.
2. It will be a matter for subsequent agreement as to which territories in the foregoing categories will be brought under the trusteeship system and upon what terms.

Article 78

The trusteeship system shall not apply to territories which have become Members of the United Nations, relationship among which shall be based on respect for the principle of sovereign equality.

Article 79

The terms of trusteeship for each territory to be placed under the trusteeship system, including any alteration or amendment, shall be agreed upon by the states directly concerned, including the mandatory power in the case of territories held under mandate by a Member of the United Nations, and shall be approved as provided for in Articles 83 and 85.

Article 80

1. Except as may be agreed upon in individual trusteeship agreements, made under Articles 77, 79, and 81, placing each territory under the trusteeship system, and until such agreements have been concluded, nothing in this Chapter shall be construed in or of itself to alter in any manner the rights whatsoever of any states or any peoples or the terms of existing international instruments to which Members of the United Nations may respectively be parties.
2. Paragraph 1 of this Article shall not be interpreted as giving grounds for delay or postponement of the negotiation and conclusion of agreements for placing mandated and other territories under the trusteeship system as provided for in Article 77.

Article 81

The trusteeship agreement shall in each case include the terms under which the trust territory will be administered and designate the authority which will exercise the administration of the trust territory. Such authority, hereinafter called the administering authority, may be one or more states or the Organization itself.

Article 82

There may be designated, in any trusteeship agreement, a strategic area or areas which may include part or all of the trust territory to which the agreement applies, without prejudice to any special agreement or agreements made under Article 43.

Article 83

1. All functions of the United Nations relating to strategic areas, including the approval of the terms of the trusteeship agreements and of their alteration or amendment, shall be exercised by the Security Council.

2. The basic objectives set forth in Article 76 shall be applicable to the people of each strategic area.

3. The Security Council shall, subject to the provisions of the trusteeship agreements and without prejudice to security considerations, avail itself of the assistance of the Trusteeship Council to perform those functions of the United Nations under the trusteeship system relating to political, economic, social, and educational matters in the strategic areas.

Article 84

It shall be the duty of the administering authority to ensure that the trust territory shall play its part in the maintenance of international peace and security. To this end the administering authority may make use of volunteer forces, facilities, and assistance from the trust territory in carrying out the obligations towards the Security Council undertaken in this regard by the administering authority, as well as for local defense and the maintenance of law and order within the trust territory.

Article 85

1. The functions of the United Nations with regard to trusteeship agreements for all areas not designated as strategic, including the approval of the terms of the trusteeship agreements and of their alteration or amendment, shall be exercised by the General Assembly.

2. The Trusteeship Council, operating under the authority of the General Assembly, shall assist the General Assembly in carrying out these functions.

Chapter XIII.   The Trusteeship Council

Composition

Article 86

1. The Trusteeship Council shall consist of the following Members of the United Nations:

a. those Members administering trust territories;

b. such of those Members mentioned by name in Article 23 as are not administering trust territories; and

c. as many other Members elected for three-year terms by the General Assembly as may be necessary to ensure that the total number of members of the Trusteeship Council is equally divided between those Members of the United Nations which administer trust territories and those which do not.

2. Each member of the Trusteeship Council shall designate one specially qualified person to represent it therein.

Functions and Powers

Article 87

The General Assembly and, under its authority, the Trusteeship Council, in carrying out their functions, may:

a. consider reports submitted by the administering authority;

b. accept petitions and examine them in consultation with the administering authority;

c. provide for periodic visits to the respective trust territories at times agreed upon with the administering authority; and

d. take these and other actions in conformity with the terms of the trusteeship agreements.

Article 88

The Trusteeship Council shall formulate a questionnaire on the political, economic, social, and educational advancement of the inhabitants of each trust territory, and the administering authority for each trust territory within the competence of the General Assembly shall make an annual report to the General Assembly upon the basis of such questionnaire.

Voting

Article 89

1. Each member of the Trusteeship Council shall have one vote.

2. Decisions of the Trusteeship Council shall be made by a majority of the members present and voting.

Procedure

Article 90

1. The Trusteeship Council shall adopt its own rules of procedure, including the method of selecting its President.

2. The Trusteeship Council shall meet as required in accordance with its rules, which shall include provision for the convening of meetings on the request of a majority of its members.

Article 91

The Trusteeship Council shall, when appropriate, avail itself of the assistance of the Economic and Social Council and of the specialized agencies in regard to matters with which they are respectively concerned.

Chapter XIV.   The International Court of Justice

Article 92

The International Court of Justice shall be the principal judicial organ of the United Nations. It shall function in accordance with the annexed Statute, which is based upon the Statute of the Permanent Court of International Justice and forms an integral part of the present Charter.

Article 93

1. All Members of the United Nations are *ipso facto* parties to the Statute of the International Court of Justice.

2. A state which is not a Member of the United Nations may become a party to the Statute of the International Court of Justice on conditions to be determined in each case by the General Assembly upon the recommendation of the Security Council.

Article 94

1. Each Member of the United Nations undertakes to comply with the decision of the International Court of Justice in any case to which it is a party.

2. If any party to a case fails to perform the obligations incumbent upon it under a judgment rendered by the Court, the other party may have recourse to the Security Council, which may, if it deems necessary, make recommendations or decide upon measures to be taken to give effect to the judgment.

Article 95

Nothing in the present Charter shall prevent Members of the United Nations from entrusting the solution of their differences to other tribunals by virtue of agreements already in existence or which may be concluded in the future.

Article 96

1. The General Assembly or the Security Council may request the International Court of Justice to give an advisory opinion on any legal question.

2. Other organs of the United Nations and specialized agencies, which may at any time be so authorized by the General Assembly, may also request advisory opinions of the Court on legal questions arising within the scope of their activities.

Chapter XV.   The Secretariat

Article 97

The Secretariat shall comprise a Secretary-General and such staff as the Organization may require. The Secretary-General shall be appointed by the General Assembly upon the recommendation of the Security Council. He shall be the chief administrative officer of the Organization.

Article 98

The Secretary-General shall act in that capacity in all meetings of the General Assembly, of the Security Council, of the Economic and Social Council, and of the Trusteeship Council, and shall perform such other functions as are entrusted to him by these organs. The Secretary-General shall make an annual report to the General Assembly on the work of the Organization.

Article 99

The Secretary-General may bring to the attention of the Security Council any matter which in his opinion may threaten the maintenance of international peace and security.

Article 100

1. In the performance of their duties the Secretary-General and the staff shall not seek or receive instructions from any government or from any other authority external to the Organization. They shall refrain from any action which might reflect on their position as international officials responsible only to the Organization.

2. Each Member of the United Nations undertakes to respect the exclusively international character of the responsibilities of the Secretary-General and the staff and not to seek to influence them in the discharge of their responsibilities.

Article 101

1. The staff shall be appointed by the Secretary-General under regulations established by the General Assembly.

2. Appropriate staffs shall be permanently assigned to the Economic and Social Council, the Trusteeship Council, and, as required, to other organs of the United Nations. These staffs shall form a part of the Secretariat.

3. The paramount consideration in the employment of the staff and in the determination of the conditions of service shall be the necessity of securing the highest standards of efficiency, competence, and integrity. Due regard shall be paid to the importance of recruiting the staff on as wide a geographical basis as possible.

Chapter XVI.   Miscellaneous Provisions

Article 102

1. Every treaty and every international agreement entered into by any Member of the United Nations after the present Charter comes into force shall as soon as possible be registered with the Secretariat and published by it.

2. No party to any such treaty or international agreement which has not been registered in accordance with the provisions of paragraph 1 of this Article may invoke that treaty or agreement before any organ of the United Nations.

Article 103

In the event of a conflict between the obligations of the Members of the United Nations under the present Charter and their obligations under any other international agreement, their obligations under the present Charter shall prevail.

Article 104

The Organization shall enjoy in the territory of each of its Members such legal capacity as may be necessary for the exercise of its functions and the fulfillment of its purposes.

Article 105

1. The Organization shall enjoy in the territory of each of its Members such privileges and immunities as are necessary for the fulfillment of its purposes.

2. Representatives of the Members of the United Nations and officials of the Organization shall similarly enjoy such privileges and immunities as are necessary for the independent exercise of their functions in connection with the Organization.

3. The General Assembly may make recommendations with a view to determining the details of the application of paragraphs 1 and 2 of this Article or may propose conventions to the Members of the United Nations for this purpose.

Chapter XVII.   Transitional Security Arrangements

Article 106

Pending the coming into force of such special agreements referred to in Article 43 as in the opinion of the Security Council enable it to begin the exercise of its responsibilities under Article 42, the parties to the Four-Nation Declaration, signed at Moscow, October 30, 1943, and France, shall, in accordance with the provisions of paragraph 5 of that Declaration, consult with one another and as occasion requires with other Members of the United Nations with a view to such joint action on behalf of the Organization as may be necessary for the purpose of maintaining international peace and security.

Article 107

Nothing in the present Charter shall invalidate or preclude action, in relation to any state which during the Second World War has been an enemy of any signatory to the present Charter, taken or authorized as a result of that war by the Governments having responsibility for such action.

Chapter XVIII.   Amendments

Article 108

Amendments to the present Charter shall come into force for all Members of the United Nations when they have been adopted by a vote of two thirds of the members of the General Assembly and ratified in accordance with their respective constitutional processes by two thirds of the Members of the United Nations, including all the permanent members of the Security Council.

Article 109

1. A General Conference of the Members of the United Nations for the purpose of reviewing the present Charter may be held at a date and place to be fixed by a two-thirds vote of the members of the General Assembly and by a vote of any nine members of the Security Council. Each Member of the United Nations shall have one vote in the conference.

2. Any alteration of the present Charter recommended by a two-thirds vote of the conference shall take effect when ratified in accordance with their respective constitutional processes by two thirds of the Members of the United Nations including all the permanent members of the Security Council.

3. If such a conference has not been held before the tenth annual session of the General Assembly following the coming into force of the present Charter, the proposal to call such a conference shall be placed on the agenda of that session of the General Assembly, and the conference shall be held if so decided by a majority vote of the members of the General Assembly and by a vote of any seven members of the Security Council.

Chapter XIX.   Ratification and Signature

Article 110

1. The present Charter shall be ratified by the signatory states in accordance with their respective constitutional processes.

2. The ratifications shall he deposited with the Government of the United States of America, which shall notify all the signatory states of each deposit as well as the Secretary-General of the Organization when he has been appointed.

3. The present Charter shall come into force upon the deposit of ratifications by the Republic of China, France, the Union of Soviet Socialist Republics, the United Kingdom of Great Britain and Northern Ireland, and the United States of America, and by a majority of the other signatory states. A protocol of the ratifications deposited shall thereupon be drawn up by the Government of the United States of America which shall communicate copies thereof to all the signatory states.

4. The states signatory to the present Charter which ratify it after it has come into force will become original Members of the United Nations on the date of the deposit of their respective ratifications.

Article 111

The present Charter, of which the Chinese, French, Russian, English, and Spanish texts are equally authentic, shall remain deposited in the archives of the Government of the United States of America. Duly certified copies thereof shall be transmitted by that Government to the Governments of the other signatory states.

In faith whereof the representatives of the Governments of the United Nations have signed the present Charter.

Done at the city of San Francisco the twenty-sixth day of June, one thousand nine hundred and forty-five.

STATUTE OF THE INTERNATIONAL COURT OF JUSTICE

June 26, 1945, 59 Stat. 1055, T.S. No. 993, 3 Bevans 1179*

Article 1

The International Court of Justice established by the Charter of the United Nations as the principal judicial organ of the United Nations shall be constituted and shall function in accordance with the provisions of the present Statute.

Chapter I.   Organization of the Court

Article 2

The Court shall be composed of a body of independent judges, elected regardless of their nationality from among persons of high moral character, who possess the qualifications required in their respective countries for appointment to the highest judicial offices, or are jurisconsults of recognized competence in international law.

Article 3

1. The Court shall consist of fifteen members, no two of whom may be nationals of the same state.

2. A person who for the purposes of membership in the Court could be regarded as a national of more than one state shall be deemed to be a national of the one in which he ordinarily exercises civil and political rights.

Article 4

1. The members of the Court shall be elected by the General Assembly and by the Security Council from a list of persons nominated by the national

---

*All Member States of the United Nations are automatically parties to the Statute (U.N. Charter, Art. 93).

groups in the Permanent Court of Arbitration, in accordance with the following provisions.

2. In the case of Members of the United Nations not represented in the Permanent Court of Arbitration, candidates shall be nominated by national groups appointed for this purpose by their governments under the same conditions as those prescribed for members of the Permanent Court of Arbitration by Article 44 of the Convention of The Hague of 1907 for the pacific settlement of international disputes.

3. The conditions under which a state which is a party to the present Statute but is not a Member of the United Nations may participate in electing the members of the Court shall, in the absence of a special agreement, be laid down by the General Assembly upon recommendation of the Security Council.

Article 5

1. At least three months before the date of the election, the Secretary-General of the United Nations shall address a written request to the members of the Permanent Court of Arbitration belonging to the states which are parties to the present Statute, and to the members of the national groups appointed under Article 4, paragraph 2, inviting them to undertake, within a given time, by national groups, the nomination of persons in a position to accept the duties of a member of the Court.

2. No group may nominate more than four persons, not more than two of whom shall be of their own nationality. In no case may the number of candidates nominated by a group be more than double the number of seats to be filled.

Article 6

Before making these nominations, each national group is recommended to consult its highest court of justice, its legal faculties and schools of law, and its national academies and national sections of international academies devoted to the study of law.

Article 7

1. The Secretary-General shall prepare a list in alphabetical order of all the persons thus nominated. Save as provided in Article 12, paragraph 2, these shall be the only persons eligible.

2. The Secretary-General shall submit this list to the General Assembly and to the Security Council.

Article 8

The General Assembly and the Security Council shall proceed independently of one another to elect the members of the Court.

Article 9

At every election, the electors shall bear in mind not only that the persons to be elected should individually possess the qualifications required, but also that in the body as a whole the representation of the main forms of civilization and of the principal legal systems of the world should be assured.

Article 10

1. Those candidates who obtain an absolute majority of votes in the General Assembly and in the Security Council shall be considered as elected.

2. Any vote of the Security Council, whether for the election of judges or for the appointment of members of the conference envisaged in Article 12, shall be taken without any distinction between permanent and non-permanent members of the Security Council.

3. In the event of more than one national of the same state obtaining an absolute majority of the votes both of the General Assembly and of the Security Council, the eldest of these only shall be considered as elected.

Article 11

If, after the first meeting held for the purpose of the election, one or more seats remain to be filled, a second and, if necessary, a third meeting shall take place.

Article 12

1. If, after the third meeting, one or more seats still remain unfilled, a joint conference consisting of six members, three appointed by the General Assembly and three by the Security Council, may be formed at any time at the request of either the General Assembly or the Security Council, for the purpose of choosing by the vote of an absolute majority one name for each seat still vacant, to submit to the General Assembly and the Security Council for their respective acceptance.

2. If the joint conference is unanimously agreed upon any person who fulfils the required conditions, he may be included in its list, even though he was not included in the list of nominations referred to in Article 7.

3. If the joint conference is satisfied that it will not be successful in procuring an election, those members of the Court who have already been elected shall, within a period to be fixed by the Security Council, proceed to fill the vacant seats by selection from among those candidates who have obtained votes either in the General Assembly or in the Security Council.

4. In the event of an equality of votes among the judges, the eldest judge shall have a casting vote.

Article 13

1. The members of the Court shall be elected for nine years and may be reelected; provided, however, that of the judges elected at the first election, the terms of five judges shall expire at the end of three years and the terms of five more judges shall expire at the end of six years.

2. The judges whose terms are to expire at the end of the above-mentioned initial periods of three and six years shall be chosen by lot to be drawn by the Secretary-General immediately after the first election has been completed.

3. The members of the Court shall continue to discharge their duties until their places have been filled. Though replaced, they shall finish any cases which they may have begun.

4. In the case of the resignation of a member of the Court, the resignation shall be addressed to the President of the Court for transmission to the Secretary-General. This last notification makes the place vacant.

Article 14

Vacancies shall be filled by the same method as that laid down for the first election, subject to the following provision: the Secretary-General shall, within one month of the occurrence of the vacancy, proceed to issue the invitations provided for in Article 5, and the date of the election shall be fixed by the Security Council.

Article 15

A member of the Court elected to replace a member whose term of office has not expired shall hold office for the remainder of his predecessor's term.

Article 16

1. No member of the Court may exercise any political or administrative function, or engage in any other occupation of a professional nature.

2. Any doubt on this point shall be settled by the decision of the Court.

Article 17

1. No member of the Court may act as agent, counsel, or advocate in any case.

2. No member may participate in the decision of any case in which he has previously taken part as agent, counsel, or advocate for one of the parties, or as a member of a national or international court, or of a commission of enquiry, or in any other capacity.

3. Any doubt on this point shall be settled by the decision of the Court.

Article 18

1. No member of the Court can be dismissed unless, in the unanimous opinion of the other members, he has ceased to fulfill the required conditions.

2. Formal notification thereof shall be made to the Secretary-General by the Registrar.

3. This notification makes the place vacant.

Article 19

The members of the Court, when engaged on the business of the Court, shall enjoy diplomatic privileges and immunities.

Article 20

Every member of the Court shall, before taking up his duties, make a solemn declaration in open court that he will exercise his powers impartially and conscientiously.

Article 21

1. The Court shall elect its President and Vice-President for three years; they may be re-elected.

2. The Court shall appoint its Registrar and may provide for the appointment of such other officers as may be necessary.

Article 22

1. The seat of the Court shall be established at The Hague. This, however, shall not prevent the Court from sitting and exercising its functions elsewhere whenever the Court considers it desirable.

2. The President and the Registrar shall reside at the seat of the Court.

Article 23

1. The Court shall remain permanently in session, except during the judicial vacations, the dates and duration of which shall be fixed by the Court.

2. Members of the Court are entitled to periodic leave, the dates and duration of which shall be fixed by the Court, having in mind the distance between The Hague and the home of each judge.

3. Members of the Court shall be bound, unless they are on leave or prevented from attending by illness or other serious reasons duly explained to the President, to hold themselves permanently at the disposal of the Court.

Article 24

1. If, for some special reason, a member of the Court considers that he should not take part in the decision of a particular case, he shall so inform the President.

2. If the President considers that for some special reason one of the members of the Court should not sit in a particular case, he shall give him notice accordingly.

3. If in any such case the member of the Court and the President disagree, the matter shall be settled by the decision of the Court.

Article 25

1. The full Court shall sit except when it is expressly provided otherwise in the present Statute.

2. Subject to the condition that the number of judges available to constitute the Court is not thereby reduced below eleven, the Rules of the Court may provide for allowing one or more judges, according to circumstances and in rotation, to be dispensed from sitting.

3. A quorum of nine judges shall suffice to constitute the Court.

Article 26

1. The Court may from time to time form one or more chambers, composed of three or more judges as the Court may determine, for dealing with particular categories of cases; for example, labor cases and cases relating to transit and communications.

2. The Court may at any time form a chamber for dealing with a particular case. The number of judges to constitute such a chamber shall be determined by the Court with the approval of the parties.

3. Cases shall be heard and determined by the chambers provided for in this Article if the parties so request.

Article 27

A judgment given by any of the chambers provided for in Articles 26 and 29 shall be considered as rendered by the Court.

Article 28

The chambers provided for in Articles 26 and 29 may, with the consent of the parties, sit and exercise their functions elsewhere than at The Hague.

Article 29

With a view to the speedy dispatch of business, the Court shall form annually a chamber composed of five judges which, at the request of the parties, may hear and determine cases by summary procedure. In addition, two judges shall be selected for the purpose of replacing judges who find it impossible to sit.

Article 30

1. The Court shall frame rules for carrying out its functions. In particular, it shall lay down rules of procedure.

2. The Rules of the Court may provide for assessors to sit with the Court or with any of its chambers, without the right to vote.

Article 31

1. Judges of the nationality of each of the parties shall retain their right to sit in the case before the Court.

2. If the Court includes upon the Bench a judge of the nationality of one of the parties, any other party may choose a person to sit as judge. Such person shall be chosen preferably from among those persons who have been nominated as candidates as provided in Articles 4 and 5.

3. If the Court includes upon the Bench no judge of the nationality of the parties, each of these parties may proceed to choose a judge as provided in paragraph 2 of this Article.

4. The provisions of this Article shall apply to the case of Articles 26 and 29. In such cases, the President shall request one or, if necessary, two of the members of the Court forming the chamber to give place to the members of the Court of the nationality of the parties concerned, and, failing such, or if they are unable to be present, to the judges specially chosen by the parties.

5. Should there be several parties in the same interest, they shall, for the purpose of the preceding provisions, be reckoned as one party only. Any doubt upon this point shall be settled by the decision of the Court.

6. Judges chosen as laid down in paragraphs 2, 3, and 4 of this Article shall fulfill the conditions required by Articles 2, 17 (paragraph 2), 20, and 24 of the present Statute. They shall take part in the decision on terms of complete equality with their colleagues.

Article 32

1. Each member of the Court shall receive an annual salary.

2. The President shall receive a special annual allowance.

3. The Vice-President shall receive a special allowance for every day on which he acts as President.

4. The judges chosen under Article 31, other than members of the Court, shall receive compensation for each day on which they exercise their functions.

5. These salaries, allowances, and compensation shall be fixed by the General Assembly. They may not be decreased during the term of office.

6. The salary of the Registrar shall be fixed by the General Assembly on the proposal of the Court.

7. Regulations made by the General Assembly shall fix the conditions under which retirement pensions may be given to members of the Court and to the Registrar, and the conditions under which members of the Court and the Registrar shall have their traveling expenses refunded.

8. The above salaries, allowances, and compensation shall be free of all taxation.

Article 33

The expenses of the Court shall be borne by the United Nations in such a manner as shall be decided by the General Assembly.

Chapter II.   Competence of the Court

Article 34

1. Only states may be parties in cases before the Court.

2. The Court, subject to and in conformity with its Rules, may request of public international organizations information relevant to cases before it, and shall receive such information presented by such organizations on their own initiative.

3. Whenever the construction of the constituent instrument of a public international organization or of an international convention adopted thereunder is in question in a case before the Court, the Registrar shall so notify the public international organization concerned and shall communicate to it copies of all the written proceedings.

Article 35

1. The Court shall be open to the states parties to the present Statute.

2. The conditions under which the Court shall be open to other states shall, subject to the special provisions contained in treaties in force, be laid down by the Security Council, but in no case shall such conditions place the parties in a position of inequality before the Court.

3. When a state which is not a Member of the United Nations is a party to a case, the Court shall fix the amount which that party is to contribute towards the expenses of the Court. This provision shall not apply if such state is bearing a share of the expenses of the Court.

Article 36

1. The jurisdiction of the Court comprises all cases which the parties refer to it and all matters specially provided for in the Charter of the United Nations or in treaties and conventions in force.

2. The states parties to the present Statute may at any time declare that they recognize as compulsory *ipso facto* and without special agreement, in relation to any other state accepting the same obligation, the jurisdiction of the Court in all legal disputes concerning:

    a. the interpretation of a treaty;

    b. any question of international law;

    c. the existence of any fact which, if established, would constitute a breach of an international obligation;

    d. the nature or extent of the reparation to be made for the breach of an international obligation.

3. The declarations referred to above may be made unconditionally or on condition of reciprocity on the part of several or certain states, or for a certain time.

4. Such declarations shall be deposited with the Secretary-General of the United Nations, who shall transmit copies thereof to the parties to the Statute and to the Registrar of the Court.

5. Declarations made under Article 36 of the Statute of the Permanent Court of International Justice and which are still in force shall be deemed, as between the parties to the present Statute, to be acceptances of the compulsory jurisdiction of the International Court of Justice for the period which they still have to run and in accordance with their terms.

6. In the event of a dispute as to whether the Court has jurisdiction, the matter shall be settled by the decision of the Court.

Article 37

Whenever a treaty or convention in force provides for reference of a matter to a tribunal to have been instituted by the League of Nations, or to the Permanent Court of International Justice, the matter shall, as between the parties to the present Statute, be referred to the International Court of Justice.

Article 38

1. The Court, whose function is to decide in accordance with international law such disputes as are submitted to it, shall apply:

    a. international conventions, whether general or particular, establishing rules expressly recognized by the contesting states;

    b. international custom, as evidence of a general practice accepted as law:

    c. the general principles of law recognized by civilized nations;

    d. subject to the provisions of Article 59, judicial decisions and the teachings of the most highly qualified publicists of the various nations, as subsidiary means for the determination of rules of law.

2. This provision shall not prejudice the power of the Court to decide a case *ex aequo et bono*, if the parties agree thereto.

Chapter III. Procedure

Article 39

1. The official languages of the Court shall be French and English. If the parties agree that the case shall be conducted in French, the judgment shall be delivered in French. If the parties agree that the case shall be conducted in English, the judgment shall be delivered in English.

2. In the absence of an agreement as to which language shall be employed, each party may, in the pleadings, use the language which it

prefers; the decision of the Court shall be given in French and English. In this case the Court shall at the same time determine which of the two texts shall be considered as authoritative.

3. The Court shall, at the request of any party, authorize a language other than French or English to be used by that party.

Article 40

1. Cases are brought before the Court, as the case may be, either by the notification of the special agreement or by a written application addressed to the Registrar. In either case the subject of the dispute and the parties shall be indicated.

2. The Registrar shall forthwith communicate the application to all concerned.

3. He shall also notify the Members of the United Nations through the Secretary-General, and also any other states entitled to appear before the Court.

Article 41

1. The Court shall have the power to indicate, if it considers that circumstances so require, any provisional measures which ought to be taken to preserve the respective rights of either party.

2. Pending the final decision, notice of the measures suggested shall forthwith be given to the parties and to the Security Council.

Article 42

1. The parties shall be represented by agents.

2. They may have the assistance of counsel or advocates before the Court.

3. The agents, counsel, and advocates of parties before the Court shall enjoy the privileges and immunities necessary to the independent exercise of their duties.

Article 43

1. The procedure shall consist of two parts: written and oral.

2. The written proceedings shall consist of the communication to the Court and to the parties of memorials, counter-memorials and, if necessary, replies; also all papers and documents in support.

3. These communications shall be made through the Registrar, in the order and within the time fixed by the Court.

4. A certified copy of every document produced by one party shall be communicated to the other party.

5. The oral proceedings shall consist of the hearing by the Court of witnesses, experts, agents, counsel, and advocates.

Article 44

1. For the service of all notices upon persons other than the agents, counsel, and advocates, the Court shall apply direct to the government of the state upon whose territory the notice has to be served.

2. The same provision shall apply whenever steps are to be taken to procure evidence on the spot.

Article 45

The hearing shall be under the control of the President or, if he is unable to preside, of the Vice-President; if neither is able to preside, the senior judge present shall preside.

Article 46

The hearing in Court shall be public, unless the Court shall decide otherwise, or unless the parties demand that the public be not admitted.

Article 47

1. Minutes shall be made at each hearing and signed by the Registrar and the President.

2. These minutes alone shall be authentic.

Article 48

The Court shall make orders for the conduct of the case, shall decide the form and time in which each party must conclude its arguments, and make all arrangements connected with the taking of evidence.

Article 49

The Court may, even before the hearing begins, call upon the agents to produce any document or to supply any explanations. Formal note shall be taken of any refusal.

Article 50

The Court may, at any time, entrust any individual, body, bureau, commission, or other organization that it may select, with the task of carrying out an enquiry or giving an expert opinion.

Article 51

During the hearing any relevant questions arc to be put to the witnesses and experts under the conditions laid down by the Court in the rules of procedure referred to in Article 30.

Article 52

After the Court has received the proofs and evidence within the time specified for the purpose, it may refuse to accept any further oral or written evidence that one party may desire to present unless the other side consents.

Article 53

1. Whenever one of the parties does not appear before the Court, or fails to defend its case, the other party may call upon the Court to decide in favor of its claim.

2. The Court must, before doing so, satisfy itself, not only that it has jurisdiction in accordance with Articles 36 and 37, but also that the claim is well founded in fact and law.

Article 54

1. When, subject to the control of the Court, the agents, counsel, and advocates have completed their presentation of the case, the President shall declare the hearing closed.

2. The Court shall withdraw to consider the judgment.

3. The deliberations of the Court shall take place in private and remain secret.

Article 55

1. All questions shall be decided by a majority of the judges present.

2. In the event of an equality of votes, the President or the judge who acts in his place shall have a casting vote.

Article 56

1. The judgment shall state the reasons on which it is based.

2. It shall contain the names of the judges who have taken part in the decision.

Article 57

If the judgment does not represent in whole or in part the unanimous opinion of the judges, any judge shall be entitled to deliver a separate opinion.

Article 58

The judgment shall be signed by the President and by the Registrar. It shall be read in open court, due notice having been given to the agents.

Article 59

The decision of the Court has no binding force except between the parties and in respect of that particular case.

Article 60

The judgment is final and without appeal. In the event of dispute as to the meaning or scope of the judgment, the Court shall construe it upon the request of any party.

Article 61

1. An application for revision of a judgment may be made only when it is based upon the discovery of some fact of such a nature as to be a decisive factor, which fact was, when the judgment was given, unknown to the Court and also to the party claiming revision, always provided that such ignorance was not due to negligence.

2. The proceedings for revision shall be opened by a judgment of the Court expressly recording the existence of the new fact, recognizing that it has such a character as to lay the case open to revision, and declaring the application admissible on this ground.

3. The Court may require previous compliance with the terms of the judgment before it admits proceedings in revision.

4. The application for revision must be made at latest within six months of the discovery of the new fact.

5. No application for revision may be made after the lapse of ten years from the date of the judgment.

Article 62

1. Should a state consider that it has an interest of a legal nature which may be affected by the decision in the case, it may submit a request to the Court to be permitted to intervene.

2. It shall be for the Court to decide upon this request.

Article 63

1. Whenever the construction of a convention to which states other than those concerned in the case are parties is in question, the Registrar shall notify all such states forthwith.

2. Every state so notified has the right to intervene in the proceedings; but if it uses this right, the construction given by the judgment will be equally binding upon it.

Article 64

Unless otherwise decided by the Court, each party shall bear its own costs.

Chapter IV.   Advisory Opinions

Article 65

1. The Court may give an advisory opinion on any legal question at the request of whatever body may be authorized by or in accordance with the Charter of the United Nations to make such a request.

2. Questions upon which the advisory opinion of the Court is asked shall be laid before the Court by means of a written request containing an exact statement of the question upon which an opinion is required, and accompanied by all documents likely to throw light upon the question.

Article 66

1. The Registrar shall forthwith give notice of the request for an advisory opinion to all states entitled to appear before the Court.

2. The Registrar shall also, by means of a special and direct communication, notify any state entitled to appear before the Court or international organization considered by the Court, or, should it not be sitting, by the President, as likely to be able to furnish information on the question, that the Court will be prepared to receive, within a time limit to be fixed by the President, written statements, or to hear, at a public sitting to be held for the purpose, oral statements relating to the question.

3. Should any such state entitled to appear before the Court have failed to receive the special communication referred to in paragraph 2 of this Article, such state may express a desire to submit a written statement or to be heard; and the Court will decide.

4. States and organizations having presented written or oral statements or both shall be permitted to comment on the statements made by other states or organizations in the form, to the extent, and within the time limits which the Court, or, should it not be sitting, the President, shall decide in each particular case. Accordingly, the Registrar shall in due time communicate any such written statements to states and organizations having submitted similar statements.

Article 67

The Court shall deliver its advisory opinions in open court, notice having been given to the Secretary-General and to the representatives of Members of the United Nations, of other states and of international organizations immediately concerned.

Article 68

In the exercise of its advisory functions the Court shall further be guided by the provisions of the present Statute which apply in contentious cases to the extent to which it recognizes them to be applicable.

Chapter V.   Amendment

Article 69

Amendments to the present Statute shall be effected by the same procedure as is provided by the Charter of the United Nations for amendments to that Charter, subject however to any provisions which the General Assembly upon recommendation of the Security Council may adopt concerning the participation of states which are parties to the present Statute but are not Members of the United Nations.

Article 70

The Court shall have power to propose such amendments to the present Statute as it may deem necessary, through written communications to the Secretary-General, for consideration in conformity with the provisions of Article 69.

2

Treaties and Customary International Law

VIENNA CONVENTION ON THE LAW OF TREATIES

May 23, 1969, U.N. Doc. A/CONF. 39/27*

The States Parties to the present Convention,

Considering the fundamental role of treaties in the history of international relations,

Recognizing the ever-increasing importance of treaties as a source of international law and as a means of developing peaceful co-operation among nations, whatever their constitutional and social systems,

Noting that the principles of free consent and of good faith and the *pacta sunt servanda* rule are universally recognized,

Affirming that disputes concerning treaties, like other international disputes, should be settled by peaceful means and in conformity with the principles of justice and international law,

*Concluded at Vienna on May 23, 1969. Entered into force on January 27, 1980. The United States signed the convention on April 24, 1970, but has not ratified it.

As of February 2013, the 113 parties to the convention were: Albania, Algeria, Andorra, Argentina, Armenia, Australia, Austria, Barbados, Belarus, Belgium, Bosnia and Herzegovina, Brazil, Bulgaria, Burkina Faso, Cameroon, Canada, Central African Republic, Chile, China, Colombia, Congo, Congo (Democratic Republic of), Costa Rica, Croatia, Cuba, Cyprus, Czech Republic, Denmark, Dominican Republic, Ecuador, Egypt, Estonia, Finland, Gabon, Georgia, Germany, Greece, Guatemala, Guinea, Guyana, Haiti, Holy See, Honduras, Hungary, Ireland, Italy, Jamaica, Japan, Kazakhstan, Kiribati, Korea (Republic of), Kuwait, Kyrgyzstan, Lao People's Democratic Republic, Latvia, Lesotho, Liberia, Libyan Arab Jamahiriya, Liechtenstein, Lithuania, Luxembourg, Macedonia (the former Yugoslav Republic of), Malawi, Malaysia, Maldives, Mali, Malta, Mauritius, Mexico, Moldova, Mongolia, Montenegro, Morocco, Mozambique, Myanmar, Nauru, Netherlands, New Zealand, Niger, Nigeria, Oman, Panama, Paraguay, Peru, Philippines, Poland, Portugal, Russian Federation, Rwanda, Saint Vincent and the Grenadines, Saudi Arabia, Senegal, Serbia, Slovakia, Slovenia, Solomon Islands, Spain, Sudan, Suriname, Sweden, Switzerland, Syrian Arab Republic, Tajikistan, Tanzania, Timor-Leste, Togo, Tunisia, Turkmenistan, Ukraine, United Kingdom, Uruguay, Uzbekistan, and Viet Nam. See the U.N. Web site at <http://treaties.un.org>.

Recalling the determination of the peoples of the United Nations to establish conditions under which justice and respect for the obligations arising from treaties can be maintained,

Having in mind the principles of international law embodied in the Charter of the United Nations, such as the principles of the equal rights and self-determination of peoples, of the sovereign equality and independence of all States, of non-interference in the domestic affairs of States, of the prohibition of the threat or use of force and of universal respect for, and observance of, human rights and fundamental freedoms for all,

Believing that the codification and progressive development of the law of treaties achieved in the present Convention will promote the purposes of the United Nations set forth in the Charter, namely, the maintenance of international peace and security, the development of friendly relations and the achievement of co-operation among nations,

Affirming that the rules of customary international law will continue to govern questions not regulated by the provisions of the present Convention,

Have agreed as follows:

Part I.   Introduction

Article 1.   Scope of the Present Convention

The present Convention applies to treaties between States.

Article 2.   Use of Terms

1. For the purposes of the present Convention:

(a) "treaty" means an international agreement concluded between States in written form and governed by international law, whether embodied in a single instrument or in two or more related instruments and whatever its particular designation;

(b) "ratification", "acceptance", "approval" and "accession" mean in each case the international act so named whereby a State establishes on the international plane its consent to be bound by a treaty;

(c) "full powers" means a document emanating from the competent authority of a State designating a person or persons to represent the State for negotiating, adopting or authenticating the text of a treaty, for expressing the consent of the State to be bound by a treaty, or for accomplishing any other act with respect to a treaty;

(d) "reservation" means a unilateral statement, however phrased or named, made by a State, when signing, ratifying, accepting, approving or acceding to a treaty, whereby it purports to exclude or to modify the legal effect of certain provisions of the treaty in their application to that State;

(e) "negotiating State" means a State which took part in the drawing up and adoption of the text of the treaty;

(f) "contracting State" means a State which has consented to be bound by the treaty, whether or not the treaty has entered into force;

(g) "party" means a State which has consented to be bound by the treaty and for which the treaty is in force;

(h) "third State" means a State not a party to the treaty;

(i) "international organization" means an intergovernmental organization.

2. The provisions of paragraph 1 regarding the use of terms in the present Convention are without prejudice to the use of those terms or to the meanings which may be given to them in the internal law of any State.

Article 3. International Agreements not Within the Scope of the Present Convention

The fact that the present Convention does not apply to international agreements concluded between States and other subjects of international law or between such other subjects of international law, or to international agreements not in written form, shall not affect:

(a) the legal force of such agreements;

(b) the application to them of any of the rules set forth in the present Convention to which they would be subject under international law independently of the Convention;

(c) the application of the Convention to the relations of States as between themselves under international agreements to which other subjects of international law are also parties.

Article 4. Non-Retroactivity of the Present Convention

Without prejudice to the application of any rules set forth in the present Convention to which treaties would be subject under international law independently of the Convention, the Convention applies only to treaties which are concluded by States after the entry into force of the present Convention with regard to such States.

Article 5. Treaties Constituting International Organizations and Treaties Adopted Within an International Organization

The present Convention applies to any treaty which is the constituent instrument of an international organization and to any treaty adopted within an international organization without prejudice to any relevant rules of the organization.

Part II. Conclusion and Entry into Force of Treaties

SECTION 1. CONCLUSION OF TREATIES

Article 6. Capacity of States to Conclude Treaties

Every State possesses capacity to conclude treaties.

Article 7. Full Powers

1. A person is considered as representing a State for the purpose of adopting or authenticating the text of a treaty or for the purpose of expressing the consent of the State to be bound by a treaty if:
   (a) he produces appropriate full powers; or
   (b) it appears from the practice of the States concerned or from other circumstances that their intention was to consider that person as representing the State for such purposes and to dispense with full powers.
2. In virtue of their functions and without having to produce full powers, the following are considered as representing their State:
   (a) Heads of State, Heads of Government and Ministers for Foreign Affairs, for the purpose of performing all acts relating to the conclusion of a treaty;
   (b) heads of diplomatic missions, for the purpose of adopting the text of a treaty between the accrediting State and the State to which they are accredited;
   (c) representatives accredited by States to an international conference or to an international organization or one of its organs, for the purpose of adopting the text of a treaty in that conference, organization or organ.

Article 8. Subsequent Confirmation of an Act Performed Without Authorization

An act relating to the conclusion of a treaty performed by a person who cannot be considered under article 7 as authorized to represent a State for that purpose is without legal effect unless afterwards confirmed by that State.

Article 9. Adoption of the Text

1. The adoption of the text of a treaty takes place by the consent of all the States participating in its drawing up except as provided in paragraph 2.
2. The adoption of the text of a treaty at an international conference takes place by the vote of two-thirds of the States present and voting, unless by the same majority they shall decide to apply a different rule.

Article 10. Authentication of the Text

The text of a treaty is established as authentic and definitive:
   (a) by such procedure as may be provided for in the text or agreed upon by the States participating in its drawing up; or
   (b) failing such procedure, by the signature, signature *ad referendum* or initialling by the representatives of those States of the text of the treaty or of the Final Act of a conference incorporating the text.

Article 11.   Means of Expressing Consent to Be Bound by a Treaty

The consent of a State to be bound by a treaty may be expressed by signature, exchange of instruments constituting a treaty, ratification, acceptance, approval or accession, or by any other means if so agreed.

Article 12.   Consent to Be Bound by a Treaty Expressed by Signature

1. The consent of a State to be bound by a treaty is expressed by the signature of its representative when:
(a) the treaty provides that signature shall have that effect;
(b) it is otherwise established that the negotiating States were agreed that signature should have that effect; or
(c) the intention of the State to give that effect to the signature appears from the full powers of its representative or was expressed during the negotiation.
2. For the purposes of paragraph 1:
(a) the initialling of a text constitutes a signature of the treaty when it is established that the negotiating States so agreed;
(b) the signature *ad referendum* of a treaty by a representative, if confirmed by his State, constitutes a full signature of the treaty.

Article 13.   Consent to Be Bound by a Treaty Expressed by an Exchange of Instruments Constituting a Treaty

The consent of States to be bound by a treaty constituted by instruments exchanged between them is expressed by that exchange when:
(a) the instruments provide that their exchange shall have that effect; or
(b) it is otherwise established that those States were agreed that the exchange of instruments should have that effect.

Article 14.   Consent to Be Bound by a Treaty Expressed by Ratification, Acceptance or Approval

1. The consent of a State to be bound by a treaty is expressed by ratification when:
(a) the treaty provides for such consent to be expressed by means of ratification;
(b) it is otherwise established that the negotiating States were agreed that ratification should be required;
(c) the representative of the State has signed the treaty subject to ratification; or
(d) the intention of the State to sign the treaty subject to ratification appears from the full powers of its representative or was expressed during the negotiation.

2. The consent of a State to be bound by a treaty is expressed by acceptance or approval under conditions similar to those which apply to ratification.

Article 15.   Consent to Be Bound by a Treaty Expressed by Accession

The consent of a State to be bound by a treaty is expressed by accession when:

(a) the treaty provides that such consent may be expressed by that State by means of accession;

(b) it is otherwise established that the negotiating States were agreed that such consent may be expressed by that State by means of accession; or

(c) all the parties have subsequently agreed that such consent may be expressed by that State by means of accession.

Article 16.   Exchange or Deposit of Instruments of Ratification, Acceptance, Approval or Accession

Unless the treaty otherwise provides, instruments of ratification, acceptance, approval or accession establish the consent of a State to be bound by a treaty upon:

(a) their exchange between the contracting States;

(b) their deposit with the depositary; or

(c) their notification to the contracting States or to the depositary, if so agreed.

Article 17.   Consent to Be Bound by Part of a Treaty and Choice of Differing Provisions

1. Without prejudice to articles 19 to 23, the consent of a State to be bound by part of a treaty is effective only if the treaty so permits or the other contracting States so agree.

2. The consent of a State to be bound by a treaty which permits a choice between differing provisions is effective only if it is made clear to which of the provisions the consent relates.

Article 18.   Obligation Not to Defeat the Object and Purpose of a Treaty Prior to Its Entry into Force

A State is obliged to refrain from acts which would defeat the object and purpose of a treaty when:

(a) it has signed the treaty or has exchanged instruments constituting the treaty subject to ratification, acceptance or approval, until it shall have made its intention clear not to become a party to the treaty; or

(b) it has expressed its consent to be bound by the treaty, pending the entry into force of the treaty and provided that such entry into force is not unduly delayed.

SECTION 2.   RESERVATIONS

Article 19.   Formulation of Reservations

A State may, when signing, ratifying, accepting, approving or acceding to a treaty, formulate a reservation unless:

(a) the reservation is prohibited by the treaty;

(b) the treaty provides that only specified reservations, which do not include the reservation in question, may be made; or

(c) in cases not falling under sub-paragraphs (a) and (b), the reservation is incompatible with the object and purpose of the treaty.

Article 20.   Acceptance of and Objection to Reservations

1. A reservation expressly authorized by a treaty does not require any subsequent acceptance by the other contracting States unless the treaty so provides.

2. When it appears from the limited number of the negotiating States and the object and purpose of a treaty that the application of the treaty in its entirety between all the parties is an essential condition of the consent of each one to be bound by the treaty, a reservation requires acceptance by all the parties.

3. When a treaty is a constituent instrument of an international organization and unless it otherwise provides, a reservation requires the acceptance of the competent organ of that organization.

4. In cases not falling under the preceding paragraphs and unless the treaty otherwise provides:

(a) acceptance by another contracting State of a reservation constitutes the reserving State a party to the treaty in relation to that other State if or when the treaty is in force for those States;

(b) an objection by another contracting State to a reservation does not preclude the entry into force of the treaty as between the objecting and reserving States unless a contrary intention is definitely expressed by the objecting State;

(c) an act expressing a State's consent to be bound by the treaty and containing a reservation is effective as soon as at least one other contracting State has accepted the reservation.

5. For the purposes of paragraphs 2 and 4 and unless the treaty otherwise provides, a reservation is considered to have been accepted by a State if it shall have raised no objection to the reservation by the end of a period of twelve months after it was notified of the reservation or by the date on which it expressed its consent to be bound by the treaty, whichever is later.

Article 21.   Legal Effects of Reservations and of Objections to Reservations

1. A reservation established with regard to another party in accordance with articles 19, 20 and 23:

(a) modifies for the reserving State in its relations with that other party the provisions of the treaty to which the reservation relates to the extent of the reservation; and

(b) modifies those provisions to the same extent for that other party in its relations with the reserving State.

2. The reservation does not modify the provisions of the treaty for the other parties to the treaty *inter se.*

3. When a State objecting to a reservation has not opposed the entry into force of the treaty between itself and the reserving State, the provisions to which the reservation relates do not apply as between the two States to the extent of the reservation.

Article 22. *Withdrawal of Reservations and of Objections to Reservations*

1. Unless the treaty otherwise provides, a reservation may be withdrawn at any time and the consent of a State which has accepted the reservation is not required for its withdrawal.

2. Unless the treaty otherwise provides, an objection to a reservation may be withdrawn at any time.

3. Unless the treaty otherwise provides, or it is otherwise agreed:

(a) the withdrawal of a reservation becomes operative in relation to another contracting State only when notice of it has been received by that State;

(b) the withdrawal of an objection to a reservation becomes operative only when notice of it has been received by the State which formulated the reservation.

Article 23. *Procedure Regarding Reservations*

1. A reservation, an express acceptance of a reservation and an objection to a reservation must be formulated in writing and communicated to the contracting States and other States entitled to become parties to the treaty.

2. If formulated when signing the treaty subject to ratification, acceptance or approval, a reservation must be formally confirmed by the reserving State when expressing its consent to be bound by the treaty. In such a case the reservation shall be considered as having been made on the date of its confirmation.

3. An express acceptance of, or an objection to, a reservation made previously to confirmation of the reservation does not itself require confirmation.

4. The withdrawal of a reservation or of an objection to a reservation must be formulated in writing.

SECTION 3. ENTRY INTO FORCE AND PROVISIONAL APPLICATION OF TREATIES

Article 24. *Entry into Force*

1. A treaty enters into force in such manner and upon such date as it may provide or as the negotiating States may agree.

2. Failing any such provision or agreement, a treaty enters into force as soon as consent to be bound by the treaty has been established for all the negotiating States.

3. When the consent of a State to be bound by a treaty is established on a date after the treaty has come into force, the treaty enters into force for that State on that date, unless the treaty otherwise provides.

4. The provisions of a treaty regulating the authentication of its text, the establishment of the consent of States to be bound by the treaty, the manner or date of its entry into force, reservations, the functions of the depositary and other matters arising necessarily before the entry into force of the treaty apply from the time of the adoption of its text.

Article 25. *Provisional Application*

1. A treaty or a part of a treaty is applied provisionally pending its entry into force if:

(a) the treaty itself so provides; or

(b) the negotiating States have in some other manner so agreed.

2. Unless the treaty otherwise provides or the negotiating States have otherwise agreed, the provisional application of a treaty or a part of a treaty with respect to a State shall be terminated if that State notifies the other States between which the treaty is being applied provisionally of its intention not to become a party to the treaty.

Part III.   Observance, Application and Interpretation of Treaties

Section 1.   Observance of Treaties

Article 26.   *Pacta Sunt Servanda*

Every treaty in force is binding upon the parties to it and must be performed by them in good faith.

Article 27.   *Internal Law and Observance of Treaties*

A party may not invoke the provisions of its internal law as justification for its failure to perform a treaty. This rule is without prejudice to article 46.

Section 2.   Application of Treaties

Article 28.   *Non-Retroactivity of Treaties*

Unless a different intention appears from the treaty or is otherwise established, its provisions do not bind a party in relation to any act or fact which took place or any situation which ceased to exist before the date of the entry into force of the treaty with respect to that party.

Article 29.   Territorial Scope of Treaties

Unless a different intention appears from the treaty or is otherwise established, a treaty is binding upon each party in respect of its entire territory.

Article 30.   Application of Successive Treaties Relating to the Same Subject-Matter

1. Subject to Article 103 of the Charter of the United Nations, the rights and obligations of States parties to successive treaties relating to the same subject-matter shall be determined in accordance with the following paragraphs.

2. When a treaty specifies that it is subject to, or that it is not to be considered as incompatible with, an earlier or later treaty, the provisions of that other treaty prevail.

3. When all the parties to the earlier treaty are parties also to the later treaty but the earlier treaty is not terminated or suspended in operation under article 59, the earlier treaty applies only to the extent that its provisions are compatible with those of the later treaty.

4. When the parties to the later treaty do not include all the parties to the earlier one:

(a) as between States parties to both treaties the same rule applies as in paragraph 3;

(b) as between a State party to both treaties and a State party to only one of the treaties, the treaty to which both States are parties governs their mutual rights and obligations.

5. Paragraph 4 is without prejudice to article 41, or to any question of the termination or suspension of the operation of a treaty under article 60 or to any question of responsibility which may arise for a State from the conclusion or application of a treaty the provisions of which are incompatible with its obligations towards another State under another treaty.

SECTION 3.   INTERPRETATION OF TREATIES

Article 31.   General Rule of Interpretation

1. A treaty shall be interpreted in good faith in accordance with the ordinary meaning to be given to the terms of the treaty in their context and in the light of its object and purpose.

2. The context for the purpose of the interpretation of a treaty shall comprise, in addition to the text, including its preamble and annexes:

(a) any agreement relating to the treaty which was made between all the parties in connexion with the conclusion of the treaty,

(b) any instrument which was made by one or more parties in connexion with the conclusion of the treaty and accepted by the other parties as an instrument related to the treaty.

3. There shall be taken into account, together with the context:

(a) any subsequent agreement between the parties regarding the interpretation of the treaty or the application of its provisions;

(b) any subsequent practice in the application of the treaty which establishes the agreement of the parties regarding its interpretation;

(c) any relevant rules of international law applicable in the relations between the parties.

4. A special meaning shall be given to a term if it is established that the parties so intended.

Article 32.   *Supplementary Means of Interpretation*

Recourse may be had to supplementary means of interpretation, including the preparatory work of the treaty and the circumstances of its conclusion, in order to confirm the meaning resulting from the application of article 31, or to determine the meaning when the interpretation according to article 31:

(a) leaves the meaning ambiguous or obscure; or

(b) leads to a result which is manifestly absurd or unreasonable.

Article 33.   *Interpretation of Treaties Authenticated in Two or More Languages*

1. When a treaty has been authenticated in two or more languages, the text is equally authoritative in each language, unless the treaty provides or the parties agree that, in case of divergence, a particular text shall prevail.

2. A version of the treaty in a language other than one of those in which the text was authenticated shall be considered an authentic text only if the treaty so provides or the parties so agree.

3. The terms of the treaty are presumed to have the same meaning in each authentic text.

4. Except where a particular text prevails in accordance with paragraph 1, when a comparison of the authentic texts discloses a difference of meaning which the application of articles 31 and 32 does not remove, the meaning which best reconciles the texts, having regard to the object and purpose of the treaty, shall be adopted.

SECTION 4.   TREATIES AND THIRD STATES

Article 34.   *General Rule Regarding Third States*

A treaty does not create either obligations or rights for a third State without its consent.

Article 35.   *Treaties Providing for Obligations for Third States*

An obligation arises for a third State from a provision of a treaty if the parties to the treaty intend the provision to be the means of establishing the obligation and the third State expressly accepts that obligation in writing.

Article 36.   Treaties Providing for Rights for Third States

1. A right arises for a third State from a provision of a treaty if the parties to the treaty intend the provision to accord that right either to the third State, or to a group of States to which it belongs, or to all States, and the third State assents thereto. Its assent shall be presumed so long as the contrary is not indicated, unless the treaty otherwise provides.

2. A State exercising a right in accordance with paragraph 1 shall comply with the conditions for its exercise provided for in the treaty or established inconformity with the treaty.

Article 37.   Revocation or Modification of Obligations or Rights of Third States

1. When an obligation has arisen for a third State in conformity with article 35, the obligation may be revoked or modified only with the consent of the parties to the treaty and of the third State, unless it is established that they had otherwise agreed.

2. When a right has arisen for a third State in conformity with article 36, the right may not be revoked or modified by the parties if it is established thatthe right was intended not to be revocable or subject to modification without the consent of the third State.

Article 38.   Rules in a Treaty Becoming Binding on Third States Through International Custom

Nothing in articles 34 to 37 precludes a rule set forth in a treaty from becoming binding upon a third State as a customary rule of international law, recognized as such.

Part IV.   Amendment and Modification of Treaties

Article 39.   General Rule Regarding the Amendment of Treaties

A treaty may be amended by agreement between the parties. The rules laid down in Part II apply to such an agreement except in so far as the treaty may otherwise provide.

Article 40.   Amendment of Multilateral Treaties

1. Unless the treaty otherwise provides, the amendment of multilateral treaties shall be governed by the following paragraphs.

2. Any proposal to amend a multilateral treaty as between all the parties must be notified to all the contracting States, each one of which shall have the right to take part in:

(a) the decision as to the action to be taken in regard to such proposal;

(b) the negotiation and conclusion of any agreement for the amendment of the treaty.

3. Every State entitled to become a party to the treaty shall also be entitled to become a party to the treaty as amended.

4. The amending agreement does not bind any State already a party to the treaty which does not become a party to the amending agreement; article 30, paragraph 4(b), applies in relation to such State.

5. Any State which becomes a party to the treaty after the entry into force of the amending agreement shall, failing an expression of a different intention by that State:

(a) be considered as a party to the treaty as amended; and

(b) be considered as a party to the unamended treaty in relation to any party to the treaty not bound by the amending agreement.

Article 41. Agreements to Modify Multilateral Treaties Between Certain of the Parties Only

1. Two or more of the parties to a multilateral treaty may conclude an agreement to modify the treaty as between themselves alone if:

(a) the possibility of such a modification is provided for by the treaty; or

(b) the modification in question is not prohibited by the treaty and:

(i) does not affect the enjoyment by the other parties of their rights under the treaty or the performance of their obligations;

(ii) does not relate to a provision, derogation from which is incompatible with the effective execution of the object and purpose of the treaty as a whole.

2. Unless in a case falling under paragraph 1(a) the treaty otherwise provides, the parties in question shall notify the other parties of their intention to conclude the agreement and of the modification to the treaty for which it provides.

Part V. Invalidity, Termination and Suspension of the Operation of Treaties

SECTION 1. GENERAL PROVISIONS

Article 42. Validity and Continuance in Force of Treaties

1. The validity of a treaty or of the consent of a State to be bound by a treaty may be impeached only through the application of the present Convention.

2. The termination of a treaty, its denunciation or the withdrawal of a party, may take place only as a result of the application of the provisions of

the treaty or of the present Convention. The same rule applies to suspension of the operation of a treaty.

Article 43. *Obligations Imposed by International Law Independently of a Treaty*

The invalidity, termination or denunciation of a treaty, the withdrawal of a party from it, or the suspension of its operation, as a result of the application of the present Convention or of the provisions of the treaty, shall not in any way impair the duty of any State to fulfil any obligation embodied in the treaty to which it would be subject under international law independently of the treaty.

Article 44. *Separability of Treaty Provisions*

1. A right of a party, provided for in a treaty or arising under article 56, to denounce, withdraw from or suspend the operation of the treaty may be exercised only with respect to the whole treaty unless the treaty otherwise provides or the parties otherwise agree.

2. A ground for invalidating, terminating, withdrawing from or suspending the operation of a treaty recognized in the present Convention may be invoked only with respect to the whole treaty except as provided in the following paragraphs or in article 60.

3. If the ground relates solely to particular clauses, it may be invoked only with respect to those clauses where:

(a) the said clauses are separable from the remainder of the treaty with regard to their application;

(b) it appears from the treaty or is otherwise established that acceptance of those clauses was not an essential basis of the consent of the other party or parties to be bound by the treaty as a whole; and

(c) continued performance of the remainder of the treaty would not be unjust.

4. In cases falling under articles 49 and 50 the State entitled to invoke the fraud or corruption may do so with respect either to the whole treaty or, subject to paragraph 3, to the particular clauses alone.

5. In cases falling under articles 51, 52 and 53, no separation of the provisions of the treaty is permitted.

Article 45. *Loss of a Right to Invoke a Ground for Invalidating, Terminating, Withdrawing from or Suspending the Operation of a Treaty*

A State may no longer invoke a ground for invalidating, terminating, withdrawing from or suspending the operation of a treaty under articles 46 to 50 or articles 60 and 62 if, after becoming aware of the facts:

(a) it shall have expressly agreed that the treaty is valid or remains in force or continues in operation, as the case may be; or

(b) it must by reason of its conduct be considered as having acquiesced in the validity of the treaty or in its maintenance in force or in operation, as the case may be.

SECTION 2. INVALIDITY OF TREATIES

Article 46. *Provisions of Internal Law Regarding Competence to Conclude Treaties*

1. A State may not invoke the fact that its consent to be bound by a treaty has been expressed in violation of a provision of its internal law regarding competence to conclude treaties as invalidating its consent unless that violation was manifest and concerned a rule of its internal law of fundamental importance.

2. A violation is manifest if it would be objectively evident to any State conducting itself in the matter in accordance with normal practice and in good faith.

Article 47. *Specific Restrictions on Authority to Express the Consent of a State*

If the authority of a representative to express the consent of a State to be bound by a particular treaty has been made subject to a specific restriction, his omission to observe that restriction may not be invoked as invalidating the consent expressed by him unless the restriction was notified to the other negotiating States prior to his expressing such consent.

Article 48. *Error*

1. A State may invoke an error in a treaty as invalidating its consent to be bound by the treaty if the error relates to a fact or situation which was assumed by that State to exist at the time when the treaty was concluded and formed an essential basis of its consent to be bound by the treaty.

2. Paragraph 1 shall not apply if the State in question contributed by its own conduct to the error or if the circumstances were such as to put that State on notice of a possible error.

3. An error relating only to the wording of the text of a treaty does not affect its validity; article 79 then applies.

Article 49. *Fraud*

If a State has been induced to conclude a treaty by the fraudulent conduct of another negotiating State, the State may invoke the fraud as invalidating its consent to be bound by the treaty.

Article 50. *Corruption of a Representative of a State*

If the expression of a State's consent to be bound by a treaty has been procured through the corruption of its representative directly or indirectly by another negotiating State, the State may invoke such corruption as invalidating its consent to be bound by the treaty.

Article 51.   Coercion of a Representative of a State

The expression of a State's consent to be bound by a treaty which has been procured by the coercion of its representative through acts or threats directed against him shall be without any legal effect.

Article 52.   Coercion of a State by the Threat or Use of Force

A treaty is void if its conclusion has been procured by the threat or use of force in violation of the principles of international law embodied in the Charter of the United Nations.

Article 53.   Treaties Conflicting with a Peremptory Norm of General International Law (Jus Cogens)

A treaty is void if, at the time of its conclusion, it conflicts with a peremptory norm of general international law. For the purposes of the present Convention, a peremptory norm of general international law is a norm accepted and recognized by the international community of States as a whole as a norm from which no derogation is permitted and which can be modified only by a subsequent norm of general international law having the same character.

SECTION 3.   TERMINATION AND SUSPENSION OF THE OPERATION OF TREATIES

Article 54.   Termination of or Withdrawal from a Treaty Under Its Provisions or by Consent of the Parties

The termination of a treaty or the withdrawal of a party may take place:
    (a) in conformity with the provisions of the treaty; or
    (b) at any time by consent of all the parties after consultation with the other contracting States.

Article 55.   Reduction of the Parties to a Multilateral Treaty Below the Number Necessary for Its Entry into Force

Unless the treaty otherwise provides, a multilateral treaty does not terminate by reason only of the fact that the number of the parties falls below the number necessary for its entry into force.

Article 56.   Denunciation of or Withdrawal from a Treaty Containing No Provision Regarding Termination, Denunciation or Withdrawal

1. A treaty which contains no provision regarding its termination and which does not provide for denunciation or withdrawal is not subject to denunciation or withdrawal unless:

(a) it is established that the parties intended to admit the possibility of denunciation or withdrawal; or

(b) a right of denunciation or withdrawal may be implied by the nature of the treaty.

2. A party shall give not less than twelve months' notice of its intention to denounce or withdraw from a treaty under paragraph 1.

Article 57. Suspension of the Operation of a Treaty Under its Provisions or by Consent of the Parties

The operation of a treaty in regard to all the parties or to a particular party may be suspended:

(a) in conformity with the provisions of the treaty; or

(b) at any time by consent of all the parties after consultation with the other contracting States.

Article 58. Suspension of the Operation of a Multilateral Treaty by Agreement Between Certain of the Parties Only

1. Two or more parties to a multilateral treaty may conclude an agreement to suspend the operation of provisions of the treaty, temporarily and as between themselves alone, if:

(a) the possibility of such a suspension is provided for by the treaty; or

(b) the suspension in question is not prohibited by the treaty and:

(i) does not affect the enjoyment by the other parties of their rights under the treaty or the performance of their obligations;

(ii) is not incompatible with the object and purpose of the treaty.

2. Unless in a case falling under paragraph 1(a) the treaty otherwise provides, the parties in question shall notify the other parties of their intention to conclude the agreement and of those provisions of the treaty the operation of which they intend to suspend.

Article 59. Termination or Suspension of the Operation of a Treaty Implied by Conclusion of a Later Treaty

1. A treaty shall be considered as terminated if all the parties to it conclude a later treaty relating to the same subject-matter and:

(a) it appears from the later treaty or is otherwise established that the parties intended that the matter should be governed by that treaty; or

(b) the provisions of the later treaty are so far incompatible with those of the earlier one that the two treaties are not capable of being applied at the same time.

2. The earlier treaty shall be considered as only suspended in operation if it appears from the later treaty or is otherwise established that such was the intention of the parties.

Article 60. Termination or Suspension of the Operation of a Treaty as a Consequence of Its Breach

1. A material breach of a bilateral treaty by one of the parties entitles the other to invoke the breach as a ground for terminating the treaty or suspending its operation in whole or in part.

2. A material breach of a multilateral treaty by one of the parties entitles:

(a) the other parties by unanimous agreement to suspend the operation of the treaty in whole or in part or to terminate it either:

(i) in the relations between themselves and the defaulting State, or

(ii) as between all the parties;

(b) a party specially affected by the breach to invoke it as a ground for suspending the operation of the treaty in whole or in part in the relations between itself and the defaulting State;

(c) any party other than the defaulting State to invoke the breach as a ground for suspending the operation of the treaty in whole or in part with respect to itself if the treaty is of such a character that a material breach of its provisions by one party radically changes the position of every party with respect to the further performance of its obligations under the treaty.

3. A material breach of a treaty, for the purposes of this article, consists in:

(a) a repudiation of the treaty not sanctioned by the present Convention; or

(b) the violation of a provision essential to the accomplishment of the object or purpose of the treaty.

4. The foregoing paragraphs are without prejudice to any provision in the treaty applicable in the event of a breach.

5. Paragraphs 1 to 3 do not apply to provisions relating to the protection of the human person contained in treaties of a humanitarian character, in particular to provisions prohibiting any form of reprisals against persons protected by such treaties.

Article 61. Supervening Impossibility of Performance

1. A party may invoke the impossibility of performing a treaty as a ground for terminating or withdrawing from it if the impossibility results from the permanent disappearance or destruction of an object indispensable for the execution of the treaty. If the impossibility is temporary, it may be invoked only as a ground for suspending the operation of the treaty.

2. Impossibility of performance may not be invoked by a party as a ground for terminating, withdrawing from or suspending the operation of a treaty if the impossibility is the result of a breach by that party either of an obligation under the treaty or of any other international obligation owed to any other party to the treaty.

Article 62. Fundamental Change of Circumstances

1. A fundamental change of circumstances which has occurred with regard to those existing at the time of the conclusion of a treaty, and which was not foreseen by the parties, may not be invoked as a ground for terminating or withdrawing from the treaty unless:

(a) the existence of those circumstances constituted an essential basis of the consent of the parties to be bound by the treaty; and

(b) the effect of the change is radically to transform the extent of obligations still to be performed under the treaty.

2. A fundamental change of circumstances may not be invoked as a ground for terminating or withdrawing from a treaty:

(a) if the treaty establishes a boundary; or

(b) if the fundamental change is the result of a breach by the party invoking it either of an obligation under the treaty or of any other international obligation owed to any other party to the treaty.

3. If, under the foregoing paragraphs, a party may invoke a fundamental change of circumstances as a ground for terminating or withdrawing from a treaty it may also invoke the change as a ground for suspending the operation of the treaty.

Article 63. Severance of Diplomatic or Consular Relations

The severance of diplomatic or consular relations between parties to a treaty does not affect the legal relations established between them by the treaty except in so far as the existence of diplomatic or consular relations is indispensable for the application of the treaty.

Article 64. Emergence of a New Peremptory Norm of General International Law (Jus Cogens)

If a new peremptory norm of general international law emerges, any existing treaty which is in conflict with that norm becomes void and terminates.

SECTION 4. PROCEDURE

Article 65. Procedure to be Followed with Respect to Invalidity, Termination, Withdrawal from or Suspension of the Operation of a Treaty

1. A party which, under the provisions of the present Convention, invokes either a defect in its consent to be bound by a treaty or a ground for impeaching the validity of a treaty, terminating it, withdrawing from it or suspending its operation, must notify the other parties of its claim. The notification shall indicate the measure proposed to be taken with respect to the treaty and the reasons therefor.

2. If, after the expiry of a period which, except in cases of special urgency, shall not be less than three months after the receipt of the notification, no party has raised any objection, the party making the notification may carry out in the manner provided in article 67 the measure which it has proposed.

3. If, however, objection has been raised by any other party, the parties shall seek a solution through the means indicated in Article 33 of the Charter of the United Nations.

4. Nothing in the foregoing paragraphs shall affect the rights or obligations of the parties under any provisions in force binding the parties with regard to the settlement of disputes.

5. Without prejudice to article 45, the fact that a State has not previously made the notification prescribed in paragraph 1 shall not prevent it from making such notification in answer to another party claiming performance of the treaty or alleging its violation.

Article 66. *Procedures for Judicial Settlement, Arbitration and Conciliation*

If, under paragraph 3 of article 65, no solution has been reached within a period of 12 months following the date on which the objection was raised, the following procedures shall be followed:

(a) any one of the parties to a dispute concerning the application or the interpretation of article 53 or 64 may, by a written application, submit it to the International Court of Justice for a decision unless the parties by common consent agree to submit the dispute to arbitration;

(b) any one of the parties to a dispute concerning the application or the interpretation of any of the other articles in Part V of the present Convention may set in motion the procedure specified in the Annex to the Convention by submitting a request to that effect to the Secretary-General of the United Nations.

Article 67. *Instruments for Declaring Invalid, Terminating, Withdrawing from or Suspending the Operation of a Treaty*

1. The notification provided for under article 65, paragraph 1 must be made in writing.

2. Any act declaring invalid, terminating, withdrawing from or suspending the operation of a treaty pursuant to the provisions of the treaty or of paragraphs 2 or 3 of article 65 shall be carried out through an instrument communicated to the other parties. If the instrument is not signed by the Head of State, Head of Government or Minister for Foreign Affairs, the representative of the State communicating it may be called upon to produce full powers.

Article 68.   Revocation of Notifications and Instruments Provided for in Articles 65 and 67

A notification or instrument provided for in articles 65 or 67 may be revoked at any time before it takes effect.

SECTION 5.   CONSEQUENCES OF THE INVALIDITY, TERMINATION OR SUSPENSION OF THE OPERATION OF A TREATY

Article 69.   Consequences of the Invalidity of a Treaty

1. A treaty the invalidity of which is established under the present Convention is void. The provisions of a void treaty have no legal force.

2. If acts have nevertheless been performed in reliance on such a treaty:

(a) each party may require any other party to establish as far as possible in their mutual relations the position that would have existed if the acts had not been performed;

(b) acts performed in good faith before the invalidity was invoked are not rendered unlawful by reason only of the invalidity of the treaty.

3. In cases falling under articles 49, 50, 51 or 52, paragraph 2 does not apply with respect to the party to which the fraud, the act of corruption or the coercion is imputable.

4. In the case of the invalidity of a particular State's consent to be bound by a multilateral treaty, the foregoing rules apply in the relations between that State and the parties to the treaty.

Article 70.   Consequences of the Termination of a Treaty

1. Unless the treaty otherwise provides or the parties otherwise agree, the termination of a treaty under its provisions or in accordance with the present Convention:

(a) releases the parties from any obligation further to perform the treaty;

(b) does not affect any right, obligation or legal situation of the parties created through the execution of the treaty prior to its termination.

2. If a State denounces or withdraws from a multilateral treaty, paragraph 1 applies in the relations between that State and each of the other parties to the treaty from the date when such denunciation or withdrawal takes effect.

Article 71.   Consequences of the Invalidity of a Treaty Which Conflicts with a Peremptory Norm of General International Law

1. In the case of a treaty which is void under article 53 the parties shall:

(a) eliminate as far as possible the consequences of any act performed in reliance on any provision which conflicts with the peremptory norm of general international law; and

(b) bring their mutual relations into conformity with the peremptory norm of general international law.

2. In the case of a treaty which becomes void and terminates under article 64, the termination of the treaty:

(a) releases the parties from any obligation further to perform the treaty;

(b) does not affect any right, obligation or legal situation of the parties created through the execution of the treaty prior to its termination; provided that those rights, obligations or situations may thereafter be maintained only to the extent that their maintenance is not in itself in conflict with the new peremptory norm of general international law.

Article 72. Consequences of the Suspension of the Operation of a Treaty

1. Unless the treaty otherwise provides or the parties otherwise agree, the suspension of the operation of a treaty under its provisions or in accordance with the present Convention:

(a) releases the parties between which the operation of the treaty is suspended from the obligation to perform the treaty in their mutual relations during the period of the suspension;

(b) does not otherwise affect the legal relations between the parties established by the treaty.

2. During the period of the suspension the parties shall refrain from acts tending to obstruct the resumption of the operation of the treaty.

Part VI. Miscellaneous Provisions

Article 73. Cases of State Succession, State Responsibility and Outbreak of Hostilities

The provisions of the present Convention shall not prejudge any question that may arise in regard to a treaty from a succession of States or from the international responsibility of a State or from the outbreak of hostilities between States.

Article 74. Diplomatic and Consular Relations and the Conclusion of Treaties

The severance or absence of diplomatic or consular relations between two or more States does not prevent the conclusion of treaties between those States. The conclusion of a treaty does not in itself affect the situation in regard to diplomatic or consular relations.

Article 75. Case of an Aggressor State

The provisions of the present Convention are without prejudice to any obligation in relation to a treaty which may arise for an aggressor State in consequence of measures taken in conformity with the Charter of the United Nations with reference to that State's aggression.

Part VII. Depositaries, Notifications, Corrections and Registration

Article 76. Depositaries of Treaties

1. The designation of the depositary of a treaty may be made by the negotiating States, either in the treaty itself or in some other manner. The depositary may be one or more States, an international organization or the chief administrative officer of the organization.

2. The functions of the depositary of a treaty are international in character and the depositary is under an obligation to act impartially in their performance. In particular, the fact that a treaty has not entered into force between certain of the parties or that a difference has appeared between a State and a depositary with regard to the performance of the latter's functions shall not affect that obligation.

Article 77. Functions of Depositaries

1. The functions of a depositary, unless otherwise provided in the treaty or agreed by the contracting States, comprise in particular:

(a) keeping custody of the original text of the treaty and of any full powers delivered to the depositary;

(b) preparing certified copies of the original text and preparing any further text of the treaty in such additional languages as may be required by the treaty and transmitting them to the parties and to the States entitled to become parties to the treaty;

(c) receiving any signatures to the treaty and receiving and keeping custody of any instruments, notifications and communications relating to it;

(d) examining whether the signature or any instrument, notification or communication relating to the treaty is in due and proper form and, if need be, bringing the matter to the attention of the State in question;

(e) informing the parties and the States entitled to become parties to the treaty of acts, notifications and communications relating to the treaty;

(f) informing the States entitled to become parties to the treaty when the number of signatures or of instruments of ratification, acceptance, approval or accession required for the entry into force of the treaty has been received or deposited;

(g) registering the treaty with the Secretariat of the United Nations.

(h) performing the functions specified in other provisions of the present Convention. . . .

Article 78. Notifications and Communications

Except as the treaty or the present Convention otherwise provide, any notification or communication to be made by any State under the present Convention shall:

(a) if there is no depositary, be transmitted direct to the States for which it is intended, or if there is a depositary, to the latter;

(b) be considered as having been made by the State in question only upon its receipt by the State to which it was transmitted or, as the case may be, upon its receipt by the depositary;

(c) if transmitted to a depositary, be considered as received by the State for which it was intended only when the latter State has been informed by the depositary in accordance with article 77, paragraph 1(e).

Article 79. Correction of Errors in Texts or in Certified Copies of Treaties

1. Where, after the authentication of the text of a treaty, the signatory States and the contracting States are agreed that it contains an error, the error shall, unless they decide upon some other means of correction, be corrected:

(a) by having the appropriate correction made in the text and causing the correction to be initialled by duly authorized representatives;

(b) by executing or exchanging an instrument or instruments setting out the correction which it has been agreed to make; or

(c) by executing a corrected text of the whole treaty by the same procedure as in the case of the original text.

2. Where the treaty is one for which there is a depositary, the latter shall notify the signatory States and the contracting States of the error and of the proposal to correct it and shall specify an appropriate time-limit within which objection to the proposed correction may be raised. If, on the expiry of the time-limit:

(a) no objection has been raised, the depositary shall make and initial the correction in the text and shall execute a *procé-verbal* of the rectification of the text and communicate a copy of it to the parties and to the States entitled to become parties to the treaty;

(b) an objection has been raised, the depositary shall communicate the objection to the signatory States and to the contracting States.

3. The rules in paragraphs 1 and 2 apply also where the text has been authenticated in two or more languages and it appears that there is a lack of concordance which the signatory States and the contracting States agree should be corrected.

4. The corrected text replaces the defective text *ab initio*, unless the signatory States and the contracting States otherwise decide. . . .

Article 80.   Registration and Publication of Treaties

1. Treaties shall, after their entry into force, be transmitted to the Secretariat of the United Nations for registration or filing and recording, as the case may be, and for publication.

2. The designation of a depositary shall constitute authorization for it to perform the acts specified in the preceding paragraph.

Part VIII.   Final Provisions

Article 81.   Signature

The present Convention shall be open for signature by all States Members of the United Nations or of any of the specialized agencies or of the International Atomic Energy Agency or parties to the Statute of the International Court of Justice, and by any other State invited by the General Assembly of the United Nations to become a party to the Convention, as follows: . . .

Article 82.   Ratification

The present Convention is subject to ratification. The instruments of ratification shall be deposited with the Secretary-General of the United Nations.

Article 83.   Accession

The present Convention shall remain open for accession by any State belonging to any of the categories mentioned in article 81. The instruments of accession shall be deposited with the Secretary-General of the United Nations.

Article 84.   Entry into Force . . . .

2. For each State ratifying or acceding to the Convention after the deposit of the thirty-fifth instrument of ratification or accession, the Convention shall enter into force on the thirtieth day after deposit by such State of its instrument of ratification or accession. . . .

ANNEX

1. A list of conciliators consisting of qualified jurists shall be drawn up and maintained by the Secretary-General of the United Nations. To this end, every State which is a Member of the United Nations or a party to the present Convention shall be invited to nominate two conciliators, and the names of the persons so nominated shall constitute the list. The term of a conciliator, including that of any conciliator nominated to fill a casual vacancy, shall be five years and may be renewed. . . .

2. When a request has been made to the Secretary-General under article 66 the Secretary-General shall bring the dispute before a conciliation commission constituted as follows:

The State or States constituting one of the parties to the dispute shall appoint:

(a) one conciliator of the nationality of that State or of one of those States, who may or may not be chosen from the list referred to in paragraph 1; and

(b) one conciliator not of the nationality of that State or of any of those States, who shall be chosen from the list.

The State or States constituting the other party to the dispute shall appoint two conciliators in the same way. The four conciliators chosen by the parties shall be appointed within sixty days following the date on which the Secretary-General receives the request.

The four conciliators shall, within sixty days following the date of the last of their own appointments, appoint a fifth conciliator chosen from the list, who shall be chairman.

If the appointment of the chairman or of any of the other conciliators has not been made within the period prescribed above for such appointment, it shall be made by the Secretary-General within sixty days following the expiry of that period. The appointment of the chairman may be made by the Secretary-General either from the list or from the membership of the International Law Commission. Any of the periods within which appointments must be made may be extended by agreement between the parties to the dispute.

Any vacancy shall be filled in the manner prescribed for the initial appointment.

3. The Conciliation Commission shall decide its own procedure. The Commission, with the consent of the parties to the dispute, may invite any party to the treaty to submit to it its views orally or in writing. Decisions and recommendations of the Commission shall be made by a majority vote of the five members.

4. The Commission may draw the attention of the parties to the dispute to any measures which might facilitate an amicable settlement.

5. The Commission shall hear the parties, examine the claims and objections, and make proposals to the parties with a view to reaching an amicable settlement of the dispute.

6. The Commission shall report within twelve months of its constitution. . . . The report of the Commission, including any conclusions stated therein regarding the facts or questions of law, shall not be binding upon the parties and it shall have no other character than that of recommendations submitted for the consideration of the parties in order to facilitate an amicable settlement of the dispute.

7. The Secretary-General shall provide the Commission with such assistance and facilities as it may require. The expenses of the Commission shall be borne by the United Nations.

3

International Law in the United States

THE CONSTITUTION OF THE UNITED STATES

We the People of the United States, in Order to form a more perfect Union, establish Justice, insure domestic Tranquility, provide for the common defence, promote the general Welfare, and secure the Blessings of Liberty to ourselves and our Posterity, do ordain and establish this Constitution for the United States of America.

Article I

Section 1. All legislative Powers herein granted shall be vested in a Congress of the United States, which shall consist of a Senate and House of Representatives.

Section 2. [1] The House of Representatives shall be composed of Members chosen every second Year by the People of the several States, and the Electors in each State shall have the Qualifications requisite for Electors of the most numerous Branch of the State Legislature.

[2] No Person shall be a Representative who shall not have attained to the Age of twenty five Years, and been seven Years a Citizen of the United States, and who shall not, when elected, be an Inhabitant of that State in which he shall be chosen.

[3] Representatives and direct Taxes shall be apportioned among the several States which may be included within this Union, according to their respective Numbers, which shall be determined by adding to the whole Number of free Persons, including those bound to Service for a Term of Years, and excluding Indians not taxed, three fifths of all other Persons. The actual Enumeration shall be made within three Years after the first Meeting of the Congress of the United States, and within every subsequent Term of ten Years, in such Manner as they shall by Law direct. The Number of Representatives shall not exceed one for every thirty Thousand, but each State shall

have at Least one Representative; and until such enumeration shall be made, the State of New Hampshire shall be entitled to chuse three, Massachusetts eight, Rhode Island and Providence Plantations one, Connecticut five, New York six, New Jersey four, Pennsylvania eight, Delaware one, Maryland six, Virginia ten, North Carolina five, South Carolina five, and Georgia three.

[4] When vacancies happen in the Representation from any State, the Executive Authority thereof shall issue Writs of Election to fill such Vacancies.

[5] The House of Representatives shall chuse their Speaker and other Officers; and shall have the sole Power of Impeachment.

Section 3. [1] The Senate of the United States shall be composed of two Senators from each State, chosen by the Legislature thereof, for six Years; and each Senator shall have one Vote.

[2] Immediately after they shall be assembled in Consequence of the first Election, they shall be divided as equally as may be into three Classes. The Seats of the Senators of the first Class shall be vacated at the Expiration of the second Year, of the second Class at the Expiration of the fourth Year, and of the third Class at the Expiration of the sixth Year, so that one third may he chosen every second Year; and if Vacancies happen by Resignation, or otherwise, during the Recess of the Legislature of any State, the Executive thereof may make temporary Appointments until the next Meeting of the Legislature, which shall then fill such Vacancies.

[3] No Person shall be a Senator who shall not have attained to the Age of thirty Years, and been nine Years a Citizen of the United States, and who shall not, when elected, be an Inhabitant of that State for which he shall be chosen.

[4] The Vice President of the United States shall be President of the Senate, but shall have no Vote, unless they be equally divided.

[5] The Senate shall chuse their other Officers, and also a President pro tempore, in the absence of the Vice President, or when he shall exercise the Office of President of the United States.

[6] The Senate shall have the sole Power to try all Impeachments. When sitting for that Purpose, they shall be on Oath or Affirmation. When the President of the United States is tried, the Chief Justice shall preside: And no Person shall be convicted without the Concurrence of two thirds of the Members present.

[7] Judgment in Cases of Impeachment shall not extend further than to removal from Office, and disqualification to hold and enjoy any Office of honor, Trust or Profit under the United States: but the Party convicted shall nevertheless be liable and subject to Indictment, Trial, Judgment and Punishment, according to Law.

Section 4. [1] The Times, Places and Manner of holding Elections for Senators and Representatives, shall be prescribed in each State by the Legislature thereof; but the Congress may at any time by Law make or alter such Regulations, except as to the Places of chusing Senators.

[2] The Congress shall assemble at least once in every Year, and such Meeting shall be on the first Monday in December, unless they shall by Law appoint a different Day.

Section 5. [1] Each House shall be the Judge of the Elections, Returns and Qualifications of its own Members, and a Majority of each shall constitute a Quorum to do Business; but a smaller Number may adjourn from day to day, and may be authorized to compel the Attendance of absent Members, in such Manner, and under such Penalties as each House may provide.

[2] Each House may determine the Rules of its Proceedings, punish its Members for disorderly Behavior, and, with the Concurrence of two thirds, expel a Member.

[3] Each House shall keep a Journal of its Proceedings, and from time to time publish the same, excepting such Parts as may in their Judgment require Secrecy; and the Yeas and Nays of the Members of either House on any question shall, at the Desire of one fifth of those Present, be entered on the Journal.

[4] Neither House, during the Session of Congress, shall, without the Consent of the other, adjourn for more than three days, nor to any other Place than that in which the two Houses shall be sitting.

Section 6. [1] The Senators and Representatives shall receive a Compensation for their Services, to be ascertained by Law, and paid out of the Treasury of the United States. They shall in all Cases, except Treason, Felony and Breach of the Peace, be privileged from Arrest during their Attendance at the Session of their respective Houses, and in going to and returning from the same; and for any Speech or Debate in either House, they shall not be questioned in any other Place.

[2] No Senator or Representative shall, during the Time for which he was elected, be appointed to any civil Office under the Authority of the United States, which shall have been created, or the Emoluments whereof shall have been encreased during such time; and no Person holding any Office under the United States, shall be a Member of either House during his Continuance in Office.

Section 7. [1] All Bills for raising Revenue shall originate in the House of Representatives; but the Senate may propose or concur with Amendments as on other Bills.

"revenue"?

[2] Every Bill which shall have passed the House of Representatives and the Senate, shall, before it become a Law, be presented to the President of the United States; If he approve he shall sign it, but if not he shall return it, with his Objections to the House in which it shall have originated, who shall enter the Objections at large on their Journal, and proceed to reconsider it. If after such Reconsideration two thirds of that House shall agree to pass the Bill, it shall be sent, together with the Objections, to the other House, by which it shall likewise be reconsidered, and if approved by two thirds of that House, it shall become a Law. But in all such Cases the Votes of both Houses shall be determined by yeas and Nays, and the Names of the Persons voting for and against the Bill shall be entered on the Journal of each House respectively. If any Bill shall not be returned by the President within ten Days (Sundays excepted) after it shall have been presented to him, the Same shall be a Law, in like Manner as if he had signed it, unless the Congress by their Adjournment prevents its Return, in which Case it shall not be a Law.

implementing

[3] Every Order, Resolution, or Vote to Which the Concurrence of the Senate and House of Representatives may be necessary (except on a question of Adjournment) shall be presented to the President of the United States; and before the Same shall take Effect, shall be approved by him, or being disapproved by him, shall be repassed by two thirds of the Senate and House of Representatives, according to the Rules and Limitations prescribed in the Case of a Bill.

Section 8. [1] The Congress shall have Power To lay and collect Taxes, Duties, Imposts and Excises, to pay the Debts and provide for the common Defence and general Welfare of the United States; but all Duties, Imposts and Excises shall be uniform throughout the United States;

[2] To borrow money on the credit of the United States.

[3] To regulate Commerce with foreign Nations, and among the several States, and with the Indian Tribes;

[4] To establish an uniform Rule of Naturalization, and uniform Laws on the subject of Bankruptcies throughout the United States;

[5] To coin Money, regulate the Value thereof, and of foreign Coin, and fix the Standard of Weights and Measures;

[6] To provide the Punishment of counterfeiting the Securities and current Coin of the United States;

[7] To establish Post Offices and post Roads;

[8] To promote the Progress of Science and useful Arts, by securing for limited Times to Authors and Inventors the exclusive Right to their respective Writings and Discoveries;

[9] To constitute Tribunals inferior to the supreme Court;

[10] To define and punish Piracies and Felonies committed on the high Seas, and Offenses against the Law of Nations;

[11] To declare War, grant Letters of Marque and Reprisal, and make Rules concerning Captures on Land and Water;

[12] To raise and support Armies, but no Appropriation of Money to that Use shall be for a longer Term than two Years;

[13] To provide and maintain a Navy;

[14] To make Rules for the Government and Regulation of the land and naval Forces;

[15] To provide for calling forth the Militia to execute the Laws of the Union, suppress Insurrections and repel Invasions;

[16] To provide for organizing, arming, and disciplining, the Militia, and for governing such Part of them as may be employed in the Service of the United States, reserving to the States respectively, the Appointment of the Officers, and the Authority of training the Militia according to the discipline prescribed by Congress;

[17] To exercise exclusive Legislation in all Cases whatsoever, over such District (not exceeding ten Miles square) as may, by Cession of particular States, and the Acceptance of Congress, become the Seat of the Government of the United States, and to exercise like Authority over all Places purchased by the Consent of the Legislature of the State in which the Same shall be, for

the Erection of Forts, Magazines, Arsenals, dock-Yards, and other needful Buildings;—And

[18] To make all Laws which shall be necessary and proper for carrying into Execution the foregoing Powers, and all other Powers vested by this Constitution in the Government of the United States, or in any Department or Officer thereof.

Section 9. [1] The Migration or Importation of such Persons as any of the States now existing shall think proper to admit, shall not be prohibited by the Congress prior to the Year one thousand eight hundred and eight, but a Tax or duty may be imposed on such Importation, not exceeding ten dollars for each Person.

[2] The privilege of the Writ of Habeas Corpus shall not be suspended, unless when in Cases of Rebellion or Invasion the public Safety may require it.

[3] No Bill of Attainder or ex post facto Law shall be passed.

[4] No Capitation, or other direct, Tax shall be laid, unless in Proportion to the Census or Enumeration herein before directed to be taken.

[5] No Tax or Duty shall be laid on Articles exported from any State.

[6] No Preference shall be given by any Regulation of Commerce or Revenue to the Ports of one State over those of another: nor shall Vessels bound to, or from, one State, be obliged to enter, clear, or pay Duties in another.

[7] No Money shall be drawn from the Treasury, but in Consequence of Appropriations made by Law; and a regular Statement and Account of the Receipts and Expenditures of all public Money shall be published from time to time.

[8] No Title of Nobility shall be granted by the United States: And no Person holding any Office of Profit or Trust under them, shall, without the Consent of the Congress, accept of any present, Emolument, Office, or Title, of any kind whatever, from any King, Prince, or foreign State.

Section 10. [1] No State shall enter into any Treaty, Alliance, or Confederation; grant Letters of Marque and Reprisal; coin Money; emit Bills of Credit; make any Thing but gold and silver Coin a Tender in Payment of Debts; pass any Bill of Attainder, ex post facto Law, or Law impairing the Obligation of Contracts, or grant any Title of Nobility.

[2] No State shall, without the Consent of the Congress, lay any Imposts or Duties on Imports or Exports, except what may be absolutely necessary for executing its inspection Laws: and the net Produce of all Duties and Imposts, laid by any State on Imports or Exports, shall be for the Use of the Treasury of the United States; and all such Laws shall be subject to the Revision and Controul of the Congress.

[3] No State shall, without the Consent of Congress, lay any Duty of Tonnage,keep Troops, or Ships of War in time of Peace, enter into any Agreement or Compact with another State, or with a foreign Power, or engage in War, unless actually invaded, or in such imminent Danger as will not admit of delay.

Article II

Section 1. [1] The executive Power shall be vested in a President of the United States of America. He shall hold his Office during the Term of four Years, and, together with the Vice President, chosen for the same Term, be elected, as follows:

[2] Each State shall appoint, in such Manner as the Legislature thereof may direct, a Number of Electors, equal to the whole Number of Senators and Representatives to which the State may be entitled in the Congress: but no Senator or Representative, or Person holding an Office of Trust or Profit under the United States, shall be appointed an Elector.

[3] The Electors shall meet in their respective States, and vote by Ballot for two Persons, of whom one at least shall not be an Inhabitant of the same State with themselves. And they shall make a List of all the Persons voted for, and of the Number of Votes for each; which List they shall sign and certify, and transmit sealed to the Seat of the Government of the United States, directed to the President of the Senate. The President of the Senate shall, in the Presence of the Senate and House of Representatives, open all the Certificates, and the Votes shall then be counted. The Person having the greatest Number of Votes shall be the President, if such Number be a Majority of the whole Number of Electors appointed; and if there be more than one who have such Majority, and have an equal Number of Votes, then the House of Representatives shall immediately chuse by Ballot one of them for President; and if no Person have a Majority, then from the five highest on the List the said House shall in like Manner chuse the President. But in chusing the President, the Votes shall be taken by States, the Representation from each State having one Vote; a quorum for this Purpose shall consist of a Member or Members from two thirds of the States, and a Majority of all the States shall be necessary to a Choice. In every Case, after the Choice of the President, the Person having the greatest Number of Votes of the Electors shall be the Vice President. But if there should remain two or more who have equal Votes, the Senate shall chuse from them by Ballot the Vice President.

[4] The Congress may determine the Time of chusing the Electors, and the Day on which they shall give their Votes; which Day shall be the same throughout the United States.

[5] No person except a natural born Citizen, or a Citizen of the United States, at the time of the Adoption of this Constitution, shall be eligible to the Office of President; neither shall any Person be eligible to that Office who shall not have attained to the Age of thirty five Years, and been fourteen Years a Resident within the United States.

[6] In case of the removal of the President from Office, or of his Death, Resignation or Inability to discharge the Powers and Duties of the said Office, the Same shall devolve on the Vice President, and the Congress may by Law provide for the Case of Removal, Death, Resignation or Inability, both of the President and Vice President, declaring what Officer shall then act as President, and such Officer shall act accordingly, until the Disability be removed, or a President shall be elected.

[7] The President shall, at stated Times, receive for his Services, a Compensation, which shall neither be increased nor diminished during the Period for which he shall have been elected, and he shall not receive within that Period any other Emolument from the United States, or any of them.

[8] Before he enter on the Execution of his Office, he shall take the following Oath or Affirmation: "I do solemnly swear (or affirm) that I will faithfully execute the Office of President of the United States, and will to the best of my Ability, preserve, protect and defend the Constitution of the United States."

Section 2. [1] The President shall be Commander in Chief of the Army and Navy of the United States, and of the Militia of the several States, when called into the actual Service of the United States; he may require the Opinion, in writing, of the principal Officer in each of the executive Departments, upon any subject relating to the Duties of their respective Offices, and he shall have Power to grant Reprieves and Pardons for Offenses against the United States, except in Cases of Impeachment.

[2] He shall have Power, by and with the Advice and Consent of the Senate, to make Treaties, provided two thirds of the Senators present concur; and he shall nominate, and by and with the Advice and Consent of the Senate, shall appoint Ambassadors, other public Ministers and Consuls, Judges of the supreme Court, and all other Officers of the United States, whose Appointments are not herein otherwise provided for, and which shall be established by Law; but the Congress may by Law vest the Appointment of such inferior Officers, as they think proper, in the President alone, in the Courts of Law, or in the Heads of Departments.

[3] The President shall have Power to fill up all Vacancies that may happen during the Recess of the Senate, by granting Commissions which shall expire at the End of their next Session.

Section 3. He shall from time to time give to the Congress Information of the State of the Union, and recommend to their Consideration such Measures as he shall judge necessary and expedient; he may, on extraordinary Occasions, convene both Houses, or either of them, and in Case of Disagreement between them, with Respect to the Time of Adjournment, he may adjourn them to such Time as he shall think proper; he shall receive Ambassadors and other public Ministers; he shall take Care that the Laws be faithfully executed, and shall Commission all the Officers of the United States.

Section 4. The President and all civil Officers of the United States, shall be removed from Office on Impeachment for, and Conviction of, Treason, Bribery, or other high Crimes and Misdemeanors.

Article III

Section 1. The judicial Power of the United States, shall be vested in one supreme Court, and in such inferior Courts as the Congress may from time to time ordain and establish. The Judges, both of the supreme and inferior

Courts, shall hold their Offices during good Behaviour, and shall, at stated Times, receive for their Services, a Compensation, which shall not be diminished during their Continuance in Office.

Section 2. [1] The Judicial Power shall extend to all Cases, in Law and Equity, arising under this Constitution, the Laws of the United States, and Treaties made, or which shall be made, under their Authority;—to all Cases affecting Ambassadors, other public Ministers and Consuls;—to all Cases of admiralty and maritime Jurisdiction;—to Controversies to which the United States shall be a Party;—to Controversies between two or more States;— between a State and Citizens of another State;—between Citizens of different States;—between Citizens of the same State claiming Lands under Grants of different States, and between a State, or the Citizens thereof, and foreign States, Citizens or Subjects.

[2] In all Cases affecting Ambassadors, other public Ministers and Consuls, and those in which a State shall be a Party, the supreme Court shall have original Jurisdiction. In all the other Cases before mentioned, the supreme Court shall have appellate Jurisdiction, both as to Law and Fact, with such Exceptions, and under such Regulations as the Congress shall make.

[3] The trial of all Crimes, except in Cases of Impeachment, shall be by Jury; and such Trial shall be held in the State where the said Crimes shall have been committed; but when not committed within any State, the Trial shall be at such Place or Places as the Congress may by Law have directed.

Section 3. [1] Treason against the United States, shall consist only in levying War against them, or in adhering to their Enemies, giving them Aid and Comfort. No person shall be convicted of Treason unless on the Testimony of two Witnesses to the same overt Act, or on Confession in open Court.

[2] The Congress shall have Power to declare the Punishment of Treason, but no Attainder of Treason shall work Corruption of Blood, or Forfeiture except during the Life of the Person attainted.

Article IV

Section 1. Full Faith and Credit shall be given in each State to the public Acts, Records, and judicial Proceedings of every other State. And the Congress may by general Laws prescribe the Manner in which such Acts, Records and Proceedings shall be proved, and the Effect thereof.

Section 2. [1] The Citizens of each State shall be entitled to all Privileges and Immunities of Citizens in the several States.

[2] A Person charged in any State with Treason, Felony, or other Crime, who shall flee from Justice, and be found in another State, shall on demand of the executive Authority of the State from which he fled, be delivered up, to be removed to the State having Jurisdiction of the Crime.

[3] No Person held to Service or Labour in one State, under the Laws thereof, escaping into another, shall, in Consequence of any Law or Regulation therein, be discharged from such Service or Labour, but shall be delivered up on Claim of the Party to whom such Service or Labour may be due.

Section 3. [1] New States may be admitted by the Congress into this Union; but no new State shall be formed or erected within the Jurisdiction of any other State; nor any State be formed by the Junction of two or more States, or Parts of States, without the Consent of the Legislatures of the States concerned as well as of the Congress.

[2] The Congress shall have Power to dispose of and make all needful Rules and Regulations respecting the Territory or other Property belonging to the United States; and nothing in this Constitution shall be so construed as to Prejudice any Claims of the United States, or of any particular State.

Section 4. The United States shall guarantee to every State in this Union a Republican Form of Government, and shall protect each of them against Invasion; and on Application of the Legislature, or of the Executive (when the Legislature cannot be convened) against domestic Violence.

Article V

The Congress, whenever two thirds of both Houses shall deem it necessary, shall propose Amendments to this Constitution, or, on the Application of the Legislatures of two thirds of the several States, shall call a Convention for proposing Amendments, which, in either Case, shall be valid to all Intents and Purposes, as part of this Constitution, when ratified by the Legislatures of three fourths of the several States, or by Conventions in three fourths thereof, as the one or the other Mode of Ratification may be proposed by the Congress; Provided that no Amendment which may be made prior to the Year One thousand eight hundred and eight shall in any Manner affect the first and fourth Clauses in the Ninth Section of the first Article; and that no State, without its Consent, shall be deprived of its equal Suffrage in the Senate.

Article VI

[1] All Debts contracted and Engagements entered into, before the Adoption of this Constitution, shall be as valid against the United States under this Constitution, as under the Confederation.

[2] This Constitution, and the Laws of the United States which shall be made in Pursuance thereof; and all Treaties made, or which shall be made, under the Authority of the United States, shall be the supreme Law of the Land; and the Judges in every State shall be bound thereby, any Thing in the Constitution or Laws of any State to the Contrary notwithstanding.

[3] The Senators and Representatives before mentioned, and the Members of the several State Legislatures, and all executive and judicial Officers, both of the United States and of the several States, shall be bound by Oath or Affirmation, to support this Constitution; but no religious Test shall ever be required as a Qualification to any Office or public Trust under the United States.

Article VII

The Ratification of the Conventions of nine States shall be sufficient for the Establishment of this Constitution between the States so ratifying the Same.

Done in Convention by the Unanimous Consent of the States present the Seventeenth Day of September in the Year of our Lord one thousand seven hundred and Eighty seven and of the Independence of the United States of America the Twelfth.

ARTICLES IN ADDITION TO, AND AMENDMENT OF, THE CONSTITUTION OF THE UNITED STATES OF AMERICA, PROPOSED BY CONGRESS, AND RATIFIED BY THE LEGISLATURES OF THE SEVERAL STATES, PURSUANT TO THE FIFTH ARTICLE OF THE ORIGINAL CONSTITUTION

Amendment I [1791]

Congress shall make no law respecting an establishment of religion, or prohibiting the free exercise thereof; or abridging the freedom of speech, or of the press; or the right of the people peaceably to assemble, and to petition the Government for a redress of grievances.

Amendment II [1791]

A well regulated Militia, being necessary to the security of a free State, the right of the people to keep and bear Arms, shall not be infringed.

Amendment III [1791]

No Soldier shall, in time of peace be quartered in any house, without the consent of the Owner, nor in time of war, but in a manner to be prescribed by law.

Amendment IV [1791]

The right of the people to be secure in their persons, houses, papers, and effects, against unreasonable searches and seizures, shall not be violated, and no Warrants shall issue, but upon probable cause, supported by Oath or affirmation, and particularly describing the place to be scarched, and the persons or things to be seized.

Amendment V [1791]

No person shall be held to answer for a capital, or otherwise infamous crime, unless on a presentment or indictment of a Grand Jury, except in cases arising in the land or naval forces, or in the Militia, when in actual service in time of War or public danger; nor shall any person be subject for the same offense to be twice put in jeopardy of life or limb; nor shall be compelled in any criminal case to be a witness against himself, nor be deprived of life, liberty, or property, without due process of law; nor shall private property be taken for public use, without just compensation.

Amendment VI [1791]

In all criminal prosecutions, the accused shall enjoy the right to a speedy and public trial, by an impartial jury of the State and district wherein the crime shall have been committed; which district shall have been previously ascertained by law, and to be informed of the nature and cause of the accusation; to be confronted with the witnesses against him; to have compulsory process for obtaining witnesses in his favor, and to have the Assistance of Counsel for his defence.

Amendment VII [1791]

In Suits at common law, where the value in controversy shall exceed twenty dollars, the right of trial by jury shall be preserved, and no fact tried by a jury, shall be otherwise re-examined in any Court of the United States, than according to the rules of the common law.

Amendment VIII [1791]

Excessive bail shall not be required, nor excessive fines imposed, nor cruel and unusual punishments inflicted.

Amendment IX [1791]

The enumeration in the Constitution, of certain rights, shall not be construed to deny or disparage others retained by the people.

Amendment X [1791]

The powers not delegated to the United States by the Constitution, nor prohibited by it to the States, are reserved to the States respectively, or to the people.

Amendment XI [1798]

The Judicial power of the United States shall not be construed to extend to any suit in law or equity, commenced or prosecuted against one of the United States by Citizens of another State, or by Citizens or Subjects of any Foreign State.

Amendment XII [1804]

The Electors shall meet in their respective states and vote by ballot for President and Vice-President, one of whom, at least, shall not be an inhabitant of the same state with themselves; they shall name in their ballots the person voted for as President, and in distinct ballots the person voted for as Vice-President, and they shall make distinct lists of all persons voted for as President, and of all persons voted for as Vice-President, and of the number of votes for each, which lists they shall sign and certify, and transmit scaled to the seat of the government of the United States, directed to the President of the Senate;—The President of the Senate shall, in the presence of the Senate and House of Representatives, open all the certificates and the votes shall then be counted;—The person having the greatest number of votes for

President, shall be the President, if such number be a majority of the whole number of Electors appointed; and if no person have such majority, then from the persons having the highest numbers not exceeding three on the list of those voted for as President, the House of Representatives shall choose immediately, by ballot, the President. But in choosing the President, the votes shall be taken by states, the representation from each state having one vote; a quorum for this purpose shall consist of a member or members from two-thirds of the states, and a majority of all the states shall be necessary to a choice. And if the House of Representatives shall not choose a President whenever the right of choice shall devolve upon them, before the fourth day of March next following, then the Vice-President shall act as President, as in the case of the death or other constitutional disability of the President.—The person having the greatest number of votes as Vice-President, shall be the Vice-President, if such number be a majority of the whole number of Electors appointed, and if no person have a majority, then from the two highest numbers on the list, the Senate shall choose the Vice-President; a quorum for the purpose shall consist of two-thirds of the whole number of Senators, and a majority of the whole number shall be necessary to a choice. But no person constitutionally ineligible to the office of President shall be eligible to that of Vice-President of the United States.

Amendment XIII [1865]

Section 1. Neither slavery nor involuntary servitude, except as a punishment for crime whereof the party shall have been duly convicted, shall exist within the United States, or any place subject to their jurisdiction.

Section 2. Congress shall have power to enforce this article by appropriate legislation.

Amendment XIV [1868]

Section 1. All persons born or naturalized in the United States, and subject to the jurisdiction thereof, are citizens of the United States and of the State wherein they reside. No State shall make or enforce any law which shall abridge the privileges or immunities of citizens of the United States; nor shall any State deprive any person of life, liberty, or property, without due process of law; nor deny to any person within its jurisdiction the equal protection of the laws.

Section 2. Representatives shall be apportioned among the several States according to their respective numbers, counting the whole number of persons in each State, excluding Indians not taxed. But when the right to vote at any election for the choice of electors for President and Vice President of the United States, Representatives in Congress, the Executive and Judicial officers of a State, or the members of the Legislature thereof, is denied to any of the male inhabitants of such State, being twenty-one years of age, and citizens of the United States, or in any way abridged, except for participation in rebellion, or other crime, the basis of representation therein shall be reduced in theproportion which the number of such male citizens shall bear to the whole number of male citizens twenty-one years of age in such State.

Section 3. No person shall be a Senator or Representative in Congress, or elector of President and Vice President, or hold any office, civil or military, under the United States, or under any State, who, having previously taken an oath, as a member of Congress, or as an officer of the United States, or as a member of any State legislature, or as an executive or judicial officer of any State, to support the Constitution of the United States, shall have engaged in insurrection or rebellion against the same, or given aid or comfort to the enemies thereof. But Congress may by a vote of two-thirds of each House, remove such disability.

Section 4. The validity of the public debt of the United States, authorized by law, including debts incurred for payment of pensions and bounties for services in suppressing insurrection or rebellion, shall not be questioned. But neither the United States nor any State shall assume or pay any debt or obligation incurred in aid of insurrection or rebellion against the United States, or any claim for the loss of emancipation of any slave; but all such debts, obligations and claims shall be held illegal and void.

Section 5. The Congress shall have power to enforce, by appropriate legislation, the provisions of this article.

Amendment XV [1870]

Section 1. The right of citizens of the United States to vote shall not be denied or abridged by the United States or by any State on account of race, color, or previous condition of servitude.

Section 2. The Congress shall have power to enforce this article by appropriate legislation.

Amendment XVI [1913]

The Congress shall have power to lay and collect taxes on incomes, from whatever source derived, without apportionment among the several States, and without regard to any census or enumeration.

Amendment XVII [1913]

[1] The Senate of the United States shall be composed of two Senators from each State, elected by the people thereof, for six years; and each Senator shall have one vote. The electors in each State shall have the qualifications requisite for electors of the most numerous branch of the State legislatures.

[2] When vacancies happen in the representation of any State in the Senate, the executive authority of such State shall issue writs of election to fill such vacancies: *Provided,* That the legislature of any State may empower the executive thereof to make temporary appointments until the people fill the vacancies by election as the legislature may direct.

[3] This amendment shall not be so construed as to affect the election or term of any Senator chosen before it becomes valid as part of the Constitution.

Amendment XVIII [1919]

Section 1. After one year from the ratification of this article the manufacture, sale, or transportation of intoxicating liquors within, the importation thereof into, or the exploration thereof from the United States and all territory subject to the jurisdiction thereof for beverage purposes is hereby prohibited.

Section 2. The Congress and the several States shall have concurrent power to enforce this article by appropriate legislation.

Section 3. This article shall be inoperative unless it shall have been ratified as an amendment to the Constitution by the legislatures of the several States, as provided in the Constitution, within seven years from the date of the submission hereof to the States by the Congress.

Amendment XIX [1920]

[1] The right of the citizens of the United States to vote shall not be denied or abridged by the United States or by any State on account of sex.

[2] Congress shall have power to enforce this article by appropriate legislation.

Amendment XX [1933]

Section 1. The terms of the President and Vice President shall end at noon on the 20th day of January, and the terms of Senators and Representatives at noon on the 3d day of January, of the years in which such terms would have ended if this article had not been ratified; and the terms of their successors shall then begin.

Section 2. The Congress shall assemble at least once in every year, and such meeting shall begin at noon on the 3d day of January, unless they shall by law appoint a different day.

Section 3. If, at the time fixed for the beginning of the term of the President, the President elect shall have died, the Vice President elect shall become President. If a President shall not have been chosen before the time fixed for the beginning of his term, or if the President elect shall have failed to qualify, then the Vice President elect shall act as President until a President shall have qualified; and the Congress may by law provide for the case wherein neither a President elect nor a Vice President elect shall have qualified, declaring who shall then act as President, or the manner in which one who is to act shall be selected, and such person shall act accordingly until a President or Vice President shall have qualified.

*Section 4.*The Congress may by law provide for the case of the death of any of the persons from whom the House of Representatives may choose a

President whenever the right of choice shall have devolved upon them, and for the case of the death of any of the persons from whom the Senate may choose a Vice President whenever the right of choice shall have devolved upon them.

Section 5. Sections 1 and 2 shall take effect on the 15th day of October following the ratification of this article.

Section 6. This article shall be inoperative unless it shall have been ratified as an amendment to the Constitution by the legislatures of three-fourths of the several States within seven years from the date of its submission.

Amendment XXI [1933]

Section 1. The eighteenth article of amendment to the Constitution of the United States is hereby repealed.

Section 2. The transportation or importation into any State, Territory, or possession of the United States for delivery or use therein of intoxicating liquors, in violation of the laws thereof, is hereby prohibited.

Section 3. This article shall be inoperative unless it shall have been ratified as an amendment to the Constitution by conventions in the several States, as provided in the Constitution, within seven years from the date of the submission hereof to the States by the Congress.

Amendment XXII [1951]

Section 1. No person shall be elected to the office of the President more than twice, and no person who has held the office of President, or acted as President, for more than two years of a term to which some other person was elected President shall be elected to the office of the President more than once. But this Article shall not apply to any person holding the office of President when this Article was proposed by the Congress, and shall not prevent any person who may be holding the office of President, or acting as President, during the term within which the Article becomes operative from holding the office of President or acting as President during the remainder of such term.

Section 2. This article shall be inoperative unless it shall have been ratified as an amendment to the Constitution by the legislatures of three-fourths of the several States within seven years from the date of its submission to the States by the Congress.

Amendment XXIII [1961]

Section 1. The District constituting the seat of Government of the United States shall appoint in such manner as the Congress may direct:

A number of electors of President and Vice President equal to the whole number of Senators and Representatives in Congress to which the District would be entitled if it were a State, but in no event more than the least populous State; they shall be in addition to those appointed by the States, but they shall be considered, for the purposes of the election of President and Vice President, to be electors appointed by a State; and they shall meet in the District and perform such duties as provided by the twelfth article of amendment.

Section 2. The Congress shall have power to enforce this article by appropriate legislation.

Amendment XXIV [1964]

Section 1. The right of citizens of the United States to vote in any primary or other election for President or Vice President, for electors for President or Vice President, or for Senator or Representative in Congress, shall not be denied or abridged by the United States or any State by reason of failure to pay any poll tax or other tax.

Section 2. The Congress shall have power to enforce this article by appropriate legislation.

Amendment XXV [1967]

Section 1. In case of the removal of the President from office or of his death or resignation, the Vice President shall become President.

Section 2. Whenever there is a vacancy in the office of the Vice President, the President shall nominate a Vice President who shall take office upon confirmation by a majority vote of both Houses of Congress.

Section 3. Whenever the President transmits to the President pro tempore of the Senate and the Speaker of the House of Representatives his written declaration that he is unable to discharge the powers and duties of his office, and until he transmits to them a written declaration to the contrary, such powers and duties shall be discharged by the Vice President as Acting President.

Section 4. Whenever the Vice President and a majority of either the principal officers of the executive departments or of such other body as Congress may by law provide, transmit to the President pro tempore of the Senate and the Speaker of the House of Representatives their written declaration that the President is unable to discharge the powers and duties of his office, the Vice President shall immediately assume the powers and duties of the office as Acting President.

Thereafter, when the President transmits to the President pro tempore of the Senate and the Speaker of the House of Representatives his written declaration that no inability exists, he shall resume the powers and duties of his office unless the Vice President and a majority of either the principal officers of the executive department or of such other body as Congress may by law provide, transmit within four days to the President pro tempore of the Senate and the Speaker of the House of Representatives their written declaration that the President is unable to discharge the powers and duties of his office. Thereupon Congress shall decide the issue, assembling within forty-eight hours for that purpose if not in session. If the Congress, within twenty-one days after receipt of the latter written declaration, or, if Congress is not in session, within twenty-one days after Congress is required to assemble, determines by two-thirds vote of both Houses that the President is unable to discharge the powers and duties of his office, the Vice President shall continue to discharge the same as Acting President; otherwise, the President shall resume the powers and duties of his office.

Amendment XXVI [1971]

Section 1. The right of citizens of the United States, who are eighteen years of age or older, to vote shall not be denied or abridged by the United States or by any State on account of age.

Section 2. The Congress shall have power to enforce this article by appropriate legislation.

Amendment XXVII [1992]

No law, varying the compensation for the services of the Senators and Representatives, shall take effect, until an election of Representatives shall have intervened.

TRADING WITH THE ENEMY ACT
(1917, as amended)

Act Oct. 6, 1917, C. 106, 40 Stat. 411, 50 U.S.C. App. §§1-5
(2012)

§5. Suspension of Provisions Relating to Ally of Enemy; Regulation of Transactions in Foreign Exchange of Gold or Silver, Property Transfers, Vested Interests, Enforcement and Penalties

(b) (1) During the time of war, the President may, through any agency that he may designate, and under such rules and regulations as he may prescribe, by means of instructions, licenses, or otherwise—

(A) investigate, regulate, or prohibit, any transactions in foreign exchange, transfers of credit or payments between, by, through, or to any banking institution, and the importing, exporting, hoarding, melting, or earmarking of gold or silver coin or bullion, currency or securities, and

(B) investigate, regulate, direct and compel, nullify, void, prevent or prohibit, any acquisition holding, withholding, use, transfer, withdrawal, transportation, importation or exportation of, or dealing in, or exercising any right, power, or privilege with respect to, or transactions involving, any property in which any foreign country or a national thereof has any interest, by any person, or with respect to any property, subject to the jurisdiction of the United States; and any property or interest of any foreign country or national thereof shall vest, when, as, and upon the terms, directed by the President, in such agency or person as may be designated from time to time by the President, and upon such terms and conditions as the President may prescribe such interest or property shall be held, used, administered, liquidated, sold, or otherwise dealt with in the interest of and for the benefit of the United States, and such designated agency or person may perform any and all acts incident to the accomplishment or furtherance of these purposes; and the President shall, in the manner hereinabove provided, require any person to keep a full record of, and to furnish under oath, in the form of reports or otherwise, complete information relative to any act or transaction referred to in this subdivision either before, during, or after the completion thereof, or relative to any interest in foreign property, or relative to any property in which any foreign country or any national thereof has or has had any interest, or as may be otherwise necessary to enforce the provisions of this subdivision, and in any case in which a report could be required, the President may, in the manner hereinabove provided, require the production, or if necessary to the national security or defense, the seizure, of any books of account, records, contracts, letters, memoranda, or other papers, in the custody or control of such person. . . .

(3) As used in this subdivision the term "United States" means the United States and any place subject to the jurisdiction thereof: *Provided, however,* That the foregoing shall not be construed as a limitation upon the power of the President, which is hereby conferred to prescribe from time to time, definitions, not inconsistent with the purposes of this subdivision, for any or all of the terms used in this subdivision. As used in this subdivision the term "person" means an individual, partnership, association, or corporation.

(4) The authority granted to the President by this section does not include the authority to regulate or prohibit, directly or indirectly, the importation from any country, or the exportation to any country, whether commercial or otherwise, regardless of format or medium of transmission, of any information or informational materials, including but not limited to, publications, films, posters, phonograph records, photographs, microfilms, microfiche, tapes, compact disks, CD ROMs, artworks, and news wire feeds. The exports exempted from regulation or prohibition by this paragraph do not include those which are otherwise controlled for export under section 5 of the Export Administration Act of 1979 [section 2404 of this Appendix], or under section 6 of that Act [section 2405 of this Appendix] to the extent that such controls promote the nonproliferation or antiterrorism policies of the United States, or with respect to which acts are prohibited by chapter 37 of title 18, United States Code [18 U.S.C.A. §791 et seq.].

(As amended Pub. L. 103-236, Title V, §525(b)(1), Apr. 30, 1994, 108 Stat. 474.)

NATIONAL EMERGENCIES ACT

Act Sept. 14, 1976, 90 Stat. 1255, 50 U.S.C. §§1601-1651
(2012)

Subchapter I—Terminating Existing Declared Emergencies

§1601.   Termination of Existing Declared Emergencies

(a) All powers and authorities possessed by the President, any other officer or employee of the Federal Government, or any executive agency, as defined in section 105 of Title 5, as a result of the existence of any declaration of national emergency in effect on September 14, 1976 are terminated two years from September 14, 1976. Such termination shall not affect—

(1) any action taken or proceeding pending not finally concluded or determined on such date;

(2) any action or proceeding based on any act committed prior to such date; or

(3) any rights or duties that matured or penalties that were incurred prior to such date.

(b) For the purpose of this section, the words "any national emergency in effect" means a general declaration of emergency made by the President.

Subchapter II—Declarations of Future National Emergencies

§1621.   Declaration of National Emergency by President; Publication in Federal Register; Effect on Other Laws; Superseding Legislation

(a) With respect to Acts of Congress authorizing the exercise, during the period of a national emergency, of any special or extraordinary power, the President is authorized to declare such national emergency. Such proclamation shall immediately be transmitted to the Congress and published in the Federal Register.

(b) Any provisions of law conferring powers and authorities to be exercised during a national emergency shall be effective and remain in effect

(1) only when the President (in accordance with subsection (a) of this section), specifically declares a national emergency, and (2) only in accordance with this chapter. No law enacted after September 14, 1976, shall supersede this subchapter unless it does so in specific terms, referring to this subchapter, and declaring that the new law supersedes the provisions of this subchapter.

§1622.   National Emergencies

(a)   Termination Methods

Any national emergency declared by the President in accordance with this subchapter shall terminate if—

(1) there is enacted into law a joint resolution terminating the emergency; or

(2) the President issues a proclamation terminating the emergency.

Any national emergency declared by the President shall be terminated on the date specified in any joint resolution referred to in clause (1) or on the date specified in a proclamation by the President terminating the emergency as provided in clause (2) of this subsection, whichever date is earlier, and any powers or authorities exercised by reason of said emergency shall cease to be exercised after such specified date, except that such termination shall not affect—

(A) any action taken or proceeding pending not finally concluded or determined on such date;

(B) any action or proceeding based on any act committed prior to such date; or

(C) any rights or duties that matured or penalties that were incurred prior to such date.

(b)   Termination Review of National Emergencies by Congress

Not later than six months after a national emergency is declared, and not later than the end of each six-month period thereafter that such emergency continues, each House of Congress shall meet to consider a vote on a joint resolution to determine whether that emergency shall be terminated.

(c)   Joint Resolution; Referral to Congressional Committees; Conference Committee in Event of Disagreement; Filing of Report; Termination Procedure Deemed Part of Rules of House and Senate

(1) A joint resolution to terminate a national emergency declared by the President shall be referred to the appropriate committee of the House of

Representatives or the Senate, as the case may be. One such joint resolution shall be reported out by such committee together with its recommendations within fifteen calendar days after the day on which such resolution is referred to such committee, unless such House shall otherwise determine by the yeas and nays.

(2) Any joint resolution so reported shall become the pending business of the House in question (in the case of the Senate the time for debate shall be equally divided between the proponents and the opponents) and shall be voted on within three calendar days after the day on which such resolution is reported, unless such House shall otherwise determine by yeas and nays.

(3) Such a joint resolution passed by one House shall be referred to the appropriate committee of the other House and shall be reported out by such committee together with its recommendations within fifteen calendar days after the day on which such resolution is referred to such committee and shall thereupon become the pending business of such House and shall be voted upon within three calendar days after the day on which such resolution is reported, unless such House shall otherwise determine by yeas and nays.

(4) In the case of any disagreement between the two Houses of Congress with respect to a joint resolution passed by both Houses, conferees shall be promptly appointed and the committee of conference shall make and file a report with respect to such joint resolution within six calendar days after the day on which managers on the part of the Senate and the House have been appointed. Notwithstanding any rule in either House concerning the printing of conference reports or concerning any delay in the consideration of such reports, such report shall be acted on by both Houses not later than six calendar days after the conference report is filed in the House in which such report is filed first. In the event the conferees are unable to agree within forty-eight hours, they shall report back to their respective Houses in disagreement.

(5) Paragraphs (1)-(4) of this subsection, subsection (b) of this section, and section 1651(b) of this title are enacted by Congress—

(A) as an exercise of the rulemaking power of the Senate and the House of Representatives, respectively, and as such they are deemed a part of the rules of each House, respectively, but applicable only with respect to the procedure to be followed in the House in the case of resolutions described by this subsection; and they supersede other rules only to the extent that they are inconsistent therewith; and

(B) with full recognition of the constitutional right of either House to change the rules (so far as relating to the procedure of that House) at any time, in the same manner, and to the same extent as in the case of any other rule of that House.

(d) Automatic Termination of National Emergency; Continuation Notice from President to Congress; Publication in Federal Register

Any national emergency declared by the President in accordance with this subchapter, and not otherwise previously terminated, shall terminate on the anniversary of the declaration of that emergency if, within the ninety-day period prior to each anniversary date, the President does not publish in the Federal Register and transmit to the Congress a notice stating that such emergency is to continue in effect after such anniversary.

(Pub. L. 94-412, Title II, §202, Sept. 14, 1976, 90 Stat. 1255; amended Pub. L. 99-93, Title VIII, §801, Aug. 16, 1985, 99 Stat. 448.)

1985 Amendment. Subsec. (a)(1). Pub. L. 99-93, 801(1)(A), substituted "there is enacted into law a joint resolution terminating the emergency" for "Congress terminates the emergency by concurrent resolution".

Subsec. (a). Pub. L. 99-93, §801(1)(B), in the provisions following par. (2) substituted "joint resolution" for "concurrent resolution".

Subsec. (b). Pub. L. 99-93, §801(2), substituted "joint resolution" for "concurrent resolution".

Subsec. (c)(1) to (4). Pub. L. 99-93, §801(3), substituted "joint resolution" for "concurrent resolution" wherever appearing.

Subchapter III—Exercise of Emergency Powers and Authorities

§1631. Declaration of National Emergency by Executive Order; Authority; Publication in Federal Register, Transmittal to Congress

When the President declares a national emergency, no powers or authorities made available by statute for use in the event of an emergency shall be exercised unless and until the President specifies the provisions of law under which he proposes that he, or other officers will act. Such specification may be made either in the declaration of a national emergency, or by one or more contemporaneous or subsequent Executive orders published in the Federal Register and transmitted to the Congress.

Subchapter IV—Accountability and Reporting Requirements of President

§1641. Accountability and Reporting Requirements of President

(a) Maintenance of File and Index of Presidential Orders, Rules and Regulations During National Emergency

When the President declares a national emergency, or Congress declares war, the President shall be responsible for maintaining a file and index of all significant orders of the President, including Executive orders and proclamations, and each Executive agency shall maintain a file and index of all rules and regulations, issued during such emergency or war issued pursuant to such declarations.

(b) Presidential Orders, Rules and Regulations; Transmittal to Congress

All such significant orders of the President, including Executive orders, and such rules and regulations shall be transmitted to the Congress promptly under means to assure confidentiality where appropriate.

(c) Expenditures During National Emergency; Presidential Reports to Congress

When the President declares a national emergency or Congress declares war, the President shall transmit to Congress, within ninety days after the end of each six-month period after such declaration, a report on the total expenditures incurred by the United States Government during such six-month period which are directly attributable to the exercise of powers and authorities conferred by such declaration. Not later than ninety days after the termination of each such emergency or war, the President shall transmit a final report on all such expenditures.

INTERNATIONAL EMERGENCY
ECONOMIC POWERS ACT (IEEPA)
(1977, as amended through 2012)

50 U.S.C. §§1701-1706

§1701. Unusual and Extraordinary Threat; Declaration of National Emergency; Exercise of Presidential Authorities

(a) Any authority granted to the President by section 1702 of this title may be exercised to deal with any unusual and extraordinary threat, which has its source in whole or substantial part outside the United States, to the national security, foreign policy, or economy of the United States, if the President declares a national emergency with respect to such threat.

(b) The authorities granted to the President by section 1702 of this title may only be exercised to deal with an unusual and extraordinary threat with respect to which a national emergency has been declared for purposes of this chapter and may not be exercised for any other purpose. Any exercise of such authorities to deal with any new threat shall be based on a new declaration of national emergency which must be with respect to such threat.

§1702. Presidential Authorities

(a)(1) At the times and to the extent specified in section 1701 of this title, the President may, under such regulations as he may prescribe, by means of instructions, licenses, or otherwise—

    (A) investigate, regulate, or prohibit—

        (i) any transactions in foreign exchange,

        (ii) transfers of credit or payments between, by, through, or to any banking institution, to the extent that such transfers or payments involve any interest of any foreign country or a national thereof,

        (iii) the importing or exporting of currency or securities, by any person, or with respect to any property, subject to the jurisdiction of the United States;

(B) investigate, block during the pendency of an investigation, regulate, direct and compel, nullify, void, prevent or prohibit, any acquisition, holding, withholding, use, transfer, withdrawal, transportation, importation or exportation of, or dealing in, or exercising any right, power, or privilege with respect to, or transactions involving, any property in which any foreign country or a national thereof has any interest by any person, or with respect to any property, subject to the jurisdiction of the United States; and

(C) when the United States is engaged in armed hostilities or has been attacked by a foreign country or foreign nationals, confiscate any property, subject to the jurisdiction of the United States, of any foreign person, foreign organization, or foreign country that he determines has planned, authorized, aided, or engaged in such hostilities or attacks against the United States; and all right, title, and interest in any property so confiscated shall vest, when, as, and upon the terms directed by the President, in such agency or person as the President may designate from time to time, and upon such terms and conditions as the President may prescribe, such interest or property shall be held, used, administered, liquidated, sold, or otherwise dealt with in the interest of and for the benefit of the United States, and such designated agency or person may perform any and all acts incident to the accomplishment or furtherance of these purposes.

(2) In exercising the authorities granted by paragraph (1), the President may require any person to keep a full record of, and to furnish under oath, in the form of reports or otherwise, complete information relative to any act or transaction referred to in paragraph (1) either before, during, or after the completion thereof, or relative to any interest in foreign property, or relative to any property in which any foreign country or any national thereof has or has had any interest, or as may be otherwise necessary to enforce the provisions of such paragraph. In any case in which a report by a person could be required under this paragraph, the President may require the production of any books of account, records, contracts, letters, memoranda, or other papers, in the custody or control of such person.

(3) Compliance with any regulation, instruction, or direction issued under this chapter shall to the extent thereof be a full acquittance and discharge for all purposes of the obligation of the person making the same. No person shall be held liable in any court for or with respect to anything done or omitted in good faith in connection with the administration of, or pursuant to and in reliance on, this chapter, or any regulation, instruction, or direction issued under this chapter.

(b) The authority granted to the President by this section does not include the authority to regulate or prohibit, directly or indirectly—

(1) any postal, telegraphic, telephonic, or other personal communication, which does not involve a transfer of anything of value; or

(2) donations, by persons subject to the jurisdiction of the United States, of articles, such as food, clothing, and medicine, intended to be used to relieve human suffering, except to the extent that the President determines that such donations (A) would seriously impair his ability to deal with any national emergency declared under section 1701 of this title, (B) are in

response to coercion against the proposed recipient or donor, or (C) would endanger Armed Forces of the United States which are engaged in hostilities or are in a situation where imminent involvement in hostilities is clearly indicated by the circumstances; or

(3) the importation from any country, or the exportation to any country, whether commercial or otherwise, regardless of format or medium of transmission, of any information or informational materials, including but not limited to, publications, films, posters, phonograph records, photographs, microfilms, microfiche, tapes, compact disks, CD ROMs, artworks, and news wire feeds. The exports exempted from regulation or prohibition by this paragraph do not include those which are otherwise controlled for export under section 2404 of the Appendix to this title, or under section 2405 of the Appendix to this title to the extent that such controls promote the nonproliferation or antiterrorism policies of the United States, or with respect to which acts are prohibited by chapter 37 of Tide 18; or

(4) any transactions ordinarily incident to travel to or from any country, including importation of accompanied baggage for personal use, maintenance within any country including payment of living expenses and acquisition of goods or services for personal use, and arrangement or facilitation of such travel including nonscheduled air, sea, or land voyages.

(c) Classified information.—In any judicial review of a determination made under this section, if the determination was based on classified information (as defined in section 1(a) of the Classified Information Procedures Act) such information may be submitted to the reviewing court ex parte and in camera. This subsection does not confer or imply any right to judicial review.

(As amended by Pub. L. 103-236, Title V, §525(c)(1), Apr. 30, 1994, 108 Stat. 474, and by Pub. L. 107-56, Title I, §106, Oct. 26, 2001, 115 Stat 277.)

§1703. Consultation and Reports

(a) Consultation with Congress

The President, in every possible instance, shall consult with the Congress before exercising any of the authorities granted by this chapter and shall consult regularly with the Congress so long as such authorities are exercised.

(b) Report to Congress Upon Exercise of Presidential Authorities

Whenever the President exercises any of the authorities granted by this chapter, he shall immediately transmit to the Congress a report specifying—

(1) the circumstances which necessitate such exercise of authority;

(2) why the President believes those circumstances constitute an unusual and extraordinary threat, which has its source in whole or substantial part outside the United States, to the national security, foreign policy, or economy of the United States;

(3) the authorities to be exercised and the actions to be taken in the exercise of those authorities to deal with those circumstances;

(4) why the President believes such actions are necessary to deal with those circumstances; and

(5) any foreign countries with respect to which such actions are to be taken and why such actions are to be taken with respect to those countries.

(c) Periodic Follow-up Reports

At least once during each succeeding six-month period after transmitting a report pursuant to subsection (b) of this section with respect to an exercise of authorities under this chapter, the President shall report to the Congress with respect to the actions taken, since the last such report, in the exercise of such authorities, and with respect to any changes which have occurred concerning any information previously furnished pursuant to paragraphs (1) through (5) of subsection (b) of this section.

(d) Supplemental Requirements

The requirements of this section are supplemental to those contained in title IV of the National Emergencies Act [50 U.S.C. §1641].

§1704. Authority to Issue Regulations

The President may issue such regulations, including regulations prescribing definitions, as may be necessary for the exercise of the authorities granted by this chapter.

§1705. Penalties

(a) Unlawful acts

It shall be unlawful for a person to violate, attempt to violate, conspire to violate, or cause a violation of any license, order, regulation, or prohibition issued under this chapter.

(b) Civil Penalty

A civil penalty may be imposed on any person who commits an unlawful act described in subsection (a) of this section in an amount not to exceed the greater of—
>   (1) $250,000; or
>   (2) an amount that is twice the amount of the transaction that is the basis of the violation with respect to which the penalty is imposed.

(c) Criminal penalty

A person who willfully commits, willfully attempts to commit, or willfully conspires to commit, or aids or abets in the commission of, an unlawful act described in subsection (a) of this section shall, upon conviction, be fined not more than $1,000,000, or if a natural person, may be imprisoned for not more than 20 years, or both.

(As amended by Pub.L. 102-393, Title VI, § 629, Oct. 6, 1992, 106 Stat. 1773; Pub.L. 102-396, Title IX, § 9155, Oct. 6, 1992, 106 Stat. 1943; Pub.L. 104-201, Div. A, Title XIV, § 1422, Sept. 23, 1996, 110 Stat. 2725; Pub.L. 109-177, Title IV, § 402, Mar. 9, 2006, 120 Stat. 243; Pub.L. 110-96, § 2(a), Oct. 16, 2007, 121 Stat. 1011.)

§1706. Savings Provisions

(a) Termination of National Emergencies Pursuant to National Emergencies Act

(1) Except as provided in subsection (b) of this section, notwithstanding the termination pursuant to the National Emergencies Act [50 U.S.C. §1601 et seq.] of a national emergency declared for purposes of this chapter, any authorities granted by this chapter, which are exercised on the date of such termination on the basis of such national emergency to prohibit transactions involving property in which a foreign country or national thereof has any interest, may continue to be so exercised to prohibit transactions involving that property if the President determines that the continuation of such prohibition with respect to that property is necessary on account of claims involving such country or its nationals.

(2) Notwithstanding the termination of the authorities described in section 101(b) of this Act, any such authorities, which are exercised with respect to a country on the date of such termination to prohibit transactions involving any property in which such country or any national there of has any interest, may continue to be exercised to prohibit transactions involving that property if the President determines that the continuation of such prohibition with respect to that property is necessary on account of claims involving such country or its nationals.

(b) Congressional Termination of National Emergencies by Concurrent Resolution

The authorities described in subsection (a)(1) of this section may not continue to be exercised under this section if the national emergency is terminated by the Congress by concurrent resolution pursuant to section 202 of the National Emergencies Act [50 U.S.C. §1622] and if the Congress specifies in such concurrent resolution that such authorities may not continue to be exercised under this section.

(c) Supplemental Savings Provisions; Supersedure of Inconsistent Provisions . . .

(d) Periodic Reports to Congress

If the President uses the authority of this section to continue prohibitions on transactions involving foreign property interests, he shall report to the Congress every six months on the use of such authority.

§1707. Multinational economic embargoes against governments in armed conflict with the United States

(a) Policy on the establishment of embargoes

It is the policy of the United States, that upon the use of the Armed Forces of the United States to engage in hostilities against any foreign country, the President shall, as appropriate—

(1) seek the establishment of a multinational economic embargo against such country; and

(2) seek the seizure of its foreign financial assets.

(b) Reports to Congress

Not later than 20 days after the first day of the engagement of the United States in hostilities described in subsection (a) of this section, the President shall, if the armed conflict has continued for 14 days, submit to Congress a report setting forth—

(1) the specific steps the United States has taken and will continue to take to establish a multinational economic embargo and to initiate financial asset seizure pursuant to subsection (a) of this section; and

(2) any foreign sources of trade or revenue that directly or indirectly support the ability of the adversarial government to sustain a military conflict against the United States.

ALIEN TORT STATUTE (ATS)
or ALIEN TORT CLAIMS ACT (ATCA)

28 U.S.C. §1350 (2012)

The district courts shall have original jurisdiction of any civil action by an alien for a tort only, committed in violation of the law of nations or a treaty of the United States.

TORTURE VICTIM PROTECTION ACT
(TVPA)

Act Mar. 12, 1992, Pub. L. 102-256, 106 Stat. 73 (reprinted at 28 U.S.C. §1350 note) (2012)

An Act to carry out obligations of the United States under the United Nations Charter and other international agreements pertaining to the protection of human rights by establishing a civil action for recovery of damages from an individual who engages in torture or extrajudicial killing. . . .

Sec. 2. Establishment of Civil Action.

(a) LIABILITY.—An individual who, under actual or apparent authority, or color of law, of any foreign nation—

(1) subjects an individual to torture shall, in a civil action, be liable for damages to that individual; or

(2) subjects an individual to extrajudicial killing shall, in a civil action, be liable for damages to the individual's legal representative, or to any person who may be a claimant in an action for wrongful death.

(b) EXHAUSTION OF REMEDIES.—A court shall decline to hear a claim under this section if the claimant has not exhausted adequate and available remedies in the place in which the conduct giving rise to the claim occurred.

(c) STATUTE OF LIMITATIONS.—No action shall be maintained under this section unless it is commenced within 10 years after the cause of action arose.

Sec. 3. Definitions.

(a) EXTRAJUDICIAL KILLING.—For the purposes of this Act, the term "extrajudicial killing" means a deliberated killing not authorized by a previous judgment pronounced by a regularly constituted court affording all the judicial guarantees which are recognized as indispensable by civilized peoples. Such term, however, does not include any such killing that, under international law, is lawfully carried out under the authority of a foreign nation.

(b) TORTURE.—For the purposes of this Act—

(1) the term "torture" means any act, directed against an individual in the offender's custody or physical control, by which severe pain or suffering (other than pain or suffering arising only from or inherent in, or incidental to, lawful sanctions), whether physical or mental, is intentionally inflicted on that individual for such purposes as obtaining from that individual or a third person information or a confession, punishing that individual for an act that individual or a third person has committed or is suspected of having committed, intimidating or coercing that individual or a third person, or for any reason based on discrimination of any kind; and

(2) mental pain or suffering refers to prolonged mental harm caused by or resulting from—

(A) the intentional infliction or threatened infliction of severe physical pain or suffering;

(B) the administration or application, or threatened administration or application, of mind altering substances or other procedures calculated to disrupt profoundly the senses or the personality;

(C) the threat of imminent death; or

(D) the threat that another individual will imminently be subjected to death, severe physical pain or suffering, or the administration or application of mind altering substances or other procedures calculated to disrupt profoundly the senses or personality.

4

International Dispute Resolution

INTERNATIONAL CHAMBER OF COMMERCE (ICC) 2012 RULES OF ARBITRATION*

<http://www.iccwbo.org>

Introductory Provisions

Article 1. International Court of Arbitration

1. The International Court of Arbitration (the "Court") of the International Chamber of Commerce (the "ICC") is the independent arbitration body of the ICC. The statutes of the Court are set forth in Appendix I.

2. The Court does not itself resolve disputes. It administers the resolution of disputes by arbitral tribunals, in accordance with the Rules of Arbitration of the ICC (the "Rules"). The Court is the only body authorized to administer arbitrations under the Rules, including the scrutiny and approval of awards rendered in accordance with the Rules. It draws up its own internal rules, which are set forth in Appendix II (the "Internal Rules").

3. The President of the Court (the "President") or, in the President's absence or otherwise at the President's request, one of its Vice-Presidents shall have the power to take urgent decisions on behalf of the Court, provided that any such decision is reported to the Court at its next session.

4. As provided for in the Internal Rules, the Court may delegate to one or more committees composed of its members the power to take certain decisions, provided that any such decision is reported to the Court at its next session.

---

* These current Rules of Arbitration of the International Chamber of Commerce (ICC) went into force as of January 1, 2012.

5. The Court is assisted in its work by the Secretariat of the Court (the "Secretariat") under the direction of its Secretary General (the "Secretary General").

Article 2. *Definitions*

In the Rules:

(i) "arbitral tribunal" includes one or more arbitrators;

(ii) "claimant" includes one or more claimants, "respondent" includes one or more respondents, and "additional party" includes one or more additional parties;

(iii) "party" or "parties" include claimants, respondents or additional parties;

(iv) "claim" or "claims" include any claim by any party against any other party;

(v) "award" includes, inter alia, an interim, partial or final award.

Article 3. *Written Notifications or Communications; Time Limits*

1. All pleadings and other written communications submitted by any party, as well as all documents annexed thereto, shall be supplied in a number of copies sufficient to provide one copy for each party, plus one for each arbitrator, and one for the Secretariat. A copy of any notification or communication from the arbitral tribunal to the parties shall be sent to the Secretariat. . . .

4. Periods of time specified in or fixed under the Rules shall start to run on the day following the date a notification or communication is deemed to have been made in accordance with Article 3(3). When the day next following such date is an official holiday, or a non-business day in the country where the notification or communication is deemed to have been made, the period of time shall commence on the first following business day. Official holidays and non-business days are included in the calculation of the period of time. If the last day of the relevant period of time granted is an official holiday or a non-business day in the country where the notification or communication is deemed to have been made, the period of time shall expire at the end of the first following business day.

Commencing the Arbitration

Article 4. *Request for Arbitration*

1. A party wishing to have recourse to arbitration under the Rules shall submit its Request for Arbitration (the "Request") to the Secretariat . . . . The Secretariat shall notify the claimant and respondent of the receipt of the Request and the date of such receipt.

2. The date on which the Request is received by the Secretariat shall, for all purposes, be deemed to be the date of the commencement of the arbitration.

3. The Request shall contain the following information:

(a) the name in full, description, address and other contact details of each of the parties;

(b) the name in full, address and other contact details of any person(s) representing the claimant in the arbitration;

(c) a description of the nature and circumstances of the dispute giving rise to the claims and of the basis upon which the claims are made;

(d) a statement of the relief sought, together with the amounts of any quantified claims and, to the extent possible, an estimate of the monetary value of any other claims;

(e) any relevant agreements and, in particular, the arbitration agreement(s);

(f) where claims are made under more than one arbitration agreement, an indication of the arbitration agreement under which each claim is made;

(g) all relevant particulars and any observations or proposals concerning the number of arbitrators and their choice in accordance with the provisions of Articles 12 and 13, and any nomination of an arbitrator required thereby; and

(h) all relevant particulars and any observations or proposals as to the place of the arbitration, the applicable rules of law and the language of the arbitration.

The claimant may submit such other documents or information with the Request as it considers appropriate or as may contribute to the efficient resolution of the dispute.

4. Together with the Request, the claimant shall:

(a) submit the number of copies thereof required by Article 3(1); and

(b) make payment of the filing fee required by Appendix III ("Arbitration Costs and Fees") in force on the date the Request is submitted.

In the event that the claimant fails to comply with either of these requirements, the Secretariat may fix a time limit within which the claimant must comply, failing which the file shall be closed without prejudice to the claimant's right to submit the same claims at a later date in another Request.

5. The Secretariat shall transmit a copy of the Request and the documents annexed thereto to the respondent for its Answer to the Request once the Secretariat has sufficient copies of the Request and the required filing fee.

Article 5.   *Answer to the Request; Counterclaims*

1. Within 30 days from the receipt of the Request from the Secretariat, the respondent shall submit an Answer (the "Answer") which shall contain the following information:

(a) its name in full, description, address and other contact details;

(b) the name in full, address and other contact details of any person(s) representing the respondent in the arbitration;

(c) its comments as to the nature and circumstances of the dispute giving rise to the claims and the basis upon which the claims are made;

(d) its response to the relief sought;

(e) any observations or proposals concerning the number of arbitrators and their choice in light of the claimant's proposals and in accordance with the provisions of Articles 12 and 13, and any nomination of an arbitrator required thereby; and f) any observations or proposals as to the place of the arbitration, the applicable rules of law and the language of the arbitration.

The respondent may submit such other documents or information with the Answer as it considers appropriate or as may contribute to the efficient resolution of the dispute.

2. The Secretariat may grant the respondent an extension of the time for submitting the Answer, provided the application for such an extension contains the respondent's observations or proposals concerning the number of arbitrators and their choice and, where required by Articles 12 and 13, the nomination of an arbitrator. If the respondent fails to do so, the Court shall proceed in accordance with the Rules . . . .

4. The Secretariat shall communicate the Answer and the documents annexed thereto to all other parties.

5. Any counterclaims made by the respondent shall be submitted with the Answer and shall provide:

(a) a description of the nature and circumstances of the dispute giving rise to the counterclaims and of the basis upon which the counterclaims are made;

(b) a statement of the relief sought together with the amounts of any quantified counterclaims and, to the extent possible, an estimate of the monetary value of any other counterclaims;

(c) any relevant agreements and, in particular, the arbitration agreement(s); and

(d) where counterclaims are made under more than one arbitration agreement, an indication of the arbitration agreement under which each counterclaim is made.

The respondent may submit such other documents or information with the counterclaims as it considers appropriate or as may contribute to the efficient resolution of the dispute.

6. The claimant shall submit a reply to any counterclaim within 30 days from the date of receipt of the counterclaims communicated by the Secretariat. Prior to the transmission of the file to the arbitral tribunal, the Secretariat may grant the claimant an extension of time for submitting the reply.

Article 6. *Effect of the Arbitration Agreement*

1. Where the parties have agreed to submit to arbitration under the Rules, they shall be deemed to have submitted *ipso facto* to the Rules in effect

on the date of commencement of the arbitration, unless they have agreed to submit to the Rules in effect on the date of their arbitration agreement.

2. By agreeing to arbitration under the Rules, the parties have accepted that the arbitration shall be administered by the Court.

3. If any party against which a claim has been made does not submit an Answer, or raises one or more pleas concerning the existence, validity or scope of the arbitration agreement or concerning whether all of the claims made in the arbitration may be determined together in a single arbitration, the arbitration shall proceed and any question of jurisdiction or of whether the claims may be determined together in that arbitration shall be decided directly by the arbitral tribunal, unless the Secretary General refers the matter to the Court for its decision pursuant to Article 6(4).

4. In all cases referred to the Court under Article 6(3), the Court shall decide whether and to what extent the arbitration shall proceed. The arbitration shall proceed if and to the extent that the Court is *prima facie* satisfied that an arbitration agreement under the Rules may exist. . . .

5. In all matters decided by the Court under Article 6(4), any decision as to the jurisdiction of the arbitral tribunal, except as to parties or claims with respect to which the Court decides that the arbitration cannot proceed, shall then be taken by the arbitral tribunal itself.

6. Where the parties are notified of the Court's decision pursuant to Article 6(4) that the arbitration cannot proceed in respect of some or all of them, any party retains the right to ask any court having jurisdiction whether or not, and in respect of which of them, there is a binding arbitration agreement.

7. Where the Court has decided pursuant to Article 6(4) that the arbitration cannot proceed in respect of any of the claims, such decision shall not prevent a party from reintroducing the same claim at a later date in other proceedings.

8. If any of the parties refuses or fails to take part in the arbitration or any stage thereof, the arbitration shall proceed notwithstanding such refusal or failure. . . .

Multiple Parties, Multiple Contracts and Consolidation

Article 7. *Joinder of Additional Parties*

1. A party wishing to join an additional party to the arbitration shall submit its request for arbitration against the additional party (the "Request for Joinder") to the Secretariat. The date on which the Request for Joinder is received by the Secretariat shall, for all purposes, be deemed to be the date of the commencement of arbitration against the additional party. Any such joinder shall be subject to the provisions of Articles 6(3)–6(7) and 9. No additional party may be joined after the confirmation or appointment of any arbitrator, unless all parties, including the additional party, otherwise agree.

The Secretariat may fix a time limit for the submission of a Request for Joinder.

2. The Request for Joinder shall contain the following information:

(a) the case reference of the existing arbitration;

(b) the name in full, description, address and other contact details of each of the parties, including the additional party; and

(c) the information specified in Article 4(3) subparagraphs c), d), e) and f).

The party filing the Request for Joinder may submit therewith such other documents or information as it considers appropriate or as may contribute to the efficient resolution of the dispute.

3. The provisions of Articles 4(4) and 4(5) shall apply, *mutatis mutandis*, to the Request for Joinder.

4. The additional party shall submit an Answer in accordance, *mutatis mutandis*, with the provisions of Articles 5(1)–5(4). . . .

Article 8.   Claims Between Multiple Parties

1. In an arbitration with multiple parties, claims may be made by any party against any other party, subject to the provisions of Articles 6(3)–6(7) and 9 and provided that no new claims may be made after the Terms of Reference are signed or approved by the Court without the authorization of the arbitral tribunal pursuant to Article 23(4). . . .

Article 9.   Multiple Contracts

Subject to the provisions of Articles 6(3)–6(7) and 23(4), claims arising out of or in connection with more than one contract may be made in a single arbitration, irrespective of whether such claims are made under one or more than one arbitration agreement under the Rules.

Article 10.   Consolidation of Arbitrations

The Court may, at the request of a party, consolidate two or more arbitrations pending under the Rules into a single arbitration, where: . . . .

The Arbitral Tribunal

Article 11.   General Provisions

1. Every arbitrator must be and remain impartial and independent of the parties involved in the arbitration.

2. Before appointment or confirmation, a prospective arbitrator shall sign a statement of acceptance, availability, impartiality and independence. The prospective arbitrator shall disclose in writing to the Secretariat any facts or circumstances which might be of such a nature as to call into question the arbitrator's independence in the eyes of the parties, as well as any

circumstances that could give rise to reasonable doubts as to the arbitrator's impartiality. The Secretariat shall provide such information to the parties in writing and fix a time limit for any comments from them.

3. An arbitrator shall immediately disclose in writing to the Secretariat and to the parties any facts or circumstances of a similar nature to those referred to in Article 11(2) concerning the arbitrator's impartiality or independence which may arise during the arbitration.

4. The decisions of the Court as to the appointment, confirmation, challenge or replacement of an arbitrator shall be final, and the reasons for such decisions shall not be communicated.

5. By accepting to serve, arbitrators undertake to carry out their responsibilities in accordance with the Rules.

6. Insofar as the parties have not provided otherwise, the arbitral tribunal shall be constituted in accordance with the provisions of Articles 12 and 13.

Article 12. Constitution of the Arbitral Tribunal Number of Arbitrators

1. The disputes shall be decided by a sole arbitrator or by three arbitrators.

2. Where the parties have not agreed upon the number of arbitrators, the Court shall appoint a sole arbitrator, save where it appears to the Court that the dispute is such as to warrant the appointment of three arbitrators. In such case, the claimant shall nominate an arbitrator within a period of 15 days from the receipt of the notification of the decision of the Court, and the respondent shall nominate an arbitrator within a period of 15 days from the receipt of the notification of the nomination made by the claimant. If a party fails to nominate an arbitrator, the appointment shall be made by the Court.

Sole Arbitrator

3. Where the parties have agreed that the dispute shall be resolved by a sole arbitrator, they may, by agreement, nominate the sole arbitrator for confirmation. If the parties fail to nominate a sole arbitrator within 30 days from the date when the claimant's Request for Arbitration has been received by the other party, or within such additional time as may be allowed by the Secretariat, the sole arbitrator shall be appointed by the Court.

Three Arbitrators

4. Where the parties have agreed that the dispute shall be resolved by three arbitrators, each party shall nominate in the Request and the Answer, respectively, one arbitrator for confirmation. If a party fails to nominate an arbitrator, the appointment shall be made by the Court.

5. Where the dispute is to be referred to three arbitrators, the third arbitrator, who will act as president of the arbitral tribunal, shall be appointed by the Court, unless the parties have agreed upon another procedure for such appointment, in which case the nomination will be subject to confirmation pursuant to Article 13. Should such procedure not result in a nomination within 30 days from the confirmation or appointment of the co-

arbitrators or any other time limit agreed by the parties or fixed by the Court, the third arbitrator shall be appointed by the Court.

6. Where there are multiple claimants or multiple respondents, and where the dispute is to be referred to three arbitrators, the multiple claimants, jointly, and the multiple respondents, jointly, shall nominate an arbitrator for confirmation pursuant to Article 13. . . .

Article 13. *Appointment and Confirmation of the Arbitrators*

1. In confirming or appointing arbitrators, the Court shall consider the prospective arbitrator's nationality, residence and other relationships with the countries of which the parties or the other arbitrators are nationals and the prospective arbitrator's availability and ability to conduct the arbitration in accordance with the Rules. The same shall apply where the Secretary General confirms arbitrators pursuant to Article 13(2).

2. The Secretary General may confirm as co-arbitrators, sole arbitrators and presidents of arbitral tribunals persons nominated by the parties or pursuant to their particular agreements, provided that the statement they have submitted contains no qualification regarding impartiality or independence or that a qualified statement regarding impartiality or independence has not given rise to objections. Such confirmation shall be reported to the Court at its next session. If the Secretary General considers that a co-arbitrator, sole arbitrator or president of an arbitral tribunal should not be confirmed, the matter shall be submitted to the Court.

3. Where the Court is to appoint an arbitrator, it shall make the appointment upon proposal of a National Committee or Group of the ICC that it considers to be appropriate. If the Court does not accept the proposal made, or if the National Committee or Group fails to make the proposal requested within the time limit fixed by the Court, the Court may repeat its request, request a proposal from another National Committee or Group that it considers to be appropriate, or appoint directly any person whom it regards as suitable.

4. The Court may also appoint directly to act as arbitrator any person whom it regards as suitable where:

(a) one or more of the parties is a state or claims to be a state entity; or

(b) the Court considers that it would be appropriate to appoint an arbitrator from a country or territory where there is no National Committee or Group; or

(c) the President certifies to the Court that circumstances exist which, in the President's opinion, make a direct appointment necessary and appropriate.

5. The sole arbitrator or the president of the arbitral tribunal shall be of a nationality other than those of the parties. However, in suitable circumstances and provided that none of the parties objects within the time limit fixed by the Court, the sole arbitrator or the president of the arbitral tribunal may be chosen from a country of which any of the parties is a national.

Article 14.   Challenge of Arbitrators

1. A challenge of an arbitrator, whether for an alleged lack of impartiality or independence, or otherwise, shall be made by the submission to the Secretariat of a written statement specifying the facts and circumstances on which the challenge is based.

2. For a challenge to be admissible, it must be submitted by a party either within 30 days from receipt by that party of the notification of the appointment or confirmation of the arbitrator, or within 30 days from the date when the party making the challenge was informed of the facts and circumstances on which the challenge is based if such date is subsequent to the receipt of such notification.

3. The Court shall decide on the admissibility and, at the same time, if necessary, on the merits of a challenge after the Secretariat has afforded an opportunity for the arbitrator concerned, the other party or parties and any other members of the arbitral tribunal to comment in writing within a suitable period of time. Such comments shall be communicated to the parties and to the arbitrators.

Article 15.   Replacement of Arbitrators

1. An arbitrator shall be replaced upon death, upon acceptance by the Court of the arbitrator's resignation, upon acceptance by the Court of a challenge, or upon acceptance by the Court of a request of all the parties.

2. An arbitrator shall also be replaced on the Court's own initiative when it decides that the arbitrator is prevented *de jure* or *de facto* from fulfilling the arbitrator's functions, or that the arbitrator is not fulfilling those functions in accordance with the Rules or within the prescribed time limits.

3. When, on the basis of information that has come to its attention, the Court considers applying Article 15(2), it shall decide on the matter after the arbitrator concerned, the parties and any other members of the arbitral tribunal have had an opportunity to comment in writing within a suitable period of time. Such comments shall be communicated to the parties and to the arbitrators.

4. When an arbitrator is to be replaced, the Court has discretion to decide whether or not to follow the original nominating process. Once reconstituted, and after having invited the parties to comment, the arbitral tribunal shall determine if and to what extent prior proceedings shall be repeated before the reconstituted arbitral tribunal.

5. Subsequent to the closing of the proceedings, instead of replacing an arbitrator who has died or been removed by the Court pursuant to Articles 15(1) or 15(2), the Court may decide, when it considers it appropriate, that the remaining arbitrators shall continue the arbitration. In making such determination, the Court shall take into account the views of the remaining arbitrators and of the parties and such other matters that it considers appropriate in the circumstances.

The Arbitral Proceedings

Article 16. Transmission of the File to the Arbitral Tribunal

The Secretariat shall transmit the file to the arbitral tribunal as soon as it has been constituted, provided the advance on costs requested by the Secretariat at this stage has been paid. . . .

Article 18. Place of the Arbitration

1. The place of the arbitration shall be fixed by the Court, unless agreed upon by the parties.

2. The arbitral tribunal may, after consultation with the parties, conduct hearings and meetings at any location it considers appropriate, unless otherwise agreed by the parties.

3. The arbitral tribunal may deliberate at any location it considers appropriate.

Article 19. Rules Governing the Proceedings

The proceedings before the arbitral tribunal shall be governed by the Rules and, where the Rules are silent, by any rules which the parties or, failing them, the arbitral tribunal may settle on, whether or not reference is thereby made to the rules of procedure of a national law to be applied to the arbitration.

Article 20. Language of the Arbitration

In the absence of an agreement by the parties, the arbitral tribunal shall determine the language or languages of the arbitration, due regard being given to all relevant circumstances, including the language of the contract.

Article 21. Applicable Rules of Law

1. The parties shall be free to agree upon the rules of law to be applied by the arbitral tribunal to the merits of the dispute. In the absence of any such agreement, the arbitral tribunal shall apply the rules of law which it determines to be appropriate.

2. The arbitral tribunal shall take account of the provisions of the contract, if any, between the parties and of any relevant trade usages.

3. The arbitral tribunal shall assume the powers of an amiable compositeur or decide ex aequo et bono only if the parties have agreed to give it such powers.

Article 22. Conduct of the Arbitration

1. The arbitral tribunal and the parties shall make every effort to conduct the arbitration in an expeditious and cost-effective manner, having regard to the complexity and value of the dispute.

2. In order to ensure effective case management, the arbitral tribunal, after consulting the parties, may adopt such procedural measures as it considers appropriate, provided that they are not contrary to any agreement of the parties.

3. Upon the request of any party, the arbitral tribunal may make orders concerning the confidentiality of the arbitration proceedings or of any other matters in connection with the arbitration and may take measures for protecting trade secrets and confidential information.

4. In all cases, the arbitral tribunal shall act fairly and impartially and ensure that each party has a reasonable opportunity to present its case.

5. The parties undertake to comply with any order made by the arbitral tribunal.

Article 23.   Terms of Reference

1. As soon as it has received the file from the Secretariat, the arbitral tribunal shall draw up, on the basis of documents or in the presence of the parties and in the light of their most recent submissions, a document defining its Terms of Reference. This document shall include the following particulars:

(a) the names in full, description, address and other contact details of each of the parties and of any person(s) representing a party in the arbitration;

(b) the addresses to which notifications and communications arising in the course of the arbitration may be made;

(c) a summary of the parties' respective claims and of the relief sought by each party, together with the amounts of any quantified claims and, to the extent possible, an estimate of the monetary value of any other claims;

(d) unless the arbitral tribunal considers it inappropriate, a list of issues to be determined;

(e) the names in full, address and other contact details of each of the arbitrators;

(f) the place of the arbitration; and

(g) particulars of the applicable procedural rules and, if such is the case, reference to the power conferred upon the arbitral tribunal to act as amiable compositeur or to decide ex aequo et bono.

2. The Terms of Reference shall be signed by the parties and the arbitral tribunal. Within two months of the date on which the file has been transmitted to it, the arbitral tribunal shall transmit to the Court the Terms of Reference signed by it and by the parties. The Court may extend this time limit pursuant to a reasoned request from the arbitral tribunal or on its own initiative if it decides it is necessary to do so.

3. If any of the parties refuses to take part in the drawing up of the Terms of Reference or to sign the same, they shall be submitted to the Court for approval. When the Terms of Reference have been signed in accordance with Article 23(2) or approved by the Court, the arbitration shall proceed.

4. After the Terms of Reference have been signed or approved by the Court, no party shall make new claims which fall outside the limits of the Terms of Reference unless it has been authorized to do so by the arbitral tribunal, which shall consider the nature of such new claims, the stage of the arbitration and other relevant circumstances.

Article 24.   Case Management Conference and Procedural Timetable

1. When drawing up the Terms of Reference or as soon as possible thereafter, the arbitral tribunal shall convene a case management conference to consult the parties on procedural measures that may be adopted pursuant to Article 22(2). Such measures may include one or more of the case management techniques described in Appendix IV. . . .

3. To ensure continued effective case management, the arbitral tribunal, after consulting the parties by means of a further case management conference or otherwise, may adopt further procedural measures or modify the procedural timetable. . . .

Article 25.   Establishing the Facts of the Case

1. The arbitral tribunal shall proceed within as short a time as possible to establish the facts of the case by all appropriate means.

2. After studying the written submissions of the parties and all documents relied upon, the arbitral tribunal shall hear the parties together in person if any of them so requests or, failing such a request, it may of its own motion decide to hear them.

3. The arbitral tribunal may decide to hear witnesses, experts appointed by the parties or any other person, in the presence of the parties, or in their absence provided they have been duly summoned.

4. The arbitral tribunal, after having consulted the parties, may appoint one or more experts, define their terms of reference and receive their reports. At the request of a party, the parties shall be given the opportunity to question at a hearing any such expert.

5. At any time during the proceedings, the arbitral tribunal may summon any party to provide additional evidence.

6. The arbitral tribunal may decide the case solely on the documents submitted by the parties unless any of the parties requests a hearing.

Article 26.   Hearings

1. When a hearing is to be held, the arbitral tribunal, giving reasonable notice, shall summon the parties to appear before it on the day and at the place fixed by it.

2. If any of the parties, although duly summoned, fails to appear without valid excuse, the arbitral tribunal shall have the power to proceed with the hearing.

3. The arbitral tribunal shall be in full charge of the hearings, at which all the parties shall be entitled to be present. Save with the approval of the

arbitral tribunal and the parties, persons not involved in the proceedings shall not be admitted.

4. The parties may appear in person or through duly authorized representatives. In addition, they may be assisted by advisers.

Article 27.   Closing of the Proceedings and Date for Submission of Draft Awards

As soon as possible after the last hearing concerning matters to be decided in an award or the filing of the last authorized submissions concerning such matters, whichever is later, the arbitral tribunal shall:

(a) declare the proceedings closed with respect to the matters to be decided in the award; and

(b) inform the Secretariat and the parties of the date by which it expects to submit its draft award to the Court for approval pursuant to Article 33.

After the proceedings are closed, no further submission or argument may be made, or evidence produced, with respect to the matters to be decided in the award, unless requested or authorized by the arbitral tribunal.

Article 28.   Conservatory and Interim Measures

1. Unless the parties have otherwise agreed, as soon as the file has been transmitted to it, the arbitral tribunal may, at the request of a party, order any interim or conservatory measure it deems appropriate. . . . Any such measure shall take the form of an order, giving reasons, or of an award, as the arbitral tribunal considers appropriate.

2. Before the file is transmitted to the arbitral tribunal, and in appropriate circumstances even thereafter, the parties may apply to any competent judicial authority for interim or conservatory measures. The application of a party to a judicial authority for such measures or for the implementation of any such measures ordered by an arbitral tribunal shall not be deemed to be an infringement or a waiver of the arbitration agreement and shall not affect the relevant powers reserved to the arbitral tribunal.

Any such application and any measures taken by the judicial authority must be notified without delay to the Secretariat. The Secretariat shall inform the arbitral tribunal thereof.

Article 29.   Emergency Arbitrator

1. A party that needs urgent interim or conservatory measures that cannot await the constitution of an arbitral tribunal ("Emergency Measures") may make an application for such measures pursuant to the Emergency Arbitrator Rules in Appendix V. Any such application shall be accepted only if it is received by the Secretariat prior to the transmission of the file to the arbitral tribunal pursuant to Article 16 and irrespective of whether the party making the application has already submitted its Request for Arbitration.

2. The emergency arbitrator's decision shall take the form of an order. The parties undertake to comply with any order made by the emergency arbitrator. . . .

7. The Emergency Arbitrator Provisions are not intended to prevent any party from seeking urgent interim or conservatory measures from a competent judicial authority at any time prior to making an application for such measures, and in appropriate circumstances even thereafter, pursuant to the Rules. . . .

Awards

Article 30.   Time Limit for the Final Award

1. The time limit within which the arbitral tribunal must render its final award is six months. Such time limit shall start to run from the date of the last signature by the arbitral tribunal or by the parties of the Terms of Reference or, in the case of application of Article 23(3), the date of the notification to the arbitral tribunal by the Secretariat of the approval of the Terms of Reference by the Court. The Court may fix a different time limit based upon the procedural timetable established pursuant to Article 24(2).

2. The Court may extend the time limit pursuant to a reasoned request from the arbitral tribunal or on its own initiative if it decides it is necessary to do so.

Article 31.   Making of the Award

1. When the arbitral tribunal is composed of more than one arbitrator, an award is made by a majority decision. If there is no majority, the award shall be made by the president of the arbitral tribunal alone.

2. The award shall state the reasons upon which it is based.

3. The award shall be deemed to be made at the place of the arbitration and on the date stated therein.

Article 32.   Award by Consent

If the parties reach a settlement after the file has been transmitted to the arbitral tribunal in accordance with Article 16, the settlement shall be recorded in the form of an award made by consent of the parties, if so requested by the parties and if the arbitral tribunal agrees to do so.

Article 33.   Scrutiny of the Award by the Court

Before signing any award, the arbitral tribunal shall submit it in draft form to the Court. The Court may lay down modifications as to the form of the award and, without affecting the arbitral tribunal's liberty of decision, may also draw its attention to points of substance. No award shall be rendered by the arbitral tribunal until it has been approved by the Court as to its form.

Article 34.   Notification, Deposit and Enforceability of the Award

1. Once an award has been made, the Secretariat shall notify to the parties the text signed by the arbitral tribunal, provided always that the costs of the arbitration have been fully paid to the ICC by the parties or by one of them. . . .

6. Every award shall be binding on the parties. By submitting the dispute to arbitration under the Rules, the parties undertake to carry out any award without delay and shall be deemed to have waived their right to any form of recourse insofar as such waiver can validly be made.

Article 35.   Correction and Interpretation of the Award; Remission of Awards

1. On its own initiative, the arbitral tribunal may correct a clerical, computational or typographical error, or any errors of similar nature contained in an award, provided such correction is submitted for approval to the Court within 30 days of the date of such award.

2. Any application of a party for the correction of an error of the kind referred to in Article 35(1), or for the interpretation of an award, must be made to the Secretariat within 30 days of the receipt of the award by such party, in a number of copies as stated in Article 3(1). . . .

Costs

Article 36.   Advance to Cover the Costs of the Arbitration

1. After receipt of the Request, the Secretary General may request the claimant to pay a provisional advance in an amount intended to cover the costs of the arbitration until the Terms of Reference have been drawn up. . . .

2. As soon as practicable, the Court shall fix the advance on costs in an amount likely to cover the fees and expenses of the arbitrators and the ICC administrative expenses for the claims which have been referred to it by the parties, unless any claims are made under Article 7 or 8 in which case Article 36(4) shall apply. The advance on costs fixed by the Court pursuant to this Article 36(2) shall be payable in equal shares by the claimant and the respondent. . . .

Article 37.   Decision as to the Costs of the Arbitration

1. The costs of the arbitration shall include the fees and expenses of the arbitrators and the ICC administrative expenses fixed by the Court, in accordance with the scale in force at the time of the commencement of the arbitration, as well as the fees and expenses of any experts appointed by the arbitral tribunal and the reasonable legal and other costs incurred by the parties for the arbitration.

2. The Court may fix the fees of the arbitrators at a figure higher or lower than that which would result from the application of the relevant scale should this be deemed necessary due to the exceptional circumstances of the case.

3. At any time during the arbitral proceedings, the arbitral tribunal may make decisions on costs, other than those to be fixed by the Court, and order payment.

4. The final award shall fix the costs of the arbitration and decide which of the parties shall bear them or in what proportion they shall be borne by the parties.

5. In making decisions as to costs, the arbitral tribunal may take into account such circumstances as it considers relevant, including the extent to which each party has conducted the arbitration in an expeditious and cost-effective manner. . . .

Miscellaneous

Article 39.   Waiver

A party which proceeds with the arbitration without raising its objection to a failure to comply with any provision of the Rules, or of any other rules applicable to the proceedings, any direction given by the arbitral tribunal, or any requirement under the arbitration agreement relating to the constitution of the arbitral tribunal or the conduct of the proceedings, shall be deemed to have waived its right to object.

Article 40.   Limitation of Liability

The arbitrators, any person appointed by the arbitral tribunal, the emergency arbitrator, the Court and its members, the ICC and its employees, and the ICC National Committees and Groups and their employees and representatives shall not be liable to any person for any act or omission in connection with the arbitration, except to the extent such limitation of liability is prohibited by applicable law.

Article 41.   General Rule

In all matters not expressly provided for in the Rules, the Court and the arbitral tribunal shall act in the spirit of the Rules and shall make every effort to make sure that the award is enforceable at law.

Appendix IV

CASE MANAGEMENT TECHNIQUES

The following are examples of case management techniques that can be used by the arbitral tribunal and the parties for controlling time and cost.

Appropriate control of time and cost is important in all cases. In cases of low complexity and low value, it is particularly important to ensure that time and costs are proportionate to what is at stake in the dispute.

(a) Bifurcating the proceedings or rendering one or more partial awards on key issues, when doing so may genuinely be expected to result in a more efficient resolution of the case.

(b) Identifying issues that can be resolved by agreement between the parties or their experts.

(c) Identifying issues to be decided solely on the basis of documents rather than through oral evidence or legal argument at a hearing.

(d) Production of documentary evidence:

(i) requiring the parties to produce with their submissions the documents on which they rely;

(ii) avoiding requests for document production when appropriate in order to control time and cost;

(iii) in those cases where requests for document production are considered appropriate, limiting such requests to documents or categories of documents that are relevant and material to the outcome of the case;

(iv) establishing reasonable time limits for the production of documents;

(v) using a schedule of document production to facilitate the resolution of issues in relation to the production of documents.

(e) Limiting the length and scope of written submissions and written and oral witness evidence (both fact witnesses and experts) so as to avoid repetition and maintain a focus on key issues.

(f) Using telephone or video conferencing for procedural and other hearings where attendance in person is not essential and use of IT that enables online communication among the parties, the arbitral tribunal and the Secretariat of the Court.

(g) Organizing a pre-hearing conference with the arbitral tribunal at which arrangements for a hearing can be discussed and agreed and the arbitral tribunal can indicate to the parties issues on which it would like the parties to focus at the hearing.

(h) Settlement of disputes:

(i) informing the parties that they are free to settle all or part of the dispute either by negotiation or through any form of amicable dispute resolution methods such as, for example, mediation under the ICC ADR Rules;

(ii) where agreed between the parties and the arbitral tribunal, the arbitral tribunal may take steps to facilitate settlement of the dispute, provided that every effort is made to ensure that any subsequent award is enforceable at law.

Additional techniques are described in the ICC publication entitled "Techniques for Controlling Time and Costs in Arbitration".

NEW YORK CONVENTION ON THE RECOGNITION AND ENFORCEMENT OF FOREIGN ARBITRAL AWARDS

June 10, 1958, 21 U.S.T. 2517, T.I.A.S. No. 6997, 330 U.N.T.S. 38*

Article I

1. This Convention shall apply to the recognition and enforcement of arbitral awards made in the territory of a State other than the State where the recognition and enforcement of such awards are sought, and arising out of differences between persons, whether physical or legal. It shall also apply to arbitral awards not considered as domestic awards in the State where their recognition and enforcement are sought.

2. The term "arbitral awards" shall include not only awards made by arbitrators appointed for each case but also those made by permanent arbitral bodies to which the parties have submitted.

3. When signing, ratifying or acceding to this Convention, or notifying extension under article X hereof, any State may on the basis of reciprocity declare that it will apply the Convention to the recognition and enforcement

---

* Done at New York on June 10, 1958. Entered into force on June 7, 1959, and for the United States on December 29, 1970.

As of February 2013, the 148 parties to the convention are: Afghanistan, Albania, Algeria, Antigua and Barbuda, Argentina, Armenia, Australia, Austria, Azerbaijan, Bahamas, Bahrain, Bangladesh, Barbados, Belarus, Belgium, Benin, Bolivia, Bosnia and Herzegovina, Botswana, Brazil, Brunei Darussalam, Bulgaria, Burkina Faso, Cambodia, Cameroon, Canada, Central African Republic, Chile, China, Colombia, Cook Islands, Costa Rica, Côte d'Ivoire, Croatia, Cuba, Cyprus, Czech Republic, Denmark, Djibouti, Dominica, Dominican Republic, Ecuador, Egypt, El Salvador, Estonia, Fiji, Finland, France, Gabon, Georgia, Germany, Ghana, Greece, Guatemala, Guinea, Haiti, Holy See, Honduras, Hungary, Iceland, India, Indonesia, Iran, Ireland, Israel, Italy, Jamaica, Japan, Jordan, Kazakhstan, Kenya, Korea (Republic of), Kuwait, Kyrgyzstan, Lao People's Democratic Republic, Latvia, Lebanon, Lesotho, Liberia, Liechtenstein, Lithuania, Luxembourg, Macedonia (the former Yugoslav Republic of), Madagascar, Malaysia, Mali, Malta, Marshall Islands, Mauritania, Mauritius, Mexico, Moldova, Monaco, Mongolia, Montenegro, Morocco, Mozambique, Nepal, Netherlands, New Zealand, Nicaragua, Niger, Nigeria, Norway, Oman, Pakistan, Panama, Paraguay, Peru, Philippines, Poland, Portugal, Qatar, Romania, Russian Federation, Rwanda, Saint Vincent and the Grenadines, San Marino, Sao Tome and Principe, Saudi Arabia, Senegal, Serbia, Singapore, Slovakia, Slovenia, South Africa, Spain, Sri Lanka, Sweden, Switzerland, Syrian Arab Republic, Tajikistan, Tanzania, Thailand, Trinidad and Tobago, Tunisia, Turkey, Uganda, Ukraine, United Arab Emirates, United Kingdom, United States of America, Uruguay, Uzbekistan, Venezuela, Viet Nam, Zambia, and Zimbabwe. See U.N. Web site at <http://treaties.un.org>.

of awards made only in the territory of another Contracting State. It may also declare that it will apply the Convention only to differences arising out of legal relationships, whether contractual or not, which are considered as commercial under the national law of the State making such declaration.

Article II

1. Each Contracting State shall recognize an agreement in writing under which the parties undertake to submit to arbitration all or any differences which have arisen or which may arise between them in respect of a defined legal relationship, whether contractual or not, concerning a subject matter capable of settlement by arbitration.

2. The term "agreement in writing" shall include an arbitral clause in a contract or an arbitration agreement, signed by the parties or contained in an exchange of letters or telegrams.

3. The court of a Contracting State, when seized of an action in a matter in respect of which the parties have made an agreement within the meaning of this article, shall, at the request of one of the parties, refer the parties to arbitration, unless it finds that the said agreement is null and void, inoperative or incapable of being performed.

Article III

Each Contracting State shall recognize arbitral awards as binding and enforce them in accordance with the rules of procedure of the territory where the award is relied upon, under the conditions laid down in the following articles. There shall not be imposed substantially more onerous conditions or higher fees or charges on the recognition or enforcement of arbitral awards to which this Convention applies than are imposed on the recognition or enforcement of domestic arbitral awards.

Article IV

1. To obtain the recognition and enforcement mentioned in the preceding article, the party applying for recognition and enforcement shall, at the time of the application, supply:

    (a) The duly authenticated original award or a duly certified copy thereof;

    (b) The original agreement referred to in article **II** or a duly certified copy thereof.

2. If the said award or agreement is not made in an official language of the country in which the award is relied upon, the party applying for recognition and enforcement of the award shall produce a translation of these documents into such language. The translation shall be certified by an official or sworn translator or by a diplomatic or consular agent.

Article V

1. Recognition and enforcement of the award may be refused, at the request of the party against whom it is invoked, only if that party furnishes to

the competent authority where the recognition and enforcement is sought, proof that:

(a) The parties to the agreement referred to in article II were, under the law applicable to them, under some incapacity, or the said agreement is not valid under the law to which the parties have subjected it or, failing any indication thereon, under the law of the country where the award was made; or

(b) The party against whom the award is invoked was not given proper notice of the appointment of the arbitrator or of the arbitration proceedings or was otherwise unable to present his case; or

(c) The award deals with a difference not contemplated by or not falling within the terms of the submission to arbitration, or it contains decisions on matters beyond the scope of the submission to arbitration, provided that, if the decisions on matters submitted to arbitration can be separated from those not so submitted, that part of the award which contains decisions on matters submitted to arbitration may be recognized and enforced; or

(d) The composition of the arbitral authority or the arbitral procedure was not in accordance with the agreement of the parties, or, failing such agreement, was not in accordance with the law of the country where the arbitration took place; or

(e) The award has not yet become binding on the parties, or has been set aside or suspended by a competent authority of the country in which, or under the law of which, that award was made.

2. Recognition and enforcement of an arbitral award may also be refused if the competent authority in the country where recognition and enforcement is sought finds that:

(a) The subject matter of the difference is not capable of settlement by arbitration under the law of that country; or

(b) The recognition or enforcement of the award would be contrary to the public policy of that country.

Article VI

If an application for the setting aside or suspension of the award has been made to a competent authority referred to in article V (1) *(e)*, the authority before which the award is sought to be relied upon may, if it considers it proper, adjourn the decision on the enforcement of the award and may also, on the application of the party claiming enforcement of the award, order the other party to give suitable security.

Article VII

1. The provisions of the present Convention shall not affect the validity of multilateral or bilateral agreements concerning the recognition and enforcement of arbitral awards entered into by the Contracting States nor deprive any interested party of any right he may have to avail himself of an arbitral award in the manner and to the extent allowed by the law or the treaties of the country where such award is sought to be relied upon.

120

2. The Geneva Protocol on Arbitration Clauses of 1923 and the Geneva Convention on the Execution of Foreign Arbitral Awards of 1927 shall cease to have effect between Contracting States on their becoming bound and to the extent that they become bound, by this Convention.

Article VIII

1. This Convention shall be open until 31 December 1958 for signature on behalf of any Member of the United Nations and also on behalf of any other State which is or hereafter becomes a member of any specialized agency of the United Nations, or which is or hereafter becomes a party to the Statute of the International Court of Justice, or any other State to which an invitation has been addressed by the General Assembly of the United Nations.

2. This Convention shall be ratified and the instrument of ratification shall be deposited with the Secretary-General of the United Nations.

Article IX

1. This Convention shall be open for accession to all States referred to in article VIII.

2. Accession shall be effected by the deposit of an instrument of accession with the Secretary-General of the United Nations.

Article X

1. Any State may, at the time of signature, ratification or accession, declare that this Convention shall extend to all or any of the territories for the international relations of which it is responsible. Such a declaration shall take effect when the Convention enters into force for the State concerned.

2. At any time thereafter any such extension shall be made by notification addressed to the Secretary-General of the United Nations and shall take effect as from the ninetieth day after the day of receipt by the Secretary-General of the United Nations of this notification, or as from the date of entry into force of the Convention for the State concerned, whichever is the later.

3. With respect to those territories to which this Convention is not extended at the time of signature, ratification or accession, each State concerned shall consider the possibility of taking the necessary steps in order to extend the application of this Convention to such territories, subject, where necessary for constitutional reasons, to the consent of the Governments of such territories.

Article XI

In the case of a federal or non-unitary State, the following provisions shall apply:

(a) With respect to those articles of this Convention that come within the legislative jurisdiction of the federal authority, the obligations of the federal Government shall to this extent be the same as those of Contracting States which are not federal States;

(b) With respect to those articles of this Convention that come within the legislative jurisdiction of constituent states or provinces which are not, under the constitutional system of the federation, bound to take legislative action, the federal Government shall bring such articles with a favourable recommendation to the notice of the appropriate authorities of constituent states or provinces at the earliest possible moment;

(c) A federal State Party to this Convention shall, at the request of any other Contracting State transmitted through the Secretary-General of the United Nations, supply a statement of the law and practice of the federation and its constituent units in regard to any particular provision of this Convention, showing the extent to which effect has been given to that provision by legislative or other action.

Article XII

1. This Convention shall come into force on the ninetieth day following the date of deposit of the third instrument of ratification or accession.

2. For each State ratifying or acceding to this Convention after the deposit of the third instrument of ratification or accession, this Convention shall enter into force on the ninetieth day after deposit by such State of its instrument of ratification or accession.

Article XIII

1. Any Contracting State may denounce this Convention by a written notification to the Secretary-General of the United Nations. Denunciation shall take effect one year after the date of receipt of the notification by the Secretary-General.

2. Any State which has made a declaration or notification under article X may, at any time thereafter, by notification to the Secretary-General of the United Nations, declare that this Convention shall cease to extend to the territory concerned one year after the date of the receipt of the notification by the Secretary-General.

3. This Convention shall continue to be applicable to arbitral awards in respect of which recognition or enforcement proceedings have been instituted before the denunciation takes effect.

Article XIV

A Contracting State shall not be entitled to avail itself of the present Convention against other Contracting States except to the extent that it is itself bound to apply the Convention. . . .

CONVENTION ON THE SETTLEMENT OF INVESTMENT DISPUTES BETWEEN STATES AND NATIONALS OF OTHER STATES

March 18, 1965, 17 U.S.T. 1270, T.I.A.S. No. 6090, 575 U.N.T.S. 159*

The Contracting States

Considering the need for international cooperation for economic development, and the role of private international investment therein;

Bearing in mind the possibility that from time to time disputes may arise in connection with such investment between Contracting States and nationals of other Contracting States;

Recognizing that while such disputes would usually be subject to national legal processes, international methods of settlement may be appropriate in certain cases;

Attaching particular importance to the availability of facilities for international conciliation or arbitration to which Contracting States and nationals of other Contracting States may submit such disputes if they so desire;

---

* Done at Washington on March 18, 1965. Entered into force on October 14, 1966. As of July 2012, the 147 parties to the convention as of are: Afghanistan, Albania, Algeria, Argentina, Armenia, Australia, Austria, Azerbaijan, Bahamas, Bahrain, Bangladesh, Barbados, Belarus, Belgium, Benin, Bosnia and Herzegovina, Botswana, Brunei Darussalam, Bulgaria, Burkina Faso, Burundi, Cambodia, Cameroon, Cape Verde, Central African Republic, Chad, Chile, China (People's Republic of), Colombia, Comoros, Congo, Congo (Democratic Republic of), Costa Rica, Côte d'Ivoire, Croatia, Cyprus, Czech Republic, Denmark, Egypt, El Salvador, Estonia, Ethiopia, Fiji, Finland, France, Gabon, Gambia, Georgia, Germany, Ghana, Greece, Grenada, Guatemala, Guinea, Guyana, Haiti, Honduras, Hungary, Iceland, Indonesia, Ireland, Israel, Italy, Jamaica, Japan, Jordan, Kazakhstan, Kenya, Korea (Republic of), Kosovo (Republic of), Kuwait, Latvia, Lebanon, Lesotho, Liberia, Lithuania, Luxembourg, Macedonia (the former Yugoslav Republic of), Madagascar, Malawi, Malaysia, Mali, Malta, Mauritania, Mauritius, Micronesia, Moldova, Mongolia, Morocco, Mozambique, Namibia, Nepal, Netherlands, New Zealand, Nicaragua, Niger, Nigeria, Norway, Oman, Pakistan, Panama, Papua New Guinea, Paraguay, Peru, Philippines, Portugal, Qatar, Romania, Rwanda, Saint Kitts and Nevis, Saint Lucia, Saint Vincent and the Grenadines, Samoa, Saudi Arabia, Senegal, Serbia, Seychelles, Sierra Leone, Singapore, Slovak Republic, Slovenia, Solomon Islands, Somalia, South Sudan, Spain, Sri Lanka, Sudan, Swaziland, Sweden, Switzerland, Syria, Tanzania, Thailand, Timor-Leste, Togo, Tonga, Trinidad and Tobago, Tunisia, Turkey, Turkmenistan, Uganda, Ukraine, United Arab Emirates, United Kingdom, United States of America, Uruguay, Uzbekistan, Yemen, Zambia, and Zimbabwe. See the ICSID Web site at <http:// www.icsid.worldbank.org>.

Desiring to establish such facilities under the auspices of the International Bank for Reconstruction and Development;

Recognizing that mutual consent by the parties to submit such disputes to conciliation or to arbitration through such facilities constitutes a binding agreement which requires in particular that due consideration be given to any recommendation of conciliators, and that any arbitral award be complied with; and

Declaring that no Contracting State shall by the mere fact of its ratification, acceptance or approval of this Convention and without its consent be deemed to be under any obligation to submit any particular dispute to conciliation or arbitration,

Have agreed as follows:

Chapter I.   International Centre for Settlement of Investment Disputes

Section 1.   Establishment and Organization

Article 1

(1) There is hereby established the International Centre for Settlement of Investment Disputes (hereinafter called the Centre). [Also known as ICSID.]

(2) The purpose of the Centre shall be to provide facilities for conciliation and arbitration of investment disputes between Contracting States and nationals of other Contracting States in accordance with the provisions of this Convention.

Article 2

The seat of the Centre shall be at the principal office of the International Bank for Reconstruction and Development (hereinafter called the Bank). . . .

Article 5

The President of the Bank shall be *ex officio* Chairman of the Administrative Council (hereinafter called the Chairman) but shall have no vote. During his absence or inability to act and during any vacancy in the office of President of the Bank, the person for the time being acting as President shall act as Chairman of the Administrative Council. . . .

Section 4.   The Panels

Article 12

The Panel of Conciliators and the Panel of Arbitrators shall each consist of qualified persons, designated as hereinafter provided, who are willing to serve thereon.

Article 13

(1) Each Contracting State may designate to each Panel four persons who may but need not be its nationals.

(2) The Chairman may designate ten persons to each Panel. The persons so designated to a Panel shall each have a different nationality.

Article 14

(1) Persons designated to serve on the Panels shall be persons of high moral character and recognized competence in the fields of law, commerce, industry or finance, who may he relied upon to exercise independent judgment. Competence in the field of law shall be of particular importance in the case of persons on the Panel of Arbitrators.

(2) The Chairman, in designating persons to serve on the Panels, shall in addition pay due regard to the importance of assuring representation on the Panels of the principal legal systems of the world and of the main forms of economic activity.

Article 15

(1) Panel members shall serve for renewable periods of six years.

(2) In case of death or resignation of a member of a Panel, the authority which designated the member shall have the right to designate another person to serve for the remainder of that member's term.

(3) Panel members shall continue in office until their successors have been designated.

Article 16

(1) A person may serve on both Panels.

(2) If a person shall have been designated to serve on the same Panel by more than one Contracting State, or by one or more Contracting States and the Chairman, he shall be deemed to have been designated by the authority which first designated him or, if one such authority is the State of which he is a national, by that State.

(3) All designations shall be notified to the Secretary-General and shall take effect from the date on which the notification is received. . . .

Chapter II.   Jurisdiction of the Centre

Article 25

(1) The jurisdiction of the Centre shall extend to any legal dispute arising directly out of an investment, between a Contracting State (or any constituent subdivision or agency of a Contracting State designated to the Centre by that

State) and a national of another Contracting State, which the parties to the dispute consent in writing to submit to the Centre. When the parties have given their consent, no party may withdraw its consent unilaterally.

(2) "National of another Contracting State" means:

(a) any natural person who had the nationality of a Contracting State other than the State party to the dispute on the date on which the parties consented to submit such dispute to conciliation or arbitration as well as on the date on which the request was registered pursuant to paragraph (3) of Article 28 or paragraph (3) of Article 36, but does not include any person who on either date also had the nationality of the Contracting State party to the dispute; and

(b) any juridical person which had the nationality of a Contracting State other than the State party to the dispute on the date on which the parties consented to submit such dispute to conciliation or arbitration and any juridical person which had the nationality of the Contracting State party to the dispute on that date and which, because of foreign control, the parties have agreed should be treated as a national of another Contracting State for the purposes of this Convention.

(3) Consent by a constituent subdivision or agency of a Contracting State shall require the approval of that State unless that State notifies the Centre that no such approval is required.

(4) Any Contracting State may, at the time of ratification, acceptance or approval of this Convention or at any time thereafter, notify the Centre of the class or classes of disputes which it would or would not consider submitting to the jurisdiction of the Centre. The Secretary-General shall forthwith transmit such notification to all Contracting States. Such notification shall not constitute the consent required by paragraph (1).

Article 26

Consent of the parties to arbitration under this Convention shall, unless otherwise stated, be deemed consent to such arbitration to the exclusion of any other remedy. A Contracting State may require the exhaustion of local administrative or judicial remedies as a condition of its consent to arbitration under this Convention.

Article 27

(1) No Contracting State shall give diplomatic protection, or bring an international claim, in respect of a dispute which one of its nationals and another Contracting State shall have consented to submit or shall have submitted to arbitration under this Convention, unless such other Contracting State shall have failed to abide by and comply with the award rendered in such dispute. . . .

Chapter III.   Conciliation

SECTION 1.   REQUEST FOR CONCILIATION

Article 28

(1) Any Contracting State or any national of a Contracting State wishing to institute conciliation proceedings shall address a request to that effect in writing to the Secretary-General who shall send a copy of the request to the other party.

(2) The request shall contain information concerning the issues in dispute, the identity of the parties and their consent to conciliation in accordance with the rules of procedure for the institution of conciliation and arbitration proceedings. . . .

SECTION 2.   CONSTITUTION OF THE CONCILIATION COMMISSION

Article 29

(1) The Conciliation Commission (hereinafter called the Commission) shall be constituted as soon as possible after registration of a request pursuant to Article 28.

(2)(a) The Commission shall consist of a sole conciliator or any uneven number of conciliators appointed as the parties shall agree.

(b) Where the parties do not agree upon the number of conciliators and the method of their appointment, the Commission shall consist of three conciliators, one conciliator appointed by each party and the third, who shall be the president of the Commission, appointed by agreement of the parties.

Article 30

If the Commission shall not have been constituted within 90 days after notice of registration of the request has been dispatched by the Secretary-General in accordance with paragraph (3) of Article 28, or such other period as the parties may agree, the Chairman shall, at the request of either party and after consulting both parties as far as possible, appoint the conciliator or conciliators not yet appointed.

Article 31

(1) Conciliators may be appointed from outside the Panel of Conciliators, except in the case of appointments by the Chairman pursuant to Article 30.

(2) Conciliators appointed from outside the Panel of Conciliators shall possess the qualities stated in paragraph (1) of Article 14.

SECTION 3. CONCILIATION PROCEEDINGS

Article 32

(1) The Commission shall be the judge of its own competence.

(2) Any objection by a party to the dispute that that dispute is not within the jurisdiction of the Centre, or for other reasons is not within the competence of the Commission, shall be considered by the Commission which shall determine whether to deal with it as a preliminary question or to join it to the merits of the dispute.

Article 33

Any conciliation proceeding shall be conducted in accordance with the provisions of this Section and, except as the parties otherwise agree, in accordance with the Conciliation Rules in effect on the date on which the parties consented to conciliation. If any question of procedure arises which is not covered by this Section or the Conciliation Rules or any rules agreed by the parties, the Commission shall decide the question.

Article 34

(1) It shall be the duty of the Commission to clarify the issues in dispute between the parties and to endeavour to bring about agreement between them upon mutually acceptable terms. To that end, the Commission may at any stage of the proceedings and from time to time recommend terms of settlement to the parties. The parties shall cooperate in good faith with the Commission in order to enable the Commission to carry out its functions, and shall give their most serious consideration to its recommendations.

(2) If the parties reach agreement, the Commission shall draw up a report noting the issues in dispute and recording that the parties have reached agreement. If, at any stage of the proceedings, it appears to the Commission that there is no likelihood of agreement between the parties, it shall close the proceedings and shall draw up a report noting the submission of the dispute and recording the failure of the parties to reach agreement. If one party fails to appear or participate in the proceedings, the Commission shall close the proceedings and shall draw up a report noting that party's failure to appear or participate.

Article 35

Except as the parties to the dispute shall otherwise agree, neither party to a conciliation proceeding shall be entitled in any other proceeding, whether before arbitrators or in a court of law or otherwise, to invoke or rely on any views expressed or statements or admissions or offers of settlement made by the other party in the conciliation proceedings, or the report or any recommendations made by the Commission.

Chapter IV. Arbitration

SECTION 1. REQUEST FOR ARBITRATION

Article 36

(1) Any Contracting State or any national of a Contracting State wishing to institute arbitration proceedings shall address a request to that effect in writing to the Secretary-General who shall send a copy of the request to the other party.

(2) The request shall contain information concerning the issues in dispute, the identity of the parties and their consent to arbitration in accordance with the rules of procedure for the institution of conciliation and arbitration proceedings.

(3) The Secretary-General shall register the request unless he finds, on the basis of the information contained in the request, that the dispute is manifestly outside the jurisdiction of the Centre. He shall forthwith notify the parties of registration or refusal to register.

SECTION 2. CONSTITUTION OF THE TRIBUNAL

Article 37

(1) The Arbitral Tribunal (hereinafter called the Tribunal) shall be constituted as soon as possible after registration of a request pursuant to Article 36.

(2) (a) The Tribunal shall consist of a sole arbitrator or any uneven number of arbitrators appointed as the parties shall agree.

(b) Where the parties do not agree upon the number of arbitrators and the method of their appointment, the Tribunal shall consist of three arbitrators, one arbitrator appointed by each party and the third, who shall be the president of the Tribunal, appointed by agreement of the parties.

Article 38

If the Tribunal shall not have been constituted within 90 days after notice of registration of the request has been dispatched by the Secretary-General in accordance with paragraph (3) of Article 36, or such other period as the parties may agree, the Chairman shall, at the request of either party and after consulting both parties as far as possible, appoint the arbitrator or arbitrators not yet appointed. Arbitrators appointed by the Chairman pursuant to this Article shall not be nationals of the Contracting State party to the dispute or of the Contracting State whose national is a party to the dispute.

Article 39

The majority of the arbitrators shall be nationals of States other than the Contracting State party to the dispute and the Contracting State whose national is a party to the dispute; provided, however, that the foregoing provisions of this Article shall not apply if the sole arbitrator or each individual member of the Tribunal has been appointed by agreement of the parties.

Article 40

(1) Arbitrators may be appointed from outside the Panel of Arbitrators, except in the case of appointments by the Chairman pursuant to Article 38.

(2) Arbitrators appointed from outside the Panel of Arbitrators shall possess the qualities stated in paragraph (1) of Article 14.

SECTION 3. POWERS AND FUNCTIONS OF THE TRIBUNAL

Article 41

(1) The Tribunal shall be the judge of its own competence.

(2) Any objection by a party to the dispute that that dispute is not within the jurisdiction of the Centre, or for other reasons is not within the competence of the Tribunal, shall be considered by the Tribunal which shall determine whether to deal with it as a preliminary question or to join it to the merits of the dispute.

Article 42

(1) The Tribunal shall decide a dispute in accordance with such rules of law as may be agreed by the parties. In the absence of such agreement, the Tribunal shall apply the law of the Contracting State party to the dispute (including its rules on the conflict of laws) and such rules of international law as may be applicable.

(2) The Tribunal may not bring in a finding of *non liquet* on the ground of silence or obscurity of the law.

(3) The provisions of paragraphs (1) and (2) shall not prejudice the power of the Tribunal to decide a dispute *ex aequo et bono* if the parties so agree.

Article 43

Except as the parties otherwise agree, the Tribunal may, if it deems it necessary at any stage of the proceedings,

(a) call upon the parties to produce documents or other evidence, and

(b) visit the scene connected with the dispute, and conduct such inquiries there as it may deem appropriate.

Article 44

Any arbitration proceeding shall be conducted in accordance with the provisions of this Section and, except as the parties otherwise agree, in accordance with the Arbitration Rules in effect on the date on which the parties consented to arbitration. If any question of procedure arises which is not covered by this Section or the Arbitration Rules or any rules agreed by the parties, the Tribunal shall decide the question.

Article 45

(1) Failure of a party to appear or to present his case shall not be deemed an admission of the other party's assertions.

(2) If a party fails to appear or to present his case at any stage of the proceedings the other party may request the Tribunal to deal with the questions submitted to it and to render an award. Before rendering an award, the Tribunal shall notify, and grant a period of grace to, the party failing to appear or to present its case, unless it is satisfied that that party does not intend to do so.

Article 46

Except as the parties otherwise agree, the Tribunal shall, if requested by a party, determine any incidental or additional claims or counter-claims arising directly out of the subject-matter of the dispute provided that they are within the scope of the consent of the parties and are otherwise within the jurisdiction of the Centre.

Article 47

Except as the parties otherwise agree, the Tribunal may, if it considers that the circumstances so require, recommend any provisional measures which should be taken to preserve the respective rights of either party.

Section 4. The Award

Article 48

(1) The Tribunal shall decide questions by a majority of the votes of all its members.

(2) The award of the Tribunal shall be in writing and shall be signed by the members of the Tribunal who voted for it.

(3) The award shall deal with every question submitted to the Tribunal, and shall state the reasons upon which it is based.

(4) Any member of the Tribunal may attach his individual opinion to the award, whether he dissents from the majority or not, or a statement of his dissent.

(5) The Centre shall not publish the award without the consent of the parties.

Article 49

(1) The Secretary-General shall promptly dispatch certified copies of the award to the parties. The award shall be deemed to have been rendered on the date on which the certified copies were dispatched.

(2) The Tribunal upon the request of a party made within 45 days after the date on which the award was rendered may after notice to the other party decide any question which it had omitted to decide in the award, and shall rectify any clerical, arithmetical or similar error in the award. Its decision

shall become part of the award and shall be notified to the parties in the same manner as the award. The periods of time provided for under paragraph (2) of Article 51 and paragraph (2) of Article 52 shall run from the date on which the decision was rendered.

SECTION 5. INTERPRETATION, REVISION AND ANNULMENT OF THE AWARD

Article 50

(1) If any dispute shall arise between the parties as to the meaning or scope of an award, either party may request interpretation of the award by an application in writing addressed to the Secretary-General.

(2) The request shall, if possible, be submitted to the Tribunal which rendered the award. If this shall not be possible, a new Tribunal shall be constituted in accordance with Section 2 of this Chapter. The Tribunal may, if it considers that the circumstances so require, stay enforcement of the award pending its decision.

Article 51

(1) Either party may request revision of the award by an application in writing addressed to the Secretary-General on the ground of discovery of some fact of such a nature as decisively to affect the award, provided that when the award was rendered that fact was unknown to the Tribunal and to the applicant and that the applicant's ignorance of that fact was not due to negligence.

(2) The application shall be made within 90 days after the discovery of such fact and in any event within three years after the date on which the award was rendered.

(3) The request shall, if possible, be submitted to the Tribunal which rendered the award. If this shall not be possible, a new Tribunal shall be constituted in accordance with Section 2 of this Chapter.

(4) The Tribunal may, if it considers that the circumstances so require, stay enforcement of the award pending its decision. If the applicant requests a stay of enforcement of the award in his application, enforcement shall be stayed provisionally until the Tribunal rules on such request.

Article 52

(1) Either party may request annulment of the award by an application in writing addressed to the Secretary-General on one or more of the following grounds:

(a) that the Tribunal was not properly constituted;

(b) that the Tribunal has manifestly exceeded its powers;

(c) that there was corruption on the part of a member of the Tribunal;

(d) that there has been a serious departure from a fundamental rule of procedure; or

(e) that the award has failed to state the reasons on which it is based.

(2) The application shall be made within 120 days after the date on which the award was rendered except that when annulment is requested on the ground of corruption such application shall be made within 120 days after discovery of the corruption and in any event within three years after the date on which the award was rendered.

(3) On receipt of the request the Chairman shall forthwith appoint from the Panel of Arbitrators an *ad hoc* Committee of three persons. None of the members of the Committee shall have been a member of the Tribunal which rendered the award, shall be of the same nationality as any such member, shall be a national of the State party to the dispute or of the State whose national is a party to the dispute, shall have been designated to the Panel of Arbitrators by either of those States, or shall have acted as a conciliator in the same dispute. The Committee shall have the authority to annul the award or any part thereof on any of the grounds set forth in paragraph (1).

(4) The provisions of Articles 41-45, 48, 49, 53 and 54, and of Chapters VI and VII shall apply *mutatis mutandis* to proceedings before the Committee.

(5) The Committee may, if it considers that the circumstances so require, stay enforcement of the award pending its decision. If the applicant requests a stay of enforcement of the award in his application, enforcement shall be stayed provisionally until the Committee rules on such request.

(6) If the award is annulled the dispute shall, at the request of either party, be submitted to a new Tribunal constituted in accordance with Section 2 of this Chapter.

SECTION 6. RECOGNITION AND ENFORCEMENT OF THE AWARD

Article 53

(1) The award shall be binding on the parties and shall not be subject to any appeal or to any other remedy except those provided for in this Convention. Each party shall abide by and comply with the terms of the award except to the extent that enforcement shall have been stayed pursuant to the relevant provisions of this Convention.

(2) For the purposes of this Section, "award" shall include any decision interpreting, revising or annulling such award pursuant to Articles 50, 51, or 52.

Article 54

(1) Each Contracting State shall recognize an award rendered pursuant to this Convention as binding and enforce the pecuniary obligations imposed by that award within its territories as if it were a final judgment of a court in that State. A Contracting State with a federal constitution may enforce such an award in or through its federal courts and may provide that such courts shall treat the award as if it were a final judgment of the courts of a constituent state.

(2) A party seeking recognition or enforcement in the territories of a Contracting State shall furnish to a competent court or other authority which such State shall have designated for this purpose a copy of the award

certified by the Secretary-General. Each Contracting State shall notify the Secretary-General of the designation of the competent court or other authority for this purpose and of any subsequent change in such designation.

(3) Execution of the award shall be governed by the laws concerning the execution of judgments in force in the State in whose territories such execution is sought.

Article 55

Nothing in Article 54 shall be construed as derogating from the law in force in any Contracting State relating to immunity of that State or of any foreign State from execution.

Chapter V.   Replacement and Disqualification of Conciliators and Arbitrators

Article 56

(1) After a Commission or a Tribunal has been constituted and proceedings have begun, its composition shall remain unchanged; provided, however, that if a conciliator or an arbitrator should die, become incapacitated, or resign, the resulting vacancy shall be filled in accordance with the provisions of Section 2 of Chapter III or Section 2 of Chapter IV.

(2) A member of a Commission or Tribunal shall continue to serve in that capacity notwithstanding that he shall have ceased to be a member of the Panel.

(3) If a conciliator or arbitrator appointed by a party shall have resigned without the consent of the Commission or Tribunal of which he was a member, the Chairman shall appoint a person from the appropriate Panel to fill the resulting vacancy.

Article 57

A party may propose to a Commission or Tribunal the disqualification of any of its members on account of any fact indicating a manifest lack of the qualities required by paragraph (1) of Article 14. A party to arbitration proceedings may, in addition, propose the disqualification of an arbitrator on the ground that he was ineligible for appointment to the Tribunal under Section 2 of Chapter IV.

Article 58

The decision on any proposal to disqualify a conciliator or arbitrator shall be taken by the other members of the Commission or Tribunal as the case may be, provided that where those members are equally divided, or in the case of a proposal to disqualify a sole conciliator or arbitrator, or a majority of the conciliators or arbitrators, the Chairman shall take that decision. If it is decided that the proposal is well-founded the conciliator or arbitrator to whom the decision relates shall be replaced in accordance with the provisions of Section 2 of Chapter III or Section 2 of Chapter IV.

Chapter VI.   Cost of Proceedings

Article 59

The charges payable by the parties for the use of the facilities of the Centre shall be determined by the Secretary-General in accordance with the regulations adopted by the Administrative Council.

Article 60

(1) Each Commission and each Tribunal shall determine the fees and expenses of its members within limits established from time to time by the Administrative Council and after consultation with the Secretary-General.

(2) Nothing in paragraph (1) of this Article shall preclude the parties from agreeing in advance with the Commission or Tribunal concerned upon the fees and expenses of its members.

Article 61

(1) In the case of conciliation proceedings the fees and expenses of members of the Commission as well as the charges for the use of the facilities of the Centre, shall be borne equally by the parties. Each party shall bear any other expenses it incurs in connection with the proceedings.

(2) In the case of arbitration proceedings the Tribunal shall, except as the parties otherwise agree, assess the expenses incurred by the parties in connection with the proceedings, and shall decide how and by whom those expenses, the fees and expenses of the members of the Tribunal and the charges for the use of the facilities of the Centre shall be paid. Such decision shall form part of the award.

Chapter VII.   Place of Proceedings

Article 62

Conciliation and arbitration proceedings shall be held at the seat of the Centre except as hereinafter provided.

Article 63

Conciliation and arbitration proceedings may be held, if the parties so agree,

(a) at the seat of the Permanent Court of Arbitration or of any other appropriate institution, whether private or public, with which the Centre may make arrangements for that purpose; or

(b) at any other place approved by the Commission or Tribunal after consultation with the Secretary-General.

Chapter VIII.   Disputes Between Contracting States

Article 64

Any dispute arising between Contracting States concerning the interpretation or application of this Convention which is not settled by negotiation shall be referred to the International Court of Justice by the application of any party to such dispute, unless the States concerned agree to another method of settlement. . . .

NORTH AMERICAN FREE TRADE AGREEMENT

U.S. Government Printing Office (1992), also reprinted in
32 I.L.M. 289 (chs. 1-9) and 605 (chs. 10-22) (1993)*

Table of Contents

Preamble

Part One: General Part
Chapter 1: Objectives
Chapter 2: General Definitions

Part Two: Trade in Goods
Chapter 3: National Treatment and Market Access for Goods
Annex 300-A: Trade and Investment in the Automotive Sector
Annex 300-B: Textile and Apparel Goods
Chapter 4: Rules of Origin
Chapter 5: Customs Procedures
Chapter 6: Energy and Basic Petrochemicals
Chapter 7: Agriculture and Sanitary and Phytosanitary Measures
Section A: Agriculture
Section B: Sanitary and Phytosanitary Measures
Chapter 8: Emergency Action

Part Three: Technical Barriers to Trade
Chapter 9: Standards-Related Measures

Part Four: Government Procurement
Chapter 10: Government Procurement

Part Five: Investment, Services and Related Matters
Chapter 11: Investment
Chapter 12: Cross-Border Trade in Services

* Signed in Washington, D.C. on December 17, 1992 by the governments of the United States, Canada, and Mexico. Officially entered into force on January 1, 1994. NAFTA is implemented in the United States by the North American Free Trade Implementation Act (1993), Pub. L. No. 103-182, 107 Stat. 2060. See the NAFTA Secretariat Web site at <http://www.nafta-sec-alena.org>.

Chapter 13: Telecommunications
Chapter 14: Financial Services
Chapter 15: Competition Policy, Monopolies and State Enterprises
Chapter 16: Temporary Entry for Business Persons

Part Six: Intellectual Property
Chapter 17: Intellectual Property

Part Seven: Administrative and Institutional Provisions
Chapter 18: Publication, Notification and Administration of Laws
Chapter 19: Review and Dispute Settlement in Antidumping and Countervailing Duty Matters
Chapter 20: Institutional Arrangements and Dispute Settlement Procedures

Part Eight: Other Provisions
Chapter 21: Exceptions
Chapter 22: Final Provisions

Part One. General Part

CHAPTER ONE. OBJECTIVES

Article 101: Establishment of the Free Trade Area

The Parties to this Agreement, consistent with Article XXIV of the *General Agreement on Tariffs and Trade,* hereby establish a free trade area.

Article 102: Objectives

1. The objectives of this Agreement, as elaborated more specifically through its principles and rules, including national treatment, most-favored-nation treatment and transparency, are to:
    (a) eliminate barriers to trade in, and facilitate the cross-border movement of, goods and services between the territories of the Parties;
    (b) promote conditions of fair competition in the free trade area;
    (c) increase substantially investment opportunities in the territories of the Parties;
    (d) provide adequate and effective protection and enforcement of intellectual property rights in each Party's territory;
    (e) create effective procedures for the implementation and application of this Agreement, for its joint administration and for the resolution of disputes; and
    (f) establish a framework for further trilateral, regional and multilateral cooperation to expand and enhance the benefits of this Agreement.
2. The Parties shall interpret and apply the provisions of this Agreement in the light of its objectives set out in paragraph 1 and in accordance with applicable rules of international law.

Article 103:   Relation to Other Agreements

1. The Parties affirm their existing rights and obligations with respect to each other under the *General Agreement on Tariffs and Trade* and other agreements to which such Parties are party.

2. In the event of any inconsistency between this Agreement and such other agreements, this Agreement shall prevail to the extent of the inconsistency, except as otherwise provided in this Agreement. . . .

Article 104:   Relation to Environmental and Conservation Agreements

1. In the event of any inconsistency between this Agreement and the specific trade obligations set out in:

(a) the *Convention on International Trade in Endangered Species of Wild Fauna and Flora,* done at Washington, March 3, 1973, as amended June 22, 1979,

(b) the *Montreal Protocol on Substances that Deplete the Ozone Layer,* done at Montreal, September 16, 1987, as amended June 29, 1990,

(c) the *Basel Convention on the Control of Transboundary Movements of Hazardous Wastes and Their Disposal,* done at Basel, March 22, 1989, on its entry into force for Canada, Mexico and the United States, or

(d) the agreements set out in Annex 104.1,

such obligations shall prevail to the extent of the inconsistency, provided that where a Party has a choice among equally effective and reasonably available means of complying with such obligations, the Party chooses the alternative that is the least inconsistent with the other provisions of this Agreement.

2. The Parties may agree in writing to modify Annex 104.1 to include any amendment to an agreement referred to in paragraph 1, and any other environmental or conservation agreement.

Article 105:   Extent of Obligations

The Parties shall ensure that all necessary measures are taken in order to give effect to the provisions of this Agreement, including their observance, except as otherwise provided in this Agreement, by state and provincial governments.

Annex 104.1.   Bilateral and Other Environmental and Conservation Agreements

1. The *Agreement Between the Government of Canada and the Government of the United States of America Concerning the Transboundary Movement of Hazardous Waste,* signed at Ottawa, October 28, 1986.

2. The *Agreement Between the United States of America and the United Mexican States on Cooperation for the Protection and Improvement of the Environment of the Environment in the Border Area,* signed at La Paz, Baja California Sur, August 14, 1983.

Part Five. Investment, Services and Related Matters

CHAPTER ELEVEN. INVESTMENT

Section A. Investment

Article 1101: Scope and Coverage

1. This Chapter applies to measures adopted or maintained by a Party relating to:

(a) investors of another Party;

(b) investments of investors of another Party in the territory of the Party; and

(c) with respect to Articles 1106 and 1114, all investments in the territory of the Party.

2. A Party has the right to perform exclusively the economic activities set out in Annex III and to refuse to permit the establishment of investment in such activities.

3. This Chapter does not apply to measures adopted or maintained by a Party to the extent that they are covered by Chapter Fourteen (Financial Services).

4. Nothing in this Chapter shall be construed to prevent a Party from providing a service or performing a function such as law enforcement, correctional services, income security or insurance, social security or insurance, social welfare, public education, public training, health, and child care, in a manner that is not inconsistent with this Chapter.

Article 1102: National Treatment

1. Each Party shall accord to investors of another Party treatment no less favorable than that it accords, in like circumstances, to its own investors with respect to the establishment, acquisition, expansion, management, conduct, operation, and sale or other disposition of investments.

2. Each Party shall accord to investments of investors of another Party treatment no less favorable than that it accords, in like circumstances, to investments of its own investors with respect to the establishment, acquisition, expansion, management, conduct, operation, and sale or other disposition of investments.

3. The treatment accorded by a Party under paragraphs 1 and 2 means, with respect to a state or province, treatment no less favorable than the most favorable treatment accorded, in like circumstances, by that state or province to investors, and to investments of investors, of the Party of which it forms a part.

4. For greater certainty, no Party may:

(a) impose on an investor of another Party a requirement that a minimum level of equity in an enterprise in the territory of the Party be held by its nationals, other than nominal qualifying shares for directors or incorporators of corporations; or

(b) require an investor of another Party, by reason of its nationality, to sell or otherwise dispose of an investment in the territory of the Party.

Article 1103:   Most-Favored-Nation Treatment

1. Each Party shall accord to investors of another Party treatment no less favorable than that it accords, in like circumstances, to investors of any other Party or of a non-Party with respect to the establishment, acquisition, expansion, management, conduct, operation, and sale or other disposition of investments.

2. Each Party shall accord to investments of investors of another Party treatment no less favorable than that it accords, in like circumstances, to investments of investors of any other Party or of a non-Party with respect to the establishment, acquisition, expansion, management, conduct, operation, and sale or other disposition of investments.

Article 1104:   Standard of Treatment

Each Party shall accord to investors of another Party and to investments of investors of another Party the better of the treatment required by Articles 1102 and 1103.

Article 1105:   Minimum Standard of Treatment

1. Each Party shall accord to investments of investors of another Party treatment in accordance with international law, including fair and equitable treatment and full protection and security.

2. Without prejudice to paragraph 1 and notwithstanding Article 1108(7)(b), each Party shall accord to investors of another Party, and to investments of investors of another Party, non-discriminatory treatment with respect to measures it adopts or maintains relating to losses suffered by investments in its territory owing to armed conflict or civil strife.

3. Paragraph 2 does not apply to existing measures relating to subsidiesor grants that would be inconsistent with Article 1102 but for Article 1108(7)(b).

Article 1106:   Performance Requirements

1. No Party may impose or enforce any of the following requirements, or enforce any commitment or undertaking, in connection with the establishment, acquisition, expansion, management, conduct or operation of an investment of an investor of a Party or of a non-Party in its territory:

(a) to export a given level or percentage of goods or services;

(b) to achieve a given level or percentage of domestic content;

(c) to purchase, use or accord a preference to goods produced or services provided in its territory, or to purchase goods or services from persons in its territory;

(d) to relate in any way the volume or value of imports to the volume or value of exports or to the amount of foreign exchange inflows associated with such investment;

(e) to restrict sales of goods or services in its territory that such investment produces or provides by relating such sales in any way to the volume or value of its exports or foreign exchange earnings;

(f) to transfer technology, a production process or other proprietary knowledge to a person in its territory, except when the requirement is imposed or the commitment or undertaking is enforced by a court, administrative tribunal or competition authority to remedy an alleged violation of competition laws or to act in a manner not inconsistent with other provisions of this Agreement; or

(g) to act as the exclusive supplier of the goods it produces or services it provides to a specific region or world market.

2. A measure that requires an investment to use a technology to meet generally applicable health, safety or environmental requirements shall not be construed to be inconsistent with paragraph 1(f). For greater certainty, Articles 1102 and 1103 apply to the measure.

3. No Party may condition the receipt or continued receipt of an advantage, in connection with an investment in its territory of an investor of a Party or of a non-Party, on compliance with any of the following requirements:

(a) to achieve a given level or percentage of domestic content;

(b) to purchase, use or accord a preference to goods produced in its territory, or to purchase goods from producers in its territory;

(c) to relate in any way the volume or value of imports to the volume or value of exports or to the amount of foreign exchange inflows associated with such investment; or

(d) to restrict sales of goods or services in its territory that such investment produces or provides by relating such sales in any way to the volume or value of its exports or foreign exchange earnings.

4. Nothing in paragraph 3 shall be construed to prevent a Party from conditioning the receipt or continued receipt of an advantage, in connection with an investment in its territory of an investor of a Party or of a non-Party, on compliance with a requirement to locate production, provide a service, train or employ workers, construct or expand particular facilities, or carry out research and development, in its territory.

5. Paragraphs 1 and 3 do not apply to any requirement other than the requirements set out in those paragraphs.

6. Provided that such measures are not applied in an arbitrary or unjustifiable manner, or do not constitute a disguised restriction on international trade or investment, nothing in paragraph 1(b) or (c) or 3(a) or (b) shall be construed to prevent any Party from adopting or maintaining measures, including environmental measures:

(a) necessary to secure compliance with laws and regulations that are not inconsistent with the provisions of this Agreement;

(b) necessary to protect human, animal or plant life or health; or

(c) necessary for the conservation of living or non-living exhaustible natural resources.

Article 1107: Senior Management and Boards of Directors

1. No Party may require that an enterprise of that Party that is an investment of an investor of another Party appoint to senior management positions individuals of any particular nationality.

2. A Party may require that a majority of the board of directors, or any committee thereof, of an enterprise of that Party that is an investment of an investor of another Party, be of a particular nationality, or resident in the territory of the Party, provided that the requirement does not materially impair the ability of the investor to exercise control over its investment.

Article 1108: Reservations and Exceptions

1. Articles 1102, 1103, 1106 and 1107 do not apply to:

(a) any existing non-conforming measure that is maintained by

(i) a Party at the federal level, as set out in its Schedule to Annex I or III,

(ii) a state or province, for two years after the date of entry into force of this Agreement, and thereafter as set out by a Party in its Schedule to Annex I in accordance with paragraph 2, or

(iii) a local government;

(b) the continuation or prompt renewal of any non-conforming measure referred to in subparagraph (a); or

(c) an amendment to any non-conforming measure referred to in subparagraph (a) to the extent that the amendment does not decrease the conformity of the measure, as it existed immediately before the amendment, with Articles 1102, 1103, 1106 and 1107. . . .

7. Articles 1102, 1103 and 1107 do not apply to:

(a) procurement by a Party or a state enterprise; or

(b) subsidies or grants provided by a Party or a state enterprise, including government supported loans, guarantees and insurance. . . .

Article 1109: Transfers

1. Each Party shall permit all transfers relating to an investment of an investor of another Party in the territory of the Party to be made freely and without delay. Such transfers include:

(a) profits, dividends, interest, capital gains, royalty payments, management fees, technical assistance and other fees, returns in kind and other amounts derived from the investment;

(b) proceeds from the sale of all or any part of the investment or from the partial or complete liquidation of the investment;

(c) payments made under a contract entered into by the investor, or its investment, including payments made pursuant to a loan agreement;

(d) payments made pursuant to Article 1110; and

(e) payments arising under Section B.

2. Each Party shall permit transfers to be made in a freely usable currency at the market rate of exchange prevailing on the date of transfer with respect to spot transactions in the currency to be transferred.

3. No Party may require its investors to transfer, or penalize its investors that fail to transfer, the income, earnings, profits or other amounts derived from, or attributable to, investments in the territory of another Party. . . .

Article 1110:   Expropriation and Compensation

1. No Party may directly or indirectly nationalize or expropriate an investment of an investor of another Party in its territory or take a measure tantamount to nationalization or expropriation of such an investment ("expropriation"), except:

(a) for a public purpose;

(b) on a non-discriminatory basis;

(c) in accordance with due process of law and Article 1105(1); and

(d) on payment of compensation in accordance with paragraphs 2 through 6.

2. Compensation shall be equivalent to the fair market value of the expropriated investment immediately before the expropriation took place ("date of expropriation"), and shall not reflect any change in value occurring because the intended expropriation had become known earlier. Valuation criteria shall include going concern value, asset value including declared tax value of tangible property, and other criteria, as appropriate, to determine fair market value.

3. Compensation shall be paid without delay and be fully realizable.

4. If payment is made in a G7 currency, compensation shall include interest at a commercially reasonable rate for that currency from the date of expropriation until the date of actual payment.

5. If a Party elects to pay in a currency other than a G7 currency, the amount paid on the date of payment, if converted into a G7 currency at the market rate of exchange prevailing on that date, shall be no less than if the amount of compensation owed on the date of expropriation had been converted into that G7 currency at the market rate of exchange prevailing on that date, and interest had accrued at a commercially reasonable rate for that G7 currency from the date of expropriation until the date of payment.

6. On payment, compensation shall he freely transferable as provided in Article 1109.

Article 1112:   Relation to Other Chapters

1. In the event of any inconsistency between this Chapter and another Chapter, the other Chapter shall prevail to the extent of the inconsistency.

Article 1114:   Environmental Measures

1. Nothing in this Chapter shall be construed to prevent a Party from adopting, maintaining or enforcing any measure otherwise consistent with this Chapter that it considers appropriate to ensure that investment activity in its territory is undertaken in a manner sensitive to environmental concerns.

2. The Parties recognize that it is inappropriate to encourage investment by relaxing domestic health, safety or environmental measures. Accordingly, a Party should not waive or otherwise derogate from, or offer to waive or otherwise derogate from, such measures as an encouragement for the establishment, acquisition, expansion or retention in its territory of an investment of an investor. If a Party considers that another Party has offered such an encouragement, it may request consultations with the other Party and the two Parties shall consult with a view to avoiding any such encouragement.

Section B.   Settlement of Disputes Between a Party and an Investor of Another Party

Article 1115:   Purpose

Without prejudice to the rights and obligations of the Parties under Chapter Twenty (Institutional Arrangements and Dispute Settlement Procedures), this Section establishes a mechanism for the settlement of investment disputes that assures both equal treatment among investors of the Parties in accordance with the principle of international reciprocity and due process before an impartial tribunal.

Article 1116:   Claim by an Investor of a Party on Its Own Behalf

1. An investor of a Party may submit to arbitration under this Section a claim that another Party has breached an obligation under:
   (a) Section A . . .
and that the investor has incurred loss or damage by reason of, or arising out of, that breach.

2. An investor may not make a claim if more than three years have elapsed from the date on which the investor first acquired, or should have first acquired, knowledge of the alleged breach and knowledge that the investor has incurred loss or damage.

Article 1117:   Claim by an Investor of a Party on Behalf of an Enterprise

1. An investor of a Party, on behalf of an enterprise of another Party that is a juridical person that the investor owns or controls directly or indirectly, may submit to arbitration under this Section a claim that the other Party has breached an obligation under:
   (a) Section A . . .
and that the enterprise has incurred loss or damage by reason of, or arising out of, that breach.

2. An investor may not make a claim on behalf of an enterprise described in paragraph 1 if more than three years have elapsed from the date on which the enterprise first acquired, or should have first acquired, knowledge of the alleged breach and knowledge that the enterprise has incurred loss or damage. . . .

4. An investment may not make a claim under this Section.

Article 1118: Settlement of a Claim Through Consultation and Negotiation

The disputing parties should first attempt to settle a claim through consultation or negotiation.

Article 1119: Notice of Intent to Submit a Claim to Arbitration

The disputing investor shall deliver to the disputing Party written notice of its intention to submit a claim to arbitration at least 90 days before the claim is submitted, which notice shall specify:

(a) the name and address of the disputing investor and, where a claim is made under Article 1117, the name and address of the enterprise;

(b) the provisions of this Agreement alleged to have been breached and any other relevant provisions;

(c) the issues and the factual basis for the claim; and

(d) the relief sought and the approximate amount of damages claimed.

Article 1120: Submission of a Claim to Arbitration

1. Except as provided in Annex 1120.1, and provided that six months have elapsed since the events giving rise to a claim, a disputing investor may submit the claim to arbitration under:

(a) the ICSID Convention, provided that both the disputing Party and the Party of the investor are parties to the Convention;

(b) the Additional Facility Rules of ICSID, provided that either the disputing Party or the Party of the investor, but not both, is a party to the ICSID Convention; or

(c) the UNCITRAL Arbitration Rules.

2. The applicable arbitration rules shall govern the arbitration except to the extent modified by this Section. . . .

Article 1122: Consent to Arbitration

1. Each Party consents to the submission of a claim to arbitration in accordance with the procedures set out in this Agreement. . . .

Article 1123: Number of Arbitrators and Method of Appointment

Except in respect of a Tribunal established under Article 1126, and unless the disputing parties otherwise agree, the Tribunal shall comprise three arbitrators, one arbitrator appointed by each of the disputing parties and the third, who shall be the presiding arbitrator, appointed by agreement of the disputing parties.

Article 1124: Constitution of a Tribunal When a Party Fails to Appoint an Arbitrator or the Disputing Parties Are Unable to Agree on a Presiding Arbitrator

1. The Secretary-General shall serve as appointing authority for an arbitration under this Section.

2. If a Tribunal . . . has not been constituted within 90 days from the date that a claim is submitted to arbitration, the Secretary-General, on the request of either disputing party, shall appoint, in his discretion, the arbitrator or arbitrators not yet appointed, except that the presiding arbitrator shall be appointed in accordance with paragraph 3.

3. The Secretary-General shall appoint the presiding arbitrator from the roster of presiding arbitrators referred to in paragraph 4, provided that the presiding arbitrator shall not be a national of the disputing Party or a national of the Party of the disputing investor. In the event that no such presiding arbitrator is available to serve, the Secretary-General shall appoint, from the ICSID Panel of Arbitrators, a presiding arbitrator who is not a national of any of the Parties.

4. On the date of entry into force of this Agreement, the Parties shall establish, and thereafter maintain, a roster of 45 presiding arbitrators meeting the qualifications of the Convention and rules referred to in Article 1120 and experienced in international law and investment matters. The roster members shall be appointed by consensus and without regard to nationality. . . .

Article 1130: Place of Arbitration

Unless the disputing parties agree otherwise, a Tribunal shall hold an arbitration in the territory of a Party that is a party to the New York Convention, selected in accordance with:

(a) the ICSID Additional Facility Rules if the arbitration is under those Rules or the ICSID Convention; or

(b) the UNCITRAL Arbitration Rules if the arbitration is under those Rules.

Article 1131: Governing Law

1. A Tribunal established under this Section shall decide the issues in dispute in accordance with this Agreement and applicable rules of international law.

2. An interpretation by the Commission of a provision of this Agreement shall be binding on a Tribunal established under this Section. . . .

Article 1135: Final Award

1. Where a Tribunal makes a final award against a Party, the Tribunal may award, separately or in combination, only:
    (a) monetary damages and any applicable interest;
    (b) restitution of property, in which case the award shall provide that the disputing Party may pay monetary damages and any applicable interest in lieu of restitution.
A tribunal may also award costs in accordance with the applicable arbitration rules.
2. Subject to paragraph 1, where a claim is made under Article 1117(1):
    (a) an award of restitution of property shall provide that restitution be made to the enterprise;
    (b) an award of monetary damages and any applicable interest shall provide that the sum be paid to the enterprise; and
    (c) the award shall provide that it is made without prejudice to any right that any person may have in the relief under applicable domestic law.
3. A Tribunal may not order a Party to pay punitive damages.

Article 1136: Finality and Enforcement of an Award

1. An award made by a Tribunal shall have no binding force except between the disputing parties and in respect of the particular case.
2. Subject to paragraph 3 and the applicable review procedure for an interim award, a disputing party shall abide by and comply with an award without delay.
3. A disputing party may not seek enforcement of a final award until:
    (a) in the case of a final award made under the ICSID Convention
        (i) 120 days have elapsed from the date the award was rendered and no disputing party has requested revision or annulment of the award, or
        (ii) revision or annulment proceedings have been completed; and
    (b) in the case of a final award under the ICSID Additional Facility Rules or the UNCITRAL Arbitration Rules
        (i) three months have elapsed from the date the award was rendered and no disputing party has commenced a proceeding to revise, set aside or annul the award, or
        (ii) a court has dismissed or allowed an application to revise, set aside or annul the award and there is no further appeal.
4. Each Party shall provide for the enforcement of an award in its territory.
5. If a disputing Party fails to abide by or comply with a final award, the Commission, on delivery of a request by a Party whose investor was a party to the arbitration, shall establish a panel under Article 2008 (Request for an Arbitral Panel). The requesting Party may seek in such proceedings:
    (a) a determination that the failure to abide by or comply with the final award is inconsistent with the obligations of this Agreement; and
    (b) a recommendation that the Party abide by or comply with the final award.

6. A disputing investor may seek enforcement of an arbitration award under the ICSID Convention, the New York Convention or the Inter-American Convention regardless of whether proceedings have been taken under paragraph 5. . . .

7. A claim that is submitted to arbitration under this Section shall be considered to arise out of a commercial relationship or transaction for purposes of Article I of the New York Convention and Article I of the InterAmerican Convention.

Section C.   Definitions

Article 1139:   Definitions

For purposes of this Chapter: . . .

G7 Currency means the currency of Canada, France, Germany, Italy, Japan, the United Kingdom of Great Britain and Northern Ireland or the United States;

ICSID means the International Centre for Settlement of Investment Disputes; . . .

Inter-American Convention means the *InterAmerican Convention on International Commercial Arbitration,* done at Panama, January 30, 1975;

investment means:

(a) an enterprise;

(b) an equity security of an enterprise;

(c) a debt security of an enterprise

(i) where the enterprise is an affiliate of the investor, or

(ii) where the original maturity of the debt security is at least three years,

but does not include a debt security, regardless of original maturity, of a state enterprise;

(d) a loan to an enterprise

(i) where the enterprise is an affiliate of the investor, or

(ii) where the original maturity of the loan is at least three years,

but does not include a loan, regardless of original maturity, to a state enterprise;

(e) an interest in an enterprise that entitles the owner to share in income or profits of the enterprise;

(f) an interest in an enterprise that entitles the owner to share in the assets of that enterprise on dissolution, other than a debt security or a loan excluded from subparagraph (c) or (d);

(g) real estate or other property, tangible or intangible, acquired in the expectation or used for the purpose of economic benefit or other business purposes; and

(h) interests arising from the commitment of capital or other resources in the territory of a Party to economic activity in such territory, such as under

(i) contracts involving the presence of an investor's property in the territory of the Party, including turnkey or construction contracts, or concessions, or

(ii) contracts where remuneration depends substantially on the production, revenues or profits of an enterprise;
but investment does not mean,

(i) claims to money that arise solely from

(i) commercial contracts for the sale of goods or services by a national or enterprise in the territory of a Party to an enterprise in the territory of another Party, or

(ii) the extension of credit in connection with a commercial transaction, such as trade financing, other than a loan covered by subparagraph (d); or

(j) any other claims to money,

that do not involve the kinds of interests set out in subparagraphs (a) through (h); . . .

Part Seven.   Administrative and Institutional Provisions

CHAPTER NINETEEN.   REVIEW AND DISPUTE SETTLEMENT IN ANTIDUMPING AND COUNTERVAILING DUTY MATTERS

Article 1901:   General Provisions

1. Article 1904 applies only with respect to goods that the competent investigating authority of the importing Party, applying the importing Party's antidumping or countervailing duty law to the facts of a specific case, determines are goods of another Party.

2. For purposes of Articles 1903 and 1904, panels shall be established in accordance with the provisions of Annex 1901.2.

3. Except for Article 2203 (Entry into Force), no provision of any other Chapter of this Agreement shall be construed as imposing obligations on a Party with respect to the Party's antidumping law or countervailing duty law.

Article 1902:   Retention of Domestic Antidumping Law and Countervailing Duty Law

1. Each Party reserves the right to apply its antidumping law and countervailing duty law to goods imported from the territory of any other Party. Antidumping law and countervailing duty law include, as appropriate for each Party, relevant statutes, legislative history, regulations, administrative practice and judicial precedents.

2. Each Party reserves the right to change or modify its antidumping law or countervailing duty law, provided that in the case of an amendment to a Party's antidumping or countervailing duty statute:

(a) such amendment shall apply to goods from another Party only if the amending statute specifies that it applies to goods from that Party or from the Parties to this Agreement;

(b) the amending Party notifies in writing the Parties to which the amendment applies of the amending statute as far in advance as possible of the date of enactment of such statute;

(c) following notification, the amending Party, on request of any Party to which the amendment applies, consults with that Party prior to the enactment of the amending statute; and

(d) such amendment, as applicable to that other Party, is not inconsistent with

(i) the *General Agreement on Tariffs and Trade* (GATT), the *Agreement on Implementation of Article VI of the General Agreement on Tariffs and Trade* (the Antidumping Code) or the *Agreement on the Interpretation and Application of Articles VI, XVI and XXIII of the General Agreement on Tariffs and Trade* (the Subsidies Code), or any successor agreement to which all the original signatories to this Agreement are party, or

(ii) the object and purpose of this Agreement and this Chapter, which is to establish fair and predictable conditions for the progressive liberalization of trade between the Parties to this Agreement while maintaining effective and fair disciplines on unfair trade practices, such object and purpose to be ascertained from the provisions of this Agreement, its preamble and objectives, and the practices of the Parties.

Article 1903:   Review of Statutory Amendments

1. A Party to which an amendment of another Party's antidumping or countervailing duty statute applies may request in writing that such amendment be referred to a binational panel for a declaratory opinion as to whether:

(a) the amendment does not conform to the provisions of Article 1902(2) (d)(i) or (ii); or

(b) such amendment has the function and effect of overturning a prior decision of a panel made pursuant to Article 1904 and does not conform to the provisions of Article 1902(2) (d)(i) or (ii).

Such declaratory opinion shall have force or effect only as provided in this Article.

2. The panel shall conduct its review in accordance with the procedures of Annex 1903.2.

3. In the event that the panel recommends modifications to the amending statute to remedy a non-conformity that it has identified in its opinion:

(a) the two Parties shall immediately begin consultations and shall seek to achieve a mutually satisfactory solution to the matter within 90 days of the issuance of the panel's final declaratory opinion. Such solution may include seeking corrective legislation with respect to the statute of the amending Party;

(b) if corrective legislation is not enacted within nine months from the end of the 90-day consultation period referred to in subparagraph(a) and no other mutually satisfactory solution has been reached, the Party that requested the panel may

       (i) take comparable legislative or equivalent executive action, or

       (ii) terminate this Agreement with regard to the amending Party on 60-day written notice to that Party.

Article 1904: Review of Final Antidumping and Countervailing Duty Determinations

1. As provided in this Article, each Party shall replace judicial review of final antidumping and countervailing duty determinations with binational panel review.

2. An involved Party may request that a panel review, based on the administrative record, a final antidumping or countervailing duty determination of a competent investigating authority of an importing Party to determine whether such determination was in accordance with the antidumping or countervailing duty law of the importing Party. For this purpose, the antidumping or countervailing duty law consists of the relevant statutes, legislative history, regulations, administrative practice and judicial precedents to the extent that a court of the importing Party would rely on such materials in reviewing a final determination of the competent investigating authority. Solely for purposes of the panel review provided for in this Article, the antidumping and countervailing duty statutes of the Parties, as those statutes may be amended from time to time, are incorporated into and made a part of this Agreement.

3. The panel shall apply the standard of review set out in Annex 1911 and the general legal principles that a court of the importing Party otherwise would apply to a review of a determination of the competent investigating authority.

4. A request for a panel shall be made in writing to the other involved Party within 30 days following the date of publication of the final determination in question in the official journal of the importing Party. In the case of final determinations that are not published in the official journal of the importing Party, the importing Party shall immediately notify the other involved Party of such final determination where it involves goods from the other involved Party, and the other involved Party may request a panel within 30 days of receipt of such notice. . . .

5. An involved Party on its own initiative may request review of a final determination by a panel and shall, on request of a person who would otherwise be entitled under the law of the importing Party to commence domestic procedures for judicial review of that final determination, request such review.

6. The panel shall conduct its review in accordance with the procedures established by the Parties pursuant to paragraph 14. Where both involved Parties request a panel to review a final determination, a single panel shall review that determination.

7. The competent investigating authority that issued the final determination in question shall have the right to appear and be represented by counsel

before the panel. Each Party shall provide that other persons who, pursuant to the law of the importing Party, otherwise would have had the right to appear and be represented in a domestic judicial review proceeding concerning the determination of the competent investigating authority, shall have the right to appear and be represented by counsel before the panel.

8. The panel may uphold a final determination, or remand it for action not inconsistent with the panel's decision. Where the panel remands a final determination, the panel shall establish as brief a time as is reasonable for compliance with the remand, taking into account the complexity of the factual and legal issues involved and the nature of the panel's decision. In no event shall the time permitted for compliance with a remand exceed an amount of time equal to the maximum amount of time (counted from the date of the filing of a petition, complaint or application) permitted by statute for the competent investigating authority in question to make a final determination in an investigation. If review of the action taken by the competent investigating authority on remand is needed, such review shall be before the same panel, which shall normally issue a final decision within 90 days of the date on which such remand action is submitted to it.

9. The decision of a panel under this Article shall be binding on the involved Parties with respect to the particular matter between the Parties that is before the panel.

10. This Agreement shall not affect:
    (a) the judicial review procedures of any Party, or
    (b) cases appealed under those procedures,
with respect to determinations other than final determinations.

11. A final determination shall not be reviewed under any judicial review procedures of the importing Party if an involved Party requests a panel with respect to that determination within the time limits set out in this Article. No Party may provide in its domestic legislation for an appeal from a panel decision to its domestic courts.

12. This Article shall not apply where:
    (a) neither involved Party seeks panel review of a final determination;
    (b) a revised final determination is issued as a direct result of judicial review of the original final determination by a court of the importing Party in cases where neither involved Party sought panel review of that original final determination; or
    (c) a final determination is issued as a direct result of judicial review that was commenced in a court of the importing Party before the date of entry into force of this Agreement.

13. Where, within a reasonable time after the panel decision is issued, an involved Party alleges that:
    (a)(i) a member of the panel was guilty of gross misconduct, bias, or a serious conflict of interest, or otherwise materially violated the rules of conduct,
        (ii) the panel seriously departed from a fundamental rule of procedure, or

(iii) the panel manifestly exceeded its powers, authority or jurisdiction set out in this Article, for example by failing to apply the appropriate standard of review, and

(b) any of the actions set out in subparagraph (a) has materially affected the panel's decision and threatens the integrity of the binational panel review process,

that Party may avail itself of the extraordinary challenge procedure set out in Annex 1904.13.

14. To implement the provisions of this Article, the Parties shall adopt rules of procedure by January 1, 1994. . . . The rules shall be designed to result in final decisions within 315 days of the date on which a request for a panel is made, and shall allow:

(a) 30 days for the filing of the complaint;

(b) 30 days for designation or certification of the administrative record and its filing with the panel;

(c) 60 days for the complainant to file its brief;

(d) 60 days for the respondent to file its brief;

(e) 15 days for the filing of reply briefs;

(f) 15 to 30 days for the panel to convene and hear oral argument; and

(g) 90 days for the panel to issue its written decision.

15. In order to achieve the objectives of this Article, the Parties shall amend their antidumping and countervailing duty statutes and regulations with respect to antidumping or countervailing duty proceedings involving goods of the other Parties, and other statutes and regulations to the extent that they apply to the operation of the antidumping and countervailing duty laws. . . .

Article 1906: Prospective Application

This Chapter shall apply only prospectively to:

(a) final determinations of a competent investigating authority made after the date of entry into force of this Agreement; and

(b) with respect to declaratory opinions under Article 1903, amendments to antidumping or countervailing duty statutes enacted after the date of entry into force of this Agreement.

Article 1907: Consultations

1. The Parties shall consult annually, or on the request of any Party, to consider any problems that may arise with respect to the implementation or operation of this Chapter and recommend solutions, where appropriate. . . .

Article 1908: Special Secretariat Provisions

1. The Parties shall establish a section within the Secretariat established pursuant to Article 2002 to facilitate the operation of this Chapter, including the work of panels or committees that may be convened pursuant to this Chapter.

2. The Secretaries of the Secretariat shall act jointly to provide administrative assistance to all panels or committees established pursuant to this Chapter. . . .

Annex 1903.2.   Panel Procedures Under Article 1903

1. The panel shall establish its own rules of procedure unless the Parties otherwise agree prior to the establishment of that panel. The procedures shall ensure a right to at least one hearing before the panel, as well as the opportunity to provide written submissions and rebuttal arguments. The proceedings of the panel shall be confidential, unless the two Parties otherwise agree. The panel shall base its decisions solely on the arguments and submissions of the two Parties.

2. Unless the Parties to the dispute otherwise agree, the panel shall, within 90 days after its chairman is appointed, present to the two Parties an initial written declaratory opinion containing findings of fact and its determination pursuant to Article 1903.

3. If the findings of the panel are affirmative, the panel may include in its report its recommendations as to the means by which the amending statute could be brought into conformity with the provisions of Article 1902(2) (d). In determining what, if any, recommendations are appropriate, the panel shall consider the extent to which the amending statute affects interests under this Agreement. Individual panelists may provide separate opinions on matters not unanimously agreed. The initial opinion of the panel shall become the final declaratory opinion, unless a Party to the dispute requests a reconsideration of the initial opinion pursuant to paragraph 4.

4. Within 14 days of the issuance of the initial declaratory opinion, a Party to the dispute disagreeing in whole or in part with the opinion may present a written statement of its objections and the reasons for those objections to the panel. In such event, the panel shall request the views of both Parties and shall reconsider its initial opinion. The panel shall conduct any further examination that it deems appropriate, and shall issue a final written opinion, together with dissenting or concurring views of individual panelists, within 30 days of the request for reconsideration.

5. Unless the Parties to the dispute otherwise agree, the final declaratory opinion of the panel shall be made public, along with any separate opinions of individual panelists and any written views that either Party may wish to be published. . . .

Annex 1904.13.   Extraordinary Challenge Procedure

1. The involved Parties shall establish an extraordinary challenge committee, composed of three members, within 15 days of a request pursuant to Article 1904(13). The members shall be selected from a 15-person roster comprised of judges or former judges of a federal judicial court of the United States or a judicial court of superior jurisdiction of Canada, or a federal judicial court of Mexico. Each Party shall name five persons to this roster. Each

involved Party shall select one member from this roster and the involved Parties shall decide by lot which of them shall select the third member from the roster.

2. The Parties shall establish by the date of entry into force of the Agreement rules of procedure for committees. The rules shall provide for a decision of a committee within 90 days of its establishment.

3. Committee decisions shall be binding on the Parties with respect to the particular matter between the Parties that was before the panel. After examination of the legal and factual analysis underlying the findings and conclusions of the panel's decision in order to determine whether one of the grounds set out in Article 1904(13) has been established, and on finding that one of those grounds has been established, the committee shall vacate the original panel decision or remand it to the original panel for action not inconsistent with the committee's decision; if the grounds are not established, it shall deny the challenge and, therefore, the original panel decision shall stand affirmed. If the original decision is vacated, a new panel shall be established pursuant to Annex 1901.2.

CHAPTER TWENTY. INSTITUTIONAL ARRANGEMENTS AND DISPUTE SETTLEMENT PROCEDURES

SECTION A—INSTITUTIONS

Article 2001: The Free Trade Commission

1. The Parties hereby establish the Free Trade Commission, comprising cabinet-level representatives of the Parties or their designees.

2. The Commission shall:

    (a) supervise the implementation of this Agreement;

    (b) oversee its further elaboration;

    (c) resolve disputes that may arise regarding its interpretation or application;

    (d) supervise the work of all committees and working groups established under this Agreement, referred to in Annex 2001.2; and

    (e) consider any other matter that may affect the operation of this Agreement.

3. The Commission may:

    (a) establish, and delegate responsibilities to, ad hoc or standing committees, working groups or expert groups;

    (b) seek the advice of non-governmental persons or groups; and

    (c) take such other action in the exercise of its functions as the Parties may agree.

4. The Commission shall establish its rules and procedures. All decisions of the Commission shall be taken by consensus, except as the Commission may otherwise agree.

5. The Commission shall convene at least once a year in regular session. Regular sessions of the Commission shall be chaired successively by each Party.

Article 2002:   The Secretariat

1. The Commission shall establish and oversee a Secretariat comprising national Sections.

2. Each Party shall:

(a) establish a permanent office of its Section;

(b) be responsible for

(i) the operation and costs of its Section, and

(ii) the remuneration and payment of expenses of panelists and members of committees and scientific review boards established under this Agreement, as set out in Annex 2002.2;

(c) designate an individual to serve as Secretary for its Section, who shall be responsible for its administration and management; and

(d) notify the Commission of the location of its Section's office.

3. The Secretariat shall:

(a) provide assistance to the Commission;

(b) provide administrative assistance to

(i) panels and committees established under Chapter Nineteen (Review and Dispute Settlement in Antidumping and Countervailing Duty Matters), in accordance with the procedures established pursuant to Article 1908, and

(ii) panels established under this Chapter, in accordance with procedures established pursuant to Article 2012; and

(c) as the Commission may direct

(i) support the work of other committees and groups established under this Agreement, and

(ii) otherwise facilitate the operation of this Agreement.

Section B—Dispute Settlement

Article 2003:   Cooperation

The Parties shall at all times endeavor to agree on the interpretation and application of this Agreement, and shall make every attempt through cooperation and consultations to arrive at a mutually satisfactory resolution of any matter that might affect its operation.

Article 2004:   Recourse to Dispute Settlement Procedures

Except for the matters covered in Chapter Nineteen (Review and Dispute Settlement in Antidumping and Countervailing Duty Matters) and as otherwise provided in this Agreement, the dispute settlement provisions of this Chapter shall apply with respect to the avoidance or settlement of all disputes between the Parties regarding the interpretation or application of this Agreement or wherever a Party considers that an actual or proposed measure of another Party is or would be inconsistent with the obligations of this Agreement or cause nullification or impairment in the sense of Annex 2004.

Article 2005: GATT Dispute Settlement

1. Subject to paragraphs 2, 3, and 4, disputes regarding any matter arising under both this Agreement and the *General Agreement on Tariffs and Trade,* any agreement negotiated thereunder, or any successor agreement (GATT), may be settled in either forum at the discretion of the complaining Party.

2. Before a Party initiates a dispute settlement proceeding in the GATT against another Party on grounds that arc substantially equivalent to those available to that Party under this Agreement, that Party shall notify any third Party of its intention. If a third Party wishes to have recourse to dispute settlement procedures under this Agreement regarding the matter, it shall inform promptly the notifying Party and those Parties shall consult with a view to agreement on a single forum. If those Parties cannot agree, the dispute normally shall be settled under this Agreement.

3. In any dispute referred to in paragraph 1 where the responding Party claims that its action is subject to Article 104 (Relation to Environmental and Conservation Agreements) and requests in writing that the matter be considered under this Agreement, the complaining Party may, in respect of that matter, thereafter have recourse to dispute settlement procedures solely under this Agreement.

4. In any dispute referred to in paragraph 1 that arises under Section B of Chapter Seven (Sanitary and Phytosanitary Measures) or Chapter Nine (Standards-Related Measures):

    (a) concerning a measure adopted or maintained by a Party to protect its human, animal or plant life or health, or to protect its environment, and

    (b) that raises factual issues concerning the environment, health, safety or conservation, including directly related scientific matters,

where the responding Party requests in writing that the matter be considered under this Agreement, the complaining Party may, in respect of that matter, thereafter have recourse to dispute settlement procedures solely under this Agreement.

5. The responding Party shall deliver a copy of a request made pursuant to paragraph 3 or 4 to the other Parties and to its Section of the Secretariat. Where the complaining Party has initiated dispute settlement proceedings regarding any matter subject to paragraph 3 or 4, the responding Party shall deliver its request no later than 15 days thereafter. On receipt of such request, the complaining Party shall promptly withdraw from participation in those proceedings and may initiate dispute settlement procedures under Article 2007.

6. Once dispute settlement procedures have been initialed under Article 2007 or dispute settlement proceedings have been initiated under the GATT, the forum selected shall be used to the exclusion of the other, unless a Party makes a request pursuant to paragraph 3 or 4.

7. For purposes of this Article, dispute settlement proceedings under the GATT are deemed to be initiated by a Party's request for a panel, such as under Article XXIII:2 of the *General Agreement on Tariffs and Trade 1947,* or for a committee investigation, such as under Article 20.1 of the Customs Valuation Code.

Consultations

Article 2006: Consultations

1. Any Party may request in writing consultations with any other Party regarding any actual or proposed measure or any other matter that it considers might affect the operation of this Agreement. . . .

Initiation of Procedures

Article 2007: Commission—Good Offices, Conciliation and Mediation

1. If the consulting Parties fail to resolve a matter pursuant to Article 2006 within:

(a) 30 days of delivery of a request for consultations,

(b) 45 days of delivery of such request if any other Party has subsequently requested or has participated in consultations regarding the same matter,

(c) 15 days of delivery of a request for consultations in matters regarding perishable agricultural goods, or

(d) such other period as they may agree, any such Party may request in writing a meeting of the Commission.

2. A Party may also request in writing a meeting of the Commission where:

(a) it has initiated dispute settlement proceedings under the GATT regarding any matter subject to Article 2005(3) or (4), and has received a request pursuant to Article 2005(5) for recourse to dispute settlement procedures under this Chapter; or

(b) consultations have been held pursuant to Article 513 (Working Group on Rules of Origin), Article 723 (Sanitary and Phytosanitary Measures—Technical Consultations) and Article 914 (Standards-Related Measures—Technical Consultations).

3. The requesting Party shall state in the request the measure or other matter complained of and indicate the provisions of this Agreement that it considers relevant. . . .

4. Unless it decides otherwise, the Commission shall convene within 10 days of delivery of the request and shall endeavor to resolve the dispute promptly.

5. The Commission may:

(a) call on such technical advisers or create such working groups or expert groups as it deems necessary,

(b) have recourse to good offices, conciliation, mediation or such other dispute resolution procedures, or

(c) make recommendations,

as may assist the consulting Parties to reach a mutually satisfactory resolution of the dispute.

6. Unless it decides otherwise, the Commission shall consolidate two or more proceedings before it pursuant to this Article regarding the same measure. The Commission may consolidate two or more proceedings regarding

other matters before it pursuant to this Article that it determines are appropriate to be considered jointly.

Panel Proceedings

Article 2008: Request for an Arbitral Panel

1. If the Commission has convened pursuant to Article 2007(4), and the matter has not been resolved within:

(a) 30 days thereafter,

(b) 30 days after the Commission has convened in respect of the matter most recently referred to it, where proceedings have been consolidated pursuant to Article 2007(6), or

(c) such other period as the consulting Parties may agree,

any consulting Party may request in writing the establishment of an arbitral panel. . . .

2. On delivery of the request, the Commission shall establish an arbitral panel.

3. A third Party that considers it has a substantial interest in the matter shall be entitled to join as a complaining Party on delivery of written notice of its intention to participate to the disputing Parties and its Section of the Secretariat. . . .

4. If a third Party does not join as a complaining Party in accordance with paragraph 3, it normally shall refrain thereafter from initiating or continuing:

(a) a dispute settlement procedure under this Agreement, or

(b) a dispute settlement proceeding in the GATT on grounds that are substantially equivalent to those available to that Party under this Agreement,

regarding the same matter in the absence of a significant change in economic or commercial circumstances.

5. Unless otherwise agreed by the disputing Parties, the panel shall be established and perform its functions in a manner consistent with the provisions of this Chapter.

Article 2009: Roster

1. The Parties shall establish by January 1, 1994 and maintain a roster of up to 30 individuals who are willing and able to serve as panelists. The roster members shall be appointed by consensus for terms of three years, and may be reappointed.

2. Roster members shall:

(a) have expertise or experience in law, international trade, other matters covered by this Agreement or the resolution of disputes arising under international trade agreements, and shall be chosen strictly on the basis of objectivity, reliability and sound judgment;

(b) be independent of, and not be affiliated with or take instructions from, any Party; and

(c) comply with a code of conduct to be established by the Commission. . . .

Article 2011:   Panel Selection

1. Where there arc two disputing Parties, the following procedures shall apply:

(a) The panel shall comprise five members.

(b) The disputing Parties shall endeavor to agree on the chair of the panel within 15 days of the delivery of the request for the establishment of the panel. If the disputing Parties are unable to agree on the chair within this period, the disputing Party chosen by lot shall select within five days as chair an individual who is not a citizen of that Party.

(c) Within 15 days of selection of the chair, each disputing Party shall select two panelists who are citizens of the other disputing Party.

(d) If a disputing Party fails to select its panelists within such period, such panelists shall be selected by lot from among the roster members who are citizens of the other disputing Party.

2. Where there are more than two disputing Parties, the following procedures shall apply:

(a) The panel shall comprise five members.

(b) The disputing Parties shall endeavor to agree on the chair of the panel within 15 days of the delivery of the request for the establishment of the panel. If the disputing Parties are unable to agree on the chair within this period, the Party or Parties on the side of the dispute chosen by lot shall select within 10 days a chair who is not a citizen of such Party or Parties.

(c) Within 15 days of selection of the chair, the Party complained against shall select two panelists, one of whom is a citizen of a complaining Party, and the other of whom is a citizen of another complaining Party. The complaining Parties shall select two panelists who are citizens of the Party complained against.

(d) If any disputing Party fails to select a panelist within such period, such panelist shall be selected by lot in accordance with the citizenship criteria of subparagraph (c).

3. Panelists shall normally be selected from the roster. Any disputing Party may exercise a peremptory challenge against any individual not on the roster who is proposed as a panelist by a disputing Party within 15 days after the individual has been proposed. . . .

Article 2012:   Rules of Procedure

1. The Commission shall establish by January 1, 1994 Model Rules of Procedure, in accordance with the following principles:

(a) the procedures shall assure a right to at least one hearing before the panel as well as the opportunity to provide initial and rebuttal written submissions; and

(b) the panel's hearings, deliberations and initial report, and all written submissions to and communications with the panel shall be confidential.

2. Unless the disputing Parties otherwise agree, the panel shall conduct its proceedings in accordance with the Model Rules of Procedure.

3. Unless the disputing Parties otherwise agree within 20 days from the date of the delivery of the request for the establishment of the panel, the terms of reference shall be:

> To examine, in the light of the relevant provisions of the Agreement, the matter referred to the Commission (as set out in the request for a Commission meeting) and to make findings, determinations and recommendations as provided in Article 2016(2).

4. If a complaining Party wishes to argue that a matter has nullified or impaired benefits, the terms of reference shall so indicate.

5. If a disputing Party wishes the panel to make findings as to the degree of adverse trade effects on any Party of any measure found not to conform with the obligations of the Agreement or to have caused nullification or impairment in the sense of Annex 2004, the terms of reference shall so indicate.

Article 2013:   Third Party Participation

A Party that is not a disputing Party, on delivery of a written notice to the disputing Parties and to its Section of the Secretariat, shall be entitled to attend all hearings, to make written and oral submissions to the panel and to receive written submissions of the disputing Parties.

Article 2014:   Role of Experts

On request of a disputing Party, or on its own initiative, the panel may seek information and technical advice from any person or body that it deems appropriate, provided that the disputing Parties so agree and subject to such terms and conditions as such Parties may agree.

Article 2015:   Scientific Review Boards

1. On request of a disputing Party or, unless the disputing Parties disapprove, on its own initiative, the panel may request a written report of a scientific review board on any factual issue concerning environmental, health, safety or other scientific matters raised by a disputing Party in a proceeding, subject to such terms and conditions as such Parties may agree.

2. The board shall be selected by the panel from among highly qualified, independent experts in the scientific matters, after consultations with the disputing Parties and the scientific bodies set out in the Model Rules of Procedure established pursuant to Article 2012(1). . . .

Article 2016: Initial Report

1. Unless the disputing Parties otherwise agree, the panel shall base its report on the submissions and arguments of the Parties and on any information before it pursuant to Article 2014 or 2015.

2. Unless the disputing Parties otherwise agree, the panel shall, within 90 days after the last panelist is selected or such other period as the Model Rules of Procedure established pursuant to Article 2012(1) may provide, present to the disputing Parties an initial report containing:

(a) findings of fact, including any findings pursuant to a request under Article 2012(5);

(b) its determination as to whether the measure at issue is or would be inconsistent with the obligations of this Agreement or cause nullification or impairment in the sense of Annex 2004, or any other determination requested in the terms of reference; and

(c) its recommendations, if any, for resolution of the dispute.

3. Panelists may furnish separate opinions on matters not unanimously agreed.

4. A disputing Party may submit written comments to the panel on its initial report within 14 days of presentation of the report.

5. In such an event, and after considering such written comments, the panel, on its own initiative or on the request of any disputing Party, may:

(a) request the views of any participating Party;

(b) reconsider its report; and

(c) make any further examination that it considers appropriate.

Article 2017: Final Report

1. The panel shall present to the disputing Parties a final report, including any separate opinions on matters not unanimously agreed, within 30 days of presentation of the initial report, unless the disputing Parties otherwise agree.

2. No panel may, either in its initial report or its final report, disclose which panelists are associated with majority or minority opinions.

3. The disputing Parties shall transmit to the Commission the final report of the panel, including any report of a scientific review board established under Article 2015, as well as any written views that a disputing Party desires to be appended, on a confidential basis within a reasonable period of time after it is presented to them.

4. Unless the Commission decides otherwise, the final report of the panel shall be published 15 days after it is transmitted to the Commission.

Implementation of Panel Reports

Article 2018: Implementation of Final Report

1. On receipt of the final report of a panel, the disputing Parties shall agree on the resolution of the dispute, which normally shall conform with

the determinations and recommendations of the panel, and shall notify their Sections of the Secretariat of any agreed resolution of any dispute.

2. Wherever possible, the resolution shall be non-implementation or removal of a measure not conforming with this Agreement or causing nullification or impairment in the sense of Annex 2004 or, failing such a resolution, compensation.

Article 2019. Non-Implementation—Suspension of Benefits

1. If in its final report a panel has determined that a measure is inconsistent with the obligations of this Agreement or causes nullification or impairment in the sense of Annex 2004 and the Party complained against has not reached agreement with any complaining Party on a mutually satisfactory resolution pursuant to Article 2018(1) within 30 days of receiving the final report, such complaining Party may suspend the application to the Party complained against of benefits of equivalent effect until such time as they have reached agreement on a resolution of the dispute.

2. In considering what benefits to suspend pursuant to paragraph 1:

(a) a complaining Party should first seek to suspend benefits in the same sector or sectors as that affected by the measure or other matter that the panel has found to be inconsistent with the obligations of this Agreement or to have caused nullification or impairment in the sense of Annex 2004; and

(b) a complaining Party that considers it is not practicable or effective to suspend benefits in the same sector or sectors may suspend benefits in other sectors.

3. On the written request of any disputing Party delivered to the other Parties and its Section of the Secretariat, the Commission shall establish a panel to determine whether the level of benefits suspended by a Party pursuant to paragraph 1 is manifestly excessive.

4. The panel proceedings shall be conducted in accordance with the Model Rules of Procedure. The panel shall present its determination within 60 days after the last panelist is selected or such other period as the disputing Parties may agree. . . .

GENERAL AGREEMENT ON TARIFFS AND TRADE: ARTICLES XXII AND XXIII

(1947, as amended)*

Article XXII.   Consultation

1. Each contracting party shall accord sympathetic consideration to, and shall afford adequate opportunity for consultation regarding, such representations as may be made by another contracting party with respect to any matter affecting the operation of this Agreement.

2. The CONTRACTING PARTIES may, at the request of a contracting party, consult with any contracting party or parties in respect of any matter for which it has not been possible to find a satisfactory solution through consultation under paragraph 1.

Article XXIII.   Nullification or Impairment

1. If any contracting party should consider that any benefit accruing to it directly or indirectly under this Agreement is being nullified or impaired or that the attainment of any objective of the Agreement is being impeded as the result of

(a) the failure of another contracting party to carry out its obligations under this Agreement, or

(b) the application by another contracting party of any measure, whether or not it conflicts with the provisions of this Agreement, or

(c) the existence of any other situation,

the contracting party may, with a view to the satisfactory adjustment of the matter, make written representations or proposals to the other contracting party or parties which it considers to be concerned. Any contracting party thus approached shall give sympathetic consideration to the representations or proposals made to it.

2. If no satisfactory adjustment is effected between the contracting parties concerned within a reasonable time, or if the difficulty is of the type described in paragraph 1(c) of this Article, the matter may be referred to the CONTRACTING PARTIES. The CONTRACTING PARTIES shall promptly investigate any matter so referred to them and shall make appropriate

* BISD Vol. IV. See the WTO website at <http://www.wto.org>.

recommendations to the contracting parties which they consider to be concerned, or give a ruling on the matter, as appropriate. The CONTRACTING PARTIES may consult with contracting parties, with the Economic and Social Council of the United Nations and with any appropriate inter-governmental organization in cases where they consider such consultation necessary. If the CONTRACTING PARTIES consider that the circumstances are serious enough to justify such action, they may authorize a contracting party or parties to suspend the application to any other contracting party or parties of such concessions or other obligations under this Agreement as they determine to be appropriate in the circumstances. If the application to any contracting party of any concession or other obligation is in fact suspended, that contracting party shall then be free, not later than sixty days after such action is taken, to give written notice to the Executive Secretary to the CONTRACTING PARTIES of its intention to withdraw from this Agreement and such withdrawal shall take effect upon the sixtieth day following the day on which such notice is received by him.

URUGUAY ROUND FINAL ACT: EXCERPTS ON THE WORLD TRADE ORGANIZATION AND SETTLEMENT OF DISPUTES

33 I.L.M. 1143-53, 1224-47 (1994)*

Final Act

1. Having met in order to conclude the Uruguay Round of Multilateral Trade Negotiations, representatives of the governments and of the European Communities, members of the Trade Negotiations Committee, *agree* that the

* The Final Act was signed in Marrakesh, Morocco, on April 15, 1994, by 109 countries. It came into effect—and the World Trade Organization (WTO) was created—on January 1, 1995. The United States passed domestic implementing legislation in 1994 that included some limitations or other variations on the provisions of the Final Act. Uruguay Round Agreements Act (1994), Pub. L. No. 103-465, 108 Stat. 4809.

The 159 members to WTO (as of February 2013) were: Albania, Angola, Antigua and Barbuda, Argentina, Armenia, Australia, Austria, Bahrain, Bangladesh, Barbados, Belgium, Belize, Benin, Bolivia, Botswana, Brazil, Brunei Darussalam, Bulgaria, Burkina Faso, Burundi, Cambodia, Cameroon, Canada, Cape Verde, Central African Republic, Chad, Chile, China, Colombia, Congo, Congo (Democratic Republic of), Costa Rica, Côte d'Ivoire, Croatia, Cuba, Cyprus, Czech Republic, Denmark, Djibouti, Dominica, Dominican Republic, Ecuador, Egypt, El Salvador, Estonia, European Communities, Fiji, Finland, France, Gabon, Gambia, Georgia, Germany, Ghana, Greece, Grenada, Guatemala, Guinea, Guinea-Bissau, Guyana, Haiti, Honduras, Hong Kong—China, Hungary, Iceland, India, Indonesia, Ireland, Israel, Italy, Jamaica, Japan, Jordan, Kenya, Korea (Republic of), Kuwait, Kyrgyzstan, Lao People's Democratic Republic, Latvia, Lesotho, Liechtenstein, Lithuania, Luxembourg, Macau, Macedonia (former Yugoslav Republic of), Madagascar, Malawi, Malaysia, Maldives, Mali, Malta, Mauritania, Mauritius, Mexico, Moldova, Mongolia, Montenegro, Morocco, Mozambique, Myanmar, Namibia, Nepal, Netherlands, New Zealand, Nicaragua, Niger, Nigeria, Norway, Oman, Pakistan, Panama, Papua New Guinea, Paraguay, Peru, Philippines, Poland, Portugal, Qatar, Romania, Russian Federation, Rwanda, Saint Kitts and Nevis, Saint Lucia, Saint Vincent and the Grenadines, Samoa, Senegal, Separate Customs Territory of Taiwan, Penghu, Kinmen and Matsu (Chinese Taipei), Saudi Arabia, Sierra Leone, Singapore, Slovakia, Slovenia, Solomon Islands, South Africa, Spain, Sri Lanka, Suriname, Swaziland, Sweden, Switzerland, Tajikistan, Tanzania, Thailand, Togo, Tonga, Trinidad and Tobago, Tunisia, Turkey, Uganda, Ukraine, United Arab Emirates, United Kingdom, United States of America, Uruguay, Vanuatu, Venezuela, Viet Nam, Zambia, and Zimbabwe.

Also, the following 25 observer governments have applied to join the WTO: Afghanistan, Algeria, Andorra, Azerbaijan, Bahamas, Belarus, Bhutan, Bosnia and Herzegovina, Comoros, Equatorial Guinea, Ethiopia, Holy See, Iran, Iraq, Kazakhstan, Lebanon, Liberia, Libya, Sao Tome and Principe, Serbia, Seychelles, Sudan, Syrian Arab Republic, Uzbekistan, and Yemen. See the WTO Web site at <http://www.wto.org>.

Agreement Establishing the World Trade Organization (referred to in this Final Act as the "WTO Agreement"), the Ministerial Declarations and Decisions, and the Understanding on Commitments in Financial Services, as annexed hereto, embody the results of their negotiations and form an integral part of this Final Act. . . .

3. The representatives *agree* on the desirability of acceptance of the WTO Agreement by all participants in the Uruguay Round of Multilateral Trade Negotiations (hereinafter referred to as "participants") with a view to its entry into force by 1 January 1995, or as early as possible thereafter. . . .

4. The representatives *agree* that the WTO Agreement shall be open for acceptance as a whole, by signature or otherwise, by all participants pursuant to Article XIV thereof. The acceptance and entry into force of a Plurilateral Trade Agreement included in Annex 4 of the WTO Agreement shall be governed by the provisions of that Plurilateral Trade Agreement.

5. Before accepting the WTO Agreement, participants which are not contracting parties to the General Agreement on Tariffs and Trade must first have concluded negotiations for their accession to the General Agreement and become contracting parties thereto. For participants which are not contracting parties to the General Agreement as of the date of the Final Act, the Schedules are not definitive and shall be subsequently completed for the purpose of their accession to the General Agreement and acceptance of the WTO Agreement. . . .

DONE at Marrakesh this fifteenth day of April one thousand nine hundred and ninety-four, in a single copy, in the English, French and Spanish languages, each text being authentic.

AGREEMENT ESTABLISHING THE WORLD TRADE ORGANIZATION

The *Parties* to this Agreement,

Recognizing that their relations in the field of trade and economic endeavour should be conducted with a view to raising standards of living, ensuring full employment and a large and steadily growing volume of real income and effective demand, and expanding the production of and trade in goods and services, while allowing for the optimal use of the world's resources in accordance with the objective of sustainable development, seeking both to protect and preserve the environment and to enhance the means for doing so in a manner consistent with their respective needs and concerns at different levels of economic development,

Recognizing further that there is need for positive efforts designed to ensure that developing countries, and especially the least developed among them, secure a share in the growth in international trade commensurate with the needs of their economic development,

Being desirous of contributing to these objectives by entering into reciprocal and mutually advantageous arrangements directed to the substantial reduction of tariffs and other barriers to trade and to the elimination of discriminatory treatment in international trade relations,

Resolved, therefore, to develop an integrated, more viable and durable multilateral trading system encompassing the General Agreement on Tariffs and Trade, the results of past trade liberalization efforts, and all of the results of the Uruguay Round of Multilateral Trade Negotiations,

Determined to preserve the basic principles and to further the objectives underlying this multilateral trading system,

Agree as follows:

Article I.   Establishment of the Organization

The World Trade Organization (hereinafter referred to as "the WTO") is hereby established.

Article II.   Scope of the WTO

1. The WTO shall provide the common institutional framework for the conduct of trade relations among its Members in matters related to the agreements and associated legal instruments included in the Annexes to this Agreement.

2. The agreements and associated legal instruments included in Annexes 1, 2 and 3 (hereinafter referred to as "Multilateral Trade Agreements") are integral parts of this Agreement, binding on all Members.

3. The agreements and associated legal instruments included in Annex 4 (hereinafter referred to as "Plurilateral Trade Agreements") arc also part of this Agreement for those Members that have accepted them, and are binding on those Members. The Plurilateral Trade Agreements do not create either obligations or rights for Members that have not accepted them.

4. The General Agreement on Tariffs and Trade 1994 as specified in Annex 1A (hereinafter referred to as "GATT 1994") is legally distinct from the General Agreement on Tariffs and Trade, dated 30 October 1947, annexed to the Final Act Adopted at the Conclusion of the Second Session of the Preparatory Committee of the United Nations Conference on Trade and Employment, as subsequently rectified, amended or modified (hereinafter referred to as "GATT 1947").

Article III.   Functions of the WTO

1. The WTO shall facilitate the implementation, administration and operation, and further the objectives, of this Agreement and of the Multilateral Trade Agreements, and shall also provide the framework for the implementation, administration and operation of the Plurilateral Trade Agreements.

2. The WTO shall provide the forum for negotiations among its Members concerning their multilateral trade relations in matters dealt with under the agreements in the Annexes to this Agreement. The WTO may also provide a forum for further negotiations among its Members concerning their multilateral trade relations, and a framework for the implementation of

the results of such negotiations, as may be decided by the Ministerial Conference.

3. The WTO shall administer the Understanding on Rules and Procedures Governing the Settlement of Disputes (hereinafter referred to as the "Dispute Settlement Understanding" or "DSU") in Annex 2 to this Agreement.

4. The WTO shall administer the Trade Policy Review Mechanism (hereinafter referred to as the "TPRM") provided for in Annex 3 to this Agreement.

5. With a view to achieving greater coherence in global economic policy-making, the WTO shall cooperate, as appropriate, with the International Monetary Fund and with the International Bank for Reconstruction and Development and its affiliated agencies.

Article IV. Structure of the WTO

1. There shall be a Ministerial Conference composed of representatives of all the Members, which shall meet at least once every two years. The Ministerial Conference shall carry out the functions of the WTO and take actions necessary to this effect. The Ministerial Conference shall have the authority to take decisions on all matters under any of the Multilateral Trade Agreements, if so requested by a Member, in accordance with the specific requirements for decision-making in this Agreement and in the relevant Multilateral Trade Agreement.

2. There shall be a General Council composed of representatives of all the Members, which shall meet as appropriate. In the intervals between meetings of the Ministerial Conference, its functions shall be conducted by the General Council. The General Council shall also carry out the functions assigned to it by this Agreement. The General Council shall establish its rules of procedure and approve the rules of procedure for the Committees provided for in paragraph 7.

3. The General Council shall convene as appropriate to discharge the responsibilities of the Dispute Settlement Body provided for in the Dispute Settlement Understanding. The Dispute Settlement Body may have its own chairman and shall establish such rules of procedure as it deems necessary for the fulfilment of those responsibilities.

4. The General Council shall convene as appropriate to discharge the responsibilities of the Trade Policy Review Body provided for in the TPRM. The Trade Policy Review Body may have its own chairman and shall establish such rules of procedure as it deems necessary for the fulfilment of those responsibilities.

5. There shall be a Council for Trade in Goods, a Council for Trade in Services and a Council for Trade-Related Aspects of Intellectual Property Rights (hereinafter referred to as the "Council for TRIPS"), which shall operate under the general guidance of the General Council. The Council for Trade in Goods shall oversee the functioning of the Multilateral Trade Agreements in Annex 1A. The Council for Trade in Services shall oversee the functioning

of the General Agreement on Trade in Services (hereinafter referred to as "GATS"). The Council for TRIPS shall oversee the functioning of the Agreement on Trade-Related Aspects of Intellectual Property Rights (hereinafter referred to as the "Agreement on TRIPS"). These Councils shall carry out the functions assigned to them by their respective agreements and by the General Council. They shall establish their respective rules of procedure subject to the approval of the General Council. Membership in these Councils shall be open to representatives of all Members. These Councils shall meet as necessary to carry out their functions.

6. The Council for Trade in Goods, the Council for Trade in Services and the Council for TRIPS shall establish subsidiary bodies as required. These subsidiary bodies shall establish their respective rules of procedure subject to the approval of their respective Councils.

7. The Ministerial Conference shall establish a Committee on Trade and Development, a Committee on Balance-of-Payments Restrictions and a Committee on Budget, Finance and Administration, which shall carry out the functions assigned to them by this Agreement and by the Multilateral Trade Agreements, and any additional functions assigned to them by the General Council, and may establish such additional Committees with such functions as it may deem appropriate. As part of its functions, the Committee on Trade and Development shall periodically review the special provisions in the Multilateral Trade Agreements in favour of the least-developed country Members and report to the General Council for appropriate action. Membership in these Committees shall be open to representatives of all Members.

8. The bodies provided for under the Plurilateral Trade Agreements shall carry out the functions assigned to them under those Agreements and shall operate within the institutional framework of the WTO. These bodies shall keep the General Council informed of their activities on a regular basis.

Article V.   Relations with Other Organizations

1. The General Council shall make appropriate arrangements for effective cooperation with other intergovernmental organizations that have responsibilities related to those of the WTO.

2. The General Council may make appropriate arrangements for consultation and cooperation with non-governmental organizations concerned with matters related to those of the WTO.

Article VI.   The Secretariat

1. There shall be a Secretariat of the WTO (hereinafter referred to as "the Secretariat") headed by a Director-General.

2. The Ministerial Conference shall appoint the Director-General and adopt regulations setting out the powers, duties, conditions of service and term of office of the Director-General.

3. The Director-General shall appoint the members of the staff of the Secretariat and determine their duties and conditions of service in accordance with regulations adopted by the Ministerial Conference.

4. The responsibilities of the Director-General and of the staff of the Secretariat shall be exclusively international in character. In the discharge of their duties, the Director-General and the staff of the Secretariat shall not seek or accept instructions from any government or any other authority external to the WTO. They shall refrain from any action which might adversely reflect on their position as international officials. The Members of the WTO shall respect the international character of the responsibilities of the Director-General and of the staff of the Secretariat and shall not seek to influence them in the discharge of their duties.

Article VII. Budget and Contributions

1. The Director-General shall present to the Committee on Budget, Finance and Administration the annual budget estimate and financial statement of the WTO. The Committee on Budget, Finance and Administration shall review the annual budget estimate and the financial statement presented by the Director-General and make recommendations thereon to the General Council. The annual budget estimate shall be subject to approval by the General Council.

2. The Committee on Budget, Finance and Administration shall propose to the General Council financial regulations which shall include provisions setting out:

    (a) the scale of contributions apportioning the expenses of the WTO among its Members; and

    (b) the measures to be taken in respect of Members in arrears.

The financial regulations shall be based, as far as practicable, on the regulations and practices of GATT 1947.

3. The General Council shall adopt the financial regulations and the annual budget estimate by a two-thirds majority comprising more than half of the Members of the WTO.

4. Each Member shall promptly contribute to the WTO its share in the expenses of the WTO in accordance with the financial regulations adopted by the General Council.

Article VIII. Status of the WTO

1. The WTO shall have legal personality, and shall be accorded by each of its Members such legal capacity as may be necessary for the exercise of its functions.

2. The WTO shall be accorded by each of its Members such privileges and immunities as are necessary for the exercise of its functions.

3. The officials of the WTO and the representatives of the Members shall similarly be accorded by each of its Members such privileges and immunities

as are necessary for the independent exercise of their functions in connection with the WTO.

4. The privileges and immunities to be accorded by a Member to the WTO, its officials, and the representatives of its Members shall be similar to the privileges and immunities stipulated in the Convention on the Privileges and Immunities of the Specialized Agencies, approved by the General Assembly of the United Nations on 21 November 1947.

5. The WTO may conclude a headquarters agreement.

Article IX.   Decision-Making

1. The WTO shall continue the practice of decision-making by consensus followed under GATT 1947.[1] Except as otherwise provided, where a decision cannot be arrived at by consensus, the matter at issue shall be decided by voting. At meetings of the Ministerial Conference and the General Council, each Member of the WTO shall have one vote. Where the European Communities exercise their right to vote, they shall have a number of votes equal to the number of their member States[2] which are Members of the WTO. Decisions of the Ministerial Conference and the General Council shall be taken by a majority of the votes cast, unless otherwise provided in this Agreement or in the relevant Multilateral Trade Agreement.[3]

2. The Ministerial Conference and the General Council shall have the exclusive authority to adopt interpretations of this Agreement and of the Multilateral Trade Agreements. In the case of an interpretation of a Multilateral Trade Agreement in Annex 1, they shall exercise their authority on the basis of a recommendation by the Council overseeing the functioning of that Agreement. The decision to adopt an interpretation shall be taken by a three-fourths majority of the Members. This paragraph shall not be used in a manner that would undermine the amendment provisions in Article X.

3. In exceptional circumstances, the Ministerial Conference may decide to waive an obligation imposed on a Member by this Agreement or any of the Multilateral Trade Agreements, provided that any such decision shall be taken by three fourths[4] of the Members unless otherwise provided for in this paragraph.

(a) A request for a waiver concerning this Agreement shall be submitted to the Ministerial Conference for consideration pursuant to the practice of

1. The body concerned shall be deemed to have decided by consensus on a matter submitted for its consideration, if no Member, present at the meeting when the decision is taken, formally objects to the proposed decision.

2. The number of votes of the European Communities and their member States shall in no case exceed the number of the member States of the European Communities.

3. Decisions by the General Council when convened as the Dispute Settlement Body shall be taken only in accordance with the provisions of paragraph 4 of Article 2 of the Dispute Settlement Understanding.

4. A decision to grant a waiver in respect of any obligation subject to a transition period or a period for staged implementation that the requesting Member has not performed by the end of the relevant period shall be taken only by consensus.

decision-making by consensus. The Ministerial Conference shall establish a time-period, which shall not exceed 90 days, to consider the request. If consensus is not reached during the time-period, any decision to grant a waiver shall be taken by three fourths of the Members.

(b) A request for a waiver concerning the Multilateral Trade Agreements in Annexes 1A or 1B or 1C and their annexes shall be submitted initially to the Council for Trade in Goods, the Council for Trade in Services or the Council for TRIPS, respectively, for consideration during a time-period which shall not exceed 90 days. At the end of the time-period, the relevant Council shall submit a report to the Ministerial Conference.

4. A decision by the Ministerial Conference granting a waiver shall state the exceptional circumstances justifying the decision, the terms and conditions governing the application of the waiver, and the date on which the waiver shall terminate. Any waiver granted for a period of more than one year shall he reviewed by the Ministerial Conference not later than one year after it is granted, and thereafter annually until the waiver terminates. In each review, the Ministerial Conference shall examine whether the exceptional circumstances justifying the waiver still exist and whether the terms and conditions attached to the waiver have been met. The Ministerial Conference, on the basis of the annual review, may extend, modify or terminate the waiver.

5. Decisions under a Plurilateral Trade Agreement, including any decisions on interpretations and waivers, shall he governed by the provisions of that Agreement.

Article X.   Amendments . . .

Article XI.   Original Membership

1. The contracting parties to GATT 1947 as of the date of entry into force of this Agreement, and the European Communities, which accept this Agreement and the Multilateral Trade Agreements and for which Schedules of Concessions and Commitments are annexed to GATT 1994 and for which Schedules of Specific Commitments are annexed to GATS shall become original Members of the WTO.

2. The least-developed countries recognized as such by the United Nations will only be required to undertake commitments and concessions to the extent consistent with their individual development, financial and trade needs or their administrative and institutional capabilities.

Article XII.   Accession

1. Any State or separate customs territory possessing full autonomy in the conduct of its external commercial relations and of the other matters provided for in this Agreement and the Multilateral Trade Agreements may accede to this Agreement, on terms to be agreed between it and the WTO. Such

accession shall apply to this Agreement and the Multilateral Trade Agreements annexed thereto.

2. Decisions on accession shall be taken by the Ministerial Conference. The Ministerial Conference shall approve the agreement on the terms of accession by a two-thirds majority of the Members of the WTO.

3. Accession to a Plurilateral Trade Agreement shall be governed by the provisions of that Agreement.

Article XIII. Non-Application of Multilateral Trade Agreements Between Particular Members

1. This Agreement and the Multilateral Trade Agreements in Annexes 1 and 2 shall not apply as between any Member and any other Member if either of the Members, at the time either becomes a Member, does not consent to such application. . . .

Article XIV. Acceptance, Entry into Force and Deposit

1. This Agreement shall be open for acceptance, by signature or otherwise, by contracting parties to GATT 1947, and the European Communities, which are eligible to become original Members of the WTO in accordance with Article XI of this Agreement. Such acceptance shall apply to this Agreement and the Multilateral Trade Agreements annexed hereto. . . .

2. A Member which accepts this Agreement after its entry into force shall implement those concessions and obligations in the Multilateral Trade Agreements that are to be implemented over a period of time starting with the entry into force of this Agreement as if it had accepted this Agreement on the date of its entry into force. . . .

Article XV. Withdrawal

1. Any Member may withdraw from this Agreement. Such withdrawal shall apply both to this Agreement and the Multilateral Trade Agreements and shall take effect upon the expiration of six months from the date on which written notice of withdrawal is received by the Director-General of the WTO.

2. Withdrawal from a Plurilateral Trade Agreement shall be governed by the provisions of that Agreement.

Article XVI. Miscellaneous Provisions

1. Except as otherwise provided under this Agreement or the Multilateral Trade Agreements, the WTO shall be guided by the decisions, procedures and customary practices followed by the CONTRACTING PARTIES to GATT 1947 and the bodies established in the framework of GATT 1947.

2. To the extent practicable, the Secretariat of GATT 1947 shall become the Secretariat of the WTO, and the Director-General to the CONTRACTING PARTIES to GATT 1947, until such time as the Ministerial Conference has

appointed a Director-General in accordance with paragraph 2 of Article VI of this Agreement, shall serve as Director-General of the WTO.

3. In the event of a conflict between a provision of this Agreement and a provision of any of the Multilateral Trade Agreements, the provision of this Agreement shall prevail to the extent of the conflict.

4. Each Member shall ensure the conformity of its laws, regulations and administrative procedures with its obligations as provided in the annexed Agreements.

5. No reservations may be made in respect of any provision of this Agreement. Reservations in respect of any of the provisions of the Multilateral Trade Agreements may only be made to the extent provided for in those Agreements. Reservations in respect of a provision of a Plurilateral Trade Agreement shall be governed by the provisions of that Agreement. . . .

DONE at Marrakesh this fifteenth day of April one thousand nine hundred and ninety-four, in a single copy, in the English, French and Spanish languages, each text being authentic.

EXPLANATORY NOTES:

The terms "country" or "countries" as used in this Agreement and the Multilateral Trade Agreements are to be understood to include any separate customs territory Member of the WTO.

In the case of a separate customs territory Member of the WTO, where an expression in this Agreement and the Multilateral Trade Agreements is qualified by the term "national", such expression shall be read as pertaining to that customs territory, unless otherwise specified.

List of Annexes

ANNEX 1 [not printed in this supplement]

ANNEX 1A: Multilateral Agreements on Trade in Goods
General Agreement on Tariffs and Trade 1994
Agreement on Agriculture
Agreement on the Application of Sanitary and Phytosanitary Measures
Agreement on Textiles and Clothing
Agreement on Technical Barriers to Trade
Agreement on Trade-Related Investment Measures
Agreement on Implementation of Article VI of the General Agreement on Tariffs and Trade 1994
Agreement on Implementation of Article VII of the General Agreement on Tariffs and Trade 1994
Agreement on Preshipment Inspection
Agreement on Rules of Origin
Agreement on Import Licensing Procedures

Agreement on Subsidies and Countervailing Measures
Agreement on Safeguards
ANNEX 1B: General Agreement on Trade in Services and Annexes
ANNEX 1C: Agreement on Trade-Related Aspects of Intellectual Property
Rights

ANNEX 2
Understanding on Rules and Procedures Governing the Settlement of
Disputes

ANNEX 3 [not printed in this supplement]
Trade Policy Review Mechanism

ANNEX 4 [not printed in this supplement]
Plurilateral Trade Agreements
Agreement on Trade in Civil Aircraft
Agreement on Government Procurement
International Dairy Agreement
International Bovine Meat Agreement

Annex 2.   Understanding on Rules and Procedures Governing the Settlement of Disputes

Members hereby *agree* as follows:

Article 1.   Coverage and Application

1. The rules and procedures of this Understanding shall apply to disputes brought pursuant to the consultation and dispute settlement provisions of the agreements listed in Appendix 1 to this Understanding (referred to in this Understanding as the "covered agreements"). The rules and procedures of this Understanding shall also apply to consultations and the settlement of disputes between Members concerning their rights and obligations under the provisions of the Agreement Establishing the World Trade Organization (referred to in this Understanding as the "WTO Agreement") and of this Understanding taken in isolation or in combination with any other covered agreement.

2. The rules and procedures of this Understanding shall apply subject to such special or additional rules and procedures on dispute settlement contained in the covered agreements as are identified in Appendix 2 to this Understanding. To the extent that there is a difference between the rules and procedures of this Understanding and the special or additional rules and procedures set forth in Appendix 2, the special or additional rules and procedures in Appendix 2 shall prevail. In disputes involving rules and

procedures under more than one covered agreement, if there is a conflict between special or additional rules and procedures of such agreements under review, and where the parties to the dispute cannot agree on rules and procedures within 20 days of the establishment of the panel, the Chairman of the Dispute Settlement Body provided for in paragraph 1 of Article 2 (referred to in this Understanding as the "DSB"), in consultation with the parties to the dispute, shall determine the rules and procedures to be followed within 10 days after a request by either Member. The Chairman shall be guided by the principle that special or additional rules and procedures should be used where possible, and the rules and procedures set out in this Understanding should be used to the extent necessary to avoid conflict.

Article 2. Administration

1. The Dispute Settlement Body is hereby established to administer these rules and procedures and, except as otherwise provided in a covered agreement, the consultation and dispute settlement provisions of the covered agreements. Accordingly, the DSB shall have the authority to establish panels, adopt panel and Appellate Body reports, maintain surveillance of implementation of rulings and recommendations, and authorize suspension of concessions and other obligations under the covered agreements. With respect to disputes arising under a covered agreement which is a Plurilateral Trade Agreement, the term "Member" as used herein shall refer only to those Members that are parties to the relevant Plurilateral Trade Agreement. Where the DSB administers the dispute settlement provisions of a Plurilateral Trade Agreement, only those Members that are parties to that Agreement may participate in decisions or actions taken by the DSB with respect to that dispute.

2. The DSB shall inform the relevant WTO Councils and Committees of any developments in disputes related to provisions of the respective covered agreements.

3. The DSB shall meet as often as necessary to carry out its functions within the time-frames provided in this Understanding.

4. Where the rules and procedures of this Understanding provide for the DSB to take a decision, it shall do so by consensus.[1]

Article 3. General Provisions

1. Members affirm their adherence to the principles for the management of disputes heretofore applied under Articles XXII and XXIII of GATT 1947, and the rules and procedures as further elaborated and modified herein.

2. The dispute settlement system of the WTO is a central element in providing security and predictability to the multilateral trading system. The Members recognize that it serves to preserve the rights and obligations of Members under the covered agreements, and to clarify the existing provisions

---

1. The DSB shall be deemed to have decided by consensus on a matter submitted for its consideration, if no Member, present at the meeting of the DSB when the decision is taken, formally objects to the proposed decision.

of those agreements in accordance with customary rules of interpretation of public international law. Recommendations and rulings of the DSB cannot add to or diminish the rights and obligations provided in the covered agreements.

3. The prompt settlement of situations in which a Member considers that any benefits accruing to it directly or indirectly under the covered agreements are being impaired by measures taken by another Member is essential to the effective functioning of the WTO and the maintenance of a proper balance between the rights and obligations of Members.

4. Recommendations or rulings made by the DSB shall be aimed at achieving a satisfactory settlement of the matter in accordance with the rights and obligations under this Understanding and under the covered agreements.

5. All solutions to matters formally raised under the consultation and dispute settlement provisions of the covered agreements, including arbitration awards, shall be consistent with those agreements and shall not nullify or impair benefits accruing to any Member under those agreements, nor impede the attainment of any objective of those agreements.

6. Mutually agreed solutions to matters formally raised under the consultation and dispute settlement provisions of the covered agreements shall be notified to the DSB and the relevant Councils and Committees, where any Member may raise any point relating thereto.

7. Before bringing a case, a Member shall exercise its judgement as to whether action under these procedures would be fruitful. The aim of the dispute settlement mechanism is to secure a positive solution to a dispute. A solution mutually acceptable to the parties to a dispute and consistent with the covered agreements is clearly to be preferred. In the absence of a mutually agreed solution, the first objective of the dispute settlement mechanism is usually to secure the withdrawal of the measures concerned if these are found to be inconsistent with the provisions of any of the covered agreements. The provision of compensation should be resorted to only if the immediate withdrawal of the measure is impracticable and as a temporary measure pending the withdrawal of the measure which is inconsistent with a covered agreement. The last resort which this Understanding provides to the Member invoking the dispute settlement procedures is the possibility of suspending the application of concessions or other obligations under the covered agreements on a discriminatory basis vis-à-vis the other Member, subject to authorization by the DSB of such measures.

8. In cases where there is an infringement of the obligations assumed under a covered agreement, the action is considered *prima facie* to constitute a case of nullification or impairment. This means that there is normally a presumption that a breach of the rules has an adverse impact on other Members parties to that covered agreement, and in such cases, it shall be up to the Member against whom the complaint has been brought to rebut the charge.

9. The provisions of this Understanding are without prejudice to the rights of Members to seek authoritative interpretation of provisions of a covered agreement through decision-making under the WTO Agreement or a covered agreement which is a Plurilateral Trade Agreement.

10. It is understood that requests for conciliation and the use of the dispute settlement procedures should not be intended or considered as contentious acts and that, if a dispute arises, all Members will engage in these procedures in good faith in an effort to resolve the dispute. It is also understood that complaints and counter-complaints in regard to distinct matters should not be linked.

11. This Understanding shall be applied only with respect to new requests for consultations under the consultation provisions of the covered agreements made on or after the date of entry into force of the WTO Agreement. With respect to disputes for which the request for consultations was made under GATT 1947 or under any other predecessor agreement to the covered agreements before the date of entry into force of the WTO Agreement, the relevant dispute settlement rules and procedures in effect immediately prior to the date of entry into force of the WTO Agreement shall continue to apply.[2] . . .

Article 4. Consultations

1. Members affirm their resolve to strengthen and improve the effectiveness of the consultation procedures employed by Members.

2. Each Member undertakes to accord sympathetic consideration to and afford adequate opportunity for consultation regarding any representations made by another Member concerning measures affecting the operation of any covered agreement taken within the territory of the former.[3]

3. If a request for consultations is made pursuant to a covered agreement, the Member to which the request is made shall, unless otherwise mutually agreed, reply to the request within 10 days after the date of its receipt and shall enter into consultations in good faith within a period of no more than 30 days after the date of receipt of the request, with a view to reaching a mutually satisfactory solution. If the Member does not respond within 10 days after the date of receipt of the request, or does not enter into consultations within a period of no more than 30 days, or a period otherwise mutually agreed, after the date of receipt of the request, then the Member that requested the holding of consultations may proceed directly to request the establishment of a panel.

4. All such requests for consultations shall be notified to the DSB and the relevant Councils and Committees by the Member which requests consultations. Any request for consultations shall he submitted in writing and shall give the reasons for the request, including identification of the measures at issue and an indication of the legal basis for the complaint.

5. In the course of consultations in accordance with the provisions of a covered agreement, before resorting to further action under this Understanding, Members should attempt to obtain satisfactory adjustment of the matter.

---

2. This paragraph shall also be applied to disputes on which panel reports have not been adopted or fully implemented.

3. Where the provisions of any other covered agreement concerning measures taken by regional or local governments or authorities within the territory of a Member contain provisions different from the provisions of this paragraph, the provisions of such other covered agreement shall prevail.

6. Consultations shall be confidential, and without prejudice to the rights of any Member in any further proceedings.

7. If the consultations fail to settle a dispute within 60 days after the date of receipt of the request for consultations, the complaining party may request the establishment of a panel. The complaining party may request a panel during the 60-day period if the consulting parties jointly consider that consultations have failed to settle the dispute.

8. In cases of urgency, including those which concern perishable goods, Members shall enter into consultations within a period of no more than 10 days after the date of receipt of the request. If the consultations have failed to settle the dispute within a period of 20 days after the date of receipt of the request, the complaining party may request the establishment of a panel.

9. In cases of urgency, including those which concern perishable goods, the parties to the dispute, panels and the Appellate Body shall make every effort to accelerate the proceedings to the greatest extent possible.

10. During consultations Members should give special attention to the particular problems and interests of developing country Members.

11. Whenever a Member other than the consulting Members considers that it has a substantial trade interest in consultations being held pursuant to paragraph 1 of Article XXII of GATT 1994, paragraph 1 of Article XXII of GATS, or the corresponding provisions in other covered agreements,[4] such Member may notify the consulting Members and the DSB, within 10 days after the date of the circulation of the request for consultations under said Article, of its desire to be joined in the consultations. Such Member shall be joined in the consultations, provided that the Member to which the request for consultations was addressed agrees that the claim of substantial interest is well-founded. In that event they shall so inform the DSB. If the request to be joined in the consultations is not accepted, the applicant Member shall be free to request consultations under paragraph 1 of Article XXII or paragraph 1 of Article XXIII of GATT 1994, paragraph I of Article XXII or paragraph 1 of Article XXIII of GATS, or the corresponding provisions in other covered agreements.

Article 5.   Good Offices, Conciliation and Mediation

1. Good offices, conciliation and mediation are procedures that are undertaken voluntarily if the parties to the dispute so agree.

---

4. The corresponding consultation provisions in the covered agreements are listed hereunder: Agreement on Agriculture, Article 19; Agreement on the Application of Sanitary and Phytosanitary Measures, paragraph 1 of Article 11; Agreement on Textiles and Clothing, paragraph 4 of Article 8; Agreement on Technical Barriers to Trade, paragraph 1 of Article 14; Agreement on Trade-Related Investment Measures, Article 8; Agreement on Implementation of Article VI of GATT 1994, paragraph 2 of Article 17; Agreement on Implementation of Article VII of GATT 1994, paragraph 2 of Article 19; Agreement on Preshipment Inspection, Article 7; Agreement on Rules of Origin, Article 7; Agreement on Import Licensing Procedures, Article 6; Agreement on Subsidies and Countervailing Measures, Article 30; Agreement on Safeguards, Article 14; Agreement on Trade-Related Aspects of Intellectual Property Rights, Article 64.1; and any corresponding consultation provisions in Plurilateral Trade Agreements as determined by the competent bodies of each Agreement and as notified to the DSB.

4. International Dispute Resolution

2. Proceedings involving good offices, conciliation and mediation, and in particular positions taken by the parties to the dispute during these proceedings, shall be confidential, and without prejudice to the rights of either party in any further proceedings under these procedures.

3. Good offices, conciliation or mediation may be requested at any time by any party to a dispute. They may begin at any time and be terminated at any time. Once procedures for good offices, conciliation or mediation are terminated, a complaining party may then proceed with a request for the establishment of a panel.

4. When good offices, conciliation or mediation are entered into within 60 days after the date of receipt of a request for consultations, the complaining party must allow a period of 60 days after the date of receipt of the request for consultations before requesting the establishment of a panel. The complaining party may request the establishment of a panel during the 60-day period if the parties to the dispute jointly consider that the good offices, conciliation or mediation process has failed to settle the dispute.

5. If the parties to a dispute agree, procedures for good offices, conciliation or mediation may continue while the panel process proceeds.

6. The Director-General may, acting in an *ex officio* capacity, offer good offices, conciliation or mediation with the view to assisting Members to settle a dispute.

Article 6.   Establishment of Panels

1. If the complaining party so requests, a panel shall be established at the latest at the DSB meeting following that at which the request first appears as an item on the DSB's agenda, unless at that meeting the DSB decides by consensus not to establish a panel.[5]

2. The request for the establishment of a panel shall be made in writing. It shall indicate whether consultations were held, identify the specific measures at issue and provide a brief summary of the legal basis of the complaint sufficient to present the problem clearly. In case the applicant requests the establishment of a panel with other than standard terms of reference, the written request shall include the proposed text of special terms of reference.

Article 7.   Terms of Reference of Panels

1. Panels shall have the following terms of reference unless the parties to the dispute agree otherwise within 20 days from the establishment of the panel:

> To examine, in the light of the relevant provisions in (name of the covered agreement(s) cited by the parties to the dispute), the matter referred to the

---

5. If the complaining party so requests, a meeting of the DSB shall be convened for this purpose within 15 days of the request, provided that at least 10 days' advance notice of the meeting is given.

DSB by (name of party) in document . . . and to make such findings as will assist the DSB in making the recommendations or in giving the rulings provided for in that/those agreement(s).

2. Panels shall address the relevant provisions in any covered agreement or agreements cited by the parties to the dispute.

3. In establishing a panel, the DSB may authorize its Chairman to draw up the terms of reference of the panel in consultation with the parties to the dispute, subject to the provisions of paragraph 1. The terms of reference thus drawn up shall be circulated to all Members. If other than standard terms of reference are agreed upon, any Member may raise any point relating thereto in the DSB.

Article 8.   Composition of Panels

1. Panels shall be composed of well-qualified governmental and/or non-governmental individuals, including persons who have served on or presented a case to a panel, served as a representative of a Member or of a contracting party to GATT 1947 or as a representative to the Council or Committee of any covered agreement or its predecessor agreement, or in the Secretariat, taught or published on international trade law or policy, or served as a senior trade policy official of a Member.

2. Panel members should be selected with a view to ensuring the independence of the members, a sufficiently diverse background and a wide spectrum of experience.

3. Citizens of Members whose governments[6] are parties to the dispute or third parties as defined in paragraph 2 of Article 10 shall not serve on a panel concerned with that dispute, unless the parties to the dispute agree otherwise.

4. To assist in the selection of panelists, the Secretariat shall maintain an indicative list of governmental and non-governmental individuals possessing the qualifications outlined in paragraph 1, from which panelists may be drawn as appropriate. . . .

5. Panels shall be composed of three panelists unless the parties to the dispute agree, within 10 days from the establishment of the panel, to a panel composed of five panelists. Members shall be informed promptly of the composition of the panel.

6. The Secretariat shall propose nominations for the panel to the parties to the dispute. The parties to the dispute shall not oppose nominations except for compelling reasons.

7. If there is no agreement on the panelists within 20 days after the date of the establishment of a panel, at the request of either party, the Director-General, in consultation with the Chairman of the DSB and the Chairman of the relevant Council or Committee, shall determine the composition of the panel by appointing the panelists whom the Director-General considers most

6. In the case where customs unions or common markets are parties to a dispute, this provision applies to citizens of all member countries of the customs unions or common markets.

appropriate in accordance with any relevant special or additional rules or procedures of the covered agreement or covered agreements which are at issue in the dispute, after consulting with the parties to the dispute. The Chairman of the DSB shall inform the Members of the composition of the panel thus formed no later than 10 days after the date the Chairman receives such a request.

8. Members shall undertake, as a general rule, to permit their officials to serve as panelists.

9. Panelists shall serve in their individual capacities and not as government representatives, nor as representatives of any organization. Members shall therefore not give them instructions nor seek to influence them as individuals with regard to matters before a panel.

10. When a dispute is between a developing country Member and a developed country Member the panel shall, if the developing country Member so requests, include at least one panelist from a developing country Member.

11. Panelists' expenses, including travel and subsistence allowance, shall be met from the WTO budget in accordance with criteria to be adopted by the General Council, based on recommendations of the Committee on Budget, Finance and Administration.

Article 9.   Procedures for Multiple Complainants

1. Where more than one Member requests the establishment of a panel related to the same matter, a single panel may be established to examine these complaints taking into account the rights of all Members concerned. A single panel should be established to examine such complaints whenever feasible.

2. The single panel shall organize its examination and present its findings to the DSB in such a manner that the rights which the parties to the dispute would have enjoyed had separate panels examined the complaints are in no way impaired. If one of the parties to the dispute so requests, the panel shall submit separate reports on the dispute concerned. The written submissions by each of the complainants shall be made available to the other complainants, and each complainant shall have the right to be present when any one of the other complainants presents its views to the panel.

3. If more than one panel is established to examine the complaints related to the same matter, to the greatest extent possible the same persons shall serve as panelists on each of the separate panels and the timetable for the panel process in such disputes shall be harmonized.

Article 10.   Third Parties

1. The interests of the parties to a dispute and those of other Members under a covered agreement at issue in the dispute shall be fully taken into account during the panel process.

2. Any Member having a substantial interest in a matter before a panel and having notified its interest to the DSB (referred to in this Understanding

as a "third party") shall have an opportunity to be heard by the panel and to make written submissions to the panel. These submissions shall also be given to the parties to the dispute and shall be reflected in the panel report.

3. Third parties shall receive the submissions of the parties to the dispute to the first meeting of the panel.

4. If a third party considers that a measure already the subject of a panel proceeding nullifies or impairs benefits accruing to it under any covered agreement, that Member may have recourse to normal dispute settlement procedures under this Understanding. Such a dispute shall be referred to the original panel wherever possible.

Article 11.   Function of Panels

The function of panels is to assist the DSB in discharging its responsibilities under this Understanding and the covered agreements. Accordingly, a panel should make an objective assessment of the matter before it, including an objective assessment of the facts of the case and the applicability of and conformity with the relevant covered agreements, and make such other findings as will assist the DSB in making the recommendations or in giving the rulings provided for in the covered agreements. Panels should consult regularly with the parties to the dispute and give them adequate opportunity to develop a mutually satisfactory solution.

Article 12.   Panel Procedures

1. Panels shall follow the Working Procedures in Appendix 3 unless the panel decides otherwise after consulting the parties to the dispute.

2. Panel procedures should provide sufficient flexibility so as to ensure high-quality panel reports, while not unduly delaying the panel process.

3. After consulting the parties to the dispute, the panelists shall, as soon as practicable and whenever possible within one week after the composition and terms of reference of the panel have been agreed upon, fix the timetable for the panel process, taking into account the provisions of paragraph 9 of Article 4, if relevant.

4. In determining the timetable for the panel process, the panel shall provide sufficient time for the parties to the dispute to prepare their submissions.

5. Panels should set precise deadlines for written submissions by the parties and the parties should respect those deadlines.

6. Each party to the dispute shall deposit its written submissions with the Secretariat for immediate transmission to the panel and to the other party or parties to the dispute. The complaining party shall submit its first submission in advance of the responding party's first submission unless the panel decides, in fixing the timetable referred to in paragraph 3 and after consultations with the parties to the dispute, that the parties should submit their first submissions simultaneously. When there are sequential arrangements for the deposit of first submissions, the panel shall establish a firm time-period for receipt of the

responding party's submission. Any subsequent written submissions shall be submitted simultaneously.

7. Where the parties to the dispute have failed to develop a mutually satisfactory solution, the panel shall submit its findings in the form of a written report to the DSB. In such cases, the report of a panel shall set out the findings of fact, the applicability of relevant provisions and the basic rationale behind any findings and recommendations that it makes. Where a settlement of the matter among the parties to the dispute has been found, the report of the panel shall be confined to a brief description of the case and to reporting that a solution has been reached.

8. In order to make the procedures more efficient, the period in which the panel shall conduct its examination, from the date that the composition and terms of reference of the panel have been agreed upon until the date the final report is issued to the parties to the dispute, shall, as a general rule, not exceed six months, In cases of urgency, including those relating to perishable goods, the panel shall aim to issue its report to the parties to the dispute within three months.

9. When the panel considers that it cannot issue its report within six months, or within three months in cases of urgency, it shall inform the DSB in writing of the reasons for the delay together with an estimate of the period within which it will issue its report. In no case should the period from the establishment of the panel to the circulation of the report to the Members exceed nine months.

10. In the context of consultations involving a measure taken by a developing country Member, . . .

11. Where one or more of the parties is a developing country Member, the panel's report shall explicitly indicate the form in which account has been taken of relevant provisions on differential and more-favourable treatment for developing country Members that form part of the covered agreements which have been raised by the developing country Member in the course of the dispute settlement procedures.

12. The panel may suspend its work at any time at the request of the complaining party for a period not to exceed 12 months. In the event of such a suspension, the time-frames set out in paragraphs 8 and 9 of this Article, paragraph 1 of Article 20, and paragraph 4 of Article 21 shall be extended by the amount of time that the work was suspended. If the work of the panel has been suspended for more than 12 months, the authority for establishment of the panel shall lapse.

Article 13. Right to Seek Information

1. Each panel shall have the right to seek information and technical advice from any individual or body which it deems appropriate. However, before a panel seeks such information or advice from any individual or body within the jurisdiction of a Member it shall inform the authorities of that Member. A Member should respond promptly and fully to any

request by a panel for such information as the panel considers necessary and appropriate. Confidential information which is provided shall not be revealed without formal authorization from the individual, body, or authorities of the Member providing the information.

2. Panels may seek information from any relevant source and may consult experts to obtain their opinion on certain aspects of the matter. With respect to a factual issue concerning a scientific or other technical matter raised by a party to a dispute, a panel may request an advisory report in writing from an expert review group. Rules for the establishment of such a group and its procedures are set forth in Appendix 4.

Article 14. *Confidentiality*

1. Panel deliberations shall be confidential.

2. The reports of panels shall be drafted without the presence of the parties to the dispute in the light of the information provided and the statements made.

3. Opinions expressed in the panel report by individual panelists shall be anonymous.

Article 15. *Interim Review Stage*

1. Following the consideration of rebuttal submissions and oral arguments, the panel shall issue the descriptive (factual and argument) sections of its draft report to the parties to the dispute. Within a period of time set by the panel, the parties shall submit their comments in writing.

2. Following the expiration of the set period of time for receipt of comments from the parties to the dispute, the panel shall issue an interim report to the parties, including both the descriptive sections and the panel's findings and conclusions. Within a period of time set by the panel, a party may submit a written request for the panel to review precise aspects of the interim report prior to circulation of the final report to the Members. At the request of a party, the panel shall hold a further meeting with the parties on the issues identified in the written comments. If no comments are received from any party within the comment period, the interim report shall be considered the final panel report and circulated promptly to the Members.

3. The findings of the final panel report shall include a discussion of the arguments made at the interim review stage. The interim review stage shall be conducted within the time-period set out in paragraph 8 of Article 12.

Article 16. *Adoption of Panel Reports*

1. In order to provide sufficient time for the Members to consider panel reports, the reports shall not be considered for adoption by the DSB until 20 days after the date they have been circulated to the Members.

2. Members having objections to a panel report shall give written reasons to explain their objections for circulation at least 10 days prior to the DSB meeting at which the panel report will be considered.

3. The parties to a dispute shall have the right to participate fully in the consideration of the panel report by the DSB, and their views shall be fully recorded.

4. Within 60 days after the date of circulation of a panel report to the Members, the report shall be adopted at a DSB meeting[7] unless a party to the dispute formally notifies the DSB of its decision to appeal or the DSB decides by consensus not to adopt the report. If a party has notified its decision to appeal, the report by the panel shall not be considered for adoption by the DSB until after completion of the appeal. This adoption procedure is without prejudice to the right of Members to express their views on a panel report.

Article 17. Appellate Review

STANDING APPELLATE BODY

1. A standing Appellate Body shall be established by the DSB. The Appellate Body shall hear appeals from panel cases. It shall be composed of seven persons, three of whom shall serve on any one case. Persons serving on the Appellate Body shall serve in rotation. Such rotation shall be determined in the working procedures of the Appellate Body.

2. The DSB shall appoint persons to serve on the Appellate Body for a four-year term, and each person may be reappointed once. However, the terms of three of the seven persons appointed immediately after the entry into force of the WTO Agreement shall expire at the end of two years, to be determined by lot Vacancies shall be filled as they arise. A person appointed to replace a person whose term of office has not expired shall hold office for the remainder of the predecessor's term.

3. The Appellate Body shall comprise persons of recognized authority, with demonstrated expertise in law, international trade and the subject matter of the covered agreements generally. They shall be unaffiliated with any government. The Appellate Body membership shall be broadly representative of membership in the WTO. All persons serving on the Appellate Body shall be available at all times and on short notice, and shall stay abreast of dispute settlement activities and other relevant activities of the WTO. They shall not participate in the consideration of any disputes that would create a direct or indirect conflict of interest.

4. Only parties to the dispute, not third parties, may appeal a panel report. Third parties which have notified the DSB of a substantial interest in the matter pursuant to paragraph 2 of Article 10 may make written submissions to, and be given an opportunity to be heard by, the Appellate Body.

5. As a general rule, the proceedings shall not exceed 60 days from the date a party to the dispute formally notifies its decision to appeal to the date the Appellate Body circulates its report. In fixing its timetable the Appellate

---

7. If a meeting of the DSB is not scheduled within this period at a time that enables the requirements of paragraphs 1 and 4 of Article 16 to be met, a meeting of the DSB shall be held for this purpose.

Body shall take into account the provisions of paragraph 9 of Article 4, if relevant. When the Appellate Body considers that it cannot provide its report within 60 days, it shall inform the DSB in writing of the reasons for the delay together with an estimate of the period within which it will submit its report. In no case shall the proceedings exceed 90 days.

6. An appeal shall be limited to issues of law covered in the panel report and legal interpretations developed by the panel.

7. The Appellate Body shall be provided with appropriate administrative and legal support as it requires.

8. The expenses of persons serving on the Appellate Body, including travel and subsistence allowance, shall be met from the WTO budget in accordance with criteria to be adopted by the General Council, based on recommendations of the Committee on Budget, Finance and Administration.

PROCEDURES FOR APPELLATE REVIEW

9. Working procedures shall be drawn up by the Appellate Body in consultation with the Chairman of the DSB and the Director-General, and communicated to the Members for their information.

10. The proceedings of the Appellate Body shall be confidential. The reports of the Appellate Body shall be drafted without the presence of the parties to the dispute and in the light of the information provided and the statements made.

11. Opinions expressed in the Appellate Body report by individuals serving on the Appellate Body shall be anonymous.

12. The Appellate Body shall address each of the issues raised in accordance with paragraph 6 during the appellate proceeding.

13. The Appellate Body may uphold, modify or reverse the legal findings and conclusions of the panel.

ADOPTION OF APPELLATE BODY REPORTS

14. An Appellate Body report shall be adopted by the DSB and unconditionally accepted by the parties to the dispute unless the DSB decides by consensus not to adopt the Appellate Body report within 30 days following its circulation to the Members.[8] This adoption procedure is without prejudice to the right of Members to express their views on an Appellate Body report.

Article 18.   Communications with the Panel or Appellate Body

1. There shall be no *ex parte* communications with the panel or Appellate Body concerning matters under consideration by the panel or Appellate Body.

---

8. If a meeting of the DSB is not scheduled during this period, such a meeting of the DSB shall be held for this purpose.

2. Written submissions to the panel or the Appellate Body shall be treated as confidential, but shall be made available to the parties to the dispute. Nothing in this Understanding shall preclude a party to a dispute from disclosing statements of its own positions to the public. Members shall treat as confidential information submitted by another Member to the panel or the Appellate Body which that Member has designated as confidential. A party to a dispute shall also, upon request of a Member, provide a non-confidential summary of the information contained in its written submissions that could be disclosed to the public.

Article 19.   Panel and Appellate Body Recommendations

1. Where a panel or the Appellate Body concludes that a measure is inconsistent with a covered agreement, it shall recommend that the Member concerned[9] bring the measure into conformity with that agreement.[10] In addition to its recommendations, the panel or Appellate Body may suggest ways in which the Member concerned could implement the recommendations.

2. In accordance with paragraph 2 of Article 3, in their findings and recommendations, the panel and Appellate Body cannot add to or diminish the rights and obligations provided in the covered agreements.

Article 20.   Time-Frame for DSB Decisions

Unless otherwise agreed to by the parties to the dispute, the period from the date of establishment of the panel by the DSB until the date the DSB considers the panel or appellate report for adoption shall as a general rule not exceed nine months where the panel report is not appealed or 12 months where the report is appealed. Where either the panel or the Appellate Body has acted, pursuant to paragraph 9 of Article 12 or paragraph 5 of Article 17, to extend the time for providing its report, the additional time taken shall be added to the above periods.

Article 21.   Surveillance of Implementation of Recommendations and Rulings

1. Prompt compliance with recommendations or rulings of the DSB is essential in order to ensure effective resolution of disputes to the benefit of all Members.

2. Particular attention should be paid to matters affecting the interests of developing country Members with respect to measures which have been subject to dispute settlement.

---

9. The "Member concerned" is the party to the dispute to which the panel or Appellate Body recommendations are directed.

10. With respect to recommendations in cases not involving a violation of GATT 1994 or any other covered agreement, see Article 26.

3. At a DSB meeting held within 30 days[11] after the date of adoption of the panel or Appellate Body report, the Member concerned shall inform the DSB of its intentions in respect of implementation of the recommendations and rulings of the DSB. If it is impracticable to comply immediately with the recommendations and rulings, the Member concerned shall have a reasonable period of time in which to do so. The reasonable period of time shall be:

(a) the period of time proposed by the Member concerned, provided that such period is approved by the DSB; or, in the absence of such approval,

(b) a period of time mutually agreed by the parties to the dispute within 45 days after the date of adoption of the recommendations and rulings; or, in the absence of such agreement,

(c) a period of time determined through binding arbitration within 90 days after the date of adoption of the recommendations and rulings.[12] In such arbitration, a guideline for the arbitrator[13] should be that the reasonable period of time to implement panel or Appellate Body recommendations should not exceed 15 months from the date of adoption of a panel or Appellate Body report. However, that time may be shorter or longer, depending upon the particular circumstances.

4. Except where the panel or the Appellate Body has extended, pursuant to paragraph 9 of Article 12 or paragraph 5 of Article 17, the time of providing its report, the period from the date of establishment of the panel by the DSB until the date of determination of the reasonable period of time shall not exceed 15 months unless the parties to the dispute agree otherwise. Where either the panel or the Appellate Body has acted to extend the time of providing its report, the additional time taken shall be added to the 15-month period; provided that unless the parties to the dispute agree that there are exceptional circumstances, the total time shall not exceed 18 months.

5. Where there is disagreement as to the existence or consistency with a covered agreement of measures taken to comply with the recommendations and rulings such dispute shall be decided through recourse to these dispute settlement procedures, including wherever possible resort to the original panel. The panel shall circulate its report within 90 days after the date of referral of the matter to it. When the panel considers that it cannot provide its report within this time frame, it shall inform the DSB in writing of the reasons for the delay together with an estimate of the period within which it will submit its report.

---

11. If a meeting of the DSB is not scheduled during this period, such a meeting of the DSB shall be held for this purpose.

12. If the parties cannot agree on an arbitrator within ten days after referring the matter to arbitration, the arbitrator shall be appointed by the Director-General within ten days, after consulting the parties.

13. The expression "arbitrator" shall be interpreted as referring either to an individual or a group.

6. The DSB shall keep under surveillance the implementation of adopted recommendations or rulings. The issue of implementation of the recommendations or rulings may be raised at the DSB by any Member at any time following their adoption. Unless the DSB decides otherwise, the issue of implementation of the recommendations or rulings shall be placed on the agenda of the DSB meeting after six months following the date of establishment of the reasonable period of time pursuant to paragraph 3 and shall remain on the DSB's agenda until the issue is resolved. At least 10 days prior to each such DSB meeting, the Member concerned shall provide the DSB with a status report in writing of its progress in the implementation of the recommendations or rulings.

7. If the matter is one which has been raised by a developing country Member, the DSB shall consider what further action it might take which would be appropriate to the circumstances.

8. If the case is one brought by a developing country Member, in considering what appropriate action might be taken, the DSB shall take into account not only the trade coverage of measures complained of, but also their impact on the economy of developing country Members concerned.

Article 22. *Compensation and the Suspension of Concessions*

1. Compensation and the suspension of concessions or other obligations are temporary measures available in the event that the recommendations and rulings are not implemented within a reasonable period of time. However, neither compensation nor the suspension of concessions or other obligations is preferred to full implementation of a recommendation to bring a measure into conformity with the covered agreements. Compensation is voluntary and, if granted, shall be consistent with the covered agreements.

2. If the Member concerned fails to bring the measure found to he inconsistent with a covered agreement into compliance therewith or otherwise comply with the recommendations and rulings within the reasonable period of time determined pursuant to paragraph 3 of Article 21, such Member shall, if so requested, and no later than the expiry of the reasonable period of time, enter into negotiations with any party having invoked the dispute settlement procedures, with a view to developing mutually acceptable compensation. If no satisfactory compensation has been agreed within 20 days after the date of expiry of the reasonable period of time, any party having invoked the dispute settlement procedures may request authorization from the DSB to suspend the application to the Member concerned of concessions or other obligations under the covered agreements.

3. In considering what concessions or other obligations to suspend, the complaining party shall apply the following principles and procedures:

    (a) the general principle is that the complaining party should first seek to suspend concessions or other obligations with respect to the same sector(s) as that in which the panel or Appellate Body has found a violation or other nullification or impairment;

(b) if that party considers that it is not practicable or effective to suspend concessions or other obligations with respect to the same sector(s), it may seek to suspend concessions or other obligations in other sectors under the same agreement;

(c) if that party considers that it is not practicable or effective to suspend concessions or other obligations with respect to other sectors under the same agreement, and that the circumstances are serious enough, it may seek to suspend concessions or other obligations under another covered agreement;

(d) in applying the above principles, that party shall take into account:

(i) the trade in the sector or under the agreement under which the panel or Appellate Body has found a violation or other nullification or impairment, and the importance of such trade to that party;

(ii) the broader economic elements related to the nullification or impairment and the broader economic consequences of the suspension of concessions or other obligations;

(e) if that party decides to request authorization to suspend concessions or other obligations pursuant to subparagraphs (b) or (c), it shall state the reasons therefor in its request. At the same time as the request is forwarded to the DSB, it also shall be forwarded to the relevant Councils and also, in the case of a request pursuant to subparagraph (b), the relevant sectoral bodies;

(f) for purposes of this paragraph, "sector" means:

(i) with respect to goods, all goods;

(ii) with respect to services, a principal sector as identified in the current "Services Sectoral Classification List" which identifies such sectors;[14]

(iii) with respect to trade-related intellectual property rights, each of the categories of intellectual property rights covered in Section 1, or Section 2, or Section 3, or Section 4, or Section 5, or Section 6, or Section 7 of Part II, or the obligations under Part III, or Part IV of the Agreement on TRIPS;

(g) for purposes of this paragraph, "agreement" means:

(i) with respect to goods, the agreements listed in Annex 1A of the WTO Agreement, taken as a whole as well as the Plurilateral Trade Agreements in so far as the relevant parties to the dispute are parties to these agreements;

(ii) with respect to services, the GATS;

(iii) with respect to intellectual property rights, the Agreement on TRIPS.

4. The level of the suspension of concessions or other obligations authorized by the DSB shall be equivalent to the level of the nullification or impairment.

---

14. The list in document MTN.GNS/W/120 identifies eleven sectors.

5. The DSB shall not authorize suspension of concessions or other obligations if a covered agreement prohibits such suspension.

6. When the situation described in paragraph 2 occurs, the DSB, upon request, shall grant authorization to suspend concessions or other obligations within 30 days of the expiry of the reasonable period of time unless the DSB decides by consensus to reject the request. However, if the Member concerned objects to the level of suspension proposed, or claims that the principles and procedures set forth in paragraph 3 have not been followed where a complaining party has requested authorization to suspend concessions or other obligations pursuant to paragraph 3(b) or (c), the matter shall be referred to arbitration. Such arbitration shall be carried out by the original panel, if members are available, or by an arbitrator[15] appointed by the Director-General and shall be completed within 60 days after the date of expiry of the reasonable period of time. Concessions or other obligations shall not be suspended during the course of the arbitration.

7. The arbitrator[16] acting pursuant to paragraph 6 shall not examine the nature of the concessions or other obligations to be suspended but shall determine whether the level of such suspension is equivalent to the level of nullification or impairment. The arbitrator may also determine if the proposed suspension of concessions or other obligations is allowed under the covered agreement. However, if the matter referred to arbitration includes a claim that the principles and procedures set forth in paragraph 3 have not been followed, the arbitrator shall examine that claim. In the event the arbitrator determines that those principles and procedures have not been followed, the complaining party shall apply them consistent with paragraph 3. The parties shall accept the arbitrator's decision as final and the parties concerned shall not seek a second arbitration. The DSB shall be informed promptly of the decision of the arbitrator and shall upon request, grant authorization to suspend concessions or other obligations where the request is consistent with the decision of the arbitrator, unless the DSB decides by consensus to reject the request.

8. The suspension of concessions or other obligations shall be temporary and shall only be applied until such time as the measure found to be inconsistent with a covered agreement has been removed, or the Member that must implement recommendations or rulings provides a solution to the nullification or impairment of benefits, or a mutually satisfactory solution is reached. In accordance with paragraph 6 of Article 21, the DSB shall continue to keep under surveillance the implementation of adopted recommendations or rulings, including those cases where compensation has been provided or concessions or other obligations have been suspended but the recommendations to bring a measure into conformity with the covered agreements have not been implemented.

---

15. The expression "arbitrator" shall be interpreted as referring either to an individual or a group.

16. The expression "arbitrator" shall be interpreted as referring either to an individual or a group or to the members of the original panel when serving in the capacity of arbitrator.

9. The dispute settlement provisions of the covered agreements may be invoked in respect of measures affecting their observance taken by regional or local governments or authorities within the territory of a Member. When the DSB has ruled that a provision of a covered agreement has not been observed, the responsible Member shall take such reasonable measures as may be available to it to ensure its observance. The provisions of the covered agreements and this Understanding relating to compensation and suspension of concessions or other obligations apply in cases where it has not been possible to secure such observance.[17]

Article 23.   Strengthening of the Multilateral System

1. When Members seek the redress of a violation of obligations or other nullification or impairment of benefits under the covered agreements or an impediment to the attainment of any objective of the covered agreements, they shall have recourse to, and abide by, the rules and procedures of this Understanding.

2. In such cases, Members shall:

(a) not make a determination to the effect that a violation has occurred, that benefits have been nullified or impaired or that the attainment of any objective of the covered agreements has been impeded, except through recourse to dispute settlement in accordance with the rules and procedures of this Understanding, and shall make any such determination consistent with the findings contained in the panel or Appellate Body report adopted by the DSB or an arbitration award rendered under this Understanding;

(b) follow the procedures set forth in Article 21 to determine the reasonable period of time for the Member concerned to implement the recommendations and rulings; and

(c) follow the procedures set forth in Article 22 to determine the level of suspension of concessions or other obligations and obtain DSB authorization in accordance with those procedures before suspending concessions or other obligations under the covered agreements in response to the failure of the Member concerned to implement the recommendations and rulings within that reasonable period of time.

Article 24.   Special Procedures Involving Least-Developed Country Members . . .

Article 25.   Arbitration

1. Expeditious arbitration within the WTO as an alternative means of dispute settlement can facilitate the solution of certain disputes that concern issues that are clearly defined by both parties.

---

17. Where the provisions of any covered agreement concerning measures taken by regional or local governments or authorities within the territory of a Member contain provisions different from the provisions of this paragraph, the provisions of such covered agreement shall prevail.

2. Except as otherwise provided in this Understanding, resort to arbitration shall be subject to mutual agreement of the parties which shall agree on the procedures to be followed. Agreements to resort to arbitration shall be notified to all Members sufficiently in advance of the actual commencement of the arbitration process.

3. Other Members may become party to an arbitration proceeding only upon the agreement of the parties which have agreed to have recourse to arbitration. The parties to the proceeding shall agree to abide by the arbitration award. Arbitration awards shall be notified to the DSB and the Council or Committee of any relevant agreement where any Member may raise any point relating thereto.

4. Articles 21 and 22 of this Understanding shall apply *mutatis mutandis* to arbitration awards.

Article 26

1. Non-Violation Complaints of the Type Described in Paragraph 1(b) of Article XXIII of GATT 1994

Where the provisions of paragraph 1(b) of Article XXIII of GATT 1994 are applicable to a covered agreement, a panel or the Appellate Body may only make rulings and recommendations where a party to the dispute considers that any benefit accruing to it directly or indirectly under the relevant covered agreement is being nullified or impaired or the attainment of any objective of that Agreement is being impeded as a result of the application by a Member of any measure, whether or not it conflicts with the provisions of that Agreement. Where and to the extent that such party considers and a panel or the Appellate Body determines that a case concerns a measure that does not conflict with the provisions of a covered agreement to which the provisions of paragraph 1(b) of Article XXIII of GATT 1994 are applicable, the procedures in this Understanding shall apply, subject to the following:

(a) the complaining party shall present a detailed justification in support of any complaint relating to a measure which does not conflict with the relevant covered agreement;

(b) where a measure has been found to nullify or impair benefits under, or impede the attainment of objectives of, the relevant covered agreement without violation thereof, there is no obligation to withdraw the measure. However, in such cases, the panel or the Appellate Body shall recommend that the Member concerned make a mutually satisfactory adjustment;

(c) notwithstanding the provisions of Article 21, the arbitration provided for in paragraph 3 of Article 21, upon request of either party, may include a determination of the level of benefits which have been nullified or impaired, and may also suggest ways and means of reaching a mutually satisfactory adjustment; such suggestions shall not be binding upon the parties to the dispute;

(d) notwithstanding the provisions of paragraph 1 of Article 22, compensation may be part of a mutually satisfactory adjustment as final settlement of the dispute.

2. COMPLAINTS OF THE TYPE DESCRIBED IN PARAGRAPH 1(c) OF ARTICLE XXIII OF GATT 1994

Where the provisions of paragraph 1(c) of Article XXIII of GATT 1994 are applicable to a covered agreement, a panel may only make rulings and recommendations where a party considers that any benefit accruing to it directly or indirectly under the relevant covered agreement is being nullified or impaired or the attainment of any objective of that Agreement is being impeded as a result of the existence of any situation other than those to which the provisions of paragraphs 1(a) and 1(b) of Article XXIII of GATT 1994 are applicable. Where and to the extent that such party considers and a panel determines that the matter is covered by this paragraph, the procedures of this Understanding shall apply only up to and including the point in the proceedings where the panel report has been circulated to the Members. The dispute settlement rules and procedures contained in the Decision of 12 April 1989 (BISD 368/61-67) shall apply to consideration for adoption, and surveillance and implementation of recommendations and rulings. The following shall also apply:

(a) the complaining party shall present a detailed justification in support of any argument made with respect to issues covered under this paragraph;

(b) in cases involving matters covered by this paragraph, if a panel finds that cases also involve dispute settlement matters other than those covered by this paragraph, the panel shall circulate a report to the DSB addressing any such matters and a separate report on matters falling under this paragraph.

Article 27. Responsibilities of the Secretariat

1. The Secretariat shall have the responsibility of assisting panels, especially on the legal, historical and procedural aspects of the matters dealt with, and of providing secretarial and technical support.

2. While the Secretariat assists Members in respect of dispute settlement at their request, there may also be a need to provide additional legal advice and assistance in respect of dispute settlement to developing country Members. To this end, the Secretariat shall make available a qualified legal expert from the WTO technical cooperation services to any developing country Member which so requests. This expert shall assist the developing country Member in a manner ensuring the continued impartiality of the Secretariat.

3. The Secretariat shall conduct special training courses for interested Members concerning these dispute settlement procedures and practices so as to enable Members' experts to be better informed in this regard.

Appendix 1.   Agreements Covered by the Understanding

(A) Agreement Establishing the World Trade Organization
(B) Multilateral Trade Agreements

    Annex 1A: Multilateral Agreements on Trade in Goods
    Annex 1B: General Agreement on Trade in Services
    Annex 1C: Agreement on Trade-Related Aspects of Intellectual Property
                Rights
    Annex 2:   Understanding on Rules and Procedures Governing the
                Settlement of Disputes

(C) Plurilateral Trade Agreements

    Annex 4:   Agreement on Trade in Civil Aircraft
                Agreement on Government Procurement
                International Dairy Agreement
                International Bovine Meat Agreement

The applicability of this Understanding to the Plurilateral Trade Agreements shall be subject to the adoption of a decision by the parties to each agreement setting out the terms for the application of the Understanding to the individual agreement, including any special or additional rules or procedures for inclusion in Appendix 2, as notified to the DSB.

Appendix 2.   Special or Additional Rules and Procedures Contained in the Covered Agreements . . .

Appendix 3.   Working Procedures

1. In its proceedings the panel shall follow the relevant provisions of this Understanding. In addition, the following working procedures shall apply.

2. The panel shall meet in closed session. The parties to the dispute, and interested parties, shall be present at the meetings only when invited by the panel to appear before it.

3. The deliberations of the panel and the documents submitted to it shall be kept confidential. Nothing in this Understanding shall preclude a party to a dispute from disclosing statements of its own positions to the public. Members shall treat as confidential information submitted by another Member to the panel which that Member has designated as confidential. Where a party to a dispute submits a confidential version of its written submissions to the panel, it shall also, upon request of a Member, provide a non-confidential summary of the information contained in its submissions that could be disclosed to the public.

4. Before the first substantive meeting of the panel with the parties, the parties to the dispute shall transmit to the panel written submissions in which they present the facts of the case and their arguments.

5. At its first substantive meeting with the parties, the panel shall ask the party which has brought the complaint to present its case. Subsequently, and

still at the same meeting, the party against which the complaint has been brought shall be asked to present its point of view.

6. All third parties which have notified their interest in the dispute to the DSB shall be invited in writing to present their views during a session of the first substantive meeting of the panel set aside for that purpose. All such third parties may be present during the entirety of this session.

7. Formal rebuttals shall be made at a second substantive meeting of the panel. The party complained against shall have the right to take the floor first to be followed by the complaining party. The parties shall submit, prior to that meeting, written rebuttals to the panel.

8. The panel may at any time put questions to the parties and ask them for explanations either in the course of a meeting with the parties or in writing.

9. The parties to the dispute and any third party invited to present its views in accordance with Article 10 shall make available to the panel a written version of their oral statements.

10. In the interest of full transparency, the presentations, rebuttals and statements referred to in paragraphs 5 to 9 shall be made in the presence of the parties. Moreover, each party's written submissions, including any comments on the descriptive part of the report and responses to questions put by the panel, shall be made available to the other party or parties.

11. Any additional procedures specific to the panel.

12. Proposed timetable for panel work:

(a)	Receipt of first written submissions of the parties:		
	(1) complaining Party:	_____	3–6 weeks
	(2) Party complained against:	_____	2–3 weeks
(b)	Date, time and place of first substantive meeting with the parties; third party session:	_____	1–2 weeks
(c)	Receipt of written rebuttals of the parties:	_____	2–3 weeks
(d)	Date, time and place of second substantive meeting with the parties:	_____	1–2 weeks
(e)	Issuance of descriptive part of the report to the parties:	_____	2–4 weeks
(f)	Receipt of comments by the parties on the descriptive part of the report:	_____	2 weeks
(g)	Issuance of the interim report, including the findings and conclusions, to the parties:	_____	2–4 weeks
(h)	Deadline for party to request review of part(s) of report:	_____	1 week
(i)	Period of review by panel, including possible additional meeting with parties:	_____	2 weeks
(j)	Issuance of final report to parties to dispute:	_____	2 weeks
(k)	Circulation of the final report to the Members:	_____	3 weeks

The above calendar may be changed in the light of unforeseen developments. Additional meetings with the parties shall be scheduled if required.

Appendix 4. Expert Review Groups

The following rules and procedures shall apply to expert review groups established in accordance with the provisions of paragraph 2 of Article 13.

1. Expert review groups are under the panel's authority. Their terms of reference and detailed working procedures shall be decided by the panel, and they shall report to the panel.

2. Participation in expert review groups shall be restricted to persons of professional standing and experience in the field in question.

3. Citizens of parties to the dispute shall not serve on an expert review group without the joint agreement of the parties to the dispute, except in exceptional circumstances when the panel considers that the need for specialized scientific expertise cannot be fulfilled otherwise. Government officials of parties to the dispute shall not serve on an expert review group. Members of expert review groups shall serve in their individual capacities and not as government representatives, nor as representatives of any organization. Governments or organizations shall therefore not give them instructions with regard to matters before an expert review group.

4. Expert review groups may consult and seek information and technical advice from any source they deem appropriate. Before an expert review group seeks such information or advice from a source within the jurisdiction of a Member, it shall inform the government of that Member. Any Member shall respond promptly and fully to any request by an expert review group for such information as the expert review group considers necessary and appropriate.

5. The parties to a dispute shall have access to all relevant information provided to an expert review group, unless it is of a confidential nature. Confidential information provided to the expert review group shall not be released without formal authorization from the government, organization or person providing the information. Where such information is requested from the expert review group but release of such information by the expert review group is not authorized, a non-confidential summary of the information will be provided by the government, organization or person supplying the information.

6. The expert review group shall submit a draft report to the parties to the dispute with a view to obtaining their comments, and taking them into account, as appropriate, in the final report, which shall also be issued to the parties to the dispute when it is submitted to the panel. The final report of the expert review group shall be advisory only.

5

States and Other Major International Entities

TREATY ON EUROPEAN UNION*

European Union Consolidated Treaties
(Official Publications of the European Union)

Table of Contents

Preamble
TITLE I   Common provisions
TITLE II   Provisions on Democratic Principles
TITLE III   Provisions on the Institutions
TITLE IV   Provisions on Enhanced Cooperation

* The original Treaty on European Union (TEU) was signed at Maastricht on February 7, 1992, and came into force on November 1, 1993.

The Treaty of Amsterdam, which was signed on October 2, 1997, and entered into force on May 1, 1999, amended the Treaty on European Union and renumbered the articles. The Treaty of Nice, which was signed on February 26, 2001, and entered into force on February 1, 2003 amended the Treaty to ease the Union's expansion to a membership of 25 states, which occurred in May 1, 2004. The treaty here has been amended further to include in its text the Protocol on the Enlargement of the European Union and the Amendments to Primary Legislation Further to the Accession of the Republic of Bulgaria and Romania to the European Union. On December 1, 2009 the Lisbon Treaty entered into force and added additional amendments to the treaty. With the changes made by the Treaty of Amsterdam, the Treaty of Nice, and the Treaty of Lisbon, the new version of the Treaty is known as the Consolidated Version of the Treaty on European Union.

As of May 1, 2013, the 27 Member States of the European Union were: Austria, Belgium, Bulgaria, Cyprus, Czech Republic, Denmark, Estonia, Finland, France, Germany, Greece, Hungary, Ireland, Italy, Latvia, Lithuania, Luxembourg, Malta, Netherlands, Poland, Portugal, Romania, Slovakia, Slovenia, Spain, Sweden, and the United Kingdom.

This treaty and the following Treaty on the Functioning of the European Union (TFEU), which superseded the Treaty Establishing the European Community (or TEC or Treaty of Rome) can be found on the EU Web site at <http://europa.eu/lisbon_treaty/full_text/index_en.htm>.

TITLE V   General Provisions on the Union's External Action
            and Specific Provisions on the Common Foreign and
            Security Policy
     Chapter 1: General provisions on the Union's external action
     Chapter 2: Specific provisions on the common foreign and
               security policy
          Section 1: Common provisions
          Section 2: Provisions on the common security and defence
                    policy
TITLE VI   Final Provisions

RESOLVED to mark a new stage in the process of European integration undertaken with the establishment of the European Communities,

DRAWING INSPIRATION from the cultural, religious and humanist inheritance of Europe, from which have developed the universal values of the inviolable and inalienable rights of the human person, freedom, democracy, equality and the rule of law,

RECALLING the historic importance of the ending of the division of the European continent and the need to create firm bases for the construction of the future Europe,

CONFIRMING their attachment to the principles of liberty, democracy and respect for human rights and fundamental freedoms and of the rule of law,

CONFIRMING their attachment to fundamental social rights as defined in the European Social Charter signed at Turin on 18 October 1961 and in the 1989 Community Charter of the Fundamental Social Rights of Workers,

DESIRING to deepen the solidarity between their peoples while respecting their history, their culture and their traditions,

DESIRING to enhance further the democratic and efficient functioning of the institutions so as to enable them better to carry out, within a single institutional framework, the tasks entrusted to them,

RESOLVED to achieve the strengthening and the convergence of their economies and to establish an economic and monetary union including, in accordance with the provisions of this Treaty and of the Treaty on the Functioning of the European Union, a single and stable currency,

DETERMINED to promote economic and social progress for their peoples, taking into account the principle of sustainable development and within the context of the accomplishment of the internal market and of reinforced cohesion and environmental protection, and to implement policies ensuring that advances in economic integration are accompanied by parallel progress in other fields,

RESOLVED to establish a citizenship common to nationals of their countries,

RESOLVED to implement a common foreign and security policy including the progressive framing of a common defence policy, which might lead to a common defence in accordance with the provisions of Article 42, thereby reinforcing the European identity and its independence in order to promote peace, security and progress in Europe and in the world,

RESOLVED to facilitate the free movement of persons, while ensuring the safety and security of their peoples, by establishing an area of freedom, security and justice, in accordance with the provisions of this Treaty and of the Treaty on the Functioning of the European Union,

RESOLVED to continue the process of creating an ever closer union among the peoples of Europe, in which decisions are taken as closely as possible to the citizen in accordance with the principle of subsidiarity,

IN VIEW of further steps to be taken in order to advance European integration,

HAVE DECIDED to establish a European Union. . . .

Title I.   Common Provisions

Article 1 (ex Article 1 TEU)*

By this Treaty, the HIGH CONTRACTING PARTIES establish among themselves a EUROPEAN UNION, hereinafter called 'the Union' on which the Member States confer competences to attain objectives they have in common.

This Treaty marks a new stage in the process of creating an ever closer union among the peoples of Europe, in which decisions are taken as openly as possible and as closely as possible to the citizen.

The Union shall be founded on the present Treaty and on the Treaty on the Functioning of the European Union (hereinafter referred to as 'the Treaties'). Those two Treaties shall have the same legal value. The Union shall replace and succeed the European Community.

Article 2

The Union is founded on the values of respect for human dignity, freedom, democracy, equality, the rule of law and respect for human rights, including the rights of persons belonging to minorities. These values are common to the Member States in a society in which pluralism, non-discrimination, tolerance, justice, solidarity and equality between women and men prevail.

Article 3 (ex Article 2 TEU)

1. The Union's aim is to promote peace, its values and the well-being of its peoples.

---

* [These parenthetical references are to the Articles in the earlier treaties before the Lisbon Treaty. These references appear in the Consolidated Version of the TEU. The EU Web site referred to on the previous page also provides tables of equivalences between the old and the new numbering of the treaties.—EDS.]

2. The Union shall offer its citizens an area of freedom, security and justice without internal frontiers, in which the free movement of persons is ensured in conjunction with appropriate measures with respect to external border controls, asylum, immigration and the prevention and combating of crime.

3. The Union shall establish an internal market. It shall work for the sustainable development of Europe based on balanced economic growth and price stability, a highly competitive social market economy, aiming at full employment and social progress, and a high level of protection and improvement of the quality of the environment. It shall promote scientific and technological advance.

It shall combat social exclusion and discrimination, and shall promote social justice and protection, equality between women and men, solidarity between generations and protection of the rights of the child.

It shall promote economic, social and territorial cohesion, and solidarity among Member States.

It shall respect its rich cultural and linguistic diversity, and shall ensure that Europe's cultural heritage is safeguarded and enhanced.

4. The Union shall establish an economic and monetary union whose currency is the euro.

5. In its relations with the wider world, the Union shall uphold and promote its values and interests and contribute to the protection of its citizens. It shall contribute to peace, security, the sustainable development of the Earth, solidarity and mutual respect among peoples, free and fair trade, eradication of poverty and the protection of human rights, in particular the rights of the child, as well as to the strict observance and the development of international law, including respect for the principles of the United Nations Charter.

6. The Union shall pursue its objectives by appropriate means commensurate with the competences which are conferred upon it in the Treaties.

Article 4

1. In accordance with Article 5, competences not conferred upon the Union in the Treaties remain with the Member States.

2. The Union shall respect the equality of Member States before the Treaties as well as their national identities, inherent in their fundamental structures, political and constitutional, inclusive of regional and local self-government. It shall respect their essential State functions, including ensuring the territorial integrity of the State, maintaining law and order and safeguarding national security. In particular, national security remains the sole responsibility of each Member State.

3. Pursuant to the principle of sincere cooperation, the Union and the Member States shall, in full mutual respect, assist each other in carrying out tasks which flow from the Treaties.

The Member States shall take any appropriate measure, general or particular, to ensure fulfilment of the obligations arising out of the Treaties or resulting from the acts of the institutions of the Union.

The Member States shall facilitate the achievement of the Union's tasks and refrain from any measure which could jeopardise the attainment of the Union's objectives.

Article 5 (ex Article 5 TEC)

1. The limits of Union competences are governed by the principle of conferral. The use of Union competences is governed by the principles of subsidiarity and proportionality.

2. Under the principle of conferral, the Union shall act only within the limits of the competences conferred upon it by the Member States in the Treaties to attain the objectives set out therein.

Competences not conferred upon the Union in the Treaties remain with the Member States.

3. Under the principle of subsidiarity, in areas which do not fall within its exclusive competence, the Union shall act only if and in so far as the objectives of the proposed action cannot be sufficiently achieved by the Member States, either at central level or at regional and local level, but can rather, by reason of the scale or effects of the proposed action, be better achieved at Union level.

The institutions of the Union shall apply the principle of subsidiarity as laid down in the Protocol on the application of the principles of subsidiarity and proportionality. National Parliaments ensure compliance with the principle of subsidiarity in accordance with the procedure set out in that Protocol.

4. Under the principle of proportionality, the content and form of Union action shall not exceed what is necessary to achieve the objectives of the Treaties.

The institutions of the Union shall apply the principle of proportionality as laid down in the Protocol on the application of the principles of subsidiarity and proportionality.

Article 6 (ex Article 6 TEU)

1. The Union recognises the rights, freedoms and principles set out in the Charter of Fundamental Rights of the European Union of 7 December 2000, as adapted at Strasbourg, on 12 December 2007, which shall have the same legal value as the Treaties.

The provisions of the Charter shall not extend in any way the competences of the Union as defined in the Treaties.

The rights, freedoms and principles in the Charter shall be interpreted in accordance with the general provisions in Title VII of the Charter governing its interpretation and application and with due regard to the explanations referred to in the Charter, that set out the sources of those provisions.

2. The Union shall accede to the European Convention for the Protection of Human Rights and Fundamental Freedoms. Such accession shall not affect the Union's competences as defined in the Treaties.

3. Fundamental rights, as guaranteed by the European Convention for the Protection of Human Rights and Fundamental Freedoms and as they result from the constitutional traditions common to the Member States, shall constitute general principles of the Union's law.

Article 7 (ex Article 7 TEU)

1. On a reasoned proposal by one third of the Member States, by the European Parliament or by the European Commission, the Council, acting by a majority of four fifths of its members after obtaining the consent of the European Parliament, may determine that there is a clear risk of a serious breach by a Member State of the values referred to in Article 2. . . .

2. The European Council, acting by unanimity on a proposal by one third of the Member States or by the Commission and after obtaining the consent of the European Parliament, may determine the existence of a serious and persistent breach by a Member State of the values referred to in Article 2, after inviting the Member State in question to submit its observations.

3. Where a determination under paragraph 2 has been made, the Council, acting by a qualified majority, may decide to suspend certain of the rights deriving from the application of the Treaties to the Member State in question, including the voting rights of the representative of the government of that Member State in the Council. . . .

The obligations of the Member State in question under this Treaty shall in any case continue to be binding on that State.

4. The Council, acting by a qualified majority, may decide subsequently to vary or revoke measures taken under paragraph 3 in response to changes in the situation which led to their being imposed.

5. The voting arrangements applying to the European Parliament, the European Council and the Council for the purposes of this Article are laid down in Article 354 of the Treaty on the Functioning of the European Union.

Article 8

1. The Union shall develop a special relationship with neighbouring countries, aiming to establish an area of prosperity and good neighbourliness, founded on the values of the Union and characterized by close and peaceful relations based on cooperation.

2. For the purposes of paragraph 1, the Union may conclude specific agreements with the countries concerned. These agreements may contain reciprocal rights and obligations as well as the possibility of undertaking activities jointly. Their implementation shall be the subject of periodic consultation.

TITLE II. PROVISIONS ON DEMOCRATIC PRINCIPLES

Article 9

In all its activities, the Union shall observe the principle of the equality of its citizens, who shall receive equal attention from its institutions, bodies, offices and agencies. Every national of a Member State shall be a citizen of the Union. Citizenship of the Union shall be additional to national citizenship and shall not replace it.

Article 10

1. The functioning of the Union shall be founded on representative democracy.

2. Citizens are directly represented at Union level in the European Parliament.
Member States are represented in the European Council by their Heads of State or Government and in the Council by their governments, themselves democratically accountable either to their national Parliaments, or to their citizens.

3. Every citizen shall have the right to participate in the democratic life of the Union. Decisions shall be taken as openly and as closely as possible to the citizen.

4. Political parties at European level contribute to forming European political awareness and to expressing the will of citizens of the Union.

Article 11

1. The institutions shall, by appropriate means, give citizens and representative associations the opportunity to make known and publicly exchange their views in all areas of Union action.

2. The institutions shall maintain an open, transparent and regular dialogue with representative associations and civil society.

3. The European Commission shall carry out broad consultations with parties concerned in order to ensure that the Union's actions are coherent and transparent.

4. Not less than one million citizens who are nationals of a significant number of Member States may take the initiative of inviting the European Commission, within the framework of its powers, to submit any appropriate proposal on matters where citizens consider that a legal act of the Union is required for the purpose of implementing the Treaties.

The procedures and conditions required for such a citizens' initiative shall be determined in accordance with the first paragraph of Article 24 of the Treaty on the Functioning of the European Union.

Article 12

National Parliaments contribute actively to the good functioning of the Union:

(a) through being informed by the institutions of the Union and having draft legislative acts of the Union forwarded to them in accordance with the Protocol on the role of national Parliaments in the European Union;

(b) by seeing to it that the principle of subsidiarity is respected in accordance with the procedures provided for in the Protocol on the application of the principles of subsidiarity and proportionality;

(c) by taking part, within the framework of the area of freedom, security and justice, in the evaluation mechanisms for the implementation of the Union policies in that area, in accordance with Article 70 of the Treaty on the Functioning of the European Union, and through being involved in the political monitoring of Europol and the evaluation of Eurojust's activities in accordance with Articles 88 and 85 of that Treaty;

(d) by taking part in the revision procedures of the Treaties, in accordance with Article 48 of this Treaty;

(e) by being notified of applications for accession to the Union, in accordance with Article 49 of this Treaty;

(f) by taking part in the inter-parliamentary cooperation between national Parliaments and with the European Parliament, in accordance with the Protocol on the role of national Parliaments in the European Union.

TITLE III. PROVISIONS ON THE INSTITUTIONS

Article 13

1. The Union shall have an institutional framework which shall aim to promote its values, advance its objectives, serve its interests, those of its citizens and those of the Member States, and ensure the consistency, effectiveness and continuity of its policies and actions.

The Union's institutions shall be:
—the European Parliament,
—the European Council,
—the Council,
—the European Commission (hereinafter referred to as 'the Commission'),
—the Court of Justice of the European Union,
—the European Central Bank,
—the Court of Auditors.

2. Each institution shall act within the limits of the powers conferred on it in the Treaties, and in conformity with the procedures, conditions and

objectives set out in them. The institutions shall practice mutual sincere cooperation.

3. The provisions relating to the European Central Bank and the Court of Auditors and detailed provisions on the other institutions are set out in the Treaty on the Functioning of the European Union.

4. The European Parliament, the Council and the Commission shall be assisted by an Economic and Social Committee and a Committee of the Regions acting in an advisory capacity.

Article 14

1. The European Parliament shall, jointly with the Council, exercise legislative and budgetary functions. It shall exercise functions of political control and consultation as laid down in the Treaties. It shall elect the President of the Commission.

2. The European Parliament shall be composed of representatives of the Union's citizens. They shall not exceed seven hundred and fifty in number, plus the President. Representation of citizens shall be degressively proportional, with a minimum threshold of six members per Member State.

No Member State shall be allocated more than ninety-six seats.

The European Council shall adopt by unanimity, on the initiative of the European Parliament and with its consent, a decision establishing the composition of the European Parliament, respecting the principles referred to in the first subparagraph.

3. The members of the European Parliament shall be elected for a term of five years by direct universal suffrage in a free and secret ballot.

4. The European Parliament shall elect its President and its officers from among its members.

Article 15

1. The European Council shall provide the Union with the necessary impetus for its development and shall define the general political directions and priorities thereof. It shall not exercise legislative functions.

2. The European Council shall consist of the Heads of State or Government of the Member States, together with its President and the President of the Commission. The High Representative of the Union for Foreign Affairs and Security Policy shall take part in its work.

3. The European Council shall meet twice every six months, convened by its President. When the agenda so requires, the members of the European Council may decide each to be assisted by a minister and, in the case of the President of the Commission, by a member of the Commission. When the situation so requires, the President shall convene a special meeting of the European Council.

4. Except where the Treaties provide otherwise, decisions of the European Council shall be taken by consensus.

5. The European Council shall elect its President, by a qualified majority, for a term of two and a half years, renewable once. In the event of an impediment or serious misconduct, the European Council can end the President's term of office in accordance with the same procedure.

6. The President of the European Council:

(a) shall chair it and drive forward its work;

(b) shall ensure the preparation and continuity of the work of the European Council in cooperation with the President of the Commission, and on the basis of the work of the General Affairs Council;

(c) shall endeavour to facilitate cohesion and consensus within the European Council;

(d) shall present a report to the European Parliament after each of the meetings of the European Council.

The President of the European Council shall, at his level and in that capacity, ensure the external representation of the Union on issues concerning its common foreign and security policy, without prejudice to the powers of the High Representative of the Union for Foreign Affairs and Security Policy.

The President of the European Council shall not hold a national office.

Article 16

1. The Council shall, jointly with the European Parliament, exercise legislative and budgetary functions. It shall carry out policy-making and coordinating functions as laid down in the Treaties.

2. The Council shall consist of a representative of each Member State at ministerial level, who may commit the government of the Member State in question and cast its vote.

3. The Council shall act by a qualified majority except where the Treaties provide otherwise.

4. As from 1 November 2014, a qualified majority shall be defined as at least 55 % of the members of the Council, comprising at least fifteen of them and representing Member States comprising at least 65 % of the population of the Union.

A blocking minority must include at least four Council members, failing which the qualified majority shall be deemed attained.

The other arrangements governing the qualified majority are laid down in Article 238(2) of the Treaty on the Functioning of the European Union.

5. The transitional provisions relating to the definition of the qualified majority which shall be applicable until 31 October 2014 and those which shall be applicable from 1 November 2014 to 31 March 2017 are laid down in the Protocol on transitional provisions.

6. The Council shall meet in different configurations, the list of which shall be adopted in accordance with Article 236 of the Treaty on the Functioning of the European Union.

The General Affairs Council shall ensure consistency in the work of the different Council configurations. It shall prepare and ensure the follow-up to meetings of the European Council, in liaison with the President of the European Council and the Commission.

The Foreign Affairs Council shall elaborate the Union's external action on the basis of strategic guidelines laid down by the European Council and ensure that the Union's action is consistent.

7. A Committee of Permanent Representatives of the Governments of the Member States shall be responsible for preparing the work of the Council.

8. The Council shall meet in public when it deliberates and votes on a draft legislative act. To this end, each Council meeting shall be divided into two parts, dealing respectively with deliberations on Union legislative acts and non-legislative activities.

9. The Presidency of Council configurations, other than that of Foreign Affairs, shall be held by Member State representatives in the Council on the basis of equal rotation, in accordance with the conditions established in accordance with Article 236 of the Treaty on the Functioning of the European Union.

Article 17

1. The Commission shall promote the general interest of the Union and take appropriate initiatives to that end. It shall ensure the application of the Treaties, and of measures adopted by the institutions pursuant to them. It shall oversee the application of Union law under the control of the Court of Justice of the European Union. It shall execute the budget and manage programmes. It shall exercise coordinating, executive and management functions, as laid down in the Treaties. With the exception of the common foreign and security policy, and other cases provided for in the Treaties, it shall ensure the Union's external representation. It shall initiate the Union's annual and multiannual programming with a view to achieving interinstitutional agreements.

2. Union legislative acts may only be adopted on the basis of a Commission proposal, except where the Treaties provide otherwise. Other acts shall be adopted on the basis of a Commission proposal where the Treaties so provide.

3. The Commission's term of office shall be five years.

The members of the Commission shall be chosen on the ground of their general competence and European commitment from persons whose independence is beyond doubt.

In carrying out its responsibilities, the Commission shall be completely independent. Without prejudice to Article 18(2), the members of the Commission shall neither seek nor take instructions from any Government or other institution, body, office or entity. They shall refrain from any action incompatible with their duties or the performance of their tasks.

4. The Commission appointed between the date of entry into force of the Treaty of Lisbon and 31 October 2014, shall consist of one national of

each Member State, including its President and the High Representative of the Union for Foreign Affairs and Security Policy who shall be one of its Vice-Presidents.

5. As from 1 November 2014, the Commission shall consist of a number of members, including its President and the High Representative of the Union for Foreign Affairs and Security Policy, corresponding to two thirds of the number of Member States, unless the European Council, acting unanimously, decides to alter this number.

The members of the Commission shall be chosen from among the nationals of the Member States on the basis of a system of strictly equal rotation between the Member States, reflecting the demographic and geographical range of all the Member States. This system shall be established unanimously by the European Council in accordance with Article 244 of the Treaty on the Functioning of the European Union.

6. The President of the Commission shall:

(a) lay down guidelines within which the Commission is to work;

(b) decide on the internal organisation of the Commission, ensuring that it acts consistently, efficiently and as a collegiate body;

(c) appoint Vice-Presidents, other than the High Representative of the Union for Foreign Affairs and Security Policy, from among the members of the Commission.

A member of the Commission shall resign if the President so requests. The High Representative of the Union for Foreign Affairs and Security Policy shall resign, in accordance with the procedure set out in Article 18(1), if the President so requests. . . .

7. Taking into account the elections to the European Parliament and after having held the appropriate consultations, the European Council, acting by a qualified majority, shall propose to the European Parliament a candidate for President of the Commission. This candidate shall be elected by the European Parliament by a majority of its component members. If he does not obtain the required majority, the European Council, acting by a qualified majority, shall within one month propose a new candidate who shall be elected by the European Parliament following the same procedure.

The Council, by common accord with the President-elect, shall adopt the list of the other persons whom it proposes for appointment as members of the Commission. They shall be selected, on the basis of the suggestions made by Member States, in accordance with the criteria set out in paragraph 3, second subparagraph, and paragraph 5, second subparagraph.

The President, the High Representative of the Union for Foreign Affairs and Security Policy and the other members of the Commission shall be subject as a body to a vote of consent by the European Parliament. On the basis of this consent the Commission shall be appointed by the European Council, acting by a qualified majority.

8. The Commission, as a body, shall be responsible to the European Parliament. In accordance with Article 234 of the Treaty on the Functioning of the European Union, the European Parliament may vote on a motion of

censure of the Commission. If such a motion is carried, the members of the Commission shall resign as a body and the High Representative of the Union for Foreign Affairs and Security Policy shall resign from the duties that he carries out in the Commission.

Article 18

1. The European Council, acting by a qualified majority, with the agreement of the President of the Commission, shall appoint the High Representative of the Union for Foreign Affairs and Security Policy. The European Council may end his term of office by the same procedure.

2. The High Representative shall conduct the Union's common foreign and security policy. He shall contribute by his proposals to the development of that policy, which he shall carry out as mandated by the Council. The same shall apply to the common security and defence policy.

3. The High Representative shall preside over the Foreign Affairs Council.

4. The High Representative shall be one of the Vice-Presidents of the Commission. He shall ensure the consistency of the Union's external action. He shall be responsible within the Commission for responsibilities incumbent on it in external relations and for coordinating other aspects of the Union's external action. . . .

Article 19

1. The Court of Justice of the European Union shall include the Court of Justice, the General Court and specialised courts. It shall ensure that in the interpretation and application of the Treaties the law is observed.

Member States shall provide remedies sufficient to ensure effective legal protection in the fields covered by Union law.

2. The Court of Justice shall consist of one judge from each Member State. It shall be assisted by Advocates-General.

The General Court shall include at least one judge per Member State.

The Judges and the Advocates-General of the Court of Justice and the Judges of the General Court shall be chosen from persons whose independence is beyond doubt and who satisfy the conditions set out in Articles 253 and 254 of the Treaty on the Functioning of the European Union. They shall be appointed by common accord of the governments of the Member States for six years. Retiring Judges and Advocates-General may be reappointed.

3. The Court of Justice of the European Union shall, in accordance with the Treaties:

(a) rule on actions brought by a Member State, an institution or a natural or legal person;

(b) give preliminary rulings, at the request of courts or tribunals of the Member States, on the interpretation of Union law or the validity of acts adopted by the institutions;

(c) rule in other cases provided for in the Treaties.

TITLE IV. PROVISIONS ON ENHANCED COOPERATION

Article 20 (ex Articles 27a to 27e , 40 to 40 b and 43 to 45 TEU and ex Articles 11 and 11a TEC)

1. Member States which wish to establish enhanced cooperation between themselves within the framework of the Union's non-exclusive competences may make use of its institutions and exercise those competences by applying the relevant provisions of the Treaties, subject to the limits and in accordance with the detailed arrangements laid down in this Article and in Articles 326 to 334 of the Treaty on the Functioning of the European Union.

Enhanced cooperation shall aim to further the objectives of the Union, protect its interests and reinforce its integration process. Such cooperation shall be open at any time to all Member States, in accordance with Article 328 of the Treaty on the Functioning of the European Union.

2. The decision authorising enhanced cooperation shall be adopted by the Council as a last resort, when it has established that the objectives of such cooperation cannot be attained within a reasonable period by the Union as a whole, and provided that at least nine Member States participate in it. The Council shall act in accordance with the procedure laid down in Article 329 of the Treaty on the Functioning of the European Union.

3. All members of the Council may participate in its deliberations, but only members of the Council representing the Member States participating in enhanced cooperation shall take part in the vote. The voting rules are set out in Article 330 of the Treaty on the Functioning of the European Union.

4. Acts adopted in the framework of enhanced cooperation shall bind only participating Member States. They shall not be regarded as part of the *acquis* which has to be accepted by candidate States for accession to the Union.

TITLE V. GENERAL PROVISIONS ON THE UNION'S EXTERNAL ACTION AND SPECIFIC PROVISIONS ON THE COMMON FOREIGN AND SECURITY POLICY

CHAPTER 1. GENERAL PROVISIONS ON THE UNION'S EXTERNAL ACTION

Article 21

1. The Union's action on the international scene shall be guided by the principles which have inspired its own creation, development and enlargement, and which it seeks to advance in the wider world: democracy, the rule of law, the universality and indivisibility of human rights and fundamental freedoms, respect for human dignity, the principles of equality and solidarity, and respect for the principles of the United Nations Charter and international law.

The Union shall seek to develop relations and build partnerships with third countries, and international, regional or global organisations which share the principles referred to in the first subparagraph. It shall promote multilateral solutions to common problems, in particular in the framework of the United Nations.

2. The Union shall define and pursue common policies and actions, and shall work for a high degree of cooperation in all fields of international relations, in order to:

(a) safeguard its values, fundamental interests, security, independence and integrity;

(b) consolidate and support democracy, the rule of law, human rights and the principles of international law;

(c) preserve peace, prevent conflicts and strengthen international security, in accordance with the purposes and principles of the United Nations Charter, with the principles of the Helsinki Final Act and with the aims of the Charter of Paris, including those relating to external borders;

(d) foster the sustainable economic, social and environmental development of developing countries, with the primary aim of eradicating poverty;

(e) encourage the integration of all countries into the world economy, including through the progressive abolition of restrictions on international trade;

(f) help develop international measures to preserve and improve the quality of the environment and the sustainable management of global natural resources, in order to ensure sustainable development;

(g) assist populations, countries and regions confronting natural or man-made disasters; and

(h) promote an international system based on stronger multilateral cooperation and good global governance.

3. The Union shall respect the principles and pursue the objectives set out in paragraphs 1 and 2 in the development and implementation of the different areas of the Union's external action covered by this Title and by Part Five of the Treaty on the Functioning of the European Union, and of the external aspects of its other policies.

The Union shall ensure consistency between the different areas of its external action and between these and its other policies. The Council and the Commission, assisted by the High Representative of the Union for Foreign Affairs and Security Policy, shall ensure that consistency and shall cooperate to that effect.

Article 22

1. On the basis of the principles and objectives set out in Article 21, the European Council shall identify the strategic interests and objectives of the Union. Decisions of the European Council on the strategic interests and objectives of the Union shall relate to the common foreign and security

policy and to other areas of the external action of the Union. Such decisions may concern the relations of the Union with a specific country or region or may be thematic in approach. They shall define their duration, and the means to be made available by the Union and the Member States.

The European Council shall act unanimously on a recommendation from the Council, adopted by the latter under the arrangements laid down for each area. Decisions of the European Council shall be implemented in accordance with the procedures provided for in the Treaties.

2. The High Representative of the Union for Foreign Affairs and Security Policy, for the area of common foreign and security policy, and the Commission, for other areas of external action, may submit joint proposals to the Council.

CHAPTER 2. SPECIFIC PROVISIONS ON THE COMMON FOREIGN AND SECURITY POLICY

Section 1. Common Provisions

Article 23

The Union's action on the international scene, pursuant to this Chapter, shall be guided by the principles, shall pursue the objectives of, and be conducted in accordance with, the general provisions laid down in Chapter 1.

Article 24 (ex Article 11 TEU)

1. The Union's competence in matters of common foreign and security policy shall cover all areas of foreign policy and all questions relating to the Union's security, including the progressive framing of a common defence policy that might lead to a common defence.

The common foreign and security policy is subject to specific rules and procedures. It shall be defined and implemented by the European Council and the Council acting unanimously, except where the Treaties provide otherwise. The adoption of legislative acts shall be excluded. The common foreign and security policy shall be put into effect by the High Representative of the Union for Foreign Affairs and Security Policy and by Member States, in accordance with the Treaties. The specific role of the European Parliament and of the Commission in this area is defined by the Treaties. The Court of Justice of the European Union shall not have jurisdiction with respect to these provisions, with the exception of its jurisdiction to monitor compliance with Article 40 of this Treaty and to review the legality of certain decisions as provided for by the second paragraph of Article 275 of the Treaty on the Functioning of the European Union.

2. Within the framework of the principles and objectives of its external action, the Union shall conduct, define and implement a common foreign and security policy, based on the development of mutual political solidarity

among Member States, the identification of questions of general interest and the achievement of an ever-increasing degree of convergence of Member States' actions.

3. The Member States shall support the Union's external and security policy actively and unreservedly in a spirit of loyalty and mutual solidarity and shall comply with the Union's action in this area.

The Member States shall work together to enhance and develop their mutual political solidarity. They shall refrain from any action which is contrary to the interests of the Union or likely to impair its effectiveness as a cohesive force in international relations.

The Council and the High Representative shall ensure compliance with these principles.

Article 25 (ex Article 12 TEU)

The Union shall conduct the common foreign and security policy by:
    (a) defining the general guidelines;
    (b) adopting decisions defining:
        (i) actions to be undertaken by the Union;
        (ii) positions to be taken by the Union;
        (iii) arrangements for the implementation of the decisions referred to in points (i) and (ii);
        and by
    (c) strengthening systematic cooperation between Member States in the conduct of policy.

Article 26 (ex Article 13 TEU)

1. The European Council shall identify the Union's strategic interests, determine the objectives of and define general guidelines for the common foreign and security policy, including for matters with defence implications. It shall adopt the necessary decisions.

If international developments so require, the President of the European Council shall convene an extraordinary meeting of the European Council in order to define the strategic lines of the Union's policy in the face of such developments.

2. The Council shall frame the common foreign and security policy and take the decisions necessary for defining and implementing it on the basis of the general guidelines and strategic lines defined by the European Council.

The Council and the High Representative of the Union for Foreign Affairs and Security Policy shall ensure the unity, consistency and effectiveness of action by the Union.

3. The common foreign and security policy shall be put into effect by the High Representative and by the Member States, using national and Union resources.

Article 27

1. The High Representative of the Union for Foreign Affairs and Security Policy, who shall chair the Foreign Affairs Council, shall contribute through his proposals towards the preparation of the common foreign and security policy and shall ensure implementation of the decisions adopted by the European Council and the Council.

2. The High Representative shall represent the Union for matters relating to the common foreign and security policy. He shall conduct political dialogue with third parties on the Union's behalf and shall express the Union's position in international organisations and at international conferences.

3. In fulfilling his mandate, the High Representative shall be assisted by a European External Action Service. This service shall work in cooperation with the diplomatic services of the Member States and shall comprise officials from relevant departments of the General Secretariat of the Council and of the Commission as well as staff seconded from national diplomatic services of the Member States. The organisation and functioning of the European External Action Service shall be established by a decision of the Council. The Council shall act on a proposal from the High Representative after consulting the European Parliament and after obtaining the consent of the Commission.

Article 28 (ex Article 14 TEU)

1. Where the international situation requires operational action by the Union, the Council shall adopt the necessary decisions. They shall lay down their objectives, scope, the means to be made available to the Union, if necessary their duration, and the conditions for their implementation. . . .

2. Decisions referred to in paragraph 1 shall commit the Member States in the positions they adopt and in the conduct of their activity. . . .

4. In cases of imperative need arising from changes in the situation and failing a review of the Council decision as referred to in paragraph 1, Member States may take the necessary measures as a matter of urgency having regard to the general objectives of that decision. The Member State concerned shall inform the Council immediately of any such measures. . . .

Article 29 (ex Article 15 TEU)

The Council shall adopt decisions which shall define the approach of the Union to a particular matter of a geographical or thematic nature. Member States shall ensure that their national policies conform to the Union positions.

Article 30 (ex Article 22 TEU)

1. Any Member State, the High Representative of the Union for Foreign Affairs and Security Policy, or the High Representative with the Commission's support, may refer any question relating to the common foreign and

security policy to the Council and may submit to it initiatives or proposals as appropriate.

2. In cases requiring a rapid decision, the High Representative, of his own motion, or at the request of a Member State, shall convene an extraordinary Council meeting within 48 hours or, in an emergency, within a shorter period.

Article 31 (ex Article 23 TEU)

1. Decisions under this Chapter shall be taken by the European Council and the Council acting unanimously, except where this Chapter provides otherwise. The adoption of legislative acts shall be excluded. . . .

2. By derogation from the provisions of paragraph 1, the Council shall act by qualified majority:

—when adopting a decision defining a Union action or position on the basis of a decision of the European Council relating to the Union's strategic interests and objectives, as referred to in Article 22(1),

—when adopting a decision defining a Union action or position, on a proposal which the High Representative of the Union for Foreign Affairs and Security Policy has presented following a specific request from the European Council, made on its own initiative or that of the High Representative,

—when adopting any decision implementing a decision defining a Union action or position . . . .

3. The European Council may unanimously adopt a decision stipulating that the Council shall act by a qualified majority in cases other than those referred to in paragraph 2.

4. Paragraphs 2 and 3 shall not apply to decisions having military or defence implications.

5. For procedural questions, the Council shall act by a majority of its members.

Article 32 (ex Article 16 TEU)

Member States shall consult one another within the European Council and the Council on any matter of foreign and security policy of general interest in order to determine a common approach. Before undertaking any action on the international scene or entering into any commitment which could affect the Union's interests, each Member State shall consult the others within the European Council or the Council. Member States shall ensure, through the convergence of their actions, that the Union is able to assert its interests and values on the international scene. Member States shall show mutual solidarity.

When the European Council or the Council has defined a common approach of the Union within the meaning of the first paragraph, the High Representative of the Union for Foreign Affairs and Security Policy and the Ministers for Foreign Affairs of the Member States shall coordinate their activities within the Council.

The diplomatic missions of the Member States and the Union delegations in third countries and at international organisations shall cooperate and shall contribute to formulating and implementing the common approach.

Article 33 (ex Article 18 TEU)

The Council may, on a proposal from the High Representative of the Union for Foreign Affairs and Security Policy, appoint a special representative with a mandate in relation to particular policy issues. The special representative shall carry out his mandate under the authority of the High Representative.

Article 34 (ex Article 19 TEU)

1. Member States shall coordinate their action in international organisations and at international conferences. They shall uphold the Union's positions in such forums. The High Representative of the Union for Foreign Affairs and Security Policy shall organise this coordination. . . .

2. In accordance with Article 24(3), Member States represented in international organisations or international conferences where not all the Member States participate shall keep the other Member States and the High Representative informed of any matter of common interest. . . .

Member States which are also members of the United Nations Security Council will concert and keep the other Member States and the High Representative fully informed. Member States which are members of the Security Council will, in the execution of their functions, defend the positions and the interests of the Union, without prejudice to their responsibilities under the provisions of the United Nations Charter.

When the Union has defined a position on a subject which is on the United Nations Security Council agenda, those Member States which sit on the Security Council shall request that the High Representative be invited to present the Union's position. . . .

Article 36 (ex Article 21 TEU)

The High Representative of the Union for Foreign Affairs and Security Policy shall regularly consult the European Parliament on the main aspects and the basic choices of the common foreign and security policy and the common security and defence policy and inform it of how those policies evolve. He shall ensure that the views of the European Parliament are duly taken into consideration. Special representatives may be involved in briefing the European Parliament. . . .

Article 37 (ex Article 24 TEU)

The Union may conclude agreements with one or more States or international organisations in areas covered by this Chapter.

Article 38 (ex Article 25 TEU)

Without prejudice to Article 240 of the Treaty on the Functioning of the European Union, a Political and Security Committee shall monitor the international situation in the areas covered by the common foreign and security policy and contribute to the definition of policies by delivering opinions to the Council at the request of the Council or of the High Representative of the Union for Foreign Affairs and Security Policy or on its own initiative. It shall also monitor the implementation of agreed policies, without prejudice to the powers of the High Representative. . . .

Within the scope of this Chapter, the Political and Security Committee shall exercise, under the responsibility of the Council and of the High Representative, the political control and strategic direction of the crisis management operations referred to in Article 43. . . .

Article 39

In accordance with Article 16 of the Treaty on the Functioning of the European Union and by way of derogation from paragraph 2 thereof, the Council shall adopt a decision laying down the rules relating to the protection of individuals with regard to the processing of personal data by the Member States when carrying out activities which fall within the scope of this Chapter, and the rules relating to the free movement of such data. Compliance with these rules shall be subject to the control of independent authorities. . . .

Section 2. Provisions on the Common Security and Defense Policy

Article 42 (ex Article 17 TEU)

1. The common security and defence policy shall be an integral part of the common foreign and security policy. It shall provide the Union with an operational capacity drawing on civilian and military assets. The Union may use them on missions outside the Union for peace-keeping, conflict prevention and strengthening international security in accordance with the principles of the United Nations Charter. The performance of these tasks shall be undertaken using capabilities provided by the Member States.

2. The common security and defence policy shall include the progressive framing of a common Union defence policy. This will lead to a common defence, when the European Council, acting unanimously, so decides. . . .

3. Member States shall make civilian and military capabilities available to the Union for the implementation of the common security and defence policy, to contribute to the objectives defined by the Council. . . .

4. Decisions relating to the common security and defence policy, including those initiating a mission as referred to in this Article, shall be adopted by the Council acting unanimously on a proposal from the High Representative of the Union for Foreign Affairs and Security Policy or an

initiative from a Member State. The High Representative may propose the use of both national resources and Union instruments, together with the Commission where appropriate.

5. The Council may entrust the execution of a task, within the Union framework, to a group of Member States in order to protect the Union's values and serve its interests. The execution of such a task shall be governed by Article 44.

6. Those Member States whose military capabilities fulfil higher criteria and which have made more binding commitments to one another in this area with a view to the most demanding missions shall establish permanent structured cooperation within the Union framework. Such cooperation shall be governed by Article 46. It shall not affect the provisions of Article 43.

7. If a Member State is the victim of armed aggression on its territory, the other Member States shall have towards it an obligation of aid and assistance by all the means in their power, in accordance with Article 51 of the United Nations Charter. This shall not prejudice the specific character of the security and defence policy of certain Member States.

Commitments and cooperation in this area shall be consistent with commitments under the North Atlantic Treaty Organisation, which, for those States which are members of it, remains the foundation of their collective defence and the forum for its implementation.

Article 43

1. The tasks referred to in Article 42(1), in the course of which the Union may use civilian and military means, shall include joint disarmament operations, humanitarian and rescue tasks, military advice and assistance tasks, conflict prevention and peace-keeping tasks, tasks of combat forces in crisis management, including peace-making and post-conflict stabilisation. All these tasks may contribute to the fight against terrorism, including by supporting third countries in combating terrorism in their territories. . . .

2. The Council shall adopt decisions relating to the tasks referred to in paragraph 1, defining their objectives and scope and the general conditions for their implementation. The High Representative of the Union for Foreign Affairs and Security Policy, acting under the authority of the Council and in close and constant contact with the Political and Security Committee, shall ensure coordination of the civilian and military aspects of such tasks.

Article 44

1. Within the framework of the decisions adopted in accordance with Article 43, the Council may entrust the implementation of a task to a group of Member States which are willing and have the necessary capability for such a task. . . .

Article 45

1. The European Defence Agency referred to in Article 42(3), subject to the authority of the Council, shall have as its task to:

(a) contribute to identifying the Member States' military capability objectives and evaluating observance of the capability commitments given by the Member States;

(b) promote harmonisation of operational needs and adoption of effective, compatible procurement methods;

(c) propose multilateral projects to fulfil the objectives in terms of military capabilities, ensure coordination of the programmes implemented by the Member States and management of specific cooperation programmes;

(d) support defence technology research, and coordinate and plan joint research activities and the study of technical solutions meeting future operational needs;

(e) contribute to identifying and, if necessary, implementing any useful measure for strengthening the industrial and technological base of the defence sector and for improving the effectiveness of military expenditure.

2. The European Defence Agency shall be open to all Member States wishing to be part of it. . . .

Article 46

1. Those Member States which wish to participate in the permanent structured cooperation referred to in Article 42(6), which fulfil the criteria and have made the commitments on military capabilities set out in the Protocol on permanent structured cooperation, shall notify their intention to the Council and to the High Representative of the Union for Foreign Affairs and Security Policy. . . .

TITLE VI.   FINAL PROVISIONS

Article 47

The Union shall have legal personality.

Article 48 (ex Article 48 TEU)

1. The Treaties may be amended in accordance with an ordinary revision procedure. They may also be amended in accordance with simplified revision procedures. . . .

Article 49 (ex Article 49 TEU)

Any European State which respects the values referred to in Article 2 and is committed to promoting them may apply to become a member of the

Union. The European Parliament and national Parliaments shall be notified of this application. The applicant State shall address its application to the Council, which shall act unanimously after consulting the Commission and after receiving the consent of the European Parliament, which shall act by a majority of its component members. The conditions of eligibility agreed upon by the European Council shall be taken into account.

The conditions of admission and the adjustments to the Treaties on which the Union is founded, which such admission entails, shall be the subject of an agreement between the Member States and the applicant State. This agreement shall be submitted for ratification by all the contracting States in accordance with their respective constitutional requirements.

Article 50

1. Any Member State may decide to withdraw from the Union in accordance with its own constitutional requirements. . . .

Article 51

The Protocols and Annexes to the Treaties shall form an integral part thereof. . . .

Article 53 (ex Article 51 TEU)

This Treaty is concluded for an unlimited period.

TREATY ON THE FUNCTIONING OF THE EUROPEAN UNION*

European Union Consolidated Treaties
(Official Publications of the European Union)

Table of Contents

I. Text of the Treaty

Preamble

Part One: Principles
TITLE I: Categories and Areas of Union Competence
TITLE II: Provisions Having General Application

Part Two: Non-Discrimination and Citizenship of the Union

* The Treaty Establishing the European Community (or Treaty of Rome) was signed on March 25, 1957, and entered into force on January 1, 1958. The separate Treaty on European Union was signed at Maastricht on February 7, 1992, and came into force on November 1, 1993.

The Treaty Establishing the European Community created the European Economic Community, which was initially one of the three European Communities and then an integral part of the European Community. The whole entity came to be known as the European Union after the Maastricht Treaty entered into force in 1993.

The Treaty Establishing the European Community was amended on January 1, 1995 by the instruments concerning the accession of Austria, Finland and Sweden to the European Union. The Treaty of Amsterdam, which was signed on October 2, 1997 and entered into force on May 1, 1999, further amended the Treaty Establishing the European Community and renumbered the articles. The Treaty of Nice, which was signed on February 26, 2001, and entered into force on February 1, 2003, once again amended the Treaty, with a view to easing the Union's expansion to a membership of 25 states, which occurred on May 1, 2004. The Treaty was further amended on January 1, 2007 by the instruments concerning the accession of Bulgaria and Romania.

On December 1, 2009, the Lisbon Treaty came into effect. With the changes made by the Lisbon Treaty, the new version of the Treaty is known as the Consolidated Version of the Treaty on the Functioning of the European Union (TFEU), which is the Treaty here. All the relevant documents can be found on the EU Web site at <http://europa.eu/lisbon_treaty/full_text/index_en.htm>.

Part Three: Union Policies and Internal Actions
   TITLE I: The Internal Market
   TITLE II: Free Movement of Goods
      Chapter 1: The customs union
      Chapter 2: Customs cooperation
      Chapter 3: Prohibition of quantitative restrictions between Member
         States
   TITLE III: Agriculture and Fisheries
   TITLE IV: Free Movement of Persons, Services and Capital
      Chapter 1: Workers
      Chapter 2: Right of establishment
      Chapter 3: Services
      Chapter 4: Capital and payments
   TITLE V: Area of Freedom, Security and Justice
      Chapter 1: General provisions
      Chapter 2: Policies on border checks, asylum and immigration
      Chapter 3: Judicial cooperation in civil matters
      Chapter 4: Judicial cooperation in criminal matters
      Chapter 5: Police cooperation
   TITLE VI: Transport
   TITLE VII: Common Rules on Competition, Taxation and
        Approximation Laws
      Chapter 1: Rules on competition
        Section 1: Rules applying to undertakings
        Section 2: Aids granted by States
      Chapter 2: Tax provisions
      Chapter 3: Approximation of laws
   TITLE VIII: Economic and Monetary Policy
      Chapter 1: Economic policy
      Chapter 2: Monetary policy
      Chapter 3: Institutional provisions
      Chapter 4: Provisions specific to Member States whose currency is
         the euro
      Chapter 5: Transitional provisions
   TITLE IX: Employment
   TITLE X: Social Policy
   TITLE XI: The European Social Fund
   TITLE XII: Education, Vocational Training, Youth and Sport
   TITLE XIII: Culture
   TITLE XIV: Public Health
   TITLE XV: Consumer Protection
   TITLE XVI: Trans-European Networks
   TITLE XVII: Industry
   TITLE XVIII: Economic, Social and Territorial Cohesion
   TITLE XIX: Research and Technological
        Development and Space

Treaty on the Functioning of the European Union

TITLE XX: Environment
TITLE XXI: Energy
TITLE XXII: Tourism
TITLE XXIII: Civil Protection
TITLE XXIV: Administrative Cooperation

Part Four: Association of the Overseas Countries and Territories

Part Five: External Action by the Union
TITLE I: General Provisions on the Union's External Action
TITLE II: Common Commercial Policy
TITLE III: Cooperation with Third Countries and
       Humanitarian Aid
  Chapter 1: Development cooperation
  Chapter 2: Economic, financial and technical cooperation with
     third countries
  Chapter 3: Humanitarian aid
TITLE IV: Restrictive Measures
TITLE V: International Agreements
TITLE VI: The Union's Relations with International Organisations
    and Third Countries and Union Delegations
TITLE VII: Solidarity Clause

Part Six: Institutional and Financial Provisions
TITLE I: Institutional Provisions
  Chapter 1: The institutions
    Section 1: The European Parliament
    Section 2: The European Council
    Section 3: The Council
    Section 4: The Commission
    Section 5: The Court of Justice of the European Union
    Section 6: The European Central Bank
    Section 7: The Court of Auditors
  Chapter 2: Legal acts of the Union, adoption procedures and other
     provisions
    Section 1: The legal acts of the Union
    Section 2: Procedures for the adoption of acts and other
     provisions
  Chapter 3: The Union's advisory bodies
    Section 1: The Economic and Social Committee
    Section 2: The Committee of the Regions
  Chapter 4: The European Investment Bank
TITLE II: Financial Provisions
  Chapter 1: The Union's own resources
  Chapter 2: The multiannual financial framework
  Chapter 3: The Union's annual budget

Chapter 4: Implementation of the budget and discharge
Chapter 5: Common provisions
Chapter 6: Combating fraud
TITLE III: Enhanced Cooperation

Part Seven: General and Final Provisions
Protocols
Protocol (No. 1) on the role of National Parliaments in the European Union
Protocol (No. 2) on the application of the principles of subsidiarity and proportionality . . . .
Protocol (No. 12) on the excessive deficit procedure . . . .

Part One.   Principles

Article 1

1. This Treaty organises the functioning of the Union and determines the areas of, delimitation of, and arrangements for exercising its competences.

2. This Treaty and the Treaty on European Union constitute the Treaties on which the Union is founded. These two Treaties, which have the same legal value, shall be referred to as "the Treaties".

TITLE I.   CATEGORIES AND AREAS OF UNION COMPETENCE

Article 2

1. When the Treaties confer on the Union exclusive competence in a specific area, only the Union may legislate and adopt legally binding acts, the Member States being able to do so themselves only if so empowered by the Union or for the implementation of Union acts.

2. When the Treaties confer on the Union a competence shared with the Member States in a specific area, the Union and the Member States may legislate and adopt legally binding acts in that area. The Member States shall exercise their competence to the extent that the Union has not exercised its competence. The Member States shall again exercise their competence to the extent that the Union has decided to cease exercising its competence.

3. The Member States shall coordinate their economic and employment policies within arrangements as determined by this Treaty, which the Union shall have competence to provide.

4. The Union shall have competence, in accordance with the provisions of the Treaty on European Union, to define and implement a common foreign and security policy, including the progressive framing of a common defence policy.

5. In certain areas and under the conditions laid down in the Treaties, the Union shall have competence to carry out actions to support, coordinate

or supplement the actions of the Member States, without thereby super-seding their competence in these areas.

Legally binding acts of the Union adopted on the basis of the provisions of the Treaties relating to these areas shall not entail harmonisation of Member States' laws or regulations.

6. The scope of and arrangements for exercising the Union's competences shall be determined by the provisions of the Treaties relating to each area.

Article 3

1. The Union shall have exclusive competence in the following areas:
  (a) customs union;
  (b) the establishing of the competition rules necessary for the functioning of the internal market;
  (c) monetary policy for the Member States whose currency is the euro;
  (d) the conservation of marine biological resources under the common fisheries policy;
  (e) common commercial policy.

2. The Union shall also have exclusive competence for the conclusion of an international agreement when its conclusion is provided for in a legislative act of the Union or is necessary to enable the Union to exercise its internal competence, or in so far as its conclusion may affect common rules or alter their scope.

Article 4

1. The Union shall share competence with the Member States where the Treaties confer on it a competence which does not relate to the areas referred to in Articles 3 and 6.

2. Shared competence between the Union and the Member States applies in the following principal areas:
  (a) internal market;
  (b) social policy, for the aspects defined in this Treaty;
  (c) economic, social and territorial cohesion;
  (d) agriculture and fisheries, excluding the conservation of marine biological resources;
  (e) environment;
  (f) consumer protection;
  (g) transport;
  (h) trans-European networks;
  (i) energy;
  (j) area of freedom, security and justice;
  (k) common safety concerns in public health matters, for the aspects defined in this Treaty.

3. In the areas of research, technological development and space, the Union shall have competence to carry out activities, in particular to define

and implement programmes; however, the exercise of that competence shall not result in Member States being prevented from exercising theirs.

4. In the areas of development cooperation and humanitarian aid, the Union shall have competence to carry out activities and conduct a common policy; however, the exercise of that competence shall not result in Member States being prevented from exercising theirs.

Article 5

1. The Member States shall coordinate their economic policies within the Union. To this end, the Council shall adopt measures, in particular broad guidelines for these policies. . . .

Specific provisions shall apply to those Member States whose currency is the euro.

2. The Union shall take measures to ensure coordination of the employment policies of the Member States, in particular by defining guidelines for these policies.

3. The Union may take initiatives to ensure coordination of Member States' social policies.

Article 6

The Union shall have competence to carry out actions to support, coordinate or supplement the actions of the Member States. The areas of such action shall, at European level, be:

    (a) protection and improvement of human health;
    (b) industry;
    (c) culture;
    (d) tourism;
    (e) education, vocational training, youth and sport;
    (f) civil protection;
    (g) administrative cooperation.

TITLE II. PROVISIONS HAVING GENERAL APPLICATION

Article 7

The Union shall ensure consistency between its policies and activities, taking all of its objectives into account and in accordance with the principle of conferral of powers.

Article 8 (ex Article 3(2) TEC)

In all its activities, the Union shall aim to eliminate inequalities, and to promote equality, between men and women.

Article 9

In defining and implementing its policies and activities, the Union shall take into account requirements linked to the promotion of a high level of employment, the guarantee of adequate social protection, the fight against social exclusion, and a high level of education, training and protection of human health.

Article 10

In defining and implementing its policies and activities, the Union shall aim to combat discrimination based on sex, racial or ethnic origin, religion or belief, disability, age or sexual orientation.

Article 11 (ex Article 6 TEC)

Environmental protection requirements must be integrated into the definition and implementation of the Union's policies and activities, in particular with a view to promoting sustainable development.

Article 12 (ex Article 153(2) TEC)

Consumer protection requirements shall be taken into account in defining and implementing other Union policies and activities.

Article 13

In formulating and implementing the Union's agriculture, fisheries, transport, internal market, research and technological development and space policies, the Union and the Member States shall, since animals are sentient beings, pay full regard to the welfare requirements of animals, while respecting the legislative or administrative provisions and customs of the Member States relating in particular to religious rites, cultural traditions and regional heritage.

Article 14 (ex Article 16 TEC)

, . . . [T]he Union and the Member States, each within their respective powers and within the scope of application of the Treaties, shall take care that such services [of general economic interest in the shared values of the Union as well as their role in promotiong social and territorial cohesion operate on the basis of principles and conditions, particularly economic and financial conditions, which enable them to fulfil their missions. . . .

Article 15 (ex Article 255 TEC)

1. In order to promote good governance and ensure the participation of civil society, the Union's institutions, bodies, offices and agencies shall conduct their work as openly as possible.

2. The European Parliament shall meet in public, as shall the Council when considering and voting on a draft legislative act.

3. Any citizen of the Union, and any natural or legal person residing or having its registered office in a Member State, shall have a right of access to documents of the Union's institutions, bodies, offices and agencies, whatever their medium, subject to the principles and the conditions to be defined in accordance with this paragraph. . . .

Article 16 (ex Article 286 TEC)

1. Everyone has the right to the protection of personal data concerning them. . . .

Article 17

1. The Union respects and does not prejudice the status under national law of churches and religious associations or communities in the Member States.

2. The Union equally respects the status under national law of philosophical and non-confessional organisations.

3. Recognising their identity and their specific contribution, the Union shall maintain an open, transparent and regular dialogue with these churches and organisations.

Part Two. Non-Discrimination and Citizenship of the Union

Article 18 (ex Article 12 TEC)

Within the scope of application of the Treaties, and without prejudice to any special provisions contained therein, any discrimination on grounds of nationality shall be prohibited. . . .

Article 19 (ex Article 13 TEC)

1. Without prejudice to the other provisions of the Treaties and within the limits of the powers conferred by them upon the Union, the Council, acting unanimously in accordance with a special legislative procedure and after obtaining the consent of the European Parliament, may take appropriate action to combat discrimination based on sex, racial or ethnic origin, religion or belief, disability, age or sexual orientation. . . .

Article 20 (ex Article 17 TEC)

1. Citizenship of the Union is hereby established. Every person holding the nationality of a Member State shall be a citizen of the Union. Citizenship of the Union shall be additional to and not replace national citizenship.

2. Citizens of the Union shall enjoy the rights and be subject to the duties provided for in the Treaties. They shall have, *inter alia*:

(a) the right to move and reside freely within the territory of the Member States;

(b) the right to vote and to stand as candidates in elections to the European Parliament and in municipal elections in their Member State of residence, under the same conditions as nationals of that State;

(c) the right to enjoy, in the territory of a third country in which the Member State of which they are nationals is not represented, the protection of the diplomatic and consular authorities of any Member State on the same conditions as the nationals of that State;

(d) the right to petition the European Parliament, to apply to the European Ombudsman, and to address the institutions and advisory bodies of the Union in any of the Treaty languages and to obtain a reply in the same language.

These rights shall be exercised in accordance with the conditions and limits defined by the Treaties and by the measures adopted thereunder.

Article 21 (ex Article 18 TEC)

1. Every citizen of the Union shall have the right to move and reside freely within the territory of the Member States, subject to the limitations and conditions laid down in the Treaties and by the measures adopted to give them effect. . . .

Article 22 (ex Article 19 TEC)

1. Every citizen of the Union residing in a Member State of which he is not a national shall have the right to vote and to stand as a candidate at municipal elections in the Member State in which he resides, under the same conditions as nationals of that State. . . .

2. Without prejudice to Article 223(1) and to the provisions adopted for its implementation, every citizen of the Union residing in a Member State of which he is not a national shall have the right to vote and to stand as a candidate in elections to the European Parliament in the Member State in which he resides, under the same conditions as nationals of that State. . . .

Article 23 (ex Article 20 TEC)

Every citizen of the Union shall, in the territory of a third country in which the Member State of which he is a national is not represented, be entitled to protection by the diplomatic or consular authorities of any Member State, on the same conditions as the nationals of that State. Member States shall adopt the necessary provisions and start the international negotiations required to secure this protection. . . .

Article 24 (ex Article 21 TEC)

The European Parliament and the Council, acting by means of regulations in accordance with the ordinary legislative procedure, shall adopt the provisions for the procedures and conditions required for a citizens' initiative within the meaning of Article 11 of the Treaty on European Union, including the minimum number of Member States from which such citizens must come.

Every citizen of the Union shall have the right to petition the European Parliament in accordance with Article 227.

Every citizen of the Union may apply to the Ombudsman established in accordance with Article 228.

Every citizen of the Union may write to any of the institutions or bodies referred to in this Article or in Article 13 of the Treaty on European Union in one of the languages mentioned in Article 55(1) of the Treaty on European Union and have an answer in the same language. . . .

Part Three. Union Policies and Internal Actions

TITLE I. THE INTERNAL MARKET

Article 26 (ex Article 14 TEC)

1. The Union shall adopt measures with the aim of establishing or ensuring the functioning of the internal market, in accordance with the relevant provisions of the Treaties.

2. The internal market shall comprise an area without internal frontiers in which the free movement of goods, persons, services and capital is ensured in accordance with the provisions of the Treaties. . . .

Article 27 (ex Article 15 TEC)

When drawing up its proposals with a view to achieving the objectives set out in Article 26, the Commission shall take into account the extent of the effort that certain economies showing differences in development will have to sustain for the establishment of the internal market and it may propose appropriate provisions. . . .

TITLE II. FREE MOVEMENT OF GOODS

Article 28 (ex Article 23 TEC)

1. The Union shall comprise a customs union which shall cover all trade in goods and which shall involve the prohibition between Member States of customs duties on imports and exports and of all charges having equivalent effect, and the adoption of a common customs tariff in their relations with third countries. . . .

2. The provisions of Article 30 and of Chapter 2 of this Title shall apply to products originating in Member States and to products coming from third countries which are in free circulation in Member States.

Article 29 (ex Article 24 TEC)

Products coming from a third country shall be considered to be in free circulation in a Member State if the import formalities have been complied with and any customs duties or charges having equivalent effect which are payable have been levied in that Member State, and if they have not benefited from a total or partial drawback of such duties or charges.

CHAPTER 1. THE CUSTOMS UNION

Article 30 (ex Article 25 TEC)

Customs duties on imports and exports and charges having equivalent effect shall be prohibited between Member States. This prohibition shall also apply to customs duties of a fiscal nature. . . .

CHAPTER 2. CUSTOMS COOPERATION

Article 33 (ex Article 135 TEC)

Within the scope of application of the Treaties, the European Parliament and the Council, acting in accordance with the ordinary legislative procedure, shall take measures in order to strengthen customs cooperation between Member States and between the latter and the Commission.

CHAPTER 3. PROHIBITION OF QUANTITATIVE RESTRICTIONS BETWEEN MEMBER STATES

Article 34 (ex Article 28 TEC)

Quantitative restrictions on imports and all measures having equivalent effect shall be prohibited between Member States.

Article 35 (ex Article 29 TEC)

Quantitative restrictions on exports, and all measures having equivalent effect, shall be prohibited between Member States.

Article 36 (ex Article 30 TEC)

The provisions of Articles 34 and 35 shall not preclude prohibitions or restrictions on imports, exports or goods in transit justified on grounds of public morality, public policy or public security; the protection of health and life of humans, animals or plants; the protection of national treasures possessing artistic, historic or archaeological value; or the protection of industrial and commercial property. Such prohibitions or restrictions shall not, however, constitute a means of arbitrary discrimination or a disguised restriction on trade between Member States. . . .

TITLE III. AGRICULTURE AND FISHERIES

Article 38 (ex Article 32 TEC)

1. The Union shall define and implement a common agriculture and fisheries policy.

The internal market shall extend to agriculture, fisheries and trade in agricultural products. . . .

Article 39 (ex Article 33 TEC)

1. The objectives of the common agricultural policy shall be:

(a) to increase agricultural productivity by promoting technical progress and by ensuring the rational development of agricultural production and the optimum utilisation of the factors of production, in particular labour;

(b) thus to ensure a fair standard of living for the agricultural community, in particular by increasing the individual earnings of persons engaged in agriculture;

(c) to stabilise markets;

(d) to assure the availability of supplies;

(e) to ensure that supplies reach consumers at reasonable prices. . . .

Article 40 (ex Article 34 TEC)

1. In order to attain the objectives set out in Article 39, a common organisation of agricultural markets shall be established. . . .

2. The common organisation established in accordance with paragraph 1 may include all measures required to attain the objectives set out in Article 39, in particular regulation of prices, aids for the production and marketing of the various products, storage and carryover arrangements and common machinery for stabilising imports or exports. . . .

TITLE IV. FREE MOVEMENT OF PERSONS, SERVICES AND CAPITAL

CHAPTER 1. WORKERS

Article 45 (ex Article 39 TEC)

1. Freedom of movement for workers shall be secured within the Union.

2. Such freedom of movement shall entail the abolition of any discrimination based on nationality between workers of the Member States as

regards employment, remuneration and other conditions of work and employment.

3. It shall entail the right, subject to limitations justified on grounds of public policy, public security or public health:

(a) to accept offers of employment actually made;

(b) to move freely within the territory of Member States for this purpose;

(c) to stay in a Member State for the purpose of employment in accordance with the provisions governing the employment of nationals of that State laid down by law, regulation or administrative action;

(d) to remain in the territory of a Member State after having been employed in that State, subject to conditions which shall be embodied in regulations to be drawn up by the Commission.

4. The provisions of this Article shall not apply to employment in the public service.

Article 46 (ex Article 40 TEC)

The European Parliament and the Council shall, acting in accordance with the ordinary legislative procedure and after consulting the Economic and Social Committee, issue directives or make regulations setting out the measures required to bring about freedom of movement for workers, as defined in Article 45. . . .

CHAPTER 2.   RIGHT OF ESTABLISHMENT

Article 49 (ex Article 43 TEC)

Within the framework of the provisions set out below, restrictions on the freedom of establishment of nationals of a Member State in the territory of another Member State shall be prohibited. Such prohibition shall also apply to restrictions on the setting-up of agencies, branches or subsidiaries by nationals of any Member State established in the territory of any Member State.

Freedom of establishment shall include the right to take up and pursue activities as self-employed persons and to set up and manage undertakings, in particular companies or firms within the meaning of the second paragraph of Article 54, under the conditions laid down for its own nationals by the law of the country where such establishment is effected, subject to the provisions of the Chapter relating to capital. . . .

Article 50 (ex Article 44 TEC)

1. In order to attain freedom of establishment as regards a particular activity, the European Parliament and the Council, acting in accordance with the ordinary legislative procedure and after consulting the Economic and Social Committee, shall act by means of directives. . . .

Article 53. (ex Article 47 TEC)

1. In order to make it easier for persons to take up and pursue activities as self-employed persons, the European Parliament and the Council shall, acting in accordance with the ordinary legislative procedure, issue directives for the mutual recognition of diplomas, certificates and other evidence of formal qualifications and for the coordination of the provisions laid down by law, regulation or administrative action in Member States concerning the taking-up and pursuit of activities as self-employed persons. . . .

Article 54 (ex Article 48 TEC)

Companies or firms formed in accordance with the law of a Member State and having their registered office, central administration or principal place of business within the Union shall, for the purposes of this Chapter, be treated in the same way as natural persons who are nationals of Member States.

"Companies or firms" means companies or firms constituted under civil or commercial law, including cooperative societies, and other legal persons governed by public or private law, save for those which are non-profit-making. . . .

CHAPTER 3.   SERVICES

Article 56 (ex Article 49 TEC)

Within the framework of the provisions set out below, restrictions on freedom to provide services within the Union shall be prohibited in respect of nationals of Member States who are established in a Member State other than that of the person for whom the services are intended. . . .

Article 57 (ex Article 50 TEC)

Services shall be considered to be "services" within the meaning of the Treaties where they are normally provided for remuneration, in so far as they are not governed by the provisions relating to freedom of movement for goods, capital and persons.

"Services" shall in particular include:
(a) activities of an industrial character;
(b) activities of a commercial character;
(c) activities of craftsmen;
(d) activities of the professions.

Without prejudice to the provisions of the Chapter relating to the right of establishment, the person providing a service may, in order to do so, temporarily pursue his activity in the Member State where the service is provided, under the same conditions as are imposed by that State on its own nationals.

Article 58 (ex Article 51 TEC)

1. Freedom to provide services in the field of transport shall be governed by the provisions of the Title relating to transport.

2. The liberalisation of banking and insurance services connected with movements of capital shall be effected in step with the liberalisation of movement of capital. . . .

Article 59 (ex Article 52 TEC)

1. In order to achieve the liberalisation of a specific service, the European Parliament and the Council, acting in accordance with the ordinary legislative procedure and after consulting the Economic and Social Committee, shall issue directives. . . .

CHAPTER 4.   CAPITAL AND PAYMENTS

Article 63 (ex Article 56 TEC)

1. Within the framework of the provisions set out in this Chapter, all restrictions on the movement of capital between Member States and between Member States and third countries shall be prohibited.

2. Within the framework of the provisions set out in this Chapter, all restrictions on payments between Member States and between Member States and third countries shall be prohibited.

Article 64 (ex Article 57 TEC)

1. The provisions of Article 63 shall be without prejudice to the application to third countries of any restrictions which exist on 31 December 1993 under national or Union law adopted in respect of the movement of capital to or from third countries involving direct investment – including in real estate – establishment, the provision of financial services or the admission of securities to capital markets. . . .

Article 66 (ex Article 59 TEC)

Where, in exceptional circumstances, movements of capital to or from third countries cause, or threaten to cause, serious difficulties for the operation of economic and monetary union, the Council, on a proposal from the Commission and after consulting the European Central Bank, may take safeguard measures with regard to third countries for a period not exceeding six months if such measures are strictly necessary.

Title V. Area of Freedom, Security and Justice

Chapter 1. General Provisions

Article 67 (ex Article 61 TEC and ex Article 29 TEU)

1. The Union shall constitute an area of freedom, security and justice with respect for fundamental rights and the different legal systems and traditions of the Member States.

2. It shall ensure the absence of internal border controls for persons and shall frame a common policy on asylum, immigration and external border control, based on solidarity between Member States, which is fair towards third-country nationals. For the purpose of this Title, stateless persons shall be treated as third-country nationals.

3. The Union shall endeavour to ensure a high level of security through measures to prevent and combat crime, racism and xenophobia, and through measures for coordination and cooperation between police and judicial authorities and other competent authorities, as well as through the mutual recognition of judgments in criminal matters and, if necessary, through the approximation of criminal laws.

4. The Union shall facilitate access to justice, in particular through the principle of mutual recognition of judicial and extrajudicial decisions in civil matters. . . .

Article 69

National Parliaments ensure that the proposals and legislative initiatives submitted under Chapters 4 and 5 comply with the principle of subsidiarity, in accordance with the arrangements laid down by the Protocol on the application of the principles of subsidiarity and proportionality. . . .

Article 71 (ex Article 36 TEU)

A standing committee shall be set up within the Council in order to ensure that operational cooperation on internal security is promoted and strengthened within the Union. . . .

Article 72 (ex Article 64(1) TEC and ex Article 33 TEU)

This Title shall not affect the exercise of the responsibilities incumbent upon Member States with regard to the maintenance of law and order and the safeguarding of internal security.

Article 73

It shall be open to Member States to organise between themselves and under their responsibility such forms of cooperation and coordination as they deem appropriate between the competent departments of their administrations responsible for safeguarding national security. . . .

CHAPTER 2. POLICIES ON BORDER CHECKS, ASYLUM AND IMMIGRATION

Article 77 (ex Article 62 TEC)

1. The Union shall develop a policy with a view to:

(a) ensuring the absence of any controls on persons, whatever their nationality, when crossing internal borders;

(b) carrying out checks on persons and efficient monitoring of the crossing of external borders;

(c) the gradual introduction of an integrated management system for external borders. . . .

Article 78 (ex Articles 63, points 1 and 2, and 64(2) TEC)

1. The Union shall develop a common policy on asylum, subsidiary protection and temporary protection with a view to offering appropriate status to any third-country national requiring international protection and ensuring compliance with the principle of *non-refoulement*. This policy must be in accordance with the Geneva Convention of 28 July 1951 and the Protocol of 31 January 1967 relating to the status of refugees, and other relevant treaties.

2. For the purposes of paragraph 1, the European Parliament and the Council, acting in accordance with the ordinary legislative procedure, shall adopt measures for a common European asylum system comprising:

(a) a uniform status of asylum for nationals of third countries, valid throughout the Union;

(b) a uniform status of subsidiary protection for nationals of third countries who, without obtaining European asylum, are in need of international protection;

(c) a common system of temporary protection for displaced persons in the event of a massive inflow;

(d) common procedures for the granting and withdrawing of uniform asylum or subsidiary protection status;

(e) criteria and mechanisms for determining which Member State is responsible for considering an application for asylum or subsidiary protection;

(f) standards concerning the conditions for the reception of applicants for asylum or subsidiary protection;

(g) partnership and cooperation with third countries for the purpose of managing inflows of people applying for asylum or subsidiary or temporary protection.

3. In the event of one or more Member States being confronted by an emergency situation characterised by a sudden inflow of nationals of third countries, the Council, on a proposal from the Commission, may adopt provisional measures for the benefit of the Member State(s) concerned. It shall act after consulting the European Parliament.

Article 79 (ex Article 63, points 3 and 4, TEC)

1. The Union shall develop a common immigration policy aimed at ensuring, at all stages, the efficient management of migration flows, fair treatment of third-country nationals residing legally in Member States, and the prevention of, and enhanced measures to combat, illegal immigration and trafficking in human beings.

2. For the purposes of paragraph 1, the European Parliament and the Council, acting in accordance with the ordinary legislative procedure, shall adopt measures in the following areas:

(a) the conditions of entry and residence, and standards on the issue by Member States of long-term visas and residence permits, including those for the purpose of family reunification;

(b) the definition of the rights of third-country nationals residing legally in a Member State, including the conditions governing freedom of movement and of residence in other Member States;

(c) illegal immigration and unauthorised residence, including removal and repatriation of persons residing without authorisation;

(d) combating trafficking in persons, in particular women and children.

3. The Union may conclude agreements with third countries for the readmission to their countries of origin or provenance of third-country nationals who do not or who no longer fulfil the conditions for entry, presence or residence in the territory of one of the Member States.

4. The European Parliament and the Council, acting in accordance with the ordinary legislative procedure, may establish measures to provide incentives and support for the action of Member States with a view to promoting the integration of third-country nationals residing legally in their territories, excluding any harmonisation of the laws and regulations of the Member States.

5. This Article shall not affect the right of Member States to determine volumes of admission of third-country nationals coming from third countries to their territory in order to seek work, whether employed or self-employed.

CHAPTER 3. JUDICIAL COOPERATION IN CIVIL MATTERS

Article 81 (ex Article 65 TEC)

1. The Union shall develop judicial cooperation in civil matters having cross-border implications, based on the principle of mutual recognition of judgments and of decisions in extrajudicial cases. Such cooperation may include the adoption of measures for the approximation of the laws and regulations of the Member States.

2. For the purposes of paragraph 1, the European Parliament and the Council, acting in accordance with the ordinary legislative procedure, shall adopt measures, particularly when necessary for the proper functioning of the internal market, aimed at ensuring:

(a) the mutual recognition and enforcement between Member States of judgments and of decisions in extrajudicial cases;

(b) the cross-border service of judicial and extrajudicial documents;

(c) the compatibility of the rules applicable in the Member States concerning conflict of laws and of jurisdiction;

(d) cooperation in the taking of evidence;

(e) effective access to justice;

(f) the elimination of obstacles to the proper functioning of civil proceedings, if necessary by promoting the compatibility of the rules on civil procedure applicable in the Member States;

(g) the development of alternative methods of dispute settlement . . . .

CHAPTER 4.   JUDICIAL COOPERATION IN CRIMINAL MATTERS

Article 82 (ex Article 31 TEU)

1. Judicial cooperation in criminal matters in the Union shall be based on the principle of mutual recognition of judgments and judicial decisions and shall include the approximation of the laws and regulations of the Member States in the areas referred to in paragraph 2 and in Article 83. . . .

2. To the extent necessary to facilitate mutual recognition of judgments and judicial decisions and police and judicial cooperation in criminal matters having a cross-border dimension, the European Parliament and the Council may, by means of directives adopted in accordance with the ordinary legislative procedure, establish minimum rules. Such rules shall take into account the differences between the legal traditions and systems of the Member States.

Article 83 (ex Article 31 TEU)

1. The European Parliament and the Council may, by means of directives adopted in accordance with the ordinary legislative procedure, establish minimum rules concerning the definition of criminal offences and sanctions in the areas of particularly serious crime with a cross-border dimension resulting from the nature or impact of such offences or from a special need to combat them on a common basis. . . .

Article 85 (ex Article 31 TEU)

1. Eurojust's mission shall be to support and strengthen coordination and cooperation between national investigating and prosecuting authorities in relation to serious crime affecting two or more Member States or requiring a prosecution on common bases, on the basis of operations conducted and information supplied by the Member States' authorities and by Europol. . . .

Article 86

1. In order to combat crimes affecting the financial interests of the Union, the Council, by means of regulations adopted in accordance with a special legislative procedure, may establish a European Public Prosecutor's Office from Eurojust. . . .

2. The European Public Prosecutor's Office shall be responsible for investigating, prosecuting and bringing to judgment, where appropriate in liaison with Europol, the perpetrators of, and accomplices in, offences against the Union's financial interests, as determined by the regulation provided for in paragraph 1. . . .

CHAPTER 5. POLICE COOPERATION

Article 87 **(ex Article 30 TEU)**

1. The Union shall establish police cooperation involving all the Member States' competent authorities, including police, customs and other specialised law enforcement services in relation to the prevention, detection and investigation of criminal offences. . . .

TITLE VI. TRANSPORT

Article 90 **(ex Article 70 TEC)**

The objectives of the Treaties shall, in matters governed by this Title, be pursued within the framework of a common transport policy. . . .

TITLE VII. COMMON RULES ON COMPETITION, TAXATION AND APPROXIMATION OF LAWS

CHAPTER 1. RULES ON COMPETITION

Section 1. Rules Applying to Undertakings

Article 101 **(ex Article 81 TEC)**

1. The following shall be prohibited as incompatible with the internal market: all agreements between undertakings, decisions by associations of undertakings and concerted practices which may affect trade between Member States and which have as their object or effect the prevention, restriction or distortion of competition within the internal market, and in particular those which:

(a) directly or indirectly fix purchase or selling prices or any other trading conditions;

(b) limit or control production, markets, technical development, or investment;

(c) share markets or sources of supply;

(d) apply dissimilar conditions to equivalent transactions with other trading parties, thereby placing them at a competitive disadvantage;

(e) make the conclusion of contracts subject to acceptance by the other parties of supplementary obligations which, by their nature or according to commercial usage, have no connection with the subject of such contracts. . . .

Article 102 (ex Article 82 TEC)

Any abuse by one or more undertakings of a dominant position within the internal market or in a substantial part of it shall be prohibited as incompatible with the internal market in so far as it may affect trade between Member States.

Such abuse may, in particular, consist in:

(a) directly or indirectly imposing unfair purchase or selling prices or other unfair trading conditions;

(b) limiting production, markets or technical development to the prejudice of consumers;

(c) applying dissimilar conditions to equivalent transactions with other trading parties, thereby placing them at a competitive disadvantage;

(d) making the conclusion of contracts subject to acceptance by the other parties of supplementary obligations which, by their nature or according to commercial usage, have no connection with the subject of such contracts. . . .

Section 2. Aids Granted by States

Article 107 (ex Article 87 TEC)

1. Save as otherwise provided in the Treaties, any aid granted by a Member State or through State resources in any form whatsoever which distorts or threatens to distort competition by favouring certain undertakings or the production of certain goods shall, in so far as it affects trade between Member States, be incompatible with the internal market. . . .

CHAPTER 2. TAX PROVISIONS

Article 110 (ex Article 90 TEC)

No Member State shall impose, directly or indirectly, on the products of other Member States any internal taxation of any kind in excess of that imposed directly or indirectly on similar domestic products.

Furthermore, no Member State shall impose on the products of other Member States any internal taxation of such a nature as to afford indirect protection to other products. . . .

CHAPTER 3. APPROXIMATION OF LAWS

Article 114 (ex Article 95 TEC)

1. . . . The European Parliament and the Council shall, acting in accordance with the ordinary legislative procedure and after consulting the Economic and Social Committee, adopt the measures for the approximation of the provisions laid down by law, regulation or administrative action in Member States which have as their object the establishment and functioning of the internal market. . . .

Article 116 (ex Article 96 TEC)

Where the Commission finds that a difference between the provisions laid down by law, regulation or administrative action in Member States is distorting the conditions of competition in the internal market and that the resultant distortion needs to be eliminated, it shall consult the Member States concerned.

If such consultation does not result in an agreement eliminating the distortion in question, the European, Parliament and the Council, acting in accordance with the ordinary legislative procedure, shall issue the necessary directives. Any other appropriate measures provided for in the Treaties may be adopted. . . .

Article 118

In the context of the establishment and functioning of the internal market, the European Parliament and the Council, acting in accordance with the ordinary legislative procedure, shall establish measures for the creation of European intellectual property rights to provide uniform protection of intellectual property rights throughout the Union and for the setting up of centralised Union-wide authorisation, coordination and supervision arrangements. . . .

TITLE VIII. ECONOMIC AND MONETARY POLICY

Article 119 (ex Article 4 TEC)

1. For the purposes set out in Article 3 of the Treaty on European Union, the activities of the Member States and the Union shall include, as provided in the Treaties, the adoption of an economic policy which is based on the close coordination of Member States' economic policies, on the internal market and on the definition of common objectives, and conducted in accordance with the principle of an open market economy with free competition.

2. Concurrently with the foregoing, and as provided in the Treaties and in accordance with the procedures set out therein, these activities shall include a single currency, the euro, and the definition and conduct of a single monetary policy and exchange-rate policy the primary objective of both of

which shall be to maintain price stability and, without prejudice to this objective, to support the general economic policies in the Union, in accordance with the principle of an open market economy with free competition.

3. These activities of the Member States and the Union shall entail compliance with the following guiding principles: stable prices, sound public finances and monetary conditions and a sustainable balance of payments.

CHAPTER 1. ECONOMIC POLICY

Article 120 **(ex Article 98 TEC)**

Member States shall conduct their economic policies with a view to contributing to the achievement of the objectives of the Union, as defined in Article 3 of the Treaty on European Union, and in the context of the broad guidelines referred to in Article 121(2). . . .

Article 121 **(ex Article 99 TEC)**

1. Member States shall regard their economic policies as a matter of common concern and shall coordinate them within the Council, in accordance with the provisions of Article 120. . . .

Article 125 **(ex Article 103 TEC)**

1. The Union shall not be liable for or assume the commitments of central governments, regional, local or other public authorities, other bodies governed by public law, or public undertakings of any Member State, without prejudice to mutual financial guarantees for the joint execution of a specific project. . . .

Article 126 **(ex Article 104 TEC)**

1. Member States shall avoid excessive government deficits.

2. The Commission shall monitor the development of the budgetary situation and of the stock of government debt in the Member States with a view to identifying gross errors. . . .

CHAPTER 2. MONETARY POLICY

Article 127 **(ex Article 105 TEC)**

1. The primary objective of the European System of Central Banks (hereinafter referred to as "the ESCB") shall be to maintain price stability. Without prejudice to the objective of price stability, the ESCB shall support the general economic policies in the Union with a view to contributing to the achievement of the objectives of the Union as laid down in Article 3 of the Treaty on European Union. The ESCB shall act in accordance with the principle of an open market economy with free competition, favouring an

efficient allocation of resources, and in compliance with the principles set out in Article 119. . . .

Article 128 (ex Article 106 TEC)

1. The European Central Bank shall have the exclusive right to authorise the issue of euro banknotes within the Union. The European Central Bank and the national central banks may issue such notes. The banknotes issued by the European Central Bank and the national central banks shall be the only such notes to have the status of legal tender within the Union. . . .

CHAPTER 4. PROVISIONS SPECIFIC TO MEMBER STATES WHOSE CURRENCY IS THE EURO

Article 136

1. In order to ensure the proper functioning of economic and monetary union, and in accordance with the relevant provisions of the Treaties, the Council shall, in accordance with the relevant procedure from among those referred to in Articles 121 and 126, with the exception of the procedure set out in Article 126(14), adopt measures specific to those Member States whose currency is the euro:

(a) to strengthen the coordination and surveillance of their budgetary discipline;

(b) to set out economic policy guidelines for them, while ensuring that they are compatible with those adopted for the whole of the Union and are kept under surveillance. . . .

CHAPTER 5. TRANSITIONAL PROVISIONS

Article 139

1. Member States in respect of which the Council has not decided that they fulfil the necessary conditions for the adoption of the euro shall hereinafter be referred to as "Member States with a derogation". . . .

Article 142 (ex Article 124(1) TEC)

Each Member State with a derogation shall treat its exchange-rate policy as a matter of common interest. In so doing, Member States shall take account of the experience acquired in cooperation within the framework of the exchange-rate mechanism.

Article 143 (ex Article 119 TEC)

1. Where a Member State with a derogation is in difficulties or is seriously threatened with difficulties as regards its balance of payments either as

a result of an overall disequilibrium in its balance of payments, or as a result of the type of currency at its disposal, and where such difficulties are liable in particular to jeopardise the functioning of the internal market or the implementation of the common commercial policy, the Commission shall immediately investigate the position of the State in question and the action which, making use of all the means at its disposal, that State has taken or may take in accordance with the provisions of the Treaties. The Commission shall state what measures it recommends the State concerned to take.

If the action taken by a Member State with a derogation and the measures suggested by the Commission do not prove sufficient to overcome the difficulties which have arisen or which threaten, the Commission shall, after consulting the Economic and Financial Committee, recommend to the Council the granting of mutual assistance and appropriate methods therefor.

The Commission shall keep the Council regularly informed of the situation and of how it is developing.

2. The Council shall grant such mutual assistance; it shall adopt directives or decisions laying down the conditions and details of such assistance . . . .

Article 144 (ex Article 120 TEC)

1. Where a sudden crisis in the balance of payments occurs and a decision within the meaning of Article 143(2) is not immediately taken, a Member State with a derogation may, as a precaution, take the necessary protective measures. Such measures must cause the least possible disturbance in the functioning of the internal market and must not be wider in scope than is strictly necessary to remedy the sudden difficulties which have arisen. . . .

TITLE IX.   EMPLOYMENT

Article 145 (ex Article 125 TEC)

Member States and the Union shall, in accordance with this Title, work towards developing a coordinated strategy for employment and particularly for promoting a skilled, trained and adaptable workforce and labour markets responsive to economic change with a view to achieving the objectives defined in Article 3 of the Treaty on European Union. . . .

TITLE X.   SOCIAL POLICY

Article 151 (ex Article 136 TEC)

The Union and the Member States, having in mind fundamental social rights such as those set out in the European Social Charter signed at Turin on 18 October 1961 and in the 1989 Community Charter of the Fundamental Social Rights of Workers, shall have as their objectives the promotion of employment, improved living and working conditions, so as to make possible their harmonisation while the improvement is being maintained, proper social protection, dialogue between management and labour, the development of human resources with a view to lasting high employment and the combating of exclusion. . . .

Article 157 (ex Article 141 TEC)

1. Each Member State shall ensure that the principle of equal pay for male and female workers for equal work or work of equal value is applied. . . .

4. With a view to ensuring full equality in practice between men and women in working life, the principle of equal treatment shall not prevent any Member State from maintaining or adopting measures providing for specific advantages in order to make it easier for the underrepresented sex to pursue a vocational activity or to prevent or compensate for disadvantages in professional careers. . . .

TITLE XI. THE EUROPEAN SOCIAL FUND

Article 162 (ex Article 146 TEC)

In order to improve employment opportunities for workers in the internal market and to contribute thereby to raising the standard of living, a European Social Fund is hereby established in accordance with the provisions set out below; it shall aim to render the employment of workers easier and to increase their geographical and occupational mobility within the Union, and to facilitate their adaptation to industrial changes and to changes in production systems, in particular through vocational training and retraining. . . .

TITLE XII. EDUCATION, VOCATIONAL TRAINING, YOUTH AND SPORT

Article 165 (ex Article 149 TEC)

1. The Union shall contribute to the development of quality education by encouraging cooperation between Member States and, if necessary, by supporting and supplementing their action, while fully respecting the responsibility of the Member States for the content of teaching and the organisation of education systems and their cultural and linguistic diversity.

The Union shall contribute to the promotion of European sporting issues, while taking account of the specific nature of sport, its structures based on voluntary activity and its social and educational function. . . .

Article 166 (ex Article 150 TEC)

1. The Union shall implement a vocational training policy which shall support and supplement the action of the Member States, while fully respecting the responsibility of the Member States for the content and organisation of vocational training. . . .

TITLE XIII. CULTURE

Article 167 (ex Article 151 TEC)

1. The Union shall contribute to the flowering of the cultures of the Member States, while respecting their national and regional diversity and at the same time bringing the common cultural heritage to the fore. . . .

TITLE XIV. PUBLIC HEALTH

Article 168 (ex Article 152 TEC)

1. A high level of human health protection shall be ensured in the definition and implementation of all Union policies and activities.

Union action, which shall complement national policies, shall be directed towards improving public health, preventing physical and mental illness and diseases, and obviating sources of danger to physical and mental health. Such action shall cover the fight against the major health scourges, by promoting research into their causes, their transmission and their prevention, as well as health information and education, and monitoring, early warning of and combating serious cross-border threats to health. . . .

TITLE XV. CONSUMER PROTECTION

Article 169 (ex Article 153 TEC)

1. In order to promote the interests of consumers and to ensure a high level of consumer protection, the Union shall contribute to protecting the health, safety and economic interests of consumers, as well as to promoting their right to information, education and to organise themselves in order to safeguard their interests. . . .

TITLE XVI. TRANS-EUROPEAN NETWORKS

Article 170 (ex Article 154 TEC)

1. To help achieve the objectives referred to in Articles 26 and 174 and to enable citizens of the Union, economic operators and regional and local communities to derive full benefit from the setting-up of an area without internal frontiers, the Union shall contribute to the establishment and development of trans-European networks in the areas of transport, telecommunications and energy infrastructures. . . .

TITLE XVII. INDUSTRY

Article 173 (ex Article 157 TEC)

1. The Union and the Member States shall ensure that the conditions necessary for the competitiveness of the Union's industry exist. . . .

TITLE XVIII. ECONOMIC, SOCIAL AND TERRITORIAL COHESION

Article 174 (ex Article 158 TEC)

In order to promote its overall harmonious development, the Union shall develop and pursue its actions leading to the strengthening of its economic, social and territorial cohesion.

In particular, the Union shall aim at reducing disparities between the levels of development of the various regions and the backwardness of the least favoured regions.

Among the regions concerned, particular attention shall be paid to rural areas, areas affected by industrial transition, and regions which suffer from severe and permanent natural or demographic handicaps such as the northernmost regions with very low population density and island, cross-border and mountain regions. . . .

TITLE XIX. RESEARCH AND TECHNOLOGICAL DEVELOPMENT AND SPACE

Article 179 (ex Article 163 TEC)

1. The Union shall have the objective of strengthening its scientific and technological bases by achieving a European research area in which researchers, scientific knowledge and technology circulate freely, and encouraging it to become more competitive, including in its industry, while promoting all the research activities deemed necessary by virtue of other Chapters of the Treaties. . . .

Article 189

1. To promote scientific and technical progress, industrial competitiveness and the implementation of its policies, the Union shall draw up a European space policy. To this end, it may promote joint initiatives, support research and technological development and coordinate the efforts needed for the exploration and exploitation of space. . . .

TITLE XX.   ENVIRONMENT

Article 191 (ex Article 174 TEC)

1. Union policy on the environment shall contribute to pursuit of the following objectives:
—preserving, protecting and improving the quality of the environment,
—protecting human health,
—prudent and rational utilisation of natural resources,
—promoting measures at international level to deal with regional or worldwide environmental problems, and in particular combating climate change. . . .

2. Union policy on the environment shall aim at a high level of protection taking into account the diversity of situations in the various regions of the Union. It shall be based on the precautionary principle and on the principles that preventive action should be taken, that environmental damage should as a priority be rectified at source and that the polluter should pay.

In this context, harmonisation measures answering environmental protection requirements shall include, where appropriate, a safeguard clause allowing Member States to take provisional measures, for non-economic environmental reasons, subject to a procedure of inspection by the Union.

Article 193 (ex Article 176 TEC)

The protective measures adopted pursuant to Article 192 shall not prevent any Member State from maintaining or introducing more stringent protective measures. Such measures must be compatible with the Treaties. . . .

TITLE XXI.   ENERGY

Article 194

1. In the context of the establishment and functioning of the internal market and with regard for the need to preserve and improve the environment, Union policy on energy shall aim, in a spirit of solidarity between Member States, to:
(a) ensure the functioning of the energy market;
(b) ensure security of energy supply in the Union;
(c) promote energy efficiency and energy saving and the development of new and renewable forms of energy; and
(d) promote the interconnection of energy networks. . . .

TITLE XXII.   TOURISM

Article 195

1. The Union shall complement the action of the Member States in the tourism sector, in particular by promoting the competitiveness of Union undertakings in that sector. . . .

TITLE XXIII. CIVIL PROTECTION

Article 196

1. The Union shall encourage cooperation between Member States in order to improve the effectiveness of systems for preventing and protecting against natural or man-made disasters. . . .

TITLE XXIV. ADMINISTRATIVE COOPERATION

Article 197

1. Effective implementation of Union law by the Member States, which is essential for the proper functioning of the Union, shall be regarded as a matter of common interest.

2. The Union may support the efforts of Member States to improve their administrative capacity to implement Union law. . . .

Part Four. Association of the Overseas Countries and Territories

Article 198 (ex Article 182 TEC)

The Member States agree to associate with the Union the non-European countries and territories which have special relations with Denmark, France, the Netherlands and the United Kingdom. These countries and territories (hereinafter called the "countries and territories") are listed in Annex II.

The purpose of association shall be to promote the economic and social development of the countries and territories and to establish close economic relations between them and the Union as a whole. . . .

Part Five. The Union's External Action

TITLE I. GENERAL PROVISIONS on THE UNION'S EXTERNAL ACTION

Article 205

The Union's action on the international scene, pursuant to this Part, shall be guided by the principles, pursue the objectives and be conducted in accordance with the general provisions laid down in Chapter 1 of Title V of the Treaty on European Union.

TITLE II. COMMON COMMERCIAL POLICY

Article 206 (ex Article 131 TEC)

By establishing a customs union in accordance with Articles 28 to 32, the Union shall contribute, in the common interest, to the harmonious development of world trade, the progressive abolition of restrictions on international trade and on foreign direct investment, and the lowering of customs and other barriers. . . .

Article 207 (ex Article 133 TEC)

1. The common commercial policy shall be based on uniform principles, particularly with regard to changes in tariff rates, the conclusion of tariff and trade agreements relating to trade in goods and services, and the commercial aspects of intellectual property, foreign direct investment, the achievement of uniformity in measures of liberalisation, export policy and measures to protect trade such as those to be taken in the event of dumping or subsidies. The common commercial policy shall be conducted in the context of the principles and objectives of the Union's external action.

2. The European Parliament and the Council, acting by means of regulations in accordance with the ordinary legislative procedure, shall adopt the measures defining the framework for implementing the common commercial policy.

3. Where agreements with one or more third countries or international organisations need to be negotiated and concluded, Article 218 shall apply, subject to the special provisions of this Article.

The Commission shall make recommendations to the Council, which shall authorise it to open the necessary negotiations. The Council and the Commission shall be responsible for ensuring that the agreements negotiated are compatible with internal Union policies and rules.

The Commission shall conduct these negotiations in consultation with a special committee appointed by the Council to assist the Commission in this task and within the framework of such directives as the Council may issue to it. The Commission shall report regularly to the special committee and to the European Parliament on the progress of negotiations.

4. For the negotiation and conclusion of the agreements referred to in paragraph 3, the Council shall act by a qualified majority.

For the negotiation and conclusion of agreements in the fields of trade in services and the commercial aspects of intellectual property, as well as foreign direct investment, the Council shall act unanimously where such agreements include provisions for which unanimity is required for the adoption of internal rules. . . .

TITLE III.   COOPERATION WITH THIRD COUNTRIES AND HUMANITARIAN AID

CHAPTER 1.   DEVELOPMENT COOPERATION

Article 208 (ex Article 177 TEC)

1. Union policy in the field of development cooperation shall be conducted within the framework of the principles and objectives of the Union's external action. The Union's development cooperation policy and that of the Member States complement and reinforce each other.

Union development cooperation policy shall have as its primary objective the reduction and, in the long term, the eradication of poverty. . . .

CHAPTER 2.   ECONOMIC, FINANCIAL AND TECHNICAL COOPERATION WITH THIRD COUNTRIES

Article 212 (ex Article 181a TEC)

1. Without prejudice to the other provisions of the Treaties, and in particular Articles 208 to 211, the Union shall carry out economic, financial and technical cooperation measures, including assistance, in particular financial assistance, with third countries other than developing countries. . . .

CHAPTER 3.   HUMANITARIAN AID

Article 214

1. The Union's operations in the field of humanitarian aid shall be conducted within the framework of the principles and objectives of the external action of the Union. Such operations shall be intended to provide *ad hoc* assistance and relief and protection for people in third countries who are victims of natural or man-made disasters, in order to meet the humanitarian needs resulting from these different situations. . . .

TITLE IV.   RESTRICTIVE MEASURES

Article 215 (ex Article 301 TEC)

1. Where a decision, adopted in accordance with Chapter 2 of Title V of the Treaty on European Union, provides for the interruption or reduction, in part or completely, of economic and financial relations with one or more third countries, the Council, acting by a qualified majority on a joint proposal from the High Representative of the Union for Foreign Affairs and Security Policy and the Commission, shall adopt the necessary measures. It shall inform the European Parliament thereof.

2. Where a decision adopted in accordance with Chapter 2 of Title V of the Treaty on European Union so provides, the Council may adopt restrictive measures under the procedure referred to in paragraph 1 against natural or legal persons and groups or non-State entities.

3. The acts referred to in this Article shall include necessary provisions on legal safeguards.

TITLE V.   INTERNATIONAL AGREEMENTS

Article 216

1. The Union may conclude an agreement with one or more third countries or international organisations where the Treaties so provide or where the conclusion of an agreement is necessary in order to achieve, within the framework of the Union's policies, one of the objectives referred to in the Treaties, or is provided for in a legally binding Union act or is likely to affect common rules or alter their scope.

2. Agreements concluded by the Union are binding upon the institutions of the Union and on its Member States.

Article 217 **(ex Article 310 TEC)**

The Union may conclude with one or more third countries or international organisations agreements establishing an association involving reciprocal rights and obligations, common action and special procedure.

Article 218 **(ex Article 300 TEC)**

1. Without prejudice to the specific provisions laid down in Article 207, agreements between the Union and third countries or international organisations shall be negotiated and concluded in accordance with the following procedure.

2. The Council shall authorize the opening of negotiations, adopt negotiating directives, authorize the signing or agreements and conclude them.

3. The Commission, or the High Representative of the Union for Foreign Affairs and Security Policy where the agreement envisaged relates exclusively or principally to the common foreign and security policy, shall submit recommendations to the Council, which shall adopt a decision authorizing the opening of negotiations and, depending on the subject of the agreement envisaged, nominating the Union negotiator or the head of the Union's negotiating team.

4. The Council may address directives to the negotiator and designate a special committee in consultation with which the negotiations must be conducted.

5. The Council, on a proposal by the negotiator, shall adopt a decision authorising the signing of the agreement and, if necessary, its provisional application before entry into force.

6. The Council, on a proposal by the negotiator, shall adopt a decision concluding the agreement.

Except where agreements relate exclusively to the common foreign and security policy, the Council shall adopt the decision concluding the agreement.

(a) after obtaining the consent of the European Parliament in the following cases: . . . .

(b) after consulting the European Parliament in other cases. . . .

8. The Council shall act by a qualified majority throughout the procedure.

However, it shall act unanimously when the agreement covers a field for which unanimity is required for the adoption of a Union act as well as for association agreements and the agreements referred to in Article 212 with the States which are candidates for accession. . . .

10. The European Parliament shall be immediately and fully informed at all stages of the procedure.

11. A Member State, the European Parliament, the Council or the Commission may obtain the opinion of the Court of Justice as to whether an agreement envisaged is compatible with the Treaties. Where the opinion of the Court is adverse, the agreement envisaged may not enter into force unless it is amended or the Treaties are revised. . . .

TITLE VI. THE UNION'S RELATIONS WITH INTERNATIONAL ORGANISATIONS AND THIRD COUNTRIES AND UNION DELEGATIONS

Article 220 (ex Articles 302 to 304 TEC)

1. The Union shall establish all appropriate forms of cooperation with the organs of the United Nations and its specialised agencies, the Council of Europe, the Organisation for Security and Cooperation in Europe and the Organisation for Economic Cooperation and Development.

The Union shall also maintain such relations as are appropriate with other international organisations. . . .

2. The High Representative of the Union for Foreign Affairs and Security Policy and the Commission shall implement this Article.

Article 221

1. Union delegations in third countries and at international organisations shall represent the Union.

2. Union delegations shall be placed under the authority of the High Representative of the Union for Foreign Affairs and Security Policy. They shall act in close cooperation with Member States' diplomatic and consular missions.

TITLE VII. SOLIDARITY CLAUSE

Article 222

1. The Union and its Member States shall act jointly in a spirit of solidarity if a Member State is the object of a terrorist attack or the victim of a natural or man-made disaster. The Union shall mobilise all the instruments at its disposal, including the military resources made available by the Member States. . . .

Part Six. Part Six. Institutional and Financial Provisions

TITLE I. INSTITUTIONAL PROVISIONS

CHAPTER 1. THE INSTITUTIONS

Section 1. The European Parliament

Article 223 (ex Article 190(4) and (5) TEC)

1. The European Parliament shall draw up a proposal to lay down the provisions necessary for the election of its Members by direct universal suffrage in accordance with a uniform procedure in all Member States or in accordance with principles common to all Member States.

The Council, acting unanimously in accordance with a special legislative procedure and after obtaining the consent of the European Parliament, which shall act by a majority of its component Members, shall lay down the necessary provisions. These provisions shall enter into force following their approval by the Member States in accordance with their respective constitutional requirements. . . .

Article 224 (ex Article 191, second subparagraph, TEC)

The European Parliament and the Council, acting in accordance with the ordinary legislative procedure, by means of regulations, shall lay down the regulations governing political parties at European level referred to in Article 10(4) of the Treaty on European Union and in particular the rules regarding their funding.

Article 225 (ex Article 192, second subparagraph, TEC)

The European Parliament may, acting by a majority of its component Members, request the Commission to submit any appropriate proposal on matters on which it considers that a Union act is required for the purpose of implementing the Treaties. If the Commission does not submit a proposal, it shall inform the European Parliament of the reasons. . . .

Article 227 (ex Article 194 TEC)

Any citizen of the Union, and any natural or legal person residing or having its registered office in a Member State, shall have the right to address, individually or in association with other citizens or persons, a petition to the European Parliament on a matter which comes within the Union's fields of activity and which affects him, her or it directly.

Article 228 (ex Article 195 TEC)

1. A European Ombudsman, elected by the European Parliament, shall be empowered to receive complaints from any citizen of the Union or any natural or legal person residing or having its registered office in a Member State concerning instances of maladministration in the activities of the Union institutions, bodies, offices or agencies, with the exception of the Court of Justice of the European Union acting in its judicial role. He or she shall examine such complaints and report on them.

In accordance with his duties, the Ombudsman shall conduct inquiries for which he finds grounds, either on his own initiative or on the basis of complaints submitted to him direct or through a Member of the European Parliament, except where the alleged facts are or have been the subject of legal proceedings. Where the Ombudsman establishes an instance of maladministration, he shall refer the matter to the institution, body, office or agency concerned, which shall have a period of three months in which to inform him of its views. The Ombudsman shall then forward a report to the European Parliament and the institution, body, office or agency concerned. The person lodging the complaint shall be informed of the outcome of such inquiries. . . .

2. The Ombudsman shall be elected after each election of the European Parliament for the duration of its term of office. The Ombudsman shall be eligible for reappointment. . . .

3. The Ombudsman shall be completely independent in the performance of his duties. In the performance of those duties he shall neither seek nor take instructions from any Government, institution, body, office or entity. The Ombudsman may not, during his term of office, engage in any other occupation, whether gainful or not. . . .

Article 231 (ex Article 198 TEC)

Save as otherwise provided in the Treaties, the European Parliament shall act by a majority of the votes cast. . . .

Article 234 (ex Article 201 TEC)

If a motion of censure on the activities of the Commission is tabled before it, the European Parliament shall not vote thereon until at least three days after the motion has been tabled and only by open vote.

If the motion of censure is carried by a two-thirds majority of the votes cast, representing a majority of the component Members of the European Parliament, the members of the Commission shall resign as a body and the High Representative of the Union for Foreign Affairs and Security Policy shall resign from duties that he or she carries out in the Commission. They shall remain in office and continue to deal with current business until they are replaced in accordance with Article 17 of the Treaty on European Union. . . .

Section 2.   The European Council

Article 235

1. Where a vote is taken, any member of the European Council may also act on behalf of not more than one other member.

Article 16(4) of the Treaty on European Union and Article 238(2) of this Treaty shall apply to the European Council when it is acting by a qualified majority. Where the European Council decides by vote, its President and the President of the Commission shall not take part in the vote.

Abstentions by members present in person or represented shall not prevent the adoption by the European Council of acts which require unanimity. . . .

Section 3.   The Council

Article 237 (ex Article 204 TEC)

The Council shall meet when convened by its President on his own initiative or at the request of one of its Members or of the Commission.

Article 238 (ex Article 205(1) and (2), TEC)

1. Where it is required to act by a simple majority, the Council shall act by a majority of its component members.

2. By way of derogation from Article 16(4) of the Treaty on European Union, as from 1 November 2014 and subject to the provisions laid down in the Protocol on transitional provisions, where the Council does not act on a proposal from the Commission or from the High Representative of the Union for Foreign Affairs and Security Policy, the qualified majority shall be defined as at least 72 % of the members of the Council, representing Member States comprising at least 65 % of the population of the Union. . . .

4. Abstentions by Members present in person or represented shall not prevent the adoption by the Council of acts which require unanimity. . . .

Article 240 (ex Article 207 TEC)

1. A committee consisting of the Permanent Representatives of the Governments of the Member States shall be responsible for preparing the

work of the Council and for carrying out the tasks assigned to it by the latter. . . .

Article 241 (ex Article 208 TEC)

The Council, acting by a simple majority, may request the Commission to undertake any studies the Council considers desirable for the attainment of the common objectives, and to submit to it any appropriate proposals. If the Commission does not submit a proposal, it shall inform the Council of the reasons. . . .

Section 4.   The Commission

Article 244

In accordance with Article 17(5) of the Treaty on European Union, the Members of the Commission shall be chosen on the basis of a system of rotation established unanimously by the European Council. . . .

Article 245 (ex Article 213 TEC)

The Members of the Commission shall refrain from any action incompatible with their duties. Member States shall respect their independence and shall not seek to influence them in the performance of their tasks. . . .

Article 250 (ex Article 219 TEC)

The Commission shall act by a majority of its Members. . . .

Section 5.   The Court of Justice of the European Union

Article 251 (ex Article 221 TEC)

The Court of Justice shall sit in chambers or in a Grand Chamber, in accordance with the rules laid down for that purpose in the Statute of the Court of Justice of the European Union.

When provided for in the Statute, the Court of Justice may also sit as a full Court.

Article 252 (ex Article 222 TEC)

The Court of Justice shall be assisted by eight Advocates-General. Should the Court of Justice so request, the Council, acting unanimously, may increase the number of Advocates-General.

It shall be the duty of the Advocate-General, acting with complete impartiality and independence, to make, in open court, reasoned submissions on cases which, in accordance with the Statute of the Court of Justice of the European Union, require his involvement.

Article 253 (ex Article 223 TEC)

The Judges and Advocates-General of the Court of Justice shall be chosen from persons whose independence is beyond doubt and who possess the qualifications required for appointment to the highest judicial offices in their respective countries or who are jurisconsults of recognised competence; they shall be appointed by common accord of the governments of the Member States for a term of six years, after consultation of the panel provided for in Article 255. . . .

The Judges shall elect the President of the Court of Justice from among their number for a term of three years. He may be re-elected.

Retiring Judges and Advocates-General may be reappointed.

Article 254 (ex Article 224 TEC)

The number of Judges of the General Court shall be determined by the Statute of the Court of Justice of the European Union. The Statute may provide for the General Court to be assisted by Advocates-General.

The members of the General Court shall be chosen from persons whose independence is beyond doubt and who possess the ability required for appointment to high judicial office. They shall be appointed by common accord of the governments of the Member States for a term of six years, after consultation of the panel provided for in Article 255. The membership shall be partially renewed every three years. Retiring members shall be eligible for reappointment. . . .

Article 256 (ex Article 225 TEC)

1. The General Court shall have jurisdiction to hear and determine at first instance actions or proceedings referred to in Articles 263, 265, 268, 270 and 272, with the exception of those assigned to a specialised court set up under Article 257 and those reserved in the Statute for the Court of Justice. The Statute may provide for the General Court to have jurisdiction for other classes of action or proceeding.

Decisions given by the General Court under this paragraph may be subject to a right of appeal to the Court of Justice on points of law only, under the conditions and within the limits laid down by the Statute.

2. The General Court shall have jurisdiction to hear and determine actions or proceedings brought against decisions of the specialised courts.

Decisions given by the General Court under this paragraph may exceptionally be subject to review by the Court of Justice, under the conditions and within the limits laid down by the Statute, where there is a serious risk of the unity or consistency of Union law being affected.

3. The General Court shall have jurisdiction to hear and determine questions referred for a preliminary ruling under Article 267, in specific areas laid down by the Statute.

Where the General Court considers that the case requires a decision of principle likely to affect the unity or consistency of Union law, it may refer the case to the Court of Justice for a ruling.

Decisions given by the General Court on questions referred for a preliminary ruling may exceptionally be subject to review by the Court of Justice, under the conditions and within the limits laid down by the Statute, where there is a serious risk of the unity or consistency of Union law being affected.

Article 257 (ex Article 225a TEC)

The European Parliament and the Council, acting in accordance with the ordinary legislative procedure, may establish specialised courts attached to the General Court to hear and determine at first instance certain classes of action or proceeding brought in specific areas. . . .

Decisions given by specialised courts may be subject to a right of appeal on points of law only or, when provided for in the regulation establishing the specialised court, a right of appeal also on matters of fact, before the General Court.

Article 258 (ex Article 226 TEC)

If the Commission considers that a Member State has failed to fulfil an obligation under the Treaties, it shall deliver a reasoned opinion on the matter after giving the State concerned the opportunity to submit its observations.

If the State concerned does not comply with the opinion within the period laid down by the Commission, the latter may bring the matter before the Court of Justice of the European Union.

Article 259 (ex Article 227 TEC)

A Member State which considers that another Member State has failed to fulfil an obligation under the Treaties may bring the matter before the Court of Justice of the European Union.

Before a Member State brings an action against another Member State for an alleged infringement of an obligation under the Treaties, it shall bring the matter before the Commission.

The Commission shall deliver a reasoned opinion after each of the States concerned has been given the opportunity to submit its own case and its observations on the other party's case both orally and in writing.

If the Commission has not delivered an opinion within three months of the date on which the matter was brought before it, the absence of such opinion shall not prevent the matter from being brought before the Court.

Article 260 (ex Article 228 TEC)

1. If the Court of Justice of the European Union finds that a Member State has failed to fulfil an obligation under the Treaties, the State shall be required to take the necessary measures to comply with the judgment of the Court.

2. If the Commission considers that the Member State concerned has not taken the necessary measures to comply with the judgment of the Court, it may bring the case before the Court after giving that State the opportunity to submit its observations. It shall specify the amount of the lump sum or penalty payment to be paid by the Member State concerned which it considers appropriate in the circumstances.

If the Court finds that the Member State concerned has not complied with its judgment it may impose a lump sum or penalty payment on it. . . .

Article 261 (ex Article 229 TEC)

Regulations adopted jointly by the European Parliament and the Council, and by the Council, pursuant to the provisions of the Treaties, may give the Court of Justice of the European Union unlimited jurisdiction with regard to the penalties provided for in such regulations.

Article 263 (ex Article 230 TEC)

The Court of Justice of the European Union shall review the legality of legislative acts, of acts of the Council, of the Commission and of the European Central Bank, other than recommendations and opinions, and of acts of the European Parliament and of the European Council intended to produce legal effects *vis-à-vis* third parties. It shall also review the legality of acts of bodies, offices or agencies of the Union intended to produce legal effects *vis-à-vis* third parties.

It shall for this purpose have jurisdiction in actions brought by a Member State, the European Parliament, the Council or the Commission on grounds of lack of competence, infringement of an essential procedural requirement, infringement of the Treaties or of any rule of law relating to their application, or misuse of powers.

The Court shall have jurisdiction under the same conditions in actions brought by the Court of Auditors, by the European Central Bank and by the Committee of the Regions for the purpose of protecting their prerogatives.

Any natural or legal person may, under the conditions laid down in the first and second paragraphs, institute proceedings against an act addressed to that person or which is of direct and individual concern to them, and against a regulatory act which is of direct concern to them and does not entail implementing measures. . . .

Article 265 (ex Article 232 TEC)

Should the European Parliament, the European Council, the Council, the Commission or the European Central Bank, in infringement of the Treaties, fail to act, the Member States and the other institutions of the Union may bring an action before the Court of Justice of the European Union to have the infringement established. . . .

Article 267 (ex Article 234 TEC)

The Court of Justice of the European Union shall have jurisdiction to give preliminary rulings concerning:
   (a) the interpretation of the Treaties;
   (b) the validity and interpretation of acts of the institutions, bodies, offices or agencies of the Union;
Where such a question is raised before any court or tribunal of a Member State, that court or tribunal may, if it considers that a decision on the question is necessary to enable it to give judgment, request the Court to give a ruling thereon.

Where any such question is raised in a case pending before a court or tribunal of a Member State against whose decisions there is no judicial remedy under national law, that court or tribunal shall bring the matter before the Court.

If such a question is raised in a case pending before a court or tribunal of a Member State with regard to a person in custody, the Court of Justice of the European Union shall act with the minimum of delay. . . .

Article 274 (ex Article 240 TEC)

Save where jurisdiction is conferred on the Court of Justice of the European Union by the Treaties, disputes to which the Union is a party shall not on that ground be excluded from the jurisdiction of the courts or tribunals of the Member States.

Article 275

The Court of Justice of the European Union shall not have jurisdiction with respect to the provisions relating to the common foreign and security policy nor with respect to acts adopted on the basis of those provisions. . . .

Article 276

In exercising its powers regarding the provisions of Chapters 4 and 5 of Title V of Part Three relating to the area of freedom, security and justice, the Court of Justice of the European Union shall have no jurisdiction to review the validity or proportionality of operations carried out by the police or other law-enforcement services of a Member State or the exercise of the responsibilities incumbent upon Member States with regard to the maintenance of law and order and the safeguarding of internal security. . . .

Section 6.   The European Central Bank

Article 282

1. The European Central Bank, together with the national central banks, shall constitute the European System of Central Banks (ESCB). The European Central Bank, together with the national central banks of the Member States whose currency is the euro, which constitute the Eurosystem, shall conduct the monetary policy of the Union. . . .

3. The European Central Bank shall have legal personality. It alone may authorise the issue of the euro. It shall be independent in the exercise of its powers and in the management of its finances. . . .

Section 7.   The Court of Auditors

Article 285 (ex Article 246 TEC)

The Court of Auditors shall carry out the Union's audit.

It shall consist of one national of each Member State. Its Members shall be completely independent in the performance of their duties, in the Union's general interest. . . .

CHAPTER 2.   LEGAL ACTS OF THE UNION, ADOPTION PROCEDURES AND OTHER PROVISIONS

Section 1.   The Legal Acts of the Union

Article 288 (ex Article 249 TEC)

To exercise the Union's competences, the institutions shall adopt regulations, directives, decisions, recommendations and opinions.

A regulation shall have general application. It shall be binding in its entirety and directly applicable in all Member States.

A directive shall be binding, as to the result to be achieved, upon each Member State to which it is addressed, but shall leave to the national authorities the choice of form and methods.

A decision shall be binding in its entirety. A decision which specifies those to whom it is addressed shall be binding only on them.

Recommendations and opinions shall have no binding force.

Article 289

1. The ordinary legislative procedure shall consist in the joint adoption by the European Parliament and the Council of a regulation, directive or decision on a proposal from the Commission. This procedure is defined in Article 294. . . .

Article 290

1. A legislative act may delegate to the Commission the power to adopt non-legislative acts of general application to supplement or amend certain non-essential elements of the legislative act. . . .

Article 291

1. Member States shall adopt all measures of national law necessary to implement legally binding Union acts.

2. Where uniform conditions for implementing legally binding Union acts are needed, those acts shall confer implementing powers on the Commission, or, in duly justified specific cases and in the cases provided for in Articles 24 and 26 of the Treaty on European Union, on the Council. . . .

Article 292

The Council shall adopt recommendations. It shall act on a proposal from the Commission in all cases where the Treaties provide that it shall adopt acts on a proposal from the Commission. It shall act unanimously in those areas in which unanimity is required for the adoption of a Union act. The Commission, and the European Central Bank in the specific cases provided for in the Treaties, shall adopt recommendations.

Section 2. Procedures for the Adoption of Acts and Other Provisions

Article 293 (ex Article 250 TEC)

1. Where, pursuant to the Treaties, the Council acts on a proposal from the Commission, it may amend that proposal only by acting unanimously, except in. . . .

Article 294 (ex Article 251 TEC)

1. Where reference is made in the Treaties to the ordinary legislative procedure for the adoption of an act, the following procedure shall apply.

2. The Commission shall submit a proposal to the European Parliament and the Council.

First reading

3. The European Parliament shall adopt its position at first reading and communicate it to the Council.

4. If the Council approves the European Parliament's position, the act concerned shall be adopted in the wording which corresponds to the position of the European Parliament.

5. If the Council does not approve the European Parliament's position, it shall adopt its position at first reading and communicate it to the European Parliament.

6. The Council shall inform the European Parliament fully of the reasons which led it to adopt its position at first reading. The Commission shall inform the European Parliament fully of its position.

Second reading

7. If, within three months of such communication, the European Parliament:

(a) approves the Council's position at first reading or has not taken a decision, the act concerned shall be deemed to have been adopted in the wording which corresponds to the position of the Council;

(b) rejects, by a majority of its component members, the Council's position at first reading, the proposed act shall be deemed not to have been adopted;

(c) proposes, by a majority of its component members, amendments to the Council's position at first reading, the text thus amended shall be forwarded to the Council and to the Commission, which shall deliver an opinion on those amendments.

8. If, within three months of receiving the European Parliament's amendments, the Council, acting by a qualified majority:

(a) approves all those amendments, the act in question shall be deemed to have been adopted;

(b) does not approve all the amendments, the President of the Council, in agreement with the President of the European Parliament, shall within six weeks convene a meeting of the Conciliation Committee.

9. The Council shall act unanimously on the amendments on which the Commission has delivered a negative opinion.

Conciliation

10. The Conciliation Committee, which shall be composed of the members of the Council or their representatives and an equal number of members representing the European Parliament, shall have the task of reaching agreement on a joint text, by a qualified majority of the members of the Council or their representatives and by a majority of the members representing the European Parliament within six weeks of its being convened, on the basis of the positions of the European Parliament and the Council at second reading.

11. The Commission shall take part in the Conciliation Committee's proceedings and shall take all necessary initiatives with a view to reconciling the positions of the European Parliament and the Council.

12. If, within six weeks of its being convened, the Conciliation Committee does not approve the joint text, the proposed act shall be deemed not to have been adopted.

Third reading

13. If, within that period, the Conciliation Committee approves a joint text, the European Parliament, acting by a majority of the votes cast, and the Council, acting by a qualified majority, shall each have a period of six weeks from that approval in which to adopt the act in question in accordance with the joint text. If they fail to do so, the proposed act shall be deemed not to have been adopted.

14. The periods of three months and six weeks referred to in this Article shall be extended by a maximum of one month and two weeks respectively at the initiative of the European Parliament or the Council.

Special provisions. . . .

Article 299 (ex Article 256 TEC)

Acts of the Council, the Commission or the European Central Bank which impose a pecuniary obligation on persons other than States, shall be enforceable. . . .

CHAPTER 3.   THE UNION'S ADVISORY BODIES

Article 300

1. The European Parliament, the Council and the Commission shall be assisted by an Economic and Social Committee and a Committee of the Regions, exercising advisory functions. . . .

CHAPTER 4.   THE EUROPEAN INVESTMENT BANK

Article 308 (ex Article 266 TEC)

The European Investment Bank shall have legal personality.

The members of the European Investment Bank shall be the Member States. . . .

Article 309 (ex Article 267 TEC)

The task of the European Investment Bank shall be to contribute, by having recourse to the capital market and utilising its own resources, to the balanced and steady development of the internal market in the interest of the Union. For this purpose the Bank shall, operating on a non-profit-making basis, grant loans and give guarantees which facilitate the financing of the following projects in all sectors of the economy . . .

TITLE II.   FINANCIAL PROVISIONS

Article 310 (ex Article 268 TEC)

1. All items of revenue and expenditure of the Union shall be included in estimates to be drawn up for each financial year and shall be shown in the budget.

The Union's annual budget shall be established by the European Parliament and the Council in accordance with Article 314.

The revenue and expenditure shown in the budget shall be in balance. . . .

CHAPTER 1.   THE UNION'S OWN RESOURCES

Article 311 (ex Article 269 TEC)

The Union shall provide itself with the means necessary to attain its objectives and carry through its policies.

Without prejudice to other revenue, the budget shall be financed wholly from own resources. . . .

CHAPTER 3.   THE UNION'S ANNUAL BUDGET. . . .

Article 314 (ex Article 272(2) to (10), TEC)

The European Parliament and the Council, acting in accordance with a special legislative procedure, shall establish the Union's annual budget. . . .

CHAPTER 4.   IMPLEMENTATION OF THE BUDGET AND DISCHARGE

Article 317 (ex Article 274 TEC)

The Commission shall implement the budget in cooperation with the Member States. . . .

TITLE III.   ENHANCED COOPERATION

Article 326 (ex Articles 27a to 27e, 40 to 40b and 43 to 45 TEU and ex Articles 11 and 11a TEC)

Any enhanced cooperation shall comply with the Treaties and Union law.

Such cooperation shall not undermine the internal market or economic, social and territorial cohesion. It shall not constitute a barrier to or discrimination in trade between Member States, nor shall it distort competition between them. . . .

Article 328 (ex Articles 27*a* to 27*e*, 40 to 40*b* and 43 to 45 TEU and ex Articles 11 and 11*a* TEC)

1. When enhanced cooperation is being established, it shall be open to all Member States, subject to compliance with any conditions of participation laid down by the authorising decision. It shall also be open to them at any other time, subject to compliance with the acts already adopted within that framework, in addition to those conditions. . . .

Part Seven.   General and Final Provisions

Article 335 (ex Article 282 TEC)

In each of the Member States, the Union shall enjoy the most extensive legal capacity accorded to legal persons under their laws; it may, in particular, acquire or dispose of movable and immovable property and may be a party to legal proceedings. To this end, the Union shall be represented by the Commission. However, the Union shall be represented by each of the institutions, by virtue of their administrative autonomy, in matters relating to their respective operation. . . .

Article 344 (ex Article 292 TEC)

Member States undertake not to submit a dispute concerning the interpretation or application of the Treaties to any method of settlement other than those provided for therein.

Article 345 (ex Article 295 TEC)

The Treaties shall in no way prejudice the rules in Member States governing the system of property ownership. . . .

Article 356 (ex Article 312 TEC)

This Treaty is concluded for an unlimited period.

Article 357 (ex Article 313 TEC)

This Treaty shall be ratified by the High Contracting Parties in accordance with their respective constitutional requirements. The Instruments of ratification shall be deposited with the Government of the Italian Republic. . . .

CHARTER OF FUNDAMENTAL RIGHTS
OF THE EUROPEAN UNION

O.J. C 364/1 (Dec. 18, 2000)*

The European Parliament, the Council and the Commission solemnly proclaim the text below as the Charter of fundamental rights of the European Union. Done at Nice on the seventh day of December in the year two thousand

Preamble

The peoples of Europe, in creating an ever closer union among them, are resolved to share a peaceful future based on common values.

Conscious of its spiritual and moral heritage, the Union is founded on the indivisible, universal values of human dignity, freedom, equality and solidarity; it is based on the principles of democracy and the rule of law. It places the individual at the heart of its activities, by establishing the citizenship of the Union and by creating an area of freedom, security and justice.

The Union contributes to the preservation and to the development of these common values while respecting the diversity of the cultures and traditions of the peoples of Europe as well as the national identities of the Member States and the organisation of their public authorities at national, regional and local levels; it seeks to promote balanced and sustainable development and ensures free movement of persons, services, goods and capital, and the freedom of establishment.

To this end, it is necessary to strengthen the protection of fundamental rights in the light of changes in society, social progress and scientific and

* At the meetings in Nice in December 2000, the Presidents of the Parliament, Council, and Commission solemnly proclaimed this new Charter of Fundamental Rights. With the Lisbon Treaty, the Charter has become legal binding and directly enforceable as of December 1, 2009. The Charter can be found on the EU Web site at <http://europa.eu/lisbon_treaty/full_text/index_en.htm>.

technological developments by making those rights more visible in a Charter.

This Charter reaffirms, with due regard for the powers and tasks of the Union and the principle of subsidiarity, the rights as they result, in particular, from the constitutional traditions and international obligations common to the Member States, the European Convention for the Protection of Human Rights and Fundamental Freedoms, the Social Charters adopted by the Union and by the Council of Europe and the case-law of the Court of Justice of the European Union and of the European Court of Human Rights.

Enjoyment of these rights entails responsibilities and duties with regard to other persons, to the human community and to future generations.

CHAPTER I. DIGNITY

Article 1. *Human Dignity*

Human dignity is inviolable. It must be respected and protected.

Article 2. *Right to Life*

1. Everyone has the right to life.
2. No one shall be condemned to the death penalty, or executed.

Article 3. *Right to the Integrity of the Person*

1. Everyone has the right to respect for his or her physical and mental integrity.
2. In the fields of medicine and biology, the following must be respected in particular:
   - the free and informed consent of the person concerned, according to the procedures laid down by law;
   - the prohibition of eugenic practices, in particular those aiming at the selection of persons;
   - the prohibition on making the human body and its parts as such a source of financial gain;
   - the prohibition of the reproductive cloning of human beings.

Article 4. *Prohibition of Torture and Inhuman or Degrading Treatment or Punishment*

No one shall be subjected to torture or to inhuman or degrading treatment or punishment.

Article 5. *Prohibition of Slavery and Forced Labour*

1. No one shall be held in slavery or servitude.
2. No one shall be required to perform forced or compulsory labour.
3. Trafficking in human beings is prohibited.

CHAPTER II. FREEDOMS

Article 6. Right to Liberty and Security

Everyone has the right to liberty and security of person.

Article 7. Respect for Private and Family Life

Everyone has the right to respect for his or her private and family life, home and communications.

Article 8. Protection of Personal Data

1. Everyone has the right to the protection of personal data concerning him or her.

2. Such data must be processed fairly for specified purposes and on the basis of the consent of the person concerned or some other legitimate basis laid down by law. Everyone has the right of access to data which has been collected concerning him or her, and the right to have it rectified.

3. Compliance with these rules shall be subject to control by an independent authority.

Article 9. Right to Marry and Right to Found a Family

The right to marry and the right to found a family shall be guaranteed in accordance with the national laws governing the exercise of these rights.

Article 10. Freedom of Thought, Conscience and Religion

1. Everyone has the right to freedom of thought, conscience and religion. This right includes freedom to change religion or belief and freedom, either alone or in community with others and in public or in private, to manifest religion or belief, in worship, teaching, practice and observance.

2. The right to conscientious objection is recognised, in accordance with the national laws governing the exercise of this right.

Article 11. Freedom of Expression and Information

1. Everyone has the right to freedom of expression. This right shall include freedom to hold opinions and to receive and impart information and ideas without interference by public authority and regardless of frontiers.

2. The freedom and pluralism of the media shall be respected.

Article 12. Freedom of Assembly and of Association

1. Everyone has the right to freedom of peaceful assembly and to freedom of association at all levels, in particular in political, trade union and civic matters, which implies the right of everyone to form and to join trade unions for the protection of his or her interests.

2. Political parties at Union level contribute to expressing the political will of the citizens of the Union.

Article 13.   Freedom of the Arts and Sciences

The arts and scientific research shall be free of constraint. Academic freedom shall be respected.

Article 14.   Right to Education

1. Everyone has the right to education and to have access to vocational and continuing training.

2. This right includes the possibility to receive free compulsory education.

3. The freedom to found educational establishments with due respect for democratic principles and the right of parents to ensure the education and teaching of their children in conformity with their religious, philosophical and pedagogical convictions shall be respected, in accordance with the national laws governing the exercise of such freedom and right.

Article 15.   Freedom to Choose an Occupation and Right to Engage in Work

1. Everyone has the right to engage in work and to pursue a freely chosen or accepted occupation.

2. Every citizen of the Union has the freedom to seek employment, to work, to exercise the right of establishment and to provide services in any Member State.

3. Nationals of third countries who are authorised to work in the territories of the Member States are entitled to working conditions equivalent to those of citizens of the Union.

Article 16.   Freedom to Conduct a Business

The freedom to conduct a business in accordance with Union law and national laws and practices is recognised.

Article 17.   Right to Property

1. Everyone has the right to own, use, dispose of and bequeath his or her lawfully acquired possessions. No one may be deprived of his or her possessions, except in the public interest and in the cases and under the conditions provided for by law, subject to fair compensation being paid in good time for their loss. The use of property may be regulated by law insofar as is necessary for the general interest.

2. Intellectual property shall be protected.

Article 18.   Right to Asylum

The right to asylum shall be guaranteed with due respect for the rules of the Geneva Convention of 28 July 1951 and the Protocol of 31 January 1967 relating to the status of refugees and in accordance with the Constitution.

Article 19.   Protection in the Event of Removal, Expulsion or Extradition

1. Collective expulsions are prohibited.
2. No one may be removed, expelled or extradited to a State where there is a serious risk that he or she would be subjected to the death penalty, torture or other inhuman or degrading treatment or punishment.

CHAPTER III.   EQUALITY

Article 20.   Equality Before the Law

Everyone is equal before the law.

Article 21.   Non-Discrimination

1. Any discrimination based on any ground such as sex, race, colour, ethnic or social origin, genetic features, language, religion or belief, political or any other opinion, membership of a national minority, property, birth, disability, age or sexual orientation shall be prohibited.
2. Within the scope of application of the Treaty establishing the European Community and of the Treaty on European Union, and without prejudice to the special provisions of those Treaties, any discrimination on grounds of nationality shall be prohibited.

Article 22.   Cultural, Religious and Linguistic Diversity

The Union shall respect cultural, religious and linguistic diversity.

Article 23.   Equality Between Women and Men

Equality between women and men must be ensured in all areas, including employment, work and pay.

The principle of equality shall not prevent the maintenance or adoption of measures providing for specific advantages in favour of the under-represented sex.

Article 24.   The Rights of the Child

1. Children shall have the right to such protection and care as is necessary for their well-being. They may express their views freely. Such views shall be taken into consideration on matters which concern them in accordance with their age and maturity.

2. In all actions relating to children, whether taken by public authorities or private institutions, the child's best interests must be a primary consideration.

3. Every child shall have the right to maintain on a regular basis a personal relationship and direct contact with both his or her parents, unless that is contrary to his or her interests.

Article 25. The Rights of the Elderly

The Union recognises and respects the rights of the elderly to lead a life of dignity and independence and to participate in social and cultural life.

Article 26. Integration of Persons with Disabilities

The Union recognises and respects the right of persons with disabilities to benefit from measures designed to ensure their independence, social and occupational integration and participation in the life of the community.

CHAPTER IV. SOLIDARITY

Article 27. Workers' Right to Information and Consultation Within the Undertaking

Workers or their representatives must, at the appropriate levels, be guaranteed information and consultation in good time in the cases and under the conditions provided for by Union law and national laws and practices.

Article 28. Right of Collective Bargaining and Action

Workers and employers, or their respective organisations, have, in accordance with Union law and national laws and practices, the right to negotiate and conclude collective agreements at the appropriate levels and, in cases of conflicts of interest, to take collective action to defend their interests, including strike action.

Article 29. Right of Access to Free Placement Services

Everyone has the right of access to a free placement service.

Article 30. Protection in the Event of Unjustified Dismissal

Every worker has the right to protection against unjustified dismissal, in accordance with Union law and national laws and practices.

Article 31. Fair and Just Working Conditions

1. Every worker has the right to working conditions which respect to his or her health, safety and dignity.

2. Every worker has the right to limitation of maximum working hours, to daily and weekly rest periods and to an annual period of paid leave.

Article 32.   Prohibition of Child Labour and Protection of Young People at Work

The employment of children is prohibited. The minimum age of admission to employment may not be lower than the minimum school-leaving age, without prejudice to such rules as may be more favourable to young people and except for limited derogations.

Young people admitted to work must have working conditions appropriate to their age and be protected against economic exploitation and any work likely to harm their safety, health or physical, mental, moral or social development or to interfere with their education.

Article 33.   Family and Professional Life

1. The family shall enjoy legal, economic and social protection.

2. To reconcile family and professional life, everyone shall have the right to protection from dismissal for a reason connected with maternity and the right to paid maternity leave and to parental leave following the birth or adoption of a child.

Article 34.   Social Security and Social Assistance

1. The Union recognises and respects the entitlement to social security benefits and social services providing protection in cases such as maternity, illness, industrial accidents, dependency or old age, and in the case of loss of employment, in accordance with the rules laid down by Union law and national laws and practices.

2. Everyone residing and moving legally within the European Union is entitled to social security benefits and social advantages in accordance with Union law and national laws and practices.

3. In order to combat social exclusion and poverty, the Union recognises and respects the right to social and housing assistance so as to ensure a decent existence for all those who lack sufficient resources, in accordance with the rules laid down by Union law and national laws and practices.

Article 35.   Health Care

Everyone has the right of access to preventive health care and the right to benefit from medical treatment under the conditions established by national laws and practices. A high level of human health protection shall be ensured in the definition and implementation of all Union policies and activities.

Article 36.   Access to Services of General Economic Interest

The Union recognises and respects access to services of general economic interest as provided for in national laws and practices, in accordance with the Treaty establishing the European Community, in order to promote the social and territorial cohesion of the Union.

Article 37.   Environmental Protection

A high level of environmental protection and the improvement of the quality of the environment must be integrated into the policies of the Union and ensured in accordance with the principle of sustainable development.

Article 38.   Consumer Protection

Union policies shall ensure a high level of consumer protection.

Chapter V.   Citizens' Rights

Article 39.   Right to Vote and to Stand as a Candidate at Elections to the European Parliament

1. Every citizen of the Union has the right to vote and to stand as a candidate at elections to the European Parliament in the Member State in which he or she resides, under the same conditions as nationals of that State.
2. Members of the European Parliament shall be elected by direct universal suffrage in a free and secret ballot.

Article 40.   Right to Vote and to Stand as a Candidate at Municipal Elections

Every citizen of the Union has the right to vote and to stand as a candidate at municipal elections in the Member State in which he or she resides under the same conditions as nationals of that State.

Article 41.   Right to Good Administration

1. Every person has the right to have his or her affairs handled impartially, fairly and within a reasonable time by the institutions, bodies, offices and agencies of the Union.
2. This right includes:
    • the right of every person to be heard, before any individual measure which would affect him or her adversely is taken;
    • the right of every person to have access to his or her file, while respecting the legitimate interests of confidentiality and of professional and business secrecy;
    • the obligation of the administration to give reasons for its decisions.
3. Every person has the right to have the Union make good any damage caused by its institutions or by its servants in the performance of their duties,

in accordance with the general principles common to the laws of the Member States.

4. Every person may write to the institutions of the Union in one of the languages of the Treaties and must have an answer in the same language.

Article 42. Right of Access to Documents

Any citizen of the Union, and any natural or legal person residing or having its registered office in a Member State, has a right of access to European Parliament, Council, and Commission documents.

Article 43. European Ombudsman

Any citizen of the Union and any natural or legal person residing or having its registered office in a Member State has the right to refer to the Ombudsman of the Union cases of maladministration in the activities of the Community institutions or bodies, with the exception of the Court of Justice and the Court of First Instance acting in their judicial role.

Article 44. Right to Petition

Any citizen of the Union and any natural or legal person residing or having its registered office in a Member State has the right to petition the European Parliament.

Article 45. Freedom of Movement and of Residence

1. Every citizen of the Union has the right to move and reside freely within the territory of the Member States.

2. Freedom of movement and residence may be granted, in accordance with the Treaty establishing the European Community, to nationals of third countries legally resident in the territory of a Member State.

Article 46. Diplomatic and Consular Protection

Every citizen of the Union shall, in the territory of a third country in which the Member State of which he or she is a national is not represented, be entitled to protection by the diplomatic or consular authorities of any Member State, on the same conditions as the nationals of that Member State.

CHAPTER VI. JUSTICE

Article 47. Right to an Effective Remedy and to a Fair Trial

Everyone whose rights and freedoms guaranteed by the law of the Union are violated has the right to an effective remedy before a tribunal in compliance with the conditions laid down in this Article.

Everyone is entitled to a fair and public hearing within a reasonable time by an independent and impartial tribunal previously established by law.

Everyone shall have the possibility of being advised, defended and represented.

Legal aid shall be made available to those who lack sufficient resources insofar as such aid is necessary to ensure effective access to justice.

Article 48. Presumption of Innocence and Right of Defence

1. Everyone who has been charged shall be presumed innocent until proved guilty according to law.

2. Respect for the rights of the defence of anyone who has been charged shall be guaranteed.

Article 49. Principles of Legality and Proportionality of Criminal Offences and Penalties

1. No one shall be held guilty of any criminal offence on account of any act or omission which did not constitute a criminal offence under national law or international law at the time when it was committed. Nor shall a heavier penalty be imposed than that which was applicable at the time the criminal offence was committed. If, subsequent to the commission of a criminal offence, the law provides for a lighter penalty, that penalty shall be applicable.

2. This Article shall not prejudice the trial and punishment of any person for any act or omission which, at the time when it was committed, was criminal according to the general principles recognised by the community of nations.

3. The severity of penalties must not be disproportionate to the criminal offence.

Article 50. Right Not to Be Tried or Punished Twice in Criminal Proceedings for the Same Criminal Offence

No one shall be liable to be tried or punished again in criminal proceedings for an offence for which he or she has already been finally acquitted or convicted within the Union in accordance with the law.

CHAPTER VII. GENERAL PROVISIONS

Article 51. Scope

1. The provisions of this Charter are addressed to the institutions and bodies, of the Union with due regard for the principle of subsidiarity and to the Member States only when they are implementing Union law. They shall therefore respect the rights, observe the principles and promote the application thereof in accordance with their respective powers.

2. This Charter does not establish any new power or task for the Community or the Union, or modify powers and tasks defined by the Treaties.

Article 52.   Scope of Guaranteed Rights

1. Any limitation on the exercise of the rights and freedoms recognised by this Charter must be provided for by law and respect the essence of those rights and freedoms. Subject to the principle of proportionality, limitations may be made only if they are necessary and genuinely meet objectives of general interest recognised by the Union or the need to protect the rights and freedoms of others.

2. Rights recognised by this Charter which are based on the Community Treaties or the Treaty on European Union shall be exercised under the conditions and within the limits defined by those Treaties.

3. Insofar as this Charter contains rights which correspond to rights guaranteed by the Convention for the Protection of Human Rights and Fundamental Freedoms, the meaning and scope of those rights shall be the same as those laid down by the said Convention. This provision shall not prevent Union law providing more extensive protection.

Article 53.   Level of Protection

Nothing in this Charter shall be interpreted as restricting or adversely affecting human rights and fundamental freedoms as recognised, in their respective fields of application, by Union law and international law and by international agreements to which the Union or all the Member States are party, including the European Convention for the Protection of Human Rights and Fundamental Freedoms, and by the Member States' constitutions.

Article 54.   Prohibition of Abuse of Rights

Nothing in this Charter shall be interpreted as implying any right to engage in any activity or to perform any act aimed at the destruction of any of the rights and freedoms recognised in this Charter or at their limitation to a greater extent than is provided for herein.

THE NORTH ATLANTIC TREATY

April 4, 1949, 63 Stat. 2241, T.I.A.S. No. 1964, 34 U.N.T.S. 243*

The Parties to this Treaty reaffirm their faith in the purposes and principles of the Charter of the United Nations and their desire to live in peace with all peoples and all governments.

They are determined to safeguard the freedom, common heritage and civilisation of their peoples, founded on the principles of democracy, individual liberty and the rule of law. They seek to promote stability and well-being in the North Atlantic area.

They are resolved to unite their efforts for collective defence and for the preservation of peace and security. They therefore agree to this North Atlantic Treaty:

Article 1

The Parties undertake, as set forth in the Charter of the United Nations, to settle any international dispute in which they may be involved by peaceful means in such a manner that international peace and security and justice are not endangered, and to refrain in their international relations from the threat or use of force in any manner inconsistent with the purposes of the United Nations.

Article 2

The Parties will contribute toward the further development of peaceful and friendly international relations by strengthening their free institutions, by bringing about a better understanding of the principles upon which these institutions are founded, and by promoting conditions of stability and well-being. They will seek to eliminate conflict in their international economic

* Signed at Washington, D.C. on April 4, 1949. Entered into force on August 24, 1949. As of April 2013, the 28 parties to the Treaty were: Albania, Belgium, Bulgaria, Canada, Croatia, Czech Republic, Denmark, Estonia, France, Germany, Greece, Hungary, Iceland, Italy, Latvia, Lithuania, Luxembourg, Netherlands, Norway, Poland, Portugal, Romania, Slovakia, Slovenia, Spain, Turkey, United Kingdom, and United States. The Web site for NATO is located at <http://www.nato.int>.

policies and will encourage economic collaboration between any or all of them.

Article 3

In order more effectively to achieve the objectives of this Treaty, the Parties, separately and jointly, by means of continuous and effective self-help and mutual aid, will maintain and develop their individual and collective capacity to resist armed attack.

Article 4

The Parties will consult together whenever, in the opinion of any of them, the territorial integrity, political independence or security of any of the Parties is threatened.

Article 5

The Parties agree that an armed attack against one or more of them in Europe or North America shall be considered an attack against them all and consequently they agree that, if such an armed attack occurs, each of them, in exercise of the right of individual or collective self-defence recognised by Article 51 of the Charter of the United Nations, will assist the Party or Parties so attacked by taking forthwith, individually, and in concert with the other Parties, such action as it deems necessary, including the use of armed force, to restore and maintain the security of the North Atlantic area.

Any such armed attack and all measures taken as a result thereof shall immediately be reported to the Security Council. Such measures shall be terminated when the Security Council has taken the measures necessary to restore and maintain international peace and security.

Article 6[1]

For the purpose of Article 5, an armed attack on one or more of the Parties is deemed to include an armed attack:

- on the territory of any of the Parties in Europe or North America, . . . on the territory of Turkey or on the islands under the jurisdiction of any of the Parties in the North Atlantic area north of the Tropic of Cancer;
- on the forces, vessels, or aircraft of any of the Parties, when in or over these territories or any area in Europe in which occupation forces of any of the Parties were stationed on the date when the Treaty entered into force or the Mediterranean Sea or the North Atlantic area north of the Tropic of Cancer.

1. The definition of the territories to which Article 5 applies was revised by Article 2 of the Protocol to the North Atlantic Treaty on the accession of Greece and Turkey signed on 22 October 1951.

Article 7

The Treaty does not affect, and shall not be interpreted as affecting, in any way the rights and obligations under the Charter of the Parties which are members of the United Nations, or the primary responsibility of the Security Council for the maintenance of international peace and security.

Article 8

Each Party declares that none of the international engagements now in force between it and any other of the Parties or any third State is in conflict with the provisions of this Treaty, and undertakes not to enter into any international engagement in conflict with this Treaty.

Article 9

The Parties hereby establish a Council, on which each of them shall be represented to consider matters concerning the implementation of this Treaty. The Council shall be so organised as to be able to meet promptly at any time. The Council shall set up such subsidiary bodies as may be necessary; in particular it shall establish immediately a defence committee which shall recommend measures for the implementation of Articles 3 and 5.

Article 10

The Parties may, by unanimous agreement, invite any other European State in a position to further the principles of this Treaty and to contribute to the security of the North Atlantic area to accede to this Treaty. Any State so invited may become a party to the Treaty by depositing its instrument of accession with the Government of the United States of America. . . .

Article 11

This Treaty shall be ratified and its provisions carried out by the Parties in accordance with their respective constitutional processes. The instruments of ratification shall be deposited as soon as possible with the Government of the United States of America, which will notify all the other signatories of each deposit. . . .

Article 12

After the Treaty has been in force for ten years, or at any time thereafter, the Parties shall, if any of them so requests, consult together for the purpose of reviewing the Treaty, having regard for the factors then affecting peace and security in the North Atlantic area, including the development of universal as well as regional arrangements under the Charter of the United Nations for the maintenance of international peace and security.

Article 13

After the Treaty has been in force for twenty years, any Party may cease to be a Party one year after its notice of denunciation has been given to the Government of the United States of America, which will inform the Governments of the other Parties of the deposit of each notice of denunciation. . . .

CHARTER OF THE ORGANIZATION
OF AMERICAN STATES (as amended)

April 30, 1948, 2 U.S.T. 2394, T.I.A.S. No. 2361; amended
effective 1970, 21 U.S.T. 607, T.I.A.S. No. 6847*

In the Name of Their Peoples, the States Represented at the Ninth
International Conference of American States,

Convinced that the historic mission of America is to offer to man a land
of liberty, and a favorable environment for the development of his personality and the realization of his just aspirations;

Conscious that that mission has already inspired numerous agreements,
whose essential value lies in the desire of the American peoples to live together in peace, and, through their mutual understanding and respect for
the sovereignty of each one, to provide for the betterment of all, in independence, in equality and under law;

Confident that the true significance of American solidarity and good
neighborliness can only mean the consolidation on this continent, within the
framework of democratic institutions, of a system of individual liberty and
social justice based on respect for the essential rights of man;

Persuaded that their welfare and their contribution to the progress and
the civilization of the world will increasingly require intensive continental cooperation;

---

* Done at Bogota on April 30, 1948. Entered into force on December 13, 1951. The 1967
Protocol of Amendment came into force on February 27, 1970. The 35 parties to the charter
are: Antigua and Barbuda, Argentina, Bahamas, Barbados, Belize, Bolivia, Brazil, Canada,
Chile, Colombia, Costa Rica, Cuba, Dominica, Dominican Republic, Ecuador, El Salvador,
Grenada, Guatemala, Guyana, Haiti, Honduras, Jamaica, Mexico, Nicaragua, Panama,
Paraguay, Peru, Saint Kitts and Nevis, Saint Lucia, Saint Vincent and the Grenadines,
Suriname, Trinidad and Tobago, United States, Uruguay, and Venezuela. The OAS suspended
Cuba's participation as a member in January 1962, on the grounds that its Marxist-Leninist
form of government was not compatible with OAS membership, but voted to lift that suspension
in June 2009. Cuba, however, has indicated it does not want to resume participation..

A 1985 Protocol, 25 I.L.M. 529 (1986), is in force for many of the parties. The 1985
Protocol, however, has not been ratified by the United States and Haiti, and some other
countries—Belize, Canada, Guyana, and Trinidad and Tobago—have neither signed nor
ratified the Protocol. Other Protocols were adopted in 1992 and 1993, have been ratified by the
United States and most other OAS members, and came into force in 1996 and 1997,
respectively. See the OAS Web site at <http://www.oas.org>.

Resolved to persevere in the noble undertaking that humanity has conferred upon the United Nations, whose principles and purposes they solemnly reaffirm;

Convinced that juridical organization is a necessary condition for security and peace founded on moral order and on justice. . . .

Have Agreed upon the following.

Part One

CHAPTER I.   NATURE AND PURPOSES
Article 1

The American States establish by this Charter the international organization that they have developed to achieve an order of peace and justice, to promote their solidarity, to strengthen their collaboration, and to defend their sovereignty, their territorial integrity, and their independence. Within the United Nations, the Organization of American States is a regional agency.

Article 2

The Organization of American States, in order to put into practice the principles on which it is founded and to fulfill its regional obligations under the Charter of the United Nations, proclaims the following essential purposes:

(a) To strengthen the peace and security of the continent;

(b) To prevent possible causes of difficulties and to ensure the pacific settlement of disputes that may arise among the Member States;

(c) To provide for common action on the part of those States in the event of aggression;

(d) To seek the solution of political, juridical, and economic problems that may arise among them; and

(e) To promote, by co-operative action, their economic, social, and cultural development.

CHAPTER II.   PRINCIPLES
Article 3

The American States reaffirm the following principles:

(a) International law is the standard of conduct of States in their reciprocal relations;

(b) International order consists essentially of respect for the personality, sovereignty, and independence of States, and the faithful fulfilment of obligations derived from treaties and other sources of international law;

(c) Good faith shall govern the relations between States;

(d) The solidarity of the American States and the high aims which are sought through it require the political organization of those States on the basis of the effective exercise of representative democracy;

(e) The American States condemn wars of aggression: victory does not give rights;

(f) An act of aggression against one American State is an act of aggression against all the other American States;

(g) Controversies of an international character arising between two or more American States shall be settled by peaceful procedures;

(h) Social justice and social security are bases of lasting peace;

(i) Economic co-operation is essential to the common welfare and prosperity of the peoples of the continent;

(j) The American States proclaim the fundamental rights of the individual without distinction as to race, nationality, creed, or sex;

(k) The spiritual unity of the continent is based on respect for the cultural values of the American countries and requires their close co-operation for the high purposes of civilization;

(l) The education of peoples should be directed toward justice, freedom, and peace.

CHAPTER III.   MEMBERS

Article 4

All American States that ratify the present Charter are Members of the Organization.

Article 5

Any new political entity that arises from the union of several Member States and that, as such, ratifies the present Charter, shall become a Member of the Organization. The entry of the new political entity into the Organization shall result in the loss of membership of each one of the States which constitute it. . . .

Article 7

The General Assembly, upon the recommendation of the Permanent Council of the Organization, shall determine whether it is appropriate that the Secretary-General be authorized to permit the applicant State to sign the Charter and to accept the deposit of the Permanent Council and the decision of the General Assembly shall require the affirmative vote of two thirds of the Member States. . . .

CHAPTER IV.   FUNDAMENTAL RIGHTS AND DUTIES OF STATES

Article 9

States are juridically equal, enjoy equal rights and equal capacity to exercise these rights, and have equal duties. The rights of each State depend not upon its power to ensure the exercise thereof, but upon the mere fact of its existence as a person under international law.

Article 10

Every American State has the duty to respect the rights enjoyed by every other State in accordance with international law.

Article 11

The fundamental rights of States may not be impaired in any manner whatsoever.

Article 12

The political existence of the State is independent of recognition by other States. Even before being recognized, the State has the right to defend its integrity and independence, to provide for its preservation and prosperity, and consequently to organize itself as it sees fit, to legislate concerning its interests, to administer its services, and to determine the jurisdiction and competence of its courts. The exercise of these rights is limited only by the exercise of the rights of other States in accordance with international law.

Article 13

Recognition implies that the State granting it accepts the personability of the new State, with all the rights and duties that international law prescribes for the two States.

Article 14

The right of each State to protect itself and to live its own life does not authorize it to commit unjust acts against another State.

Article 15

The jurisdiction of States within the limits of their national territory is exercised equally over all the inhabitants, whether nationals or aliens.

Article 16

Each State has the right to develop its cultural, political, and economic life freely and naturally. In this free development, the State shall respect the rights of the individual and the principles of universal morality. . . .

Article 18

No State or group of States has the right to intervene, directly or indirectly, for any reason whatever, in the internal or external affairs of any other State. The foregoing principle prohibits not only armed force but also any other form of interference or attempted threat against the personality of the State or against its political, economic, and cultural elements.

Article 19

No State may use or encourage the use of coercive measures of an economic or political character in order to force the sovereign will of another State and obtain from it advantages of any kind.

Article 20

The territory of a State is inviolable; it may not be the object, even temporarily, of military occupation or of other measures of force taken by another State, directly or indirectly, on any grounds whatever. No territorial acquisitions or special advantages obtained either by force or by other means of coercion shall be recognized.

Article 21

The American States bind themselves in their international relations not to have recourse to the use of force, except in the case of self-defense in accordance with existing treaties or in fulfillment thereof.

Article 22

Measures adopted for the maintenance of peace and security in accordance with existing treaties do not constitute a violation of the principles set forth in Articles 18 and 20.

CHAPTER V.   PACIFIC SETTLEMENT OF DISPUTES

Article 23

All international disputes that may arise between American States shall be submitted to the peaceful procedures set forth in this Charter, before being referred to the Security Council of the United Nations.

Article 24

The following are peaceful procedures: direct negotiation, good offices, mediation, investigation and conciliation, judicial settlement, arbitration, and those which the parties to the dispute may especially agree upon at any time.

Article 25

In the event that a dispute arises between two or more American States which, in the opinion of one of them, cannot be settled through the usual diplomatic channels, the parties shall agree on some other peaceful procedure that will enable them to reach a solution. . . .

CHAPTER VI.   COLLECTIVE SECURITY

Article 27

Every act of aggression by a State against the territorial integrity or the inviolability of the territory or against the sovereignty or political independence of an American State shall be considered an act of aggression against the other American States.

Article 28

If the inviolability or the integrity of the territory or the sovereignty or political independence of any American State should be affected by an armed attack or by an act of aggression that is not an armed attack, or by an extra-continental conflict, or by a conflict between two or more American States, or by any other fact or situation that might endanger the peace of America, the American States, in furtherance of the principles of continental solidarity or collective self-defense, shall apply the measures and procedures established in the special treaties on the subject.

CHAPTER VII.   ECONOMIC STANDARDS

Article 29

The Member States, inspired by the principles of inter-American solidarity and co-operation, pledge themselves to a united effort to ensure social justice in the Hemisphere and dynamic and balanced economic development for their peoples, as conditions essential to peace and security. . . .

Article 31

To accelerate their economic and social development, in accordance with their own methods and procedures and within the framework of the democratic principles and the institutions of the inter-American system, the Member States agree to dedicate every effort to achieve the following basic goals:

(a) Substantial and self-sustained increase in the per capita national product;

(b) Equitable distribution of national income;

(c) Adequate and equitable systems of taxation;

(d) Modernization of rural life and reforms leading to equitable and efficient land-tenure systems, increased agricultural productivity, expanded use of undeveloped land, diversification of production; and improved processing and marketing systems for agricultural products; . . .

(e) Accelerated and diversified industrialization, especially of capital and intermediate goods;

(f) Stability in the domestic price levels, compatible with sustained economic development and the attainment of social justice;

(g) Fair wages, employment opportunities, and acceptable working conditions for all;

(h) Rapid eradication of illiteracy and expansion of educational opportunities for all;

(i) Protection of man's potential through the extension and application of modern medical science;

(j) Proper nutrition, especially through the acceleration of national efforts to increase the production and availability of food;

(k) Adequate housing for all sectors of the population;

(l) Urban conditions that offer the opportunity for a healthful, productive, and full life;

(m) Promotion of private initiative and investment in harmony with action in the public sector; and

(n) Expansion and diversification of exports. . . .

CHAPTER VIII. SOCIAL STANDARDS

Article 43

The Member States, convinced that man can only achieve the full realization of his aspirations within a just social order, along with economic development and true peace, agree to dedicate every effort to the application of the following principles and mechanisms:

(a) All human beings, without distinction as to race, sex, nationality, creed, or social condition, have a right to material well-being and to their spiritual development, under circumstances of liberty, dignity, equality of opportunity, and economic security;

(b) Work is a right and a social duty, it gives dignity to the one who performs it, and it should be performed under conditions, including a system of fair wages, that ensure life, health, and a decent standard of living for the worker and his family, both during his working years and in his old age, or when any circumstance deprives him of the possibility of working;

(c) Employers and workers, both rural and urban, have the right to associate themselves freely for the defense and promotion of their interests, including the right to collective bargaining and the workers' right to strike, and recognition of the juridical personality of associations and the protection of their freedom and independence, all in accordance with applicable laws;

(d) Fair and efficient systems and procedures for consultation and collaboration among the sectors of production, . . .

(e) The operation of systems of public administration, banking and credit, enterprise, and distribution and sales, in such a way, in harmony with the private sector, as to meet the requirements and interests of the community;

(f) The incorporation and increasing participation of the marginal sectors of the population, in both rural and urban areas, in the economic, social, civic, cultural, and political life of the nation, . . .

(g) Recognition of the importance of the contribution of organizations such as labor unions, co-operatives, and cultural, professional, business, neighborhood, and community associations to the life of the society and to the development process;

(h) Development of an efficient social security policy; and

(i) Adequate provision for all persons to have due legal aid in order to secure their rights. . . .

CHAPTER IX. EDUCATIONAL, SCIENTIFIC, AND CULTURAL STANDARDS

Article 45

The Member States will give primary importance within their development plans to the encouragement of education, science, and culture, oriented toward the over-all improvement of the individual, and as a foundation for democracy, social justice, and progress. . . .

Part Two

CHAPTER X. THE ORGANS

Article 51

The Organization of American States accomplishes its purposes by means of:

(a) The General Assembly;

(b) The Meeting of Consultation of Ministers of Foreign Affairs;

(c) The Councils;

(d) The Inter-American Juridical Committee;

(e) The Inter-American Commission on Human Rights;

(f) The General Secretariat;

(g) The Specialized Conferences; . . . .

CHAPTER XI. THE GENERAL ASSEMBLY

Article 52

The General Assembly is the supreme organ of the Organization of American States. It has as its principal powers, in addition to such others as are assigned to it by the Charter, the following:

(a) To decide the general action and policy of the Organization, determine the structure and functions of its organs, and consider any matter relating to friendly relations among the American States;

(b) To establish measures for coordinating the activities of the organs, agencies, and entities of the Organization among themselves and such activities with those of the other institutions of the inter-American system;

(c) To strengthen and coordinate co-operation with the United Nations and its specialized agencies;

(d) To promote collaboration, especially in the economic, social, and cultural fields, with other international organizations whose purposes are similar to those of the Organization of American States;

(e) To approve the program-budget of the Organization and determine the quotas of the Member States;

(f) To consider the annual and special reports that shall be presented to it by the organs, agencies, and entities of the inter-American system;

(g) To adopt general standards to govern the operations of the General Secretariat; and

(h) To adopt its own rules of procedure and, by a two-thirds vote, its agenda.

The General Assembly shall exercise its powers in accordance with the provisions of the Charter and of other inter-American treaties. . . .

Article 54

All Member States have the right to be represented in the General Assembly. Each State has the right to one vote.

Article 55

The General Assembly shall convene annually during the period determined by the rules of procedure and at a place selected in accordance with the principle of rotation. . . .

Article 56

In Special circumstances and with the approval of two thirds of the Member States, the Permanent Council shall convoke a special session of the General Assembly.

CHAPTER XII. THE MEETING OF CONSULTATION OF MINISTERS OF FOREIGN AFFAIRS

Article 59

The Meeting of Consultation of Ministers of Foreign Affairs shall be held in order to consider problems of an urgent nature and of common interest to the American States, and to serve as the Organ of Consultation.

Article 60

Any Member State may request that a Meeting of Consultation be called. The request shall be addressed to the Permanent Council of the Organization, which shall decide by an absolute majority whether a meeting should be held. . . .

Article 63

In case of an armed attack within the territory of an American State or within the region of security delimited by treaties in force, a Meeting of Consultation shall be held without delay. Such Meeting shall be called immediately by the Chairman of the Permanent Council of the Organization, who shall at the same time call a meeting of the Council itself. . . .

CHAPTER XIII. THE COUNCILS OF THE ORGANIZATION COMMON PROVISIONS

Article 68

The Permanent Council of the Organization, the Inter-American Economic and Social Council, and the Inter-American Council for Education, Science, and Culture are directly responsible to the General Assembly and each has the authority granted to it in the Charter and other inter-American instruments, as well as the functions assigned to it by the General Assembly and the Meeting of Consultation of Ministers of Foreign Affairs.

Article 69

All Member States have the right to be represented on each of the Councils. Each State has the right to one vote.

Article 70

The Councils may, within the limits of the Charter and other inter-American instruments, make recommendations on matters within their authority. . . .

CHAPTER XIV. THE PERMANENT COUNCIL OF THE ORGANIZATION

Article 78

The Permanent Council of the Organization is composed of one representative of each Member State, especially appointed by the respective Government, with the rank of ambassador. . . .

Article 79

The office of Chairman of the Permanent Council shall be held by each of the representatives, in turn, following the alphabetic order in Spanish of the names of their respective countries. The office of Vice-Chairman shall be filled in the same way, following reverse alphabetic order. . . .

Article 80

Within the limits of the Charter and of inter-American treaties and agreements, the Permanent Council takes cognizance of any matter referred to it by the General Assembly or the Meeting of Consultation of Ministers of Foreign Affairs.

Article 81

The Permanent Council shall serve provisionally as the Organ of Consultation when the circumstances contemplated in Article 63 of this Charter arise. . . .

CHAPTER XVII. THE INTER-AMERICAN JURIDICAL COMMITTEE

Article 105

The purpose of the Inter-American Juridical Committee is to serve the Organization as an advisory body on juridical matters; to promote the progressive development and the codification of international law; and to study juridical problems related to the integration of the developing countries of the Hemisphere and, insofar as may appear desirable, the possibility of attaining uniformity in their legislation. . . .

CHAPTER XVIII. THE INTER-AMERICAN COMMISSION ON HUMAN RIGHTS

Article 112

There shall be an Inter-American Commission on Human Rights, whose principal function shall be to promote the observance and protection of human rights and to serve as a consultative organ of the Organization in these matters.

An inter-American convention on human rights shall determine the structure, competence, and procedure of this Commission, as well as those of other organs responsible for these matters. . . .

Part Three

CHAPTER XXII.   THE UNITED NATIONS

Article 137

None of the provisions of this Charter shall be construed as impairing the rights and obligations of the Member States under the Charter of the United Nations.

CHAPTER XXIII.   MISCELLANEOUS PROVISIONS . . .

Article 139

The Organization of American States shall enjoy in the territory of each Member such legal capacity, privileges, and immunities as are necessary for the exercise of its functions and the accomplishment of its purposes. . . .

CHAPTER XXIV.   RATIFICATION AND ENTRY INTO FORCE . . .

Article 147

Amendments to the present Charter may be adopted only at a General Assembly convened for that purpose. Amendments shall enter into force in accordance with the terms and the procedure set forth in Article 145.

Article 148

The present Charter shall remain in force indefinitely, but may be denounced by any Member State upon written notification to the General Secretariat, ...

Reservations Made at the Time of Ratifying the Charter of 1948 . . .

UNITED STATES

That the Senate give its advice and consent to ratification of the Charter with the reservation that none of its provisions shall be considered as enlarging the powers of the Federal Government of the United States or limiting the powers of the several states of the Federal Union with respect to any matters recognized under the Constitution as being within the reserved powers of the several states. . . .

6

Foreign Sovereign Immunity and the Act of State Doctrine

FOREIGN SOVEREIGN IMMUNITIES ACT OF 1976
(as codified and amended through 2010)

28 U.S.C. §§1330, 1332, 1391(f), 1441(d), 1602-1611

§1330. Actions against Foreign States

(a) The district courts shall have original jurisdiction without regard to amount in controversy of any nonjury civil action against a foreign state as defined in section 1603(a) of this title as to any claim for relief in personam with respect to which the foreign state is not entitled to immunity either under sections 1605—1607 of this title or under any applicable international agreement.

(b) Personal jurisdiction over a foreign state shall exist as to every claim for relief over which the district courts have jurisdiction under subsection (a) where service has been made under section 1608 of this title.

(c) For purposes of subsection (b), an appearance by a foreign state does not confer personal jurisdiction with respect to any claim for relief not arising out of any transaction or occurrence enumerated in sections 1605-1607 of this title.

§1332. Diversity of Citizenship; Amount in Controversy; Costs

(a) The district courts shall have original jurisdiction of all civil actions where the matter in controversy exceeds the sum or value of $75,000, exclusive of interest and costs, and is between—

(1) citizens of different States;

(2) citizens of a State and citizens or subjects of a foreign state, except that the district courts shall not have original jurisdiction under this subsection of an action between citizens of a State and citizens or subjects of a foreign state who are lawfully admitted for permanent residence in the United States and are domiciled in the same State;

(3) citizens of different States and in which citizens or subjects of a foreign state are additional parties; and

(4) a foreign state, defined in section 1603(a) of this title, as plaintiff and citizens of a State or of different States.

(b) Except when express provision therefor is otherwise made in a statute of the United States, where the plaintiff who files the case originally in the Federal courts is finally adjudged to be entitled to recover less than the sum or value of $75,000, computed without regard to any setoff or counterclaim to which the defendant may be adjudged to be entitled, and exclusive of interest and costs, the district court may deny costs to the plaintiff and, in addition, may impose costs on the plaintiff.

(c) For the purposes of this section and section 1441 of this title—

(1) a corporation shall be deemed to be a citizen of every State and foreign state by which it has been incorporated and of the State or foreign state where it has its principal place of business, except that in any direct action against the insurer of a policy or contract of liability insurance, whether incorporated or unincorporated, to which action the insured is not joined as a party-defendant, such insurer shall be deemed a citizen of

(A) every State and foreign state of which the insured is a citizen;

(B) every State and foreign state by which the insurer has been incorporated; and

(C) the State or foreign state where the insurer has its principal place of business; . . .

(e) The word "States," as used in this section, includes the Territories, the District of Columbia, and the Commonwealth of Puerto Rico.

§1391. Venue Generally. . . .

(f) Civil actions against a foreign state. A civil action against a foreign state as defined in section 1603(a) of this title may be brought—

(1) in any judicial district in which a substantial part of the events or omissions giving rise to the claim occurred, or a substantial part of property that is the subject of the action is situated;

(2) in any judicial district in which the vessel or cargo of a foreign state is situated, if the claim is asserted under section 1605(b) of this title;

(3) in any judicial district in which the agency or instrumentality is licensed to do business or is doing business, if the action is brought against an agency or instrumentality of a foreign state as defined in section 1603(b) of this title; or

(4) in the United States District Court for the District of Columbia if the action is brought against a foreign state or political subdivision thereof.

§1441. Removal of civil actions. . . .

(d) Actions against foreign states. Any civil action brought in a State court against a foreign state as defined in section 1603(a) of this title may be removed by the foreign state to the district court of the United States for the district and division embracing the place where such action is pending. Upon removal the action shall be tried by the court without jury. Where removal is based upon this subsection, the time limitations of section 1446(b) of this chapter may be enlarged at any time for cause shown. . . .

CHAPTER 97—JURISDICTIONAL IMMUNITIES OF FOREIGN STATES

Sec.
1602. Findings and declaration of purpose.
1603. Definitions.
1604. Immunity of a foreign state from jurisdiction.
1605. General exceptions to the jurisdictional immunity of a foreign state.
1606. Extent of liability.
1607. Counterclaims.
1608. Service; time to answer default.
1609. Immunity from attachment and execution of property of a foreign state.
1610. Exceptions to the immunity from attachment or execution.
1611. Certain types of property immune from execution.

§1602. Findings and Declaration of Purpose

The Congress finds that the determination by United States courts of the claims of foreign states to immunity from the jurisdiction of such courts would serve the interests of justice and would protect the rights of both foreign states and litigants in United States courts. Under international law, states are not immune from the jurisdiction of foreign courts insofar as their commercial activities are concerned, and their commercial property may be levied upon for the satisfaction of judgments rendered against them in connection with their commercial activities. Claims of foreign states to immunity should henceforth be decided by courts of the United States and of the States in conformity with the principles set forth in this chapter.

§1603. Definitions

For purposes of this chapter—

(a) A "foreign state", except as used in section 1608 of this title, includes a political subdivision of a foreign state or an agency or instrumentality of a foreign state as defined in subsection (b).

(b) An "agency or instrumentality of a foreign state" means any entity—

(1) which is a separate legal person, corporate or otherwise, and

(2) which is an organ of a foreign state or political subdivision thereof, or a majority of whose shares or other ownership interest is owned by a foreign state or political subdivision thereof, and

(3) which is neither a citizen of a State of the United States as defined in section 1332(c) and (e) of this title, nor created under the laws of any third country.

(c) The "United States" includes all territory and waters, continental or insular, subject to the jurisdiction of the United States.

(d) A "commercial activity" means either a regular course of commercial conduct or a particular commercial transaction or act. The commercial character of an activity shall be determined by reference to the nature of the course of conduct or particular transaction or act, rather than by reference to its purpose.

(e) A "commercial activity carried on in the United States by a foreign state" means commercial activity carried on by such state and having substantial contact with the United States.

§1604. Immunity of a Foreign State from Jurisdiction

Subject to existing international agreements to which the United States is a party at the time of enactment of this Act a foreign state shall be immune from the jurisdiction of the courts of the United States and of the States except as provided in sections 1605 to 1607 of this chapter.

§1605. General Exceptions to the Jurisdictional Immunity of a Foreign State

(a) A foreign state shall not be immune from the jurisdiction of courts of the United States or of the States in any case—

(1) in which the foreign state has waived its immunity either explicitly or by implication, notwithstanding any withdrawal of the waiver which the foreign state may purport to effect except in accordance with the terms of the waiver;

(2) in which the action is based upon a commercial activity carried on in the United States by the foreign state; or upon an act performed in the United States in connection with a commercial activity of the foreign state elsewhere; or upon an act outside the territory of the United States in connection with a commercial activity of the foreign state elsewhere and that act causes a direct effect in the United States;

(3) in which rights in property taken in violation of international law are in issue and that property or any property exchanged for such property is present in the United States in connection with a commercial activity carried on in the United States by the foreign state; or that property or any property exchanged for such property is owned or operated by an agency or instrumentality of the foreign state and that agency or instrumentality is engaged in a commercial activity in the United States;

(4) in which rights in property in the United States acquired by succession or gift or rights in immovable property situated in the United States are in issue;

(5) not otherwise encompassed in paragraph (2) above, in which money damages are sought against a foreign state for personal injury or death, or damage to or loss of property, occurring in the United States and caused by the tortious act or omission of that foreign state or of any official or employee of that foreign state while acting within the scope of his office or employment; except this paragraph shall not apply to—

(A) any claim based upon the exercise or performance or the failure to exercise or perform a discretionary function regardless of whether the discretion be abused, or

(B) any claim arising out of malicious prosecution, abuse of process, libel, slander, misrepresentation, deceit, or interference with contract rights; or

(6) in which the action is brought, either to enforce an agreement made by the foreign state with or for the benefit of a private party to submit to arbitration all or any differences which have arisen or which may arise between the parties with respect to a defined legal relationship, whether contractual or not, concerning a subject matter capable of settlement by arbitration under the laws of the United States, or to confirm an award made pursuant to such an agreement to arbitrate, if (A) the arbitration takes place or is intended to take place in the United States, (B) the agreement or award is or may be governed by a treaty or other international agreement in force for the United States calling for the recognition and enforcement of arbitral awards, (C) the underlying claim, save for the agreement to arbitrate, could have been brought in a United States court under this section or section 1607, or (D) paragraph (1) of this subsection is otherwise applicable; or

[(7) Repealed. Pub.L. 110-181, Div. A, §1083(b)(1)(A)(iii), Jan. 28, 2008, 122 Stat. 341]

(b) A foreign state shall not be immune from the jurisdiction of the courts of the United States in any case in which a suit in admiralty is brought to enforce a maritime lien against a vessel or cargo of the foreign state, which maritime lien is based upon a commercial activity of the foreign state: *Provided*, That—

(1) notice of the suit is given by delivery of a copy of the summons and of the complaint to the person, or his agent, having possession of the vessel or cargo against which the maritime lien is asserted; and if the vessel or cargo is arrested pursuant to process obtained on behalf of the party bringing the

suit, the service of process of arrest shall be deemed to constitute valid delivery of such notice, but the party bringing the suit shall be liable for any damages sustained by the foreign state as a result of the arrest if the party bringing the suit had actual or constructive knowledge that the vessel or cargo of a foreign state was involved; and

(2) notice to the foreign state of the commencement of suit as provided in section 1608 of this tide is initiated within ten days either of the delivery of notice as provided in paragraph (1) of this subsection or, in the case of a party who was unaware that the vessel or cargo of a foreign state was involved, of the date such party determined the existence of the foreign state's interest.

(c) Whenever notice is delivered under subsection (b)(1), the suit to enforce a maritime lien shall thereafter proceed and shall be heard and determined according to the principles of law and rules of practice of suits in rem whenever it appears that, had the vessel been privately owned and possessed, a suit in rem might have been maintained. A decree against the foreign state may include costs of the suit and, if the decree is for a money judgment, interest as ordered by the court, except that the court may not award judgment against the foreign state in an amount greater than the value of the vessel or cargo upon which the maritime lien arose. Such value shall be determined as of the time notice is served under subsection (b)(1). Decrees shall be subject to appeal and revision as provided in other cases of admiralty and maritime jurisdiction. Nothing shall preclude the plaintiff in any proper case from seeking relief in personam in the same action brought to enforce a maritime lien as provided in this section.

(d) A foreign state shall not be immune from the jurisdiction of the courts of the United States in any action brought to foreclose a preferred mortgage, as defined in section 31301 of title 46. Such action shall be brought, heard, and determined in accordance with the provisions of chapter 313 of title 46 and in accordance with the principles of law and rules of practice of suits in rem, whenever it appears that had the vessel been privately owned and possessed a suit in rem might have been maintained.

[(e), (f) Repealed. Pub.L. 110-181, Div. A, Title X, §1083(b)(1)(B), Jan. 28, 2008, 122 Stat. 341]

(g) Limitation on discovery.—

(1) In general.—(A) Subject to paragraph (2), if an action is filed that would otherwise be barred by section 1604, but for subsection (a)(7), the court, upon request of the Attorney General, shall stay any request, demand, or order for discovery on the United States that the Attorney General certifies would significantly interfere with a criminal investigation or prosecution, or a national security operation, related to the incident that gave rise to the cause of action, until such time as the Attorney General advises the court that such request, demand, or order will no longer so interfere.

(B) A stay under this paragraph shall be in effect during the 12-month period beginning on the date on which the court issues the order to stay discovery. The court shall renew the order to stay discovery for additional 12-month periods upon motion by the United States if the Attorney General certifies that discovery would significantly interfere with a criminal investigation or prosecution, or a national security operation, related to the incident that gave rise to the cause of action.

(2) Sunset.—(A) Subject to subparagraph (B), no stay shall be granted or continued in effect under paragraph (1) after the date that is 10 years after the date on which the incident that gave rise to the cause of action occurred.

(B) After the period referred to in subparagraph (A), the court, upon request of the Attorney General, may stay any request, demand, or order for discovery on the United States that the court finds a substantial likelihood would—

(i) create a serious threat of death or serious bodily injury to any person;

(ii) adversely affect the ability of the United States to work in cooperation with foreign and international law enforcement agencies in investigating violations of United States law; or

(iii) obstruct the criminal case related to the incident that gave rise to the cause of action or undermine the potential for a conviction in such case.

(3) Evaluation of evidence.—The court's evaluation of any request for a stay under this subsection filed by the Attorney General shall be conducted ex parte and in camera.

(4) Bar on motions to dismiss.—A stay of discovery under this subsection shall constitute a bar to the granting of a motion to dismiss under rules 12(b)(6) and 56 of the Federal Rules of Civil Procedure.

(5) Construction.—Nothing in this subsection shall prevent the United States from seeking protective orders or asserting privileges ordinarily available to the United States.

HISTORICAL AND STATUTORY NOTES

Civil Liability for Acts of State Sponsored Terrorism [Flatow Amendment].
Pub. L. 104-208, Div. A, Title I, §101(c) [Title V, §589], Sept. 30, 1996, 110 Stat. 3009-172, provided that:

(a) An official, employee, or agent of a foreign state designated as a state sponsor of terrorism designated under section 6(j) of the Export Administration Act of 1979 [section 2405(j) of the Appendix to Title 50, War and National Defense] while acting within the scope of his or her office, employment, or agency shall be liable to a United States national or the national's legal representative for personal injury or death caused by acts of that official, employee, or agent for which the courts of the United States may maintain jurisdiction under section 1605(a)(7) of title 28, United States Code [subsec. (a)(7) of this section] for money damages which may include economic damages, solatium, pain, and suffering, and punitive damages if the acts were among those described in section 1605(a)(7).

(b) Provisions related to statute of limitations and limitations on discovery that would apply to an action brought under 28 U.S.C. 1605(f) and (g) [subsecs. (f) and (g) of this section] shall also apply to actions brought under this section. No action shall be maintained under this action [sic] if an official, employee, or agent of the United States, while acting within the scope of his or her office, employment, or agency would not be liable for such acts if carried out within the United States.

§1605A. Terrorism Exception to the Jurisdictional Immunity of a Foreign State

(Added by Pub.L. 110-181, Div. A, Title X, § 1083(a)(1), Jan. 28, 2008, 122 Stat. 338.)

(a) In general.—

(1) No immunity.—A foreign state shall not be immune from the jurisdiction of courts of the United States or of the States in any case not otherwise covered by this chapter in which money damages are sought against a foreign state for personal injury or death that was caused by an act of torture, extrajudicial killing, aircraft sabotage, hostage taking, or the provision of material support or resources for such an act if such act or provision of material support or resources is engaged in by an official, employee, or agent of such foreign state while acting within the scope of his or her office, employment, or agency.

(2) Claim heard.—The court shall hear a claim under this section if—

(A)(i)(I) the foreign state was designated as a state sponsor of terrorism at the time the act described in paragraph (1) occurred, or was so designated as a result of such act, and, subject to subclause (II), either remains so designated when the claim is filed under this section or was so designated within the 6-month period before the claim is filed under this section; or

(II) in the case of an action that is refiled under this section by reason of section 1083(c)(2)(A) of the National Defense Authorization Act for Fiscal Year 2008 or is filed under this section by reason of section 1083(c)(3) of that Act, the foreign state was designated as a state sponsor of terrorism when the original action or the related action under section 1605(a)(7) (as in effect before the enactment of this section) or section 589 of the Foreign Operations, Export Financing, and Related Programs Appropriations Act, 1997 (as contained in section 101(c) of division A of Public Law 104-208) was filed;

(ii) the claimant or the victim was, at the time the act described in paragraph (1) occurred—

(I) a national of the United States;

(II) a member of the armed forces; or

(III) otherwise an employee of the Government of the United States, or of an individual performing a contract awarded by the United States Government, acting within the scope of the employee's employment; and

(iii) in a case in which the act occurred in the foreign state against which the claim has been brought, the claimant has afforded the foreign state a reasonable opportunity to arbitrate the claim in accordance with the accepted international rules of arbitration; or

(B) the act described in paragraph (1) is related to Case Number 1:00CV03110 (EGS) in the United States District Court for the District of Columbia.

(b) Limitations.—An action may be brought or maintained under this section if the action is commenced, or a related action was commenced under section 1605(a)(7) (before the date of the enactment of this section) or section 589 of the Foreign Operations, Export Financing, and Related Programs Appropriations Act, 1997 (as contained in section 101(c) of division A of Public Law 104-208) not later than the latter of—

(1) 10 years after April 24, 1996; or

(2) 10 years after the date on which the cause of action arose.

(c) Private right of action.—A foreign state that is or was a state sponsor of terrorism as described in subsection (a)(2)(A)(i), and any official, employee, or agent of that foreign state while acting within the scope of his or her office, employment, or agency, shall be liable to—

(1) a national of the United States,

(2) a member of the armed forces,

(3) an employee of the Government of the United States, or of an individual performing a contract awarded by the United States Government, acting within the scope of the employee's employment, or

(4) the legal representative of a person described in paragraph (1), (2), or (3), for personal injury or death caused by acts described in subsection (a)(1) of that foreign state, or of an official, employee, or agent of that foreign state, for which the courts of the United States may maintain jurisdiction under this section for money damages. In any such action, damages may include economic damages, solatium, pain and suffering, and punitive damages. In any such action, a foreign state shall be vicariously liable for the acts of its officials, employees, or agents.

(d) Additional damages.—After an action has been brought under subsection (c), actions may also be brought for reasonably foreseeable property loss, whether insured or uninsured, third party liability, and loss claims under life and property insurance policies, by reason of the same acts on which the action under subsection (c) is based.

(e) Special masters.—

(1) In general.—The courts of the United States may appoint special masters to hear damage claims brought under this section.

(2) Transfer of funds.—The Attorney General shall transfer, from funds available for the program under section 1404C of the Victims of Crime Act of 1984 (42 U.S.C. 10603c), to the Administrator of the United States district court in which any case is pending which has been brought or maintained under this section such funds as may be required to cover the costs of special masters appointed under paragraph (1). Any amount paid in compensation to any such special master shall constitute an item of court costs.

(f) Appeal.—In an action brought under this section, appeals from orders not conclusively ending the litigation may only be taken pursuant to section 1292(b) of this title.

(g) Property disposition.—

(1) In general.—In every action filed in a United States district court in which jurisdiction is alleged under this section, the filing of a notice of pending action pursuant to this section, to which is attached a copy of the complaint filed in the action, shall have the effect of establishing a lien of lis pendens upon any real property or tangible personal property that is—

   (A) subject to attachment in aid of execution, or execution, under section 1610;

   (B) located within that judicial district; and

   (C) titled in the name of any defendant, or titled in the name of any entity controlled by any defendant if such notice contains a statement listing such controlled entity.

(2) Notice.—A notice of pending action pursuant to this section shall be filed by the clerk of the district court in the same manner as any pending action and shall be indexed by listing as defendants all named defendants and all entities listed as controlled by any defendant.

(3) Enforceability.—Liens established by reason of this subsection shall be enforceable as provided in chapter 111 of this title.

(h) Definitions.—For purposes of this section—

(1) the term "aircraft sabotage" has the meaning given that term in Article 1 of the Convention for the Suppression of Unlawful Acts Against the Safety of Civil Aviation;

(2) the term "hostage taking" has the meaning given that term in Article 1 of the International Convention Against the Taking of Hostages;

(3) the term "material support or resources" has the meaning given that term in section 2339A of title 18;

(4) the term "armed forces" has the meaning given that term in section 101 of title 10;

(5) the term "national of the United States" has the meaning given that term in section 101(a)(22) of the Immigration and Nationality Act (8 U.S.C. 1101(a)(22));

(6) the term "state sponsor of terrorism" means a country the government of which the Secretary of State has determined, for purposes of section 6(j) of the Export Administration Act of 1979 (50 U.S.C. App. 2405(j)), section 620A of the Foreign Assistance Act of 1961 (22 U.S.C. 2371), section 40 of the Arms Export Control Act (22 U.S.C. 2780), or any other provision of law, is a government that has repeatedly provided support for acts of international terrorism; and

(7) the terms "torture" and "extrajudicial killing" have the meaning given those terms in section 3 of the Torture Victim Protection Act of 1991 (28 U.S.C. 1350 note).

§1606. Extent of Liability

As to any claim for relief with respect to which a foreign state is not entitled to immunity under section 1605 or 1607 of this chapter, the foreign state shall be liable in the same manner and to the same extent as a private individual under like circumstances; but a foreign state except for an agency or instrumentality thereof shall not be liable for punitive damages; if, however, in any case wherein death was caused, the law of the place where the action or omission occurred provides, or has been construed to provide, for damages only punitive in nature, the foreign state shall be liable for actual or compensatory damages measured by the pecuniary injuries resulting from such death which were incurred by the persons for whose benefit the action was brought.

§1607. Counterclaims

In any action brought by a foreign state, or in which a foreign state intervenes, in a court of the United States or of a State, the foreign state shall not be accorded immunity with respect to any counterclaim—

(a) for which a foreign state would not be entitled to immunity under section 1605 or 1605A of this chapter had such claim been brought in a separate action against the foreign state; or

(b) arising out of the transaction or occurrence that is the subject matter of the claim of the foreign state; or

(c) to the extent that the counterclaim does not seek relief exceeding in amount or differing in kind from that sought by the foreign state.

§1608. Service; Time to Answer; Default

(a) Service in the courts of the United States and of the States shall be made upon a foreign state or political subdivision of a foreign state:

(1) by delivery of a copy of the summons and complaint in accordance with any special arrangement for service between the plaintiff and the foreign state or political subdivision; or

(2) if no special arrangement exists, by delivery of a copy of the summons and complaint in accordance with an applicable international convention on service of judicial documents; or

(3) if service cannot be made under paragraphs (1) or (2), by sending a copy of the summons and complaint and a notice of suit, together with a translation of each into the official language of the foreign state, by any form of mail requiring a signed receipt, to be addressed and dispatched by the clerk of the court to the head of the ministry of foreign affairs of the foreign state concerned, or

(4) if service cannot be made within 30 days under paragraph (3), by sending two copies of the summons and complaint and a notice of suit, together with a translation of each into the official language of the foreign state, by any form of mail requiring a signed receipt, to be addressed and dispatched by the clerk of the court to the Secretary of State in Washington, District of Columbia, to the attention of the Director of Special Consular Services—and the Secretary shall transmit one copy of the papers through diplomatic channels to the foreign state and shall send to the clerk of the court a certified copy of the diplomatic note indicating when the papers were transmitted.

As used in this subsection, a "notice of suit" shall mean a notice addressed to a foreign state and in a form prescribed by the Secretary of State by regulation.

(b) Service in the courts of the United States and of the States shall be made upon an agency or instrumentality of a foreign state:

(1) by delivery of a copy of the summons and complaint in accordance with any special arrangement for service between the plaintiff and the agency or instrumentality; or

(2) if no special arrangement exists, by delivery of a copy of the summons and complaint either to an officer, a managing or general agent, or to any other agent authorized by appointment or by law to receive service of process in the United States; or in accordance with an applicable international convention on service of judicial documents; or

(3) if service cannot be made under paragraphs (1) or (2), and if reasonably calculated to give actual notice, by delivery of a copy of the summons and complaint, together with a translation of each into the official language of the foreign state—

(A) as directed by an authority of the foreign state or political subdivision in response to a letter rogatory or request or

(B) by any form of mail requiring a signed receipt, to be addressed and dispatched by the clerk of the court to the agency or instrumentality to be served, or

(C) as directed by order of the court consistent with the law of the place where service is to be made.

(c) Service shall be deemed to have been made—

(1) in the case of service under subsection (a)(4), as of the date of transmittal indicated in the certified copy of the diplomatic note; and

(2) in any other case under this section, as of the date of receipt indicated in the certification, signed and returned postal receipt, or other proof of service applicable to the method of service employed.

(d) In any action brought in a court of the United States or of a State, a foreign state, a political subdivision thereof, or an agency or instrumentality of a foreign state shall serve an answer or other responsive pleading to the complaint within sixty days after service has been made under this section.

(e) No judgment by default shall be entered by a court of the United States or of a State against a foreign state, a political subdivision thereof, or an agency or instrumentality of a foreign state, unless the claimant establishes his claim or right to relief by evidence satisfactory to the court. A copy of any such default judgment shall be sent to the foreign state or political subdivision in the manner prescribed for service in this section.

§1609. Immunity from Attachment and Execution of Property of a Foreign State

Subject to existing international agreements to which the United States is a party at the time of enactment of this Act the property in the United States of a foreign state shall be immune from attachment arrest and execution except as provided in sections 1610 and 1611 of this chapter.

§1610. Exceptions to the Immunity from Attachment or Execution*

(a) The property in the United States of a foreign state, as defined in section 1603(a) of this chapter, used for a commercial activity in the United States, shall not be immune from attachment in aid of execution, or from execution, upon a judgment entered by a court of the United States or of a State after the effective date of this Act, if—

(1) the foreign state has waived its immunity from attachment in aid of execution or from execution either explicitly or by implication, notwithstanding any withdrawal of the waiver the foreign state may purport to effect except in accordance with the terms of the waiver, or

(2) the property is or was used for the commercial activity upon which the claim is based, or

(3) the execution relates to a judgment establishing rights in property which has been taken in violation of international law or which has been exchanged for property taken in violation of international law, or

(4) the execution relates to a judgment establishing rights in property—

(A) which is acquired by succession or gift, or

(B) which is immovable and situated in the United States: *Provided,* That such property is not used for purposes of maintaining a diplomatic or consular mission or the residence of the Chief of such mission, or

(5) the property consists of any contractual obligation or any proceeds from such a contractual obligation to indemnify or hold harmless the foreign state or its employees under a policy of automobile or other liability or casualty insurance covering the claim which merged into the judgment, or

---

*See also Act of Nov. 26, 2002, Pub. L. No. 107-297, Title II, §201(a), (B), (D), 116 Stat. 2337, 2339, regarding satisfaction of judgments from blocked assets of terrorists, including presidential waivers and definitions.

(6) the judgment is based on an order confirming an arbitral award rendered against the foreign State, provided that attachment in aid of execution, or execution, would not be inconsistent with any provision in the arbitral agreement; or

(7) the judgment relates to a claim for which the foreign state is not immune under section 1605A or section 1605(a)(7) (as such section was in effect on January 27, 2008), regardless of whether the property is or was involved with the act upon which the claim is based.

(b) In addition to subsection (a), any property in the United States of an agency or instrumentality of a foreign state engaged in commercial activity in the United States shall not be immune from attachment in aid of execution, or from execution, upon a judgment entered by a court of the United States or of a State after the effective date of this Act if—

(1) the agency or instrumentality has waived its immunity from attachment in aid of execution or from execution either explicitly or implicitly, notwithstanding any withdrawal of the waiver the agency or instrumentality may purport to effect except in accordance with the terms of the waiver, or

(2) the judgment relates to a claim for which the agency or instrumentality is not immune by virtue of section 1605 (a) (2), (3), or (5), or 1605(b) of this chapter, regardless of whether the property is or was used for the activity upon which the claim is based, or

(3) the judgment relates to a claim for which the agency or instrumentality is not immune by virtue of section 1605A of this chapter or section 1605(a)(7) of this chapter (as such section was in effect on January 27, 2008), regardless of whether the property is or was involved in the act upon which the claim is based.

(c) No attachment or execution referred to in subsections (a) and (b) of this section shall be permitted until the court has ordered such attachment and execution after having determined that a reasonable period of time has elapsed following the entry of judgment and the giving of any notice required under section 1608(e) of this chapter.

(d) The property of a foreign state, as defined in section 1603(a) of this chapter, used for a commercial activity in the United States, shall not be immune from attachment prior to the entry of judgment in any action brought in a court of the United States or of a State, or prior to the elapse of the period of time provided in subsection (c) of this section, if—

(1) the foreign state has explicitly waived its immunity from attachment prior to judgment, notwithstanding any withdrawal of the waiver the foreign state may purport to effect except in accordance with the terms of the waiver, and

(2) the purpose of the attachment is to secure satisfaction of a judgment that has been or may ultimately be entered against the foreign state, and not to obtain jurisdiction.

(e) The vessels of a foreign State shall not be immune from arrest in rem, interlocutory sale, and execution in actions brought to foreclose a preferred mortgage as provided in section 1605(d).

(f)(1)(A) Notwithstanding any other provision of law, including but not limited to section 208(f) of the Foreign Missions Act (22 U.S.C. 4308(f)), and except as provided in subparagraph (B), any property with respect to which financial transactions are prohibited or regulated pursuant to section 5(b) of the Trading with the Enemy Act (50 U.S.C. App. 5(b)), section 620(a) of the Foreign Assistance Act of 1961 (22 U.S.C. 2370(a)), sections 202 and 203 of the International Emergency Economic Powers Act (50 U.S.C. 1701-1702), or any other proclamation, order, regulation, or license issued pursuant thereto, shall be subject to execution or attachment in aid of execution of any judgment relating to a claim for which a foreign state (including any agency or instrumentality or such state) claiming such property is not immune under section 1605(a)(7) (as in effect before the enactment of section 1605A) or section 1605A.

(B) Subparagraph (A) shall not apply if, at the time the property is expropriated or seized by the foreign state, the property has been held in title by a natural person or, if held in trust, has been held for the benefit of a natural person or persons.

(2)(A) At the request of any party in whose favor a judgment has been issued with respect to a claim for which the foreign state is not immune under section 1605(a)(7) (as in effect before the enactment of section 1605A) or section 1605A, the Secretary of the Treasury and the Secretary of State should make every effort to fully, promptly, and effectively assist any judgment creditor or any court that has issued any such judgment in identifying, locating, and executing against the property of that foreign state or any agency or instrumentality of such state.

(B) In providing such assistance, the Secretaries—

(i) may provide such information to the court under seal; and

(ii) should make every effort to provide the information in a manner sufficient to allow the court to direct the United States Marshal's office to promptly and effectively execute against that property.

(3) Waiver. The President may waive any provision of paragraph (1) in the interest of national security.

(g) Property in certain actions.—

(1) In general.—Subject to paragraph (3), the property of a foreign state against which a judgment is entered under section 1605A, and the property of an agency or instrumentality of such a state, including property that is a separate juridical entity or is an interest held directly or indirectly in a separate juridical entity, is subject to attachment in aid of execution, and execution, upon that judgment as provided in this section regardless of—

(A) the level of economic control over the property by the government of the foreign state;

(B) whether the profits of the property go to that government;

(C) the degree to which officials of that government manage the property or otherwise control its daily affairs;

(D) whether that government is the sole beneficiary in interest of the property; or

(E) whether establishing the property as a separate entity would entitle the foreign state to benefits in United States courts while avoiding its obligations.

(2) United States sovereign immunity inapplicable.—Any property of a foreign state, or agency or instrumentality of a foreign state, to which paragraph (1) applies shall not be immune from attachment in aid of execution, or execution, upon a judgment entered under section 1605A because the property is regulated by the United States Government by reason on action taken against that foreign state under the Trade With the Enemy Act or the International Emergency Economic Powers Act.

(3) Third-party joint property holders.—Nothing in this subsection shall be construed to supersede the authority of a court to prevent appropriately the impairment of an interest held by a person who is not liable in the action giving rise to a judgment in property subject to attachment in aid of execution, or execution, upon such judgment.

§1611. Certain Types of Property Immune from Execution

(a) Notwithstanding the provisions of section 1610 of this chapter, the property of those organizations designated by the President as being entitled to enjoy the privileges, exemptions, and immunities provided by the International Organizations Immunities Act shall not be subject to attachment or any other judicial process impeding the disbursement of funds to, or on the order of, a foreign state as the result of an action brought in the courts of the United States or of the States.

(b) Notwithstanding the provisions of section 1610 of this chapter, the property of a foreign state shall be immune from attachment and from execution, if—

(1) the property is that of a foreign central bank or monetary authority held for its own account, unless such bank or authority, or its parent foreign government, has explicitly waived its immunity from attachment in aid of execution, or from execution, notwithstanding any withdrawal of the waiver which the bank, authority or government may purport to effect except in accordance with the terms of the waiver; or

(2) the property is, or is intended to be, used in connection with a military activity and

(A) is of a military character, or

(B) is under the control of a military authority or defense agency.

(c) Notwithstanding the provisions of section 1610 of this chapter, the property of a foreign state shall be immune from attachment and from execution in an action brought under section 302 of the Cuban Liberty and Democratic Solidarity (LIBERTAD) Act of 1996 to the extent that the property is a facility or installation used by an accredited diplomatic mission for official purposes.

VIENNA CONVENTION ON
DIPLOMATIC RELATIONS

April 18, 1961, 23 U.S.T. 3227, T.I.A.S. No. 7502, 500 U.N.T.S. 95*

The States Parties to the present Convention,

Recalling that peoples of all nations from ancient times have recognized the status of diplomatic agents,

Having in mind the purposes and principles of the Charter of the United Nations concerning the sovereign equality of States, the maintenance of international peace and security, and the promotion of friendly relations among nations,

Believing that an international convention on diplomatic intercourse, privileges and immunities would contribute to the development of friendly relations among nations, irrespective of their differing constitutional and social systems,

---

*Adopted at Vienna on April 18, 1961. Entered into force on April 24, 1964. The United States ratified the convention on November 13, 1972.

As of February 2013, the 187 parties to the convention were: Afghanistan, Albania, Algeria, Andorra, Angola, Argentina, Armenia, Australia, Austria, Azerbaijan, Bahamas, Bahrain, Bangladesh, Barbados, Belarus, Belgium, Belize, Benin, Bhutan, Bolivia, Bosnia and Herzegovina, Botswana, Brazil, Bulgaria, Burkina Faso, Burundi, Cambodia, Cameroon, Canada, Cape Verde, Central African Republic, Chad, Chile, China, Colombia, Comoros, Congo, Congo (Democratic Republic of the), Costa Rica, Cote d'Ivoire, Croatia, Cuba, Cyprus, Czech Republic, Denmark, Djibouti, Dominica, Dominican Republic, Ecuador, Egypt, El Salvador, Equatorial Guinea, Eritrea, Estonia, Ethiopia, Fiji, Finland, France, Gabon, Georgia, Germany, Ghana, Greece, Grenada, Guatemala, Guinea, Guinea-Bissau, Guyana, Haiti, Holy See, Honduras, Hungary, Iceland, India, Indonesia, Iran, Iraq, Ireland, Israel, Italy, Jamaica, Japan, Jordan, Kazakhstan, Kenya, Kiribati, Korea (Democratic People's Republic of), Korea (Republic of), Kuwait, Kyrgyzstan, Lao People's Democratic Republic, Latvia, Lebanon, Lesotho, Liberia, Libyan Arab Jamahiriya, Liechtenstein, Lithuania, Luxembourg, Macedonia (the former Yugoslav Republic of), Madagascar, Malawi, Malaysia, Maldives, Mali, Malta, Marshall Islands, Mauritania, Mauritius, Mexico, Micronesia, Moldova, Monaco, Mongolia, Montenegro, Morocco, Mozambique, Myanmar, Namibia, Nauru, Nepal, Netherlands, New Zealand, Nicaragua, Niger, Nigeria, Norway, Oman, Pakistan, Panama, Papua New Guinea, Paraguay, Peru, Philippines, Poland, Portugal, Qatar, Romania, Russian Federation, Rwanda, Saint Lucia, Saint Vincent and the Grenadines, Samoa, San Marino, Sao Tome and Principe, Saudi Arabia, Serbia, Senegal, Seychelles, Singapore, Sierra Leone, Slovakia, Slovenia, Somalia, South Africa, Spain, Sri Lanka, St. Kitts and Nevis, Sudan, Suriname, Swaziland, Sweden, Switzerland, Syrian Arab Republic, Tajikistan, Tanzania, Thailand, Timor-Leste, Togo, Tonga, Trinidad and Tobago, Tunisia, Turkey, Turkmenistan, Tuvalu, Uganda, Ukraine, United Arab Emirates, United Kingdom, United States of America, Uruguay, Uzbekistan, Venezuela, Viet Nam, Yemen, Zambia, and Zimbabwe. See the U.N. Web site at <http://treaties.un.org>.

Realizing that the purpose of such privileges and immunities is not to benefit individuals but to ensure the efficient performance of the functions of diplomatic missions as representing States,

Affirming that the rules of customary international law should continue to govern questions not expressly regulated by the provisions of the present Convention,

Have agreed as follows:

Article 1

For the purpose of the present Convention, the following expressions shall have the meanings hereunder assigned to them:

(*a*) the "head of the mission" is the person charged by the sending State with the duty of acting in that capacity;

(*b*) the "members of the mission" are the head of the mission and the members of the staff of the mission;

(*c*) the "members of the staff of the mission" are the members of the diplomatic staff, of the administrative and technical staff and of the service staff of the mission;

(*d*) the "members of the diplomatic staff" are the members of the staff of the mission having diplomatic rank;

(*e*) a "diplomatic agent" is the head of the mission or a member of the diplomatic staff of the mission;

(*f*) the "members of the administrative and technical staff" are the members of the staff of the mission employed in the administrative and technical service of the mission;

(*g*) the "members of the service staff" are the members of the staff of the mission in the domestic service of the mission;

(*h*) a "private servant" is a person who is in the domestic service of a member of the mission and who is not an employee of the sending State;

(*i*) the "premises of the mission" are the buildings or parts of buildings and the land ancillary thereto, irrespective of ownership, used for the purposes of the mission including the residence of the head of the mission.

Article 2

The establishment of diplomatic relations between States, and of permanent diplomatic missions, takes place by mutual consent.

Article 3

1. The functions of a diplomatic mission consist *inter alia* in:

(*a*) representing the sending State in the receiving State;

(*b*) protecting in the receiving State the interests of the sending State and of its nationals, within the limits permitted by international law;

(*c*) negotiating with the Government of the receiving State;

(*d*) ascertaining by all lawful means conditions and developments in the receiving State, and reporting thereon to the Government of the sending State;

(*e*) promoting friendly relations between the sending State and the receiving State, and developing their economic, cultural and scientific relations.

2. Nothing in the present Convention shall be construed as preventing the performance of consular functions by a diplomatic mission.

Article 4

1. The sending State must make certain that the *agrément* of the receiving State has been given for the person it proposes to accredit as head of the mission to that State.

2. The receiving State is not obliged to give reasons to the sending State for a refusal of *agrément*.

Article 5

1. The sending State may, after it has given due notification to the receiving States concerned, accredit a head of mission or assign any member of the diplomatic staff, as the case may be, to more than one State, unless there is express objection by any of the receiving States.

2. If the sending State accredits a head of mission to one or more other States it may establish a diplomatic mission headed by a *chargé d'affaires ad interim* in each State where the head of mission has not his permanent seat.

3. A head of mission or any member of the diplomatic staff of the mission may act as representative of the sending State to any international organization.

Article 6

Two or more States may accredit the same person as head of mission to another State, unless objection is offered by the receiving State.

Article 7

Subject to the provisions of Articles 5, 8, 9 and 11, the sending State may freely appoint the members of the staff of the mission. In the case of military, naval or air attachés, the receiving State may require their names to be submitted beforehand, for its approval.

Article 8

1. Members of the diplomatic staff of the mission should in principle be of the nationality of the sending State.

2. Members of the diplomatic staff of the mission may not be appointed from among persons having the nationality of the receiving State, except with the consent of that State which may be withdrawn at any time.

3. The receiving State may reserve the same right with regard to nationals of a third State who are not also nationals of the sending State.

Article 9

1. The receiving State may at any time and without having to explain its decision, notify the sending State that the head of the mission or any member of the diplomatic staff of the mission is *persona non grata* or that any other member of the staff of the mission is not acceptable. In any such case, the sending State shall, as appropriate, either recall the person concerned or terminate his functions with the mission. A person may be declared *non grata* or not acceptable before arriving in the territory of the receiving State.

2. If the sending State refuses or fails within a reasonable period to carry out its obligations under paragraph 1 of this Article, the receiving State may refuse to recognize the person concerned as a member of the mission.

Article 10

1. The Ministry for Foreign Affairs of the receiving State, or such other ministry as may be agreed, shall be notified of:

(*a*) the appointment of members of the mission, their arrival and their final departure or the termination of their functions with the mission;

(*b*) the arrival and final departure of a person belonging to the family of a member of the mission and, where appropriate, the fact that a person becomes or ceases to be a member of the family of a member of the mission;

(*c*) the arrival and final departure of private servants in the employ of persons referred to in sub-paragraph (a) of this paragraph and, where appropriate, the fact that they are leaving the employ of such persons;

(*d*) the engagement and discharge of persons resident in the receiving State as members of the mission or private servants entitled to privileges and immunities.

2. Where possible, prior notification of arrival and final departure shall also be given.

Article 11

1. In the absence of specific agreement as to the size of the mission, the receiving State may require that the size of a mission be kept within limits considered by it to be reasonable and normal, having regard to circumstances and conditions in the receiving State and to the needs of the particular mission.

2. The receiving State may equally, within similar bounds and on a non-discriminatory basis, refuse to accept officials of a particular category.

Article 12

The sending State may not, without the prior express consent of the receiving State, establish offices forming part of the mission in localities other than those in which the mission itself is established.

Article 13

1. The head of the mission is considered as having taken up his functions in the receiving State either when he has presented his credentials or when he has notified his arrival and a true copy of his credentials has been presented to the Ministry for Foreign Affairs of the receiving State, or such other ministry as may be agreed, in accordance with the practice prevailing in the receiving State which shall be applied in a uniform manner.

2. The order of presentation of credentials or of a true copy thereof will be determined by the date and time of the arrival of the head of the mission.

Article 14

1. Heads of mission are divided into three classes, namely:

(*a*) that of ambassadors or nuncios accredited to Heads of State, and other heads of mission of equivalent rank;

(*b*) that of envoys, ministers and internuncios accredited to Heads of State;

(*c*) that of *chargés d'affaires* accredited to Ministers for Foreign Affairs.

2. Except as concerns precedence and etiquette, there shall be no differentiation between heads of mission by reason of their class.

Article 15

The class to which the heads of their missions are to be assigned shall be agreed between States.

Article 16

1. Heads of mission shall take precedence in their respective classes in the order of the date and time of taking up their functions in accordance with Article 13.

2. Alterations in the credentials of a head of mission not involving any change of class shall not affect his precedence.

3. This article is without prejudice to any practice accepted by the receiving State regarding the precedence of the representative of the Holy See.

Article 17

The precedence of the members of the diplomatic staff of the mission shall be notified by the head of the mission to the Ministry for Foreign Affairs or such other ministry as may be agreed.

Article 18

The procedure to be observed in each State for the reception of heads of mission shall be uniform in respect of each class.

Article 19

1. If the post of head of the mission is vacant, or if the head of the mission is unable to perform his functions, a *chargé d'affaires ad interim* shall act provisionally as head of the mission. The name of the *chargé d'affaires ad interim* shall be notified, either by the head of the mission or, in case he is unable to do so, by the Ministry for Foreign Affairs of the sending State to the Ministry for Foreign Affairs of the receiving State or such other ministry as may be agreed.

2. In cases where no member of the diplomatic staff of the mission is present in the receiving State, a member of the administrative and technical staff may, with the consent of the receiving State, be designated by the sending State to be in charge of the current administrative affairs of the mission.

Article 20

The mission and its head shall have the right to use the flag and emblem of the sending State on the premises of the mission, including the residence of the head of the mission, and on his means of transport.

Article 21

1. The receiving State shall either facilitate the acquisition on its territory, in accordance with its laws, by the sending State of premises necessary for its mission or assist the latter in obtaining accommodation in some other way.

2. It shall also, where necessary, assist missions in obtaining suitable accommodation for their members.

Article 22

1. The premises of the mission shall be inviolable. The agents of the receiving State may not enter them, except with the consent of the head of the mission.

2. The receiving State is under a special duty to take all appropriate steps to protect the premises of the mission against any intrusion or damage and to prevent any disturbance of the peace of the mission or impairment of its dignity.

3. The premises of the mission, their furnishings and other property thereon and the means of transport of the mission shall be immune from search, requisition, attachment or execution.

Article 23

1. The sending State and the head of the mission shall be exempt from all national, regional or municipal dues and taxes in respect of the premises

of the mission, whether owned or leased, other than such as represent payment for specific services rendered.

2. The exemption from taxation referred to in this Article shall not apply to such dues and taxes payable under the law of the receiving State by persons contracting with the sending State or the head of the mission.

Article 24

The archives and documents of the mission shall be inviolable at any time and wherever they may be.

Article 25

The receiving State shall accord full facilities for the performance of the functions of the mission.

Article 26

Subject to its laws and regulations concerning zones entry into which is prohibited or regulated for reasons of national security, the receiving State shall ensure to all members of the mission freedom of movement and travel in its territory.

Article 27

1. The receiving State shall permit and protect free communication on the part of the mission for all official purposes. In communicating with the Government and the other missions and consulates of the sending State, wherever situated, the mission may employ all appropriate means, including diplomatic couriers and messages in code or cipher. However, the mission may install and use a wireless transmitter only with the consent of the receiving State.

2. The official correspondence of the mission shall be inviolable. Official correspondence means all correspondence relating to the mission and its functions.

3. The diplomatic bag shall not be opened or detained.

4. The packages constituting the diplomatic bag must bear visible external marks of their character and may contain only diplomatic documents or articles intended for official use.

5. The diplomatic courier, who shall be provided with an official document indicating his status and the number of packages constituting the diplomatic bag, shall be protected by the receiving State in the performance of his functions. He shall enjoy personal inviolability and shall not be liable to any form of arrest or detention.

6. The sending State or the mission may designate diplomatic couriers *ad hoc*. In such cases the provisions of paragraph 5 of this Article shall also apply, except that the immunities therein mentioned shall cease to apply when such a courier has delivered to the consignee the diplomatic bag in his charge.

7. A diplomatic bag may be entrusted to the captain of a commercial aircraft scheduled to land at an authorized port of entry. He shall be provided with an official document indicating the number of packages constituting the bag but he shall not be considered to be a diplomatic courier. The mission may send one of its members to take possession of the diplomatic bag directly and freely from the captain of the aircraft.

Article 28

The fees and charges levied by the mission in the course of its official duties shall be exempt from all dues and taxes.

Article 29

The person of a diplomatic agent shall be inviolable. He shall not be liable to any form of arrest or detention. The receiving State shall treat him with due respect and shall take all appropriate steps to prevent any attack on his person, freedom or dignity.

Article 30

1. The private residence of a diplomatic agent shall enjoy the same inviolability and protection as the premises of the mission.

2. His papers, correspondence and, except as provided in paragraph 3 of Article 31, his property, shall likewise enjoy inviolability.

Article 31

1. A diplomatic agent shall enjoy immunity from the criminal jurisdiction of the receiving State. He shall also enjoy immunity from its civil and administrative jurisdiction, except in the case of:

(a) a real action relating to private immovable property situated in the territory of the receiving State, unless he holds it on behalf of the sending State for the purpose of the mission;

(b) an action relating to succession in which the diplomatic agent is involved as executor, administrator, heir or legatee as a private person and not on behalf of the sending. State:

(c) an action relating to any professional or commercial activity exercised by the diplomatic agent in the receiving State outside his official functions.

2. A diplomatic agent is not obliged to give evidence as a witness.

3. No measures of execution may be taken in respect of a diplomatic agent except in the cases coming under sub-paragraphs (a), (b) and (c) of paragraph 1 of this Article, and provided that the measures concerned can be taken without infringing the inviolability of his person or of his residence.

4. The immunity of a diplomatic agent from the jurisdiction of the receiving State does not exempt him from the jurisdiction of the sending State.

Article 32

1. The immunity from jurisdiction of diplomatic agents and of persons enjoying immunity under Article 37 may be waived by the sending State.

2. Waiver must always be express.

3. The initiation of proceedings by a diplomatic agent or by a person enjoying immunity from jurisdiction under Article 37 shall preclude him from invoking immunity from jurisdiction in respect of any counter-claim directly connected with the principal claim.

4. Waiver of immunity from jurisdiction in respect of civil or administrative proceedings shall not be held to imply waiver of immunity in respect of the execution of the judgment, for which a separate waiver shall be necessary.

Article 33

1. Subject to the provisions of paragraph 3 of this Article, a diplomatic agent shall with respect to services rendered for the sending State be exempt from social security provisions which may be in force in the receiving State.

2. The exemption provided for in paragraph 1 of this Article shall also apply to private servants who are in the sole employ of a diplomatic agent, on condition:

(a) that they are not nationals of or permanently resident in the receiving State; and

(b) that they are covered by the social security provisions which may be in force in the sending State or a third State.

3. A diplomatic agent who employs persons to whom the exemption provided for in paragraph 2 of this Article does not apply shall observe the obligations which the social security provisions of the receiving State impose upon employers.

4. The exemption provided for in paragraphs 1 and 2 of this Article shall not preclude voluntary participation in the social security system of the receiving State provided that such participation is permitted by that State.

5. The provisions of this Article shall not affect bilateral or multilateral agreements concerning social security concluded previously and shall not prevent the conclusion of such agreements in the future.

Article 34

A diplomatic agent shall be exempt from all dues and taxes, personal or real, national, regional or municipal, except:

(a) indirect taxes of a kind which are normally incorporated in the price of goods or services;

(b) dues and taxes on private immovable property situated in the territory of the receiving State, unless he holds it on behalf of the sending State for the purposes of the mission;

(*c*) estate, succession or inheritance duties levied by the receiving State, subject to the provisions of paragraph 4 of Article 39;

(*d*) dues and taxes on private income having its source in the receiving State and capital taxes on investments made in commercial undertakings in the receiving State;

(*e*) charges levied for specific services rendered;

(*f*) registration, court or record fees, mortgage dues and stamp duty, with respect to immovable property, subject to the provisions of Article 23.

Article 35

The receiving State shall exempt diplomatic agents from all personal services, from all public service of any kind whatsoever, and from military obligations such as those connected with requisitioning, military contributions and billeting.

Article 36

1. The receiving State shall, in accordance with such laws and regulations as it may adopt, permit entry of and grant exemption from all customs duties, taxes, and related charges other than charges for storage, cartage and similar services, on:

(*a*) articles for the official use of the mission;

(*b*) articles for the personal use of a diplomatic agent or members of his family forming part of his household, including articles intended for his establishment.

2. The personal baggage of a diplomatic agent shall be exempt from inspection, unless there are serious grounds for presuming that it contains articles not covered by the exemptions mentioned in paragraph 1 of this Article, or articles the import or export of which is prohibited by the law or controlled by the quarantine regulations of the receiving State. Such inspection shall be conducted only in the presence of the diplomatic agent or of his authorized representative.

Article 37

1. The members of the family of a diplomatic agent forming part of his household shall, if they are not nationals of the receiving State, enjoy the privileges and immunities specified in Articles 29 to 36.

2. Members of the administrative and technical staff of the mission, together with members of their families forming part of their respective households, shall, if they are not nationals of or permanently resident in the receiving State, enjoy the privileges and immunities specified in Articles 29 to 35, except that the immunity from civil and administrative jurisdiction of the receiving State specified in paragraph 1 of Article 31 shall not extend to acts performed outside the course of their duties. They shall also enjoy the privileges specified in Article 36, paragraph 1, in respect of articles imported at the time of first installation.

3. Members of the service staff of the mission who are not nationals of or permanently resident in the receiving State shall enjoy immunity in respect of acts performed in the course of their duties, exemption from dues and taxes on the emoluments they receive by reason of their employment and the exemption contained in Article 33.

4. Private servants of members of the mission shall, if they are not nationals of or permanently resident in the receiving State, be exempt from dues and taxes on the emoluments they receive by reason of their employment. In other respects, they may enjoy privileges and immunities only to the extent admitted by the receiving State. However, the receiving State must exercise its jurisdiction over those persons in such a manner as not to interfere unduly with the performance of the functions of the mission.

Article 38

1. Except insofar as additional privileges and immunities may be granted by the receiving State, a diplomatic agent who is a national of or permanently resident in that State shall enjoy only immunity from jurisdiction, and inviolability, in respect of official acts performed in the exercise of his functions.

2. Other members of the staff of the mission and private servants who are nationals of or permanently resident in the receiving State shall enjoy privileges and immunities only to the extent admitted by the receiving State. However, the receiving State must exercise its jurisdiction over those persons in such a manner as not to interfere unduly with the performance of the functions of the mission.

Article 39

1. Every person entitled to privileges and immunities shall enjoy them from the moment he enters the territory of the receiving State on proceeding to take up his post or, if already in its territory, from the moment when his appointment is notified to the Ministry for Foreign Affairs or such other ministry as may be agreed.

2. When the functions of a person enjoying privileges and immunities have come to an end, such privileges and immunities shall normally cease at the moment when he leaves the country, or on expiry of a reasonable period in which to do so, but shall subsist until that time, even in case of armed conflict. However, with respect to acts performed by such a person in the exercise of his functions as a member of the mission, immunity shall continue to subsist.

3. In case of the death of a member of the mission, the members of his family shall continue to enjoy the privileges and immunities to which they are entitled until the expiry of a reasonable period in which to leave the country.

4. In the event of the death of a member of the mission not a national of or permanently resident in the receiving State or a member of his family forming part of his household, the receiving State shall permit the

withdrawal of the movable property of the deceased, with the exception of any property acquired in the country the export of which was prohibited at the time of his death. . . .

Article 40

1. If a diplomatic agent passes through or is in the territory of a third State, which has granted him a passport visa if such visa was necessary, while proceeding to take up or to return to his post, or when returning to his own country, the third State shall accord him inviolability and such other immunities as may be required to ensure his transit or return. The same shall apply in the case of any members of his family enjoying privileges or immunities who are accompanying the diplomatic agent, or travelling separately to join him or to return to their country.

2. In circumstances similar to those specified in paragraph 1 of this Article, third States shall not hinder the passage of members of the administrative and technical or service staff of a mission, and of members of their families, through their territories.

3. Third States shall accord to official correspondence and other official communications in transit, including messages in code or cipher, the same freedom and protection as is accorded by the receiving State. They shall accord to diplomatic couriers, who have been granted a passport visa if such visa was necessary, and diplomatic bags in transit the same inviolability and protection as the receiving State is bound to accord.

4. The obligations of third States under paragraphs 1, 2 and 3 of this Article shall also apply to the persons mentioned respectively in those paragraphs, and to official communications and diplomatic bags, whose presence in the territory of the third State is due to *force majeure*.

Article 41

1. Without prejudice to their privileges and immunities, it is the duty of all persons enjoying such privileges and immunities to respect the laws and regulations of the receiving State. They also have a duty not to interfere in the internal affairs of that State.

2. All official business with the receiving State entrusted to the mission by the sending State shall be conducted with or through the Ministry for Foreign Affairs of the receiving State or such other ministry as may be agreed.

3. The premises of the mission must not be used in any manner incompatible with the functions of the mission as laid down in the present Convention or by other rules of general international law or by any special agreements in force between the sending and the receiving State.

Article 42

A diplomatic agent shall not in the receiving State practice for personal profit any professional or commercial activity.

Article 43

The function of a diplomatic agent comes to an end, *inter alia:*

(*a*) on notification by the sending State to the receiving State that the function of the diplomatic agent has come to an end;

(*b*) on notification by the receiving State to the sending State that, in accordance with paragraph 2 of Article 9, it refuses to recognize the diplomatic agent as a member of the mission.

Article 44

The receiving State must, even in case of armed conflict, grant facilities in order to enable persons enjoying privileges and immunities, other than nationals of the receiving State, and members of the families of such persons irrespective of their nationality, to leave at the earliest possible moment. It must, in particular, in case of need, place at their disposal the necessary means of transport for themselves and their property.

Article 45

If diplomatic relations are broken off between two States, or if a mission is permanently or temporarily recalled:

(*a*) the receiving State must, even in case of armed conflict, respect and protect the premises of the mission, together with its property and archives;

(*b*) the sending State may entrust the custody of the premises of the mission, together with its property and archives, to a third State acceptable to the receiving State;

(*c*) the sending State may entrust the protection of its interests and those of its nationals to a third State acceptable to the receiving State.

Article 46

A sending State may with the prior consent of a receiving State, and at the request of a third State not represented in the receiving State, undertake the temporary protection of the interests of the third State and of its nationals.

Article 47

1. In the application of the provisions of the present Convention, the receiving State shall not discriminate as between States.

2. However, discrimination shall not be regarded as taking place:

(*a*) where the receiving State applies any of the provisions of the present Convention restrictively because of a restrictive application of that provision to its mission in the sending State;

(*b*) where by custom or agreement States extend to each other more favourable treatment than is required by the provisions of the present Convention.

Article 48

The present Convention shall be open for signature by all States Members of the United Nations or of any of the specialized agencies or Parties to the Statute of the International Court of Justice, and by any other State invited by the General Assembly of the United Nations to become a Party to the Convention. . . .

Article 49

The present Convention is subject to ratification. The instruments of ratification shall be deposited with the Secretary-General of the United Nations.

Article 50

The present Convention shall remain open for accession by any State belonging to any of the four categories mentioned in Article 48. . . .

Article 51

1. The present Convention shall enter into force on the thirtieth day following the date of deposit of the twenty-second instrument of ratification or accession with the Secretary-General of the United Nations.

2. For each State ratifying or acceding to the Convention after the deposit of the twenty-second instrument of ratification or accession, the Convention shall enter into force on the thirtieth day after deposit by such State of its instrument of ratification or accession. . . .

VIENNA CONVENTION
ON CONSULAR RELATIONS

April 24, 1963, 21 U.S.T. 77, T.I.A.S. No. 6820, 596 U.N.T.S. 261*

The States Parties to the present Convention,

Recalling that consular relations have been established between peoples since ancient times, . . .

Considering that the United Nations Conference on Diplomatic Intercourse and Immunities adopted the Vienna Convention on Diplomatic Relations which was opened for signature on 18 April 1961,

Believing that an international convention on consular relations, privileges and immunities would also contribute to the development of friendly relations among nations, irrespective of their differing constitutional and social systems.

*Entered into force on March 19, 1967. The United States ratified the convention on November 21, 1969.

As of February 2013, the 174 parties to the convention were: Albania, Algeria, Andorra, Angola, Antigua and Barbuda, Argentina, Armenia, Australia, Austria, Azerbaijan, Bahamas, Bahrain, Bangladesh, Barbados, Belarus, Belgium, Belize, Benin, Bhutan, Bolivia, Bosnia and Herzegovina, Botswana, Brazil, Bulgaria, Burkina Faso, Cameroon, Cambodia, Canada, Cape Verde, Chile, China, Colombia, Congo (Democratic Republic of), Costa Rica, Croatia, Cuba, Cyprus, Czech Republic, Denmark, Djibouti, Dominica, Dominican Republic, Ecuador, Egypt, El Salvador, Equatorial Guinea, Eritrea, Estonia, Fiji, Finland, France, Gabon, Georgia, Germany, Ghana, Greece, Grenada, Guatemala, Guinea, Guyana, Haiti, Holy See, Honduras, Hungary, Iceland, India, Indonesia, Iran, Iraq, Ireland, Italy, Jamaica, Japan, Jordan, Kazakhstan, Kenya, Kiribati, Korea (Democratic Republic of), Korea (Republic of), Kuwait, Kyrgyzstan, Lao People's Democratic Republic, Latvia, Lebanon, Lesotho, Liberia, Libyan Arab Jamahiriya, Liechtenstein, Lithuania, Luxembourg, Macedonia (the former Yugoslav Republic of), Madagascar, Malawi, Malaysia, Maldives, Mali, Malta, Marshall Islands, Mauritania, Mauritius, Mexico, Micronesia, Moldova, Monaco, Mongolia, Montenegro, Morocco, Mozambique, Myanmar, Namibia, Nauru, Nepal, Netherlands, New Zealand, Nicaragua, Niger, Nigeria, Norway, Oman, Pakistan, Panama, Papua New Guinea, Paraguay, Peru, Philippines, Poland, Portugal, Qatar, Romania, Russian Federation, Rwanda, Saint Lucia, Saint Vincent and the Grenadines, Samoa, Sao Tome and Principe, Saudi Arabia, Serbia, Senegal, Seychelles, Singapore, Slovakia, Slovenia, Somalia, South Africa, Spain, Sri Lanka, St. Kitts and Nevis, Sudan, Suriname, Sweden, Switzerland, Syrian Arab Republic, Tajikistan, Tanzania, Thailand, Timor-Leste, Togo, Tonga, Trinidad and Tobago, Tunisia, Turkey, Turkmenistan, Tuvalu, Ukraine, United Arab Emirates, United Kingdom, United States of America, Uruguay, Uzbekistan, Vanuatu, Venezuela, Viet Nam, Yemen, and Zimbabwe. See U.N. Web site at <http://treaties.un.org>.

Realizing that the purpose of such privileges and immunities is not to benefit individuals but to ensure the efficient performance of functions by consular posts on behalf of their respective States,

Affirming that the rules of customary international law continue to govern matters not expressly regulated by the provisions of the present Convention,

Have agreed as follows:

Article 1. Definitions

1. For the purposes of the present Convention, the following expressions shall have the meanings hereunder assigned to them:

(a) "Consular post" means any consulate-general, consulate, vice-consulate or consular agency;

(b) "Consular district" means the area assigned to a consular post for the exercise of consular functions;

(c) "Head of consular post" means the person charged with the duty of acting in that capacity;

(d) "Consular officer" means any person, including the head of a consular post, entrusted in that capacity with the exercise of consular functions;

(e) "Consular employees" means any person employed in the administrative or technical service of a consular post;

(f) "Member of the service staff" means any person employed in the domestic service of a consular post;

(g) "Members of the consular post" means consular officers, consular employees and members of the service staff;

(h) "Members of the consular staff" means consular officers, other than the head of a consular post, consular employees and members of the service staff;

(i) "Member of the private staff" means a person who is employed exclusively in the private service of a member of the consular post;

(j) "Consular premises" means the buildings or parts of buildings and the land ancillary thereto, irrespective of ownership, used exclusively for the purposes of the consular post;

(k) "Consular archives" includes all the papers, documents, correspondence, books, films, tapes and registers of the consular post, together with the ciphers and codes, the card-indexes and any article of furniture intended for their protection or safekeeping.

2. Consular officers are of two categories, namely career consular officers and honorary consular officers. The provisions of Chapter II of the present Convention apply to consular posts headed by career consular officers; the provisions of Chapter III govern consular posts headed by honorary consular officers.

3. The particular status of members of the consular posts who are nationals or permanent residents of the receiving State is governed by article 71 of the present Convention.

Section I.   Establishment and Conduct of Consular Relations

Article 2.   Establishment of Consular Relations

1. The establishment of consular relations between States takes place by mutual consent.

2. The consent given to the establishment of diplomatic relations between two States implies, unless otherwise stated, consent to the establishment of consular relations.

3. The severance of diplomatic relations shall not *ipso facto* involve the severance of consular relations.

Article 3.   Exercise of Consular Functions

Consular functions are exercised by consular posts. They are also exercised by diplomatic missions in accordance with the provisions of the present Convention.

Article 4.   Establishment of a Consular Post

1. A consular post may be established in the territory of the receiving State only with that State's consent.

2. The seat of the consular post, its classification and the consular district shall be established by the sending State and shall be subject to the approval of the receiving State.

3. Subsequent changes in the seat of the consular post, its classification or the consular district may be made by the sending State only with the consent of the receiving State.

4. The consent of the receiving State shall also be required if a consulate-general or a consulate desires to open a vice-consulate or a consular agency in a locality other than that in which it is itself established.

5. The prior express consent of the receiving State shall also be required for the opening of an office forming part of an existing consular post elsewhere than at the seat thereof.

Article 5.   Consular Functions

Consular functions consist in:

(a) Protecting in the receiving State the interests of the sending State and of its nationals, both individuals and bodies corporate, within the limits permitted by international law;

(b) Furthering the development of commercial, economic, cultural and scientific relations between the sending State and the receiving State and otherwise promoting friendly relations between them in accordance with the provisions of the present Convention;

(c) Ascertaining by all lawful means conditions and developments in the commercial, economic, cultural and scientific life of the receiving State, reporting thereon to the Government of the sending State and giving information to persons interested;

(d) Issuing passports and travel documents to nationals of the sending State, and visas or appropriate documents to persons wishing to travel to the sending State;

(e) Helping and assisting nationals, both individuals and bodies corporate, of the sending State;

(f) Acting as notary and civil registrar and in capacities of a similar kind, and performing certain functions of an administrative nature, provided that there is nothing contrary thereto in the laws and regulations of the receiving State;

(g) Safeguarding the interests of nationals, both individuals and bodies corporate, of the sending State in cases of succession *mortis causa* in the territory of the receiving State, in accordance with the laws and regulations of the receiving State;

(h) Safeguarding, within the limits imposed by the laws and regulations of the receiving State, the interests of minors and other persons lacking full capacity who are nationals of the sending State, particularly where any guardianship or trusteeship is required with respect to such persons;

(i) Subject to the practices and procedures obtaining in the receiving State, representing or arranging appropriate representation for nationals of the sending State before the tribunals and other authorities of the receiving State, for the purpose of obtaining, in accordance with the laws and regulations of the receiving State, provisional measures for the preservation of the rights and interests of these nationals, where, because of absence or any other reason, such nationals are unable at the proper time to assume the defence of their rights and interests;

(j) Transmitting judicial and extra-judicial documents or executing letters rogatory or commissions to take evidence for the courts of the sending State in accordance with international agreements in force or, in the absence of such international agreements, in any other manner compatible with the laws and regulations of the receiving State;

(k) Exercising rights of supervision and inspection provided for in the laws and regulations of the sending State in respect of vessels having the nationality of the sending State, and of aircraft registered in that State, and in respect of their crews;

(l) Extending assistance to vessels and aircraft mentioned in subparagraph (k) of this article, and to their crews, taking statements regarding the voyage of a vessel, examining and stamping the ship's papers, and, without prejudice to the powers of the authorities of the receiving State, conducting investigations into any incidents which occurred during the voyage, and settling disputes of any kind between the master, the officers and the seamen in so far as this may be authorized by the laws and regulations of the sending State;

(m) Performing any other functions entrusted to a consular post by the sending State which are not prohibited by the laws and regulations of the receiving State or to which no objection is taken by the receiving State or which are referred to in the international agreements in force between the sending State and the receiving State.

Article 6. Exercise of Consular Functions Outside the Consular District

A consular officer may, in special circumstances, with the consent of the receiving State, exercise his functions outside his consular district. . . .

Article 8. Exercise of Consular Functions on Behalf of a Third State

Upon appropriate notification to the receiving State, a consular post of the sending State may, unless the receiving State objects, exercise consular functions in the receiving State on behalf of a third State.

Article 9. Classes of Heads of Consular Posts

1. Heads of consular posts are divided into four classes, namely:
   (a) Consuls-general;
   (b) Consuls;
   (c) Vice-consuls;
   (d) Consular agents.
2. Paragraph 1 of this article in no way restricts the right of any of the Contracting Parties to fix the designation of consular officers other than the heads of consular posts.

Article 10. Appointment and Admission of Heads of Consular Posts

1. Heads of consular posts are appointed by the sending State and are admitted to the exercise of their functions by the receiving State.
2. Subject to the provisions of the present Convention, the formalities for the appointment and for the admission of the head of a consular post are determined by the laws, regulations and usages of the sending State and of the receiving State respectively.

Article 11. The Consular Commission or Notification of Appointment

1. The head of a consular post shall be provided by the sending State with a document, in the form of a commission or similar instrument, made out for each appointment, certifying his capacity and showing, as a general rule, his full name, his category and class, the consular district and the seat of the consular post.
2. The sending State shall transmit the commission or similar instrument through the diplomatic or other appropriate channel to the Government of the State in whose territory the head of a consular post is to exercise his functions. . . .

Article 12.   The Exequatur

1. The head of a consular post is admitted to the exercise of his functions by an authorization from the receiving State termed an exequatur, whatever the form of this authorization.

2. A State which refuses to grant an exequatur is not obliged to give to the sending State reasons for such refusal.

3. Subject to the provisions of articles 13 and 15, the head of a consular post shall not enter upon his duties until he has received an exequatur.

Article 13.   Provisional Admission of Heads of Consular Posts

Pending delivery of the exequatur, the head of a consular post may be admitted on a provisional basis to the exercise of his functions. In that case, the provisions of the present Convention shall apply.

Article 14.   Notification to the Authorities of the Consular District

As soon as the head of a consular post is admitted even provisionally to the exercise of his functions, the receiving State shall immediately notify the competent authorities of the consular district. It shall also ensure that the necessary measures are taken to enable the head of a consular post to carry out the duties of his office and to have the benefit of the provisions of the present Convention.

Article 15.   Temporary Exercise of the Functions of the Head of a Consular Post

1. If the head of a consular post is unable to carry out his functions or the position of head of consular post is vacant, an acting head of post may act provisionally as head of the consular post.

2. The full name of the acting head of post shall be notified either by the diplomatic mission of the sending State or, if that State has no such mission in the receiving State, by the head of the consular post, or, if he is unable to do so, by any competent authority of the sending State, to the Ministry for Foreign Affairs of the receiving State or to the authority designated by that Ministry. As a general rule, this notification shall be given in advance. The receiving State may make the admission as acting head of post of a person who is neither a diplomatic agent nor a consular officer of the sending State in the receiving State conditional on its consent.

3. The competent authorities of the receiving State shall afford assistance and protection to the acting head of post. While he is in charge of the post, the provisions of the present Convention shall apply to him on the same basis as to the head of the consular post concerned. . . .

Article 16. Precedence as Between Heads of Consular Posts

1. Heads of consular posts shall rank in each class according to the date of the grant of the exequatur.

2. If, however, the head of a consular post before obtaining the exequatur is admitted to the exercise of his functions provisionally, his precedence shall be determined according to the date of the provisional admission; this precedence shall be maintained after the granting of the exequatur. . . .

4. Acting heads of posts shall rank after all heads of consular posts and, as between themselves, they shall rank according to the dates on which they assumed their functions as acting heads of posts as indicated in the notifications given under paragraph 2 of article 15.

5. Honorary consular officers who are heads of consular posts shall rank in each class after career heads of consular posts, in the order and according to the rules laid down in the foregoing paragraphs.

6. Heads of consular posts shall have precedence over consular officers not having that status.

Article 17. Performance of Diplomatic Acts by Consular Officers

1. In a State where the sending State has no diplomatic mission and is not represented by a diplomatic mission of a third State, a consular officer may, with the consent of the receiving State, and without affecting his consular status, be authorized to perform diplomatic acts. The performance of such acts by a consular officer shall not confer upon him any right to claim diplomatic privileges and immunities.

2. A consular officer may, after notification addressed to the receiving State, act as representative of the sending State to any inter-governmental organization. . . .

Article 18. Appointment of the Same Person by Two or More States as a Consular Officer

Two or more States may, with the consent of the receiving State, appoint the same person as a consular officer in that State.

Article 19. Appointment of Members of Consular Staff

1. Subject to the provisions of articles 20, 22 and 23, the sending State may freely appoint the members of the consular staff.

2. The full name, category and class of all consular officers, other than the head of a consular post, shall be notified by the sending State to the receiving State in sufficient time for the receiving State, if it so wishes, to exercise its rights under paragraph 3 of article 23.

3. The sending State may, if required by its laws and regulations, request the receiving State to grant an exequatur to a consular officer other than the head of a consular post.

4. The receiving State may, if required by its laws and regulations, grant an exequatur to a consular officer other than the head of a consular post.

Article 20. *Size of the Consular Staff*

In the absence of an express agreement as to the size of the consular staff, the receiving State may require that the size of the staff be kept within limits considered by it to be reasonable and normal, having regard to circumstances and conditions in the consular district and to the needs of the particular consular post.

Article 21. *Precedence as Between Consular Officers of a Consular Post*

The order of precedence as between the consular officers of a consular post and any change thereof shall be notified by the diplomatic mission of the sending State or, if that State has no such mission in the receiving State, by the head of the consular post, to the Ministry for Foreign Affairs of the receiving State or to the authority designated by that Ministry.

Article 22. *Nationality of Consular Officers*

1. Consular officers should, in principle, have the nationality of the sending State.

2. Consular officers may not be appointed from among persons having the nationality of the receiving State except with the express consent of that State which may be withdrawn at any time.

3. The receiving State may reserve the same right with regard to nationals of a third State who are not also nationals of the sending State.

Article 23. *Persons Declared Non Grata*

1. The receiving State may at any time notify the sending State that a consular officer is *persona non grata* or that any other member of the consular staff is not acceptable. In that event, the sending State shall, as the case may be, either recall the person concerned or terminate his functions with the consular post.

2. If the sending State refuses or fails within a reasonable time to carry out its obligations under paragraph 1 of this article, the receiving State may, as the case may be, either withdraw the exequatur from the person concerned or cease to consider him as a member of the consular staff.

3. A person appointed as a member of a consular post may be declared unacceptable before arriving in the territory of the receiving State or, if already in the receiving State, before entering on his duties with the consular post. In any such case, the sending State shall withdraw his appointment.

4. In the cases mentioned in paragraphs 1 and 3 of this article, the receiving State is not obliged to give to the sending State reasons for its decision.

Article 24. Notification to the Receiving State of Appointments, Arrivals and Departures

1. The Ministry for Foreign Affairs of the receiving State or the authority designated by that Ministry shall be notified of:

(a) The appointment of members of a consular post, their arrival after appointment to the consular post, their final departure or the termination of their functions and any other changes affecting their status that may occur in the course of their service with the consular post;

(b) The arrival and final departure of a person belonging to the family of a member of a consular post forming part of his household and, where appropriate, the fact that a person becomes or ceases to be such a member of the family;

(c) The arrival and final departure of members of the private staff and, where appropriate, the termination of their service as such;

(d) The engagement and discharge of persons resident in the receiving State as members of a consular post or as members of the private staff entitled to privileges and immunities.

2. When possible, prior notification of arrival and final departure shall also be given.

Section II.   End of Consular Functions

Article 25.   Termination of the Functions of a Member of a Consular Post

The functions of a member of a consular post shall come to an end *inter alia*:

(a) On notification by the sending State to the receiving State that his functions have come to an end;

(b) On withdrawal of the exequatur;

(c) On notification by the receiving State to the sending State that the receiving State has ceased to consider him as a member of the consular staff.

Article 26.   Departure from the Territory of the Receiving State

The receiving State shall, even in case of armed conflict, grant to members of the consular post and members of the private staff, other than nationals of the receiving State, and to members of their families forming part of their households irrespective of nationality, the necessary time and facilities to enable them to prepare their departure and to leave at the earliest possible moment after the termination of the functions of the members concerned. In particular, it shall, in case of need, place at their disposal the necessary means of transport for themselves and their property other than property acquired in the receiving State the export of which is prohibited at the time of departure.

Article 27. Protection of Consular Premises and Archives and of the Interests of the Sending State in Exceptional Circumstances

1. In the event of the severance of consular relations between two States:

(a) The receiving State shall, even in case of armed conflict, respect and protect the consular premises, together with the property of the consular post and the consular archives;

(b) The sending State may entrust the custody of the consular premises, together with the property contained therein and the consular archives, to a third State acceptable to the receiving State;

(c) The sending State may entrust the protection of its interests and those of its nationals to a third State acceptable to the receiving State.

2. In the event of the temporary or permanent closure of a consular post, the provisions of subparagraph (a) of paragraph 1 of this article shall apply. In addition:

(a) If the sending State, although not represented in the receiving State by a diplomatic mission, has another consular post in the territory of that State, that consular post may be entrusted with the custody of the premises of the consular post which has been closed, together with the property contained therein and the consular archives, and, with the consent of the receiving State, with the exercise of consular functions in the district of that consular post; or

(b) If the sending State has no diplomatic mission and no other consular post in the receiving State, the provisions of sub-paragraphs (b) and (c) of paragraph 1 of this article shall apply.

CHAPTER II. FACILITIES, PRIVILEGES AND IMMUNITIES RELATING TO CONSULAR POSTS, CAREER CONSULAR OFFICERS AND OTHER MEMBERS OF A CONSULAR POST

Section I. Facilities, Privileges and Immunities Relating to a Consular Post

Article 28. For the Work of the Consular Post

The receiving State shall accord full facilities for the performance of the functions of the consular post.

Article 29. Use of National Flag and Coat of Arms . . .

2. The national flag of the sending State may be flown and its coat of arms displayed on the building occupied by the consular post and at the entrance door thereof, on the residence of the head of the consular post and on his means of transport when used on official business. . . .

Article 30. Accommodation

1. The receiving State shall either facilitate the acquisition on its territory, in accordance with its laws and regulations, by the sending State of

premises necessary for its consular post or assist the latter in obtaining accommodation in some other way.

2. It shall also, where necessary, assist the consular post in obtaining suitable accommodation for its members.

Article 31.   Inviolability of the Consular Premises

1. Consular premises shall be inviolable to the extent provided in this article.

2. The authorities of the receiving State shall not enter that part of the consular premises which is used exclusively for the purpose of the work of the consular post except with the consent of the head of the consular post or of his designee or of the head of the diplomatic mission of the sending State. The consent of the head of the consular post may, however, be assumed in case of fire or other disaster requiring prompt protective action.

3. Subject to the provisions of paragraph 2 of this article, the receiving State is under a special duty to take all appropriate steps to protect the consular premises against any intrusion or damage and to prevent any disturbance of the peace of the consular post or impairment of its dignity.

4. The consular premises, their furnishings, the property of the consular post and its means of transport shall be immune from any form of requisition for purposes of national defence or public utility. If expropriation is necessary for such purposes, all possible steps shall be taken to avoid impeding the performance of consular functions, and prompt, adequate and effective compensation shall be paid to the sending State.

Article 32.   Exemption from Taxation of Consular Premises

1. Consular premises and the residence of the career head of consular post of which the sending State or any person acting on its behalf is the owner or lessee shall be exempt from all national, regional or municipal dues and taxes whatsoever, other than such as represent payment for specific services rendered.

2. The exemption from taxation referred to in paragraph 1 of this article shall not apply to such dues and taxes if, under the law of the receiving State, they are payable by the person who contracted with the sending State or with the person acting on its behalf.

Article 33.   Inviolability of the Consular Archives and Documents

The consular archives and documents shall be inviolable at all times and wherever they may be.

Article 34.   Freedom of Movement

Subject to its laws and regulations concerning zones entry into which is prohibited or regulated for reasons of national security, the receiving State shall ensure freedom of movement and travel in its territory to all members of the consular post.

Article 35. Freedom of Communication

1. The receiving State shall permit and protect freedom of communication on the part of the consular post for all official purposes. In communicating with the Government, the diplomatic missions and other consular posts, wherever situated, of the sending State, the consular post may employ all appropriate means, including diplomatic or consular couriers, diplomatic or consular bags and messages in code or cipher. However, the consular post may install and use a wireless transmitter only with the consent of the receiving State.

2. The official correspondence of the consular post shall be inviolable. Official correspondence means all correspondence relating to the consular post and its functions.

3. The consular bag shall be neither opened nor detained. Nevertheless, if the competent authorities of the receiving State have serious reason to believe that the bag contains something other than the correspondence, documents or articles referred to in paragraph 4 of this article, they may request that the bag be opened in their presence by an authorized representative of the sending State. If this request is refused by the authorities of the sending State, the bag shall be returned to its place of origin.

4. The packages constituting the consular bag shall bear visible external marks of their character and may contain only official correspondence and documents or articles intended exclusively for official use.

5. The consular courier shall be provided with an official document indicating his status and the number of packages constituting the consular bag. Except with the consent of the receiving State he shall be neither a national of the receiving State, nor, unless he is a national of the sending State, a permanent resident of the receiving State. In the performance of his functions he shall be protected by the receiving State. He shall enjoy personal inviolability and shall not be liable to any form of arrest or detention.

6. The sending State, its diplomatic missions and its consular posts may designate consular couriers *ad hoc*. In such cases the provisions of paragraph 5 of this article shall also apply except that the immunities therein mentioned shall cease to apply when such a courier has delivered to the consignee the consular bag in his charge.

7. A consular bag may be entrusted to the captain of a ship or of a commercial aircraft scheduled to land at an authorized port of entry. He shall be provided with an official document indicating the number of packages constituting the bag, but he shall not be considered to be a consular courier. . . .

Article 36. Communication and Contact with Nationals of the Sending State

1. With a view to facilitating the exercise of consular functions relating to nationals of the sending State:

(a) Consular officers shall be free to communicate with nationals of the sending State and to have access to them. Nationals of the sending State shall have the same freedom with respect to communication with and access to consular officers of the sending State;

(b) If he so requests, the competent authorities of the receiving State shall, without delay, inform the consular post of the sending State if, within its consular district, a national of that State is arrested or committed to prison or to custody pending trial or is detained in any other manner. Any communication addressed to the consular post by the person arrested, in prison, custody or detention shall also be forwarded by the said authorities without delay. The said authorities shall inform the person concerned without delay of his rights under this sub-paragraph;

(c) Consular officers shall have the right to visit a national of the sending State who is in prison, custody or detention, to converse and correspond with him and to arrange for his legal representation. They shall also have the right to visit any national of the sending State who is in prison, custody or detention in their district in pursuance of a judgement. Nevertheless, consular officers shall refrain from taking action on behalf of a national who is in prison, custody or detention if he expressly opposes such action.

2. The rights referred to in paragraph 1 of this article shall be exercised in conformity with the laws and regulations of the receiving State, subject to the proviso, however, that the said laws and regulations must enable full effect to be given to the purposes for which the rights accorded under this article are intended.

Article 37. Information in Cases of Deaths, Guardianship or Trusteeship, Wrecks and Air Accidents

If the relevant information is available to the competent authorities of the receiving State, such authorities shall have the duty:

(a) In the case of the death of a national of the sending State, to inform without delay the consular post in whose district the death occurred;

(b) To inform the competent consular post without delay of any case where the appointment of a guardian or trustee appears to be in the interests of a minor or other person lacking full capacity who is a national of the sending State. The giving of this information shall, however, be without prejudice to the operation of the laws and regulations of the receiving State concerning such appointments;

(c) If a vessel, having the nationality of the sending State, is wrecked or runs aground in the territorial sea or internal waters of the receiving State, or if an aircraft registered in the sending State suffers an accident on the

territory of the receiving State, to inform without delay the consular post nearest to the scene of the occurrence. . . .

Article 39.   Consular Fees and Charges

1. The consular post may levy in the territory of the receiving State the fees and charge provided by the laws and regulations of the sending State for consular acts.

2. The sums collected in the form of the fees and charges referred to in paragraph 1 of this article, and the receipts for such fees and charges, shall be exempt from all dues and taxes in the receiving State.

Section II.   Facilities, Privileges and Immunities Relating to Career Consular Officers and Other Members of a Consular Post

Article 40.   Protection of Consular Officers

The receiving State shall treat consular officers with due respect and shall take all appropriate steps to prevent any attack on their person, freedom or dignity.

Article 41.   Personal Inviolability of Consular Officers

1. Consular officers shall not be liable to arrest or detention pending trial, except in the case of a grave crime and pursuant to a decision by the competent judicial authority.

2. Except in the case specified in paragraph 1 of this article, consular officers shall not be committed to prison or be liable to any other form of restriction on their personal freedom save in execution of a judicial decision of final effect.

3. If criminal proceedings are instituted against a consular officer, he must appear before the competent authorities. Nevertheless, the proceedings shall be conducted with the respect due to him by reason of his official position and, except in the case specified in paragraph 1 of this article, in a manner which will hamper the exercise of consular functions as little as possible. When, in the circumstances mentioned in paragraph 1 of this article, it has become necessary to detain a consular officer, the proceedings against him shall be instituted with the minimum of delay.

Article 42.   Notification of Arrest, Detention or Prosecution

In the event of the arrest or detention, pending trial, of a member of the consular staff, or of criminal proceedings being instituted against him, the receiving State shall promptly notify the head of the consular post. Should the latter be himself the object of any such measure, the receiving State shall notify the sending State through the diplomatic channel.

Article 43.   Immunity from Jurisdiction

1. Consular officers and consular employees shall not be amenable to the jurisdiction of the judicial or administrative authorities of the receiving State in respect of acts performed in the exercise of consular functions.

2. The provisions of paragraph 1 of this article shall not, however, apply in respect of a civil action either:

(a) Arising out of a contract concluded by a consular officer or a consular employee in which he did not contract expressly or impliedly as an agent of the sending State; or

(b) By a third party for damage arising from an accident in the receiving State caused by a vehicle, vessel or aircraft.

Article 44.   Liability to Give Evidence

1. Members of a consular post may be called upon to attend as witnesses in the course of judicial or administrative proceedings. A consular employee or a member of the service staff shall not, except in the cases mentioned in paragraph 3 of this article, decline to give evidence. If a consular officer should decline to do so, no coercive measure or penalty may be applied to him.

2. The authority requiring the evidence of a consular officer shall avoid interference with the performance of his functions. It may, when possible, take such evidence at his residence or at the consular post or accept a statement from him in writing.

3. Members of a consular post are under no obligation to give evidence concerning matters connected with the exercise of their functions or to produce official correspondence and documents relating thereto. They are also entitled to decline to give evidence as expert witnesses with regard to the law of the sending State.

Article 45.   Waiver of Privileges and Immunities

1. The sending State may waive, with regard to a member of the consular post, any of the privileges and immunities provided for in articles 41, 43 and 44.

2. The waiver shall in all cases be express, except as provided in paragraph 3 of this article, and shall be communicated to the receiving State in writing.

3. The initiation of proceedings by a consular officer or a consular employee in a matter where he might enjoy immunity from jurisdiction under article 43 shall preclude him from invoking immunity from jurisdiction in respect of any counter-claim directly connected with the principal claim.

4. The waiver of immunity from jurisdiction for the purposes of civil or administrative proceedings shall not be deemed to imply the waiver of

immunity from the measures of execution resulting from the judicial decision; in respect of such measures, a separate waiver shall be necessary.

Article 46. Exemption from Registration of Aliens and Residence Permits

1. Consular officers and consular employees and members of their families forming part of their households shall be exempt from all obligations under the laws and regulations of the receiving State in regard to the registration of aliens and residence permits.

2. The provisions of paragraph 1 of this article shall not, however, apply to any consular employee who is not a permanent employee of the sending State or who carries on any private gainful occupation in the receiving State or to any member of the family of any such employee.

Article 47. Exemption from Work Permits

1. Members of the consular post shall, with respect to services rendered for the sending State, be exempt from any obligations in regard to work permits imposed by the laws and regulations of the receiving State concerning the employment of foreign labour.

2. Members of the private staff of consular officers and of consular employees shall, if they do not carry on any other gainful occupation in the receiving State, be exempt from the obligations referred to in paragraph 1 of this article.

Article 48. Social Security Exemption

1. Subject to the provisions of paragraph 3 of this article, members of the consular post with respect to services rendered by them for the sending State, and members of their families forming part of their households, shall be exempt from social security provisions which may be in force in the receiving State.

2. The exemption provided for in paragraph 1 of this article shall apply also to members of the private staff who are in the sole employ of members of the consular post, on condition:

(a) That they are not nationals of or permanently resident in the receiving State; and

(b) That they are covered by the social security provisions which are in force in the sending State or a third State.

3. Members of the consular post who employ persons to whom the exemption provided for in paragraph 2 of this article does not apply shall observe the obligations which the social security provisions of the receiving State impose upon employers. . . .

Article 49. Exemption from Taxation

1. Consular officers and consular employees and members of their families forming part of their households shall be exempt from all dues and taxes, personal or real, national, regional or municipal, except:

(a) Indirect taxes of a kind which are normally incorporated in the price of goods or services;

(b) Dues or taxes on private immovable property situated in the territory of the receiving State, subject to the provisions of article 32;

(c) Estate, succession or inheritance duties, and duties on transfers, levied by the receiving State, subject to the provisions of paragraph *(b)* of article 51;

(d) Dues and taxes on private income, including capital gains, having its source in the receiving State and capital taxes relating to investments made in commercial or financial undertakings in the receiving State;

(e) Charges levied for specific services rendered;

(f) Registration, court or record fees, mortgage dues and stamp duties, subject to the provisions of article 32.

2. Members of the service staff shall be exempt from dues and taxes on the wages which they receive for their services.

3. Members of the consular post who employ persons whose wages or salaries are not exempt from income tax in the receiving State shall observe the obligations which the laws and regulations of that State impose upon employers concerning the levying of income tax.

Article 50. *Exemption from Customs Duties and Inspection*

1. The receiving State shall, in accordance with such laws and regulations as it may adopt, permit entry of and grant exemption from all customs duties, taxes, and related charges other than charges for storage, cartage and similar services, on:

(a) Articles for the official use of the consular post;

(b) Articles for the personal use of a consular officer or members of his family forming part of his household, including articles intended for his establishment. The articles intended for consumption shall not exceed the quantities necessary for direct utilization by the persons concerned.

2. Consular employees shall enjoy the privileges and exemptions specified in paragraph 1 of this article in respect of articles imported at the time of first installation.

3. Personal baggage accompanying consular officers and members of their families forming part of their households shall be exempt from inspection. It may be inspected only if there is serious reason to believe that it contains articles other than those referred to in subparagraph *(b)* of paragraph 1 of this article, or articles the import or export of which is prohibited by the laws and regulations of the receiving State or which are subject to its quarantine laws and regulations. Such inspection shall be carried out in the presence of the consular officer or member of his family concerned. . . .

Article 53. *Beginning and End of Consular Privileges and Immunities*

1. Every member of the consular post shall enjoy the privileges and immunities provided in the present Convention from the moment he enters

the territory of the receiving State on proceeding to take up his post or, if already in its territory, from the moment when he enters on his duties with the consular post.

2. Members of the family of a member of the consular post forming part of his household and members of his private staff shall receive the privileges and immunities provided in the present Convention from the date from which he enjoys privileges and immunities in accordance with paragraph 1 of this article or from the date of their entry into the territory of the receiving State or from the date of their becoming a member of such family or private staff, whichever is the latest.

3. When the functions of a member of the consular post have come to an end, his privileges and immunities and those of a member of his family forming part of his household or a member of his private staff shall normally cease at the moment when the person concerned leaves the receiving State or on the expiry of a reasonable period in which to do so, whichever is the sooner, but shall subsist until that time, even in case of armed conflict. . . .

4. However, with respect to acts performed by a consular officer or a consular employee in the exercise of his functions, immunity from jurisdiction shall continue to subsist without limitation of time. . . .

Article 54. Obligations of Third States

1. If a consular officer passes through or is in the territory of a third State, which has granted him a visa if a visa was necessary, while proceeding to take up or return to his post or when returning to the sending State, the third State shall accord to him all immunities provided for by the other articles of the present Convention as may be required to ensure his transit or return. The same shall apply in the case of any member of his family forming part of his household enjoying such privileges and immunities who are accompanying the consular officer or travelling separately to join him or to return to the sending State.

2. In circumstances similar to those specified in paragraph 1 of this article, third States shall not hinder the transit through their territory of other members of the consular post or of members of their families forming part of their households.

3. Third States shall accord to official correspondence and to other official communications in transit, including messages in code or cipher, the same freedom and protection as the receiving State is bound to accord under the present Convention. They shall accord to consular couriers who have been granted a visa, if a visa was necessary, and to consular bags in transit, the same inviolability and protection as the receiving State is bound to accord under the present Convention.

4. The obligations of third States under paragraphs 1, 2 and 3 of this article shall also apply to the persons mentioned respectively in those

paragraphs, and to official communications and to consular bags, whose presence in the territory of the third State is due to *force majeure*.

Article 55. *Respect for the Laws and Regulations of the Receiving State*

1. Without prejudice to their privileges and immunities, it is the duty of all persons enjoying such privileges and immunities to respect the laws and regulations of the receiving State. They also have a duty not to interfere in the internal affairs of that State.

2. The consular premises shall not be used in any manner incompatible with the exercise of consular functions.

3. The provisions of paragraph 2 of this article shall not exclude the possibility of offices of other institutions or agencies being installed in part of the building in which the consular premises are situated, provided that the premises assigned to them are separate from those used by the consular post. In that event, the said offices shall not, for the purposes of the present Convention, be considered to form part of the consular premises.

Article 56. *Insurance Against Third Party Risks*

Members of the consular post shall comply with any requirement imposed by the laws and regulations of the receiving State in respect of insurance against third party risks arising from the use of any vehicle, vessel or aircraft.

Article 57. *Special Provisions Concerning Private Gainful Occupation*

1. Career consular officers shall not carry on for personal profit any professional or commercial activity in the receiving State.

2. Privileges and immunities provided in this chapter shall not be accorded:

(*a*) To consular employees or to members of the service staff who carry on any private gainful occupation in the receiving State;

(*b*) To members of the family of a person referred to in sub-paragraph (*a*) of this paragraph or to members of his private staff;

(*c*) To members of the family of a member of a consular post who themselves carry on any private gainful occupation in the receiving State.

CHAPTER III.   REGIME RELATING TO HONORARY CONSULAR OFFICERS AND CONSULAR POSTS HEADED BY SUCH OFFICERS

Article 58. *General Provisions Relating to Facilities, Privileges and Immunities*

1. Articles 28, 29, 30, 34. 35, 36, 37, 38 and 39, paragraph 3 of article 54 and paragraphs 2 and 3 of article 55 shall apply to consular posts headed by

an honorary consular officer. In addition, the facilities, privileges and immunities of such consular posts shall be governed by articles 59, 60, 61 and 62.

2. Articles 42 and 43, paragraph 3 of article 44, articles 45 and 53 and paragraph 1 of article 55 shall apply to honorary consular officers. In addition, the facilities, privileges and immunities of such consular officers shall be governed by articles 63, 64, 65, 66 and 67. . . .

Article 59.   Protection of the Consular Premises

The receiving State shall take such steps as may be necessary to protect the consular premises of a consular post headed by an honorary consular officer against any intrusion or damage and to prevent any disturbance of the peace of the consular post or impairment of its dignity.

Article 60.   Exemption from Taxation of Consular Premises. . . .

Article 61.   Inviolability of Consular Archives and Documents

The consular archives and documents of a consular post headed by an honorary consular officer shall be inviolable at all times and wherever they may be, provided that they are kept separate from other papers and documents . . . .

Article 62.   Exemption from Customs Duties. . . .

Article 63.   Criminal Proceedings

If criminal proceedings are instituted against an honorary consular officer, he must appear before the competent authorities. Nevertheless, the proceedings shall be conducted with the respect due to him by reason of his official position and, except when he is under arrest or detention, in a manner which will hamper the exercise of consular functions as little as possible. When it has become necessary to detain an honorary consular officer, the proceedings against him shall be instituted with the minimum of delay.

Article 64.   Protection of Honorary Consular Officers

The receiving State is under a duty to accord to an honorary consular officer such protection as may be required by reason of his official position.

Article 65.   Exemption from Registration of Aliens and Residence Permits. . . .

Article 66.   Exemption from Taxation. . . .

Article 68.   Optional Character of the Institution of Honorary Consular Officers

Each State is free to decide whether it will appoint or receive honorary consular officers.

CHAPTER IV.   GENERAL PROVISIONS

Article 69.   Consular Agents Who Are Not Heads of Consular Posts

1. Each State is free to decide whether it will establish or admit consular agencies conducted by consular agents not designated as heads of consular post by the sending State.

2. The conditions under which the consular agencies referred to in paragraph 1 of this article may carry on their activities and the privileges and immunities which may be enjoyed by the consular agents in charge of them shall be determined by agreement between the sending State and the receiving State.

Article 70.   Exercise of Consular Functions by Diplomatic Missions

1. The provisions of the present Convention apply also, so far as the context permits, to the exercise of consular functions by a diplomatic mission.

2. The names of members of a diplomatic mission assigned to the consular section or otherwise charged with the exercise of the consular functions of the mission shall be notified to the Ministry for Foreign Affairs of the receiving State or to the authority designated by that Ministry.

3. In the exercise of consular functions a diplomatic mission may address:

(a) The local authorities of the consular district;

(b) The central authorities of the receiving State if this is allowed by the laws, regulations and usages of the receiving State or by relevant international agreements.

4. The privileges and immunities of the members of a diplomatic mission referred to in paragraph 2 of this article shall continue to be governed by the rules of international law concerning diplomatic relations.

Article 71.   Nationals or Permanent Residents of the Receiving State

1. Except in so far as additional facilities, privileges and immunities may be granted by the receiving State, consular officers who are nationals

of or permanently resident in the receiving State shall enjoy only immunity from jurisdiction and personal inviolability in respect of official acts performed in the exercise of their functions, and the privilege provided in paragraph 3 of article 44. So far as these consular officers are concerned, the receiving State shall likewise be bound by the obligations laid down in article 42. If criminal proceedings are instituted against such a consular officer, the proceedings shall, except when he is under arrest or detention, be conducted in a manner which will hamper the exercise of consular functions as little as possible.

2. Other members of the consular post who are nationals of or permanently resident in the receiving State and members of their families, as well as members of the families of consular officers referred to in paragraph 1 of this article, shall enjoy facilities, privileges and immunities only in so far as these are granted to them by the receiving State. . . .

Article 72.   Non-Discrimination

1. In the application of the provisions of the present Convention the receiving State shall not discriminate as between States. . . .

Article 73.   Relationship Between the Present Convention and Other International Agreements

1. The provisions of the present Convention shall not affect other international agreements in force as between States parties to them. . . .

CHAPTER V.   FINAL PROVISIONS

Article 74.   Signature

The present Convention shall be open for signature by all States Members of the United Nations or of any of the specialized agencies or Parties to the Statute of the International Court of Justice, and by any other State invited by the General Assembly of the United Nations to become a Party to the Convention. . . .

Article 75.   Ratification

The present Convention is subject to ratification. The instruments of ratification shall be deposited with the Secretary-General of the United Nations. . . .

OPTIONAL PROTOCOL TO THE VIENNA CONVENTION ON CONSULAR RELATIONS CONCERNING THE COMPULSORY SETTLEMENT OF DISPUTES

April 24, 1963, 21 U.S.T. 325, T.I.A.S. No. 6820, 596 U.N.T.S. 487*

The States Parties to the present Protocol and to the Vienna Convention on Consular Relations, hereinafter referred to as "the Convention," adopted by the United Nations Conference held at Vienna from 4 March to 22 April 1963,

Expressing their wish to resort in all matters concerning them in respect of any dispute arising out of the interpretation or application of the Convention to the compulsory jurisdiction of the International Court of Justice, unless some other form of settlement has been agreed upon by the parties within a reasonable period,

Have agreed as follows:

Article I

Disputes arising out of the interpretation or application of the Convention shall lie within the compulsory jurisdiction of the International Court of Justice and may accordingly be brought before the Court by an application made by any party to the dispute being a Party to the present Protocol.

Article II

The parties may agree, within a period of two months after one party has notified its opinion to the other that a dispute exists, to resort not to the International Court of Justice but to an arbitral tribunal. After the expiry of

---

*Entered into force on March 19, 1967. As of February 2011, the 48 parties to the Optional Protocol were: Australia, Austria, Belgium, Botswana, Bulgaria, Burkina Faso, Denmark, Dominican Republic, Estonia, Finland, France, Gabon, Germany, Hungary, Iceland, India, Iran, Italy, Japan, Kenya, Lao People's Democratic Republic, Liechtenstein, Luxembourg, Madagascar, Malawi, Mauritius, Mexico, Nepal, Netherlands, New Zealand, Nicaragua, Niger, Norway, Oman, Pakistan, Panama, Paraguay, Peru, Philippines, Korea (Republic of), Romania, Senegal, Seychelles, Slovakia, Suriname, Sweden, Switzerland, United Kingdom, and Uruguay.

The United States had been a party to the Optional Protocol since 1969. In March 2005 the U.S. Secretary of State sent a letter to the U.N. Secretary General notifying him that the United States "hereby withdraws from the . . . Protocol. As a consequence of this withdrawal, the United States will no longer recognize the jurisdiction of the International Court of Justice reflected in that Protocol. . . ."

the said period, either party may bring the dispute before the Court by an application.

Article III

1. Within the same period of two months, the parties may agree to adopt a conciliation procedure before resorting to the International Court of Justice.

2. The conciliation commission shall make its recommendations within five months after its appointment. If its recommendations are not accepted by the parties to the dispute within two months after they have been delivered, either party may bring the dispute before the Court by an application.

7

Allocation of Legal Authority Among States

SOME U.S. ANTI-TERRORISM STATUTES

18 U.S.C. §§2331 et seq. (as amended through January 2013)

Sec. 2331.   Definitions

As used in this chapter [18 USCS §§2331 et seq.]—

(1) the term "international terrorism" means activities that—

(A) involve violent acts or acts dangerous to human life that are a violation of the criminal laws of the United States or of any State, or that would be a criminal violation if committed within the jurisdiction of the United States or of any State;

(B) appear to be intended—

(i) to intimidate or coerce a civilian population;

(ii) to influence the policy of a government by intimidation or coercion; or

(iii) to affect the conduct of a government by mass destruction, assassination, or kidnapping; and

(C) occur primarily outside the territorial jurisdiction of the United States, or transcend national boundaries in terms of the means by which they are accomplished, the persons they appear intended to intimidate or coerce, or the locale in which their perpetrators operate or seek asylum;

(2) the term "national of the United States" has the meaning given such term in section 101(a) (22) of the Immigration and Nationality Act [8 USCS §1101 (a) (22)];

(3) the term "person" means any individual or entity capable of holding a legal or beneficial interest in property;

(4) the term "act of war" means any act occurring in the course of—

(A) declared war;

(B) armed conflict, whether or not war has been declared, between two or more nations; or

(C) armed conflict between military forces of any origin; and

(5) the term "domestic terrorism" means activities that—

(A) involve acts dangerous to human life that are a violation of the criminal laws of the United States or of any State;

(B) appear to be intended—

(i) to intimidate or coerce a civilian population;

(ii) to influence the policy of a government by intimidation or coercion; or

(iii) to affect the conduct of a government by mass destruction, assassination, or kidnapping; and

(C) occur primarily within the territorial jurisdiction of the United States.

Sec. 2332. *Criminal penalties*

(a) Homicide. Whoever kills a national of the United States, while such national is outside the United States, shall—

(1) if the killing is murder (as defined in section 1111(a)), be fined under this title, punished, by death or imprisonment for any term of years or for life, or both;

(2) if the killing is a voluntary manslaughter as defined in section 1112(a) of this title, be fined under this title or imprisoned not more than ten years, or both; and

(3) if the killing is an involuntary manslaughter as defined in section 1112(a) of this title, be fined under this title or imprisoned not more than three years, or both.

(b) Attempt or conspiracy with respect to homicide. Whoever outside the United States attempts to kill, or engages in a conspiracy to kill, a national of the United States shall—

(1) in the case of an attempt to commit a killing that is a murder as defined in this chapter, be fined under this title or imprisoned not more than 20 years, or both; and

(2) in the case of a conspiracy by two or more persons to commit a killing that is a murder as defined in section 1111(a) of this title, if one or more of such persons do any overt act to effect the object of the conspiracy, be fined under this title or imprisoned for any term of years or for life, or both so fined and so imprisoned.

(c) Other conduct. Whoever outside the United States engages in physical violence—

(1) with intent to cause serious bodily injury to a national of the United States; or

(2) with the result that serious bodily injury is caused to a national of the United States;

shall be fined under this title or imprisoned not more than ten years, or both.

(d) Limitation on Prosecution. No prosecution for any offense described in this section shall be undertaken by the United States except on written certification of the Attorney General or the highest ranking subordinate of the Attorney General with responsibility for criminal prosecutions that, in the judgment of the certifying official, such offense was intended to coerce, intimidate, or retaliate against a government or a civilian population. . . .

Sec. 2333. *Civil remedies*

(a) Action and jurisdiction. Any national of the United States injured in his or her person, property, or business by reason of an act of international terrorism, or his or her estate, survivors, or heirs, may sue therefor in any appropriate district court of the United States and shall recover threefold the damages he or she sustains and the cost of the suit, including attorney's fees.

(b) Estoppel under United States law. A final judgment or decree rendered in favor of the United States in any criminal proceeding under section 1116, 1201, 1203, or 2332 of this title or section 46314, 46502, 46505, or 46506 of title 49 shall estop the defendant from denying the essential allegations of the criminal offense in any subsequent civil proceeding under this section.

(c) Estoppel under foreign law. A final judgment or decree rendered in favor of any foreign state in any criminal proceeding shall, to the extent that such judgment or decree may be accorded full faith and credit under the law of the United States, estop the defendant from denying the essential allegations of the criminal offense in any subsequent civil proceeding under this section.

Sec. 2334. *Jurisdiction and venue*

(a) General venue. Any civil action under section 2333 of this title against any person may be instituted in the district court of the United States for any district where any plaintiff resides or where any defendant resides or is served, or has an agent. Process in such a civil action may be served in any district where the defendant resides, is found, or has an agent.

(b) Special maritime or territorial jurisdiction. If the actions giving rise to the claim occurred within the special maritime and territorial jurisdiction of the United States, as defined in section 7 of this title, then any civil action under section 2333 of this title against any person may be instituted in the district court of the United States for any district in which any plaintiff resides or the defendant resides, is served, or has an agent.

(c) Service on witnesses. A witness in a civil action brought under section 2333 of this title may be served in any other district where the defendant resides, is found, or has an agent.

(d) Convenience of the forum. The district court shall not dismiss any action brought under section 2333 of this title on the grounds of the inconvenience or inappropriateness of the forum chosen, unless—

(1) the action may he maintained in a foreign court that has jurisdiction over the subject matter and over all the defendants;

(2) that foreign court is significantly more convenient and appropriate; and

(3) that foreign court offers a remedy which is substantially the same as the one available in the courts of the United States.

Sec. 2335. *Limitation of actions*

(a) In general, subject to subsection (b), a suit for recovery of damages under section 2333 of this title shall not be maintained unless commenced within 10 years after the date the cause of action accrued.

(b) Calculation of period. The time of the absence of the defendant from the United States or from any jurisdiction in which the same or a similar action arising from the same facts may be maintained by the plaintiff, or of any concealment of the defendant's whereabouts, shall not be included in the 10-year period set forth in subsection (a).

Sec. 2336. *Other limitations*

(a) Acts of war. No action shall be maintained under section 2333 of this title for injury or loss by reason of an act of war.

(b) Limitation on discovery. If a party to an action under section 2333 seeks to discover the investigative files of the Department of Justice, the Assistant Attorney General, Deputy Attorney General, or Attorney General may object on the ground that compliance will interfere with a criminal investigation or prosecution of the incident, or a national security operation related to the incident, which is the subject of the civil litigation. The court shall evaluate any such objections in camera and shall stay the discovery if the court finds that granting the discovery request will substantially interfere with a criminal investigation or prosecution of the incident or a national security operation related to the incident. The court shall consider the likelihood of criminal prosecution by the Government and other factors it deems to be appropriate. A stay of discovery under this subsection shall constitute a bar to the granting of a motion to dismiss under rules 12(b)(6) and 56 of the Federal Rules of Civil Procedure. If the court grants a stay of discovery under this subsection, it may stay the action in the interests of justice.

(c) Stay of action for civil remedies.

(1) The Attorney General may intervene in any civil action brought under section 2333 for the purpose of seeking a stay of the civil action. A stay shall be granted if the court finds that the continuation of the civil action will substantially interfere with a criminal prosecution which involves the same subject matter and in which an indictment has been

returned, or interfere with national security operations related to the terrorist incident that is the subject of the civil action. A stay may be granted for up to 6 months. The Attorney General may petition the court for an extension of the stay for additional 6-month periods until the criminal prosecution is completed or dismissed.

(2) In a proceeding under this subsection, the Attorney General may request that any order issued by the court for release to the parties and the public omit any reference to the basis on which the stay was sought.

Sec. 2337.   Suits against Government officials

No action shall be maintained under section 2333 of this title against—

(1) the United States, an agency of the United States, or an officer or employee of the United States or any agency thereof acting within his or her official capacity or under color of legal authority; or

(2) a foreign state, an agency of a foreign state, or an officer or employee of a foreign state or an agency thereof acting within his or her official capacity or under color of legal authority.

Sec. 2338.   Exclusive Federal jurisdiction

The district courts of the United States shall have exclusive jurisdiction over an action brought under this chapter [18 USCS §§2331 et seq.].

Sec. 2339.   Harboring or concealing terrorists

(a) Whoever harbors or conceals any person who he knows, or has reasonable grounds to believe, has committed, or is about to commit, an offense under section 32 (relating to destruction of aircraft or aircraft facilities), section 175 (relating to biological weapons), section 229 (relating to chemical weapons), section 831 (relating to nuclear materials), paragraph (2) or (3) of section 844(f) (relating to arson and bombing of government property risking or causing injury or death), section 1366(a) (relating to the destruction of an energy facility), section 2280 (relating to violence against maritime navigation), section 2332a (relating to weapons of mass destruction), or section 2332b (relating to acts of terrorism transcending national boundaries) of this title, section 236(a) (relating to sabotage of nuclear facilities or fuel) of the Atomic Energy Act of 1954 (42 U.S.C. 2284(a)), or section 46502 (relating to aircraft piracy) of title 49, shall be fined under this title or imprisoned not more than ten years, or both.

(b) A violation of this section may be prosecuted in any Federal judicial district in which the underlying offense was committed, or in any other Federal judicial district as provided by law.

8

State Responsibility— Injuries to Aliens and International Human Rights

TREATY BETWEEN THE GOVERNMENT OF THE UNITED STATES OF AMERICA AND THE GOVERNMENT OF THE REPUBLIC OF THE UKRAINE CONCERNING THE ENCOURAGEMENT AND RECIPROCAL PROTECTION OF INVESTMENT*

<http://www.state.gov>

The United States of America and Ukraine (hereinafter the "Parties"); Desiring to promote greater economic cooperation between them, with respect to investment by nationals and companies of one Party in the territory of the other Party;

Recognizing that agreement upon the treatment to be accorded such investment will stimulate the flow of private capital and the economic development of the Parties;

Agreeing that fair and equitable treatment of investment is desirable in order to maintain a stable framework for investment and maximum effective utilization of economic resources;

* Signed in Washington, D.C., on March 4, 1994, with annex and exchange of letters. Entered into force on November 16, 1996.

As of March 2013, the United States also had Bilateral Investment Treaties (BIT) with 41 other countries that were similar, but not identical, to its BIT with Ukraine. The countries are Albania, Argentina, Armenia, Azerbaijan, Bahrain, Bangladesh, Bolivia, Bulgaria, Cameroon, Congo (Democratic Republic of), Congo (Republic of), Croatia, Czech Republic, Ecuador, Egypt, Estonia, Georgia, Grenada, Honduras, Jamaica, Jordan, Kazakhstan, Kyrgyzstan, Latvia, Lithuania, Moldova, Mongolia, Morocco, Mozambique, Panama, Poland, Romania, Rwanda, Senegal, Slovakia, Sri Lanka, Trinidad and Tobago, Tunisia, Turkey, Ukraine, and Uruguay.

Recognizing that the development of economic and business ties can contribute to the well-being of workers in both Parties and promote respect for internationally recognized worker rights . . .

Have agreed as follows:

Article I

1. For the purposes of this Treaty,

(a) "investment" means every kind of investment in the territory of one Party owned or controlled directly or indirectly by nationals or companies of the other Party, such as equity, debt, and service and investment contracts; and includes:

(i) tangible and intangible property, including rights, such as mortgages, liens and pledges;

(ii) a company or shares of stock or other interests in a company or interests in the assets thereof;

(iii) a claim to money or a claim to performance having economic value, and associated with an investment;

(iv) intellectual property . . .

(v) any right conferred by law or contract, and any licenses and permits pursuant to law;

(b) "company" of a Party means any kind of corporation, company, association, partnership, or other organization, legally constituted under the laws and regulations of a Party or a political subdivision thereof whether or not organized for pecuniary gain, or privately or governmentally owned or controlled;

(c) "national" of a Party means a natural person who is a national of a Party under its applicable law;

(d) "return" means an amount derived from or associated with an investment, including profit; dividend; interest; capital gain; royalty payment; management, technical assistance or other fee; or returns in kind;

(e) "associated activities" include the organization, control, operation, maintenance and disposition of companies, branches, agencies, offices, factories or other facilities for the conduct of business; the making, performance and enforcement of contracts; the acquisition, use, protection and disposition of property of all kinds including intellectual property rights; the borrowing of funds; the purchase, issuance, and sale of equity shares and other securities; and the purchase of foreign exchange for imports;

(f) "state enterprise" means an enterprise owned, or controlled through ownership interests, by a Party; and

(g) "delegation" includes a legislative grant, and a government order, directive or other act transferring to a state enterprise or monopoly, or authorizing the exercise by a state enterprise or monopoly of, governmental authority.

2. Each party reserves the right to deny to any company the advantages of this Treaty if nationals of any third country control such company and, in

the case of a company of the other Party, that company has no substantial business activities in the territory of the other Party or is controlled by nationals of a third country with which the denying Party does not maintain normal economic relations.

3. Any alteration of the form in which assets are invested or reinvested shall not affect their character as investment.

Article II

1. Each Party shall permit and treat investment, and activities associated therewith, on a basis no less favorable than that accorded in like situations to investment or associated activities of its own nationals or companies, or of nationals or companies of any third country, whichever is the most favorable, subject to the right of each Party to make or maintain exceptions falling within one of the sectors or matters listed in the Annex to this Treaty. Each Party agrees to notify the other Party before or on the date of entry into force of this Treaty of all such laws and regulations of which it is aware concerning the sectors or matters listed in the Annex. Moreover, each Party agrees to notify the other of any future exception with respect to the sectors or matters listed in the Annex, and to limit such exceptions to a minimum. Any future exception by either Party shall not apply to investment existing in that sector or matter at the time the exception becomes effective. The treatment accorded pursuant to any exceptions shall, unless specified otherwise in the Annex, be not less favorable than that accorded in like situations to investments and associated activities of nationals or companies of any third country.

2. (a) Nothing in this Treaty shall be construed to prevent a Party from maintaining or establishing a state enterprise.

(b) Each Party shall ensure that any state enterprise that it maintains or establishes acts in a manner that is not inconsistent with the Party's obligations under this Treaty wherever such enterprise exercises any regulatory, administrative or other governmental authority that the Party has delegated to it, such as the power to expropriate, grant licenses, approve commercial transactions, or impose quotas, fees or other charges.

(c) Each Party shall ensure that any state enterprise that it maintains or establishes accords the better of national or most favored nation treatment in the sale of its goods or services in the Party's territory.

3. (a) Investment shall at all times be accorded fair and equitable treatment, shall enjoy full protection and security and shall in no case be accorded treatment less than that required by international law.

(b) Neither Party shall in any way impair by arbitrary or discriminatory measures the management, operation, maintenance, use, enjoyment, acquisition, expansion, or disposal of investments. For purposes of dispute resolution under Articles VI and VII, a measure may be arbitrary or discriminatory notwithstanding the fact has exercised the opportunity to review such measure in the courts or administrative tribunals of a Party.

(c) Each Party shall observe any obligation it may have entered into with regard to investments.

4. Subject to the laws relating to the entry and sojourn of aliens, nationals of either Party shall be permitted to enter and to remain in the territory of the other Party for the purpose of establishing, developing, administering or advising on the operation of an investment to which they, or a company of the first Party that employs them, have committed or are in the process of committing a substantial amount of capital or other resources.

5. Companies which are legally constituted under the applicable laws or regulations of one Party, and which are investments, shall be permitted to engage top managerial personnel of their choice, regardless of nationality.

6. Neither Party shall impose performance requirements as a condition of establishment, expansion or maintenance of investments, which require or enforce commitments to export goods produced, or which specify that goods or services must be purchased locally, or which impose any other similar requirements.

7. Each Party shall provide effective means of asserting claims and enforcing rights with respect to investment, investment agreements, and investment authorizations.

8. Each Party shall make public all laws, regulations, administrative practices and procedures, and adjudicatory decisions that pertain to or affect investments.

9. The treatment accorded by the United States of America to investments and associated activities of nationals and companies of Ukraine under the provisions of this Article shall in any State, Territory or possession of the United States of America be no less favorable than the treatment accorded therein to investments and associated activities of nationals of the United States of America resident in, and companies legally constituted under the laws and regulations of other States, Territories or possessions of the United States of America.

10. The most favored nation provisions of this Treaty shall not apply to advantages accorded by either Party to nationals or companies of any third country by virtue of:

(a) that Party's binding obligations that derive from full membership in a free trade area or customs union; or

(b) that Party's binding obligations under any multilateral international agreement under the framework of the General Agreement on Tariffs and Trade that enters into force subsequent to the signature of this Treaty.

11. The Parties acknowledge and agree that "associated activities" include without limitation, such activities as:

(a) the granting of franchises or rights under licenses;

(b) access to registrations, licenses, permits and other approvals (which shall in any event be issued expeditiously);

(c) access to financial institutions and credit markets;

(d) access to their funds held in financial institutions;

(e) the importation and installation of equipment necessary for the normal conduct of business affairs, including but not limited to, office equipment and automobiles, and the export of any equipment and automobiles so imported;

(f) the dissemination of commercial information;

(g) the conduct of market studies;

(h) the appointment of commercial representatives, including agents, consultants and distributors and their participation in trade fairs and promotion events;

(i) the marketing of goods and services, including through internal distribution and marketing systems, as well as by advertising and direct contact with individuals and companies;

(j) access to public utilities, public services and commercial rental space at nondiscriminatory prices, if the prices are set or controlled by the government; and

(k) access to raw materials, inputs and services of all types at nondiscriminatory prices, if the prices are set or controlled by the government.

Article III

1. Investments shall not be expropriated or nationalized either directly or indirectly through measures tantamount to expropriation or nationalization ("expropriation") except: for a public purpose; in a nondiscriminatory manner; upon payment of prompt, adequate and effective compensation; and in accordance with due process of law and the general principles of treatment provided for in Article II(2). Compensation shall be equivalent to the fair market value of the expropriated investment immediately before the expropriatory action was taken or became known, whichever is earlier; be calculated in a freely usable currency on the basis of the prevailing market rate of exchange at that time; be paid without delay; include interest at a commercially reasonable rate, such as LIBOR plus an appropriate margin, from the date of expropriation; be fully realizable; and be freely transferable.

2. A national or company of either Party that asserts that all or part of its investment has been expropriated shall have a right to prompt review by the appropriate judicial or administrative authorities of the other Party to determine whether any such expropriation has occurred and, if so whether any such expropriation, and any associated compensation, conforms to the principles of international law.

3. Nationals or companies of either Party whose investments suffer losses in the territory of the other Party owing to war or other armed conflict, revolution, state of national emergency, insurrection, civil disturbance or other similar events shall be accorded treatment by such other Party no less favorable than that accorded to its own nationals or companies or to nationals or companies of any third country, whichever is the most favorable treatment, as regards any measures it adopts in relation to such losses.

Article IV

1. Each Party shall permit all transfers related to an investment to be made freely and without delay into and out of its territory. Such transfers include: (a) returns; (b) compensation pursuant to Article III; (c) payments arising out of an investment dispute; (d) payments made under a contract, including amortization of principal and accrued interest payments made pursuant to a loan agreement; (e) proceeds from the sale or liquidation of all or any part of an investment; and (f) additional contributions to capital for the maintenance or development of an investment.

2. Transfers shall be made in a freely usable currency at the prevailing market rate of exchange on the date of transfer with respect to spot transactions in the currency to be transferred.

3. Notwithstanding the provisions of paragraphs 1 and 2, either Party may maintain laws and regulations (a) requiring reports of currency transfer; and (b) imposing income taxes by such means as a withholding tax applicable to dividends or other transfers. Furthermore, either Party may protect the rights of creditors, or ensure the satisfaction of judgments in adjudicatory proceedings, through the equitable, nondiscriminatory and good faith application of its law.

Article V

The Parties agree to consult promptly, on the request of either, to resolve any disputes in connection with the Treaty, or to discuss any matter relating to the interpretation or application of the Treaty.

Article VI

1. For purposes of this Article, an investment dispute is a dispute between a Party and a national or company of the other Party arising out of or relating to (a) an investment agreement between that Party and such national or company; (b) an investment authorization granted by that Party's foreign investment authority to such national or company; or (c) an alleged breach of any right conferred or created by this Treaty with respect to an investment.

2. In the event of an investment dispute, the parties to the dispute should initially seek a resolution through consultation and negotiation. If the dispute cannot be settled amicably, the national or company concerned may choose to submit the dispute for resolution:

(a) to the courts or administrative tribunals of the Party that is a party to the dispute; or

(b) in accordance with any applicable, previously agreed dispute-settlement procedures; or

(c) in accordance with the terms of paragraph 3.

3. (a) Provided that the national or company concerned has not submitted the dispute for resolution under paragraph 2 (a) or (b) and that six months have elapsed from the date on which the dispute arose, the national

or company concerned may choose to consent in writing to the submission of the dispute for settlement by binding arbitration:

(i) to the International Centre for the Settlement of Investment Disputes ("Centre") established by the Convention on the Settlement of Investment Disputes between States and Nationals of other States, done at Washington, March 18, 1965 ("ICSID Convention"), provided that the Party is a party to such Convention; or

(ii) to the Additional Facility of the Centre, if the Centre is not available; or

(iii) in accordance with the Arbitration Rules of the United Nations Commission on International Trade Law (UNCITRAL); or

(iv) to any other arbitration institution, or in accordance with any other arbitration rules, as may be mutually agreed between the parties to the dispute.

(b) Once the national or company concerned has so consented, either party to the dispute may initiate arbitration in accordance with the choice so specified in the consent.

4. Each Party hereby consents to the submission of any investment dispute for settlement by binding arbitration in accordance with the choice specified in the written consent of the national or company under paragraph 3. Such consent, together with the written consent of the national or company when given under paragraph 3 shall satisfy the requirement for:

(a) written consent of the parties to the dispute for purposes of Chapter II of the ICSID Convention (Jurisdiction of the Centre) and for purposes of the Additional Facility Rules; and

(b) an "agreement in writing" for purposes of Article II of the United Nations Convention on the Recognition and Enforcement of Foreign Arbitral Awards, done at New York, June 10, 1958 ("New York Convention").

5. Any arbitration under paragraph 3(a)(ii), (iii) or (iv) of this Article shall be held in a state that is a party to the New York Convention.

6. Any arbitral award rendered pursuant to this Article shall be final and binding on the parties to the dispute. Each Party undertakes to carry out without delay the provisions of any such award and to provide in its territory for its enforcement.

7. In any proceeding involving an investment dispute, a Party shall not assert, as a defense, counterclaim, right of set-off or otherwise, that the national or company concerned has received or will receive, pursuant to an insurance or guarantee contract, indemnification or other compensation for all or part of its alleged damages.

8. For purposes of an arbitration held under paragraph 3 of this Article, any company legally constituted under the applicable laws and regulations of a Party or a political subdivision thereof but that, immediately before the occurrence of the event or events giving rise to the dispute, was an investment of nationals or companies of the other Party, shall be treated as a national or company of such other Party in accordance with Article 25(2)(b) of the ICSID Convention.

Article VII

1. Any dispute between the Parties concerning the interpretation or application of the Treaty which is not resolved through consultations or other diplomatic channels, shall be submitted, upon the request of either Party, to an arbitral tribunal for binding decision in accordance with the applicable rules of international law. In the absence of an agreement by the Parties to the contrary, the arbitration rules of the United Nations Commission on International Trade Law (UNCITRAL), except to the extent modified by the Parties or by the arbitrators, shall govern.

2. Within two months of receipt of a request, each Party shall appoint an arbitrator. The two arbitrators shall select a third arbitrator as Chairman, who is a national of a third state. The UNCITRAL Rules for appointing members of three-member panels shall apply *mutatis mutandis* to the appointment of the arbitral panel except that the appointing authority referenced in those rules shall be the Secretary General of the Centre.

3. Unless otherwise agreed, all submissions shall be made and all hearings shall be completed within six months of the date of selection of the third arbitrator, and the Tribunal shall render its decisions within two months of the date of the final submissions or the date of the closing of the hearings, whichever is later.

4. Expenses incurred by the Chairman, the other arbitrators, and other costs of the proceedings shall be paid for equally by the Parties. The Tribunal may, however, at its discretion, direct that a higher proportion of the costs be paid by one of the Parties.

Article VIII

This Treaty shall not derogate from:
   (a) laws and regulations, administrative practices or procedures, or administrative or adjudicatory decisions of either Party;
   (b) international legal obligations; or
   (c) obligations assumed by either Party, including those contained in an investment agreement or an investment authorization,
that entitle investments or associated activities to treatment more favorable than that accorded by this Treaty in like situations.

Article IX

1. This Treaty shall not preclude the application by either Party of measures necessary for the maintenance of public order, the fulfillment of its obligations with respect to the maintenance or restoration of international peace or security, or the protection of its own essential security interests.

2. This Treaty shall not preclude either Party from prescribing special formalities in connection with the establishment of investments, but such formalities shall not impair the substance of any of the rights set forth in this Treaty.

Article X

1. With respect to its tax policies, each Party should strive to accord fairness and equity in the treatment of investment of nationals and companies of the other Party.

2. Nevertheless, the provisions of this Treaty, and in particular Articles VI and VII, shall apply to matters of taxation only with respect to the following:

(a) expropriation, pursuant to Article III;

(b) transfers, pursuant to Article IV; or

(c) the observance and enforcement of terms of an investment agreement or authorization as referred to in Article VI(1) (a) or (b),

to the extent they are not subject to the dispute settlement provisions of a Convention for the avoidance of double taxation between the two Parties, or have been raised under such settlement provisions and are not resolved within a reasonable period of time.

Article XI

This Treaty shall apply to the political subdivisions of the Parties.

Article XII

1. This Treaty shall enter into force thirty days after the date of exchange of instruments of ratification. It shall remain in force for a period of ten years and shall continue in force unless terminated in accordance with paragraph 2 of this Article. It shall apply to investments existing at the time of entry into force as well as to investments made or acquired thereafter.

2. Either Party may, by giving one year's written notice to the other Party, terminate this Treaty at the end of the initial ten year period or at any time thereafter.

3. With respect to investments made or acquired prior to the date of termination of this Treaty and to which this Treaty otherwise applies, the provisions of all of the other Articles of this Treaty shall thereafter continue to be effective for a further period of ten years from such date of termination.

4. The Annex and Side Letter shall form an integral part of the Treaty. . . .

ANNEX

1. The United States reserves the right to make or maintain limited exceptions to national treatment, as provided in Article II, paragraph 1, in the sectors or matters it has indicated below:

(a) air transportation; ocean and coastal shipping; banking; insurance; government grants; government insurance and loan programs; energy and power production; customhouse brokers; ownership of real property; ownership and operation of broadcast or common carrier radio and television stations; ownership of shares in the Communications Satellite Corporation; the provision of common carrier telephone and telegraph services; the provision of submarine cable services; use of land and natural resources; mining on the public domain; maritime services and maritime-related services; and primary dealership in United States government securities.

2. The United States reserves the right to make or maintain limited exceptions to most favored nation treatment, as provided in Article II, paragraph 1, in the sectors or matters it has indicated below:

ownership of real property; mining on the public domain; maritime services and maritime-related services; and primary dealership in United States government securities.

3. Ukraine reserves the right to make or maintain limited exceptions to national treatment, as provided in Article II, paragraph 1, in the sectors or matters it has indicated below:

production of equipment used exclusively for nuclear power plants; maritime transportation including ocean and coastal shipping; air transportation; nuclear electric energy generation; privatization of those educational, sports, medical and scientific facilities financed by the national budget; mining of salt; mining and processing of rare earth, and of uranium and other radioactive elements; ownership and operation of television and radio broadcasting stations; and ownership of land.

[TRANSLATION]

March 4, 1994

Dear Mr. Minister:

I have the honor to confirm the following understanding which was reached between the Government of the United States of America and the Government of Ukraine in the course of negotiations of the Treaty Concerning the Encouragement and Reciprocal Protection of Investment (the "Treaty"):

The Government of Ukraine agrees to designate an Office to assist U.S. nationals and companies in deriving the full benefits of the Treaty in connection with their investment and related activities.

The Office will serve as the coordinator and problem solver for investors experiencing difficulties with registration, licensing, access to utilities, regulatory and other matters.

The Office will provide the following types of services:

— information on current national and local business/investment regulations, including licensing and registration procedures, taxation, labor regulations, accounting standards, and access to credit;
— a notification procedure on proposed regulatory or legal changes affecting assistance to investors with circulation notices on regulatory changes put into force;
— coordination with Ukraine Government agencies at the national and local level to facilitate investment and resolve disputes;

— identification and dissemination of information on investment projects and their sources of finance;

— assistance to investors experiencing difficulties with repatriating profits and obtaining foreign exchange.

I understand that the Offices designated by the Government of Ukraine to assist U.S. nationals and companies in accordance with this letter are the Administration for Investment Cooperation of the Ministry of Foreign Economic Relations of Ukraine and the Department of Foreign Investments and Credits of the Ministry of the Economy of Ukraine.

I have the honor to propose that this understanding be treated as an integral part of the Treaty.

I would be grateful if you would confirm that this understanding is shared by your Government.

Sincerely,

Roman Shpek
Minister of Economy of Ukraine

DEPUTY UNITED STATES TRADE REPRESENTATIVE
EXECUTIVE OFFICE OF THE PRESIDENT

WASHINGTON, D.C. 20506

March 4, 1996

Dear Mr. Minister:

I have the honor to confirm receipt of your letter which reads as follows: "I have the honor to confirm the following understanding which was reached between the Government of the United States of America and the Government of Ukraine in the course of negotiations of the Treaty Concerning the Encouragement and Reciprocal Protection of Investment (the "Treaty"):

The Government of Ukraine agrees to designate. . . . "

I understand that the offices designated by the Government of Ukraine to assist U.S. nationals and companies in accordance with this letter are the Administration for Investment Cooperation of the Ministry of Foreign Economic Relations of Ukraine and the Department of Foreign Investments and Credits of the Ministry of the Economy of Ukraine.

I have the honor to propose that this understanding be treated as an integral part of the Treaty.

I would be grateful if you would confirm that this understanding is shared by your government.

I have the further honor to confirm that this understanding is shared by my Government and constitutes an integral part of the Treaty.

Sincerely,
Rufus Yerxa

DRAFT ARTICLES ON RESPONSIBILITY OF STATES FOR INTERNATIONALLY WRONGFUL ACTS*

by International Law Commission

Part One. The Internationally Wrongful Act of a State

CHAPTER I. GENERAL PRINCIPLES

Article 1. *Responsibility of a State for Its Internationally Wrongful Acts*

Every internationally wrongful act of a State entails the international responsibility of that State.

Article 2. *Elements of an Internationally Wrongful Act of a State*

There is an internationally wrongful act of a State when conduct consisting of an action or omission:

(a) Is attributable to the State under international law; and

(b) Constitutes a breach of an international obligation of the State.

Article 3. *Characterization of an Act of a State as Internationally Wrongful*

The characterization of an act of a State as internationally wrongful is governed by international law. Such characterization is not affected by the characterization of the same act as lawful by internal law.

CHAPTER II. ATTRIBUTION OF CONDUCT TO A STATE

Article 4. *Conduct of Organs of a State*

1. The conduct of any State organ shall be considered an act of that State under international law, whether the organ exercises legislative, executive, judicial or any other functions, whatever position it holds in the organization of the State, and whatever its character as an organ of the central government or of a territorial unit of the State.

---

* Adopted by the International Law Commission at its fifty-third session (2001). See the ILC's website at <http://www.un.org/law/ilc/index.htm>.

2. An organ includes any person or entity which has that status in accordance with the internal law of the State.

Article 5. Conduct of Persons or Entities Exercising Elements of Governmental Authority

The conduct of a person or entity which is not an organ of the State under article 4 but which is empowered by the law of that State to exercise elements of the governmental authority shall be considered an act of the State under international law, provided the person or entity is acting in that capacity in the particular instance.

Article 6. Conduct of Organs Placed at the Disposal of a State by Another State

The conduct of an organ placed at the disposal of a State by another State shall be considered an act of the former State under international law if the organ is acting in the exercise of elements of the governmental authority of the State at whose disposal it is placed.

Article 7. Excess of Authority or Contravention of Instructions

The conduct of an organ of a State or of a person or entity empowered to exercise elements of the governmental authority shall be considered an act of the State under international law if the organ, person or entity acts in that capacity, even if it exceeds its authority or contravenes instructions.

Article 8. Conduct Directed or Controlled by a State

The conduct of a person or group of persons shall be considered an act of a State under international law if the person or group of persons is in fact acting on the instructions of, or under the direction or control of, that State in carrying out the conduct.

Article 9. Conduct Carried Out in the Absence or Default of the Official Authorities

The conduct of a person or group of persons shall be considered an act of a State under international law if the person or group of persons is in fact exercising elements of the governmental authority in the absence or default of the official authorities and in circumstances such as to call for the exercise of those elements of authority.

Article 10. Conduct of an Insurrectional or Other Movement

1. The conduct of an insurrectional movement which becomes the new government of a State shall be considered an act of that State under international law.

2. The conduct of a movement, insurrectional or other, which succeeds in establishing a new State in part of the territory of a pre-existing State or in a territory under its administration shall be considered an act of the new State under international law.

3. This article is without prejudice to the attribution to a State of any conduct, however related to that of the movement concerned, which is to be considered an act of that State by virtue of articles 4 to 9.

Article 11.   Conduct Acknowledged and Adopted by a State as Its Own

Conduct which is not attributable to a State under the preceding articles shall nevertheless be considered an act of that State under international law if and to the extent that the State acknowledges and adopts the conduct in question as its own.

CHAPTER III.   BREACH OF AN INTERNATIONAL OBLIGATION

Article 12.   Existence of a Breach of an International Obligation

There is a breach of an international obligation by a State when an act of that State is not in conformity with what is required of it by that obligation, regardless of its origin or character.

Article 13.   International Obligation in Force for a State

An act of a State does not constitute a breach of an international obligation unless the State is bound by the obligation in question at the time the act occurs.

Article 14.   Extension in Time of the Breach of an International Obligation

1. The breach of an international obligation by an act of a State not having a continuing character occurs at the moment when the act is performed, even if its effects continue.

2. The breach of an international obligation by an act of a State having a continuing character extends over the entire period during which the act continues and remains not in conformity with the international obligation.

3. The breach of an international obligation requiring a State to prevent a given event occurs when the event occurs and extends over the entire period during which the event continues and remains not in conformity with that obligation.

Article 15.   Breach Consisting of a Composite Act

1. The breach of an international obligation by a State through a series of actions or omissions defined in aggregate as wrongful, occurs when the action or omission occurs which, taken with the other actions or omissions, is sufficient to constitute the wrongful act.

2. In such a case, the breach extends over the entire period starting with the first of the actions or omissions of the series and lasts for as long as these actions or omissions are repeated and remain not in conformity with the international obligation.

CHAPTER IV.   RESPONSIBILITY OF A STATE IN CONNECTION WITH THE ACT OF ANOTHER STATE

Article 16.   Aid or Assistance in the Commission of an Internationally Wrongful Act

A State which aids or assists another State in the commission of an internationally wrongful act by the latter is internationally responsible for doing so if:

(a) That State does so with knowledge of the circumstances of the internationally wrongful act; and

(b) The act would be internationally wrongful if committed by that State.

Article 17.   Direction and Control Exercised over the Commission of an Internationally Wrongful Act

A State which directs and controls another State in the commission of an internationally wrongful act by the latter is internationally responsible for that act if:

(a) That State does so with knowledge of the circumstances of the internationally wrongful act; and

(b) The act would be internationally wrongful if committed by that State.

Article 18.   Coercion of Another State

A State which coerces another State to commit an act is internationally responsible for that act if:

(a) The act would, but for the coercion, be an internationally wrongful act of the coerced State; and

(b) The coercing State does so with knowledge of the circumstances of the act.

Article 19.   Effect of This Chapter

This chapter is without prejudice to the international responsibility, under other provisions of these articles, of the State which commits the act in question, or of any other State.

CHAPTER V.   CIRCUMSTANCES PRECLUDING WRONGFULNESS

Article 20.   Consent

Valid consent by a State to the commission of a given act by another State precludes the wrongfulness of that act in relation to the former State to the extent that the act remains within the limits of that consent.

Article 21.   Self-Defence

The wrongfulness of an act of a State is precluded if the act constitutes a lawful measure of self-defence taken in conformity with the Charter of the United Nations.

Article 22.   Countermeasures in Respect of an Internationally Wrongful Act

The wrongfulness of an act of a State not in conformity with an international obligation towards another State is precluded if and to the extent that the act constitutes a countermeasure taken against the latter State in accordance with chapter II of Part Three.

Article 23.   Force Majeure

1. The wrongfulness of an act of a State not in conformity with an international obligation of that State is precluded if the act is due to *force majeure*, that is the occurrence of an irresistible force or of an unforeseen event, beyond the control of the State, making it materially impossible in the circumstances to perform the obligation.

2. Paragraph 1 does not apply if:

(a) The situation of *force majeure* is due, either alone or in combination with other factors, to the conduct of the State invoking it; or

(b) The State has assumed the risk of that situation occurring.

Article 24.   Distress

1. The wrongfulness of an act of a State not in conformity with an international obligation of that State is precluded if the author of the act in question has no other reasonable way, in a situation of distress, of saving the author's life or the lives of other persons entrusted to the author's care.

2. Paragraph 1 does not apply if:

(a) The situation of distress is due, either alone or in combination with other factors, to the conduct of the State invoking it; or

(b) The act in question is likely to create a comparable or greater peril.

Article 25.   Necessity

1. Necessity may not be invoked by a State as a ground for precluding the wrongfulness of an act not in conformity with an international obligation of that State unless the act:

(a) Is the only way for the State to safeguard an essential interest against a grave and imminent peril; and

(b) Does not seriously impair an essential interest of the State or States towards which the obligation exists, or of the international community as a whole.

2. In any case, necessity may not be invoked by a State as a ground for precluding wrongfulness if:

(a) The international obligation in question excludes the possibility of invoking necessity; or

(b) The State has contributed to the situation of necessity.

Article 26. Compliance with Peremptory Norms

Nothing in this chapter precludes the wrongfulness of any act of a State which is not in conformity with an obligation arising under a peremptory norm of general international law.

Article 27. Consequences of Invoking a Circumstance Precluding Wrongfulness

The invocation of a circumstance precluding wrongfulness in accordance with this chapter is without prejudice to:

(a) Compliance with the obligation in question, if and to the extent that the circumstance precluding wrongfulness no longer exists;

(b) The question of compensation for any material loss caused by the act in question.

Part Two. Content of the International Responsibility of a State

CHAPTER I. GENERAL PRINCIPLES

Article 28. Legal Consequences of an Internationally Wrongful Act

The international responsibility of a State which is entailed by an internationally wrongful act in accordance with the provisions of Part One involves legal consequences as set out in this Part.

Article 29. Continued Duty of Performance

The legal consequences of an internationally wrongful act under this Part do not affect the continued duty of the responsible State to perform the obligation breached.

Article 30.   Cessation and Non-Repetition

The State responsible for the internationally wrongful act is under an obligation:

(a) To cease that act, if it is continuing;

(b) To offer appropriate assurances and guarantees of non-repetition, if circumstances so require.

Article 31.   Reparation

1. The responsible State is under an obligation to make full reparation for the injury caused by the internationally wrongful act.

2. Injury includes any damage, whether material or moral, caused by the internationally wrongful act of a State.

Article 32.   Irrelevance of Internal Law

The responsible State may not rely on the provisions of its internal law as justification for failure to comply with its obligations under this Part.

Article 33.   Scope of International Obligations Set Out in This Part

1. The obligations of the responsible State set out in this Part may be owed to another State, to several States, or to the international community as a whole, depending in particular on the character and content of the international obligation and on the circumstances of the breach.

2. This Part is without prejudice to any right, arising from the international responsibility of a State, which may accrue directly to any person or entity other than a State.

CHAPTER II.   REPARATION FOR INJURY

Article 34.   Forms of Reparation

Full reparation for the injury caused by the internationally wrongful act shall take the form of restitution, compensation and satisfaction, either singly or in combination, in accordance with the provisions of this chapter.

Article 35.   Restitution

A State responsible for an internationally wrongful act is under an obligation to make restitution, that is, to re-establish the situation which existed before the wrongful act was committed, provided and to the extent that restitution:

(a) Is not materially impossible;

(b) Does not involve a burden out of all proportion to the benefit deriving from restitution instead of compensation.

Article 36.   Compensation

1. The State responsible for an internationally wrongful act is under an obligation to compensate for the damage caused thereby, insofar as such damage is not made good by restitution.

2. The compensation shall cover any financially assessable damage including loss of profits insofar as it is established.

Article 37.   Satisfaction

1. The State responsible for an internationally wrongful act is under an obligation to give satisfaction for the injury caused by that act insofar as it cannot be made good by restitution or compensation.

2. Satisfaction may consist in an acknowledgement of the breach, an expression of regret, a formal apology or another appropriate modality.

3. Satisfaction shall not be out of proportion to the injury and may not take a form humiliating to the responsible State.

Article 38.   Interest

1. Interest on any principal sum due under this chapter shall be payable when necessary in order to ensure full reparation. The interest rate and mode of calculation shall be set so as to achieve that result.

2. Interest runs from the date when the principal sum should have been paid until the date the obligation to pay is fulfilled.

Article 39.   Contribution to the Injury

In the determination of reparation, account shall be taken of the contribution to the injury by wilful or negligent action or omission of the injured State or any person or entity in relation to whom reparation is sought.

CHAPTER III.   SERIOUS BREACHES OF OBLIGATIONS UNDER PEREMPTORY NORMS OF GENERAL INTERNATIONAL LAW

Article 40.   Application of This Chapter

1. This chapter applies to the international responsibility which is entailed by a serious breach by a State of an obligation arising under a peremptory norm of general international law.

2. A breach of such an obligation is serious if it involves a gross or systematic failure by the responsible State to fulfil the obligation.

Article 41.   Particular Consequences of a Serious Breach of an Obligation Under This Chapter

1. States shall cooperate to bring to an end through lawful means any serious breach within the meaning of article 40.

2. No State shall recognize as lawful a situation created by a serious breach within the meaning of article 40, nor render aid or assistance in maintaining that situation.

3. This article is without prejudice to the other consequences referred to in this Part and to such further consequences that a breach to which this chapter applies may entail under international law.

Part Three.   The Implementation of the International Responsibility of a State

CHAPTER I.   INVOCATION OF THE RESPONSIBILITY OF A STATE

Article 42.   Invocation of Responsibility by an Injured State

A State is entitled as an injured State to invoke the responsibility of another State if the obligation breached is owed to:

(a) That State individually; or

(b) A group of States including that State, or the international community as a whole, and the breach of the obligation:

(i) Specially affects that State; or

(ii) Is of such a character as radically to change the position of all the other States to which the obligation is owed with respect to the further performance of the obligation.

Article 43.   Notice of Claim by an Injured State

1. An injured State which invokes the responsibility of another State shall give notice of its claim to that State.

2. The injured State may specify in particular:

(a) The conduct that the responsible State should take in order to cease the wrongful act, if it is continuing;

(b) What form reparation should take in accordance with the provisions of Part Two.

Article 44.   Admissibility of Claims

The responsibility of a State may not be invoked if:

(a) The claim is not brought in accordance with any applicable rule relating to the nationality of claims;

(b) The claim is one to which the rule of exhaustion of local remedies applies and any available and effective local remedy has not been exhausted.

Article 45. Loss of the Right to Invoke Responsibility

The responsibility of a State may not be invoked if:
(a) The injured State has validly waived the claim;
(b) The injured State is to be considered as having, by reason of its conduct, validly acquiesced in the lapse of the claim.

Article 46. Plurality of Injured States

Where several States are injured by the same internationally wrongful act, each injured State may separately invoke the responsibility of the State which has committed the internationally wrongful act.

Article 47. Plurality of Responsible States

1. Where several States are responsible for the same internationally wrongful act, the responsibility of each State may be invoked in relation to that act.
2. Paragraph 1:
(a) Does not permit any injured State to recover, by way of compensation, more than the damage it has suffered;
(b) Is without prejudice to any right of recourse against the other responsible States.

Article 48. Invocation of Responsibility by a State Other Than an Injured State

1. Any State other than an injured State is entitled to invoke the responsibility of another State in accordance with paragraph 2 if:
(a) The obligation breached is owed to a group of States including that State, and is established for the protection of a collective interest of the group; or
(b) The obligation breached is owed to the international community as a whole.
2. Any State entitled to invoke responsibility under paragraph 1 may claim from the responsible State:
(a) Cessation of the internationally wrongful act, and assurances and guarantees of non-repetition in accordance with article 30; and
(b) Performance of the obligation of reparation in accordance with the preceding articles, in the interest of the injured State or of the beneficiaries of the obligation breached.
3. The requirements for the invocation of responsibility by an injured State under articles 43, 44 and 45 apply to an invocation of responsibility by a State entitled to do so under paragraph 1.

Chapter II. Countermeasures

Article 49. Object and Limits of Countermeasures

1. An injured State may only take countermeasures against a State which is responsible for an internationally wrongful act in order to induce that State to comply with its obligations under Part Two.

2. Countermeasures are limited to the non-performance for the time being of international obligations of the State taking the measures towards the responsible State.

3. Countermeasures shall, as far as possible, be taken in such a way as to permit the resumption of performance of the obligations in question.

Article 50. Obligations Not Affected by Countermeasures

1. Countermeasures shall not affect:

(a) The obligation to refrain from the threat or use of force as embodied in the Charter of the United Nations;

(b) Obligations for the protection of fundamental human rights;

(c) Obligations of a humanitarian character prohibiting reprisals;

(d) Other obligations under peremptory norms of general international law.

2. A State taking countermeasures is not relieved from fulfilling its obligations:

(a) Under any dispute settlement procedure applicable between it and the responsible State;

(b) To respect the inviolability of diplomatic or consular agents, premises, archives and documents.

Article 51. Proportionality

Countermeasures must be commensurate with the injury suffered, taking into account the gravity of the internationally wrongful act and the rights in question.

Article 52. Conditions Relating to Resort to Countermeasures

1. Before taking countermeasures, an injured State shall:

(a) Call on the responsible State, in accordance with article 43, to fulfil its obligations under Part Two;

(b) Notify the responsible State of any decision to take countermeasures and offer to negotiate with that State.

2. Notwithstanding paragraph 1 (b), the injured State may take such urgent countermeasures as are necessary to preserve its rights.

3. Countermeasures may not be taken, and if already taken must be suspended without undue delay if:

(a) The internationally wrongful act has ceased; and

(b) The dispute is pending before a court or tribunal which has the authority to make decisions binding on the parties.

4. Paragraph 3 does not apply if the responsible State fails to implement the dispute settlement procedures in good faith.

Article 53. Termination of Countermeasures

Countermeasures shall be terminated as soon as the responsible State has complied with its obligations under Part Two in relation to the internationally wrongful act.

Article 54. Measures Taken by States Other Than an Injured State

This chapter does not prejudice the right of any State, entitled under article 48, paragraph 1 to invoke the responsibility of another State, to take lawful measures against that State to ensure cessation of the breach and reparation in the interest of the injured State or of the beneficiaries of the obligation breached.

Part Four.   General Provisions

Article 55. Lex Specialis

These articles do not apply where and to the extent that the conditions for the existence of an internationally wrongful act or the content or implementation of the international responsibility of a State are governed by special rules of international law.

Article 56. Questions of State Responsibility Not Regulated by These Articles

The applicable rules of international law continue to govern questions concerning the responsibility of a State for an internationally wrongful act to the extent that they are not regulated by these articles.

Article 57. Responsibility of an International Organization

These articles are without prejudice to any question of the responsibility under international law of an international organization, or of any State for the conduct of an international organization.

Article 58. Individual Responsibility

These articles are without prejudice to any question of the individual responsibility under international law of any person acting on behalf of a State.

Article 59. Charter of the United Nations

These articles are without prejudice to the Charter of the United Nations.

UNIVERSAL DECLARATION
OF HUMAN RIGHTS

G.A. Res. 217 (III), U.N. Doc. A/777 (Dec. 10, 1948)*

The General Assembly,

Proclaims this Universal Declaration of Human Rights as a common standard of achievement for all peoples and all nations, to the end that every individual and every organ of society, keeping this Declaration constantly in mind, shall strive by teaching and education to promote respect for these rights and freedoms and by progressive measures, national and international, to secure their universal and effective recognition and observance, both among the peoples of Member States themselves and among the peoples of territories under their jurisdiction.

Article 1

All human beings are born free and equal in dignity and rights. They are endowed with reason and conscience and should act towards one another in a spirit of brotherhood.

Article 2

Everyone is entitled to all the rights and freedoms set forth in this declaration, without discrimination of any kind, such as race, colour, sex, language, religion, political or other opinion, national or social origin, property, birth or other status.

Furthermore, no distinction shall be made on the basis of the political, jurisdictional or international status of the country or territory to which a person belongs, whether it be independent, trust, non-self-governing or under any other limitation of sovereignty.

Article 3

Everyone has the right to life, liberty and the security of person.

---

* The declaration was adopted by the U.N. General Assembly on December 10, 1948. Forty-eight states voted in favor, none against, and eight abstained (including Saudi Arabia, South Africa, Union of Soviet Socialist Republics, and Yugoslavia).

Article 4

No one shall be held in slavery or servitude; slavery and the slave trade shall be prohibited in all their forms.

Article 5

No one shall be subjected to torture or to cruel, inhuman or degrading treatment or punishment.

Article 6

Everyone has the right to recognition everywhere as a person before the law.

Article 7

All are equal before the law and are entitled without any discrimination to equal protection of the law. All are entitled to equal protection against any discrimination in violation of this Declaration and against any incitement to such discrimination.

Article 8

Everyone has the right to an effective remedy by the competent national tribunals for acts violating the fundamental rights granted him by the constitution or by law.

Article 9

No one shall be subjected to arbitrary arrest, detention or exile.

Article 10

Everyone is entitled in full equality to a fair and public hearing by an independent and impartial tribunal, in the determination of his rights and obligations and of any criminal charge against him.

Article 11

1. Everyone charged with a penal offence has the right to be presumed innocent until proved guilty according to law in a public trial at which he has had all the guarantees necessary for his defence.

2. No one shall be held guilty of any penal offence on account of any act or omission which did not constitute a penal offence, under national or international law, at the time when it was committed. Nor shall a heavier penalty be imposed than the one that was applicable at the time the penal offence was committed.

Article 12

No one shall be subjected to arbitrary interference with his privacy, family, home or correspondence, nor to attacks upon his honour and reputation. Everyone has the right to the protection of the law against such interference or attacks.

Article 13

1. Everyone has the right to freedom of movement and residence within the borders of each State.

2. Everyone has the right to leave any country, including his own, and to return to his country.

Article 14

1. Everyone has the right to seek and to enjoy in other countries asylum from persecution.

2. This right may not be invoked in the case of prosecutions genuinely arising from non-political crimes or from acts contrary to the purposes and principles of the United Nations.

Article 15

1. Everyone has the right to a nationality.

2. No one shall be arbitrarily deprived of his nationality nor denied the right to change his nationality.

Article 16

1. Men and women of full age, without any limitation due to race, nationality or religion, have the right to marry and to found a family. They are entitled to equal rights as to marriage, during marriage and at its dissolution.

2. Marriage shall be entered into only with the free and full consent of the intending spouses.

3. The family is the natural and fundamental group unit of society and is entitled to protection by society and the State.

Article 17

1. Everyone has the right to own property alone as well as in association with others.

2. No one shall be arbitrarily deprived of his property.

Article 18

Everyone has the right to freedom of thought, conscience and religion; this right includes freedom to change his religion or belief, and freedom, either alone or in community with others and in public or private, to manifest his religion or belief in teaching, practice, worship and observance.

Article 19

Everyone has the right to freedom of opinion and expression; this right includes freedom to hold opinions without interference and to seek, receive and impart information and ideas through any media and regardless of frontiers.

Article 20

1. Everyone has the right to freedom of peaceful assembly and association.
2. No one may be compelled to belong to an association.

Article 21

1. Everyone has the right to take part in the government of his country, directly or through freely chosen representatives.
2. Everyone has the right of equal access to public service in his country.
3. The will of the people shall be the basis of the authority of government; this will shall be expressed in periodic and genuine elections which shall be by universal and equal suffrage and shall be held by secret vote or by equivalent free voting procedures.

Article 22

Everyone, as a member of society, has the right to social security and is entitled to realization, through national effort and international cooperation and in accordance with the organization and resources of each State, of the economic, social and cultural rights indispensable for his dignity and the free development of his personality.

Article 23

1. Everyone has the right to work, to free choice of employment, to just and favorable conditions of work and to protection against unemployment.
2. Everyone, without any discrimination, has the right to equal pay for equal work.
3. Everyone who works has the right to just and favourable remuneration ensuring for himself and his family and existence worthy of human dignity, and supplemented, if necessary, by other means of social protection.
4. Everyone has the right to form and to join trade unions for the protection of his interests.

Article 24

Everyone has the right to rest and leisure, including reasonable limitation of working hours and periodic holidays with pay.

Article 25

1. Everyone has the right to a standard of living adequate for the health and well-being of himself and of his family, including food, clothing, housing

and medical care and necessary social services, and the right to security in the event of unemployment, sickness, disability, widowhood, old age or other lack of livelihood in circumstances beyond his control.

2. Motherhood and childhood are entitled to special care and assistance. All children, whether born in or out of wedlock, shall enjoy the same social protection.

Article 26

1. Everyone has the right to education. Education shall be free, at least in the elementary and fundamental stages. Elementary education shall be compulsory. Technical and professional education shall be made generally available and higher education shall be equally accessible to all on the basis of merit.

2. Education shall be directed to the full development of the human personality and to the strengthening of respect for human rights and fundamental freedoms. It shall promote understanding, tolerance and friendship among all nations, racial or religious groups, and shall further the activities of the United Nations for the maintenance of peace.

3. Parents have a right to choose the kind of education that shall be given to their children.

Article 27

1. Everyone has the right freely to participate in the cultural life of the community, to enjoy the arts and to share in scientific advancement and its benefits.

2. Everyone has the right to the protection of the moral and material interests resulting from any scientific, literary or artistic production of which he is the author.

Article 28

Everyone is entitled to a social and international order in which the rights and freedoms set forth in this Declaration can be fully realized.

Article 29

1. Everyone has duties to the community in which alone the free and full development of his personality is possible.

2. In the exercise of his rights and freedoms, everyone shall be subject only to such limitations as are determined by law solely for the purpose of securing due recognition and respect for the rights and freedoms of others and of meeting the just requirements of morality, public order and the general welfare in a democratic society.

3. These rights and freedoms may in no case be exercised contrary to the purposes and principles of the United Nations.

Article 30

Nothing in this Declaration may be interpreted as implying for any States, group or person any right to engage in any activity or to perform any act aimed at the destruction of any of the rights and freedoms set forth herein.

INTERNATIONAL COVENANT ON CIVIL AND POLITICAL RIGHTS

Dec. 16, 1966, 999 U.N.T.S. 171, 6 ILM 368*

Recognizing that these rights derive from the inherent dignity of the human person,

Recognizing that, in accordance with the Universal Declaration of Human Rights, the ideal of free human beings enjoying civil and political freedom and freedom from fear and want can only be achieved if conditions are created whereby everyone may enjoy his civil and political rights, as well as his economic, social and cultural rights,

Considering the obligation of States under the Charter of the United Nations to promote universal respect for, and observance of, human rights and freedoms,

---

* Adopted by the U.N. General Assembly at New York on December 16, 1966. G.A. Res. 2200, Entered into force on March 23, 1976. The United States ratified the covenant on June 8, 1992 with reservations, understandings, declarations, and a proviso. See the U.S. Senate Resolution following this document.

As of March 2013, the 167 parties to the covenant were: Afghanistan, Albania, Algeria, Andorra, Angola, Argentina, Armenia, Australia, Austria, Azerbaijan, Bahamas, Bahrain, Bangladesh, Barbados, Belarus, Belgium, Belize, Benin, Bolivia, Bosnia and Herzegovina, Botswana, Brazil, Bulgaria, Burkina Faso, Burundi, Cambodia, Cameroon, Canada, Cape Verde, Central African Republic, Chad, Chile, Colombia, Congo, Congo (Democratic Republic of), Costa Rica, Côte d'Ivoire, Croatia, Cyprus, Czech Republic, Denmark, Djibouti, Dominica, Dominican Republic, Ecuador, Egypt, El Salvador, Equatorial Guinea, Eritrea, Estonia, Ethiopia, Finland, France, Gabon, Gambia, Georgia, Germany, Ghana, Greece, Grenada, Guatemala, Guinea, Guinea-Bissau, Guyana, Haiti, Honduras, Hungary, Iceland, India, Indonesia, Iran, Iraq, Ireland, Israel, Italy, Jamaica, Japan, Jordan, Kazakhstan, Kenya, Korea (Democratic Republic of), Korea (Republic of), Kuwait, Kyrgyzstan, Lao (People's Democratic Republic), Latvia, Lebanon, Lesotho, Liberia, Libyan Arab Jamahiriya, Liechtenstein, Lithuania, Luxembourg, Macedonia (the former Yugoslav Republic of), Madagascar, Malawi, Maldives, Mali, Malta, Mauritania, Mauritius, Mexico, Moldova, Monaco, Mongolia, Montenegro, Morocco, Mozambique, Namibia, Nepal, Netherlands, New Zealand, Nicaragua, Niger, Nigeria, Norway, Pakistan, Panama, Papua New Guinea, Paraguay, Peru, Philippines, Poland, Portugal, Romania, Russian Federation, Rwanda, Samoa, Saint Vincent and the Grenadines, San Marino, Senegal, Serbia, Seychelles, Sierra Leone, Slovakia, Slovenia, Somalia, South Africa, Spain, Sri Lanka, Sudan, Suriname, Swaziland, Sweden, Switzerland, Syrian Arab Republic, Tajikistan, Tanzania, Thailand, Timor-Leste, Togo, Trinidad and Tobago, Tunisia, Turkey, Turkmenistan, Uganda, Ukraine, United Kingdom, United States of America, Uruguay, Uzbekistan, Vanuatu, Venezuela, Viet Nam, Yemen, Zambia, Zimbabwe. See the U.N. Web site at <http://treaties.un.org>.

Realizing that the individual, having duties to other individuals and to the community to which he belongs, is under a responsibility to strive for the promotion and observance of the rights recognized in the present Covenant,

Agree upon the following articles:

Part I

Article 1

1. All peoples have the right of self-determination. By virtue of that right they freely determine their political status and freely pursue their economic, social and cultural development.

2. All peoples may, for their own ends, freely dispose of their natural wealth and resources without prejudice to any obligations arising out of international economic co-operation, based upon the principle of mutual benefit, and international law. In no case may a people be deprived of its own means of subsistence.

3. The States Parties to the present Covenant, including those having responsibility for the administration of Non-Self-Governing and Trust Territories, shall promote the realization of the right of self-determination, and shall respect that right, in conformity with the provisions of the Charter of the United Nations.

Part II

Article 2

1. Each State Party to the present Covenant undertakes to respect and to ensure to all individuals within its territory and subject to its jurisdiction the rights recognized in the present Covenant, without distinction of any kind, such as race, colour, sex, language, religion, political or other opinion, national or social origin, property, birth or other status.

2. Where not already provided for by existing legislative or other measures, each State Party to the present Covenant undertakes to take the necessary steps, in accordance with its constitutional processes and with the provisions of the present Covenant, to adopt such legislative or other measures as may be necessary to give effect to the rights recognized in the present Covenant.

3. Each State Party to the present Covenant undertakes:

(*a*) To ensure that any person whose rights or freedoms as herein recognized are violated shall have an effective remedy, notwithstanding that the violation has been committed by persons acting in an official capacity;

(*b*) To ensure that any person claiming such a remedy shall have his right thereto determined by competent judicial, administrative or legislative authorities, or by any other competent authority provided for by the legal system of the State, and to develop the possibilities of judicial remedy;

(c) To ensure that the competent authorities shall enforce such remedies when granted,

Article 3

The States Parties to the present Covenant undertake to ensure the equal right of men and women to the enjoyment of all civil and political rights set forth in the present Covenant.

Article 4

1. In time of public emergency which threatens the life of the nation and the existence of which is officially proclaimed, the States Parties to the present Covenant may take measures derogating from their obligations under the present Covenant to the extent strictly required by the exigencies of the situation, provided that such measures are not inconsistent with their other obligations under international law and do not involve discrimination solely on the ground of race, color, sex, language, religion or social origin.

2. No derogation from articles 6, 7, 8 (paragraphs 1 and 2), 11, 15, 16 and 18 may be made under this provision.

3. Any State Party to the present Covenant availing itself of the right of derogation shall immediately inform the other States Parties to the present Covenant, through the intermediary of the Secretary-General of the United Nations, of the provisions from which it has derogated and of the reasons by which it was actuated. A further communication shall be made, through the same intermediary, on the date on which it terminates such derogation.

Article 5

1. Nothing in the present Covenant may be interpreted as implying for any State, group or person any right to engage in any activity or perform any act aimed at the destruction of any of the rights and freedoms recognized herein or at their limitation to a greater extent than is provided for in the present Covenant.

2. There shall be no restriction upon or derogation from any of the fundamental human rights recognized or existing in any State Party to the present Covenant pursuant to law, conventions, regulations or custom on the pretext that the present Covenant does not recognize such rights or that it recognizes them to a lesser extent.

Part III

Article 6

1. Every human being has the inherent right to life. This right shall be protected by law. No one shall be arbitrarily deprived of his life.

2. In countries which have not abolished the death penalty, sentence of death may be imposed only for the most serious crimes in accordance with the law in force at the time of the commission of the crime and not contrary to the provisions of the present Covenant and to the Convention on the Prevention and Punishment of the Crime of Genocide. This penalty can only be carried out pursuant to a final judgement rendered by a competent court.

3. When deprivation of life constitutes the crime of genocide, it is understood that nothing in this article shall authorize any State Party to the present Covenant to derogate in any way from any obligation assumed under the provisions of the Convention on the Prevention and Punishment of the Crime of Genocide.

4. Anyone sentenced to death shall have the right to seek pardon or commutation of the sentence. Amnesty, pardon or commutation of the sentence of death may be granted in all cases.

5. Sentence of death shall not be imposed for crimes committed by persons below eighteen years of age and shall not be carried out on pregnant women.

6. Nothing in this article shall be invoked to delay or to prevent the abolition of capital punishment by any State Party to the present Covenant.

Article 7

No one shall be subjected to torture or to cruel, inhuman or degrading treatment or punishment. In particular, no one shall be subjected without his free consent to medical or scientific experimentation.

Article 8

1. No one shall be held in slavery; slavery and the slave-trade in all their forms shall be prohibited.

2. No one shall be held in servitude.

3. (*a*) No one shall be required to perform forced or compulsory labour.

(*b*) Paragraph 3 (*a*) shall not be held to preclude, in countries where imprisonment with hard labour may be imposed as a punishment for a crime, the performance of hard labour in pursuance of a sentence to such punishment by a competent court.

(*c*) For the purpose of this paragraph the term "forced or compulsory labour" shall not include:

(i) Any work or service, not referred to in sub-paragraph (*b*), normally required of a person who is under detention in consequence of a lawful order of a court, or of a person during conditional release from such detention;

(ii) Any service of a military character and, in countries where conscientious objection is recognized, any national service required by law of conscientious objectors;

(iii) Any service exacted in cases of emergency or calamity threatening the life or well-being of the community;

(iv) Any work or service which forms part of normal civil obligations.

Article 9

1. Everyone has the right to liberty and security of person. No one shall be subjected to arbitrary arrest or detention. No one shall be deprived of his liberty except on such grounds and in accordance with such procedure as are established by law.

2. Anyone who is arrested shall be informed, at the time of arrest, of the reasons for his arrest and shall be promptly informed of any charges against him.

3. Anyone arrested or detained on a criminal charge shall be brought promptly before a judge or other officer authorized by law to exercise judicial power and shall be entitled to trial within a reasonable time or to release. It shall not be the general rule that persons awaiting trial shall be detained in custody, but release may be subject to guarantees to appear for trial, at any other stage of the judicial proceedings, and, should occasion arise, for execution of the judgement.

4. Anyone who is deprived of his liberty by arrest or detention shall be entitled to take proceedings before a court, in order that that court may decide without delay on the lawfulness of his detention and order his release if the detention is not lawful.

5. Anyone who has been the victim of unlawful arrest or detention shall have an enforceable right to compensation.

Article 10

1. All persons deprived of their liberty shall be treated with humanity and with respect for the inherent dignity of the human person.

2. (*a*) Accused persons shall, save in exceptional circumstances, be segregated from convicted persons and shall be subject to separate treatment appropriate to their status as unconvicted persons.

(*b*) Accused juvenile persons shall be separated from adults and brought as speedily as possible for adjudication.

3. The penitentiary system shall comprise treatment of prisoners the essential aim of which shall be their reformation and social rehabilitation. Juvenile offenders shall be segregated from adults and be accorded treatment appropriate to their age and legal status.

Article 11

No one shall be imprisoned merely on the ground of inability to fulfil a contractual obligation.

Article 12

1. Everyone lawfully within the territory of a State shall, within that territory, have the right to liberty of movement and freedom to choose his residence.

2. Everyone shall be free to leave any country, including his own.

3. The above-mentioned rights shall not be subject to any restrictions except those which are provided by law, are necessary to protect national security, public order (*ordre public*), public health or morals or the rights and freedoms of others, and are consistent with the other rights recognized in the present Covenant.

4. No one shall be arbitrarily deprived of the right to enter his own country.

Article 13

An alien lawfully in the territory of a State Party to the present Covenant may be expelled therefrom only in pursuance of a decision reached in accordance with law and shall, except where compelling reasons of national security otherwise require, be allowed to submit the reasons against his explusion and to have his case reviewed by, and be represented for the purpose before, the competent authority or a person or persons especially designated by the competent authority.

Article 14

1. All persons shall be equal before the courts and tribunals. In the determination of any criminal charge against him, or of his rights and obligations in a suit at law, everyone shall be entitled to a fair and public hearing by a competent, independent and impartial tribunal established by law. The Press and the public may be excluded from all or part of a trial for reasons of morals, public order (*ordre public*) or national security in a democratic society, or when the interest of the private lives of the parties so requires, or to the extent strictly necessary in the opinion of the court in special circumstances where publicity would prejudice the interests of justice; but any judgement rendered in a criminal case or in a suit at law shall be made public except where the interest of juvenile persons otherwise requires or the proceedings concern matrimonial disputes or the guardianship of children.

2. Everyone charged with a criminal offence shall have the right to be presumed innocent until proved guilty according to law.

3. In the determination of any criminal charge against him, everyone shall be entitled to the following minimum guarantees, in full equality:

(*a*) To be informed promptly and in detail in a language which he understands of the nature and cause of the charge against him;

(*b*) To have adequate time and facilities for the preparation of his defence and to communicate with counsel of his own choosing;

(*c*) To be tried without undue delay;

(*d*) To be tried in his presence, and to defend himself in person or through legal assistance of his own choosing; to be informed, if he does not have legal assistance, of this right; and to have legal assistance assigned to him, in any case where the interests of justice so require, and without payment by him in any such case if he does not have sufficient means to pay for it;

(*e*) To examine, or have examined, the witnesses against him and to obtain the attendance and examination of witnesses on his behalf under the same conditions as witnesses against him;

(*f*) To have the free assistance of an interpreter if he cannot understand or speak the language used in court;

(*g*) Not to be compelled to testify against himself or to confess guilt.

4. In the case of juvenile persons, the procedure shall be such as will take account of their age and the desirability of promoting their rehabilitation.

5. Everyone convicted of a crime shall have the right to his conviction and sentence being reviewed by a higher tribunal according to law.

6. When a person has by a final decision been convicted of a criminal offence and when subsequently his conviction has been reversed or he has been pardoned on the ground that a new or newly discovered fact shows conclusively that there has been a miscarriage of justice, the person who has suffered punishment as a result of such conviction shall be compensated according to law, unless it is proved that the non-disclosure of the unknown fact in time is wholly or partly attributable to him.

7. No one shall be liable to be tried or punished again for an offence for which he has already been finally convicted or acquitted in accordance with the law and penal procedure of each country.

Article 15

1. No one shall be held guilty of any criminal offence on account of any act or omission which did not constitute a criminal offence, under national or international law, at the time when it was committed. Nor shall a heavier penalty be imposed than the one that was applicable at the time when the criminal offence was committed. If, subsequent to the commission of the offence, provision is made by law for the imposition of a lighter penalty, the offender shall benefit thereby.

2. Nothing in this article shall prejudice the trial and punishment of any person for any act or omission which, at the time when it was committed, was criminal according to the general principles of law recognized by the community of nations.

Article 16

Everyone shall have the right to recognition everywhere as a person before the law.

Article 17

1. No one shall be subjected to arbitrary or unlawful interference with his privacy, family, home or correspondence, nor to unlawful attacks on his honour and reputation.
2. Everyone has the right to the protection of the law against such interference or attacks.

Article 18

1. Everyone shall have the right to freedom of thought, conscience and religion. This right shall include freedom to have or to adopt a religion or belief of his choice, and freedom, either individually or in community with others and in public or private, to manifest his religion or belief in worship, observance, practice and teaching.
2. No one shall be subject to coercion which would impair his freedom to have or to adopt a religion or belief of his choice.
3. Freedom to manifest one's religion or beliefs may be subject only to such limitations as are prescribed by law and are necessary to protect public safety, order, health, or morals or the fundamental rights and freedoms of others.
4. The States Parties to the present Covenant undertake to have respect for the liberty of parents and, when applicable, legal guardians to ensure the religious and moral education of their children in conformity with their own convictions.

Article 19

1. Everyone shall have the right to hold opinions without interference.
2. Everyone shall have the right to freedom of expression; this right shall include freedom to seek, receive and impart information and ideas of all kinds, regardless of frontiers, either orally, in writing or in print, in the form of art, or through any other media of his choice.
3. The exercise of the rights provided for in paragraph 2 of this article carries with it special duties and responsibilities. It may therefore be subject to certain restrictions, but these shall only be such as are provided by law and are necessary:
   (*a*) For respect of the rights or reputations of others;
   (*b*) For the protection of national security or of public order (*ordre public*), or of public health or morals.

Article 20

1. Any propaganda for war shall be prohibited by law. 2. Any advocacy of national, racial or religious hatred that constitutes incitement to discrimination, hostility or violence shall be prohibited by law.

Article 21

The right of peaceful assembly shall be recognized. No restrictions may be placed on the exercise of this right other than those imposed in conformity with the law and which are necessary in a democratic society in the interests of national security or public safety, public order (*ordre public*), the protection of public health or morals or the protection of the rights and freedoms of others.

Article 22

1. Everyone shall have the right to freedom of association with others, including the right to form and join trade unions for the protection of his interests.

2. No restrictions may be placed on the exercise of this right other than those which are prescribed by law and which are necessary in a democratic society in the interests of national security or public safety, public order (*ordre public*), the protection of public health or morals or the protection of the rights and freedoms of others. This article shall not prevent the imposition of lawful restrictions on members of the armed forces and of the police in their exercise of this right.

3. Nothing in this article shall authorize States Parties to the International Labour Organisation Convention of 1948 concerning freedom of association and protection of the right to organize to take legislative measures which would prejudice, or to apply the law in such a manner as to prejudice, the guarantees provided for in that Convention.

Article 23

1. The family is the natural and fundamental group unit of society and is entitled to protection by society and the State.

2. The right of men and women of marriageable age to marry and to found a family shall be recognized.

3. No marriage shall be entered into without the free and full consent of the intending spouses.

4. States Parties to the present Covenant shall take appropriate steps to ensure equality of rights and responsibilities of spouses as to marriage, during marriage and at its dissolution. In the case of dissolution, provision shall be made for the necessary protection of any children.

Article 24

1. Every child shall have, without any discrimination as to race, colour, sex, language, religion, national or social origin, property or birth, the right to such measures of protection as are required by his status as a minor, on the part of his family, society and the State.

2. Every child shall be registered immediately after birth and shall have a name.

3. Every child has the right to acquire a nationality.

Article 25

Every citizen shall have the right and the opportunity, without any of the distinctions mentioned in article 2 and without unreasonable restrictions:

(*a*) To take part in the conduct of public affairs, directly or through freely chosen representatives;

(*b*) To vote and to be elected at genuine periodic elections which shall be by universal and equal suffrage and shall be held by secret ballot, guaranteeing the free expression of the will of the electors;

(*c*) To have access, on general terms of equality, to public service in his country.

Article 26

All persons are equal before the law and are entitled without any discrimination to the equal protection of the law. In this respect, the law shall prohibit any discrimination and guarantee to all persons equal and effective protection against discrimination on any ground such as race, colour, sex, language, religion, political or other opinion, national or social origin, property, birth or other status.

Article 27

In those States in which ethnic, religious or linguistic minorities exist, persons belonging to such minorities shall not be denied the right, in community with the other members of their group, to enjoy their own culture, to profess and practise their own religion, or to use their own language.

Part IV

Article 28

1. There shall be established a Human Rights Committee (hereafter referred to in the present Covenant as the Committee). It shall consist of eighteen members and shall carry out the functions hereinafter provided.

2. The Committee shall be composed of nationals of the States Parties to the present Covenant who shall be persons of high moral character and recognized competence in the field of human rights, consideration being given to the usefulness of the participation of some persons having legal experience.

3. The members of the Committee shall be elected and shall serve in their personal capacity.

Article 29

1. The members of the Committee shall be elected by secret ballot from a list of persons possessing the qualifications prescribed in article 28 and nominated for the purpose by the States Parties to the present Covenant.

2. Each State Party to the present Covenant may nominate not more than two persons. These persons shall be nationals of the nominating State.

3. A person shall be eligible for renomination.

Article 30

1. The initial election shall be held no later than six months after the date of the entry into force of the present Covenant.

2. At least four months before the date of each election to the Committee, other than an election to fill a vacancy declared in accordance with article 34, the Secretary-General of the United Nations shall address a written invitation to the States Parties to the present Covenant to submit their nominations for membership of the Committee within three months.

3. The Secretary-General of the United Nations shall prepare a list in alphabetical order of all the persons thus nominated, with an indication of the States Parties which have nominated them, and shall submit it to the States Parties to the present Covenant no later than one month before the date of each election.

4. Elections of the members of the Committee shall be held at a meeting of the States Parties to the present Covenant convened by the Secretary-General of the United Nations at the Headquarters of the United Nations. At that meeting, for which two thirds of the States Parties to the present Covenant shall constitute a quorum, the persons elected to the Committee shall be those nominees who obtain the largest number of votes and an absolute majority of the votes of the representatives of States Parties present and voting.

Article 31

1. The Committee may not include more than one national of the same State.

2. In the election of the Committee, consideration shall be given to equitable geographical distribution of membership and to the representation of the different forms of civilization and of the principal legal systems.

Article 32

1. The members of the Committee shall be elected for a term of four years. They shall be eligible for re-election if renominated. However, the terms of nine of the members elected at the first election shall expire at the end of two years; immediately after the first election, the names of these nine members shall be chosen by lot by the Chairman of the meeting referred to in article 30, paragraph 4.

2. Elections at the expiry of office shall be held in accordance with the preceding articles of this part of the present Covenant.

Article 33

1. If, in the unanimous opinion of the other members, a member of the Committee has ceased to carry out his functions for any cause other than absence of a temporary character, the Chairman of the Committee shall notify the Secretary-General of the United Nations, who shall then declare the seat of that member to be vacant.

2. In the event of the death or the resignation of a member of the Committee, the Chairman shall immediately notify the Secretary-General of the United Nations, who shall declare the seat vacant from the date of death or the date on which the resignation takes effect.

Article 34

1. When a vacancy is declared in accordance with article 33 and if the term of office of the member to be replaced does not expire within six months of the declaration of the vacancy, the Secretary-General of the United Nations shall notify each of the States Parties to the present Covenant, which may within two months submit nominations in accordance with article 29 for the purpose of filling the vacancy.

2. The Secretary-General of the United Nations shall prepare a list in alphabetical order of the persons thus nominated and shall submit it to the States Parties to the present Covenant. The election to fill the vacancy shall then take place in accordance with the relevant provisions of this part of the present Covenant.

3. A member of the Committee elected to fill a vacancy declared in accordance with article 33 shall hold office for the remainder of the term of the member who vacated the seat on the Committee under the provisions of that article.

Article 35

The members of the Committee shall, with the approval of the General Assembly of the United Nations, receive emoluments from United Nations resources on such terms and conditions as the General Assembly may decide, having regard to the importance of the Committee's responsibilities.

Article 36

The Secretary-General of the United Nations shall provide the necessary staff and facilities for the effective performance of the functions of the Committee under the present Covenant.

Article 37

1. The Secretary-General of the United Nations shall convene the initial meeting of the Committee at the Headquarters of the United Nations.

2. After its initial meeting, the Committee shall meet at such times as shall be provided in its rules of procedure.

3. The Committee shall normally meet at the Headquarters of the United Nations or at the United Nations Office at Geneva.

Article 38

Every member of the Committee shall, before taking up his duties, make a solemn declaration in open committee that he will perform his functions impartially and conscientiously.

Article 39

1. The Committee shall elect its officers for a term of two years. They may be re-elected.

2. The Committee shall establish its own rules of procedure, but these rules shall provide, *inter alia*, that:

(a) Twelve members shall constitute a quorum;

(b) Decisions of the Committee shall be made by a majority vote of the members present.

Article 40

1. The States Parties to the present Covenant undertake to submit reports on the measures they have adopted which give effect to the rights recognized herein and on the progress made in the enjoyment of those rights:

(a) Within one year of the entry into force of the present Covenant for the States Parties concerned;

(b) Thereafter whenever the Committee so requests.

2. All reports shall be submitted to the Secretary-General of the United Nations, who shall transmit them to the Committee for consideration. Reports shall indicate the factors and difficulties, if any, affecting the implementation of the present Covenant.

3. The Secretary-General of the United Nations may, after consultation with the Committee, transmit to the specialized agencies concerned copies of such parts of the reports as may fall within their field of competence.

4. The Committee shall study the reports submitted by the States Parties to the present Covenant. It shall transmit its reports, and such general

comments as it may consider appropriate, to the States Parties. The Committee may also transmit to the Economic and Social Council these comments along with the copies of the reports it has received from States Parties to the present Covenant.

5. The States Parties to the present Covenant may submit to the Committee observations on any comments that may be made in accordance with paragraph 4 of this article.

Article 41

1. A State Party to the present Covenant may at any time declare under this article that it recognizes the competence of the Committee to receive and consider communications to the effect that a State Party claims that another State Party is not fulfilling its obligations under the present Covenant. Communications under this article may be received and considered only if submitted by a State Party which has made a declaration recognizing in regard to itself the competence of the Committee. No communication shall be received by the Committee if it concerns a State Party which has not made such a declaration. Communications received under this article shall be dealt with in accordance with the following procedure:

(*a*) If a State Party to the present Covenant considers that another State Party is not giving effect to the provisions of the present Covenant, it may, by written communication, bring the matter to the attention of that State Party. Within three months after the receipt of the communication, the receiving State shall afford the State which sent the communication an explanation or any other statement in writing clarifying the matter, which should include, to the extent possible and pertinent, reference to domestic procedures and remedies taken, pending, or available in the matter.

(*b*) If the matter is not adjusted to the satisfaction of both States Parties concerned within six months after the receipt by the receiving State of the initial communication, either State shall have the right to refer the matter to the Committee, by notice given to the Committee and to the other State.

(*c*) The Committee shall deal with a matter referred to it only after it has ascertained that all available domestic remedies have been invoked and exhausted in the matter, in conformity with the generally recognized principles of international law. This shall not be the rule where the application of the remedies is unreasonably prolonged.

(*d*) The Committee shall hold closed meetings when examining communications under this article.

(*e*) Subject to the provisions of sub-paragraph (*c*), the Committee shall make available its good offices to the States Parties concerned with a view to a friendly solution of the matter on the basis of respect for human rights and fundamental freedoms as recognized in the present Covenant.

(*f*) In any matter referred to it, the Committee may call upon the States Parties concerned, referred to in sub-paragraph (*b*), to supply any relevant information.

(*g*) The States Parties concerned, referred to in sub-paragraph (*b*), shall have the right to be represented when the matter is being considered in the Committee and to make submissions orally and/or in writing.

(*h*) The Committee shall, within twelve months after the date of receipt of notice under sub-paragraph (*b*), submit a report:

(i) If a solution within the terms of sub-paragraph (*e*) is reached, the Committee shall confine its report to a brief statement of the facts and of the solution reached;

(ii) If a solution within the terms of sub-paragraph (*e*) is not reached, the Committee shall confine its report to a brief statement of the facts; the written submissions and record of the oral submissions made by the States Parties concerned shall be attached to the report.

In every matter, the report shall be communicated to the States Parties concerned.

2. The provisions of this article shall come into force when ten States Parties to the present Covenant have made declarations under paragraph 1 of this article. Such declarations shall be deposited by the States Parties with the Secretary-General of the United Nations, who shall transmit copies thereof to the other States Parties. A declaration may be withdrawn at any time by notification to the Secretary-General. Such a withdrawal shall not prejudice the consideration of any matter which is the subject of a communication already transmitted under this article; no further communication by any State Party shall be received after the notification of withdrawal of the declaration has been received by the Secretary-General, unless the State Party concerned has made a new declaration.

Article 42

1. (*a*) If a matter referred to the Committee in accordance with article 41 is not resolved to the satisfaction of the States Parties concerned, the Committee may, with the prior consent of the States Parties concerned, appoint an *ad hoc* Conciliation Commission (hereinafter referred to as the Commission). The good offices of the Commission shall be made available to the States Parties concerned with a view to an amicable solution of the matter on the basis of respect for the present Covenant.

(*b*) The Commission shall consist of five persons acceptable to the States Parties concerned. If the States Parties concerned fail to reach agreement within three months on all or part of the composition of the Commission the members of the Commission concerning whom no agreement has been reached shall be elected by secret ballot by a two-thirds majority vote of the Committee from among its members.

2. The members of the Commission shall serve in their personal capacity. They shall not be nationals of the States Parties concerned, or of a

State not party to the present Covenant, or of a State Party which has not made a declaration under article 41. . . .

Article 43

The members of the Committee, and of the *ad hoc* conciliation commissions which may be appointed under article 42, shall be entitled to the facilities, privileges and immunities of experts on mission for the United Nations as laid down in the relevant sections of the Convention on the Privileges and Immunities of the United Nations.

Article 44

The provisions for the implementation of the present Covenant shall apply without prejudice to the procedures prescribed in the field of human rights by or under the constituent instruments and the conventions of the United Nations and of the specialized agencies and shall not prevent the States Parties to the present Covenant from having recourse to other procedures for settling a dispute in accordance with general or special international agreements in force between them.

Article 45

The Committee shall submit to the General Assembly of the United Nations through the Economic and Social Council, an annual report on its activities.

Part V

Article 46

Nothing in the present Covenant shall be interpreted as impairing the provisions of the Charter of the United Nations and of the constitutions of the specialized agencies which define the respective responsibilities of the various organs of the United Nations and of the specialized agencies in regard to the matters dealt with in the present Covenant.

Article 47

Nothing in the present Covenant shall be interpreted as impairing the inherent right of all peoples to enjoy and utilize fully and freely their natural wealth and resources. . . .

U.S. SENATE RESOLUTION OF ADVICE AND CONSENT TO RATIFICATION OF THE INTERNATIONAL COVENANT ON CIVIL AND POLITICAL RIGHTS

138 Cong. Rec. 8070 (1992)

RESOLVED (TWO-THIRDS OF THE SENATORS PRESENT CONCURRING THEREIN), That the Senate advise and consent to the ratification of the International Covenant on Civil and Political Rights, adopted by the United Nations General Assembly on December 16, 1966, and signed on behalf of the United States on October 5, 1977 subject to the following Reservations, Understandings, Declarations and Proviso:

I. The Senate's advice and consent is subject to the following reservations:

(1) That Article 20 does not authorize or require legislation or other action by the United States that would restrict the right of free speech and association protected by the Constitution and laws of the United States.

(2) That the United States reserves the right, subject to its Constitutional constraints, to impose capital punishment on any person (other than a pregnant woman) duly convicted under existing or future laws permitting the imposition of capital punishment, including such punishment for crimes committed by persons below eighteen years of age.

(3) That the United States considers itself bound by Article 7 to the extent that "cruel, inhuman or degrading treatment or punishment" means the cruel and unusual treatment or punishment prohibited by the Fifth, Eighth and/or Fourteenth Amendments to the Constitution of the United States.

(4) That because U.S. law generally applies to an offender the penalty in force at the time the offense was committed, the United States does not adhere to the third clause of paragraph 1 of Article 15.

(5) That the policy and practice of the United States are generally in compliance with and supportive of the Covenant's provisions regarding treatment of juveniles in the criminal justice system. Nevertheless, the United States reserves the right, in exceptional circumstances, to treat juveniles as adults, notwithstanding paragraphs 2(b) and 3 of Article 10 and paragraph 4 of Article 14. The United States further reserves to these provisions with respect to individuals who volunteer for military service prior to age 18.

II. The Senate's advice and consent is subject to the following understandings, which shall apply to the obligations of the United States under this Covenant:

(1) That the Constitution and laws of the United States guarantee all persons equal protection of the law and provide extensive protections against discrimination. The United States understands distinctions based upon race, colour, sex, language, religion, political or other opinion, national or social origin, property, birth or any other status—as those terms are used in Article 2, paragraph 1 and Article 26—to be permitted when such distinctions are, at minimum, rationally related to a legitimate governmental objective. The United States further understands the prohibition in paragraph 1 of Article 4 upon discrimination, in time of public emergency, based "solely" on the status of race, color, sex, language, religion or social origin not to bar distinctions that may have a disproportionate effect upon persons of a particular status.

(2) That the United States understands the right to compensation referred to in Articles 9 (5) and 14(6) to require the provision of effective and enforceable mechanisms by which a victim of an unlawful arrest or detention or a miscarriage of justice may seek and, where justified, obtain compensation from either the responsible individual or the appropriate governmental entity. Entitlement to compensation may be subject to the reasonable requirements of domestic law.

(3) That the United States understands the reference to "exceptional circumstances" in paragraph 2(a) of Article 10 to permit the imprisonment of an accused person with convicted persons where appropriate in light of an individual's overall dangerousness, and to permit accused persons to waive their right to segregation from convicted persons. The United States further understands that paragraph 3 of Article 10 does not diminish the goals of punishment, deterrence, and incapacitation as additional legitimate purposes for a penitentiary system.

(4) That the United States understands that subparagraphs 3(b) and (d) of Article 14 do not require the provision of a criminal defendant's counsel of choice when the defendant is provided with court-appointed counsel on grounds of indigence, when the defendant is financially able to retain alternative counsel, or when imprisonment is not imposed. The United States further understands that paragraph 3(e) does not prohibit a requirement that the defendant make a showing that any witness whose attendance he seeks to compel is necessary for his defense. The United States understands the prohibition upon double jeopardy in paragraph 7 to apply only when the judgment of acquittal has been rendered by a court of the same governmental unit, whether the Federal Government or a constituent unit, as is seeking a new trial for the same cause.

(5) That the United States understands that this Covenant shall be implemented by the Federal Government to the extent that it exercises legislative and judicial jurisdiction over the matters covered therein, and otherwise by the state and local governments; to the extent that state and

local governments exercise jurisdiction over such matters, the Federal Government shall take measures appropriate to the Federal system to the end that the competent authorities of the state or local governments may take appropriate measures for the fulfillment of the Covenant.

III. The Senate's advice and consent is subject to the following declarations:

(1) That the United States declares that the provisions of Articles 1 through 27 of the Covenant are not self-executing.

(2) That it is the view of the United States that States Party to the Covenant should wherever possible refrain from imposing any restrictions or limitations on the exercise of the rights recognized and protected by the Covenant, even when such restrictions and limitations are permissible under the terms of the Covenant. For the United States, Article 5, paragraph 2, which provides that fundamental human rights existing in any State Party may not be diminished on the pretext that the Covenant recognizes them to a lesser extent, has particular relevance to Article 19, paragraph 3, which would permit certain restrictions on the freedom of expression. The United States declares that it will continue to adhere to the requirements and constraints of its Constitution in respect to all such restrictions and limitations.

(3) That the United States declares that it accepts the competence of the Human Rights Committee to receive and consider communications under Article 41 in which a State Party claims that another State Party is not fulfilling its obligations under the Covenant

(4) That the United States declares that the right referred to in Article 47 may be exercised only in accordance with international law.

IV. The Senate's advice and consent is subject to the following proviso, which shall not be included in the instrument of ratification to be deposited by the President:

Nothing in this covenant requires or authorizes legislation, or other action, by the United States of America prohibited by the Constitution of the United States as interpreted by the United States.

FIRST OPTIONAL PROTOCOL TO THE INTERNATIONAL COVENANT ON CIVIL AND POLITICAL RIGHTS

Dec. 16, 1966, 999 U.N.T.S. 171, 6 I.L.M. 383*

The States Parties to the present Protocol,

Considering that in order further to achieve the purposes of the Covenant on Civil and Political Rights (hereinafter referred to as the Covenant) and the implementation of its provisions it would be appropriate to enable the Human Rights Committee set up in part IV of the Covenant (hereinafter referred to as the Committee) to receive and consider, as provided in the present Protocol, communications from individuals claiming to be victims of violations of any of the rights set forth in the Covenant,

Have agreed as follows:

Article 1

A State Party to the Covenant that becomes a party to the present Protocol recognizes the competence of the Committee to receive and con-

---

* Adopted by the U.N. General Assembly at New York on December 16, 1966. G.A. Res. 2200. Entered into force on March 23, 1976. The United States has not ratified this optional protocol.

As of March 2013, the 114 parties to this optional protocol were: Albania, Algeria, Andorra, Angola, Argentina, Armenia, Australia, Austria, Azerbaijan, Barbados, Belarus, Belgium, Benin, Bolivia, Bosnia and Herzegovina, Brazil, Bulgaria, Burkina Faso, Cameroon, Canada, Cape Verde, Central African Republic, Chad, Chile, Colombia, Congo, Costa Rica, Côte d'Ivoire, Croatia, Cyprus, Czech Republic, Denmark, Djibouti, Dominican Republic, Ecuador, El Salvador, Equatorial Guinea, Estonia, Finland, France, Gambia, Georgia, Germany, Ghana, Greece, Guatemala, Guinea, Guyana, Honduras, Hungary, Iceland, Ireland, Italy, Jamaica, Kazakhstan, Kyrgyzstan, Latvia, Lesotho, Libyan Arab Jamahiriya, Liechtenstein, Lithuania, Luxembourg, Macedonia (the former Yugoslav Republic of), Madagascar, Malawi, Maldives, Mali, Malta, Mauritius, Mexico, Moldova, Mongolia, Montenegro, Namibia, Nepal, Netherlands, New Zealand, Nicaragua, Niger, Norway, Panama, Paraguay, Peru, Philippines, Poland, Portugal, Romania, Russian Federation, Saint Vincent and the Grenadines, San Marino, Senegal, Serbia, Seychelles, Sierra Leone, Slovakia, Slovenia, Somalia, South Africa, Spain, Sri Lanka, Suriname, Sweden, Tajikistan, Togo, Trinidad and Tobago, Tunisia, Turkey, Turkmenistan, Uganda, Ukraine, Uruguay, Uzbekistan, Venezuela, and Zambia. See the U.N. Web site at <http://treaties.un.org>.

There is a Second Optional Protocol to the ICCPR, aiming at the abolition of the death penalty. It was adopted by the U.N. General Assembly at New York on December 15, 1989, G.A. Res. 44/128, and entered into force July 11, 1991. This optional protocol had 75 parties as of March 2013. The United States has not ratified the second optional protocol.

sider communications from individuals subject to its jurisdiction who claim to be victims of a violation by that State Party of any of the rights set forth in the Covenant. No communication shall be received by the Committee if it concerns a State Party to the Covenant which is not a party to the present Protocol.

Article 2

Subject to the provisions of article 1, individuals who claim that any of their rights enumerated in the Covenant have been violated and who have exhausted all available domestic remedies may submit a written communication to the Committee for consideration.

Article 3

The Committee shall consider inadmissible any communication under the present Protocol which is anonymous, or which it considers to be an abuse of the right of submission of such communications or to be incompatible with the provisions of the Covenant.

Article 4

1. Subject to the provisions of article 3, the Committee shall bring any communications submitted to it under the present Protocol to the attention of the State Party to the present Protocol alleged to be violating any provision of the Covenant.

2. Within six months, the receiving State shall submit to the Committee written explanations or statements clarifying the matter and the remedy, if any, that may have been taken by that State.

Article 5

1. The Committee shall consider communications received under the present Protocol in the light of all written information made available to it by the individual and by the State Party concerned.

2. The Committee shall not consider any communication from an individual unless it has ascertained that:

   (*a*) The same matter is not being examined under another procedure of international investigation or settlement;

   (*b*) The individual has exhausted all available domestic remedies.

This shall not be the rule where the application of the remedies is unreasonably prolonged.

3. The Committee shall hold closed meetings when examining communications under the present Protocol.

4. The Committee shall forward its views to the State Party concerned and to the individual.

Article 6

The Committee shall include in its annual report under article 45 of the Covenant a summary of its activities under the present Protocol.

Article 7

Pending the achievement of the objectives of resolution 1514 (XV) adopted by the General Assembly of the United Nations on 14 December 1960 concerning the Declaration on the Granting of Independence to Colonial Countries and Peoples, the provisions of the present Protocol shall in no way limit the right of petition granted to these peoples by the Charter of the United Nations and other international conventions and instruments under the United Nations and its specialized agencies. . . .

Article 10

The provisions of the present Protocol shall extend to all parts of federal States without any limitations or exceptions.

Article 11

1. Any State Party to the present Protocol may propose an amendment and file it with the Secretary-General of the United Nations. The Secretary-General shall thereupon communicate any proposed amendments to the States Parties to the present Protocol with a request that they notify him whether they favour a conference of States Parties for the purpose of considering and voting upon the proposal. In the event that at least one third of the States Parties favours such a conference, the Secretary-General shall convene the conference under the auspices of the United Nations. Any amendment adopted by a majority of the States Parties present and voting at the conference shall be submitted to the General Assembly of the United Nations for approval.

2. Amendments shall come into force when they have been approved by the General Assembly of the United Nations and accepted by a two-thirds majority of the States Parties to the present Protocol in accordance with their respective constitutional processes.

3. When amendments come into force, they shall be binding on those States Parties which have accepted them, other States Parties still being bound by the provisions of the present Protocol and any earlier amendment which they have accepted. . . .

INTERNATIONAL COVENANT ON ECONOMIC, SOCIAL AND CULTURAL RIGHTS

Dec. 16, 1966, 993 U.N.T.S. 3*

The States Parties to the present Covenant,

Considering that, in accordance with the principles proclaimed in the Charter of the United Nations, recognition of the inherent dignity and of the equal and inalienable rights of all members of the human family is the foundation of freedom, justice and peace in the world,

Recognizing that these rights derive from the inherent dignity of the human person,

Recognizing that, in accordance with the Universal Declaration of Human Rights, the ideal of free human beings enjoying freedom from fear and want can only be achieved if conditions are created whereby everyone

---

* Adopted by the U.N. General Assembly at New York on December 16, 1966. Annex to G.A. Res. 2200. Entered into force on January 3, 1976. The United States has not ratified the covenant.

The following were the 160 parties to the covenant as of March 2013: Afghanistan, Albania, Algeria, Angola, Argentina, Armenia, Australia, Austria, Azerbaijan, Bahamas, Bahrain, Bangladesh, Barbados, Belarus, Belgium, Benin, Bolivia, Bosnia and Herzegovina, Brazil, Bulgaria, Burkina Faso, Burundi, Cambodia, Cameroon, Canada, Cape Verde, Central African Republic, Chad, Chile, China, Colombia, Congo, Congo (Democratic Republic of), Costa Rica, Côte d'Ivoire, Croatia, Cyprus, Czech Republic, Denmark, Djibouti, Dominica, Dominican Republic, Ecuador, Egypt, El Salvador, Equatorial Guinea, Eritrea, Estonia, Ethiopia, Finland, France, Gabon, Gambia, Georgia, Germany, Ghana, Greece, Grenada, Guatemala, Guinea, Guinea-Bissau, Guyana, Honduras, Hungary, Iceland, India, Indonesia, Iran, Iraq, Ireland, Israel, Italy, Jamaica, Japan, Jordan, Kazakhstan, Kenya, Korea (Democratic Republic of), Korea (Republic of), Kuwait, Kyrgyzstan, Lao People's Democratic Republic, Latvia, Lebanon, Lesotho, Liberia, Libyan Arab Jamahiriya, Liechtenstein, Lithuania, Luxembourg, Macedonia (former Yugoslav Republic of), Madagascar, Malawi, Maldives, Mali, Malta, Mauritania, Mauritius, Mexico, Moldova, Monaco, Mongolia, Montenegro, Morocco, Namibia, Nepal, Netherlands, New Zealand, Nicaragua, Niger, Nigeria, Norway, Pakistan, Panama, Papua New Guinea, Paraguay, Peru, Philippines, Poland, Portugal, Romania, Russian Federation, Rwanda, Saint Vincent and the Grenadines, San Marino, Senegal, Serbia, Seychelles, Sierra Leone, Slovakia, Slovenia, Solomon Islands, Somalia, Spain, Sri Lanka, Sudan, Suriname, Swaziland, Sweden, Switzerland, Syrian Arab Republic, Tajikistan, Tanzania, Thailand, Timor-Leste, Togo, Trinidad and Tobago, Tunisia, Turkey, Turkmenistan, Uganda, Ukraine, United Kingdom, Uruguay, Uzbekistan, Venezuela, Viet Nam, Yemen, Zambia, and Zimbabwe. See the U.N. Web site at <http://treaties.un.org>.

may enjoy his economic, social and cultural rights, as well as his civil and political rights,

Considering the obligation of States under the Charter of the United Nations to promote universal respect for, and observance of, human rights and freedoms,

Realizing that the individual, having duties to other individuals and to the community to which he belongs, is under a responsibility to strive for the promotion and observance of the rights recognized in the present Covenant,

Agree upon the following articles:

Part I

Article 1

1. All peoples have the right of self-determination. By virtue of that right they freely determine their political status and freely pursue their economic, social and cultural development.

2. All peoples may, for their own ends, freely dispose of their natural wealth and resources without prejudice to any obligations arising out of international economic co-operation, based upon the principle of mutual benefit, and international law. In no case may a people be deprived of its own means of subsistence.

3. The States Parties to the present Covenant, including those having responsibility for the administration of Non-Self-Governing and Trust Territories, shall promote the realization of the right of self-determination, and shall respect that right, in conformity with the provisions of the Charter of the United Nations.

Part II

Article 2

1. Each State Party to the present Covenant undertakes to take steps, individually and through international assistance and co-operation, especially economic and technical, to the maximum of its available resources, with a view to achieving progressively the full realization of the rights recognized in the present Covenant by all appropriate means, including particularly the adoption of legislative measures.

2. The States Parties to the present Covenant undertake to guarantee that the rights enunciated in the present Covenant will be exercised without discrimination of any kind as to race, colour, sex, language, religion, political or other opinion, national or social origin, property, birth or other status.

3. Developing countries, with due regard to human rights and their national economy, may determine to what extent they would guarantee the economic rights recognized in the present Covenant to non-nationals.

Article 3

The States Parties to the present Covenant undertake to ensure the equal right of men and women to the enjoyment of all economic, social and cultural rights set forth in the present Covenant.

Article 4

The States Parties to the present Covenant recognize that, in the enjoyment of those rights provided by the State in conformity with the present Covenant, the State may subject such rights only to such limitations as are determined by law only in so far as this may be compatible with the nature of these rights and solely for the purpose of promoting the general welfare in a democratic society.

Article 5

1. Nothing in the present Covenant may be interpreted as implying for any State, group or person any right to engage in any activity or to perform any act aimed at the destruction of any of the rights or freedoms recognized herein, or at their limitation to a greater extent than is provided for in the present Covenant.

2. No restriction upon or derogation from any of the fundamental human rights recognized or existing in any country in virtue of law, conventions, regulations or custom shall be admitted on the pretext that the present Covenant does not recognize such rights or that it recognizes them to a lesser extent.

Part III

Article 6

1. The States Parties to the present Covenant recognize the right to work, which includes the right of everyone to the opportunity to gain his living by work which he freely chooses or accepts, and will take appropriate steps to safeguard this right.

2. The steps to be taken by a State Party to the present Covenant to achieve the full realization of this right shall include technical and vocational guidance and training programmes, policies and techniques to achieve steady economic, social and cultural development and full and productive employment under conditions safeguarding fundamental political and economic freedoms to the individual.

Article 7

The States Parties to the present Covenant recognize the right of everyone to the enjoyment of just and favourable conditions of work, which ensure, in particular:

(*a*) remuneration which provides all workers, as a minimum, with:

(i) fair wages and equal remuneration for work of equal value without distinction of any kind, in particular women being guaranteed conditions of work not inferior to those enjoyed by men, with equal pay for equal work;

(ii) a decent living for themselves and their families in accordance with the provisions of the present Covenant;

(*b*) safe and healthy working conditions;

(*c*) equal opportunity for everyone to be promoted in his employment to an appropriate higher level, subject to no considerations other than those of seniority and competence;

(*d*) rest, leisure and reasonable limitation of working hours and periodic holidays with pay, as well as remuneration for public holidays.

Article 8

1. The States Parties to the present Covenant undertake to ensure:

(*a*) the right of everyone to form trade unions and join the trade union of his choice, subject only to the rules of the organization concerned, for the promotion and protection of his economic and social interests. No restrictions may be placed on the exercise of this right other than those prescribed by law and which are necessary in a democratic society in the interests of national security or public order or for the protection of the rights and freedoms of others;

(*b*) the right of trade unions to establish national federations or confederations and the right of the latter to form or join international trade-union organizations;

(*c*) the right of trade unions to function freely subject to no limitations other than those prescribed by law and which are necessary in a democratic society in the interests of national security or public order or for the protection of the rights and freedoms of others;

(*d*) the right to strike, provided that it is exercised in conformity with the laws of the particular country.

2. This article shall not prevent the imposition of lawful restrictions on the exercise of these rights by members of the armed forces or of the police or of the administration of the State.

3. Nothing in this article shall authorize States Parties to the International Labour Organisation Convention of 1948 concerning Freedom of Association and Protection of the Right to Organize to take legislative measures which would prejudice, or apply the law in such a manner as would prejudice, the guarantees provided for in that Convention.

Article 9

The States Parties to the present Covenant recognize the right of everyone to social security, including social insurance.

Article 10

The States Parties to the present Covenant recognize that:

1. The widest possible protection and assistance should be accorded to the family, which is the natural and fundamental group unit of society, particularly for its establishment and while it is responsible for the care and education of dependent children. Marriage must be entered into with the free consent of the intending spouses.

2. Special protection should be accorded to mothers during a reasonable period before and after childbirth. During such period working mothers should be accorded paid leave or leave with adequate social security benefits.

3. Special measures of protection and assistance should be taken on behalf of all children and young persons without any discrimination for reasons of parentage or other conditions. Children and young persons should be protected from economic and social exploitation. Their employment in work harmful to their morals or health or dangerous to life or likely to hamper their normal development should be punishable by law. States should also set age limits below which the paid employment of child labour should be prohibited and punishable by law.

Article 11

1. The States Parties to the present Covenant recognize the right of everyone to an adequate standard of living for himself and his family, including adequate food, clothing and housing, and to the continuous improvement of living conditions. The States Parties will take appropriate steps to ensure the realization of this right, recognizing to this effect the essential importance of international co-operation based on free consent.

2. The States Parties to the present Covenant, recognizing the fundamental right of everyone to be free from hunger, shall take, individually and through international co-operation, the measures, including specific programmes, which are needed:

(*a*) to improve methods of production, conservation and distribution of food by making full use of technical and scientific knowledge, by disseminating knowledge of the principles of nutrition and by developing or reforming agrarian systems in such a way as to achieve the most efficient development and utilization of natural resources;

(*b*) taking into account the problems of both food-importing and food-exporting countries, to ensure an equitable distribution of world food supplies in relation to need.

Article 12

1. The States Parties to the present Covenant recognize the right of everyone to the enjoyment of the highest attainable standard of physical and mental health.

2. The steps to be taken by the States Parties to the present Covenant to achieve the full realization of this right shall include those necessary for:

(*a*) the provision for the reduction of the stillbirth-rate and of infant mortality and for the healthy development of the child;

(*b*) the improvement of all aspects of environmental and industrial hygiene;

(*c*) the prevention, treatment and control of epidemic, endemic, occupational and other diseases;

(*d*) the creation of conditions which would assure to all medical service and medical attention in the event of sickness.

Article 13

1. The States Parties to the present Covenant recognize the right of everyone to education. They agree that education shall be directed to the full development of the human personality and the sense of its dignity, and shall strengthen the respect for human rights and fundamental freedoms. They further agree that education shall enable all persons to participate effectively in a free society, promote understanding, tolerance and friendship among all nations and all racial, ethnic or religious groups, and further the activities of the United Nations for the maintenance of peace.

2. The States Parties to the present Covenant recognize that, with a view to achieving the full realization of this right:

(*a*) primary education shall be compulsory and available free to all;

(*b*) secondary education in its different forms, including technical and vocational secondary education, shall be made generally available and accessible to all by every appropriate means, and in particular by the progressive introduction of free education;

(*c*) higher education shall be made equally accessible to all, on the basis of capacity, by every appropriate means, and in particular by the progressive introduction of free education;

(*d*) fundamental education shall be encouraged or intensified as far as possible for those persons who have not received or completed the whole period of their primary education;

(*e*) the development of a system of schools at all levels shall be actively pursued, an adequate fellowship system shall be established, and the material conditions of teaching staff shall be continuously improved.

3. The States Parties to the present Covenant undertake to have respect for the liberty of parents and, when applicable, legal guardians, to choose for their children schools, other than those established by the public authorities, which conform to such minimum educational standards as may be laid down or approved by the State and to ensure the

religious and moral education of their children in conformity with their own convictions.

4. No part of this article shall be construed so as to interfere with the liberty of individuals and bodies to establish and direct educational institutions, subject always to the observance of the principles set forth in paragraph 1 of this article and to the requirement that the education given in such institutions shall conform to such minimum standards as may be laid down by the State.

Article 14

Each State Party to the present Covenant which, at the time of becoming a Party, has not been able to secure in its metropolitan territory or other territories under its jurisdiction compulsory primary education, free of charge, undertakes, within two years, to work out and adopt a detailed plan of action for the progressive implementation, within a reasonable number of years, to be fixed in the plan, of the principle of compulsory education free of charge for all.

Article 15

1. The States Parties to the present Covenant recognize the right of everyone:
> (*a*) to take part in cultural life;
> (*b*) to enjoy the benefits of scientific progress and its applications;
> (*c*) to benefit from the protection of the moral and material interests resulting from any scientific, literary or artistic production of which he is the author.

2. The steps to be taken by the States Parties to the present Covenant to achieve the full realization of this right shall include those necessary for the conservation, the development and the diffusion of science and culture.

3. The States Parties to the present Covenant undertake to respect the freedom indispensable for scientific research and creative activity.

4. The States Parties to the present Covenant recognize the benefits to be derived from the encouragement and development of international contacts and cooperation in the scientific and cultural fields.

Part IV

Article 16

1. The States Parties to the present Covenant undertake to submit in conformity with this part of the Covenant reports on the measures which they have adopted and the progress made in achieving the observance of the rights recognized herein.

2. (*a*) All reports shall be submitted to the Secretary-General of the United Nations, who shall transmit copies to the Economic and Social Council for consideration in accordance with the provisions of the present Covenant.

(*b*) The Secretary-General of the United Nations shall also transmit to the specialized agencies copies of the reports, or any relevant parts therefrom, from States Parties to the present Covenant which are also members of these specialized agencies in so far as these reports, or parts therefrom, relate to any matters which fall within the responsibilities of the said agencies in accordance with their constitutional instruments.

Article 17

1. The States Parties to the present Covenant shall furnish their reports in stages, in accordance with a programme to be established by the Economic and Social Council within one year of the entry into force of the present Covenant after consultation with the States Parties and the specialized agencies concerned.

2. Reports may indicate factors and difficulties affecting the degree of fulfilment of obligations under the present Covenant.

3. Where relevant information has previously been furnished to the United Nations or to any specialized agency by any State Party to the present Covenant, it will not be necessary to reproduce that information, but a precise reference to the information so furnished will suffice.

Article 18

Pursuant to its responsibilities under the Charter of the United Nations in the field of human rights and fundamental freedoms, the Economic and Social Council may make arrangements with the specialized agencies in respect of their reporting to it on the progress made in achieving the observance of the provisions of the present Covenant falling within the scope of their activities. These reports may include particulars of decisions and recommendations on such implementation adopted by their competent organs.

Article 19

The Economic and Social Council may transmit to the Commission on Human Rights for study and general recommendation or as appropriate for information the reports concerning human rights submitted by States in accordance with articles 16 and 17, and those concerning human rights submitted by the specialized agencies in accordance with article 18.

Article 20

The States Parties to the present Covenant and the specialized agencies concerned may submit comments to the Economic and Social Council on any general recommendation under article 19 or reference to such general recommendation in any report of the Commission on Human Rights or any documentation referred to therein.

Article 21

The Economic and Social Council may submit from time to time to the General Assembly reports with recommendations of a general nature and a summary of the information received from the States Parties to the present Covenant and the specialized agencies on the measures taken and the progress made in achieving general observance of the rights recognized in the present Covenant.

Article 22

The Economic and Social Council may bring to the attention of other organs of the United Nations, their subsidiary organs and specialized agencies concerned with furnishing technical assistance any matters arising out of the reports referred to in this part of the present Covenant which may assist such bodies in deciding, each within its field of competence, on the advisability of international measures likely to contribute to the effective progressive implementation of the present Covenant.

Article 23

The States Parties to the present Covenant agree that international action for the achievement of the rights recognized in the present Covenant includes such methods as the conclusion of conventions, the adoption of recommendations, the furnishing of technical assistance and the holding of regional meetings and technical meetings for the purpose of consultation and study organized in conjunction with the Governments concerned.

Article 24

Nothing in the present Covenant shall be interpreted as impairing the provisions of the Charter of the United Nations and of the constitutions of the specialized agencies which define the respective responsibilities of the various organs of the United Nations and of the specialized agencies in regard to the matters dealt with in the present Covenant.

Article 25

Nothing in the present Covenant shall be interpreted as impairing the inherent right of all peoples to enjoy and utilize fully and freely their natural wealth and resources. . . .

CONVENTION ON THE PREVENTION AND PUNISHMENT OF THE CRIME OF GENOCIDE

Dec. 9, 1948, 78 U.N.T.S. 277, 28 I.L.M. 754 *

The Contracting Parties,

Having considered the declaration made by the General Assembly of the United Nations in its resolution 96 (I) dated 11 December 1946 that genocide is a crime under international law, contrary to the spirit and aims of the United Nations and condemned by the civilized world;

Recognizing that at all periods of history genocide has inflicted great losses on humanity; and

Being convinced that, in order to liberate mankind from such an odious scourge, international co-operation is required,

Hereby agree as hereinafter provided:

---

* Adopted by the U.N. General Assembly at New York on December 9, 1948. G.A. Res. 2670. Entered into force on January 12, 1951. The United States ratified the convention on November 25, 1988. See the U.S. reservations next.

The 142 parties to the convention as of March 2013 were: Afghanistan, Albania, Algeria, Andorra, Antigua and Barbuda, Argentina, Armenia, Australia, Austria, Azerbaijan, Bahamas, Bahrain, Bangladesh, Barbados, Belarus, Belgium, Belize, Bolivia, Bosnia and Herzegovina, Brazil, Bulgaria, Burkina Faso, Burundi, Cambodia, Canada, Cape Verde, Chile, China, Colombia, Comoros, Congo (Democratic Republic of), Costa Rica, Côte d'Ivoire, Croatia, Cuba, Cyprus, Czech Republic, Denmark, Ecuador, Egypt, El Salvador, Estonia, Ethiopia, Fiji, Finland, France, Gabon, Gambia, Georgia, Germany, Ghana, Greece, Guatemala, Guinea, Haiti, Honduras, Hungary, Iceland, India, Iran, Iraq, Ireland, Israel, Italy, Jamaica, Jordan, Kazakhstan, Korea (Democratic People's Republic of), Korea (Republic of), Kuwait, Kyrgyzstan, Lao People's Democratic Republic, Latvia, Lebanon, Lesotho, Liberia, Libyan Arab Jamahiriya, Liechtenstein, Lithuania, Luxembourg, Macedonia (former Yugoslav Republic of), Malaysia, Maldives, Mali, Mexico, Moldova, Monaco, Mongolia, Montenegro, Morocco, Mozambique, Myanmar, Namibia, Nepal, Netherlands, New Zealand, Nicaragua, Nigeria, Norway, Pakistan, Panama, Papua New Guinea, Paraguay, Peru, Philippines, Poland, Portugal, Romania, Russian Federation, Rwanda, Saint Vincent and the Grenadines, Saudi Arabia, Senegal, Serbia, Seychelles, Singapore, Slovakia, Slovenia, South Africa, Spain, Sri Lanka, Sudan, Sweden, Switzerland, Syrian Arab Republic, Tanzania, Togo, Tonga, Trinidad and Tobago, Tunisia, Turkey, Uganda, Ukraine, United Arab Emirates, United Kingdom, United States of America, Uruguay, Uzbekistan, Venezuela, Viet Nam, Yemen, and Zimbabwe. See the U.N. Web site at <http://treaties.un.org>.

421

Article I

The Contracting Parties confirm that genocide, whether committed in time of peace or in time of war, is a crime under international law which they undertake to prevent and to punish.

Article II

In the present Convention, genocide means any of the following acts committed with intent to destroy, in whole or in part, a national, ethnical, racial or religious group, as such;
    (*a*) Killing members of the group;
    (*b*) Causing serious bodily or mental harm to members of the group;
    (*c*) Deliberately inflicting on the group conditions of life calculated to bring about its physical destruction in whole or in part;
    (*d*) Imposing measures intended to prevent births within the group;
    (*e*) Forcibly transferring children of the group to another group.

Article III

The following acts shall be punishable:
    (*a*) Genocide;
    (*b*) Conspiracy to commit genocide;
    (*c*) Direct and public incitement to commit genocide;
    (*d*) Attempt to commit genocide;
    (*e*) Complicity in genocide.

Article IV

Persons committing genocide or any of the other acts enumerated in article III shall be punished, whether they arc constitutionally responsible rulers, public officials or private individuals.

Article V

The Contracting Parties undertake to enact, in accordance with their respective Constitutions, the necessary legislation to give effect to the provisions of the present Convention and, in particular, to provide effective penalties for persons guilty of genocide or of any of the other acts enumerated in article III.

Article VI

Persons charged with genocide or any of the other acts enumerated in article III shall be tried by a competent tribunal of the State in the territory of which the act was committed, or by such international penal tribunal as may have jurisdiction with respect to those Contracting Parties which shall have accepted its jurisdiction.

Article VII

Genocide and the other acts enumerated in article III shall not be considered as political crimes for the purpose of extradition.

The Contracting Parties pledge themselves in such cases to grant extradition in accordance with their laws and treaties in force.

Article VIII

Any Contracting Party may call upon the competent organs of the United Nations to take such action under the Charter of the United Nations as they consider appropriate for the prevention and suppression of acts of genocide or any of the other acts enumerated in article III.

Article IX

Disputes between the Contracting Parties relating to the interpretation, application or fulfilment of the present Convention, including those relating to the responsibility of a State for genocide or for any of the other acts enumerated in article III, shall be submitted to the International Court of Justice at the request of any of the parties to the dispute. . . .

Article XIV

The present Convention shall remain in effect for a period of ten years as from the date of its coming into force.

It shall thereafter remain in force for successive periods of five years for such Contracting Parties as have not denounced it at least six months before the expiration of the current period. . . .

U.S. RESERVATIONS AND UNDERSTANDINGS TO THE GENOCIDE CONVENTION
28 I.L.M. 782 (1989)*

Reservations:

(1) That with reference to article IX of the Convention, before any dispute to which the United States is a party may be submitted to the ju-

---

* The United States ratified the Genocide Convention on November 25, 1988, subject to the following reservations and understandings.

risdiction of the International Court of Justice under this article, the specific consent of the United States is required in each case.

(2) That nothing in the Convention requires or authorizes legislation or other action by the United States of America prohibited by the Constitution of the United States as interpreted by the United States.

Understandings:

(1) That the term "intent to destroy, in whole or in part, a national, ethnical, racial, or religious group as such" appearing in article II means the specific intent to destroy, in whole or in substantial part, a national, ethnical, racial or religious group as such by the acts specified in article II.

(2) That the term "mental harm" in article II(b) means permanent impairment of mental faculties through drugs, torture or similar techniques.

(3) That the pledge to grant extradition in accordance with a state's laws and treaties in force found in article VII extends only to acts which are criminal under the laws of both the requesting and the requested state and nothing in article VI affects the right of any state to bring to trial before its own tribunals any of its nationals for acts committed outside a state.

(4) That acts in the course of armed conflicts committed without the specific intent required by article II arc not sufficient to constitute genocide as defined by this Convention.

(5) That with regard to the reference to an international penal tribunal in article VI of the Convention, the United States declares that it reserves the right to effect its participation in any such tribunal only by a treaty entered into specifically for that purpose with the advice and consent of the Senate.

INTERNATIONAL CONVENTION ON THE ELIMINATION OF ALL FORMS OF RACIAL DISCRIMINATION

660 U.N.T.S. 195, 5 I.L.M. 352 (1966)*

. . . Part I

Article 1

1. In this Convention, the term "racial discrimination" shall mean any distinction, exclusion, restriction or preference based on race, colour, descent, or national or ethnic origin which has the purpose or effect of nullifying or impairing the recognition, enjoyment or exercise, on an equal footing, of human rights and fundamental freedoms in the political, economic, social, cultural or any other field of public life.

---

* Done at New York on January 7, 1966. Entered into force on January 4, 1969.

The 175 parties to the convention as of March 2013 were: Andorra, Afghanistan, Albania, Algeria, Antigua and Barbuda, Argentina, Armenia, Australia, Austria, Azerbaijan, Bahamas, Bahrain, Bangladesh, Barbados, Belarus, Belgium, Belize, Benin, Bolivia, Bosnia and Herzegovina, Botswana, Brazil, Bulgaria, Burkina Faso, Burundi, Cambodia, Cameroon, Canada, Cape Verde, Central African Republic, Chad, Chile, China, Colombia, Comoros, Congo, Congo (Democratic Republic of), Costa Rica, Côte d'Ivoire, Croatia, Cuba, Cyprus, Czech Republic, Denmark, Djibouti, Dominican Republic, Ecuador, Egypt, El Salvador, Equatorial Guinea, Eritrea, Estonia, Ethiopia, Fiji, Finland, France, Gabon, Gambia, Georgia, Germany, Ghana, Greece, Guatemala, Guinea, Guinea-Bissau, Guyana, Haiti, Holy See, Honduras, Hungary, Iceland, India, Indonesia, Iran, Iraq, Ireland, Israel, Italy, Jamaica, Japan, Jordan, Kazakhstan, Kenya, Korea (Republic of), Kuwait, Kyrgyzstan, Lao People's Democratic Republic, Latvia, Lebanon, Lesotho, Liberia, Libyan Arab Jamahiriya, Liechtenstein, Lithuania, Luxembourg, Macedonia (the former Yugoslav Republic), Madagascar, Malawi, Maldives, Mali, Malta, Mauritania, Mauritius, Mexico, Moldova, Monaco, Mongolia, Montenegro, Morocco, Mozambique, Namibia, Nepal, Netherlands, New Zealand, Nicaragua, Niger, Nigeria, Norway, Oman, Pakistan, Panama, Papua New Guinea, Paraguay, Peru, Philippines, Poland, Portugal, Qatar, Romania, Russian Federation, Rwanda, Saint Kitts and Nevis, Saint Lucia, Saint Vincent and the Grenadines, San Marino, Saudi Arabia, Senegal, Serbia, Seychelles, Sierra Leone, Slovakia, Slovenia, Solomon Islands, Somalia, South Africa, Spain, Sri Lanka, Sudan, Suriname, Swaziland, Sweden, Switzerland, Syrian Arab Republic, Tajikistan, Thailand, Tanzania, Timor-Leste, Togo, Tonga, Trinidad and Tobago, Tunisia, Turkey, Turkmenistan, Uganda, Ukraine, United Arab Emirates, United Kingdom, United States of America, Uruguay, Uzbekistan, Venezuela, Viet Nam, Yemen, Zambia, and Zimbabwe. See the U.N. Web site at <http://treaties.un.org>.

2. This Convention shall not apply to distinctions, exclusions, restrictions or preferences made by a State Party to this Convention between citizens and non-citizens.

3. Nothing in this Convention may be interpreted as affecting in any way the legal provisions of States Parties concerning nationality, citizenship or naturalization, provided that such provisions do not discriminate against any particular nationality.

4. Special measures taken for the sole purpose of securing adequate advancement of certain racial or ethnic groups or individuals requiring such protection as may be necessary in order to ensure such groups or individuals equal enjoyment or exercise of human rights and fundamental freedoms shall not be deemed racial discrimination, provided, however, that such measures do not, as a consequence, lead to the maintenance of separate rights for different racial groups and that they shall not be continued after the objectives for which they were taken have been achieved.

Article 2

1. States Parties condemn racial discrimination and undertake to pursue by all appropriate means and without delay a policy of eliminating racial discrimination in all its forms and promoting understanding among all races, and, to this end:

(*a*) Each State Party undertakes to engage in no act or practice of racial discrimination against persons, groups of persons or institutions and to ensure that all public authorities and public institutions, national and local, shall act in conformity with this obligation;

(*b*) Each State Party undertakes not to sponsor, defend or support racial discrimination by any persons or organizations;

(*c*) Each State Party shall take effective measures to review governmental, national and local policies, and to amend, rescind or nullify any laws and regulations which have the effect of creating or perpetuating racial discrimination wherever it exists;

(*d*) Each State Party shall prohibit and bring to an end, by all appropriate means, including legislation as required by circumstances, racial discrimination by any persons, group or organization;

(*e*) Each State Party undertakes to encourage, where appropriate, integrationist multi-racial organizations and movements and other means of eliminating barriers between races, and to discourage anything which tends to strengthen racial division.

2. States Parties shall, when the circumstances so warrant, take, in the social, economic, cultural and other fields, special and concrete measures to ensure the adequate development and protection of certain racial groups or individuals belonging to them, for the purpose of guaranteeing them the full and equal enjoyment of human rights and fundamental freedoms. These measures shall in no case entail as a consequence the maintenance of

unequal or separate rights for different racial groups after the objectives for which they were taken have been achieved.

Article 3

States Parties particularly condemn racial segregation and *apartheid* and undertake to prevent, prohibit and eradicate all practices of this nature in territories under their jurisdiction.

Article 4

States Parties condemn all propaganda and all organizations which are based on ideas or theories of superiority of one race or group of persons of one colour or ethnic origin, or which attempt to justify or promote racial hatred and discrimination in any form, and undertake to adopt immediate and positive measures designed to eradicate all incitement to, or acts of, such discrimination and, to this end, with due regard to the principles embodied in the Universal Declaration of Human Rights and the rights expressly set forth in article 5 of this Convention, *inter alia:*

(*a*) Shall declare an offence punishable by law all dissemination of ideas based on racial superiority or hatred, incitement to racial discrimination, as well as all acts of violence or incitement to such acts against any race or group of persons of another colour or ethnic origin, and also the provision of any assistance to racist activities, including the financing thereof;

(*b*) Shall declare illegal and prohibit organizations, and also organized and all other propaganda activities, which promote and incite racial discrimination, and shall recognize participation in such organizations or activities as an offence punishable by law;

(*c*) Shall not permit public authorities or public institutions, national or local, to promote or incite racial discrimination.

Article 5

In compliance with the fundamental obligations laid down in article 2 of this Convention, States Parties undertake to prohibit and to eliminate racial discrimination in all its forms and to guarantee the right of everyone, without distinction as to race, colour, or national or ethnic origin, to equality before the law, notably in the enjoyment of the following rights:

(*a*) The right to equal treatment before the tribunals and all other organs administering justice;

(*b*) The right to security of person and protection by the State against violence or bodily harm, whether inflicted by government officials or by any individual, group or institution;

(*c*) Political rights, in particular the rights to participate in elections—to vote and to stand for election—on the basis of universal and equal suffrage, to take part in the Government as well as in the conduct of public affairs at any level and to have equal access to public service;

(*d*) Other civil rights, in particular:

(i) The right to freedom of movement and residence within the border of the State;

(ii) The right to leave any country, including one's own, and to return to one's country;

(iii) The right to nationality;

(iv) The right to marriage and choice of spouse;

(v) The right to own property alone as well as in association with others;

(vi) The right to inherit;

(vii) The right to freedom of thought, conscience and religion;

(viii) The right to freedom of opinion and expression;

(ix) The right to freedom of peaceful assembly and association;

(*e*) Economic, social and cultural rights, in particular:

(i) The rights to work, to free choice of employment, to just and favourable conditions of work, to protection against unemployment, to equal pay for equal work, to just and favourable remuneration;

(ii) The right to form and join trade unions;

(iii) The right to housing;

(iv) The right to public health, medical care, social security and social services;

(v) The right to education and training;

(vi) The right to equal participation in cultural activities;

(*f*) The right of access to any place or service intended for use by the general public, such as transport, hotels, restaurants, cafés, theatres and parks.

Article 6

States Parties shall assure to everyone within their jurisdiction effective protection and remedies, through the competent national tribunals and other State institutions, against any acts of racial discrimination which violate his human rights and fundamental freedoms contrary to this Convention, as well as the right to seek from such tribunals just and adequate reparation or satisfaction for any damage suffered as a result of such discrimination.

Article 7

States Parties undertake to adopt immediate and effective measures, particularly in the fields of teaching, education, culture and information, with a view to combating prejudices which lead to racial discrimination and to promoting understanding, tolerance and friendship among nations and racial or ethnical groups, as well as to propagating the purposes and principles of the Charter of the United Nations, the Universal Declaration of Human Rights, the United Nations Declaration on the Elimination of All Forms of Racial Discrimination, and this Convention.

Part II

Article 8

1. There shall be established a Committee on the Elimination of Racial Discrimination (hereinafter referred to as the Committee) consisting of eighteen experts of high moral standing and acknowledged impartiality elected by States Parties from among their nationals, who shall serve in their personal capacity, consideration being given to equitable geographical distribution and to the representation of the different forms of civilization as well as of the principal legal systems.

2. The members of the Committee shall be elected by secret ballot from a list of persons nominated by the States Parties. Each State Party may nominate one person from among its own nationals.

3. . . . At least three months before the date of each election the Secretary- General of the United Nations shall address a letter to the States Parties inviting them to submit their nominations within two months. . . .

4. Elections of the members of the Committee shall be held at a meeting of States Parties convened by the Secretary-General at United Nations Headquarters. At that meeting, for which two-thirds of the States Parties shall constitute a quorum, the persons elected to the Committee shall be those nominees who obtain the largest number of votes and an absolute majority of the votes of the representatives of States Parties present and voting.

5. (a) The members of the Committee shall be elected for a term of four years. . . .

(b) For the filling of casual vacancies, the State Party whose expert has ceased to function as a member of the Committee shall appoint another expert from among its nationals, subject to the approval of the Committee. . . .

Article 9

1. States Parties undertake to submit to the Secretary-General of the United Nations, for consideration by the Committee, a report on the legislative, judicial, administrative or other measures which they have adopted and which give effect to the provisions of this Convention:

(a) within one year after the entry into force of the Convention for the State concerned; and

(b) thereafter every two years and whenever the Committee so requests. The Committee may request further information from the States Parties.

2. The Committee shall report annually, through the Secretary-General, to the General Assembly of the United Nations on its activities and may make suggestions and general recommendations based on the examination of the reports and information received from the States Parties. . . .

Article 10

1. The Committee shall adopt its own rules of procedure.

2. The Committee shall elect its officers for a term of two years.

3. The secretariat of the Committee shall be provided by the Secretary-General of the United Nations.

4. The meetings of the Committee shall normally be held at United Nations Headquarters.

Article 11

1. If a State Party considers that another State Party is not giving effect to the provisions of this Convention, it may bring the matter to the attention of the Committee. The Committee shall then transmit the communication to the State Party concerned. Within three months, the receiving State shall submit to the Committee written explanations or statements clarifying the matter and the remedy, if any, that may have been taken by that State.

2. If the matter is not adjusted to the satisfaction of both parties, either by bilateral negotiations or by any other procedure open to them, within six months after the receipt by the receiving State of the initial communication, either State shall have the right to refer the matter again to the Committee by notifying the Committee and also the other State.

3. The Committee shall deal with a matter referred to it in accordance with paragraph 2 of this article after it has ascertained that all available domestic remedies have been invoked and exhausted in the case, in conformity with the generally recognized principles of international law. This shall not be the rule where the application of the remedies is unreasonably prolonged.

4. In any matter referred to it, the Committee may call upon the States Parties concerned to supply any other relevant information. . . .

Article 12

1. (*a*) After the Committee has obtained and collated all the information it deems necessary, the Chairman shall appoint an *ad hoc* Conciliation Commission (hereinafter referred to as the Commission) comprising five persons who may or may not be members of the Committee. The members of the Commission shall be appointed with the unanimous consent of the parties to the dispute, and its good offices shall be made available to the States concerned with a view to an amicable solution of the matter on the basis of respect for this Convention.

(*b*) If the States Parties to the dispute fail to reach agreement within three months on all or part of the composition of the Commission, the members of the Commission not agreed upon by the States parties to the dispute shall be elected by secret ballot by a two-thirds majority vote of the Committee from among its own members.

2. The members of the Commission shall serve in their personal capacity. They shall not be nationals of the States parties to the dispute or of a State not Party to this Convention.

3. The Commission shall elect its own Chairman and adopt its own rules of procedure. . . .

Article 13

1. When the Commission has fully considered the matter, it shall prepare and submit to the Chairman of the Committee a report embodying its findings on all questions of fact relevant to the issue between the parties and containing such recommendations as it may think proper for the amicable solution of the dispute.

2. The Chairman of the Committee shall communicate the report of the Commission to each of the States parties to the dispute. These States shall, within three months, inform the Chairman of the Committee whether or not they accept the recommendations contained in the report of the Commission.

3. After the period provided for in paragraph 2 of this article, the Chairman of the Committee shall communicate the report of the Commission and the declarations of the States Parties concerned to the other States Parties to this Convention.

Article 14

1. A State Party may at any time declare that it recognizes the competence of the Committee to receive and consider communications from individuals or groups of individuals within its jurisdiction claiming to be victims of a violation by that State Party of any of the rights set forth in this Convention. No communication shall be received by the Committee if it concerns a State Party which has not made such a declaration.

2. Any State Party which makes a declaration as provided for in paragraph 1 of this article may establish or indicate a body within its national legal order which shall be competent to receive and consider petitions from individuals and groups of individuals within its jurisdiction who claim to be victims of a violation of any of the rights set forth in this Convention and who have exhausted other available local remedies.

3. A declaration made in accordance with paragraph 1 of this article and the name of any body established or indicated in accordance with paragraph 2 of this article shall be deposited by the State Party concerned with the Secretary-General of the United Nations. . . . A declaration may be withdrawn at any time by notification to the Secretary-General, but such a withdrawal shall not affect communications pending before the Committee. . . .

5. In the event of failure to obtain satisfaction from the body established or indicated in accordance with paragraph 2 of this article, the petitioner shall have the right to communicate the matter to the Committee within six months.

6. (*a*) The Committee shall confidentially bring any communication referred to it to the attention of the State Party alleged to be violating any provision of this Convention, but the identity of the individual or groups of individuals concerned shall not be revealed without his or their express consent. The Committee shall not receive anonymous communications.

(*b*) Within three months, the receiving State shall submit to the Committee written explanations or statements clarifying the matter and the remedy, if any, that may have been taken by that State.

7. (*a*) The Committee shall consider communications in the light of all information made available to it by the State Party concerned and by the petitioner. The Committee shall not consider any communication from a petitioner unless it has ascertained that the petitioner has exhausted all available domestic remedies. However, this shall not be the rule where the application of the remedies is unreasonably prolonged.

(*b*) The Committee shall forward its suggestions and recommendations, if any, to the State Party concerned and to the petitioner. . . .

9. The Committee shall be competent to exercise the functions provided for in this article only when at least ten States Parties to this Convention are bound by declarations in accordance with paragraph 1 of this article. . . .

Article 20

1. The Secretary-General of the United Nations shall receive and circulate to all States which are or may become Parties to this Convention reservations made by States at the time of ratification or accession. Any State which objects to the reservation shall, within a period of ninety days from the date of the said communication, notify the Secretary-General that it does not accept it.

2. A reservation incompatible with the object and purpose of this Convention shall not be permitted, nor shall a reservation the effect of which would inhibit the operation of any of the bodies established by this Convention be allowed. A reservation shall be considered incompatible or inhibitive if at least two-thirds of the States Parties to this Convention object to it.

3. Reservations may be withdrawn at any time by notification to this effect addressed to the Secretary-General. Such notification shall take effect on the date on which it is received. . . .

Article 22

Any dispute between two or more States Parties with respect to the interpretation or application of this Convention, which is not settled by negotiation or by the procedures expressly provided for in this Convention, shall, at the request of any of the parties to the dispute, be referred to the International Court of Justice for decision, unless the disputants agree to another mode of settlement.

U.S. RESERVATIONS, UNDERSTANDING, AND DECLARATION TO THE CONVENTION ON ELIMINATION OF RACIAL DISCRIMINATION

<http://treaties.un.org>*

I. The Senate's advice and consent is subject to the following reservations:

(1) That the Constitution and laws of the United States contain extensive protections of individual freedom of speech, expression and association. Accordingly, the United States does not accept any obligation under this Convention, in particular under articles 4 and 7, to restrict those rights, through the adoption of legislation or any other measures, to the extent that they are protected by the Constitution and laws of the United States.

(2) That the Constitution and laws of the United States establish extensive protections against discrimination, reaching significant areas of nongovernmental activity. Individual privacy and freedom from governmental interference in private conduct, however, are also recognized as among the fundamental values which shape our free and democratic society. The United States understands that the identification of the rights protected under the Convention by reference in article 1 to fields of 'public life' reflects a similar distinction between spheres of public conduct that are customarily the subject of governmental regulation, and spheres of private conduct that are not. To the extent, however, that the Convention calls for a broader regulation of private conduct, the United States does not accept any obligation under this Convention to enact legislation or take other measures under paragraph (1) of article 2, subparagraphs (1) (c) and (d) of article 2, article 3 and article 5 with respect to private conduct except as mandated by the Constitution and laws of the United States.

(3) That with reference to article 22 of the Convention, before any dispute to which the United States is a party may be submitted to the

---

* The United States ratified the Convention on All Forms of Racial Discrimination on October 21, 1994, subject to the following reservations, understanding, and declaration.

jurisdiction of the International Court of Justice under this article, the specific consent of the United States is required in each case.

II. The Senate's advice and consent is subject to the following understanding, which shall apply to the obligations of the United States under this Convention:

That the United States understands that this Convention shall be implemented by the Federal Government to the extent that it exercises jurisdiction over the matters covered therein, and otherwise by the state and local governments. To the extent that state and local governments exercise jurisdiction over such matters, the Federal Government shall, as necessary, take appropriate measures to ensure the fulfilment of this Convention.

III. The Senate's advice and consent is subject to the following declaration:

That the United States declares that the provisions of the Convention are not self-executing.

CONVENTION ON THE ELIMINATION OF ALL FORMS OF DISCRIMINATION AGAINST WOMEN

Dec. 18, 1979, 1249 U.N.T.S. 13*

The States Parties to the present Convention,

Noting that the Charter of the United Nations reaffirms faith in fundamental human rights, in the dignity and worth of the human person and in the equal rights of men and women,

Noting that the Universal Declaration of Human Rights affirms the principle of the inadmissibility of discrimination and proclaims that all human beings are born free and equal in dignity and rights and that every-

---

* Adopted by the General Assembly of the United Nations on December 18, 1979. G.A. Res. 280. Entered into force on September 3, 1981. The United States signed the convention on July 17, 1980, but has not ratified it. There is an Optional Protocol of October 1999, which entered into force on December 22, 2000.

As of March 2013, the 187 parties to the convention were: Afghanistan, Albania, Algeria, Andorra, Angola, Antigua and Barbuda, Argentina, Armenia, Australia, Austria, Azerbaijan, Bahamas, Bahrain, Bangladesh, Barbados, Belarus, Belgium, Belize, Benin, Bhutan, Bolivia, Bosnia and Herzegovina, Botswana, Brazil, Brunei Darussalam, Bulgaria, Burkina Faso, Burundi, Cambodia, Cameroon, Canada, Cape Verde, Central African Republic, Chad, Chile, China, Colombia, Comoros, Congo, Congo (Democratic Republic of), Cook Islands, Costa Rica, Côte d'Ivoire, Croatia, Cuba, Cyprus, Czech Republic, Denmark, Djibouti, Dominica, Dominican Republic, Ecuador, Egypt, El Salvador, Equatorial Guinea, Eritrea, Estonia, Ethiopia, Fiji, Finland, France, Gabon, Gambia, Georgia, Germany, Ghana, Greece, Grenada, Guatemala, Guinea, Guinea-Bissau, Guyana, Haiti, Honduras, Hungary, Iceland, India, Indonesia, Iraq, Ireland, Israel, Italy, Jamaica, Japan, Jordan, Kazakhstan, Kenya, Kiribati, Korea (Republic of), Kuwait, Kyrgyzstan, Lao People's Democratic Republic, Latvia, Lebanon, Lesotho, Liberia, Libyan Arab Jamahiriya, Liechtenstein, Lithuania, Luxembourg, Macedonia (the former Yugoslav Republic of), Madagascar, Malawi, Malaysia, Maldives, Mali, Malta, Marshall Islands, Mauritania, Mauritius, Mexico, Micronesia (Federated States of), Moldova, Monaco, Mongolia, Montenegro, Morocco, Mozambique, Myanmar, Namibia, Nauru, Nepal, Netherlands, New Zealand, Nicaragua, Niger, Nigeria, Norway, Oman, Pakistan, Panama, Papua New Guinea, Paraguay, Peru, Philippines, Poland, Portugal, Qatar, Romania, Russian Federation, Rwanda, Saint Kitts and Nevis, Saint Lucia, Saint Vincent and the Grenadines, Samoa, San Marino, Sao Tome and Principe, Saudi Arabia, Senegal, Serbia, Seychelles, Sierra Leone, Singapore, Slovakia, Slovenia. Solomon Islands, South Africa, Spain, Sri Lanka, Suriname, Swaziland, Sweden, Switzerland, Syrian Arab Republic, Tajikistan, Tanzania, Thailand, Timor-Leste, Togo, Trinidad and Tobago, Tunisia, Turkey, Turkmenistan, Tuvalu, Uganda, Ukraine, United Arab Emirates, United Kingdom, Uruguay, Uzbekistan, Vanuatu, Venezuela, Viet Nam, Yemen, Zambia, and Zimbabwe. See the U.N. Web site at <http://treaties.un.org>.

one is entitled to all the rights and freedoms set forth therein, without distinction of any kind including distinction based on sex,

Noting that States Parties to the International Covenant on Human Rights have the obligation to secure the equal rights of men and women to enjoy all economic, social, cultural, civil and political rights,

Considering the international conventions concluded under the auspices of the United Nations and the specialized agencies promoting equality of rights of men and women, . . .

Concerned, however, that despite these various instruments extensive discrimination against women continues to exist,

Recalling that discrimination against women violates the principles of equality of rights and respect for human dignity, is an obstacle to the participation of women, on equal terms with men, in the political, social, economic and cultural life of their countries, hampers the growth of the prosperity of society and the family, and makes more difficult the full development of the potentialities of women in the service of their countries and of humanity,

Concerned that in situations of poverty women have the least access to food, health, education, training and opportunities for employment and other needs,

Convinced that the establishment of the new international economic order based on equity and justice will contribute significantly towards the promotion of equality between men and women,

Emphasizing that the eradication of *apartheid,* of all forms of racism, racial discrimination, colonialism, neo-colonialism, aggression, foreign occupation and domination and interference in the internal affairs of States is essential to the full enjoyment of the rights of men and women,

Convinced that the full and complete development of a country, the welfare of the world and the cause of peace require the maximum participation of women on equal terms with men in all fields,

Bearing in mind the great contribution of women to the welfare of the family and to the development of society, so far not fully recognized, the social significance of maternity and the role of both parents in the family and in the upbringing of children, and aware that the role of women in procreation should not be a basis for discrimination but that the upbringing of children requires a sharing of responsibility between men and women and society as a whole,

Aware that a change in the traditional role of men as well as the role of women in society and in the family is needed to achieve full equality between men and women,

Determined to implement the principles set forth in the Declaration on the Elimination of Discrimination against Women and, for that purpose, to adopt the measures required for the elimination of such discrimination in all its forms and manifestations,

Have agreed on the following:

Part I

Article 1

For the purposes of the present Convention, the term "discrimination against women" shall mean any distinction, exclusion or restriction made on the basis of sex which has the effect or purpose of impairing or nullifying the recognition, enjoyment or exercise by women, irrespective of their marital status, on a basis of equality of men and women, of human rights and fundamental freedoms in the political, economic, social, cultural, civil or any other field.

Article 2

States Parties condemn discrimination against women in all its forms, agree to pursue, by all appropriate means and without delay, a policy of eliminating discrimination against women and, to this end, undertake:

(a) To embody the principle of the equality of men and women in their national Constitutions or other appropriate legislation if not yet incorporated therein, and to ensure, through law and other appropriate means, the practical realization of this principle;

(b) To adopt appropriate legislative and other measures, including sanctions where appropriate, prohibiting all discrimination against women;

(c) To establish legal protection of the rights of women on an equal basis with men and to ensure through competent national tribunals and other public institutions the effective protection of women against any act of discrimination;

(d) To refrain from engaging in any act or practice of discrimination against women and to ensure that public authorities and institutions shall act in conformity with this obligation;

(e) To take all appropriate measures to eliminate discrimination against women by any person, organization or enterprise;

(f) To take all appropriate measures, including legislation, to modify or abolish existing laws, regulations, customs and practices which constitute discrimination against women;

(g) To repeal all national penal provisions which constitute discrimination against women.

Article 3

States Parties shall take in all fields, in particular in the political, social, economic and cultural fields, all appropriate measures, including legislation, to ensure the full development and advancement of women, for the purpose of guaranteeing them the exercise and enjoyment of human rights and fundamental freedoms on a basis of equality with men.

Article 4

1. Adoption by States Parties of temporary special measures aimed at accelerating *de facto* equality between men and women shall not be considered discrimination as defined in this Convention, but shall in no way entail, as a consequence, the maintenance of unequal or separate standards; these measures shall be discontinued when the objectives of equality of opportunity and treatment have been achieved.

2. Adoption by States Parties of special measures, including those measures contained in the present Convention, aimed at protecting maternity, shall not be considered discriminatory.

Article 5

States Parties shall take all appropriate measures:

(a) To modify the social and cultural patterns of conduct of men and women, with a view to achieving the elimination of prejudices and customary and all other practices which are based on the idea of the inferiority or the superiority of either of the sexes or on stereotyped roles for men and women;

(b) To ensure that family education includes a proper understanding of maternity as a social function and the recognition of the common responsibility of men and women in the upbringing and development of their children, it being understood that the interest of the children is the primordial consideration in all cases.

Article 6

States Parties shall take all appropriate measures, including legislation, to suppress all forms of traffic in women and exploitation of prostitution of women.

Part II

Article 7

States Parties shall take all appropriate measures to eliminate discrimination against women in the political and public life of the country and, in particular, shall ensure, on equal terms with men, the right:

(a) To vote in all elections and public referenda and to be eligible for election to all publicly elected bodies;

(b) To participate in the formulation of government policy and the implementation thereof and to hold public office and perform all public functions at all levels of government;

(c) To participate in non-governmental organizations and associations concerned with the public and political life of the country.

Article 8

States Parties shall take all appropriate measures to ensure to women on equal terms with men and, without any discrimination, the opportunity to represent their Governments at the international level and to participate in the work of international organizations.

Article 9

1. States Parties shall grant women equal rights with men to acquire, change or retain their nationality. They shall ensure in particular that neither marriage to an alien nor change of nationality by the husband during marriage shall automatically change the nationality of the wife, render her stateless or force upon her the nationality of the husband.

2. States Parties shall grant women equal rights with men with respect to the nationality of their children.

Part III

Article 10

States Parties shall take all appropriate measures to eliminate discrimination against women in order to ensure to them equal rights with men in the field of education and in particular to ensure, on a basis of equality of men and women:

(a) The same conditions for career and vocational guidance, for access to studies and for the achievement of diplomas in educational establishments of all categories in rural as well as in urban areas; this equality shall be ensured in pre-school, general, technical, professional and higher technical education, as well as in all types of vocational training;

(b) Access to the same curricula, the same examinations, teaching staff with qualifications of the same standard and school premises and equipment of the same quality;

(c) The elimination of any stereotyped concept of the roles of men and women at all levels and in all forms of education by encouraging coeducation and other types of education which will help to achieve this aim and, in particular, by the revision of textbooks and school programmes and the adaptation of teaching methods;

(d) The same opportunities to benefit from scholarships and other study grants;

(e) The same opportunities for access to programmes of continuing education, including adult and functional literacy programmes, particularly those aimed at reducing, at the earliest possible time, any gap in education existing between men and women;

(f) The reduction of female student drop-out rates and the organization of programmes for girls and women who have left school prematurely;

(g) The same opportunities to participate actively in sports and physical education;

(h) Access to specific educational information to help to ensure the health and well-being of families, including information and advice on family planning.

Article 11

1. States Parties shall take all appropriate measures to eliminate discrimination against women in the field of employment in order to ensure, on a basis of equality of men and women, the same rights, in particular:

(a) The right to work as an inalienable right of all human beings;

(b) The right to the same employment opportunities, including the application of the same criteria for selection in matters of employment;

(c) The right to free choice of profession and employment, the right to promotion, job security and all benefits and conditions of service and the right to receive vocational training and retraining, including apprenticeships, advanced vocational training and recurrent training;

(d) The right to equal remuneration, including benefits, and to equal treatment in respect of work of equal value, as well as equality of treatment in the evaluation of the quality of work;

(e) The right to social security, particularly in cases of retirement, unemployment, sickness, invalidity and old age and other incapacity to work, as well as the right to paid leave;

(f) The right to protection of health and to safety in working conditions, including the safeguarding of the function of reproduction.

2. In order to prevent discrimination against women on the grounds of marriage or maternity and to ensure their effective right to work, States Parties shall take appropriate measures:

(a) To prohibit, subject to the imposition of sanctions, dismissal on the grounds of pregnancy or of maternity leave and discrimination in dismissals on the basis of marital status;

(b) To introduce maternity leave with pay or with comparable social benefits without loss of former employment, seniority or social allowances;

(c) To encourage the provision of the necessary supporting social services to enable parents to combine family obligations with work responsibilities and participation in public life, in particular through promoting the establishment and development of a network of childcare facilities;

(d) To provide special protection to women during pregnancy in types of work proved to be harmful to them.

3. Protective legislation relating to matters covered in this article shall be reviewed periodically in the light of scientific and technological knowledge and shall be revised, repealed or extended as necessary.

Article 12

1. States Parties shall take all appropriate measures to eliminate discrimination against women in the field of health care in order to ensure, on a basis of equality of men and women, access to health care services, including those related to family planning.

2. Notwithstanding the provisions of paragraph 1 above, States Parties shall ensure to women appropriate services in connexion with pregnancy, confinement and the post-natal period, granting free services where necessary, as well as adequate nutrition during pregnancy and lactation.

Article 13

States Parties shall take all appropriate measures to eliminate discrimination against women in other areas of economic and social life in order to ensure, on a basis of equality of men and women, the same rights, in particular:

(a) The right to family benefits;

(b) The right to bank loans, mortgages and other forms of financial credit;

(c) The right to participate in recreational activities, sports and in all aspects of cultural life.

Article 14

1. States Parties shall take into account the particular problems faced by rural women and the significant roles which they play in the economic survival of their families, including their work in the nonmonetized sectors of the economy, and shall take all appropriate measures to ensure the application of the provisions of this Convention to women in rural areas.

2. States Parties shall take all appropriate measures to eliminate discrimination against women in rural areas in order to ensure, on a basis of equality of men and women, that they participate in and benefit from rural development and, in particular, shall ensure to such women the right:

(a) To participate in the elaboration and implementation of development planning at all levels;

(b) To have access to adequate health care facilities, including information, counselling and services in family planning;

(c) To benefit directly from social security programmes; (d) To obtain all types of training and education, formal and non-formal, including that relating to functional literacy, as well as the benefit of all community and extension services, *inter alia,* in order to increase their technical proficiency;

(e) To organize self-help groups and co-operatives in order to obtain equal access to economic opportunities through employment or self-employment;

(f) To participate in all community activities;

(g) To have access to agricultural credit and loans, marketing facilities, appropriate technology and equal treatment in land and agrarian reform as well as in land resettlement schemes;

(h) To enjoy adequate living conditions, particularly in relation to housing, sanitation, electricity and water supply, transport and communications.

Part IV

Article 15

1. States Parties shall accord to women equality with men before the law.

2. States Parties shall accord to women, in civil matters, a legal capacity identical to that of men and the same opportunities to exercise that capacity. They shall in particular give women equal rights to conclude contracts and to administer property and treat them equally in all stages of procedure in courts and tribunals.

3. States Parties agree that all contract and all other private instruments of any kind with a legal effect which is directed at restricting the legal capacity of women shall be deemed null and void.

4. States Parties shall accord to men and women the same rights with regard to the law relating to the movement of persons and the freedom to choose their residence and domicile.

Article 16

1. States Parties shall take all appropriate measures to eliminate discrimination against women in all matters relating to marriage and family relations and in particular shall ensure, on a basis of equality of men and women;

(a) The same right to enter into marriage;

(b) The same right freely to choose a spouse and to enter into marriage only with their free and full consent;

(c) The same rights and responsibilities during marriage and at its dissolution;

(d) The same rights and responsibilities as parents, irrespective of their marital status, in matters relating to their children. In all cases the interests of the children shall be paramount;

(e) The same rights to decide freely and responsibly on the number and spacing of their children and to have access to the information, education and means to enable them to exercise these rights;

(f) The same rights and responsibilities with regard to guardianship, wardship, trusteeship and adoption of children, or similar institutions where these concepts exist in national legislation. In all cases the interest of the children shall be paramount;

(g) The same personal rights as husband and wife, including the right to choose a family name, a profession and an occupation;

(h) The same rights for both spouses in respect of the ownership, acquisition, management, administration, enjoyment and disposition of property, whether free of charge or for a valuable consideration.

2. The betrothal and the marriage of a child shall have no legal effect and all necessary action, including legislation, shall be taken to specify a minimum age for marriage and to make the registration of marriages in an official registry compulsory.

Part V

Article 17

1. For the purpose of considering the progress made in the implementation of present Convention, there shall be established a Committee on the Elimination of Discrimination against Women (hereinafter referred to as the Committee) consisting . . . of 23 experts of high moral standing and competence in the field covered by the Convention. The experts shall be elected by States Parties from among their nationals and shall serve in their personal capacity, consideration being given to equitable geographical distribution and to the representation of the different forms of civilization as well as the principal legal systems.

2. The members of the Committee shall be elected by secret ballot from a list of persons nominated by States Parties. Each State Party may nominate one person from among its own nationals.

3. . . . At least three months before the date of each election the Secretary-General of the United Nations shall address a letter to the States Parties inviting them to submit their nominations within two months. . . .

4. Elections of the members of the Committee shall be held at a meeting of States Parties convened by the Secretary-General at United Nations Headquarters. At that meeting, for which two thirds of the States Parties shall constitute a quorum, the persons elected to the Committee shall be those nominees who obtain the largest number of votes and an absolute majority of the votes of the representatives of States Parties present and voting.

5. The members of the Committee shall be elected for a term of four years. . . .

7. For the filling of casual vacancies, the State Party whose expert has ceased to function as a member of the Committee shall appoint another expert from among its nationals, subject to the approval of the Committee. . . .

9. The Secretary-General of the United Nations shall provide the necessary staff and facilities for the effective performance of the functions of the Committee under the present Convention.

Article 18

1. States Parties undertake to submit to the Secretary-General of the United Nations, for consideration by the Committee, a report on the legislative, judicial, administrative or other measures which they have adopted to give effect to the provisions of the Convention and on the progress made in this respect:

(a) Within one year after the entry into force for the State concerned;

(b) Thereafter at least every four years and further whenever the Committee so requests.

2. Reports may indicate factors and difficulties affecting the degree of fulfillment of obligations under the present Convention.

Article 19

1. The Committee shall adopt its own rules of procedure.

2. The Committee shall elect its officers for a term of two years.

Article 20

1. The Committee shall normally meet for a period of not more than two weeks annually in order to consider the reports submitted in accordance with article 18 of the present Convention. . . .

Article 21

1. The Committee shall, through the Economic and Social Council, report annually to the General Assembly on its activities and may make suggestions and general recommendations based on the examination of reports and information received from the States Parties.

Part VI

Article 23

Nothing in this Convention shall affect any provisions that are more conducive to the achievement of equality between men and women which may be contained:

(a) in the legislation of a State Party; or

(b) in any other international convention, treaty or agreement in force for that State.

Article 24

States Parties undertake to adopt all necessary measures at the national level aimed at achieving the full realization of the rights recognized in the present Convention. . . .

Article 28

1. The Secretary-General of the United Nations shall receive and circulate to all States the text of reservations made by States at the time of ratification or accession.

2. A reservation incompatible with the object and purpose of the present Convention shall not be permitted. . . .

Article 29

1. Any dispute between two or more States Parties concerning the interpretation or application of the present Convention which is not settled by negotiation shall, at the request of one of them, be submitted to arbitration. If within six months from the date of the request for arbitration the parties are unable to agree on the organization of the arbitration, any one of those parties may refer the dispute to the International Court of Justice by request in conformity with the Statute of the Court.

2. Each State Party may at the time of signature or ratification of this Convention or accession thereto declare that it does not consider itself bound by paragraph 1 of this article. The other States Parties shall not be bound by paragraph 1 of this article with respect to any State Party which has made such a reservation. . . .

CONVENTION AGAINST TORTURE AND OTHER CRUEL, INHUMAN, OR DEGRADING TREATMENT OR PUNISHMENT

Dec. 10, 1984, 23 I.L.M. 1027 (1984), as modified,
24 I.L.M. 535 (1985), 1465 U.N.T.S. 85*

The States Parties to this Convention,

Considering that, in accordance with the principles proclaimed in the Charter of the United Nations, recognition of the equal and inalienable rights of all members of the human family is the foundation of freedom, justice and peace in the world,

Recognizing that those rights derive from the inherent dignity of the human person,

---

* Adopted, without a vote, by the General Assembly of the United Nations on December 10, 1984. Entered into force on June 29, 1987. The U.S. Senate advised and consented to the convention on October 29, 1990. U.S. ratification occurred on October 21, 1994, subject to reservations, understandings, and declarations (which are contained in the next document).

The 153 parties to the convention as of March 2013 were: Afghanistan, Albania, Algeria, Andorra, Antigua and Barbuda, Argentina, Armenia, Australia, Austria, Azerbaijan, Bahrain, Bangladesh, Belarus, Belgium, Belize, Benin, Bolivia, Bosnia and Herzegovina, Botswana, Brazil, Bulgaria, Burkina Faso, Burundi, Cambodia, Cameroon, Canada, Cape Verde, Chad, Chile, China, Colombia, Congo, Congo (Democratic Republic of), Costa Rica, Côte d'Ivoire, Croatia, Cuba, Cyprus, Czech Republic, Denmark, Djibouti, Dominican Republic, Ecuador, Egypt, El Salvador, Equatorial New Guinea, Estonia, Ethiopia, Finland, France, Gabon, Georgia, Germany, Ghana, Greece, Guatemala, Guinea, Guyana, Holy See, Honduras, Hungary, Iceland, Indonesia, Iraq, Ireland, Israel, Italy, Japan, Jordan, Kazakhstan, Kenya, Korea (Republic of), Kuwait, Kyrgyzstan, Lao People's Democratic Republic, Latvia, Lebanon, Lesotho, Liberia, Libyan Arab Jamahiriya, Liechtenstein, Lithuania, Luxembourg, Macedonia (the former Yugoslav Republic of), Madagascar, Malawi, Maldives, Mali, Malta, Mauritania, Mauritius, Mexico, Moldova, Monaco, Mongolia, Montenegro, Morocco, Mozambique, Namibia, Nauru, Nepal, Netherlands, New Zealand, Nicaragua, Niger, Nigeria, Norway, Pakistan, Panama, Paraguay, Peru, Philippines, Poland, Portugal, Qatar, Romania, Russian Federation, Rwanda, Saint Vincent and the Grenadines, Saudi Arabia, Senegal, Serbia, Seychelles, Sierra Leone, Slovakia, Slovenia, Somalia, South Africa, Spain, Sri Lanka, Swaziland, Sweden, Switzerland, Syrian Arab Republic, Tajikistan, Thailand, Timor-Leste, Togo, Tunisia, Turkey, Turkmenistan, Uganda, Ukraine, United Arab Emirates, United Kingdom, United States of America, Uruguay, Uzbekistan, Vanuatu, Venezuela, Yemen, and Zambia. See the U.N. Web site at <http://treaties.un.org>.

Considering the obligation of States under the Charter, in particular Article 55, to promote universal respect for, and observance of, human rights and fundamental freedoms,

Having regard to article 5 of the Universal Declaration of Human Rights and article 7 of the International Covenant on Civil and Political Rights, both of which provide that no one shall be subjected to torture or to cruel, inhuman or degrading treatment or punishment,

Having regard also to the Declaration on the Protection of All Persons from Being Subjected to Torture and Other Cruel, Inhuman or Degrading Treatment or Punishment, adopted by the General Assembly on 9 December 1975,

Desiring to make more effective the struggle against torture and other cruel, inhuman or degrading treatment or punishment throughout the world,

Have agreed as follows:

Part I

Article 1

1. For the purposes of this Convention, the term "torture" means any act by which severe pain or suffering, whether physical or mental, is intentionally inflicted on a person for such purposes as obtaining from him or a third person information or a confession, punishing him for an act he or a third person has committed or is suspected of having committed, or intimidating or coercing him or a third person, or for any reason based on discrimination of any kind, when such pain or suffering is inflicted by or at the instigation of or with the consent or acquiescence of a public official or other person acting in an official capacity. It does not include pain or suffering arising only from, inherent in or incidental to lawful sanctions.

2. This article is without prejudice to any international instrument or national legislation which does or may contain provisions of wider application.

Article 2

1. Each State Party shall take effective legislative, administrative, judicial or other measures to prevent acts of torture in any territory under its jurisdiction.

2. No exceptional circumstances whatsoever, whether a state of war or a threat of war, internal political instability or any other public emergency, may be invoked as a justification of torture.

3. An order from a superior officer or a public authority may not be invoked as a justification of torture.

Article 3

1. No State Party shall expel, return or extradite a person to another State where there are substantial grounds for believing that he would be in danger of being subjected to torture.

2. For the purpose of determining whether there are such grounds, the competent authorities shall take into account all relevant considerations including, where applicable, the existence in the State concerned of a consistent pattern of gross, flagrant or mass violations of human rights.

Article 4

1. Each State Party shall ensure that all acts of torture are offences under its criminal law. The same shall apply to an attempt to commit torture and to an act by any person which constitutes complicity or participation in torture.

2. Each State Party shall make these offences punishable by appropriate penalties which take into account their grave nature.

Article 5

1. Each State Party shall take such measures as may be necessary to establish its jurisdiction over the offences referred to in article 4 in the following cases:

(a) When the offences are committed in any territory under its jurisdiction or on board a ship or aircraft registered in that State;

(b) When the alleged offender is a national of that State;

(c) When the victim is a national of that State if that State considers it appropriate.

2. Each State Party shall likewise take such measures as may be necessary to establish its jurisdiction over such offences in cases where the alleged offender is present in any territory under its jurisdiction and it does not extradite him pursuant to article 8 to any of the States mentioned in paragraph 1 of this article.

3. This Convention does not exclude any criminal jurisdiction exercised in accordance with internal law.

Article 6

1. Upon being satisfied, after an examination of information available to it, that the circumstances so warrant, any State Party in whose territory a person alleged to have committed any offence referred to in article 4 is present shall take him into custody or take other legal measures to ensure his presence. The custody and other legal measures shall be as provided in the law of that State but may be continued only for such time as is necessary to enable any criminal or extradition proceedings to be instituted.

2. Such State shall immediately make a preliminary inquiry into the facts.

3. Any person in custody pursuant to paragraph 1 of this article shall be assisted in communicating immediately with the nearest appropriate representative of the State of which he is a national, or, if he is a stateless person, with the representative of the State where he usually resides.

4. When a State, pursuant to this article, has taken a person into custody, it shall immediately notify the States referred to in article 5, paragraph 1, of

the fact that such person is in custody and of the circumstances which warrant his detention. The State which makes the preliminary inquiry contemplated in paragraph 2 of this article shall promptly report its findings to the said States and shall indicate whether it intends to exercise jurisdiction.

Article 7

1. The State Party in the territory under whose jurisdiction a person alleged to have committed any offence referred to in article 4 is found shall in the cases contemplated in article 5, if it does not extradite him, submit the case to its competent authorities for the purpose of prosecution.

2. These authorities shall take their decision in the same manner as in the case of any ordinary offence of a serious nature under the law of that State. In the cases referred to in article 5, paragraph 2, the standards of evidence required for prosecution and conviction shall in no way be less stringent than those which apply in the cases referred to in article 5, paragraph 1.

3. Any person regarding whom proceedings are brought in connection with any of the offences referred to in article 4 shall be guaranteed fair treatment at all stages of the proceedings.

Article 8

1. The offences referred to in article 4 shall be deemed to be included as extraditable offences in any extradition treaty existing between States Parties. States Parties undertake to include such offences as extraditable offences in every extradition treaty to be concluded between them.

2. If a State Party which makes extradition conditional on the existence of a treaty receives a request for extradition from another State Party with which it has no extradition treaty, it may consider this Convention as the legal basis for extradition in respect of such offences. Extradition shall be subject to the other conditions provided by the law of the requested State.

3. States Parties which do not make extradition conditional on the existence of a treaty shall recognize such offences as extraditable offences between themselves subject to the conditions provided by the law of the requested State.

4. Such offences shall be treated, for the purpose of extradition between States Parties, as if they had been committed not only in the place in which they occurred but also in the territories of the States required to establish their jurisdiction in accordance with article 5, paragraph 1.

Article 9

1. States Parties shall afford one another the greatest measure of assistance in connection with criminal proceedings brought in respect of any of the offences referred to in article 4, including the supply of all evidence at their disposal necessary for the proceedings.

2. States Parties shall carry out their obligations under paragraph 1 of this article in conformity with any treaties on mutual judicial assistance that may exist between them.

Article 10

1. Each State Party shall ensure that education and information regarding the prohibition against torture are fully included in the training of law enforcement personnel, civil or military, medical personnel, public officials and other persons who may be involved in the custody, interrogation or treatment of any individual subjected to any form of arrest, detention or imprisonment.

2. Each State Party shall include this prohibition in the rules or instructions issued in regard to the duties and functions of any such persons.

Article 11

Each State Party shall keep under systematic review interrogation rules, instructions, methods and practices as well as arrangements for the custody and treatment of persons subjected to any form of arrest, detention or imprisonment in any territory under its jurisdiction, with a view to preventing any cases of torture.

Article 12

Each State Party shall ensure that its competent authorities proceed to a prompt and impartial investigation, wherever there is reasonable ground to believe that an act of torture has been committed in any territory under its jurisdiction.

Article 13

Each State Party shall ensure that any individual who alleges he has been subjected to torture in any territory under its jurisdiction has the right to complain to, and to have his case promptly and impartially examined by, its competent authorities. Steps shall be taken to ensure that the complainant and witnesses are protected against all ill-treatment or intimidation as a consequence of his complaint or any evidence given.

Article 14

1. Each State Party shall ensure in its legal system that the victim of an act of torture obtains redress and has an enforceable right to fair and adequate compensation, including the means for as full rehabilitation as possible. In the event of the death of the victim as a result of an act of torture, his dependents shall be entitled to compensation.

2. Nothing in this article shall affect any right of the victim or other persons to compensation which may exist under national law.

Article 15

Each State Party shall ensure that any statement which is established to have been made as a result of torture shall not be invoked as evidence in any proceedings, except against a person accused of torture as evidence that the statement was made.

Article 16

1. Each State Party shall undertake to prevent in any territory under its jurisdiction other acts of cruel, inhuman or degrading treatment or punishment which do not amount to torture as defined in article 1, when such acts are committed by or at the instigation of or with the consent or acquiescence of a public official or other person acting in an official capacity. In particular, the obligations contained in articles 10, 11, 12 and 13 shall apply with the substitution for references to torture of references to other forms of cruel, inhuman or degrading treatment or punishment.

2. The provisions of this Convention are without prejudice to the provisions of any other international instrument or national law which prohibits cruel, inhuman or degrading treatment or punishment or which relates to extradition or expulsion.

Part II

Article 17

1. There shall be established a Committee against Torture (hereinafter referred to as the Committee) which shall carry out the functions hereinafter provided. The Committee shall consist of ten experts of high moral standing and recognized competence in the field of human rights, who shall serve in their personal capacity. The experts shall be elected by the States Parties, consideration being given to equitable geographical distribution and to the usefulness of the participation of some persons having legal experience.

2. The members of the Committee shall be elected by secret ballot from a list of persons nominated by States Parties. Each State Party may nominate one person from among its own nationals. States Parties shall bear in mind the usefulness of nominating persons who are also members of the Human Rights Committee established under the International Covenant on Civil and Political Rights. . . .

5. The members of the Committee shall be elected for a term of four years. They shall be eligible for re-election if renominated. . . .

Article 18

1. The Committee shall elect its officers for a term of two years. They may be re-elected.

2. The Committee shall establish its own rules of procedure, but these rules shall provide, *inter alia,* that:

(a) Six members shall constitute a quorum;

(b) Decisions of the Committee shall be made by a majority vote of the members present.

3. The Secretary-General of the United Nations shall provide the necessary staff and facilities for the effective performance of the functions of the Committee under this Convention. . . .

Article 19

1. The States Parties shall submit to the Committee, through the Secretary-General of the United Nations, reports on the measures they have taken to give effect to their undertakings under this Convention, within one year after the entry into force of the Convention for the State Party concerned. Thereafter the States Parties shall submit supplementary reports every four years on any new measures taken and such other reports as the Committee may request.

2. The Secretary-General of the United Nations shall transmit the reports to all States Parties.

3. Each report shall be considered by the Committee which may make such general comments on the report as it may consider appropriate and shall forward these to the State Party concerned. That State Party may respond with any observations it chooses to the Committee. . . .

Article 20

1. If the Committee receives reliable information which appears to it to contain well-founded indications that torture is being systematically practised in the territory of a State Party, the Committee shall invite that State Party to co-operate in the examination of the information and to this end to submit observations with regard to the information concerned.

2. Taking into account any observations which may have been submitted by the State Party concerned, as well as any other relevant information available to it, the Committee may, if it decides that this is warranted, designate one or more of its members to make a confidential inquiry and to report to the Committee urgently.

3. If any inquiry is made in accordance with paragraph 2 of this article, the Committee shall seek the co-operation of the State Party concerned. In agreement with that State Party, such an inquiry may include a visit to its territory.

4. After examining the findings of its member or members submitted in accordance with paragraph 2 of this article, the Committee shall transmit these findings to the State Party concerned together with any comments or suggestions which seem appropriate in view of the situation.

5. All the proceedings of the Committee referred to in paragraphs 1 to 4 of this article shall be confidential, and at all stages of the proceedings the

cooperation of the State Party shall be sought. After such proceedings have been completed with regard to an inquiry made in accordance with paragraph 2, the Committee may, after consultations with the State Party concerned, decide to include a summary account of the results of the proceedings in its annual report made in accordance with article 24.

Article 21

1. A State Party to this Convention may at any time declare under this article that it recognizes the competence of the Committee to receive and consider communications to the effect that a State Party claims that another State Party is not fulfilling its obligations under this Convention. Such communications may be received and considered according to the procedures laid down in this article only if submitted by a State Party which has made a declaration recognizing in regard to itself the competence of the Committee. No communication shall be dealt with by the Committee under this article if it concerns a State Party which has not made such a declaration. Communications received under this article shall be dealt with in accordance with the following procedure:

(a) If a State Party considers that another State Party is not giving effect to the provisions of this Convention, it may, by written communication, bring the matter to the attention of that State Party. Within three months after the receipt of the communication the receiving State shall afford the State which sent the communication an explanation or any other statement in writing clarifying the matter, which should include, to the extent possible and pertinent, reference to domestic procedures and remedies taken, pending or available in the matter;

(b) If the matter is not adjusted to the satisfaction of both States Parties concerned within six months after the receipt by the receiving State of the initial communication, either State shall have the right to refer the matter to the Committee, by notice given to the Committee and to the other State;

(c) The Committee shall deal with a matter referred to it under this article only after it has ascertained that all domestic remedies have been invoked and exhausted in the matter, in conformity with the generally recognized principles of international law. This shall not be the rule where the application of the remedies is unreasonably prolonged or is unlikely to bring effective relief to the person who is the victim of the violation of this Convention;

(d) The Committee shall hold closed meetings when examining communications under this article;

(e) Subject to the provisions of subparagraph (c), the Committee shall make available its good offices to the States Parties concerned with a view to a friendly solution of the matter on the basis of respect for the obligations provided for in this Convention. For this purpose, the Committee may, when appropriate, set up an *ad hoc* conciliation commission;

(f) In any matter referred to it under this article, the Committee may call upon the States Parties concerned, referred to in subparagraph (b), to supply any relevant information;

(g) The States Parties concerned, referred to in subparagraph (b), shall have the right to be represented when the matter is being considered by the Committee and to make submissions orally and/or in writing;

(h) The Committee shall, within twelve months after the date of receipt of notice under subparagraph (b), submit a report:

(i) If a solution within the terms of subparagraph (e) is reached, the Committee shall confine its report to a brief statement of the facts and of the solution reached;

(ii) If a solution within the terms of subparagraph (e) is not reached, the Committee shall confine its report to a brief statement of the facts; the written submissions and record of the oral submissions made by the States Parties concerned shall be attached to the report. In every matter, the report shall be communicated to the States Parties concerned.

2. The provisions of this article shall come into force when five States Parties to this Convention have made declarations under paragraph 1 of this article. . . . A declaration may be withdrawn at any time by notification to the Secretary-General. Such a withdrawal shall not prejudice the consideration of any matter which is the subject of a communication already transmitted under this article. . . .

Article 22

1. A State Party to this Convention may at any time declare under this article that it recognizes the competence of the Committee to receive and consider communications from or on behalf of individuals subject to its jurisdiction who claim to be victims of a violation by a State Party of the provisions of the Convention. No communication shall be received by the Committee if it concerns a State Party which has not made such a declaration.

2. The Committee shall consider inadmissible any communication under this article which is anonymous or which it considers to be an abuse of the right of submission of such communications or to be incompatible with the provisions of this Convention.

3. Subject to the provisions of paragraph 2, the Committee shall bring any communications submitted to it under this article to the attention of the State Party to this Convention which has made a declaration under paragraph 1 and is alleged to be violating any provisions of the Convention. Within six months, the receiving State shall submit to the Committee written explanations or statements clarifying the matter and the remedy, if any, that may have been taken by that State.

4. The Committee shall consider communications received under this article in the light of all information made available to it by or on behalf of the individual and by the State Party concerned.

5. The Committee shall not consider any communications from an individual under this article unless it has ascertained that:

(a) The same matter has not been, and is not being, examined under another procedure of international investigation or settlement;

(b) The individual has exhausted all available domestic remedies; this shall not be the rule where the application of the remedies is unreasonably prolonged or is unlikely to bring effective relief to the person who is the victim of the violation of this Convention.

6. The Committee shall hold closed meetings when examining communications under this article.

7. The Committee shall forward its views to the State Party concerned and to the individual.

8. The provisions of this article shall come into force when five States Parties to this Convention have made declarations under paragraph 1 of this article. . . .

Article 23

The members of the Committee and of the ad hoc conciliation commissions which may be appointed under article 21, paragraph 1(e), shall be entitled to the facilities, privileges and immunities of experts on mission for the United Nations as laid down in the relevant sections of the Convention on the Privileges and Immunities of the United Nations. . . .

Part III . . .

Article 30

1. Any dispute between two or more States Parties concerning the interpretation or application of this Convention which cannot be settled through negotiation shall, at the request of one of them, be submitted to arbitration. If within six months from the date of the request for arbitration the Parties are unable to agree on the organization of the arbitration, any one of those Parties may refer the dispute to the International Court of Justice by request in conformity with the Statute of the Court.

2. Each State may, at the time of signature or ratification of this Convention or accession thereto, declare that it does not consider itself bound by paragraph 1 of this article. The other States Parties shall not be bound by paragraph 1 of this article with respect to any State Party having made such a reservation. . . .

U.S. RESERVATIONS, UNDERSTANDINGS, AND DECLARATIONS TO THE TORTURE CONVENTION

<http://treaties.un.org>*

I. The Senate's advice and consent is subject to the following reservations:

(1) That the United States considers itself bound by the obligation under article 16 to prevent "cruel, inhuman or degrading treatment or punishment", only insofar as the term "cruel, inhuman or degrading treatment or punishment" means the cruel, unusual and inhumane treatment or punishment prohibited by the Fifth, Eighth, and/or Fourteenth Amendments to the Constitution of the United States.

(2) That pursuant to article 30 (2) the United States declares that it does not consider itself bound by Article 30 (1), but reserves the right specifically to agree to follow this or any other procedure for arbitration in a particular case.

II. The Senate's advice and consent is subject to the following understandings, which shall apply to the obligations of the United States under this Convention:

(1) (a) That with reference to article 1, the United States understands that, in order to constitute torture, an act must be specifically intended to inflict severe physical or mental pain or suffering and that mental pain or suffering refers to prolonged mental harm caused by or resulting from (1) the intentional infliction or threatened infliction of severe physical pain or suffering; (2) the administration or application, or threatened administration or application, of mind altering substances or other procedures calculated to disrupt profoundly the senses or the personality; (3) the threat of imminent death; or (4) the threat that another person will imminently be subjected to death, severe physical pain or suffering, or the administration or application of mind altering substances or other procedures calculated to disrupt profoundly the senses or personality.

---

*The United States ratified the Torture Convention (see the previous document) on October 21, 1994, subject to the following reservations, understandings, and declarations.

(b) That the United States understands that the definition of torture in article 1 is intended to apply only to acts directed against persons in the offender's custody or physical control.

(c) That with reference to article 1 of the Convention, the United States understands that "sanctions" includes judicially-imposed sanctions and other enforcement actions authorized by United States law or by judicial interpretation of such law. Nonetheless, the United States understands that a State Party could not through its domestic sanctions defeat the object and purpose of the Convention to prohibit torture.

(d) That with reference to article 1 of the Convention, the United States understands that the term "acquiescence" requires that the public official, prior to the activity constituting torture, have awareness of such activity and thereafter breach his legal responsibility to intervene to prevent such activity.

(e) That with reference to article 1 of the Convention, the Unites States understands that noncompliance with applicable legal procedural standards does not *per se* constitute torture.

(2) That the United States understands the phrase, "where there are substantial grounds for believing that he would be in danger of being subjected to torture," as used in article 3 of the Convention, to mean "if it is more likely than not that he would be tortured."

(3) That it is the understanding of the United States that article 14 requires a State Party to provide a private right of action for damages only for acts of torture committed in territory under the jurisdiction of that State Party.

(4) That the United States understands that international law does not prohibit the death penalty, and does not consider this Convention to restrict or prohibit the United States from applying the death penalty consistent with the Fifth, Eighth and/or Fourteenth Amendments to the Constitution of the United States, including any constitutional period of confinement prior to the imposition of the death penalty.

(5) That the United States understands that this Convention shall be implemented by the United States Government to the extent that it exercises legislative and judicial jurisdiction over the matters covered by the Convention and otherwise by the state and local governments. Accordingly, in implementing articles 10-14 and 16, the United States Government shall take measures appropriate to the Federal system to the end that the competent authorities of the constituent units of the United States of America may take appropriate measures for the fulfillment of the Convention.

III. The Senate's advice and consent is subject to the following declarations:

(1) That the United States declares that the provisions of articles 1 through 16 of the Convention are not self-executing.

CONVENTION ON THE RIGHTS
OF THE CHILD

Nov. 20, 1989, 1577 U.N.T.S. 3*

Preamble

The States Parties to the present Convention,
Considering that, in accordance with the principles proclaimed in the Charter of the United Nations, recognition of the inherent dignity and of the equal and inalienable rights of all members of the human family is the foundation of freedom, justice and peace in the world,

---

* Adopted by the U.N. General Assembly at New York on November 28, 1989. Entered into force on September 2, 1990. The United States has not ratified the convention. There are two Optional Protocols from May 2000, which entered into force in 2002. The United States has ratified those protocols. The two protocols follow the convention below.

As of March 2013, the 193 parties to the convention were: Afghanistan, Albania, Algeria, Andorra, Angola, Antigua and Barbuda, Argentina, Armenia, Australia, Austria, Azerbaijan, Bahamas, Bahrain, Bangladesh, Barbados, Belarus, Belgium, Belize, Benin, Bhutan, Bolivia, Bosnia and Herzegovina, Botswana, Brazil, Brunei Darussalam, Bulgaria, Burkina Faso, Burundi, Cambodia, Cameroon, Canada, Cape Verde, Central African Republic, Chad, Chile, China, Colombia, Comoros, Congo, Congo (Democratic Republic of), Cook Islands, Costa Rica, Côte d'Ivoire, Croatia, Cuba, Cyprus, Czech Republic, Denmark, Djibouti, Dominica, Dominican Republic, Ecuador, Egypt, El Salvador, Equatorial Guinea, Eritrea, Estonia, Ethiopia, Fiji, Finland, France, Gabon, Gambia, Georgia, Germany, Ghana, Greece, Grenada, Guatemala, Guinea, Guinea-Bissau, Guyana, Haiti, Holy See, Honduras, Hungary, Iceland, India, Indonesia, Iran, Iraq, Ireland, Israel, Italy, Jamaica, Japan, Jordan, Kazakhstan, Kenya, Kiribati, Korea (Democratic People's Republic of), Korea (Republic of), Kuwait, Kyrgyzstan, Lao People's Democratic Republic, Latvia, Lebanon, Lesotho, Liberia, Libyan Arab Jamahiriya, Liechtenstein, Lithuania, Luxembourg, Macedonia (the former Yugoslav Republic of), Madagascar, Malawi, Malaysia, Maldives, Mali, Malta, Marshall Islands, Mauritania, Mauritius, Mexico, Micronesia, Moldova, Monaco, Mongolia, Montenegro, Morocco, Mozambique, Myanmar, Namibia, Nauru, Nepal, Netherlands, New Zealand, Nicaragua, Niger, Nigeria, Niue, Norway, Oman, Pakistan, Palau, Panama, Papua New Guinea, Paraguay, Peru, Philippines, Poland, Portugal, Qatar, Romania, Russian Federation, Rwanda, Saint Kitts and Nevis, Saint Lucia, Saint Vincent and the Grenadines, Samoa, San Marino, Sao Tome and Principe, Saudi Arabia, Senegal, Serbia, Seychelles, Sierra Leone, Singapore, Slovakia, Slovenia, Solomon Islands, South Africa, Spain, Sri Lanka, Sudan, Suriname, Swaziland, Sweden, Switzerland, Syrian Arab Republic, Tajikistan, Tanzania, Thailand, Timor-Leste, Togo, Tonga, Trinidad and Tobago, Tunisia, Turkey, Turkmenistan, Tuvalu, Uganda, Ukraine, United Arab Emirates, United Kingdom, Uruguay, Uzbekistan, Vanuatu, Venezuela, Viet Nam, Yemen, Zambia, and Zimbabwe. See the U.N. Web site at <http://treaties.un.org>.

Bearing in mind, that the peoples of the United Nations have, in the Charter, reaffirmed their faith in fundamental human rights and in the dignity and worth of the human person, and have determined to promote social progress and better standards of life in larger freedom,

Recognizing that the United Nations has, in the Universal Declaration of Human Rights and in the International Covenants on Human Rights, proclaimed and agreed that everyone is entitled to all the rights and freedoms set forth therein, without distinction of any kind, such as race, colour, sex, language, religion, political or other opinion, national or social origin, property, birth or other status,

Recalling that, in the Universal Declaration of Human Rights, the United Nations has proclaimed that childhood is entitled to special care and assistance,

Convinced that the family, as the fundamental group of society and the natural environment for the growth and well-being of all its members and particularly children, should be afforded the necessary protection and assistance so that it can fully assume its responsibilities within the community,

Recognizing that the child, for the full and harmonious development of his or her personality, should grow up in a family environment, in an atmosphere of happiness, love and understanding,

Considering that the child should be fully prepared to live an individual life in society, and brought up in the spirit of the ideals proclaimed in the Charter of the United Nations, and in particular in the spirit of peace, dignity, tolerance, freedom, equality and solidarity,

Bearing in mind that the need to extend particular care to the child has been stated in the Geneva Declaration of the Rights of the Child of 1924 and in the Declaration of the Rights of the Child adopted by the General Assembly on 20 November 1959 and recognized in the Universal Declaration of Human Rights, in the International Covenant on Civil and Political Rights (in particular in articles 23 and 24), in the International Covenant on Economic, Social and Cultural Rights (in particular in article 10). . . .

Taking due account of the importance of the traditions and cultural values of each people for the protection and harmonious development of the child, . . .

Have agreed as follows:

Part I

Article 1

For the purposes of the present Convention, a child means every human being below the age of eighteen years unless, under the law applicable to the child, majority is attained earlier.

Article 2

1. States Parties shall respect and ensure the rights set forth in the present Convention to each child within their jurisdiction without discrimination of any kind, irrespective of the child's or his or her parent's or legal guardian's race, colour, sex, language, religion, political or other opinion, national, ethnic or social origin, property, disability, birth or other status.

2. States Parties shall take all appropriate measures to ensure that the child is protected against all forms of discrimination or punishment on the basis of the status, activities, expressed opinions, or beliefs of the child's parents, legal guardians, or family members.

Article 3

1. In all actions concerning children, whether undertaken by public or private social welfare institutions, courts of law, administrative authorities or legislative bodies, the best interests of the child shall be a primary consideration,

2. States Parties undertake to ensure the child such protection and care as is necessary for his or her well-being, taking into account the rights and duties of his or her parents, legal guardians, or other individuals legally responsible for him or her, and, to this end, shall take all appropriate legislative and administrative measures.

3. States Parties shall ensure that the institutions, services and facilities responsible for the care or protection of children shall conform with the standards established by competent authorities, particularly in the areas of safety, health, in the number and suitability of their staff, as well as competent supervision.

Article 4

States Parties shall undertake all appropriate legislative, administrative, and other measures for the implementation of the rights recognized in the present Convention. With regard to economic, social and cultural rights, States Parties shall undertake such measures to the maximum extent of their available resources and, where needed, within the framework of international co-operation.

Article 5

States Parties shall respect the responsibilities, rights and duties of parents or, where applicable, the members of the extended family or community as provided for by local custom, legal guardians or other persons legally responsible for the child, to provide, in a manner consistent with the evolving capacities of the child, appropriate direction and guidance in the exercise by the child of the rights recognized in the present Convention.

Article 6

1. States Parties recognize that every child has the inherent right to life.

2. States Parties shall ensure to the maximum extent possible the survival and development of the child.

Article 7

1. The child shall be registered immediately after birth and shall have the right from birth to a name, the right to acquire a nationality and, as far as possible, the right to know and be cared for by his or her parents.

2. States Parties shall ensure the implementation of these rights in accordance with their national law and their obligations under the relevant international instruments in this field, in particular where the child would otherwise be stateless.

Article 8

1. States Parties undertake to respect the right of the child to preserve his or her identity, including nationality, name and family relations as recognized by law without unlawful interference.

2. Where a child is illegally deprived of some or all of the elements of his or her identity, States Parties shall provide appropriate assistance and protection, with a view to speedily re-establishing his or her identity.

Article 9

1. States Parties shall ensure that a child shall not be separated from his or her parents against their will, except when competent authorities subject to judicial review determine, in accordance with applicable law and procedures, that such separation is necessary for the best interests of the child. Such determination may be necessary in a particular case such as one involving abuse or neglect of the child by the parents, or one where the parents are living separately and a decision must be made as to the child's place of residence.

2. In any proceedings pursuant to paragraph 1 of the present article, all interested parties shall be given an opportunity to participate in the proceedings and make their views known.

3. States Parties shall respect the right of the child who is separated from one or both parents to maintain personal relations and direct contact with both parents on a regular basis, except if it is contrary to the child's best interests. . . .

Article 11

1. States Parties shall take measures to combat the illicit transfer and non-return of children abroad. . . .

Article 12

1. States Parties shall assure to the child who is capable of forming his or her own views the right to express those views freely in all matters affecting the child, the views of the child being given due weight in accordance with the age and maturity of the child.

2. For this purpose, the child shall in particular be provided the opportunity to be heard in any judicial and administrative proceedings affecting the child, either directly, or through a representative or an appropriate body, in a manner consistent with the procedural rules of national law.

Article 13

1. The child shall have the right to freedom of expression; this right shall include freedom to seek, receive and impart information and ideas of all kinds, regardless of frontiers, either orally, in writing or in print, in the form of art, or through any other media of the child's choice.

2. The exercise of this right may be subject to certain restrictions, but these shall only be such as are provided by law and are necessary:

(a) For respect of the rights or reputations of others; or

(b) For the protection of national security or of public order (ordre public), or of public health or morals.

Article 14

1. States Parties shall respect the right of the child to freedom of thought, conscience and religion.

2. States Parties shall respect the rights and duties of the parents and, when applicable, legal guardians, to provide direction to the child in the exercise of his or her right in a manner consistent with the evolving capacities of the child.

3. Freedom to manifest one's religion or beliefs may be subject only to such limitations as are prescribed by law and are necessary to protect public safety, order, health or morals, or the fundamental rights and freedoms of others.

Article 15

1. States Parties recognize the rights of the child to freedom of association and to freedom of peaceful assembly.

2. No restrictions may be placed on the exercise of these rights other than those imposed in conformity with the law and which are necessary in a democratic society in the interests of national security or public safety, public order (*ordre public*), the protection of public health or morals or the protection of the rights and freedoms of others.

Article 16

1. No child shall be subjected to arbitrary or unlawful interference with his or her privacy, family, home or correspondence, nor to unlawful attacks on his or her honour and reputation.

2. The child has the right to the protection of the law against such interference or attacks.

Article 17

States Parties recognize the important function performed by the mass media and shall ensure that the child has access to information and material from a diversity of national and international sources, especially those aimed at the promotion of his or her social, spiritual and moral well-being and physical and mental health. To this end, States Parties shall:

(*a*) Encourage the mass media to disseminate information and material of social and cultural benefit to the child and in accordance with the spirit of article 29;

(*b*) Encourage international co-operation in the production, exchange and dissemination of such information and material from a diversity of cultural, national and international sources;

(*c*) Encourage the production and dissemination of children's books;

(*d*) Encourage the mass media to have particular regard to the linguistic needs of the child who belongs to a minority group or who is indigenous;

(*e*) Encourage the development of appropriate guidelines for the protection of the child from information and material injurious to his or her well-being, bearing in mind the provisions of articles 13 and 18.

Article 18

1. States Parties shall use their best efforts to ensure recognition of the principle that both parents have common responsibilities for the upbringing and development of the child. Parents or, as the case may be, legal guardians, have the primary responsibility for the upbringing and development of the child. The best interests of the child will be their basic concern.

2. For the purpose of guaranteeing and promoting the rights set forth in the present Convention, States Parties shall render appropriate assistance to parents and legal guardians in the performance of their child-rearing

responsibilities and shall ensure the development of institutions, facilities and services for the care of children.

3. States Parties shall take all appropriate measures to ensure that children of working parents have the right to benefit from child-care services and facilities for which they are eligible.

Article 19

1. States Parties shall take all appropriate legislative, administrative, social and educational measures to protect the child from all forms of physical or mental violence, injury or abuse, neglect or negligent treatment, maltreatment or exploitation, including sexual abuse, while in the care of parent(s), legal guardian(s) or any other person who has the care of the child. . . .

Article 27

1. States Parties recognize the right of every child to a standard of living adequate for the child's physical, mental, spiritual, moral and social development. . . .

Article 28

1. States Parties recognize the right of the child to education, and with a view to achieving this right progressively and on the basis of equal opportunity, they shall, in particular:

(*a*) Make primary education compulsory and available free to all;

(*b*) Encourage the development of different forms of secondary education, including general and vocational education, make them available and accessible to every child, and take appropriate measures such as the introduction of free education and offering financial assistance in case of need;

(*c*) Make higher education accessible to all on the basis of capacity by every appropriate means;

(*d*) Make educational and vocational information and guidance available and accessible to all children;

(*e*) Take measures to encourage regular attendance at schools and the reduction of drop-out rates. . . .

Article 30

In those States in which ethnic, religious or linguistic minorities or persons of indigenous origin exist, a child belonging to such a minority or who is indigenous shall not be denied the right, in community with other members of his or her group, to enjoy his or her own culture, to profess and practise his or her own religion, or to use his or her own language. . . .

Article 40

1. States Parties recognize the right of every child alleged as, accused of, or recognized as having infringed the penal law to be treated in a manner consistent with the promotion of the child's sense of dignity and worth, which reinforces the child's respect for the human rights and fundamental freedoms of others and which takes into account the child's age and the desirability of promoting the child's reintegration and the child's assuming a constructive role in society.

2. To this end, and having regard to the relevant provisions of international instruments, States Parties shall, in particular, ensure that:

(a) No child shall be alleged as, be accused of, or recognized as having infringed the penal law by reason of acts or omissions that were not prohibited by national or international law at the time they were committed;

(b) Every child alleged as or accused of having infringed the penal law has at least the following guarantees:

(i) To be presumed innocent until proven guilty according to law;

(ii) To be informed promptly and directly of the charges against him or her, and, if appropriate, through his or her parents or legal guardians, and to have legal or other appropriate assistance in the preparation and presentation of his or her defence;

(iii) To have the matter determined without delay by a competent, independent and impartial authority or judicial body in a fair hearing according to law, in the presence of legal or other appropriate assistance and, unless it is considered not to be in the best interest of the child, in particular, taking into account his or her age or situation, his or her parents or legal guardians;

(iv) Not to be compelled to give testimony or to confess guilt; to examine or have examined adverse witnesses and to obtain the participation and examination of witnesses on his or her behalf under conditions of equality;

(v) If considered to have infringed the penal law, to have this decision and any measures imposed in consequence thereof reviewed by a higher competent, independent and impartial authority or judicial body according to law;

(vi) To have the free assistance of an interpreter if the child cannot understand or speak the language used;

(vii) To have his or her privacy fully respected at all stages of the proceedings.

3. States Parties shall seek to promote the establishment of laws, procedures, authorities and institutions specifically applicable to children alleged as, accused of, or recognized as having infringed the penal law, and, in particular:

(a) The establishment of a minimum age below which children shall be presumed not to have the capacity to infringe the penal law;

(*b*) Whenever appropriate and desirable, measures for dealing with such children without resorting to judicial proceedings, providing that human rights and legal safeguards are fully respected. . . .

Article 41

Nothing in the present Convention shall affect any provisions which are more conducive to the realization of the rights of the child and which may he contained in:

(*a*) The law of a State Party; or

(*b*) International law in force for that State.

Part II . . . .

Article 43

1. For the purpose of examining the progress made by States Parties in achieving the realization of the obligations undertaken in the present Convention, there shall be established a Committee on the Rights of the Child, which shall carry out the functions hereinafter provided.

2. The Committee shall consist of eighteen* experts of high moral standing and recognized competence in the field covered by this Convention. The members of the Committee shall be elected by States Parties from among their nationals and shall serve in their personal capacity, consideration being given to equitable geographical distribution, as well as to the principal legal systems.

3. The members of the Committee shall be elected by secret ballot from a list of persons nominated by States Parties. Each State Party may nominate one person from among its own nationals. . . .

6. The members of the Committee shall be elected for a term of four years. They shall be eligible for re-election if renominated. . . .

Article 44

1. States Parties undertake to submit to the Committee, through the Secretary-General of the United Nations, reports on the measures they have adopted which give effect to the rights recognized herein and on the progress made on the enjoyment of those rights. . . .

---

* An amendment to replace the word "ten" with "eighteen" was made in accordance with Article 50(1) of the Convention. It was accepted by 143 parties and entered into force on 18 November 2002.

OPTIONAL PROTOCOL TO THE CONVENTION ON THE RIGHTS OF THE CHILD ON THE INVOLVEMENT OF CHILDREN IN ARMED CONFLICT

Feb. 12, 2002, 2173 U.N.T.S. 222*

The States Parties to the present Protocol,

Encouraged by the overwhelming support for the Convention on the Rights of the Child, demonstrating the widespread commitment that exists to strive for the promotion and protection of the rights of the child,

Reaffirming that the rights of children require special protection, and calling for continuous improvement of the situation of children without distinction, as well as for their development and education in conditions of peace and security,

---

* Adopted by the U.N. General Assembly at New York on May 25, 2000. Entered into force on February 12, 2002.

As of March 2013, the 151 parties to the protocol were: Afghanistan, Albania, Algeria, Andorra, Angola, Argentina, Armenia, Australia, Austria, Azerbaijan, Bahrain, Bangladesh, Belarus, Belgium, Belize, Benin, Bhutan, Bolivia, Bosnia and Herzegovina, Botswana, Brazil, Bulgaria, Burkina Faso, Burundi, Cambodia, Cameroon, Canada, Cape Verde, Chad, Chile, China, Colombia, Congo, Congo (Democratic Republic of), Costa Rica, Côte d'Ivoire, Croatia, Cuba, Cyprus, Czech Republic, Denmark, Djibouti, Dominica, Ecuador, Egypt, El Salvador, Eritrea, Finland, France, Gabon, Georgia, Germany, Greece, Grenada, Guatemala, Guyana, Holy See, Honduras, Hungary, Iceland, India, Indonesia, Iraq, Ireland, Israel, Italy, Jamaica, Japan, Jordan, Kazakhstan, Kenya, Korea (Republic of), Kuwait, Kyrgyzstan, Lao People's Democratic Republic, Latvia, Lesotho, Libyan Arab Jamahiriya, Liechtenstein, Lithuania, Luxembourg, Macedonia (the former Yugoslav Republic of), Madagascar, Malawi, Malaysia, Maldives, Mali, Malta, Mauritius, Mexico, Moldova, Monaco, Mongolia, Montenegro, Morocco, Mozambique, Namibia, Nepal, Netherlands, New Zealand, Nicaragua, Niger, Nigeria, Norway, Oman, Panama, Paraguay, Peru, Philippines, Poland, Portugal, Qatar, Romania, Russia, Rwanda, Saint Vincent and the Grenadines, San Marino, Saudi Arabia, Senegal, Serbia, Seychelles, Sierra Leone, Singapore, Slovakia, Slovenia, South Africa, Spain, Sri Lanka, Sudan, Swaziland, Sweden, Switzerland, Syrian Arab Republic, Tajikistan, Tanzania, Thailand, Timor-Leste, Togo, Tunisia, Turkey, Turkmenistan, Uganda, Ukraine, United Kingdom, United States of America, Uruguay, Uzbekistan, Vanuatu, Venezuela, Viet Nam, and Yemen. See the U.N. Web site at <http://treaties.un.org.>.

Disturbed by the harmful and widespread impact of armed conflict on children and the long-term consequences it has for durable peace, security and development,

Condemning the targeting of children in situations of armed conflict and direct attacks on objects protected under international law, including places that generally have a significant presence of children, such as schools and hospitals,

Noting the adoption of the Rome Statute of the International Criminal Court, in particular, the inclusion therein as a war crime, of conscripting or enlisting children under the age of 15 years or using them to participate actively in hostilities in both international and non-international armed conflicts,

Considering therefore that to strengthen further the implementation of rights recognized in the Convention on the Rights of the Child there is a need to increase the protection of children from involvement in armed conflict,

Noting that article 1 of the Convention on the Rights of the Child specifies that, for the purposes of that Convention, a child means every human being below the age of 18 years unless, under the law applicable to the child, majority is attained earlier,

Convinced that an optional protocol to the Convention that raises the age of possible recruitment of persons into armed forces and their participation in hostilities will contribute effectively to the implementation of the principle that the best interests of the child are to be a primary consideration in all actions concerning children, . . .

Welcoming the unanimous adoption, in June 1999, of International Labour Organization Convention No. 182 on the Prohibition and Immediate Action for the Elimination of the Worst Forms of Child Labour, which prohibits, inter alia, forced or compulsory recruitment of children for use in armed conflict,

Condemning with the gravest concern the recruitment, training and use within and across national borders of children in hostilities by armed groups distinct from the armed forces of a State, and recognizing the responsibility of those who recruit, train and use children in this regard,

Recalling the obligation of each party to an armed conflict to abide by the provisions of international humanitarian law,

Stressing that the present Protocol is without prejudice to the purposes and principles contained in the Charter of the United Nations, including Article 51, and relevant norms of humanitarian law,

Bearing in mind that conditions of peace and security based on full respect of the purposes and principles contained in the Charter and observance of applicable human rights instruments are indispensable for the full protection of children, in particular during armed conflicts and foreign occupation,

Recognizing the special needs of those children who are particularly vulnerable to recruitment or use in hostilities contrary to the present Protocol owing to their economic or social status or gender,

Mindful of the necessity of taking into consideration the economic, social and political root causes of the involvement of children in armed conflicts,

Optional Protocol to the Convention on the Rights of the Child

Convinced of the need to strengthen international cooperation in the implementation of the present Protocol, as well as the physical and psychosocial rehabilitation and social reintegration of children who are victims of armed conflict, . . .

Have agreed as follows:

Article 1

States Parties shall take all feasible measures to ensure that members of their armed forces who have not attained the age of 18 years do not take a direct part in hostilities.

Article 2

States Parties shall ensure that persons who have not attained the age of 18 years are not compulsorily recruited into their armed forces.

Article 3

1. States Parties shall raise the minimum age for the voluntary recruitment of persons into their national armed forces from that set out in article 38, paragraph 3, of the Convention on the Rights of the Child, taking account of the principles contained in that article and recognizing that under the Convention persons under the age of 18 years are entitled to special protection.

2. Each State Party shall deposit a binding declaration upon ratification of or accession to the present Protocol that sets forth the minimum age at which it will permit voluntary recruitment into its national armed forces and a description of the safeguards it has adopted to ensure that such recruitment is not forced or coerced.

3. States Parties that permit voluntary recruitment into their national armed forces under the age of 18 years shall maintain safeguards to ensure, as a minimum, that:

(a) Such recruitment is genuinely voluntary;

(b) Such recruitment is carried out with the informed consent of the person's parents or legal guardians;

(c) Such persons are fully informed of the duties involved in such military service;

(d) Such persons provide reliable proof of age prior to acceptance into national military service.

4. Each State Party may strengthen its declaration at any time by notification to that effect addressed to the Secretary-General of the United Nations, who shall inform all States Parties. Such notification shall take effect on the date on which it is received by the Secretary-General.

5. The requirement to raise the age in paragraph 1 of the present article does not apply to schools operated by or under the control of the armed forces of the States Parties, in keeping with articles 28 and 29 of the Convention on the Rights of the Child.

Article 4

1. Armed groups that are distinct from the armed forces of a State should not, under any circumstances, recruit or use in hostilities persons under the age of 18 years.

2. States Parties shall take all feasible measures to prevent such recruitment and use, including the adoption of legal measures necessary to prohibit and criminalize such practices.

3. The application of the present article shall not affect the legal status of any party to an armed conflict.

Article 5

Nothing in the present Protocol shall be construed as precluding provisions in the law of a State Party or in international instruments and international humanitarian law that are more conducive to the realization of the rights of the child.

Article 6

1. Each State Party shall take all necessary legal, administrative and other measures to ensure the effective implementation and enforcement of the provisions of the present Protocol within its jurisdiction.

2. States Parties undertake to make the principles and provisions of the present Protocol widely known and promoted by appropriate means, to adults and children alike.

3. States Parties shall take all feasible measures to ensure that persons within their jurisdiction recruited or used in hostilities contrary to the present Protocol are demobilized or otherwise released from service. States Parties shall, when necessary, accord to such persons all appropriate assistance for their physical and psychological recovery and their social reintegration.

Article 7

1. States Parties shall cooperate in the implementation of the present Protocol, including in the prevention of any activity contrary thereto and in the rehabilitation and social reintegration of persons who are victims of acts contrary thereto, including through technical cooperation and financial assistance. Such assistance and cooperation will be undertaken in consultation with the States Parties concerned and the relevant international organizations.

2. States Parties in a position to do so shall provide such assistance through existing multilateral, bilateral or other programmes or, inter alia, through a voluntary fund established in accordance with the rules of the General Assembly.

Article 8

1. Each State Party shall, within two years following the entry into force of the present Protocol for that State Party, submit a report to the Committee on the Rights of the Child providing comprehensive information on the measures it has taken to implement the provisions of the Protocol, including the measures taken to implement the provisions on participation and recruitment.

2. Following the submission of the comprehensive report, each State Party shall include in the reports it submits to the Committee on the Rights of the Child, in accordance with article 44 of the Convention, any further information with respect to the implementation of the Protocol. Other States Parties to the Protocol shall submit a report every five years.

3. The Committee on the Rights of the Child may request from States Parties further information relevant to the implementation of the present Protocol.

Article 9

1. The present Protocol is open for signature by any State that is a party to the Convention or has signed it. . . .

Article 11

1. Any State Party may denounce the present Protocol at any time by written notification to the Secretary-General of the United Nations, who shall thereafter inform the other States Parties to the Convention and all States that have signed the Convention. The denunciation shall take effect one year after the date of receipt of the notification by the Secretary-General. If, however, on the expiry of that year the denouncing State Party is engaged in armed conflict, the denunciation shall not take effect before the end of the armed conflict. . . .

Article 12

1. Any State Party may propose an amendment and file it with the Secretary-General of the United Nations. The Secretary-General shall thereupon communicate the proposed amendment to States Parties with a request that they indicate whether they favour a conference of States Parties for the purpose of considering and voting upon the proposals. In the event that, within four months from the date of such communication, at least one third of the States Parties favour such a conference, the Secretary-General shall convene the conference under the auspices of the United Nations. Any amendment adopted by a majority of States Parties present and voting at the conference shall be submitted to the General Assembly of the United Nations for approval.

2. An amendment adopted in accordance with paragraph 1 of the present article shall enter into force when it has been approved by the General Assembly and accepted by a two-thirds majority of States Parties.

3. When an amendment enters into force, it shall be binding on those States Parties that have accepted it, other States Parties still being bound by the provisions of the present Protocol and any earlier amendments they have accepted. . . .

OPTIONAL PROTOCOL TO THE CONVENTION ON THE RIGHTS OF THE CHILD ON THE SALE OF CHILDREN, CHILD PROSTITUTION AND CHILD PORNOGRAPHY

Jan. 18, 2002, 2171 U.N.T.S. 227*

The States Parties to the present Protocol,

Considering that, in order further to achieve the purposes of the Convention on the Rights of the Child and the implementation of its provisions, especially articles 1, 11, 21, 32, 33, 34, 35 and 36, it would be appropriate to extend the measures that States Parties should undertake in order to guarantee the protection of the child from the sale of children, child prostitution and child pornography,

Considering also that the Convention on the Rights of the Child recognizes the right of the child to be protected from economic exploitation and from performing any work that is likely to be hazardous or to interfere with

---

* Adopted by the U.N. General Assembly at New York on May 25, 2000. Entered into force on January 18, 2002.

As of March 2013, the 163 parties to the protocol were: Afghanistan, Albania, Algeria, Andorra, Angola, Antigua and Barbuda, Argentina, Armenia, Australia, Austria, Azerbaijan, Bahrain, Bangladesh, Belarus, Belgium, Belize, Benin, Bhutan, Bolivia, Bosnia and Herzegovina, Botswana, Brazil, Brunei Darussalam, Bulgaria, Burkina Faso, Burundi, Cambodia, Canada, Cape Verde, Central African Republic, Chad, Chile, China, Colombia, Comoros, Congo, Congo (Democratic Republic of), Costa Rica, Côte d'Ivoire, Croatia, Cuba, Cyprus, Denmark, Djibouti, Dominica, Dominican Republic, Ecuador, Egypt, El Salvador, Equatorial Guinea, Eritrea, Estonia, Finland, France, Gabon, Gambia, Georgia, Germany, Greece, Grenada, Guatemala, Guinea, Guinea-Bissau, Guyana, Holy See, Honduras, Hungary, Iceland, India, Indonesia, Iran, Iraq, Israel, Italy, Jamaica, Japan, Jordan, Kazakhstan, Korea (Republic of), Kuwait, Kyrgyzstan, Lao People's Democratic Republic, Latvia, Lebanon, Lesotho, Libyan Arab Jamahiriya, Liechtenstein, Lithuania, Luxembourg, Macedonia (the former Yugoslav Republic of), Madagascar, Malawi, Malaysia, Maldives, Mali, Malta, Mauritania, Mauritius, Mexico, Micronesia, Moldova, Monaco, Mongolia, Montenegro, Morocco, Mozambique, Myanmar, Namibia, Nepal, Netherlands, New Zealand, Nicaragua, Niger, Nigeria, Norway, Oman, Pakistan, Panama, Paraguay, Peru, Philippines, Poland, Portugal, Qatar, Romania, Rwanda, San Marino, Saudi Arabia, Senegal, Serbia, Seychelles, Sierra Leone, Slovakia, Slovenia, South Africa, Spain, Sri Lanka, St. Vincent and the Grenadines, Sudan, Suriname, Swaziland, Sweden, Switzerland, Syrian Arab Republic, Tajikistan, Thailand, Timor-Leste, Togo, Tunisia, Turkey, Turkmenistan, Uganda, Ukraine, United Kingdom of Great Britain and Northern Ireland, United States of America, Uruguay, Uzbekistan, Vanuatu, Venezuela, Vietnam, Yemen, and Zimbabwe. See the U.N. Web site at <http://treaties.un.org>.

the child's education, or to be harmful to the child's health or physical, mental, spiritual, moral or social development,

Gravely concerned at the significant and increasing international traffic in children for the purpose of the sale of children, child prostitution and child pornography,

Deeply concerned at the widespread and continuing practice of sex tourism, to which children are especially vulnerable, as it directly promotes the sale of children, child prostitution and child pornography,

Recognizing that a number of particularly vulnerable groups, including girl children, are at greater risk of sexual exploitation and that girl children are disproportionately represented among the sexually exploited,

Concerned about the growing availability of child pornography on the Internet and other evolving technologies, and recalling the International Conference on Combating Child Pornography on the Internet, held in Vienna in 1999, in particular its conclusion calling for the worldwide criminalization of the production, distribution, exportation, transmission, importation, intentional possession and advertising of child pornography, and stressing the importance of closer cooperation and partnership between Governments and the Internet industry,

Believing that the elimination of the sale of children, child prostitution and child pornography will be facilitated by adopting a holistic approach, addressing the contributing factors, including underdevelopment, poverty, economic disparities, inequitable socio-economic structure, dysfunctioning families, lack of education, urban-rural migration, gender discrimination, irresponsible adult sexual behaviour, harmful traditional practices, armed conflicts and trafficking in children,

Believing that efforts to raise public awareness are needed to reduce consumer demand for the sale of children, child prostitution and child pornography, and believing further in the importance of strengthening global partnership among all actors and of improving law enforcement at the national level,

Noting the provisions of international legal instruments relevant to the protection of children, including the Hague Convention on Protection of Children and Cooperation in Respect of Intercountry Adoption, the Hague Convention on the Civil Aspects of International Child Abduction, the Hague Convention on Jurisdiction, Applicable Law, Recognition, Enforcement and Cooperation in Respect of Parental Responsibility and Measures for the Protection of Children, and International Labour Organization Convention No. 182 on the Prohibition and Immediate Action for the Elimination of the Worst Forms of Child Labour,

Encouraged by the overwhelming support for the Convention on the Rights of the Child, demonstrating the widespread commitment that exists for the promotion and protection of the rights of the child, . . .

Taking due account of the importance of the traditions and cultural values of each people for the protection and harmonious development of the child,

Have agreed as follows:

Optional Protocol to the Convention on the Rights of the Child

Article 1

States Parties shall prohibit the sale of children, child prostitution and child pornography as provided for by the present Protocol.

Article 2

For the purposes of the present Protocol:

(a) Sale of children means any act or transaction whereby a child is transferred by any person or group of persons to another for remuneration or any other consideration;

(b) Child prostitution means the use of a child in sexual activities for remuneration or any other form of consideration;

(c) Child pornography means any representation, by whatever means, of a child engaged in real or simulated explicit sexual activities or any representation of the sexual parts of a child for primarily sexual purposes.

Article 3

1. Each State Party shall ensure that, as a minimum, the following acts and activities are fully covered under its criminal or penal law, whether such offences are committed domestically or transnationally or on an individual or organized basis:

(a) In the context of sale of children as defined in article 2:

(i) Offering, delivering or accepting, by whatever means, a child for the purpose of:

a. Sexual exploitation of the child;

b. Transfer of organs of the child for profit;

c. Engagement of the child in forced labour;

(ii) Improperly inducing consent, as an intermediary, for the adoption of a child in violation of applicable international legal instruments on adoption;

(b) Offering, obtaining, procuring or providing a child for child prostitution, as defined in article 2;

(c) Producing, distributing, disseminating, importing, exporting, offering, selling or possessing for the above purposes child pornography as defined in article 2.

2. Subject to the provisions of the national law of a State Party, the same shall apply to an attempt to commit any of the said acts and to complicity or participation in any of the said acts.

3. Each State Party shall make such offences punishable by appropriate penalties that take into account their grave nature.

4. Subject to the provisions of its national law, each State Party shall take measures, where appropriate, to establish the liability of legal persons for offences established in paragraph 1 of the present article. Subject to the legal principles of the State Party, such liability of legal persons may be criminal, civil or administrative.

5. States Parties shall take all appropriate legal and administrative measures to ensure that all persons involved in the adoption of a child act in conformity with applicable international legal instruments.

Article 4

1. Each State Party shall take such measures as may be necessary to establish its jurisdiction over the offences referred to in article 3, paragraph 1, when the offences are committed in its territory or on board a ship or aircraft registered in that State.

2. Each State Party may take such measures as may be necessary to establish its jurisdiction over the offences referred to in article 3, paragraph 1, in the following cases:

(a) When the alleged offender is a national of that State or a person who has his habitual residence in its territory;

(b) When the victim is a national of that State.

3. Each State Party shall also take such measures as may be necessary to establish its jurisdiction over the aforementioned offences when the alleged offender is present in its territory and it does not extradite him or her to another State Party on the ground that the offence has been committed by one of its nationals.

4. The present Protocol does not exclude any criminal jurisdiction exercised in accordance with internal law.

Article 5

1. The offences referred to in article 3, paragraph 1, shall be deemed to be included as extraditable offences in any extradition treaty existing between States Parties and shall be included as extraditable offences in every extradition treaty subsequently concluded between them, in accordance with the conditions set forth in such treaties.

2. If a State Party that makes extradition conditional on the existence of a treaty receives a request for extradition from another State Party with which it has no extradition treaty, it may consider the present Protocol to be a legal basis for extradition in respect of such offences. Extradition shall be subject to the conditions provided by the law of the requested State.

3. States Parties that do not make extradition conditional on the existence of a treaty shall recognize such offences as extraditable offences between themselves subject to the conditions provided by the law of the requested State.

4. Such offences shall be treated, for the purpose of extradition between States Parties, as if they had been committed not only in the place in which they occurred but also in the territories of the States required to establish their jurisdiction in accordance with article 4.

5. If an extradition request is made with respect to an offence described in article 3, paragraph 1, and the requested State Party does not or will not extradite on the basis of the nationality of the offender, that State shall take

suitable measures to submit the case to its competent authorities for the purpose of prosecution.

Article 6

1. States Parties shall afford one another the greatest measure of assistance in connection with investigations or criminal or extradition proceedings brought in respect of the offences set forth in article 3, paragraph 1, including assistance in obtaining evidence at their disposal necessary for the proceedings.

2. States Parties shall carry out their obligations under paragraph 1 of the present article in conformity with any treaties or other arrangements on mutual legal assistance that may exist between them. In the absence of such treaties or arrangements, States Parties shall afford one another assistance in accordance with their domestic law.

Article 7

States Parties shall, subject to the provisions of their national law:

(a) Take measures to provide for the seizure and confiscation, as appropriate, of:

(i) Goods, such as materials, assets and other instrumentalities used to commit or facilitate offences under the present protocol;

(ii) Proceeds derived from such offences;

(b) Execute requests from another State Party for seizure or confiscation of goods or proceeds referred to in subparagraph (a) (i) and (ii);

(c) Take measures aimed at closing, on a temporary or definitive basis, premises used to commit such offences.

Article 8

1. States Parties shall adopt appropriate measures to protect the rights and interests of child victims of the practices prohibited under the present Protocol at all stages of the criminal justice process, in particular by:

(a) Recognizing the vulnerability of child victims and adapting procedures to recognize their special needs, including their special needs as witnesses;

(b) Informing child victims of their rights, their role and the scope, timing and progress of the proceedings and of the disposition of their cases;

(c) Allowing the views, needs and concerns of child victims to be presented and considered in proceedings where their personal interests are affected, in a manner consistent with the procedural rules of national law;

(d) Providing appropriate support services to child victims throughout the legal process;

(e) Protecting, as appropriate, the privacy and identity of child victims and taking measures in accordance with national law to avoid the inappropriate dissemination of information that could lead to the identification of child victims;

(f) Providing, in appropriate cases, for the safety of child victims, as well as that of their families and witnesses on their behalf, from intimidation and retaliation;

(g) Avoiding unnecessary delay in the disposition of cases and the execution of orders or decrees granting compensation to child victims.

2. States Parties shall ensure that uncertainty as to the actual age of the victim shall not prevent the initiation of criminal investigations, including investigations aimed at establishing the age of the victim.

3. States Parties shall ensure that, in the treatment by the criminal justice system of children who are victims of the offences described in the present Protocol, the best interest of the child shall be a primary consideration.

4. States Parties shall take measures to ensure appropriate training, in particular legal and psychological training, for the persons who work with victims of the offences prohibited under the present Protocol.

5. States Parties shall, in appropriate cases, adopt measures in order to protect the safety and integrity of those persons and/or organizations involved in the prevention and/or protection and rehabilitation of victims of such offences.

6. Nothing in the present article shall be construed to be prejudicial to or inconsistent with the rights of the accused to a fair and impartial trial.

Article 9

1. States Parties shall adopt or strengthen, implement and disseminate laws, administrative measures, social policies and programmes to prevent the offences referred to in the present Protocol. Particular attention shall be given to protect children who are especially vulnerable to such practices.

2. States Parties shall promote awareness in the public at large, including children, through information by all appropriate means, education and training, about the preventive measures and harmful effects of the offences referred to in the present Protocol. In fulfilling their obligations under this article, States Parties shall encourage the participation of the community and, in particular, children and child victims, in such information and education and training programmes, including at the international level.

3. States Parties shall take all feasible measures with the aim of ensuring all appropriate assistance to victims of such offences, including their full social reintegration and their full physical and psychological recovery.

4. States Parties shall ensure that all child victims of the offences described in the present Protocol have access to adequate procedures to seek,

without discrimination, compensation for damages from those legally responsible.

5. States Parties shall take appropriate measures aimed at effectively prohibiting the production and dissemination of material advertising the offences described in the present Protocol.

Article 10

1. States Parties shall take all necessary steps to strengthen international cooperation by multilateral, regional and bilateral arrangements for the prevention, detection, investigation, prosecution and punishment of those responsible for acts involving the sale of children, child prostitution, child pornography and child sex tourism. States Parties shall also promote international cooperation and coordination between their authorities, national and international non-governmental organizations and international organizations.

2. States Parties shall promote international cooperation to assist child victims in their physical and psychological recovery, social reintegration and repatriation.

3. States Parties shall promote the strengthening of international cooperation in order to address the root causes, such as poverty and underdevelopment, contributing to the vulnerability of children to the sale of children, child prostitution, child pornography and child sex tourism.

4. States Parties in a position to do so shall provide financial, technical or other assistance through existing multilateral, regional, bilateral or other programmes.

Article 11

Nothing in the present Protocol shall affect any provisions that are more conducive to the realization of the rights of the child and that may be contained in:
  (a) The law of a State Party;
  (b) International law in force for that State.

Article 12

1. Each State Party shall, within two years following the entry into force of the present Protocol for that State Party, submit a report to the Committee on the Rights of the Child providing comprehensive information on the measures it has taken to implement the provisions of the Protocol.

2. Following the submission of the comprehensive report, each State Party shall include in the reports they submit to the Committee on the Rights of the Child, in accordance with article 44 of the Convention, any further information with respect to the implementation of the present Protocol. Other States Parties to the Protocol shall submit a report every five years.

3. The Committee on the Rights of the Child may request from States Parties further information relevant to the implementation of the present Protocol.

Article 13 . . .

2. The present Protocol is subject to ratification and is open to accession by any State that is a party to the Convention or has signed it. Instruments of ratification or accession shall be deposited with the Secretary-General of the United Nations. . . .

Article 15

1. Any State Party may denounce the present Protocol at any time by written notification to the Secretary-General of the United Nations, who shall thereafter inform the other States Parties to the Convention and all States that have signed the Convention. The denunciation shall take effect one year after the date of receipt of the notification by the Secretary-General. . . .

Article 16

1. Any State Party may propose an amendment and file it with the Secretary-General of the United Nations. The Secretary-General shall thereupon communicate the proposed amendment to States Parties with a request that they indicate whether they favour a conference of States Parties for the purpose of considering and voting upon the proposals. In the event that, within four months from the date of such communication, at least one third of the States Parties favour such a conference, the Secretary-General shall convene the conference under the auspices of the United Nations. Any amendment adopted by a majority of States Parties present and voting at the conference shall be submitted to the General Assembly of the United Nations for approval.

2. An amendment adopted in accordance with paragraph 1 of the present article shall enter into force when it has been approved by the General Assembly and accepted by a two-thirds majority of States Parties.

3. When an amendment enters into force, it shall be binding on those States Parties that have accepted it, other States Parties still being bound by the provisions of the present Protocol and any earlier amendments they have accepted. . . .

EUROPEAN CONVENTION
FOR THE PROTECTION OF HUMAN RIGHTS
AND FUNDAMENTAL FREEDOMS

November 4, 1950, 312 U.N.T.S. 221, E.T.S. 5, as amended
by Protocol No. 3, E.T.S. 45, Protocol No. 5, E.T.S. 55, and
Protocol No. 8, E.T.S. 118, Protocol No. 11, E.T.S.155, and
Protocol No. 14, C.E.T.S. 194*

The Governments signatory hereto, being members of the Council of Europe,

Considering the Universal Declaration of Human Rights proclaimed by the General Assembly of the United Nations on 10th December 1948;

Considering that this Declaration aims at securing the universal and effective recognition and observance of the Rights therein declared;

Considering that the aim of the Council of Europe is the achievement of greater unity between its members and that one of the methods by which that aim is to be pursued is the maintenance and further realisation of human rights and fundamental freedoms;

Reaffirming their profound belief in those fundamental freedoms which are the foundation of justice and peace in the world and are best maintained on the one hand by an effective political democracy and on the other by a common understanding and observance of the human rights upon which they depend;

---

* The European Convention was signed at Rome on November 4, 1950. Entered into force on September 3, 1953. The convention was amended by Protocols Nos. 3 (entry into force September 1970), No. 5 (entry into force December 1971), No. 8 (entry into force January 1990), No. 11 (entry into force November 1998), and most recently No. 14 (entry into force June 2010). The convention, as amended, is provided here.

The 47 parties to the convention are: Albania, Andorra, Armenia, Austria, Azerbaijan, Belgium, Bosnia and Herzegovina, Bulgaria, Croatia, Cyprus, Czech Republic, Denmark, Estonia, Finland, France, Georgia, Germany, Greece, Hungary, Iceland, Ireland, Italy, Latvia, Liechtenstein, Lithuania, Luxembourg, Macedonia (the former Yugoslav Republic of), Malta, Moldova, Monaco, Montenegro, Netherlands, Norway, Poland, Portugal, Romania, Russia, San Marino, Serbia, Slovakia, Slovenia, Spain, Sweden, Switzerland. See the Council of Europe Web site at <http://conventions.coe.int>.

Being resolved, as the governments of European countries which are like-minded and have a common heritage of political traditions, ideals, freedom and the rule of law, to take the first steps for the collective enforcement of certain of the rights stated in the Universal Declaration,

Have agreed as follows:

Article 1. Obligation to Respect Human Rights

The High Contracting Parties shall secure to everyone within their jurisdiction the rights and freedoms defined in Section I of this Convention.

Section I. Rights and Freedoms

Article 2. Right to Life

1. Everyone's right to life shall be protected by law. No one shall be deprived of his life intentionally save in the execution of a sentence of a court following his conviction of a crime for which this penalty is provided by law.

2. Deprivation of life shall not be regarded as inflicted in contravention of this article when it results from the use of force which is no more than absolutely necessary:

    a. in defence of any person from unlawful violence;

    b. in order to effect a lawful arrest or to prevent the escape of a person lawfully detained;

    c. in action lawfully taken for the purpose of quelling a riot or insurrection.

Article 3. Prohibition of Torture

No one shall be subjected to torture or to inhuman or degrading treatment or punishment.

Article 4. Prohibition of Slavery and Forced Labour

1. No one shall be held in slavery or servitude.

2. No one shall be required to perform forced or compulsory labour.

3. For the purpose of this article the term "forced or compulsory labour" shall not include:

    a. any work required to be done in the ordinary course of detention imposed according to the provisions of Article 5 of this Convention or during conditional release from such detention;

    b. any service of a military character or, in case of conscientious objectors in countries where they are recognised, service exacted instead of compulsory military service;

    c. any service exacted in case of an emergency or calamity threatening the life or well-being of the community;

    d. any work or service which forms part of normal civic obligations.

Article 5.   Right to Liberty and Security

1. Everyone has the right to liberty and security of person. No one shall be deprived of his liberty save in the following cases and in accordance with a procedure prescribed by law:

a. the lawful detention of a person after conviction by a competent court;

b. the lawful arrest or detention of a person for noncompliance with the lawful order of a court or in order to secure the fulfilment of any obligation prescribed by law;

c. the lawful arrest or detention of a person effected for the purpose of bringing him before the competent legal authority on reasonable suspicion of having committed an offence or when it is reasonably considered necessary to prevent his committing an offence or fleeing after having done so;

d. the detention of a minor by lawful order for the purpose of educational supervision or his lawful detention for the purpose of bringing him before the competent legal authority;

e. the lawful detention of persons for the prevention of the spreading of infectious diseases, of persons of unsound mind, alcoholics or drug addicts or vagrants;

f. the lawful arrest or detention of a person to prevent his effecting an unauthorised entry into the country or of a person against whom action is being taken with a view to deportation or extradition.

2. Everyone who is arrested shall be informed promptly, in a language which he understands, of the reasons for his arrest and of any charge against him.

3. Everyone arrested or detained in accordance with the provisions of paragraph l.c of this article shall be brought promptly before a judge or other officer authorised by law to exercise judicial power and shall be entitled to trial within a reasonable time or to release pending trial. Release may be conditioned by guarantees to appear for trial.

4. Everyone who is deprived of his liberty by arrest or detention shall be entitled to take proceedings by which the lawfulness of his detention shall be decided speedily by a court and his release ordered if the detention is not lawful.

5. Everyone who has been the victim of arrest or detention in contravention of the provisions of this article shall have an enforceable right to compensation.

Article 6.   Right to a Fair Trial

1. In the determination of his civil rights and obligations or of any criminal charge against him, everyone is entitled to a fair and public hearing within a reasonable time by an independent and impartial tribunal established by law. Judgment shall be pronounced publicly but the press and public may be excluded from all or part of the trial in the interests of morals,

public order or national security in a democratic society, where the interests of juveniles or the protection of the private life of the parties so require, or to the extent strictly necessary in the opinion of the court in special circumstances where publicity would prejudice the interests of justice.

2. Everyone charged with a criminal offence shall be presumed innocent until proved guilty according to law.

3. Everyone charged with a criminal offence has the following minimum rights:

a. to be informed promptly, in a language which he understands and in detail, of the nature and cause of the accusation against him;

b. to have adequate time and facilities for the preparation of his defence;

c. to defend himself in person or through legal assistance of his own choosing or, if he has not sufficient means to pay for legal assistance, to be given it free when the interests of justice so require;

d. to examine or have examined witnesses against him and to obtain the attendance and examination of witnesses on his behalf under the same conditions as witnesses against him;

e. to have the free assistance of an interpreter if he cannot understand or speak the language used in court.

Article 7. No Punishment Without Law

1. No one shall be held guilty of any criminal offence on account of any act or omission which did not constitute a criminal offence under national or international law at the time when it was committed. Nor shall a heavier penalty be imposed than the one that was applicable at the time the criminal offence was committed.

2. This article shall not prejudice the trial and punishment of any person for any act or omission which, at the time when it was committed, was criminal according to the general principles of law recognised by civilised nations.

Article 8. Right to Respect for Private and Family Life

1. Everyone has the right to respect for his private and family life, his home and his correspondence.

2. There shall be no interference by a public authority with the exercise of this right except such as is in accordance with the law and is necessary in a democratic society in the interests of national security, public safety or the economic well-being of the country, for the prevention of disorder or crime, for the protection of health or morals, or for the protection of the rights and freedoms of others.

Article 9. Freedom of Thought, Conscience and Religion

1. Everyone has the right to freedom of thought, conscience and religion; this right includes freedom to change his religion or belief and freedom, either alone or in community with others and in public or private, to manifest his religion or belief, in worship, teaching, practice and observance.

2. Freedom to manifest one's religion or beliefs shall be subject only to such limitations as are prescribed by law and are necessary in a democratic society in the interests of public safety, for the protection of public order, health or morals, or for the protection of the rights and freedoms of others.

Article 10. Freedom of Expression

1. Everyone has the right to freedom of expression. This right shall include freedom to hold opinions and to receive and impart information and ideas without interference by public authority and regardless of frontiers. This article shall not prevent States from requiring the licensing of broadcasting, television or cinema enterprises.

2. The exercise of these freedoms, since it carries with it duties and responsibilities, may be subject to such formalities, conditions, restrictions or penalties as are prescribed by law and are necessary in a democratic society, in the interests of national security, territorial integrity or public safety, for the prevention of disorder or crime, for the protection of health or morals, for the protection of the reputation or rights of others, for preventing the disclosure of information received in confidence, or for maintaining the authority and impartiality of the judiciary.

Article 11. Freedom of Assembly and Association

1. Everyone has the right to freedom of peaceful assembly and to freedom of association with others, including the right to form and to join trade unions for the protection of his interests.

2. No restrictions shall be placed on the exercise of these rights other than such as are prescribed by law and are necessary in a democratic society in the interests of national security or public safety, for the prevention of disorder or crime, for the protection of health or morals or for the protection of the rights and freedoms of others. This article shall not prevent the imposition of lawful restrictions on the exercise of these rights by members of the armed forces, of the police or of the administration of the State.

Article 12. Right to Marry

Men and women of marriageable age have the right to marry and to found a family, according to the national laws governing the exercise of this right.

Article 13. Right to an Effective Remedy

Everyone whose rights and freedoms as set forth in this Convention are violated shall have an effective remedy before a national authority notwithstanding that the violation has been committed by persons acting in an official capacity.

Article 14. Prohibition of Discrimination

The enjoyment of the rights and freedoms set forth in this Convention shall be secured without discrimination on any ground such as sex, race, colour, language, religion, political or other opinion, national or social origin, association with a national minority, property, birth or other status.

Article 15. Derogation in Time of Emergency

1. In time of war or other public emergency threatening the life of the nation any High Contracting Party may take measures derogating from its obligations under this Convention to the extent strictly required by the exigencies of the situation, provided that such measures are not inconsistent with its other obligations under international law.

2. No derogation from Article 2, except in respect of deaths resulting from lawful acts of war, or from Articles 3, 4 (paragraph 1) and 7 shall be made under this provision.

3. Any High Contracting Party availing itself of this right of derogation shall keep the Secretary General of the Council of Europe fully informed of the measures which it has taken and the reasons therefor. It shall also inform the Secretary General of the Council of Europe when such measures have ceased to operate and the provisions of the Convention are again being fully executed.

Article 16. Restrictions on Political Activity of Aliens

Nothing in Articles 10, 11 and 14 shall be regarded as preventing the High Contracting Parties from imposing restrictions on the political activity of aliens.

Article 17. Prohibition of Abuse of Rights

Nothing in this Convention may be interpreted as implying for any State, group or person any right to engage in any activity or perform any act aimed at the destruction of any of the rights and freedoms set forth herein or at their limitation to a greater extent than is provided for in the Convention.

Article 18. Limitation on Use of Restrictions on Rights

The restrictions permitted under this Convention to the said rights and freedoms shall not be applied for any purpose other than those for which they have been prescribed.

Section II.   European Court of Human Rights

Article 19.   Establishment of the Court

To ensure the observance of the engagements undertaken by the High Contracting Parties in the Convention and the protocols thereto, there shall be set up a European Court of Human Rights, hereinafter referred to as "the Court". It shall function on a permanent basis.

Article 20.   Number of Judges

The Court shall consist of a number of judges equal to that of the High Contracting Parties.

Article 21.   Criteria for Office

1. The judges shall be of high moral character and must either possess the qualifications required for appointment to high judicial office or be jurisconsults of recognised competence.

2. The judges shall sit on the Court in their individual capacity.

3. During their term of office the judges shall not engage in any activity which is incompatible with their independence, impartiality or with the demands of a full-time office; all questions arising from the application of this paragraph shall be decided by the Court.

Article 22.   Election of Judges

The judges shall be elected by the Parliamentary Assembly with respect to each High Contracting Party by a majority of votes cast from a list of three candidates nominated by the High Contracting Party.

Article 23.   Terms of Office and Dismissal

1. The judges shall be elected for a period of nine years. They may not be re-elected.

2. The terms of office of judges shall expire when they reach the age of 70.

3. The judges shall hold office until replaced. They shall, however, continue to deal with such cases as they already have under consideration.

4. No judge may be dismissed from office unless the other judges decide by a majority of two-thirds that that judge has ceased to fulfil the required conditions.

Article 24.   Registry and Rapporteurs

1. The Court shall have a registry, the functions and organisation of which shall be laid down in the rules of the Court.

2. When sitting in a single-judge formation, the Court shall be assisted by rapporteurs who shall function under the authority of the President of the Court. They shall form part of the Court's registry.

Article 25.   Plenary Court

The plenary Court shall

a. elect its President and one or two Vice-Presidents for a period of three years; they may be re-elected;

b. set up Chambers, constituted for a fixed period of time;

c. elect the Presidents of the Chambers of the Court; they may be re-elected;

d. adopt the rules of the Court;

e. elect the Registrar and one or more Deputy Registrars;

f. make any request under Article 26, paragraph 2.

Article 26.   Single-judge formation, committees, Chambers and Grand Chamber

1. To consider cases brought before it, the Court shall sit in a single-judge formation, in committees of three judges, in Chambers of seven judges and in a Grand Chamber of seventeen judges. The Court's Chambers shall set up committees for a fixed period of time.

2. At the request of the plenary Court, the Committee of Ministers may, by a unanimous decision and for a fixed period, reduce to five the number of judges of the Chambers.

3. When sitting as a single judge, a judge shall not examine any application against the High Contracting Party in respect of which that judge has been elected.

4. There shall sit as an *ex officio member* of the Chamber and the Grand Chamber the judge elected in respect of the High Contracting Party concerned. If there is none or if that judge is unable to sit, a person chosen by the President of the Court from a list submitted in advance by that Party shall sit in the capacity of judge.

5. The Grand Chamber shall also include the President of the Court, the Vice-Presidents, the Presidents of the Chambers and other judges chosen in accordance with the rules of the Court. When a case is referred to the Grand Chamber under Article 43, no judge from the Chamber which rendered the judgment shall sit in the Grand Chamber, with the exception of the President of the Chamber and the judge who sat in respect of the High Contracting Party concerned.

Article 27.   Competence of single judges

1. A single judge may declare inadmissible or strike out of the Court's list of cases an application submitted under Article 34, where such a decision can be taken without further examination.

2. The decision shall be final.

3. If the single judge does not declare an application inadmissible or strike it out, that judge shall forward it to a committee or to a Chamber for further examination.

Article 28.   Competence of Committees

1. In respect of an application submitted under Article 34, a committee may, by a unanimous vote,

    a. declare it inadmissible or strike it out of its list of cases, where such decision can be taken without further examination; or

    b. declare it admissible and render at the same time a judgment on the merits, if the underlying question in the case, concerning the interpretation or the application of the Convention or the Protocols thereto, is already the subject of well-established case-law of the Court.

2. Decisions and judgments under paragraph 1 shall be final.

3. If the judge elected in respect of the High Contracting Party concerned is not a member of the committee, the committee may at any stage of the proceedings invite that judge to take the place of one of the members of the committee, having regard to all relevant factors, including whether that Party has contested the application of the procedure under paragraph 1.b.

Article 29.   Decisions by Chambers on Admissibility and Merits

1. If no decision is taken under Article 27 or 28, or no judgment rendered under Article 28, a Chamber shall decide on the admissibility and merits of individual applications submitted under Article 34. The decision on admissibility may be taken separately.

2. A Chamber shall decide on the admissibility and merits of inter-State applications submitted under Article 33. The decision on admissibility shall be taken separately unless the Court, in exceptional cases, decides otherwise.

Article 30.   Relinquishment of Jurisdiction to the Grand Chamber

Where a case pending before a Chamber raises a serious question affecting the interpretation of the Convention or the protocols thereto or where the resolution of a question before it might have a result inconsistent with a judgment previously delivered by the Court, the Chamber may, at any time before it has rendered its judgment, relinquish jurisdiction in favour of the Grand Chamber, unless one of the parties to the case objects.

Article 31.   Powers of the Grand Chamber

The Grand Chamber shall:

    a. determine applications submitted either under Article 33 or Article 34 when a Chamber has relinquished jurisdiction under Article 30 or when the case has been referred to it under Article 43;

    b. decide on issues referred to the Court by the Committee of Ministers in accordance with Article 46, paragraph 4; and

    c. consider requests for advisory opinions submitted under Article 47.

Article 32. *Jurisdiction of the Court*

1. The jurisdiction of the Court shall extend to all matters concerning the interpretation and application of the Convention and the protocols thereto which are referred to it as provided in Articles 33, 34, 46 and 47.

2. In the event of dispute as to whether the Court has jurisdiction, the Court shall decide.

Article 33. *Inter-State Cases*

Any High Contracting Party may refer to the Court any alleged breach of the provisions of the Convention and the protocols thereto by another High Contracting Party.

Article 34. *Individual Applications*

The Court may receive applications from any person, non-governmental organisation or group of individuals claiming to be the victim of a violation by one of the High Contracting Parties of the rights set forth in the Convention or the protocols thereto. The High Contracting Parties undertake not to hinder in any way the effective exercise of this right.

Article 35. *Admissibility Criteria*

1. The Court may only deal with the matter after all domestic remedies have been exhausted, according to the generally recognised rules of international law, and within a period of six months from the date on which the final decision was taken.

2. The Court shall not deal with any application submitted under Article 34 that

a. is anonymous; or

b. is substantially the same as a matter that has already been examined by the Court or has already been submitted to another procedure of international investigation or settlement and contains no relevant new information.

3. The Court shall declare inadmissible any individual application submitted under Article 34 if it considers that :

a. the application is incompatible with the provisions of the Convention or the Protocols thereto, manifestly ill-founded, or an abuse of the right of individual application; or

b. the applicant has not suffered a significant disadvantage, unless respect for human rights as defined in the Convention and the Protocols thereto requires an examination of the application on the merits and provided that no case may be rejected on this ground which has not been duly considered by a domestic tribunal.

4. The Court shall reject any application which it considers inadmissible under this Article. It may do so at any stage of the proceedings.

Article 36.   Third Party Intervention

1. In all cases before a Chamber or the Grand Chamber, a High Contracting Party one of whose nationals is an applicant shall have the right to submit written comments and to take part in hearings.

2. The President of the Court may, in the interest of the proper administration of justice, invite any High Contracting Party which is not a party to the proceedings or any person concerned who is not the applicant to submit written comments or take part in hearings.

3. In all cases before a Chamber or the Grand Chamber, the Council of Europe Commissioner for Human Rights may submit written comments and take part in hearings.

Article 37.   Striking Out Applications

1. The Court may at any stage of the proceedings decide to strike an application out of its list of cases where the circumstances lead to the conclusion that
    a. the applicant does not intend to pursue his application; or
    b. the matter has been resolved; or
    c. for any other reason established by the Court, it is no longer justified to continue the examination of the application.
However, the Court shall continue the examination of the application if respect for human rights as defined in the Convention and the protocols thereto so requires.

2. The Court may decide to restore an application to its list of cases if it considers that the circumstances justify such a course.

Article 38.   Examination of the Case

The Court shall examine the case together with the representatives of the parties and, if need be, undertake an investigation, for the effective conduct of which the High Contracting Parties concerned shall furnish all necessary facilities.

Article 39.   Friendly Settlements

1. At any stage of the proceedings, the Court may place itself at the disposal of the parties concerned with a view to securing a friendly settlement of the matter on the basis of respect for human rights as defined in the Convention and the Protocols thereto.

2. Proceedings conducted under paragraph 1 shall be confidential.

3. If a friendly settlement is effected, the Court shall strike the case out of its list by means of a decision which shall be confined to a brief statement of the facts and of the solution reached.

4. This decision shall be transmitted to the Committee of Ministers, which shall supervise the execution of the terms of the friendly settlement as set out in the decision.

Article 40. Public Hearings and Access to Documents

1. Hearings shall be public unless the Court in exceptional circumstances decides otherwise.

2. Documents deposited with the Registrar shall be accessible to the public unless the President of the Court decides otherwise.

Article 41. Just Satisfaction

If the Court finds that there has been a violation of the Convention or the protocols thereto, and if the internal law of the High Contracting Party concerned allows only partial reparation to be made, the Court shall, if necessary, afford just satisfaction to the injured party.

Article 42. Judgments of Chambers

Judgments of Chambers shall become final in accordance with the provisions of Article 44, paragraph 2.

Article 43. Referral to the Grand Chamber

1. Within a period of three months from the date of the judgment of the Chamber, any party to the case may, in exceptional cases, request that the case be referred to the Grand Chamber.

2. A panel of five judges of the Grand Chamber shall accept the request if the case raises a serious question affecting the interpretation or application of the Convention or the protocols thereto, or a serious issue of general importance.

3. If the panel accepts the request, the Grand Chamber shall decide the case by means of a judgment.

Article 44. Final Judgments

1. The judgment of the Grand Chamber shall be final.

2. The judgment of a Chamber shall become final

a. when the parties declare that they will not request that the case be referred to the Grand Chamber; or

b. three months after the date of the judgment, if reference of the case to the Grand Chamber has not been requested; or

c. when the panel of the Grand Chamber rejects the request to refer under Article 43.

3. The final judgment shall be published.

Article 45. Reasons for Judgments and Decisions

1. Reasons shall be given for judgments as well as for decisions declaring applications admissible or inadmissible.

2. If a judgment does not represent, in whole or in part, the unanimous opinion of the judges, any judge shall be entitled to deliver a separate opinion.

Article 46. *Binding force and execution of judgments*

1. The High Contracting Parties undertake to abide by the final judgment of the Court in any case to which they are parties.

2. The final judgment of the Court shall be transmitted to the Committee of Ministers, which shall supervise its execution.

3. If the Committee of Ministers considers that the supervision of the execution of a final judgment is hindered by a problem of interpretation of the judgment, it may refer the matter to the Court for a ruling on the question of interpretation. A referral decision shall require a majority vote of two thirds of the representatives entitled to sit on the Committee.

4. If the Committee of Ministers considers that a High Contracting Party refuses to abide by a final judgment in a case to which it is a party, it may, after serving formal notice on that Party and by decision adopted by a majority vote of two thirds of the representatives entitled to sit on the Committee, refer to the Court the question whether that Party has failed to fulfil its obligation under paragraph 1.

5. If the Court finds a violation of paragraph 1, it shall refer the case to the Committee of Ministers for consideration of the measures to be taken. If the Court finds no violation of paragraph 1, it shall refer the case to the Committee of Ministers, which shall close its examination of the case.

PROTOCOLS TO THE EUROPEAN CONVENTION FOR THE PROTECTION OF HUMAN RIGHTS AND FUNDAMENTAL FREEDOMS

PROTOCOL NO. 1

March 20, 1952, 213 U.N.T.S. 262, E.T.S. 9*

The Governments signatory here to, being Members of the Council of Europe, Being resolved to take steps to ensure the collective enforcement of certain rights and freedoms other than those already included in Section I of the Convention for the Protection of Human Rights and Fundamental Freedoms signed at Rome on 4th November, 1950 (hereinafter referred to as "the Convention"),

Have agreed as follows:

Article 1.   Protection of Property

Every natural or legal person is entitled to the peaceful enjoyment of his possessions. No one shall be deprived of his possessions except in the public interest and subject to the conditions provided for by law and by the general principles of international law.

The preceding provisions shall not, however, in any way impair the right of a State to enforce such laws as it deems necessary to control the use of property in accordance with the general interest or to secure the payment of taxes or other contributions or penalties.

Article 2.   Right to Education

No person shall be denied the right to education. In the exercise of any functions which it assumes in relation to education and to teaching, the State shall respect the right of parents to ensure such education and teaching in conformity with their own religious and philosophical convictions.

* Done at Paris on March 20, 1952. Entered into force on May 18, 1954. Amended by Protocol No. 11 (E.T.S. 155), which entered into force on November 1, 1998. The parties to the protocol include all the parties to the European Convention, except for Monaco and Switzerland.

Article 3. Right to Free Elections

The High Contracting Parties undertake to hold free elections at reasonable intervals by secret ballot, under conditions which will ensure the free expression of the opinion of the people in the choice of the legislature. . . .

PROTOCOL NO. 4

September 16, 1963, E.T.S. 46, 7 I.L.M. 978 (1986)*

Securing Certain Rights and Freedoms Other Than Those Already Included in the Convention and in the First Protocol Thereto

PREAMBLE . . .

Article 1. Prohibition of Imprisonment for Debt

No one shall be deprived of his liberty merely on the ground of inability to fulfil a contractual obligation.

Article 2. Freedom of Movement

1. Everyone lawfully within the territory of a state shall, within that territory, have the right to liberty of movement and freedom to choose his residence.

2. Everyone shall be free to leave any country, including his own.

3. No restrictions shall be placed on the exercise of these rights other than such as are in accordance with law and are necessary in a democratic society in the interests of national security or public safety, for the maintenance of *ordre public,* for the prevention of crime, for the protection of health or morals, or for the protection of the rights and freedoms of others.

4. The rights set forth in paragraph 1 may also be subject, in particular areas, to restrictions imposed in accordance with law and justified by the public interest in a democratic society.

Article 3. Prohibition of Expulsion of Nationals

1. No one shall be expelled, by means either of an individual or of a collective measure, from the territory of the state of which he is a national.

2. No one shall be deprived of the right to enter the territory of the state of which he is a national.

---

* Done at Strasbourg on September 16, 1963. Entered into force on May 2, 1968. Amended by Protocol No. 11, which entered into force on November 1, 1998. The parties to the protocol include all the parties to the European Convention except Greece, Switzerland, Turkey, and the United Kingdom.

Article 4. Prohibition of Collective Exclusion of Aliens

Collective expulsion of aliens is prohibited. . . .

Article 6. Relationship to the Convention

1. As between the High Contracting Parties the provisions of Articles 1 to 5 of this Protocol shall be regarded as additional articles to the Convention, and all the provisions of the Convention shall apply accordingly. . . .

PROTOCOL NO. 6

E.T.S. 114*

Article 1. Abolition of the Death Penalty

The death penalty shall be abolished. No one shall be condemned to such penalty or executed.

Article 2. Death Penalty in Time of War

A State may make provision in its law for the death penalty in respect of acts committed in time of war or of imminent threat of war; such penalty shall be applied only in the instances laid down in the law and in accordance with its provisions. The State shall communicate to the Secretary General of the Council of Europe the relevant provisions of that law.

Article 3. Prohibition of Derogations

No derogation from the provisions of this Protocol shall be made under Article 15 of the Convention.

Article 4. Prohibitions of Reservations

No reservation may be made under Article 57 of the Convention in respect of the provisions of this Protocol. . . .

---

* Done at Strasbourg on April 28, 1983. Entered into force on March 1, 1985. Text amended by Protocol No. 11, which entered into force on November 1, 1998. The parties to the protocol include all the parties to the European Convention except Russia.

PROTOCOL NO. 7

E.T.S. 117*

Article 1. Procedural Safeguards Relating to Expulsion of Aliens

1. An alien lawfully resident in the territory of a State shall not be expelled therefrom except in pursuance of a decision reached in accordance with law and shall be allowed:

   a. to submit reasons against his expulsion,

   b. to have his case reviewed, and

   c. to be represented for these purposes before the competent authority or a person or persons designated by that authority.

2. An alien may be expelled before the exercise of his rights under paragraph 1. *a, b* and *c* of this Article, when such expulsion is necessary in the interests of public order or is grounded on reasons of national security.

Article 2. Right of Appeal in Criminal Matters

1. Everyone convicted of a criminal offence by a tribunal shall have the right to have conviction or sentence reviewed by a higher tribunal. The exercise of this right, including the grounds on which it may be exercised, shall be governed by law.

2. This right may be subject to exceptions in regard to offences of a minor character, as prescribed by law, or in cases in which the person concerned was tried in the first instance by the highest tribunal or was convicted following an appeal against acquittal.

Article 3. Compensation for Wrongful Conviction

When a person has by a final decision been convicted of a criminal offence and when subsequently his conviction has been reversed, or he has been pardoned, on the ground that a new or newly discovered fact shows conclusively that there has been a miscarriage of justice, the person who has suffered punishment as a result of such conviction shall be compensated according to the law or the practice of the State concerned, unless it is proved that the nondisclosure of the unknown fact in time is wholly or partly attributable to him.

Article 4. Right Not to Be Tried or Punished Twice

1. No one shall be liable to be tried or punished again in criminal proceedings under the jurisdiction of the same State for an offence for which

---

* Done at Strasbourg on November 22, 1984. Entered into force on November 1, 1988. Text amended by Protocol No. 11, which entered into force on November 1, 1998. The parties to the protocol include all parties to the European Convention except Germany, Netherlands, Turkey, and United Kingdom.

he has already been finally acquitted or convicted in accordance with the law and penal procedure of that State.

2. The provisions of the preceding paragraph shall not prevent the reopening of the case in accordance with the law and penal procedure of the State concerned, if there is evidence of new or newly discovered facts, or if there has been a fundamental defect in the previous proceedings, which could affect the outcome of the case.

3. No derogation from this Article shall be made under Article 15 of the Convention.

Article 5.   Equality Between Spouses

Spouses shall enjoy equality of rights and responsibilities of a private law character between them, and in their relations with their children, as to marriage, during marriage and in the event of its dissolution. This Article shall not prevent States from taking such measures as are necessary in the interests of the children. . . .

Article 7.   Relationship to the Convention

As between the States Parties, the provisions of Articles 1 to 6 of this Protocol shall be regarded as additional Articles to the Convention, and all the provisions of the Convention shall apply accordingly. . . .

PROTOCOL NO. 12

E.T.S. 177*

Article 1.   General Prohibition of Discrimination

1. The enjoyment of any right set forth by law shall be secured without discrimination on any ground such as sex, race, colour, language, religion, political or other opinion, national or social origin, association with a national minority, property, birth or other status.

2. No one shall be discriminated against by any public authority on any ground such as those mentioned in paragraph 1.

* Done at Rome on April 11, 2000. Entered into force on April 1, 2005. The 18 parties to Protocol No. 12 are Albania, Andorra, Armenia, Bosnia and Herzegovina, Croatia, Cyprus, Finland, Georgia, Luxembourg, Macedonia (the former Yugoslav Republic of), Montenegro, Netherlands, Romania, San Marino, Serbia, Slovenia, Spain, and Ukraine.

Article 2.   Territorial Application

1. Any State may, at the time of signature or when depositing its instrument of ratification, acceptance or approval, specify the territory or territories to which this Protocol shall apply . . .

Article 3.   Relationship to the Convention

As between the States Parties, the provisions of Articles 1 and 2 of this Protocol shall be regarded as additional articles to the Convention, and all the provisions of the Convention shall apply accordingly. . . .

PROTOCOL NO. 13

C.E.T.S. 187*

Article 1.   Abolition of the Death Penalty

The death penalty shall be abolished. No one shall be condemned to such penalty or executed.

Article 2.   Prohibition of Derogations

No derogation from the provisions of this Protocol shall be made under Article 15 of the Convention.

Article 3.   Prohibition of Reservations

No reservation may be made under Article 57 of the Convention in respect of the provisions of this Protocol.

Article 4.   Territorial Application

1. Any State may, at the time of signature or when depositing its instrument of ratification, acceptance or approval, specify the territory or territories to which this Protocol shall apply. . . .

---

* Concerning the abolition of the death penalty in all circumstances. Done at Vilinus on May 3, 2002. Entered into force on July 1, 2003. As of March 2013, the parties to the protocol include all the parties to the European Convention except for Armenia, Azerbaijan, Poland, and Russia.

Article 5. Relationship to the Convention

As between the States Parties the provisions of Articles 1 to 4 of this Protocol shall be regarded as additional articles to the Convention, and all the provisions of the Convention shall apply accordingly.

PROTOCOL NO. 14
C.E.T.S. 194*

Preamble . . .

Considering the urgent need to amend certain provisions of the Convention in order to maintain and improve the efficiency of the control system for the long term, mainly in the light of the continuing increase in the workload of the European Court of Human Rights and the Committee of Ministers of the Council of Europe;

Considering, in particular, the need to ensure that the Court can continue to play its pre-eminent role in protecting human rights in Europe. . . .

Article 1

Paragraph 2 of Article 22 of the Convention shall be deleted.

Article 2

Article 23 of the Convention shall be amended to read as follows:

"Article 23 - Terms of Office and Dismissal

1. The judges shall be elected for a period of nine years. They may not be re-elected.

2. The terms of office of judges shall expire when they reach the age of 70.

3. The judges shall hold office until replaced. They shall, however, continue to deal with such cases as they already have under consideration.

4. No judge may be dismissed from office unless the other judges decide by a majority of two-thirds that that judge has ceased to fulfil the required conditions."

Article 3

Article 24 of the Convention shall be deleted. . . .

---

* Concerning the control system of the Convention. Signed at Strasbourg on May 15, 2004. As of March 2013, the protocol had been ratified by all the countries to the European Convention. Entered into force June 1, 2010.

Article 6

Article 27 of the Convention shall become Article 26 and its text shall be amended to read as follows:

"Article 26 - Single-Judge Formation, Committees, Chambers and Grand Chamber

1. To consider cases brought before it, the Court shall sit in a single-judge formation, in committees of three judges, in Chambers of seven judges and in a Grand Chamber of seventeen judges. The Court's Chambers shall set up committees for a fixed period of time.

2. At the request of the plenary Court, the Committee of Ministers may, by a unanimous decision and for a fixed period, reduce to five the number of judges of the Chambers.

3. When sitting as a single judge, a judge shall not examine any application against the High Contracting Party in respect of which that judge has been elected.

4. There shall sit as an *ex officio* member of the Chamber and the Grand Chamber the judge elected in respect of the High Contracting Party concerned. If there is none or if that judge is unable to sit, a person chosen by the President of the Court from a list submitted in advance by that Party shall sit in the capacity of judge.

5. The Grand Chamber shall also include the President of the Court, the Vice-Presidents, the Presidents of the Chambers and other judges chosen in accordance with the rules of the Court. When a case is referred to the Grand Chamber under Article 43, no judge from the Chamber which rendered the judgment shall sit in the Grand Chamber, with the exception of the President of the Chamber and the judge who sat in respect of the High Contracting Party concerned."

Article 7

After the new Article 26, a new Article 27 shall be inserted into the Convention, which shall read as follows:

"Article 27 - Competence of Single Judges

1. A single judge may declare inadmissible or strike out of the Court's list of cases an application submitted under Article 34, where such a decision can be taken without further examination.

2. The decision shall be final.

3. If the single judge does not declare an application inadmissible or strike it out, that judge shall forward it to a committee or to a Chamber for further examination."

Article 8

Article 28 of the Convention shall be amended to read as follows:

"Article 28 - Competence of Committees

1. In respect of an application submitted under Article 34, a committee may, by a unanimous vote,

a. declare it inadmissible or strike it out of its list of cases, where such decision can be taken without further examination; or

b. declare it admissible and render at the same time a judgment on the merits, if the underlying question in the case, concerning the interpretation or the application of the Convention or the Protocols thereto, is already the subject of well-established case-law of the Court.

2. Decisions and judgments under paragraph 1 shall be final.

3. If the judge elected in respect of the High Contracting Party concerned is not a member of the committee, the committee may at any stage of the proceedings invite that judge to take the place of one of the members of the committee, having regard to all relevant factors, including whether that Party has contested the application of the procedure under paragraph 1.b."

Article 9

Article 29 of the Convention shall be amended as follows:

1. Paragraph 1 shall be amended to read as follows: "If no decision is taken under Article 27 or 28, or no judgment rendered under Article 28, a Chamber shall decide on the admissibility and merits of individual applications submitted under Article 34. The decision on admissibility may be taken separately."

2. At the end of paragraph 2 a new sentence shall be added which shall read as follows: "The decision on admissibility shall be taken separately unless the Court, in exceptional cases, decides otherwise."

3. Paragraph 3 shall be deleted.

Article 10

Article 31 of the Convention shall be amended as follows:

1. At the end of paragraph a, the word "and" shall be deleted.

2. Paragraph b shall become paragraph c and a new paragraph b shall be inserted and shall read as follows:

"b. decide on issues referred to the Court by the Committee of Ministers in accordance with Article 46, paragraph 4; and".

Article 11

Article 32 of the Convention shall be amended as follows: At the end of paragraph 1, a comma and the number 46 shall be inserted after the number 34.

Article 12

Paragraph 3 of Article 35 of the Convention shall be amended to read as follows:

"3. The Court shall declare inadmissible any individual application submitted under Article 34 if it considers that:

a. the application is incompatible with the provisions of the Convention or the Protocols thereto, manifestly ill-founded, or an abuse of the right of individual application; or

b. the applicant has not suffered a significant disadvantage, unless respect for human rights as defined in the Convention and the Protocols thereto requires an examination of the application on the merits and provided that no case may be rejected on this ground which has not been duly considered by a domestic tribunal."

Article 13

A new paragraph 3 shall be added at the end of Article 36 of the Convention, which shall read as follows:

"3. In all cases before a Chamber or the Grand Chamber, the Council of Europe Commissioner for Human Rights may submit written comments and take part in hearings."

Article 14

Article 38 of the Convention shall be amended to read as follows:

"Article 38 - Examination of the Case

The Court shall examine the case together with the representatives of the parties and, if need be, undertake an investigation, for the effective conduct of which the High Contracting Parties concerned shall furnish all necessary facilities."

Article 15

Article 39 of the Convention shall be amended to read as follows:

"Article 39 - Friendly Settlements

1. At any stage of the proceedings, the Court may place itself at the disposal of the parties concerned with a view to securing a friendly settlement of the matter on the basis of respect for human rights as defined in the Convention and the Protocols thereto.

2. Proceedings conducted under paragraph 1 shall be confidential.

3. If a friendly settlement is effected, the Court shall strike the case out of its list by means of a decision which shall be confined to a brief statement of the facts and of the solution reached.

4. This decision shall be transmitted to the Committee of Ministers, which shall supervise the execution of the terms of the friendly settlement as set out in the decision."

Article 16

Article 46 of the Convention shall be amended to read as follows:

"Article 46 - Binding Force and Execution of Judgments

1. The High Contracting Parties undertake to abide by the final judgment of the Court in any case to which they are parties.

2. The final judgment of the Court shall be transmitted to the Committee of Ministers, which shall supervise its execution.

3. If the Committee of Ministers considers that the supervision of the execution of a final judgment is hindered by a problem of interpretation of the judgment, it may refer the matter to the Court for a ruling on the question of interpretation. A referral decision shall require a majority vote of two-thirds of the representatives entitled to sit on the Committee.

4. If the Committee of Ministers considers that a High Contracting Party refuses to abide by a final judgment in a case to which it is a party, it may, after serving formal notice on that Party and by decision adopted by a majority vote of two-thirds of the representatives entitled to sit on the Committee, refer to the Court the question whether that Party has failed to fulfil its obligation under paragraph 1.

5. If the Court finds a violation of paragraph 1, it shall refer the case to the Committee of Ministers for consideration of the measures to be taken. If the Court finds no violation of paragraph 1, it shall refer the case to the Committee of Ministers, which shall close its examination of the case."

Article 17

Article 59 of the Convention shall be amended as follows:

1. A new paragraph 2 shall be inserted which shall read as follows:

"2. The European Union may accede to this Convention."

2. Paragraphs 2, 3 and 4 shall become paragraphs 3, 4 and 5 respectively. . . .

Article 19

This Protocol shall enter into force on the first day of the month following the expiration of a period of three months after the date on which all Parties to the Convention have expressed their consent to be bound by the Protocol. . . .

AMERICAN CONVENTION
ON HUMAN RIGHTS

November 22, 1969, 9 I.L.M. 673 (1970)*

Preamble

The American states signatory to the present Convention, *Reaffirming* their intention to consolidate in this hemisphere, within the framework of democratic institutions, a system of personal liberty and social justice based on respect for the essential rights of man;

Recognizing that the essential rights of man are not derived from one's being a national of a certain state, but are based upon attributes of the human personality, and that they therefore justify international protection in the form of a convention reinforcing or complementing the protection provided by the domestic law of the American states;

Considering that these principles have been set forth in the Charter of the Organization of American States, in the American Declaration of the Rights and Duties of Man, and in the Universal Declaration of Human Rights . . . ;

Reiterating that, in accordance with the Universal Declaration of Human Rights, the ideal of free men enjoying freedom from fear and want can be achieved only if conditions are created whereby everyone may enjoy his economic, social, and cultural rights, as well as his civil and political rights; . . .

Have agreed upon the following:

---

* Signed at San Jose, Costa Rica on November 22, 1969. Entered into force on July 18, 1978. The United States signed the convention on June 1, 1977, but has not ratified it. The 24 parties to the convention as of March 2013 were: Argentina, Barbados, Bolivia, Brazil, Chile, Colombia, Costa Rica, Dominica, Dominican Republic, Ecuador, El Salvador, Grenada, Guatemala, Haiti, Honduras, Jamaica, Mexico, Nicaragua, Panama, Paraguay, Peru, Suriname, Uruguay, and Venezuela. See the OAS Web site at <http://www.oas.org>.

Part I. State Obligations and Rights Protected

CHAPTER I. GENERAL OBLIGATIONS

Article 1. Obligation to Respect Rights

1. The States Parties to this Convention undertake to respect the rights and freedoms recognized herein and to ensure to all persons subject to their jurisdiction the free and full exercise of those rights and freedoms, without any discrimination for reasons of race, color, sex, language, religion, political or other opinion, national or social origin, economic status, birth, or any other social condition.

2. For the purposes of this Convention, "person" means every human being.

Article 2. Domestic Legal Effects

Where the exercise of any of the rights or freedoms referred to in Article 1 is not already ensured by legislative or other provisions, the States Parties undertake to adopt, in accordance with their constitutional processes and the provisions of this Convention, such legislative or other measures as may be necessary to give effect to those rights or freedoms.

CHAPTER II. CIVIL AND POLITICAL RIGHTS

Article 3. Right to Juridical Personality

Every person has the right to recognition as a person before the law.

Article 4. Right to Life

1. Every person has the right to have his life respected. This right shall be protected by law and, in general, from the moment of conception. No one shall be arbitrarily deprived of his life.

2. In countries that have not abolished the death penalty, it may be imposed only for the most serious crimes and pursuant to a final judgment rendered by a competent court and in accordance with a law establishing such punishment, enacted prior to the commission of the crime. The application of such punishment shall not be extended to crimes to which it does not presently apply.

3. The death penalty shall not be reestablished in states that have abolished it.

4. In no case shall capital punishment be inflicted for political offenses or related common crimes.

5. Capital punishment shall not he imposed upon persons who, at the time the crime was committed, were under 18 years of age or over 70 years of age; nor shall it be applied to pregnant women.

6. Every person condemned to death shall have the right to apply for amnesty, pardon, or commutation of sentence, which may be granted in all cases. Capital punishment shall not be imposed while such a petition is pending decision by the competent authority.

Article 5. Right to Humane Treatment

1. Every person has the right to have his physical, mental, and moral integrity respected.

2. No one shall be subjected to torture or to cruel, inhuman, or degrading punishment or treatment. All persons deprived of their liberty shall be treated with respect for the inherent dignity of the human person.

3. Punishment shall not be extended to any person other than the criminal.

4. Accused persons shall, save in exceptional circumstances, be segregated from convicted persons, and shall be subject to separate treatment appropriate to their status as unconvicted persons.

5. Minors while subject to criminal proceedings shall be separated from adults and brought before specialized tribunals, as speedily as possible, so that they may be treated in accordance with their status as minors.

6. Punishments consisting of deprivation of liberty shall have as an essential aim the reform and social readaptation of the prisoners.

Article 6. Freedom from Slavery

1. No one shall be subject to slavery or to involuntary servitude, which are prohibited in all their forms, as are the slave trade and traffic in women.

2. No one shall be required to perform forced or compulsory labor. This provision shall not be interpreted to mean that, in those countries in which the penalty established for certain crimes is deprivation of liberty at forced labor, the carrying out of such a sentence imposed by a competent court is prohibited. Forced labor shall not adversely affect the dignity or the physical or intellectual capacity of the prisoner.

3. For the purposes of this article, the following do not constitute forced or compulsory labor:

a. work or service normally required of a person imprisoned in execution of a sentence or formal decision passed by the competent judicial authority. . . ;

b. military service and, in countries in which conscientious objectors are recognized, national service that the law may provide for . . . ;

c. service exacted in time of danger or calamity that threatens the existence or the well-being of the community; or

d. work or service that forms part of normal civic obligations.

Article 7. Right to Personal Liberty

1. Every person has the right to personal liberty and security.

2. No one shall be deprived of his physical liberty except for the reasons and under the conditions established beforehand by the constitution of the State Party concerned or by a law established pursuant thereto.

3. No one shall be subject to arbitrary arrest or imprisonment.

4. Anyone who is detained shall be informed of the reasons for his detention and shall be promptly notified of the charge or charges against him.

5. Any person detained shall be brought promptly before a judge or other officer authorized by law to exercise judicial power and shall be entitled to trial within a reasonable time or to be released without prejudice to the continuation of the proceedings. His release may be subject to guarantees to assure his appearance for trial.

6. Anyone who is deprived of his liberty shall be entitled to recourse to a competent court, in order that the court may decide without delay on the lawfulness of his arrest or detention order his release if the arrest or detention is unlawful. In States Parties whose laws provide that anyone who believes himself to be threatened with deprivation of his liberty is entitled to recourse to a competent court in order that it may decide on the lawfulness of such threat, this remedy may not be restricted or abolished. The interested party or another person in his behalf is entitled to seek these remedies.

7. No one shall be detained for debt. This principle shall not limit the orders of a competent judicial authority issued for nonfulfillment of duties of support.

Article 8. Right to a Fair Trial

1. Every person has the right to a hearing, with due guarantees and within a reasonable time, by a competent, independent, and impartial tribunal, previously established by law, in the substantiation of any accusation of a criminal nature made against him or for the determination of his rights and obligations of a civil, labor, fiscal, or any other nature.

2. Every person accused of a criminal offense has the right to be presumed innocent so long as his guilt has not been proven according to law. During the proceedings, every person is entitled, with full equality, to the following minimum guarantees:

　　a. the right of the accused to be assisted without charge by a translator or interpreter, if he does not understand or does not speak the language of the tribunal or court;

　　b. prior notification in detail to the accused of the charges against him;

　　c. adequate time and means for the preparation of his defense;

　　d. the right of the accused to defend himself personally or to be assisted by legal counsel of his own choosing, and to communicate freely and privately with his counsel;

　　e. the inalienable right to be assisted by counsel provided by the state, paid or not as the domestic law provides, if the accused does not defend himself personally or engage his own counsel within the time period established by law;

    f. the right of the defense to examine witnesses present in the court and to obtain the appearance, as witnesses, of experts or other persons who may throw light on the facts;

    g. the right not to be compelled to be a witness against himself or to plead guilty; and

    h. the right to appeal the judgment to a higher court.

    3. A confession of guilt by the accused shall be valid only if it is made without coercion of any kind.

    4. An accused person acquitted by a nonappealable judgment shall not be subjected to a new trial for the same cause.

    5. Criminal proceedings shall be public, except insofar as may be necessary to protect the interests of justice.

Article 9. Freedom from Ex Post Facto Laws

No one shall be convicted of any act or omission that did not constitute a criminal offense, under the applicable law, at the time it was committed. A heavier penalty shall not be imposed than the one that was applicable at the time the criminal offense was committed. If subsequent to the commission of the offense the law provides for the imposition of a lighter punishment, the guilty person shall benefit therefrom.

Article 10. Right to Compensation

Every person has the right to be compensated in accordance with the law in the event he has been sentenced by a final judgment through a miscarriage of justice.

Article 11. Right to Privacy

    1. Everyone has the right to have his honor respected and his dignity recognized.

    2. No one may be the object of arbitrary or abusive interference with his private life, his family, his home, or his correspondence, or of unlawful attacks on his honor or reputation.

    3. Everyone has the right to the protection of the law against such interference or attacks.

Article 12. Freedom of Conscience and Religion

    1. Everyone has the right to freedom of conscience and of religion. This right includes freedom to maintain or to change one's religion or beliefs, and freedom to profess or disseminate one's religion or beliefs, either individually or together with others, in public or in private.

    2. No one shall be subject to restrictions that might impair his freedom to maintain or to change his religion or beliefs.

    3. Freedom to manifest one's religion and beliefs may be subject only to the limitations prescribed by law that are necessary to protect public safety, order, health, or morals, or the rights or freedoms of others.

4. Parents or guardians, as the case may be, have the right to provide for the religious and moral education of their children or wards that is in accord with their own convictions.

Article 13.   Freedom of Thought and Expression

1. Everyone has the right to freedom of thought and expression. This right includes freedom to seek, receive, and impart information and ideas of all kinds, regardless of frontiers, either orally, in writing, in print, in the form of art, or through any other medium of one's choice.

2. The exercise of the right provided for in the foregoing paragraph shall not be subject to prior censorship but shall be subject to subsequent imposition of liability, which shall be expressly established by law to the extent necessary to ensure:

a. respect for the rights or reputations of others; or

b. the protection of national security, public order, or public health or morals.

3. The right of expression may not be restricted by indirect methods or means, such as the abuse of government or private controls over newsprint, radio broadcasting frequencies, or equipment used in the dissemination of information, or by any other means tending to impede the communication and circulation of ideas and opinions.

4. Notwithstanding the provisions of paragraph 2 above, public entertainments may be subject by law to prior censorship for the sole purpose of regulating access to them for the moral protection of childhood and adolescence.

5. Any propaganda for war and any advocacy of national, racial, or religious hatred that constitute incitements to lawless violence or to any other similar illegal action against any person or group of persons on any grounds including those of race, color, religion, language, or national origin shall be considered as offenses punishable by law.

Article 14.   Right of Reply

1. Anyone injured by inaccurate or offensive statements or ideas disseminated to the public in general by a legally regulated medium of communication has the right to reply or to make a correction using the same communications outlet, under such conditions as the law may establish.

2. The correction or reply shall not in any case remit other legal liabilities that may have been incurred.

3. For the effective protection of honor and reputation, every publisher, and every newspaper, motion picture, radio, and television company, shall have a person responsible who is not protected by immunities or special privileges.

Article 15. Right of Assembly

The right of peaceful assembly, without arms, is recognized. No restrictions may be placed on the exercise of this right other than those imposed in conformity with the law and necessary in a democratic society in the interest of national security, public safety or public order, or to protect public health or morals or the rights or freedoms of others.

Article 16. Freedom of Association

1. Everyone has the right to associate freely for ideological, religious, political, economic, labor, social, cultural, sports, or other purposes.

2. The exercise of this right shall be subject only to such restrictions established by law as may be necessary in a democratic society, in the interest of national security, public safety or public order, or to protect public health or morals or the rights and freedoms of others.

3. The provisions of this article do not bar the imposition of legal restrictions, including even deprivation of the exercise of the right of association, on members of the armed forces and the police.

Article 17. Rights of the Family

1. The family is the natural and fundamental group unit of society and is entitled to protection by society and the state.

2. The right of men and women of marriageable age to marry and to raise a family shall be recognized, if they meet the conditions required by domestic laws, insofar as such conditions do not affect the principle of nondiscrimination established in this Convention.

3. No marriage shall be entered into without the free and full consent of the intending spouses.

4. The States Parties shall take appropriate steps to ensure the equality of rights and the adequate balancing of responsibilities of the spouses as to marriage, during marriage, and in the event of its dissolution. In case of dissolution, provision shall be made for the necessary protection of any children solely on the basis of their own best interests.

5. The law shall recognize equal rights for children born out of wedlock and those born in wedlock.

Article 18. Right to a Name

Every person has the right to a given name and to the surnames of his parents or that of one of them. The law shall regulate the manner in which this right shall be ensured for all, by the use of assumed names if necessary.

Article 19. Rights of the Child

Every minor child has the right to the measures of protection required by his condition as a minor on the part of his family, society, and the state.

Article 20.   Right to Nationality

1. Every person has the right to a nationality.

2. Every person has the right to the nationality of the state in whose territory he was born if he does not have the right to any other nationality.

3. No one shall be arbitrarily deprived of his nationality or of the right to change it.

Article 21.   Right to Property

1. Everyone has the right to the use and enjoyment of his property. The law may subordinate such use and enjoyment to the interest of society.

2. No one shall be deprived of his property except upon payment of just compensation, for reasons of public utility or social interest, and in the cases and according to the forms established by law.

3. Usury and any other form of exploitation of man by man shall be prohibited by law.

Article 22.   Freedom of Movement and Residence

1. Every person lawfully in the territory of a State Party has the right to move about in it, and to reside in it subject to the provisions of the law.

2. Every person has the right to leave any country freely, including his own.

3. The exercise of the foregoing rights may be restricted only pursuant to a law to the extent necessary in a democratic society to prevent crime or to protect national security, public safety, public order, public morals, public health, or the rights or freedoms of others.

4. The exercise of the rights recognized in paragraph 1 may also be restricted by law in designated zones for reasons of public interest.

5. No one can be expelled from the territory of the state of which he is a national or be deprived of the right to enter it.

6. An alien lawfully in the territory of a State Party to this Convention may be expelled from it only pursuant to a decision reached in accordance with law.

7. Every person has the right to seek and be granted asylum in a foreign territory, in accordance with the legislation of the state and international conventions, in the event he is being pursued for political offenses or related common crimes.

8. In no case may an alien be deported or returned to a country, regardless of whether or not it is his country of origin, if in that country his right to life or personal freedom is in danger of being violated because of his race, nationality, religion, social status, or political opinions.

9. The collective expulsion of aliens is prohibited.

Article 23.   Right to Participate in Government

1. Every citizen shall enjoy the following rights and opportunities:

a. to take part in the conduct of public affairs, directly or through freely chosen representatives;

b. to vote and to be elected in genuine periodic elections, which shall be by universal and equal suffrage and by secret ballot that guarantees the free expression of the will of the voters; and

c. to have access, under general conditions of equality, to the public service of his country.

2. The law may regulate the exercise of the rights and opportunities referred to in the preceding paragraph only on the basis of age, nationality, residence, language, education, civil and mental capacity, or sentencing by a competent court in criminal proceedings.

Article 24. Right to Equal Protection

All persons are equal before the law. Consequently, they are entitled, without discrimination, to equal protection of the law.

Article 25. Right to Judicial Protection

1. Everyone has the right to simple and prompt recourse, or any other effective recourse, to a competent court or tribunal for protection against acts that violate his fundamental rights recognized by the constitution or laws of the state concerned or by this Convention, even though such violation may have been committed by persons acting in the course of their official duties.

2. The States Parties undertake:

a. to ensure that any person claiming such remedy shall have his rights determined by the competent authority provided for by the legal system of the state;

b. to develop the possibilities of judicial remedy; and

c. to ensure that the competent authorities shall enforce such remedies when granted.

CHAPTER III. ECONOMIC, SOCIAL, AND CULTURAL RIGHTS

Article 26. Progressive Development

The States Parties undertake to adopt measures, both internally and through international cooperation, especially those of an economic and technical nature, with a view to achieving progressively, by legislation or other appropriate means, the full realization of the rights implicit in the economic, social, educational, scientific, and cultural standards set forth in the Charter of the Organization of American States as amended by the Protocol of Buenos Aires.

CHAPTER IV. SUSPENSION OF GUARANTEES, INTERPRETATION, AND APPLICATION

Article 27. Suspension of Guarantees

1. In time of war, public danger, or other emergency that threatens the independence or security of a State Party, it may take measures derogating from its obligations under the present Convention to the extent and for the period of time strictly required by the exigencies of the situation, provided that such measures are not inconsistent with its other obligations under international law and do not involve discrimination on the ground of race, color, sex, language, religion, or social origin.

2. The foregoing provision does not authorize any suspension of the following articles: Article 3 (Right to Juridical Personality), Article 4 (Right to Life), Article 5 (Right to Humane Treatment), Article 6 (Freedom from Slavery), Article 9 (Freedom from *Ex Post Facto* Laws), Article 12 (Freedom of Conscience and Religion), Article 17 (Rights of the Family), Article 18 (Right to a Name), Article 19 (Rights of the Child), Article 20 (Right to Nationality), and Article 23 (Right to Participate in Government), or of the judicial guarantees essential for the protection of such rights.

3. Any State Party availing itself of the right of suspension shall immediately inform the other States Parties. . . .

Article 28. Federal Clause

1. Where a State Party is constituted as a federal state, the national government of such State Party shall implement all the provisions of the Convention over whose subject matter it exercises legislative and judicial jurisdiction.

2. With respect to the provisions over whose subject matter the constituent units of the federal state have jurisdiction, the national government shall immediately take suitable measures, in accordance with its constitution and its laws, to the end that the competent authorities of the constituent units may adopt appropriate provisions for the fulfillment of this Convention. . . .

Article 29. Restrictions Regarding Interpretation

No provision of this Convention shall be interpreted as:

a. permitting any State Party, group, or person to suppress the enjoyment or exercise of the rights and freedoms recognized in this Convention or to restrict them to a greater extent than is provided for herein;

b. restricting the enjoyment or exercise of any right or freedom recognized by virtue of the laws of any State Party or by virtue of another convention to which one of the said states is a party;

c. precluding other rights or guarantees that are inherent in the human personality or derived from representative democracy as a form of government . . . .

Article 30. Scope of Restrictions

The restrictions that, pursuant to this Convention, may be placed on the enjoyment or exercise of the rights or freedoms recognized herein may not be applied except in accordance with laws enacted for reasons of general interest and in accordance with the purpose for which such restrictions have been established.

Article 31. Recognition of Other Rights . . . .

CHAPTER V. PERSONAL RESPONSIBILITIES

Article 32. Relationship Between Duties and Rights

1. Every person has responsibilities to his family, his community, and mankind.

2. The rights of each person are limited by the rights of others, by the security of all, and by the just demands of the general welfare, in a democratic society.

Part II. Means of Protection

CHAPTER VI. COMPETENT ORGANS

Article 33

The following organs shall have competence with respect to matters relating to the fulfillment of the commitments made by the States Parties to this Convention:

a. the Inter-American Commission on Human Rights, referred to as "The Commission"; and

b. the Inter-American Court of Human Rights, referred to as "The Court."

CHAPTER VII. INTER-AMERICAN COMMISSION ON HUMAN RIGHTS

SECTION 1. ORGANIZATION

Article 34

The Inter-American Commission on Human Rights shall be composed of seven members, who shall be persons of high moral character and recognized competence in the field of human rights.

Article 35

The Commission shall represent all the member countries of the Organization of American States.

Article 36

1. The members of the Commission shall be elected in a personal capacity by the General Assembly of the Organization from a list of candidates proposed by the governments of the member states.

2. Each of those governments may propose up to three candidates, who may be nationals of the states proposing them or of any other member state of the Organization of American States. . . .

Article 37

1. The members of the Commission shall be elected for a term of four years and may be reelected only once, but the terms of three of the members chosen in the first election shall expire at the end of two years. . . .

2. No two nationals of the same state may be members of the Commission.

Article 38

Vacancies that may occur on the Commission for reasons other than the normal expiration of a term shall be filled by the Permanent Council of the Organization in accordance with the provisions of the Statute of the Commission.

Article 39

The Commission shall prepare its Statute, which it shall submit to the General Assembly for approval. It shall establish its own Regulations. . . .

SECTION 2. FUNCTIONS

Article 41

The main function of the Commission shall be to promote respect for and defense of human rights. In the exercise of its mandate, it shall have the following functions and powers:

  a. to develop an awareness of human rights among the peoples of America;

  b. to make recommendations to the governments of the member states, when it considers such action advisable, for the adoption of progressive measures in favor of human rights within the framework of their domestic law and constitutional provisions as well as appropriate measures to further the observance of those rights;

  c. to prepare such studies or reports as it considers advisable in the performance of its duties;

  d. to request the governments of the member states to supply it with information on the measures adopted by them in matters of human rights;

e. to respond, through the General Secretariat of the Organization of American States, to inquiries made by the member states on matters related to human rights and, within the limits of its possibilities, to provide those states with the advisory services they request;

f. to take action on petitions and other communications pursuant to its authority under the provisions of Articles 44 through 51 of this Convention; and

g. to submit an annual report to the General Assembly of the Organization of American States. . . .

Article 43

The States Parties undertake to provide the Commission with such information as it may request of them as to the manner in which their domestic law ensures the effective application of any provisions of this Convention.

SECTION 3. COMPETENCE

Article 44

Any person or group of persons, or any nongovernmental entity legally recognized in one or more member states of the Organization, may lodge petitions with the Commission containing denunciations or complaints of violation of this Convention by a State Party.

Article 45

1. Any State Party may . . . declare that it recognizes the competence of the Commission to receive and examine communications in which a State Party alleges that another State Party has committed a violation of a human right set forth in this Convention.

2. Communications presented by virtue of this article may be admitted and examined only if they are presented by a State Party that has made a declaration recognizing the aforementioned competence of the Commission. The Commission shall not admit any communication against a State Party that has not made such a declaration. . . .

Article 46

1. Admission by the Commission of a petition or communication lodged in accordance with Articles 44 or 45 shall be subject to the following requirements:

a. that the remedies under domestic law have been pursued and exhausted in accordance with generally recognized principles of international law;

b. that the petition or communication is lodged within a period of six months from the date on which the party alleging violation of his rights was notified of the final judgment; . . . .

Article 47

The Commission shall consider inadmissible any petition or communication submitted under Articles 44 or 45 if:

a. any of the requirements indicated in Article 46 has not been met;

b. the petition or communication does not state facts that tend to establish a violation of the rights guaranteed by this Convention;

c. the statements of the petitioner or of the state indicate that the petition or communication is manifestly groundless or obviously out of order; or

d. the petition or communication is substantially the same as one previously studied by the Commission or by another international organization.

SECTION 4. PROCEDURE

Article 48

1. When the Commission receives a petition or communication alleging violation of any of the rights protected by this Convention, it shall proceed as follows:

a. If it considers the petition or communication admissible, it shall request information from the government of the state indicated as being responsible for the alleged violations and shall furnish that government a transcript of the pertinent portions of the petition or communication. This information shall be submitted within a reasonable period . . . .

b. After the information has been received, or after the period established has elapsed and the information has not been received, the Commission shall ascertain whether the grounds for the petition or communication still exist. If they do not, the Commission shall order the record to be closed.

c. The Commission may also declare the petition or communication inadmissible or out of order on the basis of information or evidence subsequently received.

d. If the record has not been closed, the Commission shall, with the knowledge of the parties, examine the matter set forth in the petition or communication in order to verify the facts. If necessary and advisable, the Commission shall carry out an investigation, for the effective conduct of which it shall request, and the states concerned shall furnish to it, all necessary facilities.

e. The Commission may request the states concerned to furnish any pertinent information and, if so requested, shall hear oral statements or receive written statements from the parties concerned.

f. The Commission shall place itself at the disposal of the parties concerned with a view to reaching a friendly settlement of the matter on the basis of respect for the human rights recognized in this Convention.

2. However, in serious and urgent cases, only the presentation of a petition or communication that fulfills all the formal requirements of admissibility shall be necessary in order for the Commission to conduct an investigation with the prior consent of the state in whose territory a violation has allegedly been committed.

Article 49

If a friendly settlement has been reached in accordance with paragraph 1.f of Article 48, the Commission shall draw up a report. . . .

Article 50

1. If a settlement is not reached, the Commission shall . . . draw up a report setting forth the facts and stating its conclusions. If the report, in whole or in part, does not represent the unanimous agreement of the members of the Commission, any member may attach to it a separate opinion. The written and oral statements made by the parties . . . shall also be attached to the report.

2. The report shall be transmitted to the states concerned, which shall not be at liberty to publish it.

3. In transmitting the report, the Committee may make such proposals and recommendations as it sees fit.

Article 51

1. If, within a period of three months from the date of the transmittal of the report of the Commission to the states concerned, the matter has not either been settled or submitted by the Commission or by the state concerned to the Court and its jurisdiction accepted, the Commission may, by the vote of an absolute majority of its members, set forth its opinion and conclusions concerning the question submitted for its consideration.

2. Where appropriate, the Commission shall make pertinent recommendations and shall prescribe a period within which the state is to take the measures that are incumbent upon it to remedy the situation examined.

3. When the prescribed period has expired, the Commission shall decide by the vote of an absolute majority of its members whether the state has taken adequate measures and whether to publish its report.

Chapter VIII.   Inter-American Court of Human Rights

Section 1.   Organization

Article 52

1. The Court shall consist of seven judges, nationals of the member states of the Organization, elected in an individual capacity from among jurists of the highest moral authority and of recognized competence in the field of human rights, who possess the qualifications required for the exercise of the highest judicial functions in conformity with the law of the state of which they are nationals or of the state that proposes them as candidates.

2. No two judges may be nationals of the same state.

Article 53

1. The judges of the Court shall be elected by secret ballot by an absolute majority vote of the States Parties to the Convention, in the General Assembly of the Organization, from a panel of candidates proposed by those states.

2. Each of the States Parties may propose up to three candidates, nationals of the state that proposes them or of any other member state of the Organization of American States. When a slate of three is proposed, at least one of the candidates shall be a national of a state other than the one proposing the state.

Article 54

1. The judges of the Court shall be elected for a term of six years and may be reelected only once. The term of three of the judges chosen in the first election shall expire at the end of three years. Immediately after the election, the names of the three judges shall be determined by lot in the General Assembly.

2. A judge elected to replace a judge whose term has not expired shall complete the term of the latter.

3. The judges shall continue in office until the expiration of their term. However, they shall continue to serve with regard to cases that they have begun to hear and that are still pending, for which purposes they shall not be replaced by the newly elected judges.

Article 55

1. If a judge is a national of any of the States Parties to a case submitted to the Court, he shall retain his right to hear that case.

2. If one of the judges called upon to hear a case should be a national of one the States Parties to the case, any other State Party in the case may appoint a person of its choice to serve on the Court as an *ad hoc* judge.

3. If among the judges called upon to hear a case none is a national of any of the States Parties to the case, each of the latter may appoint an *ad hoc* judge.

4. An *ad hoc* judge shall possess the qualifications indicated in Article 52.

5. If several States Parties to the Convention should have the same interest in a case, they shall be considered as a single party for purposes of the above provisions. In case of doubt, the Court shall decide.

Article 56

Five judges shall constitute a quorum for the transaction of business by the Court.

Article 57

The Commission shall appear in all cases before the Court.

Article 58

1. The Court shall have its seat at the place determined by the States Parties to the Convention in the General Assembly of the Organization; however, it may convene in the territory of any member state of the Organization of American States when a majority of the Court consider it desirable, and with the prior consent of the state concerned. . . .

Article 60

The Court shall draw up its Statute which it shall submit to the General Assembly for approval. It shall adopt its own Rules of Procedure.

SECTION 2. JURISDICTION AND FUNCTIONS

Article 61

1. Only the States Parties and the Commission shall have the right to submit a case to the Court.

2. In order for the Court to hear a case, it is necessary that the procedures set forth in Articles 48 to 50 shall have been completed.

Article 62

1. A State Party may, upon depositing its instrument of ratification or adherence to this Convention, or at any subsequent time, declare that it recognizes as binding, *ipso facto*, and not requiring special agreement, the jurisdiction of the Court on all matters relating to the interpretation or application of this Convention.

2. Such declaration may be made unconditionally, on the condition of reciprocity, for a specified period, or for specific cases. . . .

3. The jurisdiction of the Court shall comprise all cases concerning the interpretation and application of the provisions of this Convention that are submitted to it, provided that the States Parties to the case recognize or have recognized such jurisdiction, whether by special declaration pursuant to the preceding paragraphs, or by a special agreement.

Article 63

1. If the Court finds that there has been a violation of a right or freedom protected by this Convention, the Court shall rule that the injured party be ensured the enjoyment of his right or freedom that was violated. It shall also rule, if appropriate, that the consequences of the measure or situation that constituted the breach of such right or freedom be remedied and that fair compensation be paid to the injured party.

2. In cases of extreme gravity and urgency, and when necessary to avoid irreparable damage to persons, the Court shall adopt such provisional measures as it deems pertinent in matters it has under consideration. With respect to a case not yet submitted to the Court, it may act at the request of the Commission.

Article 64

1. The member states of the Organization may consult the Court regarding the interpretation of this Convention or of other treaties concerning the protection of human rights in the American states. Within their spheres of competence, the organs listed in Chapter X of the Charter of the Organization of American States, as amended by the Protocol of Buenos Aires, may in like manner consult the Court.

2. The Court, at the request of a member state of the Organization, may provide that state with opinions regarding the compatibility of any of its domestic laws with the aforesaid international instruments. . . .

SECTION 3. PROCEDURE

Article 66

1. Reasons shall be given for the judgment of the Court.

2. If the judgment does not represent in whole or in part the unanimous opinion of the judges, any judge shall be entitled to have his dissenting or separate opinion attached to the judgment.

Article 67

The judgment of the Court shall be final and not subject to appeal. In case of disagreement as to the meaning or scope of the judgment, the Court shall interpret it at the request of any of the parties, provided the request is made within ninety days from the date of notification of the judgment.

Article 68

1. The States Parties to the Convention undertake to comply with the judgment of the Court in any case to which they are parties.

2. That part of a judgment that stipulates compensatory damages may be executed in the country concerned in accordance with domestic procedure governing the execution of judgments against the state. . . .

CHAPTER IX.   COMMON PROVISIONS

Article 70

1. The judges of the Court and the members of the Commission shall enjoy, from the moment of their election and throughout their term of office, the immunities extended to diplomatic agents in accordance with international law. . . .

Article 71

The position of judge of the Court or member of the Commission is incompatible with any other activity that might affect the independence or impartiality of such judge or member, as determined in the respective statutes. . . .

CONSTITUTIVE ACT OF THE
AFRICAN UNION

www.au.int/en*

We, Heads of State and Government of the Member States of the Organization of African Unity (OAU) . . .

Inspired by the noble ideals which guided the founding fathers of our Continental Organization and generations of Pan-Africanists in their determination to promote unity, solidarity, cohesion and cooperation among the peoples of Africa and African States;

Considering the principles and objectives stated in the Charter of the Organization of African Unity and the Treaty establishing the African Economic Community;

Recalling the heroic struggles waged by our peoples and our countries for political independence, human dignity and economic emancipation;

Considering that since its inception, the Organization of African Unity has played a determining and invaluable role in the liberation of the continent, the affirmation of a common identity and the process of attainment of the unity of our continent and has provided a unique framework for our collective action in Africa and in our relations with the rest of the world.

---

* The Constitutive Act entered into force in 2001. The first meeting of the AU took place on July 9, 2002. As noted in the above text, the African Union adheres to the provisions of the African Charter on Human and Peoples' Rights, which follows this excerpt.

As of March 2013, the 54 parties to the Constitutive Act are: Algeria, Angola, Benin, Botswana, Burkina Faso, Burundi, Cameroon, Cape Verdi, Central African Republic, Chad, Comoros, Congo, Congo (Democratic Republic of), Cote d'Ivoire, Djibouti, Egypt, Equatorial Guinea, Eritrea, Ethiopia, Gabon, Gambia, Ghana, Guinea Bissau, Guinea, Kenya, Lesotho, Liberia, Libyan Arab Jamahiriya, Madagascar, Malawi, Mali, Mauritania, Mauritius, Mozambique, Namibia, Niger, Nigeria, Rwanda, Western Sahara, Sao Tome and Principe, Senegal, Seychelles, Sierra Leone, Somalia, South Africa, South Sudan, Sudan, Swaziland, Tanzania, Togo, Tunisia, Uganda, Zambia, Zimbabwe.

A 2003 Protocol on the Amendments to the Constitutive Act of the African Union is pending. It requires a two-thirds majority of the 54 AU members to ratify it; as of February 28, 2013, there have been 28 ratifications/accessions.

Determine to take up the multifaceted challenges that confront our continent and peoples in the light of the social, economic and political changes taking place in the world;

Convinced of the need to accelerate the process of implementing the Treaty establishing the African Economic Community in order to promote the socio-economic development of Africa and to face more effectively the challenges posed by globalization;

Guided by our common vision of a united and strong Africa and by the need to build a partnership between governments and all segments of civil society, in particular women, youth and the private sector, in order to strengthen solidarity and cohesion among our peoples;

Conscious of the fact that the scourge of conflicts in Africa constitutes a major impediment to the socio-economic development of the continent and of the need to promote peace, security and stability as a prerequisite for the implementation of our development and integration agenda;

Determined to promote and protect human and peoples' rights, consolidate democratic institutions and culture, and to ensure good governance and the rule of law;

Further determined to take all necessary measures to strengthen our common institutions and provide them with the necessary powers and resources to enable them discharge their respective mandates effectively;

Recalling the Declaration which we adopted at the Fourth Extraordinary Session of our Assembly in Sirte, the Great Socialist People's Libyan Arab Jamahiriya, on 9.9. 99, in which we decided to establish an African Union, in conformity with the ultimate objectives of the Charter of our Continental Organization and the Treaty establishing the African Economic Community;

Have agreed as follows . . . :

Article 2 Establishment

The African Union is hereby established in accordance with the provisions of this Act.

Article 3 Objectives

The objectives of the Union shall be to:

(a) achieve greater unity and solidarity between the African countries and the peoples of Africa;

(b) defend the sovereignty, territorial integrity and independence of its Member States;

(c) accelerate the political and socio-economic integration of the continent;

(d) promote and defend African common positions on issues of interest to the continent and its peoples;

(e) encourage international cooperation, taking due account of the Charter of the United Nations and the Universal Declaration of Human Rights;

(**f**) promote peace, security, and stability on the continent;

(**g**) promote democratic principles and institutions, popular participation and good governance;

(**h**) promote and protect human and peoples' rights in accordance with the African Charter on Human and Peoples' Rights and other relevant human rights instruments;

(**i**) establish the necessary conditions which enable the continent to play its rightful role in the global economy and in international negotiations;

(**j**) promote sustainable development at the economic, social and cultural levels as well as the integration of African economies;

(**k**) promote co-operation in all fields of human activity to raise the living standards of African peoples;

(**l**) coordinate and harmonize the policies between the existing and future Regional Economic Communities for the gradual attainment of the objectives of the Union;

(**m**) advance the development of the continent by promoting research in all fields, in particular in science and technology;

(**n**) work with relevant international partners in the eradication of preventable diseases and the promotion of good health on the continent.

Article 4 Principles

The Union shall function in accordance with the following principles:

(**a**) sovereign equality and interdependence among Member States of the Union;

(**b**) respect of borders existing on achievement of independence;

(**c**) participation of the African peoples in the activities of the Union;

(**d**) establishment of a common defence policy for the African Continent;

(**e**) peaceful resolution of conflicts among Member States of the Union through such appropriate means as may be decided upon by the Assembly;

(**f**) prohibition of the use of force or threat to use force among Member States of the Union;

(**g**) non-interference by any Member State in the internal affairs of another;

(**h**) the right of the Union to intervene in a Member State pursuant to a decision of the Assembly in respect of grave circumstances, namely: war crimes, genocide and crimes against humanity;

(**i**) peaceful co-existence of Member States and their right to live in peace and security;

(**j**) the right of Member States to request intervention from the Union in order to restore peace and security;

(**k**) promotion of self-reliance within the framework of the Union;

(**l**) promotion of gender equality;

(**m**) respect for democratic principles, human rights, the rule of law and good governance;

(n) promotion of social justice to ensure balanced economic development;

(o) respect for the sanctity of human life, condemnation and rejection of impunity and political assassination, acts of terrorism and subversive activities;

(p) condemnation and rejection of unconstitutional changes of governments.

Article 5 Organs of the Union

1. The organs of the Unon shall be:
(a) The Assembly of the Union;
(b) The Executive Council;
(c) The Pan-African Parliament;
(d) The Court of Justice;
(e) The Commission; . . . .

Article 6 The Assembly

1. The Assembly shall be composed of Heads of States and Government or their duly accredited representatives.

2. The Assembly shall be the supreme organ of the Union.

3. The Assembly shall meet at least once a year in ordinary session. At the request of any Member State and on approval by a two-thirds majority of the Member States, the Assembly shall meet in extraordinary session.

4. The Office of the Chairman of the Assembly shall be held for a period of one year by a Head of State or Government elected after consultations among the Member States.

Article 7 Decisions of the Assembly

1. The Assembly shall take its decisions by consensus or, failing which, by a two-thirds majority of the Member States of the Union. However, procedural matters, including the question of whether a matter is one of procedure or not, shall be decided by a simple majority. . . .

Article 9 Powers and Functions of the Assembly

1. The functions of the Assembly shall be to:

(a) determine the common policies of the Union;

(b) receive, consider and take decisions on reports and recommendations from the other organs of the Union;

(c) consider requests for Membership of the Union;

(d) establish any organ of the Union;

(e) monitor the implementation of policies and decisions of the Union as well ensure compliance by all Member States;

(f) adopt the budget of the Union;

(g) give directives to the Executive Council on the management of conflicts, war and other emergency situations and the restoration of peace;

(h) appoint and terminate the appointment of the judges of the Court of Justice;

(i) appoint the Chairman of the Commission and his or her deputy or deputies and Commissioners of the Commission and determine their functions and terms of office. . . .

Article 18 The Court of Justice

1. A Court of Justice of the Union shall be established;

2. The statute, composition and functions of the Court of Justice shall be defined in a protocol relating thereto.

Article 19 The Financial Institutions

The Union shall have the following financial institutions whose rules and regulations shall be defined in protocols relating thereto:

(a) The African Central Bank;

(b) The African Monetary Fund;

(c) The African Investment Bank. . . .

Article 23 Imposition of Sanctions

1. The Assembly shall determine the appropriate sanctions to be imposed on any Member State that defaults in the payment of its contributions to the budget of the Union in the following manner: denial of the right to speak at meetings, to vote, to present candidates for any position or post within the Union or to benefit from any activity or commitments, therefrom;

2. Furthermore, any Member State that fails to comply with the decisions and policies of the Union may be subjected to other sanctions, such as the denial of transport and communications links with other Member States, and other measures of a political and economic nature to be determined by the Assembly.

Article 24 The Headquarters of the Union

1. The Headquarters of the Unon shall be in Addis Ababa in the Federal Democratic Republic of Ethiopia. . . .

Article 30 Suspension

Governments which shall come to power through unconstitutional means shall not be allowed to participate in the activities of the Union. . . .

AFRICAN CHARTER ON HUMAN AND PEOPLES' RIGHTS (BANJUL CHARTER)

June 27, 1981, 21 I.L.M. 59*

Preamble

The African States members of the Organization of African Unity, parties to the present convention entitled "African Charter on Human and Peoples' Rights. . . .

Reaffirming the pledge they solemnly made in Article 2 of the [O.A.U.] Charter to eradicate all forms of colonialism from Africa, to coordinate and intensify their cooperation and efforts to achieve a better life for the peoples of Africa and to promote international cooperation having due regard to the Charter of the United Nations and the Universal Declaration of Human Rights;

Taking into consideration the virtues of their historical tradition and the values of African civilization which should inspire and characterize their reflection on the concept of human and peoples' rights;

Recognizing on the one hand, that fundamental human rights stem from the attributes of human beings, which justifies their national and interna-

---

* Adopted by the Organization of African Unity at Nairobi, Kenya, on June 27, 1981. Entered into force on October 21, 1986. Later adopted by the African Union in 2001. See the African Union Web site at <http://www.africaunion.org>.

As of March 2013, the 53 parties to the charter are: Algeria, Angola, Benin, Botswana, Burkina Faso, Burundi, Cameroon, Cape Verde, Central African Republic, Chad, Comoros, Congo, Congo (Democratic Republic of), Côte d'Ivoire, Djibouti, Egypt, Equatorial Guinea, Ethiopia, Gabon, Gambia, Ghana, Guinea, Guinea-Bissau, Kenya, Lesotho, Liberia, Libyan Arab Jamahiriya, Madagascar, Malawi, Mali, Mauritania, Mauritius, Morocco, Mozambique, Namibia, Niger, Nigeria, RASD (Polisario), Rwanda, Sao Tome and Principe, Senegal, Seychelles, Sierra Leone, Somalia, South Africa, Sudan, Swaziland, Tanzania, Togo, Tunisia, Uganda, Zambia, and Zimbabwe.

Also in force is the 2003 Protocol to the African Charter on Human and Peoples' Rights on the Rights of Women in Africa. As of March 2013, there have been 28 ratifications/accessions to the Protocol.

tional protection and on the other hand that the reality and respect of people's rights should necessarily guarantee human rights;

Considering that the enjoyment of rights and freedoms also implies the performance of duties on the part of everyone;

Convinced that it is henceforth essential to pay a particular attention to the right to development and that civil and political rights cannot be dissociated from economic, social and cultural rights in their conception as well as universality and that the satisfaction of economic, social and cultural rights is a guarantee for the enjoyment of civil and political rights;

Conscious of their duty to achieve the total liberation of Africa, the peoples of which are still struggling for their dignity and genuine independence, and undertaking to eliminate colonialism, neo-colonialism, apartheid, zionism and to dismantle aggressive foreign military bases and all forms of discrimination, particularly those based on race, ethnic group, color, sex, language, religion or political opinions; . . .

Have agreed as follows:

Part I.   Rights and Duties

CHAPTER I.   HUMAN AND PEOPLES' RIGHTS

Article 1

The Member States of the Organization of African Unity parties to the present Charter shall recognize the rights, duties and freedoms enshrined in this Charter and shall undertake to adopt legislative or other measures to give effect to them.

Article 2

Every individual shall be entitled to the enjoyment of the rights and freedoms recognized and guaranteed in the present Charter without distinction of any kind such as race, ethnic group, color, sex, language, religion, political or any other opinion, national and social origin, fortune, birth or other status.

Article 3

1. Every individual shall be equal before the law.
2. Every individual shall be entitled to equal protection of the law.

Article 4

Human beings are inviolable. Every human being shall be entitled to respect for his life and the integrity of his person. No one may be arbitrarily deprived of this right.

Article 5

Every individual shall have the right to the respect of the dignity inherent in a human being and to the recognition of his legal status. All forms of exploitation and degradation of man particularly slavery, slave trade, torture, cruel, inhuman or degrading punishment and treatment shall be prohibited.

Article 6

Every individual shall have the right to liberty and to the security of his person. No one may be deprived of his freedom except for reasons and conditions previously laid down by law. In particular, no one may be arbitrarily arrested or detained.

Article 7

1. Every individual shall have the right to have his cause heard. This comprises:

(a) the right to an appeal to competent national organs against acts of violating his fundamental rights as recognized and guaranteed by conventions, laws, regulations and customs in force;

(b) the right to be presumed innocent until proved guilty by a competent court or tribunal;

(c) the right to defence, including the right to be defended by counsel of his choice;

(d) the right to be tried within a reasonable time by an impartial court or tribunal.

2. No one may be condemned for an act or omission which did not constitute a legally punishable offence at the time it was committed. No penalty, may be inflicted for an offence for which no provision was made at the time it was committed. Punishment is personal and can be imposed only on the offender.

Article 8

Freedom of conscience, the profession and free practice of religion shall be guaranteed. No one may, subject to law and order, be submitted to measures restricting the exercise of these freedoms.

Article 9

1. Every individual shall have the right to receive information.

2. Every individual shall have the right to express and disseminate his opinions within the law.

Article 10

1. Every individual shall have the right to free association provided that he abides by the law.

2. Subject to the obligation of solidarity provided for in Article 29 no one may be compelled to join an association.

Article 11

Every individual shall have the right to assemble freely with others. The exercise of this right shall be subject only to necessary restrictions provided for by law in particular those enacted in the interest of national security, the safety, health, ethics and rights and freedoms of others.

Article 12

1. Every individual shall have the right to freedom of movement and residence within the borders of a State provided he abides by the law.

2. Every individual shall have the right to leave any country including his own, and to return to his country. This right may only be subject to restrictions, provided for by law for the protection of national security, law and order, public health or morality.

3. Every individual shall have the right, when persecuted, to seek and obtain asylum in other countries in accordance with laws of those countries and international conventions.

4. A non-national legally admitted in a territory of a State Party to the present Charter, may only be expelled from it by virtue of a decision taken in accordance with the law.

5. The mass expulsion of non-nationals shall be prohibited. Mass expulsion shall be that which is aimed at national, racial, ethnic or religious groups.

Article 13

1. Every citizen shall have the right to participate freely in the government of his country, either directly or through freely chosen representatives in accordance with the provisions of the law.

2. Every citizen shall have the right of equal access to the public service of his country.

3. Every individual shall have the right of access to public property and services in strict equality of all persons before the law.

Article 14

The right to property shall be guaranteed. It may only be encroached upon in the interest of public need or in the general interest of the community and in accordance with the provisions of appropriate laws.

Article 15

Every individual shall have the right to work under equitable and satisfactory conditions, and shall receive equal pay for equal work.

Article 16

1. Every individual shall have the right to enjoy the best attainable state of physical and mental health.

2. States parties to the present Charter shall take the necessary measures to protect the health of their people and to ensure that they receive medical attention when they are sick.

Article 17

1. Every individual shall have the right to education.

2. Every individual may freely take part in the cultural life of his community.

3. The promotion and protection of morals and traditional values recognized by the community shall be the duty of the State.

Article 18

1. The family shall be the natural unit and basis of society. It shall be protected by the State which shall take care of its physical health and morals.

2. The State shall have the duty to assist the family which is the custodian of morals and traditional values recognized by the community.

3. The State shall ensure the elimination of every discrimination against women and also censure the protection of the rights of the woman and the child as stipulated in international declarations and conventions.

4. The aged and the disabled shall also have the right to special measures of protection in keeping with their physical or moral needs.

Article 19

All peoples shall be equal; they shall enjoy the same respect and shall have the same rights. Nothing shall justify the domination of a people by another.

Article 20

1. All peoples shall have the right to existence. They shall have the unquestionable and inalienable right to self-determination. They shall freely determine their political status and shall pursue their economic and social development according to the policy they have freely chosen.

2. Colonized or oppressed peoples shall have the right to free themselves from the bonds of domination by resorting to any means recognized by the international community.

3. All peoples shall have the right to the assistance of the States parties to the present Charter in their liberation struggle against foreign domination, be it political, economic or cultural.

Article 21

1. All peoples shall freely dispose of their wealth and natural resources. This right shall be exercised in the exclusive interest of the people. In no case shall a people be deprived of it.

2. In case of spoliation the dispossessed people shall have the right to the lawful recovery of its property as well as to an adequate compensation.

3. The free disposal of wealth and natural resources shall be exercised without prejudice to the obligation of promoting international economic cooperation based on mutual respect, equitable exchange and the principles of international law.

4. States parties to the present Charter shall individually and collectively exercise the right to free disposal of their wealth and natural resources with a view to strengthening African unity and solidarity.

5. States parties to the present Charter shall undertake to eliminate all forms of foreign economic exploitation particularly that practiced by international monopolies so as to enable their peoples to fully benefit from the advantages derived from their national resources.

Article 22

1. All peoples shall have the right to their economic, social and cultural development with due regard to their freedom and identity and in the equal enjoyment of the common heritage of mankind.

2. States shall have the duty, individually or collectively, to ensure the exercise of the right to development.

Article 23

1. All peoples shall have the right to national and international peace and security. The principles of solidarity and friendly relations implicitly affirmed by the Charter of the United Nations and reaffirmed by that of the Organization of African Unity shall govern relations between States.

2. For the purpose of strengthening peace, solidarity and friendly relations, States parties to the present Charter shall ensure that:

(a) any individual enjoying the right of asylum under Article 12 of the present Charter shall not engage in subversive activities against his country of origin or any other State party to the present Charter;

(b) their territories shall not be used as bases for subversive or terrorist activities against the people of any other State party to the present Charter.

Article 24

All peoples shall have the right to a general satisfactory environment favorable to their development.

Article 25

States parties to the present Charter shall have the duty to promote and ensure through teaching, education and publication, the respect of the rights and freedoms contained in the present Charter and to see to it that these freedoms and rights as well as corresponding obligations and duties are understood.

Article 26

States parties to the present Charter shall have the duty to guarantee the independence of the Courts and shall allow the establishment and improvement of appropriate national institutions entrusted with the promotion and protection of the rights and freedoms guaranteed by the present Charter.

CHAPTER II. DUTIES

Article 27

1. Every individual shall have duties towards his family and society, the State and other legally recognized communities and the international community.

2. The rights and freedoms of each individual shall be exercised with due regard to the rights of others, collective security, morality and common interest.

Article 28

Every individual shall have the duty to respect and consider his fellow beings without discrimination, and to maintain relations aimed at promoting, safeguarding and reinforcing mutual respect and tolerance.

Article 29

The individual shall also have the duty:

1. To preserve the harmonious development of the family and to work for the cohesion and respect of the family; to respect his parents at all times, to maintain them in case of need;

2. To serve his national community by placing his physical and intellectual abilities at its service;

3. Not to compromise the security of the State whose national or resident he is;

4. To preserve and strengthen social and national solidarity, particularly when the latter is threatened;

5. To preserve and strengthen the national independence and the territorial integrity of his country and to contribute to its defence in accordance with the law;

6. To work to the best of his abilities and competence, and to pay taxes imposed by law in the interest of the society;

7. To preserve and strengthen positive African cultural values in his relations with other members of the society, in the spirit of tolerance, dialogue and consultation and, in general, to contribute to the promotion of the moral well being of society;

8. To contribute to the best of his abilities, at all times and at all levels, to the promotion and achievement of African unity.

Part II.   Measures of Safeguard

CHAPTER I.   ESTABLISHMENT AND ORGANIZATION OF THE AFRICAN COMMISSION ON HUMAN AND PEOPLES' RIGHTS

Article 30

An African Commission on Human and Peoples' Rights, hereinafter called "the Commission," shall be established within the Organization of African Unity to promote human and peoples' rights and ensure their protection in Africa.

Article 31

1. The Commission shall consist of eleven members chosen from amongst African personalities of the highest reputation, known for their high morality, integrity, impartiality and competence in matters of human and peoples' rights; particular consideration being given to persons having legal experience.

2. The members of the Commission shall serve in their personal capacity.

Article 32

The Commission shall not include more than one national of the same State.

Article 33

The members of the Commission shall be elected by secret ballot by the Assembly of Heads of State and Government, from a list of persons nominated by the States parties to the present Charter. . . .

Article 36

The members of the Commission shall be elected for a six year period and shall be eligible for re-election. . . .

CHAPTER II.   MANDATE OF THE COMMISSION

Article 45

The functions of the Commission shall be:

1. To promote Human and Peoples' Rights and in particular:

(a) to collect documents, undertake studies and researches on African problems in the field of human and peoples' rights, organize seminars, symposia and conferences, disseminate information, encourage national and local institutions concerned with human and peoples' rights, and should the case arise, give its views or make recommendations to Governments.

(b) to formulate and lay down, principles and rules aimed at solving legal problems relating to human and peoples' rights and fundamental freedoms upon which African Governments may base their legislations.

(c) co-operate with other African and international institutions concerned with the promotion and protection of human and peoples' rights.

2. Ensure the protection of human and peoples' rights under conditions laid down by the present Charter.

3. Interpret all the provisions of the present Charter at the request of a State party, an institution of the OAU or an African Organization recognized by the OAU.

4. Perform any other tasks which may be entrusted to it by the Assembly of Heads of State and Government.

CHAPTER III.   PROCEDURE OF THE COMMISSION

Article 46

....The Commission may resort to any appropriate method of investigation; it may hear from the Secretary General of the Organization of African Unity or any other person capable of enlightening it. . . .

CHAPTER IV.   APPLICABLE PRINCIPLES

Article 60

The Commission shall draw inspiration from international law on human and peoples' rights, particularly from the provisions of various African instruments on human and peoples' rights, the Charter of the United

Nations, the Charter of the Organization of African Unity, the Universal Declaration of Human Rights, other instruments adopted by the United Nations and by African countries in the field of human and peoples' rights . . . .

Article 61

The Commission shall also take into consideration, as subsidiary measures to determine the principles of law, other general or special international conventions, laying down rules expressly recognized by member states of the Organization of African Unity, African practices consistent with international norms on human and peoples' rights, customs generally accepted as law, general principles of law recognized by African states as well as legal precedents and doctrine. . . .

9

Law of the Sea

UNCLOS RESOLUTION 1 RE: ESTABLISHMENT OF PREPARATORY COMMISSION

April 30, 1982, 21 I.L.M. 1253 (1982)*

Resolution 1.   Establishment of the Preparatory Commission for the International Sea-Bed Authority and for the International Tribunal for the Law of the Sea

The Third United Nations Conference on the Law of the Sea,

Having adopted the Convention on the Law of the Sea which provides for the establishment of the International Sea-Bed Authority and the International Tribunal for the Law of the Sea,

Having decided to take all possible measures to ensure the entry into effective operation without undue delay of the Authority and the Tribunal and to make the necessary arrangements for the commencement of their functions,

Having decided that a Preparatory Commission should be established for the fulfilment of these purposes,

Decides as follows: 1. There is hereby established the Preparatory Commission for the International Sea-Bed Authority and for the International Tribunal for the Law of the Sea. Upon signature of or accession to the Convention by 50 States, the Secretary-General of the United Nations shall convene the Commission, and it shall meet no sooner than 60 days and no later than 90 days thereafter.

---

* Adopted at the Third U.N. Conference on the Law of the Sea (UNCLOS) in a vote that also included the Law of the Sea Convention, *infra*, and three other resolutions. The vote on April 30, 1982 was 130 delegations in favor, 4 against, and 17 abstentions. The convention and the four resolutions, with some drafting changes (included here for Resolution 1), were later annexed to the Final Act, which was done at Montego Bay, Jamaica, on December 10, 1982.

2. The Commission shall consist of the representatives of States and of Namibia, represented by the United Nations Council for Namibia, which have signed the Convention or acceded to it. The representatives of signatories of the Final Act may participate fully in the deliberations of the Commission as observers but shall not be entitled to participate in the taking of decisions.

3. The Commission shall elect its Chairman and other officers.

4. The Rules of Procedure of the Third United Nations Conference on the Law of the Sea shall apply *mutatis mutandis* to the adoption of the rules of procedure of the Commission.

5. The Commission shall:

(a) prepare the provisional agenda for the first session of the Assembly and of the Council and, as appropriate, make recommendations relating to items thereon;

(b) prepare draft rules of procedure of the Assembly and of the Council; (c) make recommendations concerning the budget for the first financial period of the Authority;

(d) make recommendations concerning the relationship between the Authority and the United Nations and other international organizations;

(e) make recommendations concerning the Secretariat of the Authority in accordance with the relevant provisions of the Convention;

(f) undertake studies, as necessary, concerning the establishment of the headquarters of the Authority, and make recommendations relating thereto;

(g) prepare draft rules, regulations and procedures, as necessary to enable the Authority to commence its functions, including draft regulations concerning the financial management and the internal administration of the Authority;

(h) exercise the powers and functions assigned to it by resolution II of the Third United Nations Conference on the Law of the Sea relating to preparatory investment;

(i) undertake studies on the problems which would be encountered by developing land-based producer States likely to be most seriously affected by the production of minerals derived from the Area. . . .

11. The Commission shall prepare a final report on all matters within its mandate, except as provided in paragraph 10, for the presentation to the Assembly at its first session. . . .

13. The Commission shall remain in existence until the conclusion of the first session of the Assembly, at which time its property and records shall be transferred to the Authority.

14. The expenses of the Commission shall be met from the regular budget of the United Nations, subject to the approval of the General Assembly of the United Nations. . . .

CONVENTION ON THE LAW OF THE SEA

Dec. 10, 1982, 1833 U.N.T.S. 3, 21 I.L.M. 1261 (1982)*

Table of Contents

PREAMBLE

PART I. INTRODUCTION
    Article 1. Use of terms and scope

PART II. TERRITORIAL SEA AND CONTIGUOUS ZONE
    SECTION 1. GENERAL PROVISIONS
    Article 2. Legal status of the territorial sea, of the air space over the territorial sea and of its bed and subsoil
    SECTION 2. LIMITS OF THE TERRITORIAL SEA
    Article 3. Breadth of the territorial sea
    Article 4. Outer limit of the territorial sea
    Article 5. Normal baseline

---

* Done at Montego Bay, Jamaica, on December 10, 1982. Entered into force on November 16, 1994. As of March 2013, the United States has not ratified the convention.

The 165 parties to the convention are: Albania, Algeria, Angola, Antigua and Barbuda, Argentina, Armenia, Australia, Austria, Bahamas, Bahrain, Bangladesh, Barbados, Belarus, Belgium, Belize, Benin, Bolivia, Bosnia and Herzegovina, Botswana, Brazil, Brunei Darussalam, Bulgaria, Burkina Faso, Cameroon, Canada, Cape Verde, Chad, Chile, China, Comoros, Cook Islands, Congo, Congo (Democratic Republic of), Costa Rica, Côte d'Ivoire, Croatia, Cuba, Cyprus, Czech Republic, Denmark, Djibouti, Dominica, Dominican Republic, Ecuador, Egypt, Equatorial Guinea, Estonia, European Community, Fiji, Finland, France, Gabon, Gambia, Georgia, Germany, Ghana, Greece, Grenada, Guatemala, Guinea, Guinea-Bissau, Guyana, Haiti, Honduras, Hungary, Iceland, India, Indonesia, Iraq, Ireland, Italy, Jamaica, Japan, Jordan, Kenya, Kiribati, Korea (Republic of), Kuwait, Lao People's Democratic Republic, Latvia, Lebanon, Lesotho, Liberia, Lithuania, Luxembourg, Macedonia (the former Yugoslav Republic of), Madagascar, Malawi, Malaysia, Maldives, Mali, Malta, Marshall Islands, Mauritania, Mauritius, Mexico, Micronesia, Moldova, Monaco, Mongolia, Montenegro, Morocco, Mozambique, Myanmar, Namibia, Nauru, Nepal, Netherlands, New Zealand, Nicaragua, Nigeria, Niue, Norway, Oman, Pakistan, Palau, Panama, Papua New Guinea, Paraguay, Philippines, Poland, Portugal, Qatar, Romania, Russia, Saint Kitts and Nevis, Saint Lucia, Saint Vincent and the Grenadines, Samoa, Sao Tome and Principe, Saudi Arabia, Senegal, Serbia, Seychelles, Sierra Leone, Singapore, Slovakia, Slovenia, Solomon Islands, Somalia, South Africa, Spain, Sri Lanka, Sudan, Suriname, Swaziland, Sweden, Switzerland, Tanzania, Thailand, Timor-Leste, Togo, Tonga, Trinidad and Tobago, Tunisia, Tuvalu, Uganda, Ukraine, United Kingdom, Uruguay, Vanuatu, Viet Nam, Yemen, Zambia, and Zimbabwe. See the U.N. Web site at <http://treaties.un.org>.

Article 6.   Reefs
Article 7.   Straight baselines
Article 8.   Internal waters
Article 9.   Mouths of rivers
Article 10.   Bays
Article 11.   Ports
Article 12.   Roadsteads
Article 13.   Low-tide elevations
Article 14.   Combination of methods for determining baselines
Article 15.   Delimitation of the territorial sea between States with opposite or adjacent coasts
Article 16.   Charts and lists of geographical co-ordinates
SECTION 3.   INNOCENT PASSAGE IN THE TERRITORIAL SEA
SUBSECTION A.   RULES APPLICABLE TO ALL SHIPS
Article 17.   Right of innocent passage
Article 18.   Meaning of passage
Article 19.   Meaning of innocent passage
Article 20.   Submarines and other underwater vehicles
Article 21.   Laws and regulations of the coastal State relating to innocent passage
Article 22.   Sea lanes and traffic separation schemes in the territorial sea
Article 23.   Foreign nuclear-powered ships and ships carrying nuclear or other inherently dangerous or noxious substances
Article 24.   Duties of the coastal State
Article 25.   Rights of protection of the coastal State
Article 26.   Charges which may be levied upon foreign ships
SUBSECTION B.   RULES APPLICABLE TO MERCHANT SHIPS AND GOVERNMENT SHIPS OPERATED FOR COMMERCIAL PURPOSES
Article 27.   Criminal jurisdiction on board a foreign ship
Article 28.   Civil jurisdiction in relation to foreign ships
SUBSECTION C.   RULES APPLICABLE TO WARSHIPS AND OTHER GOVERNMENT SHIPS OPERATED FOR NON-COMMERCIAL PURPOSES
Article 29.   Definition of warships
Article 30.   Non-compliance by warships with the laws and regulations of the coastal State
Article 31.   Responsibility of the flag State for damage caused by a warship or other government ship operated for noncommercial purposes
Article 32.   Immunities of warships and other government ships operated for non-commercial purposes
SECTION 4.   CONTIGUOUS ZONE
Article 33.   Contiguous zone

PART III.   STRAITS USED FOR INTERNATIONAL NAVIGATION
    SECTION 1.   GENERAL PROVISIONS
        Article 34.   Legal status of waters forming straits used for
                      international navigation
        Article 35.   Scope of this Part
        Article 36.   High seas routes or routes through exclusive
                      economic zones through straits used for international
                      navigation
    SECTION 2.   TRANSIT PASSAGE
        Article 37.   Scope of this section
        Article 38.   Right of transit passage
        Article 39.   Duties of ships and aircraft during transit passage
        Article 40.   Research and survey activities
        Article 41.   Sea lanes and traffic separation schemes in straits used
                      for international navigation
        Article 42.   Laws and regulations of States bordering straits
                      relating to transit passage
        Article 43.   Navigational and safety aids and other improvements
                      and the prevention, reduction and control of pollution
        Article 44.   Duties of States bordering straits
    SECTION 3.   INNOCENT PASSAGE
        Article 45.   Innocent passage

PART IV.   ARCHIPELAGIC STATES
        Article 46.   Use of terms
        Article 47.   Archipelagic baselines
        Article 48.   Measurement of the breadth of the territorial sea, the
                      contiguous zone, the exclusive economic zone and the
                      continental shelf
        Article 49.   Legal status of archipelagic waters, of the air space
                      over archipelagic waters and of their bed and subsoil
        Article 50.   Delimitation of internal waters
        Article 51.   Existing agreements, traditional fishing rights and
                      existing submarine cables
        Article 52.   Right of innocent passage
        Article 53.   Right of archipelagic sea lanes passage
        Article 54.   Duties of ships and aircraft . . . , duties of the
                      archipelagic State and laws and regulations . . .
                      relating to . . . sea lanes passage

PART V.   EXCLUSIVE ECONOMIC ZONE
        Article 55.   Specific legal régime of the exclusive economic zone
        Article 56.   Rights, jurisdiction and duties of the coastal State in
                      the exclusive economic zone
        Article 57.   Breadth of the exclusive economic zone
        Article 58.   Rights and duties of other States in the exclusive
                      economic zone

Article 59. Basis for the resolution of conflicts regarding the attribution of rights and jurisdiction in the exclusive economic zone
Article 60. Artificial islands, installations and structures in the exclusive economic zone
Article 61. Conservation of the living resources
Article 62. Utilization of the living resources
Article 63. Stocks occurring within the exclusive economic zones of two or more coastal States . . .
Article 64. Highly migratory species
Article 65. Marine mammals
Article 66. Anadromous stocks
Article 67. Catadromous species
Article 68. Sedentary species
Article 69. Right of land-locked States
Article 70. Right of geographically disadvantaged States
Article 71. Non-applicability of articles 69 and 70
Article 72. Restrictions on transfer of rights
Article 73. Enforcement of laws and regulations of the coastal State
Article 74. Delimitation of the exclusive economic zone between States with opposite or adjacent coasts
Article 75. Charts and lists of geographical co-ordinates

PART VI.   CONTINENTAL SHELF
Article 76. Definition of the continental shelf
Article 77. Rights of the coastal State over the continental shelf
Article 78. Legal status of the superjacent waters and air space and the rights and freedoms of other States
Article 79. Submarine cables and pipelines on the continental shelf
Article 80. Artificial islands, installations and structures on the continental shelf
Article 81. Drilling on the continental shelf
Article 82. Payments and contributions with respect to the exploitation of the continental shelf beyond 200 nautical miles
Article 83. Delimitation of the continental shelf between States with opposite or adjacent coasts
Article 84. Charts and lists of geographical co-ordinates
Article 85. Tunnelling

PART VII.   HIGH SEAS
SECTION 1.   GENERAL PROVISIONS
Article 86. Application of the provisions of this Part
Article 87. Freedom of the high seas

Article 88.   Reservation of the high seas for peaceful purposes
Article 89.   Invalidity of claims of sovereignty over the high seas
Article 90.   Right of navigation
Article 91.   Nationality of ships
Article 92.   Status of ships
Article 93.   Ships flying the flag of the United Nations, its specialized agencies and the International Atomic Energy Agency
Article 94.   Duties of the flag State
Article 95.   Immunity of warships on the high seas
Article 96.   Immunity of ships used only on government non-commercial service
Article 97.   Penal jurisdiction in matters of collision or any other incident of navigation
Article 98.   Duty to render assistance
Article 99.   Prohibition of the transport of slaves
Article 100.   Duty to co-operate in the repression of piracy
Article 101.   Definition of piracy
Article 102.   Piracy by a warship, government ship or government aircraft whose crew has mutinied
Article 103.   Definition of a pirate ship or aircraft
Article 104.   Retention or loss of the nationality of a pirate ship or aircraft
Article 105.   Seizure of a pirate ship or aircraft
Article 106.   Liability for seizure without adequate grounds
Article 107.   Ships and aircraft which are entitled to seize on account of piracy
Article 108.   Illicit traffic in narcotic drugs or psychotropic substances
Article 109.   Unauthorized broadcasting from the high seas
Article 110.   Right of visit
Article 111.   Right of hot pursuit
Article 112.   Right to lay submarine cables and pipelines
Article 113.   Breaking or injury of a submarine cable or pipeline
Article 114.   Breaking or injury by owners of a submarine cable or pipeline of another submarine cable or pipeline
Article 115.   Indemnity for loss incurred in avoiding injury to a submarine cable or pipeline
SECTION 2.   CONSERVATION AND MANAGEMENT OF THE LIVING RESOURCES OF THE HIGH SEAS
Article 116.   Right to fish on the high seas
Article 117.   Duty of States to adopt with respect to their nationals measures for the conservation of the living resources of the high seas
Article 118.   Co-operation of States in the conservation and management of living resources

Article 119. Conservation of the living resources of the high seas
Article 120. Marine mammals

PART VIII.   REGIME OF ISLANDS
Article 121. Regime of islands

PART IX.   ENCLOSED OR SEMI-ENCLOSED SEAS
Article 122. Definition
Article 123. Co-operation of States bordering enclosed or semi-enclosed seas

PART X.   RIGHT OF ACCESS OF LAND-LOCKED STATES TO AND FROM THE SEA AND FREEDOM OF TRANSIT . . .

PART XI.   THE AREA
SECTION 1.   GENERAL PROVISIONS
Article 133. Use of terms
Article 134. Scope of this Part
Article 135. Legal status of the superjacent waters and air space
SECTION 2.   PRINCIPLES GOVERNING THE AREA
Article 136. Common heritage of mankind
Article 137. Legal status of the Area and its resources
Article 138. General conduct of States in relation to the Area
Article 139. Responsibility to ensure compliance and liability for damage
Article 140. Benefit of mankind
Article 141. Use of the Area exclusively for peaceful purposes
Article 142. Rights and legitimate interests of coastal States
Article 143. Marine scientific research
Article 144. Transfer of technology
Article 145. Protection of the marine environment
Article 146. Protection of human life
Article 147. Accommodation of activities in the Area and in the marine environment
Article 148. Participation of developing States in activities in the Area
Article 149. Archaeological and historical objects
SECTION 3.   DEVELOPMENT OF RESOURCES OF THE AREA
Article 150. Policies relating to activities in the Area
Article 151. Production policies
Article 152. Exercise of powers and functions by the Authority
Article 153. System of exploration and exploitation
Article 154. Periodic review
Article 155. The Review Conference

SECTION 4. THE AUTHORITY
SUBSECTION A. GENERAL PROVISIONS
  Article 156. Establishment of the Authority
  Article 157. Nature and fundamental principles of the Authority
  Article 158. Organs of the Authority
SUBSECTION B. THE ASSEMBLY
  Article 159. Composition, procedure and voting
  Article 160. Powers and functions
SUBSECTION C. THE COUNCIL
  Article 161. Composition, procedure and voting
  Article 162. Powers and functions
  Article 163. Organs of the Council . . .
SUBSECTION D. THE SECRETARIAT . . .
SUBSECTION E. THE ENTERPRISE . . .
SUBSECTION F. FINANCIAL ARRANGEMENTS OF THE AUTHORITY . . .
SUBSECTION G. LEGAL STATUS, PRIVILEGES AND IMMUNITIES . . .
SUBSECTION H. SUSPENSION OF THE EXERCISE OF RIGHTS AND PRIVILEGES OF MEMBERS . . .
SECTION 5. SETTLEMENT OF DISPUTES AND ADVISORY OPINIONS
  Article 186. Sea-Bed Disputes Chamber of the International Tribunal for the Law of the Sea
  Article 187. Jurisdiction of the Sea-Bed Disputes Chamber
  Article 188. Submission of disputes to a special chamber of the International Tribunal for the Law of the Sea or an ad hoc chamber of the Sea-Bed Disputes Chamber or to binding commercial arbitration
  Article 189. Limitation on jurisdiction with regard to decisions of the Authority
  Article 190. Participation and appearance of sponsoring States Parties in proceedings
  Article 191. Advisory opinions

PART XII. PROTECTION AND PRESERVATION OF THE MARINE ENVIRONMENT
SECTION 1. GENERAL PROVISIONS
  Article 192. General obligation
  Article 193. Sovereign right of States to exploit their natural resources
  Article 194. Measures to prevent, reduce and control pollution of the marine environment
  Article 195. Duty not to transfer damage or hazards or transform one type of pollution into another

Article 196.   Use of technologies or introduction of alien or new species

SECTION 2.   GLOBAL AND REGIONAL CO-OPERATION . . .

PART XIII.   MARINE SCIENTIFIC RESEARCH . . .

PART XIV.   DEVELOPMENT AND TRANSFER OF MARINE TECHNOLOGY . . .

PART XV.   SETTLEMENT OF DISPUTES

SECTION 1.   GENERAL PROVISIONS

Article 279.   Obligation to settle disputes by peaceful means

Article 280.   Settlement of disputes by any peaceful means chosen by the parties

Article 281.   Procedure where no settlement has been reached by the parties

Article 282.   Obligations under general, regional or bilateral agreements

Article 283.   Obligation to exchange views

Article 284.   Conciliation . . .

PART XVI.   GENERAL PROVISIONS . . .

PART XVII.   FINAL PROVISIONS

Article 305.   Signature

Article 306.   Ratification and formal confirmation

Article 307.   Accession

Article 308.   Entry into force

Article 309.   Reservations and exceptions

Article 310.   Declarations and statements

Article 311.   Relation to other conventions and international agreements

Article 312.   Amendment

Article 313.   Amendment by simplified procedure

Article 314.   Amendments to the provisions of this Convention relating exclusively to activities in the Area

Article 315.   Signature, ratification of, accession to and authentic texts of amendments

Article 316.   Entry into force of amendments

Article 317.   Denunciation

Article 318.   Status of Annexes . . .

ANNEX I.   HIGHLY MIGRATORY SPECIES

ANNEX II.   COMMISSION ON THE LIMITS OF THE CONTINENTAL SHELF

ANNEX III. BASIC CONDITIONS OF PROSPECTING, EXPLORATION AND EXPLOITATION

Article 1.   Title to minerals
Article 2.   Prospecting
Article 3.   Exploration and exploitation
Article 4.   Qualifications of applicants
Article 5.   Transfer of technology
Article 6.   Approval of plans of work
Article 7.   Selection among applicants for production authorizations
Article 8.   Reservation of areas
Article 9.   Activities in reserved areas
Article 10. Preference and priority among applicants
Article 11. Joint arrangements
Article 12. Activities carried out by the Enterprise
Article 13. Financial terms of contracts
Article 14. Transfer of data . . .
Article 16. Exclusive right to explore and exploit
Article 17. Rules, regulations and procedures of the Authority . . .

ANNEX IV. STATUTE OF THE ENTERPRISE

Article 1.   Purposes
Article 2.   Relationship to the Authority
Article 3.   Limitation of liability
Article 4.   Structure
Article 5.   Governing Board
Article 6.   Powers and functions of the Governing Board
Article 7.   Director-General and staff of the Enterprise
Article 10. Allocation of net income
Article 11. Finances
Article 12. Operations
Article 13. Legal status, privileges and immunities

ANNEX V.   CONCILIATION . . .

ANNEX VI. STATUTE OF THE INTERNATIONAL TRIBUNAL FOR THE LAW OF THE SEA

Article 1.   General provisions
SECTION 1.   ORGANIZATION OF THE TRIBUNAL
Article 2.   Composition
Article 3.   Membership
Article 4.   Nominations and elections
Article 5.   Term of office . . .
Article 13. Quorum
Article 14. Sea-Bed Disputes Chamber
Article 15. Special chambers

Article 16. Rules of the Tribunal
Article 17. Nationality of members . . .
SECTION 2. COMPETENCE
Article 20. Access to the Tribunal
Article 21. Jurisdiction
Article 22. Reference of disputes subject to other agreements
Article 23. Applicable law
SECTION 3. PROCEDURE
Article 24. Institution of proceedings
Article 25. Provisional measures
Article 26. Hearing
Article 27. Conduct of case
Article 28. Default
Article 29. Majority for decision
Article 30. Judgment
Article 31. Request to intervene
Article 32. Right to intervene in cases of interpretation or application
Article 33. Finality and binding force of decisions . . .
SECTION 4. SEA-BED DISPUTES CHAMBER
Article 35. Composition
Article 36. Ad Hoc Chambers
Article 37. Access
Article 38. Applicable law
Article 39. Enforcement of decisions of the Chamber
Article 40. Applicability of other sections of this Annex . . .

ANNEX VII. ARBITRATION
Article 1. Institution of proceedings
Article 2. List of arbitrators
Article 3. Constitution of arbitral tribunal
Article 4. Functions of arbitral tribunal
Article 5. Procedure
Article 6. Duties of parties to a dispute
Article 7. Expenses
Article 8. Required majority for decisions
Article 9. Default of appearance
Article 10. Award
Article 11. Finality of award
Article 12. Interpretation or implementation of award
Article 13. Application to entities other than States Parties

ANNEX VIII. SPECIAL ARBITRATION . . .

ANNEX IX. PARTICIPATION BY INTERNATIONAL ORGANIZATIONS . . .

The States Parties to this Convention,

Prompted by the desire to settle, in a spirit of mutual understanding and co-operation, all issues relating to the law of the sea and aware of the historic significance of this Convention as an important contribution to the maintenance of peace, justice and progress for all peoples of the world,

Noting that developments since the United Nations Conferences on the Law of the Sea held at Geneva in 1958 and 1960 have accentuated the need for a new and generally acceptable Convention on the law of the sea,

Conscious that the problems of ocean space are closely interrelated and need to be considered as a whole,

Recognizing the desirability of establishing through this Convention, with due regard for the sovereignty of all States, a legal order for the seas and oceans which will facilitate international communication, and will promote the peaceful uses of the seas and oceans, the equitable and efficient utilization of their resources, the conservation of their living resources, and the study, protection and preservation of the marine environment,

Bearing in mind that the achievement of these goals will contribute to the realization of a just and equitable international economic order which takes into account the interests and needs of mankind as a whole and, in particular, the special interests and needs of developing countries, whether coastal or land-locked,

Desiring by this Convention to develop the principles embodied in resolution 2749 (XXV) of 17 December 1970 in which the General Assembly of the United Nations solemnly declared *inter alia* that the area of the seabed and ocean floor and the subsoil thereof, beyond the limits of national jurisdiction, as well as its resources, are the common heritage of mankind, the exploration and exploitation of which shall be carried out for the benefit of mankind as a whole, irrespective of the geographical location of States,

Believing that the codification and progressive development of the law of the sea achieved in this Convention will contribute to the strengthening of peace, security, co-operation and friendly relations among all nations in conformity with the principles of justice and equal rights and will promote the economic and social advancement of all peoples of the world, in accordance with the Purposes and Principles of the United Nations as set forth in the Charter,

Affirming that matters not regulated by this Convention continue to be governed by the rules and principles of general international law,

Have agreed as follows:

Part I. Introduction

Article 1.   Use of Terms and Scope

1. For the purposes of this Convention:

(1) "Area" means the sea-bed and ocean floor and subsoil thereof, beyond the limits of national jurisdiction;

(2) "Authority" means the International Sea-Bed Authority;

(3) "activities in the Area" means all activities of exploration for, and exploitation of, the resources of the Area;

(4) "pollution of the marine environment" means the introduction by man, directly or indirectly, of substances or energy into the marine environment, including estuaries, which results or is likely to result in such deleterious effects as harm to living resources and marine life, hazards to human health, hindrance to marine activities, including fishing and other legitimate uses of the sea, impairment of quality for use of sea water and reduction of amenities;

(5) (a) "dumping" means:

(i) any deliberate disposal of wastes or other matter from vessels, aircraft, platforms or other man-made structures at sea;

(ii) any deliberate disposal of vessels, aircraft, platforms or other man-made structures at sea;

(b) "dumping" does not include:

(i) the disposal of wastes or other matter incidental to, or derived from the normal operations of vessels, aircraft, platforms or other man-made structures at sea and their equipment, other than wastes or other matter transported by or to vessels, aircraft, platforms or other man-made structures at sea, operating for the purpose of disposal of such matter or derived from the treatment of such wastes or other matter on such vessels, aircraft, platforms or structures;

(ii) placement of matter for a purpose other than the mere disposal thereof, provided that such placement is not contrary to the aims of this Convention.

2. (1) "States Parties" means States which have consented to be bound by this Convention and for which this Convention is in force.

(2) This Convention applies *mutatis mutandis* to the entities referred to in article 305, paragraph 1(b), (c), (d), (e) and (f), which become Parties to this Convention in accordance with the conditions relevant to each, and to that extent "States Parties" refers to those entities.

Part II.   Territorial Sea and Contiguous Zone

SECTION 1.   GENERAL PROVISIONS

Article 2.   *Legal Status of the Territorial Sea, of the Air Space over the Territorial Sea and of Its Bed and Subsoil*

1. The sovereignty of a coastal State extends, beyond its land territory and internal waters and, in the case of an archipelagic State, its archipelagic waters, to an adjacent belt of sea, described as the territorial sea.

2. This sovereignty extends to the air space over the territorial sea as well as to its bed and subsoil.

3. The sovereignty over the territorial sea is exercised subject to this Convention and to other rules of international law.

SECTION 2.   LIMITS OF THE TERRITORIAL SEA

Article 3.   Breadth of the Territorial Sea

Every State has the right to establish the breadth of its territorial sea up to a limit not exceeding 12 nautical miles, measured from baselines determined in accordance with this Convention.

Article 4.   Outer Limit of the Territorial Sea

The outer limit of the territorial sea is the line every point of which is at a distance from the nearest point of the baseline equal to the breadth of the territorial sea.

Article 5.   Normal Baseline

Except where otherwise provided in this Convention, the normal baseline for measuring the breadth of the territorial sea is the low-water line along the coast as marked on large-scale charts officially recognized by the coastal State.

Article 6.   Reefs

In the case of islands situated on atolls or of islands having fringing reefs, the baseline for measuring the breadth of the territorial sea is the seaward low-water line of the reef, as shown by the appropriate symbol on charts officially recognized by the coastal State.

Article 7.   Straight Baselines

1. In localities where the coastline is deeply indented and cut into, or if there is a fringe of islands along the coast in its immediate vicinity, the method of straight baselines joining appropriate points may be employed in drawing the baseline from which the breadth of the territorial sea is measured.

2. Where because of the presence of a delta and other natural conditions the coastline is highly unstable, the appropriate points may be selected along the furthest seaward extent of the low-water line and, notwithstanding subsequent regression of the low-water line, the straight baselines shall remain effective until changed by the coastal State in accordance with this Convention.

3. The drawing of straight baselines must not depart to any appreciable extent from the general direction of the coast, and the sea areas lying within the lines must be sufficiently closely linked to the land domain to be subject to the régime of internal waters.

4. Straight baselines shall not be drawn to and from low-tide elevations, unless lighthouses or similar installations which are permanently above sea level have been built on them or except in instances where the drawing of baselines to and from such elevations has received general international recognition.

5. Where the method of straight baselines is applicable under paragraph 1, account may be taken, in determining particular baselines, of economic interests peculiar to the region concerned, the reality and the importance of which are clearly evidenced by long usage.

6. The system of straight baselines may not be applied by a State in such a manner as to cut off the territorial sea of another State from the high seas or an exclusive economic zone.

Article 8.   Internal Waters

1. Except as provided in Part IV, waters on the landward side of the baseline of the territorial sea form part of the internal waters of the State.

2. Where the establishment of a straight baseline in accordance with the method set forth in article 7 has the effect of enclosing as internal water areas which had not previously been considered as such, a right of innocent passage as provided in this Convention shall exist in those waters.

Article 9.   Mouths of Rivers

If a river flows directly into the sea, the baseline shall be a straight line across the mouth of the river between points on the low-water line of its banks.

Article 10.   Bays

1. This article relates only to bays the coasts of which belong to a single State.

2. For the purposes of this Convention, a bay is a well-marked indentation whose penetration is in such proportion to the width of its mouth as to contain land-locked waters and constitute more than a mere curvature of the coast. An indentation shall not, however, be regarded as a bay unless its area is as large as, or larger than, that of the semi-circle whose diameter is a line drawn across the mouth of that indentation.

3. For the purpose of measurement, the area of an indentation is that lying between the low-water mark around the shore of the indentation and a line joining the low-water mark of its natural entrance points. Where, because of the presence of islands, an indentation has more than one mouth, the semi-circle shall be drawn on a line as long as the sum total of the lengths of the lines across the different mouths. Islands within an indentation shall be included as if they were part of the water area of the indentation.

4. If the distance between the low-water marks of the natural entrance points of a bay does not exceed 24 nautical miles, a closing line may be drawn between these two low-water marks, and the waters enclosed thereby shall be considered as internal waters.

5. Where the distance between the low-water marks of the natural entrance points of a bay exceeds 24 nautical miles, a straight baseline of 24 nautical miles shall be drawn within the bay in such a manner as to enclose the maximum area of water that is possible with a line of that length.

6. The foregoing provisions do not apply to so-called "historic" bays, or in any case where the system of straight baselines provided for in article 7 is applied.

Article 11.   Ports

For the purpose of delimiting the territorial sea, the outermost permanent harbour works which form an integral part of the harbour system are regarded as forming part of the coast. Off-shore installations and artificial islands shall not be considered as permanent harbour works.

Article 12.   Roadsteads

Roadsteads which are normally used for the loading, unloading and anchoring of ships, and which would otherwise be situated wholly or partly outside the outer limit of the territorial sea, are included in the territorial sea.

Article 13.   Low-Tide Elevations

1. A low-tide elevation is a naturally formed area of land which is surrounded by and above water at low tide but submerged at high tide. Where a low-tide elevation is situated wholly or partly at a distance not exceeding the breadth of the territorial sea from the mainland or an island, the low-water line on that elevation may be used as the baseline for measuring the breadth of the territorial sea.

2. Where a low-tide elevation is wholly situated at a distance exceeding the breadth of the territorial sea from the mainland or an island, it has no territorial sea of its own.

Article 14.   Combination of Methods for Determining Baselines

The coastal State may determine baselines in turn by any of the methods provided for in the foregoing articles to suit different conditions.

Article 15.   Delimination of the Territorial Sea Between States with Opposite or Adjacent Coasts

Where the coasts of two States are opposite or adjacent to each other, neither of the two States is entitled, failing agreement between them to the contrary, to extend its territorial sea beyond the median line every point of which is equidistant from the nearest points on the baselines from which the breadth of the territorial seas of each of the two States is measured. The above provision does not apply, however, where it is necessary by reason of historic title or other special circumstances to delimit the territorial seas of the two States in a way which is at variance therewith.

Article 16. Charts and Lists of Geographical Co-ordinates

1. The baselines for measuring the breadth of the territorial sea determined in accordance with articles 7, 9 and 10, or the limits derived therefrom, and the lines of delimitation drawn in accordance with articles 12 and 15 shall be shown on charts of a scale or scales adequate for ascertaining their position. Alternatively, a list of geographical co-ordinates of points, specifying the geodetic datum, may be substituted.

2. The coastal State shall give due publicity to such charts or lists of geographical co-ordinates and shall deposit a copy of each such chart or list with the Secretary-General of the United Nations.

SECTION 3. INNOCENT PASSAGE IN THE TERRITORIAL SEA

SUBSECTION A. RULES APPLICABLE TO ALL SHIPS

Article 17. Right of Innocent Passage

Subject to this Convention, ships of all States, whether coastal or land-locked, enjoy the right of innocent passage through the territorial sea.

Article 18. Meaning of Passage

1. Passage means navigation through the territorial sea for the purpose of:

(a) traversing that sea without entering internal waters or calling at a roadstead or port facility outside internal waters; or

(b) proceeding to or from internal waters or a call at such roadstead or port facility.

2. Passage shall be continuous and expeditious. However, passage includes stopping and anchoring, but only in so far as the same are incidental to ordinary navigation or are rendered necessary by *force majeure* or distress or for the purpose of rendering assistance to persons, ships or aircraft in danger or distress.

Article 19. Meaning of Innocent Passage

1. Passage is innocent so long as it is not prejudicial to the peace, good order or security of the coastal State. Such passage shall take place in conformity with this Convention and with other rules of international law.

2. Passage of a foreign ship shall be considered to be prejudicial to the peace, good order or security of the coastal State if in the territorial sea it engages in any of the following activities:

(a) any threat or use of force against the sovereignty, territorial integrity or political independence of the coastal State, or in any other manner in violation of the principles of international law embodied in the Charter of the United Nations;

(b) any exercise or practice with weapons of any kind;

(c) any act aimed at collecting information to the prejudice of the defence or security of the coastal State;

(d) any act of propaganda aimed at affecting the defence or security of the coastal State;

(e) the launching, landing or taking on board of any aircraft;

(f) the launching, landing or taking on board of any military device;

(g) the loading or unloading of any commodity, currency or person contrary to the customs, fiscal, immigration or sanitary laws and regulations of the coastal State;

(h) any act of wilful and serious pollution contrary to this Convention;

(i) any fishing activities;

(j) the carrying out of research or survey activities;

(k) any act aimed at interfering with any systems of communication or any other facilities or installations of the coastal State;

(l) any other activity not having a direct bearing on passage.

Article 20.   Submarines and Other Underwater Vehicles

In the territorial sea, submarines and other underwater vehicles are required to navigate on the surface and to show their flag.

Article 21.   Laws and Regulations of the Coastal State Relating to Innocent Passage

1. The coastal State may adopt laws and regulations, in conformity with the provisions of this Convention and other rules of international law, relating to innocent passage through the territorial sea, in respect of all or any of the following:

(a) the safety of navigation and the regulation of maritime traffic;

(b) the protection of navigational aids and facilities and other facilities or installations;

(c) the protection of cables and pipelines;

(d) the conservation of the living resources of the sea;

(e) the prevention of infringement of the fisheries laws and regulations of the coastal State;

(f) the preservation of the environment of the coastal State and the prevention, reduction and control of pollution thereof;

(g) marine scientific research and hydrographic surveys;

(h) the prevention of infringement of the customs, fiscal, immigration or sanitary laws and regulations of the coastal State.

2. Such laws and regulations shall not apply to the design, construction, manning or equipment of foreign ships unless they are giving effect to generally accepted international rules or standards.

3. The coastal State shall give due publicity to all such laws and regulations.

4. Foreign ships exercising the right of innocent passage through the territorial sea shall comply with all such laws and regulations and all generally accepted international regulations relating to the prevention of collisions at sea.

Article 22.   Sea Lanes and Traffic Separation Schemes in the Territorial Sea

1. The coastal State may, where necessary having regard to the safety of navigation, require foreign ships exercising the right of innocent passage through its territorial sea to use such sea lanes and traffic separation schemes as it may designate or prescribe for the regulation of the passage of ships.
2. In particular, tankers, nuclear-powered ships and ships carrying nuclear or other inherently dangerous or noxious substances or materials may be required to confine their passage to such sea lanes.
3. In the designation of sea lanes and the prescription of traffic separation schemes under this article, the coastal State shall take into account:
   (a) the recommendations of the competent international organization;
   (b) any channels customarily used for international navigation;
   (c) the special characteristics of particular ships and channels; and
   (d) the density of traffic.
4. The coastal State shall clearly indicate such sea lanes and traffic separation schemes on charts to which due publicity shall be given.

Article 23.   Foreign Nuclear-Powered Ships and Ships Carrying Nuclear or Other Inherently Dangerous or Noxious Substances

Foreign nuclear-powered ships and ships carrying nuclear or other inherently dangerous or noxious substances shall, when exercising the right of innocent passage through the territorial sea, carry documents and observe special precautionary measures established for such ships by international agreements.

Article 24.   Duties of the Coastal State

1. The coastal State shall not hamper the innocent passage of foreign ships through the territorial sea except in accordance with this Convention. In particular, in the application of this Convention or of any laws or regulations adopted in conformity with this Convention, the coastal State shall not:
   (a) impose requirements on foreign ships which have the practical effect of denying or impairing the right of innocent passage; or
   (b) discriminate in form or in fact against the ships of any State or against ships carrying cargoes to, from or on behalf of any State.
2. The coastal State shall give appropriate publicity to any danger to navigation, of which it has knowledge, within its territorial sea.

Article 25.   Rights of Protection of the Coastal State

1. The coastal State may take the necessary steps in its territorial sea to prevent passage which is not innocent.

2. In the case of ships proceeding to internal waters or a call at a port facility outside internal waters, the coastal State also has the right to take the necessary steps to prevent any breach of the conditions to which admission of those ships to internal waters or such a call is subject.

3. The coastal State may, without discrimination in form or in fact among foreign ships, suspend temporarily in specified areas of its territorial sea the innocent passage of foreign ships if such suspension is essential for the protection of its security, including weapons exercises. Such suspension shall take effect only after having been duly published.

Article 26. Charges Which May Be Levied upon Foreign Ships

1. No charge may be levied upon foreign ships by reason only of their passage through the territorial sea.

2. Charges may be levied upon a foreign ship passing through the territorial sea as payment only for specific services rendered to the ship. These charges shall be levied without discrimination.

SUBSECTION B.   RULES APPLICABLE TO MERCHANT SHIPS AND GOVERNMENT SHIPS OPERATED FOR COMMERCIAL PURPOSES

Article 27. Criminal Jurisdiction on Board a Foreign Ship

1. The criminal jurisdiction of the coastal State should not be exercised on board a foreign ship passing through the territorial sea to arrest any person or to conduct any investigation in connection with any crime committed on board the ship during its passage, save only in the following cases:

(a) if the consequences of the crime extend to the coastal State;

(b) if the crime is of a kind to disturb the peace of the country or the good order of the territorial sea;

(c) if the assistance of the local authorities has been requested by the master of the ship or by a diplomatic agent or consular officer of the flag State; or

(d) if such measures are necessary for the suppression of illicit traffic in narcotic drugs or psychotropic substances.

2. The above provisions do not affect the right of the coastal State to take any steps authorized by its laws for the purpose of an arrest or investigation on board a foreign ship passing through the territorial sea after leaving internal waters.

3. In the cases provided for in paragraphs 1 and 2, the coastal State shall, if the master so requests, notify a diplomatic agent or consular officer of the flag State before taking any steps, and shall facilitate contact between such agent or officer and the ship's crew. In cases of emergency this notification may be communicated while the measures are being taken.

4. In considering whether or in what manner an arrest should be made, the local authorities shall have due regard to the interests of navigation.

5. Except as provided in Part XII or with respect to violations of laws and regulations adopted in accordance with Part V, the coastal State may not take any steps on board a foreign ship passing through the territorial sea to arrest any person or to conduct any investigation in connection with any crime committed before the ship entered the territorial sea, if the ship, proceeding from a foreign port, is only passing through the territorial sea without entering internal waters.

Article 28.   *Civil Jurisdiction in Relation to Foreign Ships*

1. The coastal State should not stop or divert a foreign ship passing through the territorial sea for the purpose of exercising civil jurisdiction in relation to a person on board the ship.

2. The coastal State may not levy execution against or arrest the ship for the purpose of any civil proceedings, save only in respect of obligations or liabilities assumed or incurred by the ship itself in the course or for the purpose of its voyage through the waters of the coastal State.

3. Paragraph 2 is without prejudice to the right of the coastal State, in accordance with its laws, to levy execution against or to arrest, for the purpose of any civil proceedings, a foreign ship lying in the territorial sea, or passing through the territorial sea after leaving internal waters.

SUBSECTION C.   RULES APPLICABLE TO WARSHIPS AND OTHER GOVERNMENT SHIPS OPERATED FOR NON-COMMERCIAL PURPOSES

Article 29.   *Definition of Warships*

For the purposes of this Convention, "warship" means a ship belonging to the armed forces of a State bearing the external marks distinguishing such ships of its nationality, under the command of an officer duly commissioned by the government of the State and whose name appears in the appropriate service list or its equivalent, and manned by a crew which is under regular armed forces discipline.

Article 30.   *Non-Compliance by Warships with the Laws and Regulations of the Coastal State*

If any warship does not comply with the laws and regulations of the coastal State concerning passage through the territorial sea and disregards any request for compliance therewith which is made to it, the coastal State may require it to leave the territorial sea immediately.

Article 31.   *Responsibility of the Flag State for Damage Caused by a Warship or Other Government Ship Operated for Non-Commercial Purposes*

The flag State shall bear international responsibility for any loss or damage to the coastal State resulting from the non-compliance by a warship or other government ship operated for non-commercial purposes with the laws and regulations of the coastal State concerning passage through the territorial sea or with the provisions of this Convention or other rules of international law.

Article 32. Immunities of Warships and Other Government Ships Operated for Non-Commercial Purposes

With such exceptions as are contained in subsection A and in articles 30 and 31, nothing in this Convention affects the immunities of warships and other government ships operated for non-commercial purposes.

SECTION 4. CONTIGUOUS ZONE

Article 33. Contiguous Zone

1. In a zone contiguous to its territorial sea, described as the contiguous zone, the coastal State may exercise the control necessary to:
    (a) prevent infringement of its customs, fiscal, immigration or sanitary laws and regulations within its territory or territorial sea;
    (b) punish infringement of the above laws and regulations committed within its territory or territorial sea.
2. The contiguous zone may not extend beyond 24 nautical miles from the baselines from which the breadth of the territorial sea is measured.

Part III. Straits Used for International Navigation

SECTION 1. GENERAL PROVISIONS

Article 34. Legal Status of Waters Forming Straits Used for International Navigation

1. The régime of passage through straits used for international navigation established in this Part shall not in other respects affect the legal status of the waters forming such straits or the exercise by the States bordering the straits of their sovereignty or jurisdiction over such waters and their air space, bed and subsoil.
2. The sovereignty or jurisdiction of the States bordering the straits is exercised subject to this Part and to other rules of international law.

Article 35. Scope of This Part

Nothing in this Part affects:
    (a) any areas of internal waters within a strait, except where the establishment of a straight baseline in accordance with the method set forth in article 7 has the effect of enclosing as internal waters areas which had not previously been considered as such;

(b) the legal status of the waters beyond the territorial seas of States bordering straits as exclusive economic zones or high seas; or

(c) the legal régime in straits in which passage is regulated in whole or in part by long-standing international conventions in force specifically relating to such straits.

Article 36. High Seas Routes or Routes Through Exclusive Economic Zones Through Straits Used for International Navigation

This Part does not apply to a strait used for international navigation if there exists through the strait a route through the high seas or through an exclusive economic zone of similar convenience with respect to navigational and hydrographical characteristics; in such routes, the other relevant Parts of this Convention, including the provisions regarding the freedoms of navigation and overflight, apply.

SECTION 2. TRANSIT PASSAGE

Article 37. Scope of This Section

This section applies to straits which are used for international navigation between one part of the high seas or an exclusive economic zone and another part of the high seas or an exclusive economic zone.

Article 38. Right of Transit Passage

1. In straits referred to in article 37, all ships and aircraft enjoy the right of transit passage, which shall not be impeded; except that, if the strait is formed by an island of a State bordering the strait and its mainland, transit passage shall not apply if there exists seaward of the island a route through the high seas or through an exclusive economic zone of similar convenience with respect to navigational and hydrographical characteristics.

2. Transit passage means the exercise in accordance with this Part of the freedom of navigation and overflight solely for the purpose of continuous and expeditious transit of the strait between one part of the high seas or an exclusive economic zone and another part of the high seas or an exclusive economic zone. However, the requirement of continuous and expeditious transit does not preclude passage through the strait for the purpose of entering, leaving or returning from a State bordering the strait, subject to the conditions of entry to that State.

3. Any activity which is not an exercise of the right of transit passage through a strait remains subject to the other applicable provisions of this Convention.

Article 39. Duties of Ships and Aircraft During Transit Passage

1. Ships and aircraft, while exercising the right of transit passage, shall:
   (a) proceed without delay through or over the strait;

(b) refrain from any threat or use of force against the sovereignty, territorial integrity or political independence of States bordering the strait, or in any other manner in violation of the principles of international law embodied in the Charter of the United Nations;

(c) refrain from any activities other than those incident to their normal modes of continuous and expeditious transit unless rendered necessary by *force majeure* or by distress;

(d) comply with other relevant provisions of this Part.

2. Ships in transit passage shall:

(a) comply with generally accepted international regulations, procedures and practices for safety at sea, including the International Regulations for Preventing Collisions at Sea;

(b) comply with generally accepted international regulations, procedures and practices for the prevention, reduction and control of pollution from ships.

3. Aircraft in transit passage shall:

(a) observe the Rules of the Air established by the International Civil Aviation Organization as they apply to civil aircraft; state aircraft will normally comply with such safety measures and will at all times operate with due regard for the safety of navigation;

(b) at all times monitor the radio frequency assigned by the competent internationally designated air traffic control authority or the appropriate international distress radio frequency.

Article 40. Research and Survey Activities

During transit passage, foreign ships, including marine scientific research and hydrographic survey ships, may not carry out any research or survey activities without the prior authorization of the States bordering straits.

Article 41. Sea Lanes and Traffic Separation Schemes in Straits Used for International Navigation

1. In conformity with this Part, States bordering straits may designate sea lanes and prescribe traffic separation schemes for navigation in straits where necessary to promote the safe passage of ships.

2. Such States may, when circumstances require, and after giving due publicity thereto, substitute other sea lanes or traffic separation schemes for any sea lanes or traffic separation schemes previously designated or prescribed by them.

3. Such sea lanes and traffic separation schemes shall conform to generally accepted international regulations.

4. Before designating or substituting sea lanes or prescribing or substituting traffic separation schemes, States bordering straits shall refer proposals to the competent international organization with a view to their

adoption. The organization may adopt only such sea lanes and traffic separation schemes as may be agreed with the States bordering the straits, after which the States may designate, prescribe or substitute them.

5. In respect of a strait where sea lanes or traffic separation schemes through the waters of two or more States bordering the strait are being proposed, the States concerned shall co-operate in formulating proposals in consultation with the competent international organization.

6. States bordering straits shall clearly indicate all sea lanes and traffic separation schemes designated or prescribed by them on charts to which due publicity shall be given.

7. Ships in transit passage shall respect applicable sea lanes and traffic separation schemes established in accordance with this article.

Article 42.   Laws and Regulations of States Bordering Straits Relating to Transit Passage

1. Subject to the provisions of this section, States bordering straits may adopt laws and regulations relating to transit passage through straits, in respect of all or any of the following:

(a) the safety of navigation and the regulation of maritime traffic, as provided in article 41;

(b) the prevention, reduction and control of pollution, by giving effect to applicable international regulations regarding the discharge of oil, oily wastes and other noxious substances in the strait;

(c) with respect to fishing vessels, the prevention of fishing, including the stowage of fishing gear;

(d) the loading or unloading of any commodity, currency or person in contravention of the customs, fiscal, immigration or sanitary laws and regulations of States bordering straits.

2. Such laws and regulations shall not discriminate in form or in fact among foreign ships or in their application have the practical effect of denying, hampering or impairing the right of transit passage as defined in this section.

3. States bordering straits shall give due publicity to all such laws and regulations.

4. Foreign ships exercising the right of transit passage shall comply with such laws and regulations.

5. The flag State of a ship or the State of registry of an aircraft entitled to sovereign immunity which acts in a manner contrary to such laws and regulations or other provisions of this Part shall bear international responsibility for any loss or damage which results to States bordering straits. . . .

Article 44.   Duties of States Bordering Straits

States bordering straits shall not hamper transit passage and shall give appropriate publicity to any danger to navigation or overflight within or over the strait of which they have knowledge. There shall be no suspension of transit passage.

SECTION 3. INNOCENT PASSAGE

Article 45. Innocent Passage

1. The régime of innocent passage, in accordance with Part II, section 3, shall apply in straits used for international navigation:

(a) excluded from the application of the régime of transit passage under article 38, paragraph 1; or

(b) between a part of the high seas or an exclusive economic zone and the territorial sea of a foreign State.

2. There shall be no suspension of innocent passage through such straits.

Part IV. Archipelagic States

Article 46. Use of Terms

For the purposes of this Convention:

(a) "archipelagic State" means a State constituted wholly by one or more archipelagos and may include other islands;

(b) "archipelago" means a group of islands, including parts of islands, interconnecting waters and other natural features which are so closely interrelated that such islands, waters and other natural features form an intrinsic geographical, economic and political entity, or which historically have been regarded as such.

Article 47. Archipelagic Baselines

1. An archipelagic State may draw straight archipelagic baselines joining the outermost points of the outermost islands and drying reefs of the archipelago provided that within such baselines are included the main islands and an area in which the ratio of the area of the water to the area of the land, including atolls, is between 1 to 1 and 9 to 1.

2. The length of such baselines shall not exceed 100 nautical miles, except that up to 3 per cent of the total number of baselines enclosing any archipelago may exceed that length, up to a maximum length of 125 nautical miles.

3. The drawing of such baselines shall not depart to any appreciable extent from the general configuration of the archipelago.

4. Such baselines shall not be drawn to and from low-tide elevations, unless lighthouses or similar installations which are permanently above sea level have been built on them or where a low-tide elevation is situated wholly or partly at a distance not exceeding the breadth of the territorial sea from the nearest island.

5. The system of such baselines shall not be applied by an archipelagic State in such a manner as to cut off from the high seas or the exclusive economic zone the territorial sea of another State.

6. If a part of the archipelagic waters of an archipelagic State lies between two parts of an immediately adjacent neighbouring State, existing rights and all other legitimate interests which the latter State has traditionally exercised in such waters and all rights stipulated by agreement between those States shall continue and be respected.

7. For the purpose of computing the ratio of water to land under paragraph 1, land areas may include waters lying within the fringing reefs of islands and atolls, including that part of a steep-sided oceanic plateau which is enclosed or nearly enclosed by a chain of limestone islands and drying reefs lying on the perimeter of the plateau.

8. The baselines drawn in accordance with this article shall be shown on charts of a scale or scales adequate for ascertaining their position. Alternatively, lists of geographical co-ordinates of points, specifying the geodetic datum, may be substituted. . . .

Article 48.   Measurement of the Breadth of the Territorial Sea, the Contiguous Zone, the Exclusive Economic Zone and the Continental Shelf

The breadth of the territorial sea, the contiguous zone, the exclusive economic zone and the continental shelf shall be measured from archipelagic baselines drawn in accordance with article 47.

Article 49.   Legal Status of Archipelagic Waters, of the Air Space over Archipelagic Waters and of Their Bed and Subsoil

1. The sovereignty of an archipelagic State extends to the waters enclosed by the archipelagic baselines drawn in accordance with article 47, described as archipelagic waters, regardless of their depth or distance from the coast.

2. This sovereignty extends to the air space over the archipelagic waters, as well as to their bed and subsoil, and the resources contained therein.

3. This sovereignty is exercised subject to this Part. 4. The régime of archipelagic sea lanes passage established in this Part shall not in other respects affect the status of the archipelagic waters, including the sea lanes, or the exercise by the archipelagic State of its sovereignty over such waters and their air space, bed and subsoil, and the resources contained therein.

Article 50.   Delimitation of Internal Waters

Within its archipelagic waters, the archipelagic State may draw closing lines for the delimitation of internal waters, in accordance with articles 9, 10 and 11.

Article 51. Existing Agreements, Traditional Fishing Rights and Existing Submarine Cables

1. Without prejudice to article 49, an archipelagic State shall respect existing agreements with other States and shall recognize traditional fishing rights and other legitimate activities of the immediately adjacent neighbouring States in certain areas falling within archipelagic waters. The terms and conditions for the exercise of such rights and activities, including the nature, the extent and the areas to which they apply, shall, at the request of any of the States concerned, be regulated by bilateral agreements between them. Such rights shall not be transferred to or shared with third States or their nationals.

2. An archipelagic State shall respect existing submarine cables laid by other States and passing through its waters without making a landfall. . . .

Article 52. Right of Innocent Passage

1. Subject to article 53 and without prejudice to article 50, ships of all States enjoy the right of innocent passage through archipelagic waters, in accordance with Part II, section 3.

2. The archipelagic State may, without discrimination in form or in fact among foreign ships, suspend temporarily in specified areas of its archipelagic waters the innocent passage of foreign ships if such suspension is essential for the protection of its security. Such suspension shall take effect only after having been duly published.

Article 53. Right of Archipelagic Sea Lanes Passage

1. An archipelagic State may designate sea lanes and air routes thereabove, suitable for the continuous and expeditious passage of foreign ships and aircraft through or over its archipelagic waters and the adjacent territorial sea.

2. All ships and aircraft enjoy the right of archipelagic sea lanes passage in such sea lanes and air routes.

3. Archipelagic sea lanes passage means the exercise in accordance with this Convention of the rights of navigation and overflight in the normal mode solely for the purpose of continuous, expeditious and unobstructed transit between one part of the high seas or an exclusive economic zone and another part of the high seas or an exclusive economic zone.

4. Such sea lanes and air routes shall traverse the archipelagic waters and the adjacent territorial sea and shall include all normal passage routes used as routes for international navigation or overflight through or over archipelagic waters and, within such routes, so far as ships are concerned, all normal navigational channels, . . .

Article 54.   Duties of Ships and Aircraft During Their Passage, Research and Survey Activities, Duties of the Archipelagic State and Laws and Regulations of the Archipelagic State Relating to Archipelagic Sea Lanes Passage

Articles 39, 40, 42 and 44 apply mutatis mutandis to archipelagic sea lanes passage.

Part V.   Exclusive Economic Zone

Article 55.   Specific Legal Régime of the Exclusive Economic Zone

The exclusive economic zone is an area beyond and adjacent to the territorial sea, subject to the specific legal régime established in this Part, under which the rights and jurisdiction of the coastal State and the rights and freedoms of other States are governed by the relevant provisions of this Convention.

Article 56.   Rights, Jurisdiction and Duties of the Coastal State in the Exclusive Economic Zone

1. In the exclusive economic zone, the coastal State has:

(a) sovereign rights for the purpose of exploring and exploiting, conserving and managing the natural resources, whether living or non-living, of the waters superjacent to the sea-bed and of the sea-bed and its subsoil, and with regard to other activities for the economic exploitation and exploration of the zone, such as the production of energy from the water, currents and winds;

(b) jurisdiction as provided for in the relevant provisions of this Convention with regard to:

(i) the establishment and use of artificial islands, installations and structures;

(ii) marine scientific research;

(iii) the protection and preservation of the marine environment;

(c) other rights and duties provided for in this Convention.

2. In exercising its rights and performing its duties under this Convention in the exclusive economic zone, the coastal State shall have due regard to the rights and duties of other States and shall act in a manner compatible with the provisions of this Convention.

3. The rights set out in this article with respect to the sea-bed and subsoil shall be exercised in accordance with Part VI.

Article 57.   Breadth of the Exclusive Economic Zone

The exclusive economic zone shall not extend beyond 200 nautical miles from the baselines from which the breadth of the territorial sea is measured.

Article 58. Rights and Duties of Other States
in the Exclusive Economic Zone

1. In the exclusive economic zone, all States, whether coastal or land-locked, enjoy, subject to the relevant provisions of this Convention, the freedoms referred to in article 87 of navigation and overflight and of the laying of submarine cables and pipelines, and other internationally lawful uses of the sea related to these freedoms, such as those associated with the operation of ships, aircraft and submarine cables and pipelines, and compatible with the other provisions of this Convention.

2. Articles 88 to 115 and other pertinent rules of international law apply to the exclusive economic zone in so far as they are not incompatible with this Part.

3. In exercising their rights and performing their duties under this Convention in the exclusive economic zone, States shall have due regard to the rights and duties of the coastal State and shall comply with the laws and regulations adopted by the coastal State in accordance with the provisions of this Convention and other rules of international law in so far as they are not incompatible with this Part.

Article 59. Basis for the Resolution of Conflicts Regarding the Attribution
of Rights and Jurisdiction in the Exclusive Economic Zone

In cases where this Convention does not attribute rights or jurisdiction to the coastal State or to other States within the exclusive economic zone, and a conflict arises between the interests of the coastal State and any other State or States, the conflict should be resolved on the basis of equity and in the light of all the relevant circumstances, taking into account the respective importance of the interests involved to the parties as well as to the international community as a whole.

Article 60. Artificial Islands, Installations and Structures
in the Exclusive Economic Zone

1. In the exclusive economic zone, the coastal State shall have the exclusive right to construct and to authorize and regulate the construction, operation and use of:

(a) artificial islands;

(b) installations and structures for the purposes provided for in article 56 and other economic purposes;

(c) installations and structures which may interfere with the exercise of the rights of the coastal State in the zone.

2. The coastal State shall have exclusive jurisdiction over such artificial islands, installations and structures, including jurisdiction with regard to customs, fiscal, health, safety and immigration laws and regulations.

3. Due notice must be given of the construction of such artificial islands, installations or structures, and permanent means for giving warning of their

presence must be maintained. Any installations or structures which are abandoned or disused shall be removed to ensure safety of navigation, taking into account any generally accepted international standards established in this regard by the competent international organization. Such removal shall also have due regard to fishing, the protection of the marine environment and the rights and duties of other States. Appropriate publicity shall be given to the depth, position and dimensions of any installations or structures not entirely removed.

4. The coastal State may, where necessary, establish reasonable safety zones around such artificial islands, installations and structures in which it may take appropriate measures to ensure the safety both of navigation and of the artificial islands, installations and structures.

5. The breadth of the safety zones shall be determined by the coastal State, taking into account applicable international standards. Such zones shall be designed to ensure that they are reasonably related to the nature and function of the artificial islands, installations or structures, and shall not exceed a distance of 500 metres around them, measured from each point of their outer edge, except as authorized by generally accepted international standards or as recommended by the competent international organization. Due notice shall be given of the extent of safety zones.

6. All ships must respect these safety zones and shall comply with generally accepted international standards regarding navigation in the vicinity of artificial islands, installations, structures and safety zones.

7. Artificial islands, installations and structures and the safety zones around them may not be established where interference may be caused to the use of recognized sea lanes essential to international navigation.

8. Artificial islands, installations and structures do not possess the status of islands. They have no territorial sea of their own, and their presence does not affect the delimitation of the territorial sea, the exclusive economic zone or the continental shelf.

Article 61. Conservation of the Living Resources

1. The coastal State shall determine the allowable catch of the living resources in its exclusive economic zone.

2. The coastal State, taking into account the best scientific evidence available to it, shall ensure through proper conservation and management measures that the maintenance of the living resources in the exclusive economic zone is not endangered by over-exploitation. As appropriate, the coastal State and competent international organizations, whether subregional, regional or global, shall co-operate to this end.

3. Such measures shall also be designed to maintain or restore populations of harvested species at levels which can produce the maximum sustainable yield, as qualified by relevant environmental and economic factors, including the economic needs of coastal fishing communities and the special requirements of developing States, and taking into account fishing patterns,

the interdependence of stocks and any generally recommended international minimum standards, whether subregional, regional or global. . . .

Article 62.   Utilization of the Living Resources

1. The coastal State shall promote the objective of optimum utilization of the living resources in the exclusive economic zone without prejudice to article 61.

2. The coastal State shall determine its capacity to harvest the living resources of the exclusive economic zone. Where the coastal State does not have the capacity to harvest the entire allowable catch, it shall, through agreements or other arrangements and pursuant to the terms, conditions, laws and regulations referred to in paragraph 4, give other States access to the surplus of the allowable catch, having particular regard to the provisions of articles 69 and 70, especially in relation to the developing States mentioned therein.

3. In giving access to other States to its exclusive economic zone under this article, the coastal State shall take into account all relevant factors, including, *inter alia*, the significance of the living resources of the area to the economy of the coastal State concerned and its other national interests, the provisions of articles 69 and 70, the requirements of developing States in the subregion or region in harvesting part of the surplus and the need to minimize economic dislocation in States whose nationals have habitually fished in the zone or which have made substantial efforts in research and identification of stocks.

4. Nationals of other States fishing in the exclusive economic zone shall comply with the conservation measures and with the other terms and conditions established in the laws and regulations of the coastal State. These laws and regulations shall be consistent with this Convention and may relate, inter alia, to the following:

(a) licensing of fishermen, fishing vessels and equipment, including payment of fees and other forms of remuneration, which, in the case of developing coastal States, may consist of adequate compensation in the field of financing, equipment and technology relating to the fishing industry;

(b) determining the species which may be caught, and fixing quotas of catch, whether in relation to particular stocks or groups of stocks or catch per vessel over a period of time or to the catch by nationals of any State during a specified period;

(c) regulating seasons and areas of fishing, the types, sizes and amount of gear, and the types, sizes and number of fishing vessels that may be used;

(d) fixing the age and size of fish and other species that may be caught;

(e) specifying information required of fishing vessels, including catch and effort statistics and vessel position reports;

(f) requiring, under the authorization and control of the coastal State, the conduct of specified fisheries research programmes and regulating the conduct of such research, including the sampling of catches, disposition of samples and reporting of associated scientific data;

(g) the placing of observers or trainees on board such vessels by the coastal State;

(h) the landing of all or any part of the catch by such vessels in the ports of the coastal State;

(i) terms and conditions relating to joint ventures or other cooperative arrangements;

(j) requirements for the training of personnel and the transfer of fisheries technology, including enhancement of the coastal State's capability of undertaking fisheries research;

(k) enforcement procedures. . . .

Article 63.   Stocks Occurring Within the Exclusive Economic Zones of Two or More Coastal States or Both Within the Exclusive Economic Zone and in an Area Beyond and Adjacent to It

1. Where the same stock or stocks of associated species occur within the exclusive economic zones of two or more coastal States, these States shall seek, either directly or through appropriate subregional or regional organizations, to agree upon the measures necessary to co-ordinate and ensure the conservation and development of such stocks without prejudice to the other provisions of this Part. . . .

Article 64.   Highly Migratory Species

1. The coastal State and other States whose nationals fish in the region for the highly migratory species listed in Annex I shall co-operate directly or through appropriate international organizations with a view to ensuring conservation and promoting the objective of optimum utilization of such species throughout the region, both within and beyond the exclusive economic zone. . . .

Article 65.   Marine Mammals

Nothing in this Part restricts the right of a coastal State or the competence of an international organization, as appropriate, to prohibit, limit or regulate the exploitation of marine mammals more strictly than provided for in this Part. States shall co-operate with a view to the conservation of marine mammals and in the case of cetaceans shall in particular work through the appropriate international organizations for their conservation, management and study.

Article 66.   Anadromous Stocks

1. States in whose rivers anadromous stocks originate shall have the primary interest in and responsibility for such stocks.

2. The State of origin of anadromous stocks shall ensure their conservation by the establishment of appropriate regulatory measures for fishing in all waters landward of the outer limits of its exclusive economic zone and for fishing provided for in paragraph 3(b). . . .

Article 67. Catadromous Species

1. A coastal State in whose waters catadromous species spend the greater part of their life cycle shall have responsibility for the management of these species and shall ensure the ingress and egress of migrating fish.

2. Harvesting of catadromous species shall be conducted only in waters landward of the outer limits of exclusive economic zones. When conducted in exclusive economic zones, harvesting shall be subject to this article and the other provisions of this Convention concerning fishing in these zones. . . .

Article 68. Sedentary Species

This Part does not apply to sedentary species as defined in article 77, paragraph 4.

Article 69. Right of Land-Locked States

1. Land-locked States shall have the right to participate, on an equitable basis, in the exploitation of an appropriate part of the surplus of the living resources of the exclusive economic zones of coastal States of the same subregion or region, taking into account the relevant economic and geographical circumstances of all the States concerned and in conformity with the provisions of this article and of articles 61 and 62.

2. The terms and modalities of such participation shall be established by the States concerned through bilateral, subregional or regional agreements. . . .

Article 70. Right of Geographically Disadvantaged States

1. Geographically disadvantaged States shall have the right to participate, on an equitable basis, in the exploitation of an appropriate part of the surplus of the living resources of the exclusive economic zones of coastal States of the same subregion or region, taking into account the relevant economic and geographical circumstances of all the States concerned and in conformity with the provisions of this article and of articles 61 and 62.

2. For the purposes of this Part, "geographically disadvantaged States" means coastal States, including States bordering enclosed or semi-enclosed seas, whose geographical situation makes them dependent upon the exploitation of the living resources of the exclusive economic zones of other States in the subregion or region for adequate supplies of fish for the

nutritional purposes of their populations or parts thereof, and coastal States which can claim no exclusive economic zones of their own.

3. The terms and modalities of such participation shall be established by the States concerned through bilateral, subregional or regional agreements. . . .

Article 72.   Restrictions on Transfer of Rights

1. Rights provided under articles 69 and 70 to exploit living resources shall not be directly or indirectly transferred to third States or their nationals. . . .

Article 73.   Enforcement of Laws and Regulations of the Coastal State

1. The coastal State may, in the exercise of its sovereign rights to explore, exploit, conserve and manage the living resources in the exclusive economic zone, take such measures, including boarding, inspection, arrest and judicial proceedings, as may be necessary to ensure compliance with the laws and regulations adopted by it in conformity with this Convention.

2. Arrested vessels and their crews shall be promptly released upon the posting of reasonable bond or other security.

3. Coastal State penalties for violations of fisheries laws and regulations in the exclusive economic zone may not include imprisonment, in the absence of agreements to the contrary by the States concerned, or any other form of corporal punishment.

4. In cases of arrest or detention of foreign vessels the coastal State shall promptly notify the flag State, through appropriate channels, of the action taken and of any penalties subsequently imposed.

Article 74.   Delimitation of the Exclusive Economic Zone Between States with Opposite or Adjacent Coasts

1. The delimitation of the exclusive economic zone between States with opposite or adjacent coasts shall be effected by agreement on the basis of international law, as referred to in Article 38 of the Statute of the International Court of Justice, in order to achieve an equitable solution.

2. If no agreement can be reached within a reasonable period of time, the States concerned shall resort to the procedures provided for in Part XV.

3. Pending agreement as provided for in paragraph 1, the States concerned, in a spirit of understanding and co-operation, shall make every effort to enter into provisional arrangements of a practical nature and, during this transitional period, not to jeopardize or hamper the reaching of the final agreement. Such arrangements shall be without prejudice to the final delimitation.

4. Where there is an agreement in force between the States concerned, questions relating to the delimitation of the exclusive economic zone shall be determined in accordance with the provisions of that agreement. . . .

Part VI. Continental Shelf

Article 76. Definition of the Continental Shelf

1. The continental shelf of a coastal State comprises the sea-bed and subsoil of the submarine areas that extend beyond its territorial sea throughout the natural prolongation of its land territory to the outer edge of the continental margin, or to a distance of 200 nautical miles from the baselines from which the breadth of the territorial sea is measured where the outer edge of the continental margin does not extend up to that distance.

2. The continental shelf of a coastal State shall not extend beyond the limits provided for in paragraphs 4 to 6.

3. The continental margin comprises the submerged prolongation of the land mass of the coastal State, and consists of the sea-bed and subsoil of the shelf, the slope and the rise. It does not include the deep ocean floor with its oceanic ridges or the subsoil thereof.

4. (a) For the purposes of this Convention, the coastal State shall establish the outer edge of the continental margin wherever the margin extends beyond 200 nautical miles from the baselines from which the breadth of the territorial sea is measured, by either:

(i) a line delineated in accordance with paragraph 7 by reference to the outermost fixed points at each of which the thickness of sedimentary rocks is at least 1 per cent of the shortest distance from such point to the foot of the continental slope; or

(ii) a line delineated in accordance with paragraph 7 by reference to fixed points not more than 60 nautical miles from the foot of the continental slope.

(b) In the absence of evidence to the contrary, the foot of the continental slope shall be determined as the point of maximum change in the gradient at its base.

5. The fixed points comprising the line of the outer limits of the continental shelf on the sea-bed, drawn in accordance with paragraph 4(a)(i) and (ii), either shall not exceed 350 nautical miles from the baselines from which the breadth of the territorial sea is measured or shall not exceed 100 nautical miles from the 2,500 metre isobath, which is a line connecting the depth of 2,500 metres.

6. Notwithstanding the provisions of paragraph 5, on submarine ridges, the outer limit of the continental shelf shall not exceed 350 nautical miles from the baselines from which the breadth of the territorial sea is measured. This paragraph does not apply to submarine elevations that are natural components of the continental margin, such as its plateaux, rises, caps, hanks and spurs.

7. The coastal State shall delineate the outer limits of its continental shelf, where that shelf extends beyond 200 nautical miles from the baselines from which the breadth of the territorial sea is measured, by straight lines not exceeding 60 nautical miles in length, connecting fixed points, defined by co-ordinates of latitude and longitude.

8. Information on the limits of the continental shelf beyond 200 nautical miles from the baselines from which the breadth of the territorial sea is measured shall be submitted by the coastal State to the Commission on the Limits of the Continental Shelf set up under Annex II on the basis of equitable geographical representation. The Commission shall make recommendations to coastal States on matters related to the establishment of the outer limits of their continental shelf. The limits of the shelf established by a coastal State on the basis of these recommendations shall be final and binding. . . .

10. The provisions of this article are without prejudice to the question of delimitation of the continental shelf between States with opposite or adjacent coasts.

Article 77. Rights of the Coastal State over the Continental Shelf

1. The coastal State exercises over the continental shelf sovereign rights for the purpose of exploring it and exploiting its natural resources.

2. The rights referred to in paragraph 1 are exclusive in the sense that if the coastal State does not explore the continental shelf or exploit its natural resources, no one may undertake these activities without the express consent of the coastal State.

3. The rights of the coastal State over the continental shelf do not depend on occupation, effective or notional, or on any express proclamation.

4. The natural resources referred to in this Part consist of the mineral and other non-living resources of the sea-bed and subsoil together with living organisms belonging to sedentary species, that is to say, organisms which, at the harvestable stage, either are immobile on or under the sea-bed or are unable to move except in constant physical contact with the sea-bed or the subsoil.

Article 78. Legal Status of the Superjacent Waters and Air Space and the Rights and Freedoms of Other States

1. The rights of the coastal State over the continental shelf do not affect the legal status of the superjacent waters or of the air space above those waters.

2. The exercise of the rights of the coastal State over the continental shelf must not infringe or result in any unjustifiable interference with navigation and other rights and freedoms of other States as provided for in this Convention.

Article 79.   Submarine Cables and Pipelines on the Continental Shelf

1. All States are entitled to lay submarine cables and pipelines on the continental shelf, in accordance with the provisions of this article.

2. Subject to its right to take reasonable measures for the exploration of the continental shelf, the exploitation of its natural resources and the prevention, reduction and control of pollution from pipelines, the coastal State may not impede the laying or maintenance of such cables or pipelines.

3. The delineation of the course for the laying of such pipelines on the continental shelf is subject to the consent of the coastal State.

4. Nothing in this Part affects the right of the coastal State to establish conditions for cables or pipelines entering its territory or territorial sea, or its jurisdiction over cables and pipelines constructed or used in connection with the exploration of its continental shelf or exploitation of its resources or the operations of artificial islands, installations and structures under its jurisdiction. . . .

Article 80.   Artificial Islands, Installations and Structures on the Continental Shelf

Article 60 applies *mutatis mutandis* to artificial islands, installations and structures on the continental shelf.

Article 81.   Drilling on the Continental Shelf

The coastal State shall have the exclusive right to authorize and regulate drilling on the continental shelf for all purposes.

Article 82.   Payments and Contributions with Respect to the Exploitation of the Continental Shelf Beyond 200 Nautical Miles

1. The coastal State shall make payments or contributions in kind in respect of the exploitation of the non-living resources of the continental shelf beyond 200 nautical miles from the baselines from which the breadth of the territorial sea is measured.

2. The payments and contributions shall be made annually with respect to all production at a site after the first five years of production at that site. For the sixth year, the rate of payment or contribution shall be 1 per cent of the value or volume of production at the site. The rate shall increase by 1 per cent for each subsequent year until the twelfth year and shall remain at 7 per cent thereafter. Production does not include resources used in connection with exploitation.

3. A developing State which is a net importer of a mineral resource produced from its continental shelf is exempt from making such payments or contributions in respect of that mineral resource.

4. The payments or contributions shall be made through the Authority, which shall distribute them to States Parties to this Convention, on the basis of equitable sharing criteria, taking into account the interests and needs of

developing States, particularly the least developed and the land-locked among them.

Article 83. Delimitation of the Continental Shelf Between States with Opposite or Adjacent Coasts

1. The delimitation of the continental shelf between States with opposite or adjacent coasts shall be effected by agreement on the basis of international law, as referred to in Article 38 of the Statute of the International Court of Justice, in order to achieve an equitable solution.

2. If no agreement can be reached within a reasonable period of time, the States concerned shall resort to the procedures provided for in Part XV.

3. Pending agreement as provided for in paragraph 1, the States concerned, in a spirit of understanding and co-operation, shall make every effort to enter into provisional arrangements of a practical nature and, during this transitional period, not to jeopardize or hamper the reaching of the final agreement. Such arrangements shall be without prejudice to the final delimitation.

4. Where there is an agreement in force between the States concerned, questions relating to the delimitation of the continental shelf shall be determined in accordance with the provisions of that agreement.

Article 84. Charts and Lists of Geographical Co-ordinates

1. Subject to this Part, the outer limit lines of the continental shelf and the lines of delimitation drawn in accordance with article 83 shall be shown on charts of a scale or scales adequate for ascertaining their position. . . .

Part VII.   High Seas

SECTION 1.   GENERAL PROVISIONS

Article 86.   Application of the Provisions of This Part

The provisions of this Part apply to all parts of the sea that are not included in the exclusive economic zone, in the territorial sea or in the internal waters of a State, or in the archipelagic waters of an archipelagic State. This article does not entail any abridgement of the freedoms enjoyed by all States in the exclusive economic zone in accordance with article 58.

Article 87.   Freedom of the High Seas

1. The high seas are open to all States, whether coastal or land-locked. Freedom of the high seas is exercised under the conditions laid down by this

Convention and by other rules of international law. It comprises, *inter alia*, both for coastal and land-locked States:

    (a) freedom of navigation;

    (b) freedom of overflight;

    (b) freedom to lay submarine cables and pipelines, subject to Part VI;

    (d) freedom to construct artificial islands and other installations permitted under international law, subject to Part VI;

    (e) freedom of fishing, subject to the conditions laid down in section 2;

    (f) freedom of scientific research, subject to Parts VI and XIII.

2. These freedoms shall be exercised by all States with due regard for the interests of other States in their exercise of the freedom of the high seas, and also with due regard for the rights under this Convention with respect to activities in the Area.

Article 88. *Reservation of the High Seas for Peaceful Purposes*

The high seas shall be reserved for peaceful purposes.

Article 89. *Invalidity of Claims of Sovereignty over the High Seas*

No State may validly purport to subject any part of the high seas to its sovereignty.

Article 90. *Right of Navigation*

Every State, whether coastal or land-locked, has the right to sail ships flying its flag on the high seas.

Article 91. *Nationality of Ships*

1. Every State shall fix the conditions for the grant of its nationality to ships, for the registration of ships in its territory, and for the right to fly its flag. Ships have the nationality of the State whose flag they are entitled to fly. There must exist a genuine link between the State and the ship.

2. Every State shall issue to ships to which it has granted the right to fly its flag documents to that effect.

Article 92. *Status of Ships*

1. Ships shall sail under the flag of one State only and, save in exceptional cases expressly provided for in international treaties or in this Convention, shall be subject to its exclusive jurisdiction on the high seas. A ship may not change its flag during a voyage or while in a port of call, save in the case of a real transfer of ownership or change of registry.

2. A ship which sails under the flags of two or more States, using them according to convenience, may not claim any of the nationalities in question with respect to any other State, and may be assimilated to a ship without nationality. . . .

Article 94. Duties of the Flag State

1. Every State shall effectively exercise its jurisdiction and control in administrative, technical and social matters over ships flying its flag.

2. In particular every State shall:

(a) maintain a register of ships containing the names and particulars of ships flying its flag, except those which are excluded from generally accepted international regulations on account of their small size; and

(b) assume jurisdiction under its internal law over each ship flying its flag and its master, officers and crew in respect of administrative, technical and social matters concerning the ship.

3. Every State shall take such measures for ships flying its flag as are necessary to ensure safety at sea with regard, *inter alia*, to:

(a) the construction, equipment and seaworthiness of ships;

(b) the manning of ships, labour conditions and the training of crews, taking into account the applicable international instruments;

(c) the use of signals, the maintenance of communications and the prevention of collisions.

4. Such measures shall include those necessary to ensure:

(a) that each ship, before registration and thereafter at appropriate intervals, is surveyed by a qualified surveyor of ships, and has on board such charts, nautical publications and navigational equipment and instruments as are appropriate for the safe navigation of the ship;

(b) that each ship is in the charge of a master and officers who possess appropriate qualifications, in particular in seamanship, navigation, communications and marine engineering, and that the crew is appropriate in qualification and numbers for the type, size, machinery and equipment of the ship;

(c) that the master, officers and, to the extent appropriate, the crew are fully conversant with and required to observe the applicable international regulations concerning the safety of life at sea, the prevention of collisions, the prevention, reduction and control of marine pollution, and the maintenance of communications by radio.

5. In taking the measures called for in paragraphs 3 and 4 each State is required to conform to generally accepted international regulations, procedures and practices and to take any steps which may be necessary to secure their observance.

6. A State which has clear grounds to believe that proper jurisdiction and control with respect to a ship have not been exercised may report the facts to the flag State. Upon receiving such a report, the flag State shall investigate the matter and, if appropriate, take any action necessary to remedy the situation.

7. Each State shall cause an inquiry to be held by or before a suitably qualified person or persons into every marine casualty or incident of navigation on the high seas involving a ship flying its flag and causing loss of life or serious injury to nationals of another State or serious damage to ships or installations of another State or to the marine environment. The flag State

and the other State shall co-operate in the conduct of any inquiry held by that other State into any such marine casualty or incident of navigation.

Article 95.   *Immunity of Warships on the High Sea*

Warships on the high seas have complete immunity from the jurisdiction of any State other than the flag State.

Article 96.   *Immunity of Ships Used Only on Government Non-Commercial Service*

Ships owned or operated by a State and used only on government noncommercial service shall, on the high seas, have complete immunity from the jurisdiction of any State other than the flag State.

Article 97.   *Penal Jurisdiction in Matters of Collision or Any Other Incident of Navigation*

1. In the event of a collision or any other incident of navigation concerning a ship on the high seas, involving the penal or disciplinary responsibility of the master or of any other person in the service of the ship, no penal or disciplinary proceedings may be instituted against such person except before the judicial or administrative authorities either of the flag State or of the State of which such person is a national.

2. In disciplinary matters, the State which has issued a master's certificate or a certificate of competence or licence shall alone be competent, after due legal process, to pronounce the withdrawal of such certificates, even if the holder is not a national of the State which issued them.

3. No arrest or detention of the ship, even as a measure of investigation, shall be ordered by any authorities other than those of the flag State.

Article 98.   *Duty to Render Assistance*

1. Every State shall require the master of a ship flying its flag, in so far as he can do so without serious danger to the ship, the crew or the passengers:

   (a) to render assistance to any person found at sea in danger of being lost;

   (b) to proceed with all possible speed to the rescue of persons in distress, if informed of their need of assistance, in so far as such action may reasonably be expected of him;

   (c) after a collision, to render assistance to the other ship, its crew and its passengers and, where possible, to inform the other ship of the name of his own ship, its port of registry and the nearest port at which it will call.

2. Every coastal State shall promote the establishment, operation and maintenance of an adequate and effective search and rescue service regarding safety on and over the sea and, where circumstances so require, by way of mutual regional arrangements co-operate with neighbouring States for this purpose.

Article 99. Prohibition of the Transport of Slaves

Every State shall take effective measures to prevent and punish the transport of slaves in ships authorized to fly its flag and to prevent the unlawful use of its flag for that purpose. Any slave taking refuge on board any ship, whatever its flag, shall *ipso facto* be free.

Article 100. Duty to Co-operate in the Repression of Piracy

All States shall co-operate to the fullest possible extent in the repression of piracy on the high seas or in any other place outside the jurisdiction of any State.

Article 101. Definition of Piracy

Piracy consists of any of the following acts:

(a) any illegal acts of violence or detention, or any act of depredation, committed for private ends by the crew or the passengers of a private ship or a private aircraft, and directed:

(i) on the high seas, against another ship or aircraft, or against persons or property on board such ship or aircraft;

(ii) against a ship, aircraft, persons or property in a place outside the jurisdiction of any State;

(b) any act of voluntary participation in the operation of a ship or of an aircraft with knowledge of facts making it a pirate-ship or aircraft;

(c) any act of inciting or of intentionally facilitating an act described in subparagraph (a) or (b).

Article 102. Piracy by a Warship, Government Ship or Government Aircraft Whose Crew Has Mutinied

The acts of piracy, as defined in article 101, committed by a warship, government ship or government aircraft whose crew has mutinied and taken control of the ship or aircraft are assimilated to acts committed by a private ship or aircraft.

Article 103. Definition of a Pirate Ship or Aircraft

A ship or aircraft is considered a pirate ship or aircraft if it is intended by the persons in dominant control to be used for the purpose of committing one of the acts referred to in article 101. The same applies if the ship or aircraft has been used to commit any such act, so long as it remains under the control of the persons guilty of that act.

Article 104. Retention or Loss of the Nationality of a Pirate Ship or Aircraft

A ship or aircraft may retain its nationality although it has become a pirate ship or aircraft. The retention or loss of nationality is determined by the law of the State from which such nationality was derived.

Article 105.   Seizure of a Pirate Ship or Aircraft

On the high seas, or in any other place outside the jurisdiction of any State, every State may seize a pirate ship or aircraft, or a ship or aircraft taken by piracy and under the control of pirates, and arrest the persons and seize the property on board. The courts of the State which carried out the seizure may decide upon the penalties to be imposed, and may also determine the action to be taken with regard to the ships, aircraft or property, subject to the rights of third parties acting in good faith.

Article 106.   Liability for Seizure Without Adequate Grounds

Where the seizure of a ship or aircraft on suspicion of piracy has been effected without adequate grounds, the State making the seizure shall be liable to the State the nationality of which is possessed by the ship or aircraft for any loss or damage caused by the seizure.

Article 107.   Ships and Aircraft Which Are Entitled to Seize on Account of Piracy

A seizure on account of piracy may be carried out only by warships or military aircraft, or other ships or aircraft clearly marked and identifiable as being on government service and authorized to that effect.

Article 108.   Illicit Traffic in Narcotic Drugs or Psychotropic Substances

1. All States shall co-operate in the suppression of illicit traffic in narcotic drugs and psychotropic substances engaged in by ships on the high seas contrary to international conventions.

2. Any State which has reasonable grounds for believing that a ship flying its flag is engaged in illicit traffic in narcotic drugs or psychotropic substances may request the co-operation of other States to suppress such traffic.

Article 109.   Unauthorized Broadcasting from the High Seas

1. All States shall co-operate in the suppression of unauthorized broadcasting from the high seas.

2. For the purposes of this Convention, "unauthorized broadcasting" means the transmission of sound radio or television broadcasts from a ship or installation on the high seas intended for reception by the general public contrary to international regulations, but excluding the transmission of distress calls.

3. Any person engaged in unauthorized broadcasting may be prosecuted before the court of:

(a) the flag State of the ship;

(b) the State of registry of the installation;

(c) the State of which the person is a national;

(d) any State where the transmissions can be received; or

(e) any State where authorized radio communication is suffering interference. . . .

Article 110. Right of Visit

1. Except where acts of interference derive from powers conferred by treaty, a warship which encounters on the high seas a foreign ship, other than a ship entitled to complete immunity in accordance with articles 95 and 96, is not justified in boarding it unless there is reasonable ground for suspecting that:

(a) the ship is engaged in piracy;

(b) the ship is engaged in the slave trade;

(c) the ship is engaged in unauthorized broadcasting and the flag State of the warship has jurisdiction under article 109;

(d) the ship is without nationality; or

(e) though flying a foreign flag or refusing to show its flag, the ship is, in reality, of the same nationality as the warship.

2. In the cases provided for in paragraph 1, the warship may proceed to verify the ship's right to fly its flag. To this end, it may send a boat under the command of an officer to the suspected ship. If suspicion remains after the documents have been checked, it may proceed to a further examination on board the ship, which must be carried out with all possible consideration.

3. If the suspicions prove to be unfounded, and provided that the ship boarded has not committed any act justifying them, it shall be compensated for any loss or damage that may have been sustained.

4. These provisions apply *mutatis mutandis* to military aircraft.

5. These provisions also apply to any other duly authorized ships or aircraft clearly marked and identifiable as being on government service.

Article 111. Right of Hot Pursuit

1. The hot pursuit of a foreign ship may be undertaken when the competent authorities of the coastal State have good reason to believe that the ship has violated the laws and regulations of that State. Such pursuit must be commenced when the foreign ship or one of its boats is within the internal waters, the archipelagic waters, the territorial sea or the contiguous zone of the pursuing State, and may only be continued outside the territorial sea or the contiguous zone if the pursuit has not been interrupted. It is not necessary that, at the time when the foreign ship within the territorial sea or the contiguous zone receives the order to stop, the ship giving the order should likewise be within the territorial sea or the contiguous zone. If the foreign ship is within a contiguous zone, as defined in article 33, the pursuit may only be undertaken if there has been a violation of the rights for the protection of which the zone was established.

2. The right of hot pursuit shall apply mutatis mutandis to violations in the exclusive economic zone or on the continental shelf, including safety zones around continental shelf installations, of the laws and regulations of the coastal State applicable in accordance with this Convention to the exclusive economic zone or the continental shelf, including such safety zones.

3. The right of hot pursuit ceases as soon as the ship pursued enters the territorial sea of its own State or of a third State.

4. Hot pursuit is not deemed to have begun unless the pursuing ship has satisfied itself by such practicable means as may be available that the ship pursued or one of its boats or other craft working as a team and using the ship pursued as a mother ship is within the limits of the territorial sea, or, as the case may be, within the contiguous zone or the exclusive economic zone or above the continental shelf. The pursuit may only be commenced after a visual or auditory signal to stop has been given at a distance which enables it to be seen or heard by the foreign ship.

5. The right of hot pursuit may be exercised only by warships or military aircraft, or other ships or aircraft clearly marked and identifiable as being on government service and authorized to that effect.

6. Where hot pursuit is effected by an aircraft:

(a) the provisions of paragraphs 1 to 4 shall apply mutatis mutandis;

(b) the aircraft giving the order to stop must itself actively pursue the ship until a ship or another aircraft of the coastal State, summoned by the aircraft, arrives to take over the pursuit, unless the aircraft is itself able to arrest the ship. It does not suffice to justify an arrest outside the territorial sea that the ship was merely sighted by the aircraft as an offender or suspected offender, if it was not both ordered to stop and pursued by the aircraft itself or other aircraft or ships which continue the pursuit without interruption. . . .

8. Where a ship has been stopped or arrested outside the territorial sea in circumstances which do not justify the exercise of the right of hot pursuit, it shall be compensated for any loss or damage that may have been thereby sustained.

Article 112.   Right to Lay Submarine Cables and Pipelines

1. All States are entitled to lay submarine cables and pipelines on the bed of the high seas beyond the continental shelf.

2. Article 79, paragraph 5, applies to such cables and pipelines. . . .

SECTION 2. CONSERVATION AND MANAGEMENT OF THE LIVING RESOURCES OF THE HIGH SEAS

Article 116. Right to Fish on the High Seas

All States have the right for their nationals to engage in fishing on the high seas subject to:

(a) their treaty obligations;

(b) the rights and duties as well as the interests of coastal States provided for, *inter alia*, in article 63, paragraph 2, and articles 64 to 67; and

(c) the provisions of this section.

Article 117. Duty of States to Adopt with Respect to Their Nationals Measures for the Conservation of the Living Resources of the High Seas

All States have the duty to take, or to co-operate with other States in taking, such measures for their respective nationals as may be necessary for the conservation of the living resources of the high seas. . . .

Article 120. Marine Mammals

Article 65 also applies to the conservation and management of marine mammals in the high seas.

Part VIII. Regime of Islands

Article 121. Régime of Islands

1. An island is a naturally formed area of land, surrounded by water, which is above water at high tide.

2. Except as provided for in paragraph 3, the territorial sea, the contiguous zone, the exclusive economic zone and the continental shelf of an island are determined in accordance with the provisions of this Convention applicable to other land territory.

3. Rocks which cannot sustain human habitation or economic life of their own shall have no exclusive economic zone or continental shelf.

Part IX. Enclosed or Semi-Enclosed Seas

Article 122. Definition

For the purposes of this Convention, "enclosed or semi-enclosed sea" means a gulf, basin or sea surrounded by two or more States and connected to another sea or the ocean by a narrow outlet or consisting entirely or primarily of the territorial seas and exclusive economic zones of two or more coastal States.

Article 123.   Co-operation of States Bordering Enclosed or Semi-Enclosed Seas

States bordering an enclosed or semi-enclosed sea should co-operate with each other in the exercise of their rights and in the performance of their duties under this Convention. To this end they shall endeavour, directly or through an appropriate regional organization: . . . .

Part X.   Right of Access of Land-Locked States to and from the Sea and Freedom of Transit

Article 124.   Use of Terms

1. For the purposes of this Convention:
   (a) "land-locked State" means a State which has no sea-coast;
   (b) "transit State" means a State, with or without a sea-coast, situated between a land-locked State and the sea, through whose territory traffic in transit passes;
   (c) "traffic in transit" means transit of persons, baggage, goods and means of transport across the territory of one or more transit States, when the passage across such territory, with or without trans-shipment, warehousing, breaking bulk or change in the mode of transport, is only a portion of a complete journey which begins or terminates within the territory of the land-locked State;
   (d) "means of transport" means:
      (i) railway rolling stock, sea, lake and river craft and road vehicles;
      (ii) where local conditions so require, porters and pack animals. . . .

Article 125.   Right of Access to and from the Sea and Freedom of Transit

1. Land-locked States shall have the right of access to and from the sea for the purpose of exercising the rights provided for in this Convention including those relating to the freedom of the high seas and the common heritage of mankind. To this end, land-locked States shall enjoy freedom of transit through the territory of transit States by all means of transport.

2. The terms and modalities for exercising freedom of transit shall be agreed between the land-locked States and transit States concerned through bilateral, subregional or regional agreements.

3. Transit States, in the exercise of their full sovereignty over their territory, shall have the right to take all measures necessary to ensure that the rights and facilities provided for in this Part for land-locked States shall in no way infringe their legitimate interests. . . .

Article 127.   Customs Duties, Taxes and Other Charges

1. Traffic in transit shall not be subject to any customs duties, taxes or other charges except charges levied for specific services rendered in connection with such traffic. . . .

Part XI.   The Area

SECTION 1.   GENERAL PROVISIONS

Article 133.   Use of Terms

For the purposes of this Part:

(a) "resources" means all solid, liquid or gaeous mineral resources *in situ* in the Area at or beneath the sea-bed, including polymetallic nodules;

(b) resources, when recovered from the Area, are referred to as "minerals".

Article 134.   Scope of This Part

1. This Part applies to the Area.

2. Activities in the Area shall be governed by the provisions of this Part.

3. The requirements concerning deposit of, and publicity to be given to, the charts or lists of geographical co-ordinates showing the limits referred to in article 1, paragraph 1(1) are set forth in Part VI.

4. Nothing in this article affects the establishment of the outer limits of the continental shelf in accordance with Part VI or the validity of agreements relating to delimitation between States with opposite or adjacent coasts.

Article 135.   Legal Status of the Superjacent Waters and Air Space

Neither this Part nor any rights granted or exercised pursuant thereto shall affect the legal status of the waters superjacent to the Area or that of the air space above those waters.

SECTION 2.   PRINCIPLES GOVERNING THE AREA

Article 136.   Common Heritage of Mankind

The Area and its resources are the common heritage of mankind.

Article 137.   Legal Status of the Area and Its Resources

1. No State shall claim or exercise sovereignty or sovereign rights over any part of the Area or its resources, nor shall any State or natural or juridical person appropriate any part thereof. No such claim or exercise of sovereignty or sovereign rights nor such appropriation shall be recognized.

2. All rights in the resources of the Area are vested in mankind as a whole, on whose behalf the Authority shall act. These resources are not subject to alienation. The minerals recovered from the Area, however, may only be alienated in accordance with this Part and the rules, regulations and procedures of the Authority.

3. No State or natural or juridical person shall claim, acquire or exercise rights with respect to the minerals recovered from the Area except in accordance with this Part. Otherwise, no such claim, acquisition or exercise of such rights shall be recognized.

Article 138.   General Conduct of States in Relation to the Area

The general conduct of States in relation to the Area shall be in accordance with the provisions of this Part, the principles embodied in the Charter of the United Nations and other rules of international law in the interests of maintaining peace and security and promoting international cooperation and mutual understanding.

Article 139.   Responsibility to Ensure Compliance and Liability for Damage

1. States Parties shall have the responsibility to ensure that activities in the Area, whether carried out by States Parties, or state enterprises or natural or juridical persons which possess the nationality of States Parties or are effectively controlled by them or their nationals, shall be carried out in conformity with this Part. The same responsibility applies to international organizations for activities in the Area carried out by such organizations.

2. Without prejudice to the rules of international law and Annex III, article 22, damage caused by the failure of a State Party or international organization to carry out its responsibilities under this Part shall entail liability; States Parties or international organizations acting together shall bear joint and several liability. . . .

Article 140.   Benefit of Mankind

1. Activities in the Area shall, as specifically provided for in this Part, be carried out for the benefit of mankind as a whole, irrespective of the geographical location of States, whether coastal or land-locked, and taking into particular consideration the interests and needs of developing States and of peoples who have not attained full independence or other self-governing status recognized by the United Nations. . . .

2. The Authority shall provide for the equitable sharing of financial and other economic benefits derived from activities in the Area through any appropriate mechanism, on a non-discriminatory basis, in accordance with article 160, paragraph 2(f)(i).

Article 141. Use of the Area Exclusively for Peaceful Purposes

The Area shall be open to use exclusively for peaceful purposes by all States, whether coastal or land-locked, without discrimination and without prejudice to the other provisions of this Part.

Article 142. Rights and Legitimate Interests of Coastal States

1. Activities in the Area, with respect to resource deposits in the Area which lie across limits of national jurisdiction, shall be conducted with due regard to the rights and legitimate interests of any coastal State across whose jurisdiction such deposits lie. . . .

3. Neither this Part nor any rights granted or exercised pursuant thereto shall affect the rights of coastal States to take such measures consistent with the relevant provisions of Part XII as may be necessary to prevent, mitigate or eliminate grave and imminent danger to their coastline, or related interests from pollution or threat thereof or from other hazardous occurrences resulting from or caused by any activities in the Area.

Article 143. Marine Scientific Research

1. Marine scientific research in the Area shall be carried out exclusively for peaceful purposes and for the benefit of mankind as a whole, in accordance with Part XIII. . . .

Article 144. Transfer of Technology

1. The Authority shall take measures in accordance with this Convention:

(a) to acquire technology and scientific knowledge relating to activities in the Area; and

(b) to promote and encourage the transfer to developing States of such technology and scientific knowledge so that all States Parties benefit there from.

2. To this end the Authority and States Parties shall co-operate in promoting the transfer of technology and scientific knowledge relating to activities in the Area so that the Enterprise and all States Parties may benefit therefrom. . . .

Article 145. Protection of the Marine Environment

Necessary measures shall be taken in accordance with this Convention with respect to activities in the Area to ensure effective protection for the marine environment . . .

Article 147.   Accommodation of Activities in the Area and in the Marine Environment

1. Activities in the Area shall be carried out with reasonable regard for other activities in the marine environment.

2. Installations used for carrying out activities in the Area shall be subject to the following conditions:

(a) such installations shall be erected, emplaced and removed solely in accordance with this Part and subject to the rules, regulations and procedures of the Authority . . . ;

(b) such installations may not be established where interference may be caused to the use of recognized sea lanes essential to international navigation or in areas of intense fishing activity;

(c) safety zones shall be established around such installations with appropriate markings to ensure the safety of both navigation and the installations . . . ;

(d) such installations shall be used exclusively for peaceful purposes;

(e) such installations do not possess the status of islands. They have no territorial sea of their own, and their presence does not affect the delimitation of the territorial sea, the exclusive economic zone or the continental shelf. . . .

Article 149.   Archaeological and Historical Objects

All objects of an archaeological and historical nature found in the Area shall be preserved or disposed of for the benefit of mankind as a whole, particular regard being paid to the preferential rights of the State or country of origin, or the State of cultural origin, or the State of historical and archaeological origin.

SECTION 3.   DEVELOPMENT OF RESOURCES OF THE AREA

Article 150.   Policies Relating to Activities in the Area

Activities in the Area shall, as specifically provided for in this Part, be carried out in such a manner as to foster healthy development of the world economy and balanced growth of international trade, and to promote international cooperation for the over-all development of all countries, especially developing States, and with a view to ensuring:

(a) the development of the resources of the Area;

(b) orderly, safe and rational management of the resources of the Area, including the efficient conduct of activities in the Area and, in accordance with sound principles of conservation, the avoidance of unnecessary waste;

(c) the expansion of opportunities for participation in such activities consistent in particular with articles 144 and 148;

(d) participation in revenues by the Authority and the transfer of technology to the Enterprise and developing States as provided for in this Convention;

(e) increased availability of the minerals derived from the Area as needed in conjunction with minerals derived from other sources, to ensure supplies to consumers of such minerals;

(f) the promotion of just and stable prices remunerative to producers and fair to consumers for minerals derived both from the Area and from other sources, and the promotion of long-term equilibrium between supply and demand;

(g) the enhancement of opportunities for all States Parties, irrespective of their social and economic systems or geographical location, to participate in the development of the resources of the Area and the prevention of monopolization of activities in the Area;

(h) the protection of developing countries from adverse effects on their economies or on their export earnings resulting from a reduction in the price of an affected mineral, or in the volume of exports of that mineral, to the extent that such reduction is caused by activities in the Area, as provided in article 151;

(i) the development of the common heritage for the benefit of mankind as a whole; and

(j) conditions of access to markets for the imports of minerals produced from the resources of the Area and for imports of commodities produced from such minerals shall not be more favourable than the most favourable applied to imports from other sources.

Article 151.   Production Policies . . .

10. Upon the recommendation of the Council on the basis of advice from the Economic Planning Commission, the Assembly shall establish a system of compensation or take other measures of economic adjustment assistance including co-operation with specialized agencies and other international organizations to assist developing countries which suffer serious adverse effects on their export earnings or economies resulting from a reduction in the price of an affected mineral or in the volume of exports of that mineral, to the extent that such reduction is caused by activities in the Area. . . .

Article 152.   Exercise of Powers and Functions by the Authority

1. The Authority shall avoid discrimination in the exercise of its powers and functions, including the granting of opportunities for activities in the Area.

2. Nevertheless, special consideration for developing States, including particular consideration for the land-locked and geographically disadvantaged among them, specifically provided for in this Part shall be permitted.

Article 153.   System of Exploration and Exploitation

1. Activities in the Area shall be organized, carried out and controlled by the Authority on behalf of mankind as a whole in accordance with this article as well as other relevant provisions of this Part and the relevant Annexes, and the rules, regulations and procedures of the Authority.

2. Activities in the Area shall be carried out as prescribed in paragraph 3:

(a) by the Enterprise, and

(b) in association with the Authority by States Parties, or state enterprises or natural or juridical persons which possess the nationality of States Parties or are effectively controlled by them or their nationals, when sponsored by such States, or any group of the foregoing which meets the requirements provided in this Part and in Annex III.

3. Activities in the Area shall be carried out in accordance with a formal written plan of work drawn up in accordance with Annex III and approved by the Council after review by the Legal and Technical Commission. . . .

Article 154.   Periodic Review

Every five years from the entry into force of this Convention, the Assembly shall undertake a general and systematic review of the manner in which the international régime of the Area established in this Convention has operated in practice. . . .

Article 155.   The Review Conference . . .

2. The Review Conference shall ensure the maintenance of the principle of the common heritage of mankind, the international régime designed to ensure equitable exploitation of the resources of the Area for the benefit of all countries, especially the developing States, and an Authority to organize, conduct and control activities in the Area. It shall also ensure the maintenance of the principles laid down in this Part with regard to the exclusion of claims or exercise of sovereignty over any part of the Area, the rights of States and their general conduct in relation to the Area, and their participation in activities in the Area in conformity with this Convention, the prevention of monopolization of activities in the Area, the use of the Area exclusively for peaceful purposes, economic aspects of activities in the Area, marine scientific research, transfer of technology, protection of the marine environment, protection of human life, rights of coastal States, the legal status of the waters superjacent to the Area and that of the air space above those waters and accommodation between activities in the Area and other activities in the marine environment. . . .

5. Amendments adopted by the Review Conference pursuant to this article shall not affect rights acquired under existing contracts.

SECTION 4. THE AUTHORITY

SUBSECTION A. GENERAL PROVISIONS

Article 156. Establishment of the Authority

1. There is hereby established the International Sea-Bed Authority, which shall function in accordance with this Part.

2. All States Parties are *ipso facto* members of the Authority.

3. Observers at the Third United Nations Conference on the Law of the Sea who have signed the Final Act and who are not referred to in article 305, paragraph 1(c), (d), (e) or (f), shall have the right to participate in the Authority as observers, in accordance with its rules, regulations and procedures.

4. The seat of the Authority shall be in Jamaica . . .

Article 157. Nature and Fundamental Principles of the Authority

1. The Authority is the organization through which States Parties shall, in accordance with this Part, organize and control activities in the Area, particularly with a view to administering the resources of the Area.

2. The powers and functions of the Authority shall be those expressly conferred upon it by this Convention. The Authority shall have such incidental powers, consistent with this Convention, as are implicit in and necessary for the exercise of those powers and functions with respect to activities in the Area.

3. The Authority is based on the principle of the sovereign equality of all its members. . . .

Article 158. Organs of the Authority

1. There are hereby established, as the principal organs of the Authority, an Assembly, a Council and a Secretariat.

2. There is hereby established the Enterprise, the organ through which the Authority shall carry out the functions referred to in article 170, paragraph 1.

3. Such subsidiary organs as may be found necessary may be established in accordance with this Part. . . .

SUBSECTION B. THE ASSEMBLY

Article 159. Composition, Procedure and Voting

1. The Assembly shall consist of all the members of the Authority. Each member shall have one representative in the Assembly, who may be accompanied by alternates and advisers.

2. The Assembly shall meet in regular annual sessions and in such special sessions as may be decided by the Assembly, or convened by the Secretary-General at the request of the Council or of a majority of the members of the Authority.

3. Sessions shall take place at the seat of the Authority unless otherwise decided by the Assembly.

4. The Assembly shall adopt its rules of procedure. At the beginning of each regular session, it shall elect its President and such other officers as may be required. They shall hold office until a new President and other officers are elected at the next regular session.

5. A majority of the members of the Assembly shall constitute a quorum.

6. Each member of the Assembly shall have one vote.

7. Decisions on questions of procedure, including decisions to convene special sessions of the Assembly, shall be taken by a majority of the members present and voting.

8. Decisions on questions of substance shall be taken by a two-thirds majority of the members present and voting, provided that such majority includes a majority of the members participating in the session. When the issue arises as to whether a question is one of substance or not, that question shall be treated as one of substance unless otherwise decided by the Assembly by the majority required for decisions on questions of substance.

9. When a question of substance comes up for voting for the first time, the President may, and shall, if requested by at least one fifth of the members of the Assembly, defer the issue of taking a vote on that question for a period not exceeding five calendar days. This rule may be applied only once to any question, and shall not be applied so as to defer the question beyond the end of the session.

10. Upon a written request addressed to the President and sponsored by at least one fourth of the members of the Authority for an advisory opinion on the conformity with this Convention of a proposal before the Assembly on any matter, the Assembly shall request the Sea-Bed Disputes Chamber of the International Tribunal for the Law of the Sea to give an advisory opinion thereon and shall defer voting on that proposal pending receipt of the advisory opinion by the Chamber. . . .

Article 160.   Powers and Functions

1. The Assembly, as the sole organ of the Authority consisting of all the members, shall be considered the supreme organ of the Authority to which the other principal organs shall be accountable as specifically provided for in this Convention. The Assembly shall have the power to establish general policies in conformity with the relevant provisions of this Convention on any question or matter within the competence of the Authority.

2. In addition, the powers and functions of the Assembly shall be:

(a) to elect the members of the Council in accordance with article 161;

(b) to elect the Secretary-General from among the candidates proposed by the Council;

(c) to elect, upon the recommendation of the Council, the members of the Governing Board of the Enterprise and the Director-General of the Enterprise;

(d) to establish such subsidiary organs as it finds necessary for the exercise of its functions in accordance with this Part. In the composition of these subsidiary organs due account shall be taken of the principle of equitable geographical distribution and of special interests and the need for members qualified and competent in the relevant technical questions dealt with by such organs;

(e) to assess the contributions of members to the administrative budget of the Authority in accordance with an agreed scale of assessment based upon the scale used for the regular budget of the United Nations until the Authority shall have sufficient income from other sources to meet its administrative expenses;

(f) (i) to consider and approve, upon the recommendation of the Council, the rules, regulations and procedures on the equitable sharing of financial and other economic benefits derived from activities in the Area and the payments and contributions made pursuant to article 82. . . . If the Assembly does not approve the recommendations of the Council, the Assembly shall return them to the Council for reconsideration in the light of the views expressed by the Assembly;

(ii) to consider and approve the rules, regulations and procedures of the Authority, and any amendments thereto, provisionally adopted by the Council pursuant to article 162, paragraph 2(o) (ii). These rules, regulations and procedures shall relate to prospecting, exploration and exploitation in the Area, the financial management and internal administration of the Authority . . . ;

(g) to decide upon the equitable sharing of financial and other economic benefits derived from activities in the Area, consistent with this Convention and the rules, regulations and procedures of the Authority;

(h) to consider and approve the proposed annual budget of the Authority submitted by the Council;

(i) to examine periodic reports from the Council and from the Enterprise and special reports requested from the Council or any other organ of the Authority; . . .

(k) to consider problems of a general nature in connection with activities in the Area . . . ;

(l) to establish, upon the recommendation of the Council, on the basis of advice from the Economic Planning Commission, a system of compensation or other measures of economic adjustment assistance as provided in article 151, paragraph 10;

(m) to suspend the exercise of rights and privileges of membership pursuant to article 185;

(n) to discuss any question or matter within the competence of the Authority and to decide as to which organ of the Authority shall deal with any such question or matter not specifically entrusted to a particular organ. . . .

SUBSECTION C.   THE COUNCIL

Article 161.   Composition, Procedure and Voting...

2. In electing the members of the Council in accordance with paragraph 1, the Assembly shall ensure that:

(a) land-locked and geographically disadvantaged States are represented to a degree which is reasonably proportionate to their representation in the Assembly;

(b) coastal States, especially developing States, which do not qualify under paragraph 1(a), (b), (c) or (d) are represented to a degree which is reasonably proportionate to their representation in the Assembly;

(c) each group of States Parties to be represented on the Council is represented by those members, if any, which are nominated by that group.

3. Elections shall take place at regular sessions of the Assembly. Each member of the Council shall be elected for four years. At the first election, however, the term of one half of the members of each group referred to in paragraph 1 shall be two years.

4. Members of the Council shall be eligible for re-election, but due regard should be paid to the desirability of rotation of membership.

5. The Council shall function at the seat of the Authority, and shall meet as often as the business of the Authority may require, but not less than three times a year.

6. A majority of the members of the Council shall constitute a quorum.

7. Each member of the Council shall have one vote.

8. (a) Decisions on questions of procedure shall be taken by a majority of the members present and voting. . . .

(d) Decisions on questions of substance arising under the following provisions shall be taken by consensus: article 162, paragraph 2(m) and (o); adoption of amendments to Part XI.

(e) For the purposes of subparagraphs (d), (f) and (g), "consensus" means the absence of any formal objection. . . . If the President determines that there would be such an objection, the President shall establish and convene, within three days following such determination, a conciliation committee consisting of not more than nine members of the Council, with the President as chairman, for the purpose of reconciling the differences and producing a proposal which can be adopted by consensus. The committee shall work expeditiously and report to the Council within 14 days following its establishment. If the committee is unable to recommend a proposal which can be adopted by consensus, it shall set out in its report the grounds on which the proposal is being opposed.

(f) Decisions on questions not listed above which the Council is authorized to take by the rules, regulations and procedures of the Authority or otherwise shall be taken pursuant to the subparagraphs of this paragraph specified in the rules, regulations and procedures or, if not specified therein, then pursuant to the subparagraph determined by the Council if possible in advance, by consensus.

(g) When the issue arises as to whether a question is within subparagraph (a), (b), (c) or (d), the question shall be treated as being within the subparagraph requiring the higher or highest majority or consensus as the case may be, unless otherwise decided by the Council by the said majority or by consensus.

9. The Council shall establish a procedure whereby a member of the Authority not represented on the Council may send a representative to attend a meeting of the Council when a request is made by such member, or a matter particularly affecting it is under consideration. Such a representative shall be entitled to participate in the deliberations but not to vote.

Article 162. Powers and Functions

1. The Council is the executive organ of the Authority. The Council shall have the power to establish, in conformity with this Convention and the general policies established by the Assembly, the specific policies to be pursued by the Authority on any question or matter within the competence of the Authority.

2. In addition, the Council shall:

(a) supervise and co-ordinate the implementation of the provisions of this Part on all questions and matters within the competence of the Authority and invite the attention of the Assembly to cases of non-compliance;

(b) propose to the Assembly a list of candidates for the election of the Secretary-General;

(c) recommend to the Assembly candidates for the election of the members of the Governing Board of the Enterprise and the Director-General of the Enterprise;

(d) establish, as appropriate, and with due regard to economy and efficiency, such subsidiary organs as it finds necessary for the exercise of its functions in accordance with this Part . . . ;

(e) adopt its rules of procedure including the method of selecting its president;

(f) enter into agreements with the United Nations or other international organizations on behalf of the Authority and within its competence, subject to approval by the Assembly;

(g) consider the reports of the Enterprise and transmit them to the Assembly with its recommendations; . . .

(i) issue directives to the Enterprise in accordance with article 170; . . .

(i) if the Commission recommends the approval of a plan of work, it shall be deemed to have been approved by the Council if no member of the Council submits in writing to the President within 14 days a specific objection alleging non-compliance with the requirements of Annex III, article 6. If there is an objection, the conciliation procedure set forth in article 161, paragraph 8(e), shall apply . . . ;

(ii) if the Commission recommends the disapproval of a plan of work or does not make a recommendation, the Council may approve the plan of work by a three-fourths majority of the members present and voting, provided that such majority includes a majority of the members participating in the session; . . .

(k) approve plans of work submitted by the Enterprise in accordance with Annex IV, article 12, applying, mutatis mutandis, the procedures set forth in subparagraph (j);

(l) exercise control over activities in the Area in accordance with article 153, paragraph 4, and the rules, regulations and procedures of the Authority; . . .

(n) make recommendations to the Assembly, on the basis of advice from the Economic Planning Commission, for a system of compensation or other measures of economic adjustment assistance as provided in article 151, paragraph 10;

(o) (i) recommend to the Assembly rules, regulations and procedures on the equitable sharing of financial and other economic benefits derived from activities in the Area and the payments and contributions made pursuant to article 82, . . . ;

(ii) adopt and apply provisionally, pending approval by the Assembly, the rules, regulations and procedures of the Authority, and any amendments thereto . . .

(r) submit the proposed annual budget of the Authority to the Assembly for its approval; . . .

(t) make recommendations to the Assembly concerning suspension of the exercise of the rights and privileges of membership pursuant to article 185;

(u) institute proceedings on behalf of the Authority before the Sea-Bed Disputes Chamber in cases of non-compliance; . . .

(w) issue emergency orders, which may include orders for the suspension or adjustment of operations, to prevent serious harm to the marine environment arising out of activities in the Area;

(x) disapprove areas for exploitation by contractors or the Enterprise in cases where substantial evidence indicates the risk of serious harm to the marine environment; . . .

Article 163. Organs of the Council

1. There are hereby established the following organs of the Council:
   (a) an Economic Planning Commission;
   (b) a Legal and Technical Commission.
2. Each Commission shall be composed of 15 members, elected by the Council from among the candidates nominated by the States Parties.

However, if necessary, the Council may decide to increase the size of either Commission having due regard to economy and efficiency. . . .

SUBSECTION D.   THE SECRETARIAT

Article 166.   The Secretariat

1. The Secretariat of the Authority shall comprise a Secretary-General and such staff as the Authority may require.

2. The Secretary-General shall be elected for four years by the Assembly from among the candidates proposed by the Council and may be re-elected.

3. The Secretary-General shall be the chief administrative officer of the Authority, and shall act in that capacity in all meetings of the Assembly, of the Council and of any subsidiary organ, and shall perform such other administrative functions as are entrusted to the Secretary-General by these organs. . . .

Article 167.   The Staff of the Authority

1. The staff of the Authority shall consist of such qualified scientific and technical and other personnel as may be required to fulfil the administrative functions of the Authority.

2. The paramount consideration in the recruitment and employment of the staff and in the determination of their conditions of service shall be the necessity of securing the highest standards of efficiency, competence and integrity. Subject to this consideration, due regard shall be paid to the importance of recruiting the staff on as wide a geographical basis as possible.

3. The staff shall be appointed by the Secretary-General. . . .

Article 168.   International Character of the Secretariat

1. In the performance of their duties the Secretary-General and the staff shall not seek or receive instructions from any government or from any other source external to the Authority. They shall refrain from any action which might reflect on their position as international officials responsible only to the Authority. Each State Party undertakes to respect the exclusively international character of the responsibilities of the Secretary-General and the staff and not to seek to influence them in the discharge of their responsibilities. . . .

2. The Secretary-General and the staff shall have no financial interest in any activity relating to exploration and exploitation in the Area. Subject to their responsibilities to the Authority, they shall not disclose, even after the termination of their functions, any industrial secret, proprietary data which are transferred to the Authority in accordance with Annex III, article 14, or any other confidential information coming to their knowledge by reason of their employment with the Authority. . . .

SUBSECTION E. THE ENTERPRISE

Article 170. The Enterprise

1. The Enterprise shall be the organ of the Authority which shall carry out activities in the Area directly, pursuant to article 153, paragraph 2(a), as well as the transporting, processing and marketing of minerals recovered from the Area.

2. The Enterprise shall, within the framework of the International legal personality of the Authority, have such legal capacity as is provided for in the Statute set forth in Annex IV. The Enterprise shall act in accordance with this Convention and the rules, regulations and procedures of the Authority, as well as the general policies established by the Assembly, and shall be subject to the directives and control of the Council.

3. The Enterprise shall have its principal place of business at the seat of the Authority.

4. The Enterprise shall, in accordance with article 173, paragraph 2, and Annex IV, article 11, be provided with such funds as it may require to carry out its functions, and shall receive technology as provided in article 144 and other relevant provisions of this Convention.

SUBSECTION F. FINANCIAL ARRANGEMENTS OF THE AUTHORITY

Article 171. Funds of the Authority

The funds of the Authority shall include:

(a) assessed contributions made by members of the Authority in accordance with article 160, paragraph 2(e);

(b) funds received by the Authority pursuant to Annex III, article 13, in connection with activities in the Area;

(c) funds transferred from the Enterprise in accordance with Annex IV, article 10;

(d) funds borrowed pursuant to article 174;

(e) voluntary contributions made by members or other entities . . .

Article 172. Annual Budget of the Authority

The Secretary-General shall draft the proposed annual budget of the Authority and submit it to the Council. The Council shall consider the proposed annual budget and submit it to the Assembly, together with any recommendations thereon. The Assembly shall consider and approve the proposed annual budget in accordance with article 160, paragraph 2(h).

Article 173. Expenses of the Authority

1. The contributions referred to in article 171, subparagraph (a), shall be paid into a special account to meet the administrative expenses of the

Authority until the Authority has sufficient funds from other sources to meet those expenses.

2. The administrative expenses of the Authority shall be a first call upon the funds of the Authority. Except for the assessed contributions referred to in article 171, subparagraph (a), the funds which remain after payment of administrative expenses may, *inter alia*:

(a) be shared in accordance with article 140 and article 160, paragraph 2(g);

(b) be used to provide the Enterprise with funds in accordance with article 170, paragraph 4;

(c) be used to compensate developing States in accordance with article 151, paragraph 10, and article 160, paragraph 2(1). . . .

SUBSECTION G. LEGAL STATUS, PRIVILEGES AND IMMUNITIES

Article 176. Legal Status

The Authority shall have international legal personality and such legal capacity as may be necessary for the exercise of its functions and the fulfilment of its purposes.

Article 177. Privileges and Immunities

To enable the Authority to exercise its functions, it shall enjoy in the territory of each State Party the privileges and immunities set forth in this subsection. The privileges and immunities relating to the Enterprise shall be those set forth in Annex IV, article 13.

Article 178. Immunity from Legal Process

The Authority, its property and assets, shall enjoy immunity from legal process except to the extent that the Authority expressly waives this immunity in a particular case.

Article 179. Immunity from Search and Any Form of Seizure . . .

SUBSECTION H. SUSPENSION OF THE EXERCISE OF RIGHTS AND PRIVILEGES OF MEMBERS

Article 184. Suspension of the Exercise of Voting Rights

A State Party which is in arrears in the payment of its financial contributions to the Authority shall have no vote if the amount of its arrears equals or exceeds the amount of the contributions due from it for the preceding two full years. The Assembly may, nevertheless, permit such a member to vote if it is satisfied that the failure to pay is due to conditions beyond the control of the member. . . .

SECTION 5.   SETTLEMENT OF DISPUTES AND ADVISORY OPINIONS

Article 186.   Sea-Bed Disputes Chamber of the International Tribunal for the Law of the Sea

The establishment of the Sea-Bed Disputes Chamber and the manner in which it shall exercise its jurisdiction shall be governed by the provisions of this section, of Part XV and of Annex VI.

Article 187.   Jurisdiction of the Sea-Bed Disputes Chamber

The Sea-Bed Disputes Chamber shall have jurisdiction under this Part and the Annexes relating thereto in disputes with respect to activities in the Area falling within the following categories:

(a) disputes between States Parties concerning the interpretation or application of this Part and the Annexes relating thereto;

(b) disputes between a State Party and the Authority concerning: . . .

(c) disputes between parties to a contract, being States Parties, the Authority or the Enterprise, state enterprises and natural or juridical persons referred to in article 153, paragraph 2(b), concerning:

(i) the interpretation or application of a relevant contract or a plan of work; or

(ii) acts or omissions of a party to the contract relating to activities in the Area and directed to the other party or directly affecting its legitimate interests;

(d) disputes between the Authority and a prospective contractor . . . concerning the refusal of a contract or a legal issue arising in the negotiation of the contract;

(e) disputes between the Authority and a State Party, a state enterprise or a natural or juridical person sponsored by a State Party as provided for in article 153, paragraph 2(b), where it is alleged that the Authority has incurred liability as provided in Annex III, article 22;

(f) any other disputes for which the jurisdiction of the Chamber is specifically provided in this Convention.

Article 188.   Submission of Disputes to a Special Chamber of the International Tribunal for the Law of the Sea or an Ad Hoc Chamber of the Sea-Bed Disputes Chamber or to Binding Commercial Arbitration

1. Disputes between States Parties referred to in article 187, subparagraph (a), may be submitted:

(a) at the request of the parties to the dispute, to a special chamber of the International Tribunal for the Law of the Sea to be formed in accordance with Annex VI, articles 15 and 17; or

(b) at the request of any party to the dispute, to an ad hoc chamber of the Sea-Bed Disputes Chamber to be formed in accordance with Annex VI, article 36.

2. (a) Disputes concerning the interpretation or application of a contract referred to in article 187, subparagraph (c) (i), shall be submitted, at the request of any party to the dispute, to binding commercial arbitration, unless the parties otherwise agree. A commercial arbitral tribunal to which the dispute is submitted shall have no jurisdiction to decide any question of interpretation of this Convention. When the dispute also involves a question of the interpretation of Part XI and the Annexes relating thereto, with respect to activities in the Area, that question shall be referred to the Sea-Bed Disputes Chamber for a ruling.

(b) If, at the commencement of or in the course of such arbitration, the arbitral tribunal determines, either at the request of any party to the dispute or *proprio motu*, that its decision depends upon a ruling of the Sea-Bed Disputes Chamber, the arbitral tribunal shall refer such question to the Sea-Bed Disputes Chamber for such ruling. The arbitral tribunal shall then proceed to render its award in conformity with the ruling of the Sea-Bed Disputes Chamber.

(c) In the absence of a provision in the contract on the arbitration procedure to be applied in the dispute, the arbitration shall be conducted in accordance with the UNCITRAL Arbitration Rules or such other arbitration rules as may be prescribed in the rules, regulations and procedures of the Authority, unless the parties to the dispute otherwise agree.

Article 189. *Limitation on Jurisdiction with Regard to Decisions of the Authority*

The Sea-Bed Disputes Chamber shall have no jurisdiction with regard to the exercise by the Authority of its discretionary powers in accordance with this Part; in no case shall it substitute its discretion for that of the Authority. Without prejudice to article 191, in exercising its jurisdiction pursuant to article 187, the Sea-Bed Disputes Chamber shall not pronounce itself on the question of whether any rules, regulations and procedures of the Authority are in conformity with this Convention. . . . Its jurisdiction in this regard shall be confined to deciding claims that the application of any rules, regulations and procedures of the Authority in individual cases would be in conflict with the contractual obligations of the parties to the dispute or their obligations under this Convention, claims concerning excess of jurisdiction or misuse of power, and to claims for damages to be paid or other remedy to be given to the party concerned for the failure of the other party to comply with its contractual obligations or its obligations under this Convention.

Article 190. *Participation and Appearance of Sponsoring States Parties in Proceedings*

1. If a natural or juridical person is a party to a dispute referred to in article 187, the sponsoring State shall be given notice thereof and shall have the right to participate in the proceedings by submitting written or oral statements.

2. If an action is brought against a State Party by a natural or juridical person sponsored by another State Party in a dispute referred to in article 187, subparagraph (c), the respondent State may request the State sponsoring that person to appear in the proceedings on behalf of that person. Failing such appearance, the respondent State may arrange to be represented by a juridical person of its nationality.

Article 191. Advisory Opinions

The Sea-Bed Disputes Chamber shall give advisory opinions at the request of the Assembly or the Council on legal questions arising within the scope of their activities. Such opinions shall be given as a matter of urgency.

Part XII. Protection and Preservation of the Marine Environment

SECTION 1. GENERAL PROVISIONS

Article 192. General Obligation

States have the obligation to protect and preserve the marine environment.

Article 193. Sovereign Right of States to Exploit Their Natural Resources

States have the sovereign right to exploit their natural resources pursuant to their environmental policies and in accordance with their duty to protect and preserve the marine environment.

Article 194. Measures to Prevent, Reduce and Control Pollution of the Marine Environment

1. States shall take, individually or jointly as appropriate, all measures consistent with this Convention that are necessary to prevent, reduce and control pollution of the marine environment from any source, using for this purpose the best practicable means at their disposal and in accordance with their capabilities, and they shall endeavour to harmonize their policies in this connection.

2. States shall take all measures necessary to ensure that activities under their jurisdiction or control are so conducted as not to cause damage by pollution to other States and their environment, and that pollution arising from incidents or activities under their jurisdiction or control does not spread beyond the areas where they exercise sovereign rights in accordance with this Convention.

3. The measures taken pursuant to this Part shall deal with all sources of pollution of the marine environment. . . .

5. The measures taken in accordance with this Part shall include those necessary to protect and preserve rare or fragile ecosystems as well as the habitat of depleted, threatened or endangered species and other forms of marine life. . . .

SECTION 2. GLOBAL AND REGIONAL CO-OPERATION . . .

Article 198. Notification of Imminent or Actual Damage

When a State becomes aware of cases in which the marine environment is in imminent danger of being damaged or has been damaged by pollution, it shall immediately notify other States it deems likely to be affected by such damage, as well as the competent international organizations. . . .

SECTION 5. INTERNATIONAL RULES AND NATIONAL LEGISLATION TO PREVENT, REDUCE AND CONTROL POLLUTION OF THE MARINE ENVIRONMENT

Article 207. Pollution from Land-Based Sources

1. States shall adopt laws and regulations to prevent, reduce and control pollution of the marine environment from land-based sources, including rivers, estuaries, pipelines and outfall structures, taking into account internationally agreed rules, standards and recommended practices and procedures. . . .

Article 208. Pollution from Sea-Bed Activities Subject to National Jurisdiction

1. Coastal States shall adopt laws and regulations to prevent, reduce and control pollution of the marine environment arising from or in connection with sea-bed activities subject to their jurisdiction and from artificial islands, installations and structures under their jurisdiction, pursuant to articles 60 and 80. . . .

3. Such laws, regulations and measures shall be no less effective than international rules, standards and recommended practices and procedures. . . .

Article 209. Pollution from Activities in the Area

1. International rules, regulations and procedures shall be established in accordance with Part XI to prevent, reduce and control pollution of the marine environment from activities in the Area. . . .

2. Subject to the relevant provisions of this section, States shall adopt laws and regulations to prevent, reduce and control pollution of the marine environment from activities in the Area undertaken by vessels, installations, structures and other devices flying their flag or of their registry or operating under their authority, as the case may be. The requirements of such laws and regulations shall be no less effective than the international rules, regulations and procedures referred to in paragraph 1.

Article 210.   Pollution by Dumping

1. States shall adopt laws and regulations to prevent, reduce and control pollution of the marine environment by dumping. . . .

4. States, acting especially through competent international organizations or diplomatic conference, shall endeavour to establish global and regional rules, standards and recommended practices and procedures to prevent, reduce and control such pollution. . . .

5. Dumping within the territorial sea and the exclusive economic zone or onto the continental shelf shall not be carried out without the express prior approval of the coastal State, . . .

Article 211.   Pollution from Vessels

1. States, acting through the competent international organization or general diplomatic conference, shall establish international rules and standards to prevent, reduce and control pollution of the marine environment from vessels and promote the adoption, in the same manner, wherever appropriate, of routing systems designed to minimize the threat of accidents which might cause pollution of the marine environment, including the coastline, and pollution damage to the related interests of coastal States. . . .

2. States shall adopt laws and regulations for the prevention, reduction and control of pollution of the marine environment from vessels flying their flag or of their registry. Such laws and regulations shall at least have the same effect as that of generally accepted international rules and standards. . . .

4. Coastal States may, in the exercise of their sovereignty within their territorial sea, adopt laws and regulations for the prevention, reduction and control of marine pollution from foreign vessels, including vessels exercising the right of innocent passage. Such laws and regulations shall, in accordance with Part II, section 3, not hamper innocent passage of foreign vessels. . . .

SECTION 6.   ENFORCEMENT

Article 213.   Enforcement with Respect to Pollution from Land-Based Sources

States shall enforce their laws and regulations adopted in accordance with article 207 and shall adopt laws and regulations and take other measures necessary to implement applicable international rules and standards established through competent international organizations or diplomatic conference to prevent, reduce and control pollution of the marine environment from land-based sources.

Article 214.   Enforcement with Respect to Pollution from Sea-Bed Activities

States shall enforce their laws and regulations adopted in accordance with article 208 and shall adopt laws and regulations and take other measures necessary to implement applicable international rules and standards established through competent international organizations or diplomatic conference to prevent, reduce and control pollution of the marine environment arising from or in connection with sea-bed activities subject to their jurisdiction and from artificial islands, installations and structures under their jurisdiction, pursuant to articles 60 and 80. . . .

Article 216. *Enforcement with Respect to Pollution by Dumping*

1. Laws and regulations adopted in accordance with this Convention and applicable international rules and standards established through competent international organizations or diplomatic conference for the prevention, reduction and control of pollution of the marine environment by dumping shall be enforced:

(a) by the coastal State with regard to dumping within its territorial sea or its exclusive economic zone or onto its continental shelf;

(b) by the flag State with regard to vessels flying its flag or vessels or aircraft of its registry;

(c) by any State with regard to acts of loading of wastes or other matter occurring within its territory or at its off-shore terminals. . . .

Article 217. *Enforcement by Flag States*

1. States shall ensure compliance by vessels flying their flag or of their registry with applicable international rules and standards, established through the competent international organization or general diplomatic conference, and with their laws and regulations adopted in accordance with this Convention for the prevention, reduction and control of pollution of the marine environment from vessels and shall accordingly adopt laws and regulations and take other measures necessary for their implementation. Flag States shall provide for the effective enforcement of such rules, standards, laws and regulations, irrespective of where a violation occurs.

2. States shall, in particular, take appropriate measures in order to ensure that vessels flying their flag or of their registry are prohibited from sailing, until they can proceed to sea in compliance with the requirements of the international rules and standards referred to in paragraph 1, including requirements in respect of design, construction, equipment and manning of vessels. . . .

6. States shall, at the written request of any State, investigate any violation alleged to have been committed by vessels flying their flag. . . .

7. Flag States shall promptly inform the requesting State and the competent international organization of the action taken and its outcome. . . .

Article 219. *Measures Relating to Seaworthiness of Vessels to Avoid Pollution*

Subject to section 7, States which, upon request or on their own initiative, have ascertained that a vessel within one of their ports or at one of their offshore terminals is in violation of applicable international rules and standards relating to seaworthiness of vessels and thereby threatens damage to the marine environment shall, as far as practicable, take administrative measures to prevent the vessel from sailing. Such States may permit the vessel to proceed only to the nearest appropriate repair yard and, upon removal of the causes of the violation, shall permit the vessel to continue immediately.

Article 220. *Enforcement by Coastal States*

1. When a vessel is voluntarily within a port or at an off-shore terminal of a State, that State may, subject to section 7, institute proceedings in respect of any violation of its laws and regulations adopted in accordance with this Convention or applicable international rules and standards for the prevention, reduction and control of pollution from vessels when the violation has occurred within the territorial sea or the exclusive economic zone of that State.

2. Where there are clear grounds for believing that a vessel navigating in the territorial sea of a State has, during its passage therein, violated laws and regulations of that State adopted in accordance with this Convention or applicable international rules and standards for the prevention, reduction and control of pollution from vessels, that State, without prejudice to the application of the relevant provisions of Part II, section 3, may undertake physical inspection of the vessel relating to the violation and may, where the evidence so warrants, institute proceedings, including detention of the vessel, in accordance with its laws, subject to the provisions of section 7. . . .

Article 221. *Measures to Avoid Pollution Arising from Maritime Casualties*

1. Nothing in this Part shall prejudice the right of States, pursuant to international law, both customary and conventional, to take and enforce measures beyond the territorial sea proportionate to the actual or threatened damage to protect their coastline or related interests, including fishing, from pollution or threat of pollution following upon a maritime casualty or acts relating to such a casualty, which may reasonably be expected to result in major harmful consequences.

2. For the purposes of this article, "maritime casualty" means a collision of vessels, stranding or other incident of navigation, or other occurrence on board a vessel or external to it resulting in material damage or imminent threat of material damage to a vessel or cargo. . . .

SECTION 7. SAFEGUARDS . . .

Article 226. *Investigation of Foreign Vessels*

1. (a) States shall not delay a foreign vessel longer than is essential for purposes of the investigations provided for in articles 216, 218 and 220. Any

physical inspection of a foreign vessel shall be limited to an examination of such certificates, records or other documents as the vessel is required to carry by generally accepted international rules and standards or of any similar documents which it is carrying; further physical inspection of the vessel may be undertaken only after such an examination and only when:

(i) there are clear grounds for believing that the condition of the vessel or its equipment does not correspond substantially with the particulars of those documents;

(ii) the contents of such documents are not sufficient to confirm or verify a suspected violation; or

(iii) the vessel is not carrying valid certificates and records. . . .

SECTION 9.   RESPONSIBILITY AND LIABILITY

Article 235.   Responsibility and Liability

1. States are responsible for the fulfilment of their international obligations concerning the protection and preservation of the marine environment. They shall be liable in accordance with international law.

2. States shall ensure that recourse is available in accordance with their legal systems for prompt and adequate compensation or other relief in respect of damage caused by pollution of the marine environment by natural or juridical persons under their jurisdiction. . . .

SECTION 10.   SOVEREIGN IMMUNITY

Article 236.   Sovereign Immunity

The provisions of this Convention regarding the protection and preservation of the marine environment do not apply to any warship, naval auxiliary, other vessels or aircraft owned or operated by a State and used, for the time being, only on government non-commercial service. However, each State shall ensure, by the adoption of appropriate measures not impairing operations or operational capabilities of such vessels or aircraft owned or operated by it, that such vessels or aircraft act in a manner consistent, so far as is reasonable and practicable, with this Convention.

Part XIII.   Marine Scientific Research

SECTION 1.   GENERAL PROVISIONS

Article 238.   Right to Conduct Marine Scientific Research

All States, irrespective of their geographical location, and competent international organizations have the right to conduct marine scientific research subject to the rights and duties of other States as provided for in this Convention. . . .

Article 240.   General Principles for the Conduct
of Marine Scientific Research

In the conduct of marine scientific research the following principles shall apply:

(a) marine scientific research shall be conducted exclusively for peaceful purposes; . . .

(c) marine scientific research shall not unjustifiably interfere with other legitimate uses of the sea compatible with this Convention and shall be duly respected in the course of such uses; . . .

SECTION 3.   CONDUCT AND PROMOTION OF MARINE
SCIENTIFIC RESEARCH

Article 245.   Marine Scientific Research in the Territorial Sea

Coastal States, in the exercise of their sovereignty, have the exclusive right to regulate, authorize and conduct marine scientific research in their territorial sea. Marine scientific research therein shall be conducted only with the express consent of and under the conditions set forth by the coastal State.

Article 246.   Marine Scientific Research in the Exclusive Economic Zone
and on the Continental Shelf

1. Coastal States, in the exercise of their jurisdiction, have the right to regulate, authorize and conduct marine scientific research in their exclusive economic zone and on their continental shelf in accordance with the relevant provisions of this Convention. . . .

Part XIV.   Development and Transfer
of Marine Technology

SECTION 1.   GENERAL PROVISIONS

Article 266.   Promotion of the Development and Transfer of Marine
Technology

1. States, directly or through competent international organizations, shall co-operate in accordance with their capabilities to promote actively the development and transfer of marine science and marine technology on fair and reasonable terms and conditions. . . .

Part XV.   Settlement of Disputes

SECTION 1.   GENERAL PROVISIONS

Article 279.   Obligation to Settle Disputes by Peaceful Means

States Parties shall settle any dispute between them concerning the interpretation or application of this Convention by peaceful means. . . .

Article 280.   Settlement of Disputes by Any Peaceful Means Chosen by the Parties

Nothing in this Part impairs the right of any States Parties to agree at any time to settle a dispute between them concerning the interpretation or application of this Convention by any peaceful means of their own choice.

Article 281.   Procedure Where No Settlement Has Been Reached by the Parties

1. If the States Parties which are parties to a dispute concerning the interpretation or application of this Convention have agreed to seek settlement of the dispute by a peaceful means of their own choice, the procedures provided for in this Part apply only where no settlement has been reached by recourse to such means and the agreement between the parties does not exclude any further procedure . . .

Article 282.   Obligations Under General, Regional or Bilateral Agreements

If the States Parties which are parties to a dispute concerning the interpretation or application of this Convention have agreed, through a general, regional or bilateral agreement or otherwise, that such dispute shall, at the request of any party to the dispute, be submitted to a procedure that entails a binding decision, that procedure shall apply in lieu of the procedures provided for in this Part, unless the parties to the dispute otherwise agree. . . .

Article 284.   Conciliation

1. A State Party which is a party to a dispute concerning the interpretation or application of this Convention may invite the other party or parties to submit the dispute to conciliation in accordance with the procedure under Annex V, section 1, or another conciliation procedure. . . .

3. If the invitation is not accepted or the parties do not agree upon the procedure, the conciliation proceedings shall be deemed to be terminated. . . .

SECTION 2. COMPULSORY PROCEDURES ENTAILING BINDING DECISIONS

Article 286. Application of Procedures Under This Section

Subject to section 3, any dispute concerning the interpretation or application of this Convention shall, where no settlement has been reached by recourse to section 1, be submitted at the request of any party to the dispute to the court or tribunal having jurisdiction under this section.

Article 287. Choice of Procedure

1. When signing, ratifying or acceding to this Convention or at any time thereafter, a State shall be free to choose, by means of a written declaration, one or more of the following means for the settlement of disputes concerning the interpretation or application of this Convention:

(a) the International Tribunal for the Law of the Sea established in accordance with Annex VI;

(b) the International Court of Justice;

(c) an arbitral tribunal constituted in accordance with Annex VII;

(d) a special arbitral tribunal constituted in accordance with Annex VIII for one or more of the categories of disputes specified therein.

2. A declaration made under paragraph 1 shall not affect or be affected by the obligation of a State Party to accept the jurisdiction of the Sea-Bed Disputes Chamber of the International Tribunal for the Law of the Sea to the extent and in the manner provided for in Part XI, section 5.

3. A State Party which is a party to a dispute not covered by a declaration in force, shall be deemed to have accepted arbitration in accordance with Annex VII.

4. If the parties to a dispute have accepted the same procedure for the settlement of the dispute, it may be submitted only to that procedure, unless the parties otherwise agree.

5. If the parties to a dispute have not accepted the same procedure for the settlement of the dispute, it may be submitted only to arbitration in accordance with Annex VII, unless the parties otherwise agree. . . .

7. A new declaration, a notice of revocation or the expiry of a declaration does not in any way affect proceedings pending before a court or tribunal having jurisdiction under this article, unless the parties otherwise agree. . . .

Article 288. Jurisdiction

1. A court or tribunal referred to in article 287 shall have jurisdiction over any dispute concerning the interpretation or application of this Convention which is submitted to it in accordance with this Part.

2. A court or tribunal referred to in article 287 shall also have jurisdiction over any dispute concerning the interpretation or application of an

international agreement related to the purposes of this Convention, which is submitted to it in accordance with the agreement.

3. The Sea-Bed Disputes Chamber of the International Tribunal for the Law of the Sea established in accordance with Annex VI, and any other chamber or arbitral tribunal referred to in Part XI, section 5, shall have jurisdiction in any matter which is submitted to it in accordance therewith.

4. In the event of a dispute as to whether a court or tribunal has jurisdiction, the matter shall be settled by decision of that court or tribunal.

Article 289.   Experts

In any dispute involving scientific or technical matters, a court or tribunal exercising jurisdiction under this section may, at the request of a party or *proprio motu*, select in consultation with the parties no fewer than two scientific or technical experts chosen preferably from the relevant list prepared in accordance with Annex VIII, article 2, to sit with the court or tribunal but without the right to vote.

Article 290.   Provisional Measures

1. If a dispute has been duly submitted to a court or tribunal which considers that *prima facie* it has jurisdiction under this Part or Part XI, section 5, the court or tribunal may prescribe any provisional measures which it considers appropriate under the circumstances to preserve the respective rights of the parties to the dispute or to prevent serious harm to the marine environment, pending the final decision. . . .

6. The parties to the dispute shall comply promptly with any provisional measures prescribed under this article.

Article 291.   Access

1. All the dispute settlement procedures specified in this Part shall be open to States Parties.

2. The dispute settlement procedures specified in this Part shall be open to entities other than States Parties only as specifically provided for in this Convention.

Article 292.   Prompt Release of Vessels and Crews

1. Where the authorities of a State Party have detained a vessel flying the flag of another State Party and it is alleged that the detaining State has not complied with the provisions of this Convention for the prompt release of the vessel or its crew upon the posting of a reasonable bond or other financial security, the question of release from detention may be submitted to any court or tribunal agreed upon by the parties or, failing such agreement within 10 days from the time of detention, to a court or tribunal accepted by the detaining State under article 287 or to the International Tribunal for the Law of the Sea, unless the parties otherwise agree.

2. The application for release may be made only by or on behalf of the flag State of the vessel.

3. The court or tribunal shall deal without delay with the application for release and shall deal only with the question of release, without prejudice to the merits of any case before the appropriate domestic forum against the vessel, its owner or its crew. . . .

Article 293. Applicable Law

1. A court or tribunal having jurisdiction under this section shall apply this Convention and other rules of international law not incompatible with this Convention.

2. Paragraph 1 does not prejudice the power of the court or tribunal having jurisdiction under this section to decide a case *ex aequo et bono*, if the parties so agree. . . .

Article 295. Exhaustion of Local Remedies

Any dispute between States Parties concerning the interpretation or application of this Convention may be submitted to the procedures provided for in this section only after local remedies have been exhausted where this is required by international law.

Article 296. Finality and Binding Force of Decisions

1. Any decision rendered by a court or tribunal having jurisdiction under this section shall be final and shall be complied with by all the parties to the dispute.

2. Any such decision shall have no binding force except between the parties and in respect of that particular dispute.

SECTION 3. LIMITATIONS AND EXCEPTIONS TO APPLICABILITY OF SECTION 2

Article 297. Limitations on Applicability of Section 2

1. Disputes concerning the interpretation or application of this Convention with regard to the exercise by a coastal State of its sovereign rights or jurisdiction provided for in this Convention shall be subject to the procedures provided for in section 2 in the following cases:

(a) when it is alleged that a coastal State has acted in contravention of the provisions of this Convention in regard to the freedoms and rights of navigation, overflight or the laying of submarine cables and pipelines, or in regard to other internationally lawful uses of the sea specified in article 58;

(b) when it is alleged that a State in exercising the aforementioned freedoms, rights or uses has acted in contravention of this Convention or of laws or regulations adopted by the coastal State in conformity with this

Convention and other rules of international law not incompatible with this Convention; or

(c) when it is alleged that a coastal State has acted in contravention of specified international rules and standards for the protection and preservation of the marine environment which are applicable to the coastal State and which have been established by this Convention or through a competent international organization or diplomatic conference in accordance with this Convention. . . .

3. (a) Disputes concerning the interpretation or application of the provisions of this Convention with regard to fisheries shall be settled in accordance with section 2, except that the coastal State shall not be obliged to accept the submission to such settlement of any dispute relating to its sovereign rights with respect to the living resources in the exclusive economic zone. . . .

(b) Where no settlement has been reached by recourse to section 1 of this Part, a dispute shall be submitted to conciliation under Annex V, section 2, at the request of any party to the dispute, when it is alleged that: . . .

Article 298. Optional Exceptions to Applicability of Section 2

1. When signing, ratifying or acceding to this Convention or at any time thereafter, a State may, without prejudice to the obligations arising under section 1, declare in writing that it does not accept any one or more of the procedures provided for in section 2 with respect to one or more of the following categories of disputes:

(a) (i) disputes concerning the interpretation or application of articles 15, 74 and 83 relating to sea boundary delimitations, or those involving historic bays or titles, provided that a State having made such a declaration shall, when such a dispute arises subsequent to the entry into force of this Convention and where no agreement within a reasonable period of time is reached in negotiations between the parties, at the request of any party to the dispute, accept submission of the matter to conciliation under Annex V, section 2; . . .

(b) disputes concerning military activities, . . . , and disputes concerning law enforcement activities in regard to the exercise of sovereign rights or jurisdiction excluded from the jurisdiction of a court or tribunal under article 297, paragraph 2 or 3; . . .

Article 299. Right of the Parties to Agree upon a Procedure . . . .

Part XVI.   General Provisions

Article 300.   Good Faith and Abuse of Rights

States Parties shall fulfil in good faith the obligations assumed under this Convention and shall exercise the rights, jurisdiction and freedoms recognized in this Convention in a manner which would not constitute an abuse of right. . . .

Article 302.   Disclosure of Information . . . .

Article 303.   Archaeological and Historical Objects Found at Sea

1. States have the duty to protect objects of an archaeological and historical nature found at sea and shall co-operate for this purpose. . . .

3. Nothing in this article affects the rights of identifiable owners, the law of salvage or other rules of admiralty, or laws and practices with respect to cultural exchanges.

4. This article is without prejudice to other international agreements and rules of international law . . . .

Article 304.   Responsibility and Liability for Damage

The provisions of this Convention regarding responsibility and liability for damage are without prejudice to the application of existing rules and the development of further rules regarding responsibility and liability under international law.

Part XVII.   Final Provisions

Article 305.   Signature

1. This Convention shall be open for signature by:
   (a) all States; . . .
   (c) all self-governing associated States which have chosen that status in an art of self-determination supervised and approved by the United Nations in accordance with General Assembly resolution 1514 (XV) and which have competence over the matters governed by this Convention, including the competence to enter into treaties in respect of those matters;
   (d) all self-governing associated States which, in accordance with their respective instruments of association, have competence over the matters governed by this Convention . . . ;

(e) all territories which enjoy full internal self-government, recognized as such by the United Nations, but have not attained full independence in accordance with General Assembly resolution 1514 (XV) and which have competence over the matters governed by this Convention . . . ;

(f) international organizations, in accordance with Annex IX. . . .

Article 308. Entry into Force

1. This Convention shall enter into force 12 months after the date of deposit of the sixtieth instrument of ratification or accession.

2. For each State ratifying or acceding to this Convention after the deposit of the sixieth instrument of ratification or accession, the Convention shall enter into force on the thirtieth day following the deposit of its instrument of ratification or accession, subject to paragraph 1. . . .

Article 309. Reservations and Exceptions

No reservations or exceptions may be made to this Convention unless expressly permitted by other articles of this Convention.

Article 310. Declarations and Statements

Article 309 does not preclude a State, when signing, ratifying or acceding to this Convention, from making declarations or statements, however phrased or named, with a view, *inter alia*, to the harmonization of its laws and regulations with the provisions of this Convention, provided that such declarations or statements do not purport to exclude or to modify the legal effect of the provisions of this Convention in their application to that State.

Article 311. Relation to Other Conventions and International Agreements

1. This Convention shall prevail, as between States Parties, over the Geneva Conventions on the Law of the Sea of 29 April 1958.

2. This Convention shall not alter the rights and obligations of States Parties which arise from other agreements compatible with this Convention and which do not affect the enjoyment by other States Parties of their rights or the performance of their obligations under this Convention.

3. Two or more States Parties may conclude agreements modifying or suspending the operation of provisions of this Convention, applicable solely to the relations between them, provided that such agreements do not relate to a provision derogation from which is incompatible with the effective execution of the object and purpose of this Convention, and provided further that such agreements shall not affect the application of the basic principles embodied herein, and that the provisions of such agreements do not affect the enjoyment by other States Parties of their rights or the performance of their obligations under this Convention.

4. States Parties intending to conclude an agreement referred to in paragraph 3 shall notify the other States Parties. . . .

5. This article does not affect international agreements expressly permitted or preserved by other articles of this Convention.

6. States Parties agree that there shall be no amendments to the basic principle relating to the common heritage of mankind set forth in article 136 and that they shall not be party to any agreement in derogation thereof.

Article 312.   Amendment

1. After the expiry of a period of 10 years from the date of entry into force of this Convention, a State Party may . . . propose specific amendments to this Convention, other than those relating to activities in the Area, and request the convening of a conference to consider such proposed amendments. The Secretary-General shall circulate such communication to all States Parties. If, within 12 months from the date of the circulation of the communication, not less than one half of the States Parties reply favourably to the request, the Secretary-General shall convene the conference.

2. The decision-making procedure applicable at the amendment conference shall be the same as that applicable at the Third United Nations Conference on the Law of the Sea unless otherwise decided by the conference. The conference should make every effort to reach agreement on any amendments by way of consensus and there should be no voting on them until all efforts at consensus have been exhausted.

Article 313.   Amendment by Simplified Procedure

1. A State Party may . . . propose an amendment to this Convention, other than an amendment relating to activities in the Area, to be adopted by the simplified procedure set forth in this article without convening a conference. The Secretary-General shall circulate the communication to all States Parties.

2. If, within a period of 12 months from the date of the circulation of the communication, a State Party objects to the proposed amendment or to the proposal for its adoption by the simplified procedure, the amendment shall be considered rejected. The Secretary-General shall immediately notify all States Parties accordingly.

3. If, 12 months from the date of the circulation of the communication, no State Party has objected to the proposed amendment or to the proposal for its adoption by the simplified procedure, the proposed amendment shall be considered adopted. The Secretary-General shall notify all States Parties that the proposed amendment has been adopted.

Article 314.   Amendments to the Provisions of this Convention Relating Exclusively to Activities in the Area

1. A State Party may . . . propose an amendment to the provisions of this Convention relating exclusively to activities in the Area, including Annex VI, section 4. . . . The proposed amendment shall be subject to approval by the

Assembly following its approval by the Council. Representatives of States Parties in those organs shall have full powers to consider and approve the proposed amendment. The proposed amendment as approved by the Council and the Assembly shall be considered adopted. . . .

Article 315.   Signature, Ratification of, Accession to and Authentic Texts of Amendments

1. Once adopted, amendments to this Convention shall be open for signature by States Parties for 12 months from the date of adoption . . . , unless otherwise provided in the amendment itself. . . .

Article 316.   Entry into Force of Amendments

1. Amendments to this Convention, other than those referred to in paragraph 5, shall enter into force for the States Parties ratifying or acceding to them on the thirtieth day following the deposit of instruments of ratification or accession by two thirds of the States Parties or by 60 States Parties, whichever is greater. Such amendments shall not affect the enjoyment by other States Parties of their rights or the performance of their obligations under this Convention.

2. An amendment may provide that a larger number of ratifications or accessions shall be required for its entry into force than are required by this article.

3. For each State Party ratifying or acceding to an amendment referred to in paragraph 1 after the deposit of the required number of instruments of ratification or accession, the amendment shall enter into force on the thirtieth day following the deposit of its instrument of ratification or accession.

4. A State which becomes a Party to this Convention after the entry into force of an amendment in accordance with paragraph 1 shall, failing an expression of a different intention by that State:

    (a) be considered as a Party to this Convention as so amended; and

    (b) be considered as a Party to the unamended Convention in relation to any State Party not bound by the amendment.

5. Any amendment relating exclusively to activities in the Area and any amendment to Annex VI shall enter into force for all States Parties one year following the deposit of instruments of ratification or accession by three fourths of the States Parties.

6. A State which becomes a Party to this Convention after the entry into force of amendments in accordance with paragraph 5 shall be considered as a Party to this Convention as so amended. . . .

Annex I.   Highly Migratory Species

1.   Albacore tuna: *Thunnus alalunga.*
2.   Bluefin tuna: *Thunnus thynnus. . . .*

9. Frigate mackerel: *Auxis thazard; Auxis rochei.*
10. Pomfrets: *Family Bramidae.*
11. Marlins. . . .
12. Sail-fishes: *Istiophorus platypterus; Istiophorus albicans.*
13. Swordfish: *Xiphias gladius.*
14. Sauries. . . .
15. Dolphin: *Coryphaena hippurus; Coryphaena equiselis.*
16. Oceanic sharks. . . .
17. Cetaceans. . . .

Annex II. Commission on the Limits of the Continental Shelf

Article 1

In accordance with the provisions of article 76, a Commission on the Limits of the Continental Shelf beyond 200 nautical miles shall be established in conformity with the following articles. . . .

Annex III. Basic Conditions of Prospecting, Exploration and Exploitation

Article 1. *Title to Minerals*

Title to minerals shall pass upon recovery in accordance with this Convention.

Article 2. *Prospecting*

1.(a) The Authority shall encourage prospecting in the Area.

(b) Prospecting shall be conducted only after the Authority has received a satisfactory written undertaking that the proposed prospector will comply with this Convention and the relevant rules, regulations and procedures of the Authority. . . .

(c) Prospecting may be conducted simultaneously by more than one prospector in the same area or areas.

2. Prospecting shall not confer on the prospector any rights with respect to resources. . . .

Article 3. *Exploration and Exploitation*

1. The Enterprise, States Parties, and the other entities referred to in article 153, paragraph 2(b), may apply to the Authority for approval of plans of work for activities in the Area. . . .

3. Exploration and exploitation shall be carried out only in areas specified in plans of work referred to in article 153, paragraph 3, and

approved by the Authority in accordance with this Convention and the relevant rules, regulations and procedures of the Authority.

4. Every approved plan of work shall: . . .

(c) confer on the operator, in accordance with the rules, regulations and procedures of the Authority, the exclusive right to explore for and exploit the specified categories of resources in the area covered by the plan of work. . . .

5. Upon its approval by the Authority, every plan of work, except those presented by the Enterprise, shall be in the form of a contract concluded between the Authority and the applicant or applicants.

Article 4. *Qualifications of Applicants*

1. Applicants, other than the Enterprise, shall be qualified if they have the nationality or control and sponsorship required by article 153, paragraph 2(b), and if they follow the procedures and meet the qualification standards set forth in the rules, regulations and procedures of the Authority. . . .

Article 5. *Transfer of Technology . . .*

Article 6. *Approval of Plans of Work. . . .*

Article 8. *Reservation of Areas*

Each application, other than those submitted by the Enterprise or by any other entities for reserved areas, shall cover a total area, which need not be a single continuous area, sufficiently large and of sufficient estimated commercial value to allow two mining operations. The applicant shall indicate the co-ordinates dividing the area into two parts of equal estimated commercial value and submit all the data obtained by him with respect to both parts. Without prejudice to the powers of the Authority pursuant to article 17 of this Annex, the data to be submitted concerning polymetallic nodules shall relate to mapping, sampling, the abundance of nodules, and their metal content. Within 45 days of receiving such data, the Authority shall designate which part is to be reserved solely for the conduct of activities by the Authority through the Enterprise or in association with developing States. . . .

Article 9. *Activities in Reserved Areas*

1. The Enterprise shall be given an opportunity to decide whether it intends to carry out activities in each reserved area. . . .

2. The Enterprise may conclude contracts for the execution of part of its activities in accordance with Annex IV, article 12. It may also enter into joint ventures for the conduct of such activities with any entities which are eligible to carry out activities in the Area pursuant to article 153, paragraph 2(b). . . .

Article 10. Preference and Priority Among Applicants. . . .

Article 11. Joint Arrangements

1. Contracts may provide for joint arrangements between the contractor and the Authority through the Enterprise, in the form of joint ventures or production sharing, as well as any other form of joint arrangement. . . .

Article 13. Financial Terms of Contracts

1. In adopting rules, regulations and procedures concerning the financial terms of a contract between the Authority and the entities referred to in article 153, paragraph 2(b), and in negotiating those financial terms in accordance with Part XI and those rules, regulations and procedures, the Authority shall be guided by the following objectives:

(a) to ensure optimum revenues for the Authority from the proceeds of commercial production;

(b) to attract investments and technology to the exploration and exploitation of the Area;

(c) to ensure equality of financial treatment and comparable financial obligations for contractors;

(d) to provide incentives on a uniform and non-discriminatory basis for contractors to undertake joint arrangements with the Enterprise and developing States or their nationals, to stimulate the transfer of technology thereto, and to train the personnel of the Authority and of developing States;

(e) to enable the Enterprise to engage in sea-bed mining effectively at the same time as the entities referred to in article 153, paragraph 2(b); and

(f) to ensure that, as a result of the financial incentives provided to contractors under paragraph 14, under the terms of contracts reviewed in accordance with article 19 of this Annex or under the provisions of article 11 of this Annex with respect to joint ventures, contractors are not subsidized so as to be given an artificial competitive advantage with respect to land-based miners.

2. A fee shall be levied for the administrative cost of processing an application for approval of a plan of work. . . .

15. In the event of a dispute between the Authority and a contractor over the interpretation or application of the financial terms of a contract, either party may submit the dispute to binding commercial arbitration, unless both parties agree to settle the dispute by other means, in accordance with article 188, paragraph 2. . . .

Article 16. Exclusive Right to Explore and Exploit

The Authority shall, pursuant to Part XI and its rules, regulations and procedures, accord the operator the exclusive right to explore and exploit the area covered by the plan of work in respect of a specified category of resources and shall ensure that no other entity operates in the same area for a different category of resources in a manner which might interfere with the operations of the operator. The operator shall have security of tenure in accordance with article 153, paragraph 6. . . .

Article 18.   Penalties

1. A contractor's rights under the contract may be suspended or terminated only in the following cases:

(a) if, in spite of warnings by the Authority, the contractor has conducted his activities in such a way as to result in serious, persistent and wilful violations of the fundamental terms of the contract, Part XI and the rules, regulations and procedures of the Authority; or

(b) if the contractor has failed to comply with a final binding decision of the dispute settlement body applicable to him.

2. In the case of any violation of the contract not covered by paragraph 1(a), or in lieu of suspension or termination under paragraph 1(a), the Authority may impose upon the contractor monetary penalties proportionate to the seriousness of the violation. . . .

Article 21.   Applicable Law

1. The contract shall be governed by the terms of the contract, the rules, regulations and procedures of the Authority, Part XI and other rules of international law not incompatible with this Convention.

2. Any final decision rendered by a court or tribunal having jurisdiction under this Convention relating to the rights and obligations of the Authority and of the contractor shall be enforceable in the territory of each State Party. . . .

Article 22.   Responsibility

The contractor shall have responsibility or liability for any damage arising out of wrongful acts in the conduct of its operations, account being taken of contributory acts or omissions by the Authority. Similarly, the Authority shall have responsibility or liability for any damage arising out of wrongful acts in the exercise of its powers and functions, including violations under article 168, paragraph 2, account being taken of contributory acts or omissions by the contractor. Liability in every case shall be for the actual amount of damage.

Annex IV.   Statute of the Enterprise

Article 1.   Purposes

1. The Enterprise is the organ of the Authority which shall carry out activities in the Area directly, pursuant to article 153, paragraph 2(a), as well

as the transporting, processing and marketing of minerals recovered from the Area. . . .

Article 2.   Relationship to the Authority

1. Pursuant to article 170, the Enterprise shall act in accordance with the general policies of the Assembly and the directives of the Council.

2. Subject to paragraph 1, the Enterprise shall enjoy autonomy in the conduct of its operations.

3. Nothing in this Convention shall make the Enterprise liable for the acts or obligations of the Authority, or make the Authority liable for the acts or obligations of the Enterprise. . . .

Article 4.   Structure

The Enterprise shall have a Governing Board, a Director-General and the staff necessary for the exercise of its functions.

Article 5.   Governing Board

1. The Governing Board shall be composed of 15 members elected by the Assembly in accordance with article 160, paragraph 2(c). In the election of the members of the Board, due regard shall be paid to the principle of equitable geographical distribution. In submitting nominations of candidates for election to the Board, members of the Authority shall bear in mind the need to nominate candidates of the highest standard of competence, with qualifications in relevant fields, so as to ensure the viability and success of the Enterprise.

2. Members of the Board shall be elected for four years and may be re-elected; and due regard shall be paid to the principle of rotation of membership. . . .

4. Members of the Board shall act in their personal capacity. In the performance of their duties they shall not seek or receive instructions from any government or from any other source. . . .

7. Two thirds of the members of the Board shall constitute a quorum.

8. Each member of the Board shall have one vote. All matters before the Board shall be decided by a majority of its members. If a member has a conflict of interest on a matter before the Board he shall refrain from voting on that matter. . . .

Article 6.   Powers and Functions of the Governing Board

The Governing Board shall direct the operations of the Enterprise. Subject to this Convention, the Governing Board shall exercise the powers necessary to fulfil the purposes of the Enterprise, including powers:

   (a) to elect a Chairman from among its members;
   (b) to adopt its rules of procedure;

(c) to draw up and submit formal written plans of work to the Council in accordance with article 153, paragraph 3, and article 162, paragraph 2(j);

(d) to develop plans of work and programmes for carrying out the activities specified in article 170;

(e) to prepare and submit to the Council applications for production authorizations in accordance with article 151, paragraphs 2 to 7;

(f) to authorize negotiations concerning the acquisition of technology, including those provided for in Annex III, article 5, paragraph 3(a), (c) and (d), and to approve the results of those negotiations;

(g) to establish terms and conditions, and to authorize negotiations, concerning joint ventures and other forms of joint arrangements referred to in Annex III, articles 9 and 11, and to approve the results of such negotiations;

(h) to recommend to the Assembly what portion of the net income of the Enterprise should be retained as its reserves in accordance with article 160, paragraph 2(f), and article 10 of this Annex;

(i) to approve the annual budget of the Enterprise;

(j) to authorize the procurement of goods and services in accordance with article 12, paragraph 3, of this Annex; . . .

(l) to submit to the Council for the approval of the Assembly draft rules in respect of the organization, management, appointment and dismissal of the staff of the Enterprise and to adopt regulations to give effect to such rules; . . . .

(n) to enter into any legal proceedings, agreements and transactions and to take any other actions in accordance with article 13 of this Annex; . . . .

Article 7. *Director-General and Staff of the Enterprise*

1. The Assembly shall, upon the recommendation of the Council and the nomination of the Governing Board, elect the Director-General of the Enterprise who shall not be a member of the Board. The Director-General shall hold office for a fixed term, not exceeding five years, and may be re-elected for further terms.

2. The Director-General shall be the legal representative and chief executive of the Enterprise and shall be directly responsible to the Board for the conduct of the operations of the Enterprise. . . .

3. The paramount consideration in the recruitment and employment of the staff and in the determination of their conditions of service shall be the necessity of securing the highest standards of efficiency and of technical competence. Subject to this consideration, due regard shall he paid to the importance of recruiting the staff on an equitable geographical basis.

4. In the performance of their duties the Director-General and the staff shall not seek or receive instructions from any government or from any other source external to the Enterprise. . . .

Article 10.   Allocation of Net Income

1. Subject to paragraph 3, the Enterprise shall make payments to the Authority under Annex III, article 13, or their equivalent.

2. The Assembly shall, upon the recommendation of the Governing Board, determine what portion of the net income of the Enterprise shall be retained as reserves of the Enterprise. The remainder shall be transferred to the Authority.

3. During an initial period required for the Enterprise to become self-supporting, which shall not exceed 10 years from the commencement of commercial production by it, the Assembly shall exempt the Enterprise from the payments referred to in paragraph 1, and shall leave all of the net income of the Enterprise in its reserves.

Article 11.   Finances

1. The funds of the Enterprise shall include:

(a) amounts received from the Authority in accordance with article 173, paragraph 2(b);

(b) voluntary contributions made by States Parties for the purpose of financing activities of the Enterprise;

(c) amounts borrowed by the Enterprise in accordance with paragraphs 2 and 3;

(d) income of the Enterprise from its operations;

(e) other funds made available to the Enterprise to enable it to commence operations as soon as possible and to carry out its functions.

2. (a) The Enterprise shall have the power to borrow funds and to furnish such collateral or other security as it may determine. . . .

Article 12.   Operations

1. The Enterprise shall propose to the Council projects for carrying out activities in accordance with article 170. Such proposals shall include a formal written plan of work for activities in the Area in accordance with article 153, paragraph 3, and all such other information and data as may be required. . . .

2. Upon approval by the Council, the Enterprise shall execute the project on the basis of the formal written plan of work referred to in paragraph 1. . . .

4. The Enterprise shall have title to all minerals and processed substances produced by it.

5. The Enterprise shall sell its products on a non-discriminatory basis. It shall not give non-commercial discounts. . . .

7. . . . Only commercial considerations shall be relevant to its decisions. . . .

Article 13. Legal Status, Privileges and Immunities

1. To enable the Enterprise to exercise its functions, the status, privileges and immunities set forth in this article shall be accorded to the Enterprise in the territories of States Parties. . . .

Annex VI. Statute of the International Tribunal for the Law of the Sea

Article 1. General Provisions

1. The International Tribunal for the Law of the Sea is constituted and shall function in accordance with the provisions of this Convention and this Statute.

2. The seat of the Tribunal shall be in the Free and Hanseatic City of Hamburg in the Federal Republic of Germany.

3. The Tribunal may sit and exercise its functions elsewhere whenever it considers this desirable.

4. A reference of a dispute to the Tribunal shall be governed by the provisions of Parts XI and XV.

SECTION 1. ORGANIZATION OF THE TRIBUNAL

Article 2. Composition

1. The Tribunal shall be composed of a body of 21 independent members, elected from among persons enjoying the highest reputation for fairness and integrity and of recognized competence in the field of the law of the sea.

2. In the Tribunal as a whole the representation of the principal legal systems of the world and equitable geographical distribution shall be assured.

Article 3. Membership

1. No two members of the Tribunal may be nationals of the same State. A person who for the purposes of membership in the Tribunal could be regarded as a national of more than one State shall be deemed to be a national of the one in which he ordinarily exercises civil and political rights.

2. There shall be no fewer than three members from each geographical group as established by the General Assembly of the United Nations.

Article 4. Nominations and Elections

1. Each State Party may nominate not more than two persons having the qualifications prescribed in article 2 of this Annex. The members of the Tribunal shall be elected from the list of persons thus nominated. . . .

4. The members of the Tribunal shall be elected by secret ballot. Elections shall be held at a meeting of the States Parties convened . . . by a procedure agreed to by the States Parties. . . . The persons elected to the Tribunal shall be those nominees who obtain the largest number of votes and a two-thirds majority of the States Parties present and voting, provided that such majority includes a majority of the States Parties.

Article 5.   Term of Office

1. The members of the Tribunal shall be elected for nine years and may be re-elected. . . .

Article 6.   Vacancies

1. Vacancies shall be filled by the same method as that laid down for the first election. . . .

Article 7.   Incompatible Activities

1. No member of the Tribunal may exercise any political or administrative function, or associate actively with or be financially interested in any of the operations of any enterprise concerned with the exploration for or exploitation of the resources of the sea or the sea-bed or other commercial use of the sea or the sea-bed.

2. No member of the Tribunal may act as agent, counsel or advocate in any case.

3. Any doubt on these points shall be resolved by decision of the majority of the other members of the Tribunal present.

Article 8.   Conditions Relating to Participation of Members in a Particular Case

1. No member of the Tribunal may participate in the decision of any case in which he has previously taken part as agent, counsel or advocate for one of the parties, or as a member of a national or international court or tribunal, or in any other capacity. . . .

Article 10.   Privileges and Immunities

The members of the Tribunal, when engaged on the business of the Tribunal, shall enjoy diplomatic privileges and immunities.

Article 11.   Solemn Declaration by Members

Every member of the Tribunal shall, before taking up his duties, make a solemn declaration in open session that he will exercise his powers impartially and conscientiously.

Article 12. President, Vice-President and Registrar

1. The Tribunal shall elect its President and Vice-President for three years; they may be re-elected. . . .

Article 13. Quorum

1. All available members of the Tribunal shall sit; a quorum of 11 elected members shall be required to constitute the Tribunal. . . .

3. All disputes and applications submitted to the Tribunal shall be heard and determined by the Tribunal, unless article 14 of this Annex applies, or the parties request that it shall be dealt with in accordance with article 15 of this Annex.

Article 14. Sea-Bed Disputes Chamber

A Sea-Bed Disputes Chamber shall be established in accordance with the provisions of section 4 of this Annex. Its jurisdiction, powers and functions shall be as provided for in Part XI, section 5.

Article 15. Special Chambers

1. The Tribunal may form such chambers, composed of three or more of its elected members, as it considers necessary for dealing with particular categories of disputes.

2. The Tribunal shall form a chamber for dealing with a particular dispute submitted to it if the parties so request. The composition of such a chamber shall be determined by the Tribunal with the approval of the parties.

3. With a view to the speedy dispatch of business, the Tribunal shall form annually a chamber composed of five of its elected members which may hear and determine disputes by summary procedure. Two alternative members shall be selected for the purpose of replacing members who are unable to participate in a particular proceeding.

4. Disputes shall be heard and determined by the chambers provided for in this article if the parties so request.

5. A judgment given by any of the chambers provided for in this article and in article 14 of this Annex shall be considered as rendered by the Tribunal.

Article 16. Rules of the Tribunal

The Tribunal shall frame rules for carrying out its functions. In particular it shall lay down rules of procedure.

Article 17. Nationality of Members

1. Members of the Tribunal of the nationality of any of the parties to a dispute shall retain their right to participate as members of the Tribunal.

2. If the Tribunal, when hearing a dispute, includes upon the bench a member of the nationality of one of the parties, any other party may choose a person to participate as a member of the Tribunal.

3. If the Tribunal, when hearing a dispute, does not include upon the bench a member of the nationality of the parties, each of those parties may choose a person to participate as a member of the Tribunal.

4. This article applies to the chambers referred to in articles 14 and 15 of this Annex. In such cases, the President, in consultation with the parties, shall request specified members of the Tribunal forming the chamber, as many as necessary, to give place to the members of the Tribunal of the nationality of the parties concerned, and, failing such, or if they are unable to be present, to the members specially chosen by the parties.

5. Should there be several parties in the same interest, they shall, for the purpose of the preceding provisions, be considered as one party only. Any doubt on this point shall be settled by the decision of the Tribunal.

6. Members chosen in accordance with paragraphs 2, 3 and 4 shall fulfil the conditions required by articles 2, 8 and 11 of this Annex. . . .

Article 19.   Expenses of the Tribunal

1. The expenses of the Tribunal shall be borne by the States Parties and by the Authority on such terms and in such a manner as shall be decided at meetings of the States Parties.

2. When an entity other than a State Party or the Authority is a party to a case submitted to it, the Tribunal shall fix the amount which that party is to contribute towards the expenses of the Tribunal.

SECTION 2.   COMPETENCE

Article 20.   Access to the Tribunal

1. The Tribunal shall be open to States Parties.

2. The Tribunal shall be open to entities other than States Parties in any case expressly provided for in Part XI or in any case submitted pursuant to any other agreement conferring jurisdiction on the Tribunal which is accepted by all the parties to that case.

Article 21.   Jurisdiction

The jurisdiction of the Tribunal comprises all disputes and all applications submitted to it in accordance with this Convention and all matters specifically provided for in any other agreement which confers jurisdiction on the Tribunal.

Article 22. Reference of Disputes Subject to Other Agreements

If all the parties to a treaty or convention already in force and concerning the subject-matter covered by this Convention so agree, any disputes concerning the interpretation or application of such treaty or convention may, in accordance with such agreement, be submitted to the Tribunal.

Article 23. Applicable Law

The Tribunal shall decide all disputes and applications in accordance with article 293.

SECTION 3. PROCEDURE

Article 24. Institution of Proceedings

1. Disputes are submitted to the Tribunal, as the case may be, either by notification of a special agreement or by written application, addressed to the Registrar. In either case, the subject of the dispute and the parties shall be indicated.

2. The Registrar shall forthwith notify the special agreement or the application to all concerned. . . .

Article 25. Provisional Measures

1. In accordance with article 290, the Tribunal and its Sea-Bed Disputes Chamber shall have the power to prescribe provisional measures.

2. If the Tribunal is not in session or a sufficient number of members is not available to constitute a quorum, the provisional measures shall be prescribed by the chamber of summary procedure formed under article 15, paragraph 3, of this Annex. . . . They shall be subject to review and revision by the Tribunal.

Article 26. Hearing

1. The hearing shall be under the control of the President or, if he is unable to preside, of the Vice-President. . . .

2. The hearing shall be public, unless the Tribunal decides otherwise or unless the parties demand that the public be not admitted.

Article 27. Conduct of Case

The Tribunal shall make orders for the conduct of the case, decide the form and time in which each party must conclude its arguments, and make all arrangements connected with the taking of evidence.

Article 28. Default

When one of the parties does not appear before the Tribunal or fails to defend its case, the other party may request the Tribunal to continue the proceedings and make its decision. . . . Before making its decision, the

Tribunal must satisfy itself not only that it has jurisdiction over the dispute, but also that the claim is well founded in fact and law.

Article 29. Majority for Decision

1. All questions shall be decided by a majority of the members of the Tribunal who are present.

2. In the event of an equality of votes, the President or the member of the Tribunal who acts in his place shall have a casting vote.

Article 30. Judgment

1. The judgment shall state the reasons on which it is based.

2. It shall contain the names of the members of the Tribunal who have taken part in the decision.

3. If the judgment does not represent in whole or in part the unanimous opinion of the members of the Tribunal, any member shall be entitled to deliver a separate opinion. . . .

Article 31. Request to Intervene

1. Should a State Party consider that it has an interest of a legal nature which may be affected by the decision in any dispute, it may submit a request to the Tribunal to be permitted to intervene.

2. It shall be for the Tribunal to decide upon this request.

3. If a request to intervene is granted, the decision of the Tribunal in respect of the dispute shall be binding upon the intervening State Party in so far as it relates to matters in respect of which that State Party intervened.

Article 32. Right to Intervene in Cases of Interpretation or Application

1. Whenever the interpretation or application of this Convention is in question, the Registrar shall notify all States Parties forthwith.

2. Whenever pursuant to article 21 or 22 of this Annex the interpretation or application of an international agreement is in question, the Registrar shall notify all the parties to the agreement.

3. Every party referred to in paragraphs 1 and 2 has the right to intervene in the proceedings; if it uses this right, the interpretation given by the judgment will be equally binding upon it.

Article 33. Finality and Binding Force of Decisions

1. The decision of the Tribunal is final and shall be complied with by all the parties to the dispute.

2. The decision shall have no binding force except between the parties in respect of that particular dispute.

3. In the event of dispute as to the meaning or scope of the decision, the Tribunal shall construe it upon the request of any party.

Article 34.   Costs

Unless otherwise decided by the Tribunal, each party shall bear its own costs.

SECTION 4.   SEA-BED DISPUTES CHAMBER

Article 35.   Composition

1. The Sea-Bed Disputes Chamber referred to in article 14 of this Annex shall be composed of 11 members, selected by a majority of the elected members of the Tribunal from among them.

2. In the selection of the members of the Chamber, the representation of the principal legal systems of the world and equitable geographical distribution shall be assured. . . .

3. The members of the Chamber shall be selected every three years and may be selected for a second term.

4. The Chamber shall elect its President from among its members, who shall serve for the term for which the Chamber has been selected.

5. If any proceedings are still pending at the end of any three-year period for which the Chamber has been selected, the Chamber shall complete the proceedings in its original composition. . . .

7. A quorum of seven of the members selected by the Tribunal shall be required to constitute the Chamber.

Article 36.   Ad Hoc Chambers

1. The Sea-Bed Disputes Chamber shall form an ad hoc chamber, composed of three of its members, for dealing with a particular dispute submitted to it in accordance with article 188, paragraph 1(b). The composition of such a chamber shall be determined by the Sea-Bed Disputes Chamber with the approval of the parties.

2. If the parties do not agree on the composition of an ad hoc chamber, each party to the dispute shall appoint one member, and the third member shall be appointed by them in agreement. If they disagree, or if any party fails to make an appointment, the President of the Sea-Bed Disputes Chamber shall promptly make the appointment or appointments from among its members, after consultation with the parties.

3. Members of the *ad hoc* chamber must not be in the service of, or nationals of, any of the parties to the dispute.

Article 37.   Access

The Chamber shall be open to the States Parties, the Authority and the other entities referred to in Part XI, section 5.

Article 38.   Applicable Law

In addition to the provisions of article 293, the Chamber shall apply:
(a) the rules, regulations and procedures of the Authority adopted in accordance with this Convention; and
(b) the terms of contracts concerning activities in the Area in matters relating to those contracts.

Article 39.   Enforcement of Decisions of the Chamber

The decisions of the Chamber shall be enforceable in the territories of the States Parties in the same manner as judgments or orders of the highest court of the State Party in whose territory the enforcement is sought.

Article 40.   Applicability of Other Sections of This Annex

1. The other sections of this Annex which are not incompatible with this section apply to the Chamber. . . .

SECTION 5.   AMENDMENTS

Article 41.   Amendment

1. Amendments to this Annex, other than amendments to section 4, may be adopted only in accordance with article 313 or by consensus at a conference convened in accordance with this Convention.

2. Amendments to section 4 may be adopted only in accordance with article 314. . . .

Annex VII.   Arbitration

Article 1.   Institution of Proceedings

Subject to the provisions of Part XV, any party to a dispute may submit the dispute to the arbitral procedure provided for in this Annex by written notification addressed to the other party or parties to the dispute. The notification shall be accompanied by a statement of the claim and the grounds on which it is based.

Article 2.   List of Arbitrators

1. A list of arbitrators shall be drawn up and maintained by the Secretary-General of the United Nations. Every State Party shall be entitled to

nominate four arbitrators, each of whom shall be a person experienced in maritime affairs and enjoying the highest reputation for fairness, competence and integrity. The names of the persons so nominated shall constitute the list. . . .

Article 3. Constitution of Arbitral Tribunal

For the purpose of proceedings under this Annex, the arbitral tribunal shall, unless the parties otherwise agree, be constituted as follows:

(a) Subject to subparagraph (g), the arbitral tribunal shall consist of five members.

(b) The party instituting the proceedings shall appoint one member to be chosen preferably from the list referred to in article 2 of this Annex, who may be its national. The appointment shall be included in the notification referred to in article 1 of this Annex.

(c) The other party to the dispute shall, within 30 days of receipt of the notification referred to in article 1 of this Annex, appoint one member to be chosen preferably from the list, who may be its national. . . .

(d) The other three members shall be appointed by agreement between the parties. They shall be chosen preferably from the list and shall be nationals of third States unless the parties otherwise agree. The parties to the dispute shall appoint the President of the arbitral tribunal from among those three members. If, within 60 days of receipt of the notification referred to in article 1 of this Annex, the parties are unable to reach agreement on the appointment of one or more of the members of the tribunal to be appointed by agreement, or on the appointment of the President, the remaining appointment or appointments shall be made in accordance with subparagraph (e), at the request of a party to the dispute. . . .

(e) Unless the parties agree that any appointment under subparagraphs (c) and (d) be made by a person or a third State chosen by the parties, the President of the International Tribunal for the Law of the Sea shall make the necessary appointments. . . . The appointments referred to in this subparagraph shall be made from the list referred to in article 2 of this Annex within a period of 30 days of the receipt of the request and in consultation with the parties. The members so appointed shall be of different nationalities and may not be in the service of, ordinarily resident in the territory of, or nationals of, any of the parties to the dispute.

(f) Any vacancy shall be filled in the manner prescribed for the initial appointment.

(g) Parties in the same interest shall appoint one member of the tribunal jointly by agreement. Where there are several parties having separate interests or where there is disagreement as to whether they are of the same interest, each of them shall appoint one member of the tribunal. . . .

(h) In disputes involving more than two parties, the provisions of subparagraphs (a) to (f) shall apply to the maximum extent possible.

Article 4.   Functions of Arbitral Tribunal

An arbitral tribunal constituted under article 3 of this Annex shall function in accordance with this Annex and the other provisions of this Convention.

Article 5.   Procedure

Unless the parties to the dispute otherwise agree, the arbitral tribunal shall determine its own procedure, assuring to each party a full opportunity to be heard and to present its case.

Article 6.   Duties of Parties to a Dispute

The parties to the dispute shall facilitate the work of the arbitral tribunal and, in particular, in accordance with their law and using all means at their disposal, shall:

(a) provide it with all relevant documents, facilities and information; and

(b) enable it when necessary to call witnesses or experts and receive their evidence and to visit the localities to which the case relates.

Article 7.   Expenses

Unless the arbitral tribunal decides otherwise because of the particular circumstances of the case, the expenses of the tribunal, including the remuneration of its members, shall be borne by the parties to the dispute in equal shares.

Article 8.   Required Majority for Decisions

Decisions of the arbitral tribunal shall be taken by a majority vote of its members. The absence or abstention of less than half of the members shall not constitute a bar to the tribunal reaching a decision. In the event of an equality of votes, the President shall have a casting vote.

Article 9.   Default of Appearance . . . .

Article 10.   Award

The award of the arbitral tribunal shall be confined to the subject-matter of the dispute and state the reasons on which it is based. It shall contain the names of the members who have participated and the date of the award. Any member of the tribunal may attach a separate or dissenting opinion to the award.

Article 11.   Finality of Award

The award shall be final and without appeal, unless the parties to the dispute have agreed in advance to an appellate procedure. It shall be complied with by the parties to the dispute.

Article 12.   Interpretation or Implementation of Award

1. Any controversy which may arise between the parties to the dispute as regards the interpretation or manner of implementation of the award may be submitted by either party for decision to the arbitral tribunal which made the award. For this purpose, any vacancy in the tribunal shall be filled in the manner provided for in the original appointments of the members of the tribunal.

2. Any such controversy may be submitted to another court or tribunal under article 287 by agreement of all the parties to the dispute.

Article 13.   Application to Entities Other Than States Parties

The provisions of this Annex shall apply *mutatis mutandis* to any dispute involving entities other than States Parties.

Annex VIII.   Special Arbitration

Article 1.   Institution of Proceedings

Subject to Part XV, any party to a dispute concerning the interpretation or application of the articles of this Convention relating to (1) fisheries, (2) protection and preservation of the marine environment, (3) marine scientific research, or (4) navigation, including pollution from vessels and by dumping, may submit the dispute to the special arbitral procedure provided for in this Annex by written notification addressed to the other party or parties to the dispute. The notification shall be accompanied by a statement of the claim and the grounds on which it is based. . . .

Article 4.   General Provisions

Annex VII, articles 4 to 13, apply *mutatis mutandis* to the special arbitration proceedings in accordance with this Annex. . . .

AGREEMENT RELATING TO THE IMPLEMENTATION OF PART XI OF THE UNITED NATIONS CONVENTION ON THE LAW OF THE SEA OF 10 DECEMBER 1

July 28, 1994*

The General Assembly, . . .

Welcoming the report of the Secretary-General on the outcome of his informal consultations, including the draft of an agreement. . . .

1. *Expresses its appreciation* to the Secretary-General for his report on the informal consultations;

2. *Reaffirms* the unified character of the United Nations Convention on the Law of the Sea of 10 December 1982;

3. *Adopts* the Agreement relating to the implementation of Part XI of the United Nations Convention on the Law of the Sea of 10 December 1982 (hereinafter referred to as the "Agreement"), [the text is attached] . . . ;

4. *Affirms* that the Agreement shall be interpreted and applied together with Part XI as a single instrument;

---

* General Assembly Resolution 48/263 included the Agreement as an Annex. The resolution was adopted on July 28, 1994, by a vote of 121 in favor to none against, with seven abstentions. On July 29, 1994, the Agreement was opened for states to become signatories. The United States signed that day, but has yet to ratify it. The Agreement entered into force on July 28, 1996.

As of March 2013, the 144 parties to the Agreement were: Albania, Algeria, Angola, Argentina, Armenia, Australia, Austria, Bahamas, Bangladesh, Barbados, Belarus, Belgium, Belize, Benin, Bolivia, Botswana, Brazil, Brunei Darussalam, Bulgaria, Burkina Faso, Cameroon, Canada, Cape Verde, Chad, Chile, China, Congo, Cook Islands, Costa Rica, Côte d'Ivoire, Croatia, Cuba, Cyprus, Czech Republic, Denmark, Dominican Republic, Equatorial Guinea, Ecuador, Estonia, European Community, Fiji, Finland, France, Gabon, Georgia, Germany, Greece, Grenada, Guatemala, Guinea, Guyana, Haiti, Honduras, Hungary, Iceland, India, Indonesia, Ireland, Italy, Jamaica, Japan, Jordan, Kenya, Kiribati, Korea (Republic of), Kuwait, Lao People's Democratic Republic, Latvia, Lebanon, Lesotho, Liberia, Lithuania, Luxembourg, Macedonia (the former Yugoslav Republic of), Madagascar, Malawi, Malaysia, Maldives, Malta, Mauritania, Mauritius, Mexico, Micronesia, Moldova, Monaco, Mongolia, Montenegro, Morocco, Mozambique, Myanmar, Namibia, Nauru, Nepal, Netherlands, New Zealand, Nicaragua, Nigeria, Niue, Norway, Oman, Pakistan, Palau, Panama, Papua New Guinea, Paraguay, Philippines, Poland, Portugal, Qatar, Romania, Russian Federation, Samoa, Saudi Arabia, Senegal, Serbia, Seychelles, Sierra Leone, Singapore, Slovakia, Slovenia, Solomon Islands, South Africa, Spain, Sri Lanka, Suriname, Swaziland, Sweden, Switzerland, Tanzania (United Republic of), Thailand, Timor-Leste, Togo, Tonga, Trinidad and Tobago, Tunisia, Tuvalu, Uganda, Ukraine, United Kingdom, Uruguay, Vanuatu, Viet Nam, Zambia, and Zimbabwe. See the U.N. Web site at <http://treaties.un.org>.

5. Considers that future ratifications or formal confirmations of or accessions to the Convention shall represent also consent to be bound by the Agreement and that no State or entity may establish its consent to be bound by the Agreement unless it has previously established or establishes at the same time its consent to be bound by the Convention; . . .

Annex
Agreement Relating to the Implementation of Part XI of the United Nations Convention on the Law of the Sea of 10 December 1982

The States Parties to this Agreement,

Recognizing the important contribution of the United Nations Convention on the Law of the Sea of 10 December 1982 (hereinafter referred to as "the Convention") to the maintenance of peace, justice and progress for all peoples of the world,

Reaffirming that the seabed and ocean floor and subsoil thereof, beyond the limits of national jurisdiction (hereinafter referred to as "the Area"), as well as the resources of the Area, are the common heritage of mankind,

Mindful of the importance of the Convention for the protection and preservation of the marine environment and of the growing concern for the global environment,

Having considered the report of the Secretary-General of the United Nations on the results of the informal consultations among States held from 1990 to 1994 on outstanding issues relating to Part XI and related provisions of the Convention (hereinafter referred to as "Part XI"),

Noting the political and economic changes, including market-oriented approaches, affecting the implementation of Part XI,

Wishing to facilitate universal participation in the Convention, Considering that an agreement relating to the implementation of Part XI would best meet that objective,

Have agreed as follows:

Article 1.   Implementation of Part XI

1. The States Parties to this Agreement undertake to implement Part XI in accordance with this Agreement.

2. The Annex forms an integral part of this Agreement.

Article 2.   Relationship Between this Agreement and Part XI

1. The provisions of this Agreement and Part XI shall be interpreted and applied together as a single instrument. In the event of any inconsistency

between this Agreement and Part XI, the provisions of this Agreement shall prevail.

2. Articles 309 to 319 of the Convention shall apply to this Agreement as they apply to the Convention. . . .

Article 4.   Consent to be Bound

1. After the adoption of this Agreement, any instrument of ratification or formal confirmation of or accession to the Convention shall also represent consent to be bound by this Agreement.

2. No State or entity may establish its consent to be bound by this Agreement unless it has previously established or establishes at the same time its consent to be bound by the Convention.

3. A State or entity referred to in article 3 may express its consent to be bound by this Agreement by:

(a) Signature not subject to ratification, formal confirmation or the procedure set out in article 5;

(b) Signature subject to ratification or formal confirmation, followed by ratification or formal confirmation;

(c) Signature subject to the procedure set out in article 5; or

(d) Accession. . . .

Article 5.   Simplified Procedure

1. A State or entity which has deposited before the date of the adoption of this Agreement an instrument of ratification or formal confirmation of or accession to the Convention and which has signed this Agreement in accordance with article 4, paragraph 3(c), shall be considered to have established its consent to be bound by this Agreement 12 months after the date of its adoption, unless that State or entity notifies the depositary in writing before that date that it is not availing itself of the simplified procedure set out in this article.

2. In the event of such notification, consent to be bound by this Agreement shall be established in accordance with article 4, paragraph 3(b). . . .

Article 8.   States Parties

1. For the purposes of this Agreement, "States Parties" means States which have consented to be bound by this Agreement and for which this Agreement is in force.

2. This Agreement applies *mutatis mutandis* to the entities referred to in article 305, paragraph 1(c), (d), (e) and (f), of the Convention which become Parties to this Agreement in accordance with the conditions relevant to each, and to that extent "States Parties" refers to those entities. . . .

Annex

SECTION 1. COSTS TO STATES PARTIES AND INSTITUTIONAL ARRANGEMENTS

1. The International Seabed Authority (hereinafter referred to as "the Authority") is the organization through which States Parties to the Convention shall, in accordance with the regime for the Area established in Part XI and this Agreement, organize and control activities in the Area, particularly with a view to administering the resources of the Area. The powers and functions of the Authority shall be those expressly conferred upon it by the Convention. The Authority shall have such incidental powers, consistent with the Convention, as are implicit in, and necessary for, the exercise of those powers and functions with respect to activities in the Area.

2. In order to minimize costs to States Parties, all organs and subsidiary bodies to be established under the Convention and this Agreement shall be cost-effective. This principle shall also apply to the frequency, duration and scheduling of meetings.

3. The setting up and the functioning of the organs and subsidiary bodies of the Authority shall be based on an evolutionary approach, taking into account the functional needs of the organs and subsidiary bodies concerned in order that they may discharge effectively their respective responsibilities at various stages of the development of activities in the Area.

4. The early functions of the Authority upon entry into force of the Convention shall be carried out by the Assembly, the Council, the Secretariat, the Legal and Technical Commission and the Finance Committee. The functions of the Economic Planning Commission shall be performed by the Legal and Technical Commission until such time as the Council decides otherwise or until the approval of the first plan of work for exploitation.

5. Between the entry into force of the Convention and the approval of the first plan of work for exploitation, the Authority shall concentrate on:

(a) Processing of applications for approval of plans of work for exploration in accordance with Part XI and this Agreement;

(b) Implementation of decisions of the Preparatory Commission for the International Seabed Authority and for the International Tribunal for the Law of the Sea (hereinafter referred to as "the Preparatory Commission") relating to the registered pioneer investors and their certifying States, including their rights and obligations, in accordance with article 308, paragraph 5, of the Convention and resolution II, paragraph 13; . . .

(f) Adoption of rules, regulations and procedures necessary for the conduct of activities in the Area as they progress. Notwithstanding the provisions of Annex III, article 17, paragraph 2(b) and (c), of the Convention, such rules, regulations and procedures shall take into account the terms of this Agreement, the prolonged delay in commercial deep seabed mining and the likely pace of activities in the Area; . . .

6. (a) An application for approval of a plan of work for exploration shall be considered by the Council following the receipt of a recommendation on the application from the Legal and Technical Commission. The processing of an application for approval of a plan of work for exploration shall be in accordance with the provisions of the Convention, including Annex III thereof, and this Agreement, and subject to the following:

(i) A plan of work for exploration submitted on behalf of a State or entity, or any component of such entity, referred to in resolution II, paragraph 1(a)(ii) or (iii), other than a registered pioneer investor, which had already undertaken substantial activities in the Area prior to the entry into force of the Convention, or its successor in interest, shall be considered to have met the financial and technical qualifications necessary for approval of a plan of work if the sponsoring State or States certify that the applicant has expended an amount equivalent to at least US$ 30 million in research and exploration activities and has expended no less than 10 per cent of that amount in the location, survey and evaluation of the area referred to in the plan of work. If the plan of work otherwise satisfies the requirements of the Convention and any rules, regulations and procedures adopted pursuant thereto, it shall be approved by the Council in the form of a contract. The provisions of section 3, paragraph 11, of this Annex shall be interpreted and applied accordingly;

(ii) Notwithstanding the provisions of resolution II, paragraph 8(a), a registered pioneer investor may request approval of a plan of work for exploration within 36 months of the entry into force of the Convention. The plan of work for exploration shall consist of documents, reports and other data submitted to the Preparatory Commission both before and after registration and shall be accompanied by a certificate of compliance, consisting of a factual report describing the status of fulfilment of obligations under the pioneer investor regime, issued by the Preparatory Commission in accordance with resolution II, paragraph 11(a). Such a plan of work shall be considered to be approved. Such an approved plan of work shall be in the form of a contract concluded between the Authority and the registered pioneer investor in accordance with Part XI and this Agreement. The fee of US$ 250,000 paid pursuant to resolution II, paragraph 7(a), shall be deemed to be the fee relating to the exploration phase pursuant to section 8, paragraph 3, of this Annex. Section 3, paragraph 11, of this Annex shall be interpreted and applied accordingly;

(iii) In accordance with the principle of non-discrimination, a contract with a State or entity or any component of such entity referred to in subparagraph (a)(i) shall include arrangements which shall be similar to and no less favourable than those agreed with any registered pioneer investor referred to in subparagraph (a)(ii). . . .

(b) The approval of a plan of work for exploration shall be in accordance with article 153, paragraph 3, of the Convention. . . .

8. An application for approval of a plan of work for exploration, subject to paragraph 6(a)(i) or (ii), shall be processed in accordance with the procedures set out in section 3, paragraph 11, of this Annex.

9. A plan of work for exploration shall be approved for a period of 15 years. Upon the expiration of a plan of work for exploration, the contractor shall apply for a plan of work for exploitation unless the contractor has already done so or has obtained an extension for the plan of work for exploration. Contractors may apply for such extensions for periods of not more than five years each. Such extensions shall be approved if the contractor has made efforts in good faith to comply with the requirements of the plan of work but for reasons beyond the contractor's control has been unable to complete the necessary preparatory work for proceeding to the exploitation stage or if the prevailing economic circumstances do not justify proceeding to the exploitation stage.

10. Designation of a reserved area for the Authority in accordance with Annex III, article 8, of the Convention shall take place in connection with approval of an application for a plan of work for exploration or approval of an application for a plan of work for exploration and exploitation.

11. Notwithstanding the provisions of paragraph 9, an approved plan of work for exploration which is sponsored by at least one State provisionally applying this Agreement shall terminate if such a State ceases to apply this Agreement provisionally and has not become a member on a provisional basis in accordance with paragraph 12 or has not become a State Party.

12. Upon the entry into force of this Agreement, States and entities referred to in article 3 of this Agreement which have been applying it provisionally in accordance with article 7 and for which it is not in force may continue to be members of the Authority on a provisional basis pending its entry into force for such States and entities, in accordance with the following sub-paragraphs: . . .

(d) Notwithstanding the provisions of paragraph 9, an approved plan of work in the form of a contract for exploration which was sponsored pursuant to subparagraph (c)(ii) by a State which was a member on a provisional basis shall terminate if such membership ceases and the State or entity has not become a State Party;

(e) If such a member has failed to make its assessed contributions or otherwise failed to comply with its obligations in accordance with this paragraph, its membership on a provisional basis shall be terminated.

13. The reference in Annex III, article 10, of the Convention to performance which has not been satisfactory shall be interpreted to mean that the contractor has failed to comply with the requirements of an approved plan of work in spite of a written warning or warnings from the Authority to the contractor to comply therewith.

14. The Authority shall have its own budget. Until the end of the year following the year during which this Agreement enters into force, the administrative expenses of the Authority shall be met through the budget of the United Nations. Thereafter, the administrative expenses of the Authority shall be met by assessed contributions of its members, including any

members on a provisional basis, in accordance with articles 171, subparagraph (a), and 173 of the Convention and this Agreement, until the Authority has sufficient funds from other sources to meet those expenses. The Authority shall not exercise the power referred to in article 174, paragraph 1, of the Convention to borrow funds to finance its administrative budget.

15. The Authority shall elaborate and adopt, in accordance with article 162, paragraph 2(o)(ii), of the Convention, rules, regulations and procedures based on the principles contained in sections 2, 5, 6, 7 and 8 of this Annex, as well as any additional rules, regulations and procedures necessary to facilitate the approval of plans of work for exploration or exploitation, in accordance with the following subparagraphs: . . .

17. The relevant provisions of Part XI, section 4, of the Convention shall be interpreted and applied in accordance with this Agreement.

SECTION 2. THE ENTERPRISE

1. The Secretariat of the Authority shall perform the functions of the Enterprise until it begins to operate independently of the Secretariat. The Secretary-General of the Authority shall appoint from within the staff of the Authority an interim Director-General to oversee the performance of these functions by the Secretariat. . . .

2. The Enterprise shall conduct its initial deep seabed mining operations through joint ventures. Upon the approval of a plan of work for exploitation for an entity other than the Enterprise, or upon receipt by the Council of an application for a joint-venture operation with the Enterprise, the Council shall take up the issue of the functioning of the Enterprise independently of the Secretariat of the Authority. If joint-venture operations with the Enterprise accord with sound commercial principles, the Council shall issue a directive pursuant to article 170, paragraph 2, of the Convention providing for such independent functioning.

3. The obligation of States Parties to fund one mine site of the Enterprise as provided for in Annex IV, article 11, paragraph 3, of the Convention shall not apply and States Parties shall be under no obligation to finance any of the operations in any mine site of the Enterprise or under its joint-venture arrangements.

4. The obligations applicable to contractors shall apply to the Enterprise. Notwithstanding the provisions of article 153, paragraph 3, and Annex III, article 3, paragraph 5, of the Convention, a plan of work for the Enterprise upon its approval shall be in the form of a contract concluded between the Authority and the Enterprise.

5. A contractor which has contributed a particular area to the Authority as a reserved area has the right of first refusal to enter into a joint-venture arrangement with the Enterprise for exploration and exploitation of that area. If the Enterprise does not submit an application for a plan of work for activities in respect of such a reserved area within 15 years of the commencement of its functions independent of the Secretariat of the Authority or within 15 years of the date on which that area is reserved for the

Authority, whichever is the later, the contractor which contributed the area shall be entitled to apply for a plan of work for that area provided it offers in good faith to include the Enterprise as a joint-venture partner.

6. Article 170, paragraph 4, Annex IV and other provisions of the Convention relating to the Enterprise shall be interpreted and applied in accordance with this section.

SECTION 3. DECISION-MAKING

1. The general policies of the Authority shall be established by the Assembly in collaboration with the Council.

2. As a general rule, decision-making in the organs of the Authority should be by consensus.

3. If all efforts to reach a decision by consensus have been exhausted, decisions by voting in the Assembly on questions of procedure shall be taken by a majority of members present and voting, and decisions on questions of substance shall be taken by a two-thirds majority of members present and voting, as provided for in article 159, paragraph 8, of the Convention.

4. Decisions of the Assembly on any matter for which the Council also has competence or on any administrative, budgetary or financial matter shall be based on the recommendations of the Council. If the Assembly does not accept the recommendation of the Council on any matter, it shall return the matter to the Council for further consideration. The Council shall reconsider the matter in the light of the views expressed by the Assembly.

5. If all efforts to reach a decision by consensus have been exhausted, decisions by voting in the Council on questions of procedure shall be taken by a majority of members present and voting, and decisions on questions of substance, except where the Convention provides for decisions by consensus in the Council, shall be taken by a two-thirds majority of members present and voting, provided that such decisions are not opposed by a majority in any one of the chambers referred to in paragraph 9. . . .

6. The Council may defer the taking of a decision in order to facilitate further negotiation whenever it appears that all efforts at achieving consensus on a question have not been exhausted.

7. Decisions by the Assembly or the Council having financial or budgetary implications shall be based on the recommendations of the Finance Committee.

8. The provisions of article 161, paragraph 8(b) and (c), of the Convention shall not apply.

9. (a) Each group of States elected under paragraph 15(a) to (c) shall be treated as a chamber for the purposes of voting in the Council. The developing States elected under paragraph 15(d) and (e) shall be treated as a single chamber for the purposes of voting in the Council.

(b) Before electing the members of the Council, the Assembly shall establish lists of countries fulfilling the criteria for membership in the groups of States in paragraph 15(a) to (d). If a State fulfils the criteria for membership in more than one group, it may only be proposed by one group for election to the Council and it shall represent only that group in voting in the Council.

10. Each group of States in paragraph 15(a) to (d) shall be represented in the Council by those members nominated by that group. Each group shall nominate only as many candidates as the number of seats required to be filled by that group. When the number of potential candidates in each of the groups referred to in paragraph 15(a) to (e) exceeds the number of seats available in each of those respective groups, as a general rule, the principle of rotation shall apply. States members of each of those groups shall determine how this principle shall apply in those groups.

11. (a) The Council shall approve a recommendation by the Legal and Technical Commission for approval of a plan of work unless by a two-thirds majority of its members present and voting, including a majority of members present and voting in each of the chambers of the Council, the Council decides to disapprove a plan of work. If the Council does not make a decision on a recommendation for approval of a plan of work within a prescribed period, the recommendation shall be deemed to have been approved by the Council at the end of that period. . . .

   (b) The provisions of article 162, paragraph 2(j), of the Convention shall not apply.

12. Where a dispute arises relating to the disapproval of a plan of work, such dispute shall be submitted to the dispute settlement procedures set out in the Convention.

13. Decisions by voting in the Legal and Technical Commission shall be by a majority of members present and voting.

14. Part XI, section 4, subsections B and C, of the Convention shall be interpreted and applied in accordance with this section.

15. The Council shall consist of 36 members of the Authority elected by the Assembly in the following order:

   (a) Four members from among those States Parties which, during the last five years for which statistics are available, have either consumed more than 2 per cent in value terms of total world consumption or have had net imports of more than 2 per cent in value terms of total world imports of the commodities produced from the categories of minerals to be derived from the Area, provided that the four members shall include one State from the Eastern European region having the largest economy in that region in terms of gross domestic product and the State, on the date of entry into force of the Convention, having the largest economy in terms of gross domestic product, if such States wish to be represented in this group;

   (b) Four members from among the eight States Parties which have made the largest investments in preparation for and in the conduct of activities in the Area, either directly or through their nationals;

   (c) Four members from among States Parties which, on the basis of production in areas under their jurisdiction, are major net exporters ofthe categories of minerals to be derived from the Area, including at least two developing States whose exports of such minerals have a substantial bearing upon their economies;

(d) Six members from among developing States Parties, representing special interests. The special interests to be represented shall include those of States with large populations, States which are land-locked or geographically disadvantaged, island States, States which are major importers of the categories of minerals to be derived from the Area, States which are potential producers of such minerals and least developed States;

(e) Eighteen members elected according to the principle of ensuring an equitable geographical distribution of seats in the Council as a whole, provided that each geographical region shall have at least one member elected under this subparagraph. For this purpose, the geographical regions shall be Africa, Asia, Eastern Europe, Latin America and the Caribbean and Western Europe and Others.

16. The provisions of article 161, paragraph 1, of the Convention shall not apply.

SECTION 4.   REVIEW CONFERENCE

The provisions relating to the Review Conference in article 155, paragraphs 1, 3 and 4, of the Convention shall not apply. Notwithstanding the provisions of article 314, paragraph 2, of the Convention, the Assembly, on the recommendation of the Council, may undertake at any time a review of the matters referred to in article 155, paragraph 1, of the Convention. Amendments relating to this Agreement and Part XI shall be subject to the procedures contained in articles 314, 315 and 316 of the Convention, provided that the principles, regime and other terms referred to in article 155, paragraph 2, of the Convention shall be maintained and the rights referred to in paragraph 5 of that article shall not be affected.

SECTION 5.   TRANSFER OF TECHNOLOGY

1. In addition to the provisions of article 144 of the Convention, transfer of technology for the purposes of Part XI shall be governed by the following principles:

(a) The Enterprise, and developing States wishing to obtain deep seabed mining technology, shall seek to obtain such technology on fair and reasonable commercial terms and conditions on the open market, or through joint-venture arrangements;

(b) If the Enterprise or developing States are unable to obtain deep seabed mining technology, the Authority may request all or any of the contractors and their respective sponsoring State or States to cooperate with it in facilitating the acquisition of deep seabed mining technology by the Enterprise or its joint venture, or by a developing State or States seeking to acquire such technology on fair and reasonable commercial terms and conditions, consistent with the effective protection of intellectual property rights. . . .

2. The provisions of Annex III, article 5, of the Convention shall not apply.

SECTION 6. PRODUCTION POLICY

1. The production policy of the Authority shall be based on the following principles:

(a) Development of the resources of the Area shall take place in accordance with sound commercial principles;

(b) The provisions of the General Agreement on Tariffs and Trade, its relevant codes and successor or superseding agreements shall apply with respect to activities in the Area;

(c) In particular, there shall be no subsidization of activities in the Area except as may be permitted under the agreements referred to in subparagraph (b). Subsidization for the purpose of these principles shall be defined in terms of the agreements referred to in subparagraph (b);

(d) There shall be no discrimination between minerals derived from the Area and from other sources. There shall be no preferential access to markets for such minerals or for imports of commodities produced from such minerals, in particular:

(i) By the use of tariff or non-tariff barriers; and

(ii) Given by States Parties to such minerals or commodities produced by their state enterprises or by natural or juridical persons which possess their nationality or are controlled by them or their nationals;

(e) The plan of work for exploitation approved by the Authority in respect of each mining area shall indicate an anticipated production schedule which shall include the estimated maximum amounts of minerals that would be produced per year under the plan of work;

(f) The following shall apply to the settlement of disputes concerning the provisions of the agreements referred to in subparagraph (b):

(i) Where the States Parties concerned are parties to such agreements, they shall have recourse to the dispute settlement procedures of those agreements;

(ii) Where one or more of the States Parties concerned are not parties to such agreements, they shall have recourse to the dispute settlement procedures set out in the convention;

(g) In circumstances where a determination is made under the agreements referred to in subparagraph (b) that a State Party has engaged in subsidization which is prohibited or has resulted in adverse effects on the interests of another State Party and appropriate steps have not been taken by the relevant State Party or States Parties, a State Party may request the Council to take appropriate measures.

2. The principles contained in paragraph 1 shall not affect the rights and obligations under any provision of the agreements referred to in

paragraph 1(b), as well as the relevant free trade and customs union agreements, in relations between States Parties which are parties to such agreements.

3. The acceptance by a contractor of subsidies other than those which may be permitted under the agreements referred to in paragraph 1(b) shall constitute a violation of the fundamental terms of the contract forming a plan of work for the carrying out of activities in the Area.

4. Any State Party which has reason to believe that there has been a breach of the requirements of paragraphs 1(b) to (d) or 3 may initiate dispute settlement procedures in conformity with paragraph 1(f) or (g). . . .

7. The provisions of article 151, paragraphs 1 to 7 and 9, article 162, paragraph 2(q), article 165, paragraph 2(n), and Annex III, article 6, paragraph 5, and article 7, of the Convention shall not apply.

SECTION 7. ECONOMIC ASSISTANCE

1. The policy of the Authority of assisting developing countries which suffer serious adverse effects on their export earnings or economies resulting from a reduction in the price of an affected mineral or in the volume of exports of that mineral, to the extent that such reduction is caused by activities in the Area, shall be based on the following principles:

(a) The Authority shall establish an economic assistance fund from a portion of the funds of the Authority which exceeds those necessary to cover the administrative expenses of the Authority. The amount set aside for this purpose shall be determined by the Council from time to time, upon the recommendation of the Finance Committee. Only funds from payments received from contractors, including the Enterprise, and voluntary contributions shall be used for the establishment of the economic assistance fund;

(b) Developing land-based producer States whose economics have been determined to be seriously affected by the production of minerals from the deep seabed shall be assisted from the economic assistance fund of the Authority;

(c) The Authority shall provide assistance from the fund to affected developing land-based producer States, where appropriate, in cooperation with existing global or regional development institutions which have the infrastructure and expertise to carry out such assistance programmes;

(d) The extent and period of such assistance shall be determined on a case-by-case basis. In doing so, due consideration shall be given to the nature and magnitude of the problems encountered by affected developing land-based producer States.

2. Article 151, paragraph 10, of the Convention shall be implemented by means of measures of economic assistance referred to in paragraph 1. Article 160, paragraph 2(l), article 162, paragraph 2(n), article 164, paragraph 2(d), article 171, subparagraph (f), and article 173, paragraph 2(c), of the Convention shall be interpreted accordingly.

SECTION 8. FINANCIAL TERMS OF CONTRACTS

1. The following principles shall provide the basis for establishing rules, regulations and procedures for financial terms of contracts:

(a) The system of payments to the Authority shall be fair both to the contractor and to the Authority and shall provide adequate means of determining compliance by the contractor with such system;

(b) The rates of payments under the system shall be within the range of those prevailing in respect of land-based mining of the same or similar minerals in order to avoid giving deep seabed miners an artificial competitive advantage or imposing on them a competitive disadvantage;

(c) The system should not be complicated and should not impose major administrative costs on the Authority or on a contractor. Consideration should be given to the adoption of a royalty system or a combination of a royalty and profit-sharing system. If alternative systems are decided upon, the contractor has the right to choose the system applicable to its contract. Any subsequent change in choice between alternative systems, however, shall be made by agreement between the Authority and the contractor;

(d) An annual fixed fee shall be payable from the date of commencement of commercial production. This fee may be credited against other payments due under the system adopted in accordance with subparagraph (c). The amount of the fee shall be established by the Council;

(e) The system of payments may be revised periodically in the light of changing circumstances. Any changes shall be applied in a nondiscriminatory manner. Such changes may apply to existing contracts only at the election of the contractor. Any subsequent change in choice between alternative systems shall be made by agreement between the Authority and the contractor;

(f) Disputes concerning the interpretation or application of the rules and regulations based on these principles shall be subject to the dispute settlement procedures set out in the Convention.

2. The provisions of Annex III, article 13, paragraphs 3 to 10, of the Convention shall not apply.

3. With regard to the implementation of Annex III, article 13, paragraph 2, of the Convention, the fee for processing applications for approval of a plan of work limited to one phase, either the exploration phase or the exploitation phase, shall be US$ 250,000.

SECTION 9. THE FINANCE COMMITTEE

1. There is hereby established a Finance Committee. The Committee shall be composed of 15 members with appropriate qualifications relevant to financial matters. States Parties shall nominate candidates of the highest standards of competence and integrity.

2. No two members of the Finance Committee shall be nationals of the same State Party.

3. Members of the Finance Committee shall be elected by the Assembly and due account shall be taken of the need for equitable geographical distribution and the representation of special interests. Each group of States referred to in section 3, paragraph 15(a), (b), (c) and (d), of this Annex shall be represented on the Committee by at least one member. Until the Authority has sufficient funds other than assessed contributions to meet its administrative expenses, the membership of the Committee shall include representatives of the five largest financial contributors to the administrative budget of the Authority. Thereafter, the election of one member from each group shall be on the basis of nomination by the members of the respective group, without prejudice to the possibility of further members being elected from each group.

4. Members of the Finance Committee shall hold office for a term of five years. They shall be eligible for re-election for a further term. . . .

7. Decisions by the Assembly and the Council on the following issues shall take into account recommendations of the Finance Committee:

(a) Draft financial rules, regulations and procedures of the organs of the Authority and the financial management and internal financial administration of the Authority;

(b) Assessment of contributions of members to the administrative budget of the Authority in accordance with article 160, paragraph 2(e), of the Convention;

(c) All relevant financial matters, including the proposed annual budget prepared by the Secretary-General of the Authority in accordance with article 172 of the Convention and the financial aspects of the implementation of the programmes of work of the Secretariat;

(d) The administrative budget;

(e) Financial obligations of States Parties arising from the implementation of this Agreement and Part XI as well as the administrative and budgetary implications of proposals and recommendations involving expenditure from the funds of the Authority;

(f) Rules, regulations and procedures on the equitable sharing of financial and other economic benefits derived from activities in the Area and the decisions to be made thereon.

8. Decisions in the Finance Committee on questions of procedure shall be taken by a majority of members present and voting. Decisions on questions of substance shall be taken by consensus.

9. The requirement of article 162, paragraph 2(y), of the Convention to establish a subsidiary organ to deal with financial matters shall be deemed to have been fulfilled by the establishment of the Finance Committee in accordance with this section.

ANTARCTIC TREATY

Dec. 1, 1959, 12 U.S.T. 794, T.I.A.S. No. 4780, 402 U.N.T.S. 71*

The governments . . .
Have agreed as follows:

Article I

1. Antarctica shall be used for peaceful purposes only. There shall be prohibited, *inter alia*, any measures of a military nature, such as the establishment of military bases and fortifications, the carrying out of military maneuvers, as well as the testing of any type of weapons.

2. The present Treaty shall not prevent the use of military personnel or equipment for scientific research or for any other peaceful purpose.

Article II

Freedom of scientific investigation in Antarctica and cooperation toward that end, as applied during the International Geophysical Year, shall continue, subject to the provisions of the present Treaty.

Article III

1. In order to promote international cooperation in scientific investigation in Antarctica, as provided for in Article II of the present Treaty, the Contracting Parties agree that, to the greatest extent feasible and practicable:

    (a) information regarding plans for scientific programs in Antarctica shall be exchanged to permit maximum economy and efficiency of operations;

---

* Signed at Washington, D.C. on December 1, 1959. Entered into force on June 23, 1961. The 50 parties to the treaty as of March 2013 were: Argentina, Australia, Austria, Belarus, Belgium, Brazil, Bulgaria, Canada, Chile, China, Colombia, Cuba, Czech Republic, Denmark, Ecuador, Estonia, Finland, France, Germany, Greece, Guatemala, Hungary, India, Italy, Japan, Korea (Democratic People's Republic of), Korea (Republic of), Malaysia, Monaco, Netherlands, New Zealand, Norway, Pakistan, Papua New Guinea, Portugal, Peru, Poland, Romania, Russian Federation, Slovakia, South Africa, Spain, Sweden, Switzerland, Turkey, Ukraine, United Kingdom, United States of America, Uruguay, and Venezuela. See the Antarctic Treaty Secretariat Web site at <http://www.ats.aq/e/ats.htm>.

(b) scientific personnel shall be exchanged in Antarctica between expeditions and stations;

(c) scientific observations and results from Antarctica shall be exchanged and made freely available.

2. In implementing this Article, every encouragement shall be given to the establishment of cooperative working relations with those Specialized Agencies of the United Nations and other international organizations having a scientific or technical interest in Antarctica.

Article IV

1. Nothing contained in the present Treaty shall be interpreted as:

(a) a renunciation by any Contracting Party of previously asserted rights of or claims to territorial sovereignty in Antarctica;

(b) a renunciation or diminution by any Contracting Party of any basis of claim to territorial sovereignty in Antarctica which it may have whether as a result of its activities or those of its nationals in Antarctica, or otherwise;

(c) prejudicing the position of any Contracting Party as regards its recognition or non-recognition of any other State's right of or claim or basis of claim to territorial sovereignty in Antarctica.

2. No acts or activities taking place while the present Treaty is in force shall constitute a basis for asserting, supporting or denying a claim to territorial sovereignty in Antarctica or create any rights of sovereignty in Antarctica. No new claim, or enlargement of an existing claim, to territorial sovereignty in Antarctica shall be asserted while the present Treaty is in force.

Article V

1. Any nuclear explosions in Antarctica and the disposal there of radioactive waste material shall be prohibited.

2. In the event of the conclusion of international agreements concerning the use of nuclear energy, including nuclear explosions and the disposal of radioactive waste material, to which all of the Contracting Parties whose representatives are entitled to participate in the meetings provided for under Article IX are parties, the rules established under such agreements shall apply in Antarctica.

Article VI

The provisions of the present Treaty shall apply to the area south of 60° South Latitude, including all ice shelves, but nothing in the present Treaty shall prejudice or in any way affect the rights, or the exercise of the rights, of any State under international law with regard to the high seas within that area.

Article VII

1. In order to promote the objectives and ensure the observance of the provisions of the present Treaty, each Contracting Party whose representatives

are entitled to participate in the meetings referred to in Article IX of the Treaty shall have the right to designate observers to carry out any inspection provided for by the present Article. Observers shall be nationals of the Contracting Parties which designate them. The names of observers shall be communicated to every other Contracting Party having the right to designate observers, and like notice shall be given of the termination of their appointment.

2. Each observer designated in accordance with the provisions of paragraph 1 of this Article shall have complete freedom of access at any time to any or all areas of Antarctica.

3. All areas of Antarctica, including all stations, installations and equipment within those areas, and all ships and aircraft at points of discharging or embarking cargoes or personnel in Antarctica, shall be open at all times to inspection by any observers designated in accordance with paragraph 1 of this Article.

4. Aerial observation may be carried out at any time over any or all areas of Antarctica by any of the Contracting Parties having the right to designate observers.

5. Each Contracting Party shall, at the time when the present Treaty enters into force for it, inform the other Contracting Parties, and thereafter shall give them notice in advance, of

(a) all expeditions to and within Antarctica, on the part of its ships or nationals, and all expeditions to Antarctica organized in or proceeding from its territory;

(b) all stations in Antarctica occupied by its nationals; and

(c) any military personnel or equipment intended to be introduced by it into Antarctica subject to the conditions prescribed in paragraph 2 of Article I of the present Treaty.

Article VIII

1. In order to facilitate the exercise of their functions under the present Treaty, and without prejudice to the respective positions of the Contracting Parties relating to jurisdiction over all other persons in Antarctica, observers designated under paragraph 1 of Article VII and scientific personnel exchanged under subparagraph 1(b) of Article III of the Treaty, and members of the staffs accompanying any such persons, shall be subject only to the jurisdiction of the Contracting Party of which they are nationals in respect of all acts or omissions occurring while they are in Antarctica for the purpose of exercising their functions.

2. Without prejudice to the provisions of paragraph 1 of this Article, and pending the adoption of measures in pursuance of subparagraph 1(e) of Article IX, the Contracting Parties concerned in any case of dispute with regard to the exercise of jurisdiction in Antarctica shall immediately consult together with a view to reaching a mutually acceptable solution.

Article IX

1. Representatives of the Contracting Parties named in the preamble to the present Treaty shall meet at the City of Canberra within two months after the date of entry into force of the Treaty, and thereafter at suitable intervals and places, for the purpose of exchanging information, consulting together on matters of common interest pertaining to Antarctica, and formulating and considering, and recommending to their Governments, measures in furtherance of the principles and objectives of the Treaty, including measures regarding:

  (a) use of Antarctica for peaceful purposes only;

  (b) facilitation of scientific research in Antarctica;

  (c) facilitation of international scientific cooperation in Antarctica;

  (d) facilitation of the exercise of the rights of inspection provided for in Article VII of the Treaty;

  (e) questions relating to the exercise of jurisdiction in Antarctica;

  (f) preservation and conservation of living resources in Antarctica.

2. Each Contracting Party which has become a party to the present Treaty by accession under Article XIII shall be entitled to appoint representatives to participate in the meetings referred to in paragraph 1 of the present Article, during such time as that Contracting Party demonstrates its interest in Antarctica by conducting substantial scientific research activity there, such as the establishment of a scientific station or the despatch of a scientific expedition.

3. Reports from the observers referred to in Article VII of the present Treaty shall be transmitted to the representatives of the Contracting Parties participating in the meetings referred to in paragraph 1 of the present Article.

4. The measures referred to in paragraph 1 of this Article shall become effective when approved by all the Contracting Parties whose representatives were entitled to participate in the meetings held to consider those measures.

5. Any or all of the rights established in the present Treaty may be exercised as from the date of entry into force of the Treaty whether or not any measures facilitating the exercise of such rights have been proposed, considered or approved as provided in this Article.

Article X

Each of the Contracting Parties undertakes to exert appropriate efforts, consistent with the Charter of the United Nations, to the end that no one engages in any activity in Antarctica contrary to the principles or purposes of the present Treaty.

Article XI

1. If any dispute arises between two or more of the Contracting Parties concerning the interpretation or application of the present Treaty, those

Contracting Parties shall consult among themselves with a view to having the dispute resolved by negotiation, inquiry, mediation, conciliation, arbitration, judicial settlement or other peaceful means of their own choice.

2. Any dispute of this character not so resolved shall, with the consent, in each case, of all parties to the dispute, be referred to the International Court of Justice for settlement; but failure to reach agreement on reference to the International Court shall not absolve parties to the dispute from the responsibility of continuing to seek to resolve it by any of the various peaceful means referred to in paragraph 1 of this Article.

Article XII

1. (a) The present Treaty may be modified or amended at any time by unanimous agreement of the Contracting Parties whose representatives are entitled to participate in the meetings provided for under Article IX. Any such modification or amendment shall enter into force when the depositary Government has received notice from all such Contracting Parties that they have ratified it.

(b) Such modification or amendment shall thereafter enter into force as to any other Contracting Party when notice of ratification by it has been received by the depositary Government. Any such Contracting Party from which no notice of ratification is received within a period of two years from the date of entry into force of the modification or amendment in accordance with the provisions of subparagraph 1(a) of this Article shall be deemed to have withdrawn from the present Treaty on the date of the expiration of such period. . . .

10

International Environmental Law

STOCKHOLM DECLARATION, OR THE DECLARATION OF THE UNITED NATIONS CONFERENCE ON THE HUMAN ENVIRONMENT

June 16, 1972, U.N. Doc. A/CONF. 48/14, 11 I.L.M. 1416 (1972)*

The United Nations Conference on the Human Environment,
Having met at Stockholm from 5 to 16 June 1972,
Having considered the need for a common outlook and for common principles to inspire and guide the peoples of the world in the preservation and enhancement of the human environment, . . .

II.   Principles

States the common conviction that:

Principle 1

Man has the fundamental right to freedom, equality and adequate conditions of life, in an environment of a quality that permits a life of dignity and well-being, and he bears a solemn responsibility to protect and improve the environment for present and future generations. In this respect, policies promoting or perpetuating *apartheid*, racial segregation, discrimination, colonial and other forms of oppression and foreign domination stand condemned and must be eliminated.

* More formally known as the Report of the U.N. Conference on the Human Environment, from the U.N. Conference in Stockholm, Sweden, June 5-16, 1972. The document can also be found through <http://www.unep.org>.

Principle 2

The natural resources of the earth including the air, water, land, flora and fauna and especially representative samples of natural ecosystems must be safeguarded for the benefit of present and future generations through careful planning or management, as appropriate.

Principle 3

The capacity of the earth to produce vital renewable resources must be maintained and, wherever practicable, restored or improved.

Principle 4

Man has a special responsibility to safeguard and wisely manage the heritage of wildlife and its habitat which are now gravely imperilled by a combination of adverse factors. Nature conservation including wildlife must therefore receive importance in planning for economic development.

Principle 5

The non-renewable resources of the earth must be employed in such a way as to guard against the danger of their future exhaustion and to ensure that benefits from such employment are shared by all mankind.

Principle 6

The discharge of toxic substances or of other substances and the release of heat, in such quantities or concentrations as to exceed the capacity of the environment to render them harmless, must be halted in order to ensure that serious or irreversible damage is not inflicted upon ecosystems. The just struggle of the peoples of all countries against pollution should be supported.

Principle 7

States shall take all possible steps to prevent pollution of the seas by substances that are liable to create hazards to human health, to harm living resources and marine life, to damage amenities or to interfere with other legitimate uses of the sea.

Principle 8

Economic and social development is essential for ensuring a favourable living and working environment for man and for creating conditions on earth that are necessary for the improvement of the quality of life.

Principle 9

Environmental deficiencies generated by the conditions of underdevelopment and natural disasters pose grave problems and can best be remedied by accelerated development through the transfer of substantial quantities of financial and technological assistance as a supplement to the domestic effort of the developing countries and such timely assistance as may be required.

Principle 10

For the developing countries, stability of prices and adequate earnings for primary commodities and raw material are essential to environmental management since economic factors as well as ecological processes must be taken into account.

Principle 11

The environmental policies of all States should enhance and not adversely affect the present or future development potential of developing countries, nor should they hamper the attainment of better living conditions for all, and appropriate steps should be taken by States and international organizations with a view to reaching agreement on meeting the possible national and international economic consequences resulting from the application of environmental measures.

Principle 12

Resources should be made available to preserve and improve the environment, taking into account the circumstances and particular requirements of developing countries and any costs which may emanate from their incorporating environmental safeguards into their development planning and the need for making available to them, upon their request, additional international technical and financial assistance for this purpose.

Principle 13

In order to achieve a more rational management of resources and thus to improve the environment, States should adopt an integrated and coordinated approach to their development planning so as to ensure that development is compatible with the need to protect and improve the human environment for the benefit of their population.

Principle 14

Rational planning constitutes an essential tool for reconciling any conflict between the needs of development and the need to protect and improve the environment.

Principle 15

Planning must be applied to human settlements and urbanization with a view to avoiding adverse effects on the environment and obtaining maximum social, economic and environmental benefits for all. In this respect projects which are designed for colonialist and racist domination must be abandoned.

Principle 16

Demographic policies, which are without prejudice to basic human rights and which are deemed appropriate by Governments concerned, should be applied in those regions where the rate of population growth or excessive population concentrations are likely to have adverse effects on the environment or development, or where low population density may prevent improvement of the human environment and impede development.

Principle 17

Appropriate national institutions must be entrusted with the task of planning, managing or controlling the environmental resources of States with the view to enhancing environmental quality.

Principle 18

Science and technology, as part of their contribution to economic and social development, must be applied to the identification, avoidance and control of environmental risks and the solution of environmental problems and for the common good of mankind.

Principle 19

Education in environmental matters, for the younger generation as well as adults, giving due consideration to the underprivileged, is essential in order to broaden the basis for an enlightened opinion and responsible conduct by individuals, enterprises and communities in protecting and improving the environment in its full human dimension. . . .

Principle 20

Scientific research and development in the context of environmental problems, both national and multinational, must be promoted in all countries, especially the developing countries. In this connexion, the free flow of up-to-date scientific information and transfer of experience must be supported and assisted, to facilitate the solution of environmental problems; environmental technologies should be made available to developing countries on terms which would encourage their wide dissemination without constituting an economic burden on the developing countries.

Principle 21

States have, in accordance with the Charter of the United Nations and the principle of international law, the sovereign right to exploit their own resources pursuant to their own environmental policies, and the responsibility to ensure that activities within their jurisdiction or control do not cause damage to the environment of other States or of areas beyond the limits of national jurisdiction.

Principle 22

States shall co-operate to develop further the international law regarding liability and compensation for the victims of pollution and other environmental damage caused by activities within the jurisdiction or control of such States to areas beyond their jurisdiction.

Principle 23

Without prejudice to such criteria as may be agreed upon by the international community, or to standards which will have to be determined nationally, it will be essential in all cases to consider the systems of values prevailing in each country and the extent of the applicability of standards which are valid for the most advanced countries but which may be inappropriate and of unwarranted social cost for the developing countries.

Principle 24

International matters concerning the protection and improvement of the environment should be handled in a co-operative spirit by all countries, big or small, on an equal footing. Co-operation through multilateral or bilateral arrangements or other appropriate means is essential to effectively control, prevent, reduce and eliminate adverse environmental effects resulting from activities conducted in all spheres, in such a way that due account is taken of the sovereignty and interests of all States.

Principle 25

States shall ensure that international organizations play a co-ordinated, efficient and dynamic role for the protection and improvement of the environment.

Principle 26

Man and his environment must be spared the effects of nuclear weapons and all other means of mass destruction. States must strive to reach prompt agreement, in the relevant international organs, on the elimination and complete destruction of such weapons. . . .

RIO DECLARATION ON ENVIRONMENT AND DEVELOPMENT

<http://www.unep.org>*

The United Nations Conference on Environment and Development,

Having met at Rio de Janeiro from 3 to 14 June 1992,

Reaffirming the Declaration of the United Nations Conference on the Human Environment, adopted at Stockholm on 16 June 1972, and seeking to build upon it,

With the goal of establishing a new and equitable global partnership through the creation of new levels of cooperation among States, key sectors of societies and people,

Working towards international agreements which respect the interests of all and protect the integrity of the global environmental and developmental system,

Recognizing the integral and interdependent nature of the Earth, our home,

Proclaims that:

Principle 1

Human beings are at the centre of concerns for sustainable development. They are entitled to a healthy and productive life in harmony with nature.

Principle 2

States have, in accordance with the Charter of the United Nations and the principles of international law, the sovereign right to exploit their own resources pursuant to their own environmental and developmental policies, and the responsibility to ensure that activities within their jurisdiction or control do not cause damage to the environment of other States or of areas beyond the limits of national jurisdiction.

---

* Adopted by over 178 governments at the U.N. Conference on Environment and Development (UNCED), held in Rio de Janerio, Brazil, June 3-14, 1992. The document can also be found at 31 I.L.M. 874 (1992), June 14, 1992, UN Doc A/CONF.151/26 (vol. 1).

Principle 3

The right to development must be fulfilled so as to equitably meet developmental and environmental needs of present and future generations.

Principle 4

In order to achieve sustainable development, environmental protection shall constitute an integral part of the development process and cannot be considered in isolation from it.

Principle 5

All States and all people shall cooperate in the essential task of eradicating poverty as an indispensable requirement for sustainable development, in order to decrease the disparities in standards of living and better meet the needs of the majority of the people of the world.

Principle 6

The special situation and needs of developing countries, particularly the least developed and those most environmentally vulnerable, shall be given special priority. International actions in the field of environment and development should also address the interests and needs of all countries.

Principle 7

States shall cooperate in a spirit of global partnership to conserve, protect and restore the health and integrity of the Earth's ecosystem. In view of the different contributions to global environmental degradation, States have common but differentiated responsibilities. The developed countries acknowledge the responsibility that they bear in the international pursuit to sustainable development in view of the pressures their societies place on the global environment and of the technologies and financial resources they command.

Principle 8

To achieve sustainable development and a higher quality of life for all people, States should reduce and eliminate unsustainable patterns of production and consumption and promote appropriate demographic policies.

Principle 9

States should cooperate to strengthen endogenous capacity-building for sustainable development by improving scientific understanding through exchanges of scientific and technological knowledge, and by enhancing the development, adaptation, diffusion and transfer of technologies, including new and innovative technologies.

Principle 10

Environmental issues are best handled with participation of all concerned citizens, at the relevant level. At the national level, each individual shall have appropriate access to information concerning the environment that is held by public authorities, including information on hazardous materials and activities in their communities, and the opportunity to participate in decision-making processes. States shall facilitate and encourage public awareness and participation by making information widely available. Effective access to judicial and administrative proceedings, including redress and remedy, shall be provided.

Principle 11

States shall enact effective environmental legislation. Environmental standards, management objectives and priorities should reflect the environmental and development context to which they apply. Standards applied by some countries may be inappropriate and of unwarranted economic and social cost to other countries, in particular developing countries.

Principle 12

States should cooperate to promote a supportive and open international economic system that would lead to economic growth and sustainable development in all countries, to better address the problems of environmental degradation. Trade policy measures for environmental purposes should not constitute a means of arbitrary or unjustifiable discrimination or a disguised restriction on international trade. Unilateral actions to deal with environmental challenges outside the jurisdiction of the importing country should be avoided. Environmental measures addressing transboundary or global environmental problems should, as far as possible, be based on an international consensus.

Principle 13

States shall develop national law regarding liability and compensation for the victims of pollution and other environmental damage. States shall also cooperate in an expeditious and more determined manner to develop further international law regarding liability and compensation for adverse effects of environmental damage caused by activities within their jurisdiction or control to areas beyond their jurisdiction.

Principle 14

States should effectively cooperate to discourage or prevent the relocation and transfer to other States of any activities and substances that cause severe environmental degradation or are found to be harmful to human health.

Principle 15

In order to protect the environment, the precautionary approach shall be widely applied by States according to their capabilities. Where there are threats of serious or irreversible damage, lack of full scientific certainty shall not be used as a reason for postponing cost-effective measures to prevent environmental degradation.

Principle 16

National authorities should endeavour to promote the internalization of environmental costs and the use of economic instruments, taking into account the approach that the polluter should, in principle, bear the cost of pollution, with due regard to the public interest and without distorting international trade and investment.

Principle 17

Environmental impact assessment, as a national instrument, shall be undertaken for proposed activities that are likely to have a significant adverse impact on the environment and are subject to a decision of a competent national authority.

Principle 18

States shall immediately notify other States of any natural disasters or other emergencies that are likely to produce sudden harmful effects on the environment of those States. Every effort shall be made by the international community to help States so afflicted.

Principle 19

States shall provide prior and timely notification and relevant information to potentially affected States on activities that may have a significant adverse transboundary environmental effect and shall consult with those States at an early stage and in good faith.

Principle 20

Women have a vital role in environmental management and development. Their full participation is therefore essential to achieve sustainable development.

Principle 21

The creativity, ideals and courage of the youth of the world should be mobilized to forge a global partnership in order to achieve sustainable development and ensure a better future for all.

Principle 22

Indigenous people and their communities and other local communities have a vital role in environmental management and development because of their knowledge and traditional practices. States should recognize and duly support their identity, culture and interests and enable their effective participation in the achievement of sustainable development.

Principle 23

The environment and natural resources of people under oppression, domination and occupation shall be protected.

Principle 24

Warfare is inherently destructive of sustainable development. States shall therefore respect international law providing protection for the environment in times of armed conflict and cooperate in its further development, as necessary.

Principle 25

Peace, development and environmental protection are interdependent and indivisible.

Principle 26

States shall resolve all their environmental disputes peacefully and by appropriate means in accordance with the Charter of the United Nations.

Principle 27

States and people shall cooperate in good faith and in a spirit of partnership in the fulfilment of the principles embodied in this Declaration and in the further development of international law in the field of sustainable development.

VIENNA CONVENTION FOR THE PROTECTION OF THE OZONE LAYER

Mar. 22, 1985, 1513 U.N.T.S. 293, T.I.A.S. No. 11,097, 26 I.L.M. 1516 (1987)*

PREAMBLE

The Parties to this Convention,

Aware of the potentially harmful impact on human health and the environment through modification of the ozone layer,

Recalling the pertinent provisions of the Declaration of the United Nations Conference on the Human Environment, and in particular principle 21, which provides that "States have, in accordance with the Charter of the United Nations and the principles of international law, the sovereign right to exploit their own resources pursuant to their own environmental policies,

---

* Done at Vienna on March 22, 1985. Entered into force on September 22, 1988. The United States ratified the convention on August 27, 1986.

As of March 2013, the 197 parties to the convention were: Afghanistan, Albania, Algeria, Andorra, Angola, Antigua and Barbuda, Argentina, Armenia, Australia, Austria, Azerbaijan, Bahamas, Bahrain, Bangladesh, Barbados, Belarus, Belgium, Belize, Benin, Bhutan, Bolivia, Bosnia and Herzegovina, Botswana, Brazil, Brunei Darussalam, Bulgaria, Burkina Faso, Burundi, Cambodia, Cameroon, Canada, Cape Verde, Central African Republic, Chad, Chile, China, Colombia, Comoros, Congo, Congo (Democratic Republic of), Cook Islands, Costa Rica, Côte d'Ivoire, Croatia, Cuba, Cyprus, Czech Republic, Denmark, Djibouti, Dominica, Dominican Republic, Ecuador, Egypt, El Salvador, Equatorial Guinea, Eritrea, Estonia, Ethiopia, European Community, Fiji, Finland, France, Gabon, Gambia, Georgia, Germany, Ghana, Greece, Grenada, Guatemala, Guinea, Guinea-Bissau, Guyana, Haiti, Holy See, Honduras, Hungary, Iceland, India, Indonesia, Iran, Iraq, Ireland, Israel, Italy, Jamaica, Japan, Jordan, Kazakhstan, Kenya, Kiribati, Korea (Democratic People's Republic of), Korea (Republic of), Kuwait, Kyrgyzstan, Lao People's Democratic Republic, Latvia, Lebanon, Lesotho, Liberia, Libyan Arab Jamahiriya, Liechtenstein, Lithuania, Luxembourg, Macedonia (the former Yugoslav Republic of), Madagascar, Malawi, Malaysia, Maldives, Mali, Malta, Marshall Islands, Mauritania, Mauritius, Mexico, Micronesia,, Moldova, Monaco, Mongolia, Montenegro, Morocco, Mozambique, Myanmar, Namibia, Nauru, Nepal, Netherlands, New Zealand, Nicaragua, Niger, Nigeria, Niue, Norway, Oman, Pakistan, Palau, Panama, Papua New Guinea, Paraguay, Peru, Philippines, Poland, Portugal, Qatar, Romania, Russian Federation, Rwanda, Saint Kitts and Nevis, Saint Lucia, Saint Vincent and the Grenadines, Samoa, San Marino, Sao Tome and Principe, Saudi Arabia, Senegal, Serbia, Seychelles, Sierra Leone, Singapore, Slovakia, Slovenia, Solomon Islands, Somalia, South Africa, South Sudan, Spain, Sri Lanka, Sudan, Suriname, Swaziland, Sweden, Switzerland, Syrian Arab Republic, Tajikistan, Tanzania, Thailand, Timor-Leste, Togo, Tonga, Trinidad and Tobago, Tunisia, Turkey, Turkmenistan, Tuvalu, Uganda, Ukraine, United Arab Emirates, United Kingdom, United States of America, Uruguay, Uzbekistan, Vanuatu, Venezuela, Viet Nam, Yemen, Zambia, and Zimbabwe. See the U.N. Web site at <http://treaties.un.org> or <http://ozone.unep.org>.

and the responsibility to ensure that activities within their jurisdiction or control do not cause damage to the environment of other States or of areas beyond the limits of national jurisdiction,"

Taking into account the circumstances and particular requirements of developing countries,

Mindful of the work and studies proceeding within both international and national organizations and, in particular, of the World Plan of Action on the Ozone Layer of the United Nations Environment Programme,

Mindful also of the precautionary measures for the protection of the ozone layer which have already been taken at the national and international levels,

Aware that measures to protect the ozone layer from modifications due to human activities require international co-operation and action, and should be based on relevant scientific and technical considerations,

Aware also of the need for further research and systematic observations to further develop scientific knowledge of the ozone layer and possible adverse effects resulting from its modification,

Determined to protect human health and the environment against adverse effects resulting from modifications of the ozone layer,

HAVE AGREED AS FOLLOWS:

Article 1.   Definitions

For the purposes of this Convention:

1. "The ozone layer" means the layer of atmospheric ozone above the planetary boundary layer.

2. "Adverse effects" means changes in the physical environment or biota, including changes in climate, which have significant deleterious effects on human health or on the composition, resilience and productivity of natural and managed ecosystems, or on materials useful to mankind.

3. "Alternative technologies or equipment" means technologies or equipment the use of which makes it possible to reduce or effectively eliminate emissions of substances which have or are likely to have adverse effects on the ozone layer.

4. "Alternative substances" means substances which reduce, eliminate or avoid adverse effects on the ozone layer.

5. "Parties" means, unless the text otherwise indicates, Parties to this Convention.

6. "Regional economic integration organization" means an organization constituted by sovereign States of a given region which has competence in respect of matters governed by this Convention or its protocols and has been duly authorized, in accordance with its internal procedures, to sign, ratify, accept, approve or accede to the instruments concerned.

7. "Protocols" means protocols to this Convention.

Article 2.   General Obligations

1. The Parties shall take appropriate measures in accordance with the provisions of this Convention and of those protocols in force to which they

are party to protect human health and the environment against adverse effects resulting or likely to result from human activities which modify or are likely to modify the ozone layer.

2. To this end the Parties shall, in accordance with the means at their disposal and their capabilities:

(a) Co-operate by means of systematic observations, research and information exchange in order to better understand and assess the effects of human activities on the ozone layer and the effects on human health and the environment from modification of the ozone layer;

(b) Adopt appropriate legislative or administrative measures and co-operate in harmonizing appropriate policies to control, limit, reduce or prevent human activities under their jurisdiction or control should it be found that these activities have or are likely to have adverse effects resulting from modification or likely modification of the ozone layer;

(c) Co-operate in the formulation of agreed measures, procedures and standards for the implementation of this Convention, with a view to the adoption of protocols and annexes;

(d) Co-operate with competent international bodies to implement effectively this Convention and protocols to which they are party.

3. The provisions of this Convention shall in no way affect the right of Parties to adopt, in accordance with international law, domestic measures additional to those referred to in paragraphs 1 and 2 above, nor shall they affect additional domestic measures already taken by a Party, provided that these measures are not incompatible with their obligations under this Convention.

4. The application of this article shall be based on relevant scientific and technical considerations.

Article 3. Research and Systematic Observations

1. The Parties undertake, as appropriate, to initiate and co-operate in, directly or through competent international bodies, the conduct of research and scientific assessments on:

(a) The physical and chemical processes that may affect the ozone layer;

(b) The human health and other biological effects deriving from any modifications of the ozone layer, particularly those resulting from changes in ultra-violet solar radiation having biological effects (UV-B);

(c) Climatic effects deriving from any modifications of the ozone layer;

(d) Effects deriving from any modifications of the ozone layer and any consequent change in UV-B radiation on natural and synthetic materials useful to mankind;

(e) Substances, practices, processes and activities that may affect the ozone layer, and their cumulative effects;

(f) Alternative substances and technologies;

(g) Related socio-economic matters; and as further elaborated in annexes I and II.

2. The Parties undertake to promote or establish, as appropriate, directly or through competent international bodies and taking fully into account national legislation and relevant ongoing activities at both the national and international levels, joint or complementary programmes for systematic observation of the state of the ozone layer and other relevant parameters, as elaborated in annex I.

3. The Parties undertake to co-operate, directly or through competent international bodies, in ensuring the collection, validation and transmission of research and observational data through appropriate world data centres in a regular and timely fashion.

Article 4. Co-operation in the Legal, Scientific and Technical Fields

1. The Parties shall facilitate and encourage the exchange of scientific, technical, socio-economic, commercial and legal information relevant to this Convention as further elaborated in annex II. Such information shall be supplied to bodies agreed upon by the Parties. Any such body receiving information regarded as confidential by the supplying Party shall ensure that such information is not disclosed and shall aggregate it to protect its confidentiality before it is made available to all Parties.

2. The Parties shall co-operate, consistent with their national laws, regulations and practices and taking into account in particular the needs of the developing countries, in promoting, directly or through competent international bodies, the development and transfer of technology and knowledge. Such co-operation shall be carried out particularly through:

(a) Facilitation of the acquisition of alternative technologies by other Parties;

(b) Provision of information on alternative technologies and equipment, and supply of special manuals or guides to them;

(c) The supply of necessary equipment and facilities for research and systematic observations;

(d) Appropriate training of scientific and technical personnel.

Article 5. Transmission of Information

The Parties shall transmit, through the secretariat, to the Conference of the Parties established under article 6 information on the measures adopted by them in implementation of this Convention and of protocols to which they are party in such form and at such intervals as the meetings of the parties to the relevant instruments may determine.

Article 6. Conference of the Parties

1. A Conference of the Parties is hereby established. The first meeting of the Conference of the Parties shall be convened by the secretariat designated

on an interim basis under article 7 not later than one year after entry into force of this Convention. Thereafter, ordinary meetings of the Conference of the Parties shall be held at regular intervals to be determined by the Conference at its first meeting.

2. Extraordinary meetings of the Conference of the Parties shall be held at such other times as may be deemed necessary by the Conference, or at the written request of any Party, provided that, within six months of the request being communicated to them by the secretariat, it is supported by at least one third of the Parties.

3. The Conference of the Parties shall by consensus agree upon and adopt rules of procedure and financial rules for itself and for any subsidiary bodies it may establish, as well as financial provisions governing the functioning of the secretariat.

4. The Conference of the Parties shall keep under continuous review the implementation of this Convention, and, in addition, shall:

(a) Establish the form and the intervals for transmitting the information to be submitted in accordance with article 5 and consider such information as well as reports submitted by any subsidiary body;

(b) Review the scientific information on the ozone layer, on its possible modification and on possible effects of any such modification;

(c) Promote, in accordance with article 2, the harmonization of appropriate policies, strategies and measures for minimizing the release of substances causing or likely to cause modification of the ozone layer, and make recommendations on any other measures relating to this Convention;

(d) Adopt, in accordance with articles 3 and 4, programmes for research, systematic observations, scientific and technological co-operation, the exchange of information and the transfer of technology and knowledge;

(e) Consider and adopt, as required, in accordance with articles 9 and 10, amendments to this Convention and its annexes;

(f) Consider amendments to any protocol, as well as to any annexes thereto, and, if so decided, recommend their adoption to the parties to the protocol concerned;

(g) Consider and adopt, as required, in accordance with article 10, additional annexes to this Convention;

(h) Consider and adopt, as required, protocols in accordance with article 8;

(i) Establish such subsidiary bodies as are deemed necessary for the implementation of this Convention;

(j) Seek, where appropriate, the services of competent international bodies and scientific committees, in particular the World Meteorological Organization and the World Health Organization, as well as the Coordinating Committee on the Ozone Layer, in scientific research, systematic observations and other activities pertinent to the objectives of this Convention, and make use as appropriate of information from these bodies and committees;

(k) Consider and undertake any additional action that may be required for the achievement of the purposes of this Convention.

5. The United Nations, its specialized agencies and the International Atomic Energy Agency, as well as any State not party to this Convention, may be represented at meetings of the Conference of the Parties by observers. Any body or agency, whether national or international, governmental or nongovernmental, qualified in fields relating to the protection of the ozone layer which has informed the secretariat of its wish to be represented at a meeting of the Conference of the Parties as an observer may be admitted unless at least one-third of the Parties present object. The admission and participation of observers shall be subject to the rules of procedure adopted by the Conference of the Parties.

Article 7. *Secretariat*

1. The functions of the secretariat shall be:

(a) To arrange for and service meetings provided for in articles 6, 8, 9 and 10;

(b) To prepare and transmit reports based upon information received in accordance with articles 4 and 5, as well as upon information derived from meetings of subsidiary bodies established under article 6;

(c) To perform the functions assigned to it by any protocol;

(d) To prepare reports on its activities carried out in implementation of its functions under this Convention and present them to the Conference of the Parties;

(e) To ensure the necessary co-ordination with other relevant international bodies, and in particular to enter into such administrative and contractual arrangements as may be required for the effective discharge of its functions;

(f) To perform such other functions as may be determined by the Conference of the Parties.

2. The secretariat functions will be carried out on an interim basis by the United Nations Environment Programme until the completion of the first ordinary meeting of the Conference of the Parties held pursuant to article 6. At its first ordinary meeting, the Conference of the Parties shall designate the secretariat from amongst those existing competent international organizations which have signified their willingness to carry out the secretariat functions under this Convention.

Article 8. *Adoption of Protocols*

1. The Conference of the Parties may at a meeting adopt protocols pursuant to article 2.

2. The text of any proposed protocol shall be communicated to the Parties by the secretariat at least six months before such a meeting.

Article 9.   Amendment of the Convention or Protocols

1. Any Party may propose amendments to this Convention or to any protocol. Such amendments shall take due account, *inter alia*, of relevant scientific and technical considerations.

2. Amendments to this Convention shall be adopted at a meeting of the Conference of the Parties. Amendments to any protocol shall be adopted at a meeting of the Parties to the protocol in question. The text of any proposed amendment to this Convention or to any protocol, except as may otherwise be provided in such protocol, shall be communicated to the Parties by the secretariat at least six months before the meeting at which it is proposed for adoption. The secretariat shall also communicate proposed amendments to the signatories to this Convention for information.

3. The Parties shall make every effort to reach agreement on any proposed amendment to this Convention by consensus. If all efforts at consensus have been exhausted, and no agreement reached, the amendment shall as a last resort be adopted by a three-fourths majority vote of the Parties present and voting at the meeting, and shall be submitted by the Depositary to all Parties for ratification, approval or acceptance.

4. The procedure mentioned in paragraph 3 above shall apply to amendments to any protocol, except that a two-thirds majority of the parties to that protocol present and voting at the meeting shall suffice for their adoption.

5. Ratification, approval or acceptance of amendments shall he notified to the Depositary in writing. Amendments adopted in accordance with paragraphs 3 or 4 above shall enter into force between parties having accepted them on the ninetieth day after the receipt by the Depositary of notification of their ratification, approval or acceptance by at least three-fourths of the Parties to this Convention or by at least two-thirds of the parties to the protocol concerned, except as may otherwise be provided in such protocol. Thereafter the amendments shall enter into force for any other Party on the ninetieth day after that Party deposits its instrument of ratification, approval or acceptance of the amendments.

6. For the purposes of this article, "Parties present and voting" means Parties present and casting an affirmative or negative vote.

Article 10.   Adoption and Amendment of Annexes

1. The annexes to this Convention or to any protocol shall form an integral part of this Convention or of such protocol, as the case may be, and, unless expressly provided otherwise, a reference to this Convention or its protocols constitutes at the same time a reference to any annexes thereto. Such annexes shall be restricted to scientific, technical and administrative matters.

2. Except as may be otherwise provided in any protocol with respect to its annexes, the following procedure shall apply to the proposal, adoption and entry into force of additional annexes to this Convention or of annexes to a protocol:

(a) Annexes to this Convention shall be proposed and adopted according to the procedure laid down in article 9, paragraphs 2 and 3, while annexes to any protocol shall be proposed and adopted according to the procedure laid down in article 9, paragraphs 2 and 4;

(b) Any party that is unable to approve an additional annex to this Convention or an annex to any protocol to which it is party shall so notify the Depositary, in writing, within six months from the date of the communication of the adoption by the Depositary. The Depositary shall without delay notify all Parties of any such notification received. A Party may at any time substitute an acceptance for a previous declaration of objection and the annexes shall thereupon enter into force for that Party;

(c) On the expiry of six months from the date of the circulation of the communication by the Depositary, the annex shall become effective for all Parties to this Convention or to any protocol concerned which have not submitted a notification in accordance with the provision of subparagraph (b) above.

3. The proposal, adoption and entry into force of amendments to annexes to this Convention or to any protocol shall be subject to the same procedure as for the proposal, adoption and entry into force of annexes to the Convention or annexes to a protocol. Annexes and amendments thereto shall take due account, *inter alia*, of relevant scientific and technical considerations.

4. If an additional annex or an amendment to an annex involves an amendment to this Convention or to any protocol, the additional annex or amended annex shall not enter into force until such time as the amendment to this Convention or to the protocol concerned enters into force.

Article 11. Settlement of Disputes

1. In the event of a dispute between Parties concerning the interpretation or application of this Convention, the parties concerned shall seek solution by negotiation.

2. If the parties concerned cannot reach agreement by negotiation, they may jointly seek the good offices of, or request mediation by, a third party.

3. When ratifying, accepting, approving or acceding to this Convention. or at any time thereafter, a State or regional economic integration organization may declare in writing to the Depositary that for a dispute not resolved in accordance with paragraph 1 or paragraph 2 above, it accepts one or both of the following means of dispute settlement as compulsory:

(a) Arbitration in accordance with procedures to be adopted by the Conference of the Parties at its first ordinary meeting;

(b) Submission of the dispute to the International Court of Justice.

4. If the parties have not, in accordance with paragraph 3 above, accepted the same or any procedure, the dispute shall be submitted to conciliation in accordance with paragraph 5 below unless the parties otherwise agree.

5. A conciliation commission shall be created upon the request of one of the parties to the dispute. The commission shall be composed of an equal number of members appointed by each party concerned and a chairman chosen jointly by the members appointed by each party. The commission shall render a final and recommendatory award, which the parties shall consider in good faith.

6. The provisions of this article shall apply with respect to any protocol except as otherwise provided in the protocol concerned. . . .

Article 15.   Right to Vote

1. Each Party to this Convention or to any protocol shall have one vote.

2. Except as provided for in paragraph 1 above, regional economic intergration organizations, in matters within their competence, shall exercise their right to vote with a number of votes equal to the number of their member States which are Parties to the Convention or the relevant protocol. Such organizations shall not exercise their right to vote if their member States exercise theirs, and vice versa. . . .

Article 18.   Reservations

No reservations may be made to this Convention. . . .

Annex I.   Research and Systematic Observations

1. The Parties to the Convention recognize that the major scientific issues are:

(a) Modification of the ozone layer which would result in a change in the amount of solar ultra-violet radiation having biological effects (UV-B) that reaches the Earth's surface and the potential consequences for human health, for organisms, ecosystems and materials useful to mankind;

(b) Modification of the vertical distribution of ozone, which could change the temperature structure of the atmosphere and the potential consequences for weather and climate.

2. The Parties to the Convention, in accordance with article 3, shall co-operate in conducting research and systematic observations and in formulating recommendations for future research and observation in such areas as:

(a) *Research into the physics and chemistry of the atmosphere* . . .

(b) *Research into health, biological and photodegradation effects* . . .

(c) *Research on effects on climate* . . .

(d) *Systematic observation on:*

(i) The status of the ozone layer (i.e. the spatial and temporal variability of the total column content and vertical distribution) by making the Global Ozone Observing System, based on the integration of satellite and ground-based systems, fully operational; . . .

4. The following chemical substances of natural and anthropogenic origin, not listed in order of priority, are thought to have the potential to modify the chemical and physical properties of the ozone layer.

(a) **Carbon substances**

(i) *Carbon monoxide (CO)*

Carbon monoxide has significant natural and anthropogenic sources, and is thought to play a major direct role in tropospheric photochemistry, and an indirect role in stratospheric photochemistry.

(ii) *Carbon dioxide (CO_2)*

Carbon dioxide has significant natural and anthropogenic sources, and affects stratospheric ozone by influencing the thermal structure of the atmosphere.

(iii) *Methane (CH_4)*

Methane has both natural and anthropogenic sources, and affects both tropospheric and stratospheric ozone.

(iv) *Non-methane hydrocarbon species . . .*

(b) **Nitrogen substances**

(i) *Nitrous oxide (N_2O)*

The dominant sources of N_2O are natural, but anthropogenic contributions are becoming increasingly important. Nitrous oxide is the primary source of stratospheric NO_x, which play a vital role in controlling the abundance of stratospheric ozone.

(ii) *Nitrogen oxides (NO_x)*

Ground-level sources of NO_x play a major direct role only in tropospheric photochemical processes and an indirect role in stratosphere photochemistry, whereas injection of NO_x close to the tropopause may lead directly to a change in upper tropospheric and stratospheric ozone.

(c) **Chlorine substances** . . .

(d) **Bromine substances** . . .

(e) **Hydrogen substances** . . .

HELSINKI DECLARATION ON THE PROTECTION OF THE OZONE LAYER

May 2, 1989, 28 I.L.M. 1335*

The Governments and the European Communities Represented at the First Meetings of the Parties to the Vienna Convention and the Montreal Protocol

Aware of the wide agreement among scientists that depletion of the ozone layer will threaten present and future generations unless more stringent control measures are adopted

Mindful that some ozone depleting substances are powerful greenhouse gases leading to global warming

Aware also of the extensive and rapid technological development of environmentally acceptable substitutes for the substances that deplete the ozone layer and the urgent need to facilitate the transfer of technologies of such substitutes especially to developing countries

ENCOURAGE all states that have not done so to join the Vienna Convention for the Protection of the Ozone Layer and its Montreal Protocol

AGREE to phase out the production and the consumption of CFC's controlled by the Montreal Protocol as soon as possible but not later than the year 2000 and for that purpose to tighten the timetable agreed upon in the Montreal Protocol taking due account of the special situation of developing countries

AGREE to both phase out halons and control and reduce other ozone-depleting substances which contribute significantly to ozone depletion as soon as feasible

AGREE to commit themselves, in proportion to their means and resources, to accelerate the development of environmentally acceptable

---

* Done at Helsinki, Finland, on May 2, 1989. The declaration was adopted by a consensus at a meeting of the states participating in the Vienna Convention for the Protection of the Ozone Layer, *supra*, and the Montreal Protocol on Substances that Deplete the Ozone Layer, *infra*. The declaration expresses the intent of the parties. A 1990 meeting was scheduled to discuss amendments. Those amendments are provided next. See United Nations Environment Programme Web site at <http://ozone.unep.org>.

substituting chemicals, products and technologies AGREE to facilitate the access of developing countries to relevant scientific information, research results and training and to seek to develop appropriate funding mechanisms to facilitate the transfer of technology and replacement of equipment at minimum cost to developing countries.

MONTREAL PROTOCOL ON SUBSTANCES THAT DEPLETE THE OZONE LAYER (AS AMENDED)

<http://ozone.unep.org>*

The Parties to this Protocol,

Being Parties to the Vienna Convention for the Protection of the Ozone Layer.

Mindful of their obligation under that Convention to take appropriate measures to protect human health and the environment against adverse effects resulting or likely to result from, human activities which modify or are likely to modify the ozone layer,

Recognizing that world-wide emissions of certain substances can significantly deplete and otherwise modify the ozone layer in a manner that is likely to result in adverse effects on human health and the environment,

Conscious of the potential climatic effect of emissions of these substances,

Aware that measures taken to protect the ozone layer from depletion should be based on relevant scientific knowledge, taking into account technical and economic considerations,

---

* Composite Text of the Protocol as either adjusted or amended in London in 1990, Copenhagen in 1992, Vienna in 1995, Montreal in 1997, and Beijing in 1999. The amendments are in accordance with paragraph 4 of Article 9 of the Vienna Convention for the Protection of the Ozone Layer (excerpted earlier). In accordance with paragraphs 4 and 9 of Article 2 of the Montreal Protocol, the meetings also adopted the adjustments and reductions of production and consumption of controlled substances listed in the Annexes. Source: the United Nations Environment Programme (UNEP) at <http://ozone.unep.org>.

The Protocol was concluded at Montreal on September 16, 1987, and entered into force on January 1, 1989. As of February 2013, there were 197 parties to the Protocol.

They are the same parties as for the Vienna Convention, *infra*. At the Second Meeting of the Parties at London on June 29, 1990, amendments were adopted. These amendments entered into force August 10, 1992. As of February 2013, there were 197 parties to the amendments. At the Fourth Meeting of the Parties at Copenhagen on November 25, 1992, amendments were also adopted. These amendments entered into force on June 14, 1994. There are 197 parties to these amendments. At the Parties' Ninth Meeting at Montreal in September 1997, an amendment was adopted, which came into force on November 10, 1999. There are 194 parties to this amendment. At the Parties' Eleventh Meeting at Beijing in 1999, an amendment was adopted, which came into force on February 25, 2002. There are 188 parties to this amendment. The United States is a party to the Protocol and all the amendments. See the U.N. document Web site at <http://treaties.un.org> or the United Nations Environment Programme Ozone Secretariat at <http://ozone.unep.org>.

Determined to protect the ozone layer by taking precautionary measures to control equitably total global emissions of substances that deplete it, with the ultimate objective of their elimination on the basis of developments in scientific knowledge, taking into account technical and economic considerations and bearing in mind the developmental needs of developing countries,

Acknowledging that special provision is required to meet the needs of developing countries, including the provision of additional financial resources and access to relevant technologies, bearing in mind that the magnitude of funds necessary is predictable, and the funds can be expected to make a substantial difference in the world's ability to address the scientifically established problem of ozone depletion and its harmful effects,

Noting the precautionary measures for controlling emissions of certain chlorofluorocarbons that have already been taken at national and regional levels,

Considering the importance of promoting international cooperation in the research, development and transfer of alternative technologies relating to the control and reduction of emissions of substances that deplete the ozone layer, bearing in mind in particular the needs of developing countries,

HAVE AGREED AS FOLLOWS:

Article 1. Definitions

For the purposes of this Protocol:

1. "Convention" means the Vienna Convention for the Protection of the Ozone Layer, adopted on 22 March 1985.

2. "Parties" means, unless the text otherwise indicates, Parties to this Protocol.

3. "Secretariat" means the secretariat of the Convention.

4. "Controlled substance" means a substance listed in Annex A, Annex B, Annex C, or Annex E to this Protocol, whether existing alone or in a mixture. It includes the isomers of any such substance, except as specified in the relevant Annex, but excludes any controlled substance or mixture which is in a manufactured product other than a container used for the transportation or storage of that substance.

5. "Production" means the amount of controlled substances produced minus the amount destroyed by technologies to be approved by the Parties and minus the amount entirely used as feedstock in the manufacture of other chemicals. The amount recycled and reused is not to be considered as "production".

6. "Consumption" means production plus imports minus exports of controlled substances.

7. "Calculated levels" of production, imports, exports and consumption means levels determined in accordance with Article 3.

8. "Industrial rationalization" means the transfer of all or a portion of the calculated level of production of one Party to another, for the purpose of

achieving economic efficiencies or responding to anticipated shortfalls in supply as a result of plant closures.

Article 2. Control Measures . . .

5. Any Party may, for any one or more control periods, transfer to another Party any portion of its calculated level of production set out in Articles 2A to 2F and Article 2H, provided that the total combined calculated levels of production of the Parties concerned for any group of controlled substances do not exceed the production limits set out in those Articles for that group. Such transfer of production shall be notified to the Secretariat by each of the Parties concerned, stating the terms of such transfer and the period for which it is to apply.

5. *bis.* Any Party not operating under paragraph 1 of Article 5 may, for one or more control periods, transfer to another such Party any portion of its calculated level of consumption set out in Article 2F, provided that the calculated level of consumption of controlled substances in Group I of Annex A of the Party transferring the portion of its calculated level of consumption did not exceed 0.25 kilograms per capita in 1989 and that the total combined calculated levels of consumption of the Parties concerned do not exceed the consumption limits set out in Article 2F. Such transfer of consumption shall be notified to the Secretariat by each of the Parties concerned, stating the terms of such transfer and the period for which it is to apply.

6. Any Party not operating under Article 5, that has facilities for the production of Annex A or Annex B controlled substances under construction, or contracted for, prior to 16 September 1987, and provided for in national legislation prior to 1 January 1987, may add the production from such facilities to its 1986 production of such substances for the purposes of determining its calculated level of production for 1986, provided that such facilities are completed by 31 December 1990 and that such production does not raise that Party's annual calculated level of consumption of the controlled substances above 0.5 kilograms per capita.

7. Any transfer of production pursuant to paragraph 5 or any addition to production pursuant to paragraph 6 shall be notified to the secretariat, no later than the time of the transfer or addition.

8. (a) Any Parties which are Member States of a regional economic integration organization as defined in Article 1(6) of the Convention may agree that they shall jointly fulfill their obligations respecting consumption under this Article and Articles 2A to 2I provided that their total combined calculated level of consumption does not exceed the levels required by this Article and Articles 2A to 2I.

(b) The Parties to any such agreement shall inform the secretariat of the terms of the agreement before the date of the reduction in consumption with which the agreement is concerned.

(c) Such agreement will become operative only if all Member States of the regional economic integration organization and the organization concerned are Parties to the Protocol and have notified the secretariat of their manner of implementation.

9. (a) Based on the assessments made pursuant to Article 6, the Parties may decide whether:

(i) Adjustments to the ozone depleting potentials specified in Annex A, Annex B, Annex C and/or Annex E should be made, and, if so, what the adjustments should be; and

(ii) Further adjustments and reductions of production or consumption of the controlled substances should be undertaken and, if so, what the scope, amount and timing of any such adjustments and reductions should be;

(b) Proposals for such adjustments shall be communicated to the Parties by the secretariat at least six months before the meeting of the Parties at which they are proposed for adoption;

(c) In taking such decisions, the Parties shall make every effort to reach agreement by consensus. If all efforts at consensus have been exhausted, and no agreement reached, such decisions shall, as a last resort, be adopted by a two-thirds majority vote of the Parties present and voting representing a majority of the Parties operating under paragraph 1 of Article 5 present and voting and a majority of Parties not so operating present and voting.

(d) The decisions, which shall be binding on all Parties, shall forthwith be communicated to the Parties by the Depositary. Unless otherwise provided in the decisions, they shall enter into force on the expiry of six months from the date of the circulation of the communication by the Depositary.

10. Based on the assessments made pursuant to Article 6 of this Protocol and in accordance with the procedure set out in Article 9 of the Convention, the Parties may decide:

(a) whether any substances, and if so which, should be added to or removed from any annex to this Protocol; and

(b) the mechanism, scope and timing of the control measures that should apply to those substances.

11. Notwithstanding the provisions contained in this Article and Articles 2A to 2I, Parties may take more stringent measures than those required by this Article and Articles 2A to 2I.

Article 2A. CFCs

1. Each Party shall ensure that for the twelve-month period commencing on the first day of the seventh month following the date of the entry into force of this Protocol, and in each twelve-month period thereafter, its calculated level of consumption of the controlled substances in Group I of Annex A does not exceed its calculated level of consumption in 1986. By the end of the same period, each Party producing one or more of these substances shall ensure that its calculated level of production of the substances

does not exceed its calculated level of production in 1986, except that such level may have increased by no more than ten per cent based on the 1986 level. Such increase shall be permitted only so as to satisfy the basic domestic needs of the Parties operating under Article 5 and for the purposes of industrial rationalization between Parties.

2. Each Party shall ensure that for the period from 1 July 1991 to 31 December 1992 its calculated levels of consumption and production of the controlled substances in Group I of Annex A do not exceed 150 per cent of its calculated levels of production and consumption of those substances in 1986. . . .

3. Each Party shall ensure that for the twelve-month period commencing on 1 January 1994, and in each twelve-month period thereafter, its calculated level of consumption of the controlled substances in Group I of Annex A does not exceed, annually, twenty-five per cent of its calculated level of consumption in 1986. . . .

4. Each Party shall ensure that for the twelve-month period commencing on 1 January 1996, and in each twelve-month period thereafter, its calculated level of consumption of the controlled substances in Group I of Annex A does not exceed zero. . . .

5. Each Party shall ensure that for the twelve-month period commencing on 1 January 2003, and in each twelve-month period thereafter, its calculated level of production of the controlled substances in Group I of Annex A for the basic domestic needs of the Parties operating under paragraph 1 of Article 5 does not exceed eighty per cent of the annual average of its production of those substances for basic domestic needs for the period 1995 to 1997 inclusive.

6. Each Party shall ensure that for the twelve-month period commencing on 1 January 2005, and in each twelve-month period thereafter, its calculated level of production of the controlled substances in Group I of Annex A for the basic domestic needs of the Parties operating under paragraph 1 of Article 5 does not exceed fifty per cent of the annual average of its production of those substances for basic domestic needs for the period 1995 to 1997 inclusive.

7. Each Party shall ensure that for the twelve-month period commencing on 1 January 2007, and in each twelve-month period thereafter, its calculated level of production of the controlled substances in Group I of Annex A for the basic domestic needs of the Parties operating under paragraph 1 of Article 5 does not exceed fifteen per cent of the annual average of its production of those substances for basic domestic needs for the period 1995 to 1997 inclusive.

8. Each Party shall ensure that for the twelve-month period commencing on 1 January 2010, and in each twelve-month period thereafter, its calculated level of production of the controlled substances in Group I of Annex A for the basic domestic needs of the Parties operating under paragraph 1 of Article 5 does not exceed zero. . . .

Article 2B. Halons

1. Each Party shall ensure that for the twelve-month period commencing on 1 January 1992, and in each twelve-month period thereafter, its calculated level of consumption of the controlled substances in Group II of Annex A does not exceed, annually, its calculated level of consumption in 1986. . . .

3. Each Party shall ensure that for the twelve-month period commencing on 1 January 2005, and in each twelve-month period thereafter, its calculated level of production of the controlled substances in Group II of Annex A for the basic domestic needs of the Parties operating under paragraph 1 of Article 5 does not exceed fifty per cent of the annual average of its production of those substances for basic domestic needs for the period 1995 to 1997 inclusive.

4. Each Party shall ensure that for the twelve-month period commencing on 1 January 2010, and in each twelve-month period thereafter, its calculated level of production of the controlled substances in Group II of Annex A for the basic domestic needs of the Parties operating under paragraph 1 of Article 5 does not exceed zero.

Article 2C. Other Fully Halogenated CFCs

1. Each Party shall ensure that for the twelve-month period commencing on 1 January 1993, and in each twelve-month period thereafter, its calculated level of consumption of the controlled substances in Group I of Annex B does not exceed, annually, eighty per cent of its calculated level of consumption in 1989. . . .

2. Each Party shall ensure that for the twelve-month period commencing on 1 January 1994, and in each twelve-month period thereafter, its calculated level of consumption of the controlled substances in Group I of Annex B does not exceed, annually, twenty-five per cent of its calculated level of consumption in 1989. . . .

3. Each Party shall ensure that for the twelve-month period commencing on 1 January 1996, and in each twelve-month period thereafter, its calculated level of consumption of the controlled substances in Group I of Annex B does not exceed zero. Each Party producing one or more of these substances shall, for the same periods, ensure that its calculated level of production of the substances does not exceed zero. However, in order to satisfy the basic domestic needs of the Parties operating under paragraph 1 of Article 5, its calculated level of production may exceed that limit by up to fifteen per cent of its calculated level of production in 1989. . . .

4. Each party shall ensure that for the twelve-month period commencing on 1 January 2007, and in each twelve-month period thereafter, its calculated level of production of the controlled substances in Group I of Annex B for the basic domestic needs of the Parties operating under paragraph 1 of Article 5 does not exceed fifteen per cent of the annual average of

its production of those substances for basic domestic needs for the period 1998 to 2000 inclusive.

5. Each Party shall ensure that for the twelve-month period commencing on 1 January 2010, and in each twelve-month period thereafter, its calculated level of production of the controlled substances in Group I of Annex B for the basic domestic needs of the Parties operating under paragraph 1 of Article 5 does not exceed zero.

Article 2D.   Carbon Tetrachloride

1. Each Party shall ensure that for the twelve-month period commencing on 1 January 1995, its calculated level of consumption of the controlled substances in Group II of Annex B does not exceed, annually, fifteen per cent of its calculated level of consumption in 1989. Each Party producing the substance shall, for the same period, ensure that its calculated level of production of the substance does not exceed, annually, fifteen per cent of its calculated level of production in 1989. However, in order to satisfy the basic domestic needs of the Parties operating under paragraph 1 of Article 5, its calculated level of production may exceed that limit by up to ten per cent of its calculated level of production in 1989.

2. Each Party shall ensure that for the twelve-month period commencing on 1 January 1996, and in each twelve-month period thereafter, its calculated level of consumption of the controlled substances in Group II of Annex B does not exceed zero. Each Party producing the substance shall, for the same periods, ensure that its calculated level of production of the substance does not exceed zero. However, in order to satisfy the basic domestic needs of the Parties operating under paragraph 1 of Article 5, its calculated level of production may exceed that limit by up to fifteen per cent of its calculated level of production in 1989. This paragraph will apply save to the extent that the Parties decide to permit the level of production or consumption that is necessary to satisfy uses agreed by them to be essential.

Article 2E.   1,1,1-Trichloroethane (Methyl Chloroform)

1. Each Party shall ensure that for the twelve-month period commencing on 1 January 1993, its calculated level of consumption of the controlled substance in Group III of Annex B does not exceed, annually, its calculated level of consumption in 1989. . . .

2. Each Party shall ensure that for the twelve-month period commencing on 1 January 1994, and in each twelve-month period thereafter, its calculated level of consumption of the controlled substance in Group III of Annex B does not exceed, annually, fifty per cent of its calculated level of consumption in 1989. . . .

3. Each Party shall ensure that for the twelve-month period commencing on 1 January 1996, and in each twelve-month period thereafter, its calculated level of consumption of the controlled substance in Group III of Annex B does not exceed zero. Each Party producing the substance shall, for

the same periods, ensure that its calculated level of production of the substance does not exceed zero. However, in order to satisfy the basic domestic needs of the Parties operating under paragraph 1 of Article 5, its calculated level of production may exceed that limit by up to fifteen per cent of its calculated level of production for 1989. This paragraph will apply save to the extent that the Parties decide to permit the level of production or consumption that is necessary to satisfy uses agreed by them to be essential.

Article 2F. *Hydrochlorofluorocarbons*

1. Each Party shall ensure that for the twelve-month period commencing on 1 January 1996, and in each twelve-month period thereafter, its calculated level of consumption of the controlled substances in Group I of Annex C does not exceed, annually, the sum of:

(a) 3.1 percent of its calculated level of consumption in 1989 of the controlled substances in Group I of Annex A; and

(b) Its calculated level of consumption in 1989 of the controlled substances in Group I of Annex C.

2. Each Party shall ensure that for the twelve-month period commencing on 1 January 2004, and in each twelve-month period thereafter, its calculated level of consumption of the controlled substances in Group I of Annex C does not exceed, annually, sixty-five per cent of the sum referred to in paragraph 1 of this Article.

3. Each Party shall ensure that for the twelve-month period commencing on 1 January 2010, and in each twelve-month period thereafter, its calculated level of consumption of the controlled substances in Group I of Annex C does not exceed, annually, thirty-five per cent of the sum referred to in paragraph 1 of this Article.

4. Each Party shall ensure that for the twelve-month period commencing on 1 January 2015, and in each twelve-month period thereafter, its calculated level of consumption of the controlled substances in Group I of Annex C does not exceed, annually, ten per cent of the sum referred to in paragraph 1 of this Article.

5. Each Party shall ensure that for the twelve-month period commencing on 1 January 2020, and in each twelve-month period thereafter, its calculated level of consumption of the controlled substances in Group I of Annex C does not exceed, annually, zero point five (0.5) percent of the sum referred to in paragraph 1 of this Article.

6. Each Party shall ensure that for the twelve-month period commencing on 1 January 2030, and in each twelve-month period thereafter, its calculated level of consumption of the controlled substances in Group I of Annex C does not exceed zero.

7. As of 1 January 1996, each Party shall endeavour to ensure that:

(a) The use of controlled substances in Group I of Annex C is limited to those applications where other more environmentally suitable alternative substances or technologies are not available;

(b) The use of controlled substances in Group I of Annex C is not outside the areas of application currently met by controlled substances in Annexes A, B and C, except in rare cases for the protection of human life or human health; and

(c) Controlled substances in Group I of Annex C are selected for use in a manner that minimizes ozone depletion, in addition to meeting other environmental, safety and economic considerations.

8. Each Party producing one or more of these substances shall ensure that for the twelve-month period commencing on 1 January 2004, and in each twelve-month period thereafter, its calculated level of production of the controlled substances in Group I of Annex C does not exceed, annually, the average of:

(a) The sum of its calculated level of consumption in 1989 of the controlled substances in Group I of Annex C and two point eight per cent of its calculated level of consumption in 1989 and of the controlled substances in Group I of Annex A; and

(b) The sum of its calculated level of production in 1989 of the controlled substances in Group I of Annex C and two point eight per cent of its calculated level of production in 1989 of the controlled substance in Group I of Annex A.

However, in order the satisfy the basic domestic needs of the Parties operating under paragraph 1 of Article 5, its calculated level of production may exceed that limit by up to fifteen per cent of its calculated level of production of the controlled substances in Group I of Annex C as defined above.

Article 2G.   Hydrobromofluorocarbons

Each Party shall ensure that for the twelve-month period commencing on 1 January 1996, and in each twelve-month period thereafter, its calculated level of consumption of the controlled substances in Group II of Annex C does not exceed zero. Each Party producing the substances shall, for the same periods, ensure that its calculated level of production of the substances does not exceed zero. This paragraph will apply save to the extent that the Parties decide to permit the level of production or consumption that is necessary to satisfy uses agreed by them to be essential.

Article 2H.   Methyl Bromide . . .

Article 2I.   Bromochloromethane . . .

Article 3.   Calculation of Control Levels

For the purposes of Articles 2, 2A to 2I, and 5, each Party shall, for each group of substances in Annex A, Annex B, Annex C or Annex E determine its calculated level of:

(a) Production by:

(i) Multiplying its annual production of each controlled substance by the ozone depleting potential specified in respect of it in Annex A, Annex B, Annex C or Annex E; and

(ii) Adding together, for each such group, the resulting figures;

(b) Imports and exports, respectively, by following, *mutatis mutandis,* the procedure set out in sub-paragraph (a); and

(c) Consumption by adding together its calculated levels of production and imports and subtracting its calculated level of exports as determined in accordance with subparagraphs (a) and (b). However, beginning on 1 January 1993, any export of controlled substances to non-Parties shall not be subtracted in calculating the consumption level of the exporting Party.

Article 4. *Control of Trade with Non-Parties*

1. As of 1 January 1990, each Party shall ban the import of the controlled substances in Annex A from any State not party to this Protocol.

1. *bis.* Within one year of the date of the entry into force of this paragraph, each Party shall ban the import of the controlled substances in Annex B from any State not party to this Protocol.

1. *ter.* Within one year of the date of entry into force of this paragraph, each Party shall ban the import of any controlled substances in Group II of Annex C from any State not party to this Protocol.

1. *qua.* Within one year of the date of entry into force of this paragraph, each Party shall ban the import of the controlled substance in Annex E from any State not party to the Protocol.

1. *quin.* As of January 1, 2004, each Party shall ban the import of the controlled substances in Group I of Annex C from any State not party to this Protocol.

1. *sex.* Within one year of the date of entry into force of this paragraph, each Party shall ban the import of the controlled substance in Group III of Annex C from any State not party to this Protocol.

2. As of 1 January 1993, each party shall ban the export of any controlled substances in Annex A to any State not party to this Protocol.

2. *bis.* Commencing one year after the date of entry into force of this paragraph, each Party shall ban the export of any controlled substances in Annex B to any State not party to this Protocol.

2. *ter.* Commencing one year after the date of entry into force of this paragraph, each Party shall ban the export of any controlled substances in Group II of Annex C to any State not party to this Protocol.

2. *qua.* Commencing one year after the date of entry into force of this paragraph, each Party shall ban the export of the controlled substance in Annex E to any State not party to this Protocol.

2. *quin.* As of 1 January 2004, each Party shall ban the export of the controlled substances in Group I of Annex C to any State not party to this Protocol.

2. *sex.* Within one year of the date of entry into force of this paragraph, each Party shall ban the export of the controlled substance in Group III of Annex C to any State not party to this Protocol.

3. By 1 January 1992, the Parties shall, following the procedures in Article 10 of the Convention, elaborate in an annex a list of products containing controlled substances in Annex A. Parties that have not objected to the annex in accordance with those procedures shall ban, within one year of the annex having become effective, the import of those products from any State not party to this Protocol.

3. *bis.* Within three years of the date of the entry into force of this paragraph, the Parties shall, following the procedures in Article 10 of the Convention, elaborate in an annex a list of products containing controlled substances in Annex B. Parties that have not objected to the annex in accordance with those procedures shall ban, within one year of the annex having become effective, the import of those products from any State not party to this Protocol.

3. *ter.* Within three years of the date of entry into force of this paragraph, the Parties shall, following the procedures in Article 10 of the Convention, elaborate in an annex a list of products containing controlled substances in Group II of Annex C. Parties that have not objected to the annex in accordance with those procedures shall ban, within one year of the annex having become effective, the import of those products from any State not party to this Protocol.

4. By 1 January 1994, the Parties shall determine the feasibility of banning or restricting, from States not party to this Protocol, the import of products produced with, but not containing, controlled substances in Annex A. If determined feasible, the Parties shall, following the procedures in Article 10 of the Convention, elaborate in an annex a list of such products. Parties that have not objected to the annex in accordance with those procedures shall ban, within one year of the annex having become effective, the import of those products from any State not party to this Protocol.

4. *bis.* Within five years of the date of the entry into force of this paragraph, the Parties shall determine the feasibility of banning or restricting, from States not party to this Protocol, the import of products produced with, but not containing, controlled substances in Annex B. If determined feasible, the Parties shall, following the procedures in Article 10 of the Convention, elaborate in an annex a list of such products. Parties that have not objected to the annex in accordance with those procedures shall ban or restrict, within one year of the annex having become effective, the import of those products from any State not party to this Protocol.

4. *ter.* Within five years of the date of entry into force of this paragraph, the Parties shall determine feasibility of banning or restricting, from States not party to this Protocol, the import of products produced with, but not containing, controlled substances in Group II of Annex C. If determined feasible, the Parties shall, following the procedures in Article 10 of the Convention, elaborate in an annex a list of such products. Parties that have not objected to the annex in accordance with those procedures shall ban or restrict, within one year of the annex having become effective, the import of those products from any State not party to this Protocol.

5. Each Party undertakes to the fullest practicable extent to discourage the export to any State not party to this Protocol of technology for producing or utilizing controlled substances in Annexes A, B, C and E.

6. Each Party shall refrain from providing new subsidies, aid, credits, guarantees or insurance programmes for the export to States not party to this Protocol of products, equipment, plants or technology that would facilitate the production of controlled substances in Annexes A, B, C and E.

7. Paragraphs 5 and 6 shall not apply to products, equipment, plants or technology that improve the containment, recovery, recycling, or destruction of controlled substances, promote the development of alternative substances, or otherwise contribute to the reduction of emissions of controlled substances in Annexes A, B, C and E.

8. Notwithstanding the provisions of this Article, imports and exports referred to in paragraphs 1 to 4 *ter* of this Article may be permitted from, or to, any State not party to this Protocol, if that State is determined by a meeting of the Parties to be in full compliance with Article 2, Articles 2A to 2I, and this Article and have submitted data to that effect as specified in Article 7.

9. For the purposes of this Article, the term "State not party to this Protocol" shall include, with respect to a particular controlled substance, a State or regional economic integration organization that has not agreed to be bound by the control measures in effect for that substance.

10. By 1 January 1996, the Parties shall consider whether to amend this Protocol in order to extend the measures in this Article to trade in controlled substances in Group I of Annex C and in Annex E with States not party to the Protocol.

Article 4A.   *Control of Trade with Parties*

1. Where, after the phase-out date applicable to it for a controlled substance, a Party is unable, despite having taken all practicable steps to comply with its obligations under the Protocol, to cease production of that substance for domestic consumption, other than for uses agreed by the Parties to be essential, it shall ban the export of used, recycled and reclaimed quantities of that substance, other than for the purpose of destruction.

2. Paragraph 1 of this Article shall apply without prejudice to the operation of Article 11 of the Convention and the non-compliance procedure developed under Article 8 of the Protocol.

Article 4B.   *Licensing*

1. Each Party shall, by 1 January 2000, or within three months of the date of entry into force of this Article for it, whichever is the later, establish and implement a system for licensing the import and export of new, used, recycled and reclaimed controlled substances in Annexes A, B, C and E.

2. Notwithstanding paragraph 1 of this Article, any Party operating under paragraph 1 of Article 5 which decides it is not in a position to

establish and implement a system for licensing the import and export of controlled substances in Annexes C and E, may delay taking those actions until 1 January 2005, and 1 January 2002, respectively.

3. Each Party shall, within three months of the date of introducing its licensing system, report to the Secretariat on the establishment and operation of that system.

4. The Secretariat shall periodically prepare and circulate to all Parties a list of the Parties that have reported to it on their licensing systems and shall forward this information to the Implementation Committee for consideration and appropriate recommendations to the Parties.

Article 5. Special Situation of Developing Countries

1. Any Party that is a developing country and whose annual calculated level of consumption of the controlled substances in Annex A is less than 0.3 kilograms per capita on the date of the entry into force of the Protocol for it, or any time thereafter until 1 January 1999, shall, in order to meet its basic domestic needs, be entitled to delay for ten years its compliance with the control measures set out in Articles 2A to 2E, provided that any further amendments to the adjustments or amendments adopted at the Second Meeting of the Parties in London, 29 June 1990, shall apply to the Parties operating under this paragraph after the review provided for in paragraph 8 of this Article has taken place and shall be based on the conclusions of that review.

1. bis. The Parties shall, taking into account the review referred to in paragraph 8 of this Article, the assessments made pursuant to Article 6 and any other relevant information, decide by 1 January 1996, through the procedure set forth in paragraph 9 of Article 2:

(a) With respect to paragraphs 1 to 6 of Article 2F, what base year, initial levels, control schedules and phase-out date for consumption of the controlled substances in Group I of Annex C will apply to Parties operating under paragraph 1 of this Article;

(b) With respect to Article 2G, what phase-out date for production and consumption of the controlled substances in Group II of Annex C will apply to Parties operating under paragraph 1 of this Article; and

(c) With respect to Article 2H, what base year, initial levels and control schedules for consumption and production of the controlled substance in Annex E will apply to Parties operating under paragraph 1 of this Article.

2. However, any Party operating under paragraph 1 of this Article shall exceed neither an annual calculated level of consumption of the controlled substances in Annex A of 0.3 kilograms per capita nor an annual calculated level of consumption of the controlled substances of Annex B of 0.2 kilograms per capita.

3. When implementing the control measures set out in Articles 2A to 2E, any Party operating under paragraph 1 of this Article shall be entitled to use:

(a) For controlled substances under Annex A, either the average of its annual calculated level of consumption for the period 1995 to 1997 inclusive or a calculated level of consumption of 0.3 kilograms per capita, whichever is the lower, as the basis for determining its compliance with the control measures relating to consumption. . . .

(c) For controlled substances under Annex A, either the average of its annual calculated level of production for the period 1995 to 1997 inclusive or a calculated level of production of 0.3 kilograms per capita, whichever is lower, as the basis for determining its compliance with the control measures relating to production. . . .

4. If a Party operating under paragraph 1 of this Article, at any time before the control measures obligations in Articles 2A to 2I become applicable to it, finds itself unable to obtain an adequate supply of controlled substances, it may notify this to the Secretariat. The Secretariat shall forthwith transmit a copy of such notification to the Parties, which shall consider the matter at their next Meeting, and decide upon appropriate action to be taken.

5. Developing the capacity to fulfill the obligations of the Parties operating under paragraph 1 of Article 5 to comply with the control measures set out in Articles 2A to 2E and Article 2I, and any control measures in Articles 2F to 2H that are decided pursuant to paragraph 1 *bis* of this Article, and their implementation by those same Parties will depend upon the effective implementation of the financial co-operation as provided by Article 10 and transfer of technology as provided by Article 10A.

6. Any Party operating under paragraph 1 of this article may, at any time, notify the Secretariat in writing that, having taken all practicable steps, it is unable to implement any or all of the obligations laid down in Articles 2A to 2E and Article 2I, or any or all obligations in Articles 2F to 2H that are decided pursuant to paragraph 1 *bis* of this Article, due to the inadequate implementation of Articles 10 and 10A. The Secretariat shall forthwith transmit a copy of the notification to the Parties, which shall consider the matter at their next Meeting, giving due recognition to paragraph 5 of this Article, and shall decide upon appropriate action to be taken.

7. During the period between notification and the Meeting of the Parties at which the appropriate action referred to in paragraph 6 of this Article is to be decided, or for a further period, if the Meeting of Parties so decides, the non-compliance procedures referred to in Article 8 shall not be invoked against the notifying Party. . . .

9. Decisions of the Parties referred to in paragraphs 4, 6 and 7 of this Article shall be taken according to the same procedure applied to decision-making under Article 10.

Article 6. Assessment and Review of Control Measures

Beginning in 1990, and at least every four years thereafter, the Parties shall assess the control measures provided for in Article 2 and Articles 2A to 2I, on the basis of available scientific, environmental, technical and economic information. At least one year before each assessment, the Parties shall convene appropriate panels of experts qualified in the fields mentioned and determine the composition and terms of reference of any such panels. Within one year of being convened, the panels will report their conclusions, through the secretariat, to the Parties.

Article 7. Reporting of Data

1. Each Party shall provide to the Secretariat, within three months of becoming a Party, statistical data on its production, imports and exports of each of the controlled substances in Annex A for the year 1986, or the best possible estimates of such data where actual data arc not available.

2. Each Party shall provide to the Secretariat statistical data on its production, imports and exports of each of the controlled substances

—in Annexes B and Groups I and II of Annex C, for the year 1989;

—in Annex E, for the year 1991

or the best possible estimates of such data where actual data are not available, not later than three months after the date when the provisions set out in the Protocol with regard to the substances in Annexes B, C and E respectively enter into force for that Party.

3. Each Party shall provide to the Secretariat statistical data on its annual production (as defined in paragraph 5 of Article 1) of each of the controlled substances listed in Annexes A, B, C and E and, separately, for each substance,

—Amounts used for feedstocks,

—Amounts destroyed by technologies approved by the Parties, and

—Imports from and exports to Parties and non-Parties respectively, for the year during which provisions concerning the substances in Annexes A, B, C and E respectively entered into force for that Party and for each year thereafter . . . . Data shall be forwarded not later than nine months after the end of the year to which the data relate.

3. *bis.* Each Party shall provide to the Secretariat separate statistical data of its annual imports and exports of each of the controlled substances listed in Group II of Annex A and Group 1 of Annex C that have been recycled.

4. For Parties operating under the provisions of paragraph 8(a) of Article 2, the requirements in paragraphs 1, 2, 3 and 3 *bis* of this Article in respect of statistical data on imports and exports shall be satisfied if the regional economic integration organization concerned provides data on imports and exports between the organization and States that are not members of that organization.

Article 8. Non-Compliance

The Parties, at their first meeting, shall consider and approve procedures and institutional mechanisms for determining noncompliance with the provisions of this Protocol and for treatment of Parties found to be in non-compliance.

Article 9. Research, Development, Public Awareness and Exchange of Information

1. The Parties shall cooperate, consistent with their national laws, regulations and practices and taking into account in particular the needs of developing countries, in promoting, directly or through competent international bodies, research, development and exchange of information on:

(a) Best technologies for improving the containment, recovery, recycling or destruction of controlled substances or otherwise reducing their emissions;

(b) Possible alternatives to controlled substances, to products containing such substances, and to products manufactured with them; and

(c) Costs and benefits of relevant control strategies.

2. The Parties, individually, jointly or through competent international bodies, shall cooperate in promoting public awareness of the environmental effects of the emissions of controlled substances and other substances that deplete the ozone layer.

3. Within two years of the entry into force of this Protocol and every two years thereafter, each Party shall submit to the secretariat a summary of the activities it has conducted pursuant to this Article.

Article 10. Financial Mechanism

1. The Parties shall establish a mechanism for the purposes of providing financial and technical cooperation, including the transfer of technologies, to Parties operating under paragraph 1 of Article 5 of this Protocol to enable their compliance with the control measures set out in Articles 2A to 2E and Article 2I, and any control measures in Articles 2F to 2H that arc decided pursuant to paragraph 1 *bis* of Article 5. The mechanism, contributions to which shall be additional to other financial transfers to Parties operating under that paragraph, shall meet all agreed incremental costs of such Parties in order to enable their compliance with the control measures of the Protocol. An indicative list of the categories of incremental costs shall be decided by the meeting of the Parties.

2. The mechanism established under paragraph 1 shall include a Multilateral Fund. It may also include other means of multilateral, regional and bilateral cooperation.

3. The Multilateral Fund shall:

(a) Meet, on a grant or concessional basis as appropriate, and according to criteria to be decided upon by the Parties, the agreed incremental costs;

(b) Finance clearing-house functions to:

(i) Assist Parties operating under paragraph 1 of Article 5, through country specific studies and other technical co-operation, to identify their needs for cooperation;

(ii) Facilitate technical co-operation to meet these identified needs;

(iii) Distribute, as provided for in Article 9, information and relevant materials, and hold workshops, training sessions, and other related activities, for the benefit of Parties that are developing countries; and

(iv) Facilitate and monitor other multilateral, regional and bilateral co-operation available to Parties that are developing countries.

(c) Finance the secretarial services of the Multilateral Fund and related support costs.

4. The Multilateral Fund shall operate under the authority of the Parties who shall decide on its overall policies.

5. The Parties shall establish an Executive Committee to develop and monitor the implementation of specific operational policies, guidelines and administrative arrangements, including the disbursement of resources, for the purpose of achieving the objectives of the Multilateral Fund. The Executive Committee shall discharge its tasks and responsibilities, specified in its terms of reference as agreed by the Parties, with the cooperation and assistance of the International Bank for Reconstruction and Development (World Bank), the United Nations Environment Programme, the United Nations Development Programme or other appropriate agencies depending on their respective areas of expertise. The members of the Executive Committee, which shall be selected on the basis of balanced representation of the Parties operating under paragraph 1 of Article 5 and of the Parties not so operating, shall be endorsed by the Parties.

6. The Multilateral Fund shall be financed by contributions from Parties not operating under paragraph 1 of Article 5 in convertible currency or, in certain circumstances, in kind and/or in national currency, on the basis of the United Nations scale of assessments. Contributions by other Parties shall be encouraged. Bilateral and, in particular cases agreed by a decision of the Parties, regional co-operation may, up to a percentage and consistent with any criteria to be specified by decision of the Parties, be considered as a contribution to the Multilateral Fund, provided that such co-operation, as a minimum:

(a) Strictly relates to compliance with the provisions of this Protocol;

(b) Provides additional resources; and

(c) Meets agreed incremental costs.

7. The Parties shall decide upon the programme budget of the Multilateral Fund for each fiscal period and upon the percentage of contributions of the individual Parties thereto.

8. Resources under the Multilateral Fund shall be disbursed with the concurrence of the beneficiary Party.

9. Decisions by the Parties under this Article shall be taken by consensus whenever possible. If all efforts at consensus have been exhausted and no agreement reached, decisions shall be adopted by a two-thirds majority of the Parties present and voting, representing a majority of the Parties operating under paragraph 1 of Article 5 present and voting and a majority of the Parties not so operating present and voting.

10. The financial mechanism set out in this Article is without prejudice to any other future arrangements that may be developed with respect to other environmental issues.

Article 10A.   Transfer of Technology

Each Party shall take every practicable step, consistent with the programmes supported by the financial mechanism, to ensure:

(a) That the best available, environmentally safe substitutes and related technologies are expeditiously transferred to Parties operating under paragraph 1 of Article 5, and

(b) That such transfers referred to in subparagraph (a) occur under fair and most favourable conditions.

Article 11.   Meeting of the Parties

1. The Parties shall hold meetings at regular intervals. The secretariat shall convene the first meeting of the Parties not later than one year after the date of the entry into force of this Protocol and in conjunction with a meeting of the Conference of the Parties to the Convention, if a meeting of the latter is scheduled within that period.

2. Subsequent ordinary meetings of the parties shall be held, unless the Parties otherwise decide, in conjunction with meetings of the Conference of the Parties to the Convention. Extraordinary meetings of the Parties shall be held at such other times as may be deemed necessary by a meeting of the Parties, or at the written request of any Party, provided that, within six months of such a request being communicated to them by the secretariat, it is supported by at least one third of the Parties.

3. The Parties, at their first meeting, shall:

(a) Adopt by consensus rules of procedure for their meetings;

(b) Adopt by consensus the financial rules referred to in paragraph 2 of Article 13;

(c) Establish the panels and determine the terms of reference referred to in Article 6;

(d) Consider and approve the procedures and institutional mechanisms specified in Article 8; and

(e) Begin preparation of workplans pursuant to paragraph 3 of Article 10.

4. The functions of the meeting of the Parties shall be to:

(a) Review the implementation of this Protocol;

(b) Decide on any adjustments or reductions referred to in paragraph 9 of Article 2;

(c) Decide on any addition to, insertion in or removal from any annex of substances and on related control measures in accordance with paragraph 10 of Article 2;

(d) Establish, where necessary, guidelines or procedures for reporting of information as provided for in Article 7 and paragraph 3 of Article 9;

(e) Review requests for technical assistance submitted pursuant to sub-paragraph (c) of Article 12;

(f) Review reports prepared by the secretariat pursuant to subparagraph (c) of Article 12;

(g) Assess, in accordance with Article 6, the control measures;

(h) Consider and adopt, as required, proposals for amendment of this Protocol or any annex and for any new annex;

(i) Consider and adopt the budget for implementing this Protocol; and

(j) Consider and undertake any additional action that may be required for the achievement of the purposes of this Protocol.

5. The United Nations, its specialized agencies and the International Atomic Energy Agency, as well as any State not party to this Protocol, may be represented at meetings of the Parties as observers. Any body or agency, whether national or international, governmental or non-governmental, qualified in fields relating to the protection of the ozone layer which has informed the secretariat of its wish to be represented at a meeting of the Parties as an observer may be admitted unless at least one third of the Parties present object The admission and participation of observers shall be subject to the rules of procedure adopted by the Parties.

Article 12. Secretariat

For the purposes of this Protocol, the secretariat shall:

(a) Arrange for and service meetings of the Parties as provided for in Article 11;

(b) Receive and make available, upon request by a Party, data provided pursuant to Article 7;

(c) Prepare and distribute regularly to the Parties reports based on information received pursuant to Articles 7 and 9;

(d) Notify the Parties of any request for technical assistance received pursuant to Article 10 so as to facilitate the provision of this Protocol;

(e) Encourage non-Parties to attend the meetings of the Parties as observers and to act in accordance with the provisions of this Protocol;

(f) Provide, as appropriate, the information and requests referred to in subparagraphs (c) and (d) to such non-party observers; and

(g) Perform such other functions for the achievement of the purposes of this Protocol as may be assigned to it by the Parties.

Article 13. Financial Provisions

1. The Funds required for the operation of this Protocol, including those for the functioning of the secretariat related to this Protocol, shall be charged exclusively against contributions from the Parties.

2. The Parties, at their first meeting, shall adopt by consensus financial rules for the operation of this Protocol.

Article 14. Relationship of this Protocol to the Convention

Except as otherwise provided in this Protocol, the provisions of the Convention relating to its protocols shall apply to this Protocol.

Article 15. Signature . . .

Article 16. Entry into Force

1. This Protocol shall enter into force on 1 January 1989, provided that at least eleven instruments of ratification, acceptance, approval of the Protocol or accession thereto have been deposited by States or regional economic integration organizations representing at least two-thirds of 1986 estimated global consumption of the controlled substances, and the provisions of paragraph 1 of Article 17 of the Convention have been fulfilled. In the event that these conditions have not been fulfilled by that date, the Protocol shall enter into force on the ninetieth day following the date on which the conditions have been fulfilled.

2. For the purposes of paragraph 1, any such instrument deposited by a regional economic integration organization shall not be counted as additional to those deposited by member States of such organization.

3. After the entry into force of this Protocol, any State or regional economic integration organization shall become a Party to it on the ninetieth day following the date of deposit of its instrument of ratification, acceptance, approval or accession.

Article 17. Parties Joining After Entry into Force

Subject to Article 5, any State or regional economic integration organization which becomes a Party to this Protocol after the date of its entry into force, shall fulfill forthwith the sum of the obligations under Article 2, as well as under Articles 2A to 2I, and Article 4, that apply at that date to the States and regional economic integration organizations that became Parties on the date the Protocol entered into force.

Article 18. Reservations

No reservations may be made to this Protocol.

Article 19. Withdrawal

Any Party may withdraw from this Protocol by giving written notification to the Depositary at any time after four years of assuming the obligations specified in paragraph 1 of Article 2A. Any such withdrawal shall take effect upon expiry of one year after the date of its receipt by the Depositary, or on such later date as may be specified in the notification of the withdrawal. . . .

Annex A.   Controlled Substances

Group	Substance	Ozone Depleting Potential*
Group I		
$CFCl_3$	(CFC-11)	1.0
CF_2Cl_2	(CFC-12)	1.0
$C_2F_3Cl_3$	(CFC-113)	0.8
$C_2F_4Cl_2$	(CFC-114)	1.0
C_2F_6Cl	(CFC-115)	0.6
Group II		
CF_2BrCl	(halon-1211)	3.0
CF_3Br	(halon-1301)	10.0
$C_2F_4Br_2$	(halon-2402)	6.0

*These ozone depleting potentials are estimates based on existing knowledge and will be reviewed and revised periodically.

Annex B.   Controlled Substances

Group	Substance	Ozone-Depleting Potential
Group I		
CF_3Cl	(CFC-13)	1.0
C_2FCl_5	(CFC-111)	1.0
$C_2F_2Cl_4$	(CFC-112)	1.0
C_3FCl_7	(CFC-211)	1.0
$C_3F_2Cl_6$	(CFC-212)	1.0
$C_3F_3Cl_5$	(CFC-213)	1.0
$C_3F_4Cl_4$	(CFC-214)	1.0
$C_3F_5Cl_3$	(CFC-215)	1.0
$C_3F_6Cl_2$	(CFC-216)	1.0
C_3F_7Cl	(CFC-217)	1.0
Group II		
CCl_4	carbon tetrachloride	1.1
Group III		
$C_2H_3Cl_3$*	1,1,1-trichloroethane (methyl chloroform)	0.1

*This formula does not refer to 1,1,2-trichloroethane.

Annex C.   Controlled Substances

Group	Substance	Number of Isomers	Ozone Depleting Potential*
Group I			
$CHFCl_2$	(HCFC-21)**	1	0.04
CHF_2Cl	(HCFC-22)**	1	0.055
CH_2FCl	(HCFC-31)	1	0.02
C_2HFCl_4	(HCFC-121)	2	0.01-0.04
$C_2HF_2Cl_3$	(HCFC-122)	3	0.02-0.08
$C_2HF_3Cl_2$	(HCFC-123)	3	0.02-0.06
$CHCl_2CF_3$	(HCFC-123)**	—	0.02
C_2HF_4Cl	(HCFC-124)	2	0.02-0.04

[Thirty-two more substances were on this List for Group I—EDS.]

Group	Substance	Number of Isomers	Ozone Depleting Potential*
Group II			
$CHFBr_2$		1	1.00
CHF_2Br	(HBFC-22B1)	1	0.74
CH_2FBr		1	0.73
C_2HFBr_4		2	0.3-0.8
$C_2HF_2Br_3$		3	0.5-1.8
$C_2HF_3Br_2$		3	0.4-1.6
C_2HF_4Br		2	0.7-1.2
$C_2H_2FBr_3$		3	0.1-1.1

[Twenty-six more Substances were in Group II—EDS.]

Group	Substance	Number of Isomers	Ozone Depleting Potential*
Group III			
CH_2BrC_l	bromochloro-methane	1	0.12

*Where a range of ODPs is indicated, the highest value in that range shall be used for the purposes of the Protocol. The ODPs listed as a single value have been determined from calculations based on laboratory measurements. Those listed as a range are based on estimates and are less certain. The range pertains to an isomeric group. The upper value is the estimate of the ODP of the isomer with the highest ODP, and the lower value is the estimate of the ODP of the isomer with the lowest ODP.

**Identifies the most commercially viable substances with ODP values listed against them to be used for the purposes of the Protocol.

Annex D.   A List of Products* Containing Controlled Substances Specified in Annex A

1. Automobile and truck air conditioning units (whether incorporated in vehicles or not)
2. Domestic and commercial refrigeration and air conditioning/ heat pump equipment**
   e.g. Refrigerators
      Freezers
      Dehumidifiers
      Water coolers
      Ice machines
      Air conditioning and heat pump units
3. Aerosol products, except medical aerosols
4. Portable fire extinguishers
5. Insulation boards, panels and pipe covers
6. Pre-polymers

   *Though not when transported in consignments of personal or household effects or in similar non-commercial situations normally exempted from customs attention.
   **When containing controlled substances in Annex A as a refrigerant and/ or in insulating material of the product.

Annex E.   Controlled Substance

Group	Substance	Ozone Depleting Potential
Group I		
CH_3Br	methyl bromide	0.6

FRAMEWORK CONVENTION ON CLIMATE CHANGE

May 9, 1992, 31 I.L.M. 849 (1992)*

[Preamble omitted.]

Article 1.   Definitions**

For the purposes of this Convention:

1. "Adverse effects of climate change" means changes in the physical environment or biota resulting from climate change which have significant deleterious effects on the composition, resilience or productivity of natural and managed ecosystems or on the operation of socio-economic systems or on human health and welfare.

---

* Signed at New York on May 9, 1992. Entered into force March 21, 1994. As of March 2013, the 195 parties to the convention were: Afghanistan, Albania, Algeria, Andorra, Angola, Antigua and Barbuda, Argentina, Armenia, Australia, Austria, Azerbaijan, Bahamas, Bahrain, Bangladesh, Barbados, Belarus, Belgium, Belize, Benin, Bhutan, Bolivia, Bosnia and Herzegovina, Botswana, Brazil, Brunei Darussalam, Bulgaria, Burkina Faso, Burundi, Cambodia, Cameroon, Canada, Cape Verde, Central African Republic, Chad, Chile, China, Colombia, Comoros, Congo, Congo (Democratic Republic of), Cook Islands, Costa Rica, Côte d'Ivoire, Croatia, Cuba, Cyprus, Czech Republic, Denmark, Djibouti, Dominica, Dominican Republic, Ecuador, Egypt, El Salvador, Equatorial Guinea, Eritrea, Estonia, Ethiopia, European Community, Fiji, Finland, France, Gabon, Gambia, Georgia, Germany, Ghana, Greece, Grenada, Guatemala, Guinea, Guinea-Bissau, Guyana, Haiti, Honduras, Hungary, Iceland, India, Indonesia, Iran, Iraq, Ireland, Israel, Italy, Jamaica, Japan, Jordan, Kazakhstan, Kenya, Kiribati, Korea (Democratic People's Republic of), Korea (Republic of), Kuwait, Kyrgyzstan, Lao People's Democratic Republic, Latvia, Lebanon, Lesotho, Liberia, Libyan Arab Jamahiriya, Liechtenstein, Lithuania, Luxembourg, Macedonia (the former Yugoslav Republic of), Madagascar, Malawi, Malaysia, Maldives, Mali, Malta, Marshall Islands, Mauritania, Mauritius, Mexico, Micronesia, Moldova, Monaco, Mongolia, Montenegro, Morocco, Mozambique, Myanmar, Namibia, Nauru, Nepal, Netherlands, New Zealand, Nicaragua, Niger, Nigeria, Niue, Norway, Oman, Pakistan, Palau, Panama, Papua New Guinea, Paraguay, Peru, Philippines, Poland, Portugal, Qatar, Romania, Russian Federation, Rwanda, Saint Kitts and Nevis, Saint Lucia, Saint Vincent and the Grenadines, Samoa, San Marino, Sao Tome and Principe, Saudi Arabia, Senegal, Serbia, Seychelles, Sierra Leone, Singapore, Slovakia, Slovenia, Solomon Islands, Somalia, South Africa, Spain, Sri Lanka, Sudan, Suriname, Swaziland, Sweden, Switzerland, Syrian Arab Republic, Tajikistan, Tanzania, Thailand, Timor-Leste, Togo, Tonga, Trinidad and Tobago, Tunisia, Turkey, Turkmenistan, Tuvalu, Uganda, Ukraine, United Arab Emirates, United Kingdom, United States of America, Uruguay, Uzbekistan, Vanuatu, Venezuela, Viet Nam, Yemen, Zambia, and Zimbabwe. See the U.N. Web site at <http://treaties.un.org> or <http://unfccc.int>.

** Titles of articles are included solely to assist the reader.

2. "Climate change" means a change of climate which is attributed directly or indirectly to human activity that alters the composition of the global atmosphere and which is in addition to natural climate variability observed over comparable time periods.

3. "Climate system" means the totality of the atmosphere, hydrosphere, biosphere and geosphere and their interactions.

4. "Emissions" means the release of greenhouse gases and/or their precursors into the atmosphere over a specified area and period of time.

5. "Greenhouse gases" means those gaseous constituents of the atmosphere, both natural and anthropogenic, that absorb and re-emit infrared radiation.

6. "Regional economic integration organization" means an organization constituted by sovereign States of a given region which has competence in respect of matters governed by this Convention or its protocols and has been duly authorized, in accordance with its internal procedures, to sign, ratify, accept, approve or accede to the instruments concerned.

7. "Reservoir" means a component or components of the climate system where a greenhouse gas or a precursor of a greenhouse gas is stored.

8. "Sink" means any process, activity or mechanism which removes a greenhouse gas, an aerosol or a precursor of a greenhouse gas from the atmosphere.

9. "Source" means any process or activity which releases a greenhouse gas, an aerosol or a precursor of a greenhouse gas into the atmosphere.

Article 2.   Objective

The ultimate objective of this Convention and any related legal instruments that the Conference of the Parties may adopt is to achieve, in accordance with the relevant provisions of the Convention, stabilization of greenhouse gas concentrations in the atmosphere at a level that would prevent dangerous anthropogenic interference with the climate system. Such a level should be achieved within a time-frame sufficient to allow ecosystems to adapt naturally to climate change, to ensure that food production is not threatened and to enable economic development to proceed in a sustainable manner.

Article 3.   Principles

In their actions to achieve the objective of the Convention and to implement its provisions, the Parties shall be guided, *inter alia*, by the following:

1. The Parties should protect the climate system for the benefit of present and future generations of humankind, on the basis of equity and in accordance with their common but differentiated responsibilities and respective capabilities. Accordingly, the developed country Parties should take the lead in combating climate change and the adverse effects thereof.

2. The specific needs and special circumstances of developing country Parties, especially those that are particularly vulnerable to the adverse effects of climate change, and of those Parties, especially developing country Parties,

that would have to bear a disproportionate or abnormal burden under the Convention, should be given full consideration.

3. The Parties should take precautionary measures to anticipate, prevent or minimize the causes of climate change and mitigate its adverse effects. Where there are threats of serious or irreversible damage, lack of full scientific certainty should not be used as a reason for postponing such measures, taking into account that policies and measures to deal with climate change should be cost-effective so as to ensure global benefits at the lowest possible cost. To achieve this, such policies and measures should take into account different socio-economic contexts, be comprehensive, cover all relevant sources, sinks and reservoirs of greenhouse gases and adaptation, and comprise all economic sectors. Efforts to address climate change may be carried out cooperatively by interested Parties.

4. The Parties have a right to, and should, promote sustainable development. Policies and measures to protect the climate system against human-induced change should be appropriate for the specific conditions of each Party and should be integrated with national development programmes, taking into account that economic development is essential for adopting measures to address climate change.

5. The Parties should cooperate to promote a supportive and open international economic system that would lead to sustainable economic growth and development in all Parties, particularly developing country Parties, thus enabling them better to address the problems of climate change. Measures taken to combat climate change, including unilateral ones, should not constitute a means of arbitrary or unjustifiable discrimination or a disguised restriction on international trade.

Article 4.   Commitments

1. All Parties, taking into account their common but differentiated responsibilities and their specific national and regional development priorities, objectives and circumstances, shall:

(a) Develop, periodically update, publish and make available to the Conference of the Parties, in accordance with Article 12, national inventories of anthropogenic emissions by sources and removals by sinks of all greenhouse gases not controlled by the Montreal Protocol, using comparable methodologies to be agreed upon by the Conference of the Parties;

(b) Formulate, implement, publish and regularly update national and, where appropriate, regional programmes containing measures to mitigate climate change by addressing anthropogenic emissions by sources and removals by sinks of all greenhouse gases not controlled by the Montreal Protocol, and measures to facilitate adequate adaptation to climate change;

(c) Promote and cooperate in the development, application and diffusion, including transfer, of technologies, practices and processes that control, reduce or prevent anthropogenic emissions of greenhouse gases not controlled by the Montreal Protocol in all relevant sectors, including the energy, transport, industry, agriculture, forestry and waste management sectors;

(d) Promote sustainable management, and promote and cooperate in the conservation and enhancement, as appropriate, of sinks and reservoirs of all greenhouse gases not controlled by the Montreal Protocol, including biomass, forests and oceans as well as other terrestrial, coastal and marine ecosystems;

(e) Cooperate in preparing for adaptation to the impacts of climate change; develop and elaborate appropriate and integrated plans for coastal zone management, water resources and agriculture, and for the protection and rehabilitation of areas, particularly in Africa, affected by drought and desertification, as well as floods;

(f) Take climate change considerations into account, to the extent feasible, in their relevant social, economic and environmental policies and actions, and employ appropriate methods, for example impact assessments, formulated and determined nationally, with a view to minimizing adverse effects on the economy, on public health and on the quality of the environment, of projects or measures undertaken by them to mitigate or adapt to climate change;

(g) Promote and cooperate in scientific, technological, technical, socio-economic and other research, systematic observation and development of data archives related to the climate system and intended to further the understanding and to reduce or eliminate the remaining uncertainties regarding the causes, effects, magnitude and timing of climate change and the economic and social consequences of various response strategies;

(h) Promote and cooperate in the full, open and prompt exchange of relevant scientific, technological, technical, socio-economic and legal information related to the climate system and climate change, and to the economic and social consequences of various response strategies;

(i) Promote and cooperate in education, training and public awareness related to climate change and encourage the widest participation in this process, including that of non-governmental organizations; and

(j) Communicate to the Conference of the Parties information related to implementation, in accordance with Article 12.

2. The developed country Parties and other Parties included in annex I commit themselves specifically as provided for in the following:

(a) Each of these Parties shall adopt national[1] policies and take corresponding measures on the mitigation of climate change, by limiting its anthropogenic emissions of greenhouse gases and protecting and enhancing its greenhouse gas sinks and reservoirs. These policies and measures will demonstrate that developed countries are taking the lead in modifying longer-term trends in anthropogenic emissions consistent with

---

1. This includes policies and measures adopted by regional economic integration organizations.

the objective of the Convention, recognizing that the return by the end of the present decade to earlier levels of anthropogenic emissions of carbon dioxide and other greenhouse gases not controlled by the Montreal Protocol would contribute to such modification, and taking into account the differences in these Parties' starting points and approaches, economic structures and resource bases, the need to maintain strong and sustainable economic growth, available technologies and other individual circumstances, as well as the need for equitable and appropriate contributions by each of these Parties to the global effort regarding that objective. . . .

(b) In order to promote progress to this end, each of these Parties shall communicate, within six months of the entry into force of the Convention for it and periodically thereafter, and in accordance with Article 12, detailed information on its policies and measures referred to in subparagraph (a) above, as well as on its resulting projected anthropogenic emissions by sources and removals by sinks of greenhouse gases not controlled by the Montreal Protocol for the period referred to in subparagraph (a), with the aim of returning individually or jointly to their 1990 levels these anthropogenic emissions of carbon dioxide and other greenhouse gases not controlled by the Montreal Protocol. This information will be reviewed by the Conference of the Parties, at its first session and periodically thereafter, in accordance with Article 7;

(c) Calculations of emissions by sources and removals by sinks of greenhouse gases for the purposes of subparagraph (b) above should take into account the best available scientific knowledge, including of the effective capacity of sinks and the respective contributions of such gases to climate change. The Conference of the Parties shall consider and agree on methodologies for these calculations at its first session and review them regularly thereafter;

(d) The Conference of the Parties shall, at its first session, review the adequacy of subparagraphs (a) and (b) above. Such review shall be carried out in the light of the best available scientific information and assessment on climate change and its impacts, as well as relevant technical, social and economic information. Based on this review, the Conference of the Parties shall take appropriate action, which may include the adoption of amendments to the commitments in subparagraphs (a) and (b) above. The Conference of the Parties, at its first session, shall also take decisions regarding criteria for joint implementation as indicated in subparagraph (a) above. A second review of subparagraphs (a) and (b) shall take place not later than 31 December 1998, and thereafter at regular intervals determined by the Conference of the Parties, until the objective of the Convention is met;

(e) Each of these Parties shall:

(i) coordinate as appropriate with other such Parties, relevant economic and administrative instruments developed to achieve the objective of the Convention; and

(ii) identify and periodically review its own policies and practices which encourage activities that lead to greater levels of anthropogenic emissions of greenhouse gases not controlled by the Montreal Protocol than would otherwise occur;

(f) The Conference of the Parties shall review, not later than 31 December 1998, available information with a view to taking decisions regarding such amendments to the lists in annexes I and II as may be appropriate, with the approval of the Party concerned;

(g) Any Party not included in annex I may, in its instrument of ratification, acceptance, approval or accession, or at any time thereafter, notify the Depositary that it intends to be bound by subparagraphs (a) and (b) above. The Depositary shall inform the other signatories and Parties of any such notification.

3. The developed country Parties and other developed Parties included in annex II shall provide new and additional financial resources to meet the agreed full costs incurred by developing country Parties in complying with their obligations under Article 12, paragraph 1. They shall also provide such financial resources, including for the transfer of technology, needed by the developing country Parties to meet the agreed full incremental costs of implementing measures that are covered by paragraph 1 of this Article and that are agreed between a developing country Party and the international entity or entities referred to in Article 11, in accordance with that Article. The implementation of these commitments shall take into account the need for adequacy and predictability in the flow of funds and the importance of appropriate burden sharing among the developed country Parties.

4. The developed country Parties and other developed Parties included in annex II shall also assist the developing country Parties that are particularly vulnerable to the adverse effects of climate change in meeting costs of adaptation to those adverse effects.

5. The developed country Parties and other developed Parties included in annex II shall take all practicable steps to promote, facilitate and finance, as appropriate, the transfer of, or access to, environmentally sound technologies and know-how to other Parties, particularly developing country Parties, to enable them to implement the provisions of the Convention. In this process, the developed country Parties shall support the development and enhancement of endogenous capacities and technologies of developing country Parties. Other Parties and organizations in a position to do so may also assist in facilitating the transfer of such technologies.

6. In the implementation of their commitments under paragraph 2 above, a certain degree of flexibility shall be allowed by the Conference of the Parties to the Parties included in annex I undergoing the process of transition to a market economy. . . .

7. The extent to which developing country Parties will effectively implement their commitments under the Convention will depend on the effective implementation by developed country Parties of their commitments under the Convention related to financial resources and transfer of technology and will take fully into account that economic and social development

and poverty eradication are the first and overriding priorities of the developing country Parties.

8. In the implementation of the commitments in this Article, the Parties shall give full consideration to what actions are necessary under the Convention, including actions related to funding, insurance and the transfer of technology, to meet the specific needs and concerns of developing country Parties arising from the adverse effects of climate change and/or the impact of the implementation of response measures, especially on:

(a) Small island countries;

(b) Countries with low-lying coastal areas;

(c) Countries with arid and semi-arid areas, forested areas and areas liable to forest decay;

(d) Countries with areas prone to natural disasters;

(e) Countries with areas liable to drought and desertification;

(f) Countries with areas of high urban atmospheric pollution;

(g) Countries with areas with fragile ecosystems, including mountainous ecosystems;

(h) Countries whose economies are highly dependent on income generated from the production, processing and export, and/or on consumption of fossil fuels and associated energy-intensive products; and

(i) Land-locked and transit countries.

Further, the Conference of the Parties may take actions, as appropriate, with respect to this paragraph.

9. The Parties shall take full account of the specific needs and special situations of the least developed countries in their actions with regard to funding and transfer of technology.

10. The Parties shall, in accordance with Article 10, take into consideration in the implementation of the commitments of the Convention the situation of Parties, particularly developing country Parties, with economies that are vulnerable to the adverse effects of the implementation of measures to respond to climate change. This applies notably to Parties with economies that are highly dependent on income generated from the production, processing and export, and/or consumption of fossil fuels and associated energy-intensive products and/or the use of fossil fuels for which such Parties have serious difficulties in switching to alternatives.

Article 5. Research and Systematic Observation . . .

Article 6. Education, Training and Public Awareness . . .

Article 7. Conference of the Parties

1. A Conference of the Parties is hereby established.

2. The Conference of the Parties, as the supreme body of this Convention, shall keep under regular review the implementation of the Convention and any related legal instruments that the Conference of the Parties may adopt, and shall make, within its mandate, the decisions necessary to promote the effective implementation of the Convention. To this end, it shall:

(a) Periodically examine the obligations of the Parties and the institutional arrangements under the Convention, in the light of the objective of the Convention, the experience gained in its implementation and the volution of scientific and technological knowledge;

(b) Promote and facilitate the exchange of information on measures adopted by the Parties to address climate change and its effects, taking into account the differing circumstances, responsibilities and capabilities of the Parties and their respective commitments under the Convention;

(c) Facilitate, at the request of two or more Parties, the coordination of measures adopted by them to address climate change and its effects, taking into account the differing circumstances, responsibilities and capabilities of the Parties and their respective commitments under the Convention;

(d) Promote and guide, in accordance with the objective and provisions of the Convention, the development and periodic refinement of comparable methodologies, to be agreed on by the Conference of the Parties, *inter alia*, for preparing inventories of greenhouse gas emissions by sources and removals by sinks, and for evaluating the effectiveness of measures to limit the emissions and enhance the removals of these gases;

(e) Assess, on the basis of all information made available to it in accordance with the provisions of the Convention, the implementation of the Convention by the Parties, the overall effects of the measures taken pursuant to the Convention, in particular environmental, economic and social effects as well as their cumulative impacts and the extent to which progress towards the objective of the Convention is being achieved;

(f) Consider and adopt regular reports on the implementation of the Convention and ensure their publication;

(g) Make recommendations on any matters necessary for the implementation of the Convention;

(h) Seek to mobilize financial resources in accordance with Article 4, paragraphs 3, 4 and 5, and Article 11;

(i) Establish such subsidiary bodies as are deemed necessary for the implementation of the Convention;

(j) Review reports submitted by its subsidiary bodies and provide guidance to them;

(k) Agree upon and adopt, by consensus, rules of procedure and financial rules for itself and for any subsidiary bodies;

(l) Seek and utilize, where appropriate, the services and cooperation of, and information provided by, competent international organizations and intergovernmental and non-governmental bodies; and

(m) Exercise such other functions as are required for the achievement of the objective of the Convention as well as all other functions assigned to it under the Convention.

3. The Conference of the Parties shall, at its first session, adopt its own rules of procedure as well as those of the subsidiary bodies established by the Convention, which shall include decision-making procedures for matters not already covered by decision-making procedures stipulated in the

Convention. Such procedures may include specified majorities required for the adoption of particular decisions.

4. The first session of the Conference of the Parties shall be convened by the interim secretariat referred to in Article 21 and shall take place not later than one year after the date of entry into force of the Convention. Thereafter, ordinary sessions of the Conference of the Parties shall be held every year unless otherwise decided by the Conference of the Parties.

5. Extraordinary sessions of the Conference of the Parties shall be held at such other times as may be deemed necessary by the Conference, or at the written request of any Party, provided that, within six months of the request being communicated to the Parties by the secretariat, it is supported by at least one-third of the Parties.

6. The United Nations, its specialized agencies and the International Atomic Energy Agency, as well as any State member thereof or observers thereto not Party to the Convention, may be represented at sessions of the Conference of the Parties as observers. Any body or agency, whether national or international, governmental or non-governmental, which is qualified in matters covered by the Convention, and which has informed the secretariat of its wish to be represented . . . as an observer, may be so admitted unless at least one-third of the Parties present object. The admission and participation of observers shall be subject to the rules of procedure adopted by the Conference of the Parties.

Article 8. Secretariat

1. A secretariat is hereby established.

2. The functions of the secretariat shall be:

(a) To make arrangements for sessions of the Conference of the Parties and its subsidiary bodies established under the Convention and to provide them with services as required;

(b) To compile and transmit reports submitted to it;

(c) To facilitate assistance to the Parties, particularly developing country Parties, on request, in the compilation and communications of information required in accordance with the provisions of the Convention;

(d) To prepare reports on its activities and present them to the Conference of the Parties; . . .

Article 9. Subsidiary Body for Scientific and Technological Advice

1. A subsidiary body for scientific and technological advice is hereby established to provide the Conference of the Parties and, as appropriate, its other subsidiary bodies with timely information and advice on scientific and technological matters relating to the Convention. This body shall be open to participation by all Parties and shall be multidisciplinary. It shall comprise government representatives competent in the relevant field of expertise. . . .

3. The functions and terms of reference of this body may be further elaborated by the Conference of the Parties.

Article 10. Subsidiary Body for Implementation

1. A subsidiary body for implementation is hereby established to assist the Conference of the Parties in the assessment and review of the effective implementation of the Convention. This body shall be open to participation by all Parties and comprise government representatives who are experts on matters related to climate change. It shall report regularly to the Conference of the Parties on all aspects of its work.

2. Under the guidance of the Conference of the Parties, this body shall:

(a) Consider the information communicated in accordance with Article 12, paragraph 1, to assess the overall aggregated effect of the steps taken by the Parties in the light of the latest scientific assessments concerning climate change;

(b) Consider the information communicated in accordance with Article 12, paragraph 2, in order to assist the Conference of the Parties in carrying out the reviews required by Article 4, paragraph 2(d); and

(c) Assist the Conference of the Parties, as appropriate, in the preparation and implementation of its decisions.

Article 11. Financial Mechanism

1. A mechanism for the provision of financial resources on a grant or concessional basis, including for the transfer of technology, is hereby defined. It shall function under the guidance of and be accountable to the Conference of the Parties, which shall decide on its policies, programme priorities and eligibility criteria related to this Convention. Its operation shall be entrusted to one or more existing international entities.

2. The financial mechanism shall have an equitable and balanced representation of all Parties within a transparent system of governance.

3. The Conference of the Parties and the entity or entities entrusted with the operation of the financial mechanism shall agree upon arrangements to give effect to the above paragraphs, which shall include the following:

(a) Modalities to ensure that the funded projects to address climate change are in conformity with the policies, programme priorities and eligibility criteria established by the Conference of the Parties;

(b) Modalities by which a particular funding decision may be reconsidered in light of these policies, programme priorities and eligibility criteria;

(c) Provision by the entity or entities of regular reports to the Conference of the Parties on its funding operations, which is consistent with the requirement for accountability set out in paragraph 1 above; and

(d) Determination in a predictable and identifiable manner of the amount of funding necessary and available for the implementation of this Convention and the conditions under which that amount shall be periodically reviewed.

713

4. The Conference of the Parties shall make arrangements to implement the above-mentioned provisions at its first session, reviewing and taking into account the interim arrangements referred to in Article 21, paragraph 3. . . . Within four years thereafter, the Conference of the Parties shall review the financial mechanism and take appropriate measures. . . .

Article 12.   Communication of Information Related to Implementation

1. In accordance with Article 4, paragraph 1, each Party shall communicate to the Conference of the Parties, through the secretariat, the following elements of information:

(a) A national inventory of anthropogenic emissions by sources and removals by sinks of all greenhouse gases not controlled by the Montreal Protocol, to the extent its capacities permit; using comparable methodologies to be promoted and agreed upon by the Conference of the Parties;

(b) A general description of steps taken or envisaged by the Party to implement the Convention; and

(c) Any other information that the Party considers relevant to the achievement of the objective of the Convention and suitable for inclusion in its communication, including, if feasible, material relevant for calculations of global emission trends.

2. Each developed country Party and each other Party included in annex I shall incorporate in its communication the following elements of information:

(a) A detailed description of the policies and measures that it has adopted to implement its commitment under Article 4, paragraphs 2(a) and 2(b); and

(b) A specific estimate of the effects that the policies and measures referred to in subparagraph (a) immediately above will have on anthropogenic emissions by its sources and removals by its sinks of greenhouse gases during the period referred to in Article 4, paragraph 2(a).

3. In addition, each developed country Party and each other developed Party included in annex II shall incorporate details of measures taken in accordance with Article 4, paragraphs 3, 4 and 5.

4. Developing country Parties may, on a voluntary basis, propose projects for financing, including specific technologies, materials, equipment, techniques or practices that would be needed to implement such projects, along with, if possible, an estimate of all incremental costs, of the reductions of emissions and increments of removals of greenhouse gases, as well as an estimate of the consequent benefits.

5. Each developed country Party and each other Party included in annex I shall make its initial communication within six months of the entry into force of the Convention for that Party. Each Party not so listed shall make its initial communication within three years of the entry into force of the Convention for that Party, or of the availability of financial resources in accordance with Article 4, paragraph 3. Parties that are least developed

countries may make their initial communication at their discretion. The frequency of subsequent communications by all Parties shall be determined by the Conference of the Parties . . . .

6. Information communicated by Parties under this Article shall be transmitted by the secretariat as soon as possible to the Conference of the Parties and to any subsidiary bodies concerned. . . .

7. From its first session, the Conference of the Parties shall arrange for the provision to developing country Parties of technical and financial support, on request, in compiling and communicating information under this Article, as well as in identifying the technical and financial needs associated with proposed projects and response measures under Article 4. . . .

8. Any group of Parties may, subject to guidelines adopted by the Conference of the Parties, and to prior notification to the Conference of the Parties, make a joint communication in fulfillment of their obligations under this Article. . . .

9. Information received by the secretariat that is designated by a Party as confidential, in accordance with criteria to be established by the Conference of the Parties, shall be aggregated by the secretariat to protect its confidentiality before being made available to any of the bodies involved in the communication and review of information. . . .

Article 13. Resolution of Questions Regarding Implementation

The Conference of the Parties shall, at its first session, consider the establishment of a multilateral consultative process . . . for the resolution of questions regarding the implementation of the Convention.

Article 14. Settlement of Disputes

1. In the event of a dispute between any two or more Parties concerning the interpretation or application of the Convention, the Parties concerned shall seek a settlement of the dispute through negotiation or any other peaceful means of their own choice.

2. When ratifying, accepting, approving or acceding to the Convention, or at any time thereafter, a Party which is not a regional economic integration organization may declare in a written instrument submitted to the Depositary that, in respect of any dispute concerning the interpretation or application of the Convention, it recognizes as compulsory ipso facto and without special agreement, in relation to any Party accepting the same obligation:

(a) Submission of the dispute to the International Court of Justice, and/or

(b) Arbitration in accordance with procedures to be adopted by the Conference of the Parties as soon as practicable, in an annex on arbitration.

A Party which is a regional economic integration organization may make a declaration with like effect in relation to arbitration in accordance with the procedures referred to in subparagraph (b) above.

3. A declaration made under paragraph 2 above shall remain in force until it expires in accordance with its terms or until three months after written notice of its revocation has been deposited with the Depositary.

4. A new declaration, a notice of revocation or the expiry of a declaration shall not in any way affect proceedings pending before the International Court of Justice or the arbitral tribunal, unless the parties to the dispute otherwise agree.

5. Subject to the operation of paragraph 2 above, if after twelve months following notification by one Party to another that a dispute exists between them, the Parties concerned have not been able to settle their dispute through the means mentioned in paragraph 1 above, the dispute shall be submitted, at the request of any of the parties to the dispute, to conciliation.

6. A conciliation commission shall be created upon the request of one of the parties to the dispute. The commission shall be composed of an equal number of members appointed by each party concerned and a chairman chosen jointly by the members appointed by each party. The commission shall render a recommendatory award, which the parties shall consider in good faith. . . .

8. The provisions of this Article shall apply to any related legal instrument which the Conference of the Parties may adopt, unless the instrument provides otherwise. . . .

Annex I

Australia
Austria
Belarus[a]
Belgium
Bulgaria[a]
Canada
Croatia[a][*]
Czech Republic[a][*]
Denmark
European Economic Community
Estonia[a]
Finland
France
Germany
Greece
Hungary[a]
Iceland
Ireland
Italy
Japan
Latvia[a]

Liechtenstein[*]
Lithuania[a]
Luxembourg
Monaco[*]
Netherlands
New Zealand
Norway
Poland[a]
Portugal
Romania[a]
Russian Federation[a]
Slovakia[a][*]
Slovenia[a][*]
Spain
Sweden
Switzerland
Turkey
Ukraine[a]
United Kingdom of Great Britain
    and Northern Ireland
United States of America

[a]Countries that are undergoing the process of transition to a market economy.
[*]Countries added to Annex I by an amendment that entered into force on 13 August 1998, pursuant to decision 4/CP.3 adopted at COP.3.

Annex II

Australia
Austria
Belgium
Canada
Denmark
European Economic Community
Finland
France
Germany
Greece
Iceland
Ireland
Italy

Japan
Luxembourg
Netherlands
New Zealand
Norway
Portugal
Spain
Sweden
Switzerland
United Kingdom of Great
   Britain and Northern Ireland
United States of America

Note: Turkey was deleted from Annex II by an amendment that entered into force 28 June 2002, pursuant to decision 26/CP.7 adopted at COP.7.

KYOTO PROTOCOL TO THE
U.N. FRAMEWORK CONVENTION
ON CLIMATE CHANGE

Dec. 11, 1997, FCCC/CP/1997/7/Add.1 (March 25, 1998)*

The Parties to this Protocol,

Being Parties to the United Nations Framework convention on Climate Change, hereinafter referred to as "the Convention",

In pursuit of the ultimate objective of the Convention as stated in its Article 2,

---

* Signed at Kyoto, Japan, on December 11, 1997, at the end of the Third Session of the Conference of the Parties of the Framework Convention on Climate Change. This Protocol entered into force on February 16, 2005. The United States is not a party to the Protocol. After the United States signed the Protocol on November 12, 1998 during the Clinton Administration, the Bush Administration indicated in 2001 that it opposed the Protocol and had no intention of trying to ratify it. The present commitments under the Protocal expire on December 31, 2012.

As of March 2013, the 191 parties to the Protocol were: Albania, Algeria, Angola, Antigua and Barbuda, Argentina, Armenia, Australia, Austria, Azerbaijan, Bahamas, Bahrain, Bangladesh, Barbados, Belarus, Belgium, Belize, Benin, Bhutan, Bolivia, Bosnia and Herzegovina, Botswana, Brazil, Brunei Darussalam, Bulgaria, Burkina Faso, Burundi, Cambodia, Cameroon, Cape Verde, Central African Republic, Chad, Chile, China, Colombia, Comoros, Congo (Democratic Republic of), Congo (Republic of), Cook Islands, Costa Rica, Côte d'Ivoire, Croatia, Cuba, Cyprus, Czech Republic, Denmark, Djibouti, Dominica, Dominican Republic, Ecuador, Egypt, El Salvador, Equatorial Guinea, Eritrea, Estonia, Ethiopia, European Community, Fiji, Finland, France, Gabon, Gambia, Georgia, Germany, Ghana, Greece, Grenada, Guatemala, Guinea, Guinea-Bissau, Guyana, Haiti, Honduras, Hungary, Iceland, India, Indonesia, Iran, Iraq, Ireland, Israel, Italy, Jamaica, Japan, Jordan, Kazakhstan, Kenya, Kiribati, Korea (Democratic People's Republic of), Korea (Republic of), Kuwait, Kyrgyzstan, Lao People's Democratic Republic, Latvia, Lebanon, Lesotho, Liberia, Libyan Arab Jamahiriya, Liechtenstein, Lithuania, Luxembourg, Macedonia (the former Yugoslav Republic of), Madagascar, Malawi, Malaysia, Maldives, Mali, Malta, Marshall Islands, Mauritania, Mauritius, Mexico, Micronesia, Moldova, Monaco, Mongolia, Montenegro, Morocco, Mozambique, Myanmar, Namibia, Nauru, Nepal, Netherlands, New Zealand, Nicaragua, Niger, Nigeria, Niue, Norway, Oman, Pakistan, Palau, Panama, Papua New Guinea, Paraguay, Peru, Philippines, Poland, Portugal, Qatar, Romania, Russian Federation, Rwanda, Saint Kitts and Nevis, Saint Lucia, Saint Vincent and the Grenadines, Samoa, San Marino, Sao Tome and Principe, Saudi Arabia, Senegal, Serbia, Seychelles, Sierra Leone, Singapore, Slovakia, Slovenia, Solomon Islands, Somalia, South Africa, Spain, Sri Lanka, Sudan, Suriname, Swaziland, Sweden, Switzerland, Syrian Arab Republic, Tajikistan, Tanzania, Thailand, Timor-Leste, Togo, Tonga, Trinidad and Tobago, Tunisia, Turkey, Turkmenistan, Tuvalu, Uganda, Ukraine, United Arab Emirates, United Kingdom, Uruguay, Uzbekistan, Vanuatu, Venezuela, Viet Nam, Yemen, and Zambia, Zimbabwe. See U.N. Web site at <http://treaties..un.org> or <http://unfccc.int>.

Recalling the provisions of the Convention,

Being guided by Article 3 of the Convention,

Pursuant to the Berlin Mandate adopted by decision 1/CP.1 of the Conference of the Parties to the Convention at its first session,

Have agreed as follows:

Article 1

For the purposes of this Protocol, the definitions contained in Article 1 of the convention shall apply. In addition:

1. "Conference of the Parties" means the Conference of the Parties to the Convention.

2. "Convention" means the United Nations Framework Convention on Climate Change, adopted in New York on 9 May 1992.

3. "Intergovernmental Panel on Climate Change" means the Intergovernmental Panel on Climate Change established in 1988 jointly by the World Meteorological Organization and the United Nations Environment Programme.

4. "Montreal Protocol" means the Montreal Protocol on Substances that Deplete the Ozone Layer, adopted in Montreal on 16 September 1987 and as subsequently adjusted and amended.

5. "Parties present and voting" means Parties present and casting an affirmative or negative vote.

6. "Party" means, unless the context otherwise indicates, a Party to this Protocol.

7. "Party included in Annex I" means a Party included in Annex I to the Convention, as may be amended, or a Party which has made a notification under Article 4, paragraph 2(g), of the Convention.

Article 2

1. Each Party included in Annex I in achieving its quantified emission limitation and reduction commitments under Article 3, in order to promote sustainable development, shall:

(a) Implement and/or further elaborate policies and measures in accordance with its national circumstances, such as:

(i) Enhancement of energy efficiency in relevant sectors of the national economy;

(ii) Protection and enhancement of sinks and reservoirs of greenhouse gases not controlled by the Montreal Protocol, taking into account its commitments under relevant international environmental agreements; promotion of sustainable forest management practices, afforestation and reforestation;

(iii) Promotion of sustainable forms of agriculture in light of climate change considerations;

(iv) Research on, and promotion, development and increased use of, new and renewable forms of energy, of carbon dioxide sequestration technologies and of advanced and innovative environmentally sound technologies;

(v) Progressive reduction or phasing out of market imperfections, fiscal incentives, tax and duty exemptions and subsidies in all greenhouse gas emitting sectors that run counter to the objective of the Convention and application of market instruments;

(vi) Encouragement of appropriate reforms in relevant sectors aimed at promoting policies and measures which limit or reduce emissions of greenhouse gases not controlled by the Montreal Protocol;

(vii) Measures to limit and/or reduce emissions of greenhouse gases not controlled by the Montreal Protocol in the transport sector;

(viii) Limitation and/or reduction of methane emissions through recovery and use in waste management, as well as in the production, transport and distribution of energy;

(b) Cooperate with other such Parties to enhance the individual and combined effectiveness of their policies and measures adopted under this Article, pursuant to Article 4, paragraph 2(e)(i), of the Convention. To this end, these Parties shall take steps to share their experience and exchange information on such policies and measures, including developing ways of improving their comparability, transparency and effectiveness. The Conference of the Parties serving as the meeting of the Parties to this Protocol shall, at its first session or as soon as practicable thereafter, consider ways to facilitate such cooperation, taking into account all relevant information.

2. The Parties included in Annex I shall pursue limitation or reduction of emissions of greenhouse gases not controlled by the Montreal Protocol from aviation and marine bunker fuels, working through the International Civil Aviation Organization and the International Maritime Organization, respectively.

3. The Parties included in Annex I shall strive to implement policies and measures under this Article in such a way as to minimize adverse effects, including the adverse effects of climate change, effects on international trade, and social, environmental and economic impacts on other Parties, especially developing country Parties and in particular those identified in Article 4, paragraphs 8 and 9, of the Convention, taking into account Article 3 of the Convention. The Conference of the Parties serving as the meeting of the Parties to this Protocol may take further action, as appropriate, to promote the implementation of the provisions of this paragraph.

4. The Conference of the Parties serving as the meeting of the Parties to this Protocol, if it decides that it would be beneficial to coordinate any of the policies and measures in paragraph 1(a) above, taking into account different national circumstances and potential effects, shall consider ways and means to elaborate the coordination of such policies and measures.

Article 3

1. The Parties included in Annex I shall, individually or jointly, ensure that their aggregate anthropogenic carbon dioxide equivalent emissions of

the greenhouse gases listed in Annex A do not exceed their assigned amounts, calculated pursuant to their quantified emission limitation and reduction commitments inscribed in Annex B and in accordance with the provisions of this Article, with a view to reducing their overall emissions of such gases by at least 5 per cent below 1990 levels in the commitment period 2008 to 2012.

2. Each Party included in Annex I shall, by 2005, have made demonstrable progress in achieving its commitments under this Protocol.

3. The net changes in greenhouse gas emissions from sources and removals by sinks resulting from direct human-induced land-use change and forestry activities, limited to afforestation, reforestation and deforestation since 1990, measured as verifiable changes in carbon stocks in each commitment period, shall be used to meet the commitments under this Article of each Party included in Annex I. The greenhouse gas emissions by sources and removals by sinks associated with those activities shall be reported in a transparent and verifiable manner and reviewed in accordance with Articles 7 and 8.

4. Prior to the first session of the Conference of the Parties serving as the meeting of the Parties to this Protocol, each Party included in Annex I shall provide, for consideration by the Subsidiary Body for Scientific and Technological Advice, data to establish its level of carbon stocks in 1990 and to enable an estimate to be made of its changes in carbon stocks in subsequent years. The Conference of the Parties serving as the meeting of the Parties to this Protocol shall, at its first session or as soon as practicable thereafter, decide upon modalities, rules and guidelines as to how, and which, additional human-induced activities related to changes in greenhouse gas emissions by sources and removals by sinks in the agricultural soil and land-use change and forestry categories shall be added to, or subtracted from, the assigned amount for Parties included in Annex I, taking into account uncertainties, transparency in reporting, verifiability, the methodological work of the Intergovernmental Panel on Climate Change, the advice provided by the Subsidiary Body for Scientific and Technological Advice in accordance with Article 5 and the decisions of the Conference of the Parties. Such a decision shall apply in the second and subsequent commitment periods. A Party may choose to apply such a decision on these additional human-induced activities for its first commitment period, provided that these activities have taken place since 1990.

5. The Parties included in Annex I undergoing the process of transition to a market economy whose base year or period was established pursuant to decision 9/CP.2 of the Conference of the Parties at its second session, shall use that base year or period for the implementation of their commitments under this Article. Any other Party included in Annex I undergoing the process of transition to a market economy which has not yet submitted its first national communication under Article 12 of the Convention may also notify the Conference of the Parties serving as the meeting of the Parties to this Protocol that it intends to use an historical base year or period other

than 1990 for the implementation of its commitments under this Article. The Conference of the Parties serving as the meeting of the Parties to this Protocol shall decide on the acceptance of such notification.

6. Taking into account Article 4, paragraph 6, of the Convention, in the implementation of their commitments under this Protocol other than those under this Article, a certain degree of flexibility shall be allowed by the Conference of the Parties serving as the meeting of the Parties to this Protocol to the Parties included in Annex I undergoing the process of transition to a market economy.

7. In the first quantified emission limitation and reduction commitment period, from 2008 to 2012, the assigned amount for each Party included in Annex I shall be equal to the percentage inscribed for it in Annex B of its aggregate anthropogenic carbon dioxide equivalent emissions of the greenhouse gases listed in Annex A in 1990, or the base year or period determined in accordance with paragraph 5 above, multiplied by five. Those Parties included in Annex I for whom land-use change and forestry constituted a net source of greenhouse gas emissions in 1990 shall include in their 1990 emissions base year or period the aggregate anthropogenic carbon dioxide equivalent emissions by sources minus removals by sinks in 1990 from land-use change for the purposes of calculating their assigned amount.

8. Any Party included in Annex I may use 1995 as its base year for hydro-fluorocarbons, perfluorocarbons and sulphur hexafluoride, for the purposes of the calculation referred to in paragraph 7 above.

9. Commitments for subsequent periods for Parties included in Annex I shall be established in amendments to Annex B to this Protocol, which shall be adopted in accordance with the provisions of Article 21, paragraph 7. The Conference of the Parties serving as the meeting of the Parties to this Protocol shall initiate the consideration of such commitments at least seven years before the end of the first commitment period referred to in paragraph 1 above.

10. Any emission reduction units, or any part of an assigned amount, which a Party acquires from another Party in accordance with the provisions of Article 6 or of Article 17 shall be added to the assigned amount for the acquiring Party.

11. Any emission reduction units, or any part of an assigned amount, which a Party transfers to another Party in accordance with the provisions of Article 6 or of Article 17 shall be subtracted from the assigned amount for the transferring Party.

12. Any certified emission reductions which a Party acquires from another Party in accordance with the provisions of Article 12 shall be added to the assigned amount for that Party.

13. If the emissions of a Party included in Annex I in a commitment period are less than its assigned amount under this Article, this difference shall, on request of that Party, be added to the assigned amount for that Party for subsequent commitment periods.

14. Each Party included in Annex I shall strive to implement the commitments mentioned in paragraph 1 above in such a way as to minimize adverse social, environment and economic impacts on developing country Parties, particularly those identified in Article 4, paragraphs 8 and 9, of the Convention. In line with relevant decisions of the Conference of the Parties on the implementation of those paragraphs, the Conference of the Parties serving as the meeting of the Parties to this Protocol shall, at its first session, consider what actions are necessary to minimize the adverse effects of climate change and/or the impacts of response measures on Parties referred to in those paragraphs. Among the issues to be considered shall be the establishment of funding, insurance and transfer of technology.

Article 4

1. Any Parties included in Annex I that have reached an agreement to fulfil their commitments under Article 3 jointly, shall be deemed to have met those commitments provided that their total combined aggregate anthropogenic carbon dioxide equivalent emissions of the greenhouse gases listed in Annex A do not exceed their assigned amounts calculated pursuant to their quantified emission limitation and reduction commitments inscribed in Annex B and in accordance with the provisions of Article 3. The respective emission level allocated to each of the Parties to the agreement shall be set out in that agreement.

2. The Parties to any such agreement shall notify the secretariat of the terms of the agreement on the date of deposit of their instruments of ratification, acceptance or approval of this Protocol, or accession thereto. The secretariat shall in turn inform the Parties and signatories to the Convention of the terms of the agreement.

3. Any such agreement shall remain in operation for the duration of the commitment period specified in Article 3, paragraph 7.

4. If Parties acting jointly do so in the framework of, and together with, a regional economic integration organization, any alteration in the composition of the organization after adoption of this Protocol shall not affect existing commitments under this Protocol. Any alteration in the composition of the organization shall only apply for the purposes of those commitments under Article 3 that are adopted subsequent to that alteration.

5. In the event of failure by the Parties to such an agreement to achieve their total combined level of emission reductions, each Party to that agreement shall be responsible for its own level of emissions set out in the agreement.

6. If Parties acting jointly do so in the framework of, and together with, a regional economic integration organization which is itself a Party to this Protocol, each member State of that regional economic integration organization individually, and together with the regional economic integration organization acting in accordance with Article 24, shall, in the event of

failure to achieve the total combined level of emission reductions, be responsible for its level of emissions as notified in accordance with this Article.

Article 5

1. Each Party included in Annex I shall have in place, no later than one year prior to the start of the first commitment period, a national system for the estimation of anthropogenic emissions by sources and removals by sinks of all greenhouse gases not controlled by the Montreal Protocol. Guidelines for such national systems, which shall incorporate the methodologies specified in paragraph 2 below, shall be decided upon by the Conference of the Parties serving as the meeting of the Parties to this Protocol at its first session.

2. Methodologies for estimating anthropologic emissions by sources and removals by sinks of all greenhouse gases not controlled by the Montreal Protocol shall be those accepted by the Intergovernmental Panel on Climate Change and agreed upon by the Conference of the Parties at its third session. Where such methodologies are not used, appropriate adjustments shall be applied according to methodologies agreed upon by the Conference of the Parties serving as the meeting of the Parties to this Protocol at its first session. Based on the work of, *inter alia,* the Intergovernmental Panel on Climate Change and advice provided by the Subsidiary Body for Scientific and Technological Advice, the Conference of the Parties serving as the meeting of the parties to this Protocol shall regularly review and, as appropriate, revise such methodologies and adjustments, taking fully into account any relevant decisions by the Conference of the Parties. Any revision to methodologies or adjustments shall be used only for the purposes of ascertaining compliance with commitments under Article 3 in respect of any commitment period adopted subsequent to that revision.

3. The global warming potentials used to calculate the carbon dioxide equivalence of anthropogenic emissions by sources and removals by sinks of greenhouse gases listed in Annex A shall be those accepted by the Intergovernmental Panel on Climate Change and agreed upon by the Conference of the Parties at its third session. Based on the work of, *inter alia,* the Intergovernmental Panel on Climate Change and advice provided by the Subsidiary Body for Scientific and Technological Advice, the Conference of the Parties serving as the meeting of the Parties to this Protocol shall regularly review and, as appropriate, revise the global warming potential of each greenhouse gas, taking fully into account any relevant decisions by the Conference of the Parties. Any revision to a global warming potential shall apply only to commitments under Article 3 in respect of any commitment period adopted subsequent to that revision.

Article 6

1. For the purpose of meeting its commitments under Article 3, any Party included in Annex I may transfer to, or acquire from, any other such

Party emission reduction units resulting from projects aimed at reducing anthropogenic emissions by sources or enhancing anthropogenic removals by sinks of greenhouse gases in any sector of the economy, provided that:

(a) Any such project has the approval of the Parties involved;

(b) Any such project provides a reduction in emissions by sources, or an enhancement of removals by sinks, that is additional to any that would otherwise occur;

(c) It does not acquire any emission reduction units if it is not in compliance with its obligations under Articles 5 and 7; and

(d) The acquisition of emission reduction units shall be supplemental to domestic actions for the purposes of meeting commitments under Article 3.

2. The Conference of the Parties serving as the meeting of the Parties to this Protocol may, at its first session or as soon as practicable thereafter, further elaborate guidelines for the implementation of this Article for verification and reporting.

3. A Party included in Annex I may authorize legal entities to participate, under its responsibility, in actions leading to the generation, transfer or acquisition under this Article of emission reduction units.

4. If a question of implementation by a Party included in Annex I of the requirements referred to in this Article is identified in accordance with the relevant provisions of Article 8, transfers and acquisitions of emission reduction units may continue to be made after the question has been identified, provided that any such units may not be used by a Party to meet its commitments under Article 3 until any issue of compliance is resolved.

Article 7

1. Each Party included in Annex I shall incorporate in its annual inventory of anthropogenic emissions by sources and removals by sinks of greenhouse gases not controlled by the Montreal Protocol, submitted in accordance with the relevant decisions of the Conference of the Parties, the necessary supplementary information for the purposes of ensuring compliance with Article 3, to be determined in accordance with paragraph 4 below.

2. Each Party included in Annex I shall incorporate in its national communication, submitted under Article 12 of the Convention, the supplementary information necessary to demonstrate compliance with its commitments under this Protocol, to be determined in accordance with paragraph 4 below.

3. Each Party included in Annex I shall submit the information required under paragraph 1 above annually, beginning with the first inventory due under the Convention for the first year of the commitment period after this Protocol has entered into force for that Party. Each such Party shall submit the information required under paragraph 2 above as part of the first national communication due under the Convention after this Protocol has entered into force for it and after the adoption of guidelines as provided for in paragraph 4 below. . . .

4. The Conference of the Parties serving as the meeting of the Parties to this Protocol shall adopt at its first session, and review periodically thereafter, guidelines for the preparation of the information required under this Article, taking into account guidelines for the preparation of national communications by Parties . . . .

Article 8

1. The information submitted under Article 7 by each Party included in Annex I shall be reviewed by expert review teams pursuant to the relevant decisions of the Conference of the Parties and in accordance with guidelines adopted for this purpose by the Conference of the Parties serving as the meeting of the Parties to this Protocol under paragraph 4 below. The information submitted under Article 7, paragraph 1, by each Party included in Annex I shall be reviewed as part of the annual compilation and accounting of emissions inventories and assigned amounts. Additionally, the information submitted under Article 7, paragraph 2, by each Party included in Annex I shall be reviewed as part of the review of communications.

2. Expert review teams shall be coordinated by the secretariat and shall be composed of experts selected from those nominated by Parties to the Convention and, as appropriate, by intergovernmental organizations, in accordance with guidance provided for this purpose by the Conference of the Parties.

3. The review process shall provide a thorough and comprehensive technical assessment of all aspects of the implementation by a Party of this Protocol. The expert review teams shall prepare a report to the Conference of the Parties serving as the meeting of the Parties to this Protocol, assessing the implementation of the commitments of the Party and identifying any potential problems in, and factors influencing, the fulfilment of commitments. Such reports shall be circulated by the secretariat to all Parties to the Convention. The secretariat shall list those questions of implementation indicated in such reports for further consideration by the Conference of the Parties serving as the meeting of the Parties to this Protocol.

4. The Conference of the Parties serving as the meeting of the Parties to this Protocol shall adopt at its first session, and review periodically thereafter, guidelines for the review of implementation of this Protocol by expert review teams. . . .

5. The Conference of the Parties serving as the meeting of the Parties to this Protocol shall, with the assistance of the Subsidiary Body for Implementation and, as appropriate, the Subsidiary Body for Scientific and Technological Advice, consider:

(a) The information submitted by the Parties under Article 7 and the reports of the expert reviews thereon conducted under this Article; and

(b) Those questions of implementation listed by the secretariat under paragraph 3 above, as well as any questions raised by Parties.

6. Pursuant to its consideration of the information referred to in paragraph 5 above, the Conference of the Parties serving as the meeting of the Parties to this Protocol shall take decisions on any matter required for the implementation of this Protocol.

Article 9

1. The Conference of the Parties serving as the meeting of the Parties to this Protocol shall periodically review this Protocol in the light of the best available scientific information and assessments on climate change and its impacts, as well as relevant technical, social and economic information. Such reviews shall be coordinated with pertinent reviews under the Convention, in particular those required by Article 4, paragraph 2(d), and Article 7, paragraph 2(a), of the Convention. Based on these reviews, the Conference of the Parties serving as the meeting of the Parties to this Protocol shall take appropriate action. . . .

Article 10

All Parties, taking into account their common but differentiated responsibilities and their specific national and regional development priorities, objectives and circumstances, without introducing any new commitments for Parties not included in Annex I, but reaffirming existing commitments in Article 4, paragraph 1, of the Convention, and continuing to advance the implementation of these commitments in order to achieve sustainable development, taking into account Article 4, paragraphs 3, 5 and 7, of the Convention, shall:

(a) Formulate, where relevant and to the extent possible, cost-effective national and, where appropriate, regional programmes to improve the quality of local emission factors, activity data and/or models which reflect the socio-economic conditions of each Party for the preparation and periodic updating of national inventories of anthropogenic emissions by sources and removals by sinks of all greenhouse gases not controlled by the Montreal Protocol, using comparable methodologies to be agreed upon by the Conference of the Parties, and consistent with the guidelines for national communications adopted by the Conference of the Parties;

(b) Formulate, implement, publish and regularly update national and, where appropriate, regional programmes containing measures to mitigate climate change and measures to facilitate adequate adaptation to climate change;

(i) Such programmes would, *inter alia*, concern the energy, transport, and industry sectors as well as agriculture, forestry and waste management. Furthermore, adaption technologies and methods for improving spatial planning would improve adaption to climate change; and

(ii) Parties included in Annex I shall submit information on action under this Protocol, including national programmes, in accordance with Article 7, and other Parties shall seek to include in their national communications, as appropriate, information on programmes which contain measures that the Party believes contribute to addressing climate change and its adverse impacts, including the abatement of increases in greenhouse gas emissions, and enhancement of and removals by sinks, capacity building and adaptation measures;

(c) Cooperate in the promotion of effective modalities for the development, application and diffusion of, and take all practicable steps to promote, facilitate and finance, as appropriate, the transfer of, or access to, environmentally sound technologies, know-how, practices and processes pertinent to climate change, in particular to developing countries, including the formulation of policies and programmes for the effective transfer of environmentally sound technologies that are publicly owned or in the public domain and the creation of an enabling environment for the private sector, to promote and enhance access to, and transfer of, environmentally sound technologies;

(d) Cooperate in scientific and technical research and promote the maintenance and the development of systematic observation systems and development of data archives to reduce uncertainties related to the climate system, the adverse impacts of climate change and the economic and social consequences of various response strategies, and promote the development and strengthening of endogenous capacities and capabilities to participate in international and intergovernmental efforts, programmes and networks on research and systematic observation, taking into account Article 5 of the Convention;

(e) Cooperate in and promote at the international level, and, where appropriate, using existing bodies, the development and implementation of education and training programmes . . . . Suitable modalities should be developed to implement these activities through the relevant bodies of the Convention . . . ;

(f) Include in their national communications information on programmes and activities undertaken pursuant to this Article in accordance with relevant decisions of the Conference of the Parties; and

(g) Give full consideration, in implementing the commitments under this Article, to Article 4, paragraph 8, of the Convention.

Article 11

1. In the implementation of Article 10, Parties shall take into account the provisions of Article 4, paragraphs 4, 5, 7, 8 and 9, of the Convention.

2. In the context of the implementation of Article 4, paragraph 1, of the Convention, in accordance with the provisions of Article 4, paragraph 3, and Article 11 of the Convention, and through the entity or entities entrusted with the operation of the financial mechanism of the Convention, the developed country Parties and other developed Parties included in Annex II to the Convention shall:

(a) Provide new and additional financial resources to meet the agreed full costs incurred by developing country Parties in advancing the implementation of existing commitments under Article 4, paragraph 1(a), of the Convention that are covered in Article 10, subparagraph (a); and

(b) Also provide such financial resources, including for the transfer of technology, needed by the developing country Parties to meet the agreed full incremental costs of advancing the implementation of existing commitments in Article 4, paragraph 1, of the Convention that are covered by Article 10 and that are agreed between a developing country Party and the international entity or entities referred to in Article 10 of the Convention, in accordance with that Article.

The implementation of these existing commitments shall take into account the need for adequacy and predictability in the flow of funds and the importance of appropriate burden sharing among developed country Parties. The guidance to the entity or entities entrusted with the operation of the financial mechanism of the Convention in relevant decisions of the Conference of the Parties, including those agreed before the adoption of this Protocol, shall apply *mutatis mutandis* to the provisions of this paragraph.

3. The developed country Parties and other developed Parties in Annex II to the Convention may also provide, and developing country Parties avail themselves of, financial resources for the implementation of Article 10, through bilateral, regional and other multilateral channels.

Article 12

1. A clean development mechanism is hereby defined.

2. The purpose of the clean development mechanism shall be to assist Parties not included in Annex I in achieving sustainable development and in contributing to the ultimate objective of the Convention, and to assist Parties included in Annex I in achieving compliance with their quantified emission limitation and reduction commitments under Article 3.

3. Under the clean development mechanism:

(a) Parties not included in Annex I will benefit from project activities resulting in certified emission reductions; and

(b) Parties included in Annex I may use the certified emission reductions accruing from such project activities to contribute to compliance with part of their quantified emission limitation and reduction commitments under Article 3, as determined by the Conference of the Parties serving as the meeting of the Parties to this Protocol.

4. The clean development mechanism shall be subject to the authority and guidance of the Conference of the Parties serving as the meeting of the Parties to this Protocol and be supervised by an executive board of the clean development mechanism.

5. Emission reductions resulting from each project activity shall be certified by operational entities to be designated by the Conference of the Parties serving as the meeting of the Parties to this Protocol, on the basis of:

(a) Voluntary participation approved by each Party involved;

(b) Real, measurable, and long-term benefits related to the mitigation of climate change; and

(c) Reductions in emissions that are additional to any that would occur in the absence of the certified project activity.

6. The clean development mechanism shall assist in arranging funding of certified project activities as necessary.

7. The Conference of Parties serving as the meeting of the Parties to this Protocol shall, at its first session, elaborate modalities and procedures with the objective of ensuring transparency, efficiency and accountability through independent auditing and verification of project activities.

8. The Conference of the Parties serving as the meeting of the Parties to this Protocol shall ensure that a share of the proceeds from certified project activities is used to cover administrative expenses as well as to assist developing country Parties that are particularly vulnerable to the adverse effects of climate change to meet the costs of adaptation.

9. Participation under the clean development mechanism, including in activities mentioned in paragraph 3(a) above and acquisition of certified emission reductions, may involve private and/or public entities, and is to be subject to whatever guidance may be provided by the executive board of the clean development mechanism.

10. Certified emission reductions obtained during the period from the year 2000 up to the beginning of the first commitment period can be used to assist in achieving compliance in the first commitment period.

Article 13

1. The Conference of the Parties, the supreme body of the Convention, shall serve as the meeting of the Parties to this Protocol.

2. Parties to the Convention that are not Parties to this Protocol may participate as observers in the proceedings of any session of the Conference of the Parties serving as the meeting of the Parties to this Protocol. When the Conference of the Parties serves as the meeting of the Parties to this Protocol, decisions under this Protocol shall be taken only by those that are Parties to this Protocol.

3. When the Conference of the Parties serves as the meeting of the Parties to this Protocol, any member of the Bureau of the Conference of the Parties representing a Party to the Convention but, at that time, not a Party to this Protocol, shall be replaced by an additional member to be elected by and from amongst the Parties to this Protocol.

4. The Conference of the Parties serving as the meeting of the Parties to this Protocol shall keep under regular review the implementation of this Protocol and shall make, within its mandate, the decisions necessary to promote its effective implementation. It shall perform the functions assigned to it by this Protocol and shall:

(a) Assess, on the basis of all information made available to it in accordance with the provisions of this Protocol, the implementation of this

Protocol by the Parties, the overall effects of the measures taken pursuant to this Protocol, in particular environmental, economic and social effects as well as their cumulative impacts and the extent to which progress towards the objective of the Convention is being achieved;

(b) Periodically examine the obligations of the Parties under this Protocol, giving due consideration to any reviews required by Article 4, paragraph 2(d), and Article 7, paragraph 2, of the Convention, in the light of the objective of the Convention, the experience gained in its implementation and the evolution of scientific and technological knowledge, and in this respect consider and adopt regular reports on the implementation of this Protocol;

(c) Promote and facilitate the exchange of information on measures adopted by the Parties to address climate change and its effects, taking into account the differing circumstances, responsibilities and capabilities of the Parties and their respective commitments under this Protocol;

(d) Facilitate, at the request of two or more Parties, the coordination of measures adopted by them to address climate change and its effects, taking into account the differing circumstances, responsibilities and capabilities of the Parties and their respective commitments under this Protocol;

(e) Promote and guide, in accordance with the objective of the Convention and the provisions of this Protocol, and taking fully into account the relevant decisions by the Conference of the Parties, the development and periodic refinement of comparable methodologies for the effective implementation of this Protocol, to be agreed on by the Conference of the Parties serving as the meeting of the Parties to this Protocol;

(f) Make recommendations on any matters necessary for the implementation of this Protocol;

(g) Seek to mobilize additional financial resources in accordance with Article 11, paragraph 2;

(h) Establish such subsidiary bodies as are deemed necessary for the implementation of this Protocol;

(i) Seek and utilize, where appropriate, the services and cooperation of, and information provided by, competent international organizations and intergovernmental and non-governmental bodies; and

(j) Exercise such other functions as may be required for the implementation of this Protocol, and consider any assignment resulting from a decision by the Conference of the Parties.

5. The rules of procedure of the Conference of the Parties and financial procedures applied under the Convention shall be applied *mutatis mutandis* under this Protocol, except as may be otherwise decided by consensus by the Conference of the Parties serving as the meeting of the Parties to this Protocol.

6. The first session of the Conference of the Parties serving as the meeting of the Parties to this Protocol shall be convened by the secretariat in conjunction with the first session of the Conference of the Parties that is

scheduled after the date of the entry into force of this Protocol. Subsequent ordinary sessions of the Conference of the Parties serving as the meeting of the Parties to this Protocol shall be held every year and in conjunction with ordinary sessions of the Conference of the Parties unless otherwise decided by the Conference of the Parties serving as the meeting of the Parties to this Protocol.

7. Extraordinary sessions of the Conference of the Parties serving as the meeting of the Parties to this Protocol shall be held at such other times as may be deemed necessary by the Conference of the Parties. . . .

8. The United Nations, its specialized agencies and the International Atomic Energy Agency, as well as any State member thereof or observers thereto not party to the Convention, may be represented at sessions of the Conference of the Parties serving as the meeting of the Parties to this Protocol as observers. Any body or agency, whether national or international, governmental or non-governmental, which is qualified in matters covered by this Protocol and which has informed the secretariat of its wish to be represented at a session of the Conference of the Parties serving as the meeting of the Parties to this Protocol as an observer, may be so admitted unless at least one third of the Parties present object. . . .

Article 14

1. The secretariat established by Article 8 of the Convention shall serve as the secretariat of this Protocol. . . .

Article 15

1. The Subsidiary Body for Scientific and Technological Advice and the Subsidiary Body for Implementation established by Articles 9 and 10 of the Convention shall serve as, respectively, the Subsidiary Body for Scientific and Technological Advice and the Subsidiary Body for Implementation of this Protocol. . . .

Article 16

The Conference of the Parties serving as the meeting of the Parties to this Protocol shall, as soon as practicable, consider the application to this Protocol of, and modify as appropriate, the multilateral consultative process referred to in Article 13 of the Convention, in the light of relevant decisions that may be taken by the Conference of the Parties. . . .

Article 17

The Conference of the Parties shall define the relevant principles, modalities, rules and guidelines, in particular for verification, reporting and accountability for emissions trading. The Parties included in Annex B may participate in emissions trading for the purposes of fulfilling their commitments under Article 3. Any such trading shall be supplemental to domestic actions for the purpose of meeting quantified emission limitation and reduction commitments under that Article.

Article 18

The Conference of the Parties serving as the meeting of the Parties to this Protocol shall, at its first session, approve appropriate and effective procedures and mechanisms to determine and to address cases of non-compliance with the provisions of this Protocol, . . . Any procedures and mechanisms under this Article entailing binding consequences shall be adopted by means of an amendment to this Protocol.

Article 19

The provision of Article 14 of the Convention on settlement of disputes shall apply *mutatis mutandis* to this Protocol.

Article 20

1. Any party may propose amendments to this Protocol.

2. Amendments to this Protocol shall be adopted at an ordinary session of the Conference of the Parties serving as the meeting of the Parties to this Protocol. The text of any proposed amendment to this Protocol shall be communicated to the Parties by the secretariat at least six months before the meeting at which it is proposed for adoption. . . .

3. The Parties shall make every effort to reach agreement on any proposed amendment to this Protocol by consensus. If all efforts at consensus have been exhausted, and no agreement reached, the amendment shall as a last resort be adopted by a three-fourths majority vote of the Parties present and voting at the meeting. The adopted amendment shall be communicated by the secretariat to the Depositary, who shall circulate it to all Parties for their acceptance. . . .

Article 21

1. Annexes to this Protocol shall form an integral part thereof and, unless otherwise expressly provided, a reference to this Protocol constitutes at the same time a reference to any annexes thereto. Any annexes adopted after the entry into force of this Protocol shall be restricted to lists, forms and any other material of a descriptive nature that is of a scientific, technical, procedural or administrative character.

2. Any Party may make proposals for an annex to this Protocol and may propose amendments to annexes to this Protocol.

3. Annexes to this Protocol and amendments to annexes to this Protocol shall be adopted at an ordinary session of the Conference of the Parties serving as the meeting of the Parties to this Protocol. The text of any proposed annex or amendment to an annex shall be communicated to the

Parties by the secretariat at least six months before the meeting at which it is proposed for adoption. . . .

4. The Parties shall make every effort to reach agreement on any proposed annex or amendment to an annex by consensus. If all efforts at consensus have been exhausted, and no agreement reached, the annex or amendment to an annex shall as a last resort be adopted by a three-fourths majority vote of the Parties present and voting at the meeting. . . .

5. An annex, or amendment to an annex other than Annex A or B, that has been adopted in accordance with paragraphs 3 and 4 above shall enter into force for all Parties to this Protocol six months after the date of the communication by the Depositary to such Parties of the adoption of the annex or adoption of the amendment to the annex, except for those Parties that have notified the Depositary, in writing, within that period of their non-acceptance of the annex or amendment to the annex. The annex or amendment to an annex shall enter into force for Parties which withdraw their notification of non-acceptance on the ninetieth day after the date on which withdrawal of such notification has been received by the Depositary.

6. If the adoption of an annex or an amendment to an annex involves an amendment to this Protocol, that annex or amendment to an annex shall not enter into force until such time as the amendment to this Protocol enters into force.

7. Amendments to Annexes A and B to this Protocol shall be adopted and enter into force in accordance with the procedure set out in Article 20, provided that any amendment to Annex B shall be adopted only with the written consent of the Party concerned.

Article 22

1. Each Party shall have one vote, except as provided for in paragraph 2 below.

2. Regional economic integration organizations, in matters within their competence, shall exercise their right to vote with a number of votes equal to the number of their member States that are Parties to this Protocol. Such an organization shall not exercise its right to vote if any of its member States exercises its right, and vice versa.

Article 23

The Secretary-General of the United Nations shall be the Depositary. . . .

Article 24

1. This Protocol shall be open for signature and subject to ratification, acceptance or approval by States and regional economic integration organizations which are Parties to the Convention . . . . Instruments of ratification, acceptance, approval or accession shall be deposited with the Depositary. . . .

Article 25

1. This Protocol shall enter into force on the ninetieth day after the date on which not less than 55 Parties to the Convention, incorporating Parties included in Annex I which accounted in total for at least 55 per cent of the total carbon dioxide emissions for 1990 of the Parties included in Annex I, have deposited their instruments of ratification, acceptance, approval or accession.

2. For the purposes of this Article, "the total carbon dioxide emissions for 1990 of the Parties included in Annex I" means the amount communicated on or before the date of adoption of this Protocol by the Parties included in Annex I in their first national communications submitted in accordance with Article 12 of the Convention.

3. For each State or regional economic integration organization that ratifies, accepts or approves this Protocol or accedes thereto after the conditions set out in paragraph 1 above for the entry into force have been fulfilled, this Protocol shall enter into force on the ninetieth day following the date of deposit of its instrument of ratification, acceptance, approval or accession. . . .

Article 26

No reservations may be made to this Protocol.

Article 27

1. At any time after three years from the date on which this Protocol has entered into force for a Party, that Party may withdraw from this Protocol by giving written notification to the Depositary.

2. Any such withdrawal shall take effect upon expiry of one year from the date of receipt by the Depositary of the notification of withdrawal, or on such later date as may be specified in the notification of withdrawal.

3. Any Party that withdraws from the Convention shall be considered as also having withdrawn from this Protocol. . . .

Annex A

Greenhouse gases
Carbon dioxide (CO_2)
Methane (CH_4)
Nitrous oxide (N_2O)
Hydrofluorocarbons (HFCs)
Perfluorocarbons (PFCs)
Sulphur hexafluoride (SF_6)

Sectors/source categories
Energy
   Fuel combustion
      Energy industries
      Manufacturing industries and construction
      Transport
      Other sectors
      Other
   Fugitive emissions from fuels
      Solid fuels
      Oil and natural gas
      Other
Industrial processes
      Mineral products
      Chemical industry
      Metal production
      Other production
      Production of halocarbons and sulphur hexafluoride
      Consumption of halocarbons and sulphur hexafluoride
      Other
Solvent and other product use
Agriculture
      Enteric fermentation
      Manure management
      Rice cultivation
      Agricultural soils
      Prescribed burning of savannas
      Field burning of agricultural residues
      Other
Waste
Solid waste disposal on land
Wastewater handling
Waste incineration
Other

Annex B

Party	Quantified emission limitation or reduction committment (percentage of base year or period)
Australia	108
Austria	92
Belgium	92
Bulgaria*	92
Canada	94
Croatia*	95
Czech Republic*	92
Denmark	92
Estonia*	92
European Community	92
Finland	92
France	92
Germany	92
Greece	92
Hungary*	94
Iceland	110
Ireland	92
Italy	92
Japan	94
Latvia*	92
Liechtenstein	92
Lithuania*	92
Luxembourg	92
Monaco	92
Netherlands	92
New Zealand	100
Norway	101
Poland*	94
Portugal	92
Romania*	92
Russian Federation*	100
Slovakia*	92
Slovenia*	92
Spain	92
Sweden	92
Switzerland	92
Ukraine*	100

Party	Quantified emission limitation or reduction committment (percentage of base year or period)
United Kingdom of Great Britain and Northern Ireland	92
United States of America	93

*Countries that are undergoing the process of transition to a market economy.

11

Use of Force and Arms Control

U.N. "UNITING FOR PEACE" RESOLUTION
U.N. G.A. Res. 337A (V 1950)*

A

The General Assembly,

Recognizing that the first two stated Purposes of the United Nations are:

> To maintain international peace and security, and to that end: to take effective collective measures for the prevention and removal of threats to the peace, and for the suppression of acts of aggression or other breaches of the peace, and to bring about by peaceful means, and in conformity with the principles of justice and international law, adjustment or settlement of international disputes or situations which might lead to a breach of the peace, and
> To develop friendly relations among nations based on respect for the principle of equal rights and self-determination of peoples, and to take other appropriate measures to strengthen universal peace,

Reaffirming that it remains the primary duty of all Members of the United Nations, when involved in an international dispute, to seek settlement of such a dispute by peaceful means through the procedures laid down in Chapter VI of the Charter, and recalling the successful achievements of the United Nations in this regard on a number of previous occasions,

Finding that international tension exists on a dangerous scale,

Recalling its resolution 290 (IV) entitled "Essentials of peace", which states that disregard of the Principles of the Charter of the United Nations is

---

* Adopted by the U.N. General Assembly on November 3, 1950. The vote was 52 states for, 5 against (Byelorussion S.S.R., Czechoslovakia, Poland, Ukrainian S.S.R., and the U.S.S.R.), and 2 abstaining (Argentina and India).

primarily responsible for the continuance of international tension, and desiring to contribute further to the objectives of that resolution,

Reaffirming the importance of the exercise by the Security Council of its primary responsibility for the maintenance of international peace and security, and the duty of the permanent members to seek unanimity and to exercise restraint in the use of the veto,

Reaffirming that the initiative in negotiating the agreements for armed forces provided for in Article 43 of the Charter belongs to the Security Council, and desiring to ensure that, pending the conclusion of such agreements, the United Nations has at its disposal means for maintaining international peace and security,

Conscious that failure of the Security Council to discharge its responsibilities on behalf of all the Member States, particularly those responsibilities referred to in the two preceding paragraphs, does not relieve Member States of their obligations or the United Nations of its responsibility under the Charter to maintain international peace and security,

Recognizing in particular that such failure does not deprive the General Assembly of its rights or relieve it of its responsibilities under the Charter in regard to the maintenance of international peace and security,

Recognizing that discharge by the General Assembly of its responsibilities in these respects calls for possibilities of observation which would ascertain the facts and expose aggressors; for the existence of armed forces which could be used collectively; and for the possibility of timely recommendation by the General Assembly to Members of the United Nations for collective action which, to be effective, should be prompt,

A

1. Resolves that if the Security Council, because of lack of unanimity of the permanent members, fails to exercise its primary responsibility for the maintenance of international peace and security in any case where there appears to be a threat to the peace, breach of the peace, or act of aggression, the General Assembly shall consider the matter immediately with a view to making appropriate recommendations to Members for collective measures, including in the case of a breach of the peace or act of aggression the use of armed force when necessary, to maintain or restore international peace and security. If not in session at the time, the General Assembly may meet in emergency special session within twenty-four hours of the request therefor. Such emergency special session shall be called if requested by the Security Council on the vote of any seven members, or by a majority of the Members of the United Nations;

2. Adopts for this purpose the amendments to its rules of procedure set forth in the annex to the present resolution;

B

3. Establishes a Peace Observation Commission which, for the calendar years 1951 and 1952, shall be composed of fourteen Members, namely:

China, Colombia, Czechoslovakia, France, India, Iraq, Israel, New Zealand, Pakistan, Sweden, the Union of Soviet Socialist Republics, the United Kingdom of Great Britain and Northern Ireland, the United States of America and Uruguay, and which could observe and report on the situation in any area where there exists international tension the continuance of which is likely to endanger the maintenance of international peace and security. Upon the invitation or with the consent of the State into whose territory the Commission would go, the General Assembly, or the Interim Committee when the Assembly is not in session, may utilize the Commission if the Security Council is not exercising the functions assigned to it by the Charter with respect to the matter in question. Decisions to utilize the Commission shall be made on the affirmative vote of two-thirds of the members present and voting. The Security Council may also utilize the Commission in accordance with its authority under the Charter; . . .

C

7. *Invites* each Member of the United Nations to survey its resources in order to determine the nature and scope of the assistance it may be in a position to render in support of any recommendations of the Security Council or of the General Assembly for the restoration of international peace and security;

8. *Recommends* to the States Members of the United Nations that each Member maintain within its national armed forces elements so trained, organized and equipped that they could promptly be made available, in accordance with its constitutional processes, for service as a United Nations unit or units, upon recommendation by the Security Council or the General Assembly, without prejudice to the use of such elements in exercise of the right of individual or collective self-defence recognized in Article 51 of the Charter;

9. *Invites* the Members of the United Nations to inform the Collective Measures Committee provided for in paragraph 11 as soon as possible of the measures taken in implementation of the preceding paragraph;

10. Requests the Secretary-General to appoint, with the approval of the Committee provided for in paragraph 11, a panel of military experts who could be made available, on request, to Member States wishing to obtain technical advice regarding the organization, training, and equipment for prompt service as United Nations units of the elements referred to in paragraph 8;

D

11. *Establishes* a Collective Measures Committee consisting of fourteen Members, namely: Australia, Belgium, Brazil, Burma, Canada, Egypt, France, Mexico, Philippines, Turkey, the United Kingdom of Great Britain and Northern Ireland, the United States of America, Venezuela and Yugoslavia, and directs the Committee, in consultation with the Secretary-General and with

such Member States as the Committee finds appropriate, to study and make a report to the Security Council and the General Assembly, not later than 1 September 1951, on methods, including those in section C of the present resolution, which might be used to maintain and strengthen international peace and security in accordance with the Purposes and Principles of the Charter, taking account of collective self-defence and regional arrangements (Articles 51 and 52 of the Charter); . . .

13. *Requests* the Secretary-General to furnish the staff and facilities necessary for the effective accomplishment of the purposes set forth in sections C and D of the present resolution;

E

14. Is fully conscious that, in adopting the proposals set forth above, enduring peace will not be secured solely by collective security arrangements against breaches of international peace and acts of aggression, but that a genuine and lasting peace depends also upon the observance of all the Principles and Purposes established in the Charter of the United Nations, upon the implementation of the resolutions of the Security Council, the General Assembly and other principal organs of the United Nations intended to achieve the maintenance of international peace and security, and especially upon respect for and observance of human rights and fundamental freedoms for all and on the establishment and maintenance of conditions of economic and social well-being in all countries; and accordingly

15. Urges Member States to respect fully, and to intensify, joint action, in co-operation with the United Nations, to develop and stimulate universal respect for and observance of human rights and fundamental freedoms, and to intensify individual and collective efforts to achieve conditions of economic stability and social progress, particularly through the development of under-developed countries and areas.

Annex

The rules of procedure of the General Assembly are amended in the following respects:

1. The present text of rule 8 shall become paragraph (*a*) of that rule, and a new paragraph (b) shall be added to read as follows:

"Emergency special sessions pursuant to resolution 377A (V) shall be convened within twenty-four hours of the receipt by the Secretary-General of a request for such a session from the Security Council, on the vote of any seven members thereof, or of a request from a majority of the Members of the United Nations expressed by vote in the Interim Committee or otherwise, or of the concurrence of a majority of Members as provided in rule 9."

2. The present text of rule 9 shall become paragraph (a) of that rule and a new paragraph (b) shall be added to read as follows:

"This rule shall apply also to a request by any Member for an emergency special session pursuant to resolution 377A (V). In such a case the Secretary-General shall communicate with other Members by the most expeditious means of communication available."

3. Rule 10 is amended by adding at the end thereof the following:

"... In the case of an emergency special session convened pursuant to rule 8(*b*), the Secretary-General shall notify the Members of the United Nations at least twelve hours in advance of the opening of the session."

4. Rule 16 is amended by adding at the end thereof the following:

"... The provisional agenda of an emergency special session shall be communicated to the Members of the United Nations simultaneously with the communication summoning the session."

5. Rule 19 is amended by adding at the end thereof the following:

"... During an emergency special session additional items concerning the matters dealt with in resolution 377A (V) may be added to the agenda by a two-thirds majority of the Members present and voting."

6. There is added a new rule to precede rule 65 to read as follows:

"Notwithstanding the provisions of any other rule and unless the General Assembly decides otherwise, the Assembly, in case of an emergency special session, shall convene in plenary session only and proceed directly to consider the item proposed for consideration in the request for the holding of the session, without previous reference to the General Committee or to any other Committee; the President and Vice-Presidents for such emergency special sessions shall be, respectively, the Chairman of those delegations from which were elected the President and Vice-Presidents of the previous session."

B

For the purpose of maintaining international peace and security, in accordance with the Charter of the United Nations, and, in particular, with Chapters V, VI and VII of the Charter,

The General Assembly

Recommends to the Security Council:

That it should take the necessary steps to ensure that the action provided for under the Charter is taken with respect to threats to the peace, breaches of the peace or acts of aggression and with respect to the peaceful settlement of disputes or situations likely to endanger the maintenance of international peace and security;

That it should devise measures for the earliest application of Articles 43, 45, 46 and 47 of the Charter of the United Nations regarding the placing of armed forces at the disposal of the Security Council by the States Members of the United Nations and the effective functioning of the Military Staff Committee;

The above dispositions should in no manner prevent the General Assembly from fulfilling its functions under resolution 377A (V).

C

The General Assembly,

Recognizing that the primary function of the United Nations Organization is to maintain and promote peace, security and justice among all nations, . . .

Recognizing that the Charter charges the Security Council with the primary responsibility for maintaining international peace and security,

Reaffirming the importance of unanimity among the permanent members of the Security Council on all problems which are likely to threaten world peace.

Recalling General Assembly resolution 190 (III) entitled "Appeal to the Great Powers to renew their efforts to compose their differences and establish a lasting peace",

Recommends to the permanent members of the Security Council that:

(*a*) They meet and discuss, collectively or otherwise, and, if necessary, with other States concerned, all problems which are likely to threaten international peace and hamper the activities of the United Nations, with a view to their resolving fundamental differences and reaching agreement in accordance with the spirit and letter of the Charter;

(*b*) They advise the General Assembly and, when it is not in session, the Members of the United Nations, as soon as appropriate, of the results of their consultations.

U.N. DEFINITION OF AGGRESSION RESOLUTION

U.N. G.A. Res. 3314 (XIXX)*

The General Assembly,

Having considered the report of the Special Committee on the Question of Defining Aggression, . . . including the draft Definition of Aggression adopted by the Special Committee by consensus and recommended for adoption by the General Assembly,

Deeply convinced that the adoption of the Definition of Aggression would contribute to the strengthening of international peace and security,

1. *Approves* the Definition of Aggression, the text of which is annexed to the present resolution;

2. *Expresses its appreciation* to the Special Committee on the Question of Defining Aggression for its work which resulted in the elaboration of the Definition of Aggression;

3. *Calls upon* all States to refrain from all acts of aggression and other uses of force contrary to the Charter of the United Nations and the Declaration on Principles of International Law concerning Friendly Relations and Co-operation among States in accordance with the Charter of the United Nations;

4. *Calls the attention* of the Security Council to the Definition of Aggression, as set out below, and recommends that it should, as appropriate, take account of that Definition as guidance in determining, in accordance with the Charter, the existence of an act of aggression.

2319th plenary meeting
14 December 1974

Annex

Definition of Aggression

The General Assembly,

Basing itself on the fact that one of the fundamental purposes of the United Nations is to maintain international peace and security and to take effective collective measures for the prevention and removal of threats to the

* Adopted without vote by the U.N. General Assembly on December 14, 1974.

peace, and for the suppression of acts of aggression or other breaches of the peace,

Recalling that the Security Council, in accordance with Article 39 of the Charter of the United Nations, shall determine the existence of any threat to the peace, breach of the peace or act of aggression and shall make recommendations, or decide what measures shall be taken in accordance with Articles 41 and 42, to maintain or restore international peace and security,

Recalling also the duty of States under the Charter to settle their international disputes by peaceful means in order not to endanger international peace, security and justice,

Bearing in mind that nothing in this Definition shall be interpreted as in any way affecting the scope of the provisions of the Charter with respect to the functions and powers of the organs of the United Nations,

Considering also that, since aggression is the most serious and dangerous form of the illegal use of force, being fraught, in the conditions created by the existence of all types of weapons of mass destruction, with the possible threat of a world conflict and all its catastrophic consequences, aggression should he defined at the present stage,

Reaffirming the duty of States not to use armed force to deprive peoples of their right to self-determination, freedom and independence, or to disrupt territorial integrity,

Reaffirming also that the territory of a State shall not be violated by being the object, even temporarily, of military occupation or of other measures of force taken by another State in contravention of the Charter, and that it shall not be the object of acquisition by another State resulting from such measures or the threat thereof,

Reaffirming also the provisions of the Declaration on Principles of International Law concerning Friendly Relations and Co-operation among States in accordance with the Charter of the United Nations,

Convinced that the adoption of a definition of aggression ought to have the effect of deterring a potential aggressor, would simplify the determination of acts of aggression and the implementation of measures to suppress them and would also facilitate the protection of the rights and lawful interests of, and the rendering of assistance to, the victim,

Believing that, although the question whether an act of aggression has been committed must be considered in the light of all the circumstances of each particular case, it is nevertheless desirable to formulate basic principles as guidance for such determination,

Adopts the following Definition of Aggression:

Article 1

Aggression is the use of armed force by a State against the sovereignty, territorial integrity or political independence of another State, or in any other manner inconsistent with the Charter of the United Nations, as set out in this Definition.

Explanatory note: In this Definition the term "State":

(*a*) Is used without prejudice to questions of recognition or to whether a State is a member of the United Nations;

(*b*) Includes the concept of a "group of States" where appropriate.

Article 2

The first use of armed force by a State in contravention of the Charter shall constitute prima facie evidence of an act of aggression although the Security Council may, in conformity with the Charter, conclude that a determination that an act of aggression has been committed would not be justified in the light of other relevant circumstances, including the fact that the acts concerned or their consequences are not of sufficient gravity.

Article 3

Any of the following acts, regardless of a declaration of war, shall, subject to and in accordance with the provisions of article 2, qualify as an act of aggression:

(*a*) The invasion or attack by the armed forces of a State of the territory of another State, or any military occupation, however temporary, resulting from such invasion or attack, or any annexation by the use of force of the territory of another State or part thereof;

(*b*) Bombardment by the armed forces of a State against the territory of another State or the use of any weapons by a State against the territory of another State;

(*c*) The blockade of the ports or coasts of a State by the armed forces of another State;

(*d*) An attack by the armed forces of a State on the land, sea or air forces, or marine and air fleets of another State;

(*e*) The use of armed forces of one State which are within the territory of another State with the agreement of the receiving State, in contravention of the conditions provided for in the agreement or any extension of their presence in such territory beyond the termination of the agreement;

(*f*) The action of a State in allowing its territory, which it has placed at the disposal of another State, to be used by that other State for perpetrating an act of aggression against a third State;

(*g*) The sending by or on behalf of a State of armed bands, groups, irregulars or mercenaries, which carry out acts of armed force against another State of such gravity as to mount to the acts listed above, or its substantial involvement therein.

Article 4

The acts enumerated above are not exhaustive and the Security Council may determine that other acts constitute aggression under the provisions of the Charter.

Article 5

1. No consideration of whatever nature, whether political, economic, military or otherwise, may serve as a justification for aggression.

2. A war of aggression is a crime against international peace. Aggression gives rise to international responsibility.

3. No territorial acquisition or special advantage resulting from aggression is or shall be recognized as lawful.

Article 6

Nothing in this Definition shall be construed as in any way enlarging or diminishing the scope of the Charter, including its provisions concerning cases in which the use of force is lawful.

Article 7

Nothing in this Definition, and in particular article 3, could in any way prejudice the right to self-determination, freedom and independence, as derived from the Charter, of peoples forcibly deprived of that right and referred to in the Declaration on Principles of International Law concerning Friendly Relations and Co-operation among States in accordance with the Charter of the United Nations, particularly peoples under colonial and racist régimes or other forms of alien domination; nor the right of these peoples to struggle to that end and to seek and receive support, in accordance with the principles of the Charter and in conformity with the above-mentioned Declaration.

Article 8

In their interpretation and application the above provisions are inter-related and each provision should be construed in the context of the other provisions.

U.N. PARTICIPATION ACT

22 U.S.C. §287 c-d (2013)

§287c. Economic and Communication Sanctions Pursuant to United Nations Security Council Resolution

(a) Enforcement Measures; Importation of Rhodesian Chromium

Notwithstanding the provisions of any other law, whenever the United States is called upon by the Security Council to apply measures which said Council has decided, pursuant to article 41 of said Charter, are to be employed to give effect to its decisions under said Charter, the President may, to the extent necessary to apply such measures, through any agency which he may designate, and under such orders, rules, and regulations as may be prescribed by him, investigate, regulate, or prohibit, in whole or in part, economic relations or rail, sea, air, postal, telegraphic, radio, and other means of communication between any foreign country or any national thereof or any person therein and the United States or any person subject to the jurisdiction thereof, or involving any property subject to the jurisdiction of the United States. Any Executive order which is issued under this subsection and which applies measures against Southern Rhodesia pursuant to any United Nations Security Council Resolution may be enforced, notwithstanding the provisions of any other law. The President may exempt from such Executive order any shipment of chromium in any form which is in transit to the United States on March 18, 1977.

(b) Penalties

Any person who willfully violates or evades or attempts to violate or evade any order, rule, or regulation issued by the President pursuant to subsection (a) of this section shall, upon conviction, be fined not more than $1,000,000 or, if a natural person, be imprisoned for not more than ten years, or both.

(Dec. 20, 1945, c.583, §5, 59 Stat. 620; Oct. 10, 1949, c.660, §3, 63 Stat. 735; Mar. 18, 1977, Pub. L. 95-12, §1, 91 Stat. 22.) (As amended July 1, 2010, Pub. L. 111-195, Title I, §107(a)(1), 124 Stat. 1337.)

§287d. Use of Armed Forces; Limitations

The President is authorized to negotiate a special agreement or agreements with the Security Council which shall be subject to the approval of the Congress by appropriate Act or joint resolution, providing for the numbers and types of armed forces, their degree of readiness and general location, and the nature of facilities and assistance, including rights of passage, to be made available to the Security Council on its call for the purpose of maintaining international peace and security in accordance with article 43 of said Charter. The President shall not be deemed to require the authorization of the Congress to make available to the Security Council on its call in order to take action under article 42 of said Charter and pursuant to such special agreement or agreements the armed forces, facilities, or assistance provided for therein: Provided, That, except as authorized in section 287 d-1 of this title, nothing herein contained shall be construed as an authorization to the President by the Congress to make available to the Security Council for such purpose armed forces, facilities, or assistance in addition to the forces, facilities, and assistance provided for in such special agreement or agreements.

(Dec. 20, 1945, c.583, §6, 59 Stat. 621; Oct. 10, 1949, c.660, §4, 63 Stat. 735.)

§287 d-1. Noncombatant Assistance to United Nations

(a) Armed Forces Details; Supplies and Equipment; Obligation of Funds; Procurement and Replacement of Requested Items

Notwithstanding the provisions of any other law, the President, upon the request by the United Nations for cooperative action, and to the extent that he finds that it is consistent with the national interest to comply with such request, may authorize, in support of such activities of the United Nations as are specifically directed to the peaceful settlement of disputes and not involving the employment of armed forces contemplated by chapter VII of the United Nations Charter—

(1) the detail to the United Nations, under such terms and conditions as the President shall determine, of personnel of the armed forces of the United States to serve as observers, guards, or in any non-combatant capacity, but in no event shall more than a total of one thousand of such personnel be so detailed at any one time: Provided, That while so detailed, such personnel shall be considered for all purposes as acting in the line of duty including the receipt of pay and allowances as personnel of the armed forces of the United States, credit for longevity and retirement, and all other perquisites appertaining to such duty: Provided further, That upon authorization or approval by the President, such personnel may accept directly from the United Nations (a) any or all of the allowances or perquisites to which

they are entitled under the first proviso hereof, and (b) extraordinary expenses and perquisites incident to such detail;

(2) the furnishing of facilities, services, or other assistance and the loan of the agreed fair share of the United States of any supplies and equipment to the United Nations by the Department of Defense, under such terms and conditions as the President shall determine;

(3) the obligation, insofar as necessary to carry out the purposes of clauses (1) and (2) of this subsection, of any funds appropriated to the Department of Defense or any department therein, the procurement of such personnel, supplies, equipment, facilities, services, or other assistance as may be made available in accordance with the request of the United Nations, and the replacement of such items, when necessary, where they are furnished from stocks.

(b)   Reimbursement from United Nations; Waiver of Reimbursement

Whenever personnel or assistance is made available pursuant to the authority contained in subsection (a)(1) and (2) of this section, the President shall require reimbursement from the United Nations for the expense thereby incurred by the United States: *Provided*, That in exceptional circumstances, or when the President finds it to be in the national interest, he may waive, in whole or in part, the requirement of such reimbursement: *Provided further*, That when any such reimbursement is made, it shall be credited, at the option of the appropriate department of the Department of Defense, either to the appropriation, fund, or account utilized in incurring the obligation, or to an appropriate appropriation, fund, or account currently available for the purposes for which expenditures were made.

(c)   Additional Appropriation Authorizations

In addition to the authorization of appropriations to the Department of State contained in section 287e of this title, there is hereby authorized to be appropriated to the Department of Defense, or any department therein, such sums as may be necessary to reimburse such departments in the event that reimbursement from the United Nations is waived in whole or in part pursuant to authority contained in subsection (b) of this section. . . .

(Dec. 20, 1945, c.583, §7, as added Oct. 10, 1949, c.660, §5, 63 Stat. 735, and amended Aug. 10, 1949, c.412, §12(a), 63 Stat. 591.)

WAR POWERS RESOLUTION

November 7, 1973, Pub. L. No. 93-148, 87 Stat. 555, 50 U.S.C. §§1541-1548
(as amended)

§1541.   Purpose and Policy [§2]

(a)   *Congressional Declaration*

It is the purpose of this chapter to fulfill the intent of the framers of the Constitution of the United States and insure that the collective judgment of both the Congress and the President will apply to the introduction of United States Armed Forces into hostilities, or into situations where imminent involvement in hostilities is clearly indicated by the circumstances, and to the continued use of such forces in hostilities or in such situations.

(b)   *Congressional Legislative Power Under Necessary and Proper Clause*

Under article I, section 8, of the Constitution, it is specifically provided that the Congress shall have the power to make all laws necessary and proper for carrying into execution, not only its own powers but also all other powers vested by the Constitution in the Government of the United States, or in any department or officer hereof.

(c)   *Presidential Executive Power as Commander-in-Chief; Limitation*

The constitutional powers of the President as Commander-in-Chief to introduce United States Armed Forces into hostilities, or into situations where imminent involvement in hostilities is clearly indicated by the circumstances, are exercised only pursuant to (1) a declaration of war, (2) specific statutory authorization, or (3) a national emergency created by attack upon the United States, its territories or possessions, or its armed forces.

(Pub. L. 93-148, §2.)

§1542.   Consultation; Initial and Regular Consultations [§3]

The President in every possible instance shall consult with Congress before introducing United States Armed Forces into hostilities or into situations where imminent involvement in hostilities is clearly indicated by the circumstances, and after every such introduction shall consult regularly with the Congress until United States Armed Forces are no longer engaged in hostilities or have been removed from such situations.

(Pub. L. 93-148, §3.)

§1543.   Reporting Requirement [§4]

(a)   Written Report; Time of Submission; Circumstances Necessitating Submission; Information Reported

In the absence of a declaration of war, in any case in which United States Armed Forces are introduced—

(1) into hostilities or into situations where imminent involvement in hostilities is clearly indicated by the circumstances;

(2) into the territory, airspace or waters of a foreign nation, while equipped for combat, except for deployments which relate solely to supply, replacement, repair, or training of such forces; or

(3) in numbers which substantially enlarge United States Armed Forces equipped for combat already located in a foreign nation; the President shall submit within 48 hours to the Speaker of the House of Representatives and to the President pro tempore of the Senate a report, in writing, setting forth—

(A) the circumstances necessitating the introduction of United States Armed Forces;

(B) the constitutional and legislative authority under which such introduction took place; and

(C) the estimated scope and duration of the hostilities or involvement.

(b)   Other Information Reported

The President shall provide such other information as the Congress may request in the fulfillment of its constitutional responsibilities with respect to committing the Nation to war and to the use of United States Armed Forces abroad.

(c)   Periodic Reports; Semiannual Requirement

Whenever United States Armed Forces arc introduced into hostilities or into any situation described in subsection (a) of this section, the President shall, so long as such armed forces continue to be engaged in such hostilities or situation, report to the Congress periodically on the status of such hostilities or situation as well as on the scope and duration of such hostilities or situation, but in no event shall be report to the Congress less often than once every six months.

(Pub. L. 93-148, §4.)

§1544. Congressional Action [§5]

(a) Transmittal of Report and Referral to Congressional Committees; Joint Request for Convening Congress

Each report submitted pursuant to section 1543(a)(1) of this title shall be transmitted to the Speaker of the House of Representatives and to the President pro tempore of the Senate on the same calendar day. Each report so transmitted shall be referred to the Committee on Foreign Affairs of the House of Representatives and to the Committee on Foreign Relations of the Senate for appropriate action. If, when the report is transmitted, the Congress has adjourned sine die or has adjourned for any period in excess of three calendar days, the Speaker of the House of Representatives and the President pro tempore of the Senate, if they deem it advisable (or if petitioned by at least 30 percent of the membership of their respective Houses) shall jointly request the President to convene Congress in order that it may consider the report and take appropriate action pursuant to this section.

(b) Termination of Use of United States Armed Forces; Exceptions; Extension Period

Within sixty calendar days after a report is submitted or is required to be submitted pursuant to section 1543(a)(1) of this title, whichever is earlier, the President shall terminate any use of United States Armed Forces with respect to which such report was submitted (or required to be submitted), unless the Congress (1) has declared war or has enacted a specific authorization for such use of United States Armed Forces, (2) has extended by law such sixty-day period, or (3) is physically unable to meet as a result of an armed attack upon the United States. Such sixty-day period shall be extended for not more than an additional thirty days if the President determines and certifies to the Congress in writing that unavoidable military necessity respecting the safety of United States Armed Forces requires the continued use of such armed forces in the course of bringing about a prompt removal of such forces.

(c) Concurrent Resolution for Removal by President of United States Armed Forces

Notwithstanding subsection (b) of this section, at any time that United States Armed Forces are engaged in hostilities outside the territory of the United States, its possessions and territories without a declaration of war or specific statutory authorization, such forces shall be removed by the President if the Congress so directs by concurrent resolution.

(Pub. L. 93-148, §5.)

§1545. Congressional Priority Procedures for Joint Resolution or Bill [§6]

(a) Time Requirement; Referral to Congressional Committee; Single Report

Any joint resolution or bill introduced pursuant to section 1544(b) of this title at least thirty calendar days before the expiration of the sixty-day period specified in such section shall be referred to the Committee on Foreign Affairs of the House of Representatives or the Committee on Foreign Relations of the Senate, as the case may be, and such committee shall report one such joint resolution or bill, together with its recommendations, not later than twenty-four calendar days before the expiration of the sixty-day period specified in such section, unless such House shall otherwise determine by the years and nays.

(b) Pending Business; Vote

Any joint resolution or bill so reported shall become the pending business of the House in question (in the case of the Senate the time for debate shall be equally divided between the proponents and the opponents), and shall be voted on within three calendar days thereafter, unless such House shall otherwise determine by yeas and nays.

(c) Referral to Other House Committee

Such a joint resolution or bill passed by one House shall be referred to the committee of the other House named in subsection (a) of this section and shall be reported out not later than fourteen calendar days before the expiration of the sixty-day period specified in section 1544(b) of this title. The joint resolution or bill so reported shall become the pending business of the House in question and shall be voted on within three calendar days after it has been reported, unless such House shall otherwise determine by yeas and nays.

(d) Disagreement Between Houses

In the case of any disagreement between the two Houses of Congress with respect to a joint resolution or bill passed by both Houses, conferees shall be promptly appointed and the committee of conference shall make and file a report with respect to such resolution or bill not later than four calendar days before the expiration of the sixty-day period specified in section 1544(b) of this title. In the event the conferees are unable to agree within 48 hours, they shall report back to their respective Houses in disagreement. Notwithstanding any rule in either House concerning the printing of conference reports in the Record or concerning any delay in the consideration of such reports, such report shall be acted on by both Houses not later than the expiration of such sixty-day period.

(Pub. L. 93-148, §6.)

§1546.   Congressional Priority Procedures for Concurrent Resolution [§7]

(a)   *Referral to Congressional Committee; Single Report*

Any concurrent resolution introduced pursuant to section 1544(c) of this title shall be referred to the Committee on Foreign Affairs of the House of Representatives or the Committee on Foreign Relations of the Senate, as the case may be, and one such concurrent resolution shall be reported out by such committee together with its recommendations within fifteen calendar days, unless such House shall otherwise determine by the yeas and nays.

(b)   *Pending Business; Vote*

Any concurrent resolution so reported shall become the pending business of the House in question (in the case of the Senate the time for debate shall be equally divided between the proponents and the opponents) and shall be voted on within three calendar days thereafter, unless such House shall otherwise determine by yeas and nays.

(c)   *Referral to Other House Committee*

Such a concurrent resolution passed by one House shall be referred to the committee of the other House named in subsection (a) of this section and shall be reported out by such committee together with its recommendations within fifteen calendar days and shall thereupon become the pending business of such House and shall be voted upon within three calendar days, unless such House shall otherwise determine by yeas and nays.

(d)   *Disagreement Between Houses*

In the case of any disagreement between the two Houses of Congress with respect to a concurrent resolution passed by both Houses, conferees shall be promptly appointed and the committee of conference shall make and file a report with respect to such concurrent resolution within six calendar days after the legislation is referred to the committee of conference. Notwithstanding any rule in either House concerning the printing of conference reports in the Record or concerning any delay in the consideration of such reports, such report shall be acted on by both Houses not later than six calendar days after the conference report is filed. In the event the conferees are unable to agree within 48 hours, they shall report back to their respective Houses in disagreement.

(Pub. L. 93-148, §7.)

§1546a. Expedited Procedures for Certain Joint Resolutions and Bills

Any joint resolution or bill introduced in either House which requires the removal of United States Armed Forces engaged in hostilities outside the territory of the United States, its possessions and territories, without a declaration of war or specific statutory authorization shall be considered in accordance with the procedures of section 601(b) of the International Security Assistance and Arms Export Control Act of 1976, except that any such resolution or bill shall be amendable. If such a joint resolution or bill should be vetoed by the President, the time for debate in consideration of the veto message on such measure shall be limited to twenty hours in the Senate and in the House shall be determined in accordance with the Rules of the House.

(Pub. L. 98-164, Title X, §1013, Nov. 22, 1983, 97 Stat. 1062.)

§1547. Interpretation of Joint Resolution [§8]

(a) Inferences from Any Law or Treaty

Authority to introduce United States Armed Forces into hostilities or into situations wherein involvement in hostilities is clearly indicated by the circumstances shall not be inferred—

(1) from any provision of law (whether or not in effect before November 7, 1973), including any provision contained in any appropriation Act, unless such provision specifically authorizes the introduction of United States Armed Forces into hostilities or into such situations and states that it is intended to constitute specific statutory authorization within the meaning of this chapter; or

(2) from any treaty heretofore or hereafter ratified unless such treaty is implemented by legislation specifically authorizing the introduction of United States Armed Forces into hostilities or into such situations and stating that it is intended to constitute specific statutory authorization within the meaning of this chapter.

(b) Joint Headquarters Operations of High-level Military Commands

Nothing in this chapter shall be construed to require any further specific statutory authorization to permit members of United States Armed Forces to participate jointly with members of the armed forces of one or more foreign countries in the headquarters operations of high-level military commands which were established prior to November 7, 1973, and pursuant to the United Nations Charter or any treaty ratified by the United States prior to such date.

(c) Introduction of United States Armed Forces

For purposes of this chapter, the term "introduction of United States Armed Forces" includes the assignment of members of such armed forces to command, coordinate, participate in the movement of, or accompany the regular or irregular military forces of any foreign country or government when such military forces are engaged, or there exists an imminent threat that such forces will become engaged, in hostilities.

(d) Constitutional Authorities or Existing Treaties Unaffected; Construction Against Grant of Presidential Authority Respecting Use of United States Armed Forces

Nothing in this chapter—

(1) is intended to alter the constitutional authority of the Congress or of the President, or the provisions of existing treaties; or

(2) shall be construed as granting any authority to the President with respect to the introduction of United States Armed Forces into hostilities or into situations wherein involvement in hostilities is clearly indicated by the circumstances which authority he would not have had in the absence of this chapter.

(Pub. L. 93-148, §8.)

§1548. Separability of Provisions [§9]

If any provision of this chapter or the application thereof to any person or circumstance is held invalid, the remainder of the chapter and the application of such provision to any other person or circumstance shall not be affected thereby.

(Pub. L. 93-148, 9.)

MATERIALS RE: IRAQ

U.N. SECURITY COUNCIL RES. 660
August 2, 1990*

The Security Council,

Alarmed by the invasion of Kuwait on 2 August 1990 by the military forces of Iraq,

Determining that there exists a breach of international peace and security as regards the Iraqi invasion of Kuwait,

Acting under Articles 39 and 40 of the Charter of the United Nations,

1. *Condemns* the Iraqi invasion of Kuwait;

2. *Demands* that Iraq withdraw immediately and unconditionally all its forces to the positions in which they were located on 1 August 1990;

3. *Calls upon* Iraq and Kuwait to begin immediately intensive negotiations for the resolution of their differences and supports all efforts in this regard, and especially those of the League of Arab States;

4. *Decides* to meet again as necessary to consider further steps to ensure compliance with the present resolution.

U.N. SECURITY COUNCIL RES. 661
August 6, 1990**

The Security Council,

Reaffirming its resolution 660 (1990) of 2 August 1990,

Deeply concerned that that resolution has not been implemented and that the invasion by Iraq of Kuwait continues with further loss of human life and material destruction,

Determined to bring the invasion and occupation of Kuwait by Iraq to an end and to restore the sovereignty, independence and territorial integrity of Kuwait, . . .

Mindful of its responsibilities under the Charter of the United Nations for the maintenance of international peace and security,

---

* Adopted by a vote of 14-0, with Yemen abstaining.
** Adopted by a vote of 13-0, with Cuba and Yemen abstaining.

Affirming the inherent right of individual or collective self-defence, in response to the armed attack by Iraq against Kuwait, in accordance with Article 51 of the Charter,

Acting under Chapter VII of the Charter of the United Nations,

1. Determines that Iraq so far has failed to comply with paragraph 2 of resolution 660 (1990) and has usurped the authority of the legitimate Government of Kuwait;

2. Decides, as a consequence, to take the following measures to secure compliance of Iraq with paragraph 2 of resolution 660 (1990) and to restore the authority of the legitimate Government of Kuwait;

3. Decides that all States shall prevent:

(a) The import into their territories of all commodities and products originating in Iraq or Kuwait exported therefrom after the date of the present resolution;

(b) Any activities by their nationals or in their territories which would promote or are calculated to promote the export or trans-shipment of any commodities or products from Iraq or Kuwait; and any dealings by their nationals or their flag vessels or in their territories in any commodities or products originating in Iraq or Kuwait and exported therefrom after the date of the present resolution, including in particular any transfer of funds to Iraq or Kuwait for the purposes of such activities or dealings;

(c) The sale or supply by their nationals or from their territories or using their flag vessels of any commodities or products, including weapons or any other military equipment, whether or not originating in their territories but not including supplies intended strictly for medical purposes, and, in humanitarian circumstances, foodstuffs, to any person or body in Iraq or Kuwait or to any person or body for the purposes of any business carried on in or operated from Iraq or Kuwait . . . ;

4. Decides that all States shall not make available to the Government of Iraq or to any commercial, industrial or public utility undertaking in Iraq or Kuwait, any funds or any other financial or economic resources and shall prevent their nationals and any persons within their territories from removing from their territories or otherwise making available to that Government or to any such undertaking any such funds or resources and from remitting any other funds to persons or bodies within Iraq or Kuwait, except payments exclusively for strictly medical or humanitarian purposes and, in humanitarian circumstances, foodstuffs;

5. Calls upon all States, including States non-members of the United Nations, to act strictly in accordance with the provisions of the present resolution notwithstanding any contract entered into or licence granted before the date of the present resolution;

6. Decides to establish, in accordance with rule 28 of the provisional rules of procedure of the Security Council, a Committee of the Security Council consisting of all the members of the Council, to undertake the following tasks and to report on its work to the Council with its observations and recommendations:

(a) To examine the reports on the progress of the implementation of the present resolution which will be submitted by the Secretary General;

(b) To seek from all States further information regarding the action taken by them concerning the effective implementation of the provisions laid down in the present resolution;

7. *Calls upon* all States to co-operate fully with the Committee in the fulfilment of its task, including supplying such information as may be sought by the Committee in pursuance of the present resolution; . . .

9. *Decides* that, notwithstanding paragraphs 4 through 8 above, nothing in the present resolution shall prohibit assistance to the legitimate Government of Kuwait, and *calls upon* all States:

(a) To take appropriate measures to protect assets of the legitimate Government of Kuwait and its agencies;

(b) Not to recognize any regime set up by the occupying Power;

10. *Requests* the Secretary-General to report to the Council on the progress of the implementation of the present resolution, the first report to be submitted within thirty days; . . .

U.N. SECURITY COUNCIL RES. 678
November 29, 1990*

The Security Council,

Recalling and reaffirming its Resolutions 660 (1990), 661 (1990), 662 (1990), 664 (1990), 665 (1990), 666 (1990), 667 (1990), 669 (1990), 670 (1990), 674 (1990) and 677 (1990),

Noting that, despite all efforts by the United Nations, Iraq refuses to comply with its obligation to implement Resolution 660 (1990) and subsequent resolutions, in flagrant contempt of the Council,

Mindful of its duties and responsibilities under the Charter of the United Nations for the maintenance and preservation of international peace and security,

Determined to secure full compliance with its decisions,

Acting under Chapter VII of the Charter of the United Nations,

1. *Demands* that Iraq comply fully with Resolution 660 (1990) and all subsequent relevant resolutions and decides, while maintaining all its decisions, to allow Iraq one final opportunity, as a pause of good will, to do so;

2. *Authorizes* member states cooperating with the Government of Kuwait, unless Iraq on or before Jan. 15, 1991, fully implements, as set forth in paragraph 1 above, the foregoing resolutions, to use all necessary means to uphold and implement the Security Council Resolution 660 and all subsequent relevant resolutions and to restore international peace and security in the area;

3. *Requests* all states to provide appropriate support for the actions undertaken in pursuance of paragraph 2 of this resolution; and

---

* S.C. Res. 678. Adopted by a vote of 12-2, with Cuba and Yemen opposed and China abstaining.

4. Requests the states concerned to keep the Council regularly informed on the progress of actions undertaken pursuant to paragraphs 2 and 3 of this resolution;

5. Decides to remain seized of the matter.

AUTHORIZATION FOR USE OF MILITARY FORCE AGAINST IRAQ RESOLUTION

H.J. Res. 77, 102d Cong., 1st Sess. (January 12, 1991)*

To authorize the use of United States Armed Forces pursuant to United Nations Security Council Resolution 678.

Whereas the Government of Iraq without provocation invaded and occupied the territory of Kuwait on August 2, 1990; and

Whereas both the House of Representatives (in H.J. Res. 658 of the 101st Congress) and the Senate (in S. Con. Res. 147 of the 101st Congress) have condemned Iraq's invasion of Kuwait and declared their support for international action to reverse Iraq's aggression; and

Whereas Iraq's conventional, chemical, biological, and nuclear weapons and ballistic missile programs and its demonstrated willingness to use weapons of mass destruction pose a grave threat to world peace; and

Whereas the international community has demanded that Iraq withdraw unconditionally and immediately from Kuwait and that Kuwait's independence and legitimate government be restored; and

Whereas the U.N. Security Council repeatedly affirmed the inherent right of individual or collective self-defense in response to the armed attack by Iraq against Kuwait in accordance with Article 51 of the U.N. Charter; and

Whereas, in the absence of full compliance by Iraq with its resolutions, the U.N. Security Council in Resolution 678 has authorized member states of the United Nations to use all necessary means, after January 15, 1991, to uphold and implement all relevant Security Council resolutions and to restore international peace and security in the area; and

Whereas Iraq has persisted in its illegal occupation of, and brutal aggression against Kuwait: Now, therefore, be it

Resolved by the Senate and House of Representatives of the United States of America in Congress assembled,

Section 1.   Short Title.

This joint resolution may be cited as the "Authorization for Use of Military Force Against Iraq Resolution."

---

* This joint resolution was passed by Congress on January 12,1991. The Senate vote was 52-47, and the vote in the Home of Representatives was 250-183.

Section 2.   Authorization for Use of United States Armed Forces.

(a) AUTHORIZATION.—The President is authorized, subject to sub-section (b), to use United States Armed Forces pursuant to United Nations Security Council Resolution 678 (1990) in order to achieve implementation of Security Council Resolutions 660, 661, 662, 664, 665, 666, 667, 669, 670, 674, and 677.

(b) REQUIREMENT FOR DETERMINATION THAT USEOFMILITARY FORCE IS NECESSARY.—Before exercising the authority granted in subsection (a), the President shall make available to the Speaker of the House of Representatives and the President pro tempore of the Senate his determination that—

(1) the United States has used all appropriate diplomatic and other peaceful means to obtain compliance by Iraq with the United Nations Security Council resolutions cited in subsection (a); and (2) that those efforts have not been and would not be successful in obtaining such compliance.

(c) WAR POWERS RESOLUTION REQUIREMENTS.—

(1) SPECIFIC STATUTORY AUTHORIZATION.—Consistent with section 8(a)(1) of the War Powers Resolution, the Congress declares that this section is intended to constitute specific statutory authorization within the meaning of section 5(b) of the War Powers Resolution.

(2) APPLICABILITY OF OTHER REQUIREMENTS.—Nothing in this resolution supersedes any requirement of the War Powers Resolution.

Section 3.   Reports to Congress.

At least once every 60 days, the President shall submit to the Congress a summary on the status of efforts to obtain compliance by Iraq with the resolutions adopted by the United Nations Security Council in response to Iraq's aggression.

PRESIDENT BUSH'S LETTER TO CONGRESS RE: ATTACK ON IRAQ

January 16, 1991*

Dear Mr. Speaker:
[Dear Mr. President:]

* President Bush sent this letter and report to House Speaker Thomas S. Foley (D.-Wash.) and Senate President Pro Tem Robert C. Byrd (D-W.Va.) at the opening of hostilities against Iraq on Wednesday, January 16, 1991.

Pursuant to section 2(b) of the Authorization for Use of Military Force Against Iraq Resolution (H.J. Res. 77, Public Law 102-1), I have concluded that:

1. the United States has used all appropriate diplomatic and other peaceful means to obtain compliance by Iraq with U.N. Security Council Resolutions 660, 661, 662, 664, 665, 666, 667, 669, 670, 674, 677, and 678; and

2. that those efforts have not been and would not be successful in obtaining such compliance.

Enclosed is a report that supports my decision.

Sincerely,

George Bush

U.N. SECURITY COUNCIL RES. 687

(April 3, 1991)*

The Security Council, . . .

Welcoming the restoration to Kuwait of its sovereignty, independence and territorial integrity and the return of its legitimate Government,

Affirming the commitment of all Member States to the sovereignty, territorial integrity and political independence of Kuwait and Iraq, and noting the intention expressed by the Member States cooperating with Kuwait under paragraph 2 of resolution 678 (1990) to bring their military presence in Iraq to an end an soon as possible consistent with paragraph 8 of resolution 686 (1991), . . .

Taking note of the letter sent by the Minister for Foreign Affairs of Iraq on 27 February 1991 and those sent pursuant to resolution 686 (1991),

Noting that Iraq and Kuwait, as independent sovereign States, signed at Baghdad on 4 October 1963 "Agreed Minutes Between the State of Kuwait and the Republic of Iraq Regarding the Restoration of Friendly Relations, Recognition and Related Matters", thereby recognizing formally the boundary between Iraq and Kuwait and the allocation of islands, . . .

Conscious of the need for demarcation of the said boundary,

Conscious also of the statements by Iraq threatening to use weapons in violation of its obligations under the Geneva Protocol for the Prohibition of the Use in War of Asphyxiating, Poisonous or Other Cases, and of Bacteriological Methods of Warfare, signed at Geneva on17 June 1925, and of its prior use of chemical weapons and affirming that grave consequences would follow any further use by Iraq of such weapons,

Recalling that Iraq has subscribed to the Declaration adopted by all States participating in the Conference of States Parties to the 1925 Geneva Protocol and Other Interested States . . . , establishing the objective of universal elimination of chemical and biological weapons,

* Adopted by a vote of 15-0.

Recalling also that Iraq has signed the Convention on the Prohibition of the Development, Production and Stockpiling of Bacteriological (Biological) and Toxin Weapons and on Their Destruction, of 10 April 1972, . . .

Aware of the use by Iraq of ballistic missiles in unprovoked attacks and therefore of the need to take specific measures in regard to such missiles located in Iraq,

Concerned by the reports in the hands of Member States that Iraq has attempted to acquire materials for a nuclear-weapons programme contrary to its obligations under the Treaty on the Non-Proliferation of Nuclear Weapons of 1 July 1968, . . .

Conscious of the threat that all weapons of mass destruction pose to peace and security in the area and of the need to work towards the establishment in the Middle East of a zone free of such weapons, . . .

Noting that resolution 686 (1991) marked the lifting of the measures imposed by resolution 661 (1990) in so far as they applied to Kuwait,

Noting that despite the progress being made in fulfilling the obligations of resolution 686 (1991), many Kuwaiti and third country nationals are still not accounted for and property remains unreturned,

Recalling the International Convention against the Taking of Hostages . . . , which categorizes all acts of taking hostages as manifestations of international terrorism, . . .

Bearing in mind its objective of restoring international peace and security in the area as set out in recent resolutions of the Security Council,

Conscious of the need to take the following measures acting under Chapter VII of the Charter,

1. *Affirms* all thirteen resolutions noted above, except as expressly changed below to achieve the goals of this resolution, including a formal cease-fire;

A

2. *Demands* that Iraq and Kuwait respect the inviolability of the international boundary and the allocation of islands set out in the "Agreed Minutes Between the State of Kuwait and the Republic of Iraq Regarding the Restoration of Friendly Relations, Recognition and Related Matters," signed by them in the exercise of their sovereignty at Baghdad on 4 October 1963 . . .

4. *Decides* to guarantee the inviolability of the above-mentioned international boundary and to take as appropriate all necessary measures to that end in accordance with the Charter of the United Nations; . . .

C

7. *Invites* Iraq to reaffirm unconditionally its obligations under the Geneva Protocol for the Prohibition of the Use in War of Asphyxiating, Poisonous or Other Gases, and of Bacteriological Methods of Warfare, . . .

and to ratify the Convention on the Prohibition of the Development, Production and Stockpiling of Bacteriological (Biological) and Toxin Weapons and on Their Destruction . . . ;

8. *Decides* that Iraq shall unconditionally accept the destruction, removal, or rendering harmless, under international supervision, of;

(a) All chemical and biological weapons and all stocks of agents and all related subsystems and components and all research, development, support and manufacturing facilities;

(b) All ballistic missiles with a range greater than 150 kilometres and related major parts, and repair and production facilities;

9. *Decides*, for the implementation of paragraph 8 above, the following:

(a) Iraq shall submit to the Secretary-General, within fifteen days of the adoption of the present resolution, a declaration of the locations, amounts and types of all items specified in paragraph 8 and agree to urgent, on-site inspection as specified below;

(b) The Secretary-General, in consultation with the appropriate Governments . . . shall develop, and submit to the Council for approval, a plan calling for the completion of the following acts within forty-five days of such approval:

(i) The forming of a Special Commission, which shall carry out immediate on-site inspection of Iraq's biological, chemical and missile capabilities, based on Iraq's declarations and the designation of any additional locations by the Special Commission itself;

(ii) The yielding by Iraq of possession to the Special Commission for destruction, removal or rendering harmless, taking into account the requirements of public safety, of all items specified under paragraph 8(a) above, . . . and the destruction by Iraq, under the supervision of the Special Commission, of all its missile capabilities, including launchers, as specified under paragraph 8(b) above; . . .

10. *Decides* that Iraq shall unconditionally undertake not to use, develop, construct or acquire any of the items specified in paragraphs 8 and 9 above and requests the Secretary-General, in consultation with the Special Commission, to develop a plan for the future ongoing monitoring and verification of Iraq's compliance with this paragraph . . . :

11. *Invites* Iraq to reaffirm unconditionally its obligations under the Treaty on the Non-Proliferation of Nuclear Weapons of 1 July 1968;

12. Decides that Iraq shall unconditionally agree not to acquire or develop nuclear weapons or nuclear-weapons-usable material or any subsystems or components or any research, development, support or manufacturing facilities related to the above; to submit to the Secretary-General and the Director-General of the International Atomic Energy Agency . . . a declaration of the locations, amounts, and types of all items specified above; to place all of its nuclear-weapons-usable materials under the exclusive control, for custody and removal, of the International Atomic Energy Agency, . . . ; to accept, in accordance with the arrangements provided for in paragraph 13 below, urgent on-site inspection and the destruction, removal or rendering harmless as appropriate of all items specified above; and to accept the plan discussed in paragraph 13 below for the future ongoing monitoring and verification of its compliance with these undertakings;

13. Requests the Director-General of the International Atomic Energy Agency, through the Secretary-General, with the assistance and cooperation of the Special Commission . . . , to carry out immediate onsite inspection of Iraq's nuclear capabilities based on Iraq's declarations and the designation of any additional locations by the Special Commission; to develop a plan for submission to the Security Council within forty-five days calling for the destruction, removal, or rendering harmless as appropriate of all items listed in paragraph 12 above; to carry out the plan within forty-five days following approval by the Security Council; and to develop a plan, taking into account the rights and obligations of Iraq under the Treaty on the Non-Proliferation of Nuclear Weapons of 1 July 1968, for the future ongoing monitoring and verification of Iraq's compliance with paragraph 12 above . . . :

D

15. *Requests* the Secretary-General to report to the Security Council on the steps taken to facilitate the return of all Kuwaiti property seized by Iraq . . . ;

E

16. Reaffirms that Iraq, without prejudice to the debts and obligations of Iraq arising prior to 2 August 1990, which will be addressed through the normal mechanisms, is liable under international law for any direct loss, damage, including environmental damage and the depletion of natural resources, or injury to foreign Governments, nationals and corporations, as a result of Iraq's unlawful invasion and occupation of Kuwait;

17. Decides that all Iraqi statements made since 2 August 1990 repudiating its foreign debt are null and void, and demands that Iraq adhere scrupulously to all of its obligations concerning servicing and repayment of its foreign debt;

18. Decides also to create a fund to pay compensation for claims that fall within paragraph 16 above and to establish a Commission that will administer the fund;

19. Directs the Secretary-General to develop and present to the Security Council for decision . . . recommendations for the fund to meet the requirement for the payment of claims established in accordance with paragraph 18 above and for a programme to implement the decisions in paragraphs 16, 17 and 18 above, including: administration of the fund; mechanisms for determining the appropriate level of Iraq's contribution to the fund based on a percentage of the value of the exports of petroleum and petroleum products from Iraq not to exceed a figure to be suggested to the Council by the Secretary-General, taking into account the requirements of the people of Iraq, Iraq's payment capacity as assessed in conjunction with the international financial institutions taking into consideration external debt service, and the needs of the Iraqi economy; arrangements for ensuring that payments are made to the fund; the process by which funds will be allocated and claims paid; appropriate procedures for evaluating losses, listing claims and verifying their validity and resolving disputed claims in respect of Iraq's liability as specified in paragraph 16 above; and the composition of the Commission designated above;

F

20. *Decides*, effective immediately, that the prohibitions against the sale or supply to Iraq of commodities or products, other than medicine and health supplies, and prohibitions against financial transactions related thereto contained in resolution 661 (1990) shall not apply to foodstuffs notified to the Security Council Committee established by resolution 661 (1990) concerning the situation between Iraq and Kuwait or, with the approval of that Committee, under the simplified and accelerated "no-objection" procedure, to materials and supplies for essential civilian needs as identified in the report of the Secretary-General dated 20 March 1991, and in any further findings of humanitarian need by the Committee;

21. *Decides* that the Security Council shall review the provisions of paragraph 20 above every sixty days . . . for the purpose of determining whether to reduce or lift the prohibitions referred to therein;

22. *Decides* that upon the approval by the Security Council of the programme called for in paragraph 19 above and upon Council agreement that Iraq has completed all actions contemplated in paragraphs 8, 9, 10, 11, 12 and 13 above, the prohibitions against the import of commodities and products originating in Iraq and the prohibitions against financial transactions related thereto contained in resolution 661 (1990) shall have no further force or effect; . . .

24. *Decides* that, in accordance with resolution 661 (1990) and subsequent related resolutions and until a further decision is taken by the Security Council, all States shall continue to prevent the sale or supply, or the promotion or facilitation of such sale or supply, to Iraq by their nationals, or from their territories or using their flag vessels or aircraft, of:

(a) Arms and related *materiel* of all types, specifically including the sale or transfer through other means of all forms of conventional military equipment, including for paramilitary forces, and spare parts and components and their means of production, for such equipment;

(b) Items specified and defined in paragraphs 8 and 12 above not otherwise covered above;

(c) Technology under licensing or other transfer arrangements used in the production, utilization or stockpiling of items specified in subparagraphs (a) and (b) above;

(d) Personnel or materials for training or technical support services relating to the design, development, manufacture, use, maintenance or support of items specified in subparagraphs (a) and (b) above;

25. *Calls upon* all States and international organizations to act strictly in accordance with paragraph 24 above, notwithstanding the existence of any contracts, agreements, licences or any other arrangements; . . .

27. *Calls upon* all States to maintain such national controls and procedures and to take such other actions consistent with the guidelines to be established by the Security Council under paragraph 26 above as may be necessary to ensure compliance with the terms of paragraph 24 above . . . ;

28. *Agrees* to review its decisions in paragraphs 22, 23, 24 and 25 above, except for the items specified and defined in paragraphs 8 and 12 above, on a regular basis . . . , taking into account Iraq's compliance with the resolution and general progress towards the control of armaments in the region;

29. *Decides* that all States, including Iraq, shall take the necessary measures to ensure that no claim shall lie at the instance of the Government of Iraq, or of any person or body in Iraq, or of any person claiming through or for the benefit of any such person or body, in connection with any contract or other transaction where its performance was affected by reason of the measures taken by the Security Council in resolution 661 (1990) and related resolutions;

G

30. *Decides* that, in furtherance of its commitment to facilitate the repatriation of all Kuwaiti and third country nationals, Iraq shall extend all necessary cooperation to the International Committee of the Red Cross. . . .

H

32. *Requires* Iraq to inform the Security Council that it will not commit or support any act of international terrorism or allow any organization directed towards commission of such acts to operate within its territory and to condemn unequivocally and renounce all acts, methods and practices of terrorism;

I

33. *Declares* that, upon official notification by Iraq to the Secretary-General and to the Security Council of its acceptance of the provisions above, a formal cease-fire is effective between Iraq and Kuwait and the Member States cooperating with Kuwait in accordance with resolution 678 (1990);

34. *Decides* to remain seized of the matter and to take such further steps as may be required for the implementation of the present resolution and to secure peace and security in the area.

U.N. SECURITY COUNCIL RES. 688
(April 5, 1991)*

The Security Council,

Mindful of its duties and its responsibilities under the Charter of the United Nations for the maintenance of international peace and security,

Recalling Article 2, paragraph 7, of the Charter of the United Nations,

Gravely concerned by the repression of the Iraqi civilian population in many parts of Iraq, including most recently in Kurdish populated areas which led to a massive flow of refugees towards and across international frontiers and to cross border incursions, which threaten international peace and security in the region.

Deeply disturbed by the magnitude of the human suffering involved, . . .

Reaffirming the commitment of all Member States to the sovereignty, territorial integrity and political independence of Iraq and of all States in the area,

Bearing in mind the Secretary-General's report of 20 March 1991 . . . ,

1. Condemns the repression of the Iraqi civilian population in many parts of Iraq, including most recently in Kurdish populated areas, the consequences of which threaten international peace and security in the region;

2. Demands that Iraq, as a contribution to removing the threat to international peace and security in the region, immediately end this repression and expresses the hope in the same context that an open dialogue will take place to ensure that the human and political rights of all Iraqi citizens are respected;

3. Insists that Iraq allow immediate access by international humanitarian organizations to all those in need of assistance in all parts of Iraq and to make available all necessary facilities for their operations;

4. Requests the Secretary-General to pursue his humanitarian efforts in Iraq. . . .

7. Demands that Iraq cooperate with the Secretary-General to these ends;

8. Decides to remain seized of the matter.

CONGRESSIONAL AUTHORIZATION FOR USE OF MILITARY FORCE AGAINST IRAQ
Pub. L. No. 107-243, 116 Stat. 1498 (October 16, 2002)

Whereas in 1990 in response to Iraq's war of aggression against and illegal occupation of Kuwait, the United States forged a coalition of nations to liberate Kuwait and its people in order to defend the national security of the United States and enforce United Nations Security Council resolutions relating to Iraq;

---

* Adopted by a vote of 10-3, with Cuba, Yemen, and Zimbabwe dissenting, and China and India abstaining.

Whereas after the liberation of Kuwait in 1991, Iraq entered into a United Nations sponsored cease-fire agreement pursuant to which Iraq unequivocally agreed, among other things, to eliminate its nuclear, biological, and chemical weapons programs and the means to deliver and develop them, and to end its support for international terrorism;

Whereas the efforts of international weapons inspectors, United States intelligence agencies, and Iraqi defectors led to the discovery that Iraq had large stockpiles of chemical weapons and a large scale biological weapons program, and that Iraq had an advanced nuclear weapons development program that was much closer to producing a nuclear weapon than intelligence reporting had previously indicated;

Whereas Iraq, in direct and flagrant violation of the cease-fire, attempted to thwart the efforts of weapons inspectors to identify and destroy Iraq's weapons of mass destruction stockpiles and development capabilities, which finally resulted in the withdrawal of inspectors from Iraq on October 31, 1998;

Whereas in Public Law 105-235 (August 14, 1998), Congress concluded that Iraq's continuing weapons of mass destruction programs threatened vital United States interests and international peace and security, declared Iraq to be in "material and unacceptable breach of its international obligations" and urged the President "to take appropriate action, in accordance with the Constitution and relevant laws of the United States, to bring Iraq into compliance with its international obligations";

Whereas Iraq both poses a continuing threat to the national security of the United States and international peace and security in the Persian Gulf region and remains in material and unacceptable breach of its international obligations by, among other things, continuing to possess and develop a significant chemical and biological weapons capability, actively seeking a nuclear weapons capability, and supporting and harboring terrorist organizations; . . .

Whereas the current Iraqi regime has demonstrated its continuing hostility toward, and willingness to attack, the United States, including by attempting in 1993 to assassinate former President Bush and by firing on many thousands of occasions on United States and Coalition Armed Forces engaged in enforcing the resolutions of the United Nations Security Council;

Whereas members of al Qaida, an organization bearing responsibility for attacks on the United States, its citizens, and interests, including the attacks that occurred on September 11, 2001, are known to be in Iraq;

Whereas Iraq continues to aid and harbor other international terrorist organizations, including organizations that threaten the lives and safety of United States citizens;

Whereas the attacks on the United States of September 11, 2001, underscored the gravity of the threat posed by the acquisition of weapons of mass destruction by international terrorist organizations;

Whereas Iraq's demonstrated capability and willingness to use weapons of mass destruction, the risk that the current Iraqi regime will either employ those weapons to launch a surprise attack against the United States or its

Armed Forces or provide them to international terrorists who would do so, and the extreme magnitude of harm that would result to the United States and its citizens from such an attack, combine to justify action by the United States to defend itself;

Whereas United Nations Security Council Resolution 678 (1990) authorizes the use of all necessary means to enforce United Nations Security Council Resolution 660 (1990) and subsequent relevant resolutions and to compel Iraq to cease certain activities that threaten international peace and security, including the development of weapons of mass destruction and refusal or obstruction of United Nations weapons inspections in violation of United Nations Security Council Resolution 687 (1991), repression of its civilian population in violation of United Nations Security Council Resolution 688 (1991), and threatening its neighbors or United Nations operations in Iraq in violation of United Nations Security Council Resolution 949 (1994);

Whereas in the Authorization for Use of Military Force Against Iraq Resolution (Public Law 102-1), Congress has authorized the President "to use United States Armed Forces pursuant to United Nations Security Council Resolution 678 (1990) in order to achieve implementation of Security Council Resolution 660, 661, 662, 664, 665, 666, 667, 669, 670, 674, and 677";

Whereas in December 1991, Congress expressed its sense that it "supports the use of all necessary means to achieve the goals of United Nations Security Council Resolution 687 as being consistent with the Authorization of Use of Military Force Against Iraq Resolution (Public Law 102-1)," that Iraq's repression of its civilian population violates United Nations Security Council Resolution 688 and "constitutes a continuing threat to the peace, security, and stability of the Persian Gulf region," and that Congress, "supports the use of all necessary means to achieve the goals of United Nations Security Council Resolution 688"; . . .

Whereas on September 12, 2002, President Bush committed the United States to "work with the United Nations Security Council to meet our common challenge" posed by Iraq and to "work for the necessary resolutions," while also making clear that "the Security Council resolutions will be enforced, and the just demands of peace and security will be met, or action will be unavoidable";

Whereas the United States is determined to prosecute the war on terrorism and Iraq's ongoing support for international terrorist groups combined with its development of weapons of mass destruction in direct violation of its obligations under the 1991 cease-fire and other United Nations Security Council resolutions make clear that it is in the national security interests, of the United States and in furtherance of the war on terrorism that all relevant United Nations Security Council resolutions be enforced, including through the use of force if necessary; . . .

Whereas the President and Congress are determined to continue to take all appropriate actions against international terrorists and terrorist organizations, including those nations, organizations, or persons who planned, authorized, committed, or aided the terrorist attacks that occurred on September 11, 2001, or harbored such persons or organizations;

Whereas the President has authority under the Constitution to take action in order to deter and prevent acts of international terrorism against the United States, as Congress recognized in the joint resolution on Authorization for Use of Military Force (Public Law 107-40); and

Whereas it is in the national security interests of the United States to restore international peace and security to the Persian Gulf region: Now, therefore, be it

Resolved by the Senate and House of Representatives of the United States of America in Congress assembled,

[*1] Section 1.   Short Title.

This joint resolution may be cited as the "Authorization for Use of Military Force Against Iraq Resolution of 2002."

[*2] Sec. 2.   Support for United States Diplomatic Efforts.

The Congress of the United States supports the efforts by the President to—

(1) strictly enforce through the United Nations Security Council all relevant Security Council resolutions regarding Iraq and encourages him in those efforts; and

(2) obtain prompt and decisive action by the Security Council to ensure that Iraq abandons its strategy of delay, evasion and noncompliance and promptly and strictly complies with all relevant Security Council resolutions regarding Iraq.

[*3] Sec. 3.   Authorization for Use of United States Armed Forces.

(a) Authorization.—The President is authorized to use the Armed Forces of the United States as he determines to be necessary and appropriate in order to—

(1) defend the national security of the United States against the continuing threat posed by Iraq; and

(2) enforce all relevant United Nations Security Council resolutions regarding Iraq.

(b) Presidential Determination.—In connection with the exercise of the authority granted in subsection (a) to use force the President shall, prior to such exercise or as soon thereafter as may be feasible, but no later than 48 hours after exercising such authority, make available to the Speaker of the House of Representatives and the President pro tempore of the Senate his determination that—

(1) reliance by the United States on further diplomatic or other peaceful means alone either (A) will not adequately protect the national security of the United States against the continuing threat posed by Iraq or (B) is not likely to lead to enforcement of all relevant United Nations Security Council resolutions regarding Iraq; and

(2) acting pursuant to this joint resolution is consistent with the United States and other countries continuing to take the necessary actions against international terrorist and terrorist organizations, including those nations, organizations, or persons who planned, authorized, committed or aided the terrorist attacks that occurred on September 11, 2001.

(c) War Powers Resolution Requirements.—

(1) Specific statutory authorization.—Consistent with section 8(a)(1) of the War Powers Resolution, the Congress declares that this section is intended to constitute specific statutory authorization within the meaning of section 5(b) of the War Powers Resolution.

(2) Applicability of other requirements.—Nothing in this joint resolution supersedes any requirement of the War Powers Resolution.

[*4] Sec. 4. Reports to Congress.

(a) Reports.—The President shall, at least once every 60 days, submit to the Congress a report on matters relevant to this joint resolution, including actions taken pursuant to the exercise of authority granted in section 3 and the status of planning for efforts that are expected to be required after such actions are completed, including those actions described in section 7 of the Iraq Liberation Act of 1998 (Public Law 105-338).

(b) Single Consolidated Report.—To the extent that the submission of any report described in subsection (a) coincides with the submission of any other report on matters relevant to this joint resolution otherwise required to be submitted to Congress pursuant to the reporting requirements of the War Powers Resolution (Public Law 93-148), all such reports may be submitted as a single consolidated report to the Congress.

(c) Rule of Construction.—To the extent that the information required by section 3 of the Authorization for Use of Military Force Against Iraq Resolution (Public Law 102-1) is included in the report, required by this section, such report shall be considered as meeting the requirements of section 3 of such resolution.

U.N. SECURITY COUNCIL RES. 1441
(November 8, 2002)*

The Security Council,

Recalling all its previous relevant resolutions, in particular its resolutions 661 (1990) of 6 August 1990, 678 (1990) of 29 November 1990, 686 (1991) of 2 March 1991, 687 (1991) of 3 April 1991, 688 (1991) of 5 April 1991, 707 (1991) of 15 August 1991, 715 (1991) of 11 October 1991, 986 (1995) of 14 April 1995, and 1284 (1999) of 17 December 1999, and all the relevant statements of its President,

* Adopted by a vote of 15-0.

Recalling also its resolution 1382 (2001) of 29 November 2001 and its intention to implement it fully,

Recognizing the threat Iraq's non-compliance with Council resolutions and proliferation of weapons of mass destruction and long-range missiles poses to international peace and security,

Recalling that its resolution 678 (1990) authorized Member States to use all necessary means to uphold and implement its resolution 660 (1990) of 2 August 1990 and all relevant resolutions subsequent to resolution 660 (1990) and to restore international peace and security in the area,

Further recalling that its resolution 687 (1991) imposed obligations on Iraq . . . ,

Deploring the fact that Iraq has not provided an accurate, full, final, and complete disclosure, as required by resolution 687 (1991), of all aspects of its programmes to develop weapons of mass destruction and ballistic missiles with a range greater than one hundred and fifty kilometres, and of all holdings of such weapons, their components and production facilities and locations, as well as all other nuclear programmes . . . ,

Deploring further that Iraq repeatedly obstructed immediate, unconditional, and unrestricted access to sites designated by the United Nations Special Commission (UNSCOM) and the International Atomic Energy Agency (IAEA), failed to cooperate fully and unconditionally with UNSCOM and IAEA weapons inspectors, as required by resolution 687 (1991), and ultimately ceased all cooperation with UNSCOM and the IAEA in 1998,

Deploring the absence, since December 1998, in Iraq of international monitoring, inspection, and verification, as required by relevant resolutions, of weapons of mass destruction and ballistic missiles, in spite of the Council's repeated demands that Iraq provide immediate, unconditional, and unrestricted access to the United Nations Monitoring, Verification and Inspection Commission (UNMOVIC), established in resolution 1284 (1999) as the successor organization to UNSCOM, and the IAEA . . . ,

Deploring also that the Government of Iraq has failed to comply with its commitments pursuant to resolution 687 (1991) with regard to terrorism, pursuant to resolution 688 (1991) to end repression of its civilian population and to provide access by international humanitarian organizations to all those in need of assistance in Iraq, and pursuant to resolutions 686 (1991), 687 (1991), and 1284 (1999) to return or cooperate in accounting for Kuwaiti and third country nationals wrongfully detained by Iraq . . . ,

Recalling that in its resolution 687 (1991) the Council declared that a ceasefire would be based on acceptance by Iraq of the provisions of that resolution, including the obligations on Iraq contained therein,

Determined to ensure full and immediate compliance by Iraq without conditions or restrictions with its obligations under resolution 687 (1991) and other relevant resolutions . . . ,

Determined to secure full compliance with its decisions,

Acting under Chapter VII of the Charter of the United Nations,

1. *Decides* that Iraq has been and remains in material breach of its obligations under relevant resolutions, including resolution 687 (1991), in particular through Iraq's failure to cooperate with United Nations inspectors and the IAEA, and to complete the actions required under paragraphs 8 to 13 of resolution 687 (1991);

2. *Decides*, while acknowledging paragraph 1 above, to afford Iraq, by this resolution, a final opportunity to comply with its disarmament obligations under relevant resolutions of the Council; and accordingly decides to set up an enhanced inspection regime with the aim of bringing to full and verified completion the disarmament process established by resolution 687 (1991) and subsequent resolutions of the Council;

3. *Decides* that . . . the Government of Iraq shall provide to UNMOVIC, the IAEA, and the Council, not later than 30 days from the date of this resolution, a currently accurate, full, and complete declaration of all aspects of its programmes to develop chemical, biological, and nuclear weapons, ballistic missiles, and other delivery systems such as unmanned aerial vehicles and dispersal systems designed for use on aircraft, including any holdings and precise locations of such weapons, components, sub-components, stocks of agents, and related material and equipment, the locations and work of its research, development and production facilities, as well as all other chemical, biological, and nuclear programmes . . . ;

4. *Decides* that false statements or omissions in the declarations submitted by Iraq pursuant to this resolution and failure by Iraq at any time to comply with, and cooperate fully in the implementation of, this resolution shall constitute a further material breach of Iraq's obligations . . . ;

5. *Decides* that Iraq shall provide UNMOVIC and the IAEA immediate, unimpeded, unconditional, and unrestricted access to any and all, including underground, areas, facilities, buildings, equipment, records, and means of transport which they wish to inspect, as well as immediate, unimpeded, unrestricted, and private access to all officials and other persons whom UNMOVIC or the IAEA wish to interview in the mode or location of UNMOVIC's or the IAEA's choice pursuant to any aspect of their mandates; further decides that UNMOVIC and the IAEA may at their discretion conduct interviews inside or outside of Iraq, may facilitate the travel of those interviewed and family members outside of Iraq, and that, at the sole, discretion of UNMOVIC and the IAEA, such interviews may occur without the presence of observers from the Iraqi Government; and instructs UNMOVIC and requests the IAEA to resume inspections no later than 45 days following adoption of this resolution and to update the Council 60 days thereafter; . . .

7. *Decides* further that, in view of the prolonged interruption by Iraq of the presence of UNMOVIC and the IAEA and in order for them to accomplish the tasks set forth in this resolution and all previous relevant resolutions and notwithstanding prior understandings, the Council hereby establishes the following revised or additional authorities, which shall be binding upon Iraq, to facilitate their work in Iraq:

— UNMOVIC and the IAEA shall determine the composition of their inspection teams and ensure that these teams are composed of the most qualified and experienced experts available; . . .

— UNMOVIC and the IAEA shall have unrestricted rights of entry into and out of Iraq, the right to free, unrestricted, and immediate movement to and from inspection sites, and the right to inspect any sites and buildings, including immediate, unimpeded, unconditional, and unrestricted access to Presidential Sites equal to that at other sites, notwithstanding the provisions of resolution 1154 (1998) of 2 March 1998;

— UNMOVIC and the IAEA shall have the right to be provided by Iraq the names of all personnel currently and formerly associated with Iraq's chemical, biological, nuclear, and ballistic missile programmes and the associated, research, development, and production facilities; . . .

— UNMOVIC and the IAEA shall have the right to declare, for the purposes of freezing a site to be inspected, exclusion zones, including surrounding areas and transit corridors, in which Iraq will suspend ground and aerial movement so that nothing is changed in or taken out of a site being inspected;

— UNMOVIC and the IAEA shall have the free and unrestricted use and landing of fixed- and rotary-winged aircraft, including manned and unmanned reconnaissance vehicles;

— UNMOVIC and the IAEA shall have the right at their sole discretion verifiably to remove, destroy, or render harmless all prohibited weapons, subsystems, components, records, materials, and other related items, and the right to impound or close any facilities or equipment for the production thereof; and

— UNMOVIC and the IAEA shall have the right to free import and use of equipment or materials for inspections and to seize and export any equipment, materials, or documents taken during inspections, without search of UNMOVIC or IAEA personnel or official or personal baggage; . . .

9. *Requests* the Secretary-General immediately to notify Iraq of this resolution, which is binding on Iraq; demands that Iraq confirm within seven days of that notification its intention to comply fully with this resolution; and demands further that Iraq cooperate immediately, unconditionally, and actively with UNMOVIC and the IAEA;

10. *Requests* all Member States to give full support to UNMOVIC and the IAEA in the discharge of their mandates, including by providing any information related to prohibited programmes or other aspects of their mandates, including on Iraqi attempts since 1998 to acquire prohibited items, and by recommending sites to be inspected, persons to be interviewed, conditions of such interviews, and data to be collected, the results of which shall be reported to the Council by UNMOVIC and the IAEA;

11. Directs the Executive Chairman of UNMOVIC and the Director-General of the IAEA to report immediately to the Council any interference by Iraq with inspection activities, as well as any failure by Iraq to comply with its disarmament obligations, including its obligations regarding inspections under this resolution;

12. Decides to convene immediately upon receipt of a report in accordance with paragraphs 4 or 11 above, in order to consider the situation and the need for full compliance with all of the relevant Council resolutions in order to secure international peace and security;

13. Recalls, in that context, that the Council has repeatedly warned Iraq that it will face serious consequences as a result of its continued violations of its obligations;

14. Decides to remain seized of the matter.

LETTER FROM PRESIDENT BUSH TO CONGRESSIONAL LEADERS REPORTING ON THE COMMENCEMENT OF MILITARY OPERATIONS AGAINST IRAQ

(March 21, 2003)*

Dear Mr. Speaker: (Dear Mr. President:)

On March 18, 2003, I made available to you, consistent with section 3(b) of the Authorization for Use of Military Force Against Iraq Resolution of 2002 (Public Law 107-243), my determination that further diplomatic and other peaceful means alone will neither adequately protect the national security of the United States against the continuing threat posed by Iraq, nor lead to enforcement of all relevant United Nations Security Council resolutions regarding Iraq.

I have reluctantly concluded, along with other coalition leaders, that only the use of armed force will accomplish these objectives and restore international peace and security in the area. I have also determined that the use of armed force against Iraq is consistent with the United States and other countries continuing to take the necessary actions against international terrorists and terrorist organizations, including those nations, organizations, or persons who planned, authorized, committed, or aided the terrorist attacks that occurred on September 11, 2001. United States objectives also support a transition to democracy in Iraq, as contemplated by the Iraq Liberation Act of 1998 (Public Law 105-338).

Consistent with the War Powers Resolution (Public Law 93-148), I now inform you that pursuant to my authority as Commander in Chief and consistent with the Authorization for Use of Military Force Against Iraq

---

* Identical letters were sent to J. Dennis Hastert, Speaker of the House of Representatives, and Ted Stevens, President pro tempore of the Senate.

Resolution (Public Law 102-1) and the Authorization for Use of Military Force Against Iraq Resolution of 2002 (Public Law 107-243), I directed U.S. Armed Forces, operating with other coalition forces, to commence combat operations on March 19, 2003, against Iraq.

These military operations have been carefully planned to accomplish our goals with the minimum loss of life among coalition military forces and to innocent civilians. It is not possible to know at this time either the duration of active combat operations or the scope or duration of the deployment of U.S. Armed Forces necessary to accomplish our goals fully.

As we continue our united efforts to disarm Iraq in pursuit of peace, stability, and security both in the Gulf region and in the United States, I look forward to our continued consultation and cooperation.

Sincerely,
GEORGE W. BUSH

LETTER FROM THE U.S. PERMANENT REPRESENTATIVE TO THE UNITED NATIONS TO THE PRESIDENT OF THE SECURITY COUNCIL
(March 20, 2003)

Coalition forces have commenced military operations in Iraq. These operations are necessary in view of Iraq's continued material breaches of its disarmament obligations under relevant Security Council resolutions, including resolution 1441 (2002). The operations are substantial and will secure compliance with those obligations. In carrying out these operations, our forces will take all reasonable precautions to avoid civilian casualties.

The actions being taken are authorized under existing Council resolutions, including its resolutions 678 (1990) and 687 (1991). Resolution 687 (1991) imposed a series of obligations on Iraq, including, most importantly, extensive disarmament obligations, that were conditions of the ceasefire established under it. It has been long recognized and understood that a material breach of these obligations removes the basis of the ceasefire and revives the authority to use force under resolution 678 (1990). This has been the basis for coalition use of force in the past and has been accepted by the Council, as evidenced, for example, by the Secretary-General's public announcement in January 1993 following Iraq's material breach of resolution 687 (1991) that coalition forces had received a mandate from the Council to use force according to resolution 678 (1990).

Iraq continues to be in material breach of its disarmament obligations under resolution 687 (1991), as the Council affirmed in its resolution 1441 (2002). Acting under the authority of Chapter VII of the Charter of the United Nations, the Council unanimously decided that Iraq has been and remained in material breach of its obligations and recalled its repeated warnings to Iraq that it will face serious consequences as a result of its continued violations of its obligations. The resolution then provided Iraq a "final opportunity" to comply, but stated specifically that violations by Iraq of its obligations under resolution 1441 (2002) to present a currently accurate, full and complete declaration of all aspects of its weapons of mass destruction programmes and to comply with and cooperate fully in the implementation of the resolution would constitute a further material breach.

The Government of Iraq decided not to avail itself of its final opportunity under resolution 1441 (2002) and has clearly committed additional violations. In view of Iraq's material breaches, the basis for the ceasefire has been removed and use of force is authorized under resolution 678 (1990).

Iraq repeatedly has refused, over a protracted period of time, to respond to diplomatic overtures, economic sanctions and other peaceful means, designed to help bring about Iraqi compliance with its obligations to disarm and to permit full inspection of its weapons of mass destruction and related programmes. The actions that coalition forces are undertaking are an appropriate response. They are necessary steps to defend the United States and the international community from the threat posed by Iraq and to restore international peace and security in the area. Further delay would simply allow Iraq to continue its unlawful and threatening conduct.

It is the Government of Iraq that bears full responsibility for the serious consequences of its defiance of the Council's decisions.

I would be grateful if you could circulate the text of the present letter as a document of the Security Council.

(Signed) John D. Negroponte

U.K. GOVERNMENT STATEMENT: LEGAL BASIS FOR USE OF FORCE AGAINST IRAQ
(March 2003)

The Attorney General, Lord Goldsmith, has set out his view of the legal basis for the use of force against Iraq:

Authority to use force against Iraq exists from the combined effect of resolutions 678, 687, and 1441. All of these resolutions were adopted under Chapter VII of the UN Charter which allows the use of force for the express purpose of restoring international peace and security:

1. In resolution 678 the Security Council authorised force against Iraq, to eject it from Kuwait and to restore peace and security in the area.

2. In resolution 687, which set out the ceasefire conditions after Operation Desert Storm, the Security Council imposed continuing obligations on Iraq to eliminate its weapons of mass destruction in order to restore international peace and security in the area. Resolution 687 suspended but did not terminate the authority to use force under resolution 687.

3. A material breach of resolution 687 revives the authority to use force under resolution 678.

4. In resolution 1441 the Security Council determined that Iraq has been and remains in material breach of resolution 587, because it has not fully complied with its obligations to disarm under that resolution.

5. The Security Council in resolution 1441 gave Iraq "a final opportunity to comply with its disarmament obligations" and warned Iraq of the "serious consequences" if it did not.

6. The Security Council also decided in resolution 1441 that, if Iraq failed at any time to comply with and cooperate fully in the implementation of resolution 1441, that would constitute a further material breach.

7. It is plain that Iraq has failed so to comply and therefore Iraq was at the time of resolution 1441 and continues to be in material breach.

8. Thus, the authority to use force under resolution 678 has revived and so continues today.

9. Resolution 1441 would in terms have provided that a further decision of the Security Council to sanction force was required if that had been intended. Thus, all that resolution 1441 requires is reporting to and discussion by the Security Council of Iraq's failures, but not an express further decision to authorise force.

I have lodged a copy of this answer, together with resolutions 678, 687 and 1441 in the Library of both Houses.

U.N. SECURITY COUNCIL RES. 1483

(May 22, 2003)*

The Security Council,

Recalling all its previous relevant resolutions,

Reaffirming the sovereignty and territorial integrity of Iraq,

Reaffirming also the importance of the disarmament of Iraqi weapons of mass destruction and of eventual confirmation of the disarmament of Iraq,

Stressing the right of the Iraqi people freely to determine their own political future and control their own natural resources . . . ,

Encouraging efforts by the people of Iraq to form a representative government based on the rule of law that affords equal rights and justice to all Iraqi citizens without regard to ethnicity, religion, or gender . . . ,

Welcoming the first steps of the Iraqi people in this regard, and *noting* in this connection the 15 April 2003 Nasiriyah statement and the 28 April 2003 Baghdad statement,

Resolved that the United Nations should play a vital role in humanitarian relief, the reconstruction of Iraq, and the restoration and establishment of national and local institutions for representative governance,

---

* Adopted by a vote of 14-0, with Syria not present.

Noting the statement of 12 April 2003 by the Ministers of Finance and Central Bank Governors of the Group of Seven Industrialized Nations in which the members recognized the need for a multilateral effort to help rebuild and develop Iraq and for the need for assistance from the International Monetary Fund and the World Bank in these efforts,

Welcoming also the resumption of humanitarian assistance . . . ,

Affirming the need for accountability for crimes and atrocities committed by the previous Iraqi regime,

Stressing the need for respect for the archaeological, historical, cultural, and religious heritage of Iraq, . . .

Noting the letter of 8 May 2003 from the Permanent Representatives of the United States of America and the United Kingdom of Great Britain and Northern Ireland to the President of the Security Council . . . and recognizing the specific authorities, responsibilities, and obligations under applicable international law of these states as occupying powers under unified command (the "Authority"), . . .

Concerned that many Kuwaitis and Third-State Nationals still are not accounted for since 2 August 1990,

Determining that the situation in Iraq, although improved, continues to constitute a threat to international peace and security,

Acting under Chapter VII of the Charter of the United Nations,

1. *Appeals* to Member States and concerned organizations to assist the people of Iraq in their efforts to reform their institutions and rebuild their country, and to contribute to conditions of stability and security in Iraq in accordance with this resolution; . . .

3. *Appeals* to Member States to deny safe haven to those members of the previous Iraqi regime who are alleged to be responsible for crimes and atrocities and to support actions to bring them to justice;

4. *Calls upon* the Authority, consistent with the Charter of the United Nations and other relevant international law, to promote the welfare of the Iraqi people through the effective administration of the territory, including in particular working towards the restoration of conditions of security and stability and the creation of conditions in which the Iraqi people can freely determine their own political future; . . .

7. *Decides* that all Member States shall take appropriate steps to facilitate the safe return to Iraqi institutions of Iraqi cultural property and other items of archaeological, historical, cultural, rare scientific, and religious importance illegally removed from the Iraq National Museum, the National Library, and other locations in Iraq since the adoption of resolution 661 (1990) . . . , including by establishing a prohibition on trade in or transfer of such items and items with respect to which reasonable suspicion exists that they have been illegally removed, and calls upon the United Nations Educational, Scientific, and Cultural Organization, Interpol, and other international organizations, as appropriate, to assist in the implementation of this paragraph;

8. *Requests* the Secretary-General to appoint a Special Representative for Iraq whose independent responsibilities shall involve reporting regularly to

the Council on his activities under this resolution, coordinating activities of the United Nations in post-conflict processes in Iraq, coordinating among United Nations and international agencies engaged in humanitarian assistance and reconstruction activities in Iraq, and, in coordination with the Authority, assisting the people of Iraq . . . ;

9. *Supports* the formation, by the people of Iraq with the help of the Authority and working with the Special Representative, of an Iraqi interim administration as a transitional administration run by Iraqis, until an internationally recognized, representative government is established by the people of Iraq and assumes the responsibilities of the Authority;

10. *Decides* that, with the exception of prohibitions related to the sale or supply to Iraq of arms and related materiel other than those arms and related materiel required by the Authority to serve the purposes of this and other related resolutions, all prohibitions related to trade with Iraq and the provision of financial or economic resources to Iraq established by resolution 661 (1990) and subsequent relevant resolutions, including resolution 778 (1992) . . . , shall no longer apply;

11. *Reaffirms* that Iraq must meet its disarmament obligations, . . . and underlines the intention of the Council to revisit the mandates of the United Nations Monitoring, Verification, and Inspection Commission and the International Atomic Energy Agency as set forth in resolutions 687 (1991) . . . , 1284 (1999) . . . , and 1441 (2002) . . . ;

12. *Notes* the establishment of a Development Fund for Iraq to be held by the Central Bank of Iraq and to be audited by independent public accountants approved by the International Advisory and Monitoring Board of the Development Fund for Iraq and looks forward to the early meeting of that International Advisory and Monitoring Board, whose members shall include duly qualified representatives of the Secretary-General, of the Managing Director of the International Monetary Fund, of the Director-General of the Arab Fund for Social and Economic Development, and of the President of the World Bank;

13. *Notes further* that the funds in the Development Fund for Iraq shall be disbursed at the direction of the Authority, in consultation with the Iraqi interim administration, for the purposes set out in paragraph 14 below;

14. *Underlines* that the Development Fund for Iraq shall be used in a transparent manner to meet the humanitarian needs of the Iraqi people, for the economic reconstruction and repair of Iraq's infrastructure, for the continued disarmament of Iraq, and for the costs of Iraqi civilian administration, and for other purposes benefiting the people of Iraq;

15. *Calls upon* the international financial institutions to assist the people of Iraq in the reconstruction and development of their economy and to facilitate assistance by the broader donor community, and *welcomes* the readiness of creditors, including those of the Paris Club, to seek a solution to Iraq's sovereign debt problems;

16. *Requests* also that the Secretary-General, in coordination with the Authority, continue the exercise of his responsibilities under Security Council

resolution 1472 (2003) ... and 1476 (2003) ..., for a period of six months following the adoption of this resolution, and terminate within this time period, in the most cost effective manner, the ongoing operations of the "Oil-for-Food" Programme (the "Programme") ... transferring responsibility for the administration of any remaining activity under the Programme to the Authority, including by taking the following necessary measures: ...

(c) to provide the Security Council within 21 days following the adoption of this resolution, for the Security Council's review and consideration, an estimated operating budget based on funds already set aside in the account established pursuant to paragraph 8(d) of resolution 986 (1995) ...;

17. Requests further that the Secretary-General transfer as soon as possible to the Development Fund for Iraq 1 billion United States dollars from unencumbered funds in the accounts established pursuant to paragraphs 8(a) and 8(b) of resolution 986 (1995), restore Government of Iraq funds that were provided by Member States to the Secretary-General as requested in paragraph 1 of resolution 778 (1992), and decides that, after deducting all relevant United Nations expenses associated with the shipment of authorized contracts and costs to the Programme outlined in paragraph 16(c) above, including residual obligations, all surplus funds in the escrow accounts established pursuant to paragraphs 8(a), 8(b), 8(d), and 8(f) of resolution 986 (1995) shall be transferred at the earliest possible time to the Development Fund for Iraq; ...

20. *Decides* that all export sales of petroleum, petroleum products, and natural gas from Iraq following the date of the adoption of this resolution shall be made consistent with prevailing international market best practices, to be audited by independent public accountants reporting to the International Advisory and Monitoring Board referred to in paragraph 12 above in order to ensure transparency, and decides further that, except as provided in paragraph 21 below, all proceeds from such sales shall be deposited into the Development Fund for Iraq until such time as an internationally recognized, representative government of Iraq is properly constituted;

21. Decides further that 5 per cent of the proceeds referred to in paragraph 20 above shall be deposited into the Compensation Fund established in accordance with resolution 687 (1991) and subsequent relevant resolutions and that, unless an internationally recognized, representative government of Iraq and the Governing Council of the United Nations Compensation Commission, in the exercise of its authority over methods of ensuring that payments are made into the Compensation Fund, decide otherwise, this requirement shall be binding on a properly constituted, internationally recognized, representative government of Iraq and any successor thereto;

22. *Noting* the relevance of the establishment of an internationally recognized, representative government of Iraq and the desirability of prompt completion of the restructuring of Iraq's debt as referred to in paragraph 15 above, further decides that, until December 31, 2007, unless the Council decides otherwise, petroleum, petroleum products, and natural gas originating in Iraq shall be immune, until title passes to the initial purchaser from

legal proceedings against them and not be subject to any form of attachment, garnishment, or execution, and that all States shall take any steps that may be necessary under their respective domestic legal systems to assure this protection, and that proceeds and obligations arising from sales thereof, as well as the Development Fund for Iraq, shall enjoy privileges and immunities equivalent to those enjoyed by the United Nations . . . ;

23. Decides that all Member States in which there are:

(a) funds or other financial assets or economic resources of the previous Government of Iraq or its state bodies, corporations, or agencies, located outside Iraq as of the date of this resolution, or

(b) funds or other financial assets or economic resources that have been removed from Iraq, or acquired, by Saddam Hussein or other senior officials of the former Iraqi regime and their immediate family members, . . . shall freeze without delay those funds or other financial assets or economic resources and, unless these funds or other financial assets or economic resources are themselves the subject of a prior judicial, administrative, or arbitral lien or judgement, immediately shall cause their transfer to the Development Fund for Iraq, it being understood that, unless otherwise addressed, claims made by private individuals or non-government entities on those transferred funds or other financial assets may be presented to the internationally recognized, representative government of Iraq; and decides further that all such funds or other financial assets or economic resources shall enjoy the same privileges, immunities, and protections as provided under paragraph 22;

24. Requests the Secretary-General to report to the Council at regular intervals on the work of the Special Representative . . . and encourages the United Kingdom of Great Britain and Northern Ireland and the United States of America to inform the Council at regular intervals of their efforts under this resolution; . . .

26. Calls upon Member States and international and regional organizations to contribute to the implementation of this resolution;

27. Decides to remain seized of this matter.

MATERIALS RE: KOSOVO

U.S. AMBASSADOR PETER BURLEIGH, STATEMENT TO THE U.N. SECURITY COUNCIL
March 24, 1999, U.N. Doc. S/PV.3988 (1999)

The current situation in Kosovo is of grave concern to all of us. We and our allies have begun military action only with the greatest reluctance. But we believe that such action is necessary to respond to Belgrade's brutal persecution of Kosovo Albanians, violations of international law, excessive and indiscriminate use of force, refusal to negotiate to resolve the issue peacefully and recent military build-up in Kosovo—all of which foreshadow a humanitarian catastrophe of immense proportions.

We have begun today's action to avert this humanitarian catastrophe and to deter further aggression and repression in Kosovo. Serb forces numbering 40,000 are now in action in and around Kosovo. . . . As a result of Serb action in the last five weeks, there are more than 60,000 new refugees and displaced persons. The total number of displaced persons is approaching a quarter of a million.

The continuing offensive by the Federal Republic of Yugoslavia is generating refugees and creating pressures on neighbouring countries, threatening the stability of the region. . . . Recent actions by Belgrade also constitute a threat to the safety of international observers and humanitarian workers in Kosovo.

Security Council resolutions 1199 (1998) and 1203 (1998) recognized that the situation in Kosovo constitutes a threat to peace and security in the region and invoked Chapter VII of the Charter. In resolution 1199 (1998), the Council demanded that Serbian forces take immediate steps to improve the humanitarian situation and avert the impending humanitarian catastrophe.

In October 1998, Belgrade entered into agreements and understandings with the North Atlantic Treaty Organization (NATO) and the Organization for Security and Cooperation in Europe (OSCE) to verify its compliance with Security Council demands, particularly on reduction of security forces, cooperation with international observers, cooperation with humanitarian relief agencies and negotiations on a political settlement for substantial autonomy. Belgrade has refused to comply.

The actions of the Federal Republic of Yugoslavia also violate its commitments under the Helsinki Final Act, as well as its obligations under the international law of human rights. Belgrade's actions in Kosovo cannot be dismissed as an internal matter.

For months, Serb actions have led to escalating explosions of violence. It is imperative that the international community take quick measures to avoid humanitarian suffering and widespread destruction, ...

I reiterate that we have initiated action today with the greatest reluctance. Our preference has been to achieve our objectives in the Balkans through peaceful means. Since fighting erupted in February 1998, we have been actively engaged in seeking resolution of the conflict through diplomacy under the auspices of the Contact Group backed by NATO. These efforts led to talks in Rambouillet and Paris, which produced a fair, just and balanced agreement. The Kosovar Albanians signed that agreement, but Belgrade rejected all efforts to achieve a peaceful resolution.

We are mindful that violations of the ceasefire and provocations by the Kosovo Liberation Army have also contributed to this situation. However, it is Belgrade's systematic policy of undermining last October's agreements and thwarting all diplomatic efforts to resolve the situation which have prevented a peaceful solution and have led us to today's action.

In this context, we believe that action by NATO is justified and necessary to stop the violence and prevent an even greater humanitarian disaster. As President Clinton said today,

> "We and our allies have a chance to leave our children a Europe that is free, peaceful and stable. But we must act now to do that."

SIR JEREMY GREENSTOCK (U.K.), STATEMENT TO THE U.N. SECURITY COUNCIL

March 24, 1999, U.N. Doc. S/PV.3988 (1999)

. . . In defiance of the international community, President Milosevic has refused to accept the interim political settlement negotiated at Rambouillet, to observe the limits on security-force levels agreed on 25 October, and to end the excessive and disproportionate use of force in Kosovo. Because of his failure to meet these demands, we face a humanitarian catastrophe. NATO has been forced to take military action because all other means of preventing a humanitarian catastrophe have been frustrated by Serb behaviour.

We have taken this action with regret, in order to save lives. It will be directed towards disrupting the violent attacks being perpetrated by the Serb security forces and towards weakening their ability to create a humanitarian catastrophe. In the longer term, the International Criminal Tribunal for the Former Yugoslavia, whose mandate extends to Kosovo, will hold those responsible for violations of international humanitarian law accountable for their actions.

The action being taken is legal. It is justified as an exceptional measure to prevent an overwhelming humanitarian catastrophe. Under present circumstances in Kosovo, there is convincing evidence that such a catastrophe is imminent. Renewed acts of repression by the authorities of the Federal Republic of Yugoslavia would cause further loss of civilian life and would lead to displacement of the civilian population on a large scale and in hostile conditions.

Every means short of force has been tried to avert this situation. In these circumstances, and as an exceptional measure on grounds of overwhelming humanitarian necessity, military intervention is legally justifiable. The force now proposed is directed exclusively to averting a humanitarian catastrophe, and is the minimum judged necessary for that purpose. . . .

LETTER FROM PRESIDENT CLINTON TO THE SPEAKER OF THE HOUSE OF REPRESENTATIVES AND THE PRESIDENT PRO TEMPORE OF THE SENATE

(March 26, 1999)

Dear Mr. Speaker: (Dear Mr. President:)

At approximately 1:30 P.M. eastern standard time, on March 24, 1999, U.S. military forces, at my direction and in coalition with our NATO allies, began a series of air strikes in the Federal Republic of Yugoslavia (FRY) in response to the FRY government's continued campaign of violence and repression against the ethnic Albanian population in Kosovo. The mission of the air strikes is to demonstrate the seriousness of NATO's purpose so that the Serbian leaders understand the imperative of reversing course; to deter an even bloother offensive against innocent civilians in Kosovo; and, if necessary, to seriously damage the Serbian military's capacity to harm the people of Kosovo. In short, if President Milosevic will not make peace, we will limit his ability to make war.

As you are aware, the Government of the FRY has been engaged in a brutal conflict in Kosovo. In this conflict, thousands of innocent Kosovar civilians have been killed or injured by FRY government security forces. The continued repression of Kosovars by the FRY military and security police forces constitutes a threat to regional security, particularly to Albania and Macedonia and, potentially, to Greece and to Turkey. Tens of thousands of others have been displaced from their homes, and many of them have fled to the neighboring countries . . . .

The United States, working closely with our European allies and Russia, have pursued a diplomatic solution to this crisis since last fall. The Kosovar leaders agreed to the interim settlement negotiated at Rambouillet, but the FRY government refused even to discuss key elements of the peace agreement. Instead, the Government of the FRY continues its attacks on the Kosovar population and has deployed 40,000 troops in and around Kosovo in preparation for a major offensive and in clear violation of the commitments it had made.

The FRY government has failed to comply with U.N. Security Council resolutions, and its actions are in violation of its obligations under the U.N. Charter and its other international commitments. The FRY government's actions in Kosovo are not simply an internal matter. The Security Council has condemned FRY actions as a threat to regional peace and security. The FRY government's violence creates a conflict with no natural boundaries, pushing refugees across borders and potentially drawing in neighboring countries. The Kosovo region is a tinderbox that could ignite a wider European war with dangerous consequences to the United Suites.

United States and NATO forces have targeted the FRY government's integrated air defense system, military and security police command and control elements, and military and security police facilities and infrastructure. United States naval ships and aircraft and U.S. Air Force aircraft are participating in these operations. Many of our NATO allies are also contributing aircraft and other forces. . . .

We cannot predict with certainty how long these operations will need to continue. Milosevic must stop his offensive, stop the repression, and agree to a peace accord based on the framework from Rambouillet. If he does not comply with the demands of the international community, NATO operations will seriously damage Serbia's military capacity to harm the people of Kosovo. NATO forces will also use such force as is necessary to defend themselves in the accomplishment of their mission.

I have taken these actions pursuant to my constitutional authority to conduct U.S. foreign relations and as Commander in Chief and Chief Executive. In doing so, I have taken into account the views and support expressed by the Congress in S. Con. Res. 21 and H. Con. Res. 42.

I am providing this report as part of my efforts to keep the Congress fully informed, consistent with the War Powers Resolution. I appreciate the support of the Congress in this action.

Sincerely,
WILLIAM J. CLINTON

WRITTEN ANSWER FROM PRIME MINISTER TONY BLAIR TO THE HOUSE OF COMMONS

April 29, 1999

Mr. Mackinlay: To ask the Prime Minister on what authority a state, or regional organisation of states, can be empowered to intervene in the territory of another UN member state, under the United Nations Charter, on the basis of its intervention being in response to a humanitarian catastrophe; and if he will make a statement.

The Prime Minister: Under international law a limited use of force can be justifiable in support purposes laid down by the Security Council but without the Council's express authorisation when that is the only means to avert an immediate and overwhelming humanitarian catastrophe. Any such case would in the nature of things be exceptional and would depend on an objective. . . .

U.N. SECURITY COUNCIL RES. 1244
June 10, 1999*

The Security Council,

Bearing in mind the purposes and principles of the Charter of the United Nations, and the primary responsibility of the Security Council for the maintenance of international peace and security,

Recalling its resolutions . . .

Determined to resolve the grave humanitarian situation in Kosovo, Federal Republic of Yugoslavia, and to provide for the safe and free return of all refugees and displaced persons to their homes, . . .

Welcoming the general principles on a political solution to the Kosovo crisis adopted on 6 May 1999 (S/1999/516 . . .) and welcoming also the acceptance by the Federal Republic of Yugoslavia of the principles set forth in points 1 to 9 of the paper presented in Belgrade on 2 June 1999 (S/1999/649 . . .), and the Federal Republic of Yugoslavia's agreement to that paper,

Reaffirming the commitment of all Member States to the sovereignty and territorial integrity of the Federal Republic of Yugoslavia and the other States of the region, as set out in the Helsinki Final Act and annex 2,

Reaffirming the call in previous resolutions for substantial autonomy and meaningful self-administration for Kosovo,

Determining that the situation in the region continues to constitute a lineal to international peace and security,

Determined to ensure the safety and security of international personnel and the implementation by all concerned of their responsibilities under the present resolution, and *acting* for these purposes under Chapter VII of the Charter of the United Nations,

1. Decides that a political solution to the Kosovo crisis shall be based on the general principles in annex 1 and as further elaborated in the principles and other required elements in annex 2;

2. Welcomes the acceptance by the Federal Republic of Yugoslavia of the principles and other required elements referred to in paragraph 1 above, and *demands* the full cooperation of the Federal Republic of Yugoslavia in their rapid implementation;

3. Demands in particular that the Federal Republic of Yugoslavia put an immediate and verifiable end to violence and repression in Kosovo, and begin

---

* Adopted by a vote of 14-0, with China abstaining.

and complete verifiable phased withdrawal from Kosovo of all military, police and paramilitary forces according to a rapid timetable, with which the deployment of the international security presence in Kosovo will be synchronized;

4. *Confirms* that after the withdrawal an agreed number of Yugoslav and Serb military and police personnel will be permitted to return to Kosovo to perform the functions in accordance with annex 2;

5. *Decides* on the deployment in Kosovo, under United Nations auspices, of international civil and security presences, with appropriate equipment and personnel as required, and welcomes the agreement of the Federal Republic of Yugoslavia to such presences; . . .

7. *Authorizes* Member States and relevant international organizations to establish the international security presence in Kosovo as set out in point 4 of annex 2 with all necessary means to fulfil its responsibilities under paragraph 9 below;

8. *Affirms* the need for the rapid early deployment of effective international civil and security presences to Kosovo, and *demands* that the parties cooperate fully in their deployment;

9. *Decides* that the responsibilities of the international security presence to be deployed and acting in Kosovo will include:

(a) Deterring renewed hostilities, maintaining and where necessary enforcing a ceasefire, and ensuring the withdrawal and preventing the return into Kosovo of Federal and Republic military, police and paramilitary forces, except as provided in point 6 of annex 2;

(b) Demilitarizing the Kosovo Liberation Army (KLA) and other armed Kosovo Albanian groups as required in paragraph 15 below;

(c) Establishing a secure environment in which refugees and displaced persons can return home in safety, the international civil presence can operate, a transitional administration can be established, and humanitarian aid can be delivered;

(d) Ensuring public safety and order until the international civil presence can take responsibility for this task;

(e) Supervising demining until the international civil presence can, as appropriate, take over responsibility for this task;

(f) Supporting, as appropriate, and coordinating closely with the work of the international civil presence;

(g) Conducting border monitoring duties as required;

(h) Ensuring the protection and freedom of movement of itself, the international civil presence, and other international organizations;

10. *Authorizes* the Secretary-General, with the assistance of relevant international organizations, to establish an international civil presence in Kosovo in order to provide an interim administration for Kosovo under which the people of Kosovo can enjoy substantial autonomy within the Federal Republic of Yugoslavia, and which will provide transitional administration while establishing and overseeing the development of provisional democratic self-governing institutions to ensure conditions for a peaceful and normal life for all inhabitants of Kosovo;

11. *Decides* that the main responsibilities of the international civil presence will include:

(a) Promoting the establishment, pending a final settlement, of substantial autonomy and self-government in Kosovo, taking full account of annex 2 and of the Rambouillet accords (S/1999/648);

(b) Performing basic civilian administrative functions where and as long as required;

(c) Organizing and overseeing the development of provisional institutions for democratic and autonomous self-government pending a political settlement, including the holding of elections;

(d) Transferring, as these institutions are established, its administrative responsibilities while overseeing and supporting the consolidation of Kosovo's local provisional institutions and other peace-building activities;

(e) Facilitating a political process designed to determine Kosovo's future status, taking into account the Rambouillet accords (S/1999/648);

(f) In a final stage, overseeing the transfer of authority from Kosovo's provisional institutions to institutions established under a political settlement;

(g) Supporting the reconstruction of key infrastructure and other economic reconstruction;

(h) Supporting, in coordination with international humanitarian organizations, humanitarian and disaster relief aid;

(i) Maintaining civil law and order, including establishing local police forces and meanwhile through the deployment of international police personnel to serve in Kosovo;

(j) Protecting and promoting human rights;

(k) Assuring the safe and unimpeded return of all refugees and displaced persons to their homes in Kosovo; . . .

15. *Demands* that the KLA and other armed Kosovo Albanian groups end immediately all offensive actions and comply with the requirements for demilitarization . . .

16. *Decides* that the prohibitions imposed by paragraph 8 of resolution 1160 (1998) shall not apply to arms and related *materiel* for the use of the international civil and security presences; . . .

18. *Demands* that all States in the region cooperate fully in the implementation of all aspects of this resolution;

19. *Decides* that the international civil and security presences are established for an initial period of 12 months, to continue thereafter unless the Security Council decides otherwise; . . .

21. *Decides* to remain actively seized of the matter.

MATERIALS ON SEPTEMBER 11
AND THE WORLD'S RESPONSE

U.N. GENERAL ASSEMBLY RES. 56/1

(September 12, 2001)*

56/1. Condemnation of terrorist attacks in the United States of America

The General Assembly,

Guided by the purposes and principles of the Charter of the United Nations,

1. *Strongly condemns* the heinous acts of terrorism, which have caused enormous loss of human life, destruction and damage in the cities of New York, host city of the United Nations, Washington, D.C., and in Pennsylvania;

2. *Expresses its condolences and solidarity* with the people and Government of the United States of America in these said and tragic circumstances;

3. *Urgently calls* for international cooperation to bring to justice the perpetrators, organizers and sponsors of the outrages of 11 September 2001;

4. *Also Urgently calls* for international cooperation to prevent and eradicate acts of terrorism, and stresses that those responsible for aiding, supporting or harbouring the perpetrators, organizers and sponsors of such acts will be held accountable.

1st plenary meeting
12 September 2001

U.N. SECURITY COUNCIL RES. 1368

(September 12, 2001)**

The Security Council,

Reaffirming the principles and purposes of the Charter of the United Nations,

* Adopted without a vote.
** Adopted by a vote of 15-0.

Determined to combat by all means threats to international peace and security caused by terrorist acts,

Recognizing the inherent right of individual or collective self-defence in accordance with the Charter,

1. Unequivocally condemns in the strongest terms the horrifying terrorist attacks which took place on 11 September 2001 in New York, Washington, D.C. and Pennsylvania and *regards* such acts, like any act of international terrorism, as a threat to international peace and security;

2. Expresses its deepest sympathy and condolences to the victims and their families and to the people and Government of the United States of America;

3. Calls on all States to work together urgently to bring to justice the perpetrators, organizers and sponsors of these terrorist attacks and *stresses* that those responsible for aiding, supporting or harbouring the perpetrators, organizers and sponsors of these acts will be held accountable;

4. Calls also on the international community to redouble their efforts to prevent and suppress terrorist acts including by increased cooperation and full implementation of the relevant international anti-terrorist conventions and Security Council resolutions, in particular resolution 1269 (1999) of 19 October 1999;

5. Expresses its readiness to take all necessary steps to respond to the terrorist attacks of 11 September 2001, and to combat all forms of terrorism, in accordance with its responsibilities under the Charter of the United Nations;

6. Decides to remain seized of the matter.

U.S. CONGRESSIONAL JOINT RESOLUTION: AUTHORIZATION OF USE OF MILITARY FORCE

(September 14, 2001)

To authorize the use of United States Armed Forces against those responsible for the recent attacks launched against the United States.

WHEREAS, on September 11, 2001, acts of treacherous violence were committed against the United States and its citizens; and

WHEREAS, such acts render it both necessary and appropriate that the United States exercise its right to self-defense and to protect United States citizens both at home and abroad; and

WHEREAS, in light of the threat to the national security and foreign policy of the United States posed by these grave acts of violence; and

WHEREAS, such acts continue to pose an unusual and extraordinary threat to the national security and foreign policy of the United States.

WHEREAS, the President has authority under the Constitution to take action to deter and prevent acts of international terrorism against the United States.

Resolved by the Senate and the House of Representatives of the United States of America in Congress assembled,

Section 1.   Short Title

This joint resolution may be cited as the "Authorization of Use of Military Force."

Section 2.   Authorization for Use of United States Armed Forces

(a) That the President is authorized to use all necessary and appropriate force against those nations, organizations, or persons he determines planned, authorized, committed, or aided the terrorist attacks that occurred on September 11, 2001, or harbored such organization or persons, in order to prevent any future acts of international terrorism against the United States by such nations, organizations or persons.

(b) War Powers Resolution Requirements

(1) SPECIFIC STATUTORY AUTHORIZATION: Consistent with Section 8(a)(1) of the War Powers Resolution, the Congress declares that this section is intended to constitute specific statutory authorization within the meaning of Section 5(b) of the War Powers Resolution.

(2) APPLICABILITY OF OTHER REQUIREMENTS: Nothing in this resolution supercedes any requirement of the War Powers Resolution.

U.N. SECURITY COUNCIL RES. 1373

(September 28, 2001)*

The Security Council,

Reaffirming its resolutions 1269 (1999) of 19 October 1999 and 1368 (2001) of 12 September 2001,

Reaffirming also its unequivocal condemnation of the terrorist attacks which took place in New York, Washington, D.C. and Pennsylvania on 11 September 2001, and expressing its determination to prevent all such acts,

Reaffirming further that such acts, like any act of international terrorism, constitute a threat to international peace and security,

Reaffirming the inherent right of individual or collective self-defence as recognized by the Charter of the United Nations as reiterated in resolution 1368 (2001),

Reaffirming the need to combat by all means, in accordance with the Charter of the United Nations, threats to international peace and security caused by terrorist acts,

Deeply concerned by the increase, in various regions of the world, of acts of terrorism motivated by intolerance or extremism,

---

* Adopted by a vote of 15-0.

Calling on States to work together urgently to prevent and suppress terrorist acts, including through increased cooperation and full implementation of the relevant international conventions relating to terrorism,

Recognizing the need for States to complement international cooperation by taking additional measures to prevent and suppress, in their territories through all lawful means, the financing and preparation of any acts of terrorism,

Reaffirming the principle established by the General Assembly in its declaration of October 1970 (resolution 2625 (XXV)) and reiterated by the Security Council in its resolution 1189 (1998) of 13 August 1998, namely that every State has the duty to refrain from organizing, instigating, assisting or participating in terrorist acts in another State or acquiescing in organized activities within its territory directed towards the commission of such acts,

Acting under Chapter VII of the Charter of the United Nations,

1. *Decides* that all States shall:

(a) Prevent and suppress the financing of terrorist acts;

(b) Criminalize the wilful provision or collection, by any means, directly or indirectly, of funds by their nationals or in their territories with the intention that the funds should be used, or in the knowledge that they are to be used, in order to carry out terrorist acts;

(c) Freeze without delay funds and other financial assets or economic resources of persons who commit, or attempt to commit, terrorist acts or participate in or facilitate the commission of terrorist acts; of entities owned or controlled directly or indirectly by such persons; and of persons and entities acting on behalf of, or at the direction of such persons and entities, including funds derived or generated from property owned or controlled directly or indirectly by such persons and associated persons and entities;

(d) Prohibit their nationals or any persons arid entities within their territories from making any funds, financial assets or economic resources or financial or other related services available, directly or indirectly, for the benefit of persons who commit or attempt to commit or facilitate or participate in the commission of terrorist acts, of entities owned or controlled, directly or indirectly, by such persons and of persons and entities acting on behalf of or at the direction of such persons;

2. *Decides also* that all States shall:

(a) Refrain from providing any form of support, active or passive, to entities or persons involved in terrorist acts, including by suppressing recruitment of members of terrorist groups and eliminating the supply of weapons to terrorists;

(b) Take the necessary steps to prevent the commission of terrorist acts, including by provision of early warning to other States by exchange of information;

(c) Deny safe haven to those who finance, plan, support, or commit terrorist acts, or provide safe havens;

(d) Prevent those who finance, plan, facilitate or commit terrorist acts from using their respective territories for those purposes against other States or their citizens;

(e) Ensure that any person, who participates in the financing, planning, preparation or perpetration of terrorist acts or in supporting terrorist acts is brought to justice and ensure that, in addition to any other measures against them, such terrorist acts are established as serious criminal offences in domestic laws and regulations and that the punishment duly reflects the seriousness of such terrorist acts;

(f) Afford one another the greatest measure of assistance in connection with criminal investigations or criminal proceedings relating to the financing or support of terrorist acts, including assistance in obtaining evidence in their possession necessary for the proceedings;

(g) Prevent the movement of terrorists or terrorist groups by effective border controls and controls on issuance of identity papers and travel documents, and through measures for preventing counterfeiting, forgery or fraudulent use of identity papers and travel documents;

3. *Calls* upon all States to:

(a) Find ways of intensifying and accelerating the exchange of operational information, especially regarding actions or movements of terrorist persons or networks; forged or falsified travel documents; traffic in arms, explosives or sensitive materials; use of communications technologies by terrorist groups; and the threat posed by the possession of weapons of mass destruction by terrorist groups;

(b) Exchange information in accordance with international and domestic law and cooperate on administrative and judicial matters to prevent the commission of terrorist acts;

(c) Cooperate, particularly through bilateral and multilateral arrangements and agreements, to prevent and suppress terrorist attacks and take action against perpetrators of such acts;

(d) Become parties as soon as possible to the relevant international conventions and protocols relating to terrorism, including the International Convention for the Suppression of the Financing of Terrorism of 9 December 1999;

(e) Increase cooperation and fully implement the relevant international conventions and protocols relating to terrorism and Security Council resolutions 1269 (1999) and 1368 (2001);

(f) Take appropriate measures in conformity with the relevant provisions of national and international law, including international standards of human rights, before granting refugee status, for the purpose of ensuring that the asylum-seeker has not planned, facilitated or participated in the commission of terrorist acts;

(g) Ensure, in conformity with international law, that refugee status is not abused by the perpetrators, organizers or facilitators of terrorist acts, and that claims of political motivation are not recognized as grounds for refusing requests for the extradition of alleged terrorists; . . .

5. *Declares* that acts, methods, and practices of terrorism are contrary to the purposes and principles of the United Nations and that knowingly financing, planning and inciting terrorist acts are also contrary to the purposes and principles of the United Nations;

6. Decides to establish, in accordance with rule 28 of its provisional rules of procedure, a Committee of the Security Council, consisting of all the members of the Council, to monitor implementation of this resolution, with the assistance of appropriate expertise, and *calls upon* all States to report to the Committee, no later than 90 days from the date of adoption of this resolution and thereafter according to a timetable to be proposed by the Committee, on the steps they have taken to implement this resolution;

7. Directs the Committee to delineate its tasks, submit a work programme within 30 days of the adoption of this resolution, and to consider the support it requires, in consultation with the Secretary-General;

8. Expresses its determination to take all necessary steps in order to ensure the full implementation of this resolution, in accordance with its responsibilities under the Charter;

9. Decides to remain seized of this matter.

LETTER FROM PRESIDENT BUSH TO CONGRESSIONAL LEADERS REPORTING ON COMBAT ACTION IN AFGHANISTAN

(October 9, 2001)*

Dear Mr. Speaker: (Dear Mr. President:)

At approximately 12:30 p.m. (EDT) on October 7, 2001, on my orders, U.S. Armed Forces began combat action in Afghanistan against Al Qaida terrorists and their Taliban supporters. This military action is a part of our campaign against terrorism and is designed to disrupt the use of Afghanistan as a terrorist base of operations.

We are responding to the brutal September 11 attacks on our territory, our citizens, and our way of life, and to the continuing threat of terrorist acts against the United States and our friends and allies. This follows the deployment of various combat-equipped and combat support forces to a number of locations in the Central and Pacific Command areas of operations, as I reported to the Congress on September 24, to prepare for the campaign to prevent and deter terrorism.

I have taken these actions pursuant to my constitutional authority to conduct U.S. foreign relations as Commander in Chief and Chief Executive. It is not possible to know at this time either the duration of combat operations or the scope and duration of the deployment of U.S. Armed Forces necessary to counter the terrorist threat to the United States. As I have stated previously, it is likely that the American campaign against terrorism will be lengthy. I will direct such additional measures as necessary in exercise of our right to self-defense and to protect U.S citizens and interests.

* Identical letters were sent to J. Dennis Hastert, Speaker of the House of Representatives, and Robert C. Byrd, President pro tempore of the Senate.

I am providing this report as part of my efforts to keep the Congress informed, consistent with the War Powers Resolution and Public Law 107-40. Officials of my Administration and I have been communicating regularly with the leadership and other members of Congress, and we will continue to do so. I appreciate the continuing support of the Congress, including its enactment of Public Law 107-40, in these actions to protect the security of the United States of America and its citizens, civilian and military, here and abroad.

Sincerely,
GEORGE W. BUSH

LETTER FROM THE U.S. PERMANENT REPRESENTATIVE TO THE UNITED NATIONS ADDRESSED TO THE PRESIDENT OF THE SECURITY COUNCIL

(October 7, 2001)

In accordance with Article 51 of the Charter of the United Nations, I wish, on behalf of my Government, to report that the United States of America, together with other States, has initiated actions in the exercise of its inherent right of individual and collective self-defence following the armed attacks that were carried out against the United States on 11 September 2001.

On 11 September 2001, the United States was the victim of massive and brutal attacks in the states of New York, Pennsylvania and Virginia. These attacks were specifically designed to maximize the loss of life; they resulted in the death of more than 5,000 persons, including nationals of 81 countries, as well as the destruction of four civilian aircraft, the World Trade Center towers and a section of the Pentagon. Since 11 September, my Government has obtained clear and compelling information that the Al-Qaeda organization, which is supported by the Taliban regime in Afghanistan, had a central role in the attacks. There is still much we do not know. Our inquiry is in its early stages. We may find that our self-defence requires further actions with respect to other organizations and other States.

The attacks on 11 September 2001 and the ongoing threat to the United States and its nationals posed by the Al-Qaeda organization have been made possible by the decision of the Taliban regime to allow the parts of Afghanistan that it controls to be used by this organization as a base of operation. Despite every effort by the United States and the international community, the Taliban regime has refused to change its policy. From the territory of Afghanistan, the Al-Qaeda organization continues to train and support agents of terror who attack innocent people throughout the world and target United States nationals and interests in the United States and abroad.

In response to these attacks, and in accordance with the inherent right of individual and collective self-defence, United States armed forces have initiated actions designed to prevent and deter further attacks on the United States. These actions include measures against Al-Qaeda terrorist training camps and military installations of the Taliban regime in Afghanistan. In carrying out these actions, the United States is committed to minimizing civilian casualties and damage to civilian property. In addition, the United States will continue its humanitarian efforts to alleviate the suffering of the people of Afghanistan. We are providing them with food, medicine and supplies. . . .

(Signed) John D. Negroponte

U.N. SECURITY COUNCIL RES. 1378

(November 14, 2001)*

The Security Council,

Reaffirming its previous resolutions on Afghanistan . . . ,

Supporting international efforts to root out terrorism, in keeping with the Charter of the United Nations, and *reaffirming* also its resolutions 1368 (2001) of 12 September 2001 and 1373 (2001) of 28 September 2001,

Recognizing the urgency of the security and political situation in Afghanistan in light of the most recent developments, particularly in Kabul,

Condemning the Taliban for allowing Afghanistan to be used as a base for the export of terrorism by the Al-Qaida network and other terrorist groups and for providing safe haven to Usama Bin Laden, Al-Qaida and others associated with them, and in this context supporting the efforts of the Afghan people to replace the Taliban regime,

Welcoming the intention of the Special Representative to convene an urgent meeting of the various Afghan processes at an appropriate venue and *calling on* the United Front and all Afghans represented in those processes to accept his invitation to that meeting without delay . . . ,

Reaffirming its strong commitment to the sovereignty, independence, territorial integrity and national unity of Afghanistan,

Deeply concerned by the grave humanitarian situation and the continuing serious violations by the Taliban of human rights and international humanitarian law,

1. *Expresses* its strong support for the efforts of the Afghan people to establish a new and transitional administration leading to the formation of a government, . . . both of which:

— should be broad-based, multi-ethnic and fully representative of all the Afghan people and committed to peace with Afghanistan's neighbours,

— should respect the human rights of all Afghan people, regardless of gender, ethnicity or religion,

---

* Adopted by a vote of 15-0.

— should respect Afghanistan's international obligations, including by cooperating fully in international efforts to combat terrorism and illicit drug trafficking within and from Afghanistan, and

— should facilitate the urgent delivery of humanitarian assistance and the orderly return of refugees and internally displaced persons, when the situation permits; . . .

3. *Affirms* that the United Nations should play a central role in supporting the efforts of the Afghan people to establish urgently such a new and transitional administration leading to the formation of a new government . . . ;

4. *Calls* on Member States to provide:

— support for such an administration and government, including through the implementation of quick-impact projects,

— urgent humanitarian assistance to alleviate the suffering of Afghan people both inside Afghanistan and Afghan refugees . . . , and

— long-term assistance for the social and economic reconstruction and rehabilitation of Afghanistan and welcomes initiatives towards this end; . . .

6. *Decides* to remain actively seized of the matter.

U.N. SECURITY COUNCIL RES. 1383
(December 6, 2001)*

The Security Council,

Reaffirming its previous resolutions on Afghanistan . . . ,

Reaffirming its strong commitment to the sovereignty, independence, territorial integrity and national unity of Afghanistan,

Stressing the inalienable right of the Afghan people themselves freely to determine their own political future,

Determined to help the people of Afghanistan to bring to an end the tragic conflicts in Afghanistan and promote national reconciliation, lasting peace, stability and respect for human rights, as well as to cooperate with the international community to put an end to the use of Afghanistan as a base for terrorism,

Welcoming the letter of 5 December 2001 from the Secretary-General informing the Council . . . of the Agreement on provisional arrangements in Afghanistan pending the reestablishment of permanent government institutions . . . ,

* Adopted by a vote of 15-0.

Noting that the provisional arrangements are intended as a first step towards the establishment of a broad-based, gender sensitive, multi-ethnic and fully representative government,

1. Endorses the Agreement on provisional arrangements in Afghanistan pending the re-establishment of permanent government institutions . . . :

2. Calls on all Afghan groups to implement this Agreement in full, in particular through full cooperation with the Interim Authority which is due to take office on 22 December 2001; . . .

4. Declares its willingness to take further action . . . to support the Interim institutions established by the abovementioned Agreement and . . . to support the implementation of the Agreement and its annexes;

5. Calls on all Afghan groups to support full and unimpeded access by humanitarian organizations to people in need and to ensure the safety and security of humanitarian workers;

6. Calls on all bilateral and multilateral donors . . . to reaffirm, strengthen and implement their commitment to assist with the rehabilitation, recovery and reconstruction of Afghanistan, in coordination with the Interim Authority and as long as the Afghan groups fulfil their commitments;

7. Decides to remain actively seized of the matter.

U.N. SECURITY COUNCIL RES. 1386
(December 20, 2001)*

The Security Council,

Reaffirming its previous resolutions on Afghanistan . . . ,

Supporting international efforts to root out terrorism, in keeping with the Charter of the United Nations, and reaffirming also its resolutions 1368 (2001) of 12 September 2001 and 1373 (2001) of 28 September 2001,

Welcoming developments in Afghanistan that will allow for all Afghans to enjoy inalienable rights and freedom unfettered by oppression and terror, . . .

Reiterating its endorsement of the Agreement on provisional arrangements in Afghanistan pending the re-establishment of permanent government institutions, signed in Bonn on 5 December 2001 . . . ,

Taking note of the request to the Security Council . . . to consider authorizing the early deployment to Afghanistan of an international security force, as well as the briefing . . . by the Special Representative of the Secretary-General on his contacts with the Afghan authorities in which they welcome the deployment to Afghanistan of a United Nations-authorized international security force, . . .

[T]aking note of the United Kingdom offer contained therein to take the lead in organizing and commanding an International Security Assistance Force,

* Adopted by a vote of 15-0.

Stressing that all Afghan forces must adhere strictly to their obligations under human rights law, including respect for the rights of women, and under international humanitarian law,

Reaffirming its strong commitment to the sovereignty, independence, territorial integrity and national unity of Afghanistan,

Determining that the situation in Afghanistan still constitutes a threat to international peace and security,

Determined to ensure the full implementation of the mandate of the International Security Assistance Force, in consultation with the Afghan Interim Authority established by the Bonn Agreement,

Acting for these reasons under Chapter VII of the Charter of the United Nations,

1. Authorizes, as envisaged in Annex 1 to the Bonn Agreement, the establishment for 6 months of an International Security Assistance Force to assist the Afghan Interim Authority in the maintenance of security in Kabul and its surrounding areas, so that the Afghan Interim Authority as well as the personnel of the United Nations can operate in a secure environment;

2. Calls upon Member States to contribute personnel, equipment and other resources to the International Security Assistance Force . . . ;

3. Authorizes the Member States participating in the International Security Assistance Force to take all necessary measures to fulfil its mandate;

4. Calls upon the International Security Assistance Force to work in close consultation with the Afghan Interim Authority in the implementation of the force mandate . . . ;

5. Calls upon all Afghans to cooperate with the International Security Assistance Force and relevant international governmental and non-governmental organizations, and welcomes the commitment of the parties to the Bonn Agreement to do all within their means and influence to ensure security, including to ensure the safety, security and freedom of movement of all United Nations personnel and all other personnel of international governmental and non-governmental organizations deployed in Afghanistan;

6. Takes note of the pledge made by the Afghan parties to the Bonn Agreement in Annex 1 to that Agreement to withdraw all military units from Kabul, and calls upon them to implement this pledge in cooperation with the International Security Assistance Force;

7. Encourages neighbouring States and other Member States to provide to the International Security Assistance Force such necessary assistance as may be requested, including the provision of overflight clearances and transit;

8. Stresses that the expenses of the International Security Assistance Force will be borne by the participating Member States concerned, *requests* the Secretary-General to establish a trust fund through which contributions could be channelled to the Member States or operations concerned, and encourages Member States to contribute to such a fund; . . .

10. Calls on Member States participating in the International Security Assistance Force to provide assistance to help the Afghan Interim Authority in the establishment and training of new Afghan security and armed forces;

11. Decides to remain actively seized of the matter.

MATERIALS RE: INTERNATIONAL HUMANITARIAN LAW

GENEVA CONVENTION RELATIVE TO THE TREATMENT OF PRISONERS OF WAR (III)

International Committee of the Red Cross*

The undersigned Plenipotentiaries of the Governments represented at the Diplomatic Conference held at Geneva from April 21 to August 12, 1949, for the purpose of revising the Convention concluded at Geneva on July 27, 1929, relative to the Treatment of Prisoners of War, have agreed as follows:

---

* Concluded in Geneva on August 12, 1949. The four Geneva Conventions entered into force on October 21, 1950. As of November 2012, there were 194 parties to the Conventions. The parties were: Afghanistan, Albania, Algeria, Andorra, Angola, Antigua and Barbuda, Argentina, Armenia, Australia, Austria, Azerbaijan, Bahamas, Bahrain, Bangladesh, Barbados, Belarus, Belgium, Belize, Benin, Bhutan, Bolivia, Bosnia-Herzegovina, Botswana, Brazil, Brunei Darussalam, Bulgaria, Burkina Faso, Burundi, Cambodia, Cameroon, Canada, Cape Verde, Central African Republic, Chad, Chile, China, Colombia, Comoros, Congo, Congo (Democratic Republic of), Cook Islands, Costa Rica, Côte d'Ivoire, Croatia, Cuba, Cyprus, Czech, Republic, Denmark, Djibouti, Dominica, Dominican Republic, Ecuador, Egypt, El Salvador, Equatorial Guinea, Eritrea, Estonia, Ethiopia, Fiji, Finland, France, Gabon, Gambia, Georgia, Germany, Ghana, Greece, Grenada, Guatemala, Guinea, Guinea-Bissau. Guyana, Haiti, Holy See, Honduras, Hungary, Iceland, India, Indonesia, Iran, Iraq, Ireland, Israel, Italy, Jamaica, Japan, Jordan, Kazakhstan, Kenya, Kiribati, Korea (Democratic People's Republic of), Korea (Republic of), Kuwait, Kyrgyzstan, Lao People's Democratic Republic, Latvia, Lebanon, Lesotho, Liberia, Libyan Arab Jamahiriya, Liechtenstein, Lithuania, Luxembourg, Macedonia, Madagascar, Malawi, Malaysia, Maldives, Mali, Malta, Marshall Islands, Mauritania, Mauritius, Mexico, Micronesia, Moldova, Monaco, Mongolia, Montenegro, Morocco, Mozambique, Myanmar, Namibia, Nepal, Netherlands, New Zealand, Nicaragua, Niger, Nigeria, Norway, Oman, Pakistan, Palau, Panama, Papua New Guinea, Paraguay, Peru, Philippines, Poland, Portugal, Qatar, Romania, Russian Federation, Rwanda, Saint Kitts and Nevis, Saint Lucia, Saint Vincent and the Grenadines, Samoa, San Marino, Sao Tome and Principe, Saudi Arabia, Senegal, Serbia, Seychelles, Sierra Leone, Singapore, Slovakia, Slovenia, Solomon Islands, Somalia, South Africa, South Sudan, Spain, Sri Lanka, Sudan, Suriname, Swaziland, Sweden, Switzerland, Syrian Arab Republic, Tajikistan, Tanzania, Thailand, Timor-Leste, Togo, Tonga, Trinidad and Tobago, Tunisia, Turkey, Turkmenistan, Tuvalu, Uganda, Ukraine, United Arab Emirates, United Kingdom, United States, Uruguay, Uzbekistan, Vanuatu, Venezuela, Viet Nam, Yemen, Zambia, Zimbabwe. See the International Committee of the Red Cross Web site at <http://www.icrc.org>.

Part I.   General Provisions

Article 1

The High Contracting Parties undertake to respect and to ensure respect for the present Convention in all circumstances.

Article 2

In addition to the provisions which shall be implemented in peace time, the present Convention shall apply to all cases of declared war or of any other armed conflict which may arise between two or more of the High Contracting Parties, even if the state of war is not recognized by one of them.

The Convention shall also apply to all cases of partial or total occupation of the territory of a High Contracting Party, even if the said occupation meets with no armed resistance.

Although one of the Powers in conflict may not be a party to the present Convention, the Powers who are parties thereto shall remain bound by it in their mutual relations. They shall furthermore be bound by the Convention in relation to the said Power, if the latter accepts and applies the provisions thereof.

Article 3

In the case of armed conflict not of an international character occurring in the territory of one of the High Contracting Parties, each Party to the conflict shall be bound to apply, as a minimum, the following provisions:

(1) Persons taking no active part in the hostilities, including members of armed forces who have laid down their arms and those placed hors de combat by sickness, wounds, detention, or any other cause, shall in all circumstances be treated humanely, without any adverse distinction founded on race, colour, religion or faith, sex, birth or wealth, or any other similar criteria. To this end the following acts are and shall remain prohibited at any time and in any place whatsoever with respect to the above-mentioned persons:
   (a) violence to life and person, in particular murder of all kinds, mutilation, cruel treatment and torture;
   (b) taking of hostages;
   (c) outrages upon personal dignity, in particular, humiliating and degrading treatment;
   (d) the passing of sentences and the carrying out of executions without previous judgment pronounced by a regularly constituted court affording all the judicial guarantees which are recognized as indispensable by civilized peoples.
(2) The wounded and sick shall be collected and cared for.

An impartial humanitarian body, such as the International Committee of the Red Cross, may offer its services to the Parties to the conflict.

The Parties to the conflict should further endeavour to bring into force, by means of special agreements, all or part of the other provisions of the present Convention.

The application of the preceding provisions shall not affect the legal status of the Parties to the conflict.

Article 4

A. Prisoners of war, in the sense of the present Convention, are persons belonging to one of the following categories, who have fallen into the power of the enemy:

(1) Members of the armed forces of a Party to the conflict, as well as members of militias or volunteer corps forming part of such armed forces.

(2) Members of other militias and members of other volunteer corps, including those of organized resistance movements, belonging to a Party to the conflict and operating in or outside their own territory, even if this territory is occupied, provided that such militias or volunteer corps, including such organized resistance movements, fulfill the following conditions:

    (a) that of being commanded by a person responsible for his subordinates;

    (b) that of having a fixed distinctive sign recognizable at a distance;

    (c) that of carrying arms openly;

    (d) that of conducting their operations in accordance with the laws and customs of war.

(3) Members of regular armed forces who profess allegiance to a government or an authority not recognized by the Detaining Power.

(4) Persons who accompany the armed forces without actually being members thereof, such as civilian members of military aircraft crews, war correspondents, supply contractors, members of labour units or of services responsible for the welfare of the armed forces, provided that they have received authorization, from the armed forces which they accompany, who shall provide them for that purpose with an identity card similar to the annexed model.

(5) Members of crews, including masters, pilots and apprentices, of the merchant marine and the crews of civil aircraft of the Parties to the conflict, who do not benefit by more favourable treatment under any other provisions of international law.

(6) Inhabitants of a non-occupied territory, who on the approach of the enemy spontaneously take up arms to resist the invading forces, without having had time to form themselves into regular armed units, provided they carry arms openly and respect the laws and customs of war.

B. The following shall likewise be treated as prisoners of war under the present Convention:

(1) Persons belonging, or having belonged, to the armed forces of the occupied country, if the occupying Power considers it necessary by reason of such allegiance to intern them, even though it has originally liberated them while hostilities were going on outside the territory it occupies, in particular where such persons have made an unsuccessful attempt to rejoin the armed forces to which they belong and which are engaged in combat, or where they fail to comply, with a summons made to them with a view to internment.

(2) The persons belonging to one of the categories enumerated in the present Article, who have been received by neutral or nonbelligerent Powers on their territory and whom these Powers are required to intern under international law, without prejudice to any more favourable treatment which these Powers may choose to give and with the exception of Articles 8, 10, 15, 30, fifth paragraph, 58-67, 92, 126 and, where diplomatic relations exist between the Parties to the conflict and the neutral or non-belligerent Power concerned, those Articles concerning the Protecting Power. . . .

C. This Article shall in no way affect the status of medical personnel and chaplains as provided for in Article 33 of the present Convention.

Article 5

The present Convention shall apply to the persons referred to in Article 4 from the time they fall into the power of the enemy and until their final release and repatriation.

Should any doubt arise as to whether persons, having committed a belligerent act and having fallen into the hands of the enemy, belong to any of the categories enumerated in Article 4, such persons shall enjoy the protection of the present Convention until such time as their status has been determined by a competent tribunal.

Article 6

In addition to the agreements expressly provided for in Articles 10, 23, 28, 33, 60, 65, 66, 67, 72, 73, 75, 109, 110, 118, 119, 122 and 132, the High Contracting Parties may conclude other special agreements for all matters concerning which they may deem it suitable to make separate provision. No special agreement shall adversely affect the situation of prisoners of war, as defined by the present Convention, nor restrict the rights which it confers upon them.

Prisoners of war shall continue to have the benefit of such agreements as long as the Convention is applicable to them, except where express provisions to the contrary are contained in the aforesaid or in subsequent agreements, or where more favourable measures have been taken with regard to them by one or other of the Parties to the conflict.

Article 7

Prisoners of war may in no circumstances renounce in part or in entirety the rights secured to them by the present Convention, and by the special agreements referred to in the foregoing Article, if such there be.

Article 8

The present Convention shall be applied with the cooperation and under the scrutiny of the Protecting Powers whose duty it is to safeguard the interests of the Parties to the conflict. For this purpose, the Protecting Powers may appoint, apart from their diplomatic or consular staff, delegates from amongst their own nationals or the nationals of other neutral Powers. The said delegates shall be subject to the approval of the Power with which they are to carry out their duties. . . .

Article 9

The provisions of the present Convention constitute no obstacle to the humanitarian activities which the International Committee of the Red Cross or any other impartial humanitarian organization may, subject to the consent of the Parties to the conflict concerned, undertake for the protection of prisoners of war and for their relief.

Article 10

The High Contracting Parties may at any time agree to entrust to an organization which offers all guarantees of impartiality and efficacy the duties incumbent on the Protecting Powers by virtue of the present Convention.

When prisoners of war do not benefit or cease to benefit, no matter for what reason, by the activities of a Protecting Power or of an organization provided for in the first paragraph above, the Detaining Power shall request a neutral State, or such an organization, to undertake the functions performed under the present Convention by a Protecting Power designated by the Parties to a conflict. . . .

Article 11

In cases where they deem it advisable in the interest of protected persons, particularly in cases of disagreement between the Parties to the conflict as to the application or interpretation of the provisions of the present Convention, the Protecting Powers shall lend their good offices with a view to settling the disagreement. . . .

Part II. General Protection of Prisoners of War

Article 12

Prisoners of war are in the hands of the enemy Power, but not of the individuals or military units who have captured them. Irrespective of the individual responsibilities that may exist, the Detaining Power is responsible for the treatment given them.

Prisoners of war may only be transferred by the Detaining Power to a Power which is a party to the Convention and after the Detaining Power has satisfied itself of the willingness and ability of such transferee Power to apply the Convention. When prisoners of war are transferred under such circumstances, responsibility for the application of the Convention rests on the Power accepting them while they are in its custody. . . .

Article 13

Prisoners of war must at all times be humanely treated. Any unlawful act or omission by the Detaining Power causing death or seriously endangering the health of a prisoner of war in its custody is prohibited, and will be regarded as a serious breach of the present Convention. In particular, no prisoner of war may be subjected to physical mutilation or to medical or scientific experiments of any kind which are not justified by the medical, dental or hospital treatment of the prisoner concerned and carried out in his interest.

Likewise, prisoners of war must at all times be protected, particularly against acts of violence or intimidation and against insults and public curiosity.

Measures of reprisal against prisoners of war are prohibited.

Article 14

Prisoners of war are entitled in all circumstances to respect for their persons and their honour.

Women shall be treated with all the regard due to their sex and shall in all cases benefit by treatment as favourable as that granted to men. . . .

Article 15

The Power detaining prisoners of war shall be bound to provide free of charge for their maintenance and for the medical attention required by their state of health.

Article 16

Taking into consideration the provisions of the present Convention relating to rank and sex, and subject to any privileged treatment which may be accorded to them by reason of their slate of health, age or professional qualifications, all prisoners of war shall he treated alike by the Detaining Power, without any adverse distinction based on race, nationality, religious belief or political opinions, or any other distinction founded on similar criteria.

Part III. Captivity

SECTION 1. BEGINNING OF CAPTIVITY

Article 17

Every prisoner of war, when questioned on the subject, is bound to give only his surname, first names and rank, date of birth, and army, regimental, personal or serial number, or failing this, equivalent information.

If he wilfully infringes this rule, he may render himself liable to a restriction of the privileges accorded to his rank or status.

Each Party to a conflict is required to furnish the persons under its jurisdiction who are liable to become prisoners of war, with an identity card showing the owner's surname, first names, rank, army, regimental, personal or serial number or equivalent information, and date of birth. The identity card may, furthermore, bear the signature or the fingerprints, or both, of the owner, and may bear, as well, any other information the Party to the conflict may wish to add concerning persons belonging to its armed forces. As far as possible the card shall measure 6.5 × 10 cm. and shall be issued in duplicate. The identity card shall be shown by the prisoner of war upon demand, but may in no case be taken away from him.

No physical or mental torture, nor any other form of coercion, may be inflicted on prisoners of war to secure from them information of any kind whatever. Prisoners of war who refuse to answer may not be threatened, insulted, or exposed to unpleasant or disadvantageous treatment of any kind. . . .

The questioning of prisoners of war shall be carried out in a language which they understand.

Article 18

All effects and articles of personal use, except arms, horses, military equipment and military documents, shall remain in the possession of prisoners of war, likewise their metal helmets and gas masks and like articles issued for personal protection. Effects and articles used for their clothing or feeding shall likewise remain in their possession, even if such effects and articles belong to their regulation military equipment.

At no time should prisoners of war be without identity documents. The Detaining Power shall supply such documents to prisoners of war who possess none.

Badges of rank and nationality, decorations and articles having above all a personal or sentimental value may not be taken from prisoners of war. . . .

Article 19

Prisoners of war shall be evacuated, as soon as possible after their capture, to camps situated in an area far enough from the combat zone for them to be out of danger. . . .

Article 20

The evacuation of prisoners of war shall always be effected humanely and in conditions similar to those for the forces of the Detaining Power in their changes of station. . . .

SECTION II. INTERNMENT OF PRISONERS OF WAR

CHAPTER I. GENERAL OBSERVATIONS

Article 21

The Detaining Power may subject prisoners of war to internment. It may impose on them the obligation of not leaving, beyond certain limits, the camp where they are interned, or if the said camp is fenced in, of not going outside its perimeter. Subject to the provisions of the present Convention relative to penal and disciplinary sanctions, prisoners of war may not be held in close confinement except where necessary to safeguard their health and then only during the continuation of the circumstances which make such confinement necessary. . . .

CHAPTER II. QUARTERS, FOOD AND CLOTHING OF PRISONERS OF WAR

Article 25

Prisoners of war shall be quartered under conditions as favourable as those for the forces of the Detaining Power who are billeted in the same area. The said conditions shall make allowance for the habits and customs of the prisoners and shall in no case be prejudicial to their health.

The foregoing provisions shall apply in particular to the dormitories of prisoners of war as regards both total surface and minimum cubic space, and the general installations, bedding and blankets. . . .

SECTION V. RELATIONS OF PRISONERS OF WAR WITH THE EXTERIOR

Article 69

Immediately upon prisoners of war falling into its power, the Detaining Power shall inform them and the Powers on which they depend, through the Protecting Power, of the measures taken to carry out the provisions of the present Section. They shall likewise inform the parties concerned of any subsequent modifications of such measures.

Article 70

Immediately upon capture, or not more than one week after arrival at a camp, even if it is a transit camp, likewise in case of sickness or transfer to hospital or to another camp, every prisoner of war shall be enabled to write direct to his family, on the one hand, and to the Central Prisoners of War

Agency provided for in Article 123, on the other hand, a card similar, if possible, to the model annexed to the present Convention, informing his relatives of his capture, address and state of health. The said cards shall be forwarded as rapidly as possible and may not be delayed in any manner.

Article 71

Prisoners of war shall be allowed to send and receive letters and cards. If the Detaining Power deems it necessary to limit the number of letters and cards sent by each prisoner of war, the said number shall not be less than two letters and four cards monthly, exclusive of the capture cards provided for in Article 70, and conforming as closely as possible to the models annexed to the present Convention. . . .

III. Judicial Proceedings

Article 99

No prisoner of war may be tried or sentenced for an act which is not forbidden by the law of the Detaining Power or by international law, in force at the time the said act was committed.

No moral or physical coercion may be exerted on a prisoner of war in order to induce him to admit himself guilty of the act of which he is accused.

No prisoner of war may be convicted without having had an opportunity to present his defence and the assistance of a qualified advocate or counsel.

Article 100

Prisoners of war and the Protecting Powers shall be informed as soon as possible of the offences which are punishable by the death sentence under the laws of the Detaining Power.

Other offences shall not thereafter be made punishable by the death penalty without the concurrence of the Power on which the prisoners of war depend.

The death sentence cannot be pronounced on a prisoner of war unless the attention of the court has, in accordance with Article 87, second paragraph, been particularly called to the fact that since the accused is not a national of the Detaining Power, he is not bound to it by any duty of allegiance, and that he is in its power as the result of circumstances independent of his own will.

Article 101

If the death penalty is pronounced on a prisoner of war, the sentence shall not be executed before the expiration of a period of at least six months from the date when the Protecting Power receives, at an indicated address, the detailed communication provided for in Article 107.

Article 102

A prisoner of war can be validly sentenced only if the sentence has been pronounced by the same courts according to the same procedure as in the case of members of the armed forces of the Detaining Power, and if, furthermore, the provisions of the present Chapter have been observed.

Article 103

Judicial investigations relating to a prisoner of war shall be conducted as rapidly as circumstances permit and so that his trial shall take place as soon as possible. A prisoner of war shall not be confined while awaiting trial unless a member of the armed forces of the Detaining Power would be so confined if he were accused of a similar offence, or if it is essential to do so in the interests of national security. In no circumstances shall this confinement exceed three months.

Any period spent by a prisoner of war in confinement awaiting trial shall be deducted from any sentence of imprisonment passed upon him and taken into account in fixing any penalty. . . .

Article 104

In any case in which the Detaining Power has decided to institute judicial proceedings against a prisoner of war, it shall notify the Protecting Power as soon as possible and at least three weeks before the opening of the trial. . . .

The said notification shall contain the following information:

(1) Surname and first names of the prisoner of war, his rank, his army, regimental, personal or serial number, his date of birth, and his profession or trade, if any;
(2) Place of internment or confinement;
(3) Specification of the charge or charges on which the prisoner of war is to be arraigned, giving the legal provisions applicable;
(4) Designation of the court which will try the case, likewise the date and place fixed for the opening of the trial.

The same communication shall be made by the Detaining Power to the prisoners' representative. . . .

Article 105

The prisoner of war shall be entitled to assistance by one of his prisoner comrades, to defence by a qualified advocate or counsel of his own choice, to the calling of witnesses and, if he deems necessary, to the services of a competent interpreter. He shall be advised of these rights by the Detaining Power in due time before the trial.

Failing a choice by the prisoner of war, the Protecting Power shall find him an advocate or counsel, and shall have at least one week at its disposal for the purpose. The Detaining Power shall deliver to the said Power, on request, a list of persons qualified to present the defence. Failing a choice of an advocate or counsel by the prisoner of war or the Protecting Power, the Detaining Power shall appoint a competent advocate or counsel to conduct the defence.

The advocate or counsel conducting the defence on behalf of the prisoner of war shall have at his disposal a period of two weeks at least before the opening of the trial, as well as the necessary facilities to prepare the defence of the accused. He may, in particular, freely visit the accused and interview him in private. He may also confer with any witnesses for the defence, including prisoners of war. He shall have the benefit of these facilities until the term of appeal or petition has expired.

Particulars of the charge or charges on which the prisoner of war is to be arraigned, as well as the documents which are generally communicated to the accused by virtue of the laws in force in the armed forces of the Detaining Power, shall be communicated to the accused prisoner of war in a language which he understands, and in good time before the opening of the trial. The same communication in the same circumstances shall be made to the advocate or counsel conducting the defence on behalf of the prisoner of war.

The representatives of the Protecting Power shall be entitled to attend the trial of the case, unless, exceptionally, this is held in camera in the interest of State security. In such a case the Detaining Power shall advise the Protecting Power accordingly.

Article 106

Every prisoner of war shall have, in the same manner as the members of the armed forces of the Detaining Power, the right of appeal or petition from any sentence pronounced upon him, with a view to the quashing or revising of the sentence or the reopening of the trial. . . .

Article 107

Any judgment and sentence pronounced upon a prisoner of war shall be immediately reported to the Protecting Power in the form of a summary communication, which shall also indicate whether he has the right of appeal with a view to the quashing of the sentence or the reopening of the trial. This communication shall likewise be sent to the prisoners' representative concerned. It shall also be sent to the accused prisoner of war in a language he understands, if the sentence was not pronounced in his presence. . . .

Furthermore, if a prisoner of war is finally convicted or if a sentence pronounced on a prisoner of war in the first instance is a death sentence, the Detaining Power shall as soon as possible address to the Protecting Power a detailed communication containing:

(1) the precise wording of the finding and sentence;
(2) a summarized report of any preliminary investigation and of the trial, emphasizing in particular the elements of the prosecution and the defence;

(3) notification, where applicable, of the establishment where the sentence will be served. . . .

Article 108

Sentences pronounced on prisoners of war after a conviction has become duly enforceable, shall be served in the same establishments and under the same conditions as in the case of members of the armed forces of the Detaining Power. These conditions shall in all cases conform to the requirements of health and humanity.

A woman prisoner of war on whom such a sentence has been pronounced shall be confined in separate quarters and shall be under the supervision of women.

In any case, prisoners of war sentenced to a penalty depriving them of their liberty shall retain the benefit of the provisions of Articles 78 and 126 of the present Convention. Furthermore, they shall be entitled to receive and despatch correspondence, to receive at least one relief parcel monthly, to take regular exercise in the open air, to have the medical care required by their state of health, and the spiritual assistance they may desire. Penalties to which they may be subjected shall be in accordance with the provisions of Article 87, third paragraph. . . .

SECTION II. RELEASE AND REPATRIATION OF PRISONERS OF WAR AT THE CLOSE OF HOSTILITIES

Article 118

Prisoners of war shall be released and repatriated without delay after the cessation of active hostilities. . . .

Part VI. Execution of the Convention

SECTION I. GENERAL PROVISIONS

Article 126

Representatives or delegates of the Protecting Powers shall have permission to go to all places where prisoners of war may be, particularly to places of internment, imprisonment and labour, and shall have access to all premises occupied by prisoners of war. . . . They shall be able to interview the prisoners, and in particular the prisoners' representatives, without witnesses, either personally or through an interpreter.

Representatives and delegates of the Protecting Powers shall have full liberty to select the places they wish to visit. The duration and frequency of these visits shall not be restricted. Visits may not be prohibited except for reasons of imperative military necessity, and then only as an exceptional and temporary measure.

The Detaining Power and the Power on which the said prisoners of war depend may agree, if necessary, that compatriots of these prisoners of war be permitted to participate in the visits.

The delegates of the International Committee of the Red Cross shall enjoy the same prerogatives. The appointment of such delegates shall be submitted to the approval of the Power detaining the prisoners of war to be visited. . . .

Article 129

The High Contracting Parties undertake to enact any legislation necessary to provide effective penal sanctions for persons committing, or ordering to be committed, any of the grave breaches of the present Convention defined in the following Article.

Each High Contracting Party shall be under the obligation to search for persons alleged to have committed, or to have ordered to be committed, such grave breaches, and shall bring such persons, regardless of their nationality, before its own courts. It may also, if it prefers, and in accordance with the provisions of its own legislation, hand such persons over for trial to another High Contracting Party concerned, provided such High Contracting Party has made out a prima facie case.

Each High Contracting Party shall take measures necessary for the suppression of all acts contrary to the provisions of the present Convention other than the grave breaches defined in the following Article.

In all circumstances, the accused persons shall benefit by safeguards of proper trial and defence, which shall not be less favourable than those provided by Article 105 and those following of the present Convention.

Article 130

Grave breaches to which the preceding Article relates shall be those involving any of the following acts, if committed against persons or property protected by the Convention: wilful killing, torture or inhuman treatment, including biological experiments, wilfully causing great suffering or serious injury to body or health, compelling a prisoner of war to serve in the forces of the hostile Power, or wilfully depriving a prisoner of war of the rights of fair and regular trial prescribed in this Convention.

Article 131

No High Contracting Party shall be allowed to absolve itself or any other High Contracting Party of any liability incurred by itself or by another High Contracting Party in respect of breaches referred to in the preceding Article.

Article 132

At the request of a Party to the conflict, an enquiry shall be instituted, in a manner to be decided between the interested Parties, concerning any alleged violation of the Convention.

If agreement has not been reached concerning the procedure for the enquiry, the Parties should agree on the choice of an umpire who will decide upon the procedure to be followed.

Once the violation has been established, the Parties to the conflict shall put an end to it and shall repress it with the least possible delay.

Section II.   FINAL PROVISIONS...

Article 142

Each of the High Contracting Parties shall be at liberty to denounce the present Convention.

The denunciation shall be notified in writing to the Swiss Federal Council, which shall transmit it to the Governments of all the High Contracting Parties.

The denunciation shall take effect one year after the notification thereof has been made to the Swiss Federal Council. However, a denunciation of which notification has been made at a time when the denouncing Power is involved in a conflict shall not take effect until peace has been concluded, and until after operations connected with release and repatriation of the persons protected by the present Convention have been terminated.

The denunciation shall have effect only in respect of the denouncing Power. It shall in no way impair the obligations which the Parties to the conflict shall remain bound to fulfil by virtue of the principles of the law of nations, as they result from the usages established among civilized peoples, from the laws of humanity and the dictates of the public conscience. . . .

GENEVA CONVENTION RELATIVE TO THE PROTECTION OF CIVILIAN PERSONS IN TIME OF WAR (IV)

International Committee of the Red Cross*

Part I.   General Provisions

Article 1

The High Contracting Parties undertake to respect and to ensure respect for the present Convention in all circumstances.

Article 2

In addition to the provisions which shall be implemented in peacetime, the present Convention shall apply to all cases of declared war or of any other armed conflict which may arise between two or more of the High Contracting Parties, even if the state of war is not recognized by one of them.

The Convention shall also apply to all cases of partial or total occupation of the territory of a High Contracting Party, even if the said occupation meets with no armed resistance.

Although one of the Powers in conflict may not be a party to the present Convention, the Powers who are parties thereto shall remain bound by it in their mutual relations. They shall furthermore be bound by the Convention in relation to the said Power, if the latter accepts and applies the provisions thereof.

Article 3

In the case of armed conflict not of an international character occurring in the territory of one of the High Contracting Parties, each Party to the conflict shall be bound to apply, as a minimum, the following provisions:

(1) Persons taking no active part in the hostilities, including members of armed forces who have laid down their arms and those placed, hors de combat by sickness, wounds, detention, or any other cause, shall in all

---

* See the footnote at the start of the prior Geneva Convention (III). It is also applicable here.

819

circumstances be treated humanely, without any adverse distinction founded on race, colour, religion or faith, sex, birth or wealth, or any other similar criteria.

    To this end the following acts are and shall remain prohibited at any time and in any place whatsoever with respect to the above-mentioned persons:

(a) violence to life and person, in particular murder of all kinds, mutilation, cruel treatment and torture;

(b) taking of hostages:

(c) outrages upon personal dignity, in particular humiliating and degrading treatment;

(d) the passing of sentences and the carrying out of executions without previous judgment pronounced by a regularly constituted court, affording all the judicial guarantees which are recognized as indispensable by civilized peoples.

(2) The wounded and sick shall be collected and cared for.

An impartial humanitarian body, such as the International Committee of the Red Cross, may offer its services to the Parties to the conflict.

The Parties to the conflict should further endeavour to bring into force, by means of special agreements, all or part of the other provisions of the present Convention.

The application of the preceding provisions shall not affect the legal status of the Parties to the conflict.

Article 4

Persons protected by the Convention are those who, at a given moment and in any manner whatsoever, find themselves, in case of a conflict or occupation, in the hands of a Party to the conflict or Occupying Power of which they are not nationals.

Nationals of a State which is not bound by the Convention are not protected by it. Nationals of a neutral State who find themselves in the territory of a belligerent State, and nationals of a co-belligerent State, shall not be regarded as protected persons while the State of which they are nationals has normal diplomatic representation in the State in whose hands they are.

The provisions of Part II are, however, wider in application, as defined in Article 13.

Persons protected by the [other three Geneva Conventions of 1949] . . . shall not be considered as protected persons within the meaning of the present Convention.

Article 5

Where in the territory of a Party to the conflict, the latter is satisfied that an individual protected person is definitely suspected of or engaged in activities hostile to the security of the State, such individual person shall not be entitled to claim such rights and privileges under the present Convention as would, if exercised in the favour of such individual person, be prejudicial to the security of such State.

Where in occupied territory an individual protected person is detained as a spy or saboteur, or as a person under definite suspicion of activity hostile to the security of the Occupying Power, such person shall, in those cases where absolute military security so requires, be regarded as having forfeited rights of communication under the present Convention.

In each case, such persons shall nevertheless be treated with humanity and, in case of trial, shall not be deprived of the rights of fair and regular trial prescribed by the present Convention. They shall also be granted the full rights and privileges of a protected person under the present Convention at the earliest date consistent with the security of the State or Occupying Power, as the case may be.

Article 6

The present Convention shall apply from the outset of any conflict or occupation mentioned in Article 2.

In the territory of Parties to the conflict, the application of the present Convention shall cease on the general close of military operations.

In the case of occupied territory, the application of the present Convention shall cease one year after the general close of military operations; however, the Occupying Power shall be bound, for the duration of the occupation, to the extent that such Power exercises the functions of government in such territory, by the provisions of the following Articles of the present Convention: 1 to 12, 27, 29 to 34, 47, 49, 51, 52, 53, 59, 61 to 77, 143.

Protected persons whose release, repatriation or re-establishment may take place after such dates shall meanwhile continue to benefit by the present Convention.

Article 7

In addition to the agreements expressly provided for in Articles 11, 14, 15, 17, 36, 108, 109, 132, 133 and 149, the High Contracting Parties may conclude other special agreements for all matters. . . . No special agreement shall adversely affect the situation of protected persons, as defined by the present Convention, nor restrict the rights which it confers upon them.

Article 8

Protected persons may in no circumstances renounce in part or in entirety the rights secured to them by the present Convention, and by the special agreements referred to in the foregoing Article, if such there be.

Article 9

The present Convention shall be applied with the cooperation and under the scrutiny of the Protecting Powers whose duty it is to safeguard the interests of the Parties to the conflict. For this purpose, the Protecting Powers may appoint, apart from their diplomatic or consular staff, delegates from amongst their own nationals or the nationals of other neutral Powers. The said delegates shall be subject to the approval of the Power with which they are to carry out their duties.

The Parties to the conflict shall facilitate to the greatest extent possible the task of the representatives or delegates of the Protecting Powers. . . .

Article 10

The provisions of the present Convention constitute no obstacle to the humanitarian activities which the International Committee of the Red Cross or any other impartial humanitarian organization may, subject to the consent of the Parties to the conflict concerned, undertake for the protection of civilian persons and for their relief.

Article 11

The High Contracting Parties may at any time agree to entrust to an international organization which offers all guarantees of impartiality and efficacy the duties incumbent on the Protecting Powers by virtue of the present Convention.

Whenever in the present Convention mention is made of a Protecting Power, such mention applies to substitute organizations in the sense of the present Article.

The provisions of this Article shall extend and be adapted to cases of nationals of a neutral State who are in occupied territory or who find themselves in the territory of a belligerent State in which the State of which they are nationals has not normal diplomatic representation.

Article 12

In cases where they deem it advisable in the interest of protected persons, particularly in cases of disagreement between the Parties to the conflict as to the application or interpretation of the provisions of the present Convention, the Protecting Powers shall lend their good offices with a view to settling the disagreement. . . .

Part II.   General Protection of Populations Against Certain Consequences of War

Article 13

The provisions of Part II cover the whole of the populations of the countries in conflict, without any adverse distinction based, in particular, on race, nationality, religion or political opinion, and are intended to alleviate the sufferings caused by war.

Article 14

In time of peace, the High Contracting Parties and, after the outbreak of hostilities, the Parties thereto, may establish in their own territory and, if the need arises, in occupied areas, hospital and safety zones and localities so organized as to protect from the effects of war, wounded, sick and aged persons, children under fifteen, expectant mothers and mothers of children under seven. . . .

Article 15

Any Party to the conflict may, either direct or through a neutral State or some humanitarian organization, propose to the adverse Party to establish, in the regions where fighting is taking place, neutralized zones intended to shelter from the effects of war the following persons, without distinction:

(*a*) wounded and sick combatants or non-combatants;

(*b*) civilian persons who take no part in hostilities, and who, while they reside in the zones, perform no work of a military character. . . .

Article 16

The wounded and sick, as well as the infirm, and expectant mothers, shall be the object of particular protection and respect. . . .

Article 18

Civilian hospitals organized to give care to the wounded and sick, the infirm and maternity cases, may in no circumstances be the object of attack but shall at all times be respected and protected by the Parties to the conflict. . . .

Part III.   Status and Treatment of Protected Persons

SECTION I.   PROVISIONS COMMON TO THE TERRITORIES OF THE PARTIES TO THE CONFLICT AND TO OCCUPIED TERRITORIES

Article 27

Protected persons are entitled, in all circumstances, to respect for their persons, their honour, their family rights, their religious convictions and practices, and their manners and customs. They shall at all times be humanely treated, and shall be protected especially against all acts of violence or threats thereof and against insults and public curiosity.

Women shall be especially protected against any attack on their honour, in particular against rape, enforced prostitution, or any form of indecent assault.

Without prejudice to the provisions relating to their state of health, age and sex, all protected persons shall be treated with the same consideration by the Party to the conflict in whose power they are, without any adverse distinction based, in particular, on race, religion or political opinion.

However, the Parties to the conflict may take such measures of control and security in regard to protected persons as may be necessary as a result of the war.

Article 28

The presence of a protected person may not be used to render certain points or areas immune from military operations.

Article 29

The Party to the conflict in whose hands protected persons may be, is responsible for the treatment accorded to them by its agents, irrespective of any individual responsibility which may be incurred.

Article 30

Protected persons shall have every facility for making application to the Protecting Powers, the International Committee of the Red Cross, the National Red Cross (Red Crescent, Red Lion and Sun) Society of the country where they may be, as well as to any organization that might assist them. . . .

Apart from the visits of the delegates of the Protecting Powers and of the International Committee of the Red Cross, provided for by Article 143, the Detaining or Occupying Powers shall facilitate, as much as possible, visits to protected persons by the representatives of other organizations whose object is to give spiritual aid or material relief to such persons.

Article 31

No physical or moral coercion shall be exercised against protected persons, in particular to obtain information from them or from third parties.

Article 32

The High Contracting Parties specifically agree that each of them is prohibited from taking any measure of such a character as to cause the physical suffering or extermination of protected persons in their hands. This prohibition applies not only to murder, torture, corporal punishments, mutilation and medical or scientific experiments not necessitated by the medical treatment of a protected person, but also to any other measures of brutality whether applied by civilian or military agents.

Article 33

No protected person may be punished for an offence he or she has not personally committed. Collective penalties and likewise all measures of intimidation or of terrorism are prohibited.

Pillage is prohibited.

Reprisals against protected persons and their property are prohibited.

Article 34

The taking of hostages is prohibited. . . .

SECTION III. OCCUPIED TERRITORIES

Article 47

Protected persons who are in occupied territory shall not be deprived, in any case or in any manner whatsoever, of the benefits of the present Convention by any change introduced, as the result of the occupation of a territory, into the institutions or government of the said territory, nor by any agreement concluded between the authorities of the occupied territories and the Occupying Power, nor by any annexation by the latter of the whole or part of the occupied territory.

Article 48

Protected persons who are not nationals of the Power whose territory is occupied, may avail themselves of the right to leave the territory subject to the provisions of Article 35, and decisions thereon shall be taken according to the procedure which the Occupying Power shall establish in accordance with the said Article.

Article 49

Individual or mass forcible transfers, as well as deportations of protected persons from occupied territory to the territory of the Occupying Power or to that of any other country, occupied or not, are prohibited, regardless of their motive.

Nevertheless, the Occupying Power may undertake total or partial evacuation of a given area if the security of the population or imperative military reasons so demand. Such evacuations may not involve the displacement of protected persons outside the bounds of the occupied territory except when for material reasons it is impossible to avoid such displacement. Persons thus evacuated shall be transferred back to their homes as soon as hostilities in the area in question have ceased. . . .

Article 50

The Occupying Power shall, with the cooperation of the national and local authorities, facilitate the proper working of all institutions devoted to the care and education of children. . . .

Article 51

The Occupying Power may not compel protected persons to work unless they are over eighteen years of age, and then only on work which is necessary either for the needs of the army of occupation, or for the public utility services, or for the feeding, sheltering, clothing, transportation or health of the population of the occupied country. . . .

Article 53

Any destruction by the Occupying Power of real or personal property belonging individually or collectively to private persons, or to the State, or to other public authorities, or to social or cooperative organizations, is prohibited, except where such destruction is rendered absolutely necessary by military operations.

Article 54

The Occupying Power may not alter the status of public officials or judges in the occupied territories, or in any way apply sanctions to or take any measures of coercion or discrimination against them, should they abstain from fulfilling their functions for reasons of conscience.

This prohibition . . . does not affect the right of the Occupying Power to remove public officials from their posts.

Article 55

To the fullest extent of the means available to it, the Occupying Power has the duty of ensuring the food and medical supplies of the population; it should, in particular, bring in the necessary foodstuffs, medical stores and other articles if the resources of the occupied territory are inadequate. . . .

Article 64

The penal laws of the occupied territory shall remain in force, with the exception that they may be repealed or suspended by the Occupying Power in cases where they constitute a threat to its security or an obstacle to the application of the present Convention. Subject to the latter consideration and to the necessity for ensuring the effective administration of justice, the tribunals of the occupied territory shall continue to function in respect of all offences covered by the said laws.

The Occupying Power may, however, subject the population of the occupied territory to provisions which are essential to enable the Occupying Power to fulfil its obligations under the present Convention, to maintain the orderly government of the territory, and to ensure the security of the Occupying Power, of the members and property of the occupying forces or administration, and likewise of the establishments and lines of communication used by them.

Article 65

The penal provisions enacted by the Occupying Power shall not come into force before they have been published and brought to the knowledge of the inhabitants in their own language. The effect of these penal provisions shall not be retroactive.

Article 66

In case of a breach of the penal provisions promulgated by it by virtue of the second paragraph of Article 64 the Occupying Power may hand over the accused to its properly constituted, non-political military courts, on condition that the said courts sit in the occupied country. Courts of appeal shall preferably sit in the occupied country.

Article 67

The courts shall apply only those provisions of law which were applicable prior to the offence, and which are in accordance with general principles of law, in particular the principle that the penalty shall be proportionate to the offence. They shall take into consideration the fact that the accused is not a national of the Occupying Power.

Article 68

Protected persons who commit an offence which is solely intended to harm the Occupying Power, but which does not constitute an attempt on the life or limb of members of the occupying forces or administration, nor a grave collective danger, nor seriously damage the property of the occupying forces or administration or the installations used by them, shall be liable to internment or simple imprisonment, provided the duration of such internment or imprisonment is proportionate to the offence committed. Furthermore, internment or imprisonment shall, for such offences, be the only measure adopted for depriving protected persons of liberty. . . .

The penal provisions promulgated by the Occupying Power in accordance with Articles 64 and 65 may impose the death penalty against a protected person only in cases where the person is guilty of espionage, of serious acts of sabotage against the military installations of the Occupying Power or of intentional offences which have caused the death of one or more persons, provided that such offences were punishable by death under the law of the occupied territory in force before the occupation began. . . .

In any case, the death penalty may not be pronounced on a protected person who was under eighteen years of age at the time of the offence.

Article 69

In all cases the duration of the period during which a protected person accused of an offence is under arrest awaiting trial or punishment shall be deducted from any period of imprisonment awarded.

Article 70

Protected persons shall not be arrested, prosecuted or convicted by the Occupying Power for acts committed or for opinions expressed before the occupation, or during a temporary interruption thereof, with the exception of breaches of the laws and customs of war. . . .

Article 71

No sentence shall be pronounced by the competent courts of the Occupying Power except after a regular trial.

Accused persons who are prosecuted by the Occupying Power shall be promptly informed, in writing, in a language which they understand, of the particulars of the charges preferred against them, and shall be brought to trial as rapidly as possible. The Protecting Power shall be informed of all proceedings instituted by the Occupying Power against protected persons in respect of charges involving the death penalty or imprisonment for two years or more; it shall be enabled, at any time, to obtain information regarding the state of such proceedings. Furthermore, the Protecting Power shall be entitled, on request, to be furnished with all particulars of these and of any other proceedings instituted by the Occupying Power against protected persons. . . .

Article 72

Accused persons shall have the right to present evidence necessary to their defence and may, in particular, call witnesses. They shall have the right to be assisted by a qualified advocate or counsel of their own choice, who shall be able to visit them freely and shall enjoy the necessary facilities for preparing the defence.

Failing a choice by the accused, the Protecting Power may provide him with an advocate or counsel. When an accused person has to meet a serious charge and the Protecting Power is not functioning, the Occupying Power, subject to the consent of the accused, shall provide an advocate or counsel.

Accused persons shall, unless they freely waive such assistance, be aided by an interpreter, both during preliminary investigation and during the hearing in court. They shall have the right at any time to object to the interpreter and to ask for his replacement.

Article 73

A convicted person shall have the right of appeal provided for by the laws applied by the court. He shall be fully informed of his right to appeal or petition and of the time limit within which he may do so.

The penal procedure provided in the present Section shall apply, as far as it is applicable, to appeals. . . .

Article 74

Representatives of the Protecting Power shall have the right to attend the trial of any protected person, unless the hearing has, as an exceptional measure, to be held in camera in the interests of the security of the Occupying Power, which shall then notify the Protecting Power. A notification in respect of the date and place of trial shall be sent to the Protecting Power.

Any judgment involving a sentence of death, or imprisonment for two years or more, shall be communicated, with the relevant grounds, as rapidly as possible to the Protecting Power. The notification shall contain a reference to the notification made under Article 71 and, in the case of sentences of imprisonment, the name of the place where the sentence is to be served. A record of judgments other than those referred to above shall be kept by the court and shall be open to inspection by representatives of the Protecting Power. . . .

Article 75

In no case shall persons condemned to death be deprived of the right of petition for pardon or reprieve.

No death sentence shall be carried out before the expiration of a period of a least six months from the date of receipt by the Protecting Power of the notification of the final judgment confirming such death sentence, or of an order denying pardon or reprieve.

The six months period of suspension of the death sentence herein prescribed may be reduced in individual cases in circumstances of grave emergency involving an organized threat to the security of the Occupying Power or its forces, provided always that the Protecting Power is notified of such reduction and is given reasonable time and opportunity to make representations to the competent occupying authorities in respect of such death sentences.

Article 76

Protected persons accused of offences shall be detained in the occupied country, and if convicted they shall serve their sentences therein. They shall, if possible, be separated from other detainees and shall enjoy conditions of food and hygiene which will be sufficient to keep them in good health, and which will be at least equal to those obtaining in prisons in the occupied country.

They shall receive the medical attention required by their state of health.

They shall also have the right to receive any spiritual assistance which they may require.

Women shall be confined in separate quarters and shall be under the direct supervision of women.

Proper regard shall be paid to the special treatment due to minors.

Protected persons who are detained shall have the right to be visited by delegates of the Protecting Power and of the International Committee of the Red Cross, in accordance with the provisions of Article 143. . . .

Article 77

Protected persons who have been accused of offences or convicted by the courts in occupied territory, shall be handed over at the close of occupation, with the relevant records, to the authorities of the liberated territory.

Article 78

If the Occupying Power considers it necessary, for imperative reasons of security, to take safety measures concerning protected persons, it may, at the most, subject them to assigned residence or to internment.

Decisions regarding such assigned residence or internment shall be made according to a regular procedure to be prescribed by the Occupying Power in accordance with the provisions of the present Convention. . . .

Protected persons made subject to assigned residence and thus required to leave their homes shall enjoy the full benefit of Article 39 of the present Convention. . . .

Part IV. Execution of the Convention

SECTION I. GENERAL PROVISIONS

Article 142

Subject to the measures which the Detaining Powers may consider essential to ensure their security or to meet any other reasonable need, the representatives of religious organizations, relief societies, or any other organizations assisting the protected persons, shall receive from these Powers, for themselves or their duly accredited agents, all facilities for visiting the protected persons, for distributing relief supplies and material from any source, intended for educational, recreational or religious purposes, or for assisting them in organizing their leisure time within the places of internment. . . .

The special position of the International Committee of the Red Cross in this field shall be recognized and respected at all times.

Article 143

Representatives or delegates of the Protecting Powers shall have permission to go to all places where protected persons are, particularly to places of internment, detention and work.

They shall have access to all premises occupied by protected persons and shall be able to interview the latter without witnesses, personally or through an interpreter.

Such visits may not be prohibited except for reasons of imperative military necessity, and then only as an exceptional and temporary measure. Their duration and frequency shall not be restricted.

Such representatives and delegates shall have full liberty to select the places they wish to visit. . . .

The delegates of the International Committee of the Red Cross shall also enjoy the above prerogatives. . . .

Article 145

The High Contracting Parties shall communicate to one another through the Swiss Federal Council and, during hostilities, through the Protecting Powers, the official translations of the present Convention, as well as the laws and regulations which they may adopt to ensure the application thereof.

Article 146

The High Contracting Parties undertake to enact any legislation necessary to provide effective penal sanctions for persons committing, or ordering to be committed, any of the grave breaches of the present Convention defined in the following Article.

Each High Contracting Party shall be under the obligation to search for persons alleged to have committed, or to have ordered to be committed, such grave breaches, and shall bring such persons, regardless of their nationality, before its own courts. It may also, if it prefers, and in accordance with the provisions of its own legislation, hand such persons over for trial to another High Contracting Party concerned, provided such High Contracting Party has made out a prima facie case. . . .

In all circumstances, the accused persons shall benefit by safeguards of proper trial and defence, which shall not be less favourable than those provided by Article 105 and those following of the Geneva Convention relative to the Treatment of Prisoners of War of 12 August 1949.

Article 147

Grave breaches to which the preceding Article relates shall be those involving any of the following acts, if committed against persons or property protected by the present Convention: wilful killing, torture or inhuman treatment, including biological experiments, wilfully causing great suffering or serious injury to body or health, unlawful deportation or transfer or unlawful confinement of a protected person, compelling a protected person to serve in the forces of a hostile Power, or wilfully depriving a protected person of the rights of fair and regular trial prescribed in the present Convention, taking of hostages and extensive destruction and appropriation of property, not justified by military necessity and carried out unlawfully and wantonly.

Article 148

No High Contracting Party shall be allowed to absolve itself or any other High Contracting Party of any liability incurred by itself or by another High Contracting Party in respect of breaches referred to in the preceding Article.

Article 149

At the request of a Party to the conflict, an enquiry shall be instituted, in a manner to be decided between the interested Parties, concerning any alleged violation of the Convention. . . .

Once the violation has been established, the Parties to the conflict shall put an end to it and shall repress it with the least possible delay.

SECTION II. FINAL PROVISIONS . . .

Article 158

Each of the High Contracting Parties shall be at liberty to denounce the present Convention.

The denunciation shall be notified in writing to the Swiss Federal Council, which shall transmit it to the Governments of all the High Contracting Parties.

The denunciation shall take effect one year after the notification thereof has been made to the Swiss Federal Council. However, a denunciation of which notification has been made at a time when the denouncing Power is involved in a conflict shall not take effect until peace has been concluded, and until after operations connected with the release, repatriation and re-establishment of the persons protected by the present Convention have been terminated.

The denunciation shall have effect only in respect of the denouncing Power. It shall in no way impair the obligations which the Parties to the conflict shall remain bound to fulfil by virtue of the principles of the law of nations, as they result from the usages established among civilized peoples, from the laws of humanity and the dictates of the public conscience.

Article 159

The Swiss Federal Council shall register the present Convention with the Secretariat of the United Nations. . . .

PROTOCOL ADDITIONAL TO THE GENEVA CONVENTIONS OF 1949 (PROTOCOL I)

International Committee of the Red Cross*

The High Contracting Parties,

Proclaiming their earnest wish to see peace prevail among peoples,

Recalling that every State has the duty, in conformity with the Charter of the United Nations, to refrain in its international relations from the threat or use of force against the sovereignty, territorial integrity or political independence of any State, or in any other manner inconsistent with the purposes of the United Nations,

---

* The Protocol Additional to the Geneva Conventions of 12 August 1949, and relating to the Protection of Victims of International Armed Conflicts (Protocol I) was concluded in Geneva on June 8, 1977. It entered into force on December 12, 1978. The United States signed the Protocol on December 12, 1977, but has not ratified it.

As of November 2012, there were 172 parties to the Protocol. The parties were: Afghanistan, Albania, Algeria, Angola, Antigua and Barbuda, Argentina, Armenia, Australia, Austria, Bahamas, Bahrain, Bangladesh, Barbados, Belarus, Belgium, Belize, Benin, Bolivia, Bosnia and Herzegovina, Botswana, Brazil, Brunei Darussalam, Bulgaria, Burkina Faso, Burundi, Cambodia, Cameroon, Canada, Cape Verde, Central African Republic, Chad, Chile, China, Colombia, Comoros, Congo (Democratic Republic of), Congo, Cook Islands, Costa Rica, Côte d'Ivoire, Croatia, Cuba, Cyprus, Czech Republic, Denmark, Djibouti, Dominican Republic, Dominica, Ecuador, Egypt, El Salvador, Equatorial Guinea, Estonia, Ethiopia, Fiji, Finland, France, Gabon, Gambia, Georgia, Germany, Ghana, Greece, Grenada, Guatemala, Guinea, Guinea-Bissau, Guyana, Haiti, Holy See, Honduras, Hungary, Iceland, Iraq, Ireland, Italy, Jamaica, Japan, Jordan, Kazakhstan, Kenya, Korea (Democratic People's Republic of), Korea (Republic of), Kuwait, Kyrgyzstan, Lao People's Democratic Republic, Latvia, Lebanon, Lesotho, Liberia, Libyan Arab Jamahiriya, Liechtenstein, Lithuania, Luxembourg, Macedonia (the former Yugoslav Republic of), Madagascar, Malawi, Maldives, Mali, Malta, Mauritania, Mauritius, Mexico, Micronesia, Moldova, Monaco, Mongolia, Morocco, Montenegro, Mozambique, Namibia, Nauru, Netherlands, New Zealand, Nicaragua, Nigeria, Niger, Norway, Oman, Palau, Panama, Paraguay, Peru, Philippines, Poland, Portugal, Qatar, Romania, Russian Federation, Rwanda, Saint Kitts and Nevis, Saint Lucia, Saint Vincent Grenadines, Samoa, San Marino, Sao Tome and Principe, Saudi Arabia, Senegal, Serbia, Seychelles, Sierra Leone, Slovakia, Slovenia, Solomon Islands, South Africa, South Sudan, Spain, Sudan, Suriname, Swaziland, Sweden, Switzerland, Syrian Arab Republic, Tajikistan, Tanzania, Timor-Leste, Togo, Tonga, Trinidad and Tobago, Tunisia, Turkmenistan, Uganda, Ukraine, United Arab Emirates, United Kingdom, Uruguay, Uzbekistan, Vanuatu, Venezuela, Viet Nam, Yemen, Zambia, Zimbabwe. See the International Committee of the Red Cross Web site at <http://www.icrc.org>.

Believing it necessary nevertheless to reaffirm and develop the provisions protecting the victims of armed conflicts and to supplement measures intended to reinforce their application,

Expressing their conviction that nothing in this Protocol or in the Geneva Conventions of 12 August 1949 can be construed as legitimizing or authorizing any act of aggression or any other use of force inconsistent with the Charter of the United Nations,

Reaffirming further that the provisions of the Geneva Conventions of 12 August 1949 and of this Protocol must be fully applied in all circumstances to all persons who are protected by those instruments, without any adverse distinction based on the nature or origin of the armed conflict or on the causes espoused by or attributed to the Parties to the conflict,

Have agreed on the following:

Part I.   General Provisions

Art 1.   General principles and scope of application

1. The High Contracting Parties undertake to respect and to ensure respect for this Protocol in all circumstances.

2. In cases not covered by this Protocol or by other international agreements, civilians and combatants remain under the protection and authority of the principles of international law derived from established custom, from the principles of humanity and from dictates of public conscience.

3. This Protocol, which supplements the Geneva Conventions of 12 August 1949 for the protection of war victims, shall apply in the situations referred to in Article 2 common to those Conventions.

4. The situations referred to in the preceding paragraph include armed conflicts which peoples are fighting against colonial domination and alien occupation and against racist regimes in the exercise of their right of self-determination, as enshrined in the Charter of the United Nations and the Declaration on Principles of International Law concerning Friendly Relations and Co-operation among States in accordance with the Charter of the United Nations.

Art 2.   Definitions

For the purposes of this Protocol

(a) "First Convention," "Second Convention," "Third Convention" and "Fourth Convention" mean, respectively, the Geneva Convention for the Amelioration of the Condition of the Wounded and Sick in Armed Forces in the Field of 12 August 1949; the Geneva Convention for the Amelioration of the Condition of Wounded, Sick and Ship-wrecked Members of Armed Forces at Sea of 12 August 1949; the Geneva Convention relative to the Treatment of Prisoners of War of 12 August 1949; the Geneva Convention relative to the Protection of Civilian Persons in Time of War of 12 August

1949; "the Conventions" means the four Geneva Conventions of 12 August 1949 for the protection of war victims;

(b) "Rules of international law applicable in armed conflict" means the rules applicable in armed conflict set forth in international agreements to which the Parties to the conflict are Parties and the generally recognized principles and rules of international law which are applicable to armed conflict;

(c) "Protecting Power" means a neutral or other State not a Party to the conflict which has been designated by a Party to the conflict and accepted by the adverse Party and has agreed to carry out the functions assigned to a Protecting Power under the Conventions and this Protocol;

(d) "Substitute" means an organization acting in place of a Protecting Power in accordance with Article 5.

Art 3. Beginning and end of application

Without prejudice to the provisions which are applicable at all times:

(a) the Conventions and this Protocol shall apply from the beginning of any situation referred to in Article 1 of this Protocol.

(b) the application of the Conventions and of this Protocol shall cease, in the territory of Parties to the conflict, on the general close of military operations and, in the case of occupied territories, on the termination of the occupation, except, in either circumstance, for those persons whose final release, repatriation or re-establishment takes place thereafter. These persons shall continue to benefit from the relevant provisions of the Conventions and of this Protocol until their final release repatriation or re-establishment.

Art 4. Legal status of the Parties to the conflict

The application of the Conventions and of this Protocol, as well as the conclusion of the agreements provided for therein, shall not affect the legal status of the Parties to the conflict. Neither the occupation of a territory nor the application of the Conventions and this Protocol shall affect the legal status of the territory in question.

Art 5. Appointment of Protecting Powers and of their substitute

1. It is the duty of the Parties to a conflict from the beginning of that conflict to secure the supervision and implementation of the Conventions and of this Protocol by the application of the system of Protecting Powers, including inter alia the designation and acceptance of those Powers, in accordance with the following paragraphs. Protecting Powers shall have the duty of safeguarding the interests of the Parties to the conflict.

2. From the beginning of a situation referred to in Article 1, each Party to the conflict shall without delay designate a Protecting Power for the purpose of applying the Conventions and this Protocol and shall, likewise without delay and for the same purpose, permit the activities or a Protecting

Power which has been accepted by it as such after designation by the adverse Party.

3. If a Protecting Power has not been designated or accepted from the beginning of a situation referred to in Article 1, the International Committee of the Red Cross, without prejudice to the right of any other impartial humanitarian organization to do likewise, shall offer its good offices to the Parties to the conflict with a view to the designation without delay of a Protecting Power to which the Parties to the conflict consent. . . .

4. If, despite the foregoing, there is no Protecting Power, the Parties to the conflict shall accept without delay an offer which may be made by the International Committee of the Red Cross or by any other organization which offers all guarantees of impartiality and efficacy, after due consultations with the said Parties and taking into account the result of these consultations, to act as a substitute. . . .

Art 6. Qualified persons

1. The High Contracting Parties shall, also in peacetime, endeavour, with the assistance of the national Red Cross (Red Crescent, Red Lion and Sun) Societies, to train qualified personnel to facilitate the application of the Conventions and of this Protocol, and in particular the activities of the Protecting Powers.

2. The recruitment and training of such personnel are within domestic jurisdiction. . . .

Part II. Wounded, Sick and Shipwrecked

SECTION I. GENERAL PROTECTION

Art 8. Terminology

For the purposes of this Protocol:

(a) "Wounded" and "sick" mean persons, whether military or civilian, who, because of trauma, disease or other physical or mental disorder or disability, are in need of medical assistance or care and who refrain from any act of hostility. These terms also cover maternity cases, new-born babies and other persons who may be in need of immediate medical assistance or care, such as the infirm or expectant mothers, and who refrain from any act of hostility;

(b) "Shipwrecked" means persons, whether military or civilian, who are in peril at sea or in other waters as a result of misfortune affecting them or the vessel or aircraft carrying them and who refrain from any act of hostility. These persons, provided that they continue to refrain from any act of hostility, shall continue to be considered shipwrecked during their rescue until they acquire another status under the Conventions or this Protocol;

(c) "Medical personnel" means those persons assigned, by a Party to the conflict, exclusively to the medical purposes enumerated under e) or to the administration of medical units or to the operation or administration of medical transports. Such assignments may be either permanent or temporary. . . .

(d) "Religious personnel" means military or civilian persons, such as chaplains, who are exclusively engaged in the work of their ministry and attached:

(i) to the armed forces of a Party to the conflict;

(ii) to medical units or medical transports of a Party to the conflict; . . .

or

(iv) to civil defence organizations of a Party to the conflict. . . .

(e) "Medical units" means establishments and other units, whether military or civilian, organized for medical purposes, namely the search for, collection, transportation, diagnosis or treatment including first-aid treatment of the wounded, sick and shipwrecked, or for the prevention of disease. The term includes for example, hospitals and other similar units, blood transfusion centres, preventive medicine centres and institutes, medical depots and the medical and pharmaceutical stores of such units. Medical units may be fixed or mobile, permanent or temporary; . . .

(l) "Distinctive emblem" means the distinctive emblem of the red cross, red crescent or red lion and sun on a white ground when used for the protection of medical units and transports, or medical and religious personnel, equipment or supplies;

(m) "Distinctive signal" means any signal or message specified for the identification exclusively of medical units or transports in Chapter III of Annex I to this Protocol.

Art 9. Field of application

1. This Part, the provisions of which are intended to ameliorate the condition of the wounded, sick and shipwrecked, shall apply to all those affected by a situation referred to in Article 1, without any adverse distinction founded on race, colour, sex, language, religion or belief political or other opinion, national or social origin, wealth, birth or other status, or on any other similar criteria. . . .

Art 10. Protection and care

1. All the wounded, sick and shipwrecked, to whichever Party they belong, shall be respected and protected.

2. In all circumstances they shall be treated humanely and shall receive, to the fullest extent practicable and with the least possible delay, the medical care and attention required by their condition. There shall be no distinction among them founded on any grounds other than medical ones.

Art 11. Protection of persons

1. The physical or mental health and integrity of persons who are in the power of the adverse Party or who are interned, detained or otherwise deprived of liberty as a result of a situation referred to in Article 1 shall not be endangered by any unjustified act or omission. Accordingly, it is prohibited to subject the persons described in this Article to any medical procedure which is not indicated by the state of health of the person concerned and which is not consistent with generally accepted medical standards which would be applied under similar medical circumstances to persons who are nationals of the Party conducting the procedure and who are in no way deprived of liberty.

2. It is, in particular, prohibited to carry out on such persons, even with their consent:

(a) physical mutilations;

(b) medical or scientific experiments;

(c) removal of tissue or organs for transplantation, except where these acts are justified in conformity with the conditions provided for in paragraph 1.

3. Exceptions to the prohibition in paragraph 2 (c) may be made only in the case of donations of blood for transfusion or of skin for grafting, provided that they are given voluntarily and without any coercion or inducement, and then only for therapeutic purposes. . . .

4. Any wilful act or omission which seriously endangers the physical or mental health or integrity of any person who is in the power of a Party other than the one on which he depends and which either violates any of the prohibitions in paragraphs 1 and 2 or fails to comply with the requirements of paragraph 3 shall be a grave breach of this Protocol.

5. The persons described in paragraph 1 have the right to refuse any surgical operation. . . .

Part III. Methods and Means of Warfare, Combatant and Prisoners-of-War

SECTION I. METHODS AND MEANS OF WARFARE

Art 35. Basic rules

1. In any armed conflict, the right of the Parties to the conflict to choose methods or means of warfare is not unlimited.

2. It is prohibited to employ weapons, projectiles and material and methods of warfare of a nature to cause superfluous injury or unnecessary suffering.

3. It is prohibited to employ methods or means of warfare which are intended, or may be expected, to cause widespread, long-term and severe damage to the natural environment.

Art 36. New weapons

In the study, development, acquisition or adoption of a new weapon, means or method of warfare, a High Contracting Party is under an obligation to determine whether its employment would, in some or all circumstances, be prohibited by this Protocol or by any other rule of international law applicable to the High Contracting Party.

Art 37. Prohibition of Perfidy

1. It is prohibited to kill, injure or capture an adversary by resort to perfidy. Acts inviting the confidence of an adversary to lead him to believe that he is entitled to, or is obliged to accord, protection under the rules of international law applicable in armed conflict, with intent to betray that confidence, shall constitute perfidy. The following acts are examples of perfidy:

(a) the feigning of an intent to negotiate under a flag of truce or of a surrender;

(b) the feigning of an incapacitation by wounds or sickness;

(c) the feigning of civilian, non-combatant status; and

(d) the feigning of protected status by the use of signs, emblems or uniforms of the United Nations or of neutral or other States not Parties to the conflict.

2. Ruses of war are not prohibited. Such ruses are acts which are intended to mislead an adversary or to induce him to act recklessly but which infringe no rule of international law applicable in armed conflict and which are not perfidious because they do not invite the confidence of an adversary with respect to protection under that law. The following are examples of such ruses: the use of camouflage, decoys, mock operations and misinformation.

Art 38. Recognized emblems

1. It is prohibited to make improper use of the distinctive emblem of the redcross, red crescent or red lion and sun or of other emblems, signs or signals provided for by the Conventions or by this Protocol. It is also prohibited to misuse deliberately in an armed conflict other internationally recognized protective emblems, signs or signals, including the flag of truce, and the protective emblem of cultural property.

2. It is prohibited to make use of the distinctive emblem of the United Nations, except as authorized by that Organization.

Art 39. Emblems of nationality

1. It is prohibited to make use in an armed conflict of the flags or military emblems, insignia or uniforms of neutral or other States not Parties to the conflict.

2. It is prohibited to make use of the flags or military emblems, insignia or uniforms of adverse Parties while engaging in attacks or in order to shield, favour, protect or impede military operations.

3. Nothing in this Article or in Article 37, paragraph 1 (d), shall affect the existing generally recognized rules of international law applicable to espionage or to the use of flags in the conduct of armed conflict at sea.

Art 40.   Quarter

It is prohibited to order that there shall be no survivors, to threaten an adversary therewith or to conduct hostilities on this basis.

Art 41.   Safeguard of an enemy hors de combat

1. A person who is recognized or who, in the circumstances, should be recognized to be hors de combat shall not be made the object of attack.
2. A person is hors de combat if:
   (a) he is in the power of an adverse Party;
   (b) he clearly expresses an intention to surrender; or
   (c) he has been rendered unconscious or is otherwise incapacitated by wounds or sickness, and therefore is incapable of defending himself;
   provided that in any of these cases he abstains from any hostile act and does not attempt to escape. . . .

SECTION II.   COMBATANTS AND PRISONERS OF WAR

Art 43.   Armed forces

1. The armed forces of a Party to a conflict consist of all organized armed forces, groups and units which are under a command responsible to that Party for the conduct or its subordinates, even if that Party is represented by a government or an authority not recognized by an adverse Party. Such armed forces shall be subject to an internal disciplinary system which, inter alia, shall enforce compliance with the rules of international law applicable in armed conflict.
2. Members of the armed forces of a Party to a conflict (other than medical personnel and chaplains covered by Article 33 of the Third Convention) are combatants, that is to say, they have the right to participate directly in hostilities.
3. Whenever a Party to a conflict incorporates a paramilitary or armed law enforcement agency into its armed forces it shall so notify the other Parties to the conflict.

Art 44.   Combatants and prisoners of war

1. Any combatant, as defined in Article 43, who falls into the power of an adverse Party shall be a prisoner of war.
2. While all combatants are obliged to comply with the rules of international law applicable in armed conflict, violations of these rules shall not deprive a combatant of his right to be a combatant or, if he falls into the

power of an adverse Party, of his right to be a prisoner of war, except as provided in paragraphs 3 and 4.

3. In order to promote the protection of the civilian population from the effects of hostilities, combatants are obliged to distinguish themselves from the civilian population while they are engaged in an attack or in a military operation preparatory to an attack. Recognizing, however, that there are situations in armed conflicts where, owing to the nature of the hostilities an armed combatant cannot so distinguish himself, he shall retain his status as a combatant, provided that, in such situations, he carries his arms openly:

(a) during each military engagement, and

(b) during such time as he is visible to the adversary while he is engaged in a military deployment preceding the launching of an attack in which he is to participate.

Acts which comply with the requirements of this paragraph shall not be considered as perfidious within the meaning of Article 37, paragraph 1 (c).

4. A combatant who falls into the power of an adverse Party while failing to meet the requirements set forth in the second sentence of paragraph 3 shall forfeit his right to be a prisoner of war, but he shall, nevertheless, be given protections equivalent in all respects to those accorded to prisoners of war by the Third Convention and by this Protocol. This protection includes protections equivalent to those accorded to prisoners of war by the Third Convention in the case where such a person is tried and punished for any offences he has committed.

5. Any combatant who falls into the power of an adverse Party while not engaged in an attack or in a military operation preparatory to an attack shall not forfeit his rights to be a combatant and a prisoner of war by virtue of his prior activities.

6. This Article is without prejudice to the right of any person to be a prisoner of war pursuant to Article 4 of the Third Convention.

7. This Article is not intended to change the generally accepted practice of States with respect to the wearing of the uniform by combatants assigned to the regular, uniformed armed units of a Party to the conflict.

8. In addition to the categories of persons mentioned in Article 13 of the First and Second Conventions, all members of the armed forces of a Party to the conflict, as defined in Article 43 of this Protocol, shall be entitled to protection under those Conventions if they are wounded or sick or, in the case of the Second Convention, shipwrecked at sea or in other waters.

Art 45.   Protection of persons who have taken part in hostilities

1. A person who takes part in hostilities and falls into the power of an adverse Party shall be presumed to be a prisoner of war, and therefore shall be protected by the Third Convention, if he claims the status of prisoner of war, or if he appears to be entitled to such status, or if the Party on which he depends claims such status on his behalf by notification to the detaining Power or to the Protecting Power. Should any doubt arise as to whether any such person is entitled to the status of prisoner of war, he shall continue to

have such status and, therefore, to be protected by the Third Convention and this Protocol until such time as his status has been determined by a competent tribunal.

2. If a person who has fallen into the power of an adverse Party is not held as a prisoner of war and is to be tried by that Party for an offence arising out of the hostilities, he shall have the right to assert his entitlement to prisoner-of-war status before a judicial tribunal and to have that question adjudicated. Whenever possible under the applicable procedure, this adjudication shall occur before the trial for the offence. The representatives of the Protecting Power shall be entitled to attend the proceedings in which that question is adjudicated, unless, exceptionally, the proceedings are held in camera in the interest of State security. In such a case the detaining Power shall advise the Protecting Power accordingly.

3. Any person who has taken part in hostilities, who is not entitled to prisoner-of-war status and who does not benefit from more favourable treatment in accordance with the Fourth Convention shall have the right at all times to the protection of Article 75 of this Protocol. In occupied territory, any such person, unless he is held as a spy, shall also be entitled, notwithstanding Article 5 of the Fourth Convention, to his rights of communication under that Convention.

Art 46. Spies

1. Notwithstanding any other provision of the Conventions or of this Protocol, any member of the armed forces of a Party to the conflict who falls into the power of an adverse Party while engaging in espionage shall not have the right to the status of prisoner of war and may be treated as a spy.

2. A member of the armed forces of a Party to the conflict who, on behalf of that Party and in territory controlled by an adverse Party, gathers or attempts to gather information shall not be considered as engaging in espionage if, while so acting, he is in the uniform of his armed forces.

3. A member of the armed forces of a Party to the conflict who is a resident of territory occupied by an adverse Party and who, on behalf of the Party on which he depends, gathers or attempts to gather information of military value within that territory shall not be considered as engaging in espionage unless he does so through an act of false pretences or deliberately in a clandestine manner. Moreover, such a resident shall not lose his right to the status of prisoner of war and may not be treated as a spy unless he is captured while engaging in espionage.

4. A member of the armed forces of a Party to the conflict who is not a resident of territory occupied by an adverse Party and who has engaged in espionage in that territory shall not lose his right to the status of prisoner of war and may not be treated as a spy unless he is captured before he has rejoined the armed forces to which he belongs.

Art 47. Mercenaries

1. A mercenary shall not have the right to be a combatant or a prisoner of war.

2. A mercenary is any person who:

(a) is specially recruited locally or abroad in order to fight in an armed conflict;

(b) does, in fact, take a direct part in the hostilities;

(c) is motivated to take part in the hostilities essentially by the desire for private gain and, in fact, is promised, by or on behalf of a Party to the conflict, material compensation substantially in excess of that promised or paid to combatants of similar ranks and functions in the armed forces of that Party;

(d) is neither a national of a Party to the conflict nor a resident of territory controlled by a Party to the conflict;

(e) is not a member of the armed forces of a Party to the conflict; and

(f) has not been sent by a State which is not a Party to the conflict on official duty as a member of its armed forces.

Part IV.   Civilian Population

SECTION I.   GENERAL PROTECTION AGAINST EFFECTS OF HOSTILITIES

CHAPTER I.   BASIC RULE AND FIELD OF APPLICATION

Art 48.   Basic rule

In order to ensure respect for and protection of the civilian population and civilian objects, the Parties to the conflict shall at all times distinguish between the civilian population and combatants and between civilian objects and military objectives and accordingly shall direct their operations only against military objectives.

Art 49.   Definition of attacks and scope of application

1. "Attacks" means acts of violence against the adversary, whether in offence or in defence.

2. The provisions of this Protocol with respect to attacks apply to all attacks in whatever territory conducted, including the national territory belonging to a Party to the conflict but under the control of an adverse Party.

3. The provisions of this section apply to any land, air or sea warfare which may affect the civilian population, individual civilians or civilian objects on land. They further apply to all attacks from the sea or from the air against objectives on land but do not otherwise affect the rules of international law applicable in armed conflict at sea or in the air.

4. The provisions of this section are additional to the rules concerning humanitarian protection contained in the Fourth Convention, particularly in

part II thereof, and in other international agreements binding upon the High Contracting Parties, as well as to other rules of international law relating to the protection of civilians and civilian objects on land, at sea or in the air against the effects of hostilities.

CHAPTER II. CIVILIANS AND CIVILIAN POPULATION

Art 50. *Definition of civilians and civilian population*

1. A civilian is any person who does not belong to one of the categories of persons referred to in Article 4 (A) (1), (2), (3) and (6) of the Third Convention and in Article 43 of this Protocol. In case of doubt whether a person is a civilian, that person shall be considered to be a civilian.

2. The civilian population comprises all persons who are civilians.

3. The presence within the civilian population of individuals who do not come within the definition of civilians does not deprive the population of its civilian character.

Art 51. *Protection of the civilian population*

1. The civilian population and individual civilians shall enjoy general protection against dangers arising from military operations. To give effect to this protection, the following rules, which are additional to other applicable rules of international law, shall be observed in all circumstances.

2. The civilian population as such, as well as individual civilians, shall not be the object of attack. Acts or threats of violence the primary purpose of which is to spread terror among the civilian population are prohibited.

3. Civilians shall enjoy the protection afforded by this section, unless and for such time as they take a direct part in hostilities.

4. Indiscriminate attacks are prohibited. Indiscriminate attacks are:

(a) those which are not directed at a specific military objective;

(b) those which employ a method or means of combat which cannot be directed at a specific military objective; or

(c) those which employ a method or means of combat the effects of which cannot be limited as required by this Protocol; and consequently, in each such case, are of a nature to strike military objectives and civilians or civilian objects without distinction.

5. Among others, the following types of attacks are to be considered as indiscriminate:

(a) an attack by bombardment by any methods or means which treats as a single military objective a number of clearly separated and distinct military objectives located in a city, town, village or other area containing a similar concentration of civilians or civilian objects; and

(b) an attack which may be expected to cause incidental loss of civilian life, injury to civilians, damage to civilian objects, or a combination thereof, which would be excessive in relation to the concrete and direct military advantage anticipated.

6. Attacks against the civilian population or civilians by way of reprisals are prohibited.

7. The presence or movements of the civilian population or individual civilians shall not be used to render certain points or areas immune from military operations, in particular in attempts to shield military objectives from attacks or to shield, favour or impede military operations. The Parties to the conflict shall not direct the movement of the civilian population or individual civilians in order to attempt to shield military objectives from attacks or to shield military operations.

8. Any violation of these prohibitions shall not release the Parties to the conflict from their legal obligations with respect to the civilian population and civilians, including the obligation to take the precautionary measures provided for in Article 57.

CHAPTER III. CIVILIAN OBJECTS

Art 52. General Protection of civilian objects

1. Civilian objects shall not be the object of attack or of reprisals. Civilian objects are all objects which are not military objectives as defined in paragraph 2.

2. Attacks shall be limited strictly to military objectives. In so far as objects are concerned, military objectives are limited to those objects which by their nature, location, purpose or use make an effective contribution to military action and whose total or partial destruction, capture or neutralization, in the circumstances ruling at the time, offers a definite military advantage.

3. In case of doubt whether an object which is normally dedicated to civilian purposes, such as a place of worship, a house or other dwelling or a school, is being used to make an effective contribution to military action, it shall be presumed not to be so used.

Art 53. Protection of cultural objects and of places of worship

Without prejudice to the provisions of the Hague Convention for the Protection of Cultural Property in the Event of Armed Conflict of 14 May 1954, and of other relevant international instruments, it is prohibited:

(a) to commit any acts of hostility directed against the historic monuments, works of art or places of worship which constitute the cultural or spiritual heritage of peoples;

(b) to use such objects in support of the military effort;

(c) to make such objects the object of reprisals.

Art 54. Protection of objects indispensable to the survival of the civilian population

1. Starvation of civilians as a method of warfare is prohibited.

2. It is prohibited to attack, destroy, remove or render useless objects indispensable to the survival of the civilian population, such as food-stuffs,

agricultural areas for the production of food-stuffs, crops, livestock, drinking water installations and supplies and irrigation works, for the specific purpose of denying them for their sustenance value to the civilian population or to the adverse Party, whatever the motive, whether in order to starve out civilians, to cause them to move away, or for any other motive.

3. The prohibitions in paragraph 2 shall not apply to such of the objects covered by it as are used by an adverse Party:

(a) as sustenance solely for the members of its armed forces; or

(b) if not as sustenance, then in direct support of military action, provided, however, that in no event shall actions against these objects be taken which may be expected to leave the civilian population with such inadequate food or water as to cause its starvation or force its movement.

4. These objects shall not be made the object of reprisals.

5. In recognition of the vital requirements of any Party to the conflict in the defence of its national territory against invasion, derogation from the prohibitions contained in paragraph 2 may be made by a Party to the conflict within such territory under its own control where required by imperative military necessity.

Art 55. *Protection of the natural environment*

1. Care shall be taken in warfare to protect the natural environment against widespread, long-term and severe damage. This protection includes a prohibition of the use of methods or means of warfare which are intended or may be expected to cause such damage to the natural environment and thereby to prejudice the health or survival of the population.

2. Attacks against the natural environment by way of reprisals are prohibited.

Art 56. *Protection of works and installations containing dangerous forces*

1. Works or installations containing dangerous forces, namely dams, dykes and nuclear electrical generating stations, shall not be made the object of attack, even where these objects are military objectives, if such attack may cause the release of dangerous forces and consequent severe losses among the civilian population. Other military objectives located at or in the vicinity of these works or installations shall not be made the object of attack if such attack may cause the release of dangerous forces from the works or installations and consequent severe losses among the civilian population.

2. The special protection against attack provided by paragraph 1 shall cease:

(a) for a dam or a dyke only if it is used for other than its normal function and in regular, significant and direct support of military operations and if such attack is the only feasible way to terminate such support;

(b) for a nuclear electrical generating station only if it provides electric power in regular, significant and direct support of military operations and if such attack is the only feasible way to terminate such support;

(c) for other military objectives located at or in the vicinity of these works or installations only if they are used in regular, significant and direct support of military operations and if such attack is the only feasible way to terminate such support.

3. In all cases, the civilian population and individual civilians shall remain entitled to all the protection accorded them by international law, including the protection of the precautionary measures provided for in Article 57. If the protection Ceases and any of the works, installations or military objectives mentioned in paragraph 1 is attacked, all practical precautions shall be taken to avoid the release of the dangerous forces. . . .

7. In order to facilitate the identification of the objects protected by this article, the Parties to the conflict may mark them with a special sign consisting of a group of three bright orange circles placed on the same axis, as specified in . . . Annex I to this Protocol. The absence of such marking in no way relieves any Party to the conflict of its obligations under this Article.

CHAPTER IV.   PRECAUTIONARY MEASURES

Art 57.   Precautions in attack

1. In the conduct of military operations, constant care shall be taken to spare the civilian population, civilians and civilian objects.

2. With respect to attacks, the following precautions shall be taken:

(a) those who plan or decide upon an attack shall:

(i) do everything feasible to verify that the objectives to be attacked are neither civilians nor civilian objects and are not subject to special protection but are military objectives within the meaning of paragraph 2 of Article 52 and that it is not prohibited by the provisions of this Protocol to attack them;

(ii) take all feasible precautions in the choice of means and methods of attack with a view to avoiding, and in any event to minimizing, incidental loss or civilian life, injury to civilians and damage to civilian objects;

(iii) refrain from deciding to launch any attack which may be expected to cause incidental loss of civilian life, injury to civilians, damage to civilian objects, or a combination thereof, which would be excessive in relation to the concrete and direct military advantage anticipated;

(b) an attack shall be cancelled or suspended if it becomes apparent that the objective is not a military one or is subject to special protection or that the attack may be expected to cause incidental loss of civilian life, injury to civilians, damage to civilian objects, or a combination thereof, which would be excessive in relation to the concrete and direct military advantage anticipated;

(c) effective advance warning shall be given of attacks which may affect the civilian population, unless circumstances do not permit.

3. When a choice is possible between several military objectives for obtaining a similar military advantage, the objective to be selected shall be that the attack on which may be expected to cause the least danger to civilian lives and to civilian objects.

4. In the conduct of military operations at sea or in the air, each Party to the conflict shall, in conformity with its rights and duties under the rules of international law applicable in armed conflict, take all reasonable precautions to avoid losses of civilian lives and damage to civilian objects.

5. No provision of this article may be construed as authorizing any attacks against the civilian population, civilians or civilian objects.

Art 58. *Precautions against the effects of attacks*

The Parties to the conflict shall, to the maximum extent feasible:

(a) without prejudice to Article 49 of the Fourth Convention, endeavour to remove the civilian population, individual civilians and civilian objects under their control from the vicinity of military objectives;

(b) avoid locating military objectives within or near densely populated areas;

(c) take the other necessary precautions to protect the civilian population, individual civilians and civilian objects under their control against the dangers resulting from military operations. . . .

SECTION III.   TREATMENT OF PERSONS IN THE POWER OF A PARTY TO THE CONFLICT

CHAPTER I.   FIELD OF APPLICATION AND PROTECTION OF PERSONS AND OBJECTS

Art 72.   *Field of application*

The provisions of this Section are additional to the rules concerning humanitarian protection of civilians and civilian objects in the power of a Party to the conflict contained in the Fourth Convention, particularly Parts I and III thereof, as well as to other applicable rules of international law relating to the protection of fundamental human rights during international armed conflict.

Art 73.   *Refugees and stateless persons*

Persons who, before the beginning of hostilities, were considered as stateless persons or refugees under the relevant international instruments accepted by the Parties concerned or under the national legislation of the State of refuge or State of residence shall be protected persons within the meaning of Parts I and III of the Fourth Convention, in all circumstances and without any adverse distinction. . . .

Art 75. *Fundamental guarantees*

1. In so far as they are affected by a situation referred to in Article 1 of this Protocol, persons who are in the power of a Party to the conflict and who do not benefit from more favourable treatment under the Conventions or under this Protocol shall be treated humanely in all circumstances and shall enjoy, as a minimum, the protection provided by this Article without any adverse distinction based upon race, colour, sex, language, religion or belief, political or other opinion, national or social origin, wealth, birth or other status, or on any other similar criteria. Each Party shall respect the person, honour, convictions and religious practices of all such persons.

2. The following acts are and shall remain prohibited at any time and in any place whatsoever, whether committed by civilian or by military agents:

(a) violence to the life, health, or physical or mental well-being of persons, in particular:

(i) murder;

(ii) torture of all kinds, whether physical or mental;

(iii) corporal punishment; and

(iv) mutilation;

(b) outrages upon personal dignity, in particular humiliating and degrading treatment, enforced prostitution and any form of indecent assault;

(c) the taking of hostages;

(d) collective punishments; and

(e) threats to commit any of the foregoing acts.

3. Any person arrested, detained or interned for actions related to the armed conflict shall be informed promptly, in a language he understands, of the reasons why these measures have been taken. Except in cases of arrest or detention for penal offences, such persons shall be released with the minimum delay possible and in any event as soon as the circumstances justifying the arrest, detention or internment have ceased to exist.

4. No sentence may be passed and no penalty may be executed on a person found guilty of a penal offence related to the armed conflict except pursuant to a conviction pronounced by an impartial and regularly constituted court respecting the generally recognized principles of regular judicial procedure, which include the following:

(a) the procedure shall provide for an accused to be informed without delay of the particulars of the offence alleged against him and shall afford the accused before and during his trial all necessary rights and means of defence;

(b) no one shall be convicted of an offence except on the basis of individual penal responsibility;

(c) no one shall be accused or convicted of a criminal offence on account of any act or omission which did not constitute a criminal offence under the national or international law to which he was subject at the time when it was committed; nor shall a heavier penalty be imposed than that which was applicable at the time when the criminal offence was committed; if, after the commission of the offence, provision is made by law for the imposition of a lighter penalty, the offender shall benefit thereby;

(d) anyone charged with an offence is presumed innocent until proved guilty according to law;

(e) anyone charged with an offence shall have the right to be tried in his presence;

(f) no one shall be compelled to testify against himself or to confess guilt;

(g) anyone charged with an offence shall have the right to examine, or have examined, the witnesses against him and to obtain the attendance and examination of witnesses on his behalf under the same conditions as witnesses against him;

(h) no one shall be prosecuted or punished by the same Party for an offence in respect of which a final judgement acquitting or convicting that person has been previously pronounced under the same law and judicial procedure;

(i) anyone prosecuted for an offence shall have the right to have the judgement pronounced publicly; and

(j) a convicted person shall be advised on conviction of his judicial and other remedies and of the time-limits within which they may be exercised.

5. Women whose liberty has been restricted for reasons related to the armed conflict shall be held in quarters separated from men's quarters. They shall be under the immediate supervision of women. Nevertheless, in cases where families are detained or interned, they shall, whenever possible, be held in the same place and accommodated as family units.

6. Persons who are arrested, detained or interned for reasons related to the armed conflict shall enjoy the protection provided by this Article until their final release, repatriation or re-establishment, even after the end of the armed conflict.

7. In order to avoid any doubt concerning the prosecution and trial of persons accused of war crimes or crimes against humanity, the following principles shall apply:

(a) persons who are accused of such crimes should be submitted for the purpose of prosecution and trial in accordance with the applicable rules of international law; and

(b) any such persons who do not benefit from more favourable treatment under the Conventions or this Protocol shall be accorded the treatment provided by this Article, whether or not the crimes of which they are accused constitute grave breaches of the Conventions or of this Protocol.

8. No provision of this Article may be construed as limiting or infringing any other more favourable provision granting greater protection, under any applicable rules of international law, to persons covered by paragraph 1.

CHAPTER II. MEASURES IN FAVOUR OF WOMEN AND CHILDREN

Protection of women

1. Women shall be the object of special respect and shall be protected in particular against rape, forced prostitution and any other form of indecent assault.

2. Pregnant women and mothers having dependent infants who are arrested, detained or interned for reasons related to the armed conflict, shall have their cases considered with the utmost priority.

3. To the maximum extent feasible, the Parties to the conflict shall endeavour to avoid the pronouncement of the death penalty on pregnant women or mothers having dependent infants, for an offence related to the armed conflict. The death penalty for such offences shall not be executed on such women.

Art 77. Protection of children

1. Children shall be the object of special respect and shall be protected against any form of indecent assault. The Parties to the conflict shall provide them with the care and aid they require, whether because of their age or for any other reason.

2. The Parties to the conflict shall take all feasible measures in order that children who have not attained the age of fifteen years do not take a direct part in hostilities and, in particular, they shall refrain from recruiting them into their armed forces. In recruiting among those persons who have attained the age of fifteen years but who have not attained the age of eighteen years the Parties to the conflict shall endeavour to give priority to those who are oldest.

3. If, in exceptional cases, despite the provisions of paragraph 2, children who have not attained the age of fifteen years take a direct part in hostilities and fall into the power of an adverse Party, they shall continue to benefit from the special protection accorded by this Article, whether or not they are prisoners of war.

4. If arrested, detained or interned for reasons related to the armed conflict, children shall be held in quarters separate from the quarters of adults, except where families are accommodated as family units as provided in Article 75, paragraph 5.

5. The death penalty for an offence related to the armed conflict shall not be executed on persons who had not attained the age of eighteen years at the time the offence was committed.

Part V. Execution of the Conventions and Its Protocols

SECTION I. GENERAL PROVISIONS

Art 80. Measures for execution

1. The High Contracting Parties and the Parties to the conflict shall without delay take all necessary measures for the execution of their obligations under the Conventions and this Protocol.

2. The High Contracting Parties and the Parties to the conflict shall give orders and instructions to ensure observance of the Conventions and this Protocol, and shall supervise their execution.

Art 81. Activities of the Red Cross and other humanitarian organizations

1. The Parties to the conflict shall grant to the International Committee of the Red Cross all facilities, within their power so as to enable it to carry out the humanitarian functions assigned to it by the Conventions and this Protocol in order to ensure protection and assistance to the victims of conflicts. . . .

2. The Parties to the conflict shall grant to their respective Red Cross (Red Crescent, Red Lion and Sun) organizations the facilities necessary for carrying out their humanitarian activities in favour of the victims of the conflict, in accordance with the provisions of the Conventions and this Protocol and the fundamental principles of the Red Cross as formulated by the International Conferences of the Red Cross.

3. The High Contracting Parties and the Parties to the conflict shall facilitate in every possible way the assistance which Red Cross (Red Crescent, Red Lion and Sun) organizations and the League of Red Cross Societies extend to the victims of conflicts in accordance with the provisions of the Conventions and this Protocol and with the fundamental principles of the Red Cross as formulated by the International Conferences of the Red Cross.

4. The High Contracting Parties and the Parties to the conflict shall, as far as possible, make facilities similar to those mentioned in paragraphs 2 and 3 available to the other humanitarian organizations referred to in the Conventions and this Protocol. . . .

Art 82. Legal advisers in armed forces

The High Contracting Parties at all times, and the Parties to the conflict in time of armed conflict, shall ensure that legal advisers are available, when necessary, to advise military commanders at the appropriate level on the application of the Conventions and this Protocol and on the appropriate instruction to be given to the armed forces on this subject.

Art 83. Dissemination

1. The High Contracting Parties undertake, in time of peace as in time of armed conflict, to disseminate the Conventions and this Protocol as widely

as possible in their respective countries and, in particular, to include the study thereof in their programmes of military instruction and to encourage the study thereof by the civilian population, so that those instruments may become known to the armed forces and to the civilian population.

2. Any military or civilian authorities who, in time of armed conflict, assume responsibilities in respect of the application of the Conventions and this Protocol shall be fully acquainted with the text thereof.

Section II. Repression of Breaches of the Conventions and of this Protocol

Art 85. *Repression of breaches of this Protocol*

1. The provisions of the Conventions relating to the repression of breaches and grave breaches, supplemented by this Section, shall apply to the repression of breaches and grave breaches of this Protocol.

2. Acts described as grave breaches in the Conventions are grave breaches of this Protocol if committed against persons in the power of an adverse Party protected by Articles 44, 45 and 73 of this Protocol, or against the wounded, sick and shipwrecked of the adverse Party who are protected by this Protocol, or against those medical or religious personnel, medical units or medical transports which are under the control of the adverse Party and are protected by this Protocol.

3. In addition to the grave breaches defined in Article 11, the following acts shall be regarded as grave breaches of this Protocol, when committed wilfully, in violation of the relevant provisions of this Protocol, and causing death or serious injury to body or health:

(a) making the civilian population or individual civilians the object of attack;

(b) launching an indiscriminate attack affecting the civilian population or civilian objects in the knowledge that such attack will cause excessive loss of life, injury to civilians or damage to civilian objects, as defined in Article 57, paragraph 2 (a)(iii);

(c) launching an attack against works or installations containing dangerous forces in the knowledge that such attack will cause excessive loss of life, injury to civilians or damage to civilian objects, as defined in Article 57, paragraph 2 (a)(iii);

(d) making non-defended localities and demilitarized zones the object of attack;

(e) making a person the object of attack in the knowledge that he is hors de combat;

(f) the perfidious use, in violation of Article 37, of the distinctive emblem of the red cross, red crescent or red lion and sun or of other protective signs recognized by the Conventions or this Protocol.

4. In addition to the grave breaches defined in the preceding paragraphs and in the Conventions, the following shall be regarded as grave

breaches of this Protocol, when committed wilfully and in violation of the Conventions or the Protocol:

(a) the transfer by the occupying Power of parts of its own civilian population into the territory it occupies, or the deportation or transfer of all or parts of the population of the occupied territory within or outside this territory, in violation of Article 49 of the Fourth Convention;

(b) unjustifiable delay in the repatriation of prisoners of war or civilians;

(c) practices of apartheid and other inhuman and degrading practices involving outrages upon personal dignity, based on racial discrimination;

(d) making the clearly-recognized historic monuments, works of art or places of worship which constitute the cultural or spiritual heritage of peoples and to which special protection has been given by special arrangement, for example, within the framework of a competent international organization, the object of attack, causing as a result extensive destruction thereof, where there is no evidence of the violation by the adverse Party of Article 53, subparagraph (b), and when such historic monuments, works of art and places of worship are not located in the immediate proximity of military objectives;

(e) depriving a person protected by the Conventions or referred to in paragraph 2 of this Article of the rights of fair and regular trial.

5. Without prejudice to the application of the Conventions and of this Protocol, grave breaches of these instruments shall be regarded as war crimes.

Art 86. Failure to act

1. The High Contracting Parties and the Parties to the conflict shall repress grave breaches, and take measures necessary to suppress all other breaches, of the Conventions or of this Protocol which result from a failure to act when under a duty to do so.

2. The fact that a breach of the Conventions or of this Protocol was committed by a subordinate does not absolve his superiors from penal or disciplinary responsibility, as the case may be, if they knew, or had information which should have enabled them to conclude in the circumstances at the time, that he was committing or was going to commit such a breach and if they did not take all feasible measures within their power to prevent or repress the breach.

Art 87. Duty of commanders

1. The High Contracting Parties and the Parties to the conflict shall require military commanders, with respect to members of the armed forces under their command and other persons under their control, to prevent and, where necessary, to suppress and to report to competent authorities breaches of the Conventions and of this Protocol.

2. In order to prevent and suppress breaches, High Contracting Parties and Parties to the conflict shall require that, commensurate with their level

of responsibility, commanders ensure that members of the armed forces under their command are aware of their obligations under the Conventions and this Protocol.

3. The High Contracting Parties and Parties to the conflict shall require any commander who is aware that subordinates or other persons under his control are going to commit or have committed a breach of the Conventions or of this Protocol, to initiate such steps as are necessary to prevent such violations of the Conventions or this Protocol, and, where appropriate, to initiate disciplinary or penal action against violators thereof.

Art 88. *Mutual assistance in criminal matters*

1. The High Contracting Parties shall afford one another the greatest measure of assistance in connexion with criminal proceedings brought in respect of grave breaches of the Conventions or of this Protocol.

2. Subject to the rights and obligations established in the Conventions and in Article 85, paragraph 1 of this Protocol, and when circumstances permit, the High Contracting Parties shall co-operate in the matter of extradition. They shall give due consideration to the request of the State in whose territory the alleged offence has occurred.

3. The law of the High Contracting Party requested shall apply in all cases. The provisions of the preceding paragraphs shall not, however, affect the obligations arising from the provisions of any other treaty of a bilateral or multilateral nature which governs or will govern the whole or part of the subject of mutual assistance in criminal matters. . . .

Art 90. *International Fact-Finding Commission*

1. (a) An International Fact-Finding Commission (hereinafter referred to as "the Commission") consisting of 15 members of high moral standing and acknowledged impartiality shall be established;

(b) When not less than 20 High Contracting Parties have agreed to accept the competence of the Commission pursuant to paragraph 2. . . .

(c) The members of the Commission shall serve in their personal capacity and shall hold office until the election of new members at the ensuing meeting. . . .

2. . . .

(c) The Commission shall be competent to:

(i) inquire into any facts alleged to be a grave breach as defined in the Conventions and this Protocol or other serious violation of the Conventions or of this Protocol;

(ii) facilitate, through its good offices, the restoration of an attitude of respect for the Conventions and this Protocol;

(d) In other situations, the Commission shall institute an inquiry at the request of a Party to the conflict only with the consent of the other Party or Parties concerned;

3. (a) Unless otherwise agreed by the Parties concerned, all inquiries shall be undertaken by a Chamber consisting of seven members. . . .

4. (a) The Chamber set up under paragraph 3 to undertake an inquiry shall invite the Parties to the conflict to assist it and to present evidence. The Chamber may also seek such other evidence as it deems appropriate and may carry out an investigation of the situation in loco. . . .

5. (a) The Commission shall submit to the Parties a report on the findings of fact of the Chamber, with such recommendations as it may deem appropriate; . . .

(c) The Commission shall not report its findings publicly, unless all the Parties to the conflict have requested the Commission to do so.

6. The Commission shall establish its own rules. . . .

Art 91. *Responsibility*

A Party to the conflict which violates the provisions of the Conventions or of this Protocol shall, if the case demands, be liable to pay compensation. It shall be responsible for all acts committed by persons forming part of its armed forces.

Part IV.   Final Resolutions

Art 92. *Signature*

This Protocol shall be open for signature by the Parties to the Conventions six months after the signing of the Final Act and will remain open for a period of twelve months.

Art 93.   *Ratification*

. . . The instruments of ratification shall be deposited with the Swiss Federal Council, depositary of the Conventions.

Art 94.   *Accession*

This Protocol shall be open for accession by any Party to the Conventions which has not signed it. The instruments of accession shall be deposited with the depositary. . . .

Art 96.   *Treaty relations upon entry into force of this Protocol*

1. When the Parties to the Conventions are also Parties to this Protocol, the Conventions shall apply as supplemented by this Protocol.

2. When one of the Parties to the conflict is not bound by this Protocol, the Parties to the Protocol shall remain bound by it in their mutual relations. They shall furthermore be bound by this Protocol in relation to each of the

Parties which are not bound by it, if the latter accepts and applies the provisions thereof.

3. The authority representing a people engaged against a High Contracting Party in an armed conflict of the type referred to in Article 1, paragraph 4, may undertake to apply the Conventions and this Protocol in relation to that conflict by means of a unilateral declaration addressed to the depositary. Such declaration shall, upon its receipt by the depositary, have in relation to that conflict the following effects:

(a) the Conventions and this Protocol are brought into force for the said authority as a Party to the conflict with immediate effect;

(b) the said authority assumes the same rights and obligations as those which have been assumed by a High Contracting Party to the Conventions and this Protocol; and

(c) the Conventions and this Protocol are equally binding upon all Parties to the conflict.

Art 97.   Amendment

1. Any High Contracting Party may propose amendments to this Protocol. The text of any proposed amendment shall be communicated to the depositary, which shall decide, after consultation . . . , whether a conference should be convened to consider the proposed amendment. . . .

Art 99.   Denunciation

1. In case a High Contracting Party should denounce this Protocol, the denunciation shall only take effect one year after receipt of the instrument of denunciation. If, however, on the expiry of that year the denouncing Party is engaged in one of the situations referred to in Article I, the denunciation shall not take effect before the end of the armed conflict or occupation and not, in any case, before operations connected with the final release, repatriation or re-establishment of the persons protected by the Convention or this Protocol have been terminated. . . .

4. Any denunciation under paragraph 1 shall not affect the obligations already incurred, by reason of the armed conflict, under this Protocol by such denouncing Party in respect of any act committed before this denunciation becomes effective.

ANNEX I as amended on 30 November 1993: Regulations Concerning Identification. [Not included here.]
ANNEX II: Identity Card for Journalists on Dangerous Professional Missions [Not included.]

PRESIDENT OBAMA, ENSURING LAWFUL INTERROGATIONS

Exec. Order No. 13,491 (Jan. 22. 2009), 74 Fed. Reg. 4893

By the authority vested in me by the Constitution and the laws of the United States of America, in order to improve the effectiveness of human intelligence-gathering, to promote the safe, lawful, and humane treatment of individuals in United States custody and of United States personnel who are detained in armed conflicts, to ensure compliance with the treaty obligations of the United States, including the Geneva Conventions, and to take care that the laws of the United States are faithfully executed, I hereby order as follows:

Section 1. *Revocation.* Executive Order 13440 of July 20, 2007, is revoked. All executive directives, orders, and regulations inconsistent with this order, including but not limited to those issued to or by the Central Intelligence Agency (CIA) from September 11, 2001, to January 20, 2009, concerning detention or the interrogation of detained individuals, are revoked to the extent of their inconsistency with this order. Heads of departments and agencies shall take all necessary steps to ensure that all directives, orders, and regulations of their respective departments or agencies are consistent with this order. Upon request, the Attorney General shall provide guidance about which directives, orders, and regulations are inconsistent with this order.

Sec. 2. *Definitions.* As used in this order:

(a) "Army Field Manual 2-22.3" means FM 2-22.3, Human Intelligence Collector Operations, issued by the Department of the Army on September 6, 2006.

(b) "Army Field Manual 34-52" means FM 34-52, Intelligence Interrogation, issued by the Department of the Army on May 8, 1987.

(c) "Common Article 3" means Article 3 of each of the Geneva Conventions.

(d) "Convention Against Torture" means the Convention Against Torture and Other Cruel, Inhuman or Degrading Treatment or Punishment, December 10, 1984, 1465 U.N.T.S. 85, S. Treaty Doc. No. 100-20 (1988).

(e) "Geneva Conventions" means:

(i) the Convention for the Amelioration of the Condition of the Wounded and Sick in Armed Forces in the Field, August 12, 1949 (6 UST 3114);

(ii) the Convention for the Amelioration of the Condition of Wounded, Sick and Shipwrecked Members of Armed Forces at Sea, August 12, 1949 (6 UST 3217);

(iii) the Convention Relative to the Treatment of Prisoners of War, August 12, 1949 (6 UST 3316); and

(iv) the Convention Relative to the Protection of Civilian Persons in Time of War, August 12, 1949 (6 UST 3516).

(f) "Treated humanely," "violence to life and person," "murder of all kinds," "mutilation," "cruel treatment," "torture," "outrages upon personal dignity," and "humiliating and degrading treatment" refer to, and have the same meaning as, those same terms in Common Article 3.

(g) The terms "detention facilities" and "detention facility" in section 4(a) of this order do not refer to facilities used only to hold people on a short-term, transitory basis. [*4894]

Sec. 3. *Standards and Practices for Interrogation of Individuals in the Custody or Control of the United States in Armed Conflicts.*

(a) **Common Article 3 Standards as a Minimum Baseline.** Consistent with the requirements of the Federal torture statute, 18 U.S.C. 2340-2340A, section 1003 of the Detainee Treatment Act of 2005, 42 U.S.C. 2000dd, the Convention Against Torture, Common Article 3, and other laws regulating the treatment and interrogation of individuals detained in any armed conflict, such persons shall in all circumstances be treated humanely and shall not be subjected to violence to life and person (including murder of all kinds, mutilation, cruel treatment, and torture), nor to outrages upon personal dignity (including humiliating and degrading treatment), whenever such individuals are in the custody or under the effective control of an officer, employee, or other agent of the United States Government or detained within a facility owned, operated, or controlled by a department or agency of the United States.

(b) **Interrogation Techniques and Interrogation-Related Treatment.** Effective immediately, an individual in the custody or under the effective control of an officer, employee, or other agent of the United States Government, or detained within a facility owned, operated, or controlled by a department or agency of the United States, in any armed conflict, shall not be subjected to any interrogation technique or approach, or any treatment related to interrogation, that is not authorized by and listed in Army Field Manual 2-22.3 (Manual). Interrogation techniques, approaches, and treatments described in the Manual shall be implemented strictly in accord with the principles, processes, conditions, and limitations the Manual prescribes. Where processes required by the Manual, such as a requirement of approval by specified Department of Defense officials, are inapposite to a department or an agency other than the Department of Defense, such a department or agency shall use processes that are substantially equivalent to the processes the Manual prescribes for the Department of Defense. Nothing in this section shall preclude the Federal Bureau of Investigation, or other Federal law enforcement agencies, from continuing to use authorized, non-coercive techniques of interrogation that are designed to elicit voluntary statements and do not involve the use of force, threats, or promises.

(c) **Interpretations of Common Article 3 and the Army Field Manual.** From this day forward, unless the Attorney General with appropriate consultation provides further guidance, officers, employees, and other agents of the United States Government may, in conducting interrogations, act in reliance upon Army Field Manual 2-22.3, but may not, in conducting interrogations, rely upon any interpretation of the law governing interrogation—including interpretations of Federal criminal laws, the Convention Against Torture, Common Article 3, Army Field Manual 2-22.3, and its predecessor document, Army Field Manual 34-52. . . .

Sec. 4. *Prohibition of Certain Detention Facilities, and Red Cross Access to Detained Individuals.*

(a) **CIA Detention.** The CIA shall close as expeditiously as possible any detention facilities that it currently operates and shall not operate any such detention facility in the future.

(b) **International Committee of the Red Cross Access to Detained Individuals.** All departments and agencies of the Federal Government shall provide the International Committee of the Red Cross with notification of, and timely access to, any individual detained in any armed conflict in the custody or under the effective control of an officer, employee, or other agent of the United States Government or detained within a facility owned, operated, or controlled by a department or agency of the United States Government, consistent with Department of Defense regulations and policies.

Sec. 5. *Special Interagency Task Force on Interrogation and Transfer Policies.* [*4895]

(a) **Establishment of Special Interagency Task Force.** There shall be established a Special Task Force on Interrogation and Transfer Policies (Special Task Force) to review interrogation and transfer policies.

(b) **Membership.** The Special Task Force shall consist of the following members, or their designees:

(i) the Attorney General, who shall serve as Chair;

(ii) the Director of National Intelligence, who shall serve as Co-Vice-Chair;

(iii) the Secretary of Defense, who shall serve as Co-Vice-Chair;

(iv) the Secretary of State;

(v) the Secretary of Homeland Security;

(vi) the Director of the Central Intelligence Agency;

(vii) the Chairman of the Joint Chiefs of Staff; and

(viii) other officers or full-time or permanent part-time employees of the United States, as determined by the Chair, with the concurrence of the head of the department or agency concerned.

(c) **Staff** . . .

(d) **Operation.** The Chair shall convene meetings of the Special Task Force, determine its agenda, and direct its work. . . .

(e) **Mission.** The mission of the Special Task Force shall be:

(i) to study and evaluate whether the interrogation practices and techniques in Army Field Manual 2-22.3, when employed by departments or agencies outside the military, provide an appropriate means of acquiring the intelligence necessary to protect the Nation, and, if warranted, to recommend any additional or different guidance for other departments or agencies; and

(ii) to study and evaluate the practices of transferring individuals to other nations in order to ensure that such practices comply with the domestic laws, international obligations, and policies of the United States and do not result in the transfer of individuals to other nations to face torture or otherwise for the purpose, or with the effect, of undermining or circumventing the commitments or obligations of the United States to ensure the humane treatment of individuals in its custody or control.

(f) **Administration.** The Special Task Force shall be established for administrative purposes within the Department of Justice. . . .

(g) **Recommendations.** The Special Task Force shall provide a report to the President . . . on the matters set forth in subsection (d) within 180 days of the date of this order . . . .

(h) **Termination.** The Chair shall terminate the Special Task Force upon the completion of its duties.

Sec. 6. *Construction with Other Laws.* Nothing in this order shall be construed to affect the obligations of officers, employees, and other agents of the United States Government to comply with all pertinent laws and treaties of the United States governing detention and interrogation, including but not limited to: the Fifth and Eighth Amendments to the United States Constitution; the Federal torture statute, 18 U.S.C. 2340-2340A; the War Crimes Act, 18 U.S.C. 2441; the Federal assault statute, 18 U.S.C. 113; the Federal maiming statute, 18 U.S.C. 114; the Federal "stalking" statute, 18 U.S.C. 2261A; articles 93, 124, 128, and 134 of the Uniform Code of Military Justice, 10 U.S.C. 893, 924, 928, and 934; section 1003 of the Detainee Treatment Act of 2005, 42 U.S.C. 2000dd; section 6(c) of the Military Commissions Act of 2006, Public Law 109-366; the Geneva Conventions; and the Convention Against Torture. Nothing in this order shall be construed to diminish any rights that any individual may have under these or other laws and treaties. This order is not intended to, and does not, create any right or benefit, substantive or procedural, enforceable at law or in equity against the United States, its departments, agencies, or other entities, its officers or employees, or any other person.

/S/ Barack Obama
THE WHITE HOUSE,
    January 22, 2009.

PRESIDENT OBAMA, PERIODIC REVIEW OF INDIVIDUALS DETAINED AT GUANTÁNAMO BAY NAVAL STATION PURSUANT TO THE AUTHORIZATION FOR USE OF MILITARY FORCE

Exec. Order No. 13,567 (March 7, 2011), 76 Fed. Reg. 13,277

By the authority vested in me as President by the Constitution and the laws of the United States of America, including the Authorization for Use of Military Force of September 2001 (AUMF), Public Law 107-40, and in order to ensure that military detention of individuals now held at the U.S. Naval Station, Guantánamo Bay, Cuba (Guantánamo), who were subject to the interagency review under section 4 of Executive Order 13492 of January 22, 2009, continues to be carefully evaluated and justified, consistent with the national security and foreign policy interests of the United States and the interests of justice, I hereby order as follows:

Section 1. *Scope and Purpose.*

(a) The periodic review described in section 3 of this order applies only to those detainees held at Guantánamo on the date of this order, whom the interagency review established by Executive Order 13492 has (i) designated for continued law of war detention; or (ii) referred for prosecution, except for those detainees against whom charges are pending or a judgment of conviction has been entered.

(b) This order is intended solely to establish, as a discretionary matter, a process to review on a periodic basis the executive branch's continued, discretionary exercise of existing detention authority in individual cases. It does not create any additional or separate source of detention authority, and it does not affect the scope of detention authority under existing law. Detainees at Guantánamo have the constitutional privilege of the writ of habeas corpus, and nothing in this order is intended to affect the jurisdiction of Federal courts to determine the legality of their detention.

(c) In the event detainees covered by this order are transferred from Guantánamo to another U.S. detention facility where they remain in law of war detention, this order shall continue to apply to them.

Sec. 2. *Standard for Continued Detention.* Continued law of war detention is warranted for a detainee subject to the periodic review in section 3 of this order if it is necessary to protect against a significant threat to the security of the United States.

Sec. 3. *Periodic Review.* The Secretary of Defense shall coordinate a process of periodic review of continued law of war detention for each detainee described in section 1(a) of this order. In consultation with the Attorney General, the Secretary of Defense shall issue implementing guidelines governing the process, consistent with the following requirements:

(a) **Initial Review.** For each detainee, an initial review shall commence as soon as possible but no later than 1 year from the date of this order. The initial review will consist of a hearing before a Periodic Review Board (PRB). The review and hearing shall follow a process that includes the following requirements:

(1) Each detainee shall be provided, in writing and in a language the detainee understands, with advance notice of the PRB review and an unclassified summary of the factors and information the PRB will consider in evaluating whether the detainee meets the standard set forth in section 2 of this order. The written summary shall be sufficiently comprehensive to provide adequate notice to the detainee of the reasons for continued detention.

(2) The detainee shall be assisted in proceedings before the PRB by a Government-provided personal representative (representative) who possesses the security clearances necessary for access to the information described in subsection (a)(4) of this section. The representative shall advocate on behalf of the detainee before the PRB and shall be responsible for challenging the Government's information and introducing information on behalf of the detainee. In addition to the representative, the detainee may be assisted in proceedings before the PRB by private counsel, at no expense to the Government.

(3) The detainee shall be permitted to (i) present to the PRB a written or oral statement; (ii) introduce relevant information, including written declarations; (iii) answer any questions posed by the PRB; and (iv) call witnesses who are reasonably available and willing to provide information that is relevant and material to the standard set forth in section 2 of this order.

(4) The Secretary of Defense, in coordination with other relevant Government agencies, shall compile and provide to the PRB all information in the detainee disposition recommendations produced by the Task Force established under Executive Order 13492 that is relevant to the determination whether the standard in section 2 of this order has been met and on which the Government seeks to rely for that determination. In addition, the Secretary of Defense, in coordination with other relevant Government agencies, shall compile any additional information relevant to that determination, and on which the Government seeks to rely for that determination, that has become available since the conclusion of the Executive Order 13492 review. All mitigating information relevant to that determination must be provided to the PRB.

(5) The information provided in subsection (a)(4) of this section shall be provided to the detainee's representative. In exceptional circumstances . . . the PRB may determine that the representative must receive a sufficient substitute or summary, rather than the underlying information. If the detainee is represented by private counsel, the information provided in subsection (a)(4) of this section shall be provided to such counsel unless the Government determines that the need to protect national security, including intelligence sources and methods, or law enforcement or privilege concerns, requires the Government to provide counsel with a sufficient substitute or summary of the information. . . .

(6) The PRB shall conduct a hearing to consider the information described in subsection (a)(4) of this section, and other relevant information provided by the detainee or the detainee's representative or counsel, to determine whether the standard in section 2 of this order is met. . . .

(7) The PRB shall make a prompt determination, by consensus and in writing, as to whether the detainee's continued detention is warranted under the standard in section 2 of this order. If the PRB determines that the standard is not met, the PRB shall also recommend any conditions that relate to the detainee's transfer. The PRB shall provide a written summary of any final determination in unclassified form to the detainee, in a language the detainee understands . . .

(8) The Secretary of Defense shall establish a secretariat to administer the PRB review and hearing process. The Director of National Intelligence shall assist in preparing the unclassified notice and the substitutes or summaries described above. Other executive departments and agencies shall assist. . . .

(b) **Subsequent Full Review.** The continued detention of each detainee shall be subject to subsequent full reviews and hearings by the PRB on a triennial basis. Each subsequent review shall employ the procedures set forth in section 3(a) of this order.

(c) **File Reviews.** The continued detention of each detainee shall also be subject to a file review every 6 months in the intervening years between full reviews. This file review will be conducted by the PRB and shall consist of a review of any relevant new information related to the detainee compiled by the Secretary of Defense, in coordination with other relevant agencies, since the last review and, as appropriate, information considered during any prior PRB review. The detainee shall be permitted to make a written submission in connection with each file review. If, during the file review, a significant question is raised as to whether the detainee's continued detention is warranted under the standard in section 2 of this order, the PRB will promptly convene a full review pursuant to the standards in section 3(a) of this order.

(d) **Review of PRB Determinations.** The Review Committee (Committee), as defined in section 9(d) of this order, shall conduct a review if (i) a member of the Committee seeks review of a PRB determination within 30 days of that determination; or (ii) consensus within the PRB cannot be reached.

Sec. 4. *Effect of Determination to Transfer.*

(a) If a final determination is made that a detainee does not meet the standard in section 2 of this order, the Secretaries of State and Defense shall be responsible for ensuring that vigorous efforts are undertaken to identify a suitable transfer location for any such detainee, outside of the United States, consistent with the national security and foreign policy interests of the United States and the commitment set forth in section 2242(a) of the Foreign Affairs Reform and Restructuring Act of 1998 (Public Law 105-277).

(b) The Secretary of State, in consultation with the Secretary of Defense, shall be responsible for obtaining appropriate security and humane treatment assurances regarding any detainee to be transferred to another country, and for determining, after consultation with members of the Committee, that it is appropriate to proceed with the transfer.

(c) The Secretary of State shall evaluate humane treatment assurances in all cases. . . .

Sec. 5. *Annual Committee Review.*

(a) The Committee shall conduct an annual review of sufficiency and efficacy of transfer efforts, including:

(1) the status of transfer efforts for any detainee who has been subject to the periodic review under section 3 of this order, whose continued detention has been determined not to be warranted, and who has not been transferred more than 6 months after the date of such determination;

(2) the status of transfer efforts for any detainee whose petition for a writ of habeas corpus has been granted by a U.S. Federal court with no pending appeal and who has not been transferred;

(3) the status of transfer efforts for any detainee who has been designated for transfer or conditional detention by the Executive Order 13492 review and who has not been transferred; and

(4) the security and other conditions in the countries to which detainees might be transferred. . . .

(b) After completion of the initial reviews under section 3(a) of this order, and at least once every 4 years thereafter, the Committee shall review whether a continued law of war detention policy remains consistent with the interests of the United States, including national security interests.

Sec. 6. *Continuing Obligation of the Departments of Justice and Defense to Assess Feasibility of Prosecution.* As to each detainee whom the interagency review established by Executive Order 13492 has designated for continued law of war detention, the Attorney General and the Secretary of Defense shall continue to assess whether prosecution of the detainee is feasible and in the national security interests of the United States, and shall refer detainees for prosecution, as appropriate.

Sec. 7. *Obligation of Other Departments and Agencies to Assist the Secretary of Defense.* All departments, agencies, entities, and officers of the United States, to the maximum extent permitted by law, shall provide the Secretary of Defense such assistance as may be requested to implement this order.

Sec. 8. *Legality of Detention.* The process established under this order does not address the legality of any detainee's law of war detention. . . .

Sec. 9. *Definitions.*

(a) "Law of War Detention" means: detention authorized by the Congress under the AUMF, as informed by the laws of war.

(b) "Periodic Review Board" means: a board composed of senior officials tasked with fulfilling the functions described in section 3 of this order, one appointed by each of the following departments and offices: the Departments of State, Defense, Justice, and Homeland Security, as well as the Offices of the Director of National Intelligence and the Chairman of the Joint Chiefs of Staff.

(c) "Conditional Detention" means: the status of those detainees designated by the Executive Order 13492 review as eligible for transfer if one of the following conditions is satisfied: (1) the security situation improves in Yemen; (2) an appropriate rehabilitation program becomes available; or (3) an appropriate third-country resettlement option becomes available.

(d) "Review Committee" means: a committee composed of the Secretary of State, the Secretary of Defense, the Attorney General, the Secretary of Homeland Security, the Director of National Intelligence, and the Chairman of the Joint Chiefs of Staff.

Sec. 10. *General Provisions.*

(a) Nothing in this order shall prejudice the authority of the Secretary of Defense or any other official to determine the disposition of any detainee not covered by this order.

(b) This order shall be implemented subject to the availability of necessary appropriations and consistent with applicable law including: the Convention Against Torture; Common Article 3 of the Geneva Conventions; the Detainee Treatment Act of 2005; and other laws relating to the transfer, treatment, and interrogation of individuals detained in an armed conflict.

(c) This order is not intended to, and does not, create any right or benefit, substantive or procedural, enforceable at law or in equity by any party against the United States, its departments, agencies, or entities, its officers, employees, or agents, or any other person.

(d) Nothing in this order, and no determination made under this order, shall be construed as grounds for release of detainees covered by this order into the United States.

/s/ Barack Obama
THE WHITE HOUSE,
   March 7, 2011.

MATERIALS RE: PROLIFERATION, INCLUDING NORTH KOREA AND IRAN

U.N. SECURITY COUNCIL RES. 1540

April 28, 2004*

The Security Council,

Affirming that proliferation of nuclear, chemical and biological weapons, as well as their means of delivery,** constitutes a threat to international peace and security,

Reaffirming, in this context, the Statement of its President adopted at the Council's meeting at the level of Heads of State and Government on 31 January 1992 . . . , including the need for all Member States to fulfill their obligations in relation to arms control and disarmament and to prevent proliferation in all its aspects of all weapons of mass destruction, . . .

Affirming its resolve to take appropriate and effective actions against any threat to international peace and security caused by the proliferation of nuclear, chemical and biological weapons and their means of delivery, in conformity with its primary responsibilities, as provided for in the United Nations Charter,

Affirming its support for the multilateral treaties whose aim is to eliminate or prevent the proliferation of nuclear, chemical or biological weapons and the importance for all States parties to these treaties to implement them fully in order to promote international stability, . . .

Affirming that prevention of proliferation of nuclear, chemical and biological weapons should not hamper international cooperation in materials,

---

* Adopted by a vote of 15-0.

** Definitions for the purpose of this resolution only:

Means of delivery: missiles, rockets and other unmanned systems capable of delivering nuclear, chemical, or biological weapons, that are specially designed for such use.

Non-State actor: individual or entity, not acting under the lawful authority of any State in conducting activities which come within the scope of this resolution.

Related materials: materials, equipment and technology covered by relevant multilateral treaties and arrangements, or included on national control lists, which could be used for the design, development, production or use of nuclear, chemical and biological weapons and their means of delivery.

equipment and technology for peaceful purposes while goals of peaceful utilization should not be used as a cover for proliferation,

Gravely concerned by the threat of terrorism and the risk that non-State actors such as those identified in the United Nations list established and maintained by the Committee established under Security Council resolution 1267 and those to whom resolution 1373 applies, may acquire, develop, traffic in or use nuclear, chemical and biological weapons and their means of delivery,

Gravely concerned by the threat of illicit trafficking in nuclear, chemical, or biological weapons and their means of delivery, and related materials, which adds a new dimension to the issue of proliferation of such weapons and also poses a threat to international peace and security,

Recognizing the need to enhance coordination of efforts on national, sub-regional, regional and international levels in order to strengthen a global response to this serious challenge and threat to international security,

Recognizing that most States have undertaken binding legal obligations under treaties to which they are parties, or have made other commitments aimed at preventing the proliferation of nuclear, chemical or biological weapons, and have taken effective measures to account for, secure and physically protect sensitive materials, such as those required by the Convention on the Physical Protection of Nuclear Materials and those recommended by the IAEA Code of Conduct on the Safety and Security of Radioactive Sources,

Recognizing further the urgent need for all States to take additional effective measures to prevent the proliferation of nuclear, chemical or biological weapons and their means of delivery, . . .

Reaffirming the need to combat by all means, in accordance with the Charter of the United Nations, threats to international peace and security caused by terrorist acts,

Determined to facilitate henceforth an effective response to global threats in the area of non-proliferation,

Acting under Chapter VII of the Charter of the United Nations,

1. *Decides that* all States shall refrain from providing any form of support to non-State actors that attempt to develop, acquire, manufacture, possess, transport, transfer or use nuclear, chemical or biological weapons and their means of delivery;

2. *Decides also* that all States, in accordance with their national procedures, shall adopt and enforce appropriate effective laws which prohibit any non-State actor to manufacture, acquire, possess, develop, transport, transfer or use nuclear, chemical or biological weapons and their means of delivery, in particular for terrorist purposes, as well as attempts to engage in any of the foregoing activities, participate in them as an accomplice, assist or finance them;

3. *Decides also* that all States shall take and enforce effective measures to establish domestic controls to prevent the proliferation of nuclear, chemical, or biological weapons and their means of delivery, including by establishing appropriate controls over related materials and to this end shall:

(a) Develop and maintain appropriate effective measures to account for and secure such items in production, use, storage or transport;

(b) Develop and maintain appropriate effective physical protection measures;

(c) Develop and maintain appropriate effective border controls and law enforcement efforts to detect, deter, prevent and combat, including through international cooperation when necessary, the illicit trafficking and brokering in such items in accordance with their national legal authorities and legislation and consistent with international law;

(d) Establish, develop, review and maintain appropriate effective national export and trans-shipment controls over such items, including appropriate laws and regulations to control export, transit, trans-shipment and re-export and controls on providing funds and services related to such export and trans-shipment such as financing, and transporting that would contribute to proliferation, as well as establishing end-user controls; and establishing and enforcing appropriate criminal or civil penalties for violations of such export control laws and regulations;

4. Decides to establish, in accordance with rule 28 of its provisional rules of procedure, for a period of no longer than two years, a Committee of the Security Council, consisting of all members of the Council, which will, calling as appropriate on other expertise, report to the Security Council for its examination, on the implementation of this resolution, and to this end calls upon States to present a first report no later than six months from the adoption of this resolution to the Committee on steps they have taken or intend to take to implement this resolution;

5. Decides that none of the obligations set forth in this resolution shall be interpreted so as to conflict with or alter the rights and obligations of State Parties to the Nuclear Non-Proliferation Treaty, the Chemical Weapons Convention and the Biological and Toxin Weapons Convention or alter the responsibilities of the International Atomic Energy Agency or the Organization for the Prohibition of Chemical Weapons;

6. Recognizes the utility in implementing this resolution of effective national control lists and calls upon all Member States, when necessary, to pursue at the earliest opportunity the development of such lists;

7. Recognizes that some States may require assistance in implementing the provisions of this resolution within their territories and invites States in a position to do so to offer assistance as appropriate in response to specific requests to the States lacking the legal and regulatory infrastructure, implementation experience and/or resources for fulfilling the above provisions;

8. Calls upon all States:

(a) To promote the universal adoption and full implementation, and, where necessary, strengthening of multilateral treaties to which they are parties, whose aim is to prevent the proliferation of nuclear, biological or chemical weapons;

(b) To adopt national rules and regulations, where it has not yet been done, to ensure compliance with their commitments under the key multilateral nonproliferation treaties;

(c) To renew and fulfill their commitment to multilateral cooperation, in particular within the framework of the International Atomic Energy Agency, the Organization for the Prohibition of Chemical Weapons and the Biological and Toxin Weapons Convention, as important means of pursuing and achieving their common objectives in the area of non-proliferation and of promoting international cooperation for peaceful purposes;

(d) To develop appropriate ways to work with and inform industry and the public regarding their obligations under such laws; . . .

10. Further to counter that threat, *calls upon* all States, in accordance with their national legal authorities and legislation and consistent with international law, to take cooperative action to prevent illicit trafficking in nuclear, chemical or biological weapons, their means of delivery, and related materials; . . .

12. *Decides* to remain seized of the matter.

A. North Korea

U.N. SECURITY COUNCIL RES. 1718 [re: North Korea]
October 14, 2006*

The Security Council,

Recalling its previous relevant resolutions . . . ,

Reaffirming that proliferation of nuclear, chemical and biological weapons, as well as their means of delivery, constitutes a threat to international peace and security,

Expressing the gravest concern at the claim by the Democratic People's Republic of Korea (DPRK) that it has conducted a test of a nuclear weapon on 9 October 2006, and at the challenge such a test constitutes to the Treaty on the Non-Proliferation of Nuclear Weapons and to international efforts aimed at strengthening the global regime of non-proliferation of nuclear weapons, and the danger it poses to peace and stability in the region and beyond, . . .

Deploring the DPRK's announcement of withdrawal from the Treaty on the Non-Proliferation of Nuclear Weapons and its pursuit of nuclear weapons, . . .

Endorsing the Joint Statement issued on 19 September 2005 by China, the DPRK, Japan, the Republic of Korea, the Russian Federation and the United States, . . .

Expressing profound concern that the test claimed by the DPRK has generated increased tension in the region and beyond, and *determining* therefore that there is a clear threat to international peace and security,

---

* Adopted by a vote of 15-0.

Acting under Chapter VII of the Charter of the United Nations, and taking measures under its Article 41,

1. Condemns the nuclear test proclaimed by the DPRK on 9 October 2006 in flagrant disregard of its relevant resolutions . . .

2. Demands that the DPRK not conduct any further nuclear test or launch of a ballistic missile;

3. Demands that the DPRK immediately retract its announcement of withdrawal from the Treaty on the Non-Proliferation of Nuclear Weapons; . . .

5. Decides that the DPRK shall suspend all activities related to its ballistic missile programme and in this context re-establish its pre-existing commitments to a moratorium on missile launching;

6. Decides that the DPRK shall abandon all nuclear weapons and existing nuclear programmes in a complete, verifiable and irreversible manner, shall act strictly in accordance with the obligations applicable to parties under the Treaty on the Non-Proliferation of Nuclear Weapons and the terms and conditions of its International Atomic Energy Agency (IAEA) Safeguards Agreement . . . and shall provide the IAEA transparency measures extending beyond these requirements, including such access to individuals, documentation, equipments and facilities as may be required and deemed necessary by the IAEA;

7. Decides also that the DPRK shall abandon all other existing weapons of mass destruction and ballistic missile programme in a complete, verifiable and irreversible manner;

8. Decides that:

(a) All Member States shall prevent the direct or indirect supply, sale or transfer to the DPRK, through their territories or by their nationals, or using their flag vessels or aircraft, and whether or not originating in their territories, of:

(i) Any battle tanks, armoured combat vehicles, large calibre artillery systems, combat aircraft, attack helicopters, warships, missiles or missile systems as defined for the purpose of the United Nations Register on Conventional Arms, or related materiel including spare parts, or items as determined by the Security Council or the Committee established by paragraph 12 below (the Committee);

(ii) All items, materials, equipment, goods and technology as set out in the lists in documents S/2006/814 and S/2006/815, unless within 14 days of adoption of this resolution the Committee has amended or completed their provisions also taking into account the list in document S/ 2006/816, as well as other items, materials, equipment, goods and technology, determined by the Security Council or the Committee, which could contribute to DPRK's nuclear-related, ballistic missile-related or other weapons of mass destruction-related programmes;

(iii) Luxury goods;

(b) The DPRK shall cease the export of all items covered in subparagraphs (a) (i) and (a) (ii) above and that all Member States shall prohibit the procurement of such items from the DPRK by their nationals, or using their flagged vessels or aircraft, and whether or not originating in the territory of the DPRK;

(c) All Member States shall prevent any transfers to the DPRK by their nationals or from their territories, or from the DPRK by its nationals or from its territory, of technical training, advice, services or assistance related to the provision, manufacture, maintenance or use of the items in subparagraphs (a) (i) and (a) (ii) above;

(d) All Member States shall, in accordance with their respective legal processes, freeze immediately the funds, other financial assets and economic resources which are on their territories at the date of the adoption of this resolution or at any time thereafter, that are owned or controlled, directly or indirectly, by the persons or entities designated by the Committee or by the Security Council as being engaged in or providing support for, including through other illicit means, DPRK's nuclear-related, other weapons of mass destruction-related and ballistic missile-related programmes, or by persons or entities acting on their behalf or at their direction, and ensure that any funds, financial assets or economic resources are prevented from being made available by their nationals or by any persons or entities within their territories, to or for the benefit of such persons or entities;

(e) All Member States shall take the necessary steps to prevent the entry into or transit through their territories of the persons designated by the Committee or by the Security Council as being responsible for, including through supporting or promoting, DPRK policies in relation to the DPRK's nuclear-related, ballistic missile-related and other weapons of mass destruction-related programmes, together with their family members, provided that nothing in this paragraph shall oblige a state to refuse its own nationals entry into its territory;

(f) In order to ensure compliance with the requirements of this paragraph, and thereby preventing illicit trafficking in nuclear, chemical or biological weapons, their means of delivery and related materials, all Member States are called upon to take, in accordance with their national authorities and legislation, and consistent with international law, cooperative action including through inspection of cargo to and from the DPRK, as necessary;

9. *Decides* that the provisions of paragraph 8 (d) above do not apply to financial or other assets or resources that have been determined by relevant States:

(a) To be necessary for basic expenses, including payment for foodstuffs, rent or mortgage, medicines and medical treatment, taxes, insurance premiums, and public utility charges, or exclusively for payment of reasonable professional fees and reimbursement of incurred expenses associated with the provision of legal services, or fees or service charges, in accordance with national laws, for routine holding or maintenance of frozen funds, other financial assets and economic resources, after notification by the relevant States to the Committee . . . and in the absence of a negative decision by the Committee within five working days of such notification;

(b) To be necessary for extraordinary expenses, provided that such determination . . . and has been approved by the Committee; or

(c) To be subject of a judicial, administrative or arbitral lien or judgement, in which case the funds, other financial assets and economic resources may be used to satisfy that lien or judgement provided that the lien or judgement was entered prior to the date of the present resolution, is not for the benefit of a person referred to in paragraph 8 (d) above or an individual or entity identified by the Security Council or the Committee, and has been notified by the relevant States to the Committee;

10. Decides that the measures imposed by paragraph 8 (e) above shall not apply where the Committee determines on a case-by-case basis that such travel is justified on the grounds of humanitarian need, including religious obligations, or where the Committee concludes that an exemption would otherwise further the objectives of the present resolution;

11. Calls upon all Member States to report to the Security Council within thirty days of the adoption of this resolution on the steps they have taken with a view to implementing effectively the provisions of paragraph 8 above;

12. Decides to establish . . . a Committee of the Security Council consisting of all the members of the Council, to undertake the following tasks:

(a) To seek from all States, in particular those producing or possessing the items, materials, equipment, goods and technology referred to in paragraph 8 (a) above, information regarding the actions taken by them to implement effectively the measures imposed by paragraph 8 above of this resolution . . . ;

(b) To examine and take appropriate action on information regarding alleged violations of measures imposed by paragraph 8 of this resolution;

(c) To consider and decide upon requests for exemptions set out in paragraphs 9 and 10 above;

(d) To determine additional items, materials, equipment, goods and technology to be specified for the purpose of paragraphs 8 (a) (i) and 8 (a) (ii) above;

(e) To designate additional individuals and entities subject to the measures imposed by paragraphs 8 (d) and 8 (e) above;

(f) To promulgate guidelines as may be necessary to facilitate the implementation of the measures imposed by this resolution;

(g) To report at least every 90 days to the Security Council on its work, with its observations and recommendations, in particular on ways to strengthen the effectiveness of the measures imposed by paragraph 8 above;

13. Welcomes and encourages further the efforts by all States concerned to intensify their diplomatic efforts, to refrain from any actions that might aggravate tension and to facilitate the early resumption of the Six-Party Talks, with a view to the expeditious implementation of the Joint Statement issued on 19 September 2005 by China, the DPRK, Japan, the Republic of Korea, the Russian Federation and the United States, to achieve the verifiable denuclearization of the Korean Peninsula and to maintain peace and stability on the Korean Peninsula and in north-east Asia;

14. *Calls upon* the DPRK to return immediately to the Six-Party Talks without precondition and to work towards the expeditious implementation of the Joint Statement issued on 19 September 2005 by China, the DPRK, Japan, the Republic of Korea, the Russian Federation and the United States;

15. *Affirms* that it shall keep DPRK's actions under continuous review . . .

16. *Underlines* that further decisions will be required, should additional measures be necessary;

17. *Decides* to remain actively seized of the matter.

U.N. SECURITY COUNCIL STATEMENT CONDEMNING NORTH KOREAN MISSILE LAUNCH

U.N. Press Release (April 13, 2009)

The Security Council this afternoon condemned the launch carried out on 5 April by the Democratic People's Republic of Korea, in contravention of Security Council resolution 1718 (2006), which barred the East Asian country from conducting missile-related activities.

In a statement read by its President for the month of April, . . . the Security Council demanded that Democratic People's Republic of Korea conduct no further such launches, and reiterated the country's obligation to comply fully with resolution 1718, which was passed shortly after its nuclear-weapon test in October 2006.

By that earlier text, the Democratic People's Republic of Korea was forbidden to launch ballistic missiles or carry out further nuclear tests. The resolution also prevented a range of goods from entering or leaving the country and imposed an asset freeze and travel ban on persons related to its nuclear-weapon programme. . . .

The full text of the presidential statement . . . reads as follows:

The Security Council bears in mind the importance of maintaining peace and stability on the Korean peninsula and in North-East Asia as a whole. The Security Council condemns the 5 April 2009 (local time) launch by the Democratic People's Republic of Korea, which is in contravention of Security Council resolution 1718 (2006).

The Security Council reiterates that the Democratic People's Republic of Korea must comply fully with its obligations under Security Council resolution 1718 (2006).

The Security Council demands that the Democratic People's Republic of Korea not conduct any further launch.

The Security Council also calls upon all Member States to comply fully with their obligations under resolution 1718 (2006).

The Security Council agrees to adjust the measures imposed by paragraph 8 of resolution 1718 (2006) through the designation of entities and goods, and directs the Committee established pursuant to resolution 1718 (2006) to undertake its tasks to this effect and to report to the Security Council by 24 April 2009. . . .

The Security Council supports the six-party talks, calls for their early resumption and urges all the participants to intensify their efforts on the full implementation of the 19 September 2005 Joint Statement. . . .

The Security Council expresses its desire for a peaceful and diplomatic solution to the situation and welcomes efforts by Council members as well as other Member States to facilitate a peaceful and comprehensive solution through dialogue.

The Security Council will remain actively seized of the matter.

U.N. SECURITY COUNCIL RES. 2087 [re: North Korea]
January 22, 2013[*]

The Security Council,

Recalling its previous relevant resolutions . . .

Recognizing the freedom of all States to explore and use outer space in accordance with international law, including restrictions imposed by relevant Security Council resolutions,

1. *Condemns* the DPRK's launch of 12 December 2012, which used ballistic missile technology and was in violation of resolutions 1718 (2006) and 1874 (2009);

2. *Demands* that the DPRK not proceed with any further launches using ballistic missile technology, and comply with resolutions 1718 (2006) and 1874 (2009) by suspending all activities related to its ballistic missile program and in this context re-establish its pre-existing commitments to a moratorium on missile launches;

3. *Demands* that the DPRK immediately comply fully with its obligations under resolutions 1718 (2006) and 1874 (2009), including that it: abandon all nuclear weapons and existing nuclear programs in a complete, verifiable and irreversible manner; immediately cease all related activities; and not conduct any further launches that use ballistic missile technology, nuclear test or any further provocation;

4. *Reaffirms* its current sanctions measures contained in resolutions 1718 (2006) and 1874 (2009);

5. *Recalls* the measures imposed by paragraph 8 of resolution 1718 (2006), as modified by resolution 1874 (2009), and *determines* that:

   (a) The measures specified in paragraph 8(d) of resolution 1718 (2006) shall apply to the individuals and entities listed in Annex I and II,

---

[*] Adopted by a vote of 15-0.

and the measures specified in paragraph 8(e) of resolution 1718 (2006) shall apply to the individuals listed in Annex I; and,

(b) The measures imposed in paragraph 8(a), 8(b) and 8(c) of resolution 1718 (2006) shall apply to the items in INFCIRC/254/Rev.11/ Part 1 . . . ;

7. *Directs* the Committee established pursuant to resolution 1718 (2006) to issue an Implementation Assistance Notice regarding situations where a vessel has refused to allow an inspection after such an inspection has been authorized by the vessel's Flag State or if any DPRK-flagged vessel has refused to be inspected pursuant to paragraph 12 of resolution 1874 (2009);

8. *Recalls* paragraph 14 of resolution 1874 (2009), *recalls* further that States may seize and dispose of items consistent with the provisions of resolutions 1718 (2006), 1874 (2009) and this resolution . . . ;

10. *Calls upon* Member States which have not yet done so to report on the measures they have taken to implement the provisions of resolutions 1718 (2006) and 1874 (2009), *encourages* other Member States to submit, if any, additional information on implementing the provisions of resolutions 1718 (2006) and 1874 (2009); . . .

15. *Reaffirms* its support to the Six Party Talks, *calls* for their resumption, *urges* all the participants to intensify their efforts on the full and expeditious implementation of the 19 September 2005 Joint Statement issued by China, the DPRK, Japan, the Republic of Korea, the Russian Federation and the United States, with a view to achieving the verifiable denuclearization of the Korean Peninsula in a peaceful manner and to maintaining peace and stability on the Korean Peninsula and in northeast Asia;

16. *Calls upon* all Member States to implement fully their obligations pursuant to resolutions 1718 (2006) and 1874 (2009); . . .

18. *Underlines* that measures imposed by resolutions 1718 (2006) and 1874 (2009) are not intended to have adverse humanitarian consequences for the civilian population of the DPRK;

19. *Affirms* that it shall keep the DPRK's actions under continuous review and is prepared to strengthen, modify, suspend or lift the measures as may be needed in light of the DPRK's compliance, and, in this regard, *expresses its determination* to take significant action in the event of a further DPRK launch or nuclear test;

20. *Decides* to remain actively seized of the matter.

Annex I

Travel Ban/Asset Freeze

1. PAEK CHANG-HO . . .
2. CHANG MYONG-CHIN . . .
3. RA KY'ONG-SU
4. KIM KWANG-IL

Annex II

Asset Freeze

1. KOREAN COMMITTEE FOR SPACE TECHNOLOGY . . .
2. BANK OF EAST LAND . . .
3. KOREA KUMRYONG TRADING CORPORATION . . .
4. TOSONG TECHNOLOGY TRADING CORPORATION . . .
5. KOREA RYONHA MACHINERY JOINT VENTURE CORPORATION . . .
6. LEADER (HONG KONG) INTERNATIONAL . . .

U.N. SECURITY COUNCIL RES. 2094 [re: North Korea]
March 7, 2013[*]

The Security Council,

Recalling its previous relevant resolutions . . .

Reaffirming that proliferation of nuclear, chemical and biological weapons, as well as their means of delivery, constitutes a threat to international peace and security,

Underlining once again the importance that the DPRK respond to other security and humanitarian concerns of the international community,

Expressing the gravest concern at the nuclear test conducted by the Democratic People's Republic of Korea ("the DPRK") on 12 February 2013 (local time) in violation of resolutions 1718 (2006), 1874 (2009) and resolution 2087 (2013), and at the challenge such a test constitutes to the Treaty on Non-Proliferation of Nuclear Weapons ("the NPT") and to international efforts aimed at strengthening the global regime of non-proliferation of nuclear weapons, and the danger it poses to peace and stability in the region and beyond,

Concerned that the DPRK is abusing the privileges and immunities accorded under the Vienna Convention on Diplomatic and Consular Relations,

Welcoming the Financial Action Task Force's (FATF) new Recommendation 7 on targeted financial sanctions related to proliferation, and *urging* Member States to apply FATF's Interpretative Note to Recommendation 7 and related guidance papers for effective implementation of targeted financial sanctions related to proliferation,

Expressing its gravest concern that the DPRK's ongoing nuclear and ballistic missile-related activities have further generated increased tension in the region and beyond, and *determining* that there continues to exist a clear threat to international peace and security,

[*] Adopted by a vote of 15-0.

Acting under Chapter VII of the Charter of the United Nations, and taking measures under its Article 41,

1. *Condemns* in the strongest terms the nuclear test conducted by the DPRK on 12 February 2013 (local time) in violation and flagrant disregard of the Council's relevant resolutions;

2. *Decides* that the DPRK shall not conduct any further launches that use ballistic missile technology, nuclear tests or any other provocation;

3. *Demands* that the DPRK immediately retract its announcement of withdrawal from the NPT;

4. *Demands further* that the DPRK return at an early date to the NPT and International Atomic Energy Agency (IAEA) safeguards, bearing in mind the rights and obligations of States parties to the NPT, and underlines the need for all States parties to the NPT to continue to comply with their Treaty obligations;

5. *Condemns* all the DPRK's ongoing nuclear activities, including its uranium enrichment, *notes* that all such activities are in violation of resolutions 1718 (2006), 1874 (2009) and 2087 (2013), *reaffirms* its decision that the DPRK shall abandon all nuclear weapons and existing nuclear programmes, in a complete, verifiable and irreversible manner and immediately cease all related activities and shall act strictly in accordance with the obligations applicable to parties under the NPT and the terms and conditions of the IAEA Safeguards Agreement (IAEA INFCIRC/403);

6. *Reaffirms* its decision that the DPRK shall abandon all other existing weapons of mass destruction and ballistic missile programmes in a complete, verifiable and irreversible manner;

7. *Reaffirms* that the measures imposed in paragraph 8(c) of resolution 1718 (2006) apply to items prohibited by paragraphs 8(a)(i), 8 (a)(ii) of resolution 1718 (2006) and paragraphs 9 and 10 of resolution 1874 (2009), *decides* that the measures imposed in paragraph 8(c) of resolution 1718 (2006) also apply to paragraphs 20 and 22 of this resolution, and *notes* that these measures apply also to brokering or other intermediary services, including when arranging for the provision, maintenance or use of prohibited items in other States or the supply, sale or transfer to or exports from other States;

8. *Decides further* that measures specified in paragraph 8(d) of resolution 1718 (2006) shall apply also to the individuals and entities listed in annexes I and II of this resolution and to any individuals or entities acting on their behalf or at their direction, and to entities owned or controlled by them, including through illicit means, and *decides further* that the measures specified in paragraph 8(d) of resolution 1718 (2006) shall apply to any individuals or entities acting on the behalf or at the direction of the individuals and entities that have already been designated, to entities owned or controlled by them, including through illicit means;

9. *Decides* that the measures specified in paragraph 8(e) of resolution 1718 (2006) shall also apply to the individuals listed in annex I of this resolution and to individuals acting on their behalf or at their direction;

10. *Decides* that the measures specified in paragraph 8(e) of resolution 1718 (2006) and the exemptions set forth in paragraph 10 of resolution 1718 (2006) shall also apply to any individual whom a State determines is working on behalf or at the direction of a designated individual or entity or individuals assisting the evasion of sanctions or violating the provisions of resolutions 1718 (2006), 1874 (2009), 2087 (2013), and this resolution . . . ;

11. *Decides* that Member States shall, in addition to implementing their obligations pursuant to paragraphs 8(d) and (e) of resolution 1718 (2006), prevent the provision of financial services or the transfer to, through, or from their territory, or to or by their nationals or entities organized under their laws (including branches abroad), or persons or financial institutions in their territory, of any financial or other assets or resources, including bulk cash, that could contribute to the DPRK's nuclear or ballistic missile programmes, or other activities prohibited by resolutions 1718 (2006), 1874 (2009), 2087 (2013), or this resolution, or to the evasion of measures imposed by resolutions 1718 (2006), 1874 (2009), 2087 (2013), or this resolution, including by freezing any financial or other assets or resources on their territories or that hereafter come within their territories, or that are subject to their jurisdiction or that hereafter become subject to their jurisdiction, that are associated with such programmes or activities and applying enhanced monitoring to prevent all such transactions in accordance with their national authorities and legislation;

12. *Calls upon* States to take appropriate measures to prohibit in their territories the opening of new branches, subsidiaries, or representative offices of DPRK banks, . . . if they have information that provides reasonable grounds to believe that these activities could contribute to the DPRK's nuclear or ballistic missile programmes, or other activities prohibited by resolutions . . . ;

14. *Expresses* concern that transfers to the DPRK of bulk cash may be used to evade the measures imposed in resolutions 1718 (2006), 1874 (2009), 2087 (2013), and this resolution, and *clarifies* that all States shall apply the measures set forth in paragraph 11 of this resolution to the transfers of cash, including through cash couriers, transiting to and from the DPRK so as to ensure such transfers of bulk cash do not contribute to the DPRK's nuclear or ballistic missile programmes, or other activities prohibited by resolutions . . . ;

15. *Decides* that all Member States shall not provide public financial support for trade with the DPRK (including the granting of export credits, guarantees or insurance to their nationals or entities involved in such trade) where such financial support could contribute to the DPRK's nuclear or ballistic missile programmes, or other activities prohibited by resolutions . . . ;

16. *Decides* that all States shall inspect all cargo within or transiting through their territory that has originated in the DPRK, or that is destined for the DPRK, or has been brokered or facilitated by the DPRK or its nationals, or by individuals or entities acting on their behalf, if the State

concerned has credible information that provides reasonable grounds to believe the cargo contains items the supply, sale, transfer, or export of which is prohibited by resolutions . . . for the purpose of ensuring strict implementation of those provisions;

17. *Decides* that, if any vessel has refused to allow an inspection after such an inspection has been authorized by the vessel's flag State, or if any DPRK-flagged vessel has refused to be inspected pursuant to paragraph 12 of resolution 1874 (2009), all States shall deny such a vessel entry to their ports, unless entry is required for the purpose of an inspection, in the case of emergency or in the case of return to its port of origination . . . ;

18. *Calls upon* States to deny permission to any aircraft to take off from, land in or overfly their territory, if they have information that provides reasonable grounds to believe that the aircraft contains items the supply, sale, transfer or export of which is prohibited by resolutions . . . , except in the case of an emergency landing; . . .

20. *Decides* that the measures imposed in paragraphs 8(a) and 8(b) of resolution 1718 (2006) shall also apply to the items, materials, equipment, goods and technology listed in annex III of this resolution; . . .

22. *Calls upon* and allows all States to prevent the direct or indirect supply, sale or transfer to or from the DPRK or its nationals, through their territories or by their nationals, or using their flag vessels or aircraft, and whether or not originating in their territories of any item if the State determines that such item could contribute to the DPRK's nuclear or ballistic missile programmes, activities prohibited by resolutions . . . and *directs* the Committee to issue an Implementation Assistance Notice regarding the proper implementation of this provision;

23. *Reaffirms* the measures imposed in paragraph 8(a)(iii) of resolution 1718 (2006) regarding luxury goods, and *clarifies* that the term "luxury goods" includes, but is not limited to, the items specified in annex IV of this resolution;

24. *Calls upon* States to exercise enhanced vigilance over DPRK diplomatic personnel so as to prevent such individuals from contributing to the DPRK's nuclear or ballistic missile programmes, or other activities prohibited by resolutions . . .

25. *Calls upon* all States to report to the Security Council within ninety days of the adoption of this resolution, and thereafter upon request by the Committee, on concrete measures they have taken in order to implement effectively the provisions of this resolution . . . ;

27. *Directs* the Committee to respond effectively to violations of the measures decided in resolutions 1718 (2006), 1874 (2009), 2087 (2013), and this resolution, *directs* the Committee to designate additional individuals and entities to be subject to the measures imposed in resolutions 1718 (2006), 1874 (2009), 2087 (2013), and this resolution . . . :

29. *Recalls* the creation, pursuant to paragraph 26 of resolution 1874 (2009), of a Panel of Experts, under the direction of the Committee, to carry out the tasks provided for by that paragraph, *decides* to extend until 7 April

2014 the Panel's mandate, as renewed by resolution 2050 (2012), *decides further* that this mandate shall apply with respect to the measures imposed in this resolution, . . . *requests* the Secretary-General to create a group of up to eight experts and to take the necessary administrative measures to this effect, and *requests* the Committee, in consultation with the Panel, to adjust the Panel's schedule of reporting; . . .

31. *Underlines* that measures imposed by resolutions 1718 (2006), 1874 (2009), 2087 (2013) and this resolution are not intended to have adverse humanitarian consequences for the civilian population of the DPRK; . . .

33. *Expresses* its commitment to a peaceful, diplomatic and political solution to the situation and welcomes efforts by Council members as well as other States to facilitate a peaceful and comprehensive solution through dialogue and to refrain from any actions that might aggravate tensions;

34. *Reaffirms* its support to the Six-Party Talks, *calls for* their resumption, *urges* all the participants to intensify their efforts on the full and expeditious implementation of the 19 September 2005 Joint Statement issued by China, the DPRK, Japan, the Republic of Korea, the Russian Federation and the United States, with a view to achieving the verifiable denuclearization of the Korean Peninsula in a peaceful manner and to maintaining peace and stability on the Korean Peninsula and in north-east Asia;

35. *Reiterates* the importance of maintaining peace and stability on the Korean Peninsula and in north-east Asia at large;

36. *Affirms* that it shall keep the DPRK's actions under continuous review and is prepared to strengthen, modify, suspend or lift the measures as may be needed in light of the DPRK's compliance, and, in this regard, *expresses its determination* to take further significant measures in the event of a further DPRK launch or nuclear test;

37. *Decides* to remain seized of the matter.

Annex I

Travel ban/asset freeze

1. YO'N CHO'NG NAM . . .
2. KO CH'O'L-CHAE . . .
3. MUN CHO'NG-CH'O'L . . .

Annex II

Asset freeze

1. SECOND ACADEMY OF NATURAL SCIENCES . . .
2. KOREA COMPLEX EQUIPMENT IMPORT CORPORATION . . .

Annex III

Items, materials, equipment, goods and technology
Nuclear items

1. Perfluorinated Lubricants . . .
2. UF6 Corrosion Resistant Bellow-sealed Valves . . .

Missile items

1. Special corrosion resistant steels . . .
2. Ultra high-temperature ceramic composite materials in solid form (i.e. blocks, cylinders, tubes or ingots) in any of the following form factors: . . . .
3. Pyrotechnically Actuated Valves.
4. Measurement and control equipment usable for wind tunnels (balance, thermal stream measurement, flow control).
5. Sodium Perchlorate.

Chemical weapons list

1. Vacuum pumps with a manufacturer's specified maximum flow-rate greater than 1 m3/h (under standard temperature and pressure conditions), casings (pump bodies), preformed casing-liners. . . .

Annex IV

Luxury goods

1. Jewelry:
   (a) Jewelry with pearls;
   (b) Gems;
   (c) Precious and semi-precious stones (including diamonds, sapphires, rubies, and emeralds);
   (d) Jewelry of precious metal or of metal clad with precious metal.
2. Transportation items, as follows:
   (a) Yachts;
   (b) Luxury automobiles (and motor vehicles): automobiles and other motor vehicles to transport people (other than public transport), including station wagons;
   (c) Racing cars.

B. Iran

U.N. SECURITY COUNCIL RES. 1737 [re: Iran]
December 23, 2006*

The Security Council,

Recalling the Statement of its President . . . of 29 March 2006, and its resolution 1696 (2006) of 31 July 2006,

Reaffirming its commitment to the Treaty on the Non-Proliferation of Nuclear Weapons, and recalling the right of States Party, in conformity with Articles I and II of that Treaty, to develop research, production and use of nuclear energy for peaceful purposes without discrimination,

Reiterating its serious concern over the many reports of the IAEA Director General and resolutions of the IAEA Board of Governors related to Iran's nuclear programme . . . ,

Reiterating its serious concern that the IAEA Director General's report of 27 February 2006 . . . lists a number of outstanding issues and concerns on Iran's nuclear programme, including topics which could have a military nuclear dimension, and that the IAEA is unable to conclude that there are no undeclared nuclear materials or activities in Iran,

Reiterating its serious concern over the IAEA Director General's report of 28 April 2006 . . . and its findings, including that, after more than three years of Agency efforts to seek clarity about all aspects of Iran's nuclear programme, the existing gaps in knowledge continue to be a matter of concern, and that the IAEA is unable to make progress in its efforts to provide assurances about the absence of undeclared nuclear material and activities in Iran,

Noting with serious concern that, as confirmed by the IAEA Director General's reports . . . , Iran has not established full and sustained suspension of all enrichment-related and reprocessing activities as set out in resolution 1696 . . . , nor resumed its cooperation with the IAEA under the Additional Protocol, nor taken the other steps required of it by the IAEA Board of Governors, nor complied with the provisions of Security Council resolution 1696 . . . and which are essential to build confidence, and deploring Iran's refusal to take these steps,

Emphasizing the importance of political and diplomatic efforts to find a negotiated solution guaranteeing that Iran's nuclear programme is exclusively for peaceful purposes, . . .

Determined to give effect to its decisions by adopting appropriate measures to persuade Iran to comply with resolution 1696 (2006) and with the requirements of the IAEA, and also to constrain Iran's development of sensitive technologies in support of its nuclear and missile programmes,

---

* Adopted by a vote of 15-0.

until such time as the Security Council determines that the objectives of this resolution have been met,

Concerned by the proliferation risks presented by the Iranian nuclear programme . . . ,

Acting under Article 41 of Chapter VII of the Charter of the United Nations,

1. *Affirms* that Iran shall without further delay take the steps required by the IAEA Board of Governors in its resolution GOV/2006/14, which are essential to build confidence in the exclusively peaceful purpose of its nuclear programme and to resolve outstanding questions;

2. *Decides,* in this context, that Iran shall without further delay suspend the following proliferation sensitive nuclear activities:

(a) all enrichment-related and reprocessing activities, including research and development, to be verified by the IAEA; and

(b) work on all heavy water-related projects, including the construction of a research reactor moderated by heavy water, also to be verified by the IAEA;

3. *Decides* that all States shall take the necessary measures to prevent the supply, sale or transfer directly or indirectly from their territories, or by their nationals or using their flag vessels or aircraft to, or for the use in or benefit of, Iran, and whether or not originating in their territories, of all items, materials, equipment, goods and technology which could contribute to Iran's enrichment-related, reprocessing or heavy water-related activities, or to the development of nuclear weapon delivery systems, namely . . . :

4. *Decides* that all States shall take the necessary measures to prevent the supply, sale or transfer directly or indirectly from their territories, or by their nationals or using their flag vessels or aircraft to, or for the use in or benefit of, Iran, and whether or not originating in their territories, of the following items, materials, equipment, goods and technology . . . ;

6. *Decides* that all States shall also take the necessary measures to prevent the provision to Iran of any technical assistance or training, financial assistance, investment, brokering or other services, and the transfer of financial resources or services, related to the supply, sale, transfer, manufacture or use of the prohibited items, materials, equipment, goods and technology specified in paragraphs 3 and 4 above;

7. *Decides* that Iran shall not export any of the items in documents S/2006/814 and S/2006/815 and that all Member States shall prohibit the procurement of such items from Iran by their nationals, or using their flag vessels or aircraft, and whether or not originating in the territory of Iran; . . .

10. *Calls upon* all States to exercise vigilance regarding the entry into or transit through their territories of individuals who are engaged in, *directly* associated with or providing support for Iran's proliferation sensitive nuclear activities or for the development of nuclear weapon delivery systems, and decides in this regard that all States shall notify the Committee of the

entry into or transit through their territories of the persons designated in the Annex to this resolution (herein "the Annex"), as well as of additional persons designated by the Security Council or the Committee . . . ;

12. Decides that all States shall freeze the funds, other financial assets and economic resources which are on their territories at the date of adoption of this resolution or at any time thereafter, that are owned or controlled by the persons or entities designated in the Annex, as well as those of additional persons or entities designated by the Security Council or by the Committee as being engaged in, directly associated with or providing support for Iran's proliferation sensitive nuclear activities or the development of nuclear weapon delivery systems, or by persons or entities acting on their behalf or at their direction, or by entities owned or controlled by them, including through illicit means, and that the measures in this paragraph shall cease to apply in respect of such persons or entities if, and at such time as, the Security Council or the Committee removes them from the Annex, and *decides further* that all States shall ensure that any funds, financial assets or economic resources are prevented from being made available by their nationals or by any persons or entities within their territories, to or for the benefit of these persons and entities;

13. Decides that the measures imposed by paragraph 12 above do not apply to funds, other financial assets or economic resources that have been determined by relevant States:

(a) to be necessary for basic expenses, including payment for food-stuffs, rent or mortgage, medicines and medical treatment, taxes, insurance premiums, and public utility charges, . . . after notification by the relevant States to the Committee of the intention to authorize, where appropriate, access to such funds . . . and in the absence of a negative decision by the Committee within five working days of such notification;

(b) to be necessary for extraordinary expenses, provided that such determination has been notified by the relevant States to the Committee and has been approved by the Committee; . . .

15. Decides that the measures in paragraph 12 above shall not prevent a designated person or entity from making payment due under a contract entered into prior to the listing of such a person or entity . . . ;

18. Decides to establish, in accordance with rule 28 of its provisional rules of procedure, a Committee of the Security Council consisting of all the members of the Council, to undertake the following tasks:

(a) to seek from all States, in particular those in the region and those producing the items, materials, equipment, goods and technology referred to in paragraphs 3 and 4 above, information regarding the actions taken by them to implement effectively the measures imposed by paragraphs 3, 4, 5, 6, 7, 8, 10 and 12 of this resolution and whatever further information it may consider useful in this regard;

(b) to seek from the secretariat of the IAEA information regarding the actions taken by the IAEA to implement effectively the measures imposed by paragraph 16 of this resolution and whatever further information it may consider useful in this regard;

(c) to examine and take appropriate action on information regarding alleged violations of measures . . . ;

(d) to consider and decide upon requests for exemptions set out in paragraphs 9, 13 and 15 above;

(e) to determine as may be necessary additional items, materials, equipment, goods and technology to be specified for the purpose of paragraph 3 above;

(f) to designate as may be necessary additional individuals and entities subject to the measures imposed by paragraphs 10 and 12 above;

(g) to promulgate guidelines as may be necessary to facilitate the implementation of the measures imposed by this resolution . . . ;

(h) to report at least every 90 days to the Security Council on its work and on the implementation of this resolution . . . ;

19. *Decides that* all States shall report to the Committee within 60 days of the adoption of this resolution on the steps they have taken with a view to implementing effectively paragraphs 3, 4, 5, 6, 7, 8, 10, 12 and 17 above; . . .

23. *Requests* within 60 days a report from the Director General of the IAEA on whether Iran has established full and sustained suspension of all activities mentioned in this resolution, as well as on the process of Iranian compliance with all the steps required by the IAEA Board and with the other provisions of this resolution . . . ;

24. *Affirms* that it shall review Iran's actions in the light of the report referred to in paragraph 23 above, to be submitted within 60 days, and:

(a) that it shall suspend the implementation of measures if and for so long as Iran suspends all enrichment-related and reprocessing activities, including research and development, as verified by the IAEA, to allow for negotiations;

(b) that it shall terminate the measures specified in paragraphs 3, 4, 5, 6, 7, 10 and 12 of this resolution as soon as it determines that Iran has fully complied with its obligations under the relevant resolutions of the Security Council and met the requirements of the IAEA Board of Governors, as confirmed by the IAEA Board;

(c) that it shall, in the event that the report in paragraph 23 above shows that Iran has not complied with this resolution, adopt further appropriate measures under Article 41 of Chapter VII of the Charter of the United Nations to persuade Iran to comply with this resolution and the requirements of the IAEA, and underlines that further decisions will be required should such additional measures be necessary;

25. *Decides* to remain seized of the matter.

U.N. SECURITY COUNCIL RES. 1747 [re: Iran]

March 24, 2007*

The Security Council,

Recalling the Statement of its President . . . of 29 March 2006, and its resolution 1696 (2006) . . . , and its resolution 1737 (2006) . . . , and *reaffirming* their provisions,

Reaffirming its commitment to the Treaty on the Non-Proliferation of Nuclear Weapons, the need for all States Party to that Treaty to comply fully with all their obligations, and recalling the right of States Party, in conformity with Articles I and II of that Treaty, to develop research, production and use of nuclear energy for peaceful purposes without discrimination,

Recalling its serious concern over the reports of the IAEA Director General as set out in its resolutions 1696 . . . and 1737 . . . ,

Recalling the latest report by the IAEA Director General . . . of 22 February 2007 and *deploring* that, as indicated therein, Iran has failed to comply with resolution 1696 . . . and resolution 1737 . . . ,

Emphasizing the importance of political and diplomatic efforts to find a negotiated solution guaranteeing that Iran's nuclear programme is exclusively for peaceful purposes, and noting that such a solution would benefit nuclear non-proliferation elsewhere . . .

Determined to give effect to its decisions by adopting appropriate measures to persuade Iran to comply with resolution 1696 . . . and resolution 1737 . . . and with the requirements of the IAEA, and also to constrain Iran's development of sensitive technologies in support of its nuclear and missile programmes, until such time as the Security Council determines that the objectives of these resolutions have been met, . . .

Concerned by the proliferation risks presented by the Iranian nuclear programme and, in this context, by Iran's continuing failure to meet the requirements of the IAEA Board of Governors and to comply with the provisions of Security Council resolutions 1696 . . . and 1737 . . . , mindful of its primary responsibility under the Charter of the United Nations for the maintenance of international peace and security,

Acting under Article 41 of Chapter VII of the Charter of the United Nations,

1. *Reaffirms* that Iran shall without further delay take the steps required by the IAEA Board of Governors in its resolution GOV/2006/14, which are essential to build confidence in the exclusively peaceful purpose of its nuclear programme and to resolve outstanding questions, and, in this context, *affirms* its decision that Iran shall without further delay take the steps required in paragraph 2 of resolution 1737 . . . ;

2. *Calls upon* all States also to exercise vigilance and restraint regarding the entry into or transit through their territories of individuals

---

* Adopted by a vote of 15-0.

who are engaged in, directly associated with or providing support for Iran's proliferation sensitive nuclear activities or for the development of nuclear weapon delivery systems, and *decides* in this regard that all States shall notify the Committee established pursuant to paragraph 18 of resolution 1737 . . . (herein "the Committee") of the entry into or transit through their territories of the persons designated in the Annex to resolution 1737 . . . or Annex I to this resolution . . . .

4. Decides that the measures specified in paragraphs 12, 13, 14 and 15 of resolution 1737 . . . shall apply also to the persons and entities listed in Annex I to this resolution;

5. Decides that Iran shall not supply, sell or transfer directly or indirectly from its territory or by its nationals or using its flag vessels or aircraft any arms or related materiel, and that all States shall prohibit the procurement of such items from Iran by their nationals, or using their flag vessels or aircraft, and whether or not originating in the territory of Iran;

6. Calls upon all States to exercise vigilance and restraint in the supply, sale or transfer directly or indirectly from their territories or by their nationals or using their flag vessels or aircraft of any battle tanks, armoured combat vehicles, large calibre artillery systems, combat aircraft, attack helicopters, warships, missiles or missile systems as defined for the purpose of the United Nations Register on Conventional Arms to Iran, and in the provision to Iran of any technical assistance or training, financial assistance, investment, brokering or other services, and the transfer of financial resources or services, related to the supply, sale, transfer, manufacture or use of such items in order to prevent a destabilizing accumulation of arms;

7. Calls upon all States and international financial institutions not to enter into new commitments for grants, financial assistance, and concessional loans, to the Government of the Islamic Republic of Iran, except for humanitarian and developmental purposes;

8. Calls upon all States to report to the Committee within 60 days of the adoption of this resolution on the steps they have taken with a view to implementing effectively paragraphs 2, 4, 5, 6 and 7 above; . . .

10. *Welcomes* the continuous affirmation of the commitment of China, France, Germany, the Russian Federation, the United Kingdom and the United States, with the support of the European Union's High Representative, to a negotiated solution to this issue and *encourages* Iran to engage with their June 2006 proposals . . . , which were endorsed by the Security Council in resolution 1696 . . . ,

11. Reiterates its determination to reinforce the authority of the IAEA, strongly supports the role of the IAEA Board of Governors, *commends and encourages* the Director General of the IAEA and its secretariat for their ongoing professional and impartial efforts to resolve all outstanding issues in Iran within the framework of the IAEA . . . :

12. Requests within 60 days a further report from the Director General of the IAEA . . .

13. Affirms that it shall review Iran's actions in light of the report referred to in paragraph 12 above, to be submitted within 60 days, and . . .

14. *Decides* to remain seized of the matter.

U.N. SECURITY COUNCIL RES. 1803 [re: Iran]
March 3, 2008*

The Security Council,

Recalling the statement of its President, S/PRST/2006/15, of 29 March 2006, and its resolution 1696 (2006) . . . , its resolution 1737 (2006) . . . and its resolution 1747 (2007) . . . , and *reaffirming* their provisions, . . .

Noting with serious concern that, as confirmed by the reports . . . , of the Director General of the International Atomic Energy Agency (IAEA), Iran has not established full and sustained suspension of all enrichment related and reprocessing activities and heavy-water-related projects as set out in resolution 1696 (2006), 1737 (2006) and 1747 (2007) nor resumed its co-operation with the IAEA under the Additional Protocol, nor taken the other steps required by the IAEA Board of Governors, nor complied with the provisions of Security Council resolution 1696 (2006), 1737 (2006) and 1747 (2007) and which are essential to build confidence, and *deploring* Iran's refusal to take these steps, . . .

Reiterating its determination to reinforce the authority of the IAEA, strongly supporting the role of the IAEA Board of Governors, *commending* the IAEA for its efforts to resolve outstanding issues relating to Iran's nuclear programme in the work plan between the Secretariat of the IAEA and Iran . . . , welcoming the progress in implementation of this work plan as reflected in the IAEA Director General's report of 15 November 2007 . . . , and 22 February 2008 . . .

Expressing the conviction that the suspension set out in paragraph 2 of resolution 1737 (2006) as well as full, verified Iranian compliance with the requirements set out by the IAEA Board of Governors would contribute to a diplomatic, negotiated solution, that guarantees Iran's nuclear programme is for exclusively peaceful purposes, . . .

[M]indful of its primary responsibility under the Charter of the United Nations for the maintenance of international peace and security,

Acting under Article 41 of Chapter VII of the Charter of the United Nations,

1. *Reaffirms* that Iran shall without further delay take the steps required by the IAEA Board of Governors in its resolution GOV/2006/14, which are essential to build confidence in the exclusively peaceful purpose of its nuclear programme and to resolve outstanding questions, and, in this context,

---

* Adopted by a vote of 14-0, with Indonesia abstaining.

affirms its decision that Iran shall without delay take the steps required in paragraph 2 of resolution 1737 (2006) . . . ;

3. *Calls upon* all States to exercise vigilance and restraint regarding the entry into or transit through their territories of individuals who are engaged in, directly associated with or providing support for Iran's proliferation sensitive nuclear activities or for the development of nuclear weapon delivery systems, and *decides* in this regard that all States shall notify the Committee established pursuant to paragraph 18 of resolution 1737 (2006) (herein "the Committee") of the entry into or transit through their territories of the persons designated in the Annex to resolution 1737 (2006), Annex I to resolution 1747 (2007) or Annex I to this resolution, as well as of additional persons designated by the Security Council or the Committee as being engaged in, directly associated with or providing support for Iran's proliferation sensitive nuclear activities or for the development of nuclear weapon delivery systems, including through the involvement in procurement of the prohibited items, goods, equipment, materials and technology . . .

8. *Decides* that all States shall take the necessary measures to prevent the supply, sale or transfer directly or indirectly from their territories or by their nationals or using their flag vessels or aircraft to, or for use in or benefit of, Iran, and whether or not originating in their territories, of:

(a) all items, materials, equipment, goods and technology set out in INFCIRC/254/Rev.7/Part2 of document S/2006/814, except . . . ;

(b) all items, materials, equipment, goods and technology set out in 19. A.3 of Category II of document S/2006/815;

9. *Calls upon* all States to exercise vigilance in entering into new commitments for public provided financial support for trade with Iran, including the granting of export credits, guarantees or insurance, to their nationals or entities involved in such trade, in order to avoid such financial support contributing to the proliferation sensitive nuclear activities, or to the development of nuclear weapon delivery systems, as referred to in resolution 1737 (2006);

10. *Calls upon* all States to exercise vigilance over the activities of financial institutions in their territories with all banks domiciled in Iran, in particular with Bank Melli and Bank Saderat, and their branches and subsidiaries abroad, in order to avoid such activities contributing to the proliferation sensitive nuclear activities, or to the development of nuclear weapon delivery systems, as referred to in resolution 1737 (2006);

11. *Calls upon* all States, in accordance with their national legal authorities and legislation and consistent with international law, in particular the law of the sea and relevant international civil aviation agreements, to inspect the cargoes to and from Iran, of aircraft and vessels, at their airports and seaports, owned or operated by Iran Air Cargo and Islamic Republic of Iran Shipping Line, provided there are reasonable grounds to believe that the aircraft or vessel is transporting goods prohibited under this resolution or resolution 1737 (2006) or resolution 1747 (2007);

12. *Requires* all States, in cases when inspection mentioned in the paragraph above is undertaken, to submit to the Security Council within five working days a written report on the inspection containing, in particular, explanation of the grounds for the inspection, as well as information on its time, place, circumstances, results and other relevant details;

13. *Calls upon* all States to report to the Committee within 60 days of the adoption of this resolution on the steps they have taken with a view to implementing effectively paragraphs 3, 5, 7, 8, 9, 10 and 11 above; . . .

15. *Stresses* the willingness of China, France, Germany, the Russian Federation, the United Kingdom and the United States to further enhance diplomatic efforts to promote resumption of dialogue, and consultations on the basis of their offer to Iran, with a view to seeking a comprehensive, long-term and proper solution of this issue which would allow for the development of all-round relations and wider cooperation with Iran based on mutual respect and the establishment of international confidence in the exclusively peaceful nature of Iran's nuclear programme . . . ;

17. *Emphasizes* the importance of all States, including Iran, taking the necessary measures to ensure that no claim shall lie at the instance of the Government of Iran, or of any person or entity in Iran, or of persons or entities designated pursuant to resolution 1737 (2006) and related resolutions, or any person claiming through or for the benefit of any such person or entity, in connection with any contract or other transaction where its performance was prevented by reason of the measures imposed by the present resolution, resolution 1737 (2006) or resolution 1747 (2007);

18. *Requests* within 90 days a further report from the Director General of the IAEA . . . :

19. *Reaffirms* that it shall review Iran's actions in light of the report referred to in the paragraph above, and:

(a) that it shall suspend the implementation of measures if and for so long as Iran suspends all enrichment-related and reprocessing activities . . . ;

(b) that it shall terminate the measures specified in [designated U.N. resolutions and IAEA documents] . . . ;

(c) that it shall, in the event that the report shows that Iran has not complied with resolution 1696 (2006), resolution 1737 (2006), resolution 1747 (2007) and this resolution, adopt further appropriate measures under Article 41 of Chapter VII of the Charter of the United Nations to persuade Iran to comply with these resolutions and the requirements of the IAEA, and underlines that further decisions will be required should such additional measures be necessary;

20. *Decides* to remain seized of the matter.

Resolution Annex I

1. Amir Moayyed Alai (involved in managing the assembly and engineering of centrifuges)

2. Mohammad Fedai Ashiani (involved in the production of ammonium uranyl carbonate and management of the Natanz enrichment complex)

3. Abbas Rezaee Ashtiani (a senior official at the AEOI Office of Exploration and Mining Affairs)

4. Haleh Bakhtiar (involved in the production of magnesium at a concentration of 99.9%)

5. Morteza Behzad (involved in making centrifuge components)
[8 more individuals were listed here]

Resolution Annex II

A. Individuals listed in resolution 1737 (2006)
1. Mohammad Qannadi, AEOI Vice President for Research & Development
2. Dawood Agha-Jani, Head of the PFEP (Natanz)
3. Behman Asgarpour, Operational Manager (Arak)
B. Individuals listed in resolution 1747 (2007)
1. Seyed Jaber Safdari (Manager of the Natanz Enrichment Facilities)
2. Amir Rahimi (Head of Esfahan Nuclear Fuel Research and Production Centre, which is part of the AEOI's Nuclear Fuel Production and Procurement Company, which is involved in enrichment-related activities)

Resolution Annex III

1. Abzar Boresh Kaveh Co. (BK Co.) (involved in the production of centrifuge components)

2. Barzagani Tejarat Tavanmad Saccal companies (subsidiary of Saccal System companies) (this company tried to purchase sensitive goods for an entity listed in resolution 1737 (2006))

3. Electro Sanam Company (E. S. Co./E. X. Co.) (AIO front-company, involved in the ballistic missile programme)
[9 more companies were listed here]

U.N. SECURITY COUNCIL RES. 1929 [re: Iran]
June 9, 2010*

The Security Council,

Recalling the Statement of its President . . . , and its resolutions 1696 (2006), 1737 (2006), 1747 (2007), 1803 (2008), 1835 (2008), and 1887 (2009) and *reaffirming* their provisions, . . .

---

* The vote was 12-2-1, with Brazil and Turkey voting against and Lebanon abstaining.

Noting with serious concern that, as confirmed by the reports of . . . , Iran has not established full and sustained suspension of all enrichment-related and reprocessing activities and heavy water-related projects as set out in resolutions 1696 (2006), 1737 (2006), 1747 (2007) and 1803 (2008) nor resumed its cooperation with the IAEA under the Additional Protocol, nor cooperated with the IAEA in connection with the remaining issues of concern, which need to be clarified to exclude the possibility of military dimensions of Iran's nuclear programme, nor taken the other steps required by the IAEA Board of Governors, nor complied with the provisions of Security Council resolutions 1696 (2006), 1737 (2006), 1747 (2007) and 1803 (2008) and which are essential to build confidence, and *deploring* Iran's refusal to take these steps, . . .

Noting with serious concern the role of elements of the Islamic Revolutionary Guard Corps (IRGC, also known as "Army of the Guardians of the Islamic Revolution"), including those specified in Annex D and E of resolution 1737 (2006), Annex I of resolution 1747 (2007) and Annex II of this resolution, in Iran's proliferation sensitive nuclear activities and the development of nuclear weapon delivery systems,

Noting with serious concern that Iran has constructed an enrichment facility at Qom in breach of its obligations to suspend all enrichment-related activities, and that Iran failed to notify it to the IAEA until September 2009, which is inconsistent with its obligations under the Subsidiary Arrangements to its Safeguards Agreement,

Also noting the resolution of the IAEA Board of Governors (GOV/2009/82), which urges Iran to suspend immediately construction at Qom, and to clarify the facility's purpose, chronology of design and construction, and calls upon Iran to confirm, as requested by the IAEA, that it has not taken a decision to construct, or authorize construction of, any other nuclear facility which has as yet not been declared to the IAEA,

Noting with serious concern that Iran has enriched uranium to 20 per cent, and did so without notifying the IAEA with sufficient time for it to adjust the existing safeguards procedures, . . .

Reiterating its determination to reinforce the authority of the IAEA, strongly supporting the role of the IAEA Board of Governors, and *commending* the IAEA for its efforts to resolve outstanding issues relating to Iran's nuclear programme,

Expressing the conviction that the suspension set out in paragraph 2 of resolution 1737 (2006) as well as full, verified Iranian compliance with the requirements set out by the IAEA Board of Governors would contribute to a diplomatic, negotiated solution that guarantees Iran's nuclear programme is for exclusively peaceful purposes,

Emphasizing the importance of political and diplomatic efforts to find a negotiated solution guaranteeing that Iran's nuclear programme is exclusively for peaceful purposes and *noting* in this regard the efforts of Turkey and Brazil towards an agreement with Iran on the Tehran Research Reactor that could serve as a confidence-building measure, . . .

Stressing that China, France, Germany, the Russian Federation, the United Kingdom and the United States are willing to take further concrete measures on exploring an overall strategy of resolving the Iranian nuclear issue through negotiation on the basis of their June 2006 proposals . . . and their June 2008 proposals . . . , and *noting* the confirmation by these countries that once the confidence of the international community in the exclusively peaceful nature of Iran's nuclear programme is restored it will be treated in the same manner as that of any Non-Nuclear Weapon State Party to the Treaty on the Non-Proliferation of Nuclear Weapons,

Welcoming the guidance issued by the Financial Action Task Force (FATF) to assist States in implementing their financial obligations under resolutions 1737 (2006) and 1803 (2008), and *recalling* in particular the need to exercise vigilance over transactions involving Iranian banks, including the Central Bank of Iran, so as to prevent such transactions contributing to proliferation-sensitive nuclear activities, or to the development of nuclear weapon delivery systems,

Recognizing that access to diverse, reliable energy is critical for sustainable growth and development, while noting the potential connection between Iran's revenues derived from its energy sector and the funding of Iran's proliferation-sensitive nuclear activities, and *further noting* that chemical process equipment and materials required for the petrochemical industry have much in common with those required for certain sensitive nuclear fuel cycle activities,

Having regard to States' rights and obligations relating to international trade, ...

Calling for the ratification of the Comprehensive Nuclear-Test-Ban Treaty by Iran at an early date,

Determined to give effect to its decisions by adopting appropriate measures to persuade Iran to comply with resolutions 1696 (2006), 1737 (2006), 1747 (2007) and 1803 (2008) and with the requirements of the IAEA, and also to constrain Iran's development of sensitive technologies in support of its nuclear and missile programmes, until such time as the Security Council determines that the objectives of these resolutions have been met,

Concerned by the proliferation risks presented by the Iranian nuclear programme and mindful of its primary responsibility under the Charter of the United Nations for the maintenance of international peace and security,

Stressing that nothing in this resolution compels States to take measures or actions exceeding the scope of this resolution, including the use of force or the threat of force,

Acting under Article 41 of Chapter VII of the Charter of the United Nations,

1. *Affirms* that Iran has so far failed to meet the requirements of the IAEA Board of Governors and to comply with resolutions 1696 (2006), 1737 (2006), 1747 (2007) and 1803 (2008);

2. *Affirms* that Iran shall without further delay take the steps required by the IAEA Board of Governors in its resolutions GOV/2006/14 and GOV/2009/

82, which are essential to build confidence in the exclusively peaceful purpose of its nuclear programme, to resolve outstanding questions and to address the serious concerns raised by the construction of an enrichment facility at Qom in breach of its obligations to suspend all enrichment-related activities, and, in this context, *further affirms* its decision that Iran shall without delay take the steps required in paragraph 2 of resolution 1737 (2006);

3. *Reaffirms* that Iran shall cooperate fully with the IAEA on all outstanding issues, particularly those which give rise to concerns about the possible military dimensions of the Iranian nuclear programme, including by providing access without delay to all sites, equipment, persons and documents requested by the IAEA, and *stresses* the importance of ensuring that the IAEA have all necessary resources and authority for the fulfilment of its work in Iran; . . .

5. *Decides* that Iran shall without delay comply fully and without qualification with its IAEA Safeguards Agreement, including through the application of modified Code 3.1 of the Subsidiary Arrangement to its Safeguards Agreement, *calls upon* Iran to act strictly in accordance with the provisions of the Additional Protocol to its IAEA Safeguards Agreement that it signed on 18 December 2003, *calls upon* Iran to ratify promptly the Additional Protocol, and *reaffirms* that, in accordance with Articles 24 and 39 of Iran's Safeguards Agreement, Iran's Safeguards Agreement and its Subsidiary Arrangement, including modified Code 3.1, cannot be amended or changed unilaterally by Iran, and *notes* that there is no mechanism in the Agreement for the suspension of any of the provisions in the Subsidiary Arrangement;

6. *Reaffirms* that, in accordance with Iran's obligations under previous resolutions to suspend all reprocessing, heavy water-related and enrichment-related activities, Iran shall not begin construction on any new uranium-enrichment, reprocessing, or heavy water-related facility and shall discontinue any ongoing construction of any uranium-enrichment, reprocessing, or heavy water-related facility;

7. *Decides* that Iran shall not acquire an interest in any commercial activity in another State involving uranium mining, production or use of nuclear materials and technology . . . , in particular uranium-enrichment and reprocessing activities, all heavy-water activities or technology-related to ballistic missiles capable of delivering nuclear weapons, and *further decides* that all States shall prohibit such investment in territories under their jurisdiction by Iran, its nationals, and entities incorporated in Iran or subject to its jurisdiction, or by persons or entities acting on their behalf or at their direction, or by entities owned or controlled by them;

8. *Decides* that all States shall prevent the direct or indirect supply, sale or transfer to Iran, from or through their territories or by their nationals or individuals subject to their jurisdiction, or using their flag vessels or aircraft, and whether or not originating in their territories, of any battle tanks, armoured combat vehicles, large calibre artillery systems, combat aircraft, attack helicopters, warships, missiles or missile systems . . . , decides further that all States shall prevent the provision to Iran by their nationals or from or

through their territories of technical training, financial resources or services, advice, other services or assistance related to the supply, sale, transfer, provision, manufacture, maintenance or use of such arms and related materiel, and, in this context, *calls upon* all States to exercise vigilance and restraint over the supply, sale, transfer, provision, manufacture and use of all other arms and related materiel;

9. *Decides* that Iran shall not undertake any activity related to ballistic missiles capable of delivering nuclear weapons, including launches using ballistic missile technology, and that States shall take all necessary measures to prevent the transfer of technology or technical assistance to Iran related to such activities;

10. *Decides* that all States shall take the necessary measures to prevent the entry into or transit through their territories of individuals designated in Annex C, D and E of resolution 1737 (2006), Annex I of resolution 1747 (2007), Annex I of resolution 1803 (2008) and Annexes I and II of this resolution, or by the Security Council or the Committee pursuant to paragraph 10 of resolution 1737 (2006), except . . . ;

11. *Decides* that the measures specified in paragraphs 12, 13, 14 and 15 of resolution 1737 (2006) shall apply also to the individuals and entities listed in Annex I of this resolution and to any individuals or entities acting on their behalf or at their direction, and to entities owned or controlled by them, including through illicit means, and to any individuals and entities determined by the Council or the Committee to have assisted designated individuals or entities in evading sanctions of, or in violating the provisions of, resolutions 1737 (2006), 1747 (2007), 1803 (2008) or this resolution;

12. *Decides* that the measures specified in paragraphs 12, 13, 14 and 15 of resolution 1737 (2006) shall apply also to the Islamic Revolutionary Guard Corps (IRGC, also known as "Army of the Guardians of the Islamic Revolution") individuals and entities specified in Annex II, and to any individuals or entities acting on their behalf or at their direction, and to entities owned or controlled by them, including through illicit means . . . ;

14. *Calls upon* all States to inspect, in accordance with their national authorities and legislation and consistent with international law, in particular the law of the sea and relevant international civil aviation agreements, all cargo to and from Iran, in their territory, including seaports and airports, if the State concerned has information that provides reasonable grounds to believe the cargo contains items the supply, sale, transfer, or export of which is prohibited by paragraphs 3, 4 or 7 of resolution 1737 (2006), paragraph 5 of resolution 1747 (2007), paragraph 8 of resolution 1803 (2008) or paragraphs 8 or 9 of this resolution, for the purpose of ensuring strict implementation of those provisions;

15. *Notes* that States, consistent with international law, in particular the law of the sea, may request inspections of vessels on the high seas with the consent of the flag State, and *calls upon* all States to cooperate in such inspections if there is information that provides reasonable grounds to be-

lieve the vessel is carrying items the supply, sale, transfer, or export of which is prohibited by [the U.N. resolutions cited in the paragraph above] . . .

16. *Decides* to authorize all States to, and that all States shall, seize and dispose of (such as through destruction, rendering inoperable, storage or transferring to a State other than the originating or destination States for disposal) items the supply, sale, transfer, or export of which is prohibited by [the U.N. resolutions] . . .

17. *Requires* any State, when it undertakes an inspection pursuant to paragraphs 14 or 15 above to submit to the Committee within five working days an initial written report containing, in particular, explanation of the grounds for the inspections, the results of such inspections and whether or not cooperation was provided, and, if items prohibited for transfer are found . . .

18. *Decides* that all States shall prohibit the provision by their nationals or from their territory of bunkering services, such as provision of fuel or supplies, or other servicing of vessels, to Iranian-owned or contracted vessels, including chartered vessels, if they have information that provides reasonable grounds to believe they are carrying items the supply, sale, transfer, or export of which is prohibited by [the U.N. resolutions], unless provision of such services is necessary for humanitarian purposes or until such time as the cargo has been inspected, and seized and disposed of if necessary, and *underlines* that this paragraph is not intended to affect legal economic activities; . . .

20. *Requests* all Member States to communicate to the Committee any information available on transfers or activity by Iran Air's cargo division or vessels owned or operated by the Islamic Republic of Iran Shipping Lines (IRISL) to other companies that may have been undertaken in order to evade the sanctions of, or in violation of the provisions of, resolutions 1737 (2006), 1747 (2007), 1803 (2008) or this resolution, including renaming or re-registering of aircraft, vessels or ships, and requests the Committee to make that information widely available;

21. *Calls upon* all States, in addition to implementing their obligations pursuant to resolutions 1737 (2006), 1747 (2007), 1803 (2008) and this resolution, to prevent the provision of financial services, including insurance or re-insurance, or the transfer to, through, or from their territory, or to or by their nationals or entities organized under their laws (including branches abroad), or persons or financial institutions in their territory, of any financial or other assets or resources if they have information that provides reasonable grounds to believe that such services, assets or resources could contribute to Iran's proliferation-sensitive nuclear activities, or the development of nuclear weapon delivery systems, including by freezing any financial or other assets or resources on their territories or that hereafter come within their territories, or that are subject to their jurisdiction or that hereafter become subject to their jurisdiction, that are related to such programmes or activities and applying enhanced monitoring to prevent all such transactions in accordance with their national authorities and legislation; . . .

23. *Calls upon* States to take appropriate measures that prohibit in their territories the opening of new branches, subsidiaries, or representative offices of Iranian banks, and also that prohibit Iranian banks from establishing new joint ventures, taking an ownership interest in or establishing or maintaining correspondent relationships with banks in their jurisdiction to prevent the provision of financial services if they have information that provides reasonable grounds to believe that these activities could contribute to Iran's proliferation-sensitive nuclear activities or the development of nuclear weapon delivery systems;

24. *Calls upon* States to take appropriate measures that prohibit financial institutions within their territories or under their jurisdiction from opening representative offices or subsidiaries or banking accounts in Iran if they have information that provides reasonable grounds to believe that such financial services could contribute to Iran's proliferation-sensitive nuclear activities or the development of nuclear weapon delivery systems; . . .

26. *Directs* the Committee to respond effectively to violations of the measures decided in resolutions 1737 (2006), 1747 (2007), 1803 (2008) and this resolution, and *recalls* that the Committee may designate individuals and entities who have assisted designated persons or entities in evading sanctions of, or in violating the provisions of, these resolutions;

27. *Decides* that the Committee shall intensify its efforts to promote the full implementation of resolutions 1737 (2006), 1747 (2007), 1803 (2008) and this resolution, including through a work programme covering compliance, investigations, outreach, dialogue, assistance and cooperation, to be submitted to the Council within forty-five days of the adoption of this resolution; . . .

29. *Requests* the Secretary-General to create for an initial period of one year, in consultation with the Committee, a group of up to eight experts ("Panel of Experts"), under the direction of the Committee, to carry out the following tasks: (a) assist the Committee in carrying out its mandate as specified in paragraph 18 of resolution 1737 (2006) and paragraph 28 of this resolution; (b) gather, examine and analyse information from States, relevant United Nations bodies and other interested parties regarding the implementation of the measures decided in resolutions 1737 (2006), 1747 (2007), 1803 (2008) and this resolution, in particular incidents of non-compliance; (c) make recommendations on actions the Council, or the Committee or State, may consider to improve implementation of the relevant measures; and (d) provide to the Council an interim report on its work no later than 90 days after the Panel's appointment, and a final report to the Council no later than 30 days prior to the termination of its mandate with its findings and recommendations;

30. *Urges* all States, relevant United Nations bodies and other interested parties, to cooperate fully with the Committee and the Panel of Experts, in particular by supplying any information at their disposal on the implementation of the measures decided in resolutions 1737 (2006), 1747 (2007), 1803 (2008) and this resolution, in particular incidents of non-compliance;

31. *Calls upon* all States to report to the Committee within 60 days of the adoption of this resolution on the steps they have taken with a view to implementing effectively paragraphs 7, 8, 9, 10, 11, 12, 13, 14, 15, 16, 17, 18, 19, 21, 22, 23 and 24;

32. *Stresses* the willingness of China, France, Germany, the Russian Federation, the United Kingdom and the United States to further enhance diplomatic efforts to promote dialogue and consultations, including to resume dialogue with Iran on the nuclear issue without preconditions, most recently in their meeting with Iran in Geneva on 1 October 2009, with a view to seeking a comprehensive, long-term and proper solution of this issue on the basis of the proposal made by China, France, Germany, the Russian Federation, the United Kingdom and the United States on 14 June 2008, which would allow for the development of relations and wider cooperation with Iran based on mutual respect and the establishment of international confidence in the exclusively peaceful nature of Iran's nuclear programme and, inter alia, starting formal negotiations with Iran on the basis of the June 2008 proposal, and *acknowledges with appreciation* that the June 2008 proposal, as attached in Annex IV to this resolution, remains on the table;

33. *Encourages* the High Representative of the European Union for Foreign Affairs and Security Policy to continue communication with Iran in support of political and diplomatic efforts to find a negotiated solution, . . . ;

35. *Emphasizes* the importance of all States, including Iran, taking the necessary measures to ensure that no claim shall lie at the instance of the Government of Iran, or of any person or entity in Iran, or of persons or entities designated pursuant to resolution 1737 (2006) and related resolutions, or any person claiming through or for the benefit of any such person or entity, in connection with any contract or other transaction where its performance was prevented by reason of the measures imposed by resolutions 1737 (2006), 1747 (2007), 1803 (2008) and this resolution;

36. *Requests* within 90 days a report from the Director General of the IAEA on whether Iran has established full and sustained suspension of all activities mentioned in resolution 1737 (2006), as well as on the process of Iranian compliance with all the steps required by the IAEA Board of Governors and with other provisions of resolutions 1737 (2006), 1747 (2007), 1803 (2008) and of this resolution, to the IAEA Board of Governors and in parallel to the Security Council for its consideration;

37. *Affirms* that it shall review Iran's actions in light of the report referred to in paragraph 36 above, to be submitted within 90 days, and: (a) that it shall suspend the implementation of measures if and for so long as Iran suspends all enrichment-related and reprocessing activities, including research and development, as verified by the IAEA, to allow for negotiations in good faith in order to reach an early and mutually acceptable outcome; (b) that it shall terminate the measures specified in paragraphs 3, 4, 5, 6, 7 and 12 of resolution 1737 (2006), as well as in paragraphs 2, 4, 5, 6 and 7 of resolution 1747 (2007), paragraphs 3, 5, 7, 8, 9, 10 and 11 of resolution 1803 (2008), and in paragraphs 7, 8, 9, 10, 11, 12, 13, 14, 15, 16, 17, 18, 19,

21, 22, 23 and 24 above, as soon as it determines, following receipt of the report referred to in the paragraph above, that Iran has fully complied with its obligations under the relevant resolutions of the Security Council and met the requirements of the IAEA Board of Governors, as confirmed by the IAEA Board of Governors; (c) that it shall, in the event that the report shows that Iran has not complied with resolutions 1737 (2006), 1747 (2007), 1803 (2008) and this resolution, adopt further appropriate measures under Article 41 of Chapter VII of the Charter of the United Nations to persuade Iran to comply with these resolutions and the requirements of the IAEA, and *underlines* that further decisions will be required should such additional measures be necessary;

38. *Decides* to remain seized of the matter.

Annex I

Individuals and entities involved in nuclear or ballistic missile activities

Entities

1. **Amin Industrial Complex**: Amin Industrial Complex sought temperature controllers which may be used in nuclear research and operational/production facilities. Amin Industrial Complex is owned or controlled by, or acts on behalf of, the Defense Industries Organization (DIO), which was designated in resolution 1737 (2006).

2. **Armament Industries Group**: Armament Industries Group (AIG) manufacturers and services a variety of small arms and light weapons, including large- and medium-calibre guns and related technology. AIG conducts the majority of its procurement activity through Hadid Industries Complex.

3. **Defense Technology and Science Research Center**: Defense Technology and Science Research Center (DTSRC) is owned or controlled by, or acts on behalf of, Iran's Ministry of Defense and Armed Forces Logistics (MOD-AFL), which oversees Iran's defence R&D, production, maintenance, exports, and procurement.

[Nineteen other entities are similarly listed in the Resolution.]

Individuals
Javad Rahiqi: Head of the Atomic Energy Organization of Iran (AEOI) Esfahan Nuclear Technology Center (additional information: DOB: 24 April 1954; POB: Marshad).

Annex II

Entities owned, controlled, or acting on behalf of the Islamic Revolutionary Guard Corps

1. **Fater (or Faater) Institute**: Khatam al-Anbiya (KAA) subsidiary. Fater has worked with foreign suppliers, likely on behalf of other KAA companies on IRGC projects in Iran.
2. **Gharagahe Sazandegi Ghaem**: Gharagahe Sazandegi Ghaem is owned or controlled by KAA.
3. **Ghorb Karbala**: Ghorb Karbala is owned or controlled by KAA.
[Twelve other entities are similarly listed under Annex II.]

Annex III

Entities owned, controlled, or acting on behalf of the Islamic Republic of Iran Shipping Lines (IRISL)

1. **Irano Hind Shipping Company**
   Location: 18 Mehrshad Street, Sadaghat Street, Opposite of Park Mellat, Vali-e-Asr Ave., Tehran, Iran; 265, Next to Mehrshad, Sedaghat St., Opposite of Mellat Park, Vali Asr Ave., Tehran 1A001, Iran
2. **IRISL Benelux NV** . . .
3. **South Shipping Line Iran** (SSL) . . .

Annex IV

Proposal to the Islamic Republic of Iran by China, France, Germany, the Russian Federation, the United Kingdom of Great Britain and Northern Ireland, the United States of America and the European Union

Presented to the Iranian authorities on 14 June 2008 Teheran . . . .

901

MATERIALS RE: LIBYA

U.N. SECURITY COUNCIL RES. 1970
(February 26, 2011)*

The Security Council,

Expressing grave concern at the situation in the Libyan Arab Jamahiriya and condemning the violence and use of force against civilians,

Deploring the gross and systematic violation of human rights, including the repression of peaceful demonstrators, expressing deep concern at the deaths of civilians, and rejecting unequivocally the incitement to hostility and violence against the civilian population made from the highest level of the Libyan government,

Welcoming the condemnation by the Arab League, the African Union, and the Secretary General of the Organization of the Islamic Conference of the serious violations of human rights and international humanitarian law that are being committed in the Libyan Arab Jamahiriya, . . .

Welcoming the Human Rights Council resolution A/HRC/RES/S-15/1 of 25 February 2011, including the decision to urgently dispatch an independent international commission of inquiry to investigate all alleged violations of international human rights law in the Libyan Arab Jamahiriya, to establish the facts and circumstances of such violations and of the crimes perpetrated, and where possible identify those responsible,

Considering that the widespread and systematic attacks currently taking place in the Libyan Arab Jamahiriya against the civilian population may amount to crimes against humanity,

Expressing concern at the plight of refugees forced to flee the violence in the Libyan Arab Jamahiriya,

Expressing concern also at the reports of shortages of medical supplies to treat the wounded,

Recalling the Libyan authorities' responsibility to protect its population,

Underlining the need to respect the freedoms of peaceful assembly and of expression, including freedom of the media,

* Adopted by a vote of 15-0.

Stressing the need to hold to account those responsible for attacks, including by forces under their control, on civilians,

Recalling article 16 of the Rome Statute under which no investigation or prosecution may be commenced or proceeded with by the International Criminal Court for a period of 12 months after a Security Council request to that effect,

Expressing concern for the safety of foreign nationals and their rights in the Libyan Arab Jamahiriya,

Reaffirming its strong commitment to the sovereignty, independence, territorial integrity and national unity of the Libyan Arab Jamahiriya.

Mindful of its primary responsibility for the maintenance of international peace and security under the Charter of the United Nations,

Acting under Chapter VII of the Charter of the United Nations, and taking measures under its Article 41,

1. *Demands* an immediate end to the violence and calls for steps to fulfil the legitimate demands of the population;

2. *Urges* the Libyan authorities to:

(a) Act with the utmost restraint, respect human rights and international humanitarian law, and allow immediate access for international human rights monitors;

(b) Ensure the safety of all foreign nationals and their assets and facilitate the departure of those wishing to leave the country;

(c) Ensure the safe passage of humanitarian and medical supplies, and humanitarian agencies and workers, into the country; and

(d) Immediately lift restrictions on all forms of media;

3. *Requests* all Member States, to the extent possible, to cooperate in the evacuation of those foreign nationals wishing to leave the country;

ICC referral

4. *Decides* to refer the situation in the Libyan Arab Jamahiriya since 15 February 2011 to the Prosecutor of the International Criminal Court;

5. *Decides* that the Libyan authorities shall cooperate fully with and provide any necessary assistance to the Court and the Prosecutor pursuant to this resolution and, while recognizing that States not party to the Rome Statute have no obligation under the Statute, urges all States and concerned regional and other international organizations to cooperate fully with the Court and the Prosecutor;

6. *Decides* that nationals, current or former officials or personnel from a State outside the Libyan Arab Jamahiriya which is not a party to the Rome Statute of the International Criminal Court shall be subject to the exclusive jurisdiction of that State for all alleged acts or omissions arising out of or related to operations in the Libyan Arab Jamahiriya established or authorized by the Council, unless such exclusive jurisdiction has been expressly waived by the State;

7. *Invites* the Prosecutor to address the Security Council within two months of the adoption of this resolution and every six months thereafter on actions taken pursuant to this resolution;

8. *Recognizes* that none of the expenses incurred in connection with the referral, including expenses related to investigations or prosecutions in connection with that referral, shall be borne by the United Nations and that such costs shall be borne by the parties to the Rome Statute and those States that wish to contribute voluntarily;

Arms embargo

9. *Decides* that all Member States shall immediately take the necessary measures to prevent the direct or indirect supply, sale or transfer to the Libyan Arab Jamahiriya, from or through their territories or by their nationals, or using their flag vessels or aircraft, of arms and related materiel of all types, including weapons and ammunition, military vehicles and equipment, paramilitary equipment, and spare parts for the aforementioned, and technical assistance, training, financial or other assistance, related to military activities or the provision, maintenance or use of any arms and related materiel, including the provision of armed mercenary personnel whether or not originating in their territories, and decides further that this measure shall not apply to:

(a) Supplies of non-lethal military equipment intended solely for humanitarian or protective use, and related technical assistance or training, as approved in advance by the Committee established pursuant to paragraph 24 below;

(b) Protective clothing, including flak jackets and military helmets, temporarily exported to the Libyan Arab Jamahiriya by United Nations personnel, representatives of the media and humanitarian and development workers and associated personnel, for their personal use only; or

(c) Other sales or supply of arms and related materiel, or provision of assistance or personnel, as approved in advance by the Committee;

10. *Decides* that the Libyan Arab Jamahiriya shall cease the export of all arms and related materiel and that all Member States shall prohibit the procurement of such items from the Libyan Arab Jamahiriya by their nationals, or using their flagged vessels or aircraft . . . ;

11. *Calls upon* all States, in particular States neighbouring the Libyan Arab Jamahiriya, to inspect . . . : [This paragraph was replaced by paragraph 13 of U.N. Security Council Res. 1973, which comes after this Resolution.]

12. *Decides* to authorize all Member States to, and that all Member States shall, upon discovery of items prohibited by paragraph 9 or 10 of this resolution, seize and dispose (such as through destruction, rendering inoperable, storage or transferring to a State other than the originating or destination States for disposal) items the supply, sale, transfer or export of which is prohibited by paragraphs 9 or 10 of this resolution and decides further that all Member States shall cooperate in such efforts;

13. *Requires* any Member State when it undertakes an inspection pursuant to paragraph 11 above, to submit promptly an initial written report to the Committee . . . ;

14. *Encourages* Member States to take steps to strongly discourage their nationals from travelling to the Libyan Arab Jamahiriya to participate in

activities on behalf of the Libyan authorities that could reasonably contribute to the violation of human rights;

Travel ban

15. *Decides* that all Member States shall take the necessary measures to prevent the entry into or transit through their territories of individuals listed in Annex I of this resolution or designated by the Committee established pursuant to paragraph 24 below, provided that nothing in this paragraph shall oblige a State to refuse its own nationals entry into its territory;

16. *Decides* that the measures imposed by paragraph 15 above shall not apply:

(a) Where the Committee determines on a case-by-case basis that such travel is justified on the grounds of humanitarian need, including religious obligation;

(b) Where entry or transit is necessary for the fulfilment of a judicial process;

(c) Where the Committee determines on a case-by-case basis that an exemption would further the objectives of peace and national reconciliation in the Libyan Arab Jamahiriya and stability in the region; or

(d) Where a State determines on a case-by-case basis that such entry or transit is required to advance peace and stability in the Libyan Arab Jamahiriya and the States subsequently notifies the Committee within forty-eight hours after making such a determination;

Asset freeze

17. *Decides* that all Member States shall freeze without delay all funds, other financial assets and economic resources which are on their territories, which are owned or controlled, directly or indirectly, by the individuals or entities listed in annex II of this resolution or designated by the Committee established pursuant to paragraph 24 below, or by individuals or entities acting on their behalf or at their direction, or by entities owned or controlled by them, and decides further that all Member States shall ensure that any funds, financial assets or economic resources are prevented from being made available by their nationals or by any individuals or entities within their territories, to or for the benefit of the individuals or entities listed in Annex II of this resolution or individuals designated by the Committee;

18. *Expresses* its intention to ensure that assets frozen pursuant to paragraph 17 shall at a later stage be made available to and for the benefit of the people of the Libyan Arab Jamahiriya;

19. *Decides* that the measures imposed by paragraph 17 above do not apply to funds, other financial assets or economic resources that have been determined by relevant Member States:

(a) To be necessary for basic expenses, including payment for foodstuffs, rent or mortgage, medicines and medical treatment, taxes, insurance premiums, and public utility charges or exclusively for payment of reasonable professional fees and reimbursement of incurred expenses associated with the provision of legal services in accordance with national laws, or fees or service charges, in accordance with national laws, for routine holding or maintenance of frozen funds, other financial assets and economic resources, after notification by the relevant State to the Committee of the intention to authorize, where appropriate, access to such funds, other financial assets or economic resources and in the absence of a negative decision by the Committee within five working days of such notification;

(b) To be necessary for extraordinary expenses, provided that such determination has been notified by the relevant State or Member States to the Committee and has been approved by the Committee; or

(c) To be the subject of a judicial, administrative or arbitral lien or judgment, in which case the funds, other financial assets and economic resources may be used to satisfy that lien or judgment provided that the lien or judgment was entered into prior to the date of the present resolution, is not for the benefit of a person or entity designated pursuant to paragraph 17 above, and has been notified by the relevant State or Member States to the Committee;

20. *Decides* that Member States may permit the addition to the accounts frozen pursuant to the provisions of paragraph 17 above of interests or other earnings due on those accounts or payments due under contracts, agreements or obligations that arose prior to the date on which those accounts became subject to the provisions of this resolution, provided that any such interest, other earnings and payments continue to be subject to these provisions and are frozen;

21. *Decides* that the measures in paragraph 17 above shall not prevent a designated person or entity from making payment due under a contract entered into prior to the listing of such a person or entity, provided that the relevant States have determined that the payment is not directly or indirectly received by a person or entity designated pursuant to paragraph 17 above . . . ;

Designation criteria

22. *Decides* that the measures contained in paragraphs 15 and 17 shall apply to the individuals and entities designated by the Committee, pursuant to paragraph 24 (b) and (c), respectively;

(a) Involved in or complicit in ordering, controlling, or otherwise directing, the commission of serious human rights abuses against persons in the Libyan Arab Jamahiriya, including by being involved in or complicit in planning, commanding, ordering or conducting attacks, in violation of international law, including aerial bombardments, on civilian populations and facilities; or

(b) Acting for or on behalf of or at the direction of individuals or entities identified in subparagraph (a).

23. *Strongly encourages* Member States to submit to the Committee names of individuals who meet the criteria set out in paragraph 22 above;

New Sanctions Committee

24. *Decides* to establish, in accordance with rule 28 of its provisional rules of procedure, a Committee of the Security Council consisting of all the

members of the Council (herein "the Committee"), to undertake to following tasks:

(a) To monitor implementation of the measures imposed in paragraphs 9, 10, 15, and 17;

(b) To designate those individuals subject to the measures imposed by paragraphs 15 and to consider requests for exemptions in accordance with paragraph 16 above;

(c) To designate those individuals subject to the measures imposed by paragraph 17 above and to consider requests for exemptions in accordance with paragraphs 19 and 20 above;

(d) To establish such guidelines as may be necessary to facilitate the implementation of the measures imposed above;

(e) To report within thirty days to the Security Council on its work for the first report and thereafter to report as deemed necessary by the Committee; . . .

(g) To seek from all States whatever information it may consider useful regarding the actions taken by them to implement effectively the measures imposed above;

(h) To examine and take appropriate action on information regarding alleged violations or non-compliance with the measures contained in this resolution;

25. *Calls upon* all Member States to report to the Committee within 120 days of the adoption of this resolution on the steps they have taken with a view to implementing effectively paragraphs 9, 10, 15 and 17 above;

Humanitarian assistance

26. *Calls upon* all Member States, working together and acting in cooperation with the Secretary General, to facilitate and support the return of humanitarian agencies and make available humanitarian and related assistance in the Libyan Arab Jamahiriya, and requests the States concerned to keep the Security Council regularly informed on the progress of actions undertaken pursuant to this paragraph, and expresses its readiness to consider taking additional appropriate measures, as necessary, to achieve this;

Commitment to review

27. *Affirms* that it shall keep the Libyan authorities' actions under continuous review and that it shall be prepared to review the appropriateness of the measures contained in this resolution, including the strengthening, modification, suspension or lifting of the measures, as may be needed at any time in light of the Libyan authorities' compliance with relevant provisions of this resolution;

28. *Decides* to remain actively seized of the matter.

Annex I

Travel ban

1. Al-Baghdadi, Dr Abdulqader Mohammed
   Passport number: B010574. Date of birth: 01/07/1950.
   Head of the Liaison Office of the Revolutionary Committees. Revolutionary Committees involved in violence against demonstrators.
2. Dibri, Abdulqader Yusef
   Date of birth: 1946. Place of birth: Houn, Libya.
   Head of Muammar Qadhafi's personal security. Responsibility for regime security. History of directing violence against dissidents.
3. Dorda, Abu Zayd Umar
   Director, External Security Organisation. Regime loyalist. Head of external intelligence agency.
4. Jabir, Major General Abu Bakr Yunis
   Date of birth: 1952. Place of birth: Jalo, Libya.
   Defence Minister. Overall responsibility for actions of armed forces.
5. Matuq, Matuq Mohammed
   Date of birth: 1956. Place of birth: Khoms.
   Secretary for Utilities. Senior member of regime. Involvement with Revolutionary Committees. Past history of involvement in suppression of dissent and violence.
6. Qadhaf Al-dam, Sayyid Mohammed
   Date of birth: 1948. Place of birth: Sirte, Libya.
   Cousin of Muammar Qadhafi. In the 1980s, Sayyid was involved in the dissident assassination campaign and allegedly responsible for several deaths in Europe. He is also thought to have been involved in arms procurement.
7. Qadhafi, Aisha Muammar
   Date of birth: 1978. Place of birth: Tripoli, Libya.
   Daughter of Muammar Qadhafi. Closeness of association with regime.
8. Qadhafi, Hannibal Muammar
   Passport number: B/002210. Date of birth: 20/09/1975. Place of birth: Tripoli, Libya. Son of Muammar Qadhafi. Closeness of association with regime.
9. Qadhafi, Khamis Muammar
   Date of birth: 1978. Place of birth: Tripoli, Libya.
   Son of Muammar Qadhafi. Closeness of association with regime. Command of military units involved in repression of demonstrations.
10. Qadhafi, Mohammed Muammar
   Date of birth: 1970. Place of birth: Tripoli, Libya.
   Son of Muammar Qadhafi. Closeness of association with regime.

11. Qadhafi, Muammar Mohammed Abu Minyar
    Date of birth: 1942. Place of birth: Sirte, Libya.
    Leader of the Revolution, Supreme Commander of Armed Forces.
    Responsibility for ordering repression of demonstrations, human
    rights abuses.
12. Qadhafi, Mutassim. . . .
13. Qadhafi, Saadi. . . .
14. Qadhafi, Saif al-Arab. . . .
15. Qadhafi, Saif al-Islam. . . .
16. Al-Senussi, Colonel Abdullah. . . .

Annex II

Asset freeze

1. Qadhafi, Aisha Muammar. . . .
2. Qadhafi, Hannibal Muammar. . . .
3. Qadhafi, Khamis Muammar. . . .
4. Qadhafi, Muammar Mohammed Abu Minyar. . . .
5. Qadhafi, Mutassim. . . .
6. Qadhafi, Saif al-Islam. . . .

U.N. SECURITY COUNCIL RES. 1973
(March 17, 2011)*

The Security Council,
Recalling its resolution 1970 (2011) of 26 February 2011,
Deploring the failure of the Libyan authorities to comply with resolution 1970 (2011),
Expressing grave concern at the deteriorating situation, the escalation of violence, and the heavy civilian casualties,
Reiterating the responsibility of the Libyan authorities to protect the Libyan population and *reaffirming* that parties to armed conflicts bear the primary responsibility to take all feasible steps to ensure the protection of civilians,
Condemning the gross and systematic violation of human rights, including arbitrary detentions, enforced disappearances, torture and summary executions,

---

* Adopted by a vote of 10-0, with 5 abstentions (Brazil, China, Germany, India, and Russia).

Further condemning acts of violence and intimidation committed by the Libyan authorities against journalists, media professionals and associated personnel and *urging* these authorities to comply with their obligations under international humanitarian law as outlined in resolution 1738 (2006),

Considering that the widespread and systematic attacks currently taking place in the Libyan Arab Jamahiriya against the civilian population may amount to crimes against humanity, . . .

Expressing its determination to ensure the protection of civilians and civilian populated areas and the rapid and unimpeded passage of humanitarian assistance and the safety of humanitarian personnel,

Recalling the condemnation by the League of Arab States, the African Union, and the Secretary General of the Organization of the Islamic Conference of the serious violations of human rights and international humanitarian law that have been and are being committed in the Libyan Arab Jamahiriya, . . .

Taking note also of the decision of the Council of the League of Arab States of 12 March 2011 to call for the imposition of a no-fly zone on Libyan military aviation, and to establish safe areas in places exposed to shelling as a precautionary measure that allows the protection of the Libyan people and foreign nationals residing in the Libyan Arab Jamahiriya, . . .

Recalling its decision to refer the situation in the Libyan Arab Jamahiriya since 15 February 2011 to the Prosecutor of the International Criminal Court, and *stressing* that those responsible for or complicit in attacks targeting the civilian population, including aerial and naval attacks, must be held to account,

Reiterating its concern at the plight of refugees and foreign workers forced to flee the violence in the Libyan Arab Jamahiriya, *welcoming* the response of neighbouring States, in particular Tunisia and Egypt, to address the needs of those refugees and foreign workers, and *calling on* the international community to support those efforts, . . .

Considering that the establishment of a ban on all flights in the airspace of the Libyan Arab Jamahiriya constitutes an important element for the protection of civilians as well as the safety of the delivery of humanitarian assistance and a decisive step for the cessation of hostilities in Libya,

Welcoming the appointment by the Secretary General of his Special Envoy to Libya, Mr. Abdel-Elah Mohamed Al-Khatib and supporting his efforts to find a sustainable and peaceful solution to the crisis in the Libyan Arab Jamahiriya,

Reaffirming its strong commitment to the sovereignty, independence, territorial integrity and national unity of the Libyan Arab Jamahiriya,

Determining that the situation in the Libyan Arab Jamahiriya continues to constitute a threat to international peace and security,

Acting under Chapter VII of the Charter of the United Nations,

1. *Demands* the immediate establishment of a cease-fire and a complete end to violence and all attacks against, and abuses of, civilians; . . .

3. *Demands* that the Libyan authorities comply with their obligations under international law, including international humanitarian law, human rights and refugee law and take all measures to protect civilians and meet their basic needs, and to ensure the rapid and unimpeded passage of humanitarian assistance;

Protection of civilians

4. *Authorizes* Member States that have notified the Secretary-General, acting nationally or through regional organizations or arrangements, and acting in cooperation with the Secretary-General, to take all necessary measures, notwithstanding paragraph 9 of resolution 1970 (2011), to protect civilians and civilian populated areas under threat of attack in the Libyan Arab Jamahiriya, including Benghazi, while excluding a foreign occupation force of any form on any part of Libyan territory, and *requests* the Member States concerned to inform the Secretary-General immediately of the measures they take pursuant to the authorization conferred by this paragraph which shall be immediately reported to the Security Council;

5. *Recognizes* the important role of the League of Arab States in matters relating to the maintenance of international peace and security in the region, and bearing in mind Chapter VIII of the Charter of the United Nations, requests the Member States of the League of Arab States to cooperate with other Member States in the implementation of paragraph 4;

No Fly Zone

6. *Decides* to establish a ban on all flights in the airspace of the Libyan Arab Jamahiriya in order to help protect civilians;

7. *Decides further* that the ban imposed by paragraph 6 shall not apply to flights whose sole purpose is humanitarian, such as delivering or facilitating the delivery of assistance, including medical supplies, food, humanitarian workers and related assistance, or evacuating foreign nationals from the Libyan Arab Jamahiriya, nor shall it apply to flights authorised by paragraphs 4 or 8, nor other flights which are deemed necessary by States acting under the authorisation conferred in paragraph 8 to be for the benefit of the Libyan people, and that these flights shall be coordinated with any mechanism established under paragraph 8;

8. *Authorizes* Member States that have notified the Secretary-General and the Secretary-General of the League of Arab States, acting nationally or through regional organizations or arrangements, to take all necessary measures to enforce compliance with the ban on flights imposed by paragraph 6 above, as necessary, and *requests* the States concerned in cooperation with the League of Arab States to coordinate closely with the Secretary General on the measures they are taking to implement this ban, including by establishing an appropriate mechanism for implementing the provisions of paragraphs 6 and 7 above;

9. *Calls upon* all Member States, acting nationally or through regional organizations or arrangements, to provide assistance, including any

necessary over-flight approvals, for the purposes of implementing paragraphs 4, 6, 7 and 8 above;

10. *Requests* the Member States concerned to coordinate closely with each other and the Secretary-General on the measures they are taking to implement paragraphs 4, 6, 7 and 8 above . . . ;

11. *Decides* that the Member States concerned shall inform the Secretary-General and the Secretary-General of the League of Arab States immediately of measures taken in exercise of the authority conferred by paragraph 8 above, including to supply a concept of operations;

12. *Requests* the Secretary-General to inform the Council immediately of any actions taken by the Member States concerned in exercise of the authority conferred by paragraph 8 above and to report to the Council within 7 days and every month thereafter on the implementation of this resolution . . . ;

Enforcement of the arms embargo

13. *Decides that* paragraph 11 of resolution 1970 (2011) shall be replaced by the following paragraph : "Calls upon all Member States, in particular States of the region, acting nationally or through regional organisations or arrangements, in order to ensure strict implementation of the arms embargo established by paragraphs 9 and 10 of resolution 1970 (2011), to inspect in their territory, including seaports and airports, and on the high seas, vessels and aircraft bound to or from the Libyan Arab Jamahiriya, if the State concerned has information that provides reasonable grounds to believe that the cargo contains items the supply, sale, transfer or export of which is prohibited by paragraphs 9 or 10 of resolution 1970 (2011) as modified by this resolution, including the provision of armed mercenary personnel, *calls upon* all flag States of such vessels and aircraft to cooperate with such inspections and authorises Member States to use all measures commensurate to the specific circumstances to carry out such inspections";

14. *Requests* Member States which are taking action under paragraph 13 above on the high seas to coordinate closely with each other and the Secretary-General and *further requests* the States concerned to inform the Secretary-General and the Committee established pursuant to paragraph 24 of resolution 1970 (2011) ("the Committee") immediately of measures taken . . . ;

15. *Requires* any Member State whether acting nationally or through regional organisations or arrangements, when it undertakes an inspection pursuant to paragraph 13 above, to submit promptly an initial written report to the Committee . . . ;

16. *Deplores* the continuing flows of mercenaries into the Libyan Arab Jamahiriya and *calls upon* all Member States to comply strictly with their obligations under paragraph 9 of resolution 1970 (2011) to prevent the provision of armed mercenary personnel to the Libyan Arab Jamahiriya;

Ban on flights

17. *Decides* that all States shall deny permission to any aircraft registered in the Libyan Arab Jamahiriya or owned or operated by Libyan nationals or

companies to take off from, land in or overfly their territory unless the particular flight has been approved in advance by the Committee, or in the case of an emergency landing;

18. *Decides that* all States shall deny permission to any aircraft to take off from, land in or overfly their territory, if they have information that provides reasonable grounds to believe that the aircraft contains items the supply, sale, transfer, or export of which is prohibited by paragraphs 9 and 10 of resolution 1970 (2011) as modified by this resolution, including the provision of armed mercenary personnel, except in the case of an emergency landing;

Asset freeze

19. *Decides* that the asset freeze imposed by paragraph 17, 19, 20 and 21 of resolution 1970 (2011) shall apply to all funds, other financial assets and economic resources which are on their territories, which are owned or controlled, directly or indirectly, by the Libyan authorities, as designated by the Committee, or by individuals or entities acting on their behalf or at their direction, or by entities owned or controlled by them, as designated by the Committee, and *decides further* that all States shall ensure that any funds, financial assets or economic resources are prevented from being made available by their nationals or by any individuals or entities within their territories, to or for the benefit of the Libyan authorities, as designated by the Committee, or individuals or entities acting on their behalf or at their direction, or entities owned or controlled by them, as designated by the Committee, . . . ;

20. *Affirms* its determination to ensure that assets frozen pursuant to paragraph 17 of resolution 1970 (2011) shall, at a later stage, as soon as possible be made available to and for the benefit of the people of the Libyan Arab Jamahiriya;

21. *Decides* that all States shall require their nationals, persons subject to their jurisdiction and firms incorporated in their territory or subject to their jurisdiction to exercise vigilance when doing business with entities incorporated in the Libyan Arab Jamahiriya or subject to its jurisdiction, and any individuals or entities acting on their behalf or at their direction, and entities owned or controlled by them, if the States have information that provides reasonable grounds to believe that such business could contribute to violence and use of force against civilians;

Designations

22. *Decides* that the individuals listed in Annex I shall be subject to the travel restrictions imposed in paragraphs 15 and 16 of resolution 1970 (2011), and *decides* further that the individuals and entities listed in Annex II shall be subject to the asset freeze imposed in paragraphs 17, 19, 20 and 21 of resolution 1970 (2011);

23. *Decides* that the measures specified in paragraphs 15, 16, 17, 19, 20 and 21 of resolution 1970 (2011) shall apply also to individuals and entities determined by the Council or the Committee to have violated the provisions

of resolution 1970 (2011), particularly paragraphs 9 and 10 thereof, or to have assisted others in doing so;

Panel of Experts

24. *Requests* the Secretary-General to create for an initial period of one year, in consultation with the Committee, a group of up to eight experts ("Panel of Experts"), under the direction of the Committee to carry out the following tasks:

(a) Assist the Committee in carrying out its mandate as specified in paragraph 24 of resolution 1970 (2011) and this resolution;

(b) Gather, examine and analyse information from States, relevant United Nations bodies, regional organisations and other interested parties regarding the implementation of the measures decided in resolution 1970 (2011) and this resolution, in particular incidents of non-compliance;

(c) Make recommendations on actions the Council, or the Committee or State, may consider to improve implementation of the relevant measures; . . .

25. *Urges* all States, relevant United Nations bodies and other interested parties, to cooperate fully with the Committee and the Panel of Experts, in particular by supplying any information at their disposal on the implementation of the measures decided in resolution 1970 (2011) and this resolution, in particular incidents of non-compliance;

26. *Decides* that the mandate of the Committee as set out in paragraph 24 of resolution 1970 (2011) shall also apply to the measures decided in this resolution;

27. *Decides* that all States, including the Libyan Arab Jamahiriya, shall take the necessary measures to ensure that no claim shall lie at the instance of the Libyan authorities, or of any person or body in the Libyan Arab Jamahiriya, or of any person claiming through or for the benefit of any such person or body, in connection with any contract or other transaction where its performance was affected by reason of the measures taken by the Security Council in resolution 1970 (2011), this resolution and related resolutions;

28. *Reaffirms* its intention to keep the actions of the Libyan authorities under continuous review and underlines its readiness to review at any time the measures imposed by this resolution and resolution 1970 (2011), including by strengthening, suspending or lifting those measures, as appropriate, based on compliance by the Libyan authorities with this resolution and resolution 1970 (2011).

29. *Decides* to remain actively seized of the matter.

Libya: UNSCR proposed designations

Number	Name	Justification	Identifiers
Annex I: Travel Ban			
1	QUREN SALIH QUREN AL QADHAFI	Libyan Ambassador to Chad. Has left Chad for Sabha. Involved directly in recruiting and coordinating mercenaries for the regime.	
2	Colonel AMID HUSAIN AL KUNI	Governor of Ghat (South Libya). Directly involved in recruiting mercenaries.	

Number	Name	Justification	Identifiers
Annex II: Asset Freeze			
1	Dorda, Abu Zayd Umar	Position: Director, External Security Organisation	
2	Jabir, Major General Abu Bakr Yunis	Position: Defence Minister	**Title**: Major General **DOB**: –/–/ 1952. **POB**: Jalo, Libya
3	Matuq, Matuq Mohammed	Position: Secretary for Utilities	**DOB**: –/–/1956. **POB**: Khoms
4	Qadhafi, Mohammed Muammar	Son of Muammar Qadhafi. Closeness of association with regime	**DOB**: –/–/1970. **POB**: Tripoli, Libya
5	Qadhafi, Saadi	Commander Special Forces. Son of Muammar Qadhafi. Closeness of association with regime.	

Number	Name	Justification	Identifiers
		Command of military units involved in repression of demonstrations	
6	Qadhafi, Saif al-Arab	Son of Muammar Qadhafi. Closeness of association with regime	**DOB**: –/–/1982. **POB**: Tripoli, Libya
7	Al-Senussi, Colonel Abdullah	Position: Director Military Intelligence	**Title**: Colonel **DOB**: –/–/ 1949. **POB**: Sudan

Entities

Number	Name	Justification	Identifiers
1	Central Bank of Libya	Under control of Muammar Qadhafi and his family, and potential source of funding for his regime.	
2	Libyan Investment Authority	Under control of Muammar Qadhafi and his family, and potential source of funding for his regime.	**a.k.a**: Libyan Arab Foreign Investment Company (LAFICO) . . .
3	Libyan Foreign Bank	Under control of Muammar Qadhafi and his family and a potential source of funding for his regime.	
4	Libyan Africa Investment Portfolio	Under control of Muammar Qadhafi and his family, and potential source of funding for his regime.	**Address**: Jamahiriya Street, LAP Building, PO Box 91330, Tripoli, Libya
5	Libyan National Oil Corporation	Under control of Muammar Qadhafi and his family, and potential source of funding for his regime.	**Address**: Bashir Saadwi Street, Tripoli, Tarabulus, Libya

12

International Criminal Law

TREATY ON MUTUAL LEGAL ASSISTANCE IN CRIMINAL MATTERS BETWEEN FRANCE AND THE UNITED STATES OF AMERICA

2172 U.N.T.S. 69*

The President of the French Republic and the President of the United States of America,

Desiring to establish more effective cooperation in the area of mutual legal assistance in criminal matters;

Have decided to conclude a treaty on mutual legal assistance in criminal matters . . .

Have agreed as follows:

Article 1.   Scope of Assistance

1. The Contracting States undertake to afford each other, in accordance with the provisions of this Treaty, the widest measure of mutual assistance in investigations or proceedings in respect of criminal offenses the punishment of which, at the time of the request for assistance, is a matter for the judicial authorities of the Requesting State.

2. This Treaty does not apply to:

(a) the execution of requests for provisional arrest and extradition;

(b) the enforcement of criminal judgments except for forfeiture decisions referred to in Article 11; or,

(c) offenses under military law that do not constitute offenses under ordinary criminal law.

3. This Treaty is intended solely for mutual legal assistance between the States. The provisions of the Treaty shall not affect the exercise of rights

---

*Signed in Paris on December 10, 1998. Entered into force on December 1, 2001.

otherwise available to private persons under the laws of the State presented with a claim based on such rights.

Article 2. Central Authorities

1. Each State shall designate a Central Authority to make and receive requests pursuant to this Treaty. For France, the Central Authority is the Ministry of Justice. For the United States of America, the Central Authority is the Attorney General or a person designated by the Attorney General. The Central Authorities shall communicate directly with one another for the purposes of this Treaty.

2. The Central Authorities shall consult, at times to which they mutually agree, to promote the most effective use of this Treaty. The Central Authorities shall agree on such practical measures as may be necessary to facilitate the implementation of this Treaty, in particular those related to the implementation of Article 9.

3. The Central Authorities shall provide each other with information regarding the execution of requests and each shall respond to the other's requests regarding progress toward execution of specific requests.

Article 3. Competent Authorities

The Central Authorities shall make requests emanating from competent authorities. For France, the competent authorities are the judicial authorities including the public prosecutor. For the United States of America, the competent authorities are prosecutors and authorities with statutory or regulatory responsibility for investigations of criminal offenses, including the referral of matters to prosecutors for criminal prosecution. The presentation by the Central Authority of the United States of America of a request coming from such authorities establishes the competence of those authorities.

Article 4. Contents of Requests

1. Requests for assistance shall be in writing and shall include the following information:

(a) the identity of the competent authority from whom the request emanates;

(b) a description of the nature of the investigation or proceeding, including the facts on which the request is based, and a statement of the purpose for which the assistance is sought;

(c) the text of the applicable criminal statute;

(d) insofar as possible, the identity and nationality of the person who is the subject of the investigation or proceeding;

(e) insofar as possible, the identity, nationality, and address or location of any person to be served or from whom assistance is sought;

(f) a description of the evidence or other assistance sought including, where appropriate, a list of questions if testimony of a witness or questioning of a person who is the subject of the investigation or proceeding is requested; and

(g) the details of any particular procedure that the Requesting State wishes to be followed.

2. Where appropriate, the Requesting State may indicate any time limit within which the assistance should be provided.

Article 5. Transmission of Requests

Requests shall be sent by the Central Authority of the Requesting State to the Central Authority of the Requested State. The results of execution shall be returned through the same channel unless the Central Authorities agree otherwise. . . .

Article 6. Denial of Assistance

1. Legal assistance may be denied if the Requested State considers that:

(a) the offense to which the request relates is a political offense or an offense related to a political offense; or

(b) execution of the request would prejudice its sovereignty, security, public order, or other essential interests.

2. Before denial of a request for assistance, the Central Authority of the Requested State shall consult with the Central Authority of the Requesting State to consider whether assistance can be given subject to such conditions as the Requested State deems to be necessary.

3. If a request for assistance is denied, the Central Authority of the Requested State shall inform the Central Authority of the Requesting State of the reasons for the denial.

Article 7. Postponing Execution

If the Requested State determines that execution of a request would interfere with an ongoing criminal investigation or proceeding in that State, it may, after consultations between the Central Authorities, postpone execution, including transmission, or make execution subject to conditions determined to be necessary. If the Requesting State accepts the assistance subject to the conditions, it shall comply with the conditions.

Article 8. Execution of Requests

1. Requests shall be executed in accordance with the provisions of this Treaty and the laws of the Requested State.

2. The Central Authority of the Requested State shall make all necessary arrangements for a request to be presented to its competent administrative and judicial authorities for execution. Administrative and judicial authorities charged with the execution of a request shall use all necessary measures available under the laws of the Requested State to provide any form of

assistance, not prohibited by its laws, necessary or useful for the execution of the request.

3. A person giving testimony or evidence in the Requested State may assert such claims of immunity, incapacity, or privilege as are available under its laws. If such person asserts a claim under the laws of the Requesting State, the person's testimony or evidence shall be taken and the claim recorded and preserved for consideration by the judicial authorities of the Requesting State. If, within a reasonable time prior to giving testimony or evidence, such person notifies the executing authority of the Requested State of the intention to assert such a claim, the Central Authorities may consult with respect thereto.

4. A person who gives false testimony in the execution of a request shall be subject to prosecution and punishment in the Requested State in accordance with its laws.

Article 9. Specific Procedures

1. If the Requesting State requests, the Requested State shall inform it of the dates and places of the execution of the request. The authorities and persons designated by the Requesting State may be permitted to be present at, and may assist in, the execution of the request if the Requested State consents. The Requested State shall permit such designated authorities and persons to be present at and assist in the taking of depositions for use in a judicial proceeding in the Requesting State subject to, in particular, the application of Articles 6 and 7.

2. The procedures specified in this paragraph and outlined in the request shall be carried out insofar as they are not contrary to the fundamental principles of a judicial proceeding in the Requested State. The Requested State, if the Requesting State requests, shall:

(a) take the testimony of witnesses or experts under oath, or question persons who are the subject of investigations or proceedings;

(b) allow a confrontation between a defendant, together with counsel, and a witness or expert whose testimony or evidence is taken for use against that defendant in a criminal prosecution in the Requesting State;

(c) ask questions submitted by the Requesting State, including questions proposed by authorities of the Requesting State present at the execution of the request;

(d) record or allow to be recorded the testimony, questioning, or confrontation; and

(e) produce or allow to be produced a verbatim transcript of the proceeding in which the testimony, questioning, or confrontation occurs.

3. If the Requesting State requests, the Requested State shall transmit Original documents or records to the extent possible. Otherwise, the Requested State shall transmit true copies thereof.

4. If the Requesting State requests, business records, whether originals or copies, shall be accompanied by:

(a) a certificate such as Form A appended to this Treaty; or

(b) a procés-verbal containing the essential information sought in Form A. Such records shall be admissible in evidence in the Requesting State as proof of the truth of the matters set forth therein.

Article 10. Search and Seizure

1. The Requested State shall execute a request for the search, seizure, and delivery of any item to the Requesting State if the request includes the information justifying such search under the laws of the Requested State.

2. If the Requesting State requests, a competent authority in the Requested State shall provide a certificate or procés-verbal that:

(a) identifies the item seized;

(b) identifies every official who has had custody of the item seized; and

(c) describes the circumstances of custody. If, after seizure, any transfer of custody of or material change in the item seized occurs, the competent authority in the Requested State shall provide an additional certificate or procés-verbal that describes the circumstances of such transfer of custody or material change. No further proof of the identity of the item, the continuity of custody, or the integrity of its condition shall be required. The certificates or procés-verbaux shall be admissible in evidence in the Requesting State as proof thereof.

Article 11. Proceeds of Offenses

1. Upon the request of the Requesting State, the Requested State shall provide assistance for proceedings related to the forfeiture of proceeds or instrumentalities of criminal offenses.

2. Upon the request of the Requesting State, the Requested State shall take appropriate measures, in accordance with its laws, to locate and identify proceeds or instrumentalities of offenses within the Requested State. The request shall specify the reasons for believing that proceeds or instrumentalities are within the Requested State. The Requested State shall inform the Requesting State of the results of its inquiry.

3. At the request of the Requesting State, the Requested State, based on facts that would constitute an offense under the laws of both States and to the extent permitted by its laws, may take protective measures to immobilize temporarily such proceeds or instrumentalities to ensure their availability for forfeiture.

4. At the request of the Requesting State, the Requested State may execute a final decision of forfeiture pronounced by judicial authorities of the Requesting State. The execution of such a request shall be in accordance with the laws of the Requested State.

5. The Requested State that executes a final forfeiture decision shall dispose of the forfeited proceeds and instrumentalities in accordance with its laws. As it determines appropriate, the Requested State also may transfer all or part of such assets, or the proceeds of their sale, to the Requesting

State. Insofar as cooperation between the two States contributed to a final forfeiture decision, the forfeiting State, to the extent permitted by its laws and upon such terms as it deems to be appropriate, may transfer all or part of such assets, or the proceeds of their sale, to the other State.

Article 12.   Return of Evidence

1. Articles of evidence, including original documents and records, transmitted pursuant to a request shall be retained by the Requesting State unless the Requested State asks at the time of transmission for their return.

2. The Requested State may require that the Requesting State agree to terms and conditions for the care and return of articles of evidence deemed to be necessary to protect third party interests.

Article 13.   Restitution

The States shall assist each other to the extent permitted by their respective laws to facilitate restitution.

Article 14.   Confidentiality

1. The Requested State shall use its best efforts to keep confidential a request and its contents if such confidentiality is requested by the Central Authority of the Requesting State. If the request cannot be executed without breaching such confidentiality, the Central Authority of the Requested State shall so inform the Central Authority of the Requesting State, which shall then determine whether the request should nevertheless be executed.

2. The Central Authority of the Requested State may request that information or evidence furnished under this Treaty be kept confidential or be used only subject to terms and conditions it may specify. If the Requesting State accepts the information or evidence subject to such conditions, the Requesting State shall use its best efforts to comply with the conditions.

3. The Central Authority of the Requested State may request that the Requesting State not use any information or evidence obtained under this Treaty in any investigation or proceeding other than that described in the request without the prior consent of the Requested State. In that event, the Requesting State shall comply with the condition,

4. Nothing in this Article shall preclude the use or disclosure of information or evidence to the extent that an obligation exists, for the United States under its Constitution or for France under its Constitution and general principles of its law having Constitutional value, to do so in a criminal proceeding. To the extent possible, the Requesting State shall notify the Requested State in advance of any such use or disclosure.

5. Information and evidence obtained under the conditions referred to in paragraphs 2 or 3 of this Article may be used for any purpose insofar as they have been made public within the framework of the proceeding for which they were transmitted to the Requesting State.

Article 15.   Service of Procedural Documents and Judicial Decisions

1. The Requested State shall serve procedural documents and judicial decisions sent to it for this purpose by the Requesting State.

2. Service may be effected by simple transmission of the document or decision to its addressee. If the Requesting State requests, the Requested State shall serve the document using a method, provided by or compatible with its laws.

3. Proof of service shall consist of a receipt dated and signed by the addressee or a statement by the Requested State noting the fact, the method, and the date of service. Either of these documents shall be sent immediately to the Requesting State. If service could not be effected, the Requested State shall inform the Requesting State immediately of the reason.

4. The Central Authority of the Requesting State shall transmit a document requiring the appearance of a person in the Requesting State to the Central Authority of the Requested State at least 50 days before the date of the scheduled appearance. Upon the request of the Requesting State, the Central Authority of the Requested State may waive this requirement for persons other than defendants.

Article 16.   Appearance in the Requesting State

1. If the Requesting State requests the personal appearance of a witness or an expert, the Requested State shall invite this witness or expert to appear. The Requested State shall inform the Central Authority of the Requesting State of the person's response.

2. Such a request shall mention the approximate amount of the invited person's travel and subsistence costs to be reimbursed. If the person so requests, the Requesting State may advance part or all of the funds to pay those expenses through its diplomatic or consular missions in the Requested State.

3. A witness or expert who fails to comply with a document requiring an appearance in the Requesting State, service of which has been effected pursuant to a request, shall not be subjected to any sanction or measure of restraint, even if the document contains a notice of penalty, unless the person subsequently travels voluntarily to the Requesting State, is duly served, and again fails to comply.

Article 17.   Safe Conduct

1. A witness or expert appearing in the Requesting State in response to a request shall not be subject to service of process, prosecuted, detained, or subjected to any other restriction of personal liberty in that State by reason of any acts or convictions that preceded the person's departure from the Requested State unless the Central Authority of the Requesting State limits such safe conduct and so notifies the Central Authority of the Requested State. Any such limitation of safe conduct shall be communicated to the witness or expert at the time the witness or expert is invited to appear.

2. A person appearing in the Requesting State in response to a document served to answer for acts, for which that person is the subject of a

criminal investigation or prosecution, shall not be prosecuted, detained, or subjected to any other restriction of personal liberty for acts or convictions that preceded that person's departure from the Requested State other than those specified in the document served.

3. The safe conduct provided for by this Article shall cease if the person, being free to leave, has not left the Requesting State within a period of fifteen consecutive days after being officially advised that the person's presence was no longer necessary or, having left, has returned.

Article 18.   Temporary Transfer

1. Upon the request of either State, a person in custody in either State may be temporarily transferred to the receiving State to give testimony or evidence or otherwise provide assistance in investigations or proceedings in relation to a criminal matter.

2. Such transfer may be denied:

(a) if the person in custody does not consent;

(b) if the person's period of detention might be thereby extended;

(c) if the person's presence is required for ongoing criminal proceedings; or

(d) for reasons of safety, security, or other imperative concerns.

3. Pursuant to this Treaty, the receiving State shall have the obligation and the authority to keep the person transferred in custody unless the sending State authorizes the person's release.

4. The receiving State shall require no proceeding to effect the return to the sending State of the person transferred. The return shall occur by the date specified by the sending State. This period may be extended by agreement between both States.

5. The sending State shall deduct from that person's sentence any time that the person transferred serves in the custody of the receiving State.

6. A person appearing in either State pursuant to this Article may receive the safe conduct authorized under Article 17.

Article 19.   Transit

1. Upon the request of the Requesting State, the Requested State may authorize the transit through its territory of a person held in custody by the Requesting State or a third State whose personal appearance has been requested by the Requesting State to give testimony or evidence or otherwise provide assistance in investigations or proceedings in relation to a criminal matter.

2. Pursuant to this Treaty, the Requested State shall have the obligation and the authority to keep the person in custody during transit.

Article 20.   Official Records

1. At the request of the Requesting State, the Requested State shall provide copies of records of any nature and in any form that are in the

possession of its judicial authorities or government departments or agencies and that are accessible to the public.

2. At the request of the Requesting State, the Requested State may provide copies of records of any nature and in any form that are in the possession of its judicial authorities or government departments or agencies, but that are not accessible to the public, to the same extent and under the same conditions that would apply to its own competent authorities in obtaining such copies. The Requested State may in its discretion deny a request, pursuant to this paragraph, entirely or in part.

3. Official records produced pursuant to this Article and certified by a competent authority of the Requested State as official records, or true and correct copies thereof, shall be admissible in evidence in the Requesting State as proof of the truth of the matters set forth therein. No further authentication shall be necessary.

Article 21.   Translation

The Requesting State shall translate the request and any supporting documents into the language of the Requested State.

Article 22.   Legalization

Except as otherwise provided by this Treaty, evidence, in whatever form, transmitted pursuant to this Treaty shall be exempt from all legalization formalities.

Article 23.   Costs

1. The Requested State shall meet the costs of executing requests except for:

(a) the allowances and expenses related to travel of witnesses and experts pursuant to Article 16 and the travel of persons in custody pursuant to Articles 18 and 19;

(b) the costs of interpretation and translation;

(c) the costs of services provided by private parties at the request of the Requesting State; and

(d) the fees of experts needed to fulfill a request.

2. If during the execution of a request it becomes apparent that execution will entail expenses of an extraordinary nature, the Central Authorities shall consult to determine the terms and conditions according to which execution may continue.

Article 24.   Sanitation of Criminal Proceedings in the Requested State

1. Each State may provide to the other State information and evidence relating to criminal acts and request that the other State submit the information and evidence to its competent authorities for the purpose of criminal investigation and prosecution where both States have jurisdiction to

investigate and prosecute those acts. Such requests shall be transmitted through the respective Central Authorities.

2. The Requested State shall consider initiating an investigation or prosecution as appropriate under its laws.

3. The Requested State shall notify the Requesting State of any action taken pursuant to the request and transmit a copy of any decision rendered. . . .

Article 26. Termination

Either State may terminate this Treaty at any time by forwarding through the diplomatic channel written notice of termination. Termination shall take effect six months after receipt of this notification.

IN WITNESS WHEREOF, the respective Plenipotentiaries have signed this Treaty and affixed their seals thereto.

DONE at Paris this tenth day of December, 1998, in duplicate, in the French and English languages, both texts being equally authentic.

MADELEINE K. ALBRIGHT
ELISABETH GUIGOU

Explanatory Note on the Treaty on Mutual Legal Assistance in Criminal Matters Between the United States of America and France

The following understandings regarding the application of certain provisions of the treaty are agreed between the Parties.

Article 1(3)

Both Parties understand that, for the United States, the provisions of the Treaty do not create a new right on the part of a private person to obtain assistance, to suppress or exclude any testimony or evidence, or to impede the execution of a request. However, such rights of private persons as otherwise exist under United States law in this regard continue in effect.

Article 3

During the negotiation of Article 3 of the Treaty, both Parties discussed the competent authorities from whom requests under the Treaty must emanate. The Parties noted the substantial number of authorities for the United States, aside from prosecutors, that were capable of being competent to initiate requests for mutual legal assistance. These authorities are not judicial authorities but are comparable to them since their requests, in accordance with Paragraph I of Article 1, are presented in the framework of "investigations or proceedings in respect of criminal offenses the punishment of which, at the time of the request for assistance, is a matter for the judicial authorities of the Requesting State." Under United States law, these authorities are those that are responsible for the investigations of criminal offenses, including the referral of matters to prosecutors for criminal prosecution. The Parties accordingly agreed not to attempt to list exhaustively in the Treaty the numerous state and federal authorities that fall under this definition, particularly because the inadvertent omission of one from the list could diminish the value of the Treaty to the United States. To illustrate this diversity, the United States, however, has agreed to provide, for the purposes of illustration only, the following short list:

> Bureau of Alcohol, Tobacco, and Firearms
> Commodity Futures Trading Commission
> Drug Enforcement Administration
> Federal Bureau of Investigation
> Federal Trade Commission
> Food and Drug Administration
> Immigration and Naturalization Service
> Internal Revenue Service
> Securities and Exchange Commission
> Trustees in Bankruptcy.

In any case, to facilitate in the identification of competent authorities of the United States by France, the two States agreed that the requests that are presented by the Central Authority of the United States of America will establish the competence of the requesting authorities for the purposes of this Treaty.

Article 9

The first part of paragraph 1 sets forth the principle that, with the consent of the Requested State, persons designated by the Requesting State (for example, the requesting authority, the defendant, and the counsel for such persons) shall be allowed to travel to the territory of the Requested State to be present and to assist during the execution of the request. The request for legal assistance should request the presence of these persons. For purposes of this Article, the term "Requested State" refers to the authorities in the Requested State who are authorized to approve or consent to the requested presence. The second part of paragraph 1 commits the two Parties to accommodate such a request so that the deposition obtained in the Requested State may be used in the Requesting State in compliance with its internal procedure. The scope of this commitment, however, may be limited, notably by the application of Articles 6 and 7 relating respectively to the denial of requests for legal assistance and to postponement of execution of such requests.

This commitment does not preclude that, in certain cases, which in practice shall be most exceptional, the authority entrusted with the execution of the request may determine that the presence and assistance of the designated persons are not possible in a specific case.

Article 23(1)

The discussion relating to Article 23 demonstrated the Parties' concerns to execute requests for mutual legal assistance in the least expensive manner, in particular those requests to obtain depositions in the United States. As a result, the Parties agreed that the United States will arrange and pay for the audio recording of a deposition requested by French authorities and its transmission to French authorities. Sealed in a container, the audio recording will be accompanied by a report or a declaration of the competent authority in the United States certifying the circumstances in which the deposition was taken. This document will mention the name of the authority conducting the proceeding, the identity of the person being deposed, and a statement whether or not the person was deposed under oath. The document should be signed by the deponent or, in case the deponent refuses or is unable to sign the document, the document should contain a statement to that effect. On the other hand, the costs of services furnished by private parties, such as those resulting from the transcription of depositions by a "court reporter," will be paid for by French authorities.

EXTRADITION TREATY BETWEEN THE GOVERNMENT OF THE UNITED KINGDOM OF GREAT BRITAIN AND NORTHERN IRELAND AND THE GOVERNMENT OF THE UNITED STATES OF AMERICA

March 31, 2003, _____ U.S.T. _____*

The Government of the United Kingdom of Great Britain and Northern Ireland and the Government of the United States of America,

Recalling the Extradition Treaty between the Government of the United States of America and the Government of the United Kingdom of Great Britain and Northern Ireland signed at London, June 8, 1972, as amended by the Supplementary Treaty between the two States, signed at Washington, June 25, 1985; and

Desiring to provide for more effective cooperation between the two States in the suppression of crime, and, for that purpose, to conclude a new treaty for the extradition of offenders;

Have agreed as follows:

Article 1.   Obligation to Extradite

The Parties agree to extradite to each other, pursuant to the provisions of this Treaty, persons sought by the authorities in the Requesting State for trial or punishment for extraditable offences.

Article 2.   Extraditable Offences

1. An offence shall be an extraditable offence if the conduct on which the offence is based is punishable under the laws in both States by deprivation of liberty for a period of one year or more or by a more severe penalty.

2. An offence shall also be an extraditable offence if it consists of an attempt or a conspiracy to commit, participation in the commission of, aiding or abetting, counseling or procuring the commission of, or being an accessory before or after the fact to any offence described in paragraph 1 of this Article.

---

*Signed in Washington on March 31, 2003. Entered into force on April 26, 2007.

3. For the purposes of this Article, an offence shall be an extraditable offence:

(a) whether or not the laws in the Requesting and Requested States place the offence within the same category of offences or describe the offence by the same terminology; or

(b) whether or not the offence is one for which United States federal law requires the showing of such matters as interstate transportation, or use of the mails or of other facilities affecting interstate or foreign commerce, such matters being jurisdictional only.

4. If the offence has been committed outside the territory of the Requesting State, extradition shall be granted in accordance with the provisions of the Treaty if the laws in the Requested State provide for the punishment of such conduct committed outside its territory in similar circumstances. If the laws in the Requested State do not provide for the punishment of such conduct committed outside of its territory in similar circumstances, the executive authority of the Requested State, in its discretion, may grant extradition provided that all other requirements of this Treaty are met.

5. If extradition has been granted for an extraditable offence, it may also be granted for any other offence specified in the request if the latter offence is punishable by less than one year's deprivation of liberty, provided that all other requirements for extradition are met.

Article 3. Nationality

Extradition shall not be refused based on the nationality of the person sought.

Article 4. Political and Military Offences

1. Extradition shall not be granted if the offence for which extradition is requested is a political offence.

2. For the purposes of this Treaty, the following offences shall not be considered political offences:

(a) an offence for which both Parties have the obligation pursuant to a multilateral international agreement to extradite the person sought or to submit the case to their competent authorities for decision as to prosecution;

(b) a murder or other violent crime against the person of a Head of State of one of the Parties, or of a member of the Head of State's family;

(c) murder, manslaughter, malicious wounding, or inflicting grievous bodily harm;

(d) an offence involving kidnapping, abduction, or any form of unlawful detention, including the taking of a hostage;

(e) placing or using, or threatening the placement or use of, an explosive, incendiary, or destructive device or firearm capable of endangering life, of causing grievous bodily harm, or of causing substantial property damage;

(f) possession of an explosive, incendiary, or destructive device capable of endangering life, of causing grievous bodily harm, or of causing substantial property damage;

(g) an attempt or a conspiracy to commit, participation in the commission of, aiding or abetting, counseling or procuring the commission of, or being an accessory before or after the fact to any of the foregoing offences.

3. Notwithstanding the terms of paragraph 2 of this Article, extradition shall not be granted if the competent authority of the Requested State determines that the request was politically motivated. In the United States, the executive branch is the competent authority for the purposes of this Article.

4. The competent authority of the Requested State may refuse extradition for offences under military law that are not offences under ordinary criminal law. In the United States, the executive branch is the competent authority for the purposes of this Article.

Article 5.   Prior Prosecution

1. Extradition shall not be granted when the person sought has been convicted or acquitted in the Requested State for the offence for which extradition is requested.

2. The Requested State may refuse extradition when the person sought has been convicted or acquitted in a third state in respect of the conduct for which extradition is requested.

3. Extradition shall not be precluded by the fact that the competent authorities of the Requested State:

(a) have decided not to prosecute the person sought for the acts for which extradition is requested;

(b) have decided to discontinue any criminal proceedings which have been instituted against the person sought for those acts; or

(c) are still investigating the person sought for the same acts for which extradition is sought.

Article 6.   Statute of Limitations

The decision by the Requested State whether to grant the request for extradition shall be made without regard to any statute of limitations in either State.

Article 7.   Capital Punishment

When the offence for which extradition is sought is punishable by death under the laws in the Requesting State and is not punishable by death under the laws in the Requested State, the executive authority in the Requested State may refuse extradition unless the Requesting State provides an assurance that the death penalty will not be imposed or, if imposed, will not be carried out.

Article 8. Extradition Procedures and Required Documents

1. All requests for extradition shall be submitted through the diplomatic channel.

2. All requests for extradition shall be supported by:

(a) as accurate a description as possible of the person sought, together with any other information that would help to establish identity and probable location;

(b) a statement of the facts of the offence(s);

(c) the relevant text of the law(s) describing the essential elements of the offence for which extradition is requested;

(d) the relevant text of the law(s) prescribing punishment for the offence for which extradition is requested; and

(e) documents, statements, or other types of information specified in paragraphs 3 or 4 of this Article, as applicable.

3. In addition to the requirements in paragraph 2 of this Article, a request for extradition of a person who is sought for prosecution shall be supported by:

(a) a copy of the warrant or order of arrest issued by a judge or other competent authority;

(b) a copy of the charging document, if any; and

(c) for requests to the United States, such information as would provide a reasonable basis to believe that the person sought committed the offence for which extradition is requested.

4. In addition to the requirements in paragraph 2 of this Article, a request for extradition relating to a person who has been convicted of the offence for which extradition is sought shall be supported by:

(a) information that the person sought is the person to whom the finding of guilt refers;

(b) a copy of the judgment or memorandum of conviction or, if a copy is not available, a statement by a judicial authority that the person has been convicted;

(c) a copy of the sentence imposed, if the person sought has been sentenced, and a statement establishing to what extent the sentence has been carried out; and

(d) in the case of a person who has been convicted *in absentia*, information regarding the circumstances under which the person was voluntarily absent from the proceedings.

Article 9. Authentication of Documents

The documents that support an extradition request shall be deemed to be authentic and shall be received in evidence in extradition proceedings without further proof if:

(a) regarding a request from the United States

(i) they are authenticated by the oath of a witness, or

(ii) they purport to be signed by a judge, magistrate, or officer of the United States and they purport to be certified by being sealed with the official seal of the Secretary of State of the United States;

(b) regarding a request from the United Kingdom, they are certified by the principal diplomatic or principal consular officer of the United States resident in the United Kingdom, as provided by the extradition laws of the United States;

(c) regarding a request from a territory of the United Kingdom, they are certified either by the principal diplomatic or principal consular officer of the United States responsible for that territory; or

(d) regarding a request from either Party, they are certified or authenticated in any other manner acceptable under the law in the Requested State.

Article 10. Additional Information

If the Requested State requires additional information to enable a decision to be taken on the request for extradition, the Requesting State shall respond to the request within such time as the Requested State requires.

Article 11. Translation

All documents submitted under this Treaty by the Requesting State shall be in English or accompanied by a translation into English.

Article 12. Provisional Arrest

1. In an urgent situation, the Requesting State may request the provisional arrest of the person sought pending presentation of the request for extradition. A request for provisional arrest may be transmitted through the diplomatic channel or directly between the United States Department of Justice and such competent authority as the United Kingdom may designate for the purposes of this Article.

2. The application for provisional arrest shall contain:

(a) a description of the person sought;

(b) the location of the person sought, if known;

(c) a brief statement of the facts of the case including, if possible, the date and location of the offence(s);

(d) a description of the law(s) violated;

(e) a statement of the existence of a warrant or order of arrest or a finding of guilt or judgment of conviction against the person sought; and

(f) a statement that the supporting documents for the person sought will follow within the time specified in this Treaty.

3. The Requesting State shall be notified without delay of the disposition of its request for provisional arrest and the reasons for any inability to proceed with the request.

4. A person who is provisionally arrested may be discharged from custody upon the expiration of sixty (60) days from the date of provisional arrest pursuant to this Treaty if the executive authority of the Requested State has not received the formal request for extradition and the documents supporting the extradition request as required in Article 8. . . .

5. The fact that the person sought has been discharged from custody pursuant to paragraph 4 of this Article shall not prejudice the subsequent re-arrest and extradition of that person if the extradition request and supporting documents are delivered at a later date.

Article 13.   *Decision and Surrender*

1. The Requested State shall promptly notify the Requesting State of its decision on the request for extradition. Such notification should be transmitted directly to the competent authority designated by the Requesting State to receive such notification and through the diplomatic channel.

2. If the request is denied in whole or in part, the Requested State shall provide reasons for the denial. The Requested State shall provide copies of pertinent judicial decisions upon request.

3. If the request for extradition is granted, the authorities of the Requesting and Requested States shall agree on the time and place for the surrender of the person sought.

4. If the person sought is not removed from the territory of the Requested State within the time period prescribed by the law of that State, that person may be discharged from custody, and the Requested State, in its discretion, may subsequently refuse extradition for the same offence(s).

Article 14.   *Temporary and Deferred Surrender*

1. If the extradition request is granted for a person who is being proceeded against or is serving a sentence in the Requested State, the Requested State may temporarily surrender the person sought to the Requesting State for the purpose of prosecution. If the Requested State requests, the Requesting State shall keep the person so surrendered in custody and shall return that person to the Requested State after the conclusion of the proceedings against that person, in accordance with conditions to be determined by mutual agreement of the States.

2. The Requested State may postpone the extradition proceedings against a person who is being prosecuted or who is serving a sentence in that State. The postponement may continue until the prosecution of the person sought has been concluded or until such person has served any sentence imposed.

Article 15.   *Requests for Extradition Made by Several States*

If the Requested State receives requests from two or more States for the extradition of the same person, either for the same offence or for different offences, the executive authority of the Requested State shall determine to which State, if any, it will surrender the person. In making its decision, the Requested State shall consider all relevant factors, including but not limited to:

(a) whether the requests were made pursuant to a treaty;

(b) the place where each offence was committed;

(c) the gravity of the offences;

(d) the possibility of any subsequent extradition between the respective Requesting States; and

(e) the chronological order in which the requests were received from the respective Requesting States.

Article 16. Seizure and Surrender of Property

1. To the extent permitted under its law, the Requested State may seize and surrender to the Requesting State all items in whatever form, and assets, including proceeds, that are connected with the offence in respect of which extradition is granted. The items and assets mentioned in this Article may be surrendered even when the extradition cannot be effected due to the death, disappearance, or escape of the person sought.

2. The Requested State may condition the surrender of the items upon satisfactory assurances from the Requesting State that the property will be returned to the Requested State as soon as practicable. The Requested State may also defer the surrender of such items if they are needed as evidence in the Requested State.

Article 17. Waiver of Extradition

If the person sought waives extradition and agrees to be surrendered to the Requesting State, the Requested State may surrender the person as expeditiously as possible without further proceedings.

Article 18. Rule of Specialty

1. A person extradited under this Treaty may not be detained, tried, or punished in the Requesting State except for:

(a) any offence for which extradition was granted, or a differently denominated offence based on the same facts as the offence on which extradition was granted, provided such offence is extraditable, or is a lesser included offence;

(b) any offence committed after the extradition of the person; or

(c) any offence for which the executive authority of the Requested State waives the rule of specialty and thereby consents to the person's detention, trial, or punishment. For the purpose of this subparagraph:

(i) the executive authority of the Requested State may require the submission of the documentation called for in Article 8; and

(ii) the person extradited may be detained by the Requesting State for 90 days, or for such longer period of time as the Requested State may authorize, while the request for consent is being processed.

2. A person extradited under this Treaty may not be the subject of onward extradition or surrender for any offence committed prior to extradition to the Requesting State unless the Requested State consents.

3. Paragraphs 1 and 2 of this Article shall not prevent the detention, trial, or punishment of an extradited person, or the extradition of the person to a third State, if the person:

(a) leaves the territory of the Requesting State after extradition and voluntarily returns to it; or

(b) does not leave the territory of the Requesting State within 20 days of the day on which that person is free to leave.

4. If the person sought waives extradition pursuant to Article 17, the specialty provisions in this Article shall not apply.

Article 19. Transit

1. Either State may authorize transportation through its territory of a person surrendered to the other State by a third State or from the other State to a third State. A request for transit shall contain a description of the person being transported and a brief statement of the facts of the case. A person in transit shall be detained in custody during the period of transit.

2. Authorization is not required when air transportation is used by one State and no landing is scheduled on the territory of the other State. If an unscheduled landing does occur, the State in which the unscheduled landing occurs may require a request for transit pursuant to paragraph 1 of this Article, and it may detain the person until the request for transit is received and the transit is effected, as long as the request is received within 96 hours of the unscheduled landing.

Article 20. Representation and Expenses

1. The Requested State shall advise, assist, and appear on behalf of, the Requesting State in any proceedings in the courts of the Requested State arising out of a request for extradition or make all necessary arrangements for the same.

2. The Requesting State shall pay all the expenses related to the translation of extradition documents and the transportation of the person surrendered. The Requested State shall pay all other expenses incurred in that State in connection with the extradition proceedings.

3. Neither State shall make any pecuniary claim against the other State arising out of the arrest, detention, examination, or surrender of persons under this Treaty.

Article 21. Consultation

The Parties may consult with each other in connection with the processing of individual cases and in furtherance of efficient implementation of this Treaty.

Article 22.   Application

1. This Treaty shall apply to offences committed before as well as after the date it enters into force.

2. This Treaty shall apply:

(a) in relation to the United Kingdom: to Great Britain and Northern Ireland, the Channel Islands, the Isle of Man; and to any territory for whose international relations the United Kingdom is responsible and to which this agreement has been extended by agreement of the Parties; and

(b) to the United States of America.

3. The application of this Treaty to any territory in respect of which extension has been made in accordance with paragraph 2 of this Article may be terminated by either State giving six months' written notice to the other through the diplomatic channel.

4. A request by the United States for the extradition of an offender who is found in any of the territories to which this Treaty applies in accordance with paragraph 2 of this Article may be made to the Governor or other competent authority of that territory, who may take the decision himself or refer the matter to the Government of the United Kingdom for its decision. A request on the part of any of the territories to which this Treaty applies in accordance with paragraph 2 of this Article for the extradition of an offender who is found in the United States of America may be made to the Government of the United States by the Governor or other competent authority of that territory.

Article 23.   Ratification and Entry into Force . . .

2. This Treaty shall enter into force upon the exchange of the instruments of ratification.

3. Upon the entry into force of this Treaty, the Extradition Treaty signed at London on June 8, 1972, and the Supplementary Treaty signed at Washington on June 25, 1985, (together, "the prior Treaty") shall cease to have any effect as between the United States and the United Kingdom, except as otherwise provided below. The prior Treaty shall apply to any extradition proceedings in which the extradition documents have already been submitted to the courts of the Requested State at the time this Treaty enters into force, except that Article 18 of this Treaty shall apply to persons found extraditable under the prior Treaty.

4. The prior Treaty shall also apply to any territory to which it has been extended in accordance with Article II of that Treaty, until such time as the provisions of this Treaty have been extended to such a territory under Article 22(2).

Article 24.   Termination

Either State may terminate this Treaty at any time by giving written notice to the other State through the diplomatic channel, and the termination shall be effective six months after the date of receipt of such notice.

DONE at Washington, in duplicate, this 31st day of March, 2003.

U.N. SECURITY COUNCIL RESOLUTIONS ESTABLISHING WAR CRIMES TRIBUNALS FOR THE FORMER YUGOSLAVIA AND RWANDA

U.N. SECURITY COUNCIL RES. 827

(May 25, 1993)*

The Security Council, . . .

Having considered the report of the Secretary-General (S/25704 and Add.1) pursuant to paragraph 2 of resolution 808 (1993),

Expressing once again its grave alarm at continuing reports of widespread and flagrant violations of international humanitarian law occurring within the territory of the former Yugoslavia, and especially in the Republic of Bosnia and Herzegovina, including reports of mass killings, massive, organized and systematic detention and rape of women, and the continuance of the practice of "ethnic cleansing", including for the acquisition and the holding of territory,

Determining that this situation continues to constitute a threat to international peace and security,

Determined to put an end to such crimes and to take effective measures to bring to justice the persons who are responsible for them,

Convinced that in the particular circumstances of the former Yugoslavia the establishment as an ad hoc measure by the Council of an international tribunal and the prosecution of persons responsible for serious violations of international humanitarian law would enable this aim to be achieved and would contribute to the restoration and maintenance of peace,

Believing that the establishment of an international tribunal and the prosecution of persons responsible for the above-mentioned violations of international humanitarian law will contribute to ensuring that such violations are halted and effectively redressed, . . .

Reaffirming in this regard its decision in resolution 808 (1993) that an international tribunal shall be established for the prosecution of persons

---

*Adopted by a vote of 15-0.

responsible for serious violations of international humanitarian law committed in the territory of the former Yugoslavia since 1991,*Considering* that, pending the appointment of the Prosecutor of the International Tribunal, the Commission of Experts established pursuant to resolution 780 (1992) should continue on an urgent basis the collection of information relating to evidence of grave breaches of the Geneva Conventions and other violations of international humanitarian law as proposed in its interim report (S/25274),

Acting under Chapter VII of the Charter of the United Nations,

1. *Approves* the report of the Secretary-General;

2. *Decides* hereby to establish an international tribunal for the sole purpose of prosecuting persons responsible for serious violations of international humanitarian law committed in the territory of the former Yugoslavia between 1 January 1991 and a date to be determined by the Security Council upon the restoration of peace and to this end to adopt the Statute of the International Tribunal annexed to the above-mentioned report; . . .

4. *Decides* that all States shall cooperate fully with the International Tribunal and its organs in accordance with the present resolution and the Statute of the International Tribunal and that consequently all States shall take any measures necessary under their domestic law to implement the provisions of the present resolution and the Statute, including the obligation of States to comply with requests for assistance or orders issued by a Trial Chamber under Article 29 of the Statute; . . .

6. *Decides* that the determination of the seat of the International Tribunal is subject to the conclusion of appropriate arrangements between the United Nations and the Netherlands acceptable to the Council, and that the International Tribunal may sit elsewhere when it considers it necessary for the efficient exercise of its functions;

7. *Decides* also that the work of the International Tribunal shall be carried out without prejudice to the right of the victims to seek, through appropriate means, compensation for damages incurred as a result of violations of international humanitarian law;

8. *Requests* the Secretary-General to implement urgently the present resolution and in particular to make practical arrangements for the effective functioning of the International Tribunal at the earliest time and to report periodically to the Council;

9. *Decides* to remain actively seized of the matter.

U.N. SECURITY COUNCIL RES. 955

(November 8, 1994)*

The Security Council,

Reaffirming all its previous resolutions on the situation in Rwanda,

Having considered the reports of the Secretary-General pursuant to paragraph 3 of resolution 935 (1994) of 1 July 1994 (S/1994/879 and S/1994/906), and *having taken note* of the reports of the Special Rapporteur for Rwanda of the United Nations Commission on Human Rights . . .

Expressing appreciation for the work of the Commission of Experts established pursuant to resolution 935 (1994), in particular its preliminary report on violations of international humanitarian law in Rwanda . . . ,

Expressing once again its grave concern at the reports indicating that genocide and other systematic, widespread and flagrant violations of international humanitarian law have been committed in Rwanda,

Determining that this situation continues to constitute a threat to international peace and security,

Determined to put an end to such crimes and to take effective measures to bring to justice the persons who are responsible for them,

Convinced that in the particular circumstances of Rwanda, the prosecution of persons responsible for serious violations of international humanitarian law would enable this aim to be achieved and would contribute to the process of national reconciliation and to the restoration and maintenance of peace,

Believing that the establishment of an international tribunal for the prosecution of persons responsible for genocide and the other above-mentioned violations of international humanitarian law will contribute to ensuring that such violations are halted and effectively redressed,

Stressing also the need for international cooperation to strengthen the courts and judicial system of Rwanda, having regard in particular to the necessity for those courts to deal with large numbers of suspects, . . .

Acting under Chapter VII of the Charter of the United Nations,

1. *Decides* hereby, having received the request of the Government of Rwanda (S/1994/1115), to establish an international tribunal for the sole

---

*Adopted by a vote of 13-1, with Rwanda opposed and China abstaining.

purpose of prosecuting persons responsible for genocide and other serious violations of international humanitarian law committed in the territory of Rwanda and Rwandan citizens responsible for genocide and other such violations committed in the territory of neighbouring States, between 1 January 1994 and 31 December 1994 and to this end to adopt the Statute of the International Criminal Tribunal for Rwanda annexed hereto;

2. *Decides* that all States shall cooperate fully with the International Tribunal and its organs in accordance with the present resolution and the Statute of the International Tribunal and that consequently all States shall take any measures necessary under their domestic law to implement the provisions of the present resolution and the Statute, including the obligation of States to comply with requests for assistance or orders issued by a Trial Chamber under Article 28 of the Statute, and *requests* States to keep the Secretary-General informed of such measures;

3. *Considers* that the Government of Rwanda should be notified prior to the taking of decisions under articles 26 and 27 of the Statute;

4. *Urges* States and intergovernmental and non-governmental organizations to contribute funds, equipment and services to the International Tribunal, including the offer of expert personnel; . . .

6. *Decides* that the seat of the International Tribunal shall be determined by the Council having regard to considerations of justice and fairness as well as administrative efficiency, including access to witnesses, and economy, and subject to the conclusion of appropriate arrangements between the United Nations and the State of the seat, acceptable to the Council, having regard to the fact that the International Tribunal may meet away from its seat when it considers it necessary for the efficient exercise of its functions; and *decides* that an office will be established and proceedings will be conducted in Rwanda, where feasible and appropriate, subject to the conclusion of similar appropriate arrangements;

7. *Decides* to consider increasing the number of judges and Trial Chambers of the International Tribunal if it becomes necessary;

8. *Decides* to remain actively seized of the matter.

ROME STATUTE OF THE
INTERNATIONAL CRIMINAL COURT

<http://www.icc-cpi.int>*

Part 1.   Establishment of the Court

Article 1.   The Court

An International Criminal Court ("the Court") is hereby established. It shall be a permanent institution and shall have the power to exercise its jurisdiction over persons for the most serious crimes of international concern, as referred to in this Statute, and shall be complementary to national criminal jurisdictions. The jurisdiction and functioning of the Court shall be governed by the provisions of this Statute.

Article 2.   Relationship of the Court with the United Nations

The Court shall be brought into relationship with the United Nations through an agreement to be approved by the Assembly of States Parties to this Statute and thereafter concluded by the President of the Court on its behalf.

---

*The Rome Statute of the International Criminal Court was adopted by the United Nations Diplomatic Conference on July 17, 1998, by a vote of 120 in favor to seven against, with 21 abstentions. The Statute entered into force July 1, 2002.

As of May 2013, there were 122 parties to the Statute. The parties were: Afghanistan, Albania, Andorra, Antigua and Barbuda, Argentina, Australia, Austria, Bangladesh, Barbados, Belgium, Belize, Benin, Bolivia, Bosnia and Herzegovina, Botswana, Brazil, Bulgaria, Burkina Faso, Burundi, Cambodia, Canada, Cape Verde, Central African Republic, Chad, Chile, Colombia, Comoros, Congo (Democratic Republic of), Congo, Cook Islands, Costa Rica, Côte d'Ivoire, Croatia, Cyprus, Czech Republic, Denmark, Djibouti, Dominica, Dominican Republic, Ecuador, Estonia, Fiji, Finland, France, Gabon, Gambia, Georgia, Germany, Ghana, Greece, Grenada, Guatemala, Guinea, Guyana, Honduras, Hungary, Iceland, Ireland, Italy, Japan, Jordan, Kenya, Korea (Republic of), Latvia, Lesotho, Liberia, Liechtenstein, Lithuania, Luxembourg, Macedonia (the former Yugoslav Republic of), Madagascar, Malawi, Maldives, Mali, Malta, Marshall Islands, Mauritius, Mexico, Moldova (Republic of), Mongolia, Montenegro, Namibia, Nauru, Netherlands, New Zealand, Niger, Nigeria, Norway, Panama, Paraguay, Peru, Philippines, Poland, Portugal, Romania, Saint Kitts and Nevis, Saint Lucia, Saint Vincent and the Grenadines, Samoa, San Marino, Senegal, Serbia, Seychelles, Sierra Leone, Slovakia, Slovenia, South Africa, Spain, Surinam, Sweden, Switzerland, Tajikistan, Tanzania, Timor-Leste, Trinidad and Tobago, Tunisia, Uganda, United Kingdom, Uruguay, Vanuatu, Venezuela, and Zambia. Besides being at the Web site cited in the text, the document is at UN Doc. A/CONF. 183/9; 37 ILM 1002 (1998); 2187 UNTS 90.

Article 3. Seat of the Court

1. The seat of the Court shall be established at The Hague in the Netherlands ("the host State").

2. The Court shall enter into a headquarters agreement with the host State, to be approved by the Assembly of States Parties and thereafter concluded by the President of the Court on its behalf.

3. The Court may sit elsewhere, whenever it considers it desirable, as provided in this Statute.

Article 4. Legal Status and Powers of the Court

1. The Court shall have international legal personality. It shall also have such legal capacity as may be necessary for the exercise of its functions and the fulfilment of its purposes.

2. The Court may exercise its functions and powers, as provided in this Statute, on the territory of any State Party and, by special agreement, on the territory of any other State.

Part 2. Jurisdiction, Admissibility and Applicable Law

Article 5. Crimes Within the Jurisdiction of the Court

1. The jurisdiction of the Court shall be limited to the most serious crimes of concern to the international community as a whole. The Court has jurisdiction in accordance with this Statute with respect to the following crimes:
   (a) The crime of genocide;
   (b) Crimes against humanity;
   (c) War crimes;
   (d) The crime of aggression.

2. The Court shall exercise jurisdiction over the crime of aggression once a provision is adopted in accordance with articles 121 and 123 defining the crime and setting out the conditions under which the Court shall exercise jurisdiction with respect to this crime. Such a provision shall be consistent with the relevant provisions of the Charter of the United Nations.

Article 6. Genocide

For the purpose of this Statute, "genocide" means any of the following acts committed with intent to destroy, in whole or in part, a national, ethnical, racial or religious group, as such:
   (a) Killing members of the group;
   (b) Causing serious bodily or mental harm to members of the group;
   (c) Deliberately inflicting on the group conditions of life calculated to bring about its physical destruction in whole or in part;
   (d) Imposing measures intended to prevent births within the group;
   (e) Forcibly transferring children of the group to another group.

Article 7.   Crimes Against Humanity

1. For the purpose of this Statute, "crime against humanity" means any of the following acts when committed as part of a widespread or systematic attack directed against any civilian population, with knowledge of the attack:

(a) Murder;

(b) Extermination;

(c) Enslavement;

(d) Deportation or forcible transfer of population;

(e) Imprisonment or other severe deprivation of physical liberty in violation of fundamental rules of international law,

(f) Torture;

(g) Rape, sexual slavery, enforced prostitution, forced pregnancy, enforced sterilization, or any other form of sexual violence of comparable gravity;

(h) Persecution against any identifiable group or collectivity on political, racial, national, ethnic, cultural, religious, gender as defined in paragraph 3, or other grounds that are universally recognized as impermissible under international law, in connection with any act referred to in this paragraph or any crime within the jurisdiction of the Court;

(i) Enforced disappearance of persons;

(j) The crime of apartheid;

(k) Other inhumane acts of a similar character intentionally causing great suffering, or serious injury to body or to mental or physical health.

2. For the purpose of paragraph 1:

(a) "Attack directed against any civilian population" means a course of conduct involving the multiple commission of acts referred to in paragraph 1 against any civilian population, pursuant to or in furtherance of a State or organizational policy to commit such attack; . . .

(e) "Torture" means the intentional infliction of severe pain or suffering, whether physical or mental, upon a person in the custody or under the control of the accused; except that torture shall not include pain or suffering arising only from, inherent in or incidental to, lawful sanctions. . . .

Article 8.   War Crimes

1. The Court shall have jurisdiction in respect of war crimes in particular when committed as a part of a plan or policy or as part of a large-scale commission of such crimes.

2. For the purpose of this Statute, "war crimes" means:

(a) Grave breaches of the Geneva Conventions of 12 August 1949, namely, any of the following acts against persons or property protected under the provisions of the relevant Geneva Convention:

(i) Wilful killing;

(ii) Torture or inhuman treatment, including biological experiments;

(iii) Wilfully causing great suffering, or serious injury to body or health;

(iv) Extensive destruction and appropriation of property, not justified by military necessity and carried out unlawfully and wantonly;

(v) Compelling a prisoner of war or other protected person to serve in the forces of a hostile Power;

(vi) Wilfully depriving a prisoner of war or other protected person of the rights of fair and regular trial;

(vii) Unlawful deportation or transfer or unlawful confinement;

(viii) Taking of hostages.

(b) Other serious violations of the laws and customs applicable in international armed conflict, within the established framework of international law, namely, any of the following acts:

(i) Intentionally directing attacks against the civilian population as such or against individual civilians not taking direct part in hostilities;

(ii) Intentionally directing attacks against civilian objects, that is, objects which are not military objectives;

(iii) Intentionally directing attacks against personnel, installations, material, units or vehicles involved in a humanitarian assistance or peacekeeping mission in accordance with the Charter of the United Nations, as long as they are entitled to the protection given to civilians or civilian objects under the international law of armed conflict;

(iv) Intentionally launching an attack in the knowledge that such attack will cause incidental loss of life or injury to civilians or damage to civilian objects or widespread, long-term and severe damage to the natural environment which would be clearly excessive in relation to the concrete and direct overall military advantage anticipated;

(v) Attacking or bombarding, by whatever means, towns, villages, dwellings or buildings which are undefended and which are not military objectives;

(vi) Killing or wounding a combatant who, having laid down his arms or having no longer means of defence, has surrendered at discretion;

(vii) Making improper use of a flag of truce, of the flag or of the military insignia and uniform of the enemy or of the United Nations, as well as of the. distinctive emblems of the Geneva Conventions, resulting in death or serious personal injury;

(viii) The transfer, directly or indirectly, by the Occupying Power of parts of its own civilian population into the territory it occupies, or the deportation or transfer of all or parts of the population of the occupied territory within or outside this territory;

(ix) Intentionally directing attacks against buildings dedicated to religion, education, art, science or charitable purposes, historic monuments, hospitals and places where the sick and wounded are collected, provided they are not military objectives;

(x) Subjecting persons who are in the power of an adverse party to physical mutilation or to medical or scientific experiments of any kind which are neither justified by the medical, dental or hospital treatment of the person concerned nor carried out in his or her interest, and which cause death to or seriously endanger the health of such person or persons;

(xi) Killing or wounding treacherously individuals belonging to the hostile nation or army;

(xii) Declaring that no quarter will be given;

(xiii) Destroying or seizing the enemy's property unless such destruction or seizure be imperatively demanded by the necessities of war;

(xiv) Declaring abolished, suspended or inadmissible in a court of law the rights and actions of the nationals of the hostile party;

(xv) Compelling the nationals of the hostile party to take part in the operations of war directed against their own country, even if they were in the belligerent's service before the commencement of the war;

(xvi) Pillaging a town or place, even when taken by assault;

(xvii) Employing poison or poisoned weapons;

(xviii) Employing asphyxiating, poisonous or other gases, and all analogous liquids, materials or devices;

(xix) Employing bullets which expand or flatten easily in the human body, such as bullets with a hard envelope which does not entirely cover the core or is pierced with incisions;

(xx) Employing weapons, projectiles and material and methods of warfare which are of a nature to cause superfluous injury or unnecessary suffering or which are inherently indiscriminate in violation of the international law of armed conflict, provided that such weapons, projectiles and material and methods of warfare are the subject of a comprehensive prohibition and are included in an annex to this Statute, by an amendment in accordance with the relevant provisions set forth in articles 121 and 123;

(xxi) Committing outrages upon personal dignity, in particular humiliating and degrading treatment;

(xxii) Committing rape, sexual slavery, enforced prostitution, forced pregnancy, as defined in article 7, paragraph 2 (f), enforced sterilization, or any other form of sexual violence also constituting a grave breach of the Geneva Conventions;

(xxiii) Utilizing the presence of a civilian or other protected person to render certain points, areas or military forces immune from military operations;

(xxiv) Intentionally directing attacks against buildings, material, medical units and transport, and personnel using the distinctive emblems of the Geneva Conventions in conformity with international law;

(xxv) Intentionally using starvation of civilians as a method of warfare by depriving them of objects indispensable to their survival, including wilfully impeding relief supplies as provided for under the Geneva Conventions;

(xxvi) Conscripting or enlisting children under the age of fifteen years into the national armed forces or using them to participate actively in hostilities.

(c) In the case of an armed conflict not of an international character, serious violations of article 3 common to the four Geneva Conventions of 12 August 1949, namely, any of the following acts committed against persons taking no active part in the hostilities, including members of armed forces who have laid down their arms and those placed hors de combat by sickness, wounds, detention or any other cause:

(i) Violence to life and person, in particular murder of all kinds, mutilation, cruel treatment and torture;

(ii) Committing outrages upon personal dignity, in particular humiliating and degrading treatment;

(iii) Taking of hostages;

(iv) The passing of sentences and the carrying out of executions without previous judgement pronounced by a regularly constituted court, affording all judicial guarantees which are generally recognized as indispensable.

(d) Paragraph 2 (c) applies to armed conflicts not of an international character and thus does not apply to situations of internal disturbances and tensions, such as riots, isolated and sporadic acts of violence or other acts of a similar nature;

(e) Other serious violations of the laws and customs applicable in armed conflicts not of an international character, within the established framework of international law, namely, any of the following acts:

(i) Intentionally directing attacks against the civilian population as such or against individual civilians not taking direct part in hostilities;

(ii) Intentionally directing attacks against buildings, material, medical units and transport, and personnel using the distinctive emblems of the Geneva Conventions in conformity with international law;

(iii) Intentionally directing attacks against personnel, installations, material, units or vehicles involved in a humanitarian assistance or peacekeeping mission in accordance with the Charter of the United Nations, as long as they are entitled to the protection given to civilians or civilian objects under the law of armed conflict;

(iv) Intentionally directing attacks against buildings dedicated to religion, education, art, science or charitable purposes, historic monuments, hospitals and places where the sick and wounded are collected, provided they are not military objectives;

(v) Pillaging a town or place, even when taken by assault;

(vi) Committing rape, sexual slavery, enforced prostitution, forced pregnancy, as defined in article 7, paragraph 2 (f), enforced sterilization, and any other form of sexual violence also constituting a serious violation of article 3 common to the four Geneva Conventions;

(vii) Conscripting or enlisting children under the age of fifteen years into armed forces or groups or using them to participate actively in hostilities;

(viii) Ordering the displacement of the civilian population for reasons related to the conflict, unless the security of the civilians involved or imperative military reasons so demand;

(ix) Killing or wounding treacherously a combatant adversary;

(x) Declaring that no quarter will be given;

(xi) Subjecting persons who are in the power of another party to the conflict to physical mutilation or to medical or scientific experiments of any kind which are neither justified by the medical, dental or hospital treatment of the person concerned nor carried out in his or her interest, and which cause death to or seriously endanger the health of such person or persons;

(xii) Destroying or seizing the property of an adversary unless such destruction or seizure be imperatively demanded by the necessities of the conflict;

(f) Paragraph 2 (e) applies to armed conflicts not of an international character and thus does not apply to situations of internal disturbances and tensions, such as riots, isolated and sporadic acts of violence or other acts of a similar nature. It applies to armed conflicts that take place in the territory of a State when there is protracted armed conflict between governmental authorities and organized armed groups or between such groups.

3. Nothing in paragraphs 2 (c) and (d) shall affect the responsibility of a Government to maintain or re-establish law and order in the State or to defend the unity and territorial integrity of the State, by all legitimate means. . . .

Article 10.

Nothing in this Part shall be interpreted as limiting or prejudicing in any way existing or developing rules of international law for purposes other than this Statute.

Article 11.   Jurisdiction Ratione Temporis

1. The Court has jurisdiction only with respect to crimes committed after the entry into force of this Statute.

2. If a State becomes a Party to this Statute after its entry into force, the Court may exercise its jurisdiction only with respect to crimes committed after the entry into force of this Statute for that State, unless that State has made a declaration under article 12, paragraph 3.

Article 12.   Preconditions to the Exercise of the Jurisdiction

1. A State which becomes a Party to this Statute thereby accepts the jurisdiction of the Court with respect to the crimes referred to in article 5.

2. In the case of article 13, paragraph (a) or (c), the Court may exercise its jurisdiction if one or more of the following States are Parties to this Statute or have accepted the jurisdiction of the Court in accordance with paragraph 3:

(a) The State on the territory of which the conduct in question occurred or, if the crime was committed on board a vessel or aircraft, the State of registration of that vessel or aircraft;

(b) The State of which the person accused of the crime is a national.

3. If the acceptance of a State which is not a Party to this Statute is required under paragraph 2, that State may, by declaration lodged with the Registrar, accept the exercise of jurisdiction by the Court with respect to the crime in question. The accepting State shall cooperate with the Court without any delay or exception in accordance with Part 9.

Article 13. Exercise of Jurisdiction

The Court may exercise its jurisdiction with respect to a crime referred to in article 5 in accordance with the provisions of this Statute if:

(a) A situation in which one or more of such crimes appears to have been committed is referred to the Prosecutor by a State Party in accordance with article 14;

(b) A situation in which one or more of such crimes appears to have been committed is referred to the Prosecutor by the Security Council acting under Chapter VII of the Charter of the United Nations; or

(c) The Prosecutor has initiated an investigation in respect of such a crime in accordance with article 15.

Article 14. Referral of a Situation by a State Party

1. A State Party may refer to the Prosecutor a situation in which one or more crimes within the jurisdiction of the Court appear to have been committed requesting the Prosecutor to investigate the situation for the purpose of determining whether one or more specific persons should be charged with the commission of such crimes.

2. As far as possible, a referral shall specify the relevant circumstances and be accompanied by such supporting documentation as is available to the State referring the situation.

Article 15. Prosecutor

1. The Prosecutor may initiate investigations proprio motu on the basis of information on crimes within the jurisdiction of the Court.

2. The Prosecutor shall analyse the seriousness of the information received. For this purpose, he or she may seek additional information from States, organs of the United Nations, intergovernmental or nongovernmental organizations, or other reliable sources that he or she deems appropriate, and may receive written or oral testimony at the seat of the Court.

3. If the Prosecutor concludes that there is a reasonable basis to proceed with an investigation, he or she shall submit to the Pre-Trial Chamber a brequest for authorization of an investigation, together with any supporting material collected. Victims may make representations to the Pre-Trial Chamber, in accordance with the Rules of Procedure and Evidence.

4. If the Pre-Trial Chamber, upon examination of the request and the supporting material, considers that there is a reasonable basis to proceed with an investigation, and that the case appears to fall within the jurisdiction of the Court, it shall authorize the commencement of the investigation, without prejudice to subsequent determinations by the Court with regard to the jurisdiction and admissibility of a case.

5. The refusal of the Pre-Trial Chamber to authorize the investigation shall not preclude the presentation of a subsequent request by the Prosecutor based on new facts or evidence regarding the same situation.

6. If, after the preliminary examination referred to in paragraphs 1 and 2, the Prosecutor concludes that the information provided does not constitute a reasonable basis for an investigation, he or she shall inform those who provided the information. This shall not preclude the Prosecutor from considering further information submitted to him or her regarding the same situation in the light of new facts or evidence.

Article 16.   Deferral of Investigation or Prosecution

No investigation or prosecution may be commenced or proceeded with under this Statute for a period of 12 months after the Security Council, in a resolution adopted under Chapter VII of the Charter of the United Nations, has requested the Court to that effect; that request may be renewed by the Council under the same conditions.

Article 17.   Issues of Admissibility

1. Having regard to paragraph 10 of the Preamble and article 1, the Court shall determine that a case is inadmissible where:

(a) The case is being investigated or prosecuted by a State which has jurisdiction over it, unless the State is unwilling or unable genuinely to carry out the investigation or prosecution;

(b) The case has been investigated by a State which has jurisdiction over it and the State has decided not to prosecute the person concerned, unless the decision resulted from the unwillingness or inability of the State genuinely to prosecute;

(c) The person concerned has already been tried for conduct which is the subject of the complaint, and a trial by the Court is not permitted under article 20, paragraph 3;

(d) The case is not of sufficient gravity to justify further action by the Court.

2. In order to determine unwillingness in a particular case, the Court shall consider, having regard to the principles of due process recognized by international law, whether one or more of the following exist, as applicable:

(a) The proceedings were or are being undertaken or the national decision was made for the purpose of shielding the person concerned from criminal responsibility for crimes within the jurisdiction of the Court referred to in article 5;

(b) There has been an unjustified delay in the proceedings which in the circumstances is inconsistent with an intent to bring the person concerned to justice;

(c) The proceedings were not or are not being conducted independently or impartially, and they were or are being conducted in a manner which, in the circumstances, is inconsistent with an intent to bring the person concerned to justice.

3. In order to determine inability in a particular case, the Court shall consider whether, due to a total or substantial collapse or unavailability of its national judicial system, the State is unable to obtain the accused or the necessary evidence and testimony or otherwise unable to carry out its proceedings.

Article 18. *Preliminary Rulings Regarding Admissibility*

1. When a situation has been referred to the Court pursuant to article 13(a) and the Prosecutor has determined that there would be a reasonable basis to commence an investigation, or the Prosecutor initiates an investigation pursuant to articles 13(c) and 15, the Prosecutor shall notify all States Parties and those States which, taking into account the information available, would normally exercise jurisdiction over the crimes concerned. The Prosecutor may notify such States on a confidential basis and, where the Prosecutor believes it necessary to protect persons, prevent destruction of evidence or prevent the absconding of persons, may limit the scope of the information provided to States.

2. Within one month of receipt of that notice, a State may inform the Court that it is investigating or has investigated its nationals or others within its jurisdiction with respect to criminal acts which may constitute crimes referred to in article 5 and which relate to the information provided in the notification to States. At the request of that State, the Prosecutor shall defer to the State's investigation of those persons unless the Pre-Trial Chamber, on the application of the Prosecutor, decides to authorize the investigation.

3. The Prosecutor's deferral to a State's investigation shall be open to review by the Prosecutor six months after the date of deferral or at any time when there has been a significant change of circumstances based on the State's unwillingness or inability genuinely to carry out the investigation.

4. The State concerned or the Prosecutor may appeal to the Appeals Chamber against a ruling of the Pre-Trial Chamber, in accordance with article 82. The appeal may be heard on an expedited basis.

5. When the Prosecutor has deferred an investigation in accordance with paragraph 2, the Prosecutor may request that the State concerned periodically inform the Prosecutor of the progress of its investigations and any subsequent prosecutions. States Parties shall respond to such requests without undue delay.

6. Pending a ruling by the Pre-Trial Chamber, or at any time when the Prosecutor has deferred an investigation under this article, the Prosecutor may, on an exceptional basis, seek authority from the Pre-Trial Chamber to pursue necessary investigative steps for the purpose of preserving evidence

where there is a unique opportunity to obtain important evidence or there is a significant risk that such evidence may not be subsequently available.

7. A State which has challenged a ruling of the Pre-Trial Chamber under this article may challenge the admissibility of a case under article 19 on the grounds of additional significant facts or significant change of circumstances.

Article 19. Challenges to the Jurisdiction of the Court or the Admissibility of a Case

1. The court shall satisfy itself that it has jurisdiction in any case brought before it. The Court may, on its own motion, determine the admissibility of a case in accordance with article 17.

2. Challenges to the admissibility of a case on the grounds referred to in article 17 or challenges to the jurisdiction of the Court may be made by:

(a) An accused or a person for whom a warrant of arrest or a summons to appear has been issued under article 58;

(b) A State which has jurisdiction over a case, on the ground that it is investigating or prosecuting the case or has investigated or prosecuted; or

(c) A State from which acceptance of jurisdiction is required under article 12.

3. The Prosecutor may seek a ruling from the Court regarding a question of jurisdiction or admissibility. In proceedings with respect to jurisdiction or admissibility, those who have referred the situation under article 13, as well as victims, may also submit observations to the Court. . . .

6. Prior to the confirmation of the charges, challenges to the admissibility of a case or challenges to the jurisdiction of the Court shall be referred to the Pre-Trial Chamber. After confirmation of the charges, they shall be referred to the Trial Chamber. Decisions with respect to jurisdiction or admissibility may be appealed to the Appeals Chamber in accordance with article 82.

7. If a challenge is made by a State referred to in paragraph 2(b) or (c), the Prosecutor shall suspend the investigation until such time as the Court makes a determination in accordance with article 17. . . .

9. The making of challenge shall not affect the validity of any act performed by the Prosecutor or any order or warrant issued by the Court prior to the making of the challenge.

10. If the Court has decided that a case is inadmissible under article 17, the Prosecutor may submit a request for a review of the decision when he or she is fully satisfied that new facts have arisen which negate the basis on which the case had previously been found inadmissible under article 17.

11. If the Prosecutor, having regard to the matters referred to in article 17, defers an investigation, the Prosecutor may request that the relevant State make available to the Prosecutor information on the proceedings. That information shall, at the request of the State concerned, be confidential. If the Prosecutor thereafter decides to proceed with an investigation, he or she shall notify the State to which deferral of the proceedings has taken place.

Article 20.   Ne Bis In Idem

1. Except as provided in this Statute, no person shall be tried before the Court with respect to conduct which formed the basis of crimes for which the person has been convicted or acquitted by the Court.

2. No person shall be tried before another court for a crime referred to in article 5 for which that person has already been convicted or acquitted by the Court.

3. No person who has been tried by another court for conduct also proscribed under articles 6, 7 or 8 shall be tried by the Court with respect to the same conduct unless the proceedings in the other court:

(a) Were for the purpose of shielding the person concerned from criminal responsibility for crimes within the jurisdiction of the Court; or

(b) Otherwise were not conducted independently or impartially in accordance with the norms of due process recognized by international law and were conducted in a manner which, in the circumstances, was inconsistent with an intent to bring the person concerned to justice.

Article 21.   Applicable Law

1. The Court shall apply:

(a) In the first place, this Statute, Elements of Crimes and its Rules of Procedure and Evidence;

(b) In the second place, where appropriate, applicable treaties and the principles and rules of international law, including the established principles of the international law of armed conflict;

(c) Failing that, general principles of law derived by the Court from national laws of legal systems of the world including, as appropriate, the national laws of States that would normally exercise jurisdiction over the crime, provided that those principles are not inconsistent with this Statute and with international law and internationally recognized norms and standards.

2. The Court may apply principles and rules of law as interpreted in its previous decisions.

3. The application and interpretation of law pursuant to this article must be consistent with internationally recognized human rights, and be without any adverse distinction founded on grounds such as gender, as defined in article 7, paragraph 3, age, race, colour, language, religion or belief, political or other opinion, national, ethnic or social origin, wealth, birth or other status.

Part 3.   General Principles of Criminal Law

Article 22.   Nullum Crimen Sine Lege

1. A person shall not be criminally responsible under this Statute unless the conduct in question constitutes, at the time it takes place, a crime within the jurisdiction of the Court.

2. The definition of a crime shall be strictly construed and shall not be extended by analogy. In case of ambiguity, the definition shall be interpreted in favour of the person being investigated, prosecuted or convicted.

3. This article shall not affect the characterization of any conduct as criminal under international law independently of this Statute.

Article 23. Nulla Poena Sine Lege

A person convicted by the Court may be punished only in accordance with this Statute . . .

Article 25. Individual Criminal Responsibility

1. The Court shall have jurisdiction over natural persons pursuant to this Statute.

2. A person who commits a crime within the jurisdiction of the Court shall be individually responsible and liable for punishment in accordance with this Statute.

3. In accordance with this Statute, a person shall be criminally responsible and liable for punishment for a crime within the jurisdiction of the Court if that person:

(a) Commits such a crime, whether as an individual, jointly with another or through another person, regardless of whether that other person is criminally responsible;

(b) Orders, solicits or induces the commission of such a crime which in fact occurs or is attempted;

(c) For the purpose of facilitating the commission of such a crime, aids, abets or otherwise assists in its commission or its attempted commission, including providing the means for its commission;

(d) In any other way contributes to the commission or attempted commission of such a crime by a group of persons acting with a common purpose. Such contribution shall be intentional and shall either:

(i) Be made with the aim of furthering the criminal activity or criminal purpose of the group, where such activity or purpose involves the commission of a crime within the jurisdiction of the Court; or

(ii) Be made in the knowledge of the intention of the group to commit the crime;

(e) In respect of the crime of genocide, directly and publicly incites others to commit genocide;

(f) Attempts to commit such a crime by taking action that commences its execution by means of a substantial step, but the crime does not occur because of circumstances independent of the person's intentions. However, a person who abandons the effort to commit the crime or otherwise prevents the completion of the crime shall not be liable for punishment under this Statute for the attempt to commit that crime if that person completely and voluntarily gave up the criminal purpose.

4. No provision in this Statute relating to individual criminal responsibility shall affect the responsibility of States under international law. . . .

Article 27.   Irrelevance of Official Capacity

1. This Statute shall apply equally to all persons without any distinction based on official capacity. In particular, official capacity as a Head of State or Government, a member of a Government or parliament, an elected representative or a government official shall in no case exempt a person from criminal responsibility under this Statute, nor shall it, in and of itself, constitute a ground for reduction of sentence.

2. Immunities or special procedural rules which may attach to the official capacity of a person, whether under national or international law, shall not bar the Court from exercising its jurisdiction over such a person.

Article 28.   Responsibility of Commanders and Other Superiors

In addition to other grounds of criminal responsibility under this Statute for crimes within the jurisdiction of the Court:

1. A military commander or person effectively acting as a military commander shall be criminally responsible for crimes within the jurisdiction of the Court committed by forces under his or her effective command and control, or effective authority and control as the case may be, as a result of his or her failure to exercise control properly over such forces, where:

   (a) That military commander or person either knew or, owing to the circumstances at the time, should have known that the forces were committing or about to commit such crimes; and

   (b) That military commander or person failed to take all necessary and reasonable measures within his or her power to prevent or repress their commission or to submit the matter to the competent authorities for investigation and prosecution.

2. With respect to superior and subordinate relationships not described in paragraph 1, a superior shall be criminally responsible for crimes within the jurisdiction of the Court committed by subordinates under his or her effective authority and control, as a result of his or her failure to exercise control properly over such subordinates, where:

   (a) The superior either knew, or consciously disregarded information which clearly indicated, that the subordinates were committing or about to commit such crimes;

   (b) The crimes concerned activities that were within the effective responsibility and control of the superior; and

   (c) The superior failed to take all necessary and reasonable measures within his or her power to prevent or repress their commission or to submit the matter to the competent authorities for investigation and prosecution.

Article 29.   Non-Applicability of Statute of Limitations

The crimes within the jurisdiction of the Court shall not be subject to any statute of limitations.

Article 30.   Mental Element

1. Unless otherwise provided, a person shall be criminally responsible and liable for punishment for a crime within the jurisdiction of the Court only if the material elements are committed with intent and knowledge.
2. For the purposes of this article, a person has intent where:
(a) In relation to conduct, that person means to engage in the conduct;
(b) In relation to a consequence, that person means to cause that consequence or is aware that it will occur in the ordinary course of events.
3. For the purposes of this article, "knowledge" means awareness that a circumstance exists or a consequence will occur in the ordinary course of events. "Know" and "knowingly" shall be construed accordingly.

Article 31.   Grounds for Excluding Criminal Responsibility

1. In addition to other grounds for excluding criminal responsibility provided for in this Statute, a person shall not be criminally responsible if, at the time of that person's conduct:
(a) The person suffers from a mental disease or defect that destroys that person's capacity to appreciate the unlawfulness or nature of his or her conduct, or capacity to control his or her conduct to conform to the requirements of law;
(b) The person is in a state of intoxication that destroys that person's capacity to appreciate the unlawfulness or nature of his or her conduct, or capacity to control his or her conduct to conform to the requirements of law, unless the person has become voluntarily intoxicated under such circumstances that the person knew, or disregarded the risk, that, as a result of the intoxication, he or she was likely to engage in conduct constituting a crime within the jurisdiction of the Court;
(c) The person acts reasonably to defend himself or herself or another person or, in the case of war crimes, property which is essential for the survival of the person or another person or property which is essential for accomplishing a military mission, against an imminent and unlawful use of force in a manner proportionate to the degree of danger to the person or the other person or property protected. The fact that the person was involved in a defensive operation conducted by forces shall not in itself constitute a ground for excluding criminal responsibility under this subparagraph;
(d) The conduct which is alleged to constitute a crime within the jurisdiction of the Court has been caused by duress resulting from a threat of imminent death or of continuing or imminent serious bodily harm

against that person or another person, and the person acts necessarily and reasonably to avoid this threat, provided that the person does not intend to cause a greater harm than the one sought to be avoided. Such a threat may either be:

    (i) Made by other persons; or

    (ii) Constituted by other circumstances beyond that person's control.

2. The Court shall determine the applicability of the grounds for excluding criminal responsibility provided for in this Statute to the case before it.

3. At trial, the Court may consider a ground for excluding criminal responsibility other than those referred to in paragraph 1 where such a ground is derived from applicable law as set forth in article 21. The procedures relating to the consideration of such a ground shall be provided for in the Rules of Procedure and Evidence.

Article 32. *Mistake of Fact or Mistake of Law*

1. A mistake of fact shall be a ground for excluding criminal responsibility only if it negates the mental element required by the crime.

2. A mistake of law as to whether a particular type of conduct is a crime within the jurisdiction of the Court shall not be a ground for excluding criminal responsibility. A mistake of law may, however, be a ground for excluding criminal responsibility if it negates the mental element required by such a crime, or as provided for in article 33.

Article 33. *Superior Orders and Prescription of Law*

1. The fact that a crime within the jurisdiction of the Court has been committed by a person pursuant to an order of a Government or of a superior, whether military or civilian, shall not relieve that person of criminal responsibility unless:

    (a) The person was under a legal obligation to obey orders of the Government or the superior in question;

    (b) The person did not know that the order was unlawful; and

    (c) The order was not manifestly unlawful.

2. For the purposes of this article, orders to commit genocide or crimes against humanity are manifestly unlawful.

Part 4. Composition and Administration of the Court

Article 34. *Organs of the Court*

The Court shall be composed of the following organs:

    (a) The Presidency;

    (b) An Appeals Division, a Trial Division and a Pre-Trial Division;

(c) The Office of the Prosecutor;

(d) The Registry.

Article 35.   Service of Judges

1. All judges shall be elected as full-time members of the Court and shall be available to serve on that basis from the commencement of their terms of office.

2. The judges composing the Presidency shall serve on a full-time basis as soon as they are elected.

3. The Presidency may, on the basis of the workload of the Court and in consultation with its members, decide from time to time to what extent the remaining judges shall be required to serve on a full-time basis. Any such arrangement shall be without prejudice to the provisions of article 40.

4. The financial arrangements for judges not required to serve on a full-time basis shall be made in accordance with article 49.

Article 36.   Qualifications, Nomination and Election of Judges

1. Subject to the provisions of paragraph 2, there shall be 18 judges of the Court . . .

3. (a) The judges shall be chosen from among persona of high moral character, impartiality and integrity who possess the qualifications required in their respective States for appointment to the highest judicial offices.

(b) Every candidate for election to the Court shall:

(i) Have established competence in criminal law and procedure, and the necessary relevant experience, whether as judge, prosecutor, advocate or in other similar capacity, in criminal proceedings; or

(ii) Have established competence in relevant areas of international law such as international humanitarian law and the law of human rights, and extensive experience in a professional legal capacity which is of relevance to the judicial work of the Court;

(c) Every candidate for election to the Court shall have an excellent knowledge of and be fluent in at least one of the working languages of the Court.

4. (a) Nominations of candidates for election to the Court may be made by any State Party to this Statute, and shall be made either:

(i) By the procedure for the nomination of candidates for appointment to the highest judicial offices in the State in question; or

(ii) By the procedure provided for the nomination of candidates for the International Court of Justice in the Statute of that Court.

Nominations shall be accompanied by a statement in the necessary detail specifying how the candidate fulfills the requirements of paragraph 3.

(b) Each State Party may put forward one candidate for any given election who need not necessarily be a national of that State Party but shall in any case be a national of a State Party.

(c) The Assembly of States Parties may decide to establish, if appropriate, an Advisory Committee on nominations. In that event, the Committee's composition and mandate shall be established by the Assembly of States Parties. . . .

6. (a) The judges shall be elected by secret ballot at a meeting of the Assembly of States Parties convened for that purpose under article 112. Subject to paragraph 7, the persons elected to the Court shall be the 18 candidates who obtain the highest number of votes and a two-thirds majority of the States Parties present and voting. . . .

7. No two judges may be nationals of the same State . . .

8. (a) The States Parties shall, in the selection of judges, take into account the need, within the membership of the Court, for:

(i) The representation of the principal legal systems of the world;

(ii) Equitable geographical representation; and

(iii) A fair representation of female and male judges.

(b) States Parties shall also take into account the need to include judges with legal expertise on specific issues, including, but not limited to, violence against women or children.

9. (a) Subject to subparagraph (b), judges shall hold office for a term of nine years and, subject to subparagraph (c) and to article 37, paragraph 2, shall not be eligible for re-election.

(b) At the first election, one third of the judges elected shall be selected by lot to serve for a term of three years; one third of the judges elected shall be selected by lot to serve for a term of six years; and the remainder shall serve for a term of nine years.

(c) A judge who is selected to serve for a term of three years under subparagraph (b) shall be eligible for re-election for a full term.

10. Notwithstanding paragraph 9, a judge assigned to a Trial or Appeals Chamber in accordance with article 39 shall continue in office to complete any trial or appeal the hearing of which has already commenced before that Chamber. . . .

Article 38.   The Presidency

1. The President and the First and Second Vice-Presidents shall be elected by an absolute majority of the judges. They shall each serve for a term of three years or until the end of their respective terms of office as judges, whichever expires earlier. They shall be eligible for re-election once. . . .

Article 39.   Chambers

1. As soon as possible after the election of the judges, the Court shall organize itself into the divisions specified in article 34, paragraph (b). The Appeals Division shall be composed of the President and four other judges, the Trial Division of not less than six judges and the Pre-Trial Division of not less than six judges. . . .

2. (a) The judicial functions of the Court shall be carried out in each division by Chambers.

(b) (i) The Appeals Chamber shall be composed of all the judges of the Appeals Division;

(ii) The functions of the Trial Chamber shall be carried out by three judges of the Trial Division;

(iii) The functions of the Pre-Trial Chamber shall be carried out either by three judges of the Pre-Trial Division or by a single judge of that division in accordance with this Statute and the Rules of Procedure and Evidence;

(c) Nothing in this paragraph shall preclude the simultaneous constitution of more than one Trial Chamber or Pre-Trial Chamber when the efficient management of the Court's workload so requires. . . .

Article 40.   Independence of the Judges

1. The judges shall be independent in the performance of their functions.

2. Judges shall not engage in any activity which is likely to interfere with their judicial functions or to affect confidence in their independence.

3. Judges required to serve on a full-time basis at the seat of the Court shall not engage in any other occupation of a professional nature.

4. Any question regarding the application of paragraphs 2 and 3 shall be decided by an absolute majority of the judges. Where any such question concerns an individual judge, that judge shall not take part in the decision.

Article 41.   Excusing and Disqualification of Judges

1. The Presidency may, at the request of a judge, excuse that judge from the exercise of a function under this Statute, in accordance with the Rules of Procedure and Evidence.

2. (a) A judge shall not participate in any case in which his or her impartiality might reasonably be doubted on any ground. A judge shall be disqualified from a case in accordance with this paragraph if, inter alia, that judge has previously been involved in any capacity in that case before the Court or in a related criminal case at the national level involving the person being investigated or prosecuted. A judge shall also be disqualified on such other grounds as may be provided for in the Rules of Procedure and Evidence.

(b) The Prosecutor or the person being investigated or prosecuted may request the disqualification of a judge under this paragraph.

(c) Any question as to the disqualification of a judge shall be decided by an absolute majority of the judges. The challenged judge shall be entitled to present his or her comments on the matter, but shall not take part in the decision.

Article 42.   The Office of the Prosecutor

1. The Office of the Prosecutor shall act independently as a separate organ of the Court. It shall be responsible for receiving referrals and any substantiated information on crimes within the jurisdiction of the Court, for

examining them and for conducting investigations and prosecutions before the Court. A member of the Office shall not seek or act on instructions from any external source.

2. The Office shall be headed by the Prosecutor. The Prosecutor shall have full authority over the management and administration of the Office, including the staff, facilities and other resources thereof. The Prosecutor shall be assisted by one or more Deputy Prosecutors, who shall be entitled to carry out any of the acts required of the Prosecutor under this Statute. The Prosecutor and the Deputy Prosecutors shall be of different nationalities. They shall serve on a full-time basis.

3. The Prosecutor and the Deputy Prosecutors shall be persons of high moral character, be highly competent in and have extensive practical experience in the prosecution or trial of criminal cases. They shall have an excellent knowledge of and be fluent in at least one of the working languages of the Court.

4. The Prosecutor shall be elected by secret ballot by an absolute majority of the members of the Assembly of States Parties. The Deputy Prosecutors shall be elected in the same way from a list of candidates provided by the Prosecutor. . . .

5. Neither the Prosecutor nor a Deputy Prosecutor shall engage in any activity which is likely to interfere with his or her prosecutorial functions or to affect confidence in his or her independence. They shall not engage in any other occupation of a professional nature. . . .

7. Neither the Prosecutor nor a Deputy Prosecutor shall participate in any matter in which their impartiality might reasonably be doubted on any ground. . . .

8. Any question as to the disqualification of the Prosecutor or a Deputy Prosecutor shall be decided by the Appeals Chamber.

(a) The person being investigated or prosecuted may at any time request the disqualification of the Prosecutor or a Deputy Prosecutor on the grounds set out in this article; . . .

9. The Prosecutor shall appoint advisers with legal expertise on specific issues, including, but not limited to, sexual and gender violence and violence against children. . . .

Article 43.   The Registry

1. The Registry shall be responsible for the non-judicial aspects of the administration and servicing of the Court, without prejudice to the functions and powers of the Prosecutor in accordance with article 42.

2. The Registry shall be headed by the Registrar, who shall be the principal administrative officer of the Court. The Registrar shall exercise his or her functions under the authority of the President of the Court. . . .

6. The Registrar shall set up a Victims and Witnesses Unit within the Registry. This Unit shall provide, in consultation with the Office of the Prosecutor, protective measures and security arrangements, counselling and other appropriate assistance for witnesses, victims who appear before the

Court, and others who are at risk on account of testimony given by such witnesses. The Unit shall include staff with expertise in trauma, including trauma related to crimes of sexual violence. . . .

Article 48.   Privileges and Immunities

1. The Court shall enjoy in the territory of each State Party such privileges and immunities as are necessary for the fulfilment of its purposes.

2. The judges, the Prosecutor, the Deputy Prosecutors and the Registrar shall, when engaged on or with respect to the business of the Court, enjoy the same privileges and immunities as are accorded to heads of diplomatic missions and shall, after the expiry of their terms of office, continue to be accorded immunity from legal process of every kind in respect of words spoken or written and acts performed by them in their official capacity.

3. The Deputy Registrar, the staff of the Office of the Prosecutor and the staff of the Registry shall enjoy the privileges and immunities and facilities necessary for the performance of their functions, in accordance with the agreement on the privileges and immunities of the Court.

4. Counsel, experts, witnesses or any other person required to be present at the seat of the Court shall be accorded such treatment as is necessary for the proper functioning of the Court, in accordance with the agreement on the privileges and immunities of the Court. . . .

Article 50.   Official and Working Languages

1. The official languages of the Court shall be Arabic, Chinese, English, French, Russian and Spanish. . . .

2. The working languages of the Court shall be English and French. . . .

Article 51.   Rules of Procedure and Evidence

1. The Rules of Procedure and Evidence shall enter into force upon adoption by a two-thirds majority of the members of the Assembly of States Parties. . . .

Part 5.   Investigation and Prosecution

Article 53.   Initiation of an Investigation

1. The Prosecutor shall, having evaluated the information made available to him or her, initiate an investigation unless he or she determines that there is no reasonable basis to proceed under this Statute. In deciding whether to initiate an investigation, the Prosecutor shall consider whether:

(a) The information available to the Prosecutor provides a reasonable basis to believe that a crime within the jurisdiction of the Court has been or is being committed;

(b) The case is or would be admissible under article 17; and

(c) Taking into account the gravity of the crime and the interests of victims, there are nonetheless substantial reasons to believe that an investigation would not serve the interests of justice.

If the Prosecutor determines that there is no reasonable basis to proceed and his or her determination is based solely on subparagraph (c) above, he or she shall inform the Pre-Trial Chamber.

2. If, upon investigation, the Prosecutor concludes that there is not a sufficient basis for a prosecution because:

(a) There is not a sufficient legal or factual basis to seek a warrant or summons under article 58;

(b) The case is inadmissible under article 17; or

(c) A prosecution is not in the interests of justice, taking into account all the circumstances, including the gravity of the crime, the interests of victims and the age or infirmity of the alleged perpetrator, and his or her role in the alleged crime;

The Prosecutor shall inform the Pre-Trial Chamber and the State making a referral under article 14 or the Security Council in a case under article 13, paragraph (b), of his or her conclusion and the reasons for the conclusion.

3. (a) At the request of the State making a referral under article 14 or the Security Council under article 13, paragraph (b), the Pre-Trial Chamber may review a decision of the Prosecutor under paragraph 1 or 2 not to proceed and may request the Prosecutor to reconsider that decision.

(b) In addition, the Pre-Trial Chamber may, on its own initiative, review a decision of the Prosecutor not to proceed if it is based solely on paragraph 1(c) or 2(c). In such a case, the decision of the Prosecutor shall be effective only if confirmed by the Pre-Trial Chamber.

4. The Prosecutor may, at any time, reconsider a decision whether to initiate an investigation or prosecution based on new facts or information.

Article 54. Duties and Power of the Prosecutor with Respect to Investigations

1. The Prosecutor shall:

(a) In order to establish the truth, extend the investigation to cover all facts and evidence relevant to an assessment of whether there is criminal responsibility under this Statute, and, in doing so, investigate incriminating and exonerating circumstances equally;

(b) Take appropriate measures to ensure the effective investigation and prosecution of crimes within the jurisdiction of the Court, and in doing so, respect the interests and personal circumstances of victims and witnesses, including age, gender as defined in article 7, paragraph 3, and health, and take into account the nature of the crime, in particular where it involves sexual violence, gender violence or violence against children; and

(c) Fully respect the rights of persons arising under this Statute.

2. The Prosecutor may conduct investigations on the territory of a State:

(a) In accordance with the provisions of Part 9; or

(b) As authorized by the Pre-Trial Chamber under article 57, paragraph 3(d).

3. The Prosecutor may:

(a) Collect and examine evidence;

(b) Request the presence of and question persons being investigated, victims and witnesses;

(c) Seek the cooperation of any State or intergovernmental organization or arrangement in accordance with its respective competence and/ or mandate;

(d) Enter into such arrangements or agreements, not inconsistent with this Statute, as may be necessary to facilitate the cooperation of a State, intergovernmental organization or person;

(e) Agree not to disclose, at any stage of the proceedings, documents or information that the Prosecutor obtains on the condition of confidentiality and solely for the purpose of generating new evidence, unless the provider of the information consents; and

(f) Take necessary measures, or request that necessary measures be taken, to ensure the confidentiality of information, the protection of any person or the preservation of evidence.

Article 55. *Rights of Persons During an Investigation*

1. In respect of an investigation under this Statute, a person:

(a) Shall not be compelled to incriminate himself or herself or to confess guilt;

(b) Shall not be subjected to any form of coercion, duress or threat, to torture or to any other form of cruel, inhuman or degrading treatment or punishment; and

(c) Shall, if questioned in a language other, than a language the person fully understands and speaks, have, free of any cost, the assistance of a competent interpreter and such translations as are necessary to meet the requirements of fairness;

(d) Shall not be subjected to arbitrary arrest or detention; and shall not be deprived of his or her liberty except on such grounds and in accordance with such procedures as are established in the Statute.

2. Where there are grounds to believe that a person has committed a crime within the jurisdiction of the Court and that person is about to be questioned either by the Prosecutor, or by national authorities pursuant to a request made under Part 9 of this Statute, that person shall also have the following rights of which he or she shall be informed prior to being questioned:

(a) To be informed, prior to being questioned, that there are grounds to believe that he or she has committed a crime within the jurisdiction of the Court;

(b) To remain silent, without such silence being a consideration in the determination of guilt or innocence;

(c) To have legal assistance of the person's choosing, or, if the person does not have legal assistance, to have legal assistance assigned to him or her, in any case where the interests of justice so require, and without payment by the person in any such case if the person does not have sufficient means to pay for it;

(d) To be questioned in the presence of counsel unless the person has voluntarily waived his or her right to counsel. . . .

Part 6.   The Trial

Article 62.   Place of Trial

Unless otherwise decided, the place of the trial shall be the seat of the Court.

Article 63.   Trial in the Presence of the Accused

1. The accused shall be present during the trial.

2. If the accused, being present before the Court, continues to disrupt the trial, the Trial Chamber may remove the accused and shall make provision for him or her to observe the trial and instruct counsel from outside the courtroom, through the use of communications technology, if required. Such measures shall be taken only in exceptional circumstances after other reasonable alternatives have proved inadequate, and only for such duration as is strictly required. . . .

Article 66.   Presumption of Innocence

1. Everyone shall be presumed innocent until proved guilty before the Court in accordance with the applicable law.

2. The onus is on the Prosecutor to prove the guilt of the accused.

3. In order to convict the accused, the Court must be convinced of the guilt of the accused beyond reasonable doubt.

Article 67.   Rights of the Accused

1. In the determination of any charge, the accused shall be entitled to a public hearing, having regard to the provisions of this Statute, to a fair hearing conducted impartially, and to the following minimum guarantees, in full equality:

(a) To be informed promptly and in detail of the nature, cause and content of the charge, in a language which the accused fully understands and speaks;

(b) To have adequate time and facilities for the preparation of the defence and to communicate freely with counsel of the accused's choosing in confidence;

(c) To be tried without undue delay;

(d) Subject to article 63, paragraph 2, to be present at the trial, to conduct the defence in person or through legal assistance of the accused's choosing, to be informed, if the accused does not have legal assistance, of this right and to have legal assistance assigned by the Court in any case where the interests of justice so require, and without payment if the accused lacks sufficient means to pay for it;

(e) To examine, or have examined, the witnesses against him or her and to obtain the attendance and examination of witnesses on his or her behalf under the same conditions as witnesses against him or her. The accused shall also be entitled to raise defences and to present other evidence admissible under this Statute;

(f) To have, free of any cost, the assistance of a competent interpreter and such translations as are necessary to meet the requirements of fairness, if any of the proceedings of or documents presented to the Court are not in a language which the accused fully understands and speaks;

(g) Not to be compelled to testify or to confess guilt and to remain silent, without such silence being a consideration in the determination of guilt or innocence;

(h) To make an unsworn oral or written statement in his or her defence; and

(i) Not to have imposed on him or her any reversal of the burden of proof or any onus of rebuttal.

2. In addition to any other disclosure provided for in this Statute, the Prosecutor shall, as soon as practicable, disclose to the defence evidence in the prosecutor's possession or control which he or she believes shows or tends to show the innocence of the accused; or to mitigate the guilt of the accused, or which may affect the credibility of prosecution evidence. In case of doubt as to the application of this paragraph, the Court shall decide.

Article 68.   Protection of the Victims and Witnesses and Their Participation in the Proceedings

1. The Court shall take appropriate measures to protect the safety, physical and psychological well-being, dignity and privacy of victims and witnesses. . . .

Article 74.   Requirements for the Decision

1. All the judges of the Trial Chamber shall be present at each stage of the trial and throughout their deliberations. The Presidency may, on a case-by-case basis, designate, as available, one or more alternate judges to be present at each stage of the trial and to replace a member of the Trial Chamber if that member is unable to continue attending.

2. The Trial Chamber's decision shall be based on its evaluation of the evidence and the entire proceedings. The decision shall not exceed the facts

and circumstances described in the charges and any amendments to the charges. The Court may base its decision only on evidence submitted and discussed before it at the trial.

3. The judges shall attempt to achieve unanimity in their decision, failing which the decision shall be taken by a majority of the judges.

4. The deliberations of the Trial Chamber shall remain secret.

5. The decision shall be in writing and shall contain a full and reasoned statement of the Trial Chamber's findings on the evidence and conclusions. The Trial Chamber shall issue one decision. When there is no unanimity, the Trial Chamber's decision shall contain the views of the majority and the minority. The decision or a summary thereof shall be delivered in open court.

Article 75. *Reparations to Victims*

1. The Court shall establish principles relating to reparations to, or in respect of, victims, including restitution, compensation and rehabilitation. On this basis, in its decision the Court may, either upon request or on its own motion in exceptional circumstances, determine the scope and extent of any damage, loss and injury to, or in respect of, victims and will state the principles on which it is acting.

2. The Court may make an order directly against a convicted person specifying appropriate reparations to, or in respect of, victims including restitution, compensation and rehabilitation.

Where appropriate, the Court may order that the award for reparations be made through the Trust Fund provided for in article 79. . . .

Part 7.   Penalties

Article 77.   *Applicable Penalties*

1. Subject to article 110, the Court may impose one of the following penalties on a person convicted of a crime referred to in article 5 of this Statute:

(a) Imprisonment for a specified number of years, which may not exceed a maximum of 30 years; or

(b) A term of life imprisonment when justified by the extreme gravity of the crime and the individual circumstances of the convicted person.

2. In addition to imprisonment, the Court may order:

(a) A fine under the criteria provided for in the Rules of Procedure and Evidence;

(b) A forfeiture of proceeds, property and assets derived directly or indirectly from that crime, without prejudice to the rights of bona fide third parties. . . .

Article 79.   Trust Fund

1. A Trust Fund shall be established by decision of the Assembly of States Parties for the benefit of victims of crimes within the jurisdiction of the Court, and of the families of such victims.

2. The Court may order money and other property collected through fines or forfeiture to be transferred, by order of the Court, to the Trust Fund. . . .

Part 8.   Appeal and Revision

Article 81.   Appeal Against Decision of Acquittal or Conviction or Against Sentence

1. A decision under article 74 may be appealed in accordance with the Rules of Procedure and Evidence as follows:

   (a) The Prosecutor may make an appeal on any of the following grounds:

   (i) Procedural error,

   (ii) Error of fact, or

   (iii) Error of law;

   (b) The convicted person or the Prosecutor on that person's behalf may make an appeal on any of the following grounds:

   (i) Procedural error,

   (ii) Error of fact,

   (iii) Error of law, or

   (iv) Any on the ground that affects the fairness or reliability of the proceedings or decision.

2. (a) A sentence may be appealed, in accordance with the Rules of Procedure and Evidence, by the Prosecutor or the convicted person on the ground of disproportion between, the crime and the sentence;

   (b) If on an appeal against sentence the Court considers that there are grounds on which the conviction might be set aside, wholly or in part, it may invite the Prosecutor and the convicted person to submit grounds under article 81, paragraph 1(a) or (b), and may render a decision on conviction in accordance with article 83;

   (c) The same procedure applies when the Court, on an appeal against conviction only, considers that there are grounds to reduce the sentence under paragraph 2(a).

3. (a) Unless the Trial Chamber orders otherwise, a convicted person shall remain in custody pending an appeal;

   (b) When a convicted person's time in custody exceeds the sentence of imprisonment imposed, that person shall be released, except that if the Prosecutor is also appealing, the release may be subject to the conditions under subparagraph (c) below;

(c) In case of an acquittal, the accused shall be released immediately, subject to the following:

(i) Under exceptional circumstances, and having regard, inter alia, to the concrete risk of flight, the seriousness of the offence charged and the probability of success on appeal, the Trial Chamber, at the request of the Prosecutor, may maintain the detention of the person pending appeal;

(ii) A decision by the Trial Chamber under subparagraph (c) (i) may be appealed in accordance with the Rules of Procedure and Evidence.

4. Subject to the provisions of paragraph 3(a) and (b), execution of the decision or sentence shall be suspended during the period allowed for appeal and for the duration of the appeal proceedings.

Article 82.   Appeal Against Other Decisions

1. Either party may appeal any of the following decisions in accordance with the Rules of Procedure and Evidence:

(a) A decision with respect to jurisdiction or admissibility,

(b) A decision granting or denying release of the person being investigated or prosecuted;

(c) A decision of the Pre-Trial Chamber to act on its own initiative under article 56, paragraph 3;

(d) A decision that involves an issue that would significantly affect the fair and expeditious conduct of the proceedings or the outcome of the trial, and for which, in the opinion of the Pre-Trial or Trial Chamber, an immediate resolution by the Appeals Chamber may materially advance the proceedings.

2. A decision of the Pre-Trial Chamber under article 57, paragraph 3 (d), may be appealed against by the State concerned or by the Prosecutor, with the leave of the Pre-Trial Chamber. The appeal shall be heard on an expedited basis.

3. An appeal shall not of itself have suspensive effect unless the Appeals Chamber so orders, upon request, in accordance with the Rules of Procedure and Evidence.

4. A legal representative of the victims, the convicted person or a bona fide owner of property adversely affected by an order under article 73 may appeal against the order for reparations, as provided in the Rules of Procedure and Evidence.

Article 83.   Proceedings on Appeal

1. For the purposes of proceedings under article 81 and this article, the Appeals Chamber shall have all the powers of the Trial Chamber.

2. If the Appeals Chamber finds that the proceedings appealed from were unfair in a way that affected the reliability of the decision or sentence, or that the decision or sentence appealed from was materially affected by error of fact or law or procedural error, it may:

(a) Reverse or amend the decision or sentence; or

(b) Order a new trial before a different Trial Chamber.

For these purposes, the Appeals Chamber may remand a factual issue to the original Trial Chamber for it to determine the issue and to report back accordingly, or may itself call evidence to determine the issue. When the decision or sentence has been appealed only by the person convicted, or the Prosecutor on that person's behalf, it cannot be amended to his or her detriment.

3. If in an appeal against sentence the Appeals Chamber finds that the sentence is disproportionate to the crime, it may vary the sentence in accordance with Part 7.

4. The judgement of the Appeals Chamber shall be taken by a majority of the judges and shall be delivered in open court. The judgement shall state the reasons on which it is based. When there is no unanimity, the judgement of the Appeals Chamber shall contain the views of the majority and the minority, but a judge may deliver a separate or dissenting opinion on a question of law.

5. The Appeals Chamber may deliver its judgement in the absence of the person acquitted or convicted. . . .

Article 85.   *Compensation to an Arrested or Convicted Person*

1. Anyone who has been the victim of unlawful arrest or detention shall have an enforceable right to compensation.

2. When a person has by a final decision been convicted of a criminal offence, and when subsequently his or her conviction has been reversed on the ground that a new or newly discovered fact shows conclusively that there has been a miscarriage of justice, the person who has suffered punishment as a result of such conviction shall be compensated according to law, unless it is proved that the non-disclosure of the unknown fact in time is wholly or partly attributable to him or her. . . .

Part 9.   International Cooperation and Judicial Assistance

Article 86.   *General Obligation to Cooperate*

States Parties shall, in accordance with the provisions of this Statute, cooperate fully with the Court in its investigation and prosecution of crimes within the jurisdiction of the Court.

Article 87.   *Requests for Cooperation: General Provisions*

1. (a) The Court shall have the authority to make requests to States Parties for cooperation. The requests shall be transmitted through the diplomatic channel or any other appropriate channel as may be designated by each State Party upon ratification, acceptance, approval or accession. . . .

Article 89. Surrender of Persons to the Court

1. The Court may transmit a request for the arrest and surrender of a person, together with the material supporting the request outlined in article 91, to any State on the territory of which that person may be found and shall request the cooperation of that State in the arrest and surrender of such a person. States Parties shall, in accordance with the provisions of this Part and the procedure under their national law, comply with requests for arrest and surrender. . . .

Article 98. Cooperation with Respect to Waiver of Immunity and Consent to Surrender

1. The Court may not proceed with a request for surrender or assistance which would require the requested State to act inconsistently with its obligations under international law with respect to the State or diplomatic immunity of a person or property of a third state, unless the Court can first obtain the cooperation of that third State for the waiver of the immunity.

2. The Court may not proceed with a request for surrender which would require the requested State to act inconsistently with its obligations under international agreements pursuant to which the consent of a sending State is required to surrender a person of that State to the Court, unless the Court can first obtain the cooperation of the sending State for the giving of consent for the surrender. . . .

Part 10.   Enforcement

Article 103. Role of States in Enforcement of Sentences of Imprisonment

1. (a) A sentence of imprisonment shall be served in a State designated by the Court from a list of States which have indicated to the Court their willingness to accept sentenced persons.

(b) At the time of declaring its willingness to accept sentenced persons, a State may attach conditions to its acceptance as agreed by the Court and in accordance with this Part. . . .

Part 11.   Assembly of States Parties

Article 112. Assembly of States Parties

1. An Assembly of States Parties to this Statute is hereby established. Each State Party shall have one representative in the Assembly who may be accompanied by alternates and advisers. Other States which have signed the Statute or the Final Act may be observers in the Assembly.

2. The Assembly shall:

(a) Consider and adopt, as appropriate, recommendations of the Preparatory Commission;

(b) Provide management oversight to the Presidency, the Prosecutor and the Registrar regarding the administration of the Court;

(c) Consider the reports and activities of the Bureau established under paragraph 3 and take appropriate action in regard thereto;

(d) Consider and decide the budget for the Court;

(e) Decide whether to alter, in accordance with article 36, the number of judges;

(f) Consider pursuant to article 87, paragraphs 5 and 7, any question relating to non-cooperation;

(g) Perform any other function consistent with this Statute or the Rules of Procedure and Evidence.

3. (a) The Assembly shall have a Bureau consisting of a President, two Vice-Presidents and 18 members elected by the Assembly for three-year terms. . . .

6. The Assembly shall meet at the seal of the Court or at the Headquarters of the United Nations once a year and, when circumstances so require, hold special sessions. Except as otherwise specified in this Statute, special sessions shall be convened by the Bureau on its own initiative or at the request of one third of the States Parties.

7. Each State Party shall have one vote. Every effort shall be made to reach decisions by consensus in the Assembly and in the Bureau. If consensus cannot be reached, except as otherwise provided in the Statute:

(a) Decisions on matters of substance must be approved by a two-thirds majority of those present and voting provided that an absolute majority of States Parties constitutes the quorum for voting;

(b) Decisions on matters of procedure shall be taken by a simple majority of States Parties present and voting.

8. A State Party which is in arrears in the payment of its financial contributions towards the costs of the Court shall have no vote in the Assembly and in the Bureau if the amount of its arrears equals or exceeds the amount of the contributions due from it for the preceding two full years. The Assembly may, nevertheless, permit such a State Party to vote in the Assembly and in the Bureau if it is satisfied that the failure to pay is due to conditions beyond the control of the State Party.

9. The Assembly shall adopt its own rules of procedure. . . .

Part 12. Financing

Article 113. Financial Regulations

Except as otherwise specifically provided, all financial matters related to the Court and the meetings of the Assembly of States Parties, including its

Bureau and subsidiary bodies, shall be governed by this Statute and the Financial Regulations and Rules adopted by the Assembly of States Parties.

Article 114. Payment of Expenses

Expenses of the Court and the Assembly of States Parties, including its Bureau and subsidiary bodies, shall be paid from the funds of the Court.

Article 115. Funds of the Court and of the Assembly of States Parties

The expenses of the Court and the Assembly of States Parties, including its Bureau and subsidiary bodies, as provided for in the budget decided by the Assembly of States Parties, shall be provided by the following sources:

(a) Assessed contributions made by States Parties;

(b) Funds provided by the United Nations, subject to the approval of the General Assembly, in particular in relation to the expenses incurred due to referrals by the Security Council. . . .

Article 117. Assessment of Contributions

The contributions of States Parties shall be assessed in accordance with an agreed scale of assessment, based on the scale adopted by the United Nations for its regular budget and adjusted in accordance with the principles on which that scale is based. . . .

Part 13. Final Clauses

Article 119. Settlement of Disputes

1. Any dispute concerning the judicial functions of the Court shall be settled by the decision of the Court.

2. Any other dispute between two or more States Parties relating to the interpretation or application of this Statute which is not settled through negotiations within three months of their commencement shall be referred to the Assembly of States Parties. The Assembly may itself seek to settle the dispute or make recommendations on further means of settlement of the dispute, including referral to the International Court of Justice in conformity with the Statute of that Court.

Article 120. Reservations

No reservations may be made to this Statute.

Article 121. Amendments

1. After the expiry of seven years from the entry into force of this Statute, any State Party may propose amendments thereto. . . .

Article 126.   Entry into Force

1. This Statute shall enter into force on the first day of the month after the 60th day following the date of the deposit of the 60th instrument of ratification, acceptance, approval or accession with the Secretary-General of the United Nations.

2. For each State ratifying, accepting, approving or acceding to the Statute after the deposit of the 60th instrument of ratification, acceptance, approval or accession, the Statute shall enter into force on the first day of the month after the 60th day following the deposit by such State of its instrument of ratification, acceptance, approval or accession.

Article 127.   Withdrawal

1. A State Party may, by written notification addressed to the Secretary-General of the United Nations, withdraw from this Statute. The withdrawal shall take effect one year after the date of receipt of the notification, unless the notification specifies a later date.

2. A State shall not be discharged, by reason of its withdrawal, from the obligations arising from this Statute while it was a Party to the Statute, including any financial obligations which may have accrued. Its withdrawal shall not affect any cooperation with the Court in connection with criminal investigations and proceedings in relation to which the withdrawing State had a duty to cooperate and which were commenced prior to the date on which the withdrawal became effective, nor shall it prejudice in any way the continued consideration of any matter which was already under consideration by the Court prior to the date on which the withdrawal became effective. . . .